Crime and Criminals

Contemporary *and* Classic Readings

Frank R. Scarpitti

University of Delaware

Amie L. Nielsen

Bowling Green State University

Roxbury Publishing Company
Los Angeles, California

Library of Congress Cataloging-in-Publication Data

Scarpitti, Frank R.
  Crime and Criminals: Contemporary and Classic Readings
  [edited by] Frank R. Scarpitti, Amie L. Nielsen.
  p. cm.
  Includes bibliographical references and index.
  ISBN 1-891487-09-4
  1. Criminology.
  I. Nielsen, Amie, 1970–. II. Title.
  HV6025.S339 1999   98-18749
  364--dc21   CIP

CRIME AND CRIMINALS: CONTEMPORARY AND CLASSIC READINGS

Publisher and Editor: Claude Teweles
Copy Editor: Joyce Rappaport
Production Editors: James Ballinger, Dawn VanDercreek
Production Assistants: Renee Burkhammer, David Massengill
Typography: Synergistic Data Systems
Cover Design: Marnie Deacon Kenney
Cover Photo: Image © 1998 PhotoDisc, Inc.

Printed on acid-free paper in the United States of America. This paper meets the standards for recycling of the Environmental Protection Agency.

ISBN: 1-891487-09-4

ROXBURY PUBLISHING COMPANY
P.O. Box 491044
Los Angeles, California 90049-9044
Tel: (323) 653-1068 • Fax: (323) 653-4140
Email: roxbury@crl.com

TABLE OF CONTENTS

Edwin H. Sutherland and Donald R. Cressey

In this article criminal behavior is shown to be dependent on criminal law, a body of rules distinguished from other rules by specific characteristics.

William Chambliss

Chambliss demonstrates that law does not emerge from value consensus alone but depends largely on differences in power in various groups and conflicts created by social class divisions.

Jeffrey Reiman

The label "crime" is applied primarily to the dangerous actions of the poor while even greater dangers imposed on society by the wealthy are overlooked or justified in various ways.

Anthony Platt

This paper examines the origins of the juvenile justice movement; Platt concludes that it was the product of middle-class reformers who wanted to 'save' lower-class children from the disadvantages of their environment and early socialization by imposing state-sanctioned controls on their behavior.

Lynnell J. Simonson

The role and rights of victims in the criminal justice system are discussed and changes designed to address victims' feelings that they do not matter are reviewed and evaluated.

Section II: Extent and Nature of Crime

Section III: Correlates of Crime

Section IV: Theories of Crime

Section V: Types of Crime

Section VI: Responses to Crime

Preface

C*rime and Criminals: Contemporary and Classic Readings* is designed for courses that seek to provide students with a comprehensive introduction to the discipline of criminology. The selections deal, in one volume, with the full range of subjects typically covered in a criminology class, including how our society attempts to control crime and criminal behavior. Although the majority of the readings are written by sociologists, scholars in other disciplines, such as political science and psychology, are also represented.

We began this project with several purposes. First, we wished to compile a set of readings that would not only convey the rich history of the discipline of criminology, but also include contemporary works reflecting the new directions the field is taking and its continuing vitality and importance. Second, we wished to compile a collection of readings that would: convey the essential ideas concerning each topic in a straightforward, easy-to-read manner; enable students to understand these ideas and expose them to the criminological literature and research; and cultivate enthusiasm and excitement about the ideas and the field. Third, we wished to produce a reader that could be used as the primary text for a criminology class or could be used to supplement other course readings. In *Crime and Criminals: Contemporary and Classic Readings*, we have attempted to achieve these goals through a number of means.

Features of the Book

The 41 readings that follow represent the major areas and issues in the discipline of criminology. Some of the selections are "classics," others are contemporary pieces, and others provide what we consider to be a comprehensive overview of their respective topics. The readings have been edited to promote increased understanding, readability, and interest in the topic by undergraduate students. There are six sections in the book; at the beginning of each is an introductory chapter that provides an overview of the major issues in the area. The introductions are intended to help facilitate the student's understanding of the area, to acquaint him/her with the major issues, and to provide a broader context for the readings that follow. In addition, preceding each selection is an introduction that provides both a succinct overview of the article as well as discusses the importance of the selection for the student. Each reading is followed by a set of three discussion questions that are intended to help students to understand the main contributions of each article, to think critically about the issues each raises, and to integrate the ideas from the specific reading with those of the larger field.

Organization of the Book

The book is organized into six major sections, representing six major areas in criminology. In Section One, the readings deal with issues related to what behaviors are defined as crime and possible explanations concerning why some behaviors are criminalized and others are not. Section Two addresses the extent and nature of crime in the United States, including the types of data used to assess these issues. Section Three includes readings on the major correlates of crime, such as age and gender. The selections in Section Four represent the major theoretical approaches in criminology, with biological, psychological, and sociological approaches included. For the sociological theories, we include both a reading that provides an overview of the theory and an empirical example of the theory. Similarly, in Section Five, which deals with types of criminal behavior, we include two readings for each type, one that discusses the behavior more generally and one that provides a recent empirical example of the behavior. In the last section, Section Six, the readings deal with how our society reacts to crime and criminal behavior, focusing on various components of the criminal justice system.

Acknowledgements

We thank Carol Lenhart, Christopher Bradley, and Sean Rosenmerkel for providing research assistance. We also thank Eloise Barczak, Valerie Gerkens, and Linda Keene for their clerical support.

We are also grateful to the reviewers, whose contributions aided the development of this book: Robert Agnew, Emory University; Ronald Akers, University of Florida; John Dombrink, University of California, Irvine; Ronald Holmes, University of Louisville; Gary Jensen, Vanderbilt University; Jon'a Meyer, Rutgers University at Camden; Alex Piquero, Temple University; Thomas Winfree, New Mexico State University; and Richard A.Wright, Arkansas State University. We have benefited from the suggestions, enthusiasm, patience, and support of our editor Claude Teweles. Lastly, we thank Ellen Scarpitti and Ramiro Martinez Jr. for their understanding and continued support. ✦

About the Contributors

Robert Agnew is a professor in the Department of Sociology at Emory University.

Emilie Andersen Allan is a professor in the Department of Sociology at St. Francis College in Loretto, Pennsylvania.

Alan A. Block is a professor in the Department of Crime, Law, and Justice at Penn State University.

Katherine Hooper Briar formerly taught in the School of Social Work at the University of Washington.

Robert J. Bursik, Jr. is a professor in the Department of Criminology and Criminal Justice at the University of Missouri at St. Louis.

Kitty Calavita is a professor in the Department of Criminology, Law, and Society at the University of California at Irvine.

William Chambliss is a professor in the Department of Sociology at George Washington University.

Meda Chesney-Lind is a professor in the Women's Studies Program at the University of Hawaii at Manoa.

George F. Cole is Professor Emeritus in the Department of Political Science at the University of Connecticut.

The late **Donald R. Cressey** was a professor in the Department of Sociology at the University of California at Santa Barbara.

Steven R. Donziger is director of the National Center on Institutions and Alternatives (NCIA).

Delbert S. Elliott is a professor in the Department of Sociology and director of the Institute of Behavioral Research at the University of Colorado.

Diana H. Fishbein is an associate professor in the Department of Criminal Justice at the University of Baltimore.

Michael Geerken is the chief administrative officer in the Orleans Parish Criminal Sheriff's Department, New Orleans.

Gilbert Geis is Professor Emeritus at the University of California at Irvine.

Walter R. Gove is a professor in the Department of Sociology at Vanderbilt University.

Harold G. Grasmick is a professor in the Department of Sociology at the University of Oklahoma.

John M. Hagedorn is an assistant professor in the Department of Criminal Justice at the University of Illinois at Chicago.

Miles D. Harer is a research analyst in the Office of Research and Evaluation at the Federal Bureau of Prisons in Washington, D.C.

Darnell F. Hawkins is a professor in the Department of Sociology at the University of Illinois at Chicago.

Travis Hirschi is a Regents Professor in the Department of Sociology at the University of Arizona.

Michael Hughes is an associate professor in the Department of Sociology at Virginia Polytechnic Institute and State University.

David Huizinga is a senior research associate at the Institute of Behavioral Research, located at the University of Colorado.

James A. Inciardi is a professor in the Department of Sociology and Criminal Justice and is Director of the Center for Drug and Alcohol Studies at the University of Delaware.

Gary F. Jensen is a professor and the chair in the Department of Sociology at Vanderbilt University.

Maryaltani Karpos is an instructor in the Department of Sociology at the University of Miami in Florida.

Carl B. Klockars is a professor in the Department of Sociology and Criminal Justice at the University of Delaware.

John H. Laub is a professor in the Department of Criminal Justice and Criminology at the University of Maryland.

Paul Mazerolle is an assistant professor in the Department of Criminal Justice at the University of Cincinnati.

Joan McCord is a professor in the Department of Criminal Justice at Temple University.

The late **Henry D. McKay** was affiliated with the Department of Sociology at the University of Chicago.

Robert F. Meier is a professor in the Department of Sociology at Iowa State University.

Terrie E. Moffitt is a professor in the Department of Psychology at the University of Wisconsin at Madison.

Raymond Paternoster is a professor in the Department of Criminal Justice and Criminology at the University of Maryland.

Anthony Platt is a professor in the Department of Social Work at California State University.

Henry N. Pontell is a professor and chair of the Department of Criminology, Law, and Society at the University of California at Irvine.

JoAnn Ray is Professor Emeritus in the Inland Empire School of Social Work at Eastern Washington University.

Jeffrey Reiman is William Fraser McDowell Professor of Philosophy at American University.

Albert J. Reiss, Jr., is Professor Emeritus in the Department of Sociology at Yale University.

John Rosecrance was formerly in the Department of Criminal Justice at the University of Nevada at Reno.

Jeffrey A. Roth is a senior research analyst at the Urban Institute, in Washington, D.C.

Robert J. Sampson is a professor in the Department of Sociology at the University of Chicago.

Frank R. Scarpitti is a professor in the Department of Sociology and Criminal Justice at the University of Delaware.

The late **Clifford R. Shaw** was affiliated with the Department of Sociology at the University of Chicago.

Lynnell J. Simonson is a graduate student in the Department of Sociology at Iowa State University.

Mark Stafford is a professor in the Department of Sociology at the University of Texas at Austin.

Darrell J. Steffensmeier is a professor in the Department of Sociology at Penn State University.

Cathy Streifel teaches at Indiana University Northwest at Kokomo.

The late **Edwin H. Sutherland** was a professor in the Department of Sociology at Indiana University at Bloomington.

Charles R. Tittle is a professor in the Department of Sociology at Washington State University.

Michael Tonry is affiliated with the Castine Research Corporation in Castine, Maine.

Kenneth D. Tunnell teaches in the Department of Police Studies at Eastern Kentucky University.

Samuel Walker is a professor in the Department of Criminal Justice at the University of Nebraska at Omaha.

Mark Warr is a professor in the Department of Sociology at the University of Texas at Austin.

Cathy Spatz Widom is a professor in the School of Criminal Justice at the University at Albany.

Richard A. Wright is an assistant professor in the Department of Criminology, Sociology, Social Work, and Geography at Arkansas State University. ✦

Section I

Defining Crime

Most U.S. citizens believe there is far too much crime in our society, even if they do not know that about one major crime is committed every two seconds and one violent crime every 18 seconds. Knowing such facts would probably elevate one's already heightened fear of crime, a fear that has been growing in recent years. Fear of crime undermines the very quality of our lives, making us suspicious of one another, restricting our willingness to walk city streets, and increasing our demand for harsh penalties. But what is it that we fear? What is crime?

Ask the woman passing on the street, who may feel certain she knows what it is. An ordinary citizen would probably define crime as any one of a number of actions, such as rape, murder, robbery, assault, burglary, and a host of others. All of these might be included in the broad category of conventional, or street crime. They might also include vandalism, disturbing the peace, driving while intoxicated, and traffic offenses such as speeding, running a red light, or reckless driving. An informed citizen might even include the relatively newly defined crimes of marital and date rape, stalking, and computer fraud, as well as currently well-publicized crimes such as child abuse, spousal battering, elder abuse, nonpayment of child support, and credit card fraud. This list, in all probability, would include primarily crime featured in the popular media, which mention few, if any, white-collar, corporate, or political "crimes."

Not all crime seems to arouse the fear associated with conventional personal and property violations. Although average citizens know far less about white-collar and corporate crimes than about street crimes, they view them as less threatening and frightening even when they are aware of them. Corporate executives who rig bids on government contracts or who knowingly manufacture defective cars that may cause thousands of accidents and deaths are not defined as criminals in the same way that burglars or purse snatchers are. Similarly, public officials who accept bribes to overlook some wrongdoing or to help a friend obtain a lucrative government contract tend not to be seen as criminals, although such crimes may involve greater financial loss and greater potential personal harm than do street crimes.

The Legal Definition of Crime

This first section of the book will begin the study of crime and criminals by considering what is legally defined as crime and why. Most studies of law-violating behavior are based on a legal definition of the phenomenon; nevertheless, it is important to consider nonlegal definitions as well. Although nonlegal definitions do not determine the actions of the criminal justice system, they allow the student of crime to explore the ramifications

1

of potentially harmful, even deadly, behavior that the criminal law ignores. The same law, however, does not apply to all violators, because juveniles are governed by different statutes and treated differently by the state in view of their age. This distinction says a great deal about American society's definition of justice. Lastly, where do victims fit into the definition of crime and the application of law and order? Understanding these issues and the questions they raise provides the foundation needed for a knowledge of crime and criminals.

The legal definition of crime is relatively straightforward. Simply stated, a crime is any action that is in violation of law, or criminal statutes. Edwin H. Sutherland refers to crime as "behavior which is prohibited by the State and against which the State may react" (1949: 31). Paul W. Tappan says, "Crime is an intentional act or omission in violation of criminal law (statutory and case law), committed without defense or justification, and sanctioned by the state as a felony or misdemeanor" (1960: 10). Acts of omission, such as not reporting a felony of which one has been made aware, even if not personally involved, add a dimension to the definition of crime that the average citizen seldom thinks of.

Crime is a social construction; that is, what is defined as criminal behavior depends on the subjective meaning we attach to the behavior. No behavior is criminal until it is defined as such. Therefore, the definition of acts as criminal or non-criminal is not consistent across jurisdictions or time. That is why paparazzi in France could be charged with a crime for failing to assist persons in need (the 1997 car crash involving Princess Diana and Dodi Fayed), while in the United States such failure would not be a crime at all. It is also why actions not previously defined as criminal become crimes with the passage of new legislation (e.g., the Harrison Act, which outlawed most narcotics and cocaine), and why some actions previously considered to be crimes no longer are (e.g., distilling alcohol was no longer illegal following the repeal of Prohibition). Additionally, there is political and social ambivalence toward many crimes, which is why many crimes that have been on the books for years are no longer enforced (certain adult sexual activities) or are enforced sporadically (prostitution, small- time gambling).

Social context is an important factor that must also be considered. Some actions, such as killing, are not considered a crime in all situations—killing is not murder when carried out by police officers in the line of duty, when the state carries out the death penalty, or when carried out by soldiers in times of war. The social context and circumstances involved in a situation are thus important for whether an act is defined as a crime. As we see, even the simple legal definition of crime is fraught with inconsistencies and ambiguities. The examples above are only a small sample of the problems inherent in defining crime and reaching any agreement about these definitions.

The reason some acts are defined as crime in the first place is that they are believed to be deviant, outside society's boundaries of acceptable behavior. Although all crime is considered deviant, not all deviance is criminal. What differentiates behavior defined as crime from deviant behavior generally? Deviance is determined by a group or a society through a social and political process. Rules and laws are a response to individual behaviors and actions that the group disapproves of or perceives as harmful to its well-being. According to Kai Erickson, society imposes sanctions for actions it considered dangerous, embarrassing, or irritating to the group; society labels deviance and deviants. Deviant behavior deemed very offensive or antisocial is usually codified by law. Criminal law, therefore, addresses behavior that is considered detrimental to society in general, behavior that may compromise the "safety and order of the state" (Inciardi 1987: 50). Codified laws represent society's strongest negative feelings about individual behavior. Although it might appear from this perspective that the most harmful actions are prohibited by law, many experts think some of the worst offenses, often falling into the categories of corporate or political wrongdoing, are not defined as crime at all.

Once an action is defined as a crime, it is thought of as more precise and more specific than natural law or moral concepts. Criminal statutes share four characteristics that distinguish them from civil statutes or other rules of conduct: politicality (created by a constitutionally authorized body), penalty (a state-imposed punishment for a crime), specificity (strict definition of a crime and its penalty), and uniformity (applied equally to everyone in the jurisdiction) (see Reading 1).

Making Law

Three different perspectives suggest differing reasons that some behaviors are declared criminal and others not: conflict, pluralistic, and value consensus. Many theorists share the conflict perspective, which argues that laws in general reflect the values and protect the interests of the politicians, the wealthy, the powerful, the corporate leaders, and other elites, who have historically and overwhelmingly been white, male, older, middle or upper class, and often Protestant. According to conflict theorists, "law originated with the emergence of social inequality" (Bierne and Messerschmidt 1991: 23), and its purpose is to permit the socially powerful to control those who might challenge their privileged position. This perspective can be seen in the prevalence of civil penalties instead of criminal penalties in instances of corporate wrongdoing. It can be seen in the populations of our prisons, where most inmates have been convicted of conventional street crimes rather than white-collar or corporate crimes, and those few who are convicted of white-collar crimes tend to go to "country club" prisons, rather than maximum-security prisons, where violence, racial tensions, overcrowding, and other unsavory conditions are common. It can also be seen in the great multitude of laws created to protect private property, the cornerstone of capitalist economies, or to maintain the status quo (see reading Two). Indeed, many theorists view early rape laws as being aimed at protecting the property of the male (i.e., his wife) rather than protecting the female from harm. Whether or not one wholly subscribes to this theory, at the very least it can be observed that "those social classes who control the resources of society are more likely to have their interests represented by the state through the criminal law than are any and all other social groups" (Chambliss 1974: 8–9). At the same time, it must be acknowledged that many laws, such as those outlawing assault or murder, are good for the entire society.

According to the pluralistic perspective, law results from struggle by competing groups for the legal protection of their economic, social, and moral interests (Voigt et al. 1994). This view may be observed in the creation of Prohibition, which, according to Joseph R. Gusfield, reflected not only Protestant beliefs but also the efforts of the declining Federalist "aristocracy," as well as "native" (as opposed to immigrant or ethnic) Americans, to maintain their status by enacting laws outlawing the consumption of alcoholic beverages. Alcohol was customarily used and abused by the outgroups, such as the Irish, whose status they were attempting to diminish.

The third view of law creation, the value-consensus perspective, postulates law is based on the social contract, by which everyone concedes some freedoms in exchange for the good of the entire society. In this view, law supports the values and norms of society. Changes in the laws that uphold these norms can occur as a result of the efforts of special-interest groups, the efforts of an individual, or a triggering event and a resulting public grassroots outcry. Herbert Blumer suggests that there are five stages to this process, starting with the emergence of a problem, continuing with an awareness campaign through mass media, and ending with the implementation of a solution or response. Marital rape, a once inconceivable offense, began to be perceived as a crime after a woman in the state of Oregon brought divorce proceedings against her husband, accusing him of raping her during the course of their marriage (*State v. Rideout* 1978, Oregon). "Megan's law," requiring released sexual molesters of children to register with local law enforcement officials, came about as the result of a massive campaign spearheaded by outraged citizens when seven-year-old Megan Kanka of New Jersey was raped and murdered by a convicted sex offender living in her neighborhood.

In an ever changing society, laws are made, changed, or repealed in response to perceived needs, changing attitudes, public opinion, political rhetoric, special-interest groups, investigative reporting, and other catalysts. As technology changes and society evolves, conditions may be perceived to be a social problem, and new laws are created. According to Roscoe Pound (1994), laws grow out of "social, economic, and psychological conditions." Laws can be created as a result of political pressures, maneuvers, and campaign issues. Crime first became a major political issue in 1964, when Barry Goldwater made it a key platform plank in his presidential campaign against Lyndon Johnson. This political ploy, aimed at making Johnson appear responsible for a perceived increase in the rate of crime, caused Johnson to create his President's Commission on Law Enforcement and Administration of Justice (President's Crime Commission) in 1965 and led to the passage of the Omnibus Crime Control and Safe Streets Act of 1968. This act appeared to have the political goal of soothing the public's fear of crime and their attitudes toward recent Supreme Court decisions that were perceived as giving offenders too many rights at the expense of the police.

Laws are often a belated response to advances in technology. This delay may be seen as legislatures' and courts' struggle to deal with sophisticated computer crimes, assisted suicide, advanced fertilization techniques, surrogate parents, frozen sperm, cloning, medical procedures such as organ transplants, and the medical use of marijuana.

Some laws are created as a response to the nonuniform enforcement of other laws. Perhaps the best example is the creation of federal "violation of civil rights" laws, which compensate for the lack of convictions by state courts for racially motivated violent crimes. Because criminal laws permit a penalty only after a crime has actually been committed, stalking laws were created in an effort to charge offenders with a crime before they are able to do something much worse to their victims.

Laws are created by legislatures, both state and federal, and all laws are subject to the conditions spelled out in the federal Constitution, despite the fact that only one specific crime—treason—is mentioned in it. State laws are also subject to the constitutions of the individual state. Laws may vary from one jurisdiction to another; a crime in one state may not be a crime in another.

Laws are also clarified and refined by the courts, especially the U.S. Supreme Court. The Supreme Court interprets the Constitution, decisions from the lower courts, and previous Supreme Court cases. Although the Supreme Court, or any court, does not have the power to create the laws, the Court's interpretation of the Constitution and of legislative intent often has the same effect. Since Supreme Court justices are presidential appointees, presidents who have the opportunity to fill a number of Supreme Court vacancies have the potential to have the tenets of their particular party reflected in Supreme Court decisions for years to come.

Most of the processes mentioned above apply to laws governing an individual's behavior. Administrative law, the rules and guidelines of administrative agencies, generally governs corporate behavior. Persons staffing these agencies are often from the ranks of those who identify with big business; sometimes they are retirees from the very corporations they regulate. It is not unusual for corporate officers to be drawn from the ranks of the governing agencies. This practice gives some insight into why cases of corporate deviance are seldom treated as crime.

Nonlegal Definitions of Crime

The social philosopher Jeffrey Reiman contends that "Many of the ways in which the well-off harm their fellows (deadly pollution, unsafe working conditions, and the like) are not even defined as crimes though they do more damage to life and limb than the acts that are treated as crimes" (1998: viii) Those agreeing with him generally hold that the definition of "crime" should be much broader than the legal definition (see reading Three).

There are good reasons for this view, ranging from the altruistic to the practical. For one thing, social scientists would not then be limited to definitions provided by other fields, such as law or politics. They would be free to speculate and conduct research in areas far beyond those covered in the statutes.

They could illuminate areas of deviance and harm that could be covered by criminal laws but that are not, due to the interests of those who control the law-making process. By extending the definition of crime, social scientists would be able to "uncover injustices for purposes of reform" (Voigt et al. 1994: 36) and to discover "wrongs which are absolute and eternal rather than mere violations of a statutory and case law system which vary in time and place" (Tappan 1947: 96).

Broadening the definition of crime also frees social scientists from the biases against race and class that are inherent in the criminal law, which deals primarily with conventional, or street crimes. It allows them to look at crime not only as a working-class phenomenon, but also as misdeeds by those of upper socioeconomic status (Greenberg, 1993). In other words, a broad definition puts the relative danger or harm of conventional crimes in perspective. Above all, it keeps the field of criminology from being "a status quo handmaiden of political systems" (Hagan 1994: 17) by allowing criminologists to examine the ways in which laws are created and the forces behind the laws, instead of just accepting them at face value. In this way, social scientists are forced to look beyond the punishment of the offender to the structural elements that contribute to the definitions of what constitutes crime in the first place.

Piers Bierne and James Messerschmidt identify four specific sociological definitions of crime: "(1) crime as a violation of conduct norms, (2) crime as a social harm, (3) crime as a violation of human rights, and (4) crime as a form of deviance" (1991: 16). Conduct norms, a concept described by Thorsten Sellin, include normal and abnormal forms of conduct, varying, of course, from group to group. Although it would not be possible to study all abnormal forms, Sellin proposes that at the very least we should question why some of these are considered to be crime and some are not.

Crime as social harm incorporates Sutherland's ideas about white-collar crime, namely that since white-collar offenses cause harm and are punishable by fines, they meet the criteria for being defined as a crime. Crime as a violation of human rights would include any action violating one's "natural and inalienable rights," or injuries resulting from "imperialism, sexism, racism and poverty" (Bierne and Messerschmidt 1991: 18–19). Finally, crime as a form of deviance would include any acts violating social norms for which an individual is penalized. As pointed out, not all deviant acts are labeled as crime. But the concept brings up important questions regarding why some acts are regarded as deviant, who defines the behavior, what the consequences of an act for the individual are, and why certain deviant acts are criminal and certain other deviant acts are not.

Juvenile Justice

In the U.S. criminal justice system, juveniles constitute a special class and usually receive special treatment. This custom has not always been so. Before the sixteenth century, children were regarded as little adults (Hart 1991); as such, they were tried in adult courts and thrown into jails with adults. "Children were ignored, abandoned, abused, sold into slavery, and mutilated" (Hart 1991: 53). During the sixteenth, seventeenth, and eighteenth centuries, children were considered chattel; their value was in what they could contribute economically to the family. They were replaceable and interchangeable. During the eighteenth century, children began to be regarded as a special class, and parents were expected to assume responsibility for their maintenance, education, and protection. Schools were also given some responsibility for the welfare of children. Laws were created to handle difficult children. Children, though still regarded as property, were now regarded as valuable and vulnerable property.

In the nineteenth century, children were regarded as innately good (as Jean Jacques Rousseau taught), innately sinful (the Calvinist theory), or neither good nor evil but malleable (according to John Locke) (Hart: 1991). People began to believe that the protection and care that a child received could influence him or her one way or the other, and so the child began to assume more importance, to be regarded as not just a throwaway, interchangeable commodity, but as a person to be cared for. In the United States, a variety of public and private agencies began to work for the improvement of family life (see reading Four).

By the start of the twentieth century, the child-as-redeemer theory had come into play. From this perspective, the child was regarded as a valuable human resource who would "determine the future of society" (Hart, 1991, p. 53). This belief fostered a number of reform movements in the United States, including the advocating of a juvenile court system. The Juvenile Court Act created the first court for children and adolescents in Illinois in 1899.

The juvenile court was ushered in hand in hand with the idea of *parens patriae*. This concept determined that the child was entitled to certain rights of care and nurturing, and if the parent was not providing these things, or if there was no parent, the state would, in effect, become the parent for the purpose of protecting and providing for the child and guiding him or her in the right direction. It was this principle that caused the juvenile courts to be set up quite differently from adult courts. Where it was the purpose of adult courts to determine guilt and punish the guilty, it was the purpose of juvenile courts to protect and treat the child, without attaching the stigma of a criminal label (Drowns and Hess 1990). Originally, a child was defined as an individual under the age of eighteen, or under the age of twenty-one who had committed a delinquent act before age eighteen.

Children may be heard in a juvenile court for both offenses that would be crimes if committed by adults and in a number of states for "status offenses," or actions that would not be considered criminal if committed by an adult. Status offenses include running away from home, incorrigibility, and truancy. Under the philosophy of the juvenile justice system, proceedings are informal and private: the court does not release information to the press, and at the age of majority a child's court records are supposed to be sealed. Children cannot be sent to adult jails and prisons except under special circumstances and unique legal provisions, and in most states they cannot be given the death penalty. Correctional alternatives often include releasing them into the custody of their parents, or sending them to a facility for juveniles.

Even the language of a juvenile court differs from that of an adult court in order to avoid giving the impression of a criminal proceeding. A child is taken into custody, not arrested; has an adjudicatory hearing, not a trial; is held in detention, not jail; is petitioned, not accused or indicted; has a preliminary inquiry, not an arraignment; is found delinquent, not guilty; receives an adjudication, not a conviction; receives a disposition, not a sentence; receives aftercare, not parole, and so on (Drowns and Hess 1990).

Because the proceedings are not considered criminal and the court is cast in the role of parent, it is felt that the court is watching out for the best interests of the child; therefore, for many years, children had no constitutional procedural rights such as those guaranteed to adults. Because the court was nonadversarial, there appeared to be no need for the right to counsel, the right to remain silent, the right to confront witnesses, and other constitutional guarantees. Thus, children often received "treatment" out of proportion to their acts; they were confined to juvenile facilities for long periods for being status offenders, even for being abused or neglected (throwaways). Not only was their freedom taken away, but they were confined with more violent juvenile offenders, at risk of being bullied, abused, or injured in this setting as well.

Eventually, it came to people's attention that these children were receiving neither fair treatment nor the paternal protection of the state as had been assumed. They had the worst of both worlds: no treatment and no procedural rights. Supreme Court decisions, such as In Re *Gault, Kent v. The United States* and In Re *Winship* began to change this situation. Children received some rights, including the right to counsel, the privilege to defend themselves from self-incrimination, and the due-process right of proof beyond a reasonable doubt before being deprived of liberty. The only right they were denied (*McKeiver v. Pennsylvania*) was the right to a jury trial.

Although juveniles in the last 10 years have been receiving more of the legal rights enjoyed by adults, there has also been a shift toward the criminalization of many of the behaviors for which they are brought to court. This shift is changing the very face and function of the juvenile court. Instead of protecting the child, the court has pretty much washed its hands of the status offender, who may still need help, and has endorsed a get tough policy toward the delinquents who are left. During the 1990s many states have changed their laws to allow delinquents to be transferred to adult courts at younger and younger ages (Bartol and Bartol 1998), and some states are now allowing children to receive the death penalty. Although a growing number of states are demanding that violent offenders over fourteen years old be tried in criminal courts, there are instances of even younger children being tried as adults, usually for committing particularly heinous crimes.

According to some critics (Bartol and Bartol 1998), there are two current trends in attitudes toward justice for juveniles: (1) a law and order mentality, which includes tough new state and federal laws and a reluctance of courts to interfere with them, and (2) a retributive response toward seriously violent adolescents. From 1989 to 1993, the number of juvenile cases waived to adult court increased 41 percent. Thus the full circle can be seen, whereby children are once more regarded as little adults in the criminal justice system.

Victims of Crime

Ironically, the formal definition of crime does not mention victims, who are often considered the forgotten element in the criminal justice process. Who are the victims of crime? Statistically speaking some people have a greater likelihood than others of becoming the victims of conventional crime. (The odds even up a bit when considering white-collar crime; more people run the chance of being victimized by it.) In general, and for violent crimes in particular, victims are likely to be young (teenagers and young adults); male; African American or Latino;

poor; single, divorced, or separated; unemployed; a renter, and a city dweller (Voigt et al. 1994; see also National Commission 1969). Place of residence and socioeconomic status play a part, as does lifestyle. Lifestyles of the young make them especially vulnerable to street crime because they go out partying; use or are exposed to drugs, alcohol and gangs; and, in general, place themselves at greater risk.

Although most people are blameless in contributing to their becoming victims, others precipitate the crime in some way, either by carelessness or some deliberate act. Putting up with spousal abuse, starting a fight in a bar, or leaving one's keys in the ignition are examples of victims precipitating crimes. Such precipitation brings up some interesting possibilities. Marvin E. Wolfgang found that women are twice as likely to be the killer in victim-precipitated homicides as in homicides not precipitated by the victim. He thought that fact justified the "police thoroughly investigat[ing] every possibility of strong provocation by the male victim when he is slain by a female—and particularly . . . if the female is his wife" (1957). Studying the relationship between the victim and the offender helps society to understand, and perhaps even prevent, crimes.

Other people are victimized because they are more vulnerable, on account of their gender (female) or age (very young or old). Women are the usual victims of rapes and domestic violence. Although the elderly are not so frequently victimized compared to other age groups, they are greatly affected by the fear of crime, and when they are actually victims, the injury or loss may be more devastating because of their delicate physical condition or the marginal economic status of many elderly persons. Each year one million children are abused or neglected, one million are runaways (from dangerous situations), and one in five young females and one in ten young males are affected by sexual abuse (Voigt et al. 1994). Children who are not abused themselves are often the psychological victims of their parents' spousal abuse.

Who cares about the victim? In preindustrial societies, victims and their families played a direct role in meting out retribution or in receiving compensation for a wrong committed against them. But as society grew more complex and diverse, it was no longer in the best interests of the state to allow people to carry out personal vendettas or take the law into their own hands. Over time, the government replaced the victim as the wronged or injured party in crime. The victim's role was reduced to making the crime known and testifying in court. Punishment became the purview of the state. Victims were overlooked, and little thought was given to their pain and loss, inconvenience (missing work to appear in court), trauma, fear, stigma, medical expenses, health, and other detrimental effects of the crime. Some victims were treated so poorly by the system that it was akin to being victimized twice, first by the offender, and then by the system.

One frequent response is that of blaming the victim, a practice engaged in by almost everyone, from the offender to the victim. Domestic violence offers a particularly poignant example of this tendency. The offender invariably blames the victim ("Now see what you made me do"), the authorities often think the offender was provoked, and the victim herself (victims are usually women) begins to see herself as the problem ("If I'd just kept the kids quiet," or "If I hadn't burned the dinner," "Now look what I've made him do"). Blaming themselves is one reason why some women do not leave abusive relationships. Outsiders, too, often blame the victim, deciding it is her fault, there is something wrong with her if she does not leave, and even, perhaps subconsciously, she wishes to be beaten (Goode, 1990). If the police blame the victim, they are strongly tempted not to intervene or make an arrest.

In rape cases, blaming and attempting to discredit the victim are common. Rapists justify their actions by asserting, "All women want to be raped," "No woman can be raped against her will," or "She was asking for it," (Brownmiller, 1975, p. 311). According to Diana Scully and Joseph Marolla (1993: 103), several common themes appear in rape justification: "(1) women as seductresses; (2) women mean 'yes' when they say 'no'; (3) most women eventually relax and enjoy it; (4) nice girls don't get raped" (1993, p. 103) Un-

fortunately, it is not only rapists who blame the victims. Unsympathetic spouses, the general public, and law enforcement officials often wonder, to one degree or another, if or how the victim contributed to her victimization: Was she dressed provocatively? Did she lead him on? Did she willingly participate then cry "rape" when she was caught or regretted her decision? Often the victim wonders what she has done to provoke the rape. In court, she feels as if she is on trial, as the defense brings up things from her past and lifestyle that cast aspersion on her character. Similar facts about the victim are often reported in the media.

Police sometimes refuse to make arrests in domestic disputes (instead telling the husband to cool off) and in situations that seem to involve a homosexual relationship. A young boy would be alive today if police officers had not taken him back to a violent, homosexual (and deadly!) situation with Jeffrey Dahmer.

With the advent of the victims' rights movement, a number of advances have been made in the general attitude toward victims and the general willingness to assist them where possible (see reading Five). Stalking laws have been created in order to keep potential victims from greater harm. Victim-impact statements are often allowed in the sentencing phase of criminal trials. Victim advocacy groups, such as Mothers Against Drunk Driving (MADD), influence legislation that affects victims, and draw media attention to problems (such as drunk driving) that affect victims. Some cities have encouraged citizen groups to patrol neighborhoods at night in order to decrease crime. In some instances, victims may receive restitution (payment to the victim by the criminal) or compensation (assistance from government agencies for expenses incurred as a result of being a victim). Battered women's shelters have been opened to give women and their children a chance to escape from abusive mates. Most states have passed rape-shield laws to protect the private lives of rape victims who testify against their attackers in court.

In some cases, police departments have created victim-assistance units. For example, the Rochester (New York) Police Department has two: Victim Assistance Unit and Family Crisis Intervention Team (FACIT) (Roberts 1990). The Victim Assistance Unit, started in 1975, provides various services for victims, such as notification of legal court proceedings, transportation, filing for compensation for personal property damaged during a crime, and accompaniment to court (especially when the victim is afraid of or intimidated by the offender). FACIT is a crisis intervention unit, which follows up, often by going to victims' homes to prevent bad situations from deteriorating. FACIT counselors provide liaisons between clients and agencies that offer services and counseling pertinent to their problems, and it intervenes on the spot when necessary.

Though some people still claim that criminals enjoy more rights than victims do, victims have made headway in being acknowledged and in many instances helped. A number of recent changes in legal statutes and judicial procedures indicate that the law does care about victims. No changes, however, will prevent victims of crime from wondering why they were chosen to be victimized and why society did not protect them from harm.

Crime, the violation of legal statutes, exists because those with constitutional authority enact certain values into law. Understanding the law-making process becomes essential, then, to knowing why some behaviors are criminalized and others are not. Nonlegal definitions of crime, used mainly by researchers and those advocating social change, expand the range of behavior considered criminal and raise questions about the extent to which law serves all segments of society. Although the uniform application of criminal law is one of its tenets, it is applied differentially to juveniles because of their age. Although the definition of crime implies that an act is considered a crime because of the harm it does, victims of crime are often overlooked by the justice system. In the readings that follow, each of these issues pertaining to the question, "What is crime?" is examined in greater detail.

References

Bartol, Curt R. and Anne M. Bartol. 1998. *Delinquency and Justice: A Psychological Approach* (2nd Edition). Upper Saddle River, NJ: Prentice-Hall.

Bierne, Piers and James Messerschmidt. 1991. *Criminology*. San Diego: Harcourt Brace Jovanovich.

Blumer, Herbert. 1971. "Social Problems as Collective Behavior," *Social Problems* 18:298-306.

Brownmiller, Susan. 1975. *Against Our Will: Men, Women and Rape*. New York: Simon and Schuster.

Chambliss, William J. 1974. "The State, the Law, and the Definition of Behavior as Criminal or Delinquent." In D. Blaser (ed.), *Handbook of Criminology*, New York: Rand-McNally.

Drowns, Robert W. and Karen M. Hess. 1990. *Juvenile Justice*. Saint Paul, MI: West.

Erickson, Kai T. 1966. *Wayward Puritans: A Study in the Sociology of Deviance*. New York: Wiley.

Goode, Erich. 1990. *Deviant Behavior* (3rd Edition). Englewood Cliffs, NJ: Prentice Hall.

Greenberg, David F., ed. 1993. *Crime and Capitalism: Readings in Marxist Criminology*. Philadelphia: Temple University Press.

Gusfield, Joseph R. 1986. *Symbolic Crusade: Status Politics and the American Temperance Movement* (2nd ed.). Urbana, IL: University of Illinois Press.

Hagan, Frank E. 1994. *Introduction to Criminology* (3rd ed.). Chicago: Nelson-Hall.

Hart, Stuart N. 1991. "From Property to Person Status: Historical Perspective on Children's Rights," *American Psychologist*, 46:53-59.

Inciardi, James A. 1987. *Criminal Justice* (2nd ed.). San Diego: Harcourt Brace Jovanovich.

National Commission on the Causes and Prevention of Violence. 1969. "Violent Crime: Homicide, Assault, Rape, Robbery," *To Establish Justice and Ensure Domestic Tranquility, Final Report of the National Commission*. Washington, DC: Government Printing Office.

Pound, Roscoe. 1994. "The Scope and Purpose of Sociological Jurisprudence." In John Monahan, and Laurens Walker, eds. *Social Science in Law: Cases and Materials* (3rd ed.). Westbury, CT: The Foundation Press.

Reiman, Jeffrey. 1998. *The Rich Get Richer and the Poor Get Prison: Ideology, Class, and Criminal Justice* (5th ed.). Boston: Allyn and Bacon.

Roberts, Albert R. 1990. *Helping Crime Victims: Research, Policy, and Practice*. Newbury Park, CA: Sage.

Scully, Diana and Joseph Marolla. 1993. "Convicted Rapists' Vocabulary of Motive: Excuses and Justifications." In H. Delos Kelley, ed. *Deviant Behavior: A Text-Reader in the Sociology of Deviance* (4th ed.). New York: St. Martin's.

Sutherland, Edwin H. 1949. *White Collar Crime*. New York: Dryden.

Tappan, Paul W. 1947. "Who is the Criminal?" *American Sociological Review*, 12:92-102.

Tappan, Paul W. 1960. *Crime, Justice and Correction*. New York: McGraw-Hill.

Voigt, Lydia, William E. Thornton, Jr., Leo Barrile, Jerrol M. Seaman. 1994. *Criminology and Justice*. New York: McGraw-Hill.

Wolfgang, Marvin E. 1957. "Victim-Precipitated Criminal Homicide," *Journal of Criminal Law, Criminology, and Police Science*, 48:1-11. ✦

1

Characteristics of the Criminal Law

Edwin H. Sutherland
Donald R. Cressey

It *is fitting that the classic definition of crime, offered in the following excerpt, be presented by two legendary criminologists, Edwin H. Sutherland and Donald R. Cressey. As they explain, crime emanates from the criminal law, a body of rules containing unique characteristics that differentiate it from other rules and regulations found in a society. Although crime is the codification of social values shared by those possessing political authority, it is variable in nature, changing from time to time and place to place. Nevertheless, unlike personal grievances or individual wrongs, crime is believed to do social harm, harm that threatens the entire group or the social order. For that reason the state becomes the injured party in a crime, and it is the state that uses its power to control crime and punish criminal offenders.*

At the same time that Sutherland and Cressey present the legal definition of crime, discuss those characteristics that differentiate it from civil, or tort, law, and establish its legal parameters, they also point out that this definition represents an ideal type that may be difficult to find in reality. This definition of crime may satisfy certain legal requirements, but it is difficult to make behavioral sense of it. The term crime represents broad categories of behavior that are vastly different in nature and motive, often sharing little more than violation of the criminal code. When grouping crimes into broad, general categories, such as felony and misdemeanor, important behavioral differences are lost and offenders may be judged on inaccurate and misleading criteria. The legal definition of crime prevails, however, in structuring the discipline of criminology.

Criminal behavior is behavior in violation of the criminal law. No matter what the degree of immorality, reprehensibility, or indecency of an act, it is not a crime unless it is prohibited by the criminal law. The criminal law, in turn, is defined conventionally as a body of specific rules regarding human conduct which have been promulgated by political authority, which apply uniformly to all members of the classes to which the rules refer, and which are enforced by punishment administered by the state. The characteristics which distinguish the body of rules regarding human conduct from other rules are, therefore, *politicality, specificity, uniformity,* and *penal sanction.* However, these are characteristics of an ideal, completely rational system of criminal law; in practice the differences between the criminal law and other bodies of rules for human conduct are not clear-cut. Also, the ideal characteristics of the criminal law are only rarely features of the criminal law in action.

The vast majority of the rules which define certain behavior as crime are found in constitutions, treaties, common law, enactments by the legislatures of the state and its subdivisions, and in judicial and administrative regulations. However, the criminal law is not merely a collection of written proscriptions. The agencies of enforcement are the police and the courts, and these agencies, rather than the legislature, determine what the law is. According to one school of thought, police and courts merely "apply" the law in an evenhanded manner to all persons who come before them. However, both the techniques used by justice administrators in interpreting and applying the statutes and the body of ideals held by them are a part of the law in action, as truly as are the written statutes.

The court decision in one controversy becomes a part of the body of rules used in making decisions in other controversies. Consequently, law students must read court decisions in order to learn law. Further evidence supporting this view that the courts as well as the legislatures make law is found whenever the nation is confronted with the problem of selecting a justice of the Supreme Court. At such times it is explicitly recognized that the nature of the law itself, not merely its administration, is determined to a considerable extent by the proportion of liberals and conservatives on the supreme bench. Thus, behind the behavior of courts is public opinion. Also, between the courts and the legislature are intermediate agencies such as the police. Many statutes are never enforced; some are enforced only on rare occasions; others are enforced with a striking disregard for uniformity. Enforcement and administrative agencies are affected by shifts in public opinion, budget allocations, and in power. As a consequence, the law often changes while the statutes remain constant.

Politicality is regarded almost universally as a necessary element in criminal law. The rules of the trade union, the church, or the family are not regarded as criminal law, nor are violations of these rules regarded as crimes. Only violations of rules made by the state are crimes. This distinction between the state and other groups is not only arbitrary but also is difficult to maintain when attention is turned to societies where patriarchal power, private self-help, popular justice, and other forerunners of legislative justice are found. This may be illustrated by the gypsies, who have no territorial organization and no written law, but who do have customs, taboos, a semijudicial council which makes definite decisions regarding the propriety of behavior of members of the group and often imposes penalties. These councils have no political authority in the territory in which they happen to be operating, but they perform the same function within the gypsy group that courts perform in the political order. Similarly, early Chinese immigrants in Chicago established an unofficial court which had no political authority, but which, in practice, exercised the functions of an authorized court in controversies among the Chinese people. The American "Cosa Nostra" has a legislative and judicial system for administering the functional equivalent of the criminal law among its members.[1] Thus, the element of politicality is arbitrary and is not sharply defined. The earlier systems of law, together with the present relation between public opinion and legal precepts, raise the question, When should the rules of a group

be regarded as the law and violations of these rules as crimes?[2]

Specificity is included as an element in the definition of criminal law because of the contrast in this respect between criminal law and civil law. The civil law may be general. An old German civil code, for instance, provided that whoever intentionally injured another in a manner contrary to the common standards of right conduct was bound to indemnify him. The criminal law, on the other hand, generally gives a strict definition of a specific act, and when there is doubt as to whether a definition describes the behavior of a defendant, the judge is obligated to decide in favor of the defendant. In one famous case, for example, the behavior of a person who had taken an airplane was held to be exempt from the consequences of violating a statute regarding the taking of "self-propelled vehicles," on the ground that at the time the law was enacted "vehicles" did not include airplanes.[3] Some laws, to be sure, are quite general, as the laws in regard to nuisances, conspiracy, vagrancy, disorderly conduct, use of the mails to defraud, and official misfeasance. The criminal law, however, contains no general provision that any act which, when done with culpable intent, injures the public can be prosecuted as a punishable offense.[4] Consequently it frequently happens that one act is prohibited by law while another act, which is very similar in nature and effects, is not prohibited and is not illegal.[5]

Uniformity or regularity is included in the conventional definition of criminal law because law attempts to provide evenhanded justice without respect to persons. This means that no exceptions are made to criminal liability because of a person's social status; an act described as a crime is crime, no matter who perpetrates it. Also, uniformity means that the law-enforcement process shall be administered without regard for the status of the persons who have committed crimes or are accused of committing crimes. This ideal is rarely followed in practice, principally because it results in injustices. Rigid rule is softened by police discretion and judicial discretion. Rigid rule treats all persons in the class to which the law refers exactly alike, while police and judicial discretion take cognizance of the circumstances of the offense and the characteristics of the offender, a process which has come to be called "individualization."[6] Much of what happens to persons accused of delinquency or crime is determined in a process of negotiation. Equity, also, developed as a method of doing justice in particular situations where iron regularity would not do justice. As precedents in equity have accumulated, the decisions tend to become uniform, and thus similar to law. In line with the present tendency toward judicial discretion, authority has been conferred by legislative assemblies upon many administrative bodies to make regulations applicable to particular situations such as length of prison term and parole.

Penal sanction, as one of the elements in the orthodox definition of law, refers to the notion that violators will be punished or, at least, threatened with punishment by the state. Punishment under the law differs from that imposed by a mob in that it is to be applied dispassionately by representatives of the state in such a manner that it may win the approval of the cool judgment of impartial observers. A law which does not provide a penalty that will cause suffering is regarded as quite impotent and, in fact, no criminal law at all. However, the punishment provided may be very slight; in the courts of honor a verdict was reached, a party was declared guilty, and the disgrace of the declaration of guilt was the only punishment. In view of the difficulty of identifying the criminal law of nonliterate societies, where the institution of "the state" is not obvious, the suggestion has been made that the penal sanction is the only essential element in the definition of criminal law, and that wherever proscriptions are enforced by a penal sanction, there criminal law exists. This is in contrast to the tort law, where the court orders the defendant to reimburse the plaintiff, but does not punish him for damaging the plaintiff.

The punitive aspect of criminal law clearly is on the wane. In the juvenile court and to a smaller extent in the criminal courts, the tendency is to discover and use methods which are effective in forestalling crime, whether they are punitive or not. By using juvenile court procedures, we have attempted to avoid applying the "stigma of crime" to the acts of children. In theory, the juvenile court does not determine the guilt or innocence of a criminal; it merely acts in behalf of a child who is in need of help. The court's objective is treatment, not the meting out of penalties. However, except for children who are called delinquent because they have been neglected, or are "predelinquent," juvenile delinquencies are acts which would be crimes if committed by an adult. Consequently, juvenile delinquencies continue to be acts which are punishable by law, even if the punishment is kept in the background,[7] Similarly, the states and the federal government for a generation or two have been enacting laws for the regulation of manufacturing, commerce, agriculture, and other occupations. The persons affected by such laws are ordinarily respectable and powerful, and the legislatures have adapted the procedures to the status of these persons. Violations of these laws are crimes, but they are not always tried in the criminal courts. Instead, they are handled in civil and equity courts or in administrative commissions; the conventional penalties of fine and imprisonment are kept in the background to be used only as a last resort, and coercion in the first instance consists of injunctions and cease-and-desist orders. Thus these persons of social importance avoid the "stigma of crime," just as, to a lesser degree, juvenile delinquents do. The acts remain as crimes, however, for they are punishable by law.[8]

The conventional view is that a crime is an offense against the state, while, in contrast, a tort in violation of civil law is an offense against an individual. A particular act may be considered as an offense against an individual and also against the state, and is either a tort or a crime or both according to the way it is handled. A person who has committed an act of assault, for example, may be ordered by the civil court to pay the victim a sum of $500 for the damages to his interests, and he may also be ordered by the criminal court to pay a fine of $500 to the state. The payment of the first $500 is not punishment, but payment of the second $500 is punishment.

This distinction between individual damage and social harm is extremely difficult to make in the legal systems of nonliterate societies, where court procedures are relatively informal. Even in modern society, the distinction is dubious, for it rests upon the assumption that "individual" and "group" or "state" are mutually exclusive. For practical purposes, the individual is treated as if he were autonomous, but in fact an act which harms an individual also harms the group in which he has membership. Also, in modern society the indefiniteness of the distinction between torts and crimes is apparent when the victim of an act which is both a tort and a crime uses the criminal law as a method of forcing restitution which could not be secured with equal facility in the civil courts. Prosecutors frequently complain about the use of the criminal law as a collecting agency, especially because the victim who is reimbursed by the offender prior to trial then refuses to act as a witness. . . .

The rules of criminal law contain only definitions of specific crimes, such as burglary, robbery, and rape, but legal scholars have been able to abstract certain general principles from such definitions. These general principles are said to apply to all crimes and are the criteria ideally used in determination of whether any particular behavior is or is not criminal. They are consistent with the ideal characteristics of the whole body of the criminal law—politicality, specificity, uniformity, and penal sanction—and, in fact, they may be viewed as translations of the ideal characteristics of the criminal law into statements of the ideal characteristics of all crimes. The concern is shifted from determination of the characteristics of a body of rules to determination of the general characteristics of the many specific acts described in those rules. Thus, for example, penal sanction is a general characteristic of the criminal law, and liability to legally prescribed punishment is a characteristic of all acts or omissions properly called crime. Obviously, a set of criteria used for deciding whether or not any specific act is a crime must be more precise than statements of the general characteristics of a body of rules.

One extensive and thorough analysis of crimes has resulted in a description of seven interrelated and overlapping differentiae of crime.[9] Ideally, behavior would not be called crime unless all seven differentiae were pre-

sent. The following brief description of the differentiae is greatly simplified.

First, before behavior can be called crime there must be certain external consequences or "harm." A crime has a harmful impact on social interests; a "mental" or emotional state is not enough. Even if one decides to commit a crime but changes his mind before he does anything about it, he has committed no crime. The intention is not taken for the deed.

Second, the harm must be legally forbidden, must have been proscribed in penal law. Antisocial behavior is not crime unless it is prohibited by law. As indicated previously, the law must have specifically prohibited the harm which occurs. Penal law does not have a retroactive effect; there is a long-standing tradition against the enactment of ex post facto legislation.

Third, there must be "conduct"; that is, there must be an intentional or reckless action or inaction which brings the harmful consequences about. One who is physically forced to pull the trigger of a gun does not commit murder, even if someone dies from the bullet.

Fourth, "criminal intent," or *mens rea*, must be present. Hall suggests that legal scholars have often confused intentionality (deliberate functioning to reach a goal) and motivation (the reasons or grounds for the end-seeking).[10] *Mens rea* is identified with the former, not with the latter. The "motives" for a crime might be "good," but the intention itself might be an intention to effect a harm forbidden by the criminal law, a criminal intent. Thus if a man decides to kill his starving children because he feels that they will pass on to a better world, his motive is good, but his intention is wrong. Persons who are "insane" at the time they perpetrate legally forbidden harms do not commit crimes, for the necessary *mens rea* is not present.[11]

Fifth, there must be a fusion or concurrence of *mens rea* and conduct. This means, for example, that a policeman who goes into a house to make an arrest and who then commits a crime while still in the house after making the arrest cannot be considered a trespasser from the beginning. The criminal intent and the conduct do not fuse or concur.

Sixth, there must be a "causal" relation between the legally forbidden harm and the voluntary misconduct. The "conduct" of one who fails to file an income tax return is his failure to take pen and ink, fill out the form, etc.; the "harm" is the absence of a return in the collector's office. In this case, the "causal" relation between the two obviously is present. But if, for example, one man shot another (conduct) and the victim suffocated while in a hospital recovering from the wound, the relationship between conduct and harm (death) is not so clear-cut.

Seventh, there must be legally prescribed punishment. Not only must the harm be proscribed by law but, as indicated above, the proscription must carry a threat of punishment to violators. The voluntary conduct must be punishable by law.

These differentiae of crime are all concerned with the nature of the behavior which can properly be called crime, but in making decisions about most cases each criterion need not be considered separately but individually. If the *mens rea*, conduct, the legally proscribed harm are obviously present, for example, the "causal" relation between harm and misconduct almost certainly will be present. In sum, the differentiae represent the kinds of subject matter with which both criminal lawyers and criminal-law theorists must deal.

There are, of course, many exceptions to the generalization that these are the elements of all crimes. Criminal-law theory is not a body of precise principles, and consequently there are deviations from that which is logical and ideal. For purposes of illustration, we may cite two major exceptions to the above differentiae.

First, criminal intent, in the ordinary meaning of the concept, need not be present for some crimes. In some cases—the so-called strict-liability cases—the offender's intent is not considered. Instead, the person is held responsible for the results of his conduct, regardless of his intention. The handling of "statutory rape" is a case in point—no matter how elaborate the calculations, inquiries, or research which a male utilizes in reaching the conclusion that his female companion is above the age of consent, if he has sexual relations with her and it is subsequently shown that she was below the age

of consent, he has committed statutory rape. Certain "public welfare" offenses, such as traffic offenses and the selling of adulterated food, are handled under the same rule. Similarly, under the "felony-murder–misdemeanor-manslaughter doctrine" defendants are held criminally liable for much more serious offenses that they intended to commit. If one sets fire to a building and a fireman dies trying to extinguish the flames, the offender is liable for murder; if the offense had been a misdemeanor rather than arson, he would have been liable for manslaughter.

Hall has severely criticized this doctrine and the general conception of strict liability in the criminal law. He contends that it is "bad law," stating that "there is no avoiding the conclusion that strict liability cannot be brought within the scope of penal law."[12] A behavioristic school in jurisprudence, however, insists that the intent can be determined only by the circumstances of the act, and that a translation of these circumstances into mental terms confuses rather than clarifies the procedure. It contends that the doctrine of *mens rea* should be greatly modified or even abandoned. In criminology, the inclusion in the concept "crime" of behavior which was not intended by the actor makes general theoretical explanation of all crime extremely difficult. No current theoretical explanation of criminal behavior can account for the strict-liability offenses.

Second, "motive" and "intention" are confused in many court decisions. In the crime of libel, for instance, motive is explicitly considered. In many states, one cannot publish truthful, albeit damaging, statements about another unless his motive is good. Criminal conspiracy also frequently involves consideration and evaluation of a defendant's motives as well as his intention. In most instances, however, motivation ideally is taken into account only in the *administration* of the criminal law, i.e., in making a decision as to the severity of the punishment which should be accorded a criminal.

Crime is relative from the legal point of view and also from the social point of view. The criminal law has had a constantly changing content. Many early crimes were primarily religious offenses, and these remained important until recent times; now few religious offenses are included in penal codes.[13] It was a crime in Iceland in the Viking age for a person to write verses about another, even if the sentiment was complimentary, if the verses exceeded four stanzas in length. A Prussian law of 1784 prohibited mothers and nurses from taking children under two years of age into their beds. The English villein in the fourteenth century was not allowed to send his son to school, and no one lower than a freeholder was permitted by law to keep a dog. The following have at different times been crimes: printing a book, professing the medical doctrine of circulation of the blood, driving with reins, sale of coin to foreigners, having gold in the house, buying goods on the way to market or in the market for the purpose of selling them at a higher price, writing a check for less than one dollar. On the other hand, many of our present laws were not known to earlier generations—quarantine laws, traffic laws, sanitation laws, factory laws.

Laws differ, also, from one jurisdiction to another at a particular time. The laws of some states require automobile owners to paste certificates of ownership or inspection certificates on the windshield, while adjoining states prohibit the pasting of anything on the windshield. Georgia has a $1,000 fine or six months' incarceration as the maximum penalty for adultery, while in Louisiana adultery is not a crime at all.[14]

In a particular jurisdiction at a particular time there are wide variations in the interpretation and implementation of the law. These variations are related to the specific characteristics of the crimes, to the status of the offenders, and to the status of the enforcers. Sudnow has shown that what is "burglary" or "robbery" or almost any other crime is highly negotiable.[15] Further, gross forms of fraud, such as those committed by confidence men, are easily detected by the regular police, but expert investigators must deal with the subtler forms of fraud which flourish in many areas of business and of the professions. When such experts are provided by politicians interested in making subtle fraud "real crime," what has been mere chicanery is interpreted and dealt with as crime. In this sense, also, crime is relative to the status of the criminals and the situations in which they violate law.

Since crime is not a homogenous type of behavior, efforts have been made to classify crimes. They are frequently classified in respect to atrocity as felonies and misdemeanors. The more serious are called felonies and are usually punishable by death or by confinement in a state prison; the less serious are called misdemeanors and are usually punishable by confinement in a local prison or by fines. As a classification of crimes this is not very useful, as was pointed out long ago by Sir James Stephen, and it is difficult to make a clear-cut distinction between the classes. Though one may agree that assaults, as a class, are more serious offenses than permitting weeds to grow on a vacant lot in violation of a municipal ordinance, the effects of permitting the weeds to grow, in a particular case, may be more serious because of the hay fever produced by the pollen and the resulting incapacitation of many people. The fact that many things which are classed as felonies in one state are classed as misdemeanors in nearby states shows how difficult it is to make a real distinction between them. Even within a single state the distinction is often vague.

The greatest objection to the classification of crimes as felonies and misdemeanors is that it is used also as a classification of criminals. The individual who commits a felony is a felon; the individual who commits a misdemeanor is a misdemeanant. It is assumed that misdemeanants are less dangerous and more susceptible to rehabilitative measures than felons. But it is quite fallacious to judge either dangerousness or the probability of reformation from one act, for an individual may commit a misdemeanor one week, a felony the second week, and a misdemeanor the third. The acts do not represent changes in his character or changes in his dangerousness.

Moreover, the definition of a crime as misdemeanor or felony is influenced by various considerations other than atrocity or dangerousness. Since 1852, when a felony was first defined in Massachusetts as a crime punishable by confinement in the state prison, at least four changes have been made in the laws of that state determining the conditions under which a sentence is served in state prison rather than in a jail or house of correction. These changes, which also changed crimes from felonies to misdemeanors or the reverse, were not made because of alterations in views regarding the atrocity of crimes but for purely administrative reasons, generally to relieve the congestion of the state prison. In the administration of justice, thousands of persons charged with committing felonies successfully arrange to have the charge reduced to a misdemeanor, and the distinction between the two classes of offense is lost. Consequently there seems to be good reason to abandon this classification. . . .

Discussion Questions

1. Which group (legislature, police, courts) exerts the most influence over the definition/interpretation of what law is? Do you agree/disagree with the authors' contention that it is not the legislature that really defines the law?

2. These authors discuss a number of ways in which police and courts affect the nature and intent of criminal law. Is it desirable for this to take place, or does this undermine the purpose and effects of criminal law?

3. What are some of the problems associated with the classification of crimes by type of crime and by seriousness of crime? How might differences in classification affect the offender, the court, and the prison?

Notes

1. See Jean-Paul Clebert, *The Gypsies*, trans. Charles Duff (London: Vista Books, 1963), pp. 123-33; and Donald R. Cressey, *Theft of the Nation: The Structure and Operations of Organized Crime in America* (New York: Harper and Row, 1969), pp. 162-220.

2. See E. Adamson Hoebel, *The Law of Primitive Man: A Study in Comparative Legal Dynamics* (Cambridge: Harvard University Press, 1954).

3. *McBoyle v. United States*, 283 U.S. 25 (1931).

4. A German law of June 28, 1935, seems to be an exception to this generalization. It provided: "Whoever commits an action which the law declares to be punishable or which is deserving of punishment according to the fundamental idea of a penal law and the sound perception of the people, shall be punished. If no determinate penal law is directly applicable to the action, it shall be punished according to the law, the basic idea of which fits it best." Lawrence Preuss, "Punishment by Analogy in Nationalist Socialist Penal Law," *Journal of Criminal Law and Criminology*, 26:847, March-April, 1936. See also Frederick Hoefer, "The Nazi Penal System," *Journal of Criminal Law and Criminology*, 35:385-393, March-April, 1945, and 36:30-38, May-June, 1945.

5. See Jack P. Gibbs, "Crime and the Sociology of Law." *Sociology and Social Research*, 51:23-38, October, 1966.

6. See Donald R. Cressey, "Control of Crime and Consent of the Governed, An Introduction," chap. in Gresham M. Sykes and Thomas E. Drabeck, eds., *Law and the Lawless* (New York: Random House, 1969), pp. 271-287.

7. Edwin H. Sutherland and Donald R. Cressey, *Criminology*, 9th Edition, chap. 20, pp. 440-461. Copyright © 1974 by J.B. Lippincott: New York.

8. Edwin H. Sutherland, "Is 'White Collar Crime' Crime?" *American Sociological Review*, 10:132-139, April, 1945; idem, *White Collar Crime* (New York: Dryden Press, 1949), pp. 29-55.

9. Jerome Hall, *General Principles of Criminal Law*, 2d ed. (Indianapolis: Bobbs-Merrill, 1960). See especially pp. 14-26.

10. Ibid., pp. 84-93.

11. See Edwin Sutherland and Donald R. Cressey, *Criminology*, 9th Edition, pp. 156-157. J.B. Lippincott: New York.

12. Hall, *General Principles of Criminal Law*, p. 336. See also Jerome Hall, "Analytic Philosophy and Jurisprudence," *Ethics*, 77:14-28, October, 1966; and Colin Howard, *Strict Responsibility* (London: Sweet and Maxwell, 1963).

13. Kal T. Erikson, *Wayward Puritans: A Study in the Sociology of Deviance* (New York: John Wiley, 1966).

14. Robert C. Bensing, "A Comparative Study of American Sex Statutes," *Journal of Criminal Law, Criminology, and Police Science*, 42:57-72, May-June, 1951.

15. David Sudnow, "Normal Crimes: Sociological Features of the Penal Code in a Public Defender Office," *Social Problems*, 12:255-276, Winter, 1965.

2

The State, the Law, and the Definition of Behavior as Criminal or Delinquent

William J. Chambliss

Why are some acts considered criminal and others are not? A number of sociologists have answered this question by asserting that the violation of values that are in the public interest are the ones that are codified into the criminal code. In other words, some values are so important to the public good that they must be protected by the state from transgression. Hence, a "collective conscience" determines which acts are legislated as criminal and which are not. But maybe it is not quite that simple. The noted conflict theorist William Chambliss takes issue with that belief and concludes that a collective conscience is not important in determining law. Instead, crime is a political phenomenon and can be understood as the product of special interests seeking to gain advantage over political and economic competitors. He tells us that "The state, rather than being value-neutral, is, in fact, an agent of the side which controls the production and distribution of the society's available resources."

Answering the question posed above, then, depends upon our understanding of the relationship between the political process and social stratification. Conflicts emerging out of class divisions cause some acts to be seen as crime or delinquency by state representatives who favor the economic and political status quo. Those acts that might disrupt or threaten the position of the privileged are the ones likely to be labeled criminal. Thus, by understanding the process of creating law one is better able to understand crime. This is true whether one believes in the collective conscience or the conflict theory of why some acts are criminal and others are not.

It was fashionable, a few years back, to speak of crime and delinquency as though these were characteristics possessed by some people but not by others. In the heyday of such thinking, the search was on for physical, biological, or psychological traits and social experiences which led people to become "criminal" or "delinquent".[1] There is still a recognized need to look for characteristics and experiences of people which lead them to live lives different from those of their neighbors—whether the difference is in commitment to criminality, Catholicism, or cooking.

It is now generally recognized, however, that the starting point for the systematic study of crime is *not* to ask why some people become criminal while others do not, but to ask first why is it that some acts get defined as criminal while others do not. Criminology begins, then, with the sociology of law: the study of the institutions which create, interpret, and enforce the rules that tolerate and encourage one set of behaviors while prohibiting and discouraging another. . . .

Models of Law Creation

Until recently the prevailing view in modern social thought—both legal and social science—has centered on one or more of the following propositions:

1. The law represents the value-consensus of the society.

2. The law represents those values and perspectives which are fundamental to social order.

3. The law represents those values and perspectives which it is in the public interest to protect.

4. The state as represented in the legal system is value-neutral.

5. In pluralistic societies the law represents the interests of the society at large by mediating between competing interest groups.

Among sociologists the work of Emile Durkheim is the outstanding example of the systematic analysis of law from this perspective. It is, therefore, worth spending some time appraising Durkheim's thesis as put forth in *The Division of Labor in Society* (1893). My concern here will not be to point out contradictions, inconsistencies, or tautologies in Durkheim's work but only to explore how closely Durkheim's thesis fits with extant empirical data.

Durkheim stated his central thesis quite clearly: for an act to be a crime that is punishable by law, it must be (1) universally offensive to the collective conscience of the people, (2) strongly opposed, and (3) a clear and precise form of behavior. In his words:

the only common characteristic of crimes is that they consist . . . in acts universally disapproved of by members of each society . . . crime shocks sentiments which, for a given social system, are found in all healthy consciences (1893:73).

The collective sentiments to which crime corresponds must, therefore, singularize themselves from others by some distinctive property; they must have a certain average intensity. Not only are they engraven in all consciences, but they are strongly engraven (p. 77).

The wayward son, however, and even the most hardened egoist are not treated as criminals. It is not sufficient, then, that the sentiments be strong; they must be precise (p. 79).

An act is criminal when it offends strong and defined states of the collective conscience (p. 80).

Those acts, to offend the common conscience, need not relate " . . . to vital interests of society nor to a minimum of justice" (1893:81). Durkheim argues that a single murder may have less dire social consequences than the failure of the stock market, yet the former is a crime for the reasons stated and the latter is not.

Durkheim distinguishes two types of law: Restitutive and Repressive. Restitutive law "is not expiatory, but consists of a simple *return to state*" (1893:111). Repressive law is one which "in any degree whatever, invokes against its author the characteristic reaction which we term punishment" (p. 70). Restitutive laws, or as he sometimes says, "co-operative laws with restitutive sanctions" (p. 129), are laws that invoke rule enforcement but which (a) do not reflect the collective conscience (they reflect only the opinions of *some* of the members of society), and (b) do not reflect sentiments that are strongly felt. Therefore, these laws do *not* invoke penal sanctions but only rule enforcement. The more specialized the functions of law, the less the laws represent the common conscience. As a result, they cannot then offend the common conscience since they are in fact marginal and not common to all. Thus expiatory responses are likely. "The rules which determine them cannot have the superior force, the transcendent authority which, when offended, demands expiation" (1893:127).

There is very little evidence in the studies of the process by which laws are created that would support Durkheim's thesis. It is obvious that, contrary to Durkheim's expectations, industrial societies have tended to pass more and more repressive laws (Kadish, 1967) and that these laws have reflected special interests to a greater extent than they reflect the feelings of "all healthy consciences." Indeed, the reverse is closer to the mark: the collective conscience is largely irrelevant to the creation of laws. What relationship there is tends to be a consequence rather than a cause of new laws.

A view closely related to Durkheim's has also held considerable influence. This is the often-expressed belief that criminal law represents an attempt to control acts which it is in the "public interest" to control. Auerbach et al. attempted a listing of minimal elements of "the public interest":

a) It is in the "public interest" that our nation be free from outside dictation in determining its destiny; that it have the power of self-determination. . . .

b) It is in the public interest to preserve the legitimated institutions through which conflicts in our society are adjusted and peaceful change effected, no matter how distasteful particular decisions reached by these institutions may be to particular groups in our society. In other words, the preservation of democracy—government with the freely given consent of the governed—is in the public interest.

c) It is in the public interest that no group in our society should become so powerful that it can submerge the claims of all other groups.

d) It is in the public interest that all claims made by individuals and groups in our society should at least be heard and considered by the law-making authorities. This proposition, which calls for recognition of the freedom to speak and to associate with others in pursuit of group interests, is a fundamental assumption of the democratic order.

e) It is in the public interest that every individual enjoy a minimum decent life and that the degree of inequality in the opportunities open to individuals be lessened (1961:661).

A variety of arguments suggest that this statement of a national public interest is invalid. Even assuming that there were a value-consensus on these propositions, the range of questions that come before lawmaking agencies and the state is largely outside their scope. Such a view is not a very useful or interesting guide to the study of lawmaking, for very few questions coming before lawmakers actually touch on any of these generalized objectives. Rather, they tend to be much narrower: What should the penalty be for prostitution? Should the patron be punished? Does the law of theft include "breaking bale and carrying away"? Are amphetamines to be included as dangerous drugs? Should students engaged in disruption in state universities automatically be expelled upon conviction? The usual questions coming before lawmaking authorities only rarely touch on the large questions suggested by any list of supposed "public interests."

Second, even if one were to accept these statements of "the public interest," the actual questions coming before lawmakers that even touch on these objectives are never very simple. Whether or not the United States ought to simply turn itself over to a foreign power, for example, is a question that has never come and doubtless never will come before any legislature. Rather, the question is always partial and problematic: Is joining the United Nations, and the surrender of sovereignty *pro tanto*, for example, too serious an invasion of the "public interest" in independence? If "freedom to speak" is "a fundamental assumption of the democratic order," then it can be argued that no private individual or corporation ought to control newspapers, television, or other institutions of the mass media, which instead should be equally available to all without regard to their financial resources. That would require government control of the mass media, which might well be regarded as the negation of free speech. While, no doubt, it is in the public interest that every individual should enjoy the minimum essentials of a decent life, exactly how much is a "minimum"? Is it in the public interest to reduce the size of "big business" in order to keep that group from attaining too much power, even if it can be shown that large economic units are more efficient than smaller ones? And if one decides to reduce the size of "big business," what is to be the standard of acceptable maximum size?

Third, is it true that even this list of "the minimal elements of the public interest" would be unanimously accepted? It is notable for omitting any reference to minimum protection for property. Many members of the propertied classes, at least in the American society, would insist that such a guarantee is an essential component of the "public interest." The list omits any statement that equality of treatment before the law regardless of race or color is a necessary ingredient of "the public interest"; white racists would hardly complain of this omission but others surely would.

Fourth, what a majority conceives of as "the public interest" at any period in history is not a constant. Not so long ago a majority of the lawmakers believed that it was in the public interest to prevent any citizen from buying alcoholic beverages. Not very long before that, in the long view of history, no doubt a majority believed that it was in the public interest to burn wretched old women at the stake as witches. How can one be sure that today's perception of "the public interest" is not merely an evanescent reflection of the value-sets of the majority?

Finally, consider the second of the propositions put forward, the broadest and most overarching of all: "It is in the public interest to preserve the legitimated institutions through which conflicts in society are adjusted and peaceful change effected." So long as real poverty exists, it seems clear that the fifth assertion of "the public interest," i.e., "that every individual enjoy a minimum decent life," is sharply in conflict with the second. Which of these interests is to be overriding? The repeated phenomenon of urban rioting in the ghettos of America suggests that there is no value-consensus on the relative weight to be given to any of these propositions which purport to define "the public interest."

The reason why this or any other set of claimed "public interest" elements, a commonly held *summum bonum*, can never adequately describe the actual state of affairs can be explained philosophically as well as empirically. John Dewey (1938) has argued that a distinction must be made between *that which is prized* and the *process of valuation*. No doubt we all have general, culturally acquired objectives, i.e., things which are prized. In any specific instance, however, how we define these generalized goals depends on a complex process of considering objective constraints, relative costs and benefits, and the valuation of alternative means. In this process of valuation, our generalized objectives are necessarily modified and changed as they become concrete and definite—i.e., in Dewey's language, as they become ends-in-view. Whatever the relative cultural agreement on general, broad prizings, there is never any complete agreement on any specific end in view.

The particular norms prescribed by law always are specific. They always command the role-occupant to act in specific ways. It is always a statement, not of generalized prizings, but of a specific end in view. It is the result of a process of valuation. On that valuation there is never complete agreement, for there is no complete agreement on the relative weightings to be given the various prizings held in different strata of the society, nor on the relative valuation to be given to different means.

In short, every assertion that a specific law should have a certain content must necessarily reflect the process of valuation of its proponents, and by the same token, it will be opposed to the processes of valuation of its opponents. The nature of law as a normative system, commanding what ought to be done, necessitates that it will favor one group as against another. The proof, whatever academic model-builders may say, lies in the fact that there is some opposition to *every* proposed new rule, whether or not the lawmakers themselves are unanimous. Even a declaration of war in the face of armed attack is never supported by the *entire* population.

That the law necessarily advances the values of some groups in society and opposes others reflects the fact that in any complex, modern society there is no value-consensus that is relevant to the law. That is so because of the very nature of the different "webs of life" that exist. It is a function of society itself.

For many of the same reasons, the view that the state is a value-neutral agent which weighs competing interests and distributes the available resources equitably is equally untenable. There are, indeed, competing interests but the competitors enter the arena with vastly different resources and, therefore, much different chances of success (Reich, 1964; Domhoff, 1970). The state, rather than being value-neutral, is, in fact, an agent of the side which controls the production and distribution of the society's available resources. The criminal law is then first and foremost a reflection of the interests and ideologies of the governing class—whether that class is private industry or state bureaucracy. Only secondarily, and even then only in minor ways, does the criminal law reflect the value-consensus, the public interest, or the sifting and weighing of competing interests.

A model more consistent with the realities of legal change must take into account differences in power which stem largely from differences in control over the economic resources of the society. More importantly, an adequate model to account for the definition of behavior as criminal or delinquent must recognize that in societies with social class divisions there is inevitably conflict between social classes and it is this class conflict which is the moving force for legal changes. Actions of the ruling class or representatives thereof as well as the machinations of moral entrepreneurs and the mobilization of bias all reflect attempts by various social classes to have their own interests and ideologies implemented by the state through the legal system.[2] It is, of course, true that the conflicts that are the basis of legal changes are not fought by equals. Thus those who control the economic and political resources of the society will inevitably see their interests and ideologies more often represented in the law than will others.

There are, of course, issues that are of only minor consequence to the established economic and political relations in the society. Such issues may be described by the pluralist perspective that sees different interest groups of more or less equal power arguing in the value-neutral arena of state bureaucracies. It seems clear that such instances are rare, and, in fact, even when the issue is the wording of prostitution laws or the changes in juvenile court laws there are differences in power between groups and these differences will usually determine the outcome of the struggle.

Summary and Conclusion

From the Black Death in feudal England where the vagrancy laws emerged and were shaped, through the Star Chamber in the fifteenth century where judges defined the law of theft in order to protect the interests of the ruling classes, to the legislatures of New York and California and the appellate courts of the United States lies a vast array of criminal laws that have been created, contradicted, reformulated, and allowed to die. Constructing a general theory that can account for such a wide range of events is no simple task. It is not surprising that such efforts often fall short of their goal.

Looking only at the two most general models of rule creation: the "value-consensus" and the "ruling class" models and pitting them against the extant empirical data leave little doubt but that both fall short of the mark. The value-consensus model which suggests that community consensus is the moving force behind the definition of behavior as criminal and delinquent finds little support in the systematic study of the development of criminal law. The ruling class model falls short as an adequate explanation to the extent that it posits a monolithic ruling class which sits in jurisdiction over a passive mass of people and passes laws reflecting only the interests of those who rule.

On the other hand, the importance of the ruling class in determining the shape of the criminal law cannot be gainsaid—whether that influence is through direct involvement in the law-creating process or merely through the mobilization of bias. Nor, for that matter, can the influence of "public opinion" (especially as this is organized around moral entrepreneurs) be ignored as a source of criminal law. Thus both general models contain some valuable truths to which must be added the important role played by bureaucracies, vested interest groups, and even individuals acting virtually alone (Lewis, 1966).

An alternative model compatible with the data is best described as a conflict theory of legal change. The starting point for this theory is the recognition that modern, industrialized society is composed of numerous social classes and interest groups who compete for the favors of the state. The stratification of society into social classes where there are substantial (and at times vast) differences in wealth, power, and prestige inevitably leads to conflict between the extant classes. It is in the course of working through and living with these inherent conflicts that the law takes its particular content and form. It is out of the conflicts generated by social class divisions that the definition of some acts as criminal or delinquent emerges.

So long as class conflicts are latent, those who sit at the top of the political and economic structure of the society can manipulate the criminal laws to suit their own purposes. But when class conflict breaks into open rebellion, as it often does in such societies (Rubenstein, 1970), then the state must enact legislation and the courts reinterpret laws in ways that are perceived as solutions to the conflict. During times of manifest class conflict, legislatures and courts will simultaneously create criminal laws that provide greater control over those groups who are engaged in acts disruptive to the status quo and laws which appear to alleviate the conditions which are seen as giving rise to the social conflicts.

In between crises or perhaps as an adjunct to the legislative-judicial innovations taking place because of them, bureaucracies can mobilize and moral entrepreneurs organize to plead their case before the lawmaking bodies. Without the changes in economic structure that accompanied England's transition from feudalism to capitalism the laws of theft and vagrancy (to mention only two) would not have taken the form they did, just as the Supreme Court decisions and legislative enactments of the 1960s that effectively refocused substantial areas of the criminal law would not have taken place without the riots, rebellions, and overt social conflicts which characterized that historical period in America.

Crime is a political phenomenon. What gets defined as criminal or delinquent behavior is the result of a political process within which rules are formed which prohibit or require people to behave in certain ways. It is this process which must be understood as it bears on the definition of behavior as criminal if we are to proceed to the study of criminal *behavior*. Thus to ask "why is it that some acts get defined as criminal while others do not" is the starting point for all systematic study of crime and criminal behavior. Nothing is inherently criminal, it is only the response that makes it so. If we are to explain crime, we must first explain the social forces that cause some acts to be defined as criminal while other acts are not.

Discussion Questions

1. What is meant by the term "public interest"? How is it different from the "collective conscience"? In order to protect the "public interest," what sacrifices might individuals have to make? In your view, is that a good trade-off? Does the law really protect a "public interest"? In what areas is the concept of "public interest" impractical to achieve?

2. How do differences in power or resources affect the formation of law? How do they affect the outcome of the application of law to individuals?

3. Compare the value-consensus model of law creation with the ruling class model. Describe the theory behind each one. What are the weaknesses of each? How might the ruling class model affect law creation in subtle ways (other than direct involvement in the law-creation process)? Suggest some laws for which each model might be explanatory (what laws might reflect the value consensus model? The ruling class model?)

Notes

1. See, for example, Cohen (1955), Merton (1957), Miller (1958), and Cloward and Ohlin (1960). Donald Cressey has pointed out that an earlier generation of criminologists, particularly Sutherland (1924), Sellin (1938), and Tannenbaum (1938), were less likely to ignore the importance of the criminal lawmaking process; see Cressey (1968) and Sutherland and Cressey (1970).

2. Most broadly conceived, each of these sources of law may be summarized under the concept of "interest groups" (Quinney, 1970). But such a general concept does little more than provide an umbrella under which to put these various social processes. Further, the notion of "interest groups" often leads to the erroneous implication that competition for control of or influence over the state is a battle between equals where social class differences are largely irrelevant. It seems analytically wiser to deal with all the sources of criminal law creation and to see them as stemming from basic conflicts within the society.

References

Auerbach, D., K. Garrison, W. Hurst, and S. Mermin. 1961. *The Legal Process: An Introduction to Decision-Making by Judicial, Legislative, Executive, and Administrative Agencies.* San Francisco: Chandler.

Cloward, Richard A., and Lloyd E. Ohlin. 1960. *Delinquency and Opportunity: A Theory of Delinquent Gangs*. New York: Free Press of Glencoe.

Cohen, Albert K. 1955. *Delinquent Boys*. Glencoe, Ill.: Free Press.

Cressey, Donald R. 1968. "Culture conflict, differential association, and normative conflict." Pp. 43-54 in Marvin Wolfgang (ed.), *Crime and Culture: Essays in Honor of Thorsten Sellin*. New York: Wiley.

Dewey, John. 1938. *Logic: The Theory of Inquiry*. New York: Holt.

Domhoff, G. William. 1970. *The Higher Circles*. New York: Random House.

Durkheim, Emile. 1893. *The Division of Labor in Society*. Translation by George Simpson. Glencoe, Ill.: Free Press (1947 edition).

Kadish, Sanford H. 1967. "The crisis of overcriminalization." *Annals of the American Academy of Political and Social Science 374* (November):157-170.

Lewis, Anthony. 1966. *Gideon's Trumpet*. New York: Vintage Books.

Merton, Robert K. 1957. "Social structure and anomie." Chap. 4 in Robert K. Merton, *Social Theory and Social Structure*. Glencoe, Ill.: Free Press.

Miller, Walter B. 1958. "Lower class culture as a generating milieu of gang delinquency." *Journal of Social Issues* 14 (3): 5-19.

Quinney, Richard. 1970. *The Social Reality of Crime*. New York: Little, Brown.

Reich, Charles A. 1964. "The new property." *Yale Law Journal* 73 (April): 733-787.

Rubenstein, Richard E. 1970. *Rebels in Eden*. Boston: Little, Brown.

Sellin, Thorsten. 1938. *Culture Conflict and Crime*. New York: Social Science Research Council. Bulletin 41.

Sutherland, Edwin H. 1924. *Criminology*. Philadelphia: Lippincott.

Sutherland, Edwin H., and Donald R. Cressey. 1970. *Criminology*. Eighth Edition. Philadelphia: Lippincott.

Tannenbaum, Frank. 1938. *Crime and the Community*. New York: Columbia University Press.

3

A Crime by Any Other Name . . .

Jeffrey Reiman

Readings One and Two examined the legal definition of crime and the law-making process, observing that crime is dependent upon what is codified into the criminal law. Chambliss (reading Two) pointed out that acts that are prohibited by law may be the result of special interests wishing to protect or enhance their positions in the social order. In this reading, Jeffrey Reiman explores certain acts that do great social harm but are seldom defined as crime. Calling them "crimes by any other name," he demonstrates how they are comparable to criminal acts in the amount of suffering and harm they cause but are typically not thought of as criminal, nor are those committing these acts seen as criminal. What are these acts? Although he specifically investigates workplace safety violations, poor medical treatment and outright malpractice, air pollution, and exploitation of the poor, many other conditions of this sort could be listed. Should the air polluter be arrested and tried for doing bodily harm? Or the slum lord for contributing to human misery and taking advantage of the vulnerable poor? Or the mine owner for failing to install adequate safety equipment that might prevent a deadly accident?

Reiman's answer to all these questions would be yes, if human suffering and harm are criteria for defining an act as criminal. But that is typically not the answer of society's leaders, nor, in fact, is it the answer of most of us. Why not? Reiman believes that the well-to-do, the owners of mines and factories, the slum lords, physicians, and others like them in U.S. society are excluded from the definition of criminal because of their social status, while the poor are increasingly victimized by the criminal justice system. Whether or not the affluent are protected or the poor victimized, it is relevant to ask why the acts he demonstrates are harmful are not usually defined as criminal by the law or citizens, despite the threat they pose to society.

. . . What's In a Name?

If it takes you an hour to read this chapter, by the time you read the last page, three of your fellow citizens will have been murdered. *During that same time, at least four Americans will die as a result of unhealthy or unsafe conditions in the workplace!* Although these work-related deaths could have been prevented, they are not called murders. Why not? Doesn't a crime by any other name still cause misery and suffering? What's in a name?

The fact is that the label "crime" is not used in America to name all or the worst of the actions that cause misery and suffering to Americans. It is primarily reserved for the dangerous actions of the poor.

In the February 21, 1993, edition of the *New York Times*, an article appears with the headline: "Company in Mine Deaths Set to Pay Big Fine." It describes an agreement by the owners of a Kentucky mine to pay a fine for safety misconduct that may have led to "the worst American mining accident in nearly a decade." Ten workers died in a methane explosion, and the company pleaded guilty to "a pattern of safety misconduct" that included falsifying reports of methane levels and requiring miners to work under unsupported roofs. The company was fined $3.75 million. The acting foreman at the mine was the only individual charged by the federal government, and for his cooperation with the investigation, prosecutors were recommending that he receive the minimum sentence: probation to six months in prison. The company's president expressed regret for the tragedy that occurred. And the U.S. attorney said he hoped the case "sent a clear message that violations of Federal safety and health regulations that endanger the lives of our citizens will not be tolerated."[1]

Compare this with the story of Colin Ferguson, who prompted an editorial in the *New York Times* of December 10, 1993, with the headline: "Mass Murder on the 5:33."[2] A few days earlier, Colin had boarded a commuter train in Garden City, Long Island, and methodically shot passengers with a 9-millimeter pistol, killing five and wounding 18. Colin Ferguson was surely a murderer, maybe a mass murderer. My question is, "Why wasn't the death of the miners also murder? Why weren't those responsible for subjecting ten miners to deadly conditions also "mass murderers"?

Why do ten dead miners amount to an "accident," a "tragedy," and five dead commuters a "mass murder"? "Murder suggests a murderer, whereas "accident"and "tragedy" suggest the work of impersonal forces. But the charge against the company that owned the mine said that they "repeatedly exposed the mine's work crews to danger and that such conditions were frequently concealed from Federal inspectors responsible for enforcing the mine safety act." And the acting foreman admitted to falsifying records of methane levels only two months before the fatal blast. Someone was responsible for the conditions that led to the death of ten miners. Is that person not a murderer, even a *mass murderer?*

These questions are at this point rhetorical. My aim is not to discuss this case but rather to point to the blinders we wear when we look at such an "accident." There was an investigation. One person, the acting foreman, was held responsible for falsifying records. He is to be sentenced to six months in prison (at most). The company was fined. But no one will be tried for *murder*. No one will be thought of as a murderer. *Why not?* Would the miners not be safer if such people were treated as murderers? Might they not still be alive? Will a president of the United States address the Yale Law School and recommend mandatory prison sentences for such people? Will he mean these people when he states,

These relatively few, persistent criminals who cause so much misery and fear are really the core of the problem. The rest of the American people have a right to protection from their violence[?][3]

Didn't those miners have a right to protection from the violence that took their lives? *And if not, why not?*

Once we are ready to ask this question seriously, we are in a position to see that the reality of crime—that is, the acts we label crime, the acts we think of as crime, the actors and actions we treat was criminal—is *created:* It is an image shaped by decisions as to *what* will be called crime and *who* will be treated as a criminal.

The Carnival Mirror

It is sometimes coyly observed that the quickest and cheapest way to eliminate crime would be to throw out all the criminal laws. There is a sliver of truth to this view. Without criminal laws, there will be no "crimes." There would, however, still be dangerous acts. This is why we cannot solve our crime problem so simply. The criminal law *labels* some acts "crimes." In doing this, it identifies those acts so dangerous that we must use the extreme methods of criminal justice to protect ourselves against them. This does not mean the criminal law *creates* crime—it simply "mirrors" real dangers that threaten us. What is true of the criminal law is true of the whole justice system. If police did not arrest or prosecutors charge or juries convict, there would be no "criminals." This does not mean that police or prosecutors or juries create criminals any more than legislators do. They *react* to real dangers in society. The criminal justice system—from lawmakers to law enforcers—is just a mirror of the real dangers that lurk in our midst. *Or so we are told.*

How accurate is this mirror? We need to answer this in order to know whether or how well the criminal justice system is protecting us against the real threats to our well-being. The more accurate a mirror is, the more the image it shows is created by the reality it reflects. The more misshapen a mirror is, the more the distorted image is created by the mirror, not by the reality reflected. It is in this sense that I will argue that the image of crime is created: The American criminal justice system is a mirror that shows a distorted image of the dangers that threaten us—an image created more by the shape of the mirror than by the reality reflected. What do we see when we look in the criminal justice mirror?

On the morning of September 16, 1975, the *Washington Post* carried an article in its local news section headlined "Arrest Data Reveal Profile of a Suspect." The article reported the results of a study of crime in Prince George's County, a suburb of Washington, D.C. It read in part as follows:

> The typical suspect in serious crime in Prince George's County is a black male, aged 14 to 19, who lives the area inside the Capital Beltway where more than half of the county's 64,371 reported crimes were committed in 1974. [The study] presents a picture of persons, basically youths, committing a crime once every eight minutes in Prince George's County.[4]

This report is hardly a surprise. The portrait it paints of "the typical suspect in serious crime" is probably a pretty good rendering of the image lurking in the back of the minds of most people who fear crime. Furthermore, although the crime rate in Prince George's County is somewhat above the national average and its black population somewhat above that of the average suburban county, the portrait generally fits the national picture presented in the FBI's *Uniform Crime Reports* for the same year, 1974. In Prince George's County, "youths between the ages of 15 and 19 were accused of committing nearly half [45.5 percent] of all 1974 crimes."[5] For the nation in 1974, the FBI reported that persons in this age group accounted for 39.5 percent of arrests for the FBI Index crimes (criminal homicide, forcible rape, robbery, aggravated assault, burglary, larceny, and motor vehicle theft.)[6] These youths were male and (disproportionately) black. In Prince George's County, males "represented three of every four serious crime defendants."[7] In the nation in 1974, out of 1,289,524 persons arrested for FBI Index crimes, 1,043,155, or more than 80 percent, were males.[8] In Prince George's County, where blacks make up approximately 25 percent of the population, "blacks were accused of 58 percent of all serious crimes."[9] In the nation, where blacks made up 11.4 percent of the population in 1974, they accounted for 34.2 percent of arrests for Index crimes.[10]

That was 1974. But little has changed since. In his 1993 book, *How to Stop Crime*, retired police chief Anthony Bouza writes: "Street crime is mostly a black and poor young man's game."[11] And listen to the sad words of the Reverend Jesse Jackson: "There is nothing more painful to me at this stage of my life than to walk down the street and hear footsteps and start thinking about robbery—and then look around and see someone white and feel relieved."[12]

This, then, is the Typical Criminal, the one whose portrait President Reagan described as "that of a stark, staring face, a face that belongs to a frightening reality of our time—the face of a human predator, the face of the habitual criminal. Nothing in nature is more cruel and more dangerous."[13] This is the face that Ronald Reagan saw in the criminal justice mirror, more than a decade ago. Let us look more closely at the face in today's criminal justice mirror, and we shall see much the same Typical Criminal:

He is, first of all, a *he*. Out of 2,012,906 persons arrested for FBI Index crimes in 1991, 1,572,591, or 78 percent, were males.[14] Second, he is a *youth*. In 1991, more than half of arrests for FBI Index crimes were of individuals aged 22 and under.[15] Third, he is predominantly *urban*: "Among city population groupings, those with more than 250,000 inhabitants recorded the highest rate [of arrests], 7.579 [per 100,000 inhabitants]."[16] Fourth, he is disproportionately *black*—blacks are arrested for Index crimes at a rate three times that of their percentage in the national population. In 1991, when blacks were about 12 percent of the nation's population, they made up 34.6 percent of Index crime arrests.[17] Finally, he is *poor*: Among state prisoners in 1991, 33 percent were unemployed prior to being arrested—a rate nearly four times that of males in the general population. Among those state prisoners who had incomes prior to being arrested, 19 percent earned less that $3,000 a year (compared with 6.8 percent of males in the civilian labor force), and half earned less than $10,000 a year (compared with 25 percent of noninstitutionalized males).[18] As the President's Commission reported nearly 30 years ago: "The offender at the end of the road in prison is likely to be a member of the lowest social and economic groups in the country."[19]

This is the Typical Criminal feared by most law-abiding Americans. Poor, young, urban, (disproportionately) black males make up the core of the enemy forces in the war against crime. They are the heart of vicious, unorganized guerrilla army, threatening the lives, limbs, and possessions of the law-abiding members of society—necessitating recourse to the ultimate weapons of force and detention in our common defense.

But how do we know who the criminals are who so seriously endanger us that we must stop them with force and lock them in prisons?

"From the arrest records, probation reports, and prison statistics," the authors of *The Challenge of Crime in a Free Society* tell us, the " 'portrait' of the offender emerges."[20] *These sources are not merely objective readings taken at different stages in the criminal justice process: Each of them represents human decisions*. "Prison statistics" and "probation reports" reflect *decisions* of juries on who gets convicted and decisions of judges on who gets probation or prison and for how long. "Arrest records" reflect decisions about which crimes to investigate and which suspects to take into custody. All these decisions rest on the most fundamental of all *decisions*: the decisions of legislators as to which acts shall be labeled "crimes" in the first place.

The reality of crime as the target of our criminal justice system and as perceived by the general populace is not a simple objective threat to which the system reacts: *It is a reality that takes shape as it is filtered through a series of human decisions running the full gamut of the criminal justice system*—from the lawmakers who determine what behavior shall be in the province of criminal justice to the law enforcers who decide which individuals will be brought within that province.

Note that by emphasizing the role of "human decisions," I do not mean to suggest that the reality of crime is voluntarily and intentionally "created by individual "decision makers." Their decisions are themselves shaped by the social system, much as a child's decisions to become an engineer rather than a samurai warrior is shaped by the social system in which he or she grows up. Thus, to have a full explanation of how the reality of crime is created, we have to understand how our society is structured in a way that leads people to make the decisions they do. In other words, these decisions are part of the social phenomena to be explained—they are not the explanation.

For the present, however, I emphasize the role of the decisions themselves for the following reasons: First, they are conspicuous points in the social process, easy to spot and verify empirically. Second, because they are decisions aimed at protecting us from the dangers in our midst, we can compare the decisions with the real dangers and determine whether they are responding to the real dangers. Third, because the reality of crime—the real actions labeled crimes, the real individuals identified as criminals, the real faces we watch in the news as they travel from arrest to court to prison—results from these decisions, we can determine whether that reality corresponds to the real dangers in our society. Where that reality does correspond to real dangers, we can say that the reality of crime simply reflects the real dangers in society. Where that reality of crime does not correspond to the real dangers, we can say that it is a reality *created* by those decisions. And then we can investigate the role played by the social system in encouraging, reinforcing, and otherwise shaping those decisions.

It is to capture this way of looking at the relation between the reality of crime and the real dangers "out there" in society that I refer to the criminal justice system as a "mirror." Whom and what we see in this mirror is a function of the decisions about who and what are criminal, and so on. Our poor, young, urban, black male, who is so well represented in arrest records and prison populations, appears not simply because of the undeniable threat he poses to the rest of society. As dangerous as he may be, he would not appear in the criminal justice mirror *if* it had not been decided that the acts he performs should be labeled "crimes," *if* it had not been decided that he should be arrested for those crimes, *if* he had access to a lawyer who could persuade a jury to acquit him and perhaps a judge to expunge his arrest record, and *if* it had not been decided that he is the type of individual and his the type of crime that warrants imprisonment. *The shape of the reality we see in the criminal justice mirror is created by all these decision.* We want to know how accurately the reality we see in this mirror reflects the real dangers that threaten us in society.

It is not my view that this reality is created out of nothing. The mugger, the rapist, the murderer, the burglar, the robber all pose a definite threat to our well-being, and they ought to be dealt with in ways that effectively reduce that threat to the minimum level possible (without making the criminal justice system itself a threat to our lives and liberties). Of central importance, however, is that the threat posed by the Typical Criminal is not the greatest threat to which was are exposed. The acts of the Typical Criminal are not the only acts that endanger us, nor are they the acts that endanger us the most. As I shall show in this chapter, we have as great or sometimes even greater chance of being killed or disabled by an occupational injury or disease, by unnecessary surgery, or by shoddy emergency medical services than by aggravated assault or even homicide! Yet even though these threats to our well-being are graver than that posed by our poor young criminals, they do not show up in the FBI's Index of serious crimes. The individuals responsible for them do not turn up in arrest records or prison statistics. *They never become part of the reality reflected in the criminal justice mirror, although the danger they pose is at least as great and often greater than the danger posed by those who do!*

Similarly, the general public loses more *by far . . .* from price-fixing and monopolistic practices and from consumer deception and embezzlement than from all the property crime in the FBI's Index combined. Yet these far more costly acts are either not criminal, or if technically criminal, not prosecuted, or if prosecuted, not punished, or if punished, only mildly. In any event, although the individuals responsible for these acts take more money out of the ordinary citizen's pocket than our Typical Criminal, they rarely show up in arrest statistics and almost never in prison populations. *Their faces rarely appear in the criminal justice mirror, although the danger they pose is at least as great and often greater than that of those who do.*

The inescapable conclusion is that the criminal justice system does not simply *reflect* the reality of crime; it has a hand in *creating* the reality we see.

The criminal justice system is like a mirror in which society can see the face of evil in its midst. Because the system deals with some evil and not with others, because it treats some evils as the gravest and treats some of the gravest evils as minor, the image it throws back is distorted like the image in a carnival mirror. Thus, the image cast back is false not because it is invented out of thin air but because the proportions of the real are distorted: Large becomes small and small large; grave becomes minor and minor grave. Like a carnival mirror, although nothing is reflected that does not exist in the world, the image is more a creation of the mirror than a picture of the world.

If criminal justice really gives us a carnival-mirror image of "crime," we are doubly deceived. First, we are led to believe that the criminal justice system is protecting us against the gravest threats to our well-being when, in fact, the system is protecting us against only some threats and not necessarily the gravest ones. We are deceived about some threats and not necessarily the gravest ones. We are deceived about how much protection we are recieving and thus left vulnerable. The second deception is just the other side of this one. If people believe that the carnival mirror is a true mirror—that is, if they believe the criminal justice simply *reacts* to the gravest threats to their well-being—they come to believe that whatever is the target of the criminal justice system must be the greatest threat to their well-being. In other words, if people believe that the most drastic of society's weapons are wielded by the criminal justice system *in reaction to* the gravest dangers to society, they will believe the reverse as well: that those actions that call forth the most drastic of society's weapons *must be* those that pose the gravest dangers to society.

A strange alchemy takes place when people uncritically accept the legitimacy of their institutions: What *needs* justification becomes *proof* of justification. People come to believe that prisoners must be criminals *because* they are in prison and that the inmates of insane asylums must be *crazy* because they are in insane asylums.[21] The criminal justice system's use of extreme measures—such as force and imprisonment—is thought to be justified by the extreme gravity of the dangers it combats. By this alchemy, these extreme measures become *proof* of the extreme gravity of those dangers, and the first deception, which merely misleads the public about how much protection the criminal justice system is actually providing, is transformed into the second, which deceives the public into believing that the acts and actors that are the target of the criminal justice system pose the gravest threats to its well-being. Thus, the system may not only fail to protect us from dangers as great or greater than those listed in the FBI Crime Index; it may do still greater damage by creating the false security of the belief that only the acts on the FBI Index really threaten us and require control. . . .

A Crime by Any Other Name . . .

Think of a crime, any crime. Picture the first "crime" that comes into your mind. The odds are you are not imagining a mining company executive sitting at his desk, calculating the costs of proper safety precautions and deciding not to invest in them. Probably what you do see with your mind's eye is one person physically attacking another or robbing something from another via the threat of physical attack. Look more closely. What does the attacker look like? It's a safe bet he (and it is a *he*, of course) is not wearing a suit and tie. In fact, my hunch is that you—like me, like almost anyone else in America—picture a young, tough, lower-class male when the thought of crime first pops into your head. You (we) picture someone like the Typical Criminal described above. The crime itself is one in which the Typical Criminal sets out to attack or rob some specific person.

The last point is important. It indicates that we have a mental image not only of the Typical Criminal but also of the Typical Crime. If the Typical Criminal is a young, lower-class male, the Typical Crime is *one-on-one harm*—where harm means either physical injury or loss of something valuable or both. If you have any doubts that this is the Typical Crime, look at any random sample of police or private eye shows on television. How often do you see the cops on *NYPD Blue* investigate consumer fraud or failure to remove occupational hazards? And when Jessica Fletcher (on *Murder, She Wrote*) tracks down well-heeled criminals, it is almost always for garden-variety violent crimes like murder. A study of TV crime shows by The Media Institute in Washington, D.C., indicates that, while the fictional criminals portrayed on television are on the average both older and wealthier than the real criminals who figure in the FBI *Uniform Crime Reports*, "TV crimes are almost 12 times more likely to be violent as crimes committed in the real world."[22] TV crime shows broadcast the double-edged message that the one-on-one crimes of the poor are the typical crimes of all and thus not uniquely caused by the pressures of poverty; *and* that the criminal justice system pursues rich and poor alike—thus, when the criminal justice system happens to pounce on the poor in real life, it is not out of any class bias.[23]

In addition to the steady diet of fictionalized TV violence and crime, there has been an increase in the graphic display of crime on many TV news programs. Crimes reported on TV news are also far more frequently violent than real crimes are.[24] An article in *The Washingtonian* says that the word around two prominent local TV news programs is, "If it bleeds, it leads."[25] What's more, a new breed of nonfictional "tabloid" TV show has appeared in which viewers are shown films of actual violent crimes—blood, screams, and all—or reenactments of actual violent crimes, sometimes using the actual victims playing themselves! Among these are *Cops*, *Real Stories of the Highway Patrol*, *America's Most Wanted*, and *Unsolved Mysteries*. Here, too, the focus is on crimes of one-on-one violence, rather, than, say, corporate pollution. The *Wall Street Journal*, reporting on the phenomenon of tabloid TV, informs us the "Television has gone tabloid. The seamy underside of life is being bared in a new rash of true-crime series and contrived-confrontation talk shows."[26] Is there any surprise that a survey by *McCall's* indicates that its readers have grown more afraid of crime in the mid-1980s—even though victimization studies show a stable level of crime for most of this period?[27]

It is important to identify this model of Typical Crime because it functions like a set of blinders. It keeps us from calling a mine disaster a mass murder even if ten men are killed, even if someone is responsible for the unsafe conditions in which they worked and died. I contend that this particular piece of mental furniture so blocks our view that it keeps us from using the criminal justice system to protect ourselves from the greatest threats to our persons and possessions.

What keeps a mine disaster from being a mass murder in our eyes is that it is not a one-on-one harm. What is important in one-on-one harm is not the numbers but the *desire of someone (or ones) to harm someone (or ones) else.* An attack by a gang on one or more persons or an attack by an individual on several fits the model of one-on-one harm; that is, for each person harmed there is at least one individual who wanted to harm that person. Once he selects his victim, the rapist, the mugger, the murderer all want this person they have selected to suffer. A mine executive, on the other hand, does not want his employees to be harmed. He would truly prefer that there be no accident, no injured or dead miners. What he does want is something legitimate. It is what he has been hired to get: maximum profits at minimum costs. If he cuts corners to save a buck, he is just doing his job. If ten men die because he cut corners on safety, we may think him crude or callous but not a murderer. He is, at most, responsible for an *indirect harm*, not a one-on-one harm. For this, he may even be criminally indictable for violating safety regulations—but not for murder. The ten men are dead as an unwanted consequence of his (perhaps overzealous or undercautious) pursuit of a legitimate goal. So, unlike the Typical Criminal, he has not committed the Typical Crime—or so we generally believe. As a result, ten men are dead who might be alive now if cutting corners of the kind that leads to loss of life, whether suffering is specifically aimed at or not, were treated as murder.

This is my point. Because we accept the belief—encouraged by our politicians' statements about crime and by the media's portrayal of crime—that the model for crime is one person specifically trying to harm another, we accept a legal system that leaves us unprotected against much greater dangers to our lives and well-being than those threatened by the Typical Criminal. . . .

We are left with the conclusion that there is no moral basis for treating *one-on-one harm* as criminal and *indirect harm* as merely a regulatory affair. What matters, then, is whether the purpose of the criminal justice system will be served by including, in the category of serious crime, actions that are predictably likely to produce serious harm, yet that are done in pursuit of otherwise legitimate goals and without the aim of harming anyone.

What is the purpose of the criminal justice system? No esoteric answer is required. Norval Morris and Gordon Hawkins write that "the prime function of the criminal law is to protect our persons and our property."[28] *The Challenge of Crime in a Free Society*, the report of the President's Commission on Law Enforcement and Administration of Justice, tells us that "any criminal justice system is an apparatus society uses to enforce the standards of conduct necessary to protect individuals and the community."[29] Whatever else we think a criminal justice system should accomplish, I doubt if anyone would deny that its central purpose is to protect us against the most serious threats to our well-being. This purpose is seriously undermined by taking one-on-one harm as the model of crime. Excluding harm caused without the aim of harming someone in particular prevents the criminal justice system from protecting our persons and our property from dangers at least as great as those posed by one-on-one harm. This is so because . . . there are a large number of actions that are not labeled *criminal* but that lead to loss of life, limb, and possessions on a scale comparable to those actions that are represented in the FBI Crime Index—and a crime by any other name still causes misery and suffering. . . .

Summary

Once again, our investigations lead to the same result. The criminal justice system does not protect us against the gravest threats to life, limb, or possessions. Its definitions of crime are not simply a reflection of the objective dangers that threaten us. The workplace, the medical profession, the air we breathe, and the poverty we refuse to rectify lead to far more human suffering, far more death and disability, and take far more dollars from our pockets than the murders, aggravated assaults, and thefts reported annually by the FBI. What is more, this human suffering is preventable. A government really intent on protecting our well-being could enforce work safety regulations, police the medical profession, require that the clean air standards be met, and funnel sufficient money to the poor to alleviate the major disabilities of poverty—but it does not. Instead we hear a lot of cant about law and order and a lot of rant about crime in the streets. It is as if our leaders were not only refusing to protect us from the major threats to our well-being but trying to cover up this refusal by diverting our attention to crime—as if this were only the real threat.

As we have seen, the criminal justice system is a carnival mirror that presents a distorted image of what threatens us. The distortions do not end with the definitions of crime. . . . New distortions enter at every level of the system, so that in the end, when we look in our prisons to see who really threatens us, all we see are poor people. By that time, virtually all the well-to-do people who endanger us have been discreetly weeded out of the system. . . . All the mechanisms by which the criminal justice system comes down more frequently and more harshly on the poor criminal than on the well-off criminal take place *after* most of the dangerous acts of the well-to-do have been excluded from the definition of crime itself. The bias against the poor within the criminal justice system is all the more striking when we recognize that the door to that system is shaped in a way that excludes in advance the most dangerous acts of the well-to-do. Demonstrating this has been the purpose of the present chapter.

Discussion Questions

1. Reiman claims that the "mirror" of criminal justice is distorted. Do you agree? If so, what are some examples? If not, what examples would illustrate that the "mirror" is accurate? Which acts are not reflected in the "mirror"?

2. What are some of the responses to crime that, according to Reiman, shape the reality of crime? Exactly how do each of the responses affect the shaping of crime? In what way does the structure of society play a part?

3. How do television shows, FBI Uniform Crime Reports, and news reports create or perpetuate the public perception of crime? How do they reinforce the fact that many dangerous acts are not perceived as criminal acts?

Notes

1. "Company in Mine Deaths Set to Pay Big Fine," *New York Times*, February 21, 1993, p. A19.

2. "Mass Murder on the 5:33," *New York Times*, December 10, 1993, p. A34.

3. Gerald R. Ford, "To Insure Domestic Tranquility: Mandatory Sentence for Convicted Felons," speech delivered at the Yale Law School Sesquicentennial Convocation, New Haven, Connecticut, April 25, 1975, in *Vital Speeches of the Day* 41, no. 15 (May 15, 1975), p. 451.

4. "Arrest Data Reveal Profile of Suspect," *Washington Post*, September 16, 1975, p. C1.

5. Ibid.; see also Maryland-National Parks and Planning Commission, *Crime Analysis 1975: Prince George's County* (August 1975), p. 86.

6. *U.S. Department of Justice, Federal Bureau of Investigation, Uniform Crime Reports for the United States: 1974*, p. 186.(Washington, D.C.: U.S.Government Printing Office).

7. Maryland-National Capital Parks and Planning Commission, *Crime Analysis 1975*, p. 191.

8. See *UCR-1974*, p. 190.

9. "Arrest Data Reveal Profile of Suspect," p. C1; and Maryland-National Capital Parks and Planning Commission, *Crime Analysis 1975*, p. 86.

10. *UCR-1974*, p. 191.

11. Anthony Bouza, *How to Stop Crime* (New York: Plenum, 1993), p. 57.

12. Quoted in George Will, "A Measure of Morality," *Washington Post*, December 16, 1993, p. A25.

13. Speech to International Association of Chiefs of Police, September 28, 1981.

14. *UCR-1991*, p. 218.

15. *UCR-1991*, p. 223.

16. *UCR-1991*, p. 212.

17. U.S. Bureau of the Census, *Statistical Abstract of the United States: 1992*, 112th ed., p. 16, Table no. 15. Blacks accounted for 44.8 percent of arrests for violent crime in 1991. For "city arrests," the percentage of blacks for Index crimes is 36.9; for violent crimes it is 48.9 (*UCR-1991*, pp. 231, 240).

18. For documentation see Jeffrey Reiman, ". . . and the Poor Get Prison." In *The Rich Get Richer and the Poor Get Prison*, 4th Edition, pp. 100-137. (Allyn and Bacon, 1995).

19. *The Challenge of Crime in a Free Society: A Report by the President's Commission on Law Enforcement and Administration of Justice*, p. 44; see also p. 160. Washington, D.C.: U.S. Government Printing Office, February 1967.

20. Ibid.

21. This transformation has been noted by Erving Goffman in his sensitive description of total institutions, *Asylums* (Garden City, N.Y.: Doubleday, 1961).

> *This interpretative scheme of the total institution automatically begins to operate as soon as the inmate enters, the staff having the notion that entrance is prima facie evidence that one must be the kind of person the institution was set up to handle. A man in a political prison must be traitorous; a man in a prison must be a law-breaker; a man in a mental hospital must be sick. If not traitorous, criminal, or sick, why else would he be here? [p. 84]*

22. *Washington Post*, January 11, 1983, p. C10.

23. This answers Graeme Newman, who observes that most criminals on TV are white and wonders what the "ruling class" or conservatives "have to gain by denying the criminality of Blacks." Graeme R. Newman, "Popular Culture and Criminal Justice: A Preliminary Analysis," *Journal of Criminal Justice* 18 (1990), pp. 261-74.

24. Newman, "Popular Culture and Criminal Justice: A Preliminary Analysis," pp. 263-64.

25. Barbara Matusow, "If It Bleeds, It Leads," *Washingtonian*, January 1988, p. 102.

26. "Titillating Channels: TV is Going Tabloid As Shows Seek Sleaze and Find Profits, Too," *Wall Street Journal*, May 18, 1988, p. 1.

27. "Crime in America: The Shocking Truth," *McCall's*, March 1987, p. 144.

28. Norval Morris and Gordon Hawkins, *The Honest Politician's Guide to Crime Control* (Chicago: University of Chicago Press, 1970), p. 2.

29. *Challenge*, p. 7.

So, too, a person who calls forth the society's most drastic weapons of defense must pose the gravest danger to its well-being. Why else the reaction? The point is put well and tersely by D. Chapman: "There is a circular pattern in thinking: we are hostile to wicked people, wicked people are punished, punished people are wicked, we are hostile to punished people because they are wicked." "The Stereotype of the Criminal and the Social Consequences," *International Journal of Criminology and Penology* 1 (1973), p. 16.

Reprinted from: Jeffrey Reiman, "A Crime By Any Other Name." In *The Rich Get Richer and the Poor Get Prison*, 4th Edition, pp. 49-56, 59-61, 69, 89-99. Copyright © 1995 by Allyn and Bacon. Reprinted by permission. ✦

4

The Rise of the Child-Saving Movement: A Study in Social Policy and Correctional Reform

Anthony Platt

Until *the beginning of the twentieth century, legal distinctions were not made between adult and juvenile offenders. Children who broke the law were either overlooked or treated as adults. What Anthony Platt calls the child-saving movement changed all that, however. Made up of middle-class women desiring to reform the system, the movement succeeded in creating special laws and special courts in every state. Juveniles, typically defined as children under 18, were now treated in a special, more "humanitarian" way supposedly designed to reform the child. In so doing, the movement's impact was not entirely positive. Youthful misconduct once overlooked or handled by the family became defined as delinquency and was processed by juvenile courts and juvenile correctional facilities. Law-breaking children were denied legal rights extended to adults. This situation remained for close to seven decades. Juvenile reformatories often turned out to be as barbaric as those housing adults. All these evils were brought about in the name of reform.*

The origin and early implementation of this movement is an illustration of the relationship between law and social power. In this instance, middle-class reformers wanted to "save" children of the lower class from their disadvantaged environment and early socialization by imposing state-sanctioned controls on their behavior. To do so, they created and organized a social movement to change old laws and create new ones. In retrospect, we can say that both positive and negative consequences flowed from their success. It is interesting to note that nearly a hundred years after the work of the child savers, another social movement is advocating the return of many juvenile offenders to the adult court for processing and punishment, thus signifying the end of separate treatment for some juveniles.

This paper analyzes the nature and origins of the reform movement in juvenile justice and juvenile corrections at the end of the nineteenth century. Delinquency raises fundamental questions about the objects of social control, and it was through the child-saving movement that the modern system of delinquency-control emerged in the United States. The child-savers were responsible for creating a new legal institution for penalizing children (juvenile court) and a new correctional institution to accommodate the needs of youth (reformatory). The origins of "delinquency" are to be found in the programs and ideas of these reformers, who recognized the existence and carriers of delinquent norms.

Images of Delinquency

The child-saving movement, like most moral crusades, was characterized by a "rhetoric of legitimization,"[1] built on traditional values and imagery. From the medical profession, the child-savers borrowed the imagery of pathology, infection, and treatment; from the tenets of Social Darwinism, they derived their pessimistic views about the intractability of human nature and the innate moral defects of the working class; finally, their ideas about the biological and environmental origins of crime may be attributed to the positivist tradition in European criminology and to anti-urban sentiments associated with the rural, Protestant ethic.

American criminology in the last century was essentially a practical affair. Theoretical concepts of crime were imported from Europe, and an indiscriminating eclecticism dominated the literature. Lombrosian positivism and Social Darwinism were the major sources of intellectual justification for crime workers. The pessimism of Darwinism, however, was counterbalanced by notions of charity, religious optimism, and the dignity of suffering which were implicit components of the Protestant ethic.

. . . The first American writers on crime were physicians, like Benjamin Rush and Isaac Ray, who were trained according to European methods. The social sciences were similarly imported from Europe, and American criminologists fitted their data to the theoretical framework of criminal anthropology. Herbert Spencer's writings had an enormous impact on American intellectuals, and Cesare Lombroso, perhaps the most significant figure in nineteenth-century criminology, looked for recognition in the United States when he felt that his experiments had been neglected in Europe.[2]

Although Lombroso's theoretical and experimental studies were not translated into English until 1911, his findings were known by American academics in the early 1890's, and their popularity, like Spencer's works, was based on the fact that they confirmed popular assumptions about the character and existence of a "criminal class." Lombroso's original theory suggested the existence of a criminal type distinguishable from noncriminals by observable physical anomalies of a degenerative or atavistic nature. He proposed that the criminal was a morally inferior human species, characterized by physical traits reminiscent of apes, lower primates, and savage tribes. The criminal was thought to be morally retarded and, like a small child, instinctively aggressive and precocious unless restrained.[3] It is not difficult to see the connection between biological determinism in criminological literature and the principles of "natural selection"; both of these theoretical positions automatically justified the "eradication of elements that constituted a permanent and serious danger."[4]

Nature versus nurture

Before 1900, American writers were familiar with Lombroso's general propositions but had only the briefest knowledge of his research techniques.[5] Although the emerging doctrines of preventive criminology implied human malleability, most American penologists were preoccupied with the intractability of the "criminal classes."

. . . Confronted by the evidence of Darwin, Galton, Dugdale, Caldwell, and many other disciples of the biological image of man, correctional professionals were compelled to admit that "a large proportion of the unfortunate children that go to make up the great army of criminals are not born right."[6] Reformers adopted the rhetoric of Darwinism in order to emphasize the urgent need for confronting the "crime problem" before it got completely out of hand.[7] . . .

The organization of correctional workers through national representatives and their identification with the professions of law and medicine operated to discredit the tenets of Darwinism and Lombrosian theory. Correctional workers did not think of themselves merely as the custodians of a pariah class. The self-image of penal reformers as doctors rather than guards and the domination of criminological research in the United States by physicians helped to encourage the acceptance of "therapeutic" strategies in prisons and reformatories. . . . Perhaps what is more significant is that physicians furnished the official rhetoric of penal reform. Admittedly, the criminal was "pathological" and "diseased," but medical science offered the possibility of miraculous cures. Although there was a popular belief in the existence of a "criminal class" separated from the rest of mankind by a "vague boundary line," there was no good reason why this class could not be identified, diagnosed, segregated, changed, and controlled.[8]

By the late 1890's, most correctional administrators agreed that hereditary theories of crime were overfatalistic. The superintendent of the Kentucky Industrial School of Reform told delegates to a national conference on corrections that heredity is "unjustifiably made a bugaboo to discourage efforts at rescue. We know that physical heredity tendencies can be neutralized and often nullified by proper counteracting precautions."[9] . . .

Charles Cooley was one of the first sociologists to observe that criminal behavior depended as much upon social and economic circumstances as it did upon the inheritance of biological traits. "The criminal class," he said, "is largely the result of society's bad workmanship upon fairly good material." In support of this argument, he noted that there was a "large and fairly trustworthy body of evidence" to suggest that many "degenerates" could be converted into "useful citizens by rational treatment."[10]

Urban disenchantment

Another important influence on nineteenth-century criminology was a disenchantment with urban life . . . Immigrants were regarded as "unsocialized," and the city's impersonality compounded their isolation and degradation. "By some cruel alchemy," wrote Julia Lathrop, "we take the sturdiest of European peasantry and at once destroy in a large measure its power to rear to decent livelihood the first generation of offspring upon our soil."[11] The city symbolically embodied all the worst features of industrial life. . . .

Programs which promoted rural and primary group concepts were encouraged because slum life was regarded as unregulated, vicious, and lacking social rules. Its inhabitants were depicted as abnormal and maladjusted, living their lives in chaos and conflict.[12] It was consequently the task of social reformers to make city life more wholesome, honest, and free from depravity. . . .

Although there was a wide difference of opinion among experts as to the precipitating causes of crime, it was generally agreed that criminals were abnormally conditioned by a multitude of biological and environmental forces, some of which were permanent and irreversible. Biological theories of crime were modified to incorporate a developmental view of human behavior. If, as it was believed, criminals are conditioned by biological heritage and brutish living conditions, then prophylactic measures must be taken early in life. Criminals of the future generations must be reached. "They are born to

crime," wrote the penologist Enoch Wines in 1880, "brought up for it. They must be saved."[13]

Maternal Justice

The 1880's and 1890's represented for many middle-class intellectuals and professionals a period of discovery of the "dim attics and damp cellars in poverty-stricken sections of populous towns" and of "innumerable haunts of misery throughout the land."[14] The city was suddenly discovered to be a place of scarcity, disease, neglect, ignorance, and "dangerous influences." Its slums were the "last resorts of the penniless and the criminal"; here humanity reached its lowest level of degradation and despair.[15]

The discovery of problems posed by "delinquent" youth was greatly influenced by the role of feminist reformers in the child-saving movement. It was widely agreed that it was a woman's business to be involved in regulating the welfare of children, for women were considered the "natural caretakers" of wayward children.[16] . . .

Child-saving was a predominantly feminist movement, and it was regarded even by antifeminists as female domain. The social circumstances behind this appreciation of maternalism were women's emancipation and the accompanying changes in the character of traditional family life. Educated middle-class women now had more leisure time but a limited choice of careers. Child-saving was a reputable task for women who were allowed to extend their housekeeping functions into the community without denying antifeminist stereotypes of woman's nature and place. . . .

Child-saving may be understood as a crusade which served symbolic and status functions for native, middle-class Americans, particularly feminist groups. . . . Their traditional functions were dramatically threatened by the weakening of domestic roles and the specialized rearrangement of family life.[17] One of the main forces behind the child-saving movement was a concern for the structure of family life and the proper socialization of young persons, since it was these concerns that had traditionally given purpose to a woman's life. Professional organizations—such as Settlement Houses, Women's Clubs, Bar Associations, and penal organizations—regarded child-saving as a problem of women's rights, whereas their opponents seized upon it as an opportunity to keep women in their proper place. . . . In fact, the new role of social worker was created by deference to antifeminist stereotypes of a "woman's place."

A woman's place

Feminist involvement in child-saving was endorsed by a variety of penal and professional organizations. Their participation was usually justified as an extension of their housekeeping functions so that they did not view themselves, nor were they regarded by others, as competitors for jobs usually performed by men. Proponents of the "new penology" insisted that reformatories should resemble home life, for institutions without women were likely to do more harm than good to inmates. . . .

Female delegates to philanthropic and correctional conferences also realized that correctional work suggested the possibility of useful careers. . . . Women were exhorted by other delegates to make their lives meaningful by participating in welfare programs, volunteering their time and services, and getting acquainted with less privileged groups.[18] . . .

Although the child-savers were responsible for some minor reforms in jails and reformatories, they were more particularly concerned with extending governmental control over a whole range of youthful activities that had previously been handled on an informal basis. The main aim of the child-savers was to impose sanctions on conduct unbecoming youth and to disqualify youth from enjoying adult privileges.[19] . . .

The child-saving movement was not so much a break with the past as an affirmation of faith in traditional institutions. Parental authority, education at home, and the virtues of rural life were emphasized because they were in decline at this time. The child-saving movement was, in part, a crusade which, through emphasizing the dependence of the social order on the proper socialization of children, implicitly elevated the nuclear family and, more especially, the role of women as stalwarts of the family. The child-savers were prohibitionists, in a general sense, who believed that social progress depended on efficient law enforcement, strict supervision of children's leisure and recreation, and the regulation of illicit pleasures. What seemingly began as a movement to humanize the lives of adolescents soon developed into a program of moral absolutism through which youth was to be saved from movies, pornography, cigarettes, alcohol, and anything else which might possibly rob them of their innocence. . . .

Juvenile Court

The essential preoccupation of the child-saving movement was the recognition and control of youthful deviance. It brought attention to, and thus "invented," new categories of youthful misbehavior which had been hitherto unappreciated. The efforts of the child-savers were institutionally expressed in the juvenile court, which, despite recent legislative and constitutional reforms, is generally acknowledged as their most significant contribution to progressive penology.

The juvenile-court system was part of a general movement directed towards removing adolescents from the criminal-law process and creating special programs for delinquent, dependent, and neglected children. Regarded widely as "one of the greatest advances in child welfare that has ever occurred," the juvenile court was considered "an integral part of total welfare planning."[20] . . .

The juvenile court was a special tribunal created by statute to determine the legal status of children and adolescents. Underlying the juvenile-court movement was the concept of *parens patriae* by which the courts were authorized to handle with wide discretion the problems of "its least fortunate junior citizens."[21] The administration of juvenile justice differed in many important respects from the criminal-court processes. A child was not accused of a crime but offered assistance and guidance; intervention in his life was not supposed to carry the stigma of criminal guilt. Judicial records were not generally available to the press or public, and juvenile court hearings were conducted in relative privacy. Juvenile-court procedures were typically informal and inquisitorial. Specific criminal safeguards of due process were not applicable because juvenile proceedings were defined by statute as civil in character.[22]

The original statutes enabled the courts to investigate a wide variety of youthful needs and misbehavior. . . . Statutory definitions of "delinquency"encompassed (1) acts that would be criminal if committed by adults; (2) acts that violated county, town, or municipal ordinances; and (3) violations of vaguely defined catch-alls—such as "vicious or immoral behavior," "incorrigibility," and "truancy"— which "seem to express the notion that the adolescent, if allowed to continue, will engage in more serious conduct."[23]

The juvenile-court movement went far beyond a concern for special treatment of adolescent offenders. It brought within the ambit of governmental control a set of youthful activities that had been previously ignored or dealt with on an informal basis. It was not by accident that the behavior selected for penalizing by the child-savers—sexual license, drinking, roaming the streets, begging, frequenting dance halls and movies, fighting, and being seen in public late at night—was most directly relevant to the children of lower-class migrant and immigrant families.

The juvenile court was not perceived by its supporters as a revolutionary experiment, but rather as a culmination of traditionally valued practices.[24] The child-saving movement was "antilegal," in the sense that it derogated civil rights and procedural formalities, while relying heavily on extra-legal techniques. The judges of the new court were empowered to investigate the character and social life of predelinquent as well as delinquent children; they examined motivation rather than intent, seeking to identify the moral reputation of problematic children. The requirements of preventative penology and child-saving further justified the court's intervention in cases where no offense had actually been committed, but where, for example, a child was posing problems for some person in authority such as a parent or teacher or social worker.

The personal touch

. . . Juvenile court judges had to be carefully selected for their skills as expert diagnosticians and for their appreciation of the "helping" professions. Miriam Van Waters, for example, regarded the juvenile court as a "laboratory of human behavior" and its judges as "experts with scientific training and specialists in the art of human relations." It was the judge's task to "get the whole truth about a child" in the same way that a "physician searches for every detail that bears on the condition of a patient."[25]

The child-savers' interest in preventive strategies and treatment programs was based on the premise that delinquents possess innate or acquired characteristics which predispose them to crime and distinguish them from law-abiding youths. Delinquents were regarded as constrained by a variety of biological and environmental forces, so that their proper treatment involved discovery of the "cause of the aberration" and application of "the appropriate corrective or antidote."[26] . . .

The use of terms like "unsocialized," "maladjusted," and "pathological" to describe the behavior of delinquents implied that "socialized" and "adjusted" children conform to middle-class morality and participate in respectable institutions.[27] The failure empirically to demonstrate psychological differences between delinquents and nondelinquents did not discourage the child-savers from believing that rural and middle-class values constitute "normality." The unique character of the child-saving movement was its concern for predelinquent offenders— "children who occupy the debatable ground between criminality and innocence"—and its claim that it could transform potential criminals into respectable citizens by training them in "habits of industry, self-control and obedience to law."[28] This policy justified the diminishing of traditional procedures in juvenile court. If children were to be rescued, it was important that the rescuers be free to provide their services without legal hindrance. Delinquents had to be saved, transformed, and reconstituted. . . .

The Reformatory System

It was through the reformatory system that the child-savers hoped to demonstrate that delinquents were capable of being converted into law-abiding citizens. The reformatory was initially developed in the United States during the middle of the nineteenth century as a special form of prison discipline for adolescents and young adults. . . .

The reformatory was distinguished from the traditional penitentiary by its policy of indeterminate sentencing, the "mark" system, and "organized persuasion" rather than "coercive restraint." Its administrators assumed that abnormal and troublesome individuals could become useful and productive citizens. Wines and Dwight, in a report to the New York legislature in 1867, proposed that the ultimate aim of penal policy was reformation of the criminal, which could only be achieved

> by placing the prisoner's fate, as far as possible, in his own hand, by enabling him, through industry and good conduct to raise himself, step by step, to a position of less restraint; while idleness and bad conduct, on the other hand, keep him in a state of coercion and restraint.[29]

But, as Brockway observed at the first meeting of the National Prison Congress in 1870, the "new penology" was tough-minded and devoid of "sickly sentimentalism . . . Criminals shall either be cured, or kept under such continued restraint as gives guarantee of safety from further depredations."[30]

Reformatories, unlike penitentiaries and jails, theoretically repudiated punishments based on intimidation and repression. They took into account the fact that delinquents were "either physically or mentally below the average." The reformatory system was based on the assumption that proper training can counteract the impositions of poor family life, a corrupt environment, and poverty, while at the same time toughening and preparing delinquents for the struggle ahead. . . .

The reformatory movement spread rapidly through the United States, and European

visitors crossed the Atlantic to inspect and admire the achievements of their pragmatic colleagues. Mary Carpenter, who visited the United States in 1873, was generally satisfied with the "generous and lavish expenditures freely incurred to promote the welfare of the inmates, and with the love of religion." Most correctional problems with regard to juvenile delinquents, she advised, could be remedied if reformatories were built like farm schools or "true homes."[31] . . .

To cottage and country

Granted the assumption that "nurture" could usually overcome most of nature's defects, reformatory-administrators set about the task of establishing programs consistent with the aim of retraining delinquents for law-abiding careers. . . . The heritage of biological imagery and Social Darwinism had a lasting influence on American criminology, and penal reformers continued to regard delinquency as a problem of individual adjustment to the demands of industrial and urban life. Delinquents had to be removed from contaminating situations, segregated from their "miserable surroundings," instructed, and "put as far as possible on a footing of equality with the rest of the population."[32]

The trend from congregate housing in the city to group living in the country represented a significant change in the organization of penal institutions for young offenders. The family or cottage plan differed in several important respects from the congregate style of traditional prisons and jails. . . .

The new penology emphasized the corruptness and artificiality of the city: from progressive education, it inherited a concern for naturalism, purity, and innocence. It is not surprising, therefore, that the cottage plan also entailed a movement to a rural location. The aim of penal reformers was not merely to use the countryside for teaching agricultural skills. The confrontation between corrupt delinquents and unspoiled nature was intended to have a spiritual and regenerative effect. The romantic attachment to rural values was quite divorced from social and agricultural realities. It was based on a sentimental and nostalgic repudiation of city life. Advocates of the reformatory system generally ignored the economic attractiveness of city work and the redundancy of farming skills. As one economist cautioned reformers in 1902:

> Whatever may be said about the advantages of farm life for the youth of our land, and however much it may be regretted that young men and women are leaving the farm and flocking to the cities, there can be no doubt that the movement cityward will continue. . . . There is great danger that many who had left the home (that is, reformatory), unable to find employment in agricultural callings, would drift back to the city and not finding there an opportunity to make use of the technical training secured in the institution, would become discouraged and resume their old criminal associations and occupations.[33]

The "new" reformatory suffered, like all its predecessors, from overcrowding, mismanagement, "boodleism," understaffing, and inadequate facilities. Its distinctive features were the indeterminate sentence, the movement to cottage and country, and agricultural training. Although there was a decline in the use of brutal punishments, inmates were subjected to severe personal and physical controls: military exercises, "training of the will," and long hours of tedious labor constituted the main program of reform.

Summary and Conclusions

The child-saving movement was responsible for reforms in the ideological and institutional control of "delinquent" youth. The concept of the born delinquent was modified with the rise of a professional class of penal administrators and social servants who promoted a developmental view of human behavior and regarded most delinquent youth as salvageable. The child-savers helped to create special judicial and correctional institutions for the processing and management of "troublesome" youth.

There has been a shift during the last fifty years or so in official policies concerning delinquency. The emphasis has shifted from one emphasizing the criminal nature of delinquency to the "new humanism" which speaks of disease, illness, contagion, and the like. It is essentially a shift from a legal to a medical emphasis. The emergence of a medical emphasis is of considerable significance, since it is a powerful rationale for organizing social action in the most diverse behavioral aspects of our society. For example, the child-savers were not concerned merely with "humanizing" conditions under which children were treated by the criminal law. It was rather their aim to extend the scope of governmental control over a wide variety of personal misdeeds and to regulate potentially disruptive persons.[34] The child-savers' reforms were politically aimed at lower-class behavior and were instrumental in intimidating and controlling the poor.

The child-savers made a fact out of the norm of adolescent dependence. . . . The juvenile court reached into the private lives of youth and disguised basically punitive policies in the rhetoric of "rehabilitation."[35] The child-savers were prohibitionists, in a general sense, who believed that adolescents needed protection from even their own inclinations.

The basic conservatism of the child-saving movement is apparent in the reformatory system which proved to be as tough-minded as traditional forms of punishment. Reformatory programs were unilateral, coercive, and an invasion of human dignity. What most appealed to correctional workers were the paternalistic assumptions of the "new penology," its belief in social progress through individual reform, and its nostalgic preoccupation with the "naturalness" and intimacy of a preindustrial way of life.

The child-saving movement was heavily influenced by middle-class women who extended their housewifely roles into public service. Their contribution may also be seen as a "symbolic crusade" in defense of the nuclear family and their positions within it. They regarded themselves as moral custodians and supported programs and institutions dedicated to eliminating youthful immorality. Social service was an instrumentality for female emancipation, and it is not too unreasonable to suggest that women advanced their own fortune at the expense of the dependency of youth.

This analysis of the child-saving movement suggests the importance of (1) understanding the relationship between correctional reforms and related changes in the administration of criminal justice, (2) accounting for the motives and purposes of those enterprising groups who generate such reforms, (3) investigating the methods by which communities establish the formal machinery for regulating crime, and (4) distinguishing between idealized goals and enforced conditions in the implementation of correctional reforms. . . .

Discussion Questions

1. Explain why the child-saving movement was a predominantly feminist movement. What role did women play in this movement? Why were they involved? What social factors precipitated the movement? How was the structure of the family changing?

2. In what ways was the reformatory different than the traditional penitentiary? What were the methods of correction used in the reformatory?

3. Discuss the "shift" in the official policies concerning delinquency from the late nineteenth to the early twentieth century. What were the views of the nature of delinquency? How did they change?

Notes

1. This term is used by Donald W. Ball, "An Abortion Clinic Ethnography," 14 *Social Problems*, 1967, pp. 293-301.

2. See Lombroso's Introduction to Arthur MacDonald, *Criminology* (New York: Funk and Wagnalls, 1893).

3. Marvin E. Wolfgang, "Cesare Lombroso," in Hermann Mannheim (ed.), *Pioneers in Criminology* (London: Stevens and Sons, 1960), pp. 168-227.

4. Leon Radzinowicz, *Ideology and Crime* London: Heinemann Educational Books, (1966), p. 55.

5. See, for example, Arthur MacDonald, *Abnormal Man* (Washington, D.C.: U.S. Government Printing Office, 1893); and Robert Fletcher, *The New School of Criminal Anthropology* (Washington, D.C.: Judd and Delwiler, 1891).

6. Sarah B. Cooper, "The Kindergarten as Child-Saving Work," in National Conference of Charities and Correction, *Proceedings* (Madison, 1883), pp. 130-138.

7. I.N. Kerlin, "The Moral Imbecile," in National Conference of Charities and Correction, *Proceedings* (Baltimore, 1890), pp. 244-250.

8. See, for example, Illinois, Board of State Commissioners of Public Charities, *Second Biennial Report* (Springfield: State Journal Steam Print, 1873), pp. 195-196.

9. Peter Caldwell, "The Duty of the State to Delinquent Children," National Conference of Charities and Correction, *Proceedings* (New Haven, 1895), pp. 134-143.

10. Charles H. Cooley, "'Nature v. Nurture' in the Making of Social Careers," National Conference of Charities and Correction, *Proceedings* (Grand Rapids, Michigan, 1896), pp. 405.

11. Julia Lathrop, "The Development of the Probation System in a Large City," 13 *Charity* (January 1905), p. 348.

12. William Foote Whyte, "Social Disorganization in the Slums," 8 *American Sociological Review* (1943), pp. 34-39.

13. Enoch C. Wines, *The State of Prisons and of Child-Saving Institutions in the Civilized World* (Cambridge, MA: Harvard University Press, 1880), p. 132.

14. William P. Letchworth, "Children of the State," National Conference of Charities and Correction, *Proceedings* (St. Paul, MN, 1886), p. 138. The idea that intellectuals *discovered* poverty as a result of their own alienation from the centers of power has been fully treated by Richard Hofstadter, *The Age of Reform* (New York: Vintage Books, 1955); and Christopher Lasch, *The New Radicalism in America, 1889-1963: The Intellectual as a Social Type* (New York: Alfred A. Knopf, 1965).

15. R.W. Hill, "The Children of Shinbone Alley," National Conference of Charities and Correction, *Proceedings* (Omaha, 1887), p. 231.

16. Robert Sunley, "Early Nineteenth Century American Literature on Child-Rearing," in Margaret Mead and Martha Wolfenstein (eds.), *Childhood in Contemporary Cultures* (Chicago: University of Chicago Press, 1955), p. 152; see also Orville G. Brim, *Education for Child-Rearing* (New York: Free Press, 1965), pp. 321-349.

17. Talcott Parsons and Robert F. Baley, *Family, Socialization and Interaction Process* (Glencoe, IL: Free Press, 1955), pp. 3-33.

18. Clara T. Leonard, "Family Homes for Pauper and Dependent Children," in Annual Conference of Charities, *Proceedings*, 1879, *loc. cit.*, p. 175.

19. Bennett Berger, Review of Frank Musgrove, *Youth and the Social Order*, 32 *American Sociological Review*, 1927, p. 1021.

20. Charles L. Chute, "The Juvenile Court in Retrospect," 13 *Federal Probation* (September 1949), p. 7; Harrison A. Dobbs, "In Defense of Juvenile Courts," 13 *Federal Probation* (September 1949), p. 29.

21. Gustav L. Schramm, "The Juvenile Court Idea," 13 *Federal Probation* (September 1949), p. 21.

22. Monrad G. Paulsen, "Fairness to the Juvenile Offender," 41 *Minnesota Law Review* 1957, pp. 547-567. Note: "Rights and Rehabilitation in the Juvenile Courts," 67 *Columbia Law Review*, 1967, pp. 281-341.

23. Joel F. Handler and Margaret K. Rosenheim, "Privacy and Welfare: Public Assistance and Juvenile Justice," 31 *Law and Contemporary Problems*, 1966, pp. 377-412.

24. A reform movement, according to Herbert Blumer, is differentiated from a revolution by its inherent respectability and acceptance of an existing social order. "The primary function of the reform movement is probably not so much the bringing about of social change, as it is to reaffirm the ideal values in a given society."—Herbert Blumer, "Collective Behavior," in Alfred McClung Lee (ed.), *Principles of Sociology* (New York: Barnes and Noble, 1963), pp. 212-213.

25. Miriam Van Waters, "The Socialization of Juvenile Court Procedure," 12 *Journal of Criminal Law and Criminology*, 1922, pp. 61.

26. Illinois, Board of State Commissioners of Public Charities, *First Biennial Report* (Springfield: Illinois Journal Printing Office, 1871), p. 180.

27. C. Wright Mills, "The Professional Ideology of Social Pathologists," in Bernard Rosenberg, Israel Gerver, and F. William Howton (eds.), *Mass Society in Crisis* (New York: The Macmillan Company, 1964), pp. 92-111.

28. Illinois, Board of State Commissioners of Public Charities, *Sixth Biennial Report* (Springfield: H.W. Rokker, 1880), p. 104.

29. Max Grunhut, *Penal Reform* (Oxford, England: Clarendon Press, 1948), p. 90.

30. This speech is reprinted in Zebulon Reed Brockway, *Fifty Years of Prison Service* (New York: Charities Publication Committee, 1912), pp. 389-408.

31. Mary Carpenter, "Suggestions on Reformatory Schools and Prison Discipline, Founded on Observations Made During a Visit to the United States," National Prison Reform Congress, *Proceedings* (St. Louis, 1874), pp. 157-173.

32. Morrison, *op. cit.*, pp. 60, 276.

33. M.B. Hammond's comments at the Illinois Conference of Charities (1901), reported in Illinois, Board of State Commissioners of Public Charities, *Seventeenth Biennial Report* (Springfield: Phillips Brothers, 1902), pp. 232-233.

34. This thesis is supported by a European study of family life, Phillipe Aries, *Centuries of Childhood* (New York: Vintage Books, 1965).

35. Francis A. Allen, *The Borderland of Criminal Justice* (Chicago: University of Chicago Press, 1964), *passim*.

5

The Victim's Rights Movement: A Critical View from a Practicing Sociologist

Lynnell J. Simonson

D*o victims of crime matter? For a long time, the official answer to that question was "not much." Because the state is the injured party in a crime, the victim's role has traditionally been to help the state convict the accused by identifying him or her as the offender and testifying to that effect in court. The history of the victim's role is described by Lynnell Simonson in the following section.*

As Simonson points out, this role has been unsatisfactory for victims and has recently changed. A victim's rights movement has emerged in recent years as a result of a number of forces advocating greater participation of victims in the judicial process as well as compensation and counseling for them. Supported by both federal and state laws, victims are now often permitted to make impact statements to the judge before sentencing, are sometimes compensated for their loss, and may receive psychological help to cope with the trauma of victimization.

These changes are not perfect, however, as the author points out. Many legitimate victims are overlooked and the services offered are usually inadequate. Nevertheless, they have symbolic value, allowing victims of crime to believe that the state is concerned about them and their suffering. In other words, recent changes have led to the criminal's not receiving all of the attention and recognition that victims

do matter. While much of this change is illusory, it is important that society continue to ease the burden of victims of crime.

Throughout the centuries, the role, importance, and visibility of the crime victim has varied considerably, reflecting a variety of political and social arrangements. The Enlightenment philosophy, which argued that community, as well as the individual victim, is harmed by the crime led the criminal justice system to remove the victim from the process. This article begins with a brief historical account of the role of the victim in the American criminal justice system and the shifts in ideology that facilitated the purge of victims that has been characteristic of criminal justice in the United States. This historical review helps to illuminate the current status of victims within the criminal justice system, which must be seen from where it emerged and from what it reacted against.

The paper will then discuss the recent "victim's rights movement" and how the "reemergence" of the victim in the criminal justice system came about. I discuss the rationales given by the victim's movement for including the victim in the criminal justice process, and offer a critical assessment of the possible latent interests that might be served by this movement and its proposed reforms. This critical view reveals a possible hidden agenda within the reform movement, and thus adds a dimension to the widely held mainstream understanding of the victim's rights movement. I ask which crime victims are receiving services and whether the services are actually designed to help victims or the prosecutor's office.[1] . . .

The Victim in United States History

The American criminal justice system was shaped largely by the English system, although certain elements can also be traced to French and Dutch traditions. During the seventeenth century when the colonies were being settled, the English relied primarily on a system of private prosecution (Gittler 1984). The victim was at the center of the criminal justice process and had distinct "ownership" of the crime and the justice process. The victim or interested party was responsible for investigating the crime and apprehending the perpetrator. Law enforcement of this time relied upon "hue and cry" whereby the victim called upon neighbors and friends to assist in pursuing the criminal. Victims were also responsible for the cost of the warrant, the constable's services, and attorney's fees for the prosecution of the crime (McDonald 1976). Restitution to the victim was the primary goal of the justice system in colonial America. When the offender was indigent, the victim was authorized to sell the defendant into service for a period corresponding to the amount of damages and the costs associated with the prosecution (Nelson 1974). The victim also had the option of selling the convict's services to another individual. However, if the victim did not sell the convict, they were responsible for the costs of keeping the convict in jail (McDonald 1976).

Restitution as a goal of the criminal justice system fell out of favor in the late eighteenth century for a number of reasons, all linked to the ideas of the Enlightenment. The Enlightenment produced many individuals whose ideas changed the shape and focus of the American criminal justice system. They all shared the belief in the rationality of man, and his ability to plan his actions in order to gain power or comfort. This contrasts with the previously popular notion of original sin and divine providence. The Enlightenment theorists also were the first to focus on individual rights, which had a profound impact on the criminal justice system. Since the criminal justice system arose from the social contract, it was to serve the interests of society, not the individual victim. Victim neglect, therefore, is not just a matter of indifference, but a logical extension of a justice system that treats crime as an offense against the state (Umbreit 1985). Thus, restitution was no longer considered a legitimate goal of the criminal justice system, but the concern of the civil courts (McDonald 1976). There was a growing distinction between criminal and civil law, and the proper avenue for the victim to recover damages became the civil tort (Gittler 1984).

The changes in the way people thought about law accompanied the many changes in the social structure that were also occurring. As cities became increasingly urbanized and characterized by commercial trade, people's sense of social responsibility decreased (McDonald 1976). Although laws were passed attempting to make the community responsible for crime victims' losses, they were unpopular and were soon replaced by cash rewards for convictions of criminals. This led to informers acting as freelance policemen and "thief takers" who made their living catching criminals. There was a growing dissatisfaction with the criminal justice system, and the ideas of Bentham and Beccaria were embraced enthusiastically as models for reform.

In addition to philosophical changes, there were three major developments in the administration of criminal justice which, although they developed for reasons unrelated to victims, nonetheless had a profound affect on the role of the victim in the pursuit of justice. The growth of the office of the public prosecutor and the creation of the modern police force were the first major changes to displace the victim. This shift from private to public investigation and prosecution took control away from victims and limited their role to that of witnesses. These reforms were followed closely by the advent of "the great experiment" in corrections and rehabilitation, the penitentiary (McDonald 1976:650). It has been argued that these changes, along with the virtual elimination of restitution to the victim, were the primary factors leading to the displacement of the victim from the criminal justice system (Gittler 1984).

One of the primary rationales in the nineteenth century for the establishment of the modern police force and the expansion of the public prosecutor's office was the elimination of inequality. "Reformers were concerned about the injustice of a system in which only wealthy victims could afford to buy law enforcement and justice" (McDonald 1977: 298). It was argued that a system of public prosecution might be perceived as consistent with the colonial commitment to a more democratic society. There is also some evidence that the public prosecutor was thought to protect citizens against malicious prosecutions (Jacoby 1980).

The final factor leading to the decline in restitution was the development in the late eighteenth century of the penitentiary, originally conceived of as a humanitarian substitute for capital and corporal punishment. This was also linked to the optimistic ideas of the Enlightenment, namely that crime can be prevented by deterrence. In 1778, the first prison opened in Philadelphia. In 1805, Massachusetts opened its new prison as well. It was initially expected that victims would continue to receive treble damages (restitution and costs of prosecution), and that confinement would only be used when traditional methods were unworkable. However, incarceration soon became the preferred method of punishment and the means by which the victim's stake in the correctional process was finally eliminated. It is significant to note that 1805 was also the last time a Massachusetts court required a convict to pay treble damages to the victim (McDonald 1977).

Although some refer to colonial times as the "golden age of the victim," presumably because the victim had "ownership" of the crime, few would advocate a return to a justice system which required victims to pay for investigation and prosecution costs, not to mention the costs of incarceration. There has been, however, a growing dissatisfaction with the criminal justice system, and part of the problem is thought to lie in the removal of the victim from the process. It is ironic that innovations like the professional police force and the public prosecutor's office, originally designed to liberate an oppressed group of people (poor crime victims), had the effect of denying *all* victims "legal standing" in the criminal justice system. The following section will discuss recent attempts to change the balance of power between the victim, the offender, and the state. It will offer a mainstream view of the forces which led to the current victim's rights movement and the primary goals of the movement. One purpose here is to set the stage for the critical view of the movement offered in the final section of the paper.

The Victim's Rights Movement

Within the last two decades, a movement has developed which advocates the return of the victim to the criminal justice process. Efforts to change the treatment of victims were first initiated by feminists, acting out of concern for rape and domestic violence victims (Brownmiller 1975). Feminists were joined by "law and order groups," frustrated with increasing crime rates, and by victim's associations, who often sought to attract media attention to the "forgotten persons" of the criminal justice system. These efforts were supported by law enforcement, who argued that fewer criminals were prosecuted and convicted as a result of non-cooperation of victims (Davis 1983). Law enforcement was also responding to studies which found that crime victims were afraid of how they would be treated by the criminal justice system, and if they would be believed (Kidd and Chayet 1984; Kilpatrick et al. 1987). Many reforms were enacted in the 1980s, aimed at providing "a series of remedies" to crime victims through the establishment of Victim Assistance Programs (VAPs).

Another primary factor leading to the recent "rediscovery" of crime victims was the empirical and clinical evidence that had emerged describing a "secondary victimization," an additional emotional psychological injury suffered by crime victims when they interacted with individuals within the criminal justice process. Research found that victims were often dissatisfied, frustrated, and resentful of the criminal justice system, especially the court processes (Hagan 1982; Kelly 1984). They reported being unable to rid themselves of feelings of guilt and shame associated with the incident (Smale and Spickenheuer 1979); and they transferred a sense of disorder, powerlessness, and fear to other life spheres (Kelly 1984; McLeod 1986).

Efforts to improve the treatment of crime victims began with attempts to make financial compensation available and to increase the use of restitution as a sentencing option. In 1965, California enacted the first restitution legislation in the United States. The first formal restitution program began operations in Minnesota in 1972 and next in Georgia in

1974 (Viano 1983). This "financial" approach to impact assessment was intended to serve a restorative function in ameliorating victim loss by returning victims to precrime conditions (Edelhertz and Geis 1973; McLeod 1986). This theory of "restitutive justice" starts from the Kantian premise that restitution is the most effective means of restoring the condition of things as they were before the crime disturbed the relations between offender and victim, and between the offender and society. Additionally, some said that restitution allowed the offender to realize the harm he or she had done and to accept genuine responsibility for repairing it (Goldstein 1982; Umbreit 1985).

However, it soon became clear that restitution offered compensation to only a limited number of victims, because many offenders had no money and few prospects of future employment. The emphasis of the victim's movement then shifted from working for restitution only, to lobbying for legislative changes to provide for victim assistance services, and an insurance of sorts for crime victims (McLeod 1986). These efforts led to the passage of *Public Law 92-291*, known as the *Federal Victim Witness Protection Act of 1982*, which described the "cooperation of victims to be essential to the functioning of the criminal justice system . . . and the current criminal justice system [as] unresponsive to their real needs." The Congress declared the purpose of the legislation to "enhance and protect the necessary role of crime victims . . . [and to] provide a series of remedies, including restitution, guidelines for fair treatment of victims, and victim impact statements." Programs were then designed to respond to victims more immediate needs like child care, transportation, and notification of delays.

One of the most significant and controversial changes resulting from this legislation was the right of the victim to submit a victim impact statement. A victim impact statement (VIS) is a statement containing "information concerning any harm, including financial, social, psychological, and physical, done to or loss suffered by any victim of the offense; and any other information that may aid the court in sentencing including the restitution needs of the victim" (P.L. 92-291, S. 2420,

1982). The judge is to consult the report and consider it in light of the four purposes of sentencing identified in the *Sentencing Reform Act of 1984:* punishment, deterrence, incapacitation, and rehabilitation (Hoffman 1983, Talbert 1988). The inclusion of a VIS in the pre-sentence investigation allows the severity of the crime to be weighed in determining the length of sentence imposed, and also allows comprehensive restitution to be ordered.

The demand to bring victims back into the sentencing process centers both on the victim's right to be heard concerning the impact of the crime on his or her life, and the opportunity for the victim to express their wishes regarding the disposition of the offender and other related concerns (Erez and Tontodonato 1990). By participating in the criminal justice process, the victim reasserts a sense of control over his or her life. The "perception of control" variable has been identified as a key factor in understanding the impact of victimization (Kilpatrick and Otto 1987). However, as Goldstein (1982, p. 517) notes, "the purpose of victim participation is not only to make the victim feel better, but also to assure fuller consideration of issues of accuracy and legality where there is a risk that such issues will submerged by the pressures of bureaucracy" (Davis et al. 1984, Forst and Hernon 1985).

Currently, there are many rationales given for the increased involvement of crime victims in the criminal justice process. Most practically, enhancement of the rights and privileges of crime victims are said to encourage victim cooperation within the system, and result in improved efficiency and effectiveness of the system in general (Davis 1983; McLeod 1986). By inviting victim participation the system hopes to increase victim satisfaction, encouraging victim involvement and thereby enhancing system efficiency (Seeba 1982; McLeod 1986). Another argument in favor of victim participation, particularly in the sentencing phase, is that it will increase accuracy in sentencing proportionate to the harm done (Lamborn 1987). The effectiveness of sentencing, as the public degradation ceremony for the crime, is also thought to be increased by victim involvement

(Little 1983; Rubel 1986; Young 1987). Humanitarian and social welfare rationales for providing relief to victims are often cited, along with declarations of the system's injustice, claiming that it ignores victims' interests and treats them unfairly. A "social contract" rationale is also given for involving the victim, stressing that it is the duty of the state to protect its citizens from attack (Hudson 1984). Finally, victim involvement is recommended for the psychological healing and restoration of the crime victim (Rubel 1986; Young 1987). By participating in the prosecution process, the victim increases their perception of control, which has been shown to assist them in their recovery (Kilpatrick and Otto 1987).

The concerns of those opposed to victim input into the sentencing process represent a significant challenge. This is primarily because their arguments are based upon legal principles, whereas the arguments surrounding the inclusion of the VIS in sentencing are humanitarian or organizationally motivated. The courts, it is argued, are not in the business of making victims feel better. The courts exist to sanction someone who has broken society's rules. Therefore, when examining whether victims should be allowed input into the sentencing process, it seems logical to discuss the rationales for punishment described in the *Sentencing Reform Act of 1984:* retribution, deterrence, incapacitation, and rehabilitation. These are the concepts presumed to underlie the sentences received by offenders in the United States today.

Using a model of retribution, victim input is allowed to the extent that it provides an accurate objective measure of victim harm. However, it would not allow for the victim's suggestions for sentencing (Morris 1976). The deterrence model justifies victim input at sentencing, but only if it increases the certainty of the sentence (Talbert 1988). If allowing victim input into sentencing leads to a greater cooperation of victims with prosecutors, it is possible that victim impact statements could lead to greater certainty of the sanction. The incapacitation model only calls for input from victims when they know the defendant well and may have valuable information regarding the lifestyle and past criminal behavior of the offender.

To summarize, victim participation can be compatible with the explicit goals of sentencing. However, current sentencing goals do not provide adequate rationales for the widespread use of the VIS (Simonson 1993).

Opponents of increased victim participation in the criminal justice system argue that the state can more effectively and objectively resolve conflicts than can individuals, and that increasing involvement of the victim in the process acts to defeat the destabilizing effects of the state appropriation of conflicts (Henderson 1985; Keisel 1984). They argue that the court should be insulated from public pressures, and that victims' input would jeopardize that independence. Major concerns also arise regarding the appearance of justice and actual justice. Judges and defense attorneys tend to equate sensitivity to victim's problems with a lack of fairness to the defendant (Erez 1990; Kelly 1990; Rubel 1987). Others have voiced concerns about the possibility that victims' input could increase sentencing disparity and reduce the predictability of outcomes (Davis et al. 1984; Ranish and Shichor 1985).

The struggle over the proper role of the victim in the criminal justice system is far from over. The constitutionality of the Victim Impact Statement is still up for debate—a debate that will likely be addressed by the "new" Supreme Court. The primary funding source for VAP's, the *Victim's of Crime Act* (VOCA) will require future authorization from Congress to continue funding at current levels. Crime victims will be competing with other interests for the government's money, and victim's advocates will need to demonstrate what they have accomplished for crime victims with the money they have already received. This seems an opportune time to critically evaluate the success of the victim's rights movement.

The Victim's Rights Movement: A Critical View

As with any historical event, the "causes" of the rise of the victim's movement are subject to interpretation. While it does not entirely contradict the earlier depiction, adopting a critical perspective adds another dimension to the story. According to Quinney (1975:188), a critical perspective is "one of de-mystification, [of] the removal of the myths—the false consciousness—created by the official reality. Conventional experience is revealed for what it is—a reification of an oppressive social order." With regard to crime victims, it urges us to ask how an individual becomes defined as a victim (or client of a VAP), and what role the victim represents or symbolizes in the criminal justice system (Williams and McShane 1992). It suggests that we pay close attention to the power differentials between the victim and the other actors in the criminal justice system, and ask who is benefitting from the victim's rights movement and the reforms achieved thus far.

Why Now?

A critical perspective allows us to see that it is no coincidence that the victim's rights movement developed at much the same time as a new multi-disciplinary area of study, victimology. Grassroots programs advanced by the early feminists were fortunate that their efforts to improve the system's treatment of victims came at the same time that the justice system was becoming aware of its need for more cooperative victims. A series of victimization surveys done in the late 1960s showed that many people failed to report crime to the police (Davis and Henley 1990). In 1973, the Courts Task Force on the National Advisory Commission on Criminal Justice Standards and Goals reported, "the failure of victims/witnesses to attend court proceedings was a significant contributor to dismissal rates," and that "nearly half of the felony arrests in Washington D.C. were being rejected for prosecution because of uncooperative witnesses" (Davis and Henley 1990:158). It is not surprising that institutional efforts to improve the treatment of crime victims came only after studies suggested that the criminal justice system would benefit by such a change (Kelly 1990).

Increasing victim's "perception of control" was found to be in the state's best interest. Research on procedural justice has found that "perceived influence" was more important to satisfaction of victims and defendants than the actual outcome of the case (Smith 1985; Tyler 1984). One study found that victims were more likely to be satisfied with the criminal justice system if they were notified of the outcome of their case, and if they perceived that they had an influence on that outcome (Forst and Hernon 1985). Indeed, a sense of participation was found more critical to the victim's satisfaction with the criminal justice system than whether or not the defendants were punished (Kelly 1984). These findings suggested that giving victims a voice in the criminal justice process would increase their satisfaction with the system as a whole.

It is also no coincidence that the prevailing victim's movement was largely dominated by politically conservative policies and that it was successful in implementing victim's rights legislation during a decade of conservative executive control. Victim advocates with a critical perspective (e.g., feminist, antiracist, anticorporate) have been excluded from such government programs (Elias 1986). Consequently, the conservative crime-control line has become dominant among victim's rights groups.

Who is Served?

A critical look at the implementation of the victim's rights reforms shows us that, in fact, it is primarily those victims who are "of use" to the state and the criminal justice system who have benefitted. First, most victim/witness assistance programs which have developed as a result of the victim's rights movement get their referrals from the prosecutor's office (Hillenbrand and Smith 1989; McDaniel, n.d.; Nice 1988). For example, of the ten VAPs serving victims in North Dakota in 1992, six operated out of the State's Attorney's Office and one out of the Department of Parole and Probation, and three were sponsored by Domestic Violence Programs. VAPs which operate in association with State's Attorney's Offices tend to serve only those victims who have reported the crime to the police; and they pay particular attention to those whose cases the State's Attorney has decided to prosecute.[2] If the advocate has time, she or he will also contact victims whose cases have been dismissed or for some reason will not be prosecuted. Advocates function here as a type of public relations officer for the State's Attorney and try to make the victims feel better about getting inadequate justice. At the quarterly meetings of the North Dakota Victim's Assistance Association (NDVAA), one advocate said the police officers laughingly called her the State's Attorney's "shit deflector."

Of course, there are many victim/witness programs who also accept referrals directly from the police stations and from local social service offices, as well as "self-referrals." I was fortunate to have both the Chief of Police and the County Sheriff on the advisory board for the VAP, which helped me gain access to the police logs. I was able to use my own discretion and contact any and all of the victims who called the police, regardless of whether or not a Uniform Crime Report form was filed, or whether or not a referral was made to the State's Attorney's Office. Ideally, all victims of violent crime and all elderly, handicapped, and child victims were contacted. However, when things got hectic and it was necessary to make choices about which victims to contact immediately and which to postpone contact, cases which were going to trial (or were otherwise engaged in the system) took priority. Additionally, my office was the exception in North Dakota, where six of the offices got referrals directly from the State's Attorney's Office, and two others worked out of Domestic Violence Programs. The latter, however, had neither access to police logs nor "automatic" referrals from the State's Attorney.

In addition to the "referral bias," there is a second way that the VAPs work to advance the agenda of the criminal justice system. In order for a victim to be eligible for "Victim's Compensation" (federal and state money available to compensate victims for expenses resulting from a crime), the incident must be reported to the police. If victimization studies show that almost 50 percent of all crime does not get reported to the police, and only those victims who report crime may receive compensation, it stands to reason that most victims do not receive compensation for their losses which resulted from a crime. The percentage of crime victims actually receiving services drops even further when one consider the fact that of those cases reported to the police, only a certain percentage are ac-

tually prosecuted, and as was stated previously, most victim/witness programs get their referrals from the prosecutor. It becomes clear that although the laws may have been designed to assist all victims of crime, as they have been implemented they often serve the interests of the State's Attorney. Services are available primarily for those who cooperate with the "legitimate" institution of conflict resolution.

Thirdly, those receiving money from the "Crime Victim's Reparations Fund" (CVR), must be "innocent" victims of crime. This is a formal requirement printed on the brochure which is distributed to crime victims. When an application is submitted for CVR funds, copies of the police reports are required and letters of support from the victim/witness advocate are recommended. If these are not included with the initial application, the claims officer contacts the police station and requests them, often creating an additional delay. A conviction is not required to secure funds from CVR, nor does it necessarily guarantee the application will be accepted. If the advisory board concludes that the victim has precipitated the crime, they may and sometimes do reject the application.

A critical perspective reminds us that the artificial dichotomy between the victim and the offender is derived from a middle-class conception of crime, where the victim/offender relationship is static (Williams and McShane 1992). This is problematic for several reasons. The distinction between "innocent" and not so innocent victims fails to take into account the fact that there is often no way to discriminate between the two, and the person identified by police as the perpetrator may simply be the less injured of the two parties. It also masks the fact that many victims of crime may be also be defendants in another case, a situation which is quite common. It is so common, in fact, that the first training I received from NDVAA involved policy and procedure for dealing with victims who are also offenders in other cases.

This distinction is a crucial part of the social imagery used to gain support for victim's rights. Durkheim (1965) offered a discussion of the order maintaining function of deviance, specifically that it provides an example of an act which exceeds the boundary of acceptable behavior. Because reality does not always distinguish between the victim and the offender, it is all the more important that the imagery maintain the victim/offender dichotomy. "Failure to keep the roles separate may result in challenges to the legal system, law and ultimately to the political-legal order itself. Imagery, then, is boundary-maintaining and necessary to the existence and maintenance of any social order" (Williams and McShane 1992:263). By reinforcing the artificial dichotomy between victim and offender, the victim's rights movement masks the true dynamic nature of crime.

Who Benefits Most?

Another fact that calls into question the motives behind the victim's movement is the focus of the interventions. The services offered to crime victims may be described more accurately as "system oriented" than "victim oriented." For example, many of the services focus on assisting the victim in the role of *witness*: notification of proceedings (and cancellations), transportation to and from court, child care while the witness is needed for the case, separate waiting rooms, courtroom orientation, and support from an advocate during the proceedings. Even those services that appear to directly benefit the victim, like restitution and counseling, may be seen as beneficial to the state (Williams and McShane 1992). "Unless their emotional needs are met, many victims will either not testify—and thereby force the prosecutor to drop the case—or they will testify so poorly that the prosecutor loses the case. Thus, many prosecutors have come to value the victim/witness programs' ability to prepare the victim/witness" (Finn, n.d.). For example, at the 1993 North Dakota winter meeting of the State's Attorney's Association, a workshop was given heralding the advantages of having an advocate in the State's Attorney's Office. Public relations and dealing with "difficult" victims were seen to be the most beneficial aspects of the advocate's role in the office.

In addition to the examples of self-interest described previously, critical criminologists claim that by focusing attention on individual victimization of "innocent" people, atten-

tion is deflected from other forms of victimization which might be linked to the capitalist system (Friedrichs 1983). "The Marxist thought which underlies critical criminology suggests that the workers as a class are victims of inevitable exploitation which results from private ownership of the means of production" (p. 285). The concept of victimization is also limited by the fact that criminal law reflects the interests of the ruling class (Quinney 1974). As Viano (1983:25) observes:

> Most—if not all—of the laws reflect a middle-class sense of values. Thus, justice, crime, punishment and remedies rest on middle-class foundations. But most of the known victims belong to the lower class. Consequently, there is an inherent inequity in the criminal justice system, since the opinions of one socioeconomic class dominate and dictate the perception, assessment and disposition of matters deeply affecting another.

Thus, victim's advocates do not serve the worker who was injured due to his employer's gross negligence, nor do they offer compensation to victims of racism or sexism. They reinforce the idea that violent personal crime is the most significant threat to contemporary society.

The previous discussion should help to explain why some critical criminologists have claimed that victims have been manipulated and "co-opted" by legislators and other authorities within the criminal justice system (Elias 1986). Their criticism presents a serious challenge to the mainstream interpretation of the "significant gains" achieved by the victim's rights movement. This critical view reveals a latent agenda within the reform movement and adds a dimension to the widely held mainstream understanding of the victim's rights movement. It argues that the criminal justice system has maintained the authority to decide who is an "innocent" victim (and thus deserving of services), and then gives priority to those cases where the victim's testimony is essential to the prosecution. It points out that most of the reforms are advantageous to the criminal justice system and draws attention to the symbolic value of the victim. Finally, it argues that focusing on the victims of violent crime draws attention away from other types of crime more directly linked to the private ownership of property. . . .

Discussion Questions

1. What factors led to the decline in restitution in the eighteenth century? How did the Enlightenment affect the decline? How were victims treated in the criminal justice system?

2. In what ways were victims able to become involved in the criminal justice process as a result of the Federal Victim Witness Protection Act of 1982? Why are some opposed to victim input?

3. In what ways is the concept of victimization limited? How does this affect the functioning of our legal system? Compare this concept to the historical concept of the victim and the role the victim played in the criminal justice process.

Notes

1. To answer these questions I have relied upon my experience as the director of a community-based non-profit Victim Assistance Program in rural North Dakota. I have also relied upon the experiences of ten or so victim/witness advocates who regularly attended the quarterly meetings of the North Dakota Victim's Assistance Association from 1991 to 1993.

2. That is not to say that because VAP's are directly associated with the State's Attorney's Office, they will refuse services to victims who have not reported crime to the police. It is merely to say that they receive a great majority of their referrals from the State's Attorney and that these cases occupy a majority of the advocate's time.

References

Brownmiller, Susan. 1975. *Against Our Will: Men, Women, and Rape.* New York: Simon and Schuster.

Davis, Robert C. 1983. "Victim and Witness Noncooperation: A Second Look at a Persistent Phenomena." *Journal of Criminal Justice 1*, 11:233-87.

Davis, Robert C. and Madeline Henley. 1990. "Victim Service Programs," Pp. 157-71 in *Victims of Crime: Problems, Policies, and Programs,* edited by A. Lurigio, W. Skogen, and R. Davis. Newbury Park, CA: Sage.

Davis, Robert C., Francis Kunreuther, and Elizabeth Connick. 1984. "Expanding the Victim's Role in Criminal Court Dispositional Process: The Results of an Experiment." *Journal of Criminal Law and Criminology,* 75:491-505.

Durkheim, Emile. 1965. *The Rules of the Sociological Method,* S. Solovay and J. Mueller trans. New York: Free Press.

Edelhertz, Herbert and Gilbert Geis. 1973. "Public Compensation of Victims of Crime: A Survey of the New York Experience." *Criminal Law Bulletin,* 9:56.

Elias, Robert. 1986. *The Politics of Victimization.* New York: Oxford University Press.

Erez, Edna. 1990. "Victim Participation at Sentencing: Rhetoric or Reality." *Journal of Criminal Justice,* 18:19-31.

Erez, Edna and Pamela Tontodonato. 1990. "The Effect of Victim Participation in Sentencing on Sentence Outcome." *Criminology,* 28:451-75.

Finn, Peter. No Date. *Victims Crime File Study Guide.* Washington, DC: National Institute of Justice.

Forst, Brian E. and Jolent C. Hernon. 1985. *The Criminal Justice Response to Victim Harm.* Research in Brief (June). Washington, DC: National Institute of Justice.

Friedrichs, David. 1983. "Victimology: A Consideration of the Radical Critique." *Crime and Delinquency,* 29:283-94.

Gittler, Josephine. 1984. "Expanding the Role of the Victim in a Criminal Action: An Overview of Issues and Problems." *Pepperdine Law Review,* 11: 117-82.

Goldstein, Abraham S. 1982. "Defining the Role of the Victim in Criminal Prosecution." *Mississippi Law Journal,* 52:515-61.

Hagan, John. 1982. "Victims Before the Law: A Study of Victim's Involvement in the Criminal Justice Process." *Journal of Criminal Law and Criminology,* 73:317-29.

Henderson, Lynne N. 1985. "The Wrongs of Victim's Rights." *Stanford Law Review,* 37:937-1021.

Hillenbrand, Susan W. and Barbara E. Smith. 1989. *Victim's Rights Legislation: An Assessment of Its Impact on Criminal Justice Practitioners and Victims.* Chicago, IL: American Bar Association.

Hoffman, Martha. 1983. "Victim Impact Statements." *Western State University Law Review,* 10:221-28.

Hudson, Paul S. 1984. "The Crime Victim and the Criminal Justice System: Time for a Change." *Pepperdine Law Review,* 11:23-62.

Jacoby, Joan. 1980. *The American Prosecutor: A Search for Identity.* Lexington, MA: Lexington Books.

Keisel, D. 1984. "Crime and Punishment—Victim's Movement Presses Courts and Legislature." *American Bar Association Journal*, 70:25-28.

Kelly, Deborah P. 1984. "Victims' Perceptions of Criminal Justice." *Pepperdine Law Review*, 11:15-22.

——. 1990. "Victim Participation in the Criminal Justice System." Pp. 172-87 in *Victims of Crime: Problems, Policies, and Programs*, edited by A. Lurigio, W. Skogen, and R. Davis. Newbury Park, CA: Sage.

Kidd, R. F. and E. F. Chayet. 1984. "Why Victims' Fail to Report? The Psychology of Criminal Victimization." *Journal of Social Issues*, 40:39-50.

Kilpatrick, Dean G. and Randy K. Otto. 1987. "Constitutionally Guaranteed Participation in Criminal Proceedings for Victims: Potential Effects on Psychological Functioning." *Wayne Law Review*, 34:7-28.

Kilpatrick, Dean, Lois J. Veronen, Menjamin E. Saunders, Connie L. Best, and Judith M. Von. 1987. "Criminal Victimization: Lifetime Prevalence, Reporting to Police, and Psychological Impact." *Crime and Delinquency*, 33:479-89.

Lamborn, LeRoy L. 1987. "Victim Participation in the Criminal Justice Process: The Proposal for a Constitutional Amendment." *Wayne Law Review*, 34:125-220.

Little, Joseph W. 1983. "The Law of Sentencing as Public Ceremony." *University of Florida Law Review*, 35:1-40.

McDaniel, Suzanne. No Date. *Crime Victim Impact: The Report of The Texas Crime Victim Clearinghouse to The 71st Legislature.*

McDonald, William F. 1976. "Towards a Bicentennial Revolution in Criminal Law." *American Criminal Law Review*, 13:49-73.

——. 1977. "The Role of the Victim in America." Pp. 295-307 in *Assessing the Criminal: Restitution, Retribution, and the Legal Process*, edited by R. Barnett and J. Hogel. Cambridge, MA: Ballinger.

McLeod, Maurine. 1986. "Victim Participation at Sentencing." *Criminal Law Bulletin*, 22:501-17.

Morris, Herbert. 1976. *On Guilt and Innocence: Essays in Legal Philosophy and Moral Psychology.* Berkeley, CA: University of California Press.

Nelson, W.E. 1974. "Emerging Notions of Modern Criminal Law in the Revolutionary Era: An Historical Perspective," Pp. 100-26 in *Criminal Justice in America*, edited by R. Quinney. Boston: Little, Brown.

Nice, David C. 1988. "State Programs for Crime Victims." *Policy Studies Journal*, 17:25-41.

Quinney, Richard. 1974. "Who is the Victim?" Pp. 103-19 in *Victimology*, edited by I. Drapkin and E. Viano. Lexington, MA: Lexington Books.

——. 1975. "Crime Control in Capitalist Society: A Critical Philosophy of Legal Order." Pp. 181-202 in *Critical Criminology*, edited by I. Taylor, P. Walton, and J. Young. Boston, MA: Routledge and Kegan Paul.

Ranish, Donald R. and David Schichor. 1985. "The Victim's Role in the Penile Process: Recent Developments in California." *Federal Probation*, 49:50-57.

Rubel, Howard C. 1986. "Victim Participation at Sentencing Proceedings." *Criminal Law Quarterly*, 28:226-50.

Seeba, Leslie. 1982. "The Victim's Role in the Penile Process: A Theoretical Orientation." *American Journal of Comparative Law*, 30:217-40.

Simonson, Lynnell J. 1993. "Victim Impact Statements: Do They Make A Difference?" Paper presented at the Midwest Sociological Society meetings in Chicago, IL.

Smale, G. J. A. and H. L. P. Spickenheuer. 1979. "Feelings of Guilt and Need for Retaliation in Victims of Serious Crime." *Victimology*, 4:75-85.

Smith, Brent S. 1985. "Trends in the Victims' Rights Movement and Implications for Future Research." *Victimology*, 10:34-43.

Talbert, Phillip A. 1988. "The Relevance of Victim Impact Statements to the Criminal Sentencing Decision." *UCLA Law Review*, 36:199-232.

Tyler, Tom R. 1984. "The Role of Perceived Injustice in Defendant's Evaluations of Their Courtroom Experience." *Law and Society Review*, 18:51-74.

Umbreit, Mark. 1985. *Crime and Reconciliation: Creative Options for Victims and Offenders.* Nashville, TN: Abingdon Press.

Viano, Emilio. 1983. "Victimology: The Development of a New Perspective." *Victimology*, 8:17-30.

Williams, Frank P. and Marilyn D. McShane. 1988. *Criminological Theory.* Englewood Cliffs, NJ: Prentice-Hall.

——. 1992. "Radical Victimology: A Critique of the Concept of Victim in Traditional Victimology." *Crime and Delinquency*, 38:258-71.

Young, Marlene A. 1987. "A Constitutional Amendment for Victims of Crime: The Victims' Perspective." *Wayne Law Review*, 34:51-68.

Section II

Extent and Nature of Crime

Newspapers and television portray crime in a particular way. Local and even national evening news programs provide coverage of the most sensationalistic kinds of offenses. The media frenzy surrounding the Nicole Brown-Simpson and Ronald Goldman cases is perhaps the best example of overzealous reporting and the highly sensationalized picture of crime with which most Americans are familiar. Popular television shows also present a good deal of violence; such shows as *Homicide: Life on the Streets*, *NYPD Blue*, and numerous others depict homicide and other forms of violence as extremely prevalent crimes in the United States.

Criminologists are interested in learning more about the actual extent and nature of crime than the distorted picture portrayed in print and on radio and television. Some of the questions they study include the following: How many crimes are committed in the United States? What are the characteristics of people who commit offenses? How widespread is criminal offending? How widespread is criminal victimization? Who are the criminals? Who are the victims?

The answer to these questions, in part, is that it depends. That is, it depends on how we measure crime as well as the kinds of crimes in which we are most interested. As Section Five of this book describes, there are many different types of crime. What we measure, and how we measure it, have important implications for what we know about the nature

and extent of crime. Unfortunately, reliable and valid data are not available for many crimes, including public-order crimes, professional crimes, organized crimes, and white-collar crimes. There are a variety of reasons for this lack of data, including the nature of the offenses themselves. These matters will be dealt with in more detail in Section Five.

Unlike data for the above-mentioned offenses, "good" data are available for crimes of violence and property offenses. Even for these offenses, however, the type of data that we use is important for determining the picture of crime that we have. Criminologists typically rely on three types of data to determine the nature and extent of crime: "official" data, victimization surveys, and self-report surveys. Each type provides a different picture of crime, and much effort has been expended to identify the strengths and weaknesses of each type.

This section will consider the three different types of data and their strengths and weaknesses. It will then discuss the nature and extent of crime in the United States as revealed by these data sources. Finally, it will consider issues related to "overcriminalization," that is, whether U.S. society labels too many offenses as criminal. The four readings that follow this introduction examine the strengths and weaknesses of the three types of data, and also look at drug abuse, one of the most important Part II offenses.

Official Data

When criminologists discuss "official data," they are usually referring to information available in the Uniform Crime Reports (UCR), which are compiled and published by the Federal Bureau of Investigation (FBI). The UCR is an annual report published since 1930 that incorporates data from 95 percent of the police precincts in all 50 states. It includes crimes known to the police (either through citizen reports or through police discovery), information about the number of arrests, and some characteristics of the people arrested. Each reporting unit collects this information for its jurisdiction; this information is forwarded to the FBI, which publishes the Uniform Crime Reports (Federal Bureau of Investigation 1997).

The crimes recorded in the UCR are of two types: Part I offenses, usually called index crimes, and Part II offenses. There are eight index crimes, which are offenses that we usually think of as "serious" crimes. The four violent index crimes are murder and nonnegligent homicide, forcible rape, aggravated assault, and robbery. All these crimes include an element of force or threat of force, and include attempts to commit these crimes. The element of force differentiates them from the four property index crimes, which are larceny-theft, burglary, motor vehicle theft, and arson.

Although states have somewhat different definitions for each of the eight index crimes, the UCR data incorporate crimes that are consistent with a standard set of definitions. The definitions for the violent index crimes provided by the Federal Bureau of Investigation are as follows: murder and nonnegligent homicide is "the willful (nonnegligent) killing of one human being by another"; rape is "the carnal knowledge of a female forcibly and against her will"; aggravated assault is "an unlawful attack by one person upon another for the purpose of inflicting severe or aggravated personal injury"; robbery is "the taking or attempting to take anything of value from the care, custody, or control of a person or persons by force or threat of force or violence and/or by putting the victim in fear" (Federal Bureau of Investigation 1997: 13, 23, 31, and 26 respectively). The definitions of the index property crimes are: larceny-theft is "the unlawful taking, carrying, leading or riding away of property from the possession or constructive possession of another" and includes such crimes as shoplifting; burglary is "the unlawful entry of a structure to commit a felony or theft"; motor vehicle theft is "the [unlawful] theft or attempted theft of a motor vehicle" (p. 49); arson is "any willful or malicious burning or attempt to burn, with or without intent to defraud" the property of another (Federal Bureau of Investigation 1997: 43, 38, 49, and 53 respectively).

In addition to the number of crimes known to the police, the UCR also reports information about arrests for the index crimes. Several different types of information are reported. Clearance rates are reported for each type of index crime; these are the percentage of crimes known to the police that are "cleared" or "when at least one person is arrested, charged with the commission of the crime, and turned over to the court for prosecution" (Federal Bureau of Investigation 1997: 203). (Note that just because a crime is "cleared" does not mean that the person(s) arrested will necessarily plead guilty or be found guilty.) Also included in the UCR is the number of people arrested and the characteristics of those arrested, such as age, gender, and race.

The UCR also provides information about Part II offenses. As a whole, they are generally considered less serious than Part I index crimes. Part II offenses include a variety of crimes, such as drug abuse violations, prostitution, simple assaults, drunkenness, disorderly conduct, vagrancy, weapons offenses, and two status offenses (runaways and curfew violations). For these offenses, arrest information, rather than the number of offenses known to the police, are usually reported. This is because of the nature of the Part II offenses: many of them are not necessarily reported to the police but rather are detected through the proactive efforts of the police themselves.

The UCR is an important source of data about the nature and extent of crime in the United States. Nevertheless, the UCR data have both strengths and weaknesses that can make their use somewhat problematic. Walter R. Gove, Michael Hughes, and Michael Geerken discuss some of the problems with the UCR, as well as other sources of crime data, in reading Six, although they conclude that the UCR provides valid information about most index crimes.

The UCR provides the longest-running source of crime data in the United States. As such, we are able to measure long-term trends in crimes known to the police. With the increased professionalization of police forces over time, we can have increased confidence that many crimes reported to the police are recorded and counted as crimes. The arrest data provide some insight into the characteristics of offenders who are committing the crimes that result in arrest.

The UCR data have a number of limitations, however. A substantial number of crimes are *not* reported to the police (see the discussion below). Thus, using the UCR to determine the number of crimes that are committed seriously underestimates the true number of crimes. The crimes that are reported to the police are more serious (in terms of injury or loss) than those that are not reported. (Bureau of Justice Statistics 1997b). Further, although arrest data provide some insight into demographic characteristics of criminals, using this information is problematic. The clearance rates for violent, and particularly property, index crimes indicate that only about half of violent crimes are cleared by arrest; for property crimes, only about 20 percent. Thus, even if we assume that the persons arrested for crimes that are cleared are the actual perpetrators (a somewhat questionable assumption), in one of two cases the perpetrator of violent crimes is not apprehended; for property crimes, this number is four in five! It cannot be assumed, therefore, that the people who are arrested are representative of all offenders.

There are other problems with UCR data. The police have discretion in whom they arrest; although the seriousness of the offense is an important factor, extralegal factors also seem to play a role in the decision to arrest (Smith and Visher 1981; Lundman 1996; Worden and Shepard 1996; but see also Klinger 1994, 1996). Limited information other than demographic information is available about arrestees; for example, no information is available about their socioeconomic status (an important factor in criminological theories as discussed in Section III) or motivations for committing the offense.

Despite its weaknesses, the UCR is an important data source available to criminologists, and as discussed in reading Six, its data are generally considered valid for the index crimes.

Victimization Surveys

Partly in response to some of the problems with the UCR, however, alternative sources of crime data were developed. One of these is victimization surveys. The primary victimization survey, which is discussed here, is the National Crime Victimization Survey (NCVS). The National Crime Survey (NCS), as it was originally called, was initiated in 1973 by the Bureau of Justice Statistics (BJS). The NCVS consists of interviews with a nationally representative sample of approximately 100,000 people age twelve and over living in 50,000 households in the United States. Everyone in this sample is interviewed every six months about his or her personal experiences as a victim in the previous six months (that is, whether he or she has been the victim of a crime in the 6 months prior to the interview). In addition, one adult member of the household provides information about whether the household itself has been victimized by a property crime. Households remain in the study for three years and then are replaced (Bureau of Justice Statistics 1997b).

In the interview, respondents are asked whether they were the victims of specific crimes, such as robbery. They are asked about each crime separately, in order to obtain information about different offenses. The crimes asked about are similar to the Part I index crimes (except homicide), but identical definitions are *not* used. As indicated in readings Six and Eight, respondents were not explicitly asked about rape until 1993, when the survey was changed to address this limitation. Also obtained is information related to characteristics of respondents and households, such as socioeconomic status and number of household residents, and about the crime, such as where it occurred and whether the victim resisted (Bureau of Justice Statistics 1997b).

Although originally envisioned as a measure of the true crime rate, the NCVS is not without strengths and weaknesses. Some of these are discussed in readings Six and Eight, but they will be briefly considered here.

The NCVS has several strengths. It provides an alternative estimate of the number of crimes that occur in the United States each year. In addition, it provides information on crime and victims that is unavailable in official data. For example, when possible, NCVS respondents provide information about the perpetrator(s) (e.g., the age and the relationship to the victim), the situation (e.g., when and where the crime occurred), and the amount of damage (e.g., physical injury or financial loss). The NCVS also obtains important information about whether a crime was reported to the police and the reasons behind the decision to report it or not. Thus, the NCVS makes it possible to estimate the number of crimes that have occurred, characteristics of the victims, characteristics of the offenders, factors associated with the crime, and the percentage of crimes reported to the police and reasons why many crimes go unreported.

The NCVS also has a number of weaknesses. The interviewer can have important effects on the situation and on the respondent, thus potentially influencing whether victimizations are reported, which in turn affects the total number of victimizations. Further, respondents may be unwilling to report their experiences as victims, particularly those offenses also not reported to the police (and most likely not reported to the interviewer for the same reasons they were not reported to the police). Other problems arise because respondents may "telescope" (say an event occurred during a given time period when it actually occurred outside of it), forget that a crime occurred, or report a nonserious event as a serious one.

As a whole, the NCVS provides some important information about the nature and extent of crime that the UCR does not and therefore, is an important data source. Like the UCR, however, the NCVS is not without weaknesses, some of which are shared by self-report surveys, which are considered in the next section.

Self-Report Surveys

The third major data source widely used by criminologists is self-report surveys. Where victimization surveys ask respondents about whether they have been the victim of a crime, self-report surveys are primarily interested in obtaining information about respondents' own delinquent and criminal behavior. Use of the self-report method in criminology became popular after the publication of an article in 1958 by James F. Short and F. Ivan Nye article that used this methodology; since that time, numerous self-report surveys have been developed. The National Youth Survey (see readings 7 and 20) and the Rochester Developmental Youth Survey are but two examples. The surveys include questions not only about criminal and delinquent behavior but also about a variety of other topics, such as demographic characteristics, familial relationships, attitudes, and a host of related issues.

As with the other data sources, self-report data have strengths and weaknesses. With regard to strengths, self-report surveys give researchers access to information that official data and victimization surveys do not. Their delinquency and crime measures are generally considered reliable and valid (see reading Seven; Hindelang, Hirschi, and Weis, 1981) and allow estimation of the prevalence and incidence of offending, regardless of whether offenders are caught for the crimes. Further, these surveys allow researchers to obtain information about why an individual commits crimes, and factors associated with an individual's behavior, such as whether he or she has delinquent friends, socioeconomic status, attitudes, and a number of other topics.

Self-report studies also have important weaknesses. Responses to such surveys may have different degrees of validity, with the validity of responses from African American males about delinquent and criminal activity coming particularly under scrutiny (see reading Seven; Hindelang, Hirschi, and Weis, 1981). Self-reports rely on the willingness and ability of an individual to report his or her behavior; several factors limit this ability, such as telescoping, forgetting, and social acceptability. Further, questions related to the frequency of a behavior are particularly susceptible to problems of underreporting and overreporting; that is, a person may underestimate or overestimate the number of times he or she committed an offense. Although a number of techniques in the interview situation can be utilized to reduce these problems, they cannot completely eliminate them.

Self-reports are subject to other problems. Many items included in the surveys are trivial (nonserious) and overlap (they do not measure distinct behaviors). More important, serious persistent offenders are underrepresented for a variety of reasons, thus disallowing examination of factors associated with their offending patterns and factors that differentiate this group from other offenders (Elliott and Ageton 1980; Cernkovich, Giordano, and Pugh 1985).

Crime in the United States

An understanding of the strengths and weaknesses of the three major sources of criminological data is necessary if one is to be able to think critically about what each shows about the nature and extent of crime in the United States. As discussed in Section III, the discrepant results obtained from different data sources create controversy over the nature of the relationship between several of the correlates and crime, as well as have implications for theories of crime.

Crimes Known to the Police

The United States, in comparison to other countries, and particularly Westernized countries, has extremely high crime and violence rates (Archer and Gartner 1984; United Nations 1997). In 1996 there were 13,473,614 index crimes known to the police, or 5,079 per 100,000 people (Federal Bureau of Investigation 1997). Despite these high numbers, they reflect the fifth straight year

of decline in crime in the United States. This decline is a relatively recent pattern, however, as crime rates increased in almost every year between 1960 and 1991, the peak year of offenses known to the police. More specifically, in 1960, there were 3,384,200 offenses (1,887 per 100,000) known to the police; by 1991, there were 14,872,900 offenses known to the police (5,898 per 100,000), reflecting almost a threefold increase in the 30 year period (Maguire and Pastore 1997).

Of the index crimes, the vast majority are property crimes rather than violent crimes. In any given year, property crimes comprise approximately 88 percent and violent offenses 12 percent of index crimes known to the police. Of the index crimes, the one most often reported to the police is larceny-theft (7,894,620 known to the police in 1996); homicide, the crime that receives the most attention in the media, is the smallest category among serious offenses (with 19,645 offenses in 1996) (Federal Bureau of Investigation 1997).

Within the United States, crime is not evenly distributed; that is, crime rates vary by geographic region and by size of locale. In particular, both property and violent index crime rates are highest in the South, followed by the West (Nelsen, Corzine, and Huff-Corzine 1994; Federal Bureau of Investigation 1997). This finding is consistent with a "subculture of violence" (Wolfgang and Ferracuti 1967) often attributed to the South. In addition, index crime rates are highest in large cities and their surrounding areas (i.e., Metropolitan Statistical Areas), followed by cities outside of metropolitan areas, and then rural counties, which have the lowest crime rates (Federal Bureau of Investigation 1997).

Arrests and Characteristics of Arrestees

Despite the large number of index crimes known to the police, arrests for these crimes are fairly infrequent, as indicated by the clearance rates. In 1996, for violent crimes overall, about 47 percent were cleared, with variations ranging from 67 percent for homicide to 27 percent for robbery. Clearance rates were lower for property crimes, with 18 percent of the four crimes cleared (Federal Bureau of Investigation 1997). Despite the low clearance rates, close to 3 million people were arrested for an index crime in 1996. Not surprisingly, the majority were arrested for property crimes, with larceny-theft leading the way.

What are the characteristics of the people arrested? Although we cannot be certain that those arrested are representative of all offenders, the UCR arrest data suggest their characteristics (Federal Bureau of Investigation 1997). As a whole, arrestees are young; in 1996, 56 percent of those arrested for all index crimes were under the age of twenty-five (46 percent of violent arrestees and 59 percent of property crime arrestees). Further, juveniles (under age eighteen) accounted for almost 31 percent of all people arrested for index crimes. Over the past decade, the number of juvenile arrests has increased at a greater pace than adult arrests. This increase is particularly true of violent index crimes, with arrests for homicide for juveniles up 51 percent, arrests for robbery up 57 percent, and arrests for aggravated assault up 70 percent between 1987 and 1996; the comparable arrests for adults declined 10 percent and 3 percent and rose 39 percent, respectively (Federal Bureau of Investigation 1997).

Gender and race patterns are also evident in arrest data. Arrestees are disproportionately male: males represented 79 percent of those arrested for index crimes in 1996. The situation is even more disproportionate for violent crimes, with males making up 85 percent of such arrestees in 1996; 72 percent of those arrested for property crime were male. With regard to race, African Americans are disproportionately represented relative to their size in the population. Although they comprised approximately 12.6 percent of the U.S. population in 1996 (U.S. Bureau of Census 1997), they accounted for about 35 percent of index arrestees overall. In 1996 they represented approximately 43 percent of those arrested for violent crimes and about 32 percent of those arrested for property crime. Overall, whites accounted for the majority of all arrestees for index crimes (62 percent), violent crime arrestees (55 percent), and property crime arrestees (65 percent) (Federal Bureau of Investigation 1997). Whites, however, are almost 83 percent of the

population in the United States (because Hispanics may be of any race and are not differentiated in the UCR statistics, they are not treated separately here) (U.S. Bureau of Census 1997). The reasons for these differences across demographic groups will be discussed in more detail in Section III.

Comparison of the UCR and NCVS

Despite the seemingly large number of offenses revealed by the UCR, the NCVS reveals what is often called "the dark figure of crime." That is, the NCVS indicates that substantially more crimes are committed than are reported to the police. For example, in 1996 the NCVS estimates that there were approximately 36,800,000 crimes against persons and households. Of these, 27.3 million were property offenses and 9.1 million were personal offenses. Although there are differences in definitions and measurement, the figure of almost 37 million (Bureau of Justice Statistics 1997a) dwarfs the number of similar crimes known to the police in 1996 (about 13 million) (Federal Bureau of Investigation 1997).

A potential problem arises with regard to comparisons of the NCVS and UCR. Although the two are not directly comparable in terms of definitions used and crimes included, crime rates derived from the two sources have been compared by a number of criminologists (e.g., Blumstein, Cohen, and Rosenfeld 1991; McDowall and Loftin 1992). In many cases, the NCVS and UCR patterns are parallel, but the NCVS reveals higher rates than the UCR. When the NCVS and UCR show widely discrepant crime rates, which should criminologists use to base their estimates of the true number of crimes? This issue is discussed in reading Eight, by Gary Jensen and Maryaltani Karpos, who attempt to reconcile discrepant patterns of rape rates.

That the number estimated by the NCVS is much higher than reported in the UCR is not altogether surprising given the low percentages of people who report the offense to the police. The NCVS reveals that in 1996 for all violent crimes, only 43 percent were reported to the police; this figure varied substantially by the type of crime, with 54 percent of robberies and only 31 percent of rapes reported. For property crimes against the household, only 35 percent overall were reported, again with variations by crimes (76 percent of motor vehicle thefts, compared to only 28 percent of thefts, were reported to the police) (Bureau of Justice Statistics 1997a). The rationale for not reporting a crime to the police varies across and within the categories of violent and property crimes. For violent crimes, respondents were most likely to cite the reason for not reporting was that it was a "private or personal matter." "Object recovered; offender unsuccessful" was the most frequently cited reason for not reporting property crimes to the police (Bureau of Justice Statistics 1997b).

Victims of Crime

Who are the victims of all these crimes? The answer is related to the extent and nature of crime in society. The NCVS suggests that the characteristics of victims closely resemble those of offenders. The results of the 1996 NCVS indicate that for violent crimes (excluding homicide), victims tend to have the following characteristics: they are male (except for rape); young (between the ages of twelve and twenty-four); more likely to be African American than white; more likely to be Hispanic than non-Hispanic; poor (household incomes under $7,500); single, separated, or divorced; live in the West; and live in urban areas (Bureau of Justice Statistics 1997a).

For property crimes in 1996, the characteristics of the heads of households that were victimized resemble those of victims of violence with one notable exception. Specifically, property victimization rates are highest for households headed by African Americans rather than whites and Hispanics rather than non-Hispanics, located in the West or in an urban area, and rented rather than owned the home. Overall, however, property victimization rates are highest for households with incomes of $75,000 and over, although this figure varies by specific offense: burglaries are highest for households under $7,500, thefts for those over $75,000, and motor vehicle thefts for those in the category of $35,000 to $49,999 (Bureau of Justice Statistics 1997a). It should be noted that the characteristics of

victims are considered here separately (e.g., considering race without also considering household income), an approach that Section III reveals is problematic, but the results do suggest who tends to be victimized by conventional street crimes in U.S. society.

The relationship between offender and victim often differs from stereotypes. For example, most violent crimes are intraracial rather than interracial. This fact is particularly illustrated by homicide: in cases in which there is a single victim and a single offender who has been identified, 84 percent of whites are killed by other whites and 92 percent of African Americans are killed by other African Americans (Federal Bureau of Investigation 1997). Further, many crimes of violence are not committed by strangers but rather by people the victims know. For violent crimes (completed and attempted) overall, the NCVS indicates that the offender was a stranger in just over half the cases in 1994. For robbery, the offender was a stranger in 78 percent of cases, while for aggravated assault the offender was a stranger in 61 percent of cases. For rape, however, the victim and offender were strangers in only 36 percent of cases and were at least acquainted with each other in the remaining 64 percent (Bureau of Justice Statistics 1997b).

Self-Report Information

Self-report studies provide a picture that is fairly different from that of the UCR or NCVS. Specifically, self-report studies reveal that crime is much more prevalent, or widespread, among the general population than was generally assumed prior to extensive use of the surveys. In addition, these studies reveal that a large number of crimes are committed by people who are never caught or punished. For example, results from Monitoring the Future, an annual nationally representative self-report survey of high school students and young adults, indicate that for twelfth graders in 1996, 14 percent had "hurt someone bad enough to need bandages or a doctor," 32 percent had "taken something not belonging to you worth under $50," and 24 percent had "gone into some house or building when you weren't supposed to be there" at least once in the previous year. Overall, however, only 10 percent had "been arrested and taken to a police station" during that year, suggesting that relatively few people are caught or punished for their crimes (Maguire and Pastore 1997).

Further, self-report studies indicate that gender, race, and class differences revealed by official data on crime, and the basis of many theories, are not found in self-report studies or, if found, the relationships are smaller than indicated in official data (e.g., Huizinga and Elliott 1987; Tittle and Meier 1990). Although these findings are not always consistent and may be due to measurement issues (e.g., Elliott and Ageton 1980; Farnworth et al. 1994), they have important implications for criminology. These issues, and their implications, are discussed in more detail in Section III.

Part II Offenses and Overcriminalization

The attention in this section thus far has been primarily on the eight index crimes, which are considered the most serious and have been used to gauge crime in the United States. Recall, however, that the UCR provides information about both the index crimes and Part II offenses. The data for Part II offenses are presented in terms of arrests, rather than offenses known to the police. Reading Nine provides many insights into how the number of arrests for such offenses can be greatly influenced by social and political factors rather than simply by the number of offenses being committed. Indeed, arrests for Part II offenses largely reflect the proactive enforcement efforts of the police and other law enforcement agencies.

The Part II offenses are important to consider for several reasons. First, arrests for them are the majority of arrests made in any given year and thereby have a huge impact on the criminal justice system in terms of police, court, and prison resources. Second, many of these offenses are "victimless crimes," those that may involve harm to the person engaged in the behavior itself but not directly to others (Federal Bureau of Investigation 1997). Whether some of these offenses should be considered criminal, or whether

our society is "overcriminalized," are important issues that may be studied by examining these offenses.

Part II Offenses

In 1996 an estimated 15,168,100 people were arrested. Of these, only 18 percent were arrested for index crimes. The remaining 82 percent can be accounted for by Part II offenses. Not including the residual category of "all other offenses," drug abuse violations represent the single offense, of either Part I or Part II offenses, for which the most people were arrested in 1996. Indeed, 10 percent of all people arrested were arrested for drug abuse violations. Further, the minority of arrests for drug abuse were for sale or manufacture (25 percent) and the majority (75 percent) for possession; of the possession arrests, half were for marijuana. These figures are in stark contrast to the picture of crime portrayed on television or suggested by examination of Part I crime data. The combined categories of prostitution and commercialized vice, drug abuse, gambling, liquor law violations, drunkenness, disorderly conduct, and vagrancy, all offenses that may be considered victimless, account for more than 25 percent of all arrests (Federal Bureau of Investigation 1997).

Michael Tonry (reading 9) and Steven R. Donziger (reading 40) document some of the implications of one of these offenses—drug abuse—for the criminal justice system. The number of people arrested for drug abuse violations has increased dramatically since 1980, from 600,000 in 1980 to about 1.5 million in 1996 (Federal Bureau of Investigation 1997) and the percentage of inmates incarcerated for drug-related offenses has also increased greatly (Bureau of Justice Statistics 1992). Surveys of high school students reveal that despite the war on drugs, use of marijuana and other illicit drugs is currently on the rise, following a period of decline in the 1980s (Johnston, O'Malley, and Bachman 1996).

Overcriminalization

The point is not to argue that the use of drugs specifically should be decriminalized, although there are scholars who do argue for their legalization (see Inciardi 1991, and Trebach and Inciardi 1993, for the pros and cons of this issue). Instead, drug abuse provides a striking example which allows us to pose the question of whether the United States as a society is "overcriminalized," that is, does our society define as criminal many behaviors that are of little, if any, threat to society? Should our laws focus only on behaviors that are truly harmful to society and its citizens? Some scholars answer these questions in the affirmative. Sanford H. Kadish, for example, argues that laws have been misused to criminalize offenses such as drug use, prostitution, drunkenness, vagrancy, and others, and the "existence of these crimes and attempts at their eradication raise problems of inestimable importance for the criminal law" (1971: 57).

Overcriminalization has several important effects, according to Kadish. First, when laws are used to legislate morality, the nonenforcement of these laws undermines their intent, produces indifference and cynicism in the public, and may lead to discriminatory law enforcement. Second, such laws may result in the "diversion of police resources; encouragement of use of illegal means of police control [and] degradation of the image of law enforcement; discriminatory enforcement against the poor; and official corruption" (Kadish, 1971: 60). Additional problems may also result from such laws. Prohibiting behavior has little effect on how often people engage in it, and enforcement efforts might actually lead to more criminal behavior, since they produce greater organization and profit for those involved, thereby attracting more people and making enforcement even more difficult. With drug trafficking, increased enforcement efforts led to greater organization of the trade and the use of more sophisticated techniques and technology, resulting in traffickers being harder to detect (e.g., Johnson et al. 1990; Adler 1993). Kadish also states that there is "a cost of inestimable importance, one which tends to be a product of virtually all the misuses of criminal law. . . . That is the substantial diversion of police, prosecutorial and judicial time, personnel, and resources" from protecting society from truly harmful behaviors (1971: 63).

The implications for the extent and nature of crime are important. As outlined in Section One, the laws that are created reflect changing social attitudes and political processes. Law enforcement efforts and resources are expended to enforce laws related to victimless offenses that seem to reflect efforts to regulate morality. Further, people arrested for these offenses are taking up valuable resources, including jail and prison space, and are clogging the court system. People convicted of such offenses are labeled with a criminal record that will plague them for the rest of their lives. Despite the fact that many of these behaviors are ones that society disapproves of, defining them as crimes reflects the notion that our society may be overcriminalized.

The readings that follow deal with issues particularly related to the strengths and weaknesses of data sources available to criminologists for studying the extent and nature of crime. One article focuses on UCR data, another on the NCS, and a third on the reliability and validity of self-report data. The final article in this section deals with an important Part II offense—drug abuse—and shows some of the social and political processes involved in enforcement efforts surrounding this offense.

References

Adler, Patricia A. 1993. *Wheeling and Dealing: An Ethnography of an Upper-Level Drug Dealing and Smuggling Community.* 2nd Edition. New York: Columbia University Press.

Archer, Dane and Rosemary Gartner. 1984. *Violence and Crime in Cross-National Perspective.* New Haven, CT: Yale University Press.

Blumstein, Alfred J., Jacqueline Cohen, and Richard Rosenfeld. 1991. "Trend and Deviation in Crime Rate: A Comparison of UCR and NCS Data for Burglary and Robbery," *Criminology,* 29:237-264.

Bureau of Justice Statistics. 1992. *Prisoners in 1991.* Washington, DC: U.S. Department of Justice.

Bureau of Justice Statistics. 1997a. *Criminal Victimization 1996: Changes 1995-96 with Trends 1993-96.* Bulletin NCJ-165812. Washington, DC: U.S. Department of Justice.

Bureau of Justice Statistics. 1997b. *Criminal Victimization in the United States, 1994.* NCJ-

162126. Washington, DC: U.S. Department of Justice.

Cernkovich, Stephen A., Peggy C. Giordano, and Meredith D. Pugh. 1985. "Chronic Offenders: The Missing Cases in Self-Report Delinquency Research," *Journal of Criminal Law and Criminology*, 76:705-732.

Elliott, Delbert S. and Suzanne S. Ageton. 1980. "Reconciling Race and Class Differences in Self-Reported and Official Estimates of Delinquency," *American Sociological Review*, 45:95-110.

Farnworth, Margaret, Terence P. Thornberry, Marvin D. Krohn, and Alan J. Lizotte. 1994. "Measurement in the Study of Class and Delinquency: Integrating Theory and Research," *Journal of Research in Crime and Delinquency*, 31: 32-61.

Federal Bureau of Investigation. 1997. *Crime in the United States, 1996*. Washington, DC: U.S. Government Printing Office.

Hindelang, Michael J., Travis Hirschi, and Joseph G. Weis. 1981. *Measuring Delinquency*. Beverly Hills, CA: Sage.

Huizinga, David and Delbert S. Elliott. 1987. "Juvenile Offender Prevalence, Incidence, and Arrest Rates by Race," *Crime & Delinquency*, 33: 206-233.

Inciardi, James A. (Ed.) 1991. *The Drug Legalization Debate*. Newbury Park, CA: Sage Publications.

Johnson, Bruce D., Terry Williams, Kojo A. Die, and Harry Sanabria. 1990. "Drug Abuse in the Inner City: Impact on Hard-Drug users and the Community." In Michael Tonry and James Q. Wilson, eds., *Drugs and Crime*. Chicago: University of Chicago Press.

Johnston, Lloyd D., Patrick O'Malley, and Jerald G. Bachman. 1996. *National Survey Results on Drug Use from The Monitoring the Future Study 1975-1995*. Volume I, Secondary School Students. NIH Publication No. 96-4139. Washington, DC: U.S. Government Printing Office.

Kadish, Sanford H. 1971. "Overcriminalization." In L. Radzinowitz and M. Wolfgang (eds.), *The Criminal in Society*. New York: Basic Books.

Klinger, David A. 1994. "Demeanor or Crime? Why 'Hostile' Citizens are More Likely to Be Arrested," *Criminology*, 32:475-493.

——. 1996. "More on Demeanor and Arrest in Dade County," *Criminology*, 34:61-79.

Lundman, Richard J. 1996. "Demeanor and Arrest: Additional Evidence from Previously Unpublished Data," *Journal of Research in Crime and Delinquency*, 33:306-323.

Maguire, Kathleen and Ann L. Pastore (Eds.). 1997. *Sourcebook of Criminal Justice Statistics 1996*. U.S. Department of Justice, Bureau of Justice Statistics. Washington, DC: U.S. Government Printing Office.

McDowall, David and Colin Loftin. 1992. "Comparing the UCR and NCS Over Time," *Criminology*, 30:125-132.

Nelsen, Candice, Jay Corzine, and Lin Huff-Corzine. 1994. "The Violent West Reexamined: A Research Note on Regional Homicide Rates," *Criminology*, 32:149-161.

Short, James F., Jr. and F. Ivan Nye. 1958. "Extent of Unrecorded Juvenile Delinquency: Tentative Conclusions," *Journal of Criminal Law and Criminology*, 49:296-302.

Smith, Douglas A. and Christy Visher. 1981. "Street-Level Justice: Situational Determinants of Police Arrest Decisions," *Social Problems*, 29:167-177.

Tittle, Charles R. and Robert F. Meier. 1990. "Specifying the SES/Delinquency Relationship," *Criminology*, 28:271-299.

Trebach, Arnold S. and James A. Inciardi. 1993. *Legalize It?: Debating American Drug Policy*. Washington, DC: American University Press.

United Nations. 1997. *Demographic Yearbook 1995*. New York: United Nations.

U.S. Bureau of Census. 1997. *Statistical Abstract of the United States: 1997*. Washington, DC: U.S. Government Printing Office.

Wolfgang, Marvin E. and Franco Ferracuti. 1967. *The Subculture of Violence*. New York: Tavistock.

Worden, Robert E. and Robin L. Shepard. 1996. "Demeanor, Crime, and Police Behavior: A Reexamination of the Police Services Study Data," *Criminology*, 34:83-105. ✦

6

Are Uniform Crime Reports a Valid Indicator of the Index Crimes? An Affirmative Answer With Minor Qualifications

Walter R. Gove
Michael Hughes
Michael Geerken

The type of data used to measure crime has important implications for the picture of crime that society sees. Within criminology, there has been a great deal of debate about the merits of the three major types of data available: official data, victimization surveys, and self-report surveys. In this selection, Walter Gove, Michael Hughes, and Michael Geerken illuminate some of the issues raised in this debate.

The primary emphasis in the selection is on the validity of official data and the Uniform Crime Reports (UCR) specifically. The authors examine the validity of the UCR data for Part I index crimes, excluding arson. Their results suggest that as a whole, the UCR data provide valid measures of the index crimes, and in some cases, measures more valid than those provided by victimization surveys. Overall, the authors conclude that the UCR data are generally valid measures of the crimes that are perceived by both the police and citizens as the most serious.

A number of other issues important for criminology are also discussed. As the authors note, official data, victimization data, and self-report data all provide somewhat different pictures and, in some instances, discrepant pictures of crime, and all have important limitations that render none ideal for all types of studies in criminology. In official data, not all crimes that are known about are reported to the police, nor are all crimes reported to the police eventually recorded in the UCR. Official data are constructed, in the sense that two types of "filter" processes are involved: the victim must be aware of the crime and decide to report it to the police, and the police must determine if a crime actually occurred and record it as such, with the offense eventually counted by the FBI. A number of factors can impinge upon this process, although the authors indicate that the seriousness of the crime and the victim's wishes are two of the most important considerations.

Two recent assessments (Gibbs, 1983; Gove, 1983) of the field of criminology during the past 20 years conclude that the key methodological issue (and, in many respects, the key theoretical issue) confronting the field is a clear determination of how official crime rates are constructed and what they reflect. Both assessments hold that the field of criminology cannot substantially advance without using official crime rates for scientific purposes.

The present paper attempts to assess the validity and scientific utility of the Uniform Crime Reports (UCR). It is argued that the UCR have a clear interpretation and for most purposes are a valid measure of the FBI index crimes. In reaching this conclusion we draw on a variety of evidence including studies of citizen and police behavior, victimization studies, and, to a lesser extent, self-report studies of deviant behavior. The conclusion that the UCR are reasonable measures of the various index crimes is in part based on the proposition that official statistics provide good measures of certain types of criminal behavior, and we recognize that they are less adequate as measures of other types of criminal behavior. Thus, part of the conclusion is based on developing a fairly clear understanding of what the UCR actually measures. The conclusion also requires an understanding of what is measured by self-reports and, particularly, victimization surveys.

This position is controversial and runs counter to what has been a very common view of the UCR. . . .

Much of the justification for questioning the validity and/or utility of the Uniform Crime Reports is based on empirical evidence. Introduced by Porterfield (1946), self-report studies have shown *drastically higher rates* of unofficial delinquency and *much weaker* correlations by class and race than are disclosed by official statistics. Furthermore, victimization surveys indicate that the majority of crimes are not reported to the police (Decker, 1980: 50; Cohen and Lichbach, 1982: 261). These data are commonly interpreted as indicating that the vast majority of crime goes unrecorded, and the large number of unreported crimes, commonly called the "dark figure of crime," is used to call into question the validity of official statistics. It is also argued that the victimization surveys and the UCR appear to be measuring different things. . . .

Official Crime Statistics and Self-Reports: The Illusion of a Difference

The apparent sharp disparity between self-reports and official statistics which has plagued criminologists for a number of years has, to our satisfaction, been resolved. This resolution effectively answers one of the issues used to question the validity of official statistics and provides a step towards understanding what official statistics in general and the UCR in particular measure. Recently there have been at least four major attempts to interpret the apparent disparity between official delinquency rates and self-reported delinquency rates. . . .

These studies indicate that at least most of the apparent disparity in the rates in the self-report studies and official statistics is due to

the very high rates of nonserious crime found in the self-report studies. This suggests that a substantial part of the "dark figure of crime" involves relatively trivial criminal acts. The studies indicate that class, race, sex, and age are related to crime in the direction reported by official statistics of arrest rates, and the study by Thornberry and Farnworth (1982) suggests the strength of the relationship is roughly consistent with that found in official statistics. However, these analyses focus on offender characteristics and provide no direct evidence of the factors determining what the police record as a crime; they only tangentially touch on the central issue raised by Kitsuse and Cicourel (1963)—namely, the factors that determine how the official statistics are constructed. These studies do not tell us what the UCR means and how we should interpret them. How do the unreported crimes differ from the reported crimes? Are there systematic differences? Unless we have a fair understanding of the characteristics of crimes that become official and those that do not, we are on very tenuous ground when we use official statistics to try to determine if crime is related to such things as income, racial inequality, urban density, city size, governmental structure, or a variety of other variables, for we do not know what the crime rates measure (Booth et al., 1977; Decker, 1980; Decker et al., 1982; O'Brien, 1983).

A Critical Issue: Understanding What the Victimization Surveys Measure

In attempting to determine the validity of the UCR and to interpret what they mean, we will draw heavily on the victimization survey, analyses of the surveys, and studies of police behavior. In many respects victimization surveys can be seen as an attempt to estimate the amount of criminal behavior using techniques that are entirely independent of the process that leads to officially recorded crime. The first victimization survey of a normal population was conducted in the U.S. in 1966 (Biderman and Reiss, 1967; Biderman, 1967).

Since 1973, the U.S. Census Bureau has fielded a large national victimization survey of households (Penick and Owens, 1976; Garofalo and Skogan, 1977). There have been attempts to relate changes over time in the rates found in the national victimization survey with changes in the national rates in the UCR. Although an early study by Eck and Riccio (1978) interpreted the data as indicating that the variations over time in the UCR did not reflect real difference in the crime rate, the more recent study by Biderman, Lynch, and Peterson (1982) suggests that the variations over time in the UCR correspond to variations in the national victimization survey and thus reflect real differences.

From 1971 to 1975, the Bureau of the Census performed victimization surveys in the 26 largest United States cities, each survey consisting of a sample of 10,000 households (approximately 22,000 individuals). Residents were asked if they had been victims of certain types of crime during the preceding year. Persons over 12 years of age were questioned about crimes against the person (rape, robbery, aggravated and simple assault, and personal larceny) and one adult in each household was questioned about crimes against household (burglary, auto theft, and household theft). Information about the circumstances surrounding each incident and about characteristics of the respondent and the household were collected. Similar data were obtained from businesses, except that no questions were asked about larceny. The number of businesses sampled ranged from 1,000 to 5,000 depending on the city sampled. It should be noted that 13 of the 26 cities were sampled twice.

Because data were obtained from both individuals and businesses in the 26 cities surveyed, it is relatively easy to compare victimization crime rates with the UCR (except for larceny). Furthermore, it is possible to compare characteristics of the cities with the two crime indexes, something that is not possible with the national victimization surveys. We know of eight comparisons of the UCR and the city victimization surveys (Skogan, 1974; Clarren and Schwartz, 1976; Decker, 1980; Booth et al., 1977; Nelson, 1979; Decker et al., 1982; Cohen and Lichbach, 1982; Cohen and Land, 1984). Although Skogan (1974) in his preliminary analysis is relatively optimistic about the implications of the victimization survey for the UCR, most of the other investigators have concluded that the city victimization surveys raise serious questions about the UCR. . . .

Before turning to how the Uniform Crime Reports are constructed, and particularly the light that the victimization surveys shed on the UCR, it is necessary to discuss what the victimization surveys measure. It is particularly important to focus on the methodological problems characteristic of the victimization surveys, because they are generally viewed as a more valid indicator of the crime rate than the UCR (Decker et al., 1982; Cohen and Land, 1984).

Conceptual Issues

In the victimization surveys, "victimizations" are conceptualized as discrete incidents with a beginning and an end, which are sharply bounded in time and space. As a result the surveys do not measure well continuous processes that are not clearly delineated discrete events but that instead resemble enduring conditions. Furthermore, they only measure events that can be uniquely described and ignore classes of crimes for which victimization is quite prevalent but the frequency of individual incidents is unknown. This procedure of operationalizing victimizations implies that crimes can be understood apart from their social context, that they are discrete events which are bounded in time and space, and that crimes are knowable as discrete individual incidents (Skogan, 1981a: 7, 1981b; Biderman, 1981).

Context. The victimization survey presupposes that through description behavior can be identified as criminal or noncriminal. However, criminality is a concept which in law is not strictly defined in terms of behavior. An example will help to illustrate the problem. The UCR definition of "aggravated assault" is an unlawful attack by one person against another for the purpose of inflicting severe bodily injury, usually accompanied by the use of a weapon or other means likely to produce death or severe bodily harm (United

States Department of Justice, F.B.I., 1973: 11). A number of sources of potential confusion lie in this definition. The "attack" does not have to produce any injury or even harm, since the definition includes attempts (as we will see, the inclusion of "attempts" is especially problematic in the victimization surveys). Furthermore, the issue of intent is crucial. Yet the establishment of intent is often difficult for the average citizen and the uniformed patrolman (who usually acts on secondhand information). Whether an attack is "unlawful" is likewise a difficult decision for the average citizen to make, particularly in the case of heated disputes where both parties (and their respective friends) feel aggrieved or threatened by the other. In fact, the victimization surveys do not determine who is the "aggressor" and who is the "victim," because the issue is never even broached in the interview. It would appear that most "aggressors" would be categorized as "victims" in the surveys. Furthermore, what is a "severe injury"? Injuries obviously fall along a continuum of seriousness and gray areas will always exist. The issue is complicated by the fact that the categories such as aggravated assault, simple assault, assault and battery, and fighting specifically exclude consideration of injury (United States Department of Justice, F.B.I., 1973: 55). . . .

Such serious definitional problems exist for almost all crimes. Among the index crimes, rape and minor burglary are almost as difficult (in some cases more difficult) to define and apply to concrete situations than are definitions of aggravated assaults (Clarren and Schwartz, 1976). In fact, it is not clear that a definition of a crime can refer only to objectively measurable behavior without some reference to intent of the offender, the unique circumstances, and the general attitude or condition of the victim.

The problem of social meaning is not as important a methodological issue with street robbery or anonymous assaults, but physical aggression among family and friends, and theft and robberies in which the offender is known to the victim are much more difficult to interpret. The "crimininality" of such incidents depends heavily on the attitudes of those involved. Victimization surveys find such incidents tend not to be reported to the police and the most common reason given for not reporting is that "it was not a police matter," which suggests the victim did not wish to treat it as a crime. Nevertheless, such incidents are reported as crimes in the surveys (Hindelang, 1976; Gottfredson and Gottfredson, 1980.)

Discrete events versus continuous processes. Several crimes such as child abuse, spouse abuse, and robberies of children at school are perhaps better viewed as ongoing processes than as discrete events. Consider the family in which the father regularly comes home drunk, beats his wife, and threatens to beat his children. Occasionally, the conflict may escalate so that a family member or neighbor calls the police, so the police are apt to have an episodic record of such events. In the crime surveys these processes are treated as "series offenses." Series offenses are those incidents that are so frequent, similar in character, or otherwise difficult to separate that the victim cannot disentangle them during the interview into concrete events occurring at specific times. About 100 series incidents are recorded every month in the National Crime Surveys and they make up about 3% of all incident reports (Dodge, 1975). Overall, series incidents are disproportionately violent crimes. In the National Crime Survey and in the City Victimization Surveys, series incidents are completely excluded when the data are processed to produce crime rate estimates (Skogan, 1981a: 9). . . .

Reliance on the victims' definition of criminal acts. Because victimization surveys rely only on the report of the victims, the data may be distorted by variation in how respondents define crime. This appears to be a key issue with assaultive behavior. As Skogan (1981a: 10) notes, victimologists have always assumed the bulk of victims of assault come from the lower reaches of the social ladder because lower status persons are heavily overrepresented among victims of such crime on police files. However, in survey data, education is typically positively associated with victimization by assault. In 1976, for example, persons with college degrees recalled three times as many assaults as those with only an elementary education (U.S. Department of Justice, 1979: Table 15). This finding is extremely stable, being found in the United States (Dodge et al., 1976), Germany (Stephan, 1976), the Netherlands (Steinmetz, 1979), Norway, Finland, and Denmark (Wolf, 1976).

Skogan (1981a: 10) notes there are two competing explanations for this relationship, both of which assume that assaults tend to be more common in the lower class. The first is that educated persons are better respondents and give more complete information, and there is evidence to support this position (Skogan, 1981a: 22; Sudman and Bradburn, 1974; Sparks, Genn, and Dodd, 1977). However, it seems unlikely that this characteristic of respondents is sufficient to account for the relationship observed with education. The second is that persons in a lower-class environment may see a certain act as a normal aspect of daily life, while persons who have had very little contact with physically assaultive behavior may see the same act as a brush with criminal violence. . . .

Subcultural differences in the salience of aggressive behavior may also explain some of the perplexing racial differences in reported assault victimization. For example, white residents of Washington, D.C., reported a rate of assault victimization that was two and one half times what blacks reported, a racial difference that is entirely due to nonserious assaults (U.S. Department of Justice, 1975: Table 3, 247). . . .

Sampling and Interviewer Effects

Interviewer effects . . . The categorization of many crimes is quite sensitive to individual discretion at the lower end of the seriousness scale, whether the discretion is of police officers (in the UCR crime estimates) or of respondents and their interviewers (in the victimization surveys). In an excellent discussion of the problem, Clarren and Schwartz (1976: 129) conclude that "the upper bound for the number of 'crimes' that could be elicited is limited only by the persistence of the interviewer and the patience of the respondent." Bailey, Moore, and Bailer (1978) show that a considerable amount of

the variation in reported crime in the victimization surveys is due to interviewer effects—that is, variation due to the fact that some interviewers elicit more and/or different kinds of information from respondents than others. The extent of these effects varies both across cities and across crimes. . . .

The issue of the distribution of crime. While crime is relatively infrequent in the general population, this is not the case among certain subgroups. For example, in 1970 two thirds of the reported robberies in the United States were concentrated in 32 cities which contained 16% of the national population. Within those cities crime was very heavily concentrated within a few places (Skogan, 1979). As a result, a very small proportion of the population is exposed to extremely high levels of risk and contains a disproportionate number of victims. The relatively extreme spatial concentration of victims, especially victims of violent crime, poses a serious problem in drawing probability samples that will accurately reflect the proportion of criminal victimizations. As Skogan (1981a: 5) indicates, this problem has not been solved. A further difficulty is that factors associated with the victimization rates are also associated with the nonresponse rate, which tends to be particularly high among crime victims (Martin, 1981). . . .

Response Bias

Nonrecall. One way of checking the accuracy of victimization surveys is to take incidents from police files and to interview the victims. The San Jose reverse record check found that violent crimes of assault and rape were much less likely to be reported in the survey than property crimes (Turner, 1972); the prime determinant in whether the violent crimes were reported to the police was the relationship of the offender to the victim. . . .

Classification. Another key finding of the record checks is that the police frequently classify a crime differently than the victims do in the survey. In general, the police tend to classify the crimes as less serious than do the victims. . . . A major reason why the police classification may differ from the victim's is that the data from police records and police decisions reflect information gathered from a variety of sources other than the victim, including their own observations and reports of witnesses (Skogan, 1978, 1981a: 13).

Other sources of error. It has consistently been found that interviewing a single informant in a household produces considerably fewer victimization reports that if all residents were interviewed (Biderman and Reiss, 1967; Sudman and Bradburn, 1974; Ennis, 1967; Stephan, 1976; Dodge, 1977). This is a source of some error in the city interview, because not all household respondents were interviewed, and even when all household respondents were interviewed, not all were asked about certain crimes (Dodge, 1977; Skogan, 1981a). Furthermore, a substantial number of crimes are not recalled unless they occurred in the very recent past, and the rate at which incidents are forgotten increases with time (Skogan, 1981a; Woltman, Bushery, and Carstensen, 1975; Penick and Owens, 1976). In addition to respondents forgetting or not telling about some crimes, other crimes that occurred prior to the time frame covered in the interview (one year in the city surveys) tend to be telescoped in the interview. . . .

Assessment of the Victimization Data

Property crimes. As it is presently constructed, the National Crime Survey appears to measure serious property crimes adequately—that is, successful robberies, burglaries, and auto theft. The measure of larceny appears to be much less satisfactory because (1) most larceny involves offenses of small value, and (2) data on larceny are not obtained from businesses (Skogan, 1981a; Gottfredson and Gottfredson, 1980). For these crimes the city victimization surveys are much more problematic, in part because they occurred before many of the refinements in the current victimization surveys were made. Nevertheless, for serious robberies, burglaries, and auto thefts the estimated crime rates should have a rough correspondence with reality. By using the term seriousness we are concerned with such issues as the success of the crime, who committed it, the

loss incurred, where the crime was committed, and, with robbery, such issues as the weapon used and the extent of bodily harm. Most cases of larceny where substantial loss is incurred are probably reported. However, because larceny primarily involves items of little value (Gottfredson and Gottfredson, 1980), it is not clear that the relatively few cases of "serious larceny" that occur in a city will be closely related to the rates estimated in the victimization survey.

Assault and rape. There is substantial evidence that the data from the victimization surveys substantially underreport assaults and rapes among acquaintances, friends, and relatives. In the national survey 60% of the assaults were attributed to strangers and in the city survey 70% of interpersonal violence was attributed to strangers. As Skogan (1981a: 29) notes, these data do not correspond to what is known about the dynamics of interpersonal violence, namely that a much higher proportion of assaults and even rapes take place among family, friends, and acquaintances. Numerous studies of police homicide files suggest that strangers account for only 25% of all urban murders; homicide and assault typically are very similar in origin although the processes differ in outcome. (For review of the evidence, see Zimring, 1972; Curtis, 1974; Ennis, 1967; Skogan, 1978, 1981a; U.S. Department of Justice, F.B.I., 1971). Skogan (1981a:30) indicates that the victimization surveys are particularly suspect because police files contain three and one half times more violence between acquaintances than is reported in interviews. A study conducted in Washington, D.C., by the Law Enforcement Assistance Administration (LEAA, 1977) found that in 1973, according to the victimization survey, 30% of the victims were assaulted by nonstrangers, whereas 75% of the persons arrested for assault were nonstrangers. The LEAA data on rapes are even more striking. They found that only 9% of the rapes reported in the victimization survey included nonstrangers whereas the official statistics indicated that 57% of the rapes included nonstrangers. . . .

The LEAA (1977:19) study concludes that the data are "substantial enough to cast serious doubt on the victimization surveys' ability to measure the incidence of assault and rape between nonstrangers." The report goes on to assert that "either the survey should be restructured to obtain better information on nonstranger violence or estimates from the survey should be limited to data about assault and rape between strangers" (1977:19). . . .

It should be quite clear that for rape and assault, the measures of "crime" in the victimization surveys and in the UCR are completely different. We have focused on the issue of stranger/nonstranger violence, and to a lesser extent on the differences between blacks and whites, but probably a substantial part of the difference is due to the nature of the instruments used. In the UCR, the police must determine to their satisfaction that an assault or rape occurred. To do so they must conduct an investigation to determine if the incident fits the criteria for that particular crime. For aggravated assault, these criteria are (1) an unlawful attack of one person upon another, (2) for the purpose of inflicting severe or aggravated bodily injury, which (3) usually involves the use of a weapon or by means likely to produce death or severe bodily injury. In the victimization surveys, an aggravated assault is defined as having occurred if the respondent answers survey questions which indicate that he or she was (1) attacked with a weapon resulting in any injury, or (2) attacked without a weapon resulting either in serious injury (e.g., broken bones, loss of teeth, internal injuries, loss of consciousness) or an undetermined injury requiring two or more days of hospitalization, or (3) attacked in an attempted assault with a weapon. Note that in the victimization definition there is no determination of lawfulness or of intent.

For rape, the factors the police must determine to their satisfaction before a rape incident appears in the UCR are that a man must have had (1) carnal knowledge of a woman, (2) forcibly, and (3) against her will. In the victimization surveys a woman is never asked if she has been raped. To be recorded as rape the woman had to answer that she was raped to one of the following questions: (1) "Did anyone threaten to beat you up or threaten

you in some other way?" or (2) "Did anyone *try* to attack you in some other way?" In the interview rape is never mentioned, no definitions are given, and no follow-up or probing questions are asked to find out the nature of the rape. . . .

In summary, there is little if any reason to believe that across cities the victimization rates for aggravated assault and rape will correlate with the UCR rates. (For a more detailed discussion of this issue, see Skogan, 1978, 1981a; LEAA, 1977).

The Construction of UCR Offense Rate Statistics

UCR Index offense rates can be conceptualized as the final product of a filtering process which selects from a wide range of illicit behavior those specific acts reported to the FBI as serious crime. The most crucial step in the creation of an official crime statistic is the police becoming aware that a crime has been committed. The evidence consistently indicates that in this process the police are primarily reactive rather than proactive; that is, the crime is detected by a citizen who then notifies the police. . . . Thus, the process can most conveniently be considered as occurring in two stages: (1) a citizen detecting the offense, deciding to report it to police, and actually doing so, and (2) a police officer interpreting the reported offense, deciding to record it as an official crime, and later reporting it to the FBI under some UCR category. . . .

Citizen Reporting and Nonreporting

Detection of a criminal offense involves both observing an event and defining that event as a criminal act. An attempted burglary where the burglar leaves no sign of an attempted entry or where the potential victim misinterprets the sign will not be labeled as a crime. Further, an event might be observed, yet not reported as a crime either (1) because the illegal nature of the act is not known, (2) because the citizen disagrees with the legal definition of an act as criminal, or (3) the cost of reporting the crime is not worth the benefit. It should be noted that citizens quite often cannot make the proper legal classification of an incident. . . . Among other things, this suggests that citizens in an interview may describe an incident as in a different category than police would have. This finding is supported in the reverse record checks; it is also found in studies which attempt to match victims' reports with police records (e.g., Schneider, 1977).

Reporting. Two issues crucial to deciding if there is a systematic bias in citizen reports of crimes to the police are whether among the different segments in our society (1) there are differences in the perceived severity of various crimes, or (2) there are differences in how serious a person must perceive a crime to be before reporting it to the police. . . . In short, with regard to the first issue it appears that the different segments of society agree on the severity of the various crimes covered by the FBI index crimes and that differences in perceived severity would not be a source of systematic bias affecting citizen reports of crime to the police.[1] . . .

Thus, the evidence from the victimization surveys provides very strong support for the view that perceived seriousness of the crime is the key determinant of reporting a crime to the police and the attributes of the individual and where the person lives play only a very minor role.

Another way to assess the reasons for citizens not reporting crimes is simply to ask the respondent why the crime was not reported. The two most frequently given reasons are that the offense "was not serious enough" to report and that "the police could not be effective." For the crimes of rape, assault, and motor theft a large percent of the victims reported that the victimization was "a private matter." Fear of reprisal is infrequently given as a reason for not reporting a crime (Biderman, Johnson, McIntyre, and Weir, 1967: 154; Ennis, 1967: 44; Hawkins, 1973; Hindelang, 1976: 5; Gottfredson and Gottfredson, 1980; U.S. Department of Justice, F.B.I., 1974). . . .

In summary, the perceived seriousness of a crime appears to be the prime determinant of whether it is reported to the police. Furthermore, there is no evidence in the studies reviewed to suggest that different segments of society differ in the level of perceived seriousness (of the FBI index crimes) required before a crime is reported to the police.[2]

Police Recording and Nonrecording

The second major filter through which crime counts pass is the police organization itself, from the first patrolman's contact with the complaining citizen through the final classification of a crime into UCR categories for official recording and publication. It is the alleged bias in this screening process which has traditionally caused the most concern about the usefulness of official police statistics. As was noted, the initiation of the recording process is almost always in response to a citizen's complaint.

There are a number of ways of measuring law enforcement bias in the recording of crime. One is to look at characteristics of individuals and see if they are treated differently by legal officials. Another is to look at police departments and their reporting behavior. A third is to look at independent indicators of the crime rate.

Characteristics of individuals and police behavior. Perhaps the best direct-observation study is that of Black and Reiss (1970). The study consists of systematic observation of police-citizen transactions occurring in lower-class areas of Boston, Chicago, and Washington, D.C., during the summer of 1966. Black and Reiss (1970:76) found that

(1) Most police encounters with juveniles arise in direct response to citizens who take the initiative to mobilize the police to action.

(2) The probability of arrest increases with the legal seriousness of alleged juvenile offenses, in particular as that legal seriousness is defined in the criminal law for adults.

(3) Police sanctioning of juveniles strongly reflects the manifest preferences of citizen complainants in field encounters.

(4) The presence of situational evidence linking a juvenile to a deviant act is an important factor in the probability of arrest.

Note that the key determinants of official action were perceived seriousness of the offense and the desires of the complainant. In no instance did the police initiate official action when the complainant manifested a preference for informal action. When no complainant was present, the police very rarely initiated official action even though the suspect was found with incriminating evidence of some sort (Black and Reiss, 1970:76). Second, there was no evidence of racial discrimination on the part of the police. Third, the deference of the offender had little effect on police action, with 22% of the antagonistic suspects and 22% of the very deferential suspects being arrested.[3] These findings have recently been replicated by Lundman, Sykes, and Clark (1978).[4] . . .

Block and Block (1980), using secondary data from a victimization survey and police records in Chicago, look at the process by which robbery is transformed into statistics. Rates of victimization are based on a survey conducted in 1974 and the rates of official records are based on a sample of police records for different months in 1975, with the rates projected for the entire year. . . . Block and Block found that (1) age, sex, and race of the victim had no effect on the decision probabilities at any stage in the decision process; (2) victim and police decisions are primarily affected by the seriousness of the incident as indicated by whether a gun was used or robbery completed; (3) most of the serious cases that are eliminated are eliminated by the victim and not by the police, and in fact no crimes were eliminated by the police when a robbery was completed and a gun was used; and (4) upon responding to a robbery reported by a victim, the police "found" 79% (officially reported a robbery had occurred), while 21% received a different categorization (this most frequently occurred when the victim reported a completed robbery with no gun, and it is likely that many of these were categorized as burglaries).

By far the best studies of the validity of UCR figures regarding race, sex, and age characteristics of offenders are those by Hindelang (1978; 1981). Hindelang (1978) compared UCR estimates of the racial distribution of offenders for four common-law personal crimes—robbery, rape, aggravated assault, and simple assault—to those obtained from the national victimization survey. . . . Hindelang (1978:101) concludes that "these data suggest there is virtually no criminal justice system selection bias for either rape or robbery."

The pattern is quite different with assault, particularly aggravated assault. The UCR arrest rate for aggravated assault is 41% black, and the victimization survey rate is 30% black (Hindelang, 1978: 100). When we look at the respondents in the victimization surveys who said they had reported the crime to the police, the percent black drops to 26 (Hindelang, 1978:102), and so the disparity between the UCR and the NCS increases. . . .

More recently, Hindelang (1981) compared offender characteristics using the victimization surveys and the UCR. He looked at crime rates by sex, race, and age for personal crimes (rape, robbery, assault, and personal larceny) and for household crimes (burglary, household larceny, and vehicle theft). . . . Hindelang demonstrates a remarkable correspondence between the survey data and official statistics. Hindelang (1981: 473) concludes, "the general agreement between UCR and NCS (National Crime Survey) on the offenders' sex, race, and age characteristics increases the probability that both are acceptably valid." . . .

Other evidence also suggests that professionalism is related both to more complete and more accurate crime reporting. . . . With the increase in both federal money and federal guidelines for police departments across the country during the 1970s, it is likely there was an increase in the level and uniformity of the professionalism of police departments, and that this variable is less important as a determinant of variation in the official crime rate across cities than it was in the past. Note also that in the past three decades there has been a very sharp increase in the number of agencies reporting to the FBI and at the present time virtually all relevant agencies report. . . .

In summary, there are four factors which appear to play a significant role in whether the police, upon responding to a complaint, report a crime. The first is whether upon investigation the police conclude that the evidence fairly clearly indicates a crime has occurred (remember that the police and the citizens often differ regarding the appropriate categorization of a crime). Second, the police very rarely report a crime if the victim would prefer to treat the matter informally. Third, the more serious the crime, the more likely the police are to report it; with regard to this point it is worth emphasizing that police and citizens use very similar criteria for the "seriousness." Fourth, the more professional the police department, the more likely its officers are to report a crime. There has been a substantial increase in the professionalism of the police departments over the past four decades. In evaluating police behavior in the reporting of a crime, it is very important for the reader to keep in mind that the key determinant of whether a crime is officially recorded is the decision of the victim to notify the police, while police behavior plays a much more modest role.

A Comparison of UCR and Victimization Estimates

The best way to answer questions about the validity of the UCR is to relate them to the "true" crime rate. Since one can only estimate this rate (it can never be measured directly) and since all estimates of the true rates contain error, the next best test is to compare the UCR rates to another, maximally different indicator of the same variable, that is, to compare it to another flawed measure of the true rate. If the two measures share no method variance, if there is no common source of error which will bias both measures (in the same or in opposite directions), then the relationship between the two can be treated as a validity coefficient because the only source of common variance is taken to be the true rate (Skogan 1974). . . .

The correlations are higher for crimes involving theft (including robbery) than for purely personal crimes (aggravated assault and rape), and there tends to be less agreement among the investigators regarding the correlations for purely personal crimes. One can interpret this lack of agreement for the personal crimes among investigators as due

to different decisions about the proper categorizations in the victimization surveys. Motor theft is consistently found to have the highest correlation and all the studies find burglary and robbery to have relatively high correlations. As expected, Nelson (1979) finds higher correlations with motor theft and robbery than most of the other investigators, while Clarren and Schwartz (1976) and Decker (1980) find a higher correlation with burglary. Nelson *also* found the correlation with robberies committed with a weapon to be substantially stronger than robberies without weapons, which is consistent with the fact that when weapons are used the crimes are much more likely to be reported to the police and the police are much more likely to record that a robbery occurred. Except for the study by Decker (1980), all of the studies found essentially no correlation between the measures of rape, and all studies found a negative correlation between the two measures of aggravated assault.

Motor Theft, Robbery, and Burglary

The victimization surveys and the UCR have similar rates for motor theft, and in the victimization surveys the respondents almost always indicated that they reported the crime to the police; however, with burglary and robbery the victimization rate is approximately three times as large as the UCR and the majority of the crimes are not reported to the police (Decker, 1980: 50). We would thus expect the correlations between the victimization survey and the UCR to be higher with motor theft than with burglary and robbery. . . . In short, for these crimes our analysis indicates the UCR rates are very highly correlated with the true crime rates and are a valid measure of serious motor theft, robberies, and burglaries. . . .

Larceny

Among the FBI index crimes considered here, the larceny crime rate has received the least attention. However, it is clear that larceny is (1) the most frequent index crime, (2) the most difficult to detect, (3) the crime least likely to be reported to the police (Schneider,

1981) and (4) the crime most amenable to reporting manipulation in response to political pressures (Clarren and Schwartz, 1976). The victimization surveys clearly indicated that for larceny the greater the value of the object stolen, the greater the likelihood that the crime will be reported and recorded. . . . However, because the vast majority of larcenies involve property of modest value, the official larceny rate will not primarily reflect stolen objects of considerable value (even though these crimes are the most likely to be reported and recorded). On reverse record recall checks, larceny is considerably less likely to be recalled than robbery or burglary but much more likely to be recalled than assault or rape (Penick and Owens, 1976: 39).

. . . The results of Decker and of Cohen and Lichbach indicate that the UCR larceny rate is fairly highly correlated with the true larceny rate. In contrast, the results of Decker et al. and Cohen and Land suggest that while the UCR larceny rate is clearly correlated with the true larceny rate, the relationship is not particularly robust. Thus, all four studies provide support for the position that the UCR larceny rate is correlated with the true larceny rate, but the results are equivocal with regard to the strength of that relationship, ranging from modest to strong. . . .

Overall, unlike the other property index crimes, larceny needs more research before one can conclude that the official rate is a valid indicator. In our view the evidence is sufficient to support the position that the official larceny rate is adequate as a rough indicator of the actual larceny rate, meaning that *marked* variation in the official larceny rate will reflect real variation. However, the evidence is insufficient to conclude that modest changes in the actual larceny rate will be reflected in the official larceny rate.

Homicide

Hindelang (1974b) examined sources of homicide using data from the NORC, the Center for Health Statistics, and the UCR, and the comparisons indicated a high level of accuracy in the official homicide rates. More recently, Cantor and Cohen (1980) compared the UCR with the homicide rate measured by the vital statistic reports, and their analysis also shows that (at least since 1949) the UCRs provide an accurate measure of the homicide rate.

Aggravated Assault

There is a relatively large negative correlation between aggravated assault reported in victimization surveys and in the UCR, and in most analyses this relationship is statistically significant. Given the small sample size (n = 26), this is a remarkable finding. In the victimization surveys most of the aggravated assaults involve strangers, injury is rare, and serious injury is very rare. Furthermore, reverse record checks show that assaults by acquaintances, particularly by relatives, are rarely recalled in survey interviews. Also, official records have much higher rates of violence between acquaintances than are shown in the surveys, and many investigators have concluded that victimization surveys are unable to measure violence.

According to the U.S. Department of Justice, F.B.I. (1971:11-12), "most aggravated assaults occur within the family unit or among neighbors or acquaintances. The victim and the offender relationship as well as the nature of the attack makes this crime similar to murder." And there is an extensive literature indicating homicides and aggravated assaults typically occur among a certain segment of the population which has a very high rate of violence (Mulville, Tumin, and Curtis, 1967; Wolfgang, 1958; Curtis, 1974; Luckenbill, 1984; Skogan, 1981a: 29-31). . . . Thus, the evidence involving police behavior indicates that stranger assaults are more likely to be reported than nonstranger assaults; if this is correct, then the high rate of stranger assaults reported in the victimization surveys is even more misrepresentative than a simple comparison with official statistics indicates.

What may be occurring with aggravated assault is the following. Serious assaults typically involve significant bodily injury, or at least a serious attempt to inflict such injury. Such assaults are likely to lead to police involvement due to someone else's effort to stop a serious altercation by calling the police, or when serious injury does occur (such as a knife or gunshot wound), the police become involved when medical attention is sought. The evidence suggests that the UCR rate of aggravated assaults largely reflects such cases. . . .

It is also likely that in victimization surveys the nonreporting of aggravated assaults, particularly those committed by family members and acquaintances, occurs for the following reasons. First, such assaults typically arise over very trivial matters (Mulville et al., 1967; Curtis, 1974) and when one has a close relationship with an individual one tends, over time, to put the assault into the context of one's overall relationship with the person and as a consequence the incident tends to become normalized.[5] Second, because the assaults tend to occur in an environment where there is a high level of verbal and physical conflict, they would be fairly common experience to those involved and thus more easily forgotten and less likely to be reported to strangers.[6]

It is clear that many "aggravated assaults" are not recorded in the UCR. However, given the inability of the victimization surveys to measure non-stranger assaults and the very high proportion of "nonserious aggravated assaults" in the victimization surveys, it appears that the UCR provide a better measure. . . .

Rape

Victimization surveys appear to be unable to measure rape adequately and, according to official statistics, they vastly undercount nonstranger rape. As with other assaults, the majority of rapes reported in the victimization surveys were attempted and not completed, and in a substantial majority of the rapes reported the victims received no physical injury. Unfortunately, because the victimization surveys contain no probes for either attempted or completed rapes, it is very difficult to grasp what the victimization surveys are measuring.

According to the UCR, rape is carnal knowledge of a female against her will through the use of force or the threat of force. In 1970, 71% of the official rape offenses involved a complete rape while the remaining 29% were attempted (U.S. Department of

Justice, F.B.I., 1971: 14). According to official records rape is more likely than most of the index crimes (all except homicide and aggravated assault) to involve someone known to the victim. . . . Thus, official statistics on rape are much more likely to deal with completed rapes than are victimization surveys and report a vastly higher rate of nonstranger rapes than are reported in victimization surveys.

Of all the index crimes, rape appears to be the most problematic in terms of both the willingness of victims to contact the police and the ability to establish that the incident meets the legal criteria. That rape is difficult to prove is indicated by the fact that in 1970, for the nation as a whole, 18% of the reported rapes were determined to be unfounded (U.S. Department of Justice, F.B.I., 1971: 14), and the rate appears to be relatively costant over the years. As the UCR makes clear, the fact that upon investigation the police decided a citizen-reported rape was unfounded does not mean a rape did not occur, but that in most cases it was difficult to establish that force or threat of force was used because a prior relationship existed between the victim and the offender (U.S. Department of Justice, F.B.I., 1971: 14). . . .

It is argued that when a rape occurs it is primarily the severity of the turmoil, anguish, and bodily harm that determines whether the rape is reported to the police. Nonstranger rapes are probably less likely to be reported to the police than stranger rapes. However, it is likely that the victim's relationship with the offender tends to play a relatively modest role at the time a rape occurs but the nature of the relationship becomes increasingly important with the passage of time. Rapes reported in the UCR are probably a relatively poor indicator of rape as a social phenomenon but are probably a relatively accurate indicator of rapes which meet the established legal criteria (Lizotte, 1985).

It is not argued that only true rapes are reported in the UCR and that the victimization surveys are measuring trivial events. What is proposed is that the UCR tend to measure violent rapes where the legal evidence is clear.[7] In contrast, many of the rapes measured in the victimization surveys may be highly traumatic to the victim, but they are probably less serious in terms of violence, and in terms of legal criteria the evidence is more ambiguous. Such rapes appear to be fairly common and to be particularly difficult to contain by formal means of social control.

Conclusion

For a number of decades social scientists have recognized that the UCR are the result of a set of social processes which result in some crimes becoming "official" while other crimes do not become public "social facts." Since the recognition that the UCR were the product of a social process which selected out a large number of crimes, it has not been clear what the UCR represent. This paper, drawing on recent research, has attempted to interpret the meaning of the UCR and thus to assess their validity.

Running throughout this discussion of the factors involved in the development of crime rates are a few important themes. Both citizens and the police are involved in a decision-making process concerning the classification of an incident as an official crime. In the United States and most other democracies, the primary responsibility for serious crime detection is lodged in the citizenry rather than the police. The uniformed patrol division is geared for the reaction to citizen calls for help through a centralized radio communications system. In the majority of crime situations, the police act in response to citizens' telephone calls and give great weight to the preference of the complainant for action. The key factor in the decision of the citizen to notify the police, as well as in the police response to the complaint, is the perceived *seriousness* of the incident, especially if seriousness is defined very generally.

It appears that both the citizen and the police are in general agreement as to what is a serious crime, particularly if it involves bodily injury (or serious threat of bodily injury), if the property stolen is of high value, if the act is committed by a stranger, or it involves breaking and entering. The perceived seriousness of the crime, first and primarily as defined by the victim, and secondarily as defined by the police, appears to account for most of the variance in whether a crime is officially reported. . . .

Legal seriousness, victim-offender relationship, desires of the complainant, and the extent to which citizen and police see an incident as a public or private matter are all criteria related to reporting. They all concern the extent to which the victim of a crime sees himself or herself as substantially injured by another citizen in a way he or she cannot control. . . . Thus, official crime rates are in part a measure of the extent to which the citizens feel injured, frightened, and financially hurt by a criminal act. In this sense they may be a better measure of social disruption than are "true rates," where more objectively definable behavior is measured. In short, the rates of the index crimes presented in the UCR appear to be reasonably good approximations of true crime rates when the latter are defined as what both citizens and the police view as serious violations of the laws which codify the fundamental personal and property norms of society.[8]

Thus, the "dark figure" of crime uncovered in victimization surveys primarily involves rather trivial events; as Skogan (1978:14) states, "Most victimizations are not notable events. The majority are property crimes in which the perpetrator is never detected. The financial stakes are small, and the costs of calling the police greatly outweigh the benefits." (See also Gottfredson and Gottfredson, 1980: 28-36). For those crimes when the victim knows the offender and does not notify the police the major reason that the police are not notified is that the victim views the "crime" as a "private matter." The aggravated assaults committed by strangers that are uncovered by victimization surveys and are not officially reported almost invariably involve no injury, and it is likely that most would not meet the legal criteria in aggravated assault. Similarly, most of the rapes committed by strangers and which are not reported by the police involve rapes that were not completed and that did not cause injury. Apparently, like self-reported delinquency, the criminal behavior picked up by victimization surveys but not reported to the police involves a different domain of behavior than that which is officially recorded (Hindelang et al., 1979).

The analysis suggests that the UCR appear to reflect fairly accurately what the citizens and the police perceive as violations of the law which pose a significant threat to the social order. For motor vehicle theft, robbery, burglary, and homicide, the evidence supporting this interpretation is also quite strong. For aggravated assault and rape the evidence is quite strong, but in reaching this conclusion one must recognize that one is making choices about the validity of various pieces of conflicting evidence. In particular, we are largely ignoring the data from the victimization surveys on assaults and rape on the grounds that they vastly underreport non-stranger assaults and rape and record a large number of aggravated assaults and rapes by strangers that do not meet the legal criteria.

Although there is general support for the utility of official larceny rates, in many respects the evidence on larceny is the most equivocal. As the rate of larceny is very high, even though most larcenies are not reported to the police, the official larceny rate is substantially higher than the other index crime rates. This means that the overall index crime rate disproportionately reflects the official rate of larceny, and given our questions about the validity of the larceny rate it is probably better not to look at the overall rate but to look at the crimes separately. In summary, it is concluded that the index crimes, with the possible exception of larceny, are valid indicators of crimes which members of society perceive as serious.

Most criminologists agree that the actual or "true" crime rate should correlate with urban structural characteristics and that if we had a valid indicator of the crime rate we could determine the relationship between crime and those structural characteristics (Shaw and McKay, 1931, 1969; Lander, 1954; Chilton, 1964; Bordua, 1958-1959; Schuessler, 1962; Land and Felson, 1976; Cohen and Felson, 1979; Hughes and Carter, 1983; Crutchfield, Geerken, and Gove, 1982; Cohen and Lichbach, 1982; Blau and Blau, 1982). Furthermore, a valid indicator of the crime rate is essential to study an etiological theory of criminality (see especially Gibbs, 1981, 1983). It is clear that the UCR provide a valid indicator of the index crimes and can be used in studies of the relationship between crime and social structural characteristics and in etiological studies.

When the UCR are used it should be made clear that one is dealing with the relatively serious crimes which tend to pass through the citizen and the police filters and are officially reported. Finally, it is important to note that if one defines crime as criminal acts serious enough to be reacted to by both citizens and the police, then from the evidence reviewed above, the UCR are at least as valid and probably more valid than the data from victimization surveys. In fact, with regard to rape and aggravated assault the rates obtained from the UCR have much more validity than the victimization rates.[9]

Discussion Questions

1. What are the Uniform Crime Reports? What are the strengths of these data? What are some of their limitations?

2. In what senses are official data (Uniform Crime Reports) socially constructed? What factors are important for determining whether an offense is actually reported to the police? What factors are important for determining whether the police record an "offense" as a crime?

3. Overall, for what offenses are the UCR data valid? For what offenses are the UCR less valid? What are the implications of this for criminologists' use of official data to study crime?

Notes

1. Miethe (1982) argues that perhaps some of the apparent consensus on the perceived seriousness of crimes may be a methodological artifact. However, because his argument only applies to minor crimes, which are not part of the FBI index crimes, this possibility has no relevance to the present discussion.

2. A reviewer of this paper has suggested that different segments of society (blacks and possibly persons from the lower class in general) are less likely to report comparable crimes to the police, with those segments requiring a higher "threshold level" (that is, a more serious crime) before reporting a crime to the police. This argument suggests that, because

blacks (and possibly members of the lower class in general) are less likely to report comparable crimes to the police than other members of the population, and because there are class and ethnic variations across cities, there could be a systematic bias in the UCR statistics across cities. The studies just reviewed appear to contradict such an argument. However, many assaults and some rapes that are reported to the police are not reported in victimization surveys, and many of those reported to the police are not reported in victimization surveys, and many of those reported come from educated whites, so these data do not conclusively address the issue for auto theft, burglary, robbery, or homicide. We argue later in the paper that with regard to reporting assaults and rapes to the police, at the time the crime is committed the threshold level is relatively comparable across the different components of society. However, the evidence for this proposition is largely inferential.

3. In an earlier study, Piliavin and Briar (1964) reported that the demeanor of the juvenile had a very strong effect on the field disposition of the suspect, even stronger than the type of offense. However, as Hirschi (1980:282) notes, because offenses did not vary in this study, "anything and everything will be more important than offense in determining the severity of disposition."

4. The reader may want to look at Hirschi's (1980:295-297) discussion of the interpretation of Lundman et al.'s (1978) findings in evaluating this summary of their findings.

5. We would argue that with aggravated assault, because there is a serious threat to one's life, the issue of stranger versus acquaintance tends to be ignored at the time the crime is committed. Furthermore, when someone other than the victim reports the assault to the police, the person reporting the crime is likely to be relatively unconcerned with the issue of the relationship between the offender and the victim. Thus, if correct, the victim's relationship to the assailant often only becomes an issue after the crime has occurred.

6. This analysis is consistent with the hypothesis that a subculture of violence is causally linked to a high level of violence; however, these assumptions do not require that the "subculture of violence" hypothesis be correct. All we are assuming is that when violence is common (1) it tends to be normalized, and (2) people will tend to be more distrustful of strangers.

7. First, at the time they occur nonstranger rapes are likely to be perceived as less serious. Second, victims are aware that the issue of force is more difficult to establish when the victim has an established relationship with the offender.

8. It should be clear from the discussion that what most citizens and police perceive as serious crimes tend not to include most white-collar crime, which many sociologists see as particularly serious crimes (Chambliss and Seidman, 1971; Quinney, 1975, 1978; Johnson and Wasicklewski, 1982).

9. In recent years the second most common source of data in the study of crime has been the victimization survey. If the analysis presented here is correct, then some of those studies are of questionable value. At the minimum investigators should be as cautious in drawing conclusions from victimization studies as they are in drawing conclusions from studies based on the UCR.

References

Akman, Dogan, Andre Normandeau, and Steven Turner. 1967. "The Measurement of Delinquency in Canada" in *Journal of Criminal Law, Criminology, and Police Science* 58: 330-337.

Bailer, Barbara, Leroy Bailey, and Joyce Stevens. 1977. "Measures of Interviewer Bias and Variance" in *Journal of Marketing Research* 14: 337-343.

Bailey, Leroy, Thomas F. Moore, and Barbara A. Bailer. 1978. "An Interviewer's Variance Study of the National Crime Survey City Sample" in *Journal of the American Statistical Association* 73: 16-23.

Beattie, Ronald H. and John P. Kenney. 1966. "Aggravated Crimes" in *Annals of the American Academy of Political and Social Sciences* 364: 73-85.

Berk, Richard, Donileen Loseke, Sarah Fenstermaker Berk, and David Rauma. 1980. "Bringing the Cops Back In: In Study of Efforts to Make the Criminal Justice System More Responsive to Incidents of Family Violence" in *Social Science Research* 9: 193-215.

——. 1982. "Throwing the Cops Back Out: The Decline of a Local Program to Make the Criminal Justice System More Responsive to Incidents of Domestic Violence" in *Social Science Research*.

Berk, Sarah and Donileen Loseke. 1981. "Handling Family Violence: The Situational Determinants of Police Arrests in Domestic

Disturbances" in *Law and Society Review* 15: 317-346.

Biderman, Albert D. 1966. "Social Indicators and Goals" in Raymond A. Bauer (ed.), *Social Indicators*. Cambridge, MA: MIT Press.

——. 1967. "Surveys of Population Samples for Estimating Crime Incidence" in *The Annals* 374: 16-33.

——. 1975. *A Social Indicator of Interpersonal Harm*. Washington, D.C.: Bureau of Social Science Research.

——. 1981. "Sources of Data for Victimology" in *Journal of Criminal Law and Criminology* 72: 789-817.

Biderman, Albert D. and Albert Reiss. 1967. "On Exploring the 'Dark Figure' of Crime" in *The Annals* 374: 1-15.

Biderman, Albert D., James P. Lynch, and Joseph L. Peterson. 1982. "Why NCS Diverges From UCR Index Trends." Unpublished manuscript. Washington, D.C.: Bureau of Social Science Research.

Biderman, Albert D., Louise A. Johnson, Jennie McIntyre, and Adrianne W. Weir. 1967. "Report on a Pilot Study in the District of Columbia on Victimization and Attitudes Toward Law Enforcement." Field Surveys I. President's Commission on Law Enforcement and Administration of Justice. Washington, D.C.: U.S. Government Printing Office.

Black, Donald. 1970. "Production of Crime Rates" in *American Sociological Review* 35: 733-748.

Black, Donald and Albert Reiss, Jr. 1970. "Police Control of Juveniles" in *American Sociological Review* 35: 63-77.

Blau, Judith R. and Peter M. Blau. 1982. "Metropolitan Structure and Violent Crime" in *American Sociological Review* 47: 114-128.

Block, Richard. 1974. "Why Notify the Police? The Victim's Decision to Notify the Police of an Assault" in *Criminology* 11: 555-566.

——. 1981. "Victim-Offender Dynamics in Violent Crime" in *Journal of Criminal Law and Criminology* 74: 743-761.

Block, Richard and Carolyn Block. 1980. "Decision and Data: The Official Transformation of Robbery Incidents into Official Robbery Statistics" in *Journal of Criminal Law and Criminology* 171: 622-636.

Booth, Alan, David Johnson, and Harvey Choldin. 1977. "Correlates of the City Crime Rate: Victimization Surveys Versus Official Statistics" in *Social Problems* 25: 187-197.

Bordua, David J. 1958-1959. "Juvenile Delinquency and Anomie: An Attempt at Replication" in *Social Problems* 6: 230-238.

Bordua, David J. and Albert Reiss, Jr. 1967. "Organization and Environment: A Perspective on the Police" in David J. Bordua (ed.), *The Police: Six Sociological Essays*. New York: Wiley.

Braithwaite, John. 1981. "The Myth of Social Class and Crime Reconsidered" in *American Sociological Review* 46: 36-57.

Cantor, David and Lawrence Cohen. 1980. "Comparing Measures of Homicide Trends: Methodological and Substantive Differences in the Vital Statistics and the Uniform Crime Report Time Series (1933-1975)" in *Social Science Research* 9: 121-145.

Catlin, Gary and Susan Murry. 1979. "Report on Canadian Victimization Survey Methodological Pretests Ottawa, Canada": Government Statistics.

Chambliss, William J. and Robert B. Seidman. 1971. *Law, Order, and Power*. Reading, MA: Addison Wesley.

Chilton, Roland J. 1964. "Continuity in Delinquency Area Research: A Comparison of Studies for Baltimore, Detroit, and Indianopolis" in *American Sociological Review* 29: 71-83.

Clarren, Summer N. and Alfred I. Schwartz. 1976. "Measuring a Program's Impact: A Cautionary Note" in Wesley Skogan (ed.), *Sample Surveys of the Victims of Crime*. Cambridge, MA: Ballinger.

Clelland, Donald and Timothy Carter. 1980. "The New Myth of Class and Crime" in *Criminology* 18: 391-396.

Cohen, Larry J. and March I. Lichbach. 1982. "Alternative Measures of Crime: A Statistical Evaluation" in *The Sociological Quarterly* 23: 253-266.

Cohen, Larry J. and March I. Lichbach. 1982. "Alternative Measures of Crime: A Statistical Evaluation" in *The Sociological Quarterly* 23: 253-266.

Cohen, Lawrence E. and Marcus Felson. 1979. "Urban Social Structural Determinants of Discrepancies Between Crime Reports and Crime Surveys." Presented at the annual meeting of the American Sociological Association.

Cohen, Lawrence E. and Kenneth Land. 1984. "Discrepancies Between Crime Reports and Crime Surveys: Urban Social Structural Determinants." *Criminology* 22: 499-530.

Cohen, Lawrence E. and Rodney Stark. 1974. "Discriminatory Labelling and the Five-Finger Discount: An Empirical Analysis of Differential Shoplifting Dispositions" in *Journal of Research in Crime and Delinquency* 11: 25-39.

Crutchfield, Robert, Michael Geerken, and Walter Grove. 1982. "Crime Rate and Social Integration: The Impact of Metropolitan Mobility" in *Criminology* 20: 467-478.

Cullen, Frances T., Bruce G. Link, and Craig W. Pozanzi. 1982. "The Seriousness of Crime Revisited: Have Attitudes Toward White-Collar Crime Changed?" in *Criminology* 20: 83-102.

Curtis, Lynn A. 1974. *Criminal Violence.* Lexington, MA: D.C. Heath.

Decker, Scott. 1980. *Criminalization, Victimization and Structural Correlates of Twenty-Six American Cities.* Saratoga, CA: Century Twenty-one Publishing.

Decker, David, David Shichor, and Robert O'Brien. 1982. *Urban Structure and Victimization.* Lexington, MA: Lexington.

Dodge, Richard. 1970. *Victims Recall Pretest—Washington, D.C.* Unpublished paper. Washington, D.C.: U.S. Census Bureau.

———. 1975. *Series Victimization: What is to be Done?* Washington, D.C.: U.S. Census Bureau, Crime Statistics Analysis Staff.

———. 1977. *Analysis of Screen Questions on the National Crime Survey.* Unpublished paper. Washington, D.C.: U.S. Census Bureau, Crime Statistics Analysis Staff.

Dodge, Richard and Harold Lentzner. 1978. "Patterns of Personal Series Incidents in the National Crime Survey." Presented at the annual meeting of the American Statistical Association.

Dodge, Richard, Harold Lentzner, and Frederick Shenk. 1976. "Crime in the United States: A Report on the National Crime Survey" in Wesley Skogan (ed.), *Sample Surveys of the Victims of Crime.* Cambridge, MA: Ballinger.

Dunbow, Frederic L. and David E. Reed. 1976. "The Limits of Victims Surveys: A Community Case Study" in Wesley Skogan (ed.), *Sample Surveys of the Victims of Crime.* Cambridge, MA: Ballinger.

Eck, J. Ernst and Lucius Riccio. 1978. "Relationship Between Reported Crime Rates and Victimization Survey Results: An Empirical and Analytic Study" in *Journal of Criminal Justice* 7: 293-308.

Elliot, Delbert S. and Suzanne S. Ageton. 1980. "Reconciling Race and Class Differences in Self-Reported and Official Estimates of Delinquency" in *American Sociological Review* 45: 95-110.

Ennis, Philip H. 1967. "Criminal Victimization in the United States: A Report of a National Survey" in *Field Surveys II.* Washington, D.C.: U.S. Government Printing Office.

Figlio, Robert M. 1975. "The Seriousness of Offenses: An Evaluation by Offenders and Non-offenders" in *Journal of Criminal Law and Criminology* 66: 189-200.

Garofalo, James and Michael J. Hindelang. 1977. *An Introduction to the National Crime Survey.* Washington, D.C.: U.S. Department of Justice.

Geerken, Michael and Walter R. Gove. 1977. "Deterrence, Overload and Incapacitation: An Evaluation of Three Explanations of the Negative Correlation Between Crime and Punishment" in *Social Forces* 56: 424-27.

Gibbs, Jack. 1981. *Norms, Deviance and Social Control: Conceptual Matters.* New York: Elsevier.

———. 1983. "The State of Criminology Theory." Presented at the annual meeting of the American Society of Criminology.

Gibbs, Jack and Maynard Erickson. 1976. "Crime Rates of American Cities in an Ecological Context" in *American Journal of Sociology* 82: 605-20.

———. 1979. "Conceptions of Criminal and Delinquent Acts" in *Delinquent Behavior* 1: 71-100.

Gottfredson, Michael and Don Gottfredson. 1980. *Decisionmaking in Criminal Justice.* Cambridge: Ballinger.

Gottfredson, Michael and Michael J. Hindelang. 1979. "A Study of the Behavior of Law" in *American Sociological Review* 44: 3-18.

Gove, Walter R. 1983. "Criminology: The Current State of the Field." Presented at the annual meeting of the Southern Sociology Society.

Hagan, John. 1972. "The Labelling Perspective, the Delinquent and the Police: A Review of the Literature." *Canadian Journal of Criminology and Corrections* 14: 150-165.

Hawkins, Danell. 1980. "Perceptions of Punishment for Crime" in *Deviant Behavior* 1: 193-216.

Hawkins, Richard O. 1973. "Who Called the Cops? Decisions to Report Criminal Victimization" in *Law and Society Review* 7: 427-444.

Hindelang, Michael J. 1974a. "Decisions of Shoplifting Victims to Involve the Criminal Justice Process" in *Social Problems* 21: 580-593.

———. 1974b. "The Uniform Crime Reports Revisited" in *Journal of Criminal Justice* 2: 1-17.

———. 1976. *Criminal Victimization in Eight American Cities.* Cambridge, MA: Ballinger.

———. 1978. "Race and Involvement in Common Law Personal Crimes" in *American Sociological Review* 43: 93-109.

———. 1981. "Variation in Rates of Offending" in *American Sociological Review* 46: 461-74.

Hindelang, Michael J., Michael Gottfredson, and James Garofalo. 1978. *Victims of Personal Crime: An Empirical Foundation for a Theory of*

Personal Victimization. Cambridge, MA: Ballinger.

Hindelang, Michael J., Travis Hirschi, and Joseph G. Weis. 1979. "Correlates of Delinquency: The Illusion of Discrepancy Between Self-Report and Official Measures" in *American Sociological Review* 44: 995-1,014.

——. 1982. "Reply to 'On the Use of Self-Report Data to Determine the Class Distribution of Criminal and Delinquent Behavior" in *American Sociological Review* 47: 433-435.

Hirschi, Travis. 1980. "Labelling Theory and Juvenile Delinquency: An Assessment of the Evidence and Postscript" in Walter R. Gove (ed.), *The Labelling of Deviance* (2nd ed.). Beverly Hills: Sage.

Hsu, Marlene. 1973. "Cultural and Sexual Differences in the Judgment of Criminal Offenses: A Replication of the Measurement of Delinquency" in *Journal of Criminal Law and Criminology* 64: 348-353.

Hughes, Michael and Timothy J. Carter. 1983. "A Declining Economy and Sociological Explanation of Crime" in Kevin N. Wright (ed.), *Crime and Criminal Justice in a Declining Economy.* Cambridge, MA: Oelgeschlager, Gunn, and Hain.

Jacob, Herbert. 1975. "Crimes, Victims and Statistics: Some Words of Caution." Unpublished paper. Evanston, IL: Northwestern University.

Johnson, Kirk and Patricia Wasicklewski. 1982. "A Commentary on Victimization Research and the Importance of Meaning Structures" in *Criminology* 20: 205-222.

Kitsuse, John and Aaron Cicourel. 1963. "A Note on the Use of Official Statistics" in *Social Problems* 10: 131-139.

Kleck, Gary. 1982. "On the Use of Self-Report Data to Determine the Class Distribution of Criminal and Delinquent Behavior" in *American Sociological Review* 47: 427-433.

Land, Kenneth C. and Marcus Felson. 1976. "A General Framework for Building Dynamic Macro Social Indicator Models: Including an Analysis of Changes in Crime Rates and Police Expenditures" in *American Journal of Sociology* 82: 565-604.

Lander, Bernard. 1954. *Understanding Juvenile Delinquency.* New York: Columbia University Press.

Law Enforcement Assistance Administration. 1977. *Expanding the Perspective of Crime Data: Performance Implication for Policy Makers.* Washington, D.C.: U.S. Government Printing Office.

Lizotte, Alan. 1985. "The Uniqueness of Rape: Reporting Assaultive Behavior to the Police" in *Crime and Delinquency* 31: 169-190.

Luckenbill, David. 1984. "Murder and Assault" in Robert Meier (ed.), *Major Forms of Crime.* Beverly Hills: Sage.

Lundman, Richard. 1978. "Shoplifting and Police Referral: A Re-examination" in *Journal of Criminal Law and Criminology* 69: 395-408.

Lundman, Richard, Richard Sykes, and John Clark. 1978. "Police Control of Juveniles: A Replication" in *Journal of Research on Crime and Delinquency* 15: 74-91.

Martin, Elizabeth. 1981. "A Twist on the Heisenberg Principle—Or How Crime Affects Measurement" in *Social Indicators Research* 9: 191-223.

McCleary, Richard, Barbara Nienstedt, and James Erven. 1982. "Uniform Crime Reports on Organizational Outcomes: Three Time Series Experiments" in *Social Problems* 29: 361-372.

Miethe, Terance. 1982. "Public Consensus on Crime Seriousness" in *Criminology*: 515-526.

Miller, Frank, Robert Dawson, George E. Day, and Raymond Parnas. 1971. *Cases and Materials on Criminal Justice Administration and Related Process.* Mineola, NY: Foundation.

Miller, Walter B. 1967. "Theft Behavior in City Gangs" in Malcolm W. Klein (ed.), *Juvenile Gangs in Context: Theory, Research and Action.* Englewood Cliffs, NJ: Prentice-Hall.

Mulville, Donald, Melvin Tumin, and Lynn Curtis. 1967. *Crimes of Violence.* National Commission on the Causes and Prevention of Violence. Washington, D.C.: U.S. Government Printing Office.

Nelson, James. 1979. "Implications for the Ecological Study of Crime: A Research Note" in William Parsonage (ed.), *Perspectives of Victimology.* Beverly Hills: Sage.

Neter, John and Joseph Woksberg. 1964. "A Study of Response Errors in Expenditures Data From Household Interviews" in *Journal of American Statistical Association* 59: 17-53.

Newman, Graeme R. 1976. *Comparative Deviance: Perception and Law in Six Cultures.* New York: Elsevier.

O'Brien, Robert. 1983. "Metropolitan Structure and Violent Crime: Which Measure of Crime?" in *American Sociological Review* 48: 434-437.

Penick, Bettye, K. Eidson, and Maurice Owens. 1976. *Surveying Crime.* Washington, D.C.: National Academy of Sciences.

Piliavin, Irving and Scott Briar. 1964. "Police Encounters with Juveniles" in *American Journal of Sociology* 70: 206-214.

Pontell, Henry, Daniel Granito, Constance Keenan, and Gilbert Geis. 1984. "Seriousness of Crime: A Survey of the Nation's Chiefs of Police" in *Journal of Criminal Justice* 13: 1-13.

Porterfield, Austin. 1946. *Youth in Trouble*. Fort Worth: Leo Potishman Foundation.

Price, James. 1966. "A Test of the Accuracy of Crime Statistics" in *Social Problems* 14: 214-221.

Quinney, Richard. 1970. *The Social Reality of Crime*. Boston: Little, Brown.

———. 1975. *Criminology: Analysis and Critique of Crime in America*. Boston: Little Brown.

———. 1978. *Class, State and Crime*. New York: Longman.

Reiss, Albert J., Jr. 1967. "Studies in Crime and Law Enforcement in Major Metropolitan Areas" in *Field Surveys III*, Vol. 1. Washington, D.C.: U.S. Government Printing Office.

———. 1978. *Final Report for Analytical Studies of Victimization in Crime Using National Crime Survey Data*. New Haven, CT: Yale University, Institute for Policy Studies.

Rossi, Peter, Emily Waite, Christine Bose, and Richard Berk. 1974. "The Seriousness of Crimes: Normative Structure and Individual Differences." *American Sociological Review* 39: 224-237.

Schneider, Anne. 1977. *The Portland Forward Check of Crime Victims: Final Report*. Eugene Oregon: Institute for Policy Analysis.

———. 1981. "Methodological Problems in Victimization Surveys and Their Implications for Research in Victimology" in *Journal of Criminal Law and Criminology* 72: 818-838.

Schneider, Anne, Jaine Burcert, and L.A. Wilson. 1976. "The Role Attitudes in the Decision to Report Crimes to the Police" in William McDonald (ed.), *Criminal Justice and the Victims*. Beverly Hills: Sage.

Schrager, Laura and James F. Short, Jr. 1980. "How Serious a Crime? Perceptions of Organizational and Common Crimes" in Gilbert Geis and Ezra Stotland (eds.), *White-Collar Crime: Theory and Research*. Beverly Hills: Sage.

Schuessler, Karl. 1962. "Components of Variation in City Crime Rate" in *Social Problems* 9: 314-323.

Seidman, David and Michael Couzens. 1974. "Getting the Crime Rate Down: Political Pressure and Crime Reporting" in *Law and Society Review* 8: 457-493.

Sellin, Thorsten and Marvin Wolfgang. 1964. *The Measurement of Delinquency*. New York: Wiley.

Shaw, Clifford R. and Henry D. McKay. 1931. "Social Factors in Juvenile Delinquency" in *Report on the Causes of Crime*, Vol. 2. National Commission on Law Observance and Enforcement. Washington, D.C.: U.S. Government Printing Office.

———. 1969. *Juvenile Delinquency and Urban Areas* (revised ed.). Chicago: The University of Chicago Press.

Shenk, Frederick and William McInerney. 1978. "Issues Arising From Application of the National Crime Survey." Presented at the annual meeting of the Southwestern Political Science Association.

Skogan, Wesley. 1974. "The Validity of Official Crime Statistics: An Empirical Investigation" in *Social Science Quarterly* 55: 25-38.

———. 1976. "Crime and Crime Rates" in Wesley Skogan (ed.), *Sample Surveys of Victims of Crime*. Cambridge, MA: Ballinger.

———. 1978. *Victimization Surveys and Criminal Justice Planning*. National Institute of Law Enforcement and Criminal Justice, Washington, D.C.: U.S. Government Printing Office.

———. 1979. "Crime in Contemporary America" in Hugh Graham and Ted Gurr (eds.), *Violence in America*. Beverly Hills: Sage.

———. 1981a. *Issues in the Measurement of Victimization*. Washington, D.C.: U.S. Government Printing Office.

———. 1981b. "Assessing the Behavioral Context of Victimization" in *Journal of Criminal Law and Criminology* 72: 727-742.

Skogan, Wesley and William Klecka. 1977. *The Fear of Crime*. Washington, D.C.: American Political Science Association.

Sparks, Richard, Hazel Genn, and David Dodd. 1977. *Surveying Victims*. New York: Wiley.

Steinmetz, Carl. 1979. "An Empircally Tested Analysis of Victimization Risks." Presented at the Third International Symposium on Victimology.

Stephan, Egon. 1975. "Die ergebnisse der stuttgater opferbefrangung unter beruchksichtigung verglecichbarer Amerikanischer daten." Kriminolostatistic 5: 210-306.

———. 1976. *Die Stuttgarter Opferbefragung*. Wiesbaden, Germany: Bundeskriminalant.

Sudman, Seymour and Norman Bradburn. 1974. *Response Effects in Surveys: A Review and Synthesis*. Chicago: Aldine.

Sullivan, Peggy and Walter Gove. 1984. "The Perceived Utility of the Uniform Crime Reports: An Analysis of Current Criminology Textbooks." Unpublished paper. Nashville: Vanderbilt University.

Thornberry, Terence and Margaret Farnworth. 1982. "Social Correlates of Criminal Involvement: Further Evidence on the Relationship

Between Social Status and Criminal Behavior" in *American Sociological Review* 47: 505-518.

Tittle, Charles R., Wayne J. Villemez, and Douglas A. Smith. 1978. "The Myth of Social Class and Criminality: An Empirical Assessment of the Empirical Evidence" in *American Sociological Review* 43: 643-656.

Turk, Austin T. 1969. *Criminality and Legal Order.* Chicago: Rand-McNally.

Turner, Anthony. 1972. *The San Jose Methods Test of Known Crime Victims.* Washington, D.C.: National Criminal Justice Information and Statistics Service, U.S. Department of Justice.

U.S. Department of Justice. 1975. *Criminal Victimization in 13 American Cities.* Washington, D.C.: National Criminal Justice Information and Statistics Service.

——. 1979. *Criminal Victimization in the United States, 1976.* Washington, D.C.: National Criminal Justice Information and Statistics Service, U.S. Department of Justice.

——. 1982. *Violent Crime by Strangers.* Washington, D.C.: Bureau of Justice Statistics.

U.S. Department of Justice, Federal Bureau of Investigation. 1971. *Uniform Crime Reports, 1970.* Washington, D.C.: U.S. Government Printing Office.

——. 1973. *Uniform Crime Reports, 1971.* Washington, D.C.: U.S. Government Printing Office.

——. 1974. *Uniform Crime Reporting Handbook.* Washington, D.C.: U.S. Government Printing Office.

Velez-Dias, Angel and Edwin I. Megargee. 1970. "An Investigation of Differences in Value Judgments Between Youthful Offenders and Non-Offenders in Puerto Rico" in *Journal of Criminal Law, Criminology, and Police Science* 61: 549-553.

Wilson, James Q. 1976. *Varieties of Police Behavior.* Cambridge, MA: Harvard University Press.

Wolf, Preben. 1976. "On Individual Victims of Certain Crimes in Four Scandinavian Countries 1970-74: A Comparative Study." Presented at the Second International Symposium of Victimology.

Wolfgang, Marvin. 1958. *Patterns in Criminal Homicide.* Philadelphia: University of Pennsylvania Press.

Wolfgang, Marvin and Simon Singer. 1978. "Victim Categories of Crime" in *The Journal of Criminal Law and Criminology* 69: 779-94.

Woltman, Henry, John Bushery, and Larry Carstensen. 1975. "Recall Bias and Telescoping in the National Crime Survey." Unpublished paper. Washington, D.C.: U.S. Census Bureau, Statistical Methods Division.

Yost, Linda and Richard Dodge. 1970. "Household Survey of Victims of Crime: Second Pretest—Baltimore, Maryland. Unpublished paper. Washington, D.C.: U.S. Census Bureau.

Zimring, Franklin. 1972. "The Medium is the Message: Firearms Caliber as a Determinant of Death From Assault" in *Journal of Legal Studies* 1: 97-123.

7

Reassessing the Reliability and Validity of Self-Report Delinquency Measures

David Huizinga
Delbert S. Elliott

Extensive use of self-report data in criminology began in the 1950s and continues to be used. At the same time that this method was gaining in popularity, however, criticisms were being leveled against it. In response, numerous attempts have been made to determine if self-reports are valid and reliable measures of delinquent and criminal behavior. David Huizinga and Delbert Elliott have developed and administered the National Youth Survey, one of the best known and most widely analyzed self-report studies in criminology (see also readings 20 and 22). In this selection they address the issues of reliability and validity.

Reliability, and particularly validity, are important for all forms of measurement. Huizinga and Elliott consider several different types of reliability and validity and provide definitions for them. Reliability can be loosely defined as the ability to replicate results; although reliability varies depending on the method used to assess it, self-reports are generally considered reliable. Validity, which can be defined as whether a measure assesses what it is intended to measure, is more questionable in self-reported delinquency. Huizinga and Elliott examine several types of validity, including content validity and empirical validity. They indicate that overall, self-reports are generally valid. The evidence suggests that there is differential validity in different groups. In particular, they report that the validity of self-reports for black males is lower than for other groups, with underreporting of behavior the most serious problem. Huizinga and Elliott conclude that overall, self-reported delinquency data are generally reliable and valid, although the empirical results suggest that neither reliability nor validity is overwhelmingly high and this cannot be ignored when using such data.

Introduction

General Objectives

Few issues are as critical to the study of crime and delinquency as the question of the reliability and validity of our measures of this phenomenon. Much of the earlier debate on this issue centered on the relative merits and disadvantages of self-report measures as compared to official record measures, and for a number of years now criminologists have been polarized with respect to these two approaches to measuring crime. This resulted in part because there was limited information available on the reliability and validity of self-report measures and in part because these measures appeared to generate different basic findings regarding the volume and distribution of crime in the population and a different partitioning of subjects into criminal and noncriminal subgroups. These measure-related differences quickly became linked to ideological differences and theoretical preferences.

The concern over the measurement of crime has now taken a slightly different direction. Currently many crime and delinquency researchers consider self-report measures to have acceptable levels of reliability and validity, i.e., the reliability and validity of these measures compare favorably to those of other standard measures employed routinely by social scientists (Hindelang et al., 1981). It is also clear that official record measures of crime have *not* been replaced by self-report measures, and there is no sign that they are likely to be replaced in the near-future. Further, there is recent evidence that at least some of the earlier observed discrepancies in findings between self-report and official record measures were the result of differences in measure content and form, i.e., comparisons involving different offense sets and/or prevalence with incidence measures (Reiss, 1975; Hindelang et al., 1979, 1981; Elliott and Ageton, 1980; Elliott and Huizinga, 1983). As a result, self-reported offender measures, self-reported victimization measures, and official record measures now tend to be viewed as alternative measures of crime which compliment one another, each having some strengths or advantages which the others lack and some limitations which are better addressed by the others. Each is considered a reasonably reliable and valid measure of crime which is more appropriate for certain research purposes than others (Garofalo and Hindelang, 1977).

The accumulated research on the reliability and validity of self-report delinquency measures has consistently supported the conclusion that these measures have acceptable levels of reliability and validity as judged by conventional social-science standards (e.g., Hindelang et al., 1981; Sampson, 1985; Wyner, 1981; Hardt and Petersen-Hardt, 1977; Huizinga and Elliott, 1983). Still, the question of the reliability and validity of self-report measures continues to be a major issue. There are several reasons for this. First, the approach to validation has relied heavily (but not exclusively) upon official record measures of crime as the validation criterion. While correlation with alternative measures is a standard form of measure validation, since the validity of neither arrest nor self-report measures is beyond question, it leaves the issue of the true validity of these two measures unanswered. Second, there are conceptual, methodological, or interpretation problems with much of the earlier validation work. Third, a number of important validity issues have simply not been addressed. For example, the major emphasis has been on deliberate falsification and recall problems as sources of underreporting; relatively little attention has been given to sources of error leading to overreporting.

Fourth, there is some evidence that while self-report measures are reliable and valid in general, they are differentially valid within certain subpopulations. For example, Hindelang et al. (1981) found that self-report measures have a lower reliability and validity for blacks and delinquents than for whites and nondelinquents. There are grounds for questioning this finding (see Elliott, 1982), but if it were sustained by further research, it would seriously limit the appropriateness of self-report measures for certain research purposes. Finally, while these measures may meet minimum standards, it cannot be said that estimates of reliability and validity are uniformly high; there is an obvious need to work toward the further improvement of self-report measures of crime and delinquency.

In the following sections, several issues related to the reliability and validity of self-report delinquency measures are raised. Discussions of these issues include prior research findings and incorporate new information from the National Youth Survey.[1] In light of the problems described, some cautions about the use of self-report measures are made.

Reliability

Definition of Reliability

The reliability of a measuring instrument is commonly defined as the level of precision of the instrument. In this context, the level of precision refers to the extent to which the measuring instrument would produce identical scores if it were used to make multiple measures of the same object or, equivalently, the amount of measurement error, when each measurement is considered as the sum of true score and error components. . . .

Reported Levels of Reliability in Prior Research

In a brief and nonexhaustive review of the reliabilities reported in earlier delinquency studies, it became apparent that although only a few studies had formally examined the reliability of the SRD indices employed, those that had were reasonably consistent in reporting relatively high reliabilities for the total samples. . . . In general, it appears that the reliability of SRD indices is quite high and would be considered adequate by the prevailing standards for attitude and other social-psychological measures.

There are, however, some findings which are not as positive. In a more comprehensive study of the reliability of SRD measures, Hindelang et al. (1981) examined reliabilities of different scoring procedures within different sex, race, and police-court record groups. All but one group had test-retest reliabilities in the 0.84-0.97 range. For black males with a police record, however, the reliabilities varied from 0.62 to 0.81, depending on scoring procedure. Patterson and Loeber (1982) report on the reliabilities of various subscales of a larger general measure of SRD and note that a scale consisting of only nonserious items had a reliability of 0.69. Thus there is some indication that the high reliabilities for total samples and total scales may not carry over to certain subgroups or subscales. It should also be noted that there is an indication that when a variety measure (i.e., a count of the number of different offenses committed) is used, the reported reliabilities are slightly higher than when a frequency measure (i.e., the number of all reported offenses) is used (Belson, 1968; Hindelang et al., 1981).

In the National Youth Survey (NYS) test-retest reliabilities were obtained for a sample of respondents. The total set of respondents participating in the fifth-wave survey was stratified by race (white, black) and four levels of delinquent involvement. Within each of the eight strata, approximately 20 individuals were randomly selected to be included in the test-retest study. A total of 177 retest interviews was completed. All retest respondents were reinterviewed approximately four weeks after their initial interview. (The distribution of test-retest intervals is bell shaped, with a range of 21-35 days. The mean, median, and mode, however, all fall on the 28- to 29-day interval.) The retest interview was conducted in the same manner as the initial interview and in most cases involved identical interview situations, i.e., the same interview setting and interviewer. Complete details of the test-retest study are given by Huizinga and Elliott (1983). . . .

In general, the reliabilities of the individual items included in the NYS delinquency measure are over 0.5, with the majority of reliabilities ranging from 0.65 to 1.00. Although there are some items with low reliabilities, for the most part the reliabilities at the item level are in the same range as the reliabilities for scales. Thus, the reliabilities of the scales do not result from a fortuitous combination of item scores, but reflect the reliabilities of the underlying items. . . .

Some Empirical Evidence of the Correlation Between Scores and Magnitude of Errors

Some notion of differences in the magnitude of the errors made by less frequent and more frequent offenders is indicated by the proportions of these offender types who change their responses by more than two behaviors. . . . Defining a low-delinquency group as having five or fewer reported offenses and a high-delinquency group as having six or more reported offenses, approximately 60% of the low-delinquency group had test-retest differences on the general SRD measures that were two or less, and only about 20% of the high-delinquency group were this precise. While the exact magnitude of error is not indicated by these data, they clearly suggest that errors made by high-frequency offenders are likely, on the average, to be larger than those made by less frequent offenders. While the proportion of individuals within these two delinquent groups with difference scores of less than two varies by particular scales, the low-delinquency group always has the largest such proportions. . . .

Percentage of Persons who Change Their Response From Positive to Never or From Never to Positive

Although not directly involved in the usual examination of reliability for delinquency measures, it is of interest to examine a particular kind of change in SRD scores from test to retest. While small changes in reported delinquency would be expected, it might be anticipated that individuals will accurately remember and report whether they ever engaged in particular behaviors during the last year. Thus, it would be expected that never (or zero) responses on the original test would remain never on the retest and, similarly, that positive responses would remain positive. . . .

The magnitude of the percentages of individuals who change their mind about whether or not they have engaged in various kinds of delinquent behavior clearly suggests a moderate level of error in many of the SRD indices. Although for group analyses the positive-to-never and never-to-positive changes may "cancel" much of the error, for individual data the "error" is rather large. As noted above, this is especially true for the less serious or minor scales, where over a quarter of some subgroups changed their minds about whether they had ever (in the last year) engaged in certain minor delinquent behaviors. Thus, the lack of response consistency to the question of ever committing particular offenses suggests that at least the minor SRD indices may not be very reliable.

Summary

In the preceding it has been noted that because delinquent behavior is most likely not a homogenous domain, the use of test-retest correlations as measures of the reliability of SRD indices is more appropriate. The vast majority of studies examining the reliability of SRD indices has followed this prescription and generally has found the reliabilities to lie in the eighties and nineties. While this level of reliability is often said to be adequate in the light of prevailing standards for attitude measurement, there are some major difficulties inherent in the reliabilities of SRD indices. . . .

Clearly, the reliability of SRD scales is an issue that requires further examination and it would be inappropriate to assume on the basis of current evidence that the reliability of SRD indices is adequate for all subgroups or for all purposes. While the current evidence is promising and the reliabilities reported compare favorably with those of other social-psychological measures, further effort in determining and improving the reliability of SRD measures is necessary and some care should be taken in the use of these scales in future delinquency research. . . .

Validity

Definition

The validity of a psychological or behavioral test is commonly defined as the evidence that the test measures what it was intended to measure or that it represents what it appears to represent. Thus to determine the validity of indices of delinquent or criminal behavior, it becomes important to delineate carefully what is being measured or represented. The term delinquent has been used in various ways, e.g., to describe persons or groups, to describe illegal behaviors, and as a synonym for deviant, with the result that the meaning of the term delinquent is often ambiguous. However, what is being measured by a delinquency index for most current researchers is the commission of behaviors that are violations of criminal statutes or such violations that are actually acted upon by formal law-enforcement agencies. This definition is important not only because it is a necessary prerequisite to determining if a measure is valid but also because it indicates what ostensibly is being measured is a count of specific behaviors. Underlying the delinquency measures are, although perhaps unknowable, absolute true scores of delinquent behavior. Thus delinquency is not an abstract construct and a variety of empirical indicators can play a more prominent role in the determination of the validity of a given measure of delinquent behavior.

Given a relatively precise definition of what is being measured, three major approaches to the demonstration of validity are often described. Content validity refers to the subjective evaluation that the test items seem plausible and relevant and that the universe of behavior being measured is adequately sampled by the test items. Empirical or criterion validity refers to the relationship between test scores and some known external criterion that accurately indicates the quantity being measured. Construct validity involves the use of theoretical hypotheses about the relationship of test scores to other theoretical variables and the empirical justification of those hypotheses.

In general, based on the first or second of these indicators of validity, almost all researchers in crime and delinquency that have investigated the validity of their self-reported measures of delinquent behavior conclude that these measures are reasonably valid or are valid in the sense that they compare favorably with the validity of other measures employed in the social sciences (cf. Hindelang et al., 1981, pp. 114, 213). However, it should be carefully noted that most such researchers, including the authors of this article, have a vested interest in producing a positive evaluation of the validity of either official data or self-reports of delinquency (or both), since a negative evaluation would challenge years of individual research effort. The conclusions concerning validity are not made by disinterested parties. In the validity literature, only two articles provide strong cautionary notes. Gould (1969) suggests that given the problems inherent in both arrest and self-report data, there may be no measure of delinquent behavior in which criminologists can place a high degree of trust, and Bridges (1978) concludes from a more technical examination that biases and correlated errors may seriously distort our measures of crime and delinquency.

Construct validity has seldom, if ever, been used in delinquency research. The problem of simultaneously examining both tests of theory and validity issues within the same study generally precludes examination of construct validity. However, many variables theoretically linked to delinquency have been shown to be correlated with self-reported delinquency measures, and even when the correlations are not those specified by a given theory, the researchers have concluded that the theories are misspecified and not that the self-report measures are invalid. Thus, in a very loose sense, there is some indication of the construct validity of SRD measures.

In the following sections a brief review of findings relative to the content and empirical validity of self-reported measures of delinquency is given. A more detailed review of some of the studies cited is given by Hindelang et al. (1981).

Content Validity

Face Validity. Face validity refers to the evaluation of what the items included in an index appear to measure. Many of the indices of self-reported delinquency that have been used include items that do not involve violations of criminal statutes or involve such trivial infractions that they would rarely result in official action even if observed or discovered. Although many of the items included in some SRD indices are about criminal violations, others are not, and the summative scales or indices constructed from the total set of items thus do not appear to have a uniform or consistent face validity. More recently this problem has been recognized and at least partially corrected by the elimination of items that involve only trivial or noncriminal infractions. However, many of the SRD indices in use include such items and thus may fail the test of validity [a notable exception is the set of items employed by Hindelang et al. (1981)].

A related problem concerns the nature of responses to items which, on the surface, appear to be about serious-offense behavior. Questioning respondents about offenses they have reported reveals that some responses are about trivial events that do not match the severity of the offense described. This source of error results in inflated estimates of involvement in delinquent behavior, i.e., it constitutes a form of overreporting. . . .

The vast majority of overreporting (trivial responses) in the NYS involved items concerning minor assault. However, the remaining items, especially felony assault (including robbery) and property damage items, also had a sizable proportion of responses that were considered trivial. There was no evidence, however, of a differential distribution of trivial responses by sex, race, social class, or place of residence (urban, suburban, rural). Exactly why the interview situation, instruction sets, or wording of items causes some respondents to report trivial events to serious items is not clear, but some combination of those factors illicited reports of trivial events. . . . Since there were no sex, race, class, or age differentials in the reporting of trivial events, this overreporting problem may not be a serious one for estimating the social correlates of criminal behavior. But it poses a serious problem for comparisons of self-reported offense rates with NCS or UCR rates and potential problems for etiological studies. . . .

Empirical or Criterion Validity

In examining the empirical validity of SRD measures, various means of determining the relationship between SRD and some external criterion have been employed. These include known groups—in which the differences in SRD between groups presumed to have differences in delinquent behavior are demonstrated; correlational—in which the relationship of SRD scales with a criterion variable is examined; and official record checks—in which a check is made to determine if an individual with an officially recorded offense reports a behavior matching the offense behavior.

Known Group Validity. Differences in SRD between various groups expected to have different levels of delinquency have been examined by several studies. . . .

In all cases involving official records or self-report of official contact, the groups that would be anticipated to have higher delinquent involvement (those with greater official involvement) had substantially and usually statistically significant higher mean SRD scores. Although few formally examined the ability of the SRD measures actually to discriminate between groups, most studies would appear to allow some moderately accurate classification into the known groups. In terms of this rather minimal check in validity, self-report measures of delinquency are clearly indicated as being valid.

Differences between the mean SRD scores of groups defined by different levels of variables related to delinquent behavior have also been investigated. . . . As with official records, again all groups anticipated to have greater delinquent involvement have higher mean SRD scores. Thus, those who teachers nominate, who have a greater number of delinquent friends, who have lower socialization scores, who have a low perceived risk of punishment, who are less obedient, or who are class bullys, as groups, have higher SRD scores. As a result, in terms of the differences between the groups defined by these other variables, the SRD indices would appear to be valid.

Correlational Validity. Stronger evidence for the validity of a measure is provided by its correlation with a criterion related to the behavior being measured. A number of factors important to SRD measures affect the magnitude of the measure-criterion correlation, however. . . . Because most criterion measures used in the examination of the validity of SRD measures are not particularly accurate indicators of the volume of delinquent behavior, correlations between SRD and criterion variables are not expected to be high. . . .

The correlational validity of SRD measures has been examined using official data, other self-reported indicators of delinquent involvement, reports on respondents behavior by others, and other variables presumed to be related to SRD as criterion measures. The correlations among SRD and arrests or official contacts are generally low. . . . The relationship between SRD and self-reported official contacts is much higher, with correlations ranging in the 0.60s for various scales (Hindelang et al., 1981).

The level of these relationships between SRD and official contacts or self-reported official contacts raises a number of issues that are beyond the scope of this paper. Clearly if official data are an accurate reflection of individual involvement in delinquent behavior, then SRD measures do not appear to be very valid. It is more likely, however, that the frequency of delinquent behavior is not tied very tightly to arrests or contacts, and other problems with the accuracy of official data coupled with problems of reliability result in the low reported correlations. . . .

Record Checks. One of the most frequently used methods for investigating the validity of SRD measures has been an examination of whether offenses or official actions reported by others will be admitted on a self-report index. These examinations have included whether individuals will self-report the behaviors evidenced by peer reports of their offense behavior and whether they will self-report acts reported or known to the police. While only indirectly related to SRD indices, examinations have also been made of whether individuals will self-report known arrests, court appearances, and convictions. . . .

Record checks that examine whether offenses known to the police are reported on SRD indices have shown that a high proportion of such offenses is in fact admitted. . . .

Hindelang et al. (1981), employing a community sample of youth found that the self-reporting rate of official offenses varies by race, with whites admitting 90% of their official offenses and blacks 65% of their official offences. While there is, thus, some evidence of differential validity by offense type and by race, it appears that a high percentage of offenses known to police is reported on SRD indices.

While the above record checks have examined offense *behavior*, it is also useful to determine how many *individuals* are concealing their delinquent behavior. Conceivably, only a few individuals may account for the majority of unreported official offenses. Gibson et al. (1970), in a sample of British schoolboys, found that 83% admitted all official convictions on a SRD inventory, 9% made at least partial admissions, and only 8% made no relevant admissions. Thus only 8% deliberately concealed or failed to recall their convictions. . . .

Record checks of self-reported official contacts also provide some indication of the amount of overreporting on self-report measures. Although there is some question whether self-reported official actions that cannot be verified result from inaccuracies in the official record (see Chaiken and Chaiken, 1982) or from exaggeration on the part of respondents, high levels of overreporting would seem suspicious. Estimates of the number of individuals who report official contact when there is no official record vary from 10 to 30% (Hardt and Petersen-Hardt, 1977; Hathaway et al., 1960; Hirschi, 1969). . . . There is thus some indication of potential exaggeration on the part of respondents to self-report questionnaires. . . .

Given the findings from the various official record checks, what conclusions seem warranted? First, it appears that the majority of arrested individuals will self-report officially known offenses. The assertion that most such individuals will deliberately hide their delinquent behavior on survey instruments does not appear to be true. Second, whether self-reported measures of delinquency are seen as valid is an issue for debate. Clearly, on the basis of the official record checks, SRD measures are not perfectly valid and the degree to which the measures appear to be valid depends on whether one "sees the cup as being mostly full or partially empty." Using the NYS data, which present perhaps the lowest record-check validity estimates for juvenile studies, and assuming that the official records are accurate and that the findings from the arrested sample can be generalized to the total sample, it then appears that at least 20% of the respondents may be concealing or forgetting some part of their delinquent behavior and that, overall, approximately 20% of the delinquent behavior among respondents is not being reported on the SRD measure. If the necessary assumptions are correct, clearly this is a substantial error, and even allowing some leeway for inaccurate official records, the findings suggest a sizable level of *underreporting* on the part of youthful respondents. Third, because of potential errors in official records, the magnitude of *overreporting* in self-report instruments is difficult to determine. However, if the errors in official records are not too large, the official record checks also give some indication of *overreporting* on the part of respondents. Further, the earlier discussion of the rate of reporting trivial events suggests substantial levels of overreporting (i.e., 22-32% of all reported offenses). Overall, the magnitude of overreporting appears to be at least as great as that of underreporting. While these two sources of error tend to offset one another on a global measure of delinquency, this may not be the case on more specific scales or for particular subgroups (e.g., blacks).

Differential Validity of SRD

In the preceding review there has been some indication that the level of validity of SRD measures may differ in different subgroups. In this section the question of differential validity is examined more completely. It should be noted that most of the evidence concerning differential validity comes from record checks and is thus limited to samples of arrestees and arrest behaviors. Whether these findings can be generalized to total samples or to all offense behaviors of arrestees requires some questionable assumptions. . . .

Assuming that the findings can be generalized from arrested to general samples, several conclusions appear warranted. While it appears that there are some sex differences on particular items, overall levels of underreporting do not vary by sex. Findings concerning social class are mixed, but generally there are few substantial or consistent class differences. The two largest studies with comprehensive arrest and SRD data clearly provide evidence of differentials by race. Most extreme is the underreporting by black males and, in one study, evidence of underreporting by black females as well. In addition, there is some indication that rates of underreporting are greater for the more serious offenses. While it is possible that the magnitudes of the differentials encountered are in part dependent on police practices and errors and biases in official data, they nevertheless provide a cautionary note about the interpretation of results from SRD studies, especially results concerning race. A description of some of the factors that may influence the size of the race differential and analyses of problems arising from this differential are given by Hindelang et al. (1981).

Assuming that there is a potential for blacks, and black males in particular, to have a larger underreporting rate on record checks of official data, a major issue arises as to why this is the case. There are a number of possibilities including lying or deliberate falsification, forgetting and lower salience of events, difficulty with coding behavioral events, difficulty with "paper-and-pencil" tests, acquiescence and social desirability, and inaccurate or invalid arrest data. There is, however, relatively little evidence concerning this issue. . . .

In light of the above, unequivocal answers about why there is a white-black differential in the underreporting of officially recorded offenses are unknown, as is the exact magnitude of the differential. It is our judgment that the strength of the evidence suggests that while various factors may reduce the level of the differential, some difference in the reporting of known arrest offenses remains, and a research effort directed at understanding the reasons underlying this differential would be profitable.

Summary

As an overview of the validity of self-reported offender measures, the consideration of the content validity of these measures indicated some potential problems. Examination of the face validity of these measures suggested that they often included trivial items that either were not law violations or were such trivial infractions that in only very specialized circumstances would they result in official action. There is also evidence that items involving seriously delinquent behaviors lead to reports of trivial behaviors and thus to overreporting on some items. The sampling validity of the items contained in self-reported measures is also of concern. The construction of these measures needs to ensure that the full range of delinquent behavior is included. Often, serious offenses have not been adequately represented in prior measures.

In examining the empirical validity of the self-reported offender measures, the examination of known group validity consistently indicated substantial and often large differences on self-report measures between groups presumed to have a low or high involvement in delinquent behavior. The correlational validity of these measures, as indicated by their correlation with other criterion variables presumed to indicate levels of delinquent behavior, was generally quite small. However, none of the criterion variables that have been used are very good indicators of the level of individual delinquent behavior, and as a result, the low correlations would be anticipated. The lack of any good criterion variables provides a major obstacle to the examination of the validity of self-reported offender measures. Without such variables, no truly adequate test of validity can be made. Finally, official record checks indicate that some, and usually the majority of, "officially known" individuals will report the majority of their known offenses, including their serious offenses. However, these record checks also indicate sizable levels of underreporting, especially among blacks, and in general the rate of underreporting was larger for more serious offenses.

Conclusion

It has become customary, as Hindelang et al. (1981) note, for researchers employing self-reported offender data to preface their work with a brief review of research on the reliability and validity of these measures and to reach the general conclusion that these measures are reasonably reliable and valid or that at least the reliability and validity of these measures compare favorably with those of other social-science measures. However, the discussion of the reliability and validity of self-reported offender data presented above suggests that the quality of these measures cannot be taken for granted, nor are the reliabilities and validities sufficiently high that these measures can be used without question. Although at times the psychometric properties of SRD compare favorably with those of other social-science measures, there are instances where they clearly do not meet this criteria. Particularly problematic are the lower validities among black respondents. In addition, because these are measures of countable behaviors, not loosely defined attitudes, matching the levels of reliability and validity of other social-science variables does not mean that the SRD measures are particularly good or that they would meet the standards commonly required in other academic fields.

We believe that self-report measures are among the most promising of our measures of criminal behavior and are, perhaps, the only measures capable of meeting the needs of both descriptive and etiological research efforts. As a result, while research projects employing SRD measures are likely to be continuing, attempts to improve this methodology should be undertaken. . . . Such research is necessary if the full potential of self-report offender measures is to be realized.

Discussion Questions

1. Based on the Huizinga and Elliott article, what is the definition of reliability? What is the definition of validity? What are the different types of validity these scholars consider? Why are issues related to reliability and validity of data important to consider in criminology?

2. What do Huizinga and Elliott conclude about the reliability of self-reported delinquency? What does the empirical evidence suggest about the validity of self-reported delinquency?

3. What are the implications of Huizinga and Elliott's findings for studying race differences in offending behavior? What are the implications of these findings for studying criminal and delinquent behavior in general through use of self-reports?

Note

1. The National Youth Survey (NYS) is a projected longitudinal study of delinquent behavior, alcohol and drug use, and problem-related substance use in the American youth population. To date, six waves of data have been collected on this national youth panel ($N = 1725$), covering the period from 1976 to 1993. The NYS employed a probability sample of households in the continental United States based upon a self-weighting, multistage, cluster sampling design. Annual involvement in delinquent behavior and substance use was selfreported by members of the youth panel in confidential, personal (face-to-face) interviews. In 1980 a search of police records was completed for each respondent in each location where the respondent lived between 1976 and 1978.

References

Belson, W. A. 1969. "The extent of stealing by London boys and some of its origins." *Adv. Sci.* 25: 171-184.

Bridges, G. 1978. "Errors in the measurement of crime: An application of Joreskogs method or analysis of general covariance structures." In Wellford, C. (ed.), *Quantitative Studies in Criminology*. Sage, Beverly Hills, pp. 9-29.

Chaiken, J. M., and Chaiken, M. R. 1982. *Varieties of Criminal Behavior*. Rand Corp., Santa Monica.

Elliott, D. S. 1982. "A review essay on 'Measuring Delinquency' by M. J. Hindelang, T. Hirschi, and J. G. Weis." *Criminology*, 20: 527-537.

Elliott, D. S., and Ageton, S. S. 1980. "Reconciling race and class differences in self-reported and official estimates of delinquency." *Am. Sociol. Rev.* 45(l): 95-110.

Elliott, D. S., and Huizinga, D. 1983. "Social class and delinquent behavior in a national youth panel: 1976-1980." *Criminology*, 21: 149-177.

Garofalo, J., and Hindelang, M. J. 1977. *An Introduction to the National Crime Survey*. U.S. Government Printing Office, Washington, D.C.

Gibson, H. B., Morrison, S., and West, D. J. 1970. "The confession of known offenses in response to a self-reported delinquency schedule." *Br. J. Criminol*. 10: 277-280.

Gould, L. C. 1969. "Who defines delinquency: A comparison of self-reported and officially reported incidences of delinquency for three racial groups." *Soc. Problems*, 16: 325-336.

Hardt, R. H., and Peterson-Hardt, S. 1977. "On determining the quality of the delinquency self-report method." *J. Res. Crime Delinq*. 14: 247-261.

Hathaway, R. S., Monachesi, E. D., and Young, L. A. 1960. "Delinquency rates and personality." *J. Crim. Law Criminal. Police Sci*. 50: 433-440.

Hindelang, M. J., Hirschi, T., and Weis, J. G. 1979. "Correlates of delinquency: The illusion of discrepancy between self-report and official measures." *Am. Sociol. Rev*. 44: 995-1014.

Hindelang, M. J., Hirschi, T., and Weis, J. G. 1981. *Measuring Delinquency*. Sage, Beverly Hills.

Hirschi, T. 1969. *Causes of Delinquency*. University of California Press, Berkeley.

Huizinga, D., and Elliott, D. S. 1983. "A preliminary examination of the reliability and validity of the national youth survey self-reported delinquency indices." *National Youth Survey Project Report 27*. Behavioral Research Institute, Boulder, Colo.

Patterson, G. R., and Loeber, R. 1982. "The understanding and prediction of delinquent child behavior." *Research proposal to NIMH*. Oregon Social Learning Center, Eugene.

Reiss, A. J., Jr. 1975. "Inappropriate theories and inadequate methods as policy plaques: self-reported delinquency and the law." In Demerath, N. J., III, et al. (eds.), *Social Policy and Sociology*. Academic Press, New York.

Sampson, R. J. 1985. "Sex differences in self-reported delinquency and official records: A multiple group structural modeling approach." *J. Quani. Criminol*. 1: 345-366.

Wyner, G. A. 1981. "Response errors in self-reported number of arrests." In Bohrnstedt and Borgatta (eds.), *Social Measurement*. Sage, Beverly Hills.

8

Managing Rape: Exploratory Research on the Behavior of Rape Statistics

Gary F. Jensen
Maryaltani Karpos

Introduction

Victimization surveys originated in an attempt to measure the "true" crime rate in society and to offset the problems involved in using the UCR to measure crime rates (see reading Six). The best known and longest running such survey is the National Crime Victimization Survey (NCVS). This survey reveals that a "dark figure" of crime exists, that is, a large number of crimes occur that are not reported to the police or included in official data. Introduction of the survey did not solve all questions about the true crime rate, however. Instead, comparisons of the crime rates obtained from both the UCR and the survey have been made, with claims of one or the other being a more valid measure of crime. This selection, by Gary F. Jensen and Maryaltani Karpos, is one example of a comparison between the UCR and NCVS. The authors attempt to reconcile differences evidenced in rape rates over time that are found in the two data sources.

Jensen and Karpos demonstrate that while UCR rape rates have increased over time, those obtained in the NCVS have declined. They argue that the differences in rates may be attributable to a number of factors. Under the assumption that the NCVS rates more closely resemble the "true" rape rates, they show that the

UCR data may reflect the larger number of civilian (and particularly female) law enforcement employees and the greater number of rape crisis centers. These factors result in a higher rape rate found in official statistics, although the true rape rate may have declined over time. Although rape is perhaps the most likely of the index crimes to be affected, this selection is illuminating in that it demonstrates how social factors, as well as increased attention to a particular type of crime, can combine to produce an apparent increase in rates while the actual rate may remain stable or decline.

It is commonplace in discussions of official statistics on crime to note that variations over time and space in police-recorded crime can reflect changes in public willingness to report crimes to the police and in the police response to crime, in addition to variation in actual criminal events (see, e.g., Barlow, 1990; Conklin, 1989; Kelly, 1990; Siegel, 1989). As one technique for circumventing such influences and more directly measuring some types of criminal events, the annual National Crime Survey (NCS) of household and personal victimizations was developed and has become a major alternative to the Federal Bureau of Investigation's Uniform Crime Reports (UCR) for determining trends and spatial variations in crime.

With both types of data available since 1973, numerous analyses have assessed the degree to which the UCR and NCS measure similar or disparate phenomena. There appears to be mounting agreement that for some types of crime they yield similar results when comparing cities (see Gove et al., 1985, for a review). However, there is an ongoing debate about the degree to which they measure the same trends and fluctuations in underlying criminal events over time. . . .

The focus of this analysis is an offense for which there is either explicit agreement that NCS and UCR data are *not* measuring the same phenomenon or that methodological problems preclude an adequate comparison—forcible rape. Blumstein et al. (1992:117-118) state that, in contrast to burglary and robbery, they are prepared to accept that NCS and UCR measures of rape

Figure 8.1
UCR and NCS Crime Rates, 1973–1990

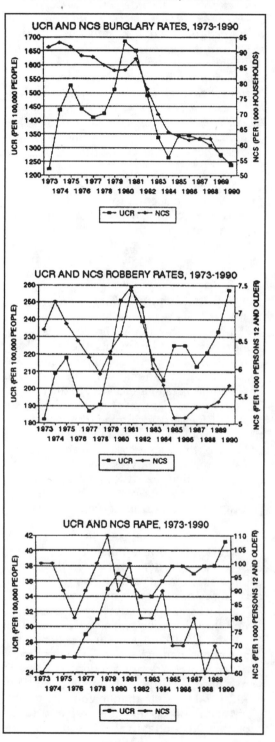

share little common variance due to sampling error (small numbers of cases for NCS rape) and systematic, nonsampling errors (e.g., upward shifts in rape reporting).

In Figure 8.1 we have plotted the NCS and UCR data for rape and the two offenses deemed to "share variance"—burglary and robbery.[1] This comparative context is important for assessing whether NCS rape statistics behave more strangely or erratically over time than statistics for other offenses and for discerning the nature and magnitude of disparities involving the two types of data. . . . In terms of the significance, direction, and fit of a linear trend, *NCS measures of rape behave the same as the burglary and robbery measures.* The NCS data may be based on a small number of victimizations compared with robbery and burglary, but they behave in an orderly manner. In fact, the upward shift of UCR rape rates, coupled with the downward shift of the NCS rates, generates a high level of "shared variance" between the series. But, in contrast to burglary and robbery, that shared variance stems from a strong inverse relationship: The greater the rate of officially recognized rape (UCR rapes "known to police"), the lower the rape victimization rate (NCS rape rates). This negative relationship could reflect a deterministic causal process at work (see concluding section) or could be totally spurious. . . .

Thus, one of a variety of issues that must be addressed in a theory of crime statistics is the disparity in rape statistics generated by an upward trend in UCR rape rates coupled with an apparent downward trend in NCS rape rates. Prior literature has concentrated on cultural and organizational factors that can cause the UCR rape rate to increase, regardless of actual rape, and we deal with that topic first. We then consider the exploratory hypothesis that the downward trend in NCS rape data reflects actual trends in rape.

Victimizations Reported to Police

The most common interpretation of the disparity in trends for rape is that the trends differ because of changes in the willingness of women to report such offenses to the police. The most often cited research on the topic (see, e.g., LaFree, 1989; Seigel, 1989) is a study by Orcutt and Faison (1988) examining trends in reporting of rape victimizations in National Crime Surveys from 1973 through 1985. Orcutt and Faison report increases in the percentage of female victims indicating that they reported the rape to the police. The increases were particularly prominent for nonstranger rape. Moreover, they report that the increase is correlated with increases in the acceptance of liberated sex role attitudes. Increases in acceptance of liberated feminist sex role definitions are thought to lead to increases in reports of rape victimizations to police, which in turn lead to increases in UCR rape rates.

Figure 8.2
NCS Rapes Reported to Police, 1973–1990

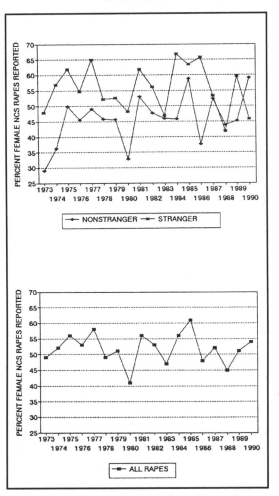

Figure 8.2 summarizes the percentage of stranger, nonstranger, and all rape victimizations involving female victims reported to police from 1973 through 1990.[2]. . .

Orcutt and Faison argue that this upward movement is a product of changes in sex role attitudes. . . .

We used data from the annual Monitoring the Future surveys (MFS) carried out among a representative sample of high school seniors to measure feminist or liberated gender beliefs in 1975 through 1988 (Johnston et al., 1975-1988). The MFS is more likely to be representative of the population of young adults than college surveys. Moreover, it includes numerous items relevant to acceptance or rejection of traditional gender stereotypes or endorsement of liberated gender beliefs. . . .

For 1975 through 1988, there is no significant correlation between gender beliefs and nonstranger victimizations reported to the police. . . . Thus, the relationship reported by Orcutt and Faison was due to either their specific measure of gender beliefs or, more likely, the more prominent upward shift in percentage of nonstranger victimizations reported for the 1973-1985 period. Endorsement of feminist gender beliefs has increased over time, and such beliefs may be relevant to the behavior of crime statistics. But, the mechanism generating that relevance does not appear to be willingness to report victimizations to the police, at least not as measured in the National Crime Survey.

While the slight upward trend in nonstranger rapes reported cannot be attributed to shifts in gender beliefs, there is a small correlation between percentage of nonstranger rape victimizations reported to police and the UCR rape rate. . . . Thus, consistent with Orcutt and Faison's argument, one possible source of the upward trend in UCR rape rates is a slight increase in reports of NCS nonstranger rape victimizations to police. However, alternative sources of the UCR trend in rape must be considered, not only because that relationship is quite weak, but because overall reporting of rape victimizations has not increased over the 1973-1990 time span.[3]

Organizational and Employee Change

Literature on the organizational management of crime has suggested a number of variables that can lead to general increases in recorded crime, and some of them are particularly relevant to rape processing. For example, McCleary et al. (1982) report that a shift to civilian dispatchers can lead to increases in "crimes-known-to-police." If that shift coincided with a shift to female civilian dispatchers and female dispatchers were found to filter out fewer potential rapes, the official recognition of rape in crime statistics would increase as a product of changes in the composition of police departments.

Data on law enforcement employees in cities of 2,500 or more population are available in the Uniform Crime Reports over a considerable period and more detailed data are available beginning with the 1971 report (Federal Bureau of Investigation, 1960-1991). . . . The percentage of police employees who are civilian . . . has increased considerably over time. In 1960, 10% of urban law enforcement employees were civilian employees as distinct from sworn police officers. By 1975 that percentage had risen to 17%, and by 1990, 22% of employees were civilian. This increase was highly correlated with an increase in female law enforcement employees. The percentage of all law enforcement personnel in the female civilian category . . . increased from 7% in 1971 to 16% in 1990. The percentage of females among sworn officers increased from 1% to 8%. Thus, when compared with NCS data on victimizations reported to police, changes in the composition of law enforcement personnel are far more promising candidates for explaining artificial increases in rape rates.

Some specific changes in the organizational management of rape victimizations occurred during the 1970s and are potentially relevant to changes in UCR rape statistics as well. While rape crisis centers are a well-publicized component of the contemporary rape enforcement scene, there were no rape crisis centers nor specialized agencies to support rape victims until late 1969. By 1970 there were six or seven such agencies, by 1973 there were 61, and by 1981 there were at least 740 such agencies around the United States. There was relatively little growth of such centers in the 1980s, and some observers consider the period since the early 1980s to be one of retrenchment and withering financial support (Harvey, 1985; Koss and Harvey, 1987). In short, the major period of growth in organizations that could affect the official management of rape was the 1970s.

Police departments also changed the internal management of rape cases by creating specialized units and changing their procedures for managing rape cases. If those changes lessened the tendency to dismiss certain type of reports as unfounded, they would have led to an increase in UCR rape rates. LaFree's analysis (1989) of rape processing in Indianapolis supports this interpretation. LaFree reports that the establishment of a special sex offender unit was followed by a decline in the percentage of cases that the police deemed "unfounded." He did not find significant changes at other stages in the processing of rape cases. . . .

Given the magnitude of bivariate relationships, it should not be surprising that when (a) female reports to police of nonstranger rape victimizations and (b) organizational or employee variables are considered simultaneously, only the latter are significantly associated with UCR rape rates.[4] Female victimizations reported to the police are not significantly related to UCR rape rates when organizational and employee variables are introduced.

Figure 8.3 illustrates the nature of the shared trends between the UCR rape rate and percent civilian from 1960 to 1990. However, the span of time in the UCR series during which the UCR rate accelerates more rapidly than percent civilian would predict is exactly the period in which organizational change also occurred. Indeed, if the sample is limited to the 1968-1990 period, both percent civilian and estimated number of rape crisis centers are significantly related to the UCR rate. . . . The UCR rape rate can be predicted with considerable accuracy based on percent civilian alone, and anomalies in the prediction can be explained by introducing organizational innovations during specific periods of time.

Figure 8.3
UCR Rape, Percent Civilian, and Crisis
Centers

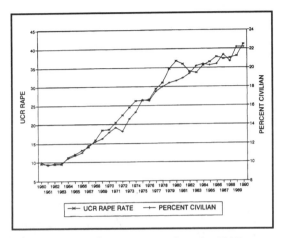

These data do not prove that the UCR rape rate is a product of changes in the management of rape cases. However, they do show that, given available measures, such changes are a far more plausible source of trends than variations in NCS victimizations reported. Moreover, since the relationships are limited to common trends, one has to be very wary of spurious correlations. However, in this instance, the coincidence of trends is consistent with prior theory and research and is presented as a counter to other, much weaker, coincidences proposed in the literature. Moreover, this deterministic interpretation is strengthened when the downward shift in the NCS rape rate is considered.

The Downward Trend in NCS Rape Rates

Despite the annual collection of two types of data on rape by separate government agencies, we cannot answer the simple question "Has the rate of rape increased, decreased, or been stable in the past two decades?" An alarmist could point to the UCR data and claim marked increases in the risk of rape in the United States. In contrast, an optimist could point to NCS data as evidence that there has been progress in reducing the risk of rape for most of the past two decades. While there are other sources of survey data

for many types of offenses,[5] there is no third measure of rape that would allow an adjudication between the two measures. Third sources have suggested that both the UCR and NCS underestimate rape (see Eigenberg, 1990), but supporting data are not available over time.

One potential indirect measure is public opinion poll data on women's fear of crime. It is not an ideal candidate for adjudicating between the two measures because it can be a product of the publicity accorded crime statistics themselves. Hence, a correspondence between trends for fear and measures of rape may reveal nothing about actual rape rates. Numerous researchers have noted that public fear of crime does not necessarily coincide with actual risks of crime (see Warr, 1991). However, there is also evidence that rape is "at the heart of fear of crime" for women (Warr, 1991:7).

The Roper Opinion Research Center has asked a question about such fears periodically since 1973 ("Is there any area right around here—that is, within a mile—where you would be afraid to walk alone at night?"), and those data have been summarized in other sources (Bureau of Justice Statistics, 1974-1991). If fear of rape is central to women's fear of walking alone and if UCR-based "increases" are more likely to be publicized and attended to by the public than news of decreases, one would anticipate an upward trend in women's fear over time. In contrast, if women are responding to publicity regarding NCS data or to a real downward trend in the risk of rape, one would expect a decrease in fear of walking alone at night.

The actual trend in women's fear of walking alone at night has been downward—from a high of 63% in the mid-1970s to about 55 percent in the late 1980s. Women do not appear to have been more fearful in the 1980s than in the 1970s, despite the higher levels of rape indicated by the Uniform Crime Reports. Indeed, the trend in the NCS rape rate and women's fear of walking alone at night are very similar. However, the shared trends are both downward and both are contrary to the trend in the UCR rape rate. While additional data would be necessary to test the implied hypotheses adequately, the data are consistent with a scenario in which women's fear can be interpreted as a response to a decline in the rate of rape—a decline that is captured by the NCS data. Advocacy of the UCR as the best data for discerning the real trend in rape would necessitate a far less parsimonious explanation of the sum total of findings. If we were to argue that the UCR data over time approximate the real trend, we would have to (a) develop an explanation for the contrary trends in fear and the UCR as well as the contrary trends in UCR and NCS rape rates, (b) ignore plausible theories and research findings that would explain why the UCR rate exhibits an upward, nonlinear trend, and (c) propose a better explanation for a downward trend in NCS rape rates. . . .

. . . In their analysis of research on NCS and UCR crime rates, Gove et al. (1985:483) cite prior research (Geerken and Gove, 1977) to defend the position that UCR data accurately reflect the true larceny rate on the grounds that "as deterrence theory predicts . . . there is a strong negative correlation between the larceny crime rate and the larceny clearance rate.". . .

The two NCS rape rates, the UCR rape rate, and the UCR percent cleared are plotted in Figure 8.4. . . . There is no significant correlation between the UCR rape rate and the percentage of rapes cleared. In contrast, there are significant negative relationships between the NCS rape rate and percent cleared. . . . Hence, regardless of measure, fluctuations in rape are negatively related to fluctuations in the percentage of rapes cleared by arrest. . . .

Since deterrence theory would predict inverse trends as well as inverse relationships for annual changes, the NCS data behave in a manner more consistent with deterrence theory than does the UCR rape rate. Following the logic of Gove et al.'s argument, we can propose that the NCS female rape rate is a closer approximation of the real rate than is the UCR rape rate. Both types of data behave as expected when annual fluctuations are considered.

There is another sense in which the NCS data on rape could be interpreted in a manner consistent with deterrence theory. Prior discussions of the disparity between UCR and

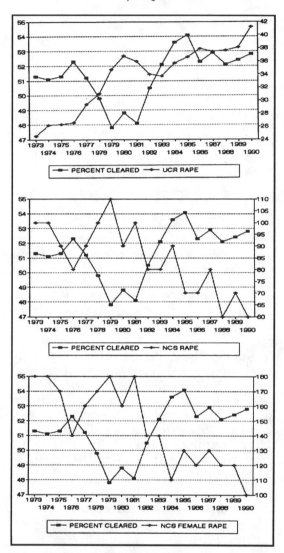

Figure 8.4
Trends in Percent Cleared and Measures of Rape

NCS data have interpreted the upward trend in UCR rates as a reflection of "systematic" errors in the form of changes in victim reporting or law enforcement procedure. While such an interpretation has been used to exclude rape from arguments that the UCR and NCS measure the same phenomenon, the full implications of such systematic errors have not been addressed. If systematic error takes the form of an upward trend in official attention to rape, we can propose that increases in

UCR rape rates can have deterministic consequences for the level of the NCS rape rate. The transformation of criminal events into "crimes known to the police" is a first step in the official recognition and control of crime. If NCS rape data and women's fear of walking alone are indicators of the actual rate of rape events, the data are consistent with the argument that the rate of rape is inversely related to the level of official recognition and attempts to control the problem. These observations are, admittedly, highly speculative, but they are quite plausible given our overall pattern of findings. Indeed, if the UCR rape rate and rape clearance are treated as measures of attempted official control, they can be used to predict the level of NCS rape with a high degree of accuracy. . . . Thus, disparate data on rape may reflect a deterministic relation between the two measures whereby an upward trend in attempted control is associated with a downward trend in the rate of rape.[6]

Summary and Conclusions

The pattern of findings reported in this paper make sense if two assumptions are made: First, the NCS rate is a better approximation of the true rate of rape over time than the UCR rate. Second, trends in UCR data primarily reflect trends in the organization and management of rape victimizations. The first assumption is consistent with findings for trends in fear and with deterrence theory. The second assumption is supported by (a) prior research (i.e., LaFree's observations), (b) the close fit of trends in organizational and employee variables thought to affect rape processing as compared with the slight relation found for nonstranger rapes reported to police, and (c) by the contrary trends in the UCR and fear data.

It is important to emphasize that while the NCS data are proposed as a closer approximation to the true rate of rape in this analysis, the NCS data do not directly measure rape. Eigenberg (1990) has stressed that since the NCS measures rape by follow-up questions on assault, one cannot be certain what the NCS is measuring.[7] However, this has been true throughout the history of the NCS, and it is plausible to assume that this problem should not lead to a systematic downward trend. If there has been a systematic change in the manner of collecting or categorizing the NCS data that would lead to a downward trend, such a change should be identified and measured.

While there is mounting evidence that the UCR rape rate is sensitive to the amount of official attention accorded rape, the NCS data are not impervious to such influences. In January 1991, Steven Dillingham (1991:iii), the director of the Bureau of Justice Statistics announced that the NCS was going to pay special attention to improving the measurement of rape in victimization surveys. . . . While UCR police statistics on rape may have increased due to increases in the amount of organized and recorded police attention to rape, the increase in interviewer attention to rape in the NCS is likely to lead to an increase in NCS rape rates as well. Indeed, the NCS is going to pay more attention specifically to rape and assault precisely because they are presumed to be underestimated. With increased interviewer attention to the problem of rape, the long, downward shift in NCS rape victimization rates is likely to end regardless of stability or change in actual rape. Thus, while victimization surveys were designed to avoid problems with variation in "official" police statistics, the NCS is itself a body of data garnered through officials who have announced their intention to vary the amount of attention accorded certain types of crimes. If the changes have their intended effect, there will be another source of systematic error to complicate analyses over the next several years. Once the changes announced are fully implemented, analysts will have a better measure of rape but it will be many years before they can hazard any statements about trends in rape events over time. Thus, the behavior of the NCS rate of rape, like the behavior of the UCR rate, is likely to be affected by changes in the collection and management of information on rape.

Discussion Questions

1. According to Jensen and Karpos, what do the UCR data reveal about rape rates over time? What do the NCS data reveal

about the rape rates in society? Based on their analysis, do you agree that rape rates have declined over time?

2. What factors influence the rising rape rates seen in the UCR data? The declining rape rates revealed by the NCS?

3. What are the potential implications of having social factors influence the data available for criminologists to use to study crime? Do you think that it will ever be possible to determine the "true" crime rate without error?

Notes

1. Basic data on victimization rates over time were compiled drawing on the 1980 and 1991 issues of the Bureau of Justice Statistics' *Sourcebook of Criminal Justice Statistics*, edited in 1980 by Hindelang, Gottfredson, and Flanagan, and in 1991 by Flanagan and Maguire. The UCR crime rates are summarized in the 1991 *Sourcebook of Criminal Justice Statistics*.

2. These more detailed data on rape were derived from the 1973 through 1990 issues of the Bureau of Justice Statistics' *Criminal Victimization in the United States*.

3. While victimizations reported to police are not correlated with gender beliefs, there is a significant correlation between liberated gender beliefs and the UCR rape rate ($b = .18$, $r^2 = +.64$, $p = .000$). However, the relation between the two disappears when first differences are used ($r^2 = .00$). Note that the absence of a significant relation between gender beliefs and victimizations reported to police does not rule out other mechanisms through which changing beliefs can affect the behavior of crime statistics. For example, if the upward shift of liberated gender beliefs is relevant to the upward shift in UCR rape rates, it may be through correlated changes in the processing of rape cases rather than through victimizations reported to police.

4. When introduced into regression analyses with any of the organizational or employee variables, the relationship of victim reporting to the UCR rape rate disappears. For 1973-1990, the number of rape crisis centers and an employee variable generated R^2s ranging from .89 to .92. Moreover, there are no relationships using differenced series. However, since gender beliefs were available for a shorter period (1975-1988) than the other variables, the results of regression analyses including such beliefs differ from the results of analyses for longer periods. However, they differ in a manner that strengthens the argument that changes in the official management of rape are a source of variation in UCR rape rates. When first differences for female reports of nonstranger rapes, crisis centers, and gender beliefs are used, the annual change in crisis centers comes very close to being a significant correlate of fluctuations in UCR rape rates ($b = .016$, $p = .06$). Hence, whether considering similarities in trends or fluctuations, organizational and employee changes are more promising candidates for explaining UCR rates than other variables suggested in the literature.

5. National poll data on assault victimizations and annual surveys of victimization and self-reported offenses involving high school seniors are available for a sufficient period of time to consider them as a third source of data (see Bureau of Justice Statistics, *Sourcebook of Criminal Justice Statistics, 1990*). The authors know of no third source of data for rape over time.

6. An alternative interpretation of UCR-NCS rape trends is that our statistics compiling agencies are "converging" on a common rate. The disparity in the two measures has been declining over time. We interpret that decline as reflecting meaningful contrary trends in disparate phenomena rather than some sort of convergence on the "real" rate. If a convergence on the "real" rate is reflected in the variations over time, the organizational and political processes that would lead to such increasing agreement in data compiled by different types of agencies and officials would have to be specified. If the NCS detected fewer rapes over time by refining its measures or training its interviewers differently, such changes should be identified and their impact studied.

7. While we have concentrated on rape, the same changes could account for other UCR-NCS disparities. For example, the only offense showing a greater negative correlation with its UCR counterpart than that found for rape is aggravated assault. Blumstein et al. (1992) did not expect a correspondence between NCS and UCR data for assault because of classification problems. With growing emphasis on domestic violence, shelters for abused women, and how spousal violence is classified, increases in UCR aggravated assault rates could reflect changes in the man-

agement of violence against women in general. In contrast, we would not expect such organizational and employee changes to make as much difference for property-oriented crimes. Considering the correlations between the organizational and employee variables and other UCR offenses, the closest relationships are found for rape and aggravated assault.

References

Barlow, Hugh. 1990. *Introduction to Criminology*. Glenview, Ill.: Scott, Foresman.

Blumstein, Alfred, Jacqueline Cohen, and Richard Rosenfeld. 1991. "Trend and deviation in crime rates: A comparison of UCR and NCS data for burglary and larceny." *Criminology*, 29:237-263.

———. 1992. "The UCR-NCS relationship revisited: A reply to Menard." *Criminology*, 30:115-124.

Bureau of Justice Statistics. 1973. *Criminal Victimization in the United States*. Washington, D.C.: Bureau of Justice Statistics.

———. 1974. *Sourcebook of Criminal Justice Statistics*. Washington, D.C.: Bureau of Justice Statistics.

Conklin, John E. 1989. *Criminology*. New York: Macmillan.

Dillingham, Steven D. 1991. Foreword. In Caroline Wolf Harlow, *Female Victims of Violent Crime*. Washington, D.C.: Bureau of Justice Statistics.

Eigenberg, Helen M. 1990. "The National Crime Survey and rape: The case of the missing question." *Justice Quarterly*, 7:655-671.

Federal Bureau of Investigation. 1960-1991. *Crime in the United States. Uniform Crime Reports*. Washington, D.C.: 1991 Federal Bureau of Investigation.

Geerken, Michael and Walter R. Gove. 1977. "Deterrence, overload and incapacitation: An evaluation of three explanations of the negative correlation between crime and punishment." *Social Forces*, 56:424-427.

Gove, Walter R., Michael Hughes, and Michael Geerken. 1985. "Are Uniform Crime Reports a valid indicator of the index crimes? An affirmative answer with minor qualifications." *Criminology*, 23:451-501.

Harvey, Mary. 1985. *Exemplary Rape Crisis Programs*. Rockville, Md.: National Institute of Mental Health.

Johnston, Lloyd D., Jerald G. Bachman, and Patrick M. O'Malley. 1975-1988. "Monitoring the Future: Questionnaire Responses from the Nation's High School Seniors." Survey Research Center. Ann Arbor, Mich.: Institute for Social Research.

Kelly, Delos H. 1990. *Criminal Behavior: Text and Readings in Criminology*. New York: St. Martin's Press.

Koss, Mary and Mary Harvey. 1987. *The Rape Victim*. Lexington, Mass.: The Stephen Greene Press.

LaFree, Gary D. 1989. *Rape and Criminal Justice: The Social Construction of Sexual Assault*. Belmont, Calif: Wadsworth.

McCleary, Richard and Richard A. Hay, Jr., with Errol E. Meidinger and David McDowall. 1980. *Applied Time Series Analysis for the Social Sciences*. Beverly Hills, Calif.: Sage.

McCleary, Richard, Barbara C. Nienstedt, and James M. Erven. 1982. "Uniform Crime Reports as organizational outcomes: Three time series experiments." *Social Problems*, 29:361-372.

McDowall, David and Colin Loftin. 1992. "Comparing the UCR and NCS over time." *Criminology*, 30:125-132.

McDowall, David, Richard McCleary, Errol E. Meidinger, and Richard A. Hay, Jr. 1980. *Interrupted Time Series Analysis*. Beverly Hills, Calif.: Sage.

Menard, Scott. 1992. "Residual gains, reliability, and the UCR-NCS relationship: A comment on Blumstein, Cohen, and Rosenfeld (1991)." *Criminology*, 30:105-113.

Orcutt, James D. and R. Faison. 1988. "Sex-role attitude change and reporting of rape victimization, 1973-1985." *The Sociological Quarterly*, 29:589-604.

Seigel, Larry J. 1989. *Criminology*. St. Paul, Minn.: West.

Warr, Mark. 1991. "America's perception of crime and punishment." In Joseph F. Sheley, *Criminology: A Contemporary Handbook*, Belmont, Calif.: Wadsworth.

9

Racial Politics, Racial Disparities, and the War on Crime

Michael Tonry

When discussing the nature and extent of crime in the United States, the emphasis tends to be on Part I offenses (index crimes). In any given year, however, arrests for these crimes comprise only about 20 percent of all arrests; 80 percent of arrests are for Part II offenses. Arrests for Part II offenses largely reflect proactive enforcement efforts in that many of them are first detected by the police rather than being reported to them by citizens; the offenses that are rigorously enforced can vary widely over time and jurisdiction.

Of the Part II offenses, drug abuse violations represents the largest single category, with about 10% of all arrestees in 1996. The "public order" or "victimless" crimes such as drug abuse violations and prostitution are offenses about which the public is ambivalent. Some argue that legally defining such behaviors as crime reflects the government's attempt to legislate morality (see also reading 41). Further, some argue that "overcriminalization" is a problem in our society, that is, we live in a society in which too many types of behaviors are considered criminal. Such behaviors that perhaps should not be defined as criminal, including drug abuse, can have an important impact on the criminal justice system when the enforcement of laws is vigorous.

Such has been true of drugs in the 1980s and 1990s. Although drug laws have been on the books since 1914, social factors have had a tremendous impact on the increased enforcement of these laws and the resulting rising number of arrests. As Michael Tonry demonstrates in this selection, increased enforcement of drug laws has significantly changed the composition of prison populations. The "War on Drugs" has resulted in increased racial disproportionality in prison populations, due primarily to more rigorous law enforcement and sentencing practices related to drug abuse. Further, these enforcement efforts have resulted in huge increases in the overall prison population (see also reading 40). Central to Tonry's argument is the discussion that the war on drugs is ineffective and disproportionately affects African Americans, both factors that were known about before this policy was pursued.

Racial disparities in arrests, jailing, and imprisonment steadily worsened after 1980 for reasons that have little to do with changes in crime patterns and almost everything to do with two political developments. First, conservative Republicans in national elections "played the race card" by using anticrime slogans (remember Willie Horton?) as a way to appeal to anti-Black sentiments of White voters. Second, conservative politicians of both parties promoted and voted for harsh crime control and drug policies that exacerbated existing racial disparities.

The worsened disparities might have been ethically defensible if they had been based on good faith beliefs that some greater policy good would thereby have been achieved. Sometimes unwanted side effects of social policy are inevitable. Traffic accidents and fatalities are a price we pay for the convenience of automobiles. Occupational injuries are a price we pay for engaging in the industries in which they occur.

The principal causes of worse racial disparities have been the War on Drugs launched by the Bush and Reagan administrations, characterized by vast increases in arrests and imprisonment of street-level drug dealers, and the continuing movement toward harsher penalties. Policies toward drug offenders are a primary cause of recent increases in jail and prison admissions and populations. Racial disparities among drug offenders are worse than among other offenders. . . .

Crime Reduction Effects of Crime Control Policy

There is no basis for a claim that recent harsh crime control policies or the enforcement strategies of the War on Drugs were based on good faith beliefs that they would achieve their ostensible purposes. In this and other countries, practitioners and scholars have long known that manipulation of penalties has few, if any, effects on crime rates.

Commissions and expert advisory bodies have been commissioned by the federal government repeatedly over the last 30 years to survey knowledge of the effects of crime control policies, and consistently they have concluded that there is little reason to believe that harsher penalties significantly enhance public safety. In 1967, the President's Commission on Law Enforcement and Administration of Justice observed that crime control efforts can have little effect on crime rates without much larger efforts being directed at crime's underlying social and economic causes. "The Commission . . . has no doubt whatever that the most significant action that can be taken against crime is action designed to eliminate slums and ghettos, to improve education, to provide jobs. . . . We shall not have dealt effectively with crime until we have alleviated the conditions that stimulate it."

In 1978, the National Academy of Sciences Panel on Research on Deterrent and Incapacitative Effects, funded by President Ford's department of justice and asked to examine the available evidence on the crime-reductive effects of sanctions, concluded: "In summary, we cannot assert that the evidence warrants an affirmative conclusion regarding deterrence" (Blumstein, Cohen, and Nagin 1978). Fifteen years later, the National Academy of Sciences Panel on the Understanding and Control of Violent Behavior, created and paid for with funds from the Reagan and Bush administration departments of justice, surveyed knowledge of the effects of harsher penalties on violent crime (Reiss and Roth 1993). A rhetorical question and answer in the panel's final report says it all: "What effect has increasing the prison population had on violent crime? Apparently very little. . . . If

tripling the average length of sentence of incarceration per crime [between 1976 and 1989] had a strong preventive effect," reasoned the panel, "then violent crime rates should have declined" (p. 7). They had not.

I mention that the two National Academy of Sciences panels were created and supported by national Republican administrations to demonstrate that skepticism about the crime-preventive effects of harsher punishments is not a fantasy of liberal Democrats. Anyone who has spent much time talking with judges or corrections officials knows that most, whatever their political affiliations, do not believe that harsher penalties significantly enhance public safety.

Likewise, outside the United States, conservative governments in other English-speaking countries have repudiated claims that harsher penalties significantly improve public safety. . . .

. . . In Brian Mulroney's Canada, the Committee on Justice and the Solicitor General (in American terms, the judiciary committee) proposed in 1993 that Canada shift from an American-style crime control system to a European-style preventive approach. In arguing for the shift in emphasis, the committee observed that "the United States affords a glaring example of the limited effect that criminal justice responses may have on crime. . . . If locking up those who violate the law contributed to safer societies then the United States should be the safest country in the world" (Standing Committee on Justice and the Solicitor General 1993). . . .

There is no better evidentiary base to justify recent drug control policies. . . . There was no reasonable basis for believing recent policies would achieve their ostensible goals. In drug policy jargon, the United States has adopted a prohibitionistic rather than a harm-reduction strategy and has emphasized supply-side over demand-side tactics (Wilson 1990). This strategic choice implies a preference for legal threats and moral denunciation of drug use and users instead of a preference for minimizing net costs and social harms to the general public, the law enforcement system, and drug users. The tactical choice is between a law enforcement emphasis on arrest and punishment of dealers, distributors, and importers, interdiction, and source-country programs or a prevention emphasis on drug treatment, drug-abuse education in schools, and mass media programs aimed at public education. The supply-side bias in recent American policies was exemplified throughout the Bush administration by its insistence that 70% of federal antidrug funds be devoted to law enforcement and only 30 percent to treatment and education (Office of National Drug Control Policy 1990).

It has been a long time since most researchers and practitioners believed that current knowledge justifies recent American drug control policies. Because the potential income from drug dealing means that willing aspirants are nearly always available to replace arrested street-level dealers, large-scale arrests have repeatedly been shown to have little or no effect on the volume of drug trafficking or on the retail prices of drugs (e.g., Chaiken 1988; Sviridoff, Sadd, Curtis, and Grine 1992). Because the United States has long and porous borders, and because an unachievably large proportion of attempted smuggling would have to be stopped to affect drug prices significantly, interdiction has repeatedly been shown to have little or no effect on volume or prices (Reuter 1988). Because cocaine, heroin, and marijuana can be grown in many parts of the world in which government controls are weak and peasant farmers' incentives are strong, source-country programs have seldom been shown to have significant influence on drug availability or price in the United States (Moore 1990).

The evidence in support of demand-side strategies is far stronger. In December 1993, the President's Commission on Model State Drug Laws, appointed by President Bush, categorically concluded, "Treatment works." That conclusion is echoed by more authoritative surveys of drug treatment evaluations by the U.S. General Accounting Office (1990), the National Institute of Medicine (Gerstein and Jarwood 1990), and in *Crime and Justice* by Anglin and Hser (1990). Because drug use and offending tend to coincide in the lives of drug-using offenders, the most effective and cost-effective way to deal with such offenders is to get and keep them in well-run treatment programs.

A sizable literature now also documents the effectiveness of school-based drug education in reducing drug experimentation and use among young people (e.g., Botvin 1990; Ellickson and Bell 1990). Although there is no credible literature that documents the effects of mass media campaigns on drug use, a judge could take judicial notice of their ubiquity. It is not unreasonable to believe that such campaigns have influenced across-the-board declines in drug use in the United States since 1980 (a date, incidentally, that precedes the launch of the War on Drugs by nearly 8 years).

That the preceding summary of our knowledge of the effectiveness of drug control methods is balanced and accurate is shown by the support it receives from leading conservative scholars. Senator-scholar Daniel Patrick Moynihan (1993) has written, "Interdiction and 'drug busts' are probably necessary symbolic acts, but nothing more." James Q. Wilson (1990), for two decades America's leading conservative crime control scholar, observed that "significant reductions in drug abuse will come only from reducing demand for those drugs. . . . The marginal product of further investment in supply reduction is likely to be small" (p. 534). He reports that "I know of no serious law-enforcement official who disagrees with this conclusion. Typically, police officials tell interviewers that they are fighting either a losing war or, at best, a holding action" (p. 534).

Thus a fair-minded survey of existing knowledge provides no grounds for believing that the War on Drugs or the harsh policies exemplified by "three strikes and you're out" laws and evidenced by a tripling in America's prison population since 1980 could achieve their ostensible purposes. . . .

Racial Disparities in Arrests, Jail, and Prison

Racial disparities, especially affecting Blacks, have long bedeviled the criminal justice system. Many hundreds of studies of disparities have been conducted and there is now widespread agreement among researchers about causes. Racial bias and stereotyping no doubt play some role, but they are not the major cause. In the longer term, disparities in jail and prison populations are mainly the result of racial differences in offending patterns. In the shorter term, the worsening disparities since 1980 are not primarily the result of racial differences in offending but were foreseeable effects of the War on Drugs and the movement toward increased use of incarceration. . . .

Figure 9.1, showing the percentages of prison inmates who were Black or White from 1960 to 1991, reveals two trends. First, for as long as prison population data have been compiled, the percentage of inmates who are black has by several times exceeded the percentage of Americans who are Black (10% to 13% during the relevant period). Second, since 1980 the Black percentage among prisoners has increased sharply.

Racial disproportions among prison inmates are inherently undesirable, and considerable energy has been expended on efforts to understand them. In 1982, Blumstein showed that around 80% of the disproportion could be explained on the basis of racial differences in arrest patterns. Of the unexplained 20%, Blumstein argued, some might represent bias and some might reflect racial differences in criminal history or arguably valid case-processing differences. Some years earlier, Hindelang (1976, 1978) had demonstrated that racial patterns in victims' identifications of their assailants closely resembled racial differences in arrests. Some years later, Langan (1985) skipped over the arrest stage altogether and showed that racial patterns in victims' identifications of their assailants explained about 80% of disparities in prison admissions. In 1990, Klein, Petersilia, and Turner showed that, after criminal history and other legitimate differences between cases were taken into account, the offender's race had no independent predictive effect in California on whether he was sent to prison or for how long. There the matter rests. Blumstein (1993a) updated his analysis and reached similar conclusions (with one important exception that is discussed below).

Although racial crime patterns explain a large part of racial imprisonment patterns, they do not explain why the Black percentage rose so rapidly after 1980. Table 9.1 shows

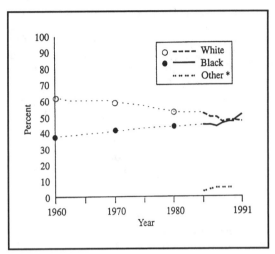

Figure 9.1
Prisoners in State and Federal Prisons on Census Date by Race, 1961–1991

SOURCES: For 1960, 1970, 1980: Cahalan 1986, table 3.31; for 1985-1991: Bureau of Justice Statistics 1993, 1991a, 1991b, 1989a, 1989b, 1987.
* = Hispanics in many states, Asians, Native Americans

Black and White percentages among people arrested for the eight serious FBI Index Crimes at 3-year intervals from 1976 to 1991 and for 1992. Within narrow bands of fluctuation, racial arrest percentages have been stable since 1976. Comparing 1976 with 1992, for example, Black percentages among people arrested for murder, robbery, and burglary were slightly up and Black percentages among those arrested for rape, aggravated assault, and theft were slightly down. Overall, the percentage among those arrested for violent crimes who were Black fell from 47.5% to 44.8%. Because prison sentences have traditionally been imposed on people convicted of violent crimes, Blumstein's and the other analyses suggest that the Black percentage among inmates should be flat or declining. That, however, is not what Figure 9.1 shows. Why not?

Part of the answer can be found in prison admissions. Figure 9.2 shows racial percentages among prison admissions from 1960 to 1992. Arrests of Blacks for violent crimes may not have increased since 1980, but the percentage of Blacks among those sent to prison has increased starkly, reaching 54% in

1991 and 1992. Why? The main explanation concerns the War on Drugs.

Table 9.2 shows racial percentages among persons arrested for drug crimes between 1976 and 1992. Blacks today make up about 13% of the U.S. population and, according to National Institute on Drug Abuse (1991) surveys of Americans' drug use, are no more likely than Whites ever to have used most drugs of abuse. Nonetheless, the percentages of Blacks among drug arrestees were in the low 20% range in the late 1970s, climbing to around 30% in the early 1980s and peaking at 42% in 1989. The number of drug arrests of Blacks more than doubled between 1985 and 1989, whereas White drug arrests increased only by 27%. Figure 9.3 shows the stark differences in drug arrest trends by race from 1976 to 1991.

Drug control policies are a major cause of worsening racial disparities in prison. In the federal prisons, for example, 22% of new admissions and 25% of the resident population were drug offenders in 1980. By 1990, 42% of new admissions were drug offenders as in 1992 were 58% of the resident population. In state prisons, 5.7% of inmates in 1979 were drug offenders, a figure that by 1991 had climbed to 21.3% to become the single largest category of prisoners (robbers, burglars, and

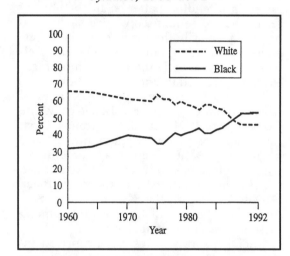

Figure 9.2
Admissions to Federal and State Prisons by Race, 1960–1992

SOURCES: Langan 1991; Gilliard 1992; Perkins 1992, 1993; Perkins and Gilliard 1992.
NOTE: Hispanics are included in Black and White populations.

murderers were next at 14.8 percent, 12.4%, and 10.6%, respectively) (Beck et al. 1993).

The effect of drug policies can be seen in prison data from a number of states. . . . In Pennsylvania, Clark (1992) reports, Black male prison admissions for drug crimes grew

Table 9.1
Percentage Black and White Arrests for Index I Offenses 1976-1991 (3-year intervals)[a]

	1976 White	1976 Black	1979 White	1979 Black	1982 White	1982 Black	1985 White	1985 Black	1988 White	1988 Black	1991 White	1991 Black	1992 White	1992 Black
Murder and nonnegligent manslaughter	45.0	53.5	49.4	47.7	48.8	49.7	50.1	48.4	45.0	53.5	43.4	54.8	43.5	55.1
Forcible rape	51.2	46.6	50.2	47.7	48.7	49.7	52.2	46.5	52.7	45.8	54.8	43.5	55.5	42.8
Robbery	38.9	59.2	41.0	56.9	38.2	60.7	37.4	61.7	36.3	62.6	37.6	61.1	37.7	60.9
Aggravated assault	56.8	41.0	60.9	37.0	59.8	38.8	58.0	40.4	57.6	40.7	60.0	38.3	59.5	38.8
Burglary	69.0	29.2	69.5	28.7	67.0	31.7	69.7	28.9	67.0	31.3	68.8	29.3	67.8	30.4
Larceny-theft	65.7	32.1	67.2	30.2	64.7	33.4	67.2	30.6	65.6	32.2	66.6	30.9	66.2	31.4
Motor vehicle theft	71.1	26.2	70.0	27.2	66.9	31.4	65.8	32.4	58.7	39.5	58.5	39.3	58.4	39.4
Arson	—	—	78.9	19.2	74.0	24.7	75.7	22.8	73.5	25.0	76.7	21.5	76.4	21.9
Violent crime[b]	50.4	47.5	53.7	44.1	51.9	46.7	51.5	47.1	51.7	46.8	53.6	44.8	53.6	44.8
Property crime[c]	67.0	30.9	68.2	29.4	65.5	32.7	67.7	30.3	65.3	32.6	66.4	31.3	65.8	31.8
Total crime index	64.1	33.8	65.3	32.4	62.7	35.6	64.5	33.7	62.4	35.7	63.2	34.6	62.7	35.2.

SOURCES: *Sourcebook of Criminal Justice Statistics.* Various years. Washington, DC: Department of Justice, Bureau of Justice Statistics; FBI 1993, Table 43.
a. Because of rounding, the percentages may not add to total.
b. Violent crimes are offenses of murder, forcible rape, robbery, and aggravated assault.
c. Property crimes are offenses of burglary, larceny-theft, motor vehicle theft, and arson.

Table 9.2
U.S.Drug Arrests by Race, 1976-1992

Year	Total Violations	White	White %	Black	Black %
1976	475,209	366,081	77	103,615	22
1977	565,371	434,471	77	122,594	22
1978	592,168	462,728	78	127,277	21
1979	516,142	396,065	77	112,748	22
1980	531,953	401,979	76	125,607	24
1981	584,776	432,556	74	146,858	25
1982	562,390	400,683	71	156,369	28
1983	615,081	423,151	69	185,601	30
1984	560,729	392,904	70	162,979	29
1985	700,009	482,486	69	210,298	30
1986	688,815	463,457	67	219,159	32
1987	809,157	511,278	63	291,177	36
1988	844,300	503,125	60	334,015	40
1989	1,074,345	613,800	57	452,574	42
1990	860,016	503,315	59	349,965	41
1991	763,340	443,596	58	312,997	41
1992	919,561	546,430	59	364,546	40

SOURCES: FBI 1993, Table 43; *Sourcebook of Criminal Justice Statistics—1978–1992.*
Various tables. Washington, DC: U.S. Department of Justice, Bureau of Justice Statistics.

four times faster (up 1,613%) between 1980 and 1990 than did White male admissions (up 477%). In California, according to Zimring and Hawkins (1994), the number of males in prison for drug crimes grew 15 fold between 1980 and 1990 and "there were more people in prison in California for drug offenses in 1991 than there were for *all* offenses at the end of 1979" (p. 89; emphasis in original).

Why, if Blacks in their lives are no more likely than Whites to use illicit drugs, are Blacks so much more likely to be arrested and imprisoned? One possible answer, which is almost certainly wrong, is that Blacks are proportionately more likely to sell drugs. We have no representative surveys of drug dealers and so cannot with confidence paint demographic pictures. However, there is little reason to suspect that drug crimes are more interracial than are most other crimes. In addition, the considerations that make arrests of Black dealers relatively easy make arrests of White dealers relatively hard.

Drug arrests are easier to make in socially disorganized inner-city minority areas than in working or middle-class urban or suburban areas for a number of reasons. First, although drug sales in working or middle-class areas are likely to take place indoors and in private spaces where they are difficult to observe, drug sales in poor minority areas are likely to take place outdoors in streets, alleys, or abandoned buildings, or indoors in public places like bars. Second, although working or middle-class drug dealers in stable areas are unlikely to sell drugs to undercover strangers, dealers in disorganized areas have little

Figure 9.3
Arrest Rates for Drug Offenses by Race, 1965–1991

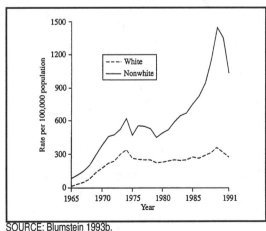

SOURCE: Blumstein 1993b.

choice but to sell to strangers and new acquaintances. These differences mean that it is easier for police to make arrests and undercover purchases in urban minority areas than elsewhere. Because arrests are fungible for purposes of both the individual officer's personnel file and the department's year-to-year statistical comparisons, more easy arrests look better than fewer hard ones. And because, as ethnographic studies of drug trafficking make clear (Fagan 1993; Padilla 1992), arrested drug dealers in disadvantaged urban minority communities are generally replaced within days, there is a nearly inexhaustible potential supply of young minority Americans to be arrested.

There is another reason why the War on Drugs worsened racial disparities in the justice system. Penalties for drug crimes were steadily made harsher since the mid-1980s. In particular, purveyors of crack cocaine, a drug used primarily by poor urban Blacks and Hispanics, are punished far more severely than are purveyors of powder cocaine, a pharmacologically indistinguishable drug used primarily by middle-class Whites. The most notorious disparity occurs under federal law which equates 1 gram of crack with 100 grams of powder. As a result, the average prison sentence served by Black federal prisoners is 40% longer than the average sentence for Whites (McDonald and Carlson 1993). Although the Minnesota Supreme Court and two federal district courts have struck down the 100-to-1 rule as a denial of constitutional equal protection to Blacks, at the time of writing, every federal court of appeals that had considered the question had upheld the provision.

The people who launched the drug wars knew all these things—that the enemy troops would mostly be young minority males, that an emphasis on supply-side antidrug strategies, particularly use of mass arrests, would disproportionately ensnare young minority males, that the 100-to-1 rule would disproportionately affect Blacks, and that there was no valid basis for believing that any of these things would reduce drug availability or prices.

Likewise, as the first section showed, there was no basis for a good faith belief that the harsher crime control policies of recent years—more and longer mandatory minimum sentences, tougher and more rigid sentencing guidelines, and three-strikes-and-you're-out laws—would reduce crime rates, and there was a good basis for predicting that they would disproportionately damage Blacks. If Blacks are more likely than Whites to be arrested, especially for drug crimes, the greater harshness of toughened penalties will disproportionately be borne by Blacks. Because much crime is intraracial, concern for Black victims might justify harsher treatment of Black offenders if there were any reason to believe that harsher penalties would reduce crime rates. Unfortunately, as the conservative national governments of Margaret Thatcher and Brian Mulroney and reports of National Academy of Sciences Panels funded by the administrations of Republican Presidents Ford, Reagan, and Bush all agree, there is no reason to believe that harsher penalties significantly reduce crime rates.

Justifying the Unjustifiable

There is no valid policy justification for the harsh drug and crime control policies of the Reagan and Bush administrations, and for their adverse differential effect on Blacks. The justification, such as it is, is entirely political. Crime is an emotional subject and visceral appeals by politicians to people's fears and resentments are difficult to counter.

It is easy to seize the low ground in political debates about crime policy. When one candidate campaigns with pictures of clanging prison gates and grief-stricken relatives of a rape or murder victim, and with disingenuous promises that newer, tougher policies will work, it is difficult for an opponent to explain that crime is a complicated problem, that real solutions must be long term, and that simplistic toughness does not reduce crime rates. This is why, as a result, candidates often compete to establish which is tougher in his views about crime. It is also why less conservative candidates often try to preempt their more conservative opponents by adopting a tough stance early in the campaign. Finally, it is why political pundits congratulate President Clinton on his acumen in proposing federal crime legislation as or more harsh than his opponents. . . .

Conservative Republican politicians have, since the late 1960s, used welfare, especially Aid to Families with Dependent Children, and crime as symbolic issues to appeal to anti-Black sentiments and resentments of White voters, as Thomas and Mary Edsall's *Chain Reaction: The Impact of Race, Rights, and Taxes on American Politics* (1991) makes clear. The Edsalls provide a history, since the mid-1960s, of "a conservative politics that had the effect of polarizing the electorate along racial lines." Anyone who observed Ronald Reagan's portrayal in several campaigns of Linda Evans, a Black Chicago woman, as the "welfare queen" or George Bush's use of Black murderer Willie Horton to caricature Michael Dukakis's criminal justice policies knows of what the Edsalls write. . . .

Public discourse about criminal justice issues has been debased by the cynicism that made Willie Horton a major participant in the 1988 presidential election. That cynicism has made it difficult to discuss or develop sensible public policies, and that cynicism explains why conservative politicians have been able year after year successfully to propose ever harsher penalties and crime control and drug policies that no informed person believes can achieve their ostensible goals.

Three final points, arguments that apologists for current policies sometimes make, warrant mention. First, it is sometimes said to be unfair to blame national Republican administrations for the failures and disparate impacts of recent crime control policies. This ignores the efforts of the Reagan and Bush administrations to encourage and, through federal mandates and funding restrictions, to coerce states to follow the federal lead. Attorney General William Barr (e.g., 1992) made the most aggressive efforts to compel state adoption of tougher criminal justice policies, and the Bush administration's final proposed crime bills restricted eligibility for federal funds to states that, like the federal government, abolished parole release and adopted sentencing standards no less severe than those in the federal sentenc-

ing guidelines. In any case, as the Edsalls' book makes clear, the use of crime control issues (among others including welfare reform and affirmative action) to elicit anti-Black sentiments from White voters has long been a stratagem of both state and federal Republican politicians.

Second, sometimes it is argued that political leaders have merely followed the public will; voters are outraged by crime and want tougher policies (Dilulio 1991). This is a half-truth that gets the causal order backwards. Various measures of public sentiment, including both representative surveys like Gallup and Harris polls and work with focus groups, have for many years consistently shown that the public is of two minds about crime (Roberts 1992). First, people are frustrated and want offenders to be punished. Second, people believe that social adversity, poverty, and a troubled home life are the principal causes of crime, and they believe government should work to rehabilitate offenders. A number of surveys have found that respondents who would oppose a tax increase to pay for more prisons would support a tax increase to pay for rehabilitative programs. These findings of voter ambivalence about crime should not be surprising. Most people have complicated views about complicated problems. For example, most judges and corrections officials have the same ambivalent feelings about offenders that the general public has. Conservative politicians have seized upon public support of punishment and ignored public support of rehabilitation and public recognition that crime presents complex, not easy, challenges. By presenting crime control issues only in emotional, stereotyped ways, conservative politicians have raised its salience as a political issue but made it impossible for their opponents to respond other than in the same stereotyped ways.

Third, sometimes it is argued that disparate impacts on Black offenders are no problem and that, because much crime is intraracial, failure to adopt tough policies would disserve the interests of Black victims. As former Attorney General Barr (1992) put it, perhaps in ill-chosen words, "the benefits of increased incarceration would be enjoyed disproportionately by Black Americans" (p. 17). This argument also is based on a half-truth. No one wants to live in unsafe neighborhoods or to be victimized by crime, and in a crisis, people who need help will seek it from the police, the public agency of last resort. Requesting help in a crisis and supporting harsh policies with racially disparate effects are not the same thing. The relevant distinction is between acute and chronic problems. A substantial body of public opinion research (e.g., National Opinion Research Center surveys conducted throughout the 1980s summarized in Wood 1990) shows that Blacks far more than Whites support establishment of more generous social welfare policies, full employment programs, and increased social spending. The congressional Black and Hispanic caucuses have consistently opposed bills calling for tougher sanctions and supported bills calling for increased spending on social programs aimed at improving conditions that cause crime. Thus, in claiming to be concerned about Black victims, conservative politicians are responding to natural human calls for help in a crisis while ignoring evidence that Black citizens would rather have government support efforts to ameliorate the chronic social conditions that cause crime and thereby make calls for help in a crisis less necessary.

The evidence on the effectiveness of recent crime control and drug abuse policies, as the first section demonstrated, cannot justify their racially disparate effects on Blacks, nor, as this section demonstrates, can the claims that such policies merely manifest the peoples' will or respect the interests of Black victims. All that is left is politics of the ugliest kind. The War on Drugs and the set of harsh crime control policies in which it was enmeshed were adopted to achieve political, not policy, objectives, and it is the adoption for political purposes of policies with foreseeable disparate impacts, the use of disadvantaged Black Americans as means to the achievement of White politicians' electoral ends, that must in the end be justified. It cannot.

Discussion Questions

1. According to Tonry, what social factors have been responsible for the increased emphasis on drug abuse violations by the criminal justice system? What have been the implications of this emphasis for the system?

2. Arrests for Part II offenses make up the majority of arrests for all crimes and are increasingly making up a large percentage of our prison populations in the United States (due primarily to drug abuse violations). Are these behaviors "overcriminalized"? That is, should drug use and other "victimless crimes" be legally defined as crimes? In a hypothetical situation, what would be the impact of eliminating certain behaviors as crimes from our legal statutes?

3. Tonry argues that the "War on Drugs" was pursued despite the knowledge that this policy would not work with regard to deterring drug use and sales and would disproportionately impact African Americans. What evidence does Tonry offer to support his position? Do you feel that the Reagan, Bush, and Clinton administrations were right to pursue the war on drugs despite its failures?

References

Anglin, M. Douglas and Yih-Ing Hser. 1990. "Treatment of Drug Abuse." In *Drugs and Crime*, edited by M. Tonry and J. Q. Wilson. Chicago: University of Chicago Press.

Austin, James and Aaron David McVey. 1989. *The Impact of the War on Drugs*. San Francisco: National Council on Crime and Delinquency.

Barr, William P. 1992. "The Case for More Incarceration." Washington, DC: U.S. Department of Justice, Office of Policy Development.

Beck, Allen et al. 1993. *Survey of State Prison Inmates, 1991*. Washington, DC: Bureau of Justice Statistics.

Blumstein, Alfred. 1982. "On the Racial Disproportionality of United States' Prison Populations." *Journal of Criminal Law and Criminology*, 73:1259-81.

———. 1993a. "Racial Disproportionality of U.S. Prison Populations Revisited." *University of Colorado Law Review*, 64:743-60.

——. 1993b. "Making Rationality Relevant—The American Society of Criminology 1992 Presidential Address." *Criminology*, 31:1-16.

Blumstein, Alfred, Jacqueline Cohen, and Daniel Nagin. 1978. *Deterrence and Incapacitation.* Report of the National Academy of Sciences Panel on Research on Deterrent and Incapacitation Effects. Washington, DC: National Academy Press.

Botvin, Gilbert J. 1990. "Substance Abuse Prevention: Theory, Practice, and Effectiveness." In *Drugs and Crime*, edited by M. Tonry and J. Q. Wilson. Chicago: University of Chicago Press.

Bureau of Justice Statistics. 1987. *Correctional Populations in the United States, 1985.* Washington, DC: U.S. Department of Justice, Bureau of Justice Statistics.

——. 1989a. *Correctional Populations in the United States, 1987.* Washington, DC: U.S. Department of Justice, Bureau of Justice Statistics.

——. 1989b. *Correctional Populations in the United States, 1986.* Washington, DC: U.S. Department of Justice, Bureau of Justice Statistics.

——. 1991a. *Correctional Populations in the United States, 1989.* Washington, DC: U.S. Department of Justice, Bureau of Justice Statistics.

——. 1991b. *Correctional Populations in the United States, 1988.* Washington, DC: U.S. Department of Justice, Bureau of Justice Statistics.

——. 1993. *Correctional Populations in the United States, 1991.* Washington, DC: U.S. Department of Justice, Bureau of Justice Statistics.

Cahalan, Margaret Wemer. 1986. *Historical Corrections Statistics in the United States, 1850-1984.* Washington, DC: U.S. Department of Justice, Bureau of Justice Statistics.

Canadian Sentencing Commission. 1987. *Sentencing Reform: A Canadian Approach.* Ottawa: Canadian Government Publishing Centre.

Chaiken, Marcia, ed. 1988. *Street Level Enforcement: Examining the Issues.* Washington, DC: U.S. Government Printing Office.

Clark, Stover. 1992. "Pennsylvania Corrections in Context." *Overcrowded Times*, 3:45.

Clarke, Stevens H. 1992. "North Carolina Prisons Growing." *Overcrowded Times* 3:1, 11-13.

Dilulio, John J. 1991. *No Escape: The Future of American Corrections.* New York: Basic Books.

Edsall, Thomas and Mary Edsall. 1991. *Chain Reaction: The Impact of Race, Rights, and Taxes on American Politics.* New York: Norton.

Ellickson, Phyllis L. and Robert M. Bell. 1990. *Prospects for Preventing Drug Use Among Young Adolescents.* Santa Monica, CA: RAND.

Fagan, Jeffrey. 1993. "The Political Economy of Drug Dealing Among Urban Gangs." In *Drugs and the Community,* edited by R. C. Davis, A. J. Lurigio, and D. P. Rosenbaum. Springfield, IL: Charles C. Thomas.

Federal Bureau of Investigation. 1993. *Uniform Crime Reports for the United States—1992.* Washington, DC: U.S. Government Printing Office.

Gerstein, Dean R. and Henrik J. Jarwood, eds. 1990. *Treating Drug Problems.* Report of the Committee for Substance Abuse Coverage Study, Division of Health Care Services, National Institute of Medicine. Washington, DC: National Academy Press.

Gilliard, Darrell K. 1992. *National Corrections Reporting Program, 1987.* Washington, DC: U.S. Department of Justice, Bureau of Justice Statistics.

Hindelang, Michael. 1976. *Criminal Victimization in Eight American Cities: A Descriptive Analysis of Common Theft and Assault.* Washington, DC: Law Enforcement Assistance Administration.

——. 1978. "Race and Involvement in Common Law Personal Crimes." *American Sociological Review*, 43:93-108.

Home Office. 1990. *Protecting the Public.* London: H. M. Stationery Office.

Klein, Stephen, Joan Petersilia, and Susan Turner. 1990. "Race and Imprisonment Decisions in California." *Science*, 247:812-16.

Langan, Patrick A. 1985. "Racism on Trial: New Evidence to Explain the Racial Composition of Prisons in the United States." *Journal of Criminal Law and Criminology*, 76:666-83.

——. 1991. *Race of Persons Admitted to State and Federal Institutions, 1926-86.* Washington, DC: U.S. Department of Justice, Bureau of Justice Statistics.

McDonald, Douglas and Ken Carlson. 1993. *Sentencing in the Federal Courts: Does Race Matter?* Washington, DC: U.S. Department of Justice, Bureau of Justice Statistics.

Moore, Mark H. 1990. "Supply Reduction and Drug Law Enforcement." In *Drugs and Crime*, edited by M. Tonry and J. Q. Wilson. Chicago: University of Chicago Press.

Moynihan, Daniel Patrick. 1993. "Iatrogenic Government Social Policy and Drug Research." *American Scholar*, 62:351-62.

National Institute on Drug Abuse. 1991. *National Household Survey on Drug Abuse: Population*

Estimates 1990. Washington, DC: U.S. Government Printing Office.

Office of National Drug Control Policy. 1990. *National Drug Control Strategy*, January 1990. Washington, DC: Author.

Padilla, Felix. 1992. *The Gang as an American Enterprise*. New Brunswick, NJ: Rutgers University Press.

Perkins, Craig. 1992. *National Corrections Reporting Program, 1989*. Washington, DC: U.S. Department of Justice, Bureau of Justice Statistics.

——. 1993. *National Corrections Reporting Program, 1990.* Washington, DC: U.S. Department of Justice, Bureau of Justice Statistics.

Perkins, Craig and Darrell K. Gilliard. 1992. *National Corrections Reporting Program, 1988*. Washington, DC: U.S. Department of Justice, Bureau of Justice Statistics.

President's Commission on Law Enforcement and Administration of Justice. 1967. *The Challenge of Crime in a Free Society*. Washington, DC: U.S. Government Printing Office.

President's Commission on Model State Drug Laws. 1993. *Final Report*. Washington, DC: U.S. Government Printing Office.

Reiss, Albert J., Jr. and Jeffrey Roth. 1993. *Understanding and Controlling Violence. Report of the National Academy of Sciences Panel on the Understanding and Control of Violence*. Washington, DC: National Academy Press.

Reuter, Peter. 1988. "Can the Borders Be Sealed?" *Public Interest*, 92:51-65.

Roberts, Julian V. 1992. "Public Opinion, Crime, and Criminal Justice." In *Crime and Justice: A Review of Research*, vol. 16, edited by M. Tonry. Chicago: University of Chicago Press.

Sourcebook of Criminal Justice Statistics. 1978–1992. Washington, DC: Department of Justice, Bureau of Justice Statistics.

Standing Committee on Justice and the Solicitor General. 1993. *Crime Prevention in Canada: Toward a National Strategy*. Ottawa: Canada Communication Group.

Sviridoff, Michele, Susan Sadd, Richard Curtis, and Randolph Grine. 1992. *The Neighborhood Effects of Street-Level Drug Enforcement*. New York: Vera Institute of Justice.

Tonry, Michael. 1994. *Malign Neglect: Race, Crime, and Punishment in America.* New York: Oxford University Press.

U.S. General Accounting Office. 1990. *Drug Abuse: Research on Treatment May Not Address Current Needs*. Washington, DC: U.S. General Accounting Office.

Wilson, James Q. 1990. "Drugs and Crime." In *Drugs and Crime*, edited by M. Tonry and J. Q. Wilson. Chicago: University of Chicago Press.

Wood, Floris W. 1990. *An American Profile: Opinions and Behavior 1972-1989*. New York: Gale Research.

Zimring, Franklin E. and Gordon Hawkins. 1994. "The Growth of Imprisonment in California." *British Journal of Criminology* 34:83-95.

Section III

Correlates of Crime

Crime is unevenly distributed through the social system. Since not all of us are criminals and crime occurs more often in some areas than in others, sociologists and criminologists have devoted much time and attention to understanding how and why crime is concentrated as it is. Even the casual observer is able to see that most conventional criminals seem to represent a constellation of social characteristics that have come to be associated with such crime. They are of lower socioeconomic status, often minority-group members, male, young, and from troubled families. Although those with quite different characteristics do commit crimes and are prosecuted in the courts, they represent a decided minority of such cases. Why? What is the relationship of class, race, gender, age, and family to crime and delinquency? These correlates of crime tell an interesting story about where crime occurs and who its perpetrators are. In many cases, the correlates of those committing the offenses closely resembles those of the victims.

Although the correlates of crime listed above are often thought of independently of one another, they seldom exert influence on behavior in isolation. More realistically, they operate in combination, reinforcing one another while affecting the person's behavior in a variety of ways. In the profile of a typical conventional offender, for example, which is more important, race, gender, age or family stability? More likely, no single factor is solely

responsible for the offender's behavior, but interacting together they have a powerful influence. In this section, each of these four factors is discussed and their contribution to criminality examined.

Social Class and Crime

Many persons who are known to commit the ordinary, or index, crimes come from lower socioeconomic backgrounds, which include unemployment, little money, and poor education. These characteristics are particularly true of young offenders. Various studies of delinquents and young adults who are arrested for street crimes confirm their lower-class status (Byrne and Sampson 1985; Thornberry and Farnsworth 1982). This finding is so prevalent that underprivileged status is an important element in many theories of the causes of crime.

But there is another view, supported by self-report studies involving subjects of all social classes, that lower-class men and women are simply more likely to be arrested and convicted, whereas middle-class and upper-class offenders often manage to avoid arrest and particularly conviction. Though social class plays a major role in most criminological theories, there is still debate over its significance in the causation of crime (see reading 10). For example, Charles R. Tittle, Wayne J. Villemez, and Douglas A. Smith (1978) believe that there is little or no inverse relationship between class and criminality and that such a relationship cannot be demonstrated in either official statistics or in self-report studies. They believe that crime is just more visible in lower-income neighborhoods. They state quite plainly that "In short, class and criminality are now, and probably never were related, at least not during the recent past." Indeed, they interpret Sutherland's differential association as being an absence of "countervailing interpersonal influences [rather] than of class position or place of residence," and they observe, as Sutherland would agree, that "definitions favorable to deviance are . . . distributed over the classes" (1978: 653). Others (Voigt et al. 1994: 93-94) point out that some self-report studies even indicate a higher incidence of serious deviant behavior among the upper class than among the lower. This finding, however, is not consistent in all such studies.

Although John Braithwaite (1981) acknowledged that not all self-report studies support a relationship between class and crime, he thought that too many of them do support a connection to be considered mere chance. He disagreed with Tittle and his associates, indicating his belief that self-report studies exaggerated the delinquency of middle-class youth. He cited the National Youth Survey to prove his point. Although there was not much difference in numbers of victimless crimes (public disorder, status offenses, drug use) committed, the lower class committed four times as many "predatory crimes against persons" and about two times as many "predatory crimes against property" as middle-class youth. Furthermore, he said, one is more likely to become the victim of certain types of crimes in lower-class neighborhoods and that social class accounts for more variance than any other urban ecological factor. Finally, he demonstrated that most studies not showing a relationship between class and crime were conducted in rural areas, where class distinctions may not be as strong.

Scholars who agree that there is a relationship between social class and crime offer various explanations. W. Bonger, for example, writing in 1916, found criminal attitudes of both the upper and the lower class to be tied to capitalism. The lower class is affected by the misery imposed upon them by the capitalists, and the upper class is influenced by a greedy desire for more wealth.

According to Thomas J. Bernard (1988), those who are the truly disadvantaged suffer from high levels of angry aggression, brought about by the urban environment (population density, noise pollution), low social position, racial or ethnic discrimination, and social isolation. As some people in these circumstances experience frequent and intense "situation arousal," they are unable to cope; they become angry and engage in some form of intentional harm.

William Julius Wilson (1996) attributes much crime to joblessness (which is rapidly increasing in urban areas) and high levels of neighborhood deterioration, partly the fault of corporations and businesses moving out. He equates this situation with high levels of social disorganization, which then lead to the problems of gang violence, drug use and drug dealing, and crime in general. Nearly 40 years earlier, Walter Miller (1958) saw the lower-class community as one which has created its own tradition of behavior and values that influences its members. These "focal concerns," as he refers to them, are trouble, toughness, smartness (ability to outsmart), excitement, fate (luck), and autonomy. These distinct concepts are part of a culture that encourages a young person to become involved in gang delinquency in order to attain these valued characteristics.

Differences in social class certainly create different opportunities for engaging in crime. One cannot commit embezzlement, for instance, when one is unemployed. As John Braithwaite (1981) points out, the lower class commits more of the conventional crimes likely to be handled by the police, whereas the middle class engages in crimes connected to their occupations. These are the same crimes, of course, that are lightly penalized.

Social class certainly affects how one is processed through the system; it is the lower class who cannot afford bail, who must depend upon public defenders, who cannot pay for private investigators. Reiman (1988: 162) sees the bias in the criminal justice system as blurring the distinction between "criminal classes" and "lower classes," creating instead the concept of the "dangerous classes." This situation results in the fact that "Fear and hostility are directed toward the predatory acts of the poor [rather] than toward the acts of the rich" (1988: 162). Although many agree that social class affects crime, almost all agree that it affects the way offenders from different backgrounds are treated by the criminal justice system.

Race, Ethnicity and Crime

Crime rates vary among African Americans, Whites, Hispanics, Asians, Native Americans, and other racial and ethnic groups. Because of data limitations, this brief discussion will be primarily limited to differences between African Americans and whites, with references made to other groups where possible. Evidence on the relationship between race and ethnicity and crime rates is often conflicting. Although they are only 12 percent of the population, African Americans represent 63 percent of those arrested for robbery, 54 percent of those arrested for homicide, and 31 percent of those arrested for burglary (LaFree, Drass, and O'Day 1992). Thus, relative to their size in the population, African Americans are disproportionately involved in crime, with the glaring exception of white-collar crime. As Marvin E. Wolfgang (1966: 46) points out, "Most corporate crime reflects not only the collar but of the skin as well, and neither becomes part of the arrest statistics available for analysis by race."

A number of critics claim that this picture of African American crime is not accurate, and they offer explanations of the existing rates that place them in a different context. Probably the two most widely held explanations are the confounding effects of social class and prejudice within the justice system. One theory is that conventional crime is highly correlated with social class, and blacks are overrepresented in the lower classes and underclasses. It is theorized that when social class is taken into consideration, the effects of race are greatly diminished (see the previous section of this introduction).

Others point out that self-report studies indicate that crime is more evenly distributed by social class than official reports show. One study of delinquency among college students found that the main difference between their delinquency and that of others who went to court seemed to be the relative immunity given them because of their status, and proportionately fewer African Americans than whites attend college (Wolfgang 1966).

Gary LaFree, Kriss A. Drass, and Patrick O'Day (1992) also challenge some common assumptions about social class pertaining to crime. Looking at economics, they found that economic stress and unemployment had little effect on African American crime, though it did have an effect on white crime rates. The deprivation of African Americans relative to whites (interracial deprivation) also had little effect on African American crime. However, they did find support for an intraracial polarization effect, based on a widening gap between middle-class and underclass African Americans. Interestingly, they found a similar effect for whites.

Bias or prejudice against African Americans in the criminal justice system can be observed at many levels. African Americans have higher rates of arrest, conviction, and imprisonment, combined with longer lengths of incarceration than other groups (Maurer 1990). They are more likely to be subject to illegal arrests and detentions, to be arrested and convicted on skimpy evidence, to go to jail rather than receive bail, and to receive harsher sentences (Kappeler, Blumberg, and Potter 1996). Adult African American males have a 1-in-5 chance of going to prison at some point in their lifetime, and for the twenty–to–twenty-nine age group there are currently more African American males under criminal justice supervision (incarceration, probation, and parole) than there are in colleges and universities (LaFree 1995). African Americans have a proportionately greater chance of receiving the death penalty than whites. African American juveniles are also more likely than whites to experience higher rates of formal processing, court referral, and adjudication as a delinquent, and are more likely to receive harsher dispositions (Bishop and Frazier 1988). La-Free and his associates (1992) confirm that African Americans usually commit crimes against other African Americans (thus creating a high victimization rate similar to rates of offending) and point out that African American men have a 1-in-21 chance of being murdered in their lifetimes (see reading 11).

Though few official statistics have been gathered on groups other than African Americans and whites, there is some evidence "that Latinos ages 15 to 19 may have the highest homicide victimization rates of any minority group" (Bartol and Bartol 1998: 41). Ramiro Martinez looked at Latino violence as related to poverty and inequality. He noted that the 1980 Latino homicide rate of 20 per 100,000 was not dissimilar to African American rates of 27 per 100,000, and twice the national rate. Like LaFree, Martinez concluded that intraracial inequality (similar to LaFree's polarization) has more impact on crime than poverty does, as a widening gap persists between poor and middle-class Latinos.

Other evidence indicates that Native Americans also have high violent crime rates, although the accuracy of official data is questionable (Bartol and Bartol 1998). Ronet Bachman looked at homicide rates per 100,000 from 1980 to 1984 and found African American rates to be 33.1, American Indian rates to be 9.6, and white rates to be 4.6, making American Indian rates much lower than African American rates, but still twice those of whites. Bachman also indicated that these numbers are somewhat deceiving, since on some reservations rates are as high as 100, even 127, per 100,000 population. A few of the contributing factors include economic deprivation, alcohol and drug use, social disorganization, and a subculture of violence. Bachman's research also discovered that during 1985, more than 15 percent of American Indians engaged in domestic violence (slightly higher than white rates at just under 15 percent); three out of every hundred women were severely assaulted by their husbands.

The relationship between race and crime is exceedingly complex, with the effects of race and ethnicity masked by complex factors that may be operating in subtle and indirect ways. The overlap between race and social class, noted earlier, may mean that race and ethnic differences in crime are the product of socioeconomic status rather than race per se. If so, we may expect the crime rates of today's minorities to decline if and when their economic circumstances improve.

Gender and Crime

It is a well-known fact that men commit a great many more crimes than women. They also commit different types of crimes. Men are more likely to commit violent crimes, such as aggravated assault. Women are seldom violent; they tend to commit such crimes as prostitution, shoplifting, and welfare fraud. They also commit child abuse and elder abuse; middle age daughters are the most common abusers of aged parents (Alston 1996). There has been a trend in the last twenty years for some women to be involved in white-collar crime, probably corresponding to their entry into business and professional careers (Simpson 1989).

Sally S. Simpson (1991) has made a distinction between African American and white females, indicating that social class greatly affects the different rates of crime found for women of different races. The African American female crime rate is quite similar to that for white males, both of which are greater than the rate for white females but much less than the rate for African American men. This fact illustrates once again that no one variable can be considered in isolation, and many variables affect crime rates among different groups. Simpson points out that both lower-class crimes and female crimes reflect the powerless status of these groups. But powerless men turn to violent street crime; powerless women turn to vice crimes such as drugs and prostitution and to nonviolent property crimes.

Until very recently, status offenses figured heavily in the labeling of young girls as delinquent (Chesney-Lind 1989). In 1983, for instance, 34 percent of girls referred to juvenile or family court were there for such offenses as truancy or running away from home, but only 12 percent of boys in the system were referred for these types of offenses, even though evidence indicates that boys engaged in these acts as frequently as girls did. Because the courts failed to recognize that many of these acts were committed as a result of girls' being physically assaulted or sexually abused in the home, the courts tended to criminalize the very acts (such as running away or stealing to survive once on the street) that facilitated their survival.

Violence among teenage girls appears to be on the rise (Kelley et al. 1997). In Denver, serious violence among thirteen- to fifteen-year-old girls is more than half that of boys, a number substantially higher than found among adults. In Rochester, at age thirteen, boys' prevalence rate for serious violence is 16 percent, and girls' is 18 percent! At age twelve, 15 percent of Rochester girls and 19 percent of boys were involved in serious violence. For every 100 fourteen-year old girls in Rochester, more than 18 had committed an average of 5.5 offenses each.

For most crimes, overall gender stability exists; men far outnumber women and have done so for a long time. Where evidence points to gender convergence, with women offenders beginning to rival men, it is for less serious property crimes and substance abuse (Belknap 1996). Where gender convergence exists, it can likely be explained by one of the following reasons: (1) changes in law enforcement practices (women are treated more like men), (2) feminization of poverty (an increasing number of poor women are forced into crime), (3) changes in data collection methods (minor offenses get recorded as major crimes), (4) increases in women's crimes with small original base numbers (it does not take much to show an increase when the base is small) (see reading 12).

Just as males commit more violent crimes, they are also more often the victims of those types of crimes, with the exception of rape. Women are more often victims of rape and domestic violence. Of criminal homicides, 36 percent are intergender and 64 percent are intragender. When one gender kills the other, two-thirds are men killing women and one-third are women killing men (Goode 1990: 232), and when women do kill, they usually kill someone they know (lovers, husbands, children). Many woman who kill have been the victims of abuse.

After years of being neglected in the study of crime and deviance, women are finally gaining a new and well-deserved level of importance in such research. Previously, when female offending was studied, female criminals were accused of being biological atavists, rebellious toward feminine roles, inferior to men, deceitful, narcissistic, dull, devoid of sexuality, and a host of other uncomplimentary descriptions (Klein 1973). Recently, feminist scholars have developed a perspective that takes into account "points of reference, underlying assumptions, and understandings about crime, victimization, and the justice process" (Simpson 1989: 606). Instead of looking at women's crime in terms of masculinization or sexuality, for example, contemporary research looks at women's economic plight, abusive backgrounds, and similar areas that give insight into differences in male and female offending. For example, rape has been reinterpreted by feminist scholars as a crime of male power and domination. Pornography, incest, battering, and sexual harassment are now examined as various ways of victimizing women. The introduction of feminist scholarship into the study of crime has changed the way criminologists think about female offenders and female victims. Theories of crime causation offered from a feminist point of view have broadened the perspective on crime and brought us closer to an explanation of female criminals and their offenses.

Age and Crime

Studies of the relationship between age and crime indicate that for most offenders, crime peaks in adolescence or young adulthood and then declines, often sharply (Steffensmeier et al. 1989). Ages of peak involvement and ages and rates of decline differ for different crimes, however. For instance, burglary peaks at age sixteen, then rapidly declines. A study of nonviolent offenses found the peak age for male involvement to be fifteen and through eighteen, with decline beginning at nineteen (Farrington 1986). Researchers have found vandalism, auto theft, arson, burglary, theft, and liquor violations most prevalent among young offenders with median ages of seventeen and eighteen. Handling stolen property, abuse of narcotics, violence, disorderly conduct, prostitution, sex offenses (other than rape or prostitution), forgery and fraud, and family abuse are found most frequently in the next group, with median ages between twenty and twenty-eight. Drunkenness, drunk driving, and gambling are most prevalent among an older group of violators, those with median ages between thirty-five and thirty-seven. Although there are slight differences in peak ages based on gender, the overall pattern is similar, with a peak age of fifteen for arson for both males and females, a peak age for murder of twenty for males and twenty-three for females, and peak ages for auto theft, burglary, and aggravated assault falling in between with a one- or two-year difference in peak age for males and females. In contrast to Darrell J. Steffensmeier and his associates, who placed peaks and declines at earlier ages, David P. Farrington concludes in his study that the average age of offenders is between twenty-five and thirty. (It must be noted that some discrepancies arise from the fact that different studies focus on a different array of crimes).

Some crimes do not decline much with age. Gambling, for instance, rises dramatically in one's twenties and then remains high into one's sixties. There is evidence (Steffensmeier et al. 1989) that older people commit less visible, less likely-to-be-reported, and more lucrative crimes, such as corporate crime, racketeering, and political corruption. Crimes that have lower risks decline with age at a slower rate. One study (Farrington 1986) indicated that the ages of victims of violent crime also peak at sixteen to nineteen.

Age affects the rate of crime in a number of ways. For example, on the one hand, the younger one is at the onset of criminal activity, the more likely one is to pursue crime in later life, and the more likely one is to be involved in serious crime (Farrington 1986). On the other hand, the older a person is when released from prison, the less likely it is that he or she will return to crime. Changes in crime patterns as one ages encompass a number of factors (see reading 13). They may be due at least partially to crime switching, in which offenders shift from burglary, for instance, to something like drug- and alcohol-related offenses. Specialization increases

with age, but seriousness of offense often does not increase.

A large number of offenders outgrow crime. This fact can be explained in a number of ways. For example, some believe that aging criminals apply a cost benefit analysis and determine that as one gets older, the cost (possibility of longer prison sentences, greater likelihood of losing family or job) outweighs the benefits (Farrington 1986). James Q. Wilson and Richard J. Herrnstein (1985) believe that as offenders age they become better at delaying gratification and considering the future consequences of their criminal actions. Other criminologists, such as Letitia T. Alston note a decrease in speed, physical stamina, and other physical characteristics as one ages.

Although burglary, robbery, and shoplifting all decrease with age, there has been an exceptional upswing in shoplifting among the elderly, as well as a general "reported increase in crimes committed by older people" (Alston 1996: 4). The elderly who are involved with crime are likely to be involved in victimless crimes, such as being drunk and disorderly ("geriatric delinquency") or body exposure. Larceny-theft accounts for 79.8 percent of the elderly arrests for index crimes. Some reasons why crime by the elderly might be increasing, besides a general decline in economic status, include their becoming a larger portion of the population (thus, even if the rate remains the same, sheer numbers will increase), their remaining healthier longer (sustained health and vigor facilitate crime commission), and the number of elderly alcohol abusers has been increasing.

Family and Crime

Sheldon Glueck and Eleanor Glueck (1950) determined that broken homes were a major contributor to juvenile delinquency. Although other studies have since confirmed their findings (Sampson and Laub 1993), their studies came under attack for problems with methodology (Drowns and Hess 1990). Since that time, it has been shown that a number of family variables, among them broken homes, have some impact on delinquency. It is believed by some that ". . . the best predictor of the onset of offending is poor parental control" (Farrington 1986: 231). Farrington is quick to point out, however, that as children near their teenage years, other influences become important in their lives, and they become influenced less by their family and more by their peers.

A number of factors relating to the family are thought to play a part in the decision to engage in delinquency and crime. Travis Hirschi believes that whether or not children commit delinquent acts depends upon the strength of their attachment to their parents and whether or not they have internalized parental standards for their behavior. A study conducted by Walter R. Gove and Robert D. Crutchfield (1982), which examined the variables of family structure, poor parental characteristics, household characteristics, and parent child relationships, supports Hirschi's contention that attachment is the strongest predictor of delinquency. Important aspects of parental attachment are the time shared between parent and child; parents' "psychological presence," even when they are not there; intimacy of their communication; and the affection, love, and respect they and their children share. Males and females appear to be affected differently by the nature of family relationships. Characteristics of the parents' marriage are more important for males, while parent-child interaction and parental control are important for females in predicting delinquency. In reviewing the literature, Gove and Crutchfield found that a number of family variables appear to be related to delinquency, including broken homes, poor marital relationships, lack of parental control, ineffectual parental behavior, and poor parent-child relationships. The authors caution, however, that many of the studies specifying these variables have severe limitations.

Joseph H. Rankin and Roger Kern (1994) took the study of attachment one step further, to determine whether it mattered if the child was attached to both parents or just one. They found that a strong attachment to both parents was a better predictor of nondelinquent behavior than a strong attachment to just one parent. This finding has implications for the single-parent home even when there is a strong attachment to the custodial parent. In addition to attachment, Lawrence Rosen lists lack of role modeling, parental conflict (with each other), large family size, and erratic discipline or the absence of direct social control as variables that might contribute to delinquency. Farrington thinks that there is no informal social control for juveniles when parents are working.

There are other hypotheses related to the absence or presence of parents in the home, as well as to their employment status. Hirschi believes that boys are more likely to engage in delinquency when their fathers are unemployed or their family is on welfare (the family is not self-sufficient). While the idea that children in households headed by women are more likely to engage in delinquent acts has been discussed, LaFree (1995) found that there was often less crime in such African American households than in two-parent households.

There are situations, of course, when families can have a totally devastating effect on the children. One such case is when a child is being physically or sexually abused in the home. Another is when the child observes spousal abuse in the home. One of the strongest predictors of the child's growing up to be an abuser is having grown up in an abusive home. Although Joan McCord cites neglect and rejection as well as abuse as predictors of delinquency and crime, her research indicates that parental rejection is a more significant factor in determining law-violating behavior (see reading 14).

Explanations of all of these relationships—class and crime, race and crime, gender and crime, age and crime, and family and crime—have been advanced in various theories of crime. As will soon be described, learning theory, strain theory, control theory, and social disorganization theory, to name the most prominent, have viewed one or more of these correlates of crime as essential parts of their explanations of crime. Indeed, knowledge of these correlates makes it easier to understand why certain groups are more likely than others to commit certain types of crimes. Nevertheless, the exact relationship between these correlates and crime remains unclear, and more research is clearly needed. The following readings illustrate some of the research that explores the relationship between class, race, gender, age, and family and crime and delinquency.

References

Alston, Letitia T. 1996. *Crime and Older Americans*. Springfield, IL: Charles C. Thomas.

Bachman, Ronet. 1992. *Death and Violence on the Reservation: Homicide, Family Violence, and Suicide in American Indian Populations*. New York: Auburn House.

Bartol, Curt R. and Anne M. Bartol. 1998. *Delinquency and Justice: A Psychological Approach* (2nd ed.). Upper Saddle River, NJ: Prentice Hall.

Belknap, Joanne. 1996. *The Invisible Woman: Gender, Crime, and Justice*. Belmont, CA: Wadsworth.

Bernard, Thomas J. 1988. "Angry Aggression Among the 'Truly Disadvantaged'," *Criminology*, 28:73-96.

Bishop, Donna M. and Charles E. Frazier. 1988. "The Influence of Race in Juvenile Justice Processing," *Journal of Research in Crime and Delinquency*, 25:242-263.

Bonger, W. 1916. *Criminality and Economic Conditions*. Boston: Little, Brown.

Braithwaite, John. 1981. "The Myth of Social Class and Criminality Reconsidered," *American Sociological Review*, 46:36-57.

Byrne, James and Robert Sampson. 1985. *The Social Ecology of Crime*. (New York: Springer-Verlag).

Chesney-Lind, Meda. 1989. "Girls' Crime and Woman's Place: Toward a Feminist Model of Female Delinquency," *Crime and Delinquency*, 35:5-29.

Drowns, Robert W. and Karen M. Hess. 1990. *Juvenile Justice*. Saint Paul, MI: West.

Farrington, David P. 1986. "Age and Crime." In Michael Tonry and Norval Morris (eds.), *Crime and Justice*. Chicago: University of Chicago Press.

Glueck, Sheldon and Eleanor T. Glueck. 1950. *Unraveling Juvenile Delinquency*. New York: Commonwealth Fund.

Goode, Erich. 1990. *Deviant Behavior* (3rd ed.). Englewood Cliffs, NJ: Prentice Hall.

Gove, Walter R. and Robert D. Crutchfield. 1982. "The Family and Juvenile Delinquency," *The Sociological Quarterly*, 23:301-319.

Hirschi, Travis. 1969. *Causes of Delinquency*. Berkeley: University of California Press.

Kappeler, Victor E., Mark Blumberg, and Gary W. Potter. 1996. *The Mythology of Crime and Criminal Justice* (2nd ed.). Prospect Heights, IL: Waveland.

Kelley, Barbara Tatem, David Huizinga, Terence P. Thornberry, and Rolf Loeber. 1997. "Epidemiology of Serious Violence," *Juvenile Justice Bulletin*, June 1997. Washington, DC: U.S. Department of Justice, Office of Juvenile Justice and Delinquency Prevention.

Klein, Dorie. 1973. "The Etiology of Female Crime: A Review of the Literature." In Susan Datesman and Frank Scarpitti (eds.), *Women, Crime and Justice*. New York: Oxford.

LaFree, Gary. 1995. "Race and Crime Trends in the United States, 1946-1990." In D.H. Hawkins (ed.), *Ethnicity, Race and Crime*. Albany: State University of New York Press.

LaFree, Gary, Kriss A. Drass, and Patrick O'Day. 1992. "Race and Crime in Postwar America: Determinants of African-American and White Rates, 1957-1988," *Criminology*, 30:157-188.

Loeber, Rolf and Thomas Dishion. 1983. "Early Predictors of Male Delinquency: A Review," *Psychological Bulletin*, 94:68-99.

Martinez, Ramiro, Jr. 1996. "Latinos and Lethal Violence: The Impact of Poverty and Inequality," *Social Problems*, 43:131-146.

Mauer, Marc. 1990. *Young Black Men and the Criminal Justice System: A Growing National Problem*. Washington, DC: The Sentencing Project.

McCord, Joan. 1991. "Family Relationships, Juvenile Delinquency, and Adult Criminality," *Criminology*, 29:397-417.

Miller, Walter B. 1958. "Lower Class Culture as a Generating Milieu of Gang Delinquency," *Journal of Social Issues*, 14:5-19.

Rankin, Joseph H. and Roger Kern. 1994. "Parental Attachments and Delinquency," *Criminology*, 32:495-515.

Reiman, Jeffrey. 1998. *The Rich Get Richer and the Poor Get Prison: Ideology, Class, and Criminal Justice* (5th ed.). Boston: Allyn and Bacon.

Rosen, Lawrence. 1985. "Family and Delinquency: Structure or Function?" *Criminology*, 23:553-573.

Sampson, Robert J. and John H. Laub. 1993. *Crime in the Making*. Cambridge: Harvard University Press.

Simpson, Sally S. 1989. "Feminist Theory, Crime, and Justice," *Criminology*, 27:605-631.

Simpson, Sally S. 1991. "Caste, Class, and Violent Crime: Explaining Difference in Female Offending," *Criminology*, 29:115-135.

Steffensmeier, Darrell J., Emilie Andersen Allan, Miles D. Harer, and Cathy Streifel. 1989. "Age and the Distribution of Crime," *American Journal of Sociology*, 94:8-3-31.

Thornberry, Terence and Margaret Farnsworth. 1982. "Social Correlates of Criminal Involvement: Further Evidence of the Relationship Between Social Status and Criminal Behavior," *American Sociological Review*, 47:505-518.

Tittle, Charles R., Wayne J. Villemez, and Douglas A. Smith. 1978. "The Myth of Social Class and Criminality: An Empirical Assessment of the Empirical Evidence," *American Sociological Review*, 43:643-656.

Voigt, Lydia, William E. Thornton, Jr., Leo Barrile, and Jerrol M. Seaman. 1994. *Criminology and Justice*. New York: McGraw-Hill.

West, Donald J. 1982. *Delinquency: Its Roots, Careers, and Prospects*. London: Heinemann.

Wilson, James Q. and Richard J. Herrnstein. 1985. *Crime and Human Nature*. New York: Simon and Schuster.

Wilson, William Julius. 1996. "Work," *The New York Times Magazine*, August 18:26-30.

Wolfgang, Marvin E. 1966. "Race and Crime." In H. Klare (ed.) *Changing Concepts of Crime and Its Treatment*. New York: Pergamon.

Wolfgang, Marvin E., Thorsten Sellin, and Robert Figlio. 1972. "Delinquency in a Birth Cohort." In Joseph E. Jacoby (ed.), *Classics of Criminology*. Prospect Heights, IL: Waveland. ✦

10

Specifying the SES/Delinquency Relationship

Charles R. Tittle
Robert F. Meier

For a long time, sociologists and criminologists believed that there was a direct relationship between socioeconomic status (SES) and crime and delinquency. Lower class persons, they believed, were more likely to break the law than middle- and upper-class persons because of the social and economic deprivations and hardships they had to endure. Official data on known crimes supported this contention. Questions began to arise, however, when self-report studies indicating offenses unknown to the police showed offending behavior to be more evenly distributed across the classes than was previously believed. As this selection by Charles Tittle and Robert Meier explains, scholars lined up on both sides of the debate that followed, often with study results supporting their chosen position. What, then, is the student to believe about the relationship between class and crime?

This selection examines several categories of studies that purport to test the relationship between socioeconomic status and delinquency. The results are both illuminating and perplexing, demonstrating that a under some conditions, SES and delinquency are significantly related, leading some scholars to proclaim a relationship between class and crime. But Tittle and Meier are more skeptical, questioning the lack of "systematic patterns whereby those relationships occur." They conclude that SES may not be as important as some researchers have believed, although its precise role in delinquency prediction remains to be deter-

mined. Actual reviews of many of the studies have been omitted.

It is no overstatement that the relationship between social class and criminal behavior is one of the most important and perennial issues in the sociology of crime. The centrality of the dispute is undeniable and on its resolution presumably hinges the fate of many theories of crime and delinquency (but see Tittle, 1983). An apparently simple question—What is the relationship between social class and criminality?—has generated a large research literature, but the results of empirical investigations are inconsistent. The relationship is said to be positive (direct), negative (inverse), conditional, or some combination of the three. Different studies have used different samples, measures of social class, measures of delinquency or crime, and analytic procedures, and some of the discrepant findings are attributable to those different methodologies. But regardless of the conceptual or methodological reasons, criminologists seem no closer to resolving the issue and identifying the nature of the relationship than 50 years ago.

Most criminological data collected prior to the 1950s seemed to demonstrate strong SES differences between delinquents and nondelinquents. Indeed, the existence of a negative relationship between SES and delinquency was accepted as fact by most social scientists, and it became the basis for several theories of delinquency. But not all scholars accepted this conventional wisdom uncritically. Some observed that the official data on which the SES/delinquency correlation was based could be biased because much delinquency was hidden from official view and those hidden acts might have been more equally distributed among the various social strata than the officially known acts. But real controversy about an SES/delinquency relationship did not emerge until self-report studies became common.

Early self-report research by Nye and Short (1957; Nye et al., 1958) suggested that there was no statistically significant relationship between delinquency and SES. Numerous subsequent studies, using a variety of techniques, measures, and analytic procedures, confirmed that conclusion (e.g., Akers, 1964; Arnold, 1966; Clark and Wenninger, 1962; Dentler and Monroe, 1961; Hirschi, 1969; Vaz, 1966; Winslow, 1967). But still other research contradicted the Nye and Short conclusion and reaffirmed the original finding of a negative relationship between SES and delinquency (e.g., McDonald, 1968; Reiss and Rhodes, 1961; Slocum and Stone, 1963; West and Farrington, 1973). In addition, by the late 1960s critics began to challenge the validity of self-report evidence (see Hindelang et al., 1981).

The controversy became acute with the publication of a paper by Tittle et al. (1978). Their meta-analysis of official data and self-report studies, which provided data reducible to a comparable, contingency-table format, revealed that the association between SES and crime/delinquency was negative and at best small, that this negative association had diminished in magnitude over four decades, and that temporal changes were mainly for results based on official statistics rather than self-reports.

There were strong reactions to the Tittle et al. paper. Some scholars challenged the conclusions and presented alternative analyses or interpretations (Braithwaite, 1981; Clelland and Carter, 1980; Kleck, 1982; Nettler, 1978, 1985; Stark, 1979; see also responses to the critics: Tittle et al., 1979, 1982; Tittle, 1985; Tittle and Villemez, 1978). Others, however, were stimulated to further thought and research, reasoning that although there may be no general correlation between SES and delinquency or criminal behavior, there might well be specific conditions under which SES and deviance are related. The product of those additional efforts is a substantial literature published in the last decade that has focused on three categories of specific conditions under which SES effects on delinquency might emerge.[1] They are (1) specific conditions of measurement, (2) specific demographic conditions, and (3) contextual conditions.

Conditions of Measurement

The Independent Variable

Several efforts to pinpoint an SES/delinquency relationship have focused on the meaning and method of measuring socioeconomic status.

The Underclass Specification. Some (e.g., Clelland and Carter, 1980) have proposed that it is only at the very lowest point on an SES Continuum that differences in delinquency can be found. They argue that research using gradational measures, which array respondents on a continuum, are inappropriate for examining the SES/delinquency relationship, and they propose instead a two-category measurement that delineates an "underclass" from all others. . . .

Notwithstanding interpretations set forth by the authors of the above studies (which are contradictory, in any case), it appears that the evidence concerning the effect of SES, as reflected in measures differentiating an underclass from others, is problematic. One study shows one significant correlation (of −.08) out of two. Another shows a range of correlations from −.11 to −.02 for five measures, none of which would likely be statistically significant in a sample of only 110. A third study shows four significant effects out of eight tests, with no measures of association (a sample of approximately 1,500 would usually show significance with only a very small correlation coefficient). A fourth study shows a higher SES/delinquency relationship using an underclass measure, but both the underclass and the conventional occupational measures revealed significant and fairly large effects of SES. Finally, a fifth study, focusing on adults, found mixed results. Thus, it appears that "underclass/overclass" measures of SES that have been used do not unambiguously specify an SES/delinquency relationship.

The Gradational Specification. It has also been argued that the SES/delinquency relationship will emerge if the correct, specific indicator of social rank, conceived in terms of a gradational continuum, is employed in the test (Thornberry and Farnworth, 1982). . . .

... Again, the evidence provides little confidence that using particular indicators of social rank will specify the SES/delinquency relationship. Of the four studies reviewed, one finds education the superior predictor, one finds occupation superior, one presents inconsistent evidence, and the fourth shows almost imperceptible differences between the two. And in no instance was the association between any of the indicators and the measures of delinquency consistently negative and strong.

Marxian Class Specification. A third approach contends that the true SES/delinquency relationship will not be found until SES is reconceptualized in terms of the parents' positions in the social structure relative to the means of production (Brownfield, 1986; Colvin and Pauly, 1983). Two studies conducted since 1978 address this potential specification. . . .

. . . The two studies employing a measure of SES based on a Marxian class conception provide no evidence that such a shift in conceptualization will specify a potential link between SES and delinquency. Indeed, if anything, the results suggest a complete negation of the expected inverse association, because most of the effects in the Hagan et al. data were positive (a result consistent with their theoretical argument) and the Brownfield data show no effects at all (it is not possible to determine directional tendencies from his presentation).

The Youth Status Specification. Fourth, it has been suggested that the SES/delinquency relationship will be discovered if SES is measured in terms of the youth's own position within the social structure of the school rather than in terms of the parents' SES (Stark, 1979). To our knowledge, no studies examining this relationship were reported within the past decade. Indeed, we are not sure any exist prior to 1978. Although Stark emphasizes that this finding is uniform in delinquency research, he refers specifically only to Hirschi's Richmond Youth Study, which shows that youths who are attached to the school are less likely to be delinquent. It is not at all clear, however, that attachment to the school or academic success is synonymous with status within "teenage society" or standing in "the status system of the school." Clearly, Stark assumes that academic success is equivalent to success in the teenage high school social system: "The better a person is doing in school, the higher a person stands among his or her peers" (p. 669). Braithwaite (1981) makes a similar assumption: "If we assign adolescents a class position of their own derived from their location on the success ladder of the school, then a powerful class-crime relationship can be demonstrated. The weight of empirical evidence that school failure is a strong correlate of delinquency is beyond question" (p. 50). Yet, research by Coleman (1961) suggests that academic success is indicative of social success in a student culture in only some type of schools. We contend, therefore, that the potential specification of the SES/delinquency relationship by measuring the status of the juvenile in the teenage social system rather than in terms of the family's SES has not really been investigated, and until the social status of youths is directly measured and related to delinquency, one cannot know if this condition will unmask the true SES/delinquency relationship.

The Dependent Variable

Various scholars have suggested that the SES/delinquency relationship is contingent on how the dependent variable, delinquency, is measured.

The Data Source Specification. It has often been suggested that a negative relationship between SES and delinquency can be shown if one uses official police or court data rather than self-report data (but see Hindelang et al., 1979, for a contrary argument), presumably because lower status persons are more likely to underreport their offenses, thereby reducing the true relationship between SES and delinquency (Kleck, 1982; Nettler, 1978), or because of other methodological artifacts of self-report data (Elliott and Ageton, 1980). Testing this specification has been difficult, however, because most official published data, particularly the Uniform Crime Reports, do not include information about the SES of the offenders. It was customary for many years to attempt to overcome this limitation by substituting areal/ecological measures of SES for individual measures or by substituting racial categorization for SES categorization. But it is now recognized that using areal measures is likely to inflate artificially the magnitude of the true associations between the individual variables of interest (Hindelang et al., 1981) and that racial proxies suppress any effects potentially attributable to low-status whites and high-status blacks. Thus, it is necessary to use data that include direct measures of the individual's SES, perhaps from survey responses, as well as measures of delinquency from official records. . . .

Overall, then, recent analyses concerning the strength of an SES/delinquency relationship as revealed by officially recorded measures relative to self-report measures show mixed results. In one case no differences are observed, in another a possibly significant difference is reported, and in the third the evidence is diffuse and contradictory. Hence, it has not been demonstrated that an SES/delinquency relationship is contingent on the source of the data.

The Seriousness Specification. Numerous scholars have asserted that an SES/delinquency relationship is contingent on whether the measure of delinquency is focused exclusively on serious, criminal acts rather than on a full range of delinquencies or mainly on less serious delinquencies. According to some observers, a negative association between SES and delinquency applies only to serious criminal acts (Clelland and Carter, 1980; Elliott and Ageton, 1980; Nettler, 1978; see also Hindelang et al., 1981, for an argument that self-report studies cover a less serious domain of behavior). Because of its plausibility, this argument has been one of the most frequently addressed specifications in the post-1978 literature, and nine studies bear on it. . . .

The nine studies relevant to the seriousness specification show no consistent support for the idea that an SES/delinquency relationship will be found when researchers measure serious delinquency. Of the nine, two provide evidence supporting the argument, four provide mixed findings, and three report evidence contrary to the argument.

The Frequency Specification. Elliott and Ageton (1980) contend that the SES/delin-

quency relationship will become clear when researchers measure delinquency in such a way that the full frequency of various offenses can be captured. In much research, investigators do not use actual frequencies at all, opting instead for such response categories as never, sometimes, often, very often, and always. And sometimes, when investigators collect information about frequency, they end up analyzing the data in terms of the proportion of the various SES levels that reports some involvement or involvement above a particular magnitude (prevalence). In other instances, researchers use numerical categories but collapse the upper one; for example, a researcher might inquire about how often the respondent committed a certain act during the past year, presenting numbers 1 through 10 and a final number of 10+ (alternatively, the researcher might collect the actual number of offenses, but code all answers above 10 as an inclusive category of 10+). Thus, if lower SES respondents commit offenses far more frequently than those of other statuses, this difference will be concealed by the manner in which the data are collected or managed. . . .

The four data sets compiled since 1978 that used measures of delinquency based on frequency of offense show inconsistent results. The two most extensive data sets—the National Youth Survey and the Philadelphia cohort follow-up—produce weak, contrary or inconsistent findings, one of the more limited studies finds contrary evidence, and the other finds weak but supportive evidence. Thus, it appears that the SES/delinquency relationship cannot be specified by focusing on the full frequency of offenses, even for serious criminal acts.

Demographic Conditions

Specification by Race

Hagan (1985:121) suggests that an SES/delinquency relationship will be greater among blacks than among whites. Recent studies based on three important data sets bear on this possibility. . . .

These three data sets do not demonstrate that an SES/delinquency relationship is specific to one race or the other. Moreover, those instances revealing some tendency toward one race or the other suggest that if a racial specification were present, an association between SES and delinquency would probably be more likely among whites than blacks— the opposite of the association suggested by Hagan.

Specification by Gender

Although no theorist, to our knowledge, has set forth a specific rationale suggesting that an SES/delinquency relationship will be confined to one gender or the other, or even that such an association will be greater for one gender than the other, three studies have examined the SES/delinquency association within categories of gender.[2] Theories usually invoked as postulating SES/delinquency relationships (see Tittle 1983), however, would logically lead to the expectation that such relationships would be more prevalent among males than among females. For instance, since males are expected to achieve more than females, one might imagine that anomie will induce males to innovate more often than females. . . .

The three studies relevant to gender specification, therefore, do not demonstrate that SES and delinquency are more highly related among one gender than the other. One study reports some evidence of greater effects among males, but the other two both show contradictory internal findings depending on the measures of SES used or the method of analysis.

Context and the SES/Delinquency Relationship

Specification by Urbanness

At least two publications (Hagan, 1985: 121; Krohn et al. 1980:314) suggest that an SES/delinquency relationship will be more evident in urban than in other places. But we were able to locate only one study reporting comparative evidence on this point.

Using a sample of youths from 15 schools (nine junior high and six senior high) in three types of communities in two states, Krohn et al. (1980) calculated correlations between respondent's individual social status, as reflected by father's occupation, and three fac-tor-score-based scales of self-reported delinquency (social and hard drug use and serious delinquent behavior), as well as an additive index of minor delinquency, separately for each of the schools. Only 10 of the 60 (17%) situations showed statistically significant correlations, but seven of the eight urban junior high schools showed significant relationships between individual SES and at least one of the four delinquency measures. No significant correlations were present for any of the other junior high schools. This seemed to indicate specification by urbanness, but the pattern was not there when the senior high schools were considered. Hence, the results are only suggestive of an urbanness specification. Although the SES/delinquency relationship is more prominent in the urban schools for the younger adolescents, the fact that even among them only seven of 32 correlations proved significant calls into question even the narrower specification by urbanness and age. Moreover, the absence of any trend along those lines among the high school students is contrary to the specification in question.

An alternative method for evaluating a possible urbanness specification is to consider the magnitude and/or consistency of associations between SES and delinquency in studies using only urban samples. Ten such data sets have been used for studies since 1978. Only three of those data sets (Cernkovich, 1978; Ouston, 1984; and Simcha-Fagan and Schwartz, 1986) show significant effects in a majority of the conditions examined. Five yield contradictory results (1— Johnson, 1980; 2—Johnstone, 1978; 3— Thornberry and Christenson, 1984; Thornberry and Farnworth, 1982; Tracy, 1987; 4— Hindelang et al., 1981; Sampson, 1986; 5— Farrington, 1983; West, 1982), and two (Cernkovich and Giordano, 1979; Hagan et al., 1985) produce no significant negative associations between SES and delinquency. Although these studies collectively fail to sustain the idea that SES and delinquency are highly related in larger sized places, one must be cautious in rejecting the urbanness specification on this basis. Not only does the diversity of the studies make interpretation difficult, but there are no reasonable comparisons with smaller sized places.

Specification by Heterogeneity

Ideas about a potential specification by the heterogeneity of the social environment were formulated even before the post-1978 flurry of research into specification. Reiss and Rhodes (1963) hypothesized greater SES/delinquency associations in SES-heterogeneous schools. They reasoned that relative deprivation among lower status youths, which was thought to motivate delinquency, would be greater in heterogeneous contexts. The hypothesis was not supported by the data, however; in fact, it was more consistent with the idea that status frustration is greater in the more homogeneous schools.

Harry (1974) hypothesized the same outcome as Reiss and Rhodes, but his reasoning focused on heterogeneity of cultural influences rather than heterogeneity of social status. He believed that a pro-law culture would permeate all students in culturally homogeneous middle-class schools regardless of any individual variation in status. This would vitiate any SES/delinquency relationship. And in mixed-class schools a homogeneous amalgamated general culture would presumably emerge to contradict any SES/delinquency association. But he contended that the middle-class culture of school officials in predominantly working-class schools would conflict with the youths working-class culture, causing such youths to form a subculture. This putative subculture would presumably cause delinquency among its members, leaving the non-subculturally involved higher status youths in such schools to be guided into conformity by school officials. The result would be a negative SES/delinquency relationship only in the culturally heterogeneous contexts.

Only the previously described Krohn et al. (1980) research has tried to test the heterogeneity specification hypothesis, however, and its data are of only indirect relevance. By aggregating individual-level information for sampled individuals within each school, Krohn et al. were able to estimate the SES characteristics of their 15 schools. The schools were then grouped into three categories based on the percentage of the sample in each school with fathers in various occupational categories. This permitted study of the associations between individual SES and four measures of self-reported delinquency within each type of school context. In trying to test the Harry hypothesis, they *assumed* more cultural heterogeneity in the working-class schools, expecting an SES/delinquency relationship among only those in the working-class schools.

The results were not favorable. Only three (15%) of the 20 associations based on those in working-class schools (5 schools and 4 measures of delinquency), proved to be statistically significant, and the middle- and upper-middle-class schools produced seven (18 percent) significant correlations out of 40. Thus, it appears that cultural or social heterogeneity is not the key to specifying the SES/delinquency relationship. But again, a firm conclusion would be premature because Krohn et al. had no actual measure of heterogeneity.

Specification by SES of the Context

Johnstone (1978) maintains that lower status youths will experience severe relative deprivation in higher status contexts, leading to high rates of delinquency, and that higher status youths, lacking deprivation, will have relatively low rates of delinquency. Conversely, lower status youths in lower status contexts will experience little deprivation because they will compare themselves with other lower status youths and will therefore commit relatively little delinquency. But higher status youths will also feel little relative deprivation in the lower status context. Although Johnstone was mainly interested in explaining variations in absolute levels of delinquency, his argument implies that the association between SES and delinquency will be confined to higher status contexts because the large discrepancy in status there should motivate lower status youths to delinquency. But in lower status contexts there will be little variation in delinquency among the SES levels because no status group is relatively deprived. By extension, modest associations between SES and delinquency should prevail in middle-status contexts.

Although various authors have measured the SES characteristics of social contexts and of the individuals therein (e.g., Sampson, 1986; Simcha-Fagan and Schwartz, 1986; Thornberry and Farnworth, 1982), only two recent studies have examined the strength of association between an individual's SES and delinquency within contexts that vary in overall SES. Although Krohn et al. (1980) interpret their data only with respect to a potential heterogeneity specification, the SES specification can also be evaluated from their data. They found slightly more instances of an SES/delinquency relationship in the middle and upper status schools, which provides some small support for the Johnstone hypothesis.

Johnstone (1978) himself reported results from a survey of 1,200 youths in the Chicago SMSA, which he combined with information from the 1970 census. Individual SES was measured with a composite, trichotomized index using weighted educational and occupational components from the survey. The SES of the census tract where the youth lived was measured by the average educational, occupational, and income characteristics as revealed in the census (each component was trichotomized and summed and the resulting sum was trichotomized). Delinquency was measured with eight indices reflecting differing types of self-reported offenses and degrees of seriousness. The relationship between SES and delinquency proved to be lowest in the low-status contexts for all eight measures of delinquency. But the highest associations between SES and delinquency were not in the high-status contexts as he predicted. Rather, they were in the medium-status contexts for seven of the eight measures. Thus, Johnstone's own data only partially confirm his hypothesized SES contextual specification. Moreover, because his method of presentation prohibits measuring associations between SES and delinquency directly (he used rank-order analysis), one cannot tell how strong even the supporting data are. These two studies, therefore, do not confirm or negate the hypothesis of an SES/delinquency specification by the SES of the context. One of them is contradictory and the other is only partially supportive.

The evidence concerning specification of an SES/delinquency relationship by characteristics of the social context is both meager and generally nonsupportive. Thus, although too little research has been done to draw a firm conclusion, it appears from the research that has been conducted that characteristics of the social context will not specify when delinquency and SES will be related.

Summary

Research published since 1978, using both official and self-reported data, suggests again (cf. Tittle et al., 1978) that there is no pervasive relationship between individual SES and delinquency. Although 18 of 21 studies (including three—Cernkovich, 1978; McCord, 1979; Wadsworth, 1979—that report the magnitude of this association only for a whole sample) report finding *at least one condition* under which there is a significant relationship between SES and delinquency,[3] the overall proportion of investigated conditions in which such relationships were found is less than 20%.[4] Nevertheless, since this figure exceeds chance, it confirms the wisdom of searching for specific circumstances under which an SES/delinquency relationship might exist. If SES is related to delinquency only sometimes, then scientific imperatives require one to look for systematic patterns whereby those relationships occur. Only then can we construct theories with statements of scope (Walker and Cohen, 1985) that enable one to account for reality.

The search for specification has so far proven disappointing, however. Our review of the recent evidence concerning 12 hypothesized specifying conditions has failed to find any hypothesized specification that is sustained by the evidence. Perhaps it is premature to conclude from this that none of the hypothesized conditions does in fact specify an SES/delinquency relationship. After all, some of the conditions have hardly been researched at all. Particularly lacking is research on contextual specifications and on the youth's status specification suggested by Stark (1979). In addition, much of the research about some of the hypothesized specifications is not directly addressed to the relevant issue, and some of the measures of the specifying conditions may be questionable. Finally, drawing general conclusions about the hypotheses requires aggregation of diverse studies, many of which may not be comparable. For all these reasons, it would be erroneous to conclude that an SES/delinquency relationship is not specifiable. However, it is correct to say that it has not yet been specified.

Discussion

Where does this leave us, then, in trying to account for delinquency with the help of SES? It appears, on the basis of the recent evidence, that SES may not be nearly so important as many seem to think (Braithwaite, 1981; Kleck, 1982; Nettler, 1978, 1985), but it may well be more important than others have concluded (Tittle et al., 1978). But the circumstances under which individual SES plays a role in delinquency production remains elusive. Sometimes SES does appear to predict delinquency; most of the time it does not.

One response to this reality is to continue to try to find the conditions under which SES predicts delinquency. Much remains to be investigated, and the quality of research can surely be improved. Moreover, scientists are always intrigued by a puzzle, and this is a puzzle of the highest order, particularly since the unruliness of the SES variable seems to challenge a number of theories (but see Tittle, 1983, for a contrary point of view).

A second approach, pioneered by Colvin and Pauly (1983) and by Hagan and his associates (1985), would reconceptualize the problem in terms of interactions among SES and other variables that ultimately have import for delinquency. The focus then is neither on whether SES is generally related to delinquency nor on the conditions wherein it might be so related. Rather, the focus is on the way in which SES sets the parameters within which social structural and other factors impinge on delinquency. Within that framework there would be little reason to expect a direct effect of SES on delinquency, although there would be many reasons to expect indirect effects that would only become

apparent after the intricate processes of social life were explicated. Once the scholarly community as a whole moves to that more sophisticated level, dogged attempts to prove that SES, in some form or circumstance, must be related to delinquency will probably seem primitive.

A third strategy would be to rethink the whole idea of SES and its potential effects on delinquency. After all, SES, no matter how conceptualized, is no more than a configurative concept, presumably amalgamating many specific attributes (Loeber and Dishion, 1983). To achieve a general summary measure of a concept like this, one must blur particular details. But in reality it may be the blurred details that are important in understanding delinquency. For instance, if SES supposedly predicts youthful misbehavior because more lower status than higher status youths are deprived, it would make more sense to measure deprivation directly than to measure SES, which is a step removed from the real variable at issue. In addition, since deprivation is usually perceived by the individual in relative terms, it may better be conceived as a subjective variable. Hence, it is quite likely that many higher status youths *feel* relatively deprived even though they may not be objectively deprived. Indeed, many higher status youths may actually be objectively deprived of intelligence, looks, athletic ability, or other attributes. Thus, SES may be a poor proxy for the numerous causal variables that are supposedly embodied within it.

If our reasoning is correct, the knotty problem of individual delinquent behavior would best be approached by attempting to build better theory that owes no allegiance to SES. This need not be an intellectually painful process, but it will require a shift from the use of a configurative concept to a more precise identification of those variables that may really matter with respect to delinquency, possibly including values, bonding, peer structure, relative deprivation, community social climate, attitudes, and others. It will also require an examination of the assumptions and underlying logic that have for generations led scholars to focus on the potential interrelationship of such factors around "social class" (see Meier, 1985). Some might see this agenda as possibly calling for dismantling extant theories, supposedly based on SES as an explanatory variable, in order to identify the crucial underlying factors that presumably affect juvenile misconduct (Cernkovich, 1978). Still others might view this agenda as preliminary to the construction of integrated models in which the variables so identified are combined with others to build new theories. But regardless of how the process is viewed, some disaggregation of the social class concept appears necessary for improvement of existing theories and development of new ones. Although involving hard conceptual and theoretical work, such an approach would appear to be in everyone's best interests.

Discussion Questions

1. Why is the evidence concerning the effect of SES on delinquency seen as "problematic"? What are the findings?

2. Discuss the ways in which the SES/delinquency relationship is contingent on how the dependent variable, delinquency, is measured.

3. What demographic conditions interact with the SES/delinquency relationship? In what ways do they affect it? How does the context affect the SES/delinquency relationship?

Notes

1. In dealing with this issue it is useful to differentiate the literature concerning delinquency from that concerning adult crime. Because overlap between the two is often incomplete, it may be misleading to generalize from one to the other. This is particularly true because studies of SES and delinquency include status offenses and/or other misbehaviors that are not criminal but are relevant to tests of theories of deviance and/or delinquency. Therefore, our concern is specifically the delinquency literature.

2. Other studies (Cernkovich and Giordano, 1979; Figueira-McDonough et al., 1981) examine gender differences in delinquency but do not examine an SES/delinquency relationship within gender categories.

3. Some scholars would regard this as overwhelming evidence of the generality of an

SES/delinquency relationship (e.g., Braithwaite, 1981). It appears to us, however, that the real issue is not whether one can usually find some condition that will yield a significant negative SES/delinquency relationship, but rather whether such a relationship is persistent across a variety of conditions, and if not, can the circumstances under which it emerges be specified in a systematic and empirically supportable way.

4. It is practically impossible to establish this figure exactly because some researchers do not report measures of significance; some researchers report their data in such a way that it is difficult to ascertain even the magnitude of association; some of the instances examined involve analyses of the same data by different researchers with contradictory results; and sometimes it appears that the failure to achieve significance is the result of researcher's having broken the samples into subgroups with N's too small to demonstrate a significant relationship even when the association is relatively large. We counted all instances in which the SES/delinquency relationship was examined by some scholar for a specific subgroup or for some specific condition of measurement and then divided into the number that were statistically significant (or appeared that they might if it were possible to calculate an appropriate statistic or the N of the subsample was of a reasonable size), using the significant finding in those cases in which different authors found contradictory results from the same data. This produced a percentage of 16%, but in order to allow for possible error we prefer to grant the possibility of as many as 20% of the instances yielding significant associations.

References

Akers, Ronald L. 1964. "Socioeconomic status and delinquent behavior: A retest." *Journal of Research in Crime and Delinquency,* 1:38-46.

Arnold, William R. 1966. "Continuities in research: Scaling delinquent behavior." *Social Problems,* 13:59-66.

Braithwaite, John. 1981. "The myth of social class and criminality reconsidered." *American Sociological Review,* 46:36-57.

Brown, Stephen E. 1984. "Social class, child maltreatment, and delinquent behavior." *Criminology,* 22:259-278.

Brownfield, David. 1986. "Social class and violent behavior." *Criminology,* 24:421-438.

Cernkovich, Steven A. 1978. "Value orientations and delinquency involvement." *Criminology,* 15:443-458.

Cernkovich, Steven and Peggy Giordano. 1979. "A comparative analysis of male and female delinquency." *Sociological Quarterly,* 20:131-14.

Clark, John P. and Eugene P. Wenninger. 1962. "Socio-economic class and area as correlates of illegal behavior among juveniles." *American Sociological Review,* 27:826-834.

Clelland, Donald and Timothy J. Carter. 1980. "The new myth of class and crime." *Criminology,* 18:319-336.

Coleman, James S. 1961. *Adolescent Society.* New York: Free Press.

Colvin, Mark and John Pauly. 1983. "A critique of criminology: Toward an integrated structural marxist theory of delinquency production." *American Journal of Sociology,* 89:513-551.

Dentler, Robert A. and Lawrence J. Monroe. 1961. "Social correlates of early adolescent theft." *American Sociological Review,* 26:733-743.

Elliott, Delbert S. and Suzanne S. Ageton. 1980. "Reconciling race and class differences in self-reported and official estimates of delinquency." *American Sociological Review,* 45:95-110.

Elliott, Delbert S. and David Huizinga. 1983. "Social class and delinquent behavior in a national youth panel." *Criminology,* 21:149-177.

Farrington, David P. 1983. "Further Analyses of a Longitudinal Survey of Crime and Delinquency." *Final report to the National Institute of Justice.* Washington, D.C.

Figueira-McDonough, Josefina, William H. Barton, and Rosemary C. Sarri. 1981. "Normal deviance: Gender similarities in adolescent subcultures." In Marguerite Q. Warren (ed.), *Comparing Female and Male Offenders.* Beverly Hills, Calif.: Sage.

Hagan, John. 1985. *Modern Criminology: Crime, Criminal Behavior, and Its Control.* New York: McGraw-Hill.

Hagan, John, A. R. Gillis, and John Simpson. 1985. "The class structure of gender and delinquency: Toward a power-control theory of common delinquent behavior." *American Journal of Sociology,* 90:1151-1178.

Harry, Joseph. 1974. "Social class and delinquency: One more time." *Sociological Quarterly,* 15:294-301..

Hindelang, Michael, Travis Hirschi, and Joseph G. Weis. 1979. "Correlates of delinquency: The illusion of discrepancy between self-report and official measures." *American Sociological Review,* 44:995-1014.

——. 1981. *Measuring Delinquency.* Beverly Hills, Calif.: Sage.

Hirschi, Travis. 1969. *Causes of Delinquency.* Berkeley: University of California Press.

Johnson, Richard E. 1980. "Social class and delinquent behavior: A new test." *Criminology,* 18:86-93.

Johnstone, John W. C. 1978. "Social class, social areas and delinquency." *Sociology and Social Research,* 63:49-72.

Kleck, Gary. 1982. "On the use of self-report to determine the class distribution of criminal and delinquent behavior." *American Sociological Review,* 47:427-433.

Krohn, Marvin D., Ronald L. Akers, Marcia J. Radosevich, and Lonn Lanza-Kaduce. 1980. "Social status and deviance." *Criminology,* 18:303-318.

Loeber, Rolf and Thomas Dishion. 1983. "Early predictors of male delinquency: A review." *Psychological Bulletin,* 94:68-99.

McCord, Joan. 1979. "Some child-rearing antecedents of criminal behavior in adult men." *Journal of Personality and Social Psychology,* 37:1477-1486.

McDonald, Lynn. 1968. *Social Class and Delinquency.* New York: Archon.

Meier, Robert F. (ed.) 1985. *Theoretical Methods in Criminology.* Beverly Hills, Calif.: Sage.

Nettler, Gwynn. 1978. "Social status and self-reported criminality." *Social Forces,* 57:304-305.

——. 1985. "Social class and crime, one more time." *Social Forces,* 63:1076-1077.

Nye, F. Ivan and James F. Short. 1957. "Scaling delinquent behavior." *American Sociological Review,* 22:326-331.

Nye, F. Ivan, James F. Short, and Virgil Olson. 1958. *Socioeconomic Review,* 63:381-389.

Ouston, Janet. 1984. "Delinquency, family background, and educational attainment." *British Journal of Criminology,* 24:2-26.

Polk, Kenneth, Christine Adler, Gordon Bazemore, Gerald Blake, Sheila Cordray, Gary Coventry, James Galvin, and Mark Temple. 1981. "Becoming Adult: An Analysis of Maturational Development from Age 16 to 30 of a Cohort of Young Men." *Final Report, Grant No. MH14806, Center for Studies of Crime and Delinquency, National Institute of Mental Health.* Washington, DC: U.S. Department of Health and Human Services.

Reiss, Albert J. and Albert L. Rhodes. 1961. "The distribution of juvenile delinquency in the social class structure." *American Sociological Review,* 26:720-732.

——. 1963. "Status deprivation and delinquent behavior." *Sociological Quarterly,* 4:135-149.

Sampson, Robert J. 1986. "Effects of socioeconomic context on official reaction to juvenile delinquency." *American Sociological Review*, 51:876-885.

Sellin, Thorsten and Marvin Wolfgang. 1978. *The Measurement of Delinquency*. 1964. Montclair, N.J.: Patterson Smith.

Simcha-Fagan, Ora and Joseph F. Schwartz. 1986. "Neighborhood and delinquency: An assessment of contextual effects." *Criminology*, 24:667-703.

Slocum, Walter L. and Carol L. Stone. 1963. "Family culture patterns and delinquent type behavior." *Journal of Marriage and Family Living*, 25:202-208.

Stark, Rodney. 1979. "Whose status counts?" *American Sociological Review*, 44:668-669.

Thornberry, Terence P. and R. L. Christenson. 1984. "Unemployment and criminal involvement: An investigation of reciprocal causal structure." *American Sociological Review*, 49:398-411.

Thornberry, Terence P. and Margaret Farnworth. 1982. "Social correlates of criminal involvement: Further evidence of the relationship between social status and criminal behavior." *American Sociological Review*, 47:505-518.

Tittle, Charles R. 1983. "Social class and criminal behavior: A critique of the theoretical foundation." *Social Forces*, 62:334-358.

——. 1985. "A plea for open minds, one more time: Response to Nettler." *Social Forces*, 63:1078-1080.

Tittle, Charles R. and Wayne J. Villemez. 1978. "Response to Gwynn Nettler." *Social Forces*, 57:306-307.

Tittle, Charles R., Wayne J. Villemez, and Douglas A. Smith. 1978. "The myth of social class and criminality: An empirical assessment of the empirical evidence." *American Sociological Review*, 43:643-656.

——. 1979. "Reply to Stark." *American Sociological Review*, 44:669-670.

——. 1982. "One step forward, two steps back: More on the class/criminality controversy." *American Sociological Review*, 47:435-438.

Tracy, Paul E., Jr. 1987. "Race and class differentials in official and self-reported delinquency." In Martin E. Wolfgang, Terence P. Thornberry, and Robert M. Figlio (eds.), *From Boy to Man, From Delinquency to Crime*. Chicago: University of Chicago Press.

Vaz, Edmund W. 1966. "Self-reported juvenile delinquency and socioeconomic status." *Canadian Journal of Corrections*, 8:20-27.

Wadsworth, Michael. 1979. *Roots of Delinquency: Infancy, Adolescence and Crime*. New York: Barnes and Noble.

Walker, Henry A. and Bernard P. Cohen. 1985. "Scope statements: Imperatives for evaluating theory." *American Sociological Review*, 50:288-301.

West, Donald J. 1982. *Delinquency: Its Roots, Careers, and Prospects*. London: Heinemann.

West, Donald J. and David P. Farrington. 1973. *Who Becomes Delinquent?* London: Heinemann.

Winslow, Robert H. 1967. "Anomie and its alternatives: A self-report study of delinquency." *Sociological Quarterly*, 8:468-480.

Wolfgang, Marvin E., Robert M. Figlio, and Thorsten Sellin. 1972. *Delinquency in a Birth Cohort*. Chicago: University of Chicago Press.

Wright, Eric O. and Luca Perrone. 1977. "Marxist class categories and income inequality." *American Sociological Review*, 42:32-55.

11

Explaining the Black Homicide Rate

Darnell F. Hawkins

Race has been a correlate of crime for as long as modern social scientists have been examining these variables. The rate of crime, especially homicide, has been and continues to be higher for African Americans than for whites. Are blacks genetically predisposed to violence or is their involvement in such crimes a vestige of slavery and the contemporary aftermath—social prejudice and discrimination? Or, is black crime and violence the result of socioeconomic conditions that have relegated so many African Americans to an underclass status that is nearly impossible to escape? In this reading, Darnell Hawkins asks and answers these questions while critically examining various theoretical explanations of the disproportionate rate of black homicide.

Until recently, explanations of black crime and violence were rooted in the ongoing effects of slavery, inequality, and discrimination. Hawkins refers to these as "external" reasons for black-white crime differences, circumstances residing outside the black community and over which African Americans had little control. Present-day theorists are just as likely, however, to emphasize "internal" conditions as well, those over which the minority community has some control. The social disorganization of black communities and the subculture of violence that some contend is perpetuated in black communities are often cited as more important than the legacy of slavery and discrimination.

Hawkins demonstrates the interaction between traditional external conditions and more contemporary internal circumstances. In so doing, he makes a strong case for the det-rimental impact of economic inequality and racial discrimination. He is emphatic in his conclusion that deprivation, whether one is black or white, is linked to high rates of homicide. Discrimination imposes an economic burden on African Americans that is not comparable to that of any other group. In the end, black violence must be understood in the context of both historical legacy and modern socioeconomic conditions.

Numerous attempts have been made to devise theories to explain the etiology of homicide. These include explanations that focus on the psychosocial traits of individual offenders as well as on group and societal characteristics. Ethnic and racial group differences in the rate of homicide have been noted in many societies, as have the effects of racial and ethnic heterogeneity on rates of violence across societies. The comparatively high rate of homicide among American Blacks has been well documented during the last half-century. Nevertheless, relatively few theories of the etiology of homicide specifically address the question of what accounts for racial differences.

In the current discussion the literature of the past 50 years on homicide in the United States is reviewed in an attempt to identify explanations that have been offered for the extremely high rate of homicide among Blacks. Although somewhat cursory, this review reveals significant patterns. First, theory-oriented discussions of this phenomenon were more common at the turn of the century than during recent decades. A notable exception may be the work of a few theorists within the "subculture" tradition. Recent literature consists primarily of quantitative assessments of rate differences. The researchers within this tradition offer few explicit explanations for the Black-White homicide differential.

On the other hand, implicit reasons for racial differences are embedded in the methods used to study homicide in the U.S. In particular, Black-White comparisons in criminology are implicitly etiological, in that they presuppose various ways that race influences group differences. These presuppositions are an integral part of the social scientific view of race relations and social life among Blacks that has persisted for most of the twentieth century.

Many of the ideas central to this implicit theorizing have been the target of increasing criticism and debate during recent years. One major area of disagreement concerns the causal significance of historical and economic factors for the persistence of current levels of sociopathology among American Blacks. Many have questioned the extent to which slavery's legacy and present-day poverty and inequality provide explanations for the current Black-White crime rate differential. We will explore these issues by first examining more closely the nature of the theory that is implicit in Black-White comparisons in American social science.

The Comparison is the Message

Social data differentiated by race has been routinely collected by governmental agencies and social researchers for many decades. Black-White comparisons have been common in social science research for most of this century. So common has this practice become that researchers frequently collect and analyze such data without any theoretically grounded reason for doing so. Such data have constituted a kind of "moral statistic" during the past, and during recent decades, its collection has been prompted by legal scrutiny of racial discrimination. Social scientists have documented racial differences in values and public opinion: the number of persons living in poverty, raised in single-parent homes, born to teen mothers, or arrested for various criminal acts. Such comparisons have been ubiquitous among both Black and White researchers and observers, making Blacks perhaps the most widely studied racial/ethnic group in the United States (Jaynes and Williams, 1989).

These differences are routinely reported and are a well-known feature of the social landscape as surveyed by social scientists or the mass media. Yet very little theory is brought to bear to explain these differences. Like any other comparisons within social science, racial comparisons are appropriate when past empirical research informs clear hypotheses about reasons for systematic group differences. But many Black-White comparisons in American social research today are made in knee-jerk fashion and without explanation, as if reasons for observed differences were "common knowledge."

It is tempting to dismiss such seemingly theoretical studies as "mindless empiricism." But dismissing them ignores the real impact that these studies have as theory-laden "moral statistics" and political documents.[1] This article argues that a vast array of presumptions, metatheory, and theory is an integral part of such comparisons. In a society such as the United States, where race and racism have so greatly affected everyday life, these race-related theoretical underpinnings have achieved the status of common knowledge. As "common knowledge," however, they are far from harmless or noncontroversial. Black-White comparisons, although obviously useful, frequently become themselves the "message" (to paraphrase Marshall McLuhan). As silent, implicit theory, this message remains an uncontested but potentially damaging aspect of American race relations and politics.

The implicit conceptualizations and theory evident in Black-White comparisons are best revealed through an examination of the "findings" and "conclusions" that have been reported by American race relations researchers. Among them are the following:

1. When analyzed in the aggregate, most measures of various social phenomena will reveal that Blacks are more "disadvantaged" than Whites.

2. Race has been a significant "causal" factor in the distribution of advantages in the United States.

3. Most Black deficits are attributable to "social" causes. These include the legacy of slavery and oppression and continuing racism and inequality. These causes may also include sociocultural factors not linked directly to slavery and oppression such as African cultural heritage or sociocultural patterns unique to American Blacks that have arisen since the end of slavery.

4. To the extent that Black-White differences are not attributable to "social" causes, genetic differences may explain variance.

In their various forms, these themes underlie most social scientific comparisons of Blacks and Whites in the United States, whether the concern is teenage pregnancy, unemployment, or crime. They are the core of liberal race relations theory and research within the American social sciences (Vander Zanden, 1973, as cited in Pettigrew, 1980, p. xxxi). Let us now turn our attention to the criminological literature and consider the origin and development of these themes in early research on homicide.

Race and Homicide Rates

In comparison to almost all other types of crime, data on homicide have been affected less by problems of reliability and validity. One of the first major social scientific inquiries devoted entirely to the analysis of homicide (Brearley, 1932) reported that the rate among Blacks was more than seven times that for Whites. Official crime and mortality data and a large number of empirical studies conducted since Brearley's have merely documented the persistence of this racial difference. The work of Wolfgang (1958), for example, and numerous follow-up studies in that tradition have been largely data-driven and nontheoretical (Hawkins, 1986). When explicit explanations are offered, they are generally derived from reasons offered by Brearley for the race differences that he observed. Much the same can be said of the significant studies of national homicide patterns by Henry and Short (1954) and Pettigrew and Spier (1962).

In a chapter entitled, "The Negro and Homicide," Brearley (1932) reviewed a range of explanations for the disproportionate incidence of homicide among Blacks that was common during the early twentieth century. He noted that these explanations range from more credible ones to those based on prejudice or hasty generalizations. Among the various explanations outlined in his chapter were the following (pp. 111-116):

1. The West African cultural heritage from which most Black Americans originally came is characterized by a disregard for the sanctity of human life. This disregard was strengthened by the brutal conditions under which Blacks were forced to live in the New World.

2. Because of their peculiar genetically-determined temperament, Blacks lack the power to control themselves in accordance with the requirements of others.

3. Blacks are characterized by excessive emotionality which can be attributed partly to their evolution in climatic conditions characterized by excessive heat.

4. "Their education and training is less; their poverty is greater and consequently their housing and living conditions are more deplorable; there is less provision made for colored defectives; they are in a more or less unstable condition because they have but lately been given freedom and many of them, especially in the cities and the North, are in a new and strange environment; they are discriminated against socially and industrially; they are often abused by the police; and sometimes, at least, not fairly treated by the courts" (p. 115, quoting Reuter, 1927, p. 363).

5. The high homicide rate of Blacks may be more apparent than real. If interracial slayings were eliminated, and a careful study made of comparable groups of Whites and Blacks of the same economic, educational, and social status and the same inability to secure justice except by recourse to violence, approximately equal homicide rates might be found for the two races.

These were the common explanations for Black sociopathology that emerged during the decades immediately following the Civil War. Some were merely popular explanations for the group crime rate differences (within and across races) during this period. Others were popular conceptions specifically of Blacks. A comparison between Brearley's list and that derived from the current literature review reveals that social scientists have rejected the more racist and nonpositivist explanations. But when attempting to explain the high rate of Black homicide, many contemporary researchers have merely repeated more acceptable items from the Brearley listing without major modification or theoretical elaboration. This practice is especially evident in the numerous post-Wolfgang case studies of homicide in selected urban areas (Block, 1975; Bourdouris, 1970; Lundsgaarde, 1977; Pokorny, 1965; Voss and Hepburn, 1968). Further, implicit in most multicity quantitative analyses is a Brearley-type listing, since measures of poverty, inequality, population density, and so forth, are often included in the multivariate models without sufficient theoretical justification (Blau and Blau, 1982; Messner, 1982, 1983; Messner and Tardiff, 1986). The result is a kind of nonfocused "shopping list" of reasons for the high rate of homicide among Blacks.

This "shopping list" approach to explaining the disproportionate rate of Black homicide—listing a range of sociocultural, historical-structural, economic, social psychological, biological and other factors that may contribute to the high incidence of homicide among Blacks—does not provide the guidance needed to shape policy. During the past several decades, the etiology of crime has been conceptualized most often in terms of multiple factor causation. Researchers typically argue that no single cause of any form of criminal behavior can be isolated, and they make little effort to assess the possible primacy of certain causal factors in comparison to others. But acknowledging the existence of multiple causes does not mean that all causal factors are equally important. Durkheim and other theorists noted that many factors contribute to the etiology of crime, but they also noted the causal primacy of certain factors in comparison to others.

Although little explicit theorizing has addressed the possible primacy of different causal factors in the etiology of Black homicide, recent investigations reveal a major change in the choice of explanations offered. Researchers examining Black-White homicide differences have noticeably shifted in their assumptions about the general "locus of causation." The tendency during recent years has been to emphasize "internal" as opposed to "external" factors. As part of this shift, a few researchers have attacked the now traditional focus on slavery and racial oppression as the major sources of explanation for the Black-White differential. These themes are explored next.

External Versus Internal Causation

The terms "internal" and "external" are useful as a heuristic device as long as they are not taken to imply the existence of mutually exclusive and unrelated phenomena. Many researchers acknowledge that certain "internal" conditions stem directly from various "external" forces. This article uses the terms to describe those causal factors that researchers appear to regard as primary—a distinction similar to the notion of proximate as opposed to less immediate causation in legal reasoning.

From Brearley through Wolfgang and into the 1960s and 1970s, the dominant explanations offered for the high rate of Black homicides were external. Although Brearley listed a number of competing explanations, he himself favored the explanation offered by Reuter (1927), cited earlier. Writing when slavery and the Reconstruction era were not distant memories and racial segregation and oppression were common in both the South and non-South, Brearley stressed the significance of social-structural factors, such as racial oppression. As Pettigrew (1980) has noted, this emphasis was evident in all areas of race relations research during this period.

Wolfgang, too, saw the high rate of Black homicide as primarily the result of the legacy of slavery and postslavery discrimination and oppression. Wolfgang and Ferracuti (1982) labeled as "subculture of violence" those social conditions that were "internal" to the Black community (e.g., social disorganization), and saw them as important contributors to sociopathology. They did, however, see these internal factors as themselves caused largely by external forces, specifically White racism.

As the 20th century wanes, no new explanations for the Black-White homicide differential (or other forms of Black sociopathology) have emerged. The internal colonialist explanations offered by Blauner (1972) has never been systematically applied to the study of crime, although the potential exists for such application. Building on ideas similar to those presented by Fanon (1963, 1967) and Memmi (1967), Blauner viewed Black Americans as a colonized people despite the legal gains of the 1960s. Fanon (1963, 1967) noted the high level of intragroup violence found among colonized peoples, and attributed it to the self-hatred that results from colonialist oppression. Marxist theorists have seldom addressed the question of what accounts for racial differences in levels of violence. Since the late 1970s and early 1980s, however, considerable debate has centered around several important questions, all generated because the rate of violent crime among Blacks has failed to decline significantly during the last half-century (see Lane, 1986).

Increasingly, researchers question the causal significance of the two most commonly cited "external" reasons for Black-White differences—slavery and its legacy, and continued inequality and discrimination. One current argument maintains that many of the most blatant forms of racial discrimination have been alleviated during the past three decades. Some researchers ask: If discrimination contributes to the Black crime rate, why haven't the two phenomena fallen off together? In addition, many researchers have questioned whether poverty explains the patterning of homicide within or across groups. They note the absence of a significant statistical correlation in some studies between area homicide and poverty rates. Some have noted that neither absolute nor relative deprivation alone or together can fully explain the distribution of homicide (Messner, 1982). Although not definitive, these and related research findings buttress arguments that the Black-White homicide differential may not result primarily from such external causes as current Black economic disadvantage. Yet these researchers provide few alternative explanations.

Similarly, many researchers are questioning the viability of the argument that this country's history of slavery affects current Black crime patterns. Even if the effects of slavery can be shown to have contributed to high rates of Black homicide during the early 20th century, these researchers ask how significant are such effects today—nearly 125 years after slavery's end? The very persistence of Black disadvantage and sociopathology has been used, among other things, to call into question explanations that emphasize the significance of slavery and past oppression. That is, the temporal distance between current social conditions and slavery is said to cast doubt on its role as a major causal factor. The legal reforms of the 1960s have been cited as further evidence of the demise of slavery-produced social institutions and practices in modern American society.

As the traditional liberal explanations for Black sociopathology have been attacked, a group of researchers sometimes identified as Black conservatives has begun to explore other possible external causes. This group has also focused on alleged causes of Black disadvantage that are presumably internal to the Black community. The most prominent among these researchers are Sowell (1981, 1986) and Loury (1985, 1987). Regardless of the merit of their arguments, their major contribution has been to address the question of Black-White difference from a more theoretical perspective. The issues they raise are not new but part of a long line of work carried on by both Black and White researchers since the turn of the century.[2]

One question argued by these investigators regards which phenomenon was the greater contributor to 20th-century Black disadvantage: slavery or the massive rural-South-to-urban-North migration of the turn of the century? Frazier (1957) posed this question and concluded that the migration was a major cause of Black social disorganization and the crime it spawned in the urban North during the first half of this century. Other researchers have noted that migration to urban America was a source of sociopathology not only for Blacks but also for various White ethnic groups entering the country. This argument was a central theme of the Chicago school of sociology (Park, Burgess, and McKenzie, 1928) and was later popularized by Banfield (1970) and Glazer (1971).

This immigrant analogy was used to predict that as Blacks became economically successful, fully socialized urban residents, their rates of sociopathology would drop. Irish Americans are frequently cited as an especially impressive example of such a transformation. After being the target of religious and ethnic prejudice for many decades and being regarded as prone to criminality, they are now said to be model Americans. Greeley (1974, pp. 42-43) and Schaefer (1979, pp. 129-143) showed that by the 1960s and 1970s, the average income earned by Irish Catholics was equal to that earned by most other major ethnic groups, nearly equal to the income of Jewish Americans, and greater than that earned by German Americans. These statistics and those for other ethnic and racial groups, including some more recent non-White immigrants, are often presented in contradistinction to data that document persisting Black disadvantage (Lane, 1986).

These and other attacks on traditional liberal explanations have left researchers without adequate explanations for the persistence of high rates of homicide among Blacks. The recent media coverage of the rapid rise in the homicide rate for the nation's capital has highlighted a paucity of theory and solutions. The current rate of Black homicide is much the same as that observed by Brearley more than 50 years ago. The failure of criminologists and other social scientists to offer explanations for this significant aspect of Black disadvantage represents a failure of both liberal and radical social theory in the United States. Liberal race relations theory is the product of reformist and activist impulses aimed at discounting biological notions of racial difference and ameliorating the social conditions of Black Americans. Given such a legacy, the high rate of crime among Blacks has been problematic—as much a political embarrassment as a topic for scientific scrutiny. Criminologists of a liberal bent have chosen to emphasize and investigate the problems of bias in the administration of justice rather than the problem of disproportionate killing among Blacks. Yet, given the continued political and scientific salience of this social problem, different lines of explanations have been pursued. Many researchers have turned to an emphasis on "internal" factors to account for the high rate of criminal violence among Blacks.

Internal Factors Cited

The self-perpetuating subculture. The concept of a subculture has a long history in sociological research. Subcultural theory of the etiology of homicide was both implicit and explicit in Brearley's 1932 work and that of later researchers, notably Henry and Short (1954), Wolfgang (1958), Wolfgang and Spier (1962), and Lundsgaarde (1977). It has been the preeminent explanation for the etiology of crime for the past 50 years. The concept has been used frequently to explain the behavior of White ethnic groups (including southern Whites), as well as that of non-Whites. Indeed, the idea of a pathological Black subculture is implicit in much social research of the last 100 years. Within criminology, Wolfgang and Ferracuti (1982) formalized this theory into the notion of a subculture of violence.

As the persuasiveness of "external" explanations for Black sociopathology has weakened, many researchers have returned to Wolfgang's "subculture of violence" thesis. They have tended, however, to leave out Wolfgang's consideration of the force of external factors in shaping the subculture. While Wolfgang and Ferracuti have been criticized for failing to give sufficient weight to external factors, more recent theorists rely on a concept of subculture that pays even less attention to the interaction of dominant culture and subculture. Indeed, many recent analysts explicitly argue that slavery and postslavery racism do not explain the Black-White crime differential. History and current economic inequalities are acknowledged, but the Black community is depicted as an isolated, wholly self-perpetuating, pathological subculture (Curtis, 1975; Silberman, 1978). Such a subculture is said to be perpetuated less by White racism than by a lack of self-help among Blacks. This line of argument has become more persuasive in a post-civil-rights-law era, in which affirmative action programs and much attention to the Black underclass have not conspicuously improved the welfare of the majority of Blacks.

Genes and violence. The other major internal explanation for both intra- and intergroup crime differentials is that different groups are genetically more or less predisposed to violence. As previously noted, Brearley (1932) mentioned the possibility that constitutional differences between Blacks and Whites may explain their differing levels of homicide. Brearley de-emphasized this explanation, however, in favor of external causes. Notions of genetic differences between the races are obviously part of the implicit theory embedded in modern Black-White comparisons. The demise of liberal and radical perspectives on Black disadvantage opens the door to explicit theory linking social behavior and biological traits.

Wilson and Herrnstein (1985) provided one of the most recent restatements of the genetic/biological theory. They discounted most external explanations, including any version of the subculture of violence theory, as inadequate for explaining the Black-White crime differential. While acknowledging the limitation of all theories, including their own, to completely account for Black-White crime differences, they argued that genetic differences cannot be ignored. Both the research credentials of the authors and the absence of counter arguments have led to much scholarly and public receptiveness to this line of explanation.

Economic Inequality and Discrimination Revisited

How convincing are these alternative explanations for the high rate of homicide among Blacks? Are they supported by empirical research? It is proposed here that we must not abandon the idea that past and present racial discrimination and economic inequality are major contributors to the high rate of homicide among Blacks. The Black-White homicide differential results from the structure of American society, not from genetic or other deficiencies originating with Blacks as a group. Neither the quantitative criminological research on homicide nor any other research has discredited the importance of these factors for understanding both historical and contemporary rates of violence among Blacks.

Indeed, many research findings and other observations argue for a continuing emphasis on inequality and discrimination as significant causal factors. Despite some findings to the contrary, a significant correlation has been shown to exist among societal inequality, discrimination, and homicide (Vold and Bernard, 1986). Deprivation, whether relative or absolute, is linked to high rates of homicide. Among all groups in the United States, regardless of race, homicide is found disproportionately among the lowest socioeconomic groups. Among Blacks, homicide is concentrated among the underclass. Given their methods, researchers have not been able to discount the importance of purely economic inequality (as opposed to its possible subcultural correlates) for explaining comparably high rates of homicide among Blacks, Native Americans, and southern Whites, as well as among many White ethnic immigrants during the years immediately following their entry into the United States.

Indeed, given the clustering of homicide among poor populations within societies with high levels of economic inequality, one can question the appropriateness of the traditional Black-White comparisons found in social research. That is, we must begin to ask such questions as these: What is the appropriate White group for comparison with the Black population? Is it poor Whites? Is it Whites of Southern heritage? Are all non-White populations appropriate comparison groups for understanding the sources of Black disadvantage in the United States? The debate concerning whether race or social class is the best predictor of one's life chances illustrates the need to ponder these questions (Wilson, 1978). Researchers have long noted that comparing the disproportionately lower-income Black population to a more affluent aggregate White population distorts and conceals many differences and similarities between the groups. It is also a comparison that is guided by little concern for theory. We must begin to rethink not only the theory embedded in Black-White comparisons but the importance of accounting for economic inequality in interpreting racial difference. This is an important concern when attempting to explain the rate of Black homicide in the United States.

However, an emphasis on economic inequality does not mean that we should ignore the historical context within which such inequality arose. The effects of historical forces upon current social conditions simply cannot be denied. No other ethnic group to whom Blacks as a group are often unfavorably compared was enslaved en masse and brought to this country by force. An internal colonialist model rather than an immigrant analogy might be most useful for conceptualizing the historical dimensions of Black-White relations in the United States. It is highly likely that slavery set into motion certain structural, social psychological, and economic forces that partly account for the Black-White crime differential, and that greatly affect in many other ways the behavior of both Blacks and Whites in the United States today. These forces may be extremely difficult to operationalize and quantify using positivistic scientific methods. But the difficulty of the task should not make us retreat. On the contrary, the difficulty should spur us to develop ever more refined, sensitive, and powerful research questions and methods in our attempt to articulate the causes and find the solutions to the continuing problem of Black homicide.

Discussion Questions

1. In "The Negro and Homicide," what were the explanations that Brearley offered for Black sociopathology? Which of these, if any, seem to have some merit? What other "shopping list" explanations have been offered since Brearley?

2. Explain Wolfgang and Ferracuti's theory of a subculture of violence. What are some "internal" and "external" causations? What is the relationship between the external and the internal causes? What aspects of the theory have more recent researchers emphasized?

3. How does the structure of society affect the Black-White homicide differential? Describe the correlation between social inequality, discretion, and Black homicide rates. To what extent is this relationship similar to that of earlier immigrant groups?

Notes

1. As in earlier European societies, crime indices in the United States are used as a measure of societal morality and the condition of the "dangerous class." In the United States, crime committed by Blacks has also been a politically volatile subject. The controversy surrounding the depiction of a Black criminal in the 1988 presidential campaign provides evidence of this phenomenon. Even more recently, the Stuart case in Boston has highlighted this phenomenon.

2. Many trace its origins to the classic debate between Booker T. Washington and W.E.B. Du Bois. Each of these men represented a point of view that was shared by many scholars and public officials, both Black and White, during the late 1800s and early 1900s. At base, the debate involved questions of the relative importance of legal reform versus self-help as methods for reducing Black social disadvantage. In more recent years, this debate has included the use of an "immigrant analogy" to discuss causes of and remedies for Black deficits. Many of the ideas of Sowell and Loury are shared by such White researchers as Glazer and Moynihan.

References

Banfield, E. 1970. *The Unheavenly City: The Nature and Future of Our Urban Crisis*. Boston: Little, Brown.

Blau, J. R., and Blau, P. M. 1982. "The Cost of Inequality: Metropolitan Structure and Violent Crime" in *American Sociological Review* 47, p. 114-129.

Blauner, R. 1972. *Racial Oppression in America*. New York: Harper & Row.

Block, R. 1975. "Homicide in Chicago: A Nine-Year Study (1965-1973)." *Journal of Criminal Law and Criminology*, 66, 496-510.

Boudouris, J. 1970. *Trends in Homicide, Detroit, 1926-68*. Unpublished doctoral dissertation, Wayne State University, Detroit, Michigan.

Brearley, H. C. 1932. *Homicide in the United States*. Chapel Hill: University of North Carolina Press.

Curtis, L. A. 1975. *Violence, Race and Culture*. Lexington, MA: D.C. Heath.

Fanon, F. 1963. *The Wretched of the Earth*. New York: Grove.

——. 1967. *Black Skin, White Masks*. New York: Macmillan.

Frazier, E. F. 1957. *The Negro in the United States*. New York: Macmillan.

Glazer, N. 1971. "Blacks and Ethnic Groups: The Difference, and the Political Difference it Makes" in N. I. Huggins, M. Kilson, & D. M. Fox (Eds.), *Key Issues in the Afro-American Experience* (Vol. 2, 193-211). New York: Harcourt Brace Jovanovich.

Greeley, A. M. 1974. *Ethnicity in the United States: A Preliminary Reconnaissance.* New York: Wiley.

Hawkins, D. F. 1986. *Homicide Among Black Americans.* Lanham, MD: University Press of America.

Henry, A. F., and Short, J. F. 1954. *Suicide and Homicide.* Glencoe, IL: Free Press.

Jaynes, G. D., and Williams, R. M., Jr. (Eds.). 1989. *A Common Destiny: Blacks and American Society.* Washington, D.C.: National Academy Press.

Lane, R. 1986. *Roots of Violence in Black Philadelphia, 1860-1900.* Cambridge, MA: Harvard University Press.

Loury, G. C. 1985. "The Moral Quandary of the Black Community" in *Public Interest* 79, 9-22.

——. 1987. "Matters of Color—Blacks and the Constitutional Order" in *Public Interest* 85, 109-123.

Lundsgaarde, H. P. 1977. *Murder in Space City: A Cultural Analysis of Houston Homicide Patterns.* New York: Oxford University Press.

Memmi, A. 1967. *The Colonizer and the Colonized.* Boston: Beacon.

Messner, S. F. 1982. "Poverty, Inequality, and the Urban Homicide Rate: Some Unexpected Findings" in *Criminology* 20, 103-114.

——. 1983. "Regional Differences in the Economic Correlates of the Urban Homicide Rate: Some Evidence on the Importance of the Cultural Context." *Criminology* 21, 477-488.

Messner, S. F., and Tardiff, K. 1986. "Economic Inequality and Levels of Homicide: An Analysis of Urban Neighborhoods" in *Criminology* 24, 297-318.

Park, R. Burgess, E. W., and McKenzie, R. D. 1928. *The City.* Chicago: University of Chicago Press.

Pettigrew, T. F. (Ed.). 1980. *The Sociology of Race Relations.* New York: Free Press.

Pettigrew, T. F. and Spier, R. B. 1962. "The Ecological Structure of Negro Homicide" in *American Journal of Sociology* 67, 621-629.

Pokorny, A. D. 1965. "A Comparison of Homicide in Two Cities" in *Journal of Criminal Law, Criminology, and Police Science* 56, 479-487.

Reuter, E. G. 1927. *American Race Problems.* New York: Crowell.

Schaefer, R. T. 1979. *Racial and Ethnic Groups.* Boston: Little, Brown.

Silberman, C. E. 1978. *Criminal Violence, Criminal Justice.* New York: Vintage.

Sowell, T. 1981. *Ethnic America.* New York: Basic Books.

——. 1986. *A Conflict of Visions.* New York: William Morrow.

Vander Zanden, J. W. 1973. "Sociological Studies of American Blacks" in *Sociological Quarterly* 14, 32.

Vold, G. B., and Bernard, T. J. 1986. *Theoretical Criminology.* New York: Oxford University Press.

Voss, H., and Hepburn, J. R. 1968. "Patterns in Criminal Homicide in Chicago" in *Journal of Criminal Law, Criminology, and Police Science,* 59, 499-508.

Wilson, J. Q., and Herrnstein, R. J. 1985. *Crime and Human Nature.* New York: Simon & Schuster.

Wilson, W. J. 1978. *The Declining Significance of Race.* Chicago: University of Chicago Press.

Wolfgang, M. E. 1958. *Patterns in Criminal Homicide.* New York: Wiley.

Wolfgang, M. E., and Ferracuti, F. 1982. *The Subculture of Violence: Towards an Integrated Theory in Criminology.* Beverly Hills, CA: Sage.

12

Trends in Women's Crime

Meda Chesney-Lind

Until the 1970s, criminologists were not particularly interested in women criminal offenders or the role they played in crime. Official crime data indicated that few women offenders were represented among conventional criminals. Women who were arrested and processed were usually accused of prostitution, child abuse, or consumer crimes, offenses traditionally committed by women because of their gender roles. Or, they were the accessories of men who led them astray. Their relatively small number and the unique nature of their offenses allowed such women to be neglected by scholars searching for explanations of criminal behavior.

This situation began to change in the 1970s with the publication of several provocative works on women criminals and the alleged increase in their numbers and the severity of their offenses. Over the next 20 years research pertaining to women criminals and their roles in crime expanded greatly. New theoretical and research questions were asked, a variety of empirical data were gathered, and new conclusions have been drawn. This selection by a leading feminist criminologist is part of the new scholarship directed at understanding women's criminal roles in crime.

Chesney-Lind examines "women's place" in American society and shows the relationship between traditional gender roles and criminality. Data indicate that women are arrested largely for the same relatively minor offenses they have always committed, despite the claim of some observers that present-day women offenders are commiting more masculine crimes. Although the number of women offenders is somewhat greater than in the past, these increases can be explained by the gen-

dered social circumstances that influence their lives. No support exists for the notion that women offenders are acting out liberated roles and adopting the criminal behavior of men. In fact, the analysis of recent arrest trends indicates that most women who commit crimes are motivated by their economic marginalization rather than by their commitment to liberated gender roles. Being poor, victimized, and dependent is more likely to explain female crime than are factors associated with women's liberation.

Women's crime, like girls' crime, is deeply affected by women's place. As a result, women's contribution to serious crime, like that of girls', is minor. Of those adults arrested for serious crimes of violence in 1994 (murder, forcible rape, robbery, and aggravated assault), only 14% were female. Indeed, women constituted only 18.8% of all arrests during that year (Federal Bureau of Investigation, 1995, p. 222). This also means that adult women are an even smaller percentage of those arrested than their girl counterparts (who now comprise about one out of four juvenile arrests).

Moreover, the majority of adult women offenders, like girls, are arrested and tried for relatively minor offenses. In 1994, women were most likely to be arrested for larceny theft (which alone accounted for 15.5% of all adult women's arrests), followed by drug abuse violations (9.3%). This means that over a quarter of all the women arrested in the United States that year were arrested for one of these two offenses. Women's offenses, then, are concentrated in just a few criminal categories, just as women's employment in the mainstream economy is concentrated in a few job categories. Furthermore, these offenses, as we shall see, are closely tied to women's economic marginality and the ways women attempt to cope with poverty.

Unruly Women: A Brief History of Women's Offenses

Women's concentration in petty offenses is not restricted to the present. A study of women's crime in 14th-century England (Hanawalt, 1982) and descriptions of the backgrounds of the women who were forcibly transported to Australia several centuries later (Beddoe, 1979) document the astonishing stability in patterns of women's lawbreaking.

The women who were transported to Australia, for example, were servants, maids, or laundresses convicted of petty theft (stealing, shoplifting, and picking pockets) or prostitution. The number of women transported for these trivial offenses is sobering. Between 1787 and 1852, no less than 24,960 women, fully a third of whom were first offenders, were sent to relieve the "shortage" of women in the colonies. Shipped in rat-infested holds, the women were systematically raped and sexually abused by the ships' officers and sailors, and the death rate in the early years was as high as one in three. Their arrival in Australia was also a nightmare; no provision was made for the women and many were forced to turn to prostitution to survive (Beddoe, 1979, pp. 11–21).

Other studies add different but important dimensions to the picture. For example, Bynum's (1992) research on "unruly" women in antebellum North Carolina adds the vital dimension of race to the picture. She notes that the marginalized members of society, particularly "free black and unmarried poor white women" were most often likely both to break social and sexual taboos *and* to face punishment by the courts. Indeed, she observes that "if North Carolina lawmakers could have done so legally, they would have rid society altogether" of these women (Bynum, 1992, p. 10). As it was, they harshly enforced laws against fornication, bastardy, and prostitution in an attempt to effect these women and their progeny.

The role of urbanization and class is further explored in Feeley and Little's (1991) research on criminal cases appearing in London courts between 1687 and 1912, and Boritch and Hagan's (1990) research on arrests in Toronto between 1859 and 1955. Both of these studies examine the effect of industrialization and women's economic roles (or economic marginalization) on women's offenses. Both works present evidence that women were drawn to urban areas, where they were employed in extremely low-paid work. As a result, this forced many into forms of offending, including disorderly conduct, drunkenness, and petty thievery. Boritch and Hagan make special note of the large numbers of women arrested for property offenses, "drunkenness" and "vagrancy," which can be seen as historical counterparts to modern drug offenses (Boritch & Hagan, 1990). But what of women who committed "serious" offenses such as murder? Jones's (1980) study of early women murderers in the United States reveals that many of America's early women murderers were indentured servants. Raped by calculating masters who understood that giving birth to a "bastard" would add 1 to 2 years to a woman's term of service, these desperate women hid their pregnancies and then committed infanticide. Jones also provides numerous historical and contemporary examples of desperate women murdering their brutal "lovers" or husbands. The less dramatic links between forced marriage, women's circumscribed options, and women's decisions to kill, often by poison, characterized the Victorian murderesses. These women, though rare, haunted the turn of the century, in part because women's participation in the methodical violence involved in arsenic poisoning was considered unthinkable (Hartman, 1977).

In short, research on the history of women's offenses, and particularly women's violence, is a valuable resource for its information on the level and character of women's crime and as a way to understand the relationship between women's crime and women's lives. Whenever a woman commits murder, particularly if she is accused of murdering a family member, people immediately ask, "How could she do that?" Given the enormous costs of being born female, that may well be the wrong question. The real question, as a review of the history of women's crime illustrates, is not why women murder but rather why so few murder.

Take a look at some facts. Every 15 seconds a woman is beaten in her own home (Bureau of Justice Statistics, 1989a). A National Institute of Mental Health study (based on urban area hospitals) estimated that 21% of all *women* using emergency surgical services had been injured in a domestic violence incident; that half of all *injuries* presented by women to emergency surgical services occurred in the context of partner abuse; and that over half of all rapes of women over the age of 30 had been perpetrated by an intimate partner (Stark et al., 1981). In the United States, for example, former Surgeon General C. Everett Koop estimated that 3 to 4 million women are battered each year; roughly half of them are single, separated, or divorced (Koop, 1989). Battering also tends to escalate and become more severe over time. Almost half of all batterers beat their partners at least three times a year (Straus, Gelles, & Steinmetz, 1980). This description of victimization doesn't address other forms of women's abuse, such as incest and sexual assault, which have rates as alarmingly high (see Center for Policy Studies, 1991).

The real question is why so few women resort to violence in the face of such horrendous victimization—even to save their lives. In 1994, in the United States, only 10.8% of those arrested for murder were women—meaning that murder, like other forms of violent crime, is almost exclusively a male activity. In fact, women murderers, as both Jones and Hartman document, are interesting precisely because of their rarity. The large number of women arrested for trivial property and morals offenses, coupled with the virtual absence of women from those arrested for serious property crimes and violent crimes, provides clear evidence that women's crime parallels their assigned role in the rest of society (Klein & Kress, 1976). In essence, women's place in the legitimate economy largely relegates them to jobs that pay poorly and are highly sex segregated (like secretarial and sales jobs); likewise, in the illicit or criminal world, they occupy fewer roles and roles that do not "pay" as well as men's crime. There is, however, little understanding of why this is the case, and, until recently, little scholarship devoted to explaining this pattern. This chapter will attempt to address both the reality of women's crime and the fascination with the atypical woman offender who is violent and defies her "conventional role" in both the mainstream and the criminal world.

Trends in Women's Arrests

Over the years, women have typically been arrested for larceny theft, drunk driving, fraud (the bulk of which is welfare fraud and naive check forgery), drug abuse violations, and buffer charges for prostitution (such as disorderly conduct and a variety of petty offenses that fall under the broad category of "other offenses") (Steffensmeier, 1980; Steffensmeier & Allan, 1990) (see Table 12. 1).

Arrest data certainly suggest that the "war on drugs" has translated into a war on women. Between 1985 and 1994, arrests of adult women for drug abuse violations increased by 100.1%, compared to 53.7% for men (Federal Bureau of Investigation, 1992, p. 222). The past decade (1985-1994) has also seen increases in arrests of women for "other assaults" (up 126%) (not unlike the pattern seen in girls' arrests). Arrest rates show much the same pattern (see Table 12.1). In the past decade, arrests of women for drug offenses and other assaults have replaced fraud and disorderly conduct as the most common offenses for which adult women are arrested.

These figures, however, should not be used to support notions of dramatic increases in women's crime. As an example, although the number of adult women arrested between 1993 and 1994 did increase by 5.8%, that increase followed a slight decline in women's arrests between 1992 and 1993 (Federal Bureau of Investigation, 1994, p. 226; Federal Bureau of Investigation, 1995, p. 226).

The arrests of women for Part One or "index" offenses (murder, rape, aggravated assault, robbery, burglary, larceny theft, motor vehicle theft, and arson) increased by 25.2% (compared to an increase in male arrests of 14.3%) between 1985 and 1994 (Federal Bureau of Investigation, 1993, p. 222). Much of this increase, however, can be explained by increases in larceny theft, which some contend often involves such minor offenses that it should not be confused with "serious" crime (see Steffensmeier & Allan, 1990).

Moreover, looking at these offenses differently reveals a picture of stability rather than change over the past decade. Women's share of these arrests (as a proportion of all those arrested for these offenses) rose from 21.8%

Table 12.1
Trends in Adult Arrest by Gender, 1985–1994

Offense	Percentage Change (1985-1994)	
	Male	Female
Total	**15.4**	**36.4**
Murder & nonnegligent manslaughter	13.4	–4.2
Forcible rape	–5.1	–4.4
Robbery	10.1	32.5
Aggravated assault	65.1	110.5
Burglary	–14.4	25.0
Larceny theft	7.5	14.1
Motor vehicle theft	29.1	77.1
Arson	–23.6	–12.4
Violent crime	42.5	89.9
Property crime	3.1	16.1
Crime index total	14.3	25.2
Other assaults	80.7	126.2
Forgery & counterfeiting	29.0	41.6
Fraud	32.0	11.4
Embezzlement	16.2	40.8
Stolen property; buy, receive, possess	18.2	37.3
Vandalism	14.9	60.7
Weapons; carrying, possessing, etc.	26.1	29.2
Prostitution & commercialized vice	8.4	–24.9
Sex offenses (except forcible rape & prostitution)	–4.5	15.5
Drug abuse violations	53.7	100.1
Gambling	–44.8	–40.5
Offenses against family & children	80.0	264.6
Driving under the influence	–24.2	–4.7
Liquor laws	–0.7	38.1
Drunkenness	–32.1	–8.0
Disorderly conduct	–5.2	1.7
Vagrancy	–43.0	29.7
All other offenses (except traffic)	45.7	78.5
Suspicion (not included in totals)	1.0	19.9
Curfew & loitering law violations	0.0	0.0
Runaway	0.0	0.0

SOURCE: Federal Bureau of Investigation. (1994). *Crime in the United States—1993.* Washington, D.C.: U.S. Department of Justice, p. 222.

to 23.4% between 1985 and 1994. Women's share of arrests for serious violent offenses rose from 10.9% to 14% during the same period (Federal Bureau of Investigation, 1994, p. 222)—hardly anything to get excited about. At the other extreme is the pattern found in arrests for prostitution—the only crime among the 29 offense categories tracked by the FBI for which arrests of women account for the majority (61.3%) of all arrests.

Overall, the increase in women's arrests is largely accounted for by more arrests of women for nonviolent property offenses, such as shoplifting (larceny theft, which was up 14.1%), check forgery (forgery/counterfeiting, which was up 41.6%), welfare fraud ("fraud," which was up 11. 4%), and, most important, drug offenses (up 100.1%) (Federal Bureau of Investigation, 1993, p. 222). Here, the increases in arrests are real, because the base numbers are large and, as a result, these offenses make up a large portion of women's official deviance. Whether they are the product of actual changes in women's

Table 12.2
Trends in Adult Arrest Rates by Gender, 1985–1994

Offense	Male		Female	
	Arrest Rate/100k (1994)	% Change in Rate (1985-1994)	Arrest rate/100k (1994)	% Change in Rate (1985-1994)
Total	13,403.9	9.4	3,119.7	29.7
Murder & nonnegligent manslaughter	24.2	7.6	2.9	–9.4
Forcible rape	42.2	–10.0	0.4	0.0
Robbery	159.3	4.5	16.3	25.4
Aggravated assault	541.3	56.6	105.6	100.0
Burglary	311.9	–18.8	38.7	18.7
Larceny theft	933.7	2.0	482.5	8.5
Motor vehicle theft	144.1	22.4	17.9	68.9
Arson	10.4	–27.8	2.3	–14.8
Violent crime	767.0	35.2	125.3	80.5
Property crime	1,400.1	–2.2	541.4	10.3
Crime index total	2,167.1	8.4	666.6	19.0
Other assaults	1,170.6	71.4	240.7	114.9
Forgery & counterfeiting	95.2	22.4	52.5	34.6
Fraud	321.2	25.2	210.7	5.9
Embezzlement	10.9	10.1	7.9	33.9
Stolen property; buy, receive, possess	143.8	12.2	23.6	30.4
Vandalism	201.3	9.0	35.8	53.0
Weapons; carrying, possessing, etc.	256.3	19.6	22.1	22.8
Prostitution & commercialized vice	58.4	2.8	92.6	–28.6
Sex offenses (except forcible rape & prostitution)	105.8	–9.4	10.2	10.9
Drug abuse violations	1,405.0	45.8	290.5	90.1
Gambling	20.9	–47.6	4.0	–43.7
Offenses against family & children	114.3	70.6	29.8	246.5
Driving under the influence	1,520.4	–28.1	251.6	–9.5
Liquor laws	459.5	–5.8	93.3	31.2
Drunkenness	851.3	–35.6	109.9	–12.6
Disorderly conduct	622.1	–10.0	157.9	–3.3
Vagrancy	24.6	–46.0	6.9	23.2
All other offenses (except traffic)	3,855.3	38.3	813.1	69.6
Suspicion (not included in totals)	13.0	–3.7	2.3	15.0
Curfew & loitering law violations	0.0	0.0	0.0	0.0
Runaway	0.0	0.0	0.0	0.0

SOURCE: Federal Bureau of Investigation. (1994). *Crime in the United States —1993*. Washington, D.C.: U.S. Department of Justice, p. 222.

behavior over the past decade or changes in law enforcement practices is an important question, and one to which we now turn.

How Could She? The Nature and Causes of Women's Crime

The pattern of women's crime, as represented in official arrest statistics, is remarkably similar to the pattern seen earlier for girls. Adult women have been, and continue to be, arrested for minor crimes (generally shoplifting and welfare fraud) and what might be called "deportment" offenses (prostitution, disorderly conduct, and, arguably, "driving under the influence"). Their younger counterparts are arrested for essentially the same crimes, in addition to status offenses (running away from home, incorrigibility, truancy, and other noncriminal offenses for which only minors can be taken into custody). Arrests of adult women, like arrests of girls, have increased for both aggravated and other assaults. Finally, and most important, adult women's arrests for drug offenses have soared.

Where there have been increases in women's arrests for offenses that sound non-traditional, such as embezzlement (or, as we shall see later in this chapter, robbery), careful examination reveals the connections between these offenses and women's place.

Embezzlement

In the case of embezzlement, for which women's arrests increased by 40.8% in the past decade, careful research disputes the notion of women moving firmly into the ranks of big-time, white-collar offenders. Because women are concentrated in low-paying clerical, sales, and service occupations (Renzetti & Curran, 1995), they are "not in a position to steal hundreds of thousands of dollars but they [are] in a position to pocket smaller amounts" (Simon & Landis, 1991, p. 56). Moreover, their motives for such theft often involve family responsibilities rather than a desire for personal gain (Daly, 1989; Zietz, 1981).

Daly's analysis of gender differences in white-collar crime is particularly useful. In a review of federal "white-collar" crime cases in seven federal districts (which included people convicted of bank embezzlement, income tax fraud, postal fraud, etc.), she found that gender played a substantial role in the differences between men's and women's offenses. For example, of those arrested for bank embezzlement, 60% of the women were tellers and 90% were in some sort of clerical position. By contrast, about half of the men charged with embezzlement held professional and managerial positions (bank officers and financial managers). Therefore it is no surprise that for each embezzlement offense, men's attempted economic gain was 10 times higher than women's (Daly, 1989). In commenting on this pattern, Daly notes, "the women's socio-economic profile, coupled with the nature of their crimes, makes one wonder if 'white collar' aptly described them or their illegalities" (Daly, 1989, p. 790).

Embezzlement is a particularly interesting offense to "unpack" because it is one of the offenses for which, if present trends continue, women may comprise about half of those charged with this offense (Renzetti &

Curran, 1995, p. 310). In fact, women composed 41.8% of those charged with embezzlement in 1994 (Federal Bureau of Investigation, 1995, p. 222). Yet these increases cannot be laid at the door of women breaking into traditionally "male" offense patterns. Women's increased share of arrests for embezzlement is probably an artifact of their presence in low-level positions that make them more vulnerable to frequent checking and hence more vulnerable to detection (Steffensmeier & Allan, 1990). Combining this with these women's lack of access to resources to "cover" their thefts prompts Steffensmeier and Allan to draw a parallel between modern women's involvement in embezzlement and increases in thefts by women in domestic service a century ago.

Driving Under the Influence

Arrests of women driving under the influence (DUI) account for almost 1 arrest in 10 of women. One study (Wells-Parker, Pang, Anderson, McMillen, & Miller, 1991) found that women arrested for DUI tended to be older than men (with nearly half of the men but less than a third of the women under 30), more likely to be "alone, divorced or separated" and to have fewer serious drinking problems and fewer extensive prior arrests for DUI or "public drunkenness" (Wells-Parker et al., 1991, p. 144). Historically, women were arrested for DUI only if "the DUI involved a traffic accident or physical/verbal abuse of a police officer" (Coles, 1991, p. 5). These patterns have probably eroded in recent years because of public outrage over drinking and driving and an increased use of roadblocks. Changes in police practices, rather than changes in women's drinking, could easily explain the prominence of this offense in women's official crime patterns.

Women tend to drink alone and deny treatment (Coles, 1991). Also, in contrast to men, they tend to drink for "escapism and psychological comfort" (Wells-Parker et al., 1991, p. 146). For these reasons, intervention programs that attempt to force women to examine their lives and the quality of relationships, which tend to work for male DUI offenders, are not successful with women. Indeed, these interventions could "exacerbate a sense of distress, helplessness and hopelessness" that could, in turn, trigger more drinking (Wells-Parker et al., 1991, p. 146).

Larceny Theft/Shoplifting

Women's arrests for larceny theft are composed largely of arrests for shoplifting. Steffensmeier (1980) estimates that perhaps as many as four fifths of all arrests on larceny charges are for shoplifting. Cameron's (1953) early study of shoplifting in Chicago explains that women's prominence among those arrested for shoplifting may not reflect greater female involvement in the offense but rather differences in the ways men and women shoplift. Her research revealed that women tend to steal more items than men, to steal items from several stores, and to steal items of lesser value. Store detectives explained this pattern by saying that people tended to "steal the same way they buy" (Cameron, 1953, p. 159). Men came to the store with one item in mind. They saw it, took it, and left the store. Women, on the other hand, shopped around. Because the chance of being arrested increases with each item stolen, Cameron felt that the stores probably underestimated the level of men's shoplifting.

Although women stole more items than men, the median value of adult male theft was significantly higher than that of women's (Cameron, 1953, p. 62). In addition, more men than women were defined as "commercial shoplifters" (people who stole merchandise for possible resale).

Perhaps as a result of women's shopping and shoplifting patterns, studies done later (Lindquist, 1988) have found that women constitute 58% of those caught shoplifting. Steffensmeier and Allan (1990) go so far as to suggest that shoplifting may be regarded as a prototypically female offense. Shopping is, after all, part of women's "second shift" of household management, housework, and child care responsibilities (Hochschild, 1989). Shoplifting can be seen as a criminal extension of expected and familiar women's work.

Even the reasons for shoplifting are gendered. Men, particularly young men, tend to view stealing as part of a broader pattern of masculine display of "badness" and steal

items that are of no particular use to them (Steffensmeier & Allan, 1990). At the other extreme, they may be professional thieves and thus more likely to escape detection (Cameron, 1953).

Girls and women, on the other hand, tend to steal items that they either need or feel they need but cannot afford. As a result, they tend to steal from stores and to take things such as clothing, cosmetics, and jewelry. Campbell (1981) notes that women—young and old— are the targets of enormously expensive advertising campaigns for a vast array of personal products. These messages, coupled with the temptations implicit in long hours spent "shopping," lead to many arrests of women for these offenses.

Despite some contentions that women actually shoplift more than men, self-report data in fact show few gender differences in the prevalence of the behavior (see Chesney-Lind & Shelden, 1992, for a review of these studies). What appears to be happening is that girls and women shoplift in different ways than men. In addition, they are more often apprehended because store detectives expect women to shoplift more than men and thus watch women more closely (Morris, 1987).

Big Time/Small Time

English (1993) approached the issue of women's crime by analyzing detailed self-report surveys she administered to a sample of 128 female and 872 male inmates in Colorado. She examined both "participation rates" and "crime frequency" figures for a wide array of different offenses. She found few differences in the participation rates of men and women, with the exception of three property crimes. Men were more likely than women to report participation in burglary, whereas women were more likely than men to have participated in theft and forgery. Exploring these differences further, she found that women "lack the specific knowledge needed to carry out a burglary" (English, 1993, p. 366).

Women were far more likely than men to be involved in "forgery" (it was the most common crime for women and fifth out of eight for men). Follow-up research on a subsample of "high crime"-rate female respondents revealed that many had worked in retail establishments and therefore "knew how much time they had" between stealing the checks or credit cards and having them reported (English, 1993, p. 370). The women said that they would target "strip malls" where credit cards and bank checks could be stolen easily and used in nearby retail establishments. The women reported that their high-frequency theft was motivated by a "big haul," which meant a purse with several hundred dollars in it, in addition to cards and checks. English concludes that "women's over representation in low-paying, low status jobs" increases their involvement in these property crimes (English, 1993, p. 171).

English's findings with regard to two other offenses, for which gender differences did not appear in participation rates, are worth exploring here. She found no difference in the "participation rates" of women and men in drug sales and assault. However, when examining the frequency data, English found that women in prison reported making significantly more drug sales than men but not because they were engaged in big-time drug selling. Instead, their high number of drug sales occurred because women's drug sales were "concentrated in the small trades (i.e., transactions of less than $10)" (English, 1993, p. 372). Because they made so little money, English found that 20% of the active women dealers reported making 20 or more drug deals per day (English, 1993, p. 372).

A reverse of the same pattern was found when she examined women's participation in assault. Here, slightly more (27.8%) of women than men (23.4%) reported assaulting someone in the past year. However, most of these women reported making only one assault during the study period (65.4%), compared to only about a third of the men (37.5%).

English found that "economic disadvantage" played a role in both women's and men's criminal careers. Beyond this, however, gender played an important role in shaping women's and men's response to poverty. Specifically, women's criminal careers reflect "gender differences in legitimate and illegitimate opportunity structures, in personal networks, and in family obligations" (English, 1993, p. 3 74).

Pathways to Women's Crime

As with girls, the links between adult women's victimization and crimes are increasingly clear. . . the backgrounds of adult women offenders hint at links between childhood victimization and adult offending. In an important study of such links, Gilfus (1992) interviewed 20 incarcerated women and documented how such childhood injuries were linked to adult crimes in women.

Gilfus extends the work of Miller (1986) and Chesney-Lind and Rodriguez (1983) on the ways in which women's backgrounds color their childhoods and ultimately their adulthoods. She conducted in-depth interviews in 1985 and 1986 with the women in a Northeastern women's facility that, at the time, served as both a jail and a prison. From these lengthy interviews, she reconstructed "life event histories" for each of the women. The group had a mean age of 30 (ranging from 20 to 41 years of age), and included 8 African American and 12 white women. All of the women had life histories of what Gilfus characterized as "street crimes"—by which she meant prostitution, shoplifting, check or credit card fraud, and drug law violations. Their current offenses included assault and battery; accessory to rape; breaking and entering; and multiple charges of drug possession, larceny, and prostitution (Gilfus, 1992, p. 68). Sentence lengths ranged, for this group, from 3 months to 20 years.

Most of the women were single mothers, three-quarters were intravenous drug users, and almost all (17) had histories of prostitution (seven of the women had begun as teenage prostitutes). Most of these women had grown up with violence; 13 of the 20 reported childhood sexual abuse and 15 had experienced "severe child abuse" (Gilfus, 1992, p. 70). There were no differences in the levels of abuse reported by black and white respondents, although African American women grew up in families that were more economically marginalized than their white counterparts. Although some women's childhood memories were totally colored by their sexual abuse, for most of the women in Gilfus's sample, coping with and surviving multiple victimization was the more normal pattern. In the words of one of these women, "I just got hit a lot. . . . 'Cause they would both drink and they wouldn't know the difference. Mmm, picked up, thrown against walls, everything, you name it" (Gilfus, 1992, p. 72).

Despite the abuse and violence, these women recall spending time trying to care for and protect others, especially younger siblings, and attempting to do housework and even care for their abusive and drug or alcohol dependent parents. They also recall teachers who ignored signs of abuse and who, in the case of African American girls, were hostile and racist. Ultimately, 16 out of the 20 dropped out of high school (Gilfus, 1992, p. 69). The failure of the schools to be responsive to these young women's problems meant that the girls could perceive no particular future for themselves. Given the violence in their lives, drugs provided these girls with a solace found nowhere else.

Many (13) ran away from home as girls. "Rape, assault, and even attempted murder" were reported by 16 of the 20, with an average of three "rape or violent rape attempts" per woman; many of these occurred in the context of prostitution but when the women attempted to report the assault, the police simply "ridiculed" the women or threatened to arrest them. In some cases, the police would demand sexual services for not arresting the woman (Gilfus, 1992, p. 79).

Violence also characterized these women's relationships with adult men; 15 of the 20 had lived with violent men. The women were expected to bring in money, generally through prostitution and shoplifting. These men functioned as the women's pimps but also sold drugs, committed robberies, or fenced the goods shoplifted by the women. Thirteen of the women had become pregnant as girls but only four kept their first baby. Most of the women had subsequent children whom they attempted to mother despite their worsening addictions, and they tended to rely on their mothers (not their boyfriends) to take care of their children while in prison. The women continued to see their criminal roles as forms of caretaking; taking care of their children and of their abusive boyfriends. As Gilfus puts it, "the women in this study consider their illegal activities to be form of *work* which is undertaken primarily from economic necessity to support partners, children, and addictions" (1992, p. 86). Gilfus further speculates that violence "may socialize women to adopt a tenacious commitment to caring for anyone who promises love, material success, and acceptance" (p. 86), which, in turn, places them at risk for further exploitation and abuse.

The interviews Arnold (1995) conducted, based on this same hypothesis, with 50 African American women serving sentences in a city jail and 10 additional interviews with African American women in prison are an important addition to the work of Gilfus. Arnold notes that African American girls are not only sexually victimized but are also the victims of "class oppression." Specifically, she notes that "to be young, black, poor and female is to be in a high-risk category for victimization and stigmatization on many levels" (Arnold, 1995, p. 139). Growing up in extreme poverty means that African American girls may turn earlier to deviant behavior, particularly stealing, to help themselves and their families. One young woman told Arnold that "my father beat my mother and neglected his children. . . . I began stealing when I was 12. I hustled to help feed and clothes the other [12] kids and help pay the rent" (Arnold, 1995, p. 139).

Thus, the caretaking role noted in women's pathways to crime is accentuated in African American families because of extreme poverty. Arnold also noted that economic need interfered with young black girls' ability to concentrate on schoolwork and attend school. Finally, Arnold noted, as had Gilfus, that African American girls were "victimized" by the school system (1995, p. 140); one of her respondents said that "some [of the teachers] were prejudiced, and one had the nerve to tell the whole class he didn't like black people" (p. 140). Most of her respondents said that even if they went to school every day, they did not learn anything. Finally, despite their desperate desire to "hold on . . . to conventional roles in society," the girls were ultimately pushed out of these, onto the streets, and into petty crime (p. 141).

The mechanics of surviving parental abuse and educational neglect were particularly hard on young African American girls, forcing them to drop out of school, on to the streets, and into permanent "structural dislocation" (Arnold, 1995, p. 143). Having no marketable skills and little education, many resorted to "prostitution and stealing" while further immersing themselves in drug addiction.

Beyond the Street Woman: Resurrecting the Liberated Female Crook?

Issues of women's violence and the relationship between that violence and other changes in women's environment are recurring themes in discussions of women's crime. . . . a persistent theme in women's criminality is the presumed link between efforts to improve women's economic and political position and levels of girls' and women's crime—particularly violent crime. . . . there is nothing particularly "new" about the concern. During the early 1970s, newspapers and periodicals were full of stories about the "new female criminal" (Foley, 1974; Klemesrud, 1978; *Los Angeles Times* Service, 1975; Nelson, 1977; Roberts, 1971). Presumably inspired by the women's movement, the female criminal supposedly sought equality in the underworld just as her more conventional counterparts pursued their rights in more acceptable arenas.

Such media accounts, like contemporary "girlz in the hood" stories, generally relied on two types of evidence to support the alleged relationship between the women's rights movement and increasing female criminality: Federal Bureau of Investigation (FBI) statistics showing dramatic increases in the number of women arrested for nontraditional crimes, and sensationalistic accounts of women's violence. In the 1970s, the activities of female political activists such as Leila Khaled, Bernardine Dohrn, and Susan Saxe were featured. Of course, women's involvement in political or terrorist activity is nothing new, as the activities of Joan of Arc and Charlotte Corday demonstrate.

Arrest data collected by the FBI seem to provide more objective evidence that dramatic changes in the number of women arrested were occurring during the years associated with the second wave of feminist activity. For example, between 1960 and 1975, arrests of adult women went up 60.2% and arrests of juvenile women increased a startling 253.9%. In specific, nontraditional crimes, the increases were even more astounding. For example, between 1960 and 1975, the number of women arrested for murder was up 105.7%, forcible rape arrests increased by 633.3%, and robbery arrests were up 380.5% (Federal Bureau of Investigation, 1973, p. 124; Federal Bureau of Investigation, 1976, p. 191).

Law enforcement officials were among the earliest to link these changes to the movement for female equality. "The women's liberation movement has triggered a crime wave like the world has never seen before," claimed Chief Ed Davis of the Los Angeles Police Department (Weis, 1976, p. 17). On another occasion, he expanded on his thesis by explaining that the "breakdown of motherhood" signaled by the women's movement could lead to "the use of dope, stealing, thieving and killing" (*Los Angeles Times* Service, 1975, p. B4). Other officials, such as Sheriff Peter Pritchess of California, made less inflammatory comments that echoed the same general theme: "As women emerge from their traditional roles as housewife and mother, entering the political and business fields previously dominated by males, there is no reason to believe that women will not also approach equality with men in the criminal activity field" (Roberts, 1971, P. 72).

Law enforcement officials were not alone in holding this position; academics like Adler (1975a, 1975b) also linked increases in the number of women arrested to women's struggle for social and economic equality. Adler noted, for example, that "in the middle of the twentieth century, we are witnessing the simultaneous rise and fall of women. Rosie the Riveter of World War II has become Robin the Rioter or Rhoda the Robber of the Vietnam era. Women have lost more than their chains. For better or worse, they have lost many of the restraints which kept them within the law" (Adler, 1975b, p. 24).

Such arguments, it turns out, are nothing new. The first wave of feminism also saw an attempt to link women's rights with women's crime. Smart (1976), for example, found the following comment by W. I. Thomas written in 1921, the year after the ratification of the 19th Amendment guaranteeing women the right to vote:

> The modern age of girls and young men is intensely immoral, and immoral seemingly without the pressure of circumstances. At whose door we may lay the fault, we cannot tell. Is it the result of what we call "the emancipation of woman," with its concomitant freedom from chaperonage, increased intimacy between the sexes in adolescence, and a more tolerant viewpoint towards all things unclean in life? (Smart, 1976, pp. 70-71)

Students of women's crime were also quick to note that the interest in the female criminal after so many years of invisibility was ironic and questioned why the new visibility was associated with "an image of a woman with a gun in hand" (Chapman, 1980, p. 68). Chapman concluded that this attention to the female criminal was "doubly ironic" because closer assessments of the trends in women's violence did not support what might be called the "liberation hypothesis" and, more to the point., data showed that the position of women in the mainstream economy during those years was "actually worsening" (Chapman, 1980, pp. 68-69).

To be specific, although what might be called the "liberation hypothesis" or "emancipation hypothesis" met with wide public acceptance, careful analyses of changes in women's arrest rate provided little support for the notion. Using national arrest data supplied by the FBI and more localized police and court statistics, Steffensmeier (1980, p. 58) examined the pattern of female criminal behavior for the years 1965 through 1977 (the years most heavily affected by the second wave of feminist activity). By weighting the arrest data for changes in population and comparing increases in women's arrests to increases in men's arrests, Steffensmeier con-

cluded that "females are not catching up with males in the commission of violent, masculine, male-dominated, serious crimes (except larceny) or in white collar crimes" (1980, p. 72). He did note increases in women's arrests in the Uniform Crime Report categories of larceny, fraud, forgery, and vagrancy, but by examining these increases more carefully, he demonstrated that they were due almost totally to increases in traditionally female crimes, such as shoplifting, prostitution, and passing bad checks (fraud).

Moreover, Steffensmeier (1980) noted that forces other than changes in female behavior were probably responsible for shifts in the numbers of adult women arrested for these traditionally female crimes. The increased willingness of stores to prosecute shoplifters, the widespread abuse of vagrancy statutes to arrest prostitutes combined with a declining use of this same arrest category to control public drunkenness, and the growing concern with "welfare fraud" were all social factors that he felt might explain changes in women's arrests without necessarily changing the numbers of women involved in these activities.

Steffensmeier's findings confirm the reservations that had been voiced earlier by Simon (1975), Rans (1975), and others about making generalizations solely from dramatic percentage increases in the number of women's arrests. These reservations are further justified by current arrest data that suggest that the sensationalistic increases of the early 1970s were not indicative of a new trend. Between 1976 and 1979, for example, the arrests of all women rose only 7.1%, only slightly higher than the male increase of 5.8% for the same period (Chesney-Lind, 1986).

Finally, women offenders of the 1970s were unlikely targets for the messages of the largely middle-class women's movement. Women offenders tend to be poor, members of minority groups, with truncated educations and spotty employment histories. These were precisely the women whose lives were largely unaffected by the gains, such as they were, of the then white, middle-class women's rights movement (Chapman, 1980; Crites, 1976). Crites, for example, noted that, "These women rather than being recipients of expanded rights and opportunities gained by the women's movement, are, instead, witnessing declining survival options" (Crites, 1976, p. 37). Research on the orientations of women offenders to the arguments of the women's movement also indicated that, if anything, these women held very traditional attitudes about gender (see Chesney-Lind & Rodriguez, 1983, for a summary of these studies).

To summarize, careful work on the arrest trends of the 1970s provided no support for the popular liberation hypothesis of women's crime. Changes in women's arrest trends, it turned out, better fit arguments of women's economic marginalization than of her liberation (Simon & Landis, 1991).

The Revival of the 'Violent Female Offender'

The failure of careful research to support notions of radical shifts in the character of women's crime went almost completely unnoticed in the popular press. As a result, there was apparently nothing to prevent a recycling of a revised "liberation" hypothesis a decade and a half later.

. . . [O]ne of the first articles to use this recycled hypothesis was a 1990 article in the *Wall Street Journal* titled, "You've Come a Long Way, Moll," that focused on increases in the number of women arrested for violent crimes. This article opened with a discussion of women in the military, noting that "the armed forces already are substantially integrated" and moved from this point to observe that "we needn't look to the dramatic example of battle for proof that violence is no longer a male domain. Women are now being arrested for violent crimes—such as robbery and aggravated assault—at a higher rate than ever before recorded in the US" (Crittenden, 1990, p. Al 4).

. . . [M]any of the articles to follow dealt with young women (particularly girls in gangs), but there were some exceptions. For example, the "Hand That Rocks the Cradle Is Taking Up Violent Crime," (Kahler, 1992) focused on increases in women's imprisonment and linked this pattern to "the growing number of women committing violent crimes" (Kahler, 1992, p. 3-1).

Comparing the arrest rates that prompted the first media surge of reporting on the "liberation" hypothesis with the arrest rates from the second wave of media interest today, it is evident that little has changed. As noted earlier in this chapter, women's share of violent crime has remained more or less stable, though arrests of women for "other assaults" did climb by 126.2% in the past decade (but the arrests of men increased by 80.7%) (Federal Bureau of Investigation, 1995). Moreover, between 1993 and 1994, the number of women arrested for serious crimes of violence increased by only 5.5% (Federal Bureau of Investigation, 1994, p. 226).

The news media were not alone in their interest in women's violence—particularly violent street crime. In a series of articles (Baskin, Sommers, & Fagan, 1993; Sommers & Baskin, 1992, 1993), the authors explore the extent and character of women's violent crime in New York. Prompted by an account in their neighborhood paper of two women who shot another woman in a robbery, the authors note that their research "has led us to the conclusion that women in New York City are becoming more and more likely to involve themselves in violent street crime" (Baskin et al., 1993, p. 401). Some of the findings that brought them to this conclusion follow.

In one study (Sommers & Baskin, 1992), they use arrest data from New York City (and arrest histories of 266 women) to argue that "black and Hispanic females exhibited high rates of offending relative to white females." They further argue that "violent offending rates of black females parallel that of white males" (Sommers & Baskin, 1992, p. 191). Included in their definition of "violent" crimes is murder, robbery, aggravated assault, and burglary (apparently classified as a violent crime in New York City, but classified as a property crime by the FBI).

The authors explain that this pattern is a product of "the effects of the social and institutional transformation of the inner city" (Sommers & Baskin, 1992, p. 198). Specifically, the authors contend that "violence and drug involvement" are adaptive strategies in underclass communities that are racked by poverty and unemployment. Both men and women, they argue, move to crime as a way of coping with "extreme social and economic deprivation" (p. 198).

A second study (Sommers & Baskin, 1993) further explores women's violent offenses by analyzing interview data from 23 women arrested for a violent felony offense (robbery or assault) and 65 women incarcerated for such an offense. Finding a high correlation between substance abuse and the rate of violent crime (particularly for those who committed robbery and robbery with assault), they also noted that "the women in our study who were involved in robbery were not crime specialists but also had a history of engagement in nonviolent theft, fraud, forgery, prostitution, and drug dealing" (p. 142). In fact, they comment that "these women are not roaming willy-nilly through the streets engaging in 'unprovoked' violence" (p. 154).

Just how involved these women were in more traditional forms of female crime was not apparent in the text of this article. In an appendix, however, the role played by a history of prostitution in the lives of these women offenders is particularly clear. As an example, the women who reported committing both robbery and assault also had the highest rate of involvement with prostitution (77%) (Baskin & Sommers, 1993, p. 159).

In a third paper, Baskin et al. (1993) explore "the political economy of street crime." This work, which appears to be based on the New York arrest data and a discussion of the explosion of crack selling in the city, explores the question, "Why do black females exhibit such relatively high rates of violence?" (Baskin et al., 1993, p. 405). Convinced that the concentration of poverty is associated positively with the level of criminal activity, regardless of race, the authors then conclude that "the growing drug markets and a marked disappearance of males" combine with other factors in underclass communities "to create social and economic opportunity structures open to women's increasing participation in violent crime" (Baskin et al., 1993, p. 406).

The authors further suggest that traditional theories of women's offenses, particularly those that emphasize gender and victimization, do not adequately explain women's violent crime. Their work, they contend, "confirms our initial sense that women in inner city neighborhoods are being pulled toward violent street crime by the same forces that have been found to affect their male counterparts (e.g., peers, opportunity structures, neighborhood effects)" (Baskin et al., 1993, p. 412). They conclude that the socioeconomic situation in the inner city, specifically as it is affected by the drug trade, creates "new dynamics of crime where gender is a far less salient factor" (Baskin et al., 1993, p. 417).

These authors argue that in economically devastated inner cities such as New York, women's violence—particularly the violence of the women of color—does not need to be considered in terms of the place of these women in patriarchal society (e.g., the effect of gender in their lives). Instead, they contend that these women (like their male counterparts) are being drawn to violence and other forms of traditionally male crimes for the same reasons as men.

This turns the "liberation" hypothesis on its head. Now it is not presumed economic gain that promoted "equality" in crime, but rather it is economic marginalization that causes women to move out of their "traditional" roles into the role of criminal. Is that really what is going on?

This chapter has already cast doubt on the notion that there has been any dramatic shift in women's share of violent crime (at least as measured by arrest statistics). This chapter has also provided evidence that women's participation in offenses that sound "non-traditional" (such as embezzlement, DUI, and larceny theft) is deeply affected by the "place" of women in society. Both of these findings cast doubt on claims for the existence of a new, violent street criminal class of women. . . .

Discussion Questions

1. A review of the history of women's crime illustrates that the real question is not why women murder, but rather why so few women murder. What motivated this comment by the author? What is the significance of the question?

2. Why are women more likely to be arrested for shoplifting than men? How do their motivations, styles and actions differ?

3. In what types of crimes are women more likely to engage? Why? What social factors affect this decision? Has the nature of women's crime changed much over the years? Why or why not? How have the trends in women's arrests changed over the years (if at all)?

References

Adler, F. (1975a). "The rise of the female crook." *Psychology Today*, 9, 42–46, 112–114.

Adler, F. (1975b). *Sisters in Crime*. New York: Mcgraw Hill.

Arnold, R. (1995). "The processes of victimization and criminalization of black women." In B.R. Price & N. Sokoloff (Eds.), *The Criminal Justice System and Women* (pp. 136–146). New York: McGraw-Hill.

Baskin, D., & Sommers, I. (1993). "Females' initiation into violent street crime." *Justice Quarterly*, 10(4), 559–581.

Baskin, D., Sommers, I., & Fagan, J. (1993). "The political economy of female violent street crime." *Fordham Urban Law Journal*, 20(3), 401–417.

Beddoe, D. (1979). *Welsh convict women*. Barry, Wales: Stewart Williams.

Boritch, H., & Hagan, J. (1990). "A century of crime in Toronto: Gender, class and patterns of social control, 1859–1955." *Criminology*, 28 (4), 567–599.

Bureau of Justice Statistics. (1989a). *Criminal victimization in the United States*. Washington, D.C.: U.S. Department of Justice.

Bynum, V.E. (1992). *Unruly women*. Chapel Hill: University of North Carolina Press.

Cameron, M.B. (1953). *Department store shoplifting*. Unpublished doctoral dissertation, Indiana University.

Campbell, A. (1981). *Girl delinquents*. New York: St. Martin's.

Center for Policy Studies. (1991). *Violence against women as bias motivate hate crime*. Washington, D.C.: Center for Women Policy Studies.

Chapman, J. R. (1980). *Economic realities and the female offender*. Lexington, MA: Lexington Books.

Chesney-Lind, M. (1986). "Women and crime: The female offender." *Signs*, 12, 78–96.

Chesney-Lind, M., & Rodriguez, N. (1983). "Women under lock and key." *The Prison Journal*, 63, 47–65.

Chesney-Lind, M., & Shelden, R. G. (1992). *Girls, delinquency, and the juvenile justice system*. Pacific Grove, CA: Brooks/Cole.

Coles, F. (1991, February). *Women, alcohol, and automobiles: A deadly cocktail*. Paper presented at the Western Society of Criminology Meetings, Berkeley, California.

Crites, L. (1976). *The female offender*. Lexington, MA: Lexington Books.

Crittenden, D. (1990, January 25). "You've come a long way, Moll." *Wall Street Journal*, p. A14.

Daly, K. (1989). "Gender and varieties of white-collar crime." *Criminology*, 27(4), 769–793.

English, K. (1993). "Self-reported crimes rates of women prisoners." *Journal of Quantitative Criminology*, 9, 357–382.

Federal Bureau of Investigation. (1973). *Crime in the United States—1972*. Washington, D.C.: U.S. Department of Justice.

Federal Bureau of Investigation. (1976). *Crime in the United States—1975*. Washington, D.C.: U.S. Department of Justice.

Federal Bureau of Investigation. (1992). *Crime in the United States—1991*. Washington, D.C.: U.S. Department of Justice.

Federal Bureau of Investigation. (1993). *Crime in the United States—1992*. Washington, D.C.: U.S. Department of Justice.

Federal Bureau of Investigation. (1994). *Crime in the United States—1993*. Washington, D.C.: U.S. Department of Justice.

Federal Bureau of Investigation. (1995). *Crime in the United States—1994*. Washington, D.C.: U.S. Department of Justice.

Feeley, M., & Little, D. L. (1991). "The vanishing female: The decline of women in the criminal process." *Law and Society Review*, 256, 719–758.

Foley, C. (1974, October 20). "Increase of women in crime and violence." *Honolulu Sunday Star-Bulletin and Advertiser*, p. 1.

Gilfus, M. (1992). "From victims to survivors to offenders: Women's routes of entry into street crime." *Women and Criminal Justice*, 4(1), 63–89.

Hanawalt, L.B. (1982). "Women before the law: Females as felons and prey in fourteenth-century England." In D. K. Weibberg (Ed.), *Women and the Law* (pp. 165–196). Cambridge, MA: Schenkman.

Hartman, M. S. (1977). *Victorian murderesses*. New York: Schoken.

Hochschild, A. (1989). *The second shift*. New York: Viking.

Jones, A. (1980). *Women who kill*. New York: Fawcett.

Kahler. K. (1992, May 17). "Hand that rocks the cradle is taking up violent crime." *Sunday Star-Ledger*, p. 3A.

Klein, D., & Kress, J. (1976). "Any woman's blues: A critical overview of women, crime and the criminal justice system." *Crime and Social Justice*, 5(Spring/Summer), 34–48.

Klemesrud, J. (1978, January 16). "Women terrorists, sisters in crime." *Honolulu Star-Bulletin*, p. C1.

Koop, C. E. (1989, May 22). *Violence against women: A global problem*. Address by the Surgeon General of the U.S. Public Health Service at a conference of the Pan American Health Organization, Washington, D.C.

Lindquist, J. (1988). *Misdemeanor crime*. Newbury Park, CA: Sage.

Los Angeles Times Service. (1975, August 7). "L.A. police chief blames libbers." *Honolulu Advertiser*, p. B4.

Miller, E. (1986). *Street woman*. Philadelphia: Temple University Press.

Morris, A. (1987). *Women, crime and criminal justice*. New York: Basil Blackwell.

Nelson, L. D. (1977, October 23). "Women make gains in shady world, too." *Honolulu Sunday Star-Bulletin and Advertiser*, p. G-8.

Rans, L. (1975). *Women's arrest statistics*. (The women offender report). Washington, D.C.: American Bar Association, Female Offender Resource Center.

Renzetti, C., & Curran, D. J. (1995). *Women, men and society*. Boston: Allyn and Bacon.

Roberts, S. (1971, June 13). "Crime rate of women up sharply over men's." *New York Times*, pp. 1, 72.

Simon, R. (1975). *Women and crime*. Lexington, MA: Lexington Books.

Simon, R. J., & Landis, J. (1991). *The crimes women commit, the punishments they receive*. Lexington, MA: Lexington Books.

Smart, C. (1976). *Women, crime and criminology: A feminist critique*. London: Routledge and Kegan Paul.

Sommers, I., & Baskin, D. (1992). "Sex, race, age, and violent offending." *Violence and Its Victims*, 7(3), 191–201.

Sommers, I., & Baskin, D. (1993). "The situational context of violent female offending." *Crime and Delinquency*, 30, 136–162.

Stark, E., Flitcraft, A., Zuckerman, D., Grey, A., Robison, J., & Frazier, W. (1981). "Wife abuse in the medical setting: An introduction for health personnel." *Domestic Violence Monograph Services, No. 7*. Rockville, MD: National Clearinghouse on Domestic Violence.

Steffensmeier, D. J. (1980). "Sex differences in patterns of adult crime, 1965—1977." *Social Forces*, 58, 1080–1108.

Steffensmeier, D., & Allen, E. (1995). "Criminal behavior: Gender and age." In J. Sheley (Ed.), *Criminology: A contemporary handbook* (pp. 83–114).

Straus, M. A., Gelles, R. J., & Steinmetz, S. (1980). *Behind closed doors: Violence in the American family*. Garden City, NY: Doubleday.

Weis, J. G. (1976). "Liberation and crime: The invention of the new female criminal." *Crime and Social Justice*, 6, 17.

Wells-Parker, E., Pang, M. G., Anderson, B. J., McMillen, D. L. & Miller, D. I. (1991). "Female DUI offenders." *Journal of Studies in Alcohol*, 52, 142–147.

Zietz, D. (1981). *Women who embezzle or defraud: A study of convicted felons*. New York, Praeger.

Reprinted from: Meda Chesney-Lind, "Trends in Women's Crime." In *The Female Offender*, pp. 95-119. Copyright © 1997 by Sage Publications. Reprinted by permission. ✦

13

Age and the Distribution of Crime

Darrell J. Steffensmeier
Emilie Andersen Allan
Miles D. Harer
Cathy Streifel

For some time criminologists have spoken of a relationship between age and crime. Crime, they have said, is principally an activity of the young, and as one ages the probability of criminal involvement decreases, a process sometimes referred to as "aging out." The reasons for the decline in crime rates as one passes from adolescence to young adulthood are many. They may include social maturation, family responsibilities, or finding a job. As one's stake in conformity rises, so does the cost of becoming involved in criminality. Some crimes, like white-collar offenses, tend to peak later, however, and appear to be subject to a different age-crime dynamic than conventional offenses.

In this selection Darrell L. Steffensmeier and his associates examine several challenges to the traditional explanation of the age-crime relationship. The authors point out "that the criminological literature as yet contains no systematic study of the age-crime distribution over time and by offense type. . . ." Their work fills that void and reveals several interesting facts about contemporary criminality. They find that today's offenders are younger than in the past, and that industrialization has played a significant role in that change. Certain common offenses of youth, such as mischief and high-risk property crimes, peak early and fall off steeply, while crimes of lower risk and even most personal crimes decline much more

slowly. They conclude that there is no single age-crime pattern but many such patterns based on the nature of the offense.

Variations in criminal activity by age should not be surprising. On the one hand, the search for thrills and adventure associated with youth often leads to crime. So does the lack of meaningful social roles for teenagers in modern society. On the other hand, opportunities to commit certain types of crime are also associated with age, hence the peaking of criminal activity at older ages for some offenses.

The proposition that involvement in crime diminishes with age is one of the oldest and most widely accepted in criminology (Quetelet 1831; Parmelee 1918). But there is disagreement about the strength and the universality of the age-crime relation. The traditional sociological view is that crime tends to peak in adolescence or early adulthood and then generally declines with age. However, while a decline in criminality is common to all age-crime distributions over time or across localities, *the parameters of the distributions may be quite different* (Mannheim 1965).

The traditional sociological explanation of the tendency for crime to decline with age (whether sharply for some crimes or slowly for others) rests on the Hobbesian assumption that human behavior is not inherently conforming and that the "problem of social order" facing any society is a recurring one. Any society capable of survival must have an institutional structure that motivates its youth to assume adult roles and responsibilities. As Ryder (1965, p. 845) observes, "Society at large is faced perennially with an invasion of barbarians . . . [and] every adult generation is faced with the task of civilizing those barbarians." This "civilizing," or pressure toward conformity, is achieved through age-related processes of socialization, social integration, and social control that raise the costs of crime and reduce its benefits.

Recently, Hirschi and Gottfredson (1983; Gottfredson and Hirschi 1986) have disputed the traditional sociological view of the age-crime relationship, arguing instead that the age distribution of crime is essentially invariant across time and space, regardless of offense. They further argue that existing explanations for the relationship between age and crime are erroneous and that the age distribution of crime cannot be explained by sociological theories currently utilized by criminologists (such as strain, differential association, or social control) because the causal variables employed in these theories are supposed to vary across time and space. In addition, Hirschi and Gottfredson contend that the identification of the causes of crime at any age will suffice to identify them at other ages as well. Thus, cohort and other types of longtitudinal research designs are not necessary in studying crime causation.

We agree with other critics (e.g., Greenberg 1985; Farrington 1986) that Hirschi and Gottfredson's contentions are overstated and misleading. First, the evidence offered by Hirschi and Gottfredson on the age-crime relation over time and across offenses is sparse. Comparisons across offense type are limited to plots displaying the age distribution for common crimes of theft and interpersonal violence. The comparison over time is limited to plots showing three age distributions: one on total indicted persons from England and Wales in 1842-44, another on total convictions from England and Wales in 1842-44, another on total convictions from England in 1913, and another on total arrests from the United States in 1979 as reported in the *Uniform Crime Reports*. "The shape or form of the distribution," Hirschi and Gottfredson (1983, p. 55) conclude, "has remained virtually unchanged for about 150 years." Unfortunately, Hirschi and Gottfredson do not provide any statistical tests, and their age-crime plots are so compressed that it is difficult, if not impossible, to discern whether, in fact, any differences in age distribution do exist.

Second, although few in number, the studies examining the age-crime relationship have had modest success in identifying social causes, despite Hirschi and Gottfredson's claim to the contrary. For example, Rowe and Tittle conclude that social processes do explain much of the age-crime relationship when the sociological variables (social integration, moral commitment, fear of sanctions, and utility of crime) are considered si-

multaneously in an *additive* model. Also, in a reanalysis of the Tittle data set aimed at overcoming statistical flaws in the original investigation (e.g., inappropriate use of γ and the introduction of control variables only one or two at a time rather than simultaneously), Kercher (1987) concludes that the Tittle data provide strong evidence that age affects crime indirectly through intervening sociological variables such as moral commitment and criminal associates. Several other studies have also supported the ability of sociological factors to explain the age-crime relationship, including Jensen's (1977) study of rule breaking among women in prison, Hollinger and Clark's (1983) self-report study of employee pilferage, and Meier and Johnson's (1977) study of marijuana smoking among adults aged 18 and older. The role of sociological factors in explaining the age-crime relationship is further supported by reasonably reliable, though fragmentary, data on factors influencing cessation of criminal careers (e.g., Shover 1985; Steffensmeier 1986; McCord and Sanchez 1983; Trasler 1979; Farrington 1986).

Furthermore, even if it were an incontrovertible fact that the age distribution generally holds across time, place, and demographic subgroup, it would not follow that age-crime distributions are not generated by social processes. One would not argue that social factors are not involved in the cultural universal that males have higher status than females in every culture.

It is no exaggeration to say that the criminological literature as yet contains no systematic study of the age-crime distribution over time and by offense type, so this paper fills a large gap. First, it provides an analysis of recent *UCR* age-specific arrest data for over 25 types of offenses for purposes of determining the homogeneity of the age curve across offense types. Second, it compares the contemporary age-crime pattern with patterns of 20 and 40 years ago for purposes of determining the stability (invariance) of the age-crime distribution over time.

Age-specific arrest data of the FBI's *Uniform Crime Reports (UCR)* covering the past half-century provide the best opportunity to test the invariance hypothesis. The *UCR* data provide fairly refined breakdowns as to offense and age grouping; yet no one has systematically analyzed the arrest data for all offense types or over the entire period for which age-specific *UCR* arrest data are available. Furthermore, Hirschi and Gottfredson explicitly claim (but do not document) that these data support their position. . . .

Expectations

Traditional research and theory on the age-crime relationship suggest some of the patterns that may be expected: (1) most crimes peak in adolescence or early adulthood, then decline fairly steadily; (2) crime types vary in peak ages of criminality and in rates of decline from the peak; (3) because of the effect of industrialization, peak ages have become younger over the past four decades, and the descent of the age curve from the peak has become steeper. Tittle (1988) points out that both labeling theory and social-control theory can contribute to an understanding of these general patterns, while Greenberg (1977) has argued the relevance of strain theory. We believe that opportunity theory and differential association/reinforcement can also help explain age-crime patterns.

For example, the general rise in rates of offending among teenagers and the peaking of rates in adolescence or young adulthood reflect the increased sources of criminogenic reinforcement experienced by young people, whereas the decline in rates of older persons reflects the powerful institutional pressures for conformity that accompany adulthood. Juveniles have not as yet developed either a well-defined sense of self or strong stakes in conformity. At the same time, they are barred from many legitimate avenues for achieving socially valued goals; their dependent status insulates them from many of the social and legal costs of illegitimate activities; and their stage of cognitive development limits prudence concerning the consequences of their behavior (Elliott, Ageton, and Canter 1979; Friday and Hage 1976; Greenberg 1977; Wilcox 1979; Kohlberg 1983). Juveniles trying to establish and test their self-identities are experimenting with many different kinds of behavior and are thus likely to obtain valued goods, portray courage or loyalty in the presence of peers, strike out at someone who is disliked, or simply "get kicks" (Gold 1970; Briar and Piliavin 1965).

It is also expected that there will be clear differences across offense types in the age distribution of arrests. In comparison with adults, juveniles have more sources of reinforcement for involvement in low-yield, high-risk types of behavior represented by such offenses as burglary, robbery, and vandalism. These crimes tend to be committed in peer groups and to be relatively unsophisticated in that the perpetrators rely more on physical strength, mobility, and daring than on skills and contacts. For most juveniles, they are also "low-yield" or exploratory offenses that, like the drug and alcohol offense categories, provide "thrills" and peer acceptance as much as or more than real financial gain (Lemert 1951; Matza 1964; McGahey 1986; Giordano, Cernkovich, and Pugh 1986; for a treatment of how most burglaries and thefts are "low-yield," see Steffensmeier 1986). The age distribution for such crimes will peak at an early age and decline rapidly among older age groups.

Because such crimes are low yield and high risk, their age-specific rates will peak at an early age and drop off quickly during the transition from adolescence to adulthood. With increased maturity, young adults shift from self-absorption to concern for others and for the broader community and rapidly come to see delinquent behaviors as childish or foolish. They also begin to lose some of the strength and agility required for certain delinquent acts. Those who remain unscathed by negative labels will have noncriminal identities confirmed at the same time as their stakes in conformity are increasing (Tittle 1988). Leaving school, entering employment, going to college, enlisting in the military, and getting married not only increase social integration and orientation to conventional society; they also diminish the opportunities for committing these offenses and increase the potential costs of legal and social sanctions—at the same time that those legal sanctions increase substantially (Zimring 1981; Elliott et al. 1979; Empey 1978).

But, since the motivation and the opportunity for different kinds of crime are age related, it is not plausible to expect every offense category to follow a pattern of early peak age and rapid decline. For example, a number of property-crime categories like embezzlement and fraud provide the possibility of greater gains and lower risk, so that the rates of offending should not peak as early or drop as fast (Coleman 1987). Various public-order offense categories (e.g., homicide and assault) have a more expressive character that is less susceptible to rational withdrawal and have greater cultural supports; such categories should therefore have "older" age curves that show continued high rates of offending into the adult years (Lemert 1951; Gibbons 1987; Steffensmeier 1987). In other words, the effects of social contingencies may vary for different crimes and age groups; if so, criminological theory must address these variations, and a single "global" explanation of the age-crime relationship may be unrealistic.

Given the massive social changes of the past half-century, traditional views suggest that, between 1940 and 1980, we may expect to find a trend toward an increased proportion of youthful offenders because of heightened status anxiety among contemporary adolescents (Friday and Hage 1976; Greenberg 1977; Glaser 1978). Although present since colonial times, the discontinuity in transition from adolescence to adulthood has accelerated in the post-World War II period with major changes in the family, education, the labor force, the military, and in adolescence more generally (Clausen 1986). In modern societies, it has become more difficult to achieve the events marking the transition to adulthood in a normatively prescribed order (Hogan 1980). The role of industrialization in changing the age-crime relation is supported by comparisons of the age-crime distribution between advanced and less industrialized nations, which reveal that the relative magnitude of youth involvement in reported crime is considerably smaller in developing nations than in advanced ones (Christie 1974; Greenberg 1977; Mannheim 1965). . . .

Findings

Gottfredson and Hirschi write: "the propensity to commit criminal acts reaches a peak in the middle to late teens and then declines rapidly throughout life. Further, this distribution is characteristic of the age-crime relation regardless of sex, race, country, time, or offense. Indeed, the persistence of this relation across time and culture is phenomenal" (1986, p. 219). Our task is to investigate their assertion of invariance with respect to offense and time. . . . [W]e examine the age distribution of crime in the recent period, using data averaged over the years 1980-91 and focusing on whether the distribution varies by offense type. . . . [Next] we examine whether the age-crime distribution is invariant over time by comparing the 1980 pattern with the patterns for 1960 and 1940. . . .

On the basis of an analysis of age patterns in crime, as revealed in *UCR* arrest statistics for more than 20 different offense types for 1980, 1960, and 1940, we reject the hypothesis that the age distribution of crime is invariant across crime types and over time. When looked at by offense type, although a decline in criminality at older ages is common to all age-crime distributions, the parameters—both in modal age and in shape—of the distributions are quite different. When looked at over time, the age curves peak earlier and become progressively steeper, so that the offenders of today tend to be younger and less variable in age than in 1940 or in 1960. The consistency of these findings with those for differences between developing and advanced nations supports the position that industrialization has played an important role in changing the age-crime relation.

During the current period, the hypothesized pattern fits the age curves for low-yield, high-risk property crimes and certain other criminal-mischief, "hell-raising" types of crimes. More remunerative property crimes with lower risks, as well as most person crimes, public-order offenses, and alcohol abuse, all have much flatter age curves and a slower drop-off in rates of offending. More than one-half of all offense categories have values of 33 or higher on the index of dissimilarity compared with our criterion crime of burglary (meaning that more than one-third of all arrests would have to be shifted for the comparison crime to achieve an age distribution identical to that of burglary). overall, the results from the index of dissimilarity and χ^2 tests identified only offenses homogenous with burglary.

Thus, there is not a single age pattern, as suggested by Hirschi and Gottfredson, but several. Unfortunately, because of the overly broad *UCR* offense categories the *UCR* data are hardly adequate for clear-cut delineation of "young" versus "middle-aged" versus "elderly" age-crime patterns, much less for systematic testing of theories of crime causation on age effects (see discussion earlier . . .). An even more serious limitation is the likelihood that older people may shift to less visible criminal roles such as loan shark, bookie, or fence (Steffensmeier 1986); or, as a spinoff of legitimate roles, they may commit surreptitious crimes unlikely to be reported to the authorities, such as business fraud, bribery, price-fixing, labor-union racketeering, or black-market activities (Clinard 1952; Clinard and Yeager 1980; Vaughn 1983; Knapp Commission 1972; Adler 1986; Pennsylvania Crime Commission 1981; Coleman 1987). Unfortunately, we know very little about the age distribution of persons who commit these and related lucrative crimes, but fragmentary evidence suggests that such crimes are likely to involve syndicate members, professional criminals, corporate officers, corrupt officials, and so on, who tend to be relatively old. In contrast to the age curves for ordinary crimes, which tend to be sharply peaked, it may be that the age curves for lucrative criminality not only peak much later but tend not to decline with age. The age curve for gambling may provide a hint.[1]

Our findings have important implications for forecasting and for aggregate research using cross-sectional or longitudinal data. First, research attempting to forecast trends in crime rates must take into account the fact that the effect of the population's age composition will vary by crime type, as some research has found (Steffensmeier and Harer 1987). For example, the age distribution of property crimes is generally younger than for person crimes, public-order offenses, or sub-

stance abuse. However, even within offense types there are substantial variations in age patterns. The patterns identified by the homogeneity tests can provide some guidance in identifying offenses that may be safely classed together.

Second, the differences in shapes of curves are also sufficient for us to recommend that, for greater accuracy, projections of future trends as well as rate adjustments for historical time-series data should incorporate all age categories rather than lump data into large age groups (e.g., 15-24). Adjustment procedures that are overly simplified can falsely overpredict or underpredict age-structure effects, depending on the skewness of the age curve and the proportion of the population falling into the extremes of the age grouping.

Third, the age-crime relationship is sufficiently robust that both cross-sectional and longitudinal research should include appropriate age-composition controls, particularly since many causal variables of interest (e.g., labor-market factors) also strongly covary by age (Allan 1985). The effects of any social contingency may vary over the life span and may vary further by type of offense, so that, when possible, research should be age stratified or should incorporate age-standardized rates for variables with strong age patterns.

There is obviously a need for more research on the age-crime issue. Unfortunately, the prospects are dim for cumulative research that examines the age-crime relation over extended historical periods. The *UCR* data used in this study, despite their shortcomings, are probably the most comprehensive and reliable age statistics available, particularly if the focus is on the United States. The results of our analysis, therefore, may be the most conclusive that are possible. These results confirm that the tendency of crime to decline with age is tenacious by offense type and over time, but that the modal age and the rate of decline from the modal age vary considerably. As it stands, therefore, the best available evidence on the age-crime relationship is more consistent with the traditional sociological position than with the Hirschi and Gottfredson view. In fact, the evidence against invariance appears incontrovertible, and efforts could more profitably be directed at explaining variations in the age-crime relationship.

There are, nonetheless, two important caveats in our interpretation of the age statistics. First, by being selective, one could produce comparisons that would support an argument of either invariance (by presenting data mainly for the property or criminal-mischief crimes, or for a shorter time period only) or variance (by presenting only the most divergent offense types or time periods). Second, we have characterized the Hirschi and Gottfredson position as being more sweeping than the traditional sociological view (for similar interpretations of their argument, see Greenberg 1985; Farrington 1986; Gove 1985). If this is an accurate portrayal of their position, the findings of this report fail to substantiate it. On the other hand, if the Hirschi and Gottfredson position is less sweeping and universalistic, it is redundant, since it does not go beyond the traditional position on the issue.

Discussion Questions

1. Explain the relationship between low-yield, high-risk crimes (such as vandalism) and age distribution. Is this consistent with the age distribution of other types of crime? Does it hold across time, place and demographic subgroup? Does the same age distribution apply to all crimes? Why or why not?

2. How do motivations to commit crime change through the maturation process? How does this process vary among types of crime committed?

3. While it is clear that there is a relationship between age and crime, why has it been difficult to study? How will it change in the future? What, if anything, can be done to improve the method of study?

Endnote

1. Since our article went to press, we became aware of Shavit and Rattner's *AJS* article, "Age, Crime, and the Early Life Course" (1988). Combining police data with demographic and life history data of a sample of 2,144 Israeli youth (ages 10–29), the authors conclude (1) that the shape of the age-crime distribution does not vary significantly across ethnic, socioeconomic, and religious orthodoxy groups and (2) that the age-crime distribution cannot be explained in terms of age variations in marital status, employment, and schooling. These findings are interpreted as supporting the Hirschi and Gottfredson invariance thesis. We believe the Shavit and Rattner study has a number of flaws and offers a poor test of the invariance position. First, they use a total index (total police contacts) that may be heavily weighted by one or two offenses. Thus the sharp decline in police contacts from age 16 to 17 may be due largely to a change in legal status of juveniles at age 17 in Israel. Second, the authors ignore the fact that the erratic multimmodal age-crime plot displayed in their fig. 1 deviates sharply from the unimodal curve touted by Hirschi and Gottfredson as "universal." Instead of dropping off steadily after a peak in late adolescence, their curve fluctuates wildly and is actually higher at age 29 than at age 17. Shavit and Rattner thus provide strong evidence of cross-national variation in the age-crime curve. Third, we question the assumption that the failure to find difference across social groups supports the Hirschi and Gottfredson view that no known sociological or economic set of variables can account for age variations in delinquency. As discussed elsewhere (Steffensmeier and Allan [1988]), for any given time and culture, we expect that a common set of social and legal factors will influence the age propensity of differing social groups in roughly equal fashion, so that cross-group variation in the age-crime curve will be slight. Fourth, the life-course variables are based on retrospective life histories and fail to take into account the importance of anticipatory socialization. After the mid teens (e.g., 17-year-olds), before youths actually assume the adult roles involved in work, marriage, college, or military service, the *anticipation* of assuming these roles contributes to greater prudence and diminishes their willingness to commit crimes—especially the high-risk, exploratory delinquencies of younger teens.

References

Adler, Patricia. 1986. "Wheeling and Dealing: A Sociological Portrait of an Upper-Level Drug-Dealing and Smuggling Community." Ph.D. dissertation. University of California, San Diego, Department of Sociology.

Allan, Emilie A. 1985. "Crime and the Labor Market." Ph.D. dissertation. Pennsylvania State University, Department of Sociology.

Briar, Scott, and Irving Piliavin. 1965. "Delinquency, Situational Inducements, and Commitment to Conformity." *Social Problems* 13:33-45.

Christie, Nils. 1974. "Criminological Data as Indicators on Contemporary Society." Pp. 144-55 in *Crime and Industrialization*. Stockholm: Scandinavian Research Council for Criminology.

Clausen, John. 1986. *The Life Course: A Sociological Perspective*. Englewood Cliffs, N.J.: Prentice-Hall.

Clinard, Marshall. 1952. *The Black Market: A Study of White Collar Crime*. New York: Rinehart.

Clinard, Marshall, and Peter Yeager. 1980. *Corporate Crime*. New York: Macmillan.

Cline, Hugh. 1980. "Criminal Behavior over the Life Span." Pp. 641-74 in *Constancy and Change in Human Development*, edited by Orville Brim and Jerome Kagan. Cambridge: Harvard University Press.

Clogg, Clifford C. 1982. "Using Association Models in Sociological Research: Some Examples." *American Journal of Sociology* 88:114-34.

Cohen, Lawrence, and Kenneth Land. 1987. "Age Structure and Crime: Symmetry versus Asymmetry and the Projection of Crime Rates through the 1990s." *American Sociological Review* 52:170-83.

Coleman, James William. 1987. "Toward an Integrated Theory of White-Collar Crime." *American Journal of Sociology* 93:406-39.

Elliott, Delbert, Suzanne Ageton, and Rachelle Canter. 1979. "An Integrated Theoretical Perspective on Delinquent Behavior." *Journal of Research in Crime and Delinquency* 16: 3-27.

Elliott, Delbert, Suzanne Ageton, David Huizinga et al. 1983. *The Prevalence and Incidence of Delinquent Behavior: 1976-1980*. Boulder, Colo.: Behavioral Research Institute.

Empey, Lamar. 1978. *American Delinquency: Its Meaning and Construction*. Homewood, Ill.: Dorsey.

Farrington, David. 1986. "Age and Crime." Pp. 189-250 in *Crime and Justice: An Annual Review of Research*, edited by Michael Tonry and Norval Morris. Chicago: University of Chicago Press.

Friday, Paul, and Jerald Hage. 1976. "Youth Crime in Postindustrial Societies: An Integrated Perspective." *Criminology* 14:347-68.

Gibbons, Don. 1987. *Society, Crime and Criminal Behavior*. Englewood Cliffs, N.J.: Prentice-Hall.

Giordano, Peggy, Stephen Cernkovich, and M.D. Pugh. 1986. "Friendships and Delinquency." *American Journal of Sociology* 91: 1170-1202.

Glaser, Daniel. 1978. *Crime in Our Changing Society*. New York: Holt, Rinehart & Winston.

Gold, Martin. 1970. *Delinquent Behavior in an American City*. Belmont, Calif.: Brooks/Cole.

Goodman, Leo. 1981. "Criteria for Determining Whether Certain Categories in a Cross-Classification Table Should Be Combined, with Special Reference to Occupational Categories in an Occupational Mobility Table." *American Journal of Sociology* 87:612-50.

Gottfredson, Michael, and Travis Hirschi. 1986. "The True Value of Lambda Would Appear to Be Zero: An Essay on Career Criminals, Criminal Careers, Selective Incapacitation, Cohort Studies, and Related Topics." *Criminology* 24:213-34.

Gove, Walter. 1985. "The Effect of Age and Gender on Deviant Behavior: A Biopsychosocial Perspective." Pp. 115-44 in *Gender and the Life Course*, edited by Alice Rossi. Hawthorne, N.Y.: Aldine.

Greenberg, David. 1977. "Delinquency and the Age Structure of Society." *Contemporary Crises* 1:189-224.

——. 1985. "Age, Crime, and Social Explanation." *American Journal of Sociology* 91:1-21.

Hirschi, Travis, and Michael Gottfredson. 1983. "Age and the Explanation of Crime." *American Journal of Sociology* 89:552-84.

Hogan, Dennis. 1980. "The Transition to Adulthood as a Career Contingency." *American Sociological Review* 45:261-75.

Hollinger, Richard, and John Clark. 1983. *Theft by Employees*. Lexington, Mass.: Lexington.

Jensen, Gary. 1977. "Age and Rule Breaking in Prison." *Criminology* 14:555-68.

Kercher, Kyle. 1987. "Explaining the Relationship Between Age and Crime: The Biological vs. Sociological Model." Presented at the annual meeting of the American Society of Criminology, Montreal.

Knapp Commission. 1972. *The Knapp Commission Report on Police Corruption*. New York: Braziller.

Kohlberg, Lawrence. 1983. *The Psychology of Moral Development*. New York: Harper & Row.

Lemert, Edwin. 1951. *Social Pathology*. New York: McGraw-Hill.

Lichter, Daniel. 1985. "Racial Concentration and Segregation Across U.S. Counties, 1950-1980." *Demography* 22:603-9.

McCord, William, and Jose Sanchez. 1983. "The Treatment of Deviant Children: A Twenty-Five Year Follow-Up Study." *Crime and Delinquency* 29:238-53.

McGahey, Richard. 1986. "Economic Conditions, Neighborhood Organization, and Urban Crime." Pp. 231-70 in *Communities and Crime*, edited by Albert Reiss, Jr., and Michael Tonry. Chicago: University of Chicago Press.

Mannheim, Hermann. 1965. *Comparative Criminology*. Boston: Houghton Mifflin.

Matza, David. 1964. *Delinquency and Drift*. New York: Wiley.

Meier, R., and W. Johnson. 1977. "Deterrence as Social Control: The Legal and Extralegal Production of Conformity." *American Sociological Review* 42:292-304.

Parmelee, Maurice. 1918. *Criminology*. New York: Macmillan.

Pennsylvania Crime Commission. 1981. *A Decade of Organized Crime, 1980 Report*. St. Davids: Commonwealth of Pennsylvania.

Quetelet, Adolphe. 1831. *Research on the Propensity to Crime of Different Ages*. Brussels: Hayez.

Reckless, Walter. 1950. *The Crime Problem*. New York: Appleton-Century-Crofts.

Rowe, Allan, and Charles Tittle. 1977. "Life Cycle Changes and Criminal Propensity." *Sociological Quarterly* 18:223-36.

Ryder, Norman. 1965. "The Cohort as a Concept in the Study of Social Change." *American Sociological Review* 30:843-61.

Shavit, Yossi, and Arye Rattner. 1988. "Age, Crime, and the Early Life Course." *American Journal of Sociology* 93:1457-70.

Shover, Neal. 1985. *Aging Criminals*. Beverly Hills: Sage.

Shryock, H., and J. Siegel. 1976. *The Methods and Materials of Demography*. New York: Academic.

Steffensmeier, Darrell. 1986. *The Fence: In the Shadow of Two Worlds*. Totowa, N.J.: Rowman & Littlefield.

Steffensmeier, Darrell, and Emilie A. Allan. 1988. "Sex Disparities in Arrests by Residence, Race, and Age: An Assessment of the Gender Convergence/Crime Hypothesis." *Justice Quarterly* 5:53-80.

Steffensmeier, Darrell, and Michael Cobb. 1981. "Sex Differences in Urban Arrest Patterns, 1934-79." *Social Problems* 29:37-49.

Steffensmeier, Darrell, and Miles Harer. 1987. "Is the Crime Rate Really Falling? An 'Aging' U.S. Population and Its Impact on the Nation's Crime Rate, 1980-1984." *Journal of Research in Crime and Delinquency* 24:23-48.

Steffensmeier, Darrell, Cathy Streifel, and Miles D. Harer. 1987. "Relative Cohort Size and Youth Crime in the United States, 1953-1984." *American Sociological Review* 52:702-10.

Sutherland, Edwin, and Donald Cressey. 1978. *Criminology*, 10th ed. Philadelphia: Lippincott.

Tittle, Charles R. 1988. "Two Empirical Regularities (Maybe) in Search of an Explanation: Commentary on the Age/Crime Debate." *Criminology* 26:75-85.

Trasler, Gordon. 1979. "Delinquency, Recidivism, and Desistance." *British Journal of Criminology* 19:314-22.

U.S. Bureau of Justice Statistics. 1987. *Criminal Victimization in the United States, 1985*. Washington, D.C.: Government Printing Office.

U.S. Federal Bureau of Investigation. 1939. *Uniform Crime Reports*. Washington, D.C.: Government Printing Office.

——. 1940. *Uniform Crime Reports*. Washington, D.C.: Government Printing Office.

——. 1960. *Uniform Crime Reports*. Washington, D.C.: Government Printing Office.

——. 1961. *Uniform Crime Reports*. Washington, D.C.: Government Printing Office.

——. 1980. *Uniform Crime Reports*. Washington, D.C.: Government Printing Office.

——. 1981. *Uniform Crime Reports*. Washington, D.C.: Government Printing Office.

Vaughan, Diane. 1983. *Controlling Unlawful Organizational Behavior: Social Structure and Corporate Misconduct*. Chicago: University of Chicago Press.

Wilcox, Mary. 1979. *Developmental Journey: A Guide to the Development of Logical and Moral Reasoning and Social Perspective*. Nashville: Abington.

Zimring, Franklin. 1981. "Kids, Groups and Crime: Some Implications of a Well-Known Secret." *Journal of Criminal Law, Criminology, and Police Science* 48:433-34.

14

Family Relationships, Juvenile Delinquency, and Adult Criminality

Joan McCord

The role of the family in juvenile delinquency has long been debated by criminologists and family sociologists. Since the family is the child's primary socializing agent, it has been natural to look there for explanations of antisocial behavior. This tendency has been strengthened by the popularity of personality-development theories, which seem to place responsibility for all behavior on early family experiences. Do bad parents create bad children who grow up to become bad adults? Some people seem to think so. Researchers have also looked at birth order to determine its impact on the behavior of children. Although personality differences can apparently be found among siblings by order of birth, this difference has not been related to delinquency and crime. Broken homes have been singled out for blame by many critics who see the family instability caused by divorce and separation as detrimental to the behavioral development of the child. And these are but a few of the family variables that have been hypothesized to be related to juvenile delinquency and even to adult crime.

This selection by Joan McCord uses longitudinal data from a classic study of delinquency to address two important questions: Do family interactions in childhood influence criminality among males, and if so, what is the nature of these interactions? Do maternal or paternal interactions influence the child's delinquency? McCord found that childhood family relationships and interactive patterns do influence criminal behavior. The mother's competence in carrying out the maternal role and the expectations the family had of the child influenced the likelihood of delinquency. Competent mothers with high expectations of their child seem to insulate him against juvenile delinquency in the adolescent years. This insulation has an impact on adult criminality as well, since boys who do not become delinquent are less likely to engage in adult crime. Although it is the mother who insulates and nurtures the child as a juvenile, it is the father who appears to provide the role model for the son as an adult. The father's interaction with the family is more probable to have a direct influence on the son's adult criminality.

McCord's work establishes the important role family relationships play in determining delinquency and crime. Although mothers appear to play the more important role in determining the juvenile's behavior, paternal influence is also important, since fathers teach sons how to behave as adults.

Theoretical Perspective

Historically, family interactions have been assumed to influence criminal behavior. Plato, for example, prescribed a regimen for rearing good citizens in the nursery. Aristotle asserted that in order to be virtuous, "we ought to have been brought up in a particular way from our very youth" (Bk.II, Ch. 3:11048). And John Locke wrote his letters on the education of children in the belief that errors "carry their afterwards-incorrigible taint with them, through all the parts and stations of life" (1693:iv).

Twentieth century theorists ranging from the analytic to the behavioral seem to concur with the earlier thinkers in assuming that parental care is critical to socialized behavior. Theorists have suggested that inadequate families fail to provide the attachments that could leverage children into socialized lifestyles (e.g., Hirschi, 1969). They note that poor home environments provide a backdrop for children to associate differentially with those who have antisocial definitions of their environments (e.g., Sutherland and Cressey, 1974). And they point out that one feature of inadequate child rearing is that it fails to reward desired behavior and fails to condemn behavior that is not desired (e.g., Akers, 1973; Bandura and Walters, 1959).

Over the past several decades, social scientists have suggested that crime is a product of broken homes (e.g., Bacon et al., 1963; Burt, 1925; Fenichel, 1945; Freud, 1953; Goode, 1956; Murdock, 1949; Parsons and Bales, 1955; Shaw and McKay, 1932; Wadsworth, 1979), maternal employment (e.g., Glueck and Glueck, 1950; Nye, 1959), and maternal rejection (Bowlby, 1940, 1951; Goldfarb, 1945; Newell, 1934, 1936). Some have linked effects from broken homes with the impact parental absence has on sex-role identity (Bacon et al., 1963; Lamb, 1976; Levy, 1937; Miller, 1958; Whiting et al., 1958), and others have suggested that parental absence and maternal employment affect crime through contributing to inadequate supervision (e.g., Dornbusch et al., 1985; Hirschi, 1969; Hoffman, 1975; Maccoby, 1958; Nye, 1958).

Despite this long tradition, empirical support demonstrating the link between child rearing and criminal behavior has been weak. Accounting for this fact, Hirschi (1983) suggested that attributing behavioral differences to socialization practiced in the family is "directly contrary to the metaphysic of our age" (p. 54). Hirschi criticized the few studies that refer to family influences for using global measures of inadequacy, noting that they cannot yield information about the practices or policies that might reduce criminality.

Most of the evidence made available since Hirschi's appraisal has depended on information from adolescents who have simultaneously reported their parents' behavior and their own delinquencies (e.g., Cernkovich and Giordano, 1987; Hagan et al., 1985; Jensen and Brownfield, 1983; van Voorhis et al., 1988). Because these studies are based on data reporting delinquency and socialization variables at the same time, they are unable to disentangle causes from effects.

Two studies based on adolescents' reports have addressed the sequencing issue. Both used data collected by the Youth in Transition Project from adolescents at ages 15 and 17 years (Bachman and O'Malley, 1984). Liska and Reed (1985) looked at changes in delinquency related to parent-adolescent interaction; their analyses suggest that friendly interaction with parents (attachment) retards delinquency, which in turn, promotes school attachment and stronger family ties. Wells and Rankin (1988) considered the efficacy of various dimensions of direct control on delinquency; their analyses suggest that restrictiveness, but not harshness, inhibits delinquency. Although the same data base was used for the two studies, neither considered variables that appeared in the other, so the issues of relative importance and of collinearity among child-rearing parameters were not examined.

Relying on adolescents to report about their parents' child-rearing behavior assumes that the adolescents have correctly perceived, accurately recalled, and honestly reported the behavior of their parents. There are grounds for questioning those assumptions.

Experimental studies show that conscious attention is unnecessary for experiences to be influential (Kellogg, 1980); thus adolescents' reports reflecting this bias would tend to blur real differences in upbringing.

In addition, studies of perception and recall suggest that reports about child rearing are likely to be influenced by the very features under study as possible consequences of faulty child rearing. For example, abused children tend to perceive their parents as less punitive than revealed by objective evidence (Dean et al., 1986; J. McCord, 1983a); aggressive children tend to perceive behavior justifying aggression (Dodge and Somberg, 1987); and painful experience tends to exaggerate recall of painful events (Eich et al., 1990). Yet, criminologists have paid little attention to measurement issues related to ascertaining the impact of socialization within families.

Studies of the impact of child rearing suffer from special problems. When the source of data is children's reports on their parents' behavior, effects and causes are likely to be confounded. When parents report on their own behavior, they are likely to have a limited and biasing perspective and to misrepresent what they are willing to reveal. These biases have been shown in a study that included home observations as well as mothers' reports. The child's compliance was related to observed, although not to reported, behavior of the mother (Forehand et al., 1978). Eron and his coworkers (1961) discovered that even when fathers and mothers reported similarly about events, "the relation to other variables was not the same for the two groups of parents" (p. 471). Additionally, regardless of the source of information, if data are collected after the onset of misbehavior, distortions of memory give rise to biases.

Attention to problems of measurement characterize two studies of juvenile crime. In one, Larzelere and Patterson (1990) combined interviews with the child and his parents, observations, and the interviewer's impressions to create measures of discipline and monitoring. They found strong collinearity and therefore used a combined measure of "parental management." Data on family management were collected when the children were approximately nine years old. This variable mediated a relationship between socioeconomic status and delinquency as reported by the boys when they were 13. Larzelere and Patterson acknowledge that their measure of delinquency may be premature, but they point out that early starters tend to become the more serious criminals.

In the other study, Laub and Sampson (1988) reanalyzed data from the files compiled by Sheldon Glueck and Eleanor Glueck (1950). They built measures of family discipline, parent-child relations, and maternal supervision from multiple sources of information. The variables indicated that child-rearing processes bore strong relations to juvenile delinquency, as measured through official records. Laub and Sampson concluded that "family process and delinquency are related not just independent of traditional sociological controls, but of biosocial controls as well" (p. 374).

Other researchers have focused on different parts of the child-rearing process. Selection seems to be more a matter of style than a result of considered evidence. In reviewing studies of family socialization, Loeber and Stouthamer-Loeber (1986) concluded that parental neglect had the largest impact on crime. They also suggested the possibility of a sleeper effect from socialization practices, although they noted that reports by different members of the family have little convergence.

Problems in collecting information make the few extant longitudinal data sets that include family interactions particularly valuable. The Cambridge-Somerville Youth Study data provided evidence about childhood milieu and family interaction collected during childhood. The data were based on observations of family processes by a variety of people over a period of several years.

Prior analyses of the data, based on a follow-up when the men were in their late twenties, have provided evidence of predictive validity for many of the measures. The results of these earlier studies suggested that child-rearing practices mediate the conditions under which sons follow the footsteps of criminal fathers (J. McCord and W. McCord, 1958). They showed that child-rearing practices are correlated with concurrent aggressive behavior among nondelinquents (W. McCord et al., 1961) and contribute to promoting antisocial directions for aggressive behavior (J. McCord et al., 1963a). Analyses also indicated that the stability of family environments mediated results of maternal employment on concurrent characteristics of dependency and sex anxiety; only among unstable families did maternal employment seem to contribute to subsequent delinquency (J. McCord et al., 1963b). Probably the most critical test of the predictive worth of the coded variables appeared in the analyses of their relation to alcoholism (W. McCord and J. McCord, 1960). Spurred on by these results, I collected additional information from and about the men two decades later.

Prior analyses from this extended data base have suggested that parental affection acts as a protective factor against crime (J. McCord, 1983b, 1986) and alcoholism (J. McCord, 1988). Analyses also suggested that how parents responded to their son's aggressive behavior influenced whether early aggression continued through adolescence and emerged as criminal behavior (J. McCord, 1983b).

In tracing the comparative results of child abuse, neglect, and rejection, analyses indicated both that parental rejection was more criminogenic than either abuse or neglect and that vulnerability to alcoholism, mental illness, early death, and serious criminality was increased by having had an alcoholic, criminal, or aggressive parent (J. McCord, 1983a).

Prior analyses from these data have also shown that single-parent families are not more criminogenic than two-parent families—provided the mother is affectionate (J. McCord, 1982). Additional analyses of family structure indicated that although parental absence had a detrimental effect on delinquency, only when compounded by other family-related stresses did it have an apparent effect on serious criminal behavior, alcoholism, or occupational achievement (J. McCord, 1990).

Theories have emphasized one or another description of family life as important to healthy child development. Research concerned with bonding to, or identification with, socialized adults has focused on affection of parents for their children (e.g., Hirschi, 1969; W. McCord and J. McCord, 1959). Research based on either conditioning or dissonance theories has emphasized discipline and controls (e.g., Bandura and Walters, 1959; Baumrind, 1968, 1978, 1983; Lewis, 1981). And differential association and social learning theories give special weight to the nature of available models (e.g., Akers, 1973; Bandura and Walters, 1963; Sutherland and Cressey, 1974).

Because criminologists have rarely gone beyond describing home environments in globally evaluative terms, the same data could be interpreted as confirming the importance of family bonding or of providing firm control. In order to distinguish among effects, equally valid and reliable measurement of the different dimensions is needed, and collinearity among the measures must be taken into account. Although it is known that child rearing influences adult criminality (J. McCord, 1979, 1983b), there is little ground for judging the extent to which one or another dimension of child rearing is important at different times. Thus, the question remains: In what ways does child rearing affect criminal behavior?

This study addresses two questions: (1) Are there particular features of child rearing that influence criminal outcomes or does only the general home atmosphere of childhood account for the relationship between conditions of socialization and crime? (2) Do similar influences operate to increase criminality at different ages?

Method

This study includes 232 boys who had been randomly selected for a treatment program that, although designed to prevent delinquency, included both well behaved and troubled youngsters. The boys were born between 1926 and 1933. They lived in congested, urban areas near Boston, Massachusetts. Counselors visited their homes about twice a month over a period of more than five years. Typically, the boys were between their tenth and sixteenth birthdays at the time of the visits.

One emphasis of the youth study was on developing sound case reports. Staff meetings included discussion of cases not only from the perspective of treatment but also to provide rounded descriptions of the child's life circumstances. After each visit with a boy or his parents, counselors dictated reports about what they saw and heard (see Powers and Witmer, 1951). The reports from visits to the boys' homes provided the raw material for subsequent analyses.

Child-Rearing Variables

In 1957, records were coded to describe the 232 families of the 253 boys who had remained in the program after an initial cut in 1941 (see W. McCord and J. McCord, 1960). Codes included ratings of family structure, family conflict, esteem of each parent for the other, parental supervision and disciplinary characteristics, parental warmth, self confidence, role, and aggressiveness. Codes also included parental alcoholism and criminality. The coding was designed for global assessments; this type of rating helps to circumvent problems that would occur when measures depend on specific items of information that might be missing from any particular data collection effort.

Among the 232 families, 130 were intact through the boys' sixteenth year. There were 60 families in which mothers were not living with a man; 23 fathers had died and 37 were living elsewhere. There were 30 families with mother substitutes and 29 with father substitutes, including 17 in which both natural parents were absent. Information about absent parents came from their concurrent interactions with the boys or their mothers. Thirteen substitute fathers and 13 substitute mothers were rated.

Ratings for the mother's self-confidence were based on how she reacted when faced with problems. If she showed signs of believing in her ability to handle problems, she was rated as self-confident (N = 66). Alternative ratings were "no indication," "victim or pawn," and "neutral."

The attitude of a parent toward the boy was classified as "affectionate" if that parent interacted frequently with the child without being generally critical. Among the parents, 110 mothers and 59 fathers were rated as affectionate. Alternative classifications were "passively affectionate" (if the parent was concerned for the boy's welfare, but there was little interaction), "passively rejecting" (if the parent was unconcerned for the boy's welfare and interacted little), "actively rejecting" (if the parent was almost constantly critical of the boy), "ambivalent" (if the parents showed marked alternation between affection and rejection of the child), and "no indication."

Parental conflict reflected reports of disagreements about the child, values, money, alcohol, or religion. Ratings could be "no indication," "apparently none," "some," or "considerable." Parents were classified as evidencing (N = 75) or not evidencing considerable conflict.

A rating of each parent's esteem for the other was based on evidence indicating whether a parent showed respect for the judgment of the other. Ratings could be "no indication," "moderate or high," or "low." In this study, each parent was classified as showing or not showing moderate or high esteem for the other. Almost an equal number of mothers (N = 109) and fathers (N = 106) revealed relatively high esteem for their spouse.

Maternal restrictiveness was rated as "subnormal" if a mother permitted her son to make virtually all his choices without her guidance (N = 83). Alternative ratings were "no indications," "normal," and "overly restrictive."

Parental supervision was measured by the degree to which the boy's activities after school were governed by an adult. Supervision could be rated "present" (N = 132) or, alternatively, "sporadic," "absent," or "no information."

Discipline by each parent was classified into one of six categories. "Consistently punitive, including very harsh verbal abuse," identified a parent who used physical force to control the boy. A parent who used praise, rewards, or reasoning to control the boy was rated as "consistent, nonpunitive." Alternative categories were "erratically punitive," "inconsistent, nonpunitive," "extremely lax, with almost no use of discipline," and "no information." Fathers were difficult to classify for consistency, so for this analysis, their discipline was coded as "punitive" (N = 39) or "other." Mother's discipline was coded as "consistent and nonpunitive" (N = 70), or "other."

A mother's role in the family was classified as "leader," "dictator," "martyr," "passive," "neglecting," or "no indication." The leadership role involved participating in family decisions. Mothers in this analysis were classified either as being (N = 144) or not being leaders.

The aggressiveness of each parent was rated as "unrestrained" if that parent regularly expressed anger by such activities as shouting abuses, yelling, throwing or breaking things, or hitting people. Thirty-seven fathers and 23 mothers were rated as aggressive. Alternative classifications were "no indication," "moderately aggressive," or "greatly inhibited." . . .

Follow Up Measures

Between 1975 and 1980, when they ranged from 45 to 53 years in age, the former youth study participants were retraced. Twenty-four were found through their death records.[1] Police and court records had been collected in 1948. Those records of juvenile delinquency were combined with records gathered in 1979 from probation departments in Massachusetts and in other states to which the men had migrated.

The measure of criminality depended on official records of convictions. Such records do not reflect all crimes committed (Murphy et al., 1946), but they do appear to identify those who commit serious crimes and those who break the law frequently (Morash, 1984). In addition, several studies show convergence between results from official records and from well-designed self-reporting instruments for measuring serious criminality (Elliott and Ageton, 1980; Farrington, 1979; Hindelang et al., 1979; Reiss and Rhodes, 1961).

A boy was considered a juvenile delinquent if he had been convicted for an index crime prior to reaching the age of 18 years. Fifty boys had been convicted for such serious crimes as auto theft, breaking and entering, and assault. Of the 50 juvenile's convicted for serious crimes, 21 also were convicted for serious crimes as adults; additionally, 29 men not convicted as juveniles were convicted for at least one index crime as an adult. . . .

Results

Comparisons for the impact of child rearing showed that Mother's Competence, Father's Interaction with the family, and Family Expectations were related to juvenile delinquency. Considered separately, poor child rearing in each of these domains reliably increased risk of delinquency . . . .

Joint effects of poor child rearing can be seen by examining their combinations in relation to juvenile delinquency. Only 5% of the boys reared by competent mothers in families with good paternal interaction and high expectations had become delinquents. In contrast, almost half (47%) had become delinquents among those who had been raised by incompetent mothers in homes that had poor paternal interaction and low expectations. . . .

Serious criminality as a juvenile was strongly related to both the mother's competence and to family expectations for the boy. Together, these accounted for 12% of the variance in juvenile delinquency, p = .0001. Father's poor interaction with the family showed a weaker relationship with juvenile delinquency; it accounted for an additional 1.5% of the variance, p = .0617.

A different picture emerges from analyses of the impact of child-rearing variables on adult criminality.[2] . . . Father's interaction with the family increased in importance. With the exception of affection, each of the variables contributing to this dimension was related to adult criminality. The impact of the mother's competence had weakened—only the mother's self confidence clearly contributed to adult criminality. The dimension of family expectations was not reliably related to adult convictions, although supervision and maternal control apparently had enduring effects. The categorical analysis of variance, controlling collinearity, indicated that only the father's interactions bore a significant independent relationship to adult criminality. . . .

Conviction as a juvenile was related to being convicted as an adult. As noted above, among the 50 boys who had been juvenile delinquents, 21 (42%) had been convicted for serious crimes as adults. In contrast, among 182 boys who had not been convicted for serious crimes as juveniles, 27 (15%) had been convicted for serious crimes as adults. . . .

Summary and Discussion

This study reexamined the ways in which family interactions during childhood influence criminal behavior. By considering families whose socioeconomic backgrounds were similar, it was possible to look beyond effects of poverty, social disorganization, and blighted urban conditions.

Case records based on repeated visits to the homes of 232 boys allowed analyses that included the dynamics of family interactions. The variables resulting from observations in the homes were reduced to three dimensions in order to minimize problems of collinearity. A reasonable conclusion from the data is that the mother's competence and family expectations influenced the likelihood that a son became a juvenile delinquent.

Competent mothers seem to insulate a child against criminogenic influences even in deteriorated neighborhoods. Competent mothers were self-confident and provided leadership; they were consistently nonpunitive in discipline and affectionate. Coupled with high family expectations, maternal competence seems to reduce the probability that sons become juvenile delinquents. The influence of these child-rearing conditions on adult criminality appears to be largely through their impact on juvenile delinquency.

Compared with the mother's influences, the father's interactions with his family appeared less important during the juvenile years. Father's interactions with the family became more important, however, as the boys matured.

Fathers who interact with their wives in ways exhibiting high mutual esteem, who are not highly aggressive, and who generally get along well with their wives provide models for socialized behavior. Conversely, fathers who undermine their wives, who fight with the family, and who are aggressive provide models of antisocial behavior. Both types of fathers, it seems, teach their sons how to behave when they become adults.

The evidence from this study raises doubts about two currently prevalent views. One view holds that regardless of age of the criminal, crime is merely a particular symptom of a single underlying "disorder." The other view holds that causes of crime are basically the same at all ages. This study indicates that the causes of juvenile crime are different from those of adult criminality. Juvenile delinquency might be explained through elements of control, as represented by maternal competence and high expectations, but adult criminality appears to hold a component based on role expectations. If these interpretations are correct, criminality cannot be attributed to a single type of cause, nor does it represent a single underlying tendency.

Discussion Questions

1. It has often been said that broken homes contribute to crime and delinquency. Does empirical data support this theory? Are broken homes linked with juvenile delinquency? What is problematic about studies on this topic?

2. What are some of the problems associated with adolescents' reporting parents' child-rearing behavior? What are some of the problems associated with parents reporting their own behavior?

3. What family characteristics do seem to have an effect on crime and delinquency? Exactly how does this work (how do certain characteristics affect crime)? Can measurement of any of these characteristics predict future criminal tendencies? Do any family characteristics seem to deter entry into crime?

Notes

1. None of the subjects died before the age of 20. Of those who died in their twenties, nine had no convictions and one was convicted only as a juvenile. Of those who died in their thirties, three had no convictions, two were convicted only as juveniles, and two were convicted only as adults. Of those who died in their forties, three were not convicted, two were convicted only as adults, and two were convicted both as juveniles and as adults.

2. The range in age among the 20 who had died prior to the follow-up and did not have criminal records as adults was 20 to 50 years. The median age was 39. Only six were under age 25. Because there was no attempt to ascertain rates of criminality, no correction was attempted for time of "exposure."

References

Akers, R.L. 1973. *Deviant Behavior: A Social Learning Approach*. Belmont, CA: Wadsworth.

Aristotle. 1941. *Ethica Nicomachea*, trans. W.D. Ross. In R. McKeon (eds.), *The Basic Works of Aristotle*. New York: Random House.

Bachman, J.G. and P.M. O'Malley. 1984. *The Youth in Transition Project*. In S.A. Mednick, M. Harway, and K.M. Finello (eds.), *Handbook of Longitudinal Research*. New York: Praeger.

Bacon, M.K., I.L. Child, and H. Barry, Jr. 1963. "A Cross-Cultural Study of Correlates of Crime" in *Journal of Abnormal and Social Psychology* 66:291-300.

Bandura, A. and R.H. Walters. 1959. *Adolescent Aggression*. New York: Ronald.

——. 1963. *Social Learning and Personality Development*. New York: Holt, Rinehart & Winston.

Baumrind, D. 1968. "Authoritarian vs. Authoritative Parental Control." *Adolescence* 3:255-272.

——. 1978. "Parental Disciplinary Patterns and Social Competence in Children." *Youth and Society* 9(3):239-276.

——. 1983. "Rejoinder to Lewis's Reinterpretation of Parental Firm Control Effects: Are Authoritative Families Really Harmonious?" *Psychological Bulletin* 94(1):132-142.

Bowlby, J. 1940. "The Influence of Early Environment on Neurosis and Neurotic Character." *International Journal of Psychoanalysis* 21:154.

——. 1951. "Maternal Care and Mental Health." *Bulletin of the World Health Organization* 3:355-534.

Burt, C. 1925. *The Youth Delinquent*. New York: Appleton & Co.

Cernkovich, S.A. and P.C. Giordano. 1987. "Family Relationships and Delinquency." *Criminology* 25(2):295-319.

Cohen, J. 1960. "A Coefficient of Agreement for Nominal Scales." *Educational and Psychological Measurement* 20:37-46.

Dean, A.L., M.M. Malik, W. Richards, and S.A. Stringer. 1986. "Effects of Parental Maltreatment on Children's Conceptions of Interpersonal Relationships." *Developmental Psychology* 22(5):617-626.

Dodge, K.Q. and D.R. Somberg. 1987. "Hostile Attributional Biases Among Aggressive Boys are Exacerbated Under Conditions of Threats to the Self." *Child Development* 58:213-224.

Dornbusch, S.M., J.M. Carlsmith, S.J. Bushwall, P.L. Ritter, H. Leiderman, A.H. Hastorf, and R.T. Gross. 1985. "Single Parents, Extended Households, and the Control of Adolescents." *Child Development* 56:326-341.

Eich, E., S. Rachman, and C. Lopatka. 1990. "Affect, Pain, and Autobiographical Memory." *Journal of Abnormal Psychology* 99(2):174-178.

Elliott, D.S. and S.S. Ageton. 1980. "Reconciling Race and Class Differences in Self-Reported and Official Estimates of Delinquency." *American Sociological Review* 45:95-110.

Eron, L.D., T.J. Banta, L.O. Walder, and J.H. Laulicht. 1961. "Comparison of Data Obtained From Mothers and Fathers on Child-Rearing Practices and Their Relation to Child Aggression." *Child Development* 32(3):455-472.

Farrington, D.P. 1979. "Environmental Stress, Delinquent Behavior, and Convictions." In I.G. Sarason and C.D. Spielberger (eds.), *Stress and Anxiety*. Vol. 6. New York: John Wiley & Sons.

Fenichel, O. 1945. *The Psychoanalytic Theory of Neurosis*. New York: Norton.

Forehand, R., K.C. Wells, and E.T. Sturgis. 1978. "Predictors of Child Noncompliant Behavior in the Home." *Journal of Consulting and Clinical Psychology* 46(1):179.

Freud, S. 1953. "Three Essays on the Theory of Sexuality." In *Standard Edition*. Vol. VII. London: Hogarth.

Glueck, S. and E.T. Glueck. 1950. *Unraveling Juvenile Delinquency*. New York: Commonwealth Fund.

Goldfarb, W. 1945. "Psychological Privation in Infancy and Subsequent Adjustment." *American Journal of Orthopsychiatry* 15:247-255.

Goode, W.J. 1956. *After Divorce*. Glencoe, IL: Free Press.

Hagan, J., A.R. Gillis, and J. Simpson. 1985. "The Class Structure of Gender and Delinquency: Toward a Power-Control Theory of Common Delinquent Behavior." *American Journal of Sociology* 90:1151-1178.

Hindelang, M.J., T. Hirschi, and J.G. Weis. 1979. "Correlates of Delinquency: The Illusion of Discrepancy Between Self-Report and Official Measures." *American Sociological Review* 44:995-1014.

Hirschi, T. 1969. *Causes of Delinquency*. Berkeley: University of California Press.

——. 1983. "Crime and the Family." In J.Q. Wilson (ed.), *Crime and Public Policy*. San Francisco: Institute for Contemporary Studies.

Hoffman, L.W. 1975. "Effects on Child." In L.W. Hoffman and F.I. Nye (eds.), *Working Mothers*. San Francisco: Jossey-Bass.

Jensen, G.F. and D. Brownfield. 1983. "Parents and Drugs." *Criminology* 21(4):543-555.

Kellogg, R.T. 1980. "Is Conscious Attention Necessary for Long-Term Storage." *Journal of Experimental Psychology* 6(4):379-390.

Lamb, M.E. 1976. "The Role of the Father: An Overview." In M.E. Lamb (ed.), *The Role of the Father in Child Development*. New York: John Wiley & Sons.

Larzelere, R.E. and G.R. Patterson. 1990. "Parental Management: Mediator of the Effect of Socioeconomic Status on Early Delinquency." *Criminology* 28(2):301-323.

Laub, J.H. and R.J. Sampson. 1988. "Unraveling Families and Delinquency: A Reanalysis of the Gluecks' Data." *Criminology* 26(3):355-380.

Levy, D. 1937. "Primary Affect Hunger." *American Journal of Psychiatry* 94:643-652.

Lewis, C. 1981. "The Effects of Parental Firm Control: A Reinterpretation of Findings." *Psychological Bulletin* 90(3):547-563.

Liska, A.E. and M.D. Reed. 1985. "Ties to Conventional Institutions and Delinquency: Estimating Reciprocal Effects." *American Sociological Review* 50(Aug):547-560.

Locke, J. 1693. "Some Thoughts Concerning Education." Vol. 8, *Collected Works*. 9th ed. London: T. Longman.

Loeber, R. and M. Stouthamer-Loeber. 1986. "Family Factors as Correlates and Predictors of Juvenile Conduct Problems and Delinquency." In M. Tonry and N. Morris (eds.), *Crime and Justice*. Vol. 7. Chicago: University of Chicago Press.

Maccoby, E.E. 1958. "Effects Upon Children of Their Mothers' Outside Employment." In National Manpower Council, Work in the Lives of Married Women. New York: Columbia University Press.

McCord, J. 1979. "Some Child-Rearing Antecedents of Criminal Behavior in Adult Men." *Journal of Personality and Social Psychology* 37:1477-1486.

———. 1982. "A Longitudinal View of the Relationship Between Paternal Absence and Crime." In J. Gunn and D.P. Farrington (eds.), *Abnormal Offenders, Delinquency, and the Criminal Justice System*. Chichester: John Wiley & Sons.

———. 1983a. "A Forty Year Perspective on Effects of Child Abuse and Neglect." *Child Abuse and Neglect* 7:265-270.

———. 1983b. "A Longitudinal Study of Aggression and Antisocial Behavior." In K.T. Van Dusen and S.A. Mednick (eds.), *Prospective Studies of Crime and Delinquency*. Boston: Kluwer-Nijhoff.

———. 1986. "Instigation and Insulation: How Families Affect Antisocial Behavior." In J. Block, D. Olweus, and M.R. Yarrow (eds.), *Development of Antisocial and Prosocial Behavior*. New York: Academic Press.

———. 1988. "Identifying Developmental Paradigms Leading to Alcoholism." *Journal of Studies on Alcohol* 49(4):357-362.

———. 1990. "Longterm Effects of Parental Absence." In L. Robins and M. Rutter (eds.), *Straight and Devious Pathways from Childhood to Adulthood*. New York: Cambridge University Press.

McCord, J. and W. McCord. 1958. "The Effects of Parental Role Model on Criminality." *Journal of Social Issues* 14(3):66-75.

———. 1962. "Cultural Stereotypes and the Validity of Interviews for Research in Child Development." *Child Development* 32(2):171-185.

McCord, J., W. McCord, and A. Howard. 1963a. "Family Interaction as Antecedent to the Direction of Male Aggressiveness." *Journal of Abnormal and Social Psychology* 66:239-242.

McCord, J., W. McCord, and E. Thurber. 1963b. "The Effects of Maternal Employment on Lower Class Boys." *Journal of Abnormal & Social Psychology* 67(1):177-182.

McCord, W. and J. McCord. 1959. *Origins of Crime*. New York: Columbia University Press.

———. 1960. *Origins of Alcoholism*. Stanford, CA: Stanford University Press.

McCord, W., J. McCord, and A. Howard. 1961. "Familial Correlates of Agression in Nondelinquent Male Children." *Journal of Abnormal & Social Psychology* 1:79-93.

Miller, W.B. 1958. "Lower Class Culture as a Generating Milieu of Gang Delinquency." *Journal of Social Issues* 14:5-19.

Morash, M. 1984. "Establishment of a Juvenile Police Record: The Influence of Individual and Peer Group Characteristics." *Criminology* 22:97-111.

Murdock, G.P. 1949. *Social Structure*. New York: Macmillan.

Murphy, F.J., M.M. Shirley, and H.L. Witmer. 1946. "The Incidence of Hidden Delinquency." *American Journal of Orthopsychiatry* 16:686-696.

Newell, H.W. 1934. "The Psycho-Dynamics of Maternal Rejection." *American Journal of Orthopsychiatry* 4:387-401.

———. 1936. "A Further Study of Maternal Rejection." *American Journal of Orthopsychiatry* 6:576-589.

Nye, F.I. 1958. *Family Relationships and Delinquent Behavior*. New York: John Wiley & Sons.

———. 1959. "Maternal Employment and the Adjustment of Adolescent Children." *Marriage and Family Living* 21(August):240-244.

Parsons, T. and R.F. Bales. 1955. *Family, Socialization and Interaction Process*. Glencoe, IL: Free Press.

Plato Laws, trans. B. Jowett. *In the Dialogues of Plato* (1937). NY: Random House.

Powers, E. and H. Witmer. 1951. *An Experiment in the Prevention of Delinquency: The Cambridge-Somerville Youth Study*. New York: Columbia University Press.

Reiss, A.J., Jr., and A.L. Rhodes. 1961. "Delinquency and Class Structure." *American Sociological Review* 26(5):720-732.

Robins, L.N. 1966. *Deviant Children Grown Up*. Baltimore: Williams & Wilkins.

SAS Institute. 1985. *SAS User's Guide: Statistics*. 1985 ed. Cary, NC: SAS Institute.

Scott, W.A. 1955. "Reliability of Content Analysis: The Case of Nominal Scale Coding." *Public Opinion Quarterly* 19(3):321-325.

Shaw, C. and H.D. McKay. 1932. "Are Broken Homes A Causative Factor in Juvenile Delinquency?" *Social Forces* 10:514-524.

Sutherland, E.H. and D.R. Cressey. 1974. *Criminology*. 1924. 9th ed. Philadelphia: Lippincott.

van Voorhis, P., F.T. Cullen, R.A. Mathers, and C.C. Garner. 1988. "The Impact of Family Structure and Quality on Delinquency: A Comparative Assessment of Structural and Functional Factors." *Criminology* 26(2):235-261.

Wadsworth, M. 1979. *Roots of Delinquency*. New York: Barnes and Noble.

Weller, L. and E. Luchterhand. 1983. "Family Relationships of 'Problem' and 'Promising' youth." *Adolescence* 18(69):43-100.

Wells, L.E. and J.H. Rankin. 1988. "Direct Parental Controls and Delinquency." *Criminology* 26(2):263-285.

Whiting, J.W.M., R. Kluckhohn, and A. Anthony. 1958. "The Function of Male Initiation Ceremonies at Puberty." In E.E. Maccoby, T.M. Newcomb, and E.L. Hartley (eds.), *Readings in Social Psychology*. New York: Holt, Rinehart & Winston.

Yarrow, M.R., J.D. Campbell, and R.V. Burton. 1970. "Recollections of Childhood: A study of the Retrospective Method." *Monographs of the Society for Research in Child Development* 35(1):1-83.

Section IV

Theories of Crime

Crime does not occur in a vacuum. Although to the untrained eye, crime may appear to be random or haphazard, numerous consistent patterns or regularities have been identified with regard to crime. For example, as revealed in Section III, certain factors or correlates are associated with crime. How can we account for such regularities and patterns? Why do they exist? To attempt to answer these questions, criminologists rely on theories.

Criminological theories are systematic, consistent sets of ideas that provide comprehensive frameworks in an attempt to understand and explain crime. To be considered a theory, a set of ideas must include testable propositions. As such, a theory can be found to be untrue or it can be supported through empirical research; however, a theory can never be definitively proven to be true and applicable under all conditions. Theories not only provide a framework for understanding crime, but they can also have important policy implications for its prevention and control. For example, if policy makers believe that crime is the result of genetic causes, the approach they would take to control and prevent crime would be very different from the approach others would take if they attributed crime to socially disorganized neighborhoods.

Criminologists have produced numerous theories to explain crime and criminal behavior. Although most theories attempt to explain "street crimes," some try to explain all types of criminal and antisocial behavior. Theories vary in terms of the factors and processes they consider important for understanding crime. Some theories attempt to explain why particular individuals engage in crime; to do so, they focus on factors at the individual level (the microlevel), such as biological or psychological abnormalities of offenders. Some sociological theories are also interested in explaining the behavior of individuals, but rather than emphasize characteristics of individuals, they tend to focus on social processes, such as interactions with peers, that influence people's behavior. Other theories attempt to explain crime rates, rather than individual behavior. Such theories thus focus on structural factors (the macrolevel), such as poverty rates or social disorganization in an area.

With few exceptions, however, theories are not strictly individualist (microlevel) or structural (macrolevel) approaches. Instead, they form a continuum, ranging from more individualistic to more structural. For example, Sutherland's theory of differential association (reading 19) focuses on individuals and the processes involved in learning to commit crime. He also includes, however, a macrolevel component (differential social organization) in describing the role of the larger social group in this learning process. In addition, different theories overlap in the types of social processes they emphasize. As an example, both differential association theory and social control theory (reading 17) consider peers and other intimates to be important for explaining an individual's criminal behavior; the theories, however, provide different explanations concerning how and why such people influence offending. The overlaps are also apparent with regard to a relatively recent trend in criminology to attempt to integrate similar theories rather than examining them as competing approaches, such as the integrated theory of Delbert S. Elliott, Susan S, Ageton, and Rachelle J. Canter and the "control balance" theory of Charles Tittle.

Criminological theories can be broadly categorized in terms of the disciplines and their respective foci. That is, the three major areas of criminological theories are biological, psychological, and sociological. Both within and across these areas there are many different approaches to understanding crime. This section provides an overview of the major traditions within each of the three broad areas.

Biological Approaches

Biological approaches posit that crime is attributable to genetic and other biological factors at the level of the individual. In general, scholars who work in this area are interested in identifying a biological basis for behavior, and they attempt to differentiate criminals and noncriminals on the basis of such factors as brain damage or genetic abnormalities. The biological factors implicated in criminal behavior may result from genetic mutations inherited from parents, from mutations occurring after conception or while the fetus is developing, or from environmental factors, such as injury or exposure to toxins, that increase the likelihood of engaging in crime (Vold, Bernard, and Snipes, 1998).

Researchers interested in identifying a genetic basis for criminal behavior conduct family, twin, or adoption studies. In family studies, the criminality of family members is examined; similarity in crime involvement may be attributable to genetic factors. Studies of twins involve comparing the similarity, or concordance, of criminality of genetically identical twins (who are genetically identical) and that of fraternal twins (who share about 50 percent of the same genes, the same as nontwin siblings). To the extent that concordance rates are higher for identical twins than for fraternal twins, this fact should support a genetic basis for criminality. For both family and twin studies, however, the similarity in offending may be the result of shared environment (and therefore social factors), and even of being treated the same (particularly identical twins), rather than reflecting a genetic basis. Adoption studies, by contrast, involve comparing the criminal offending of an adoptee with the behavior of both the adoptive parents and the biological parents. The extent of similarity in the adoptee's offending with that of the adopting parents is attributable to environmental factors; similarity in offending with biological parents is attributable to genetic factors. The results of the three types of studies—family, twin, and adoption—are summarized by Diana Fishbein in reading 15. Overall, she concludes that genetics may play a role in criminality.

Other types of biological factors have also been examined in relation to crime. Differences in responses to and levels of neurotransmitters, chemicals that play a key role in allowing electrical impulses to be transmitted in the brain, may be associated with antisocial and violent behavior. Similarly, differences in levels and responses to hormones, particularly the male androgen, testosterone (Booth and Osgood 1993), as well as hormonal changes associated with the menstrual cycle in women, may be associated with criminal and aggressive behavior. Brain irregularities, whether due to biological abnormalities or caused by injury, may also be associated with criminal behavior (Vold, Bernard, and Snipes 1998). Neuropsychological deficits, resulting from some type of brain dysfunction and manifested in terms of low verbal ability and other problems, are associated with offending behavior in adolescence (Moffitt, Lyman, and Silva 1994). In addition, the autonomic nervous system (ANS), the part of the central nervous system that controls involuntary bodily functions such as the heart rate, may play a role in crime, with some criminals having slower than average ANS responses (Vold, Bernard, and Snipes 1998; reading 15).

Other biological factors may be implicated in crime. Consumption of alcohol and/or drugs may result in irrational behavior, either due directly to consumption and its effects on behavior or to irritability associated with withdrawal symptoms (Goldstein 1985). The effects of alcohol, a legal and widely used drug in the United States, may include increased aggressiveness and disinhibition, which increase the likelihood of criminal, particularly violent, behavior (Collins 1981). Other biological factors may also promote criminal behavior. Poor diet, exposure to lead, and head injury may all result in brain damage and may increase the chances of an individual's engaging in violence, or in crime more generally (Vold, Bernard, and Snipes, 1998).

Overall, the research seems to indicate that there may be a genetic or other biological basis for some criminal behavior. Such approaches are becoming more prevalent in mainstream criminology (e.g., Ellis and Walsh 1997). However, most biological approaches, and scholars who adhere to them, recognize at some level the important role of psychological and social factors in determining whether biological "vulnerabilities," or predispositions for offending actually lead to crime.

Psychological Approaches

Psychological approaches, like biological approaches, tend to focus on processes at the individual level. Psychological approaches take a variety of forms but generally are interested in differentiating offenders from nonoffenders on psychological dimensions. The major approaches in psychology have been in the areas of psychoanalysis, personality characteristics, and psychological pathologies (such as antisocial personality disorder and psychoses). Other approaches, such as the psychological theory proposed by Terrie E. Moffitt in reading 16, focus on different factors; Moffitt, for example, considers neuropsychological deficits and developmental processes to differentiate adoles-

cence-limited and life-course persistent offenders.

Psychoanalytic theory provides one explanation for crime. Although Sigmund Freud did not focus on criminals specifically, much of the theorizing in this area is based on his work. The psychoanalytic tradition regards crime as the result of an imbalance in the workings of the three components of the self: the id, the ego, and the superego. The id is comprised of instincts and drives that seek immediate gratification; the superego is the conscience or social authority; and the ego attempts to balance the id's drives and the demands of the superego. From this perspective, crime may result from either the overdevelopment or underdevelopment of the ego or superego. Some suggest that such overdevelopment of the ego or superego produces excess feelings of guilt; crime provides a potential source of punishment that will alleviate feelings of guilt and restore balance to the individual. Other psychoanalysts argue that underdevelopment of these components produces crime because there is inadequate regulation or control of the id; involvement in crime provides a means to satisfy the desires, drives, and instincts located in the id. Later psychoanalysts have further developed some of these ideas; psychoanalytic approaches, however, suffer from several limitations, including the criticism that it is impossible to test their essential hypotheses. As a whole, then, psychoanalytic approaches have not been very useful for criminologists (Vold, Bernard, and Snipes 1998).

Another psychological approach attempts to identify personality characteristics that differentiate offenders from nonoffenders. Such efforts have been ongoing for several decades. Although a review of the literature in 1950 by Karl F. Schuessler and Donald R. Cressey suggested that no personality characteristics specifically differentiate criminals and noncriminals, other criminologists suggest that there are differences. For example, in the same year Sheldon Glueck and Eleanor Glueck differentiated a group of 500 delinquents from a matched group of 500 nondelinquents on the basis of such characteristics as extroversion, hostility, and impulsiveness. More recent efforts suggest that personality characteristics may be important. "Lifestyle criminals," offenders with long term involvement in crime, are characterized by "faulty, irrational thinking" and possession of eight cognitive traits, such as mollification (justification of criminal activity in terms of external forces operating on the criminal), entitlement (a sense of privilege; the world exists to benefit and pleasure criminals), and superoptimism (an extreme sense of self-confidence in one's ability to get away with most things) (Walters 1990). The personality characteristics of "negative emotionality" (a combination of aggression, alienation, and stress reaction) and "constraint" (a combination of harm avoidance, traditionalism, and control) are consistently associated with offending and other antisocial behaviors across countries, genders, and races (Caspi et al. 1994).

Research on personality disorders is another psychological approach to crime. Of particular interest for criminologists are people with antisocial or psychopathic personalities. Psychopaths (or sociopaths) are thought to be more likely than other people to engage in criminal and antisocial behavior, and even the definition of "antisocial personality disorder" used by the American Psychiatric Association includes law violations and aggressive behavior as two of several diagnostic criteria. Such people are asocial, aggressive, highly impulsive, feel little or no guilt for antisocial behavior, and cannot form lasting bonds of affection with others. They are present oriented, impulsive, and do not plan their crimes. It must be noted, however, that not all criminals are sociopaths, nor do all sociopaths commit crimes (Vold, Bernard, and Snipes 1998).

Two recent approaches that may be considered psychological because of their emphasis on stable individual differences have had an important impact on criminology. One approach, posited by Wilson and Herrnstein, argues that people who engage in crime are impulsive and present oriented, often paying little attention to long-term consequences or rewards. These scholars argue that "constitutional factors," such as low IQ and personality characteristics, as well as social factors, such as family and peers, play a role in the development of impulsiveness and

present orientedness. A somewhat similar approach is the "general theory" of crime proposed by Michael R. Gottfredson and Travis Hirschi. They argue that all criminals, regardless of the types of crime they commit, have little self-control. Lack of self-control is characterized by impulsiveness, risk taking, present orientedness, and other similar characteristics. Gottfredson and Hirschi argue that self-control is established early in life and is a stable trait over time; however, they posit that lack of self-control results from the family's providing the child with inadequate socialization, rather than from psychological or biological factors. The "general theory," and particularly the concept of low self-control, is currently undergoing intensive empirical testing by criminologists. As a whole, the literature suggests that lack of self-control may, in fact, be associated with criminal behavior, although this association is not unequivocal (e.g., Arneklev et al. 1993).

Sociological Approaches

With sociological theories, the focus is on social processes that affect crime, either at the individual level (microlevel theories) or at the level of the group, neighborhood, or society (macrolevel theories). As noted earlier, theories rarely fit neatly into either a micro or macro category, but instead often rely on processes ongoing at both levels. This section will consider several different sociological theories of crime, including social control theory, differential association theory, strain theory, and social disorganization theory.

Social Control Theory

Social control theories differ from most other approaches with regard to the basic question they seek to address. Although most theories attempt to determine why some people engage in crime, social control theories are interested in explaining why it is that more people do not engage in crime or, more specifically, what keeps people from committing crimes. The foundation for social control theories was provided by Walter Reckless, through his early work on containment theory, and Albert Reiss, who argued that both personal controls (factors internal to the individual) and social controls (forces external to the individual, such as the social institution of school) keep individuals from engaging in crime. The most prominent of such approaches, however, is Hirschi's social control theory; reading 17 is an excerpt from his classic statement of the theory.

Hirschi argues that social bonds between the individual and conventional institutions and conventional persons explain why people do not engage in delinquency or crime. Strong bonds induce conformity and inhibit people from engaging in crime; weak bonds enable them to engage in crime. The four bonds are attachment (affective ties to other people), commitment (commitment to conventional goals and actions that provide a "stake in conformity"), involvement (time spent engaged in conventional activities), and belief (the extent to which an individual believes he or she should obey the norms and rules of society) (see reading 17).

The bonds that are formed vary over the life course in terms of the individuals and institutions to which one is bonded. In childhood, strong bonds to family are key (Cernkovich and Giordano 1986; Sampson and Laub 1993; Rankin and Kern 1994); in adolescence, bonds to peers and school are important for explaining delinquency (Giordano, Cernkovich, and Pugh 1986; Cernkovich and Giordano 1992; Sampson and Laub 1993). Although Hirschi originally argued that delinquents have no friends and that friends exert pressure to conform, his own and subsequent research has convincingly demonstrated that being bonded to delinquent peers is associated with offending. In addition, social control theory has recently been extended by Robert J. Sampson and John H. Laub (1993; also see reading 18) to explain crime and deviance over the life-course, with spousal attachments and jobs in adulthood found by these and other scholars (Nagin, Farrington, and Moffitt 1995; Horney, Osgood, and Marshall 1995) to be important inhibitors of offending by adults.

Differential Association

The differential association tradition stems largely from the work of Edwin Sutherland and is generally categorized as a learning theory. Sutherland was interested in developing a general statement of how all types of crime are learned (Vold, Bernard, and Snipes 1998), and he later applied his theory to explain white-collar crime (Sutherland, 1983; reading 30).

Sutherland's theory has two components: differential association and differential social organization. As discussed in reading 19, differential association is delineated in a set of nine propositions that provide an explanation for how individuals learn to engage in delinquency and crime. According to Sutherland, this learning involves all of the same processes that are involved in learning conventional behavior. One learns the specific techniques for committing the crime, as well as drives, motivations, and rationalizations for behavior. The learning of both the method and the meaning occurs in the context of intimate personal groups; in most cases, these groups involve one's friends. The drives, motives, and rationalizations that an individual learns provide ways of defining the law that may support upholding it or violating it. The "principle of differential association" posits that an individual will engage in offending when the number of definitions that support violating the law is greater than the number that support conforming to the law. Differential associations (generally considered to mean contact with intimate personal groups that provide definitions concerning violation of the law) differ in terms of their priority, duration, intensity, and frequency, which helps explain why definitions provided by some people are more important than those provided by others.

Sutherland also attempted to address the question of where the definitions that support violating the law originate. He suggested that "differential social organization," a more structural element, may provide an answer. Sutherland held that groups in society are organized differently in terms of whether they support conformity to laws and law-abiding behavior or violation of the law and criminal behavior under some circumstances. In groups organized in favor of violation, delinquent traditions are initiated and perpetuated over time, providing a ready set of definitions supporting violation. According to Sutherland, those people who have contact with, or who are members of, groups organized in support of violation have the highest crime rates because of their exposure to these definitions.

Although criticized as difficult to test because of a lack of precise definitions, empirical research has generally upheld Sutherland's theory of differential association. Much of this research has focused on the role of peers in offending; having delinquent peers is one of the most consistent correlates of engaging in crime and delinquency (see reading 20). Further, tests of the theory's components, usually involving examination of the concepts of priority, intensity, frequency, and duration of differential associations, generally support the theory (e.g., Warr 1993). Other studies suggest, however, that engaging in crime may involve simply learning to commit the offending behavior without necessarily learning the drives, motives, and rationalizations for it, that is, individuals may commit offenses primarily because their friends do so (see reading 20).

Other criminologists have sought to more fully articulate the processes involved in learning criminal behavior, attempting to expand upon Sutherland's differential association theory. Most notable is the work of Robert L. Burgess and Ronald L. Akers (see also Akers 1985), which combines and extends some elements of differential association with those in the psychological tradition of social learning theory. Their theory, also known in criminology as social learning theory, integrates elements such as conditioning and reinforcement, with the latter considered the most important process involved in learning delinquents (as well as other types of) behavior. When engaging in delinquency results in some form of reinforcement for the behavior, it increases the likelihood of repeating the behavior in the future. Empirical tests of Burgess and Akers' social learning theory are generally supportive of this approach (Akers et al. 1979).

Strain Theory

Strain theory was developed by Robert K. Merton (1968). Building upon the notion of anomie (or normlessness) from Emile Durkheim's earlier work, Merton focused on conditions in American society that created "social structural strain" and thereby produced high crime rates. Merton argued that American society holds up certain goals for all individuals to aspire to, primarily monetary success. Although this goal is widely held, if not universal, in the United States, society is organized in such a way that the legitimate means—education, hard work, deferred gratification, and conventional jobs—used to attain this goal are not universally available. In fact, the opportunities to achieve financial success are unequally distributed, with members of the lower classes having few chances to accumulate wealth through legitimate means in comparison to members of the middle and upper classes. Even if one works hard and defers gratification, it is the result— monetary success—that counts, not simply working hard. The disjunction between monetary wealth as a cultural goal and the fact that the social structure limits access to the legitimate means to attain the goal, typically for the lower classes, results in "strain" (Vold, Bernard, and Snipes 1998).

Merton delineated five behavioral adaptations that individuals may use in an attempt to deal with strain: conformity, innovation, ritualism, retreatism, and rebellion. The type of adaptation used depends on the person's reaction to the cultural goal (money) and to legitimate ways to achieve it (hard work). Individuals who conform accept both the cultural goal and the legitimate means for achieving it; they continue to attempt to achieve the goal through legitimate means. Innovation is of much interest to criminologists; it involves acceptance of the cultural goal and rejection of the legitimate means. As such, innovators rely on illegal means in an attempt to achieve monetary success. The third adaptation, ritualism, entails rejection of the cultural goal and acceptance of the means, that is, ritualists work hard but do not aspire to accumulate wealth. Retreatism, the fourth adaptation involves rejection of both the cultural goals and legitimate means; these individuals, who include a variety of people such as the mentally ill or homeless, "drop out" of society and may turn to drugs or alcohol. The fifth adaptation, rebellion, not only rejects the cultural goal and legitimate means but seeks to change or replace them (Merton 1968).

In part because of criticisms and mixed empirical support, there have been several attempts to extend Merton's theory. Albert Cohen examined the delinquency of lower-class boys, positing that they fail to achieve status (especially in school), which is defined by middle-class standards. Such boys seek to deal with the strain ("status frustration") that this situation creates for them. For some, the solution is "reaction formation," or complete rejection of middle class-values and acceptance of the values of the delinquent gang, which offer an alternative avenue to achieve status.

Another extension to strain theory was put forward in 1960 by Richard Cloward and Lloyd Ohlin. They argue that on the one hand the adaptation to strain is structured by illegitimate opportunities. Boys faced with strain will become criminal, for example, if there are criminal role models available to teach them how to be criminal, and if in their neighborhood there is an integration of offenders of different ages and of criminal and conventional values. On the other hand, boys without such opportunities for illegitimate behavior will adapt in other ways. Such boys who live in disorganized neighborhoods may become involved in a conflict gang, whose focus is on using violence as a means to attain status. Youths who do not have access to illegitimate opportunity structures or who cannot achieve status through violence are essentially "double failures." Some of them turn to drugs and alcohol, in conjunction with belonging to retreatist gangs, as a means to adapt to strain.

Merton's approach was extended again by Steven Messner and Richard Rosenfeld in 1992. They examine how crime is produced by the structural and cultural arrangements in society and the emphasis on the pursuit of the "American Dream." A more social psychological extension which is currently having an important impact in criminology is offered by Robert Agnew (see reading 21), who suggests several additional sources of strain beyond a disjunction between the cultural goals and legitimate means to achieve them. Agnew also discusses nondelinquent coping responses and factors associated with choosing a delinquent rather than a nondelinquent response to strain. This extension of strain theory is currently being examined empirically, with the results of these studies generally supportive of its tenets support (Agnew and White 1992; Brezina 1996; reading 22).

Social Disorganization Theory

The social disorganization (or social ecology) perspective developed during the 1920s out of the work of several scholars at the University of Chicago. It focuses on explaining crime rates in various ecological areas, or neighborhoods, of cities. The work in this area relied on the earlier research of Robert Park and Ernest W. Burgess (c.f., Burgess, 1925). They developed the model of "The City," which depicted the processes of growth and change in the populations of various Chicago neighborhoods. In this model, there were five concentric zones, with the center located in the center of Chicago. Zone I was the "industrial area"; zone II was the "zone of transition," where new residents generally moved because of the cheap housing and access to industrial areas; zone III contained the "workingmen's homes"; zone IV contained "better residences"; and, zone V, the greatest distance from the center of Chicago, was the "commuter's zone."

Clifford Shaw and Henry D. McKay applied the concentric-zone model to the study of crime and delinquency rates in Chicago (and subsequently in other cities; see reading 22 and Shaw and McKay 1969). They found that delinquency rates varied largely by zone, with the zone of transition (II) having the highest delinquency rates. Delinquency rates declined sequentially as one moved out from zone II to zone V, which had the lowest rates.

Shaw and McKay attributed their findings to varying levels of social disorganization found in the different zones. The high- delinquency area, zone II, was characterized by a heterogeneous population, population turnover, bad housing, poverty, family disintegration, and a host of other problems. The heterogeneity and turnover undermined the strength of social institutions, such as churches, which are instrumental in maintaining the organization of the neighborhood. As a result, this zone was characterized by social disorganization, that is, a breakdown in a sense of community, or identification, among residents. Neighbors did not know one another; they may have spoken different languages and so did not communicate, had little or no interest in events that happened in the neighborhood, and were unable or unwilling to intervene in potentially troublesome situations. Under these circumstances, people living in the neighborhood were unable to exert informal social control over the behavior of other residents. As one moved toward the outer zones, the level of social disorganization declined. Neighborhoods were more stable, social institutions were stronger, and greater social control could be exerted over the behavior of residents, thereby producing lower delinquency rates.

In addition, Shaw and McKay demonstrated that zone II had the highest delinquency rates over an extended period of time. This finding held regardless of the nativity or the racial or ethnic composition of the people who lived there. During the time when a particular group lived in the zone of transition, it had very high delinquency rates. When members of this group moved out to zone III and beyond because they were financially able to do so (and because they were pushed out by new incoming groups), their delinquency rates declined. This fact led Shaw and McKay to conclude that delinquent behavior is due to the disorganized setting, produced by processes related to invasion and succession of different population groups, rather than to disorganized individuals (see reading 23).

The social disorganization theory fell out of favor for a number of years, due in part to failed delinquency-prevention policies that were based on it, although research on crime and neighborhoods continued. In the 1980s and into the 1990s, there has been renewed interest in the social disorganization perspective, both theoretically and empirically (Reiss and Tonry 1986). A number of changes have occurred in society, however, which have had a large impact on the growth and residential patterns of cities, such as economic restructuring (resulting in the loss of blue-collar industrial and manufacturing jobs and the creation of low-paying service jobs), the increasing pattern of racial and economic segregation, and the development of the underclass, a "truly disadvantaged" group characterized by extremely high rates of joblessness, unemployment, and isolation, among other problems (Massey and Denton 1993; Wilson 1987 1996).

Such changes and their effects on the structure of cities have led to a dismissal of the concentric-zone component of early social disorganization theories. Instead, different efforts to "modernize" the theory have been made in order to account for the changes and address their implications for crime. For example, Rodney Stark delineated a series of propositions that suggest why poor, overcrowded neighborhoods marked by high rates of population turnover should also have high crime and delinquency rates. Others, such as Robert J. Bursik and Harold G. Grasmick, have emphasized the importance of considering the impact of different levels of social controls, associated with the economic and political power of neighborhoods, on crime rates (see also reading 24). At present, the empirical work in social disorganization reflects both traditional and new foci, with research examining factors associated with social disorganization, demographic transitions, social-control mechanisms, and economic conditions in different neighborhoods in various cities, such as New York (Messner and Tardiff 1986), Chicago (reading 24; Morenoff and Sampson 1998), and Miami (Martinez 1997), and their impact on crime rates.

Other Approaches

In addition to the traditional criminological theories discussed above, there are several other important approaches, including labeling theory, conflict or Marxist approaches, and feminist theories. A brief description of some of these is provided, although they are not discussed in detail here.

Labeling theory emerged in the 1950s and 1960s. Particularly important to this approach was the work of Edwin Lemert, John Kitsuse, and Howard Becker, among other scholars. This approach argues that crime and delinquency result from the very processes designed to control them, that is, once someone is identified and labeled by the police and the criminal justice system as a delinquent or a criminal, the label becomes a self-fulfilling prophecy. The label results in the individual's being isolated from conventional people and pushed to associate with similarly labeled people. In addition, the individual internalizes the label and delinquent or criminal becomes his or her master (or primary) status. As a result of coming to view oneself as delinquent, the individual comes, as other people already do, to expect such behavior from him or herself and eventually begins to engage in it again. Offending that produces the initial identification by the system is "primary deviance"; offending that occurs subsequent to the labeling process is "secondary deviance."

The similar conflict and Marxist perspectives are considered together here for the sake of brevity. Unlike other approaches, which see society based on consensus, conflict and Marxist theories see society as comprised of competing groups, the powerful and the powerless. Very simply, the difference between the conflict and the Marxist approaches is that conflict theorists are interested in power relations without specifying the source of power, while Marxist scholars are interested in power derived from the economic system, specifically from ownership of the means of production. According to the early conflict and Marxist scholars, such as Thorsten Sellin, Richard Quinney, and William Chambliss and Robert Seidman, among others, those with the power in society make the laws. The behaviors that are criminalized are those that threaten the interests (particularly economic and political) of the powerful, typically behaviors engaged in by the powerless, while the behaviors that the powerful groups engage in tend to not be criminalized (see also reading 3 and the discussion in the introduction to Section One). Therefore, the less powerful groups in society are those with the highest crime rates, while the most powerful have low crime rates. In the last ten years, this approach has been re-conceptualized by several scholars, including Edmund McGarrell and Thomas Castellano and John Hagan, although they continue to focus on the role of power in determining what constitutes crime and who is punished as criminals (Vold, Bernard, and Snipes 1998).

Feminist theories are similar to conflict and Marxist theories in that they consider the role of power in relation to crime. For feminist theories, however, the source of power is patriarchy. Research and theorizing in this area began vigorously in the 1960s and 1970s, as documented in Section Three, prior to this time there was little research on the role of females in crime. In the 1970s, two books, one by Freda Adler (1975) and the other by Rita Simon (1975), were published that both represented, and led to interest in, the issue of women and crime. After these initial works, feminist scholarship in criminology evolved along several different lines (liberal, radical, socialist, and others; see Vold, Bernard, and Snipes 1998). Overall, however, feminist scholars paid attention principally to the roles of patriarchy and male dominance in society as they relate to crime, both in terms of the effect they have on the kinds of crimes females commit (those that tend to be powerless, such as shoplifting), as well as the crimes perpetrated against them, primarily by males, such as rape and spousal assault (Lilly, Cullen, and Ball 1995; Vold, Bernard, and Snipes 1998).

The readings that follow include both classic and contemporary statements of the major theoretical approaches in criminology in the three disciplines of biology, psychology, and sociology. In addition, following each of the selections of sociological theories is an example of some of the empirical research ongoing in each tradition.

References

Adler, Freda. 1975. *Sisters in Crime: The Rise of the New Female Criminal*. New York: McGraw-Hill.

Agnew, Robert and Helene Raskin White. 1992. "An Empirical Test of General Strain Theory," *Criminology*, 30: 475-499.

Akers, Ronald L. 1985. *Deviant Behavior: A Social Learning Approach* (3rd ed.). Belmont, CA: Wadsworth.

Akers, Ronald L., Marvin D. Krohn, Lonn Lanza-Kaduce, and Marcia Radosevich. 1979. "Social Learning and Deviant Behavior: A General Test of a Specific Theory," *American Sociological Review*, 44: 635-655.

Arneklev, Bruce J., Harold G. Grasmick, Charles R. Tittle, and Robert J. Bursik, Jr. 1993. "Low Self-Control and Imprudent Behavior," *Journal of Quantitative Criminology*, 9: 225-247.

Becker, Howard S. 1963. *Outsiders: Studies in the Sociology of Deviance*. New York: The Free Press.

Booth, Alan and D. Wayne Osgood. 1993. "The Influence of Testerone on Deviance in Adulthood: Assessing and Explaining the Relationship," *Criminology*, 31: 93-117.

Brezina, Timothy. 1996. "Adapting to Strain: An Examination of Delinquent Coping Responses," *Criminology*, 34: 39-60.

Burgess, Ernest W. 1925. "The Growth of the City: An Introduction to a Research Project." In R.E. Park, E.W. Burgess, and R.D. McKenzie, (eds.) *The City*. Chicago: University of Chicago Press.

Burgess, Robert L. and Ronald L. Akers. 1966. "A Differential Association-Reinforcement Theory of Criminal Behavior," *Social Problems*, 14: 128-147.

Bursik, Robert J. Jr. and Harold G. Grasmick. 1993. *Neighborhoods and Crime*. New York: Lexington Books.

Caspi, Avshalom, Terrie E. Moffitt, Phil A. Silva, Magda Stouthamer-Loeber, Robert F. Krueger, and Pamela S. Schmutte. 1994. "Are Some People Crime-Prone? Replications of the Personality-Crime Relationship Across Countries, Genders, Race and Methods," *Criminology*, 32: 163-195.

Cernkovich, Stephen A. and Peggy C. Giordano. 1986. "Family Relationships and Delinquency," *Criminology*, 25: 295-319.

——. "School Bonding, Race, and Delinquency," *Criminology*, 30: 261-291.

Chambliss, William and Robert Seidman. 1971. *Law, Order, and Power*. Reading, Mass: Addison-Wesley.

Cloward, Richard A. and Lloyd E. Ohlin. 1960. *Delinquency and Opportunity: A Theory of Delinquent Gangs*. New York: The Free Press.

Cohen, Albert K. 1955. *Delinquent Boys: The Culture of the Gang*. New York: The Free Press.

Collins, James J. 1981. "Alcohol Use and Criminal Behavior: An Empirical, Theoretical, and Methodological Overview." In J.J. Collins Jr. (ed.), *Drinking and Crime*. New York: The Guilford Press.

Elliott, Delbert S., Suzanne S. Ageton, and Rachelle J. Canter. 1979. "An Integrated Theoretical Perspective on Delinquent Behavior," *Journal of Research in Crime and Delinquency*, 16: 3-27.

Ellis, Lee and Anthony Walsh. 1997. "Gene-Based Evolutionary Theories in Criminology," *Criminology*, 35: 229-276.

Giordano, Peggy C., Stephen A. Cernkovich, and M.D. Pugh. 1986. "Friendships and Delinquency," *American Journal of Sociology*, 91: 1170-1202.

Glueck, Sheldon and Eleanor Glueck. 1950. *Unraveling Juvenile Delinquency*. New York: Commonwealth Fund.

Goldstein, Paul J. 1985. "The Drugs/Violence Nexus: A Tripartite Conceptual Framework," *Journal Of Drugs Issues*, 15: 493-506.

Gottfredson, Michael R. and Travis Hirschi. 1990. *A General Theory of Crime*. Stanford, CA: Stanford University Press.

Hagan, John. 1989. *Structural Criminology*. New Brunswick: Rutgers University Press.

Horney, Julie D., D. Wayne Osgood, and Ineke Haen Marshall. 1995. "Criminal Careers in the Short-Term: Intra-Individual Variability in Crime and Its Relation to Local Life Circumstances," *American Sociological Review*, 60: 655-673.

Kitsuse, John. 1962. "Societal Reaction to Deviance: Problems of Theory and Method," *Social Problems*, 9: 247-256.

Lemert, E.M. 1951. *Social Pathology*. New York: McGraw Hill.

Lilly, J. Robert, Francis T. Cullen, and Richard A. Ball. 1995. *Criminological Theory: Context and Consequences*. Thousand Oaks, CA: Sage Publications.

Martinez, Ramiro Jr. 1997. "Homicide Among Miami's Ethnic Groups: Anglos, Blacks and Latinos in the 1990s," *Homicide Studies*, 1: 17-34.

Massey, Douglas S. and Nancy A. Denton. 1993. *American Apartheid: Segregation and the Making of the Underclass*. Cambridge: Harvard University Press.

McGarrell, Edmund and Thomas Castellano. 1991. "An Integrative Conflict Model of the Criminal Law Formulation Process," *Journal of Research in Crime and Delinquency*, 28: 174-96.

Merton, Robert K. 1968. *Social Theory and Social Structure*. Glencoe, IL: The Free Press.

Messner, Steven F. and Richard Rosenfeld. 1992. *Crime and the American Dream*. Belmont, CA: Wadsworth.

Messner, Steven F. and Kenneth Tardiff. 1986. "Economic Inequality and Levels of Homicide: An Analysis of Urban Neighborhoods," *Criminology*, 24: 297-316.

Moffitt, Terrie E., Donald R. Lyman, and Phil A. Silva. 1994. "Neuropsychological Tests Predicting Persistent Male Delinquency," *Criminology*, 32: 277-300.

Morenoff, Jeffrey D. and Robert J. Sampson. 1997. "Violent Crime and the Spatial Dynamics of Neighborhood Transition," *Social Forces*, 76: 31-64.

Nagin, Daniel S., David P. Farrington, and Terrie E. Moffitt. 1995. "Life-Course Trajectories of Different Types of Offenders," *Criminology*, 33: 111-139.

Quinney, Richard. 1977. *Class, State and Crime*. New York: David McKay Co.

Rankin, Joseph H. and Roger Kern. 1994. "Parental Attachments and Delinquency," *Criminology*, 32: 495-515.

Reckless, Walter C. 1961. *The Crime Problem* (3rd Ed.). New York: Appleton-Century-Crofts.

Reiss, Albert J. 1951. "Delinquency as the Failure of Personal and Social Controls," *American Sociological Review*, 16: 196-207.

Reiss, Albert J. and Michael Tonry (eds.). 1986. *Communities and Crime*. Volume 8. Chicago: University of Chicago Press.

Sampson, Robert J. and John H. Laub. 1993. *Crime in the Making*. Cambridge: Harvard University Press.

Schuessler, Karl F. and Donald R. Cressey. 1950. "Personality Characteristics of Criminals," *American Journal of Sociology*, 55: 476-484.

Sellin, Thorsten. 1938. *Culture Conflict and Crime*. New York: Social Science Research Council.

Shaw, Clifford R. and Henry D. McKay. 1969. *Juvenile Delinquency and Urban Areas* (revised ed.). Chicago: University of Chicago Press.

Simon, Rita J. 1975. *Women and Crime*. Lexington, MA: Lexington.

Stark, Rodney. 1987. "Deviant Places: A Theory of the Ecology of Crime," *Criminology*, 25: 893-909.

Sutherland, Edwin H. 1983. *White Collar Crime: The Uncut Version*. New Haven, CT: Yale University Press.

Tittle, Charles R. 1995. *Control Balance: Toward a General Theory of Deviance*. Boulder, CO: Westview Press.

Vold, George B., Thomas J. Bernard, and Jeffrey B. Snipes. 1998. *Theoretical Criminology* (4th Edition). New York: Oxford.

Walters, Glenn D. 1990. *The Criminal Lifestyle: Patterns of Serious Criminal Conduct*. Newbury Park, CA: Sage.

Warr, Mark. 1993. "Age, Peers, and Delinquency," *Criminology*, 31: 17-40.

Wilson, James Q. and Richard J. Herrnstein. 1985. *Crime & Human Nature*. New York: Simon and Schuster.

Wilson, William Julius. 1987. *The Truly Disadvantaged*. Chicago: University of Chicago Press.

——. 1996. *When Work Disappears*. New York: Knopf. ✦

15

Biological Perspectives in Criminology

Diana H. Fishbein

Biological approaches in criminology focus on individual-level abnormalities to differentiate offenders and nonoffenders. Such approaches focus on a variety of issues related to genetic and other biological bases of criminal behavior, including neurological dysfunction (brain damage), poor nutrition, genetic composition (such as XYY males), and the hereditary nature of criminality. Although many of these researchers tend to be in genetics, neuroscience, and other disciplines, their findings have implications for criminology.

Diana H. Fishbein provides a recent, comprehensive overview of various biological approaches to understanding criminal behavior. She covers the areas of genetics (heredity, as demonstrated in family, twin, and adoption studies), biochemical factors (e.g., hormones and neurotransmitters), and psychological inducements (e.g., psychoactive drugs). In doing so, she demonstrates that there is a substantial body of literature that suggests the importance of considering the role of biology in crime. Fishbein also argues, however, that biology cannot be disconnected from social and psychological factors that interact with biology and that may influence whether biological predispositions and abnormalities will lead to crime. Further, she warns against implementation of biologically based crime control and prevention measures in the near future on the grounds of insufficient results from methodologically strong studies, and for ethical and moral reasons.

Wilson and Herrnstein (1985) recently published a massive evaluation of the implications of biological data for topics of interest to criminologists. Their message is that insufficient consideration has been given to biological and social interactions in criminological studies. Consistent observations that a small percentage of offenders are responsible for a preponderance of serious crime (Hamparin et al., 1978; Moffitt et al., 1989; Wolfgang, 1972) suggest that particular forces produce antisocial behavior in particular individuals. Further, much research shows that violent criminals have an early history of crime and aggression (Loeber and Dishion, 1983; Moffitt et al., 1989). The possibility that biological conditions may play a role in the development of antisocial and criminal behavior is accentuated by these reports and has spurred a search for biological markers in "vulnerable" subgroups (Mednick et al., 1987).

In the past, theories of the biological aspects of criminal behavior were marked by a general lack of knowledge regarding the human brain and by serious methodological shortcomings (see, e.g., Glueck and Glueck, 1956; Goddard, 1921; Hooten, 1939; Jacobs et al., 1965; Lombroso, 1918; Sheldon, 1949). Indeed, "biological criminology" was eventually discredited because its findings were largely unscientific, simplistic, and unicausal. Biological factors were globally rejected due to the inability of theorists to posit a rational explanation for the development of criminal behavior.

More recently, biological aspects of criminal behavior have been investigated by numerous behavioral scientists employing a multidisciplinary approach that promises to enhance substantially the rigor of the findings. Scientists in such fields as genetics, biochemistry, endocrinology, neuro-science, immunology, and psychobiology have been intensively studying aspects of human behavior that are relevant to the criminologist and the criminal justice practitioner. Due to the highly technical and field-specific language of much of this research, findings generated from these works are not usually included in the literature reviews of criminologists. The relative lack of interdisciplinary communication has resulted in a lack of awareness of data pertinent to the study of crime and criminal behavior. This paper is a small step toward filling that gap. . . .

Theoretical and Methodological Parameters

Several critical issues must be addressed in order to (1) establish the relevancy of biology to the study of crime, (2) develop the groundwork for including biological data in criminological theories, (3) design research projects using compatible measurement instruments, data sets, and statistical techniques, and (4) determine the boundaries of practical applications of biological findings. . . . Pertinent issues include nature versus nurture, free will versus determinism, identifying relevant behavioral disorders and subject populations, assumptions and conceptual framework, and finally, methodological considerations. . . .

Nature or Nurture?

The first issue that must be addressed before the parameters of biological research in criminology can be established is the age-old question of whether human behavior is a product of nature or nurture. Theoreticians of the past generally espoused one or the other viewpoint. Those who claim that nature contributes predominantly to an individual's behavior have been affiliated in the past with conservative political ideologies and were known as "hereditarians." In this circle, behavior was primarily attributed to inherited predispositions, and genetic influences were considered responsible for most of the variance in complex human behaviors.

The argument that nurture is the impetus for behavior was advocated by the "environmentalists," who were generally associated with a liberal ideology. Watson's (1925) interpretation of John Locke's *tabula rasa* (blank slate), for example, maintained that humans are born without predispositions to behave in any predetermined or predictable manner. Environmental inputs were considered primarily responsible for the final behavioral product, and manipulations of external inputs were thought to modify behavior. . . .

Few behavioral scientists today adhere to either of these extreme views. A consensus has been emerging over the past 10 to 15 years that the "truth" lies somewhere in between— a "nature plus nurture" perspective (see Plomin, 1989). Although the nurture perspective has dominated fields such as criminology for the past few decades, substantial biological findings can no longer be ignored. Several studies on alcoholism, temperament, criminality, depression, and mental illness have established a solid role for genetic and biological influences (selected recent examples are detailed below). Even though behavioral scientists have yet to determine precisely the separate, relative contributions of biology and social learning to behavior, their findings are particularly relevant to the criminologist, who should play an instrumental role in their evaluation given the potential impact on policy.

Evidence for an interaction between nature and nurture comes from both animal and clinical studies, which demonstrates the strength and importance of the dynamic link between biological and acquired traits. . . .

These illustrations remind us that as evidence for a substantial genetic influence grows we must be cautious not to replace environmental explanations with biological deterministic views. Instead, a more accommodating, balanced approach will carry more empirical weight.

Free Will or Determinism?

The acceptance of biological explanations for human behavior has been thought by many to preclude the possibility of free will. This fundamental fear has resulted in a pervasive rejection of biological contributions to behavior. Although some behavioral scientists are deterministic in their views, attributing behavior to everything from socioeconomic conditions to neurochemical events, most individuals prefer to credit their own free will for their behavior. A compromise reflecting a more accurate position on the forces behind human behavior is widely accepted, however—the theory of "conditional free will" (see Denno, 1988, for discussion of "degree determinism," a related view). . . .

In accordance with probability theory, social human behavior is contingent on a countless number of possible decisions from among which the individual may choose. Not all of those decisions are feasible, however, nor are the resources available that are required to act on them. Choosing a course of action, therefore, is limited by preset boundaries, which narrows the range of possibilities substantially. Decision-limiting factors include current circumstances and opportunities, learning experiences, physiological abilities, and genetic predispositions. Each one of these conditions collaborates internally (physically) and externally (environmentally) to produce a final action. The behavioral result is thus restricted to options available within these guidelines, yet it is "indeterminable" and cannot be precisely predicted. . . .

The principle of conditional free will does not demand a deterministic view of human behavior. Rather, it postulates that individuals choose a course of action within a preset, yet to some degree changeable, range of possibilities and that, assuming the conditions are suitable for rational thought, we are accountable for our actions. Given "rational" thought processes, calculation of risks versus benefits, and the ability to judge the realities that exist, the result is likely to be an adaptive response, that is, the behavior will be beneficial for the individual and the surrounding environment.

This theory of conditional free will predicts that if one or more conditions to which the individual is exposed are disturbed or irregular, the individual is more likely to choose a disturbed or irregular course of action. Thus, the risk of such a response increases as a function of the number of deleterious conditions. . . .

Identifying Behaviors and Populations for Study

Definitional issues are hotly debated among criminologists as a result of the growing recognition that not all "illegal" behaviors are dysfunctional or maladaptive and not all "legitimate" behaviors are moral, acceptable, or adaptive. In attempting to develop a framework for including biological perspectives in criminology, one must first identify behaviors of interest and appropriate subject populations.

The term *criminality* includes behaviors that do not necessarily offend all members of society, such as certain so-called victimless acts, and it excludes behaviors that may be antisocial or illegal but that are not detected by the criminal justice system. *Maladaptivity* includes antisocial behaviors that are costly to citizens and society overall. Such behaviors do not necessarily violate legal norms or come to official attention, however. Individuals who display maladaptive behavior do have a high probability of being labeled as delinquent or criminal, but being so labeled is not a sufficient criterion to be identified as maladaptive. . . .

Criminal behavior is not exclusively maladaptive or dysfunctional behavior; thus, biological theories are differentially relevant to various forms of criminality. Biological findings in behavioral research are of particular interest for the study and management of maladaptive behaviors, both criminal and undetected behaviors that are detrimental to individuals so affected or their milieu. . . .

Conceptual Framework

. . . Individuals are not inherently criminal, nor do they suddenly become homicidal maniacs (except under unusual circumstances). Antisocial behavior has many precursors.[1] Manifestations of a problem are frequently observed in childhood when innate tendencies toward antisocial behavior or other risk factors are compounded by suboptimal environmental and social conditions (Denno, 1988; Lewis et al., 1979, 1985; Mednick et al., 1984). These early seeds of maladaptive behavior are commonly ignored, inappropriately treated, or not recognized as complications that warrant intervention. In such cases, the severity of the condition and resultant behaviors are well advanced by adolescence and adulthood. According to this "developmental course" model of human behavior, criminal behavior is virtually always secondary to an underlying problem(s), as illustrated in Figure 15.1.

One straightforward example of this process, which pervades the criminological literature, is the link between IQ or learning disabilities and delinquent/criminal behavior.[2] Children with conduct disorders tend to have lower IQ scores than nondeviant controls (Huesmann et al., 1984; Kellam et al., 1975; Lewis et al., 1981; Robins, 1966). . . . Probable conditions that may antedate both low IQ and conduct disorder are parental psychopathology, temperamental disturbances, neurological problems, genetic susceptibilities, and disadvantaged environmental influences (Shonfeld et al., 1988). With a learning-disabled or conduct-disordered child, the existence of one or more of these deleterious conditions will increase the likelihood of further adjustment problems. Over time, behavioral difficulties become compounded and, to some extent, reinforced once the child has established mechanisms to protect himself or herself and cope with his or her liabilities. Thus, maladaptive behavior is a function of cumulative, developmental process.

Although low IQ or a learning disability is not inherently criminogenic, in the absence of proper intervention the child may become frustrated attempting to pursue mainstream goals without the skills to achieve them. . . .

Thus, the child's behavior elicits a negative response from his or her environment, which leads to further reactions from the child (see Patterson et al., 1989). Consequently, the cycle of negatively interacting forces continues and the risk of becoming delinquent and eventually criminal is heightened.

Once the individual attracts the attention of the criminal justice system, the problem is already significantly compounded and difficult to treat, and the costs to society are exorbitant. . . .

The learning process as it contributes to behavior cannot be underestimated in this model because, fundamentally, both biological and social behavior are learned. Biological traits and proclivities are not stationary characteristics; they are reinforced or, in some cases, altered through social learning processes. . . .

Humans are equipped with the innate biological capacity to learn as a product of their genetic blueprint, which is physically expressed in the structure of the brain. When an individual is exposed to a stimulus from the internal (biological) or external (social)

Figure 15.1
Developmental Course Model
(The Developmental Stages of Maladaptive Behavior)

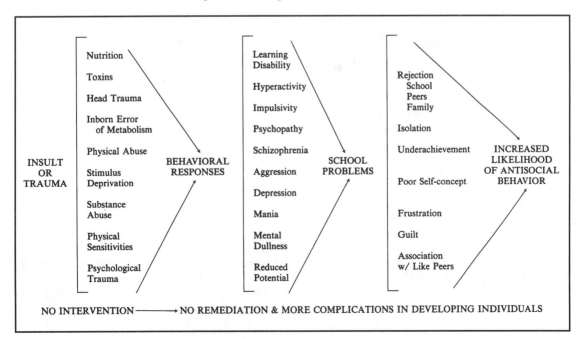

environment, permanent changes occur in the neural structure and biochemical function of the brain. This process is referred to as "memory," experiences coded and stored for retrieval in the form of chemical transformations. . . .

The learning process of comparing new information with memories to produce a response frequently results in "behavioral conditioning." There is an innate foundation for learning in our biological structure that sets contingencies for behavioral conditioning in an individual, consistent with the premise of conditional free will. . . . The two forms of behavioral conditioning, classical and instrumental, both directly involve biological mechanisms. Classical conditioning refers to the response elicited by a neutral stimulus that has been associated with the acquisition of a reward or the avoidance of harm. . . .

When an individual is instrumental in causing a stimulus to occur, operant or instrumental conditioning is at work. The stimulus being elicited either satiates a drive or permits one to avoid a noxious result. For example, if we learn that stealing results in a reward, the behavior will continue. On the other hand, if we are consistently punished for such behavior, we are unlikely to repeat the action. Thus, both forms of conditioning revolve around the same contingencies (biological dictates to avoid pain and seek pleasure, known as hedonism), which function to reinforce our behavior.

Certain behaviors are reinforced when the following conditions exist: (1) the behavior and the stimulus occur together in time and space (continuity), (2) repetition of the association strengthens the conditioned response, (3) the result either evokes pleasure or relieves pain, and (4) there is no interference, as in the form of new experiences, to weaken or extinguish the response. The concept of deterrence is founded on these principles.[3]

In general, the criminal justice system relies on the association made between specific, in this case illegal, behaviors and the application of a painful or punitive sanction, which generally involves the removal of certain freedoms and exposure to unpleasant living conditions. The painful stimulus must be temporarily associated with the behavior, consistently applied, and intense enough to prevent further such behaviors. According to the fourth condition listed above, the individual must not learn that the intrinsic reward properties of the behavior are greater or more consistent than the punishment. And finally, opportunities for preferred modes of behavior must be available. Due to the prevalence of low clearance rates, trial delays, inconsistently applied dispositions, legal loopholes, the learning of improper reward and punishment contingencies, and a lack of available legitimate opportunities, the criminal justice system and society at large have been unable to meet the criteria set above for deterrence and prevention.

The experience of a painful consequence being associated with a behavior is encoded into memory, and when we calculate the consequences of performing that behavior in the future we are deterred by the possible negative response. The impetus for such behavioral change resides in our nervous system. . . . Individuals with a properly functioning nervous system are quite effectively conditioned to avoid stressful situations given the learned contingencies discussed above. . . . Thus, we make a rational choice based on a calculation of costs and benefits and, in this case, deterrence is most likely achieved.

The learning and conditioning of behavior occur differentially among individuals given their neurological status. For example, psychopaths are relatively unemotional, impulsive, immature, thrill-seeking, and "unconditionable" (Cleckley, 1964; Moffitt, 1983; Quay, 1965; Zuckerman, 1983). . . .

In sum, social behavior is learned through the principles of conditioning, which are founded on biological and genetic dictates in accord with stimulus-response relationships. Social rewards remain secondary to biological rewards; our desire for money is social, but it is secondary to being a means for obtaining food and shelter. Thus, social behavior satisfies biological needs and drives by providing adaptive mechanisms for reproduction, mating, rearing, defense, and numerous other biological functions. Even though these strategies are fundamentally biological, how we behave to satisfy them relies heavily on learning.

Measurement and Methodological Issues

Research findings from various behavioral sciences that are relevant to the criminologist can be evaluated in the context of the parameters described above. . . . As a prelude to the discussion, this section examines some of the weaknesses common to such studies.

First, studies of incarcerated populations present obvious problems regarding the generalizability of findings in that any observed effect or correlation may be due to the effects of institutionalized offenders as subjects did not attempt to measure or control for prison conditions and influences. . . .

Second, many forms of bias in selecting subjects are evident in some studies. For example, several studies focus on criminal offenders and ignore pervasive illegal behaviors in undetected samples. There is a strong possibility that apprehended or incarcerated subjects differ from those who avoid detection in terms of their characteristics and the impact of criminal justice procedures.

Third, the use of control subjects is frequently neglected or inappropriate controls are examined. . . .

Fourth, widely divergent conceptual and methodological principles are, at times, applied across studies, which makes it difficult to compare and replicate findings. . . . Measurement instruments differ among studies and interpretations of findings are variable.

Fifth, several points of caution are particularly relevant to interpretation of studies of psychopathic subjects. The widespread use of self-report and retrospective data is problematic generally, but additional problems arise when these data sources are used to examine offenders, a population notorious for falsifying records. Psychopaths, who are depicted as crafty deceivers, offer especially unreliable data. Yet, self-report measures are frequently used to select and categorize subjects. . . .

The discussion that follows concentrates on the biological aspects of this multifaceted relationship because the criminological literature has dealt almost exclusively with sociological and legal issues to the neglect of other interacting conditions. . . .

Selected Studies of the Biology of Maladaptive Behavior

Evolutionary Dictates

Human instinctual drives (e.g., eating, reproduction, and defensive behavior) ensure our survival and are essentially stable over time. The mechanisms for acting on these drives, however, especially the brain, continuously evolve to enhance our survival capabilities and have improved substantially. With the advent of human consciousness, psychological forces and cultural values interact and sometimes compete with biological drives dictated by evolutionary trends (Thiessen, 1976). Thus, human behavior is a product of the profound and complex interaction of biological and social conditions. Due to the intricacy of this interaction and the elusiveness of evolutionary directions, the nature and outcome of this process are difficult to identify and to study.

Most behaviors have some adaptive significance (i.e., they reflect an attempt to adapt to environmental conditions) and, thus, can be studied in an evolutionary context. Aggression is one form of behavior that has been extensively studied with respect to its adaptive significance. . . . Abnormal environmental conditions characterize prisons and may contribute to the incidence of overt aggressive behavior among inmates; they may also partially explain the relationship between contacts with the criminal justice system (e.g., amount of time incarcerated) and recidivism rates. Also, the prevalence of abnormal environmental conditions has increased with the ever-increasing breakdown of the family structure, community disorganization, disparity between public policy and biological needs, crowding, learned helplessness, and other frequently cited characteristics of U.S. urbanization (Archer and Gartner, 1984: 98-117; Larson, 1984: 116-141). Investigation of how these deleterious conditions exacerbate maladaptive behavioral mechanisms may eventually lead to socioenvironmental programs to enhance, rather than detract from, adaptive capabilities. . . .

Genetic Contributions

Research on the genetic components of human behavior suffers in general from numerous methodological and interpretive flaws (Blehar et al., 1988; Clerget-Darpoux et al., 1986; DeFries and Plomin, 1978; Ghodsian-Carpey and Baker, 1987). It is difficult to isolate genetic factors from ontogenetic (developmental) events, cultural influences, early experiences, and housing conditions. As a result, most studies of human behavior have examined the transmission of socioenvironmental factors that can be more empirically observed and manipulated. . . .

As a rule, what is inherited is not a behavior; rather, it is the way in which an individual responds to the environment. It provides an orientation, predisposition, or tendency to behave in a certain fashion. Also, genetic influences on human behavior are polygenic—no single gene effect can be identified for most behaviors.

Intellectual deficits, which are closely tied to delinquent and criminal lifestyles (Hirschi and Hindelang, 1977), are understood to be largely heritable (Bouchard and McGue, 1981; Cattell, 1982). Temperamental traits and personality types, possible precursors of maladaptive or criminal behavior, have also been shown to have heritable components in humans. . . . Individuals with such personality dispositions, compared with those without, have an increased familial incidence of similar behavioral problems and show differences, along with their family members, in certain biochemical, neuropsychological, and physiological parameters (Biederman et al., 1986; Cadoret et al., 1975; DeFries and Plomin, 1978; Hare and Schalling, 1978; Plomin et al., 1990; Rushton et al., 1986; Tarter et al., 1985; Zuckerman, 1983). The behavioral outcome is contingent on various stressors in the environment, life experiences, and current opportunities. . . .

Numerous studies have attempted to estimate the genetic contribution to the development of criminality, delinquency, aggression, and antisocial behavior. . . . Overall, many of these behavioral genetic studies suffer from one or more of the methodological weaknesses discussed earlier. . . .

Family Studies. The family study seeks to identify genetic influences on behavioral traits by evaluating similarities among family members. Cross-generational linkages have been reported for personality and behavioral attributes related to criminal behavior, including temper outbursts (Mattes and Fink, 1987), sociopathy (Cloninger et al., 1975, 1978; Guze et al., 1967), delinquency (Robins et al., 1975; Rowe, 1986), hyperactivity and attention deficit disorder (Cantwell, 1979), conduct disorder, aggression, violence, and psychopathy (Bach-y-Rita et al., 1971; Stewart et al., 1980; Stewart and DeBlois, 1983; Stewart and Leone, 1978; Twito and Stewart, 1982).

Despite conclusions from many of these studies that genetic effects are largely responsible for criminal behavior, this method of study does not directly assess genetic contributions. Environmental influences on measures of behavior may be common to parents and offspring, and thus, large environmental correlations among relatives cannot be accounted for. Diet, environmental toxins, neighborhood conditions, and television-viewing habits are only a few examples of environmental factors that similarly influence family members. . . . At this point, one may only conclude that the incidence of criminal and related behaviors appears to have a familial basis. The relative influences of genetics and environmental conditions cannot, however, be estimated.

Twin Studies. The classic twin design involves the testing of identical (monozygotic or MZ) and fraternal (dizygotic or DZ) twins. MZ twins share genetic material from the biologic parents and are thus considered genetically identical. DZ twins are approximately 50% genetically alike, as are regular siblings. The extent to which MZ resemblances with respect to a characteristic are greater than DZ resemblances provides evidence for a genetic influence on the variable. To the extent that there is still some degree of DZ resemblance after genetic influences have been accounted for, there is evidence for the influence of common family environment on the variable. . . .

No definitive conclusions can be drawn from twin studies of aggressiveness or criminal behavior because no consistent pattern of genetic influence emerges. Nevertheless, twin studies of criminal and related behaviors fairly consistently provide some intriguing evidence for a genetic effect, and genetic influences warrant continued, but more rigorous, study.

Adoption Studies. Adoption studies examine individuals who were raised from infancy by nonrelated adoptive parents rather than biological relatives. To the extent that subjects resemble the biological relatives and not the nonbiological relatives, heredity is thought to play a contributory role. The adoption study method promises to provide unambiguous evidence for the relative contribution of heredity as a cause for behavioral traits and for genetics-environment interactions. Nevertheless, the method has some weaknesses (see Walters and White, 1989, for examples). . . .

Several adoption studies indicate noteworthy genetic effects on criminal or delinquent behavior and related psychopathology (i.e., psychopathy).[4] For the most part, these studies suggest that biological relatives of criminal or antisocial probands have a greater history of criminal convictions or antisocial behavior than the biological relatives of noncriminal control adoptees. In general, family environment, including such indices as social class, rearing styles, and parental attitudes, played a smaller role than did purported genetic effects. . . .

Adoption studies highlight the importance of gene-environment interactional models (Rowe and Osgood, 1984). . . . Even though these conditions interact to product antisocial behavior, many researchers attest that environmental and genetic factors differentially influence behavior and that their relative contributions may be measurable (see Plomin et al., 1990).[5]

Biological Contributions

Genetic foundations for behavioral disorders are manifested in a phenotype, which is the resulting, visible expression of a genetic trait. . . . Although researchers can rarely trace a behavioral disorder to a specific gene, they can more aptly measure the manifestation of a genetic blueprint in nervous system features. Other biological traits associated with behavioral problems are not directly genetic in origin; they may be due to mutations in a genetic constitution, biochemical exposures, or a deleterious social environment. All of these conditions, from the genetic to the environmentally precipitated, exert their influence on the nervous system and, thus, can be measured and manipulated. . . .

Biochemical Correlates. A number of biochemical differences have been found between controls and individuals with psychopathy, antisocial personality, violent behavior, conduct disorder, and other behaviors associated with criminal behavior. These groups have been discriminated on the basis of levels of certain hormones, neurotransmitters, peptides, toxins, and metabolic processes (Brown et al., 1979; Davis et al., 1983; Eichelman and Thoa, 1972; Mednick et al., 1987; Rogeness et al., 1987; Roy et al., 1986; Valzelli, 1981; Virkkunen and Narvanen, 1987).

Current investigations of biochemical mechanisms of aggressiveness focus on the study of central neurotransmitter systems. Observations from animal and human studies, for example, indicate that serotonin, a neurotransmitter, globally inhibits behavioral responses to emotional stimuli and modulates aggression (Muhlbauer, 1985; Soubrie, 1986; van Praag et al., 1987). . . . These studies indicate that serotonin functioning is altered in some types of human aggressiveness and violent suicidal behavior. Thus, a decrease in serotonergic activity may produce disinhibition in both brain mechanisms and behavior and result in increased aggressiveness or impulsivity. . . .

There is evidence that high levels of the male sex hormone testosterone may influence aggressive behavior in males (Kreuz and Rose, 1971; Olweus et al., 1988; Rada et al., 1983; Schiavi et al., 1984), although discrepant studies exist (Coe and Levine, 1983). It has been further suggested that sex hormones may also contribute to antisocial behavior in some women. The premenstrual period in particular has been associated with elevated levels of aggressivity and irritability. This phase of the hormonal cycle is marked by an imbalance in the estrogen-progesterone ratio, which may trigger both physical and psychological impairments in a subgroup of women. . . .

Exposure to toxic trace elements is yet another factor that has been shown to interfere with brain function and behavior. Chronic or acute exposure to lead, for example, has a deleterious effect on brain function by damaging organ systems, impairing intellectual development, and subsequently interfering with the regulation of behavior. . . . Because of the high correlation among school failure, learning disabilities, and delinquency, lead intoxication is a relevant criminological issue.

A growing body of research has further demonstrated that lead intoxication is significantly associated with hyperactivity and impulsivity (David et al., 1972; Needleman et al., 1979), putative precursors to delinquency, and criminal behavior (Denno, 1988). . . .

Many of these studies lack proper control groups and double blind procedures, yet accumulating evidence strongly suggests that, given other deleterious socioenvironmental conditions, an individual exposed to lead is more likely to manifest maladaptive behavior (see Rimland and Larson, 1983, for a review of studies). . . .

Psychopharmacological Inducements

Psychopharmacology is the study of the psychological and behavioral aspects of drug effects on brain metabolism and activity. Aggression, for example, can be elicited or extinguished by the administration of a pharmacologic agent. . . . Certain drugs, particularly many of the illicit drugs, are reported to increase aggressive responses, for example, amphetamines, cocaine, alcohol, and phencyclidine (PCP). The actual expression of aggressive behavior depends on the dose, route of administration, genetic factors, and type of aggression. . . .

Implications for Criminal Justice Practices

In order to determine the relevance and significance of biological perspectives for criminology, researchers must estimate the incidence of biological disorders among maladaptive populations, identify etiologic mechanisms, assess the dynamic interaction among biological and socioenvironmental factors, and determine whether improvements in behavior follow large-scale therapeutic manipulations.

At this stage of scientific inquiry in the biological sciences, researchers have yet to determine the significance of biological disorders in criminal populations. Nor are they able to speak of a causal link between biological abnormalities and specific behavioral disorders. They are beginning to identify putative correlates or markers of antisocial behavior using biological tests (e.g., EEG slowing, body lead burden, neurotransmitter imbalance). Some of those correlations may prove to be spurious, but at present, which ones cannot be identified. Seen in this light, it would be premature to apply biological findings routinely to criminal justice procedures. . . .

Closing Comments

How biological variables interact with social and psychological factors to produce human behavior generally and antisocial behavior specifically is unknown. The bulk of biological studies, both those described herein and others not included, have examined only a few isolated variables and have generally failed to evaluate dynamic interrelationships among biological and socioenvironmental conditions (see Denno, 1988, and Wilson and Herrnstein, 1985, for detailed critiques). In order to evaluate the relative significance of biological contributions to antisocial behavior, sophisticated, statistical techniques (i.e., structural equation models) must be applied to multivariate designs that use rigorous measurement instruments. Studies of biological influence would benefit greatly from adopting the methodological and statistical techniques of sociologists to increase the rigor and relevance of the findings.

Caution against the premature application of biological findings is clearly called for. The weaknesses in design, sampling techniques, and statistical procedures delineated above preclude drawing definitive conclusions, and results are frequently contested and unreliable. Policies and programs based on equivocal and controversial findings waste time and money and potentially compromise individual rights and community safety. A number of legal, ethical, and political obstacles to the acceptance and application of biological and medical information by the criminal justice system are covered extensively elsewhere (Fishbein and Thatcher, in press; Jeffery, 1985; Marsh and Katz, 1985). At the very least, care must be taken not to stigmatize or otherwise traumatize individuals or groups that are, as yet, innocent of a criminal or civil violation. As researchers, we must avoid applying labels to behaviors we do not understand. In the event that biological measures are shown to be reliable and valid predictors of behavior and mental status, several serious civil rights and constitutional issues related to early identification and intervention in the absence of a proven violation of law would demand careful consideration. . . .

Overall, evidence to suggest that biological conditions have a profound impact on the adaptive, cognitive, and emotional abilities of the individual is compelling. Investigation of the discriminants for behavioral dysfunctions indicates that the impact of these factors is substantial. When a biological disadvantage is present due to genetic influences or when a physical trauma occurs during developmental stages of childhood, the resultant deficit may be compounded over time and drastically interfere with behavioral functions throughout life. Such conditions appear to place an individual at high risk for persistent problematic behavior. Disturbances associated with poor environmental and social conditions coupled with impaired brain function may eventually be amenable to intervention. The unfortunate reality for those who come into contact with the courts by virtue of their dysfunction, however, is that the underlying causes of their disorder are inaccurately evaluated or simply unattended. . . .

Discussion Questions

1. What is the relationship between heredity and crime, according to Fishbein? What do the results of family, adoption, and twin studies indicate?

2. Fishbein indicates that biology cannot be considered without also taking into account the roles of psychological and social factors. Why does she argue this? Provide examples of situations in which social and psychological factors can have important roles in determining whether a biological predisposition leads to criminal behavior.

3. What are some of the potential implications of biologically based theories for criminology? What types of crime control efforts would be suggested by such theories? What are some of the moral and ethical problems with such policies?

Notes

1. Antisocial children have a high incidence of adjustment problems, for example, low academic achievement, temper tantrums, conduct disorders, and negative attitudes (see Patterson et al., 1989, for a summary review).

2. See Critchley (1968), Hirschi and Hindelang (1977), McGee et al. (1986), McManus et al. (1985), Perlmutter (1987), Poremba (1975), Robins (1966), Shonfeld et al. (1988), Wolff et al. (1982).

3. Moffitt (1983) provides an excellent overview of the learning process in the suppression of punished behaviors as dictated by external and internal contingencies, e.g., cognitive abilities of the individual. Although Moffitt appropriately cautions against the uncritical application of the experimental model of punishment (procedures to manipulate behavior in a laboratory setting) to the process of punishing juvenile offenders, she discusses how the data may be used in constructing more effective deterrence programs.

4. For the former see Cloninger et al. (1982), Crowe (1972), Hutchings and Mednick (1975), Mednick et al. (1984), Sigvardsson et al. (1982); for the latter see Cadoret (1978), Cadoret et al. (1985), Crowe (1974), Schulsinger (1985).

5. Plomin and Daniels (1987) provide convincing evidence that genetic influences may explain within-family resemblances and that environmental influences more aptly explain within-family differences.

References

Allen, H., L. Lewis, H. Goldman, and S. Dinitz. 1971. "Hostile and Simple Sociopaths: An Empirical Typology." *Criminology* 9(1)27-47.

American Psychological Association. 1987. *Diagnostic and Statistical Manual of Mental Disorders*. 3ʳᵈ ed., rev. (DSM-III-R). Washington, D.C.: American Psychological Association.

Archer, D. and R. Gartner. 1984. *Violence and Crime in Cross-National Perspective*. New Haven: Yale University Press.

Aronow, R., J.N. Miceli, and A.K. Done. 1980. "A Therapeutic Approach to the Acutely Overdosed Patient." *Journal of Psychedelic Drugs* 12:259-268.

Bach-y-Rita, G., J.R. Lion, and F.R. Ervin. 1970. "Pathological Intoxication." Clinical and Electroencephalographic Studies. *American Journal of Psychiatry* 127:698-703.

Bach-y-Rita, G., J.R. Lion, C.E. Climent, and F.R. Ervin. 1971. "Episodic Dyscontrol: A Study of 130 Violent Patients." *American Journal of Psychiatry* 127:1473-1478.

Benignus, V.A., D.A. Otto, K.E. Muller, and K.J. Seiple. 1981. "Effects of Age and Body Lead Burden on CNS Function in Young Children. II: EEG Spectra." *Electroencephalography and Clinical Neurophysiology* 52:240-248.

Berlin, F.S. 1983. "Sex Offenders: A Biomedical Perspective and a Status Report on Biomedical Treatment." In J.G. Greer and I.R. Stuart (eds.), *The Sexual Aggressor: Current Perspectives on Treatment*. New York: Van Nostrand Reinhold.

Berlin, F.S. and C.F. Meinecke. 1981. "Treatment of Sex Offenders With Antiandrogenic Medication: Conceptualization, Review of Treatment Modalities, and Preliminary Findings." *American Journal of Psychiatry* 138:601-607.

Biederman, J., K. Munir, D. Knee, W. Habelow, M. Armentano, S. Autor, S.K. Hoge, and C. Waternaux. 1986. "A Family Study of Patients With Attention Deficit Disorder and Normal Controls." *Journal of Psychiatric Research* 20(4):263-274.

Blackburn, R. 1978. "Psychopathy, Arousal and the Need for Stimulation." In R.D. Hare and D. Schalling (eds.), *Psychopathic Behaviour: Approaches to Research*. Chichester, England: John Wiley & Sons.

——. 1986. "Patterns of Personality Deviation Among Violent Offenders: Replication and Extension of an Empirical Taxonomy." *British Journal of Criminology* 26:254-269.

——. 1988. "On Moral Judgements and Personality Disorders: The Myth of Psychopathic Personality Revisited." *British Journal of Psychiatry* 153:505-512.

Blehar, M.C., M.M. Weissman, E.S. Gershon, and R.M.A. Hirschfeld. 1988. "Family and Genetic Studies of Affective Disorders." *Archives of General Psychiatry* 45:289-292.

Bohman, M., C.R. Cloninger, S. Sigvardsson, and A.-L. Von Knorring. 1982. "Predisposition to Petty Criminality in Swedish Adoptees: I. Genetic and Environmental Heterogeneity." *Archives of General Psychiatry* 41:872-878.

Bouchard, T.J., Jr., and M. McGue. 1981. "Familial Studies of Intelligence: A Review." *Science* 212:1055-1059.

Bradford, J. 1983. "Research on Sex Offenders." *Psychiatric Clinics of North America* 6:715-713.

Brizer, D.A. and M. Crowner. 1989. *Current Approaches to the Prediction of Violence*. Washington, D.C.: American Psychiatric Press.

Brook, J.S., S. Gordon, and M. Whiteman. 1985. "Stability of Personality During Adolescence and its Relationship to Stage of Drug Use." *Genetic, Social and General Psychology Monographs*. 111(3):317-330.

Brown, G.L., F.K. Goodwin, J.C. Ballenger, P.F. Goyer, and L.F. Major. 1979. "Aggression in Humans Correlates With Cerebrospinal Fluid Amine Metabolites." *Psychiatry Research* 1(2):131-139.

Bryant, E.T., M.L. Scott, C.J. Golden, and D.C. Tori. 1984. "Neuropsychological Deficits, Learning Disability, and Violent Behavior." *Journal of Consulting and Clinical Psychology* 52:323-324.

Bryce-Smith, D. and H.A. Waldron. 1974. "Lead, Behavior, and Criminality." *The Ecologist* 4:367-377.

Cadoret, R.J. 1978. "Psychopathology in Adopted Away Offspring of Biologic Parents With Antisocial Behavior." *Archives of General Psychiatry* 35:176-184.

Cadoret, R.J., L. Cunningham, R. Loftus, and J. Edwards. 1975. "Studies of Adoptees From Psychiatrically Disturbed Biologic Parents. II. Temperament, Hyperactive, Antisocial and Developmental Variables." *Journal of Pediatrics* 87:301-306.

Cadoret, R.J., T.W. O'Gorman, E. Troughton, and E. Heywood. 1985. "Alcoholism and Antisocial Personality: Interrelationships, Genetic and Environmental Factors." *Archives of General Psychiatry* 42:161-167.

Cantwell, D.P. 1979. "Minimal Brain Dysfunction in Adults: Evidence From Studies of Psychiatric Illness in the Families of Hyperactive Children." In L. Bellak (ed.), *Psychiatric Aspects of*

Minimal Brain Dysfunction in Adults. New York: Grune and Stratton.

Carlson, N.R. 1977. *Physiology of Behavior.* Boston: Allyn & Bacon.

Carroll, B.J. and M. Steiner. 1987. "The Psychobiology of Premenstrual Dysphoria: The Role of Prolactin." *Psychoneuroendocrinology* 3:171-180.

Cattell, R.B. 1982. *The Inheritance of Personality and Ability: Research Methods and Findings.* New York: Academic Press.

Christiansen, K.O. 1977a. "A Preliminary Study of Criminality Among Twins." In S.A. Mednick and K.O. Christiansen (eds.), *Biosocial Bases of Criminal Behavior.* New York: Gardner Press.

Clare, A.W. 1985. "Hormones, Behaviour and the Menstrual Cycle." *Journal of Psychosomatic Research* 29(3):225-233.

Cleckley, H. 1964. *The Mask of Sanity.* 4th ed. St. Louis: Mosby.

Clerget-Darpoux, F., L.R. Goldin, and E.S. Fershon. 1986. "Clinical Methods in Psychiatric Genetics. III. Environmental Stratification May Simulate a Genetic Effect in Adoption Studies." *Acta Psychiatric Scandanavia* 74:305-311.

Cloninger, C.R., T. Reich, and S.B. Guze. 1975. "The Multifactoral Model of Disease Transmission: II. Sex Differences in the Familial Transmission of Sociopathy (Antisocial Personality)." *British Journal of Psychiatry 127:11-22.*

Cloninger, C.R., K.O. Christiansen, R. Reich, and I.I. Gottesman. 1978. "Implications of Sex Differences in the Prevalences of Antisocial Personality, Alcoholism, and Criminality for Familial Transmission." *Archives of General Psychiatry* 35:941-951.

Cloninger, C.R., S. Sigvardsson, M. Bohman, and A-L. von Knorring. 1982. "Predisposition to Petty Criminality in Swedish Adoptees: II. Cross-Fostering Analysis of Gene-Environment Interaction." *Archives of General Psychiatry* 39:1242-1247.

Cocozza, J.J. and H.J. Steadman. 1974. "Some Refinements in the Measurement and Prediction of Dangerous Behavior." *American Journal of Psychiatry* 131:1012-1014.

Coe, C.L. and S. Levine. 1983. "Biology of Aggression." *Bulletin of the American Academy of Psychiatry Law* 11:131-148.

Cohen, S. 1977. "Angel Dust." *Journal of the American Medical Association* 238:515-516.

——. 1980. "Alcoholic Hypoglycemia." *Drug Abuse and Alcoholism Newsletter* 9(2):1-4.

Coid, J. 1979. "Mania a Potu: A Critical Review of Pathological Intoxication." *Psychological Medicine* 9:709-719.

Cooke, W.R. 1945. "The Differential Psychology of the American Woman." *American Journal of Obstetrics and Gynecology* 49:457-472.

Cordoba, O.A. and J.L. Chapel. 1983. "Medroxyprogesterone Acetate Antiandrogen Treatment of Hypersexuality in a Pedophiliac Sex Offender." *American Journal of Psychiatry* 140:1036-1039.

Critchley, E.M.R. 1968. "Reading Retardation, Dyslexia, and Delinquency." *British Journal of Psychiatry* 115:1537-1547.

Crowe, R.R. 1972. "The Adopted Offspring of Women Criminal Offenders: A Study of Their Arrest Records." *Archives of General Psychiatry* 27:600-603.

——. 1974. "An Adoption Study of Antisocial Personality." *Archives of General Psychiatry* 31:785-791.

Dalgard, O.S. and E. Kringler. 1976. "A Norwegian Twin Study of Criminality." *British Journal of Criminology* 16:213-232.

Dalton, K. 1964. *The Premenstrual Syndrome.* Springfield, IL: Charles C. Thomas.

——. 1966. "The Influence of Mother's Menstruation on Her Child." *Proceedings of the Royal Society of Medicine* 59:1014-1016.

David, O.J., J. Clark, and K. Voeller. 1972. "Lead and Hyperactivity." *Lancet* 2:900.

David, O.J., S.P. Hoffman, J. Sverd, J. Clark, and K. Voeller. 1976. "Lead and Hyperactivity: Behavioral Response to Chelation—A Pilot Study." *American Journal of Psychiatry* 133:1155.

Davis, B.A., P.H. Yu, A.A. Boulton, J.S. Wormith, and D. Addington. 1983. "Correlative Relationship Between Biochemical Activity and Aggressive Behavior." *Progress in Neuro-sychopharmacology and Biological Psychiatry* 7:529-535.

DeFries, J.C. and R. Plomin. 1978. "Behavioral Genetics." *Annual Reviews in Psychology* 29:473-515.

Demsky, L.S. 1984. "The Use of Depo-Provera in the Treatment of Sex Offenders." *The Journal of Legal Medicine* 5:295-322.

Denno, D.W. 1988. "Human Biology and Criminal Responsibility: Free Will or Free Ride?" *University of Pennsylvania Law Review* 137(2):615-671.

Devonshire, P.A., R.C. Howard, and C. Sellars. 1988. "Frontal Lobe Functions and Personality in Mentally Abnormal Offenders." *Personality and Individual Differences* 9:339-344.

Deykin, E.Y., J.C. Levy, and V. Wells. 1986. "Adolescent Depression, Alcohol and Drug Abuse." *American Journal of Public Health* 76:178-182.

Domino, E.F. 1978. "Neurobiology of Phencyclidine—An Update." In R.C. Peterson and R.C. Stillman (eds.), *Phencyclidine (PCP) Abuse: An*

Appraisal. NIDA Research Monograph 21. Rockville, MD: National Institute on Drug Abuse.

——. 1980. "History and Pharmacology of PCP and PCP-Related Analogs." *Journal of Psychedelic Drugs* 12:223-227.

D'Orban, P.T. and J. Dalton. 1980. "Violent Crime and the Menstrual Cycle." *Psychological Medicine* 10:353-359.

Eichelman, B.S. and N.B. Thoa. 1972. "The Aggressive Monoamines." *Biological Psychiatry* 6(2):143-163.

Ellis, L. and M.A. Ames. 1987. "Neurohormonal Functioning and Sexual Orientation: A Theory of Homosexuality-Heterosexuality." *Psychological Bulletin* 101:233-258.

Ellis, D. and P. Austin. 1971. "Menstruation and Aggressive Behavior in a Correctional Center for Women." *Journal of Criminal Law, Criminology and Police Science* 62:388-395.

Epps, P. 1962. "Women Shoplifters in Holloway Prison." In T.C.N. Gibbens, and J. Prince (eds.), *Shoplifting*. London: The Institute for the Study and Treatment of Delinquency.

Eysenck, H.J. 1977. *Crime and Personality*. Rev. ed. London: Routledge & Kegan Paul.

Fauman, M.A. and B.J. Fauman. 1980. "Chronic Phencyclidine (PCP) Abuse: A Psychiatric Perspective." *Journal of Psychedelic Drugs* 12:307-314.

Fishbein, D.H. and R. Thatcher. In press. "Legal Applications of Electrophysiological Assessments." In J. Dywan, R. Kaplan, and F. Pirozzolo (eds.), *Neuropsychology and the Law*. New York: Springer-Verlag.

Fishbein, D.H., D. Lozovsky, and J.H. Jaffe. 1989. "Impulsivity, Aggression and Neuroendocrine Responses to Serotonergic Simulation in Substance Abusers." *Biological Psychiatry* 25:1049-1066.

Geary, D.C. 1989. "A Model for Representing Gender Differences in the Pattern of Cognitive Abilities." *American Psychologist* 44:1155-1156.

Ghodsian-Carpey, J. and L.A. Baker. 1987. "Genetic and Environmental Influences on Aggression in 4 to 7 Year Old Twins." *Aggressive Behavior* 13:173-186.

Ginsburg, B.E. and B.F. Carter. 1987. *Premenstrual Syndrome: Ethical and Legal Implications in a Biomedical Perspective*. New York: Plenum.

Glueck, S. and E.T. Glueck. 1956. *Physique and Delinquency*. New York: Harper & Row.

Goddard, H.H. 1921. *Juvenile Delinquency*. New York: Dodd, Mead.

Gottfredson, S. 1986. "Statistical and Actual Considerations." In F. Dutile and C. Foust (eds.), *The Prediction of Criminal Violence*. Springfield, IL: Charles C. Thomas.

Gove, W.R. and C. Wilmoth. In press. "Risk, Crime and Physiological Highs: A Consideration of Neurological Processes Which May Act as Positive Reinforcers." In L. Ellis and H. Hoffman (eds.), *Evolution, The Brain and Criminal Behavior: A Reader in Biosocial Criminology*. New York: Praeger.

Guze, S.B., E.D. Wolfgram, J.K. McKinney, and D.P. Cantwell. 1967. "Psychiatric Illness in the Families of Convicted Criminals: A Study of 519 First-degree Relatives." *Diseases of the Nervous System* 28:651-659.

Hamparin, D.M., R. Schuster, S. Dinitz, and J.P. Conrad. 1978. *The Violent Few: A Study of Dangerous Juvenile Offenders*. Lexington, MA: Lexington Books.

Hare, R.D. 1970. *Psychopathy: Theory and Research*. New York: John Wiley & Sons.

——. 1978. "Electrodermal and Cardiovascular Correlates of Psychopathy." In R.D. Hare and D. Schalling (eds.), *Psychopathic Behavior*. New York: John Wiley & Sons.

Hare, R.D. and D. Schalling. 1978. *Psychopathic Behavior*. New York: John Wiley & Sons.

Harry, B. and C. Blacer. 1987. "Menstruation and Crime: A Critical Review of the Literature From the Clinical Criminology Perspective." *Behavioral Sciences and the Law* 5(3)307-322.

Haskett, R.F. 1987. "Premenstrual Dysphoric Disorder: Evaluation, Pathophysiology and Treatment." *Progress in Neuro-Psychopharmacology and Biological Psychiatry* 11:129-135.

Hill, D. and D. Watterson. 1942. "Electroencephalographic Studies of the Psychopathic Personality." *Journal of Neurological Psychiatry* 5:47-64.

Hirschi, T. 1969. *Causes of Delinquency*. Berkeley: University of California Press.

Hirschi, T. and M.J. Hindelang. 1977. "Intelligence and Delinquency: A Revisionist Review." *Science* 196:1393-1409.

Hooten, E.A. 1939. *The American Criminal: An Anthropological Study*. Cambridge, MA: Harvard University Press.

House, T.H. and W.L. Milligan. 1976. "Autonomic Responses to Modeled Distress in Prison Psychopaths." *Journal of Personality and Social Psychology* 34:556-560.

Howard, R.C. 1984. "The Clinical EEG and Personality in Mentally Abnormal Offenders." *Psychological Medicine* 14:569-580.

——. 1986. "Psychopathy: A Psychobiological Perspective." *Personality and Individual Differences* 7(6):795-806.

Huesmann, L.R., L.D. Eron, M.M. Lefkowitz, and L.O. Walder. 1984. "Stability of Aggression Over Time and Generations." *Developmental Psychology* 20:1120-1134.

Hurwitz, I., R.M. Bibace, P.H. Wolff, and B.M. Rowbotham. 1972. "Neuropsychological Function of Normal Boys, Delinquent Boys, and Boys With Learning Problems." *Perceptual and Motor Skills* 35(2):387-394.

Hutchings, B. and S.A. Mednick. 1975. "Registered Criminality in the Adoptive and Biological Parents of Registered Male Criminal Adoptees." In R.R. Fieve, D. Rosenthal, and H. Brill (eds.), *Genetic Research in Psychiatry*. Baltimore: John Hopkins University Press.

Jacobs, P.A., M. Brunton, M.M. Melville, R.P. Brittain, and W. McClemont. 1965. "Aggressive Behaviour, Mental Sub-Normality, and the XYY Male." *Nature* 108:1351-1352.

Jeffery, C.R. 1977. *Crime Prevention Through Environmental Design*. Beverly Hills, CA: Sage.

——. 1985. *Attacks on the Insanity Defense: Biological Psychiatry and New Perspectives on Criminal Behavior*. Springfield, IL: Charles C. Thomas.

Jutai, J.W. and R.D. Hare. 1983. "Psychopathy and Selective Attention During Performance of a Complex Perceptual-Motor Task." *Psychophysiology* 20:146-151.

Kadzin, A.E. 1987. "Treatment of Antisocial Behavior in Children: Current Status and Future Directions." *Psychological Bulletin* 102:187-203.

Kagan, J., J.S. Reznick, and N. Snidman. 1988. "Biological Bases of Childhood Shyness." *Science* 240:167-171.

Kandel, E. and S.A. Mednick. 1988. "IQ as a Protective Factor for Subjects at High Risk for Antisocial Behavior." *Journal of Consulting and Clinical Psychology* 56:224-226.

Kellam, S.G., J.D. Branch, D.C. Agrawal, and M.E. Ensminger. 1975. *Mental Health and Going to School: The Woodlawn Program of Assessment, Early Intervention and Evaluation*. Chicago: University of Chicago Press.

Kellam, S.G., M.E. Ensminger, and M.B. Simon. 1980. "Mental Health in First Grade and Teenage Drug, Alcohol, and Cigarette Use." *Drug and Alcohol Dependence* 5:273-304.

Khajawall, A.M., T.B. Erickson, and G.B. Simpson. 1982. "Chronic Phencyclidine Abuse and Physical Assault." *American Journal of Psychiatry* 139:1604-1606.

Kiloh, L.G., A.J. McComas, and J.W. Osselton. 1972. *Clinical Electroencephalography*. 3rd ed. London: Butterworths.

Kreuz, L.E. and R.M. Rose. 1971. "Assessment of Aggressive Behavior and Plasma Testosterone in a Young Criminal Population." *Psychomatic Medicine* 34:321-332.

Kuperman, S. and M. Stewart. 1987. "Use of Propranolol to Decrease Aggressive Outbursts in Younger Patients." *Psychosomatics* 28:315-319.

Larson, C.J. 1984. *Crime, Justice and Society*. New York: General Hall.

Lester, M.L. and D.H. Fishbein. 1987. "Nutrition and Neuropsychological Development in Children." In R. Tarter, D.H. Van Thiel, and K. Edwards (eds.), *Medical Neuropsychology: The Impact of Disease on Behavior*. New York: Plenum.

Lewis, D.O., S.S. Shanok, and D.A. Balla. 1979. "Perinatal Difficulties, Head and Face Trauma and Child Abuse in the Medical Histories of Serious Youthful Offenders." *American Journal of Psychiatry* 136:419-423.

Lewis, D.O., S.S. Shanok, and J.N. Pincus. 1981. "The Neuropsychiatric Status of Violent Male Delinquents." In D.O. Lewis (ed.), *Vulnerabilities to Delinquency*. New York: Spectrum.

Lewis, D.O., E. Moy, L.D. Jackson, R. Aaronson, N. Restifo, S. Serra, and A. Simos. 1985. "Biopsychosocial Characteristics of Children who Later Murder: A Prospective Study." *American Journal of Psychiatry* 143:838-845.

Lewis, D.O., J.H. Pincus, M. Feldman, L. Jackson, and B. Bard. 1986. "Psychiatric, Neurological, and Psychoeducational Characteristics of 15 Death Row Inmates in the United States." *American Journal of Psychiatry* 143:838-845.

Lewis, D.O., J.H. Pincus, B. Bard, E. Richardson, L.S. Prichep, M. Feldman, and C. Yeager. 1988. "Neuropsychiatric, Psychoeducational, and Family Characteristics of 14 Juveniles Condemned to Death in the United States." *American Journal of Psychiatry* 145:584-589.

Linder, R.L., S.E. Lerner, and R.S. Burns. 1981. "The Experience and Effects of PCP Abuse." In *The Devil's Dust: Recognition, Management, and Prevention of Phencyclidine Abuse*. Belmont, CA: Wardsworth.

Linnoila, M., M. Virkkunen, M. Scheinin, A. Nuutila, R. Rimon, and F.K. Goodwin. 1983. "Low Cerebrospinal Fluid 5-Hydroxyindoleacetic Acid Concentration Differentiates Impulsive From Nonimpulsive Violent Behavior." *Life Sciences* 33:2609-2614.

Lion, J.R. 1974. "Diagnosis and Treatment of Personality Disorders." In J.R. Lion (ed.), *Person-

ality Disorders: Diagnosis and Treatment. Baltimore: Williams and Wilkins.

——. 1979. "Benzodiazepines in the Treatment of Aggressive Patients." *Journal of Clinical Psychiatry* 40:70-71.

Loeber, R. and T. Dishion. 1983. "Early Predictors of Male Delinquency: A Review." *Psychological Bulletin* 94:68-99.

Lombroso, C. 1918. *Crimes, Its Causes and Remedies*. Boston: Little, Brown.

Lykken, D.T. 1957. "A Study of Anxiety in the Sociopathic Personality." *Journal of Abnormal and Social Psychology* 55:6-10.

Maletsky, B.M. 1976. "The Diagnosis of Pathological Intoxication." *Journal of Studies on Alcohol* 37:1215-1228.

Marinacci, A.A. 1963. "Special Types of Temporal Lobe Seizures Following Ingestion of Alcohol." *Bulletin of the Los Angeles Neurological Society* 28:241-250.

Marrs-Simon, P.A., M. Weiler, M.C. Santangelo, M.T. Perry, and J.B. Leikin. 1988. "Analysis of Sexual Disparity of Violent Behavior in PCP Intoxication." *Veterinary and Human Toxicology* 30(1):53-55.

Marsh, F.H. and J. Katz. 1985. *Biology, Crime and Ethics: A Study of Biological Explanations for Criminal Behavior*. Cincinnati: Anderson Publishing.

Mattes, J.A. and M. Fink. 1987. "A Family Study of Patients With Temper Outbursts." *Journal of Psychiatric Research* 21:249-255.

McCardle, L. and D.H. Fishbein. 1989. "The Self-Reported Effects of PCP on Human Aggression." *Addictive Behaviors* 4(4):465-472.

McGee, R., S. Williams, D.L. Share, J. Anderson, and P.A. Silva. 1986. "The Relationship Between Specific Reading Retardation, General Reading Backwardness and Behavioral Problems in a Large Sample of Dunedin Boys: A Longitudinal Study From Five to Eleven Years." *Journal of Child Psychology and Psychiatry* 27:597-610.

McManus, M., A. Brickman, N.E. Alessi, and W.L. Grapentine. 1985. "Neurological Dysfunction in Serious Delinquents." *Journal of the American Academy of Child Psychiatry* 24:481-486.

Mednick, S.A., J. Volavka, W.F. Gabrielli, and T.M. Itil. 1981. "EEG Predicts Later Delinquency." *Criminology* 19:219-229.

Mednick, S.A., V. Pollock, , J. Volavka, and W.F. Gabrielli, Jr. 1982. "Biology and Violence." In M.E. Wolfgang and N.A. Weiner (eds.), *Criminal Violence*. Beverly Hills, CA: Sage.

Mednick, S.A., W.F. Gabrielli, Jr., and B. Hutchings. 1984. "Genetic Influences in Criminal Convictions: Evidence From an Adoption Cohort." *Science* 224:891-894.

Mednick, S.A., T.E. Moffitt, and S.A. Stack. 1987. *The Causes of Crime: New Biological Approaches*. New York: Cambridge University Press.

Moffitt, T.E. 1983. "The Learning Theory Model of Punishment: Implications for Delinquency Deterrence." *Criminal Justice and Behavior* 10:131-158.

Moffitt, T.E., S.A. Mednick, W.F. Gabrielli, Jr. 1989. "Predicting Careers of Criminal Violence: Descriptive Data and Predispositional Factors." In D.A. Brizer and M. Crowner (eds.), *Current Approaches to the Prediction of Violence*. Washington, D.C.: American Psychiatric Press.

Monahan, J. 1981. *The Clinical Prediction of Violent Behavior*. Rockville, MD: U.S. Department of Health and Human Services.

Moore, L.S. and A.I. Fleischman. 1975. "Subclinical Lead Toxicity." *Orthomolecular Psychiatry* 4:61-70.

Morton, J.H., H. Additon, and R.G. Addison. 1953. "A Clinical Study of Premenstrual Tension." *American Journal of Obstetrics and Gynecology* 65:1182-1191.

Muhlbauer, H.D. 1985. "Human Aggression and the Role of Central Serotonin." *Pharmacopsychiatry* 18:218-221.

Murray, J.B. 1987. "Psychopharmacological Therapy of Deviant Sexual Behavior." *Journal of General Psychology* 115:101-110.

Needleman, H.L., C. Gunnoe, A. Leviton, P. Reed, H. Peresie, C. Maher, and P. Barrett. 1979. "Deficits in Psychologic and Classroom Performance of Children With Elevated Dentine Lead Levels." *New England Journal of Medicine* 300:689-695.

Olds, J. and P. Milner. 1954. "Positive Reinforcement Produced by Electrical Stimulation of Septal Area and Other Regions of Rat Brain." *Journal of Comparative and Physiological Psychology* 47:419-427.

Olweus, D. 1979. "Stability of Aggressive Reaction Patterns in Males: A Review." *Psychological Bulletin* 86:852-875.

Owen, D. and J.O. Sines. 1970. "Heritability of Personality in Children." *Behavior Genetics* 1:235-248.

Patterson, G.R., B.D. DeBaryshe, and E. Ramsey. 1989. "A Developmental Perspective on Antisocial Behavior." *American Psychologist* 44:329-335.

Perlmutter, B.F. 1987. "Delinquency and Learning Disabilities: Evidence for Compensatory Behaviors and Adaptation." *Journal of Youth and Adolescence* 16:89-95.

Pihl, R.O. and M. Parkes. 1977. "Hair Element Content in Learning Disabled Children." *Science* 198:204.

Pihl, R.O. and D. Ross. 1987. "Research on Alcohol Related Aggression: A Review and Implications for Understanding Aggression." In S.W. Sadava (ed.), *Drug Use and Psychological Theory*. New York: Hayworth Press.

Pihl, R.O., F. Ervin, G. Pelletier, W. Diekel, and W. Strain. 1982. "Hair Element Content of Violent Criminals." *Canadian Journal of Psychiatry* 27:533.

Pincus, J. and G. Tucker. 1974. *Behavioral Neurology*. New York: Oxford University Press.

Plomin, R. 1989. "Environment and Genes: Determinants of Behavior." *American Psychologist* 44:105-111.

Plomin, R. and D. Daniels. 1986. "Genetics and Shyness." In W.H. Jones, J.M. Cheek, and S.R. Briggs (eds.), *Shyness: Perspectives on Research and Treatment*. New York: Plenum.

——. 1987. "Why are Children in the Same Family so Different From One Another?" *Behavioral and Brain Sciences* 10:1-16.

Plomin, R., J.C. DeFries, and G.E. McClearn. 1980. *Behavioral Genetics: A Primer*. San Francisco: W.H. Freeman.

Plomin, R., T.T. Foch, and D.C. Rowe. 1981. "Bobo Clown Aggression in Childhood: Environment, Not Genes." *Journal of Research in Personality* 15:331-342.

Plomin, R., K. Nitz, and D.C. Rowe. 1990. "Behavioral Genetics and Aggressive Behavior in Childhood." In M. Lewis and S.M. Miller (eds.), *Handbook of Developmental Psychopathology*. New York: Plenum.

Pontius, A.A. and K.F. Ruttiger. 1976. "Frontal lobe system maturational lag in juvenile delinquents shown in narratives test." *Adolescence* XI (44):509-518.

Pontius, A.A. and B.S. Yudowitz. 1980. "Frontal Lobe System Dysfunction in Some Critical Actions as Shown in the Narratives Test." *The Journal of Nervous and Mental Disease* 168:111-117.

Poremba, C. 1975. "Learning Disabilities, Youth and Delinquency: Programs for Intervention." In H.R. Myklebust (ed.), *Progress in Learning Disabilities*. Vol. III. New York: Grune & Stratton.

Pugh, G.E 1977. *The Biological Origin of Human Values*. New York: Basic Books.

Quay, H.C. 1965. "Psychopathic Personality as Pathological Stimulation Seeking." *American Journal of Psychiatry* 122:180-183.

Rada, R.T., D.R. Laws, R. Kellner, L. Stivastava, and G. Peake. 1983. "Plasma Androgens in Violent and Nonviolent Sex Offenders." *Bulletin of the American Academy of Psychiatry Law* 11:149-158.

Raine, A. 1988. "Psychopathy: A Single or Dual Concept?" *Personality and Individual Differences* 9(4):825-827.

Raine, A. and P.H. Venables. 1987. "Contingent Negative Variation, P3 Evoked Potentials and Antisocial Behavior." *Psychophysiology* 24(2): 191-199.

Richman, N., J. Stevenson, and P.J. Graham. 1982. *Pre-school to School: A Behavioural Study*. London: Academic Press.

Rimland, B. and G.E. Larson. 1983. "Hair Mineral Analysis and Behavior: An Analysis of 51 Studies." *Journal of Learning Disabilities* 16:279-285.

Robins, L.N. 1966. *Deviant Children Grown Up: A Sociological and Psychiatric Study of Sociopathic Personality*. Baltimore: Williams & Wilkins.

Robins, L.N., P.A. West, and B.L. Herjanic. 1975. "Arrests and Delinquency in Two Generations: A Study of Black Urban Families and Their Children." *Journal of Child Psychology and Psychiatry* 16:125-140.

Rogeness, G.A., M.A. Javors, J.W. Maas, C.A. Macedo, and C. Fischer. 1987. "Plasma Dopamine-B-Hydroxylase, HVA, MHPG, and Conduct Disorder in Emotionally Disturbed Boys." *Biological Psychiatry* 22:1155-1158.

Rowe, D.C. 1983. "Biometrical Genetic Models of Self-Reported Delinquent Behavior: A Twin Study." *Behavior Genetics* 13:473-489.

——. 1986. "Genetic and Environmental Components of Antisocial Behavior: A Study of 265 Twin Pairs." *Criminology* 24(3):513-532.

Rowe, D.C. and D.W. Osgood. 1984. "Heredity and Sociological Theories of Delinquency: A Reconsideration." *American Sociological Review* 49:526-540.

Roy, A., M. Virkkunen, S. Guthrie, R. Poland, and M. Linnoila. 1986. "Monoamines, Glucose Metabolism, Suicidal and Aggressive Behaviors." *Psychopharmacology Bulletin* 22(3):661-665.

Rushton, J.P., D.W. Fulker, M.C. Neale, D.K.B. Nias, and H.J. Eysenck. 1986. "Altruism and Aggression: The Heritability of Individual Differences." *Journal of Personality and Social Psychology* 50(6):1192-1198.

Schiavi, R.C., A. Theilgaard, D.R. Owen, and D. White. 1984. "Sex Chromosome Anomalies, Hormones, and Aggressivity." *Archives of General Psychiatry* 39:7-13.

Schuckit, M.A. and M.A. Morrissey. 1978. "Propoxyphene and Phencyclidine (PCP) Use in Adolescents." *Journal of Clinical Psychiatry* 39:7-13.

Schulsinger, F. 1985. "The Experience from the Adoption Method in Genetic Research." *Progress in Clinical and Biological Research* 177:461-478.

Seigal, R.K. 1978. "Phencyclidine, Criminal Behavior, and the Defense of Diminished Capacity." In R.C. Peterson and R.C. Stillman (eds.), *Phencyclidine (PCP) Abuse: An Appraisal*. NIDA Research Monograph 21. Rockville, MD: National Institute on Drug Abuse.

Sheldon, W.H. 1949. *Varieties of Delinquent Youth*. New York: Harper & Row.

Shonfeld, I.S., D. Shaffer, P. O'Connor, and S. Portnoy. 1988. "Conduct Disorder and Cognitive Functioning: Testing Three Causal Hypotheses." *Child Development* 59:993-1007.

Sigvardsson, S., C.R. Cloninger, M. Bohman, and A-L von Knorring. 1982. "Predisposition to Petty Criminality in Swedish Adoptees. III. Sex Differences and Validation of the Male Typology." *Archives of General Psychiatry* 39:1248-1253.

Smith, D.E. and D.R. Weeson. 1980. "PCP Abuse: Diagnostic and Pharmacalogical Treatment Approaches." *Journal of Psychedelic Drugs* 12:293-299.

Soubrie, P. 1986. "Reconciling the Role of Central Serotonin Neurons in Human and Animal Behavior." *The Behavioral and Brain Sciences* 9:319-364.

Spodak, M.K., Z.A. Falck, and J.R. Rappeport. 1978. "The Hormonal Treatment of Paraphiliacs With Depo-Provera." *Criminal Justice and Behavior* 5:304-314.

Stein, L. and C.D. Wise. 1973. "Amphetamine and Noradrenergic Reward Pathways." In E. Usdin, and S.H. Snyder (eds.), *Frontiers in Catecholamine Research*. New York: Pergamon.

Stewart, M.A. and C.S. de Blois. 1983. "Father-son Resemblances in Aggressive and Antisocial Behavior." *British Journal of Psychiatry* 142:78-84.

Stewart, M.A. and L. Leone. 1978. "A Family Study of Unsocialized Aggressive Boys." *Biological Psychiatry* 13:107-117.

Stewart, M.A., C.S. de Blois, and C. Cummings. 1980. "Psychiatric Disorder in the Parents of Hyperactive Boys and Those With Conduct Disorder." *Journal of Child Psychology and Psychiatry* 21:283-292.

Sutker, P.B. and A.N. Allain. 1987. "Cognitive Abstraction, Shifting, and Control: Clinical Sample Comparisons of Psychopaths and Nonpsychopaths." *Journal of Abnormal Psychology* 96(1):73-75.

Syndulko, K. 1978. "Electrocortical Investigations of Sociopathy." In R.D. Hare and D.

Schalling (eds.), *Psychopathic Behavior: Approaches to Research*. Chichester, England: John Wiley & Sons.

Syndulko, K., D.A. Parker, R. Jens, I. Maltzman, and E. Ziskund. 1975. "Psychophysiology of Sociopathy: Electrocortical Measures." *Biological Psychology* 3:185-200.

Tarter, R.E., A.I. Alterman, and K.L. Edwards. 1985. "Vulnerability to Alcoholism in Men: A Behavior-Genetic Perspective." *Journal of Studies on Alcoholism* 46(4):329-356.

Tellegen, A., D.T. Lykken, T.J. Bouchard, K. Wilcox, N. Segal, and S. Rich. 1988. "Personality Similarity in Twins Reared Apart and Together." *Journal of Personality and Social Psychology* 54(6):1031-1039.

Thiessen, D.D. 1976. *The Evolution and Chemistry of Aggression*. Springfield, IL: Charles C. Thomas.

Trunnell, E.P. and C.W. Turner. 1988. "A Comparison of the Psychological and Hormonal Factors in Women With and Without Premenstrual Syndrome." *Journal of Abnormal Psychology* 97:429-436.

Twito, T.J. and M.A. Stewart. 1982. "A Half-Sibling Study of Aggressive Conduct Disorder." *Neuropsychobiology* 8:144-150.

Valzelli, L. 1981. *Psychobiology of Aggression and Violence*. New York: Raven Press.

van Praag, H.M., R.S. Kahn, G.M. Asnis, S. Wetzler, S.L. Brown, A. Bleich, and M.L. Korn. 1987. "Denosologization of Biological Psychiatry or the Specificity of 5-HT Disturbances in Psychiatric Disorders." *Journal of Affective Disorders* 13:1-8.

Venables, P.H. 1987. "Autonomic Nervous System Factors in Criminal Behavior." In S.A. Mednick, T.E. Moffitt, and S.A. Stack (eds.), *The Cause of Crime: New Biological Approaches*. New York: Cambridge University Press.

Virkkunen, M. and S. Narvanen. 1987. "Plasma Insulin, Tryptophan and Serotonin Levels During the Glucose Tolerance Test Among Habitually Violent and Impulsive Offenders." *Neuropsychobiology* 17:19-23.

Virkkunen, M., A. Nuutila, F.K. Goodwin, and M. Linnoila. 1987. "Cerebrospinal Fluid Monoamine Metabolite Levels in Male Arsonists." *Archives of General Psychiatry* 44:241-247.

Virkkunen, M., J. DeJong, J. Bartkko, F.K. Goodwin, and M. Linnoila. 1989. "Relationship of Psychobiological Variables to Recidivism in Violent Offenders and Impulsive Fire Setters." *Archives of General Psychiatry* 46:600-603.

Volavka, J. 1987. "Electroencephalogram Among Criminals." In S.A. Mednick, T.E. Moffitt, and

S.A. Stack (eds.), *The Causes of Crime: New Biological Approaches*. New York: Cambridge University Press.

Waid, W.M., M.T. Orne, and S.K. Wilson. 1979. "Socialization, Awareness and the Electrodermal Response to Deception and Self-Disclosure." *Journal of Abnormal Psychology* 88:663-666.

Wallgren, H. and H. Barry. 1970. *Action of Alcohol*. Vols. 1 and 2. New York: Elsevier.

Walters, G.D. and T.W. White. 1989. "Heredity and Crime: Bad Genes or Bad Research?" *Criminology* 27:455-486.

Watson, J.B. 1925. *Behaviorism*. New York: W.W. Norton.

Weingartner, H., M.V. Rudorfer, M.S. Buchsbaum, and M. Linnoila. 1983. "Effects of Serotonin on Memory Impairments Produced by Ethanol." *Science* 221:472-474.

Wenk, E.A., J.O. Robison, and G.W. Smith. 1972. "Can Violence be Predicted?" *Crime and Delinquency* 18:393-402.

Widom, C.S. 1978. "Toward an Understanding of Female Criminality." *Progress in Experimental Personality Research* 8:245-308.

Wilson, J.Q. and R.J. Herrnstein. 1985. *Crime and Human Nature*. New York: Simon & Schuster.

Wise, R. 1984. "Neural Mechanisms of the Reinforcing Action of Cocaine." *NIDA Research Monograph* 50. Rockville, MD: National Institute on Drug Abuse.

Wolff, P.H., D. Waber, M. Bauermeister, C. Cohen, and R. Ferber. 1982. "The Neuropsychological Status of Adolescent Delinquent Boys." *Journal of Child Psychology and Psychiatry* 23:267-279.

Wolfgang, M.E., R.M. Figlio, and T. Sellin. 1972. *Delinquency in a Birth Cohort*. Chicago: University of Chicago Press.

Yeudall, L.T., O. Fedora, and D. Fromm. 1985. "A Neuropsychosocial Theory of Persistent Criminality: Implications for Assessment and Treatment." *Research Bulletin* 97. Edmonton: Alberta Hospital.

Yudofsky, S.C., J.M. Silver, and S.E. Schneider. 1987. "Pharmacologic Treatment of Aggression." *Psychiatric Annals* 17:397-406.

Zuckerman, M. 1983. "A Biological Theory of Sensation Seeking." In Zuckerman, M. (ed.), *Biological Basis of Sensation Seeking, Impulsivity and Anxiety*. Hillsdale, N.J.: Lawrence Erlbaum Associates.

16

Adolescence-Limited and Life-Course-Persistent Antisocial Behavior: A Developmental Taxonomy

Terrie E. Moffitt

In general, psychological approaches in criminology focus on differentiating offenders and nonoffenders on the basis of individual-level psychological processes. Some scholars in this area focus on personality characteristics, others focus on issues related to intelligence or to psychological abnormalities such as psychoses, and still others do work related to the psychoanalytic tradition. In this selection Terrie E. Moffitt delineates a psychologically based theory in her attempt to explain the relationship between age and offending.

Moffitt seeks to differentiate between the majority of individuals who offend for a brief time in adolescence (adolescence-limited offenders) and the minority of those who continue to offend over a prolonged period of time (life-course-persistent offenders). She offers differing explanations for the antisocial and delinquent behavior patterns of these two groups. Life-course-persistent persons are born with or develop neuropsychological impairments that may result in problematic inter-

actions with parents. These interactions pave the way for antisocial behavior, which may then be perpetuated by later interactions in school and work. Such behavior establishes a pattern leading to continuity of antisocial behavior into adulthood that the individual is unable to relinquish. The adolescence-limited offender, however, enters delinquency as the result of a "maturity gap," in which the adolescent seeks to be treated and seen as an adult. However, as these youths near the end of adolescence, opportunities to engage in behaviors associated with adult status become available, and continued antisocial and delinquent behavior is costly in terms of coveted adult roles (e.g., an arrest limits job opportunities). They reduce or end antisocial activities; the former social behaviors of this group have prepared them to be able to move into conventional lifestyles.

There are marked individual differences in the stability of antisocial behavior. Many people behave antisocially, but their antisocial behavior is temporary and situational. In contrast, the antisocial behavior of some people is very stable and persistent. Temporary, situational antisocial behavior is quite common in the population, especially among adolescents. Persistent, stable antisocial behavior is found among a relatively small number of males whose behavior problems are also quite extreme. The central tenet of this article is that temporary versus persistent antisocial persons constitute two qualitatively distinct types of persons. In particular, I suggest that juvenile delinquency conceals two qualitatively distinct categories of individuals, each in need of its own distinct theoretical explanation. . . .

Previous antisocial classification schemes may capture the imaginations of social scientists because, although they provided more or less accurate behavioral descriptions of antisocial subtypes, they offered relatively little in the way of etiological or predictive validity (Morey, 1991). . . . In this article, I elaborate on the distinction between temporary and persistent antisocial behavior and offer a pair of new developmental theories of criminal behavior that are based on this distinction. . . .

If correct, this simple typology can serve a powerful organizing function, with important implications for theory and research on the causes of crime. For delinquents whose criminal activity is confined to the adolescent years, the causal factors may be proximal, specific to the period of adolescent development, and theory must account for the *discontinuity* in their lives. In contrast, for persons whose adolescent delinquency is merely one inflection in a continuous lifelong antisocial course a theory of antisocial behavior must locate its causal factors early in their childhoods and must explain the continuity in their troubled lives.

The dual taxonomy (and its two theories) that I propose in this article is best introduced with reference to the mysterious relationship between age and antisocial behavior. This relationship is at once the most robust and least understood empirical observation in the field of criminology.

Age and Antisocial Behavior

When official rates of crime are plotted against age, the rates for both prevalence and incidence of offending appear highest during adolescence; they peak sharply at about age 17 and drop precipitously in young adulthood. The majority of criminal offenders are teenagers; by the early 20s, the number of active offenders decreases by over 50%, and by age 28, almost 85% of former delinquents desist from offending (Blumstein & Cohen, 1987; Farrington, 1986). With slight variations, this general relationship between age and crime obtains among males and females, for most types of crimes, during recent historical periods and in numerous Western nations (Hirschi & Gottfredson, 1983). . . .

Until recently, research on age and crime has relied on official data, primarily arrest and conviction records. As a result, the left-hand side of the age-crime curve has been censored. Indeed, in many empirical comparisons between early-onset and late-onset antisocial behavior, *early* has been artifactually defined as mid-adolescence on the basis of first police arrest or court conviction (cf.

Farrington, Loeber, Elliott, et al., 1990; Tolan, 1987). However, research on childhood conduct disorder has now documented that antisocial behavior begins long before the age when it is first encoded in police data banks. Indeed, it is now known that the steep decline in antisocial behavior between ages 17 and 30 is mirrored by a steep incline in antisocial behavior between ages seven and 17 (Loeber, Stouthamer-Loeber, Van Kammen, and Farrington, 1989; Wolfgang, Figlio, and Sellin, 1972). . . . Furthermore, we may venture across disciplinary boundaries to add developmental psychologists' reports of childhood aggression (Pepler and Rubin, 1991) and mental health researchers' reports of conduct disorder (Kazdin, 1987) to criminologists' studies of self-reported delinquency and official crime. So doing, it becomes obvious that manifestations of antisocial behavior emerge very early in the life course and remain present thereafter.

With the advent of alternate measurement strategies, most notably self-reports of deviant behavior, researchers have learned that arrest statistics merely reflect the tip of the deviance iceberg (Hood and Sparks, 1970; Klein, 1989). Actual rates of illegal behavior soar so high during adolescence that participation in delinquency appears to be a normal part of teen life (Elliott, Ageton, Huizinga, Knowles, and Canter, 1983). With the liberty of some artistic license, the curved line plotted in Figure 16.1 may be taken to represent what is currently known about the prevalence of antisocial behaviors over the life course.

Although there is widespread agreement about the curve of crime over age, there are few convincing explanations for the shape of the curve. Until recently, scholars still disagreed about whether the adolescent peak represented a change in prevalence or a change in incidence: Does adolescence bring an increment in the number of people who are willing to offend or does the small and constant number of offenders simply generate more criminal acts while they are adolescent? Empirical evaluations now suggest that the former explanation is correct. In his English study of offense rates over age, Farrington (1983) showed that the adolescent peak reflects a temporary increase in the number of people involved in antisocial behavior, not a temporary acceleration in the offense rates of individuals. This finding has been replicated in American samples (Wolfgang, Thornberry, and Figlio, 1987). The small human figures under the curve of Figure 16.1 portray these changes in prevalence.

But whence the increase in the prevalence of offenders? One possibility is that some phenomenon unique to adolescent development causes throngs of new adolescent offenders to temporarily join the few stable antisocial individuals in their delinquent ways. Figure 16.1 depicts the typological thesis to be argued here. A small group of persons is shown engaging in antisocial behavior of one sort or another at every stage of life. I have labeled these persons *life-course-persistent* to reflect the continuous course of their antisocial behavior. A larger group of persons fills out the age-crime curve with crime careers of shorter duration. I have labeled these persons *adolescence-limited* to reflect their more temporary involvement in antisocial behavior. Thus, timing and duration of the course of antisocial involvement are the defining features in the natural histories of the two proposed types of offenders.

Two oft-cited rules of thumb asserted by Robins (1978) seen to simultaneously assert and deny the life-course stability of antisocial behavior: "Adult antisocial behaviour virtually *require* childhood antisocial behaviour [yet] most antisocial youths do *not* become antisocial adults" (p. 611). In fact, research has shown that antisocial behavior is remarkably stable across time and circumstance for some persons but decidedly unstable for most other people.

The stability of antisocial behavior is closely linked to its extremity. The extreme frequency of crime committed by a few males is impressive; it has been repeatedly shown that the most persistent 5% or 6% of offenders are responsible for about 50% of known crimes (see Farrington, Ohlin, and Wilson, 1986, for a review). In their study of 10,000 men, Wolfgang et al. (1972) found that 6% of offenders accounted for more than half of the crimes committed by the sample; relative to

other offenders. These high-rate offenders began their criminal careers earlier and continued them for more years. The relationship between stability and extremity is found in samples of children as well. In his analysis of a sample of third-grade boys, Patterson (1982) found that the most aggressive 5% of the boys constituted the most persistent group as well; 39% of them ranked above the 95th percentile on aggression ten years later, and 100% of them were still above the median. Similarly, Loeber (1982) has reviewed research showing that stability of youngsters' antisocial behavior across time is linked with stability across situations and that both forms of stability are characteristic of a relatively small group of persons with extremely antisocial behavior.

Thus, in defiance of regression to the

Figure 16.1
Hypothetical illustration of the changing prevalence of participation in antisocial behavior across the life course. (The solid line represents the known curve of crime over age. The arrows represent the duration of participation in antisocial behavior in individuals.)

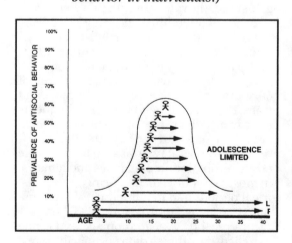

mean, a group of extremely antisocial persons remain extreme on measures taken at later ages and in different situations. Among other persons, however, temporary and situational manifestations of antisocial behavior (even to severe levels) may be quite common. . . .

I have already alluded to the small number of persons in the general population whose antisocial behavior is life-course-persistent. In fact, epidemiological research has shown that there is remarkable uniformity in the prevalence rates of different manifestations of severe antisocial behavior: Regardless of their age, under 10% of males warrant an "official" antisocial designation. . . .

It is possible, of course, that the persons who constitute these epidemiological statistics at different ages are all different individuals. However, the longitudinal data suggest otherwise: It is more likely that the remarkable constancy of prevalence rates reflects the reoccurrence of the same life-course-persistent individuals in different antisocial categories at different ages. . . .

A substantial body of longitudinal research consistently points to a very small group of males who display high rates of antisocial behavior across time and in diverse situations. The professional nomenclature may change but the faces remain the same as they drift through successive systems aimed at curbing their deviance: schools, juvenile-justice programs, psychiatric treatment centers, and prisons. The topography of their behavior may change with changing opportunities, but the underlying disposition persists throughout the life course.

Whereas a few males evidence antisocial behavior that emerges in toddlerhood and is persistent thereafter, the majority of boys who become antisocial first do so during adolescence (Elliott, Knowles. and Canter, 1981). This tidal wave of adolescent onset has been studied in the aforementioned representative sample of New Zealand boys (Moffitt, 1991). Between ages 11 and 15, about one third of the sample joined the delinquent lifestyles of the 5% of boys who had shown stable and pervasive antisocial behavior since preschool. As a group, these adolescent newcomers to antisocial ways had not formerly exceeded the normative levels of antisocial behavior for boys at ages three, five, seven, nine, or 11. Despite their lack of prior experience, by age 15, the newcomers equated their preschool-onset antisocial peers in the variety of laws they had broken, the frequency with which they broke them, and the number of times they appeared in juvenile court (Moffitt. 1991). On the basis of such commonly used indexes of adolescent delinquency the two delinquent groups were indistinguishable. Thus, if the sample was viewed only as an adolescent cross section, researchers would lose sight of the two delinquent groups' very different developmental histories, seeing only delinquents and nondelinquents.

. . . Earlier, I noted that the stability of antisocial behavior implies its extremity but that extremity does not imply stability: measures of the frequency or seriousness of adolescent offending will not discriminate very well between life-course-persistent and adolescence-limited delinquents. On the basis of their study and others, Elliott and Huizinga concluded that there is "no effective means for discriminating between the serious career offenders and nonserious offenders" (p. 98). A notable feature of the taxonomy introduced in this article is that knowledge of a subject's preadolescent behavior is *required* for making the differential diagnosis between the life-course-persistent and adolescence-limited types of antisocial teenager. Longitudinal designs are needed to collect the lifetime repeated measures that are needed to distinguish individual differences in the developmental course of antisocial behavior.[1]

I have argued in this section that juvenile delinquency conceals two categories of people. A very large group participates in antisocial behavior during adolescence. A much smaller group, who continues serious antisocial behavior throughout adulthood, is the same group whose antisocial behavior was stable across the years from early childhood. The categories remain hypothetical types, because no longitudinal study has yet repeatedly measured antisocial behavior in a representative sample of the same individuals from preschool to midlife. I describe in the next sections the two hypothetical types of antisocial youth: life-course-persistent and adolescence-limited. I argue that the two groups differ in etiology, developmental course, prognosis, and, importantly, classification of their behavior as either pathological or normative. . . .

Life-Course-Persistent Antisocial Behavior

... Continuity of Antisocial Behavior Defined

As implied by the label, continuity is the hallmark of the small group of life-course-persistent antisocial persons. Across the life course, these individuals exhibit changing manifestations of antisocial behavior: biting and hitting at age four, shoplifting and truancy at age ten, selling drugs and stealing cars at age 16, robbery and rape at age 22, and fraud and child abuse at age 30; the underlying disposition remains the same, but its expression changes form as new social opportunities arise at different points in development. This pattern of continuity across age is matched also by cross-situational consistency: Life-course-persistent antisocial persons lie at home, steal from shops, cheat at school, fight in bars, and embezzle at work (Farrington, 1991; Loeber, 1982; Loeber and Baicker-McKee, 1989; Robins, 1966, 1978; White et al., 1990).

The concept of behavioral coherence, or *heterotypic continuity*, is invoked here to extend observations of continuity beyond the mere persistence of a single behavior to encompass a variety of antisocial expressions that emerge as development affords new opportunities. Heterotypic continuity refers to continuity of an inferred trait or attribute that is presumed to underlie diverse phenotypic behaviors (Kagan, 1969). As Kagan and Moss (1962) suggested, a specific behavior in childhood might not be predictive of phenotypically similar behavior later in adulthood, but it may still be associated with behaviors that are *conceptually* consistent with the earlier behavior.

Examples of heterotypic continuities have been reported by Ryder (1967), who found that childhood aggression, physical adventurousness. and nonconformity were related to adult sexual behavior. . . . In addition, in their hallmark study, West and Farrington (1977) observed that stealing, alcohol abuse, sexual promiscuity, reckless driving, and violence were linked across the life course. The prognosis for the life-course-persistent person is bleak: Drug and alcohol addiction; unsatisfactory employment; unpaid debts; homelessness; drunk driving; violent assault; multiple and unstable relationships; spouse battery; abandoned, neglected, or abused children; and psychiatric illness have all been reported at very high rates for offenders who persist past the age of 25 (Farrington and West, 1990; Robins, 1966; Sampson and Laub, 1990). Thus, this theory of life-course-persistent antisocial behavior predicts continuity across the entire life course but allows that the underlying disposition will change its manifestation when age and social circumstances alter opportunities.

Although reports of the continuity of antisocial styles from childhood to young adulthood abound, the outcomes of antisocial individuals during midlife have seldom been examined. The pattern of official crime over age implies that criminal offending all but disappears by midlife,[2] but there is no reason to expect that life-course-persistents miraculously assume prosocial tendencies after an antisocial tenure of several decades. Indeed, criminal psychopaths decrease their number of arrestable offenses at about age 40, but the constellation of antisocial personality traits described by Cleckley (1976) persists in male samples at least until age 69 (Harpur and Hare, 1991). . . .

Beginnings: Neuropsychological Risk for Difficult Temperament and Behavioral Problems

If some individuals' antisocial behavior is stable from preschool to adulthood as the data imply, then investigators are compelled to look for its roots early in life, in factors that are present before or soon after birth. It is possible that the etiological chain begins with some factor capable of producing individual differences in the neuropsychological functions of the infant nervous system. Factors that influence infant neural development are myriad, and many of them have been empirically linked to antisocial outcomes.

One possible source of neuropsychological variation that is linked to problem behavior is disruption in the ontogenesis of the fetal brain. Minor physical anomalies, which are thought to be observable markers for hidden anomalies in neural development, have been found at elevated rates among violent offenders and subjects with antisocial personality traits (Fogel, Mednick, and Michelson, 1985; E. Kandel, Brennan, and Mednick, 1989; Paulhus and Martin, 1986). Neural development may be disrupted by maternal drug abuse, poor prenatal nutrition, or pre- or postnatal exposure to toxic agents (Needleman and Beringer, 1981; Rodning, Beckwith, and Howard, 1989; Stewart, 1983). Even brain insult suffered because of complications during delivery has been empirically linked to later violence and antisocial behavior in carefully designed longitudinal studies (E. Kandel and Mednick, 1991; Szatmari, Reitsma-Street, and Offord, 1986). In addition, some individual differences in neuropsychological health are heritable in origin (Borecki and Ashton, 1984; Martin, Jardine, and Eaves, 1984; Plomin, Nitz, and Rowe, 1990; Tambs, Sundet, and Magnus. 1984; Vandenberg, 1969). Just as parents and children share facial resemblances, they share some structural and functional similarities within their nervous systems. After birth, neural development may be disrupted by neonatal deprivation of nutrition, stimulation, and even affection (Cravioto and Arrieta, 1983: Kraemer, 1988; Meany, Aitken, van Berkel, Bhatnagar, and Sapolsky, 1988). Some studies have pointed to child abuse and neglect as possible sources of brain injury in the histories of delinquents with neuropsychological impairment (Lewis, Shanok, Pincus, and Glaser, 1979; Milner and McCanne, 1991; Tarter, Hegedus, Winsten, and Alterman, 1984).

There is good evidence that children who ultimately become persistently antisocial do suffer from deficits in neuropsychological abilities. I have elsewhere reviewed the available empirical and theoretical literatures; the link between neuropsychological impairment and antisocial outcomes is one of the most robust effects in the study of antisocial behavior (Moffitt, 1990b; Moffitt and Henry, 1991; see also Hirschi and Hindelang, 1977). Two sorts of neuropsychological deficits are empirically associated with antisocial behavior: verbal and "executive" functions. The verbal deficits of antisocial children are perva-sive, affecting receptive listening and reading, problem solving, expressive speech and writing, and memory. In addition, executive deficits produce what is sometimes referred to as a compartmental learning disability (Price, Daffner, Stowe, and Mesulam, 1990), including symptoms such as inattention and impulsivity. These cognitive deficits and antisocial behavior share variance that is independent of social class, race, test motivation, and academic attainment (Moffitt, 1990b; Lynam, Moffitt, and Stouthamer-Loeber, 1993). In addition, the relation is not an artifact of slow-witted delinquents' greater susceptibility to detection by police; undetected delinquents have weak cognitive skills too (Moffitt and Silva, 1988a).

The evidence is strong that neuropsychological deficits are linked to the kind of antisocial behavior that begins in childhood and is sustained for lengthy periods. In a series of articles (Moffitt, 1990a; Moffitt and Henry, 1989; Moffitt and Silva, 1988b), I have shown that poor verbal and executive functions are associated with antisocial behavior, if it is extreme and persistent. . . .

Neuropsychological variation and the "difficult" infant. Before describing how neuropsychological variation might constitute risk for antisocial behavior, it is useful to define what is meant here by neuropsychological. By combining *neuro* with *psychological,* I refer broadly to the extent to which anatomical structures and physiological processes within the nervous system influence psychological characteristics' such as temperament, behavioral development, cognitive abilities, or all three. For example, individual variation in brain function may engender differences between children in activity level, emotional reactivity, or self-regulation (temperament); speech, motor coordination, or impulse control (behavioral development); and attention, language, learning, memory, or reasoning (cognitive abilities).

Children with neurological difficulties severe enough to constitute autism, severe physical handicap, or profound mental retardation are usually identified and specially treated by parents and professionals. However, other infants have subclinical levels of problems that affect the difficulty of rearing them, variously referred to as difficult temperament, language or motor delays, or mild cognitive deficits. Compromised neuropsychological functions are associated with a variety of consequences for infants' cognitive and motor development as well as for their personality development (Rothbart and Derryberry, 1981). Toddlers with subtle neuropsychological deficits may be clumsy and awkward, overactive, inattentive, irritable, impulsive, hard to keep on schedule, delayed in reaching developmental milestones, poor at verbal comprehension, deficient at expressing themselves, or slow at learning new things (Rutter, 1977, 1983; Thomas and Chess, 1977; Wender, 1971). . . .

Child-environment comparison in nature: A source of interaction continuity. Up to this point, I have emphasized in this article the characteristics of the developing child as if environments were held constant. Unfortunately, children with cognitive and temperamental disadvantages are not generally born into supportive environments, nor do they even get a fair chance of being randomly assigned to good or bad environments. Unlike the aforementioned infants in Hertzig's (1983) study of temperament and neurological symptoms, most low-birth-weight infants are not born into intact, middle-class families. Vulnerable infants are disproportionately found in environments that will not be ameliorative because many sources of neural maldevelopment co-occur with family disadvantage or deviance.

Indeed, because some characteristics of parents and children tend to be correlated, parents of children who are at risk for antisocial behavior often inadvertently provide their children with criminogenic environments (Sameroff and Chandler, 1975). The intergenerational transmission of severe antisocial behavior has been carefully documented in a study of three generations (Huesmann et al., 1984). In that study of 600 subjects, the stability of individuals' aggressive behavior from eight to age 30 was exceeded by the stabillity of aggression across the generations from grandparent to parent to child. . . .

Parents and children resemble each other on temperament and personality. Thus, parents of children who are difficult to manage often lack the necessary psychological and physical resources to cope constructively with a difficult child (Scarr and McCartney, 1983; Snyder and Patterson, 1987). For example, temperamental traits such as activity level and irritability are known to be partly heritable (Plomin, Chipuer, and Loehlin, 1990). This suggests that children whose hyperactivity and angry outbursts might be curbed by firm discipline will tend to have parents who are inconsistent disciplinarians; the parents tend to be impatient and irritable too. The converse is also true: Empirical evidence has been found for a relationship between variations in parents' warmth and infants' easiness (Plomin, Chipuer, and Loehlin, 1990).

Parents and children also resemble each other on cognitive ability. The known heritability of measured intelligence (Plomin, 1990; Loehlin, 1989) implies that children who are most in need of remedial cognitive stimulation will have parents who may be least able to provide it. Moreover, parents' cognitive abilities set limits on their own educational and occupational attainment (Barrett and Depinet, 1991). As one consequence, families whose members have below-average cognitive capacities will often be least able financially to obtain professional interventions or optimal remedial schooling for their at-risk children.

Even the social and structural aspects of the environment may be stacked against children who enter the world at risk. . . . Vulnerable children are often subject to adverse homes and neighborhoods because their parents are vulnerable to problems too (cf. Lahey et al., 1990).

. . . The perverse compounding of children's vulnerabilities with their families' imperfections does not require that the child's neuropsychological risk arise from any genetic disposition. In fact, for my purposes, it is immaterial whether parent-child similarities arise from shared genes or shared homes. A home environment wherein prenatal care is haphazard, drugs are used during pregnancy, and infants' nutritional needs are neglected is a setting where sources of children's neuropsychological dysfunction that are clearly environmental coexist with a criminogenic social environment.

Problem child-problem parent interactions and the emergence of antisocial behaviors. I believe that the juxtaposition of a vulnerable and difficult infant with an adverse rearing context initiates risk for the life-course-persistent pattern of antisocial behavior. The ensuing process is a transactional one in which the challenge of coping with a difficult child evokes a chain of failed parent-child encounters (Sameroff and Chandler, 1975). The assertion that children exert important effects on their social environments is useful in understanding this hypothetical process (Bell and Chapman, 1986). It is now widely acknowledged that personality and behavior are shaped in large measure by interactions between the person and the environment (cf. Buss, 1987; Plomin, DeFries, and Loehlin, 1977; Scarr and McCartney, 1983). One form of interaction may play a particularly important role both in promoting an antisocial style and in maintaining its continuity across the life course: *Evocative* interaction occurs when a child's behavior evokes distinctive responses from others (Caspi et al., 1987).

Children with neuropsychological problems evoke a challenge to even the most resourceful, loving, and patient families. For example, Tinsley and Parke (1983) have reviewed literature showing that low-birth-weight, premature infants negatively influence the behavior of their caretakers; they arrive before parents are prepared, their crying patterns are rated as more disturbing and irritating, and parents report that they are less satisfying to feed, less pleasant to hold, and more demanding to care for than healthy babies. Many parents of preterm infants hold unrealistic expectations about their children's attainment of developmental milestones, and these may contribute to later dysfunctional parent-child relationships (Tinsley and Parke, 1983). More disturbing, an infant's neurological health status has been shown to be related to risk for maltreatment and neglect (Friedrich and Boriskin, 1976; Frodi et al., 1978; Hunter, Kilstrom, Kraybill. and Loda, 1978; Milowe and Lowrie, 1964; Sandgrund, Gaines, and Green, 1974).

Numerous studies have shown that a toddler's problem behaviors may affect the parents' disciplinary strategies as well as subsequent interactions with adults and peers (Bell and Chapman, 1986; Chess and Thomas, 1987). For example. children characterized by a difficult temperament in infancy are more likely to resist their mothers' efforts to control them in early childhood (Lee and Bates, 1985). Similarly, mothers of difficult boys experience more problems in their efforts to socialize their children. Maccoby and Jacklin (1983) showed that over time these mothers reduce their efforts to actively guide and direct their children's behavior and become increasingly less involved in the teaching process. . . . It may well be that early behavioral difficulties contribute to the development of persistent antisocial behavior by evoking responses from the interpersonal social environment, responses that exacerbate the child's tendencies (Goldsmith, Bradshaw, and Rieser-Danner, 1986; Lytton, 1990). "The child acts; the environment reacts; and the child reacts back in mutually interlocking evocative interaction" (Caspi et al., 1987, p. 308).

Such a sequence of interactions would be most likely to produce lasting antisocial behavior problems if caretaker reactions were more likely to exacerbate than to ameliorate children's problem behavior. . . . Some data suggest that children's predispositions toward antisocial behavior may be exacerbated under deviant rearing conditions. In the New Zealand longitudinal study, there was a significant interaction effect between children's neuropsychological deficit and family adversity on one type of delinquent act: aggressive confrontation with a victim or adversary. Among the 536 boys in the sample, the 75 boys who had both low neuropsychological test scores and adverse home environments earned a mean aggression score more than four times greater than that of boys with either neuropsychological problems or adverse homes (Moffitt, 1990b). . . . Behavior-genetic adoption studies of antisocial behavior often report a similar pattern of findings, wherein the highest rates of criminal outcomes are found for adoptees whose foster parents, as well as their biological parents.

214 Section IV ✦ *Theories of Crime*

were deviant (e.g., Mednick, Gabrielli, and Hutchings, 1984). Thus, children's predispositions may evoke exacerbating responses from the environment and may also render them more vulnerable to criminogenic environments.

If the child who "steps off on the wrong foot" remains on an ill-starred path, subsequent stepping-stone experiences culminate in life-course-persistent antisocial behavior. For life-course-persistent antisocial individuals, deviant behavior patterns later in life may thus reflect early individual differences that are perpetuated or exacerbated by interactions with the social environment: first at home, and later at school. Quay (1987) summarized this as "this youth is likely to be at odds with everyone in the environment, and most particularly with those who must interact with him on a daily basis to raise, educate, or otherwise control him. . . . This pattern is the most troublesome to society, seems least amenable to change, and has the most pessimistic prognosis for adult adjustment" (p. 121). . . .

Maintenance and Elaboration Over the Life Course: Cumulative Continuity, Contemporary Continuity, and Narrowing Options for Change

In the previous section, the concept of evocative person-environment interaction was called on to describe how children's difficult behaviors might affect encounters with their parents. Two additional types of interaction may help to explain how the life-course-persistent individual's problem behavior, once initiated, might promote its own continuity and pervasiveness. Reactive interaction occurs when different youngsters exposed to the same environment experience it, interpret it, and react to it in accordance with their particular style. For example, in interpersonal situations where cues are ambiguous, aggressive children are likely to mistakenly attribute harmful intent to others and then act accordingly (Dodge and Frame, 1982). *Proactive* interaction occurs when people select or create environments that support their styles. For example, antisocial individuals appear to be likely to affiliate selectively with antisocial others, even when se-

lecting a mate. Some evidence points to nonrandom mating along personality traits related to antisocial behavior (Buss, 1984), and there are significant spouse correlations on conviction for crimes (e.g., Baker, Mack, Moffitt, and Mednick, 1989).

The three types of person-environment interactions can produce two kinds of consequences in the life course: *cumulative consequences* and *contemporary consequences* (Caspi and Bem, 1990). Early individual differences may set in motion a downhill snowball of cumulative continuities. In addition, individual differences may themselves persist from infancy to adulthood, continuing to influence adolescent and adult behavior in a proximal contemporary fashion. Contemporary continuity arises if the life-course-persistent person continues to carry into adulthood the same underlying constellation of traits that got him into trouble as a child, such as high activity level, irritability, poor self-control, and low cognitive ability. . . .

Elsewhere, I describe in detail some of the patterns of interaction between persons and their social environments that may promote antisocial continuity across time and across life domains (Caspi and Moffitt, in press-b). Two sources of continuity deserve emphasis here because they narrow the options for change. These processes are (a) failing to learn conventional prosocial alternatives to antisocial behavior and (b) becoming ensnared in a deviant life-style by crime's consequences. These concepts have special implications for the questions of why life-course-persistent individuals fail to desist from delinquency as young adults and why they are so impervious to intervention.

A restricted behavioral repertoire. This theory of life-course-persistent antisocial behavior asserts that the causal sequence begins very early and the formative years are dominated by chains of cumulative and contemporary continuity. As a consequence, little opportunity is afforded for the life-course-persistent antisocial individual to learn a behavioral repertoire of prosocial alternatives. Thus, one overlooked and pernicious source of continuity in antisocial behavior is simply a lack of recourse to any other options. In keeping with this prediction, Vitaro, Gagnon, and Tremblay (1990) have shown that aggressive children whose behavioral repertoires consist almost solely of antisocial behaviors are less likely to change over years than are aggressive children whose repertoires comprise some prosocial behaviors as well.

Life-course-persistent persons miss out on opportunities to acquire and practice prosocial alternatives at each stage of development. Children with poor self-control and aggressive behavior are often rejected by peers and adults (Coie, Belding, and Underwood, 1988; Dodge, Coie, and Brakke, 1982; Vitaro et al., 1990). In turn, children who have learned to expect rejection are likely in later settings to withdraw, or strike out preemptively, precluding opportunities to affiliate with prosocial peers (Dodge and Newman, 1981; Dodge and Frame, 1982; LaFrenier and Sroufe, 1985; Nasby, Hayden, and DePaulo, 1980). Such children are robbed of chances to practice conventional social skills. Alternatively, consider this sequence of narrowing options: Behavior problems at school and failure to attain basic math and reading skills place a limit on the variety of job skills that can be acquired and thereby cut off options to pursue legitimate employment as an alternative to the underground economy (Farrington, Gallagher, Morley, Ledger, and West, 1986; Maughan, Gray, and Rutter, 1985; Moffitt, 1990a). Simply put, if social and academic skills are not mastered in childhood, it is very difficult to later recover lost opportunities.

Becoming ensnared by consequences of antisocial behavior. Personal characteristics such as poor self-control, impulsivity, and inability to delay gratification increase the risk that antisocial youngsters will make irrevocable decisions that close the doors of opportunity. Teenaged parenthood, addiction to drugs or alcohol, school dropout, disabling or disfiguring injuries, patchy work histories, and time spent incarcerated are *snares* that diminish the probabilities of later success by eliminating opportunities for breaking the chain of cumulative continuity (Cairns and Cairns, 1991; J. Q. Wilson and Hernstein, 1985). Similarly, labels accrued early in life can foreclose later opportunities; an early arrest record or a "bad" reputation

may rule out lucrative jobs, higher education, or an advantageous marriage (Farrington, 1977; Klein, 1986; West, 1982). In short, the behavior of life-course-persistent antisocial persons is increasingly maintained and supported by narrowing options for conventional behavior.

Interventions with life-course-persistent persons have met with dismal results (Lipton, Martinson, and Wilks, 1975; Palmer, 1984; Sechrest, White, and Brown, 1979). This is not surprising, considering that most interventions are begun relatively late in the chain of cumulative continuity. The forces of continuity are formidable foes (Caspi and Moffitt, in press-a). After a protracted deficient learning history, and after options for change have been eliminated, efforts to suppress antisocial behavior will not automatically bring prosocial behavior to the surface in its place. Now-classic research on learning shows conclusively that efforts to extinguish undesirable behavior will fail unless alternative behaviors are available that will attract reinforcement (Azrin and Holz, 1966). My analysis of increasingly restricted behavioral options suggests the hypothesis that opportunities for change will often be actively transformed by life-course-persistents into opportunities for continuity: Residential treatment programs provide a chance to learn from criminal peers, a new job furnishes the chance to steal, and new romance provides a partner for abuse. This analysis of life-course-persistent antisocial behavior anticipates disappointing outcomes when such antisocial persons are thrust into new situations that purportedly offer the chance "to turn over a new leaf.". . .

When in the life course does the potential for change dwindle to nil? How many person-environment interactions must accumulate before the life-course-persistent pattern becomes set? . . . The well-documented resistance of antisocial personality disorder to treatments of all kinds seems to suggest that the life-course-persistent style is fixed sometime before age 18 (Suedfeld and Landon, 1978). Studies of crime careers reveal that it is very unusual for males to first initiate crime after adolescence, suggesting that if an adult is going to be antisocial, the pattern must be established by late adolescence (Elliott, Huizinga, and Menard, 1989).[3] . . .

Life-Course-Persistent Antisocial Behavior as Psychopathology

The life-course-persistent antisocial syndrome, as described here, has many characteristics that, taken together, suggest psychopathology. . . .

The theoretical syndrome is also characterized by tenacious stability across time and in diverse circumstances. This high probability response style is relied on even in situations where it is clearly inappropriate or disadvantageous (Caspi and Moffitt, in press-b), especially if there is a very limited repertoire of alternative conventional behaviors (Tremblay, 1991). . . .

The syndrome is associated with other mental disorders. There is good evidence that such "comorbidity" is associated with long-term continuity. An impressive body of research documents an overlap between persistent forms of antisocial behavior and other conditions of childhood such as learning disabilities and hyperactivity (cf. Moffitt, 1990a). . . . This proliferation of mental disorders is common among life-course-persistent antisocial persons. For example, in the Epidemiological Catchment Area (ECA) study of mental disorders among 19,000 adults, over 90 percent of the cases with antisocial personality disorder had at least one additional psychiatric diagnosis. . . . The comorbid conditions that disproportionately affected antisocial adults were mania, schizophrenia, drug and alcohol abuse, depression, and anxiety disorders (Robins and Regier, 1991).

Adolescence-Limited Antisocial Behavior

. . . Discontinuity: The Most Common Course of Antisocial Behavior

As implied by the proffered label, discontinuity is the hallmark of teenaged delinquents who have no notable history of antisocial behavior in childhood and little future for such behavior in adulthood. However, the brief tenure of their delinquency should not obscure their prevalence in the population or the gravity of their crimes. In contrast with the rare life-course-persistent type, adolescence-limited delinquency is ubiquitous. Several studies have shown that about one third of males are arrested during their lifetime for a serious criminal offense, whereas fully four fifths of males have police contact for some minor infringement (Farrington, Ohlin, and Wilson, 1986). Most of these police contacts are made during the adolescent years. Indeed, numerous rigorous self-report studies have now documented that it is statistically aberrant to refrain from crime during adolescence (Elliott et al., 1983; Hirschi, 1969; Moffitt and Silva, 1988c).

Compared with the life-course-persistent type, adolescence-limited delinquents show relatively little continuity in their antisocial behavior. Across age, change in delinquent involvement is often abrupt, especially during the periods of onset and desistence. For example, in my aforementioned longitudinal study of a representative sample of boys, 12% of the youngsters were classified as new delinquents at age 13; they had no prior history of antisocial behavior from age 5 to age 11. Between age 11 and age 13, they changed from below the sample average to 1.5 standard deviations above average on self-reported delinquency (Moffitt, 1990a). By age 15, another 20% of this sample of boys had joined the newcomers to delinquency despite having no prior history of antisocial behavior (Moffitt, 1991). Barely into mid-adolescence, the prevalence rate of markedly antisocial boys had swollen from 5% at age 11 to 32% at age 15. When interviewed at age 18, only 7% of the boys denied all delinquent activities. By their mid-20s, at least three fourths of these new offenders are expected to cease all offending (Farrington, 1986).

Adolescence-limited delinquents may also have sporadic, crime-free periods in the midst of their brief crime "careers." Also, in contrast with the life-course-persistent type, they lack consistency in their antisocial behavior across situations. For example, they may shoplift in stores and use drugs with friends but continue to obey the rules at school. Because of the chimeric nature of their delinquency, different reporters (such as self, parent, and teacher) are less likely to agree about their behavior problems when asked to complete rating scales or clinical interviews (Loeber, Green, Lahey, and Stouthamer-Loeber, 1990; Loeber and Schmaling, 1985).

These observations about temporal *instability* and cross-situational *inconsistency* are more than merely descriptive. They have implications for a theory of the etiology of adolescence-limited delinquency. Indeed, the flexibility of most delinquents' behavior suggests that their engagement in deviant lifestyles may be under the control of reinforcement and punishment contingencies.

Unlike their life-course-persistent peers, whose behavior was described as inflexible and refractory to changing circumstances, adolescence-limited delinquents are likely to engage in antisocial behavior in situations where such responses seem profitable to them, but they are also able to abandon antisocial behavior when prosocial styles are more rewarding. They maintain control over their antisocial responses and use antisocial behavior only in situations where it may serve an instrumental function. Thus, principles of learning theory will be important for this theory of the cause of adolescence-limited delinquency.

A theory of adolescence-limited delinquency must account for several empirical observations: modal onset in early adolescence, recovery by young adulthood, widespread prevalence, and lack of continuity. Why do youngsters with no history of behavior problems in childhood suddenly become antisocial in adolescence? Why do they develop antisocial problems rather than other difficulties? Why is delinquency so common among teens? How are they able to spontaneously recover from an antisocial lifestyle within a few short years?

Just as the childhood onset of life-course-persistent persons compelled me to look for causal factors early in their lives, the coincidence of puberty with the rise in the prevalence of delinquent behavior compels me to took for clues in adolescent development. Critical features of this developmental period are variability in biological age, the increasing importance of peer relationships, and the budding of teenagers' self-conscious values, attitudes, and aspirations. These developmental tasks form the building blocks for a theory of adolescence-limited delinquency.

Beginnings: Motivation, Mimicry, and Reinforcement

Why do adolescence-limited delinquents begin delinquency? The answer advanced here is that their delinquency is "social mimicry" of the antisocial style of life-course-persistent youths. . . .

If social mimicry is to explain why adolescence-limited delinquents begin to mimic the antisocial behavior of their life-course-persistent peers, then, logically, delinquency must be a social behavior that allows access to some desirable resource. I suggest that the resource is mature status, with its consequent power and privilege.

Before modernization, biological maturity came at a later age, social adult status arrived at an earlier age, and rites of passage more clearly delineated the point at which youths assumed new roles and responsibilities. . . . Secular changes in health and work have lengthened the duration of adolescence. The ensuing gap leaves modern teenagers in a 5- to 10-year role vacuum (Erikson, 1960). They are biologically capable and compelled to be sexual beings, yet they are asked to delay most of the positive aspects of adult life (see Buchanan, Eccles, and Becker, 1992, for a review of studies of the compelling influence of pubertal hormones on teens' behavior and personality). In most American states, teens are not allowed to work or get a driver's license before age 16, marry or vote before age 18, or buy alcohol before age 21, and they are admonished to delay having children and establishing their own private dwellings until their education is completed at age 22, sometimes more than 10 years after they attain sexual maturity. They remain financially and socially dependent on their families of origin and are allowed few decisions of any real import. Yet they want desperately to establish intimate bonds with the opposite sex, to accrue material belongings, to make their own decisions, and to be regarded as consequential by adults (Csikszentmihalyi and Larson, 1984). Contemporary adolescents are thus trapped in a *maturity gap*, chronological hostages of a time warp between biological age and social age.

This emergent phenomenology begins to color the world for most teens in the first years of adolescence. . . . At the time of biological maturity, salient pubertal changes make the remoteness of ascribed social maturity painfully apparent to teens. This new awareness coincides with their promotion into a high school society that is numerically dominated by older youth. Thus, just as teens begin to feel the discomfort of the maturity gap, they enter a social reference group that has endured the gap for 3 to 4 years and has already perfected some delinquent ways of coping with it. Indeed, several researchers have noted that this life-course transition into high school society may place teens at risk for antisocial behavior. In particular, exposure to peer models, when coupled with puberty, is an important determinant of adolescence-onset cases of delinquency (Caspi, Lynam, Moffitt, and Silva, 1993; Magnusson, 1988; Simmons and Blyth, 1987).

Life-course-persistent youngsters are the vanguard of this transition. Healthy adolescents are capable of noticing that the few life-course-persistent youths in their midst do not seem to suffer much from the maturity gap. (At a prevalence rate of about 5%, one or two such experienced delinquents in every classroom might be expected.) Already adept at deviance, life-course-persistent youths are able to obtain possessions by theft or vice that are otherwise inaccessible to teens who have no independent incomes (e.g., cars, clothes, drugs, or entry into adults-only leisure settings). Life-course-persistent boys are more sexually experienced and have already initiated relationships with the opposite sex.[4] Life-course-persistent boys appear relatively free of their families of origin; they seem to go their own way, making their own rules. As evidence that they make their own decisions, they take risks and do dangerous things that parents could not possibly endorse. As evidence that they have social consequence in the adult world, they have personal attorneys, social workers, and probation officers; they operate small businesses in the underground economy; and they have fathered children (Weiher, Huizinga, Lizotte, and Van Kam-

men, 1991). Viewed from within contemporary adolescent culture, the antisocial precocity of life-course-persistent youths becomes a coveted social asset (cf. Finnegan, 1990a, 1990b; Jessor and Jessor, 1977; Silbereisen and Noack, 1988). . . . Antisocial behavior becomes a valuable technique that is demonstrated by life-course-persistents and imitated carefully by adolescence-limiteds. The effect of peer delinquency on the onset of delinquency is among the most robust facts in criminology research (Elliott and Menard, in press; Jessor and Jessor, 1977; Reiss, 1986; Sarnecki, 1986). . . .

Social mimicry and the relationships between life-course-persistent and adolescence-limited delinquents. One hypothesized by-product of the maturity gap is a shift during early adolescence by persistent antisocial youth from peripheral to more influential positions in the peer social structure. This shift should occur as aspects of the antisocial style become more interesting to other teens. In terms of its epidemiology, delinquent participation shifts from being primarily an individual psychopathology in childhood to a normative group social behavior during adolescence and then back to psychopathology in adulthood. Consider that the behavior problems of the few pioneering antisocial children in an age cohort must develop on an individual basis; such early childhood pioneers lack the influence of delinquent peers (excepting family members). However, near adolescence, a few boys join the life-course-persistent ones, then a few more, until a critical mass is reached when almost all adolescents are involved in some delinquency with age peers. . . .

Much evidence suggests that, before adolescence, life-course-persistent antisocial children are ignored and rejected by other children because of their unpredictable, aggressive behavior (Coie et al., 1988; Dodge et al., 1982). After adolescence has passed, life-course-persistent adults are often described as lacking the capacity for loyalty or friendship (Cleckley, 1976; Robins, 1985). At first, these observations may seem contrary to my assertion that life-course-persistents assume social influence over youths who admire and emulate their style during adolescence. . . . In this theory, adolescents who wish to prove their maturity need only notice that the style of life-course-persistents resembles adulthood more than it resembles childhood. Then they need only observe antisocial behavior closely enough and long enough to imitate it successfully. What is contended is that adolescence-limited youths should regard life-course-persistent youths as models, and life-course-persistent teens should regard themselves as magnets for other teens. Neither perception need involve reciprocal liking between individuals. . . .

A magnet role would imply that children who were rejected and ignored by others should experience newfound "popularity" as teens, relative to their former rejected status. That is, life-course-persistent youth should encounter more contacts with peers during adolescence when other adolescents draw near so as to imitate their lifestyle. Some research is consistent with this interpretation. . . . [A]ggressive seventh-graders in the Carolina Longitudinal Study were rated as popular as often as nonaggressive youths by both teachers and themselves and were as likely as other youths to be nuclear members of peer groups (Cairns, Cairns, Neckerman, Gest, and Gariépy, 1988). In their review of peer-relationship studies, Coie, Dodge, and Kupersmidt (1990) noted that the relationship between overt aggression and peer rejection is weaker or absent in adolescent samples compared with child samples. Findings such as these suggest that aggressive teens experience regular contacts with peers, however short-lived. . . .

Life-course-persistents serve as core members of revolving networks, by virtue of being role models or trainers for new recruits (Reiss, 1986). They exploit peers as drug customers, as fences, as lookouts, or as sexual partners. Such interactions among life-course-persistent and adolescence-limited delinquents may represent a symbiosis of mutual exploitation. Alternatively, life-course-persistent offenders need not even be aware of all of the adolescence-limited youngsters who imitate their style. Unlike adolescence-limited offenders, who appear to need peer support for crime, life-course-persistent offenders are willing to offend alone (Knight and West, 1975). The point is that the phenomena of "delinquent peer networks" and "co-offending" during the adolescent period do not necessarily connote supportive friendships that are based on intimacy, trust, and loyalty, as is sometimes assumed. Social mimicry of delinquency can take place if experienced offenders actively educate new recruits. However, it can also take place if motivated learners merely observe antisocial models from afar.

Reinforcement of delinquency by its "negative" consequences. For teens who become adolescence-limited delinquents, antisocial behavior is an effective means of knifing-off childhood apron strings and of proving that they can act independently to conquer new challenges (Erikson, 1960). Hypothetical reinforcers for delinquency include damaging the quality of intimacy and communication with parents, provoking responses from adults in positions of authority, finding ways to look older (such as by smoking cigarettes, being tattooed, playing the big spender with ill-gotten gains), and tempting fate (risking pregnancy, driving while intoxicated, or shoplifting under the noses of clerks). None of these putative reinforcers may seem very pleasurable to the middle-aged academic, but each of the aforementioned consequences is a precious resource to the teenager and can serve to reinforce delinquency. . . .

I suggest that every curfew violated, car stolen, drug taken, and baby conceived is a statement of personal independence and thus a reinforcer for delinquent involvement. Ethnographic interviews with delinquents reveal that proving maturity and autonomy are strong personal motives for offending (e.g., Goldstein, 1990). Such hypothetical reinforcing properties have not been systematically tested for most types of delinquent acts. However epidemiological studies have confirmed that adolescent initiation of tobacco, alcohol, and drug abuse are reinforced because they symbolize independence and maturity to youth (D. Kandel, 1980; Mausner and Platt, 1971). . . .

Why Doesn't Every Teenager Become Delinquent?

The proffered theory of adolescence-limited delinquency regards this sort of delinquency as an adaptive response to contextual circumstances. As a consequence, the theory seems to predict that every teen will engage in delinquency. Data from epidemiological studies using the self-report method suggest that almost all adolescents do commit some illegal acts (Elliott et al., 1983). In addition, even studies using official records of arrest by police find surprisingly high prevalence rates (for a review see Farrington, Ohlin, and Wilson, 1986). Nevertheless, some youths commit less delinquency than others, and a small minority abstains completely. Unfortunately, almost no research sheds light on the characteristics of teens who abstain from antisocial behavior altogether. Speculations are thus ill-informed by empirical observations. However, some predictions may be derived from the present theory of adolescence-limited delinquency. The predictions center on two theoretical prerequisites for adolescent-onset delinquency: the motivating maturity gap and antisocial role models. Some youths may skip the maturity gap because of late puberty or early initiation into adult roles. Others may find few opportunities for mimicking life-course-persistent delinquent models.

Some youths who refrain from antisocial behavior may, for some reason, not sense the maturity gap and therefore lack the hypothesized motivation for experimenting with crime. Perhaps such teens experience very late puberty so that the gap between biological and social adulthood is not signaled to them early in adolescence. . . . Perhaps other abstainers belong to cultural or religious subgroups in which adolescents are given legitimate access to adult privileges and accountability. . . .

Some nondelinquent teens may lack structural opportunities for modeling antisocial peers. Adolescent crime rates are generally lower in rural areas than in inner-city areas (Skogan, 1979, 1990). Teens in urban areas are surrounded by a greater density of age peers (and have readier unsupervised access to them through public transportation and meeting venues such as parks and shopping malls) than are teens in relatively isolated rural areas. . . . School structures may also constrain or facilitate access to life-course-persistent models. Caspi et al. (1993) found that early puberty was associated with delinquency in girls but only if they had access to boys through attending coed high schools. . . .

Youths may also be excluded from opportunities to mimic antisocial peers because of some personal characteristics that make them unattractive to other teens or that leave them reluctant to seek entry to newly popular delinquent groups. Shedler and Block (1990) found such an effect on the use of illegal drugs. They compared the personality styles of three adolescent groups: teens who abstained from trying any drug, teens who experimented with drugs, and teens who were frequent heavy drug users. Adolescents who experimented were the best adjusted teens in the sample. As expected, frequent users were troubled teens, who were alienated and antisocial. However, the abstainers were also problem teens. . . . Similarly, Farrington and West (1990) reported that boys from criminogenic circumstances who did not become delinquent seemed nervous and withdrawn and had few or no friends. These provocative findings remind us that deviance is defined in relationship to its normative context. During adolescence, when delinquent behavior becomes the norm, nondelinquents warrant our scientific scrutiny. . . .

Desistence From Crime: Adolescence-Limiteds Are Responsive to Shifting Reinforcement Contingencies

By definition, adolescence-limited delinquents generally do not maintain their delinquent behavior into adulthood. The account of life-course-persistent persons I made earlier in this article required an analysis of maintenance factors. In contrast, this account of adolescence-limited delinquents demands an analysis of desistance: Why do adolescence-limited delinquents desist from delinquency? This theory's answer: Healthy youths respond adaptively to changing contingencies. If motivational and learning mechanisms initiate and maintain their delinquency, then, likewise, changing contingencies can extinguish it.

Preoccupied with explaining the origins of crime, most theories of delinquency have neglected to address the massive shift in the prevalence of criminal involvement between adolescence and adulthood. . . . A general application of an amplifying process to all delinquency is inconsistent with the empirical observation that desistance from crime is the normative pattern.

Waning motivation and shifting contingencies. . . . With the inevitable progression of chronological age, more legitimate and tangible adult roles become available to teens. Adolescence-limited delinquents gradually experience a loss of motivation for delinquency as they exit the maturity gap. Moreover, when aging delinquents attain some of the privileges they coveted as teens, the consequences of illegal behavior shift from rewarding to punishing, *in their perception*. An adult arrest record will limit their job opportunities, drug abuse keeps them from getting to work on time, drunk driving is costly, and bar fights lead to accusations of unfit parenthood. Adolescence-limited delinquents have something to lose by persisting in their antisocial behavior beyond the teen years.

There is some evidence that many young adult offenders weigh the relative rewards from illegal and conventional activities when they contemplate future offending. . . . Important for this theory, research shows that "commitment costs" are among the factors weighed by young adults when they decide to discontinue offending. In the criminological subfield of perceptual deterrence research, commitment costs are defined as a person's judgment that past accomplishments will be jeopardized or that future goals will be foreclosed (Williams and Hawkins, 1986). Criminal behavior incurs commitment costs if it risks informal sanctions (disapproval by family, community, or employer) as well as formal sanctions (arrest or conviction penalty). Given that very few delinquent acts culminate in formal sanctions, perceptual deterrence theories consider informal sanctions as keys to deterrence. . . .

Options for change. Consistent with this motivational analysis, the antisocial behavior of many delinquent teens has been found to decline after they leave high school (Elliott and Voss, 1974), join the army (Elder, 1986; Mattick, 1960), marry a prosocial spouse (Sampson and Laub, 1990), move away from the old neighborhood (West, 1982), or get a full-time job (Sampson and Laub, 1990). As these citations show, links between the assumption of adult roles and criminal desistance have been observed before. The issue left unaddressed by theory is why are some delinquents able to desist when others are not? . . . Here, two positions are advanced: Unlike their life-course-persistent counterparts, adolescence-limited delinquents are relatively exempt from the forces of (a) cumulative and (b) contemporary continuity.

First, without a lifelong history of antisocial behavior, the forces of cumulative continuity have had fewer years in which to gather the momentum of a downhill snowball. Before taking up delinquency, adolescence-limited offenders had ample years to develop an accomplished repertoire of prosocial behaviors and basic academic skills. These social skills and academic achievements make them eligible for postsecondary education, good marriages, and desirable jobs.

The availability of alternatives to crime may explain why some adolescence-limited delinquents desist later than others. . . . Although the forces of cumulative continuity build up less momentum over the course of their relatively short crime careers, many adolescence-limited youths will fall prey to many of the same snares that maintain continuity among life-course-persistent persons. Those whose teen forays into delinquency inadvertently attracted damaging consequences may have more difficulty desisting. A drug habit, an incarceration, interrupted education, or a teen pregnancy are snares that require extra effort and time from which to escape. Thus, this theory predicts that variability in age at desistance from crime should be accounted for by the cumulative number and type of ensnaring life events that entangle persons in a deviant life-style.

Second, in stark contrast with the earlier account of life-course-persistent offenders, personality disorder and cognitive deficits play no part in the delinquency of adolescence-limited offenders. As a result, they are exempt from the sources of contemporary continuity that plague their life-course-persistent counterparts. In general, these young adults have adequate social skills, they have a record of average or better academic achievement, their mental health is sturdy, they still possess the capacity to forge close attachment relationships, and they retain the good intelligence they had when they entered adolescence. . . .

At the crossroads of young adulthood, adolescence-limited and life-course-persistent delinquents go different ways. This happens because the developmental histories and personal traits of adolescence-limiteds allow them the option of exploring new life pathways. The histories and traits of life-course-persistents have foreclosed their options, entrenching them in the antisocial path. . . .

Adolescence-Limited Antisocial Behavior Is Not Pathological Behavior

In an earlier section, it was contended that life-course-persistent antisocial behavior represented an especially pernicious and tenacious form of psychopathology. My view of adolescence-limited delinquency is strikingly different: Its prevalence is so great that it is normative rather than abnormal. It is flexible and adaptable rather than rigid and stable; most delinquent careers are of relatively short duration because the consequences of crime, although reinforcing for youths caught inside the maturity gap, become punishing to youths as soon as they age out of it. Instead of a biological basis in the nervous system, the origins of adolescence-limited delinquency lie in youngsters' best efforts to cope with the widening gap between biological and social maturity. Moreover, neither this theory nor the empirical evidence suggests that there are links between mental disorders and short-term adolescent delinquency. . . .

Discussion Questions

1. Define what Moffitt means by the term "adolescence limited offender." Define what Moffitt means by the term "life-

course-persistent offenders." What are some of the differences between the two types of offenders?

2. Why do life-course-persistent offenders develop? How does the environment interact with neuropsychological impairments to increase the likelihood of antisocial behavior? What factors promote the likelihood that such offenders will continue to engage in such behavior over long periods of time?

3. Why does the life-course-persistent offender not desist from involvement in delinquency and crime like the adolescence limited offenders? Why does the adolescence limited offender become involved in delinquency? Why do such offenders desist from offending at the end of adolescence?

Notes

1. It may be countered that research has distinguished delinquent subtypes that are based on cross-sectional information. For example, the delinquent behaviors of the life-course-persistent type may be distinguished by relatively more overt aggression, whereas the adolescence-limited type may show relatively more covert offending under peer influence. I agree. Factor-analytic studies have revealed an aggressive "undersocialized" factor and a "socialized" peer-oriented factor (Quay, 1964a, 1964b, 1966), and meta-analytic studies have revealed "overt" and "covert" offense patterns (Loeber and Schmaling, 1985). However, such scale pairs are highly and positively correlated in adolescent samples, in which the evidence for offense versatility outweighs evidence for offense specialization Klein, 1984: Robins, 1978). Cross-sectional classification has not proven effective at the level of the individual. My assertion that developmental history is needed for confident classification is buttressed by the repeated finding that age of onset of antisocial behavior problems is the single best predictor of adult criminal outcomes (Farrington, Loeber, Elliott, et al. 1990).

2. The conclusion that crime ceases in midlife may be premature: it is based on cross-sectional age comparisons of arrest and conviction rates. There are at least four reasons to doubt the conclusions that have been based

on this method. First, official records underestimate the amount of true crime. Second, there may be justice-system biases toward underarrest and prosecution of older persons. Third, death and imprisonment may selectively remove persistent offenders from official crime statistics. Fourth, cross-cohort comparisons may mistake generational effects for age effects (Rowe and Tittle, 1977). Thus, until longitudinal researchers collect self-reports of crime in the same individuals from adolescence to old age, the midlife disappearance of crime will remain an empirical question.

3. Between 9 and 22% of males not arrested as juveniles are arrested as adults, suggesting that adult-onset offenders constitute between 5% and 15% of all males (for a review see Farrington, Ohlin, and Wilson, 1986). However, estimates that are based on such official data are too high because most offenders engage in crime for some time before they are first arrested. Longitudinal studies of self-report delinquency show that only 1% to 4% of males commit their first criminal offense after age 17 (Elliott, Huizinga, and Menard, 1989). Adult-onset crime is not only very unusual, but it tends to be low rate, nonviolent (Blumstein and Cohen, 1987), and generally not accompanied by the many complications that attend a persistent and pervasive antisocial life-style (Farrington, Loeber, Elliott, et al., 1990).

4. Several longitudinal studies have shown that a history of antisocial behavior predicts early sexual experience for males relative to their age peers (Elliott and Morse, 1987: Jessor, Costa, Jessor, and Donovan, 1983; Weiher, Huizinga, Lizotte, and Van Kammen, 1991). Specifically, almost all of the sexual experience of an early adolescent cohort is concentrated among the most seriously delinquent 5% of its boys (Elliott and Morse, 1987).

References

Agnew, R. 1991. "The interactive effect of peer variables on delinquency." *Criminology, 29*, 47-72.

American Psychiatric Association. 1987. *Diagnostic and statistical manual of mental disorders* (3rd ed., rev.). Washington, DC: Author.

Anderson, E. 1990. *Streetwise*. Chicago: University of Chicago Press.

Anderson, K. E., Lytton, H., and Romney, D. M. 1986. "Mothers' interaction with normal and conduct-disordered boys: Who affects whom?" *Developmental Psychology, 22*, 604-609.

Azrin, N. H. and Holz, W. C. 1966. "Punishment." In W. K. Honig (Ed.), *Operant behavior: Areas of research and application*, pp. 390-477. New York: Appleton-Century Crofts.

Baker, L. A., Mack W., Moffitt, T. E., and Mednick, S. A. 1989. "Etiology of sex differences in criminal convictions in a Danish adoption cohort." *Behavior Genetics, 19*, 355-370.

Bandura, A. 1979. "The social learning perspective: Mechanisms of aggression." In H. Toch (Ed.), *Psychology of crime and criminal justice*, pp. 193-236. Prospect Heights, IL: Waveland Press.

Barrett, G. V. and Depinet, R. L. 1991. "A reconsideration of testing for competence rather than for intelligence." *American Psychologist, 46*, 1012-1024.

Becker, G. S. 1968. "Crime and punishment: An economic approach." *Journal of Political Economy, 76*, 169-217.

Bell, R. Q. and Chapman, M. 1986. "Child effects in studies using experimental or brief longitudinal approaches to socialization." *Developmental Psychology, 22*, 595-603.

Bloch, H. A. and Niederhoffer, A. 1958. *The gang: A study in adolescent behavior*. New York: Philosophical Library.

Blumstein, A. and Cohen, J. 1987. "Characterizing criminal careers." *Science, 237*, 985-991.

Blumstein, A., Cohen, I., and Farrington, D. P. 1988. "Criminal career research: Its value for criminology." *Criminology, 26*, 1-35.

Borecki, I. B. and Ashton, G. C. 1984. "Evidence for a major gene influencing performance on a vocabulary test." *Behavior Genetics, 14*, 63-80.

Bowlby, J. 1988. "Developmental psychiatry comes of age." *American Journal of Psychiatry, 145*, 1-10.

Buchanan, C. M., Eccles, J. S., and Becker, J. B. 1992. "Are adolescents the victims of raging hormones: Evidence for activational effects of hormones on moods and behavior at adolescence." *Psychological Bulletin, 111*, 62-107.

Buikhuisen, W. 1987. "Cerebral dysfunctions and persistent juvenile delinquency." In S. A. Mednick, T. E. Moffitt, and S. A. Stack (Eds.), *The causes of crime: New biological approaches*, pp. 168-184. Cambridge, England: Cambridge University Press.

Buss, D. M. 1984. "Toward a psychology of person-environment correspondence: The role of spouse selection." *Journal of Personality and Social Psychology, 47*, 361-377.

——. 1987. "Selection, evocation, and manipulation." *Journal of Personality and Social Psychology, 53*, 1214-1221.

Cairns, R. B. and Cairns, B. D. 1991. *Adolescence in our time: Lifelines and risks*. Unpublished manuscript.

Cairns, R. B., Cairns, B. D., Neckerman, H. J., Gest, S. D.. and Gariépy, J. L. 1988. "Social networks and aggressive behavior: Peer support or peer rejection?" *Developmental Psyrhology, 24*, 815-823.

Caspi, A., and Bem, D. J. 1990. "Personality continuity and change across the life course." In L. Pervin (Ed.), *Handbook of personality theory and research*, pp. 549-575. New York: Guilford Press.

Caspi, A., Bem, D. J., and Elder, G. H., Jr. 1989. "Continuities and consequences of interactional styles across the life course." *Journal of personality, 57*, 375-406.

Caspi, A., Elder, G. H., and Bem, D. J. 1987. "Moving against the world: Life-course patterns of explosive children." *Developmental Psychology, 23*, 308-313.

Caspi, A., Lynam. D., Moffitt, T. E., and Silva, P. A. 1993. "Unraveling girls' delinquency: Biological, dispositional, and contextual contributions to adolescent misbehavior." *Developmental Psychology, 29*, 19-30.

Caspi, A. and Moffitt, T. E. 1991. "Individual differences are accentuated during periods of social change: The sample case of girls at puberty." *Journal of Personality and Social Psychology, 61*, 157-168.

——. in press-a. "Continuity amidst change: A paradoxical theory of personality coherence." *Psychological Inquiry.*

——. in press-b. "The continuity of maladaptive behavior: From description to understanding in the study of antisocial behavior." In D. Cicchetti and D. Cohen (Eds.), *Manual of developmental psychopathology*. New York: Wiley.

Chaiken, M. R. and Chaiken, J. M. 1984. "Offender types and public policy." *Crime and Delinquency, 30*, 195-226.

Chess, S. and Thomas, A. 1987. *Origins and evolution of behavior disorders: From infancy to early adult life*. Cambridge, MA: Harvard University Press.

Clarke, A. D. B. and Clarke, A. M. 1984. "Constancy and change in the growth of human characteristics." *Journal of Child Psychology and Psychiatry, 25*, 191-210.

Cleckley, H. 1976. *The mask of sanity*. (5th ed.). St. Louis, MO: Mosby.

Cloninger. C. R. 1987. "A systematic method for clinical description and classification of personality variants." *Archives of General Psychology, 44*, 573-588.

Cloward, R. A. and Ohlin. L. E. 1960. *Delinquency and opportunity*. New York: Free Press of Glencoe.

Coie. J. D., Belding, M., and Underwood, M. 1988. "Aggression and peer rejection in childhood." In B. Lahey and A. Kazdin (Eds.), *Advances in clinical child psychology*, Vol. 2, pp. 125-158. New York: Plenum Press.

Coie. J. D., Dodge, K., and Kupersmidt. J. 1990. "Peer group behavior and social status." In S. R. Asher and J. D. Coie (Eds.), *Peer rejection in childhood*, pp. 17-59. Cambridge, England: Cambridge University Press.

Costello, E. J. 1989. "Developments in child psychiatric epidemiology." *Journal of the American Academy of child and adolescent psychiatry, 28*, 836-841.

Cravioto, I. and Arrieta, R. 1983. "Malnutrition in childhood." In M. Rutter (Ed.), *Developmental neuropsychiatry*, pp. 32-51. New York: Guilford Press.

Csikszentmihalyi, M. and Larson, R. 1984. *Being adolescent: Conflict and growth in the teenage years*. New York: Basic Books.

Davison. G. C. and Neale, J. M. 1990. *Abnormal psychology*, (5th ed.). New York: Wiley.

DiLalla, L. F. and Gottesman, I. I. 1989. "Heterogeneity of causes for delinquency and criminality: Lifespan perspectives." *Development and Psychopathology, 1*, 339-349.

Dishion, T. J., Patterson, G. R., Stoolmiller, M., and Skinner, M. L. 1990. *An ecological analysis of boys' drift to antisocial peers: From middle childhood to early adolescence*. Unpublished manuscript, Oregon Social Learning Center, Eugene.

——. 1991. "Family, school, and behavioral antecedents to early adolescent involvement with antisocial peers." *Developmental Psychology, 27*, 172-180.

Dodge, K. A., Coie, J. D., and Brakke, N. P. 1982. "Behavior patterns of socially rejected and neglected preadolescents: The roles of social approach and aggression." *Journal of Abnormal Child Psychology, 10*, 389-410.

Dodge, K. A., and Frame, C. L. 1982. "Social cognitive biases and deficits in aggressive boys." *Child Development, 53*, 629-635.

Dodge, K. A., and Newman, J. P. 1981. "Biased decision-making processes in aggressive boys." *Journal of Abnormal Psychology, 90*, 375-379.

Edelbrock, C., Rende. R., Plomin, R., and Thompson, L. A. in press. "Genetic and environmental effects on competence and problem behavior in childhood and early adolescence." *Journal of Child Psychology and Psychiatry.*

Elder, G. H., Jr. 1986. "Military times and turning points in men's lives. *Developmental Psychology, 22,* 233-245.

Elliott, D. S., Ageton, S. S., Huizinga, D., Knowles, B. A., and Canter, R. J. 1983. *The prevalence and incidence of delinquent behavior: 1976-1980* (The National Youth Survey Report No. 26). Boulder, CO: Behavioral Research Institute.

Elliott, D. S. and Huizinga, D. 1983. "Social class and delinquent behavior in a national youth panel: 1976-1980." *Criminology, 21,* 149-177.

———. 1984, April. *The relationship between delinquent behavior and ADM problems.* Paper presented at the ADAMHA/OJJDP State-of-the-Art Research Conference on Juvenile Offenders with Serious Drug, Alcohol, and Mental Health Problems, Rockville, MD.

Elliott, D. S., Huizinga, D., and Menard, S. 1989. *Multiple problem youth: Delinquency, substance use, and mental health problems.* New York: Springer-Verlag.

Elliott, D. S., Huizinga, D., and Morse, B. 1986. "Self-reported violent offending: A descriptive analysis of juvenile violent offenders and their offending careers." *Journal of Interpersonal Violence, 1.* 472-514.

Elliott, D. S., Knowles, B., and Canter, R. 1981. *The epidemiology of delinquent behavior and drug use among American adolescents: 1976-1980* (The National Youth Survey Project Report No. 14). Boulder, CO: Behavioral Research Institute.

Elliott, D. and Menard, S. in press. "Delinquent friends and delinquent behavior: Temporal and developmental patterns." In D. Hawkins (Ed.), *Some current theories qf deviance and crime.* New York: Springer-Verlag.

Elliott, D. S. and Morse, B. J. 1987. "Drug use, delinquency, and sexual activity." In C. Jones and E. McAnarney (Eds.), *Drug abuse and adolescent sexual activity, pregnancy, and parenthood,* pp. 32-60. Washington, DC: U.S. Government Printing Office.

Elliott. D. S. and Voss, H. L. 1974. *Delinquency and dropout.* Lexington, MA: Heath.

Empey, L. T. 1978. *American delinquency.* Homewood, IL: Dorsey Press.

Erikson, E. H. 1960. "Youth and the life cycle." *Children Today, 7,* 187-194.

Eysenck, H. J. 1977. *Crime and personality.* London: Routledge.

Fagan. J. and Wexler, S. 1987. "Crime at home and in the streets: The relationship between family and stranger violence." *Violence and Victims, 2,* 5-23.

Farrington. D. P. 1977. "The effects of public labelling." *British Journal of criminology, 17,* 112-125.

———. 1983. "Offending from 10 to 25 years of age." In K. Van Dusen and S. A. Mednick (Eds.), *Prospective studies of crime and delinquency,* pp. 17-38. Boston: Kluwer-Nijhoff.

———. 1986. "Age and crime." In M. Tonry and N. Morris (Eds.), *Crime and Justice: An Annual Review of Research,* (Vol. 7, pp. 189-250). Chicago: University of Chicago Press.

———. 1989. "Early predictors of adolescent aggression and adult violence." *Violence and Victims, 4,* 79-100.

———. 1991. "Antisocial personality from childhood to adulthood." *The Psychologist, 4,* 389-394.

Farrington, D. P., Gallagher, B., Morley. L., Ledger, R. J., and West, D. J. 1986. "Unemployment, school leaving and crime." *British Journal of Criminology, 26,* 335-356.

Farrington, D. P., Loeber. R., Elliott, D. S., Hawkins, D. J., Kandel, D. B., Klein, M. W., McCord, J., Rowe, D., and Tremblay, R. 1990. "Advancing knowledge about the onset of delinquency and crime." In B. Lahey and A. Kazdin (Eds.), *Advances in clinical child psychology* (Vol. 13, pp. 283-342). New York: Plenum Press.

Farrington, D. P., Loeber, R., and Van Kammen, W. B. 1990. "Long-term criminal outcomes of hyperactivity-impulsivity-attention deficit and conduct problems in childhood." In L. N. Robins and M. R. Rutter (Eds.), *Straight and devious pathways from childhood to adulthood,* pp. 62-81. Cambridge, England: Cambridge University Press.

Farrington, D., Ohlin. L., and Wilson, J. Q. 1986. *Understanding and controlling crime.* New York: Springer-Verlag.

Farrington, D. P. and West, D. J. 1990. "The Cambridge study of delinquent development: A long-term follow-up of 411 London males." In H. J. Kerner and G. Kaiser (Eds.), *Kriminalitat,* pp. 117-138. New York: Springer-Verlag.

Feehan, M., Stanton, W., McGee, R., Silva, P. A,, and Moffitt, T. E. 1990. "Is there an association between lateral preference and delinquent behavior?" *Journal of Abnormal Psychology, 99,* 198-201.

Fergusson, D. M., Horwood, L. J., and Lloyd, M. 1991. "A latent class model of child offending." *Criminal Behaviour and Mental Health, 1,* 90-106.

Finnegan, W. 1990a, September. "Out there, I." *The New Yorker*, pp. 51-86.

——. 1990b, November. "Out there, II." *The New Yorker*, pp. 60-90.

Fogel, C. A., Mednick, S. A., and Michelson, N. 1985. "Minor physical anomalies and hyperactivity." *Acta Psychiatrica Scandinavica*, 72, 551-556.

Friedrich, W. N. and Boriskin, J. A. 1976. "The role of the child in abuse." *American Journal of Orthopsychiatry*, 46, 580-590.

Frodi, A. M., Lamb, M. E., Leavitt, L. E., Donovan, W. L., Neff, C., and Sherry, D. 1978. "Fathers' and mothers' responses to the faces and cries of normal and premature infants." *Developmental Psychology*, 14, 490-498.

Goldsmith, H. H., Bradshaw, D. L., and Rieser-Danner, L. A. 1986. "Temperament as a potential developmental influence on attachment." In J. V. Lerner and R. M. Lerner (Eds.), *Temperament and social interaction during infancy and childhood*, pp. 5-34. San Francisco: Jossey-Bass.

Goldstein, A. P. 1990. *Delinquents on delinquency*. Champaign, IL: Research Press.

Gorenstein, E. E. and Newman, J. P. 1980. "Disinhibitory psychopathology: A new perspective and a model for research." *Psychological Review*, 87, 301-315.

Gottfredson, M. and Hirschi, T. 1986. "The value of lambda would appear to be zero: An essay on career criminals, criminal careers, selective incapacitation, cohort studies, and related topics." *Criminology*, 24, 213-234.

Gottfredson, M. and Hirschi, T. 1990. *A general theory of crime*. Stanford, CA: Stanford University Press.

Gove, W. R. 1985. "The effect of age and gender on deviant behavior: A biopsychosocial perspective." In A. Rossi (Ed.), *Gender and the life course*, pp. 115-144. Chicago: Aldine.

Greenberg, D. F. 1985. "Age, crime, and social explanation." *American Journal of Sociology*, 91, 1-21.

Hagan, J. 1987. "Class in the household: A power-control theory of gender and delinquency." *American Journal of Sociology*, 92, 788-816.

Hagan, J., Gillis, A. R., and Simpson, J. 1985. "The class structure of gender and delinquency: Toward a power-control theory of common delinquent behavior." *American Journal of Sociology*, 90, 1151-1179.

Hare, R. D., Hart, S. D., and Harpur, T. J. 1991. "Psychopathy and the DSM-IV criteria for antisocial personality disorder." *Journal of Abnormal Psychology*, 100, 391-398.

Hare, R. D. and McPherson, L. M. 1984. "Violent and aggressive behavior by criminal psychopaths." *International Journal of Law and Psychiatry*, 7, 35-50.

Harpur, T. J. and Hare, R. D. 1991. *The assessment of psychopathy as a function of age*. Unpublished manuscript, University of British Columbia, Vancouver, British Columbia, Canada.

Henry, B., Moffitt, T. E., Robins, L. N., Earls, F., and Silva, P. A. 1993. "Early family predictors of child and adolescent antisocial behavior: Who are the mothers of delinquents?" *Criminal Behavior and Mental Health*, 3, 97-118.

Hertzig, M. 1983. "Temperament and neurological status." In M. Rutter (Ed.), *Developmental neuropsychiatry*, pp. 164-180. New York: Guilford Press.

Hirschi, T. 1969. *Causes of delinquency*. Berkeley, CA: University of California Press.

Hirschi, T. and Gottfredson, M. 1983. "Age and the explanation of crime." *American Journal of Sociology*, 89, 552-584.

Hirschi, T. and Hindelang, M. J. 1977. "Intelligence and delinquency: A revisionist review." *American Sociological Review*, 42, 571-587.

Hood, R. and Sparks, R. 1970. *Key issues in criminology*. New York: McGraw-Hill.

Horan, P. M. and Hargis, P. G. 1991. "Children's work and schooling in the late nineteenth-century family economy." *American Sociological Review*, 56, 583-596.

Huesmann, L. R., Eron, L. D., Lefkowitz, M. M., and Waider, L. O. 1984. "Stability of aggression over time and generations." *Developmental Psychology*, 20, 1120-1134.

Hunter, R. S., Kilstrom, N., Kraybill, E. N., and Loda, F. 1978. "Antecedents of child abuse and neglect in premature infants: A prospective study in a newborn intensive care unit." *Pediatrics*, 61, 629-635.

Jesness, C. F. and Haapanen, R. A. 1982. *Early identification of chronic offender*. Sacramento, CA: Department of Youth Authority.

Jessor, R., Costa, F., Jessor, L., and Donovan, J. E. 1983. "Time of first intercourse: A prospective study." *Journal of Personality and Social Psychology*, 44, 608-626.

Jessor, R. and Jessor, S. L. 1977. *Problem behavior and psychosocial development: A longitudinal study of youth*. San Diego, CA: Academic Press.

Kagan, J. 1969. "The three faces of continuity in human development." In D. A. Goslin (Ed.), *Handbook of socialization theory and research*, pp. 983-1002. Chicago: Rand McNally.

Kagan, J. and Moss, H. A. 1962. *Birth to maturity*. New York: Wiley.

Kandel, D. 1980. "Drug and drinking behavior among youth." *Annual Review of Sociology, 6,* 235-285.

Kandel, E., Brennan, P. A., and Mednick, S. A. 1989. "Minor physical anomalies and parental modeling of aggression predict to violent offending." *Acta Psychiatrica Scandanavica, 78,* 1-5.

Kandel, E. and Mednick, S. A. 1991. "Perinatal complications predict violent offending." *Criminology, 29,* 519-530.

Kazdin, A. E. 1987. *Conduct disorders in childhood and adolescence.* Newbury Park, CA: Sage.

Klein, M. W. 1984. "Offense specialization and versatility among juveniles: A review of the evidence." *British Journal of Criminology, 24,* 185-194.

Klein, M. W. 1986. "Labelling theory and delinquency policy." *Criminal Justice and Behavior 13,* 47-79.

Klein, M. 1989. "Watch out for that last variable." In S. Mednick, T. Moffitt, and S. A. Stack (Eds.), *The causes of crime: New biological approaches,* pp. 25-41. Cambridge, England: Cambridge University Press.

Knight, B. J. and West, D. J. 1975. "Temporary and continuing delinquency." *British Journal of Criminology, 15,* 43-50.

Kraemer, G. W. 1988. "Speculations on the developmental neurobiology of protest and despair." In P. Simon, P. Soubrie, and D. Widlocher (Eds.), *Inquiry into schizophrenia and depression: Animal models of psychiatric disorders,* pp. 101-147. Basel, Switzerland: Karger.

LaFrenier, P. and Sroufe, L. A. 1985. "Profiles of peer competence in the preschool: Interrelations between measures, influence of social ecology, and relation to attachment history." *Developmental Psychology, 21,* 56-69.

Lahey, B. B., Frick, P. J., Loeber, R., Tannenbaum, B. A., Van Horn, Y. and Christ, M. A. G. 1990. *Oppositional and conduct disorder, I. A. meta-analytic review.* Unpublished manuscript.

Lee, C. L. and Bates, J. E. 1985. "Mother-child interaction at age two years and perceived difficult temperament." *Child Development, 56,* 1314-1323.

Lemert, E. M. 1967. *Human deviance, social problems, and social control.* Englewood Cliffs, NJ: Prentice Hall.

Lewis, D. O., Shanok, S. S., Pincus, J. H., and Glaser, G. H. 1979. "Violent juvenile delinquents: Psychiatric, neurological, psychological and abuse factors." *Journal of the American Academy of Child Psychiatry, 2,* 307-319.

Lipton, D., Martinson. R., and Wilks, J. 1975. *The effectiveness of correctional treatment: A survey of treatment evaluation studies.* New York: Praeger.

Loeber, R. 1982. "The stability of antisocial and delinquent child behavior: A review." *Child Development, 53,* 1431-1446.

Loeber, R. and Baicker-McKee, C. 1989. *The changing manifestations of disruptive/antisocial behavior from early childhood to early adulthood: Evolution or tautology?* Unpublished manuscript. Western Psychiatric Institute, University of Pittsburgh. Pittsburgh. PA.

Loeber, R., Green, S., Lahey, B., and Stouthamer-Loeber, M. 1990. "Optimal informants on childhood disruptive behaviors." *Development and Psychopathology, 1,* 317-337.

Loeber, R. and LeBlanc, M. 1990. "Toward a developmental criminology." In M. Tonry and N. Morris (Eds.), *Crime and Justice,* Vol. 12, pp. 375-473. Chicago: University of Chicago Press.

Loeber, R. and Schmaling, K. B. 1985. "Empirical evidence for overt and covert patterns of antisocial conduct problems: A metaanalysis." *Journal of Abnormal Child Psychology, 13,* 337-353.

Loeber, R., Stouthamer-Loeber, M., Van Kammen, W., and Farrington, D. P. 1989. "Development of a new measure of self-reported antisocial behavior for young children: Prevalence and reliability." In M. Klein (Ed.), *Cross-national research in self-reported crime and delinquency,* pp. 203-226. Boston: Kluwer-Nijhoff.

Loehlin, J. C. 1989. "Partitioning environmental and genetic contributions to behavioral development." *American Psychologist, 44,* 1285-1292.

Lynam, D., Moffitt, T., and Stouthamer-Loeber, M. 1993. "Explaining the relation between IQ and delinquency: Class, race, test motivation, school failure, or self-control?" *Journal of Abnormal Psychology, 102,* 187-196.

Lytton, H. 1990. "Child and parent effects in boys' conduct disorder. A reinterpretation." *Developmental Psychology, 26,* 683-697.

Maccoby, E. E. and Jacklin, C. N. 1983. "The 'person' characteristics of children and the family as environment." In D. Magnusson and V. L. Allen (Eds.), *Human development: An interactional perspective,* pp. 75-92. San Diego, CA: Academic Press.

Magnusson, D. 1988. *Individual development from an interactional perspective: A longitudinal study.* Hillsdale, NJ: Eribaum.

Martin, N. G., Jardine, R., and Eaves, L. J. 1984. "Is there only one set of genes for different abilities?" *Behavior Genetics, 14,* 355-370.

Mattick, H. W. 1960. "Parolees in the army during World War II." *Federal Probation, 24,* 49-55.

Maughan, B., Gray, G., and Rutter, M. 1985. "Reading retardation and antisocial behavior: A follow-up into employment." *Journal of Child Psychiatry and Psychology, 26,* 741-758.

Mausner, B. and Platt, E. S. 1971. *Smoking: A behavioral analysis.* Elmsford, NY: Pergamon Press.

McGee, R., Partridge, E., Williams, S. M., and Silva, P. A. 1991. "A twelve-year follow up of preschool hyperactive children." *Journal of the American Academy of Child and Adolescent Psychiatry, 30,* 224-232.

Meany, M. J., Aitken, D. H., van Berkel, C., Bhatnager, S., and Sapolsky, R. M. 1988. "Effect of neonatal handling on age-related impairments associated with the hippocampus." *Science, 239,* 766-768.

Mednick, S. A. 1977. "A bio-social theory of the learning of law-abiding behavior." In S. A. Mednick and K. 0. Christiansen (Eds.), *Biosocial bases of criminal behavior,* pp. 1-8. New York: Gardner Press.

Mednick, S. A., Gabrielli, W. F., and Hutchings, B. 1984. "Genetic influences in criminal behavior: Some evidence from an adoption cohort." *Science, 224,* 891-893.

Meehl, P. E. and Golden, R. R. 1982. "Taxometric methods." In P. C. Kendall and J. N. Butcher (Eds.), *Handbook of research methods in clinical psychology,* pp. 127-181. New York: Wiley.

Megargee, E. 1976. "The prediction of dangerous behavior." *Criminal Justice and Behavior, 3,* 3-21.

Millon, T. 1991. "Classification in psychopathology: Rationale, alternatives, and standards." *Journal of Abnormal Psychology, 100,* 245-261.

Milner, J. S. and McCanne, T. R. 1991. "Neuropsychological correlates of physical child abuse." In J. S. Milner (Ed.), *Neuropsychology of aggression,* pp. 131-145. Norwell, MA: Kluwer Academic.

Milowe, I. D. and Lowrie, R. S. 1964. "The child's role in the battered child syndrome." *Journal of Pediatrics, 65,* 1079-1081.

Modell, J., Furstenberg, F. F., and Hershberg, T. 1976. "Social change and transitions to adulthood in historical perspective." *Journal of Family History, 12,* 7-32.

Moffitt, T. E. 1990a. "Juvenile delinquency and attention-deficit disorder: Developmental trajectories from age 3 to 15." *Child Development, 61,* 893-910.

——. 1990b. "The neuropsychology of delinquency: A critical review of theory and research." In N. Morris and M. Tonry (Eds.), *Crime and justice,* Vol. 12, pp. 99-169. Chicago: University of Chicago Press.

——. 1991, September. *Juvenile delinquency: Seed of a career in violent crime, just sowing wild oats—or both?* Paper presented at the Science and Public Policy Seminars of the Federation of Behavioral, Psychological, and Cognitive Sciences. Washington, DC.

Moffitt, T. E. and Henry, B. 1989. "Neuropsychological assessment of executive functions in self-reported delinquents." *Development and Psychopathology, 1,* 105-118.

——. 1991. "Neuropsychological studies of juvenile delinquency and violence: A review." In J. Milner (Ed.), *The neuropsychology of aggression,* pp. 67-91. Norwell. MA: Kluwer Academic.

Moffitt, T. E., Mednick, S. A., and Gabrielli, W. F. 1989. "Predicting criminal violence: Descriptive data and predispositional factors." In D. Brizer and M. Crowner (Eds.), *Current approaches to the prediction of violence,* pp. 13-34. Washington, DC: American Psychiatric Association.

Moffitt, T. E. and Silva, P. A. 1988a. "IQ and delinquency: A direct test of the differential detection hypothesis." *Journal of Abnormal Psychology, 97,* 330-333.

——. 1988b. "Neuropsychological deficit and self-reported delinquency in an unselected birth cohort." *Journal of the American Academy of Child and Adolescent Psychiatry, 27,* 233-240.

——. 1988c. "Self-reported delinquency: Results from an instrument for New Zealand." *Australian and New Zealand Journal of Criminology, 21,* 227-240.

Morey, L. C. 1991. "Classification of mental disorder as a collection of hypothetical constructs." *Journal of Abnormal Psychology, 100,* 289-293.

Moynihan, M. 1968. "Social mimicry: Character convergence versus character displacement." *Evolution, 22,* 315-331.

Murray, C. A. 1976. *The line between learning disabilities and juvenile delinquency.* Washington, DC: U.S. Department of Justice.

Nagin, D. and Paternoster, R. 1991. "The preventive effects of the perceived risk of arrest: Testing an expanded conception of deterrence." *Criminology, 29,* 561-588.

Nasby, W., Hayden, B., and DePaulo, B. M. 1980. "Attributional bias among aggressive boys to interpret unambiguous social stimuli as displays of hostility." *Journal of Abnormal Psychology, 89,* 459-468.

Needleman. H. L. and Beringer. D. C. 1981. "The epidemiology of low-level lead exposure in childhood. *Journal of Child Psychiatry, 20,* 496-512.

Palmer, T. 1984. "Treatment and the role of edification: A review of basics." *Crime and Delinquency, 30,* 245-267.

Panel on Youth of the President's Science Advisory Committee. 1974. *Transition to adulthood.* Chicago: University of Chicago Press.

Parkhurst, J. T. and Asher, S. R. 1992. "Peer rejection in middle school: Subgroup differences in behavior, loneliness, and interpersonal concerns." *Developmental Psychology, 28,* 231-241.

Paternoster, R., Saltzman, L. E., Waldo, G. P., and Chiricos, T. G. 1983. "Perceived risk and social control: Do sanctions really deter?" *Law and Society Review, 17,* 457-479.

Patterson, G. R. 1982. *Coercive family process.* Eugene, OR: Castalia.

Paulhus, D. L. and Martin, C. L. 1986. "Predicting adult temperament from minor physical anomalies." *Journal of Personality and Social Psychology, 50,* 1235-1239.

Pepler, D. and Rubin, K. (Eds.). 1991. *The development and treatment of childhood aggression.* Hillsdale, NJ: Erlbaum.

Piliavin, I., Thornton, C., Gartner, R., and Matsueda, R. 1986. "Crime, deterrence, and rational choice." *American Sociological Review, 51,* 101-119.

Plomin, R. 1990. "The role of inheritance in behavior." *Science, 248,* 183-188.

Plomin, R. and Bergeman, C. S. 1990. "The nature of nurture: Genetic influence on environmental measures." *Behavioral and Brain Sciences, 14,* 373-386.

Plomin, R., Chipuer, H. M., and Loehlin, J. C. 1990. "Behavioral genetics and personality." In L. A. Pervin (Ed.), *Handbook of personality theory and research,* pp. 225-243. New York: Guilford Press.

Plomin, R., DeFries, J. C., and Loehlin, J. C. 1977. "Genotype-environment interaction and correlation in the analysis of human behavior." *Psychological Bulletin, 88,* 245-258.

Plomin, R., Nitz, K., and Rowe, D. C. 1990. "Behavioral genetics and aggressive behavior in childhood." In M. Lewis and S. M. Miller (Eds.), *Handbook of developmental psychopathology,* pp. 119-133. New York: Plenum Press.

Price, B. H., Daffner, K. R., Stowe, R. M., and Mesulam, M. M. 1990. "The compartmental learning disabilities of early frontal lobe damage." *Brain, 113,* 1383-1393.

Quay, H. C. 1964a. "Dimensions of personality in delinquent boys as inferred from the factor analysis of case history data." *Child Development, 35,* 479-484.

——. 1964b. "Personality dimensions in delinquent males as inferred from the factor analysis of behavior ratings." *Journal of Research in Crime and Delinquency, 1,* 33-37.

——. 1966. "Personality patterns in preadolescent delinquent boys." *Educational and Psychological Measurements, 6,* 99-110.

——. 1987. "Patterns of delinquent behavior." In H. C. Quay (Ed.), *Handbook of juvenile delinquency,* pp. 118-138. New York: Wiley.

Quine, W. V. O. 1977. "Natural kinds." In S. P. Schwartz (Ed.), *Naming, necessity, and natural kinds,* pp. 155-175. Ithaca, NY. Cornell University Press.

Quinton, D. and Rutter, M. 1988. *Parenting breakdown: The making and breaking of intergenerational links.* Aldershot, England: Avebury.

Reiss, A. J., Jr. 1986. "Co-offender influences on criminal careers." In A. Blumstein, J. Cohen, J. A. Roth, and C. Visher (Eds.), *Criminal careers and career criminals,* pp. 121-160. Washington, DC: National Academy Press.

Reiss, A. J., Jr.. and Farrington, D. P. 1991. "Advancing knowledge about co-offending: Results from a prospective longitudinal survey of London males." *Journal of Criminal Law and Criminology, 82,* 360-395.

Robins, L. N. 1966. *Deviant children grown up.* Baltimore, MD: Williams & Wilkins.

——. 1978. "Sturdy childhood predictors of adult antisocial behaviour: Replications from longitudinal studies." *Psychological Medicine, 8,* 611-622.

——. 1985. "Epidemiology of antisocial personality." In J. O. Cavenar (Ed.), *Psychiatry,* Vol. 3, pp. 1-14. Philadelphia: Lippincott.

Robins, L. N. and Regier, D. A. 1991. *Psychiatric disorders in America.* New York: Free Press.

Rodning, C., Beckwith, L., and Howard, J. 1989. "Characteristics of attachment organization and play organization in prenatally drug-exposed toddlers." *Development and Psychopathology, 1,* 277-289.

Rothbart, M. K. and Derryberry, D. 1981. "Development of individual differences in temperament." In M. E. Lamb and A. L. Brown (Eds.), *Advances in developmental psychology,* Vol. 1, pp. 37-66. Hillsdale, NJ: Eribaum.

Rowe, A. R. and Tittle, C. R. 1977. "Life cycle changes and criminal propensity." *The Sociological Quarterly, 18,* 223-236.

Rutter, M. 1977. "Brain damage syndromes in childhood: Concepts and findings." *Journal of Child Psychology and Psychiatry, 18,* 1-22.

——. (Ed.). 1983. *Developmental neuropsychiatry.* New York: Guilford Press.

Rutter, M., Tizard, J., and Whitmore, K. 1970. *Education, health and behaviour.* London: Longman.

Ryder, R. G. 1967. "Birth to maturity revisited: A canonical analysis." *Journal of Personality and Social Psychology, 1*, 168-172.

Sameroff, A. and Chandler, M. 1975. "Reproductive risk and the continuum of caretaking casualty." In F. Horowitz, M. Hetherington, S. Scarr-Salapatek, and G. Siegel (Eds.), *Review of child development research*, Vol. 4, pp. 187-244. Chicago: University of Chicago Press.

Sampson, R. J. and Groves, W. B. 1989. "Community structure and crime: Testing social disorganization theory." *American Journal of Sociology, 94*, 774-802.

Sampson, R. J. and Laub, J. H. 1990. "Crime and deviance over the life course: The salience of adult social bonds." *American Sociological Review, 55*, 609-627.

Sampson, R. J. and Laub, J. H. 1992. "Crime and deviance in the life course." *Annual Review of Sociology, 18*, 63-84.

Sandgrund, A. K., Gaines, R., and Green, A. 1974. "Child abuse and mental retardation: A problem of cause and effect." *American Journal of Mental Deficiency, 79*, 327-330.

Sarnecki, J. 1986. *Delinquent networks.* Stockholm: National Council for Crime Prevention.

Scarr, S. and McCartney, K. 1983. "How people make their own environments: A theory of genotype→environment effects. *Child Development, 54*, 424-435.

Schwendinger, H. and Schwendinger. J. S. 1985. *Adolescent subcultures and delinquency.* New York: Praeger.

Sechrest, L., White, S. O., and Brown, E. D. (Eds.). 1979. *The rehabilitation of criminal offenders: Problems and prospects.* Washington, DC: National Academy of Sciences.

Shaw, C. R. and McKay, H. D. 1942. *Juvenile delinquency and urban areas.* Chicago: University of Chicago Press.

Shedler, J. and Block, J. 1990. "Adolescent drug use and psychological health." *American Psychologist, 45*, 612-630.

Silbereisen, R. K. and Noack, P. 1988. "On the constructive role of problem behavior in adolescence." In N. Bolger, A. Caspi, G. Downey, and M. Moorehouse (Eds.), *Persons in context: Developmental processes*, pp. 152-180. Cambridge, England: Cambridge University Press.

Simmons, R. G. and Blyth, D. A. 1987. *Moving into adolescence: The impact of pubertal change and school context.* New York: Aldine de Gruyter.

Skogan, W. G. 1979. "Crime in contemporary America." In H. D. Graham and T R. Gurr (Eds.), *Violence in America: Historical and comparative perspectives*, pp. 375-391. Beverly Hills, CA: Sage.

——. 1990. *Disorder and decline.* New York: Free Press.

Smith, D. A. and Visher, C. A. 1980. "Sex and involvement in deviance/crime: A quantitative review of the empirical literature." *American Sociological Review, 45*, 691-701.

Snyder, J. and Patterson. G. 1987. "Family interaction and delinquent behavior." In H. Quay (Ed.), *Handbook of juvenile delinquency*, pp. 216-243. New York: Wiley.

Stattin, H. and Magnusson, D. 1984. *The role of early aggressive behavior for the frequency, the seriousness, and the types of later criminal offenses* (report). Stockholm: University of Stockholm, Department of Psychology.

Steffensmeier, D. J., Allan, E. A., Harer, M. D., and Streifel, C. 1989. "Age and the distribution of crime." *American Journal of Sociology, 94*, 803-831.

Steinberg, L. 1981. "Transformations in family relations at puberty." *Developmental Psychology, 17*, 833-840.

——. 1987. "Impact of puberty on family relations: Effects of pubertal status and pubertal timing." *Developmental Psychology, 23*, 451-460.

Steinberg, L. and Silverberg, S. B. 1986. "The vicissitudes of autonomy in early adolescence." *Child Development, 57*, 841-851.

Stewart, A. 1983. "Severe perinatal hazards." In M. Rutter (Ed.), *Developmental neuropsychiatry*, pp. 15-31. New York: Guilford Press.

Suedfeld, P., and Landon, P. B. 1978. "Approaches to treatment." In R. Hare and D. Schalling (Eds.), *Psychopathic behaviour*, pp. 347-376. New York: Wiley.

Sutherland, E. and Cressey, D. R. 1978. *Criminology.* Philadelphia: Lippincott.

Szatmari, P., Reitsma-Street, M., and Offord, D. 1986. "Pregnancy and birth complications in antisocial adolescents and their siblings." *Canadian Journal of Psychiatry, 31*, 513-516.

Tambs, K., Sundet, J. M., and Magnus, P. 1984. "Heritability analysis of the WAIS subtests: A study of twins." *Intelligence, 8*, 283-293.

Tanner, J. M. 1978. *Fetus into man.* Cambridge, MA: Harvard University Press.

Tarter, R. E., Hegedus, A. M., Winsten, N. E., and Alterman, A. L. 1984. "Neuropsychological, personality and familial characteristics of physically abused delinquents." *Journal of the*

American Academy of Child Psychiatry, 23, 668-674.

Thomas, A. and Chess, S. 1977. *Temperament and development.* New York: Brunner/Mazel.

Tinsley, B. R. and Parke, R. D. 1983. "The person-environment relationship: Lessons from families with preterm infants." In D. Magnusson and V. L. Allen (Eds.), *Human development: An interactional perspective,* pp. 93-110. San Diego, CA: Academic Press.

Tolan, P. H. 1987. "Implications of age of onset for delinquency risk." *Journal of Abnormal Child Psychology, 15,* 47-65.

Tremblay, R. E. 1991. "Aggression, prosocial behavior, and gender: Three magic words, but no magic wand." In D. Pepler and K. Rubin (Eds.), *The development and treatment of childhood aggression,* pp. 71-77. Hillsdale, NJ: Erlbaum.

Udry, J. R. 1988. "Biological predispositions and social control in adolescent sexual behavior." *American Sociological Review, 53,* 709-722.

Vandenberg, S. G. 1969. "A twin study of spatial ability." *Multivariate Behavioral Research, 4,* 273-294.

Vitaro. F, Gagnon, C., and Tremblay, R. E. 1990. "Predicting stable peer rejection from kindergarten to grade one." *Journal of Clinical Child Psychology, 19,* 257-264.

Warr, M. and Stafford, M. 1991. "The influence of delinquent peers: What they think or what they do?" *Criminology, 29,* 851-866.

Warren, M. Q. 1969. "The case for differential treatment of delinquents." *Annals of the American Academy of Political Science, 381,* 47-59.

Weiher. A., Huizinga, D., Lizotte, A. J., and Van Kammen, W. B. 1991. "The relationship between sexual activity, pregnancy, delinquency. and drug abuse." In D. Huizinga, R. Loeber, and T. Thornberry (Eds.), *Urban delinquency and substance abuse: A technical report* (Chapter 6). Washington, DC: Office of Juvenile Justice and Delinquency Prevention.

Wender, P. H. 1997. *Minimal brain dysfunction in children.* New York: Wiley.

West, D. J. 1982. *Delinquency.* Cambridge, MA: Harvard University Press.

West, D. J. and Farrington, D. P. 1977. *The delinquent way of life.* New York: Crane Russak.

White, J., Moffitt, T. E., Caspi, A., Jeglum, D., Needles, D., and Stouthamer-Loeber, M. in press. "Measuring impulsivity and examining its relationship to delinquency." *Journal of Abnormal Psychology.*

White, J., Moffitt, T. E., Earls, F., Robins, L. N., and Silva, P. A. 1990. "How early can we tell? Preschool predictors of boys' conduct disorder and delinquency." *Criminology, 28,* 507-533.

Williams, K. R. and Hawkins, R. 1986. "Perceptual research on general deterrence: A review." *Law and Society Review, 20,* 545-572.

Wilson, E. O. 1975. *Sociobiology.* Cambridge. MA: Harvard University Press.

Wilson, J. Q. 1983. "Crime and American culture." *The Public Interest, 70,* 22-48.

Wilson, J. Q. and Herrnstein, R. J. 1985. *Crime and human nature.* New York: Simon and Schuster.

Wolfgang, M. E., Figlio, R. M., and Sellin, T. 1972. *Delinquency in a birth cohort.* Chicago: University of Chicago Press.

Wolfgang, M. E., Thornberry, T. P., and Figlio, R. M. 1987. *From boy to man, from delinquency to crime.* Chicago: University of Chicago Press.

Wyshak, G. and Frisch, R. E. 1982. "Evidence for a secular trend in age of menarche." *New England Journal of Medicine, 306,* 1033-1035.

Reprinted from: Terrie E. Moffit, "Adolescence-Limited and Life-Course-Persistent Antisocial Behavior: A Developmental Taxonomy." In *Psychological Review* 100, pp. 674-692, 696-701. Copyright © 1993 by the American Psychological Association. Reprinted by permission the American Psychological Association and Terrie E. Moffit. ✦

17

A Control Theory of Delinquency

Travis Hirschi

Most *criminological theories seek to explain why some people commit crime and others do not. Control theories, sometimes referred to as social-bond theories, ask a different question. They seek to understand why more people are not offenders. To this end, they attempt to identify factors that inhibit or prevent delinquent and criminal behavior rather than factors contributing to such behavior. Travis Hirschi has provided what is perhaps the definitive statement on control theory, which is summarized in this selection.*

Hirschi's popular conceptualization of control theory posits that four social bonds to conventional institutions (e.g., schools) and people (e.g., parents) serve to explain why some individuals do not engage in delinquency and crime. The four bonds are attachment, commitment, involvement, and belief. According to his perspective, possessing strong social bonds gives the individual a "stake in conformity"; engaging in delinquency or crime involves the risk of losing those things that the individual deems valuable, such as love and respect from parents or time and effort expended in school in order to obtain a good job. Stronger social bonds are generally associated with no or lower involvement in crime; weak or nonexistent social bonds are associated with an increased likelihood of offending.

"The more weakened the groups to which [the individual] belongs, the less he depends on them, the more he consequently depends on himself and recognizes no other rules of conduct than what are founded on his private interests."[1]

Control theories assume that delinquent acts result when an individual's bond to society is weak or broken. Since these theories embrace two highly complex concepts, the *bond* of the individual to *society*, it is not surprising that they have at one time or another formed the basis of explanations of most forms of aberrant or unusual behavior. It is also not surprising that control theories have described the elements of the bond to society in many ways, and that they have focused on a variety of units as the point of control.

I begin with a classification and description of the elements of the bond to conventional society. I try to show how each of these elements is related to delinquent behavior and how they are related to each other. I then turn to the question of specifying the unit to which the person is presumably more or less tied, and to the question of the adequacy of the motivational force built into the explanation of delinquent behavior.

Elements of the Bond

Attachment

. . . Durkheim said it many years ago: "We are moral beings to the extent that we are social beings."[2] This may be interpreted to mean that we are moral beings to the extent that we have "internalized the norms" of society. But what does it mean to say that a person has internalized the norms of society? The norms of society are by definition shared by the members of society. To violate a norm is, therefore, to act contrary to the wishes and expectations of other people. If a person does not care about the wishes and expectations of other people—that is, if he is insensitive to the opinion of others—then he is to that extent not bound by the norms. He is free to deviate.

The essence of internalization of norms, conscience, or superego thus lies in the attachment of the individual to others.[3] This view has several advantages over the concept of internalization. For one, explanations of deviant behavior based on attachment do not beg the question, since the extent to which a person is attached to others can be measured independently of his deviant behavior. Furthermore, change or variation in behavior is explainable in a way that it is not when notions of internalization or superego are used.

For example, the divorced man is more likely after divorce to commit a number of deviant acts, such as suicide or forgery. If we explain these acts by reference to the superego (or internal control), we are forced to say that the man "lost his conscience" when he got a divorce; and, of course, if he remarries, we have to conclude that he gets his conscience back.

This dimension of the bond to conventional society is encountered in most social control-oriented research and theory. F. Ivan Nye's "internal control" and "indirect control" refer to the same element, although we avoid the problem of explaining changes over time by locating the "conscience" in the bond to others rather than making it part of the personality.[4] Attachment to others is just one aspect of Albert J. Reiss's "personal controls"; we avoid his problems of tautological empirical *observations* by making the relationship between attachment and delinquency problematic rather than definitional.[5] Finally, Scott Briar and Irving Piliavin's "commitment" or "stake in conformity" subsumes attachment, as their discussion illustrates, although the terms they use are more closely associated with the next element to be discussed.[6]

Commitment

"Of all passions, that which inclineth men least to break the laws, is fear. Nay, excepting some generous natures, it is the only thing, when there is the appearance of profit or pleasure by breaking the laws, that makes men keep them."[7] Few would deny that men on occasion obey the rules simply from fear of the consequences. This rational component in conformity we label commitment. What does it mean to say that a person is committed to conformity? In Howard S. Becker's formulation it means the following:

First, the individual is in a position in which his decision with regard to some particular line of action has consequences for other interests and activities not necessarily [directly] related to it. Second, he has placed himself in that position by his own prior actions. A third element is present though so obvious as not to be apparent: the committed person must be aware [of these other interests] and must recog-

nize that his decision in this case will have ramifications beyond it.[8]

The idea, then, is that the person invests time, energy, himself, in a certain line of activity—say, getting an education, building up a business, acquiring a reputation for virtue. When or whenever he considers deviant behavior, he must consider the costs of this deviant behavior, the risk he runs of losing the investment he has made in conventional behavior.

If attachment to others is the sociological counterpart of the superego or conscience, commitment is the counterpart of the ego or common sense. To the person committed to conventional lines of action, risking one to ten years in prison for a ten-dollar holdup is stupidity, because to the committed person the costs and risks obviously exceed ten dollars in value. . . . In the sociological control theory, it can be and is generally assumed that the decision to commit a criminal act may well be rationally determined—that the actor's decision was not irrational given the risks and costs he faces. Of course, as Becker points out, if the actor is capable of in some sense calculating the costs of a line of action, he is also capable of calculational errors: ignorance and error return, in the control theory, as possible explanations of deviant behavior.

The concept of commitment assumes that the organization of society is such that the interests of most persons would be endangered if they were to engage in criminal acts. Most people, simply by the process of living in an organized society, acquire goods, reputations, prospects that they do not want to risk losing. . . . Many hypotheses about the antecedents of delinquent behavior are based on this premise. For example, Arthur L. Stinchombe's hypothesis that "high school rebellion . . . Occurs when future status is not clearly related to present performance"[9] suggests that one is committed to conformity not only by what one has but also by what one hopes to obtain. Thus "ambition" and/or "aspiration" play an important role in producing conformity. The person becomes committed to a conventional line of action, and he is therefore committed to conformity.

Most lines of action in a society are of course conventional. The clearest examples are educational and occupational careers. Actions thought to jeopardize one's chances in these areas are presumably avoided. . . .

Involvement

Many persons undoubtedly owe a life of virtue to a lack of opportunity to do otherwise. Time and energy are inherently limited: "Not that I would not, if I could, be both handsome and fat and well dressed, and a great athlete, and make a million a year, be a wit, a bon vivant, and a lady killer, as well as a philosopher, a philanthropist, a statesman, warrior, and African explorer, as well as a 'tone-poet' and saint. But the thing is simply impossible."[10] The things that William James here says he would like to be or do are all, I suppose, within the realm of conventionality, but if he were to include illicit actions he would still have to eliminate some of them as simply impossible.

Involvement or engrossment in conventional activities is thus often part of a control theory. The assumption, widely shared, is that a person may be simply too busy doing conventional things to find time to engage in deviant behavior. The person involved in conventional activities is tied to appointments, deadlines, working hours, plans, and the like, so the opportunity to commit deviant acts rarely arises. To the extent that he is engrossed in conventional activities, he cannot even think about deviant acts, let alone act out his inclinations.[11]

This line of reasoning is responsible for the stress placed on recreational facilities in many programs to reduce delinquency, for much of the concern with high school dropouts, and for the idea that boys should be drafted into the Army to keep them out of trouble. So obvious and persuasive is the idea that involvement in conventional activities is a major deterrent to delinquency that it was accepted even by Sutherland: "In the general area of juvenile delinquency it is probable that the most significant difference between juveniles who engage in delinquency and those who do not is that the latter are provided abundant opportunities of a conventional type for satisfying their recreational interests, while the former lack those opportunities or facilities."[12]

The view that "idle hands are the devil's workshop" has received more sophisticated treatment in recent sociological writings on delinquency. David Matza and Gresham M. Sykes, for example, suggest that delinquents have the values of a leisure class, the same values ascribed by Veblen to *the* leisure class: a search for kicks, disdain of work, a desire for the big score, and acceptance of aggressive toughness as proof of masculinity.[13] Matza and Sykes explain delinquency by reference to this system of values, but they note that adolescents at all class levels are "to some extent" members of a leisure class, that they "move in a limbo between earlier parental domination and future integration with the social structure through the bonds of work and marriage.[14] In the end, then, the leisure of the adolescent produces a set of values, which, in turn, leads to delinquency.

Belief

Unlike the cultural deviance theory, the control theory assumes the existence of a common value system within the society or group whose norms are being violated. If the deviant is committed to a value system different from that of conventional society, there is, within the context of the theory, nothing to explain. The question is, "Why does a man violate the rules in which he believes?" It is not, "Why do men differ in their beliefs about what constitutes good and desirable conduct?" The person is assumed to have been socialized (perhaps imperfectly) into the group whose rules he is violating; deviance is not a question of one group imposing its rules on the members of another group. In other words, we not only assume the deviant *has* believed the rules, we assume he believes the rules even as he violates them.

How can a person believe it is wrong to steal at the same time he is stealing? In the strain theory, this is not a difficult problem. . . . However, given the control theory's assumptions about motivation, if both the deviant and the nondeviant believe the deviant act is wrong, how do we account for the fact that one commits it and the other does not?

Control theories have taken two approaches to this problem. In one approach, beliefs are treated as mere words that mean little or nothing if the other forms of control are missing. . . . In short, beliefs, at least insofar as they are expressed in words, drop out of the picture; since they do not differentiate between deviants and nondeviants, they are in the same class as "language" or any other characteristic common to all members of the group. Since they represent no real obstacle to the commission of delinquent acts, nothing need be said about how they are handled by those committing such acts. The control theories that do not mention beliefs (or values), and many do not, may be assumed to take this approach to the problem.

The second approach argues that the deviant rationalizes his behavior so that he can at once violate the rule and maintain his belief in it. . . . In both Cressey's and Sykes and Matza's treatments, these rationalizations (Cressey calls them "verbalizations," Sykes and Matza term them "techniques of neutralization") occur prior to the commission of the deviant act. If the neutralization is successful, the person is free to commit the act(s) in question. Both in Cressey and in Sykes and Matza, the strain that prompts the effort at neutralization also provides the motive force that results in the subsequent deviant act. Their theories are thus, in this sense, strain theories. Neutralization is difficult to handle within the context of a theory that adheres closely to control theory assumptions, because in the control theory there is no special motivational force to account for the neutralization. This difficulty is especially noticeable in Matza's later treatment of this topic, where the motivational component, the "will to delinquency" appears *after* the moral vacuum has been created by the techniques of neutralization.[15] . . .

In attempting to solve a strain theory problem with control theory tools, the control theorist is thus led into a trap. He cannot answer the crucial question. The concept of neutralization assumes the existence of moral obstacles to the commission of deviant acts. In order plausibly to account for a deviant act, it is necessary to generate motivation to deviance that is at least equivalent in force to the resistance provided by these moral obstacles. However, if the moral obstacles are removed, neutralization and special motivation are no longer required. We therefore follow the implicit logic of control theory and remove these moral obstacles by hypothesis. Many persons do not have an attitude of respect toward the rules of society: many persons feel no moral obligation to conform regardless of personal advantage. Insofar as the values and beliefs of these persons are consistent with their feelings, and there should be a tendency toward consistency, neutralization is unnecessary; it has already occurred.

Does this merely push the question back a step and at the same time produce conflict with the assumption of a common value system? I think not. . . . We do not assume, in other words, that the person constructs a system of rationalizations in order to justify commission of acts he *wants* to commit. We assume, in contrast, that the beliefs that free a man to commit deviant acts are *unmotivated* in the sense that he does not construct or adopt them in order to facilitate the attainment of illicit ends. In the second place, we do not assume, as does Matza, that "delinquents concur in the conventional assessment of delinquency."[16] We assume, in contrast, that there is *variation* in the extent to which people believe they should obey the rules of society, and, furthermore, that the less a person believes he should obey the rules, the more likely he is to violate them.[17]

In chronological order, then, a person's beliefs in the moral validity of norms are, for no teleological reason, weakened. The probability that he will commit delinquent acts is therefore increased. When and if he commits a delinquent act, we may justifiably use the weakness of his beliefs in explaining it, but no special motivation is required to explain either the weakness of his beliefs or, perhaps, his delinquent act.

The keystone of this argument is of course the assumption that there is variation in belief in the moral validity of social rules. This assumption is amenable to direct empirical test and can thus survive at least until its first confrontation with data. . . .

The idea of a common (or, perhaps better, a single) value system is consistent with the fact, or presumption, of variation in the strength of moral beliefs. We have not suggested that delinquency is based on beliefs counter to conventional morality; we have not suggested that delinquents do not believe delinquent acts are wrong. They may well believe these acts are wrong, but the meaning and efficacy of such beliefs are contingent upon other beliefs, and, indeed, on the strength of other ties to the conventional order.[18] . . .

Where is the Motivation?

The most disconcerting question the control theorist faces goes something like this: "Yes, but *why* do they do it?" In the good old days, the control theorist could simply strip away the "veneer of civilization" and expose man's "animal impulses" for all to see. These impulses appeared to him (and apparently to his audience) to provide a plausible account of the motivation to crime and delinquency. His argument was *not* that delinquents and criminals alone are animals, but that we are all animals, and thus all naturally capable of committing criminal acts. . . .

It was no longer fashionable (within sociology, at least) to refer to animal impulses. The control theorist tended more and more to deemphasize the motivational component of his theory. He might refer in the beginning to "universal human needs," or some such, but the driving force behind crime and delinquency was rarely alluded to. At the same time, his explanations of crime and delinquency increasingly left the reader uneasy. What, the reader asked, is the control theorist assuming? . . .

There are several additional accounts of "why they do it" that are to my mind persuasive and at the same time generally compatible with control theory.[19] But while all of these accounts may be compatible with control theory, they are by no means deducible from it. Furthermore, they rarely impute built-in, unusual motivation to the delinquent: he is attempting to satisfy the same desires, he is reacting to the same pressures as other boys (as is clear, for example, in the previous quotation from Briar and Piliavin). In other words, if included, these accounts of motivation would serve the same function in

the theory that "animal impulses" traditionally served: they might add to its persuasiveness and plausibility, but they would add little else, since they do not differentiate delinquents from nondelinquents.

In the end, then, control theory remains what it has always been: a theory in which deviation is not problematic. The question "Why do they do it?" is simply not the question the theory is designed to answer. The question is, "Why don't we do it?" There is much evidence that we would if we dared.

Discussion Questions

1. Hirschi argues that four social bonds serve to inhibit or prevent involvement in delinquency and crime. Identify and define each of Hirschi's four social bonds. Why does each of the bonds inhibit or prevent involvement in delinquency?

2. Two institutions that are often examined in empirical studies involving social control theory are family and school. Given your knowledge of social control theory, why should attachment to parents limit or prevent offending? Commitment to school?

3. Hirschi makes the case that control theories differ from other criminological theories. How do they differ from other types of theories? Why is this is an important difference?

Notes

1. Emile Durkheim, *Suicide*, trans. John A. Spaulding and George Simpson (New York: The Free Press, 1951), p. 209.

2. Emile Durkheim, *Moral Education*, trans. Everett K. Wilson and Herman Schnurer (New York: The Free Press, 1961), p. 64.

3. Although attachment alone does not exhaust the meaning of internalization, attachments and beliefs combined would appear to leave only a small residue of "internal control" not susceptible in principle to direct measurement.

4. F. Ivan Nye, *Family Relationships and Delinquent Behavior* (New York: Wiley, 1958), pp. 5-7.

5. Albert J. Reiss, Jr., "Delinquency as the Failure of Personal and Social Controls," *Ameri-*

can *Sociological Review*, XVI (1951), 196-207. For example, "Our observations show . . . That delinquent recidivists are less often persons with mature ego ideals or nondelinquent social roles." (p. 204).

6. Scott Briar and Irving Piliavin, "Delinquency, Situational Inducements, and Commitment to Conformity," *Social Problems*, XIII (1965), 41-42. The concept "stake in conformity" was introduced by Jackson Toby in his "Social Disorganization and Stake in Conformity: Complementary Factors in the Predatory Behavior of Hoodlums," *Journal of Criminal Law, Criminology and Police Science*, XLVIII (1957), 12-17. See also his "Hoodlum or Business Man: An American Dilemma," *The Jews*, ed. Marshall Sklare (New York: The Free Press, 1958), pp. 542-550. Throughout the text, I occasionally use "stake in conformity" in speaking in general of the strength of the bond to conventional society. So used, the concept is somewhat broader than is true for either Toby or Briar and Piliavin, where the concept is roughly equivalent to what is here called "commitment."

7. Thomas Hobbes, *Leviathan* (Oxford: Basil Blackwell, 1957), p. 195.

8. Howard S. Becker, "Notes on the Concept of Commitment," *American Journal of Sociology* LXVI (1969).

9. Arthur L. Stinchombe, *Rebellion in a High School* (Chicago: Quadrangle, 1964), p. 5.

10. William James, *Psychology* (Cleveland: World Publishing Co., 1948), p. 186.

11. Few activities appear to be so engrossing that they rule out contemplation of alternative lines of behavior, at least if estimates of the amount of time men spend plotting sexual deviations have any validity.

12. The Sutherland Papers, ed. Albert K. Cohen et al. (Bloomington: Indiana University Press, 1956), p. 37.

13. David Matza and Gresham M. Sykes, "Juvenile Delinquency and Subterranean Values,"

American Sociological Review, XXVI (1961), 712-719.

14. Ibid., p. 718.

15. David Matza, *Delinquency and Drift* (New York: Wiley, 1964), pp. 181-191.

16. *Delinquency and Drift*, p. 43.

17. This assumption is not, I think, contradicted by the evidence presented by Matza against the existence of a delinquent subculture. In comparing the attitudes and actions of delinquents with the picture painted by delinquent subculture theorists, Matza emphasizes—and perhaps exaggerates—the extent to which delinquents are tied to the conventional order. In implicitly comparing delinquents with a supermoral man, I emphasize—and perhaps exaggerate—the extent to which they are not tied to the conventional order.

18. The position taken here is therefore somewhere between the "semantic dementia" and the "neutralization" positions. Assuming variation, the delinquent is, at the extremes, freer than the neutralization argument assumes. Although the possibility of wide discrepancy between what the delinquent professes and what he practices still exists, it is presumably much rarer than is suggested by studies of articulate "psychopaths."

19. For example: Carl Wertham, "The Function of Social Definitions in the Development of Delinquent Careers," *Juvenile Delinquency and Youth Crime*, Report of the President's Commission on Law Enforcement and Administration of Justice (Washington: USGPO, 1967), pp. 155-170; Jackson Toby, "Affluence and Adolescent Crime," *ibid.*, pp. 132-144; James F. Short, Jr., and Fred L. Strodtbeck, *Group Process and Gang Delinquency* (Chicago: University of Chicago Press, 1965), pp. 248-264.

18

Crime and Deviance Over the Life Course: The Salience of Adult Social Bonds

Robert J. Sampson
John H. Laub

Hirschi's social-control theory has received somewhat mixed support in the empirical literature, and his hypotheses regarding the role of peers in offending have particularly been criticized. Nevertheless, social-control theory continues to have an important role in criminological theorizing and research, as evidenced in the recent work of Robert J. Sampson and John H. Laub.

In this selection, Sampson and Laub demonstrate that social bonds have important implications for adult offending. They take a life-course approach (one of the first such studies in criminology) and examine factors associated with continuity and change in criminal behavior over time. In their longitudinal data set, approximately half the respondents had officially been adjudicated delinquent as juveniles, while half were "nondelinquent" as juveniles. The results of the study indicate that regardless of previous offending history, developing strong social bonds to conventional institutions or people in adulthood has important implications for criminal and deviant behavior. Specifically, job stability and marital attachments were important inhibitors of criminal behavior in adulthood, both for the men

who as adolescents were nondelinquent and for those who were officially adjudicated as delinquent. These results suggest that offending trajectories over time can be modified by transitions, particularly those involving strong social bonds, and indicate that changes in social circumstances can have important implications for changes in criminal and deviant behavior over the lifecourse.

Sociological criminology has neglected early childhood characteristics, and consequently has not come to grips with the link between early childhood behaviors and later adult outcomes (Caspi, Bem, and Elder 1989; Farrington 1989; Gottfredson and Hirschi 1990). Although criminal behavior peaks in the teenage years, there is substantial evidence of early delinquency as well as continuation of criminal behavior over the life course. By concentrating on the teenage years, sociological perspectives on crime fail to address the life-span implications of childhood behavior (Wilson and Herrnstein 1985). At the same time, criminologists have not devoted much attention to what Rutter (1988, p. 3) calls "escape from the risk process," limiting our understanding of desistance from crime and the transitions from criminal to noncriminal behavior.

To address these limitations, we develop a theoretical model of age-graded informal social control to account for persistence and desistance in criminal behavior. Our basic thesis is that while continuity in deviant behavior exists, social ties in adulthood—to work, family, and community—explain changes in criminality over the life span. Our model acknowledges the importance of early childhood behaviors while rejecting the implication that later adult factors have little relevance (Wilson and Herrnstein 1985). We contend that social interaction with adult institutions of informal social control has important effects on crime and deviance. As such, ours is a "sociogenic" theoretical model of adult crime and deviance. . . .

The Life Course Perspective

The life course has been defined as "pathways through the age differentiated life span," where age differentiation "is manifested in expectations and options that impinge on decision processes and the course of events that give shape to life stages, transitions, and turning points" (Elder 1985, p. 17). Two central concepts underlie the analysis of life course dynamics. A *trajectory* is a pathway or line of development over the life span such as worklife, marriage, parenthood, self-esteem, and criminal behavior. Trajectories refer to long-term patterns of behavior and are marked by a sequence of life events and transitions (Elder 1985, pp. 31-2). *Transitions* are specific life events that are embedded in trajectories and evolve over shorter time spans (e.g., first job or first marriage). Some of them are age-graded and some are not. What is often assumed to be important is the timing and the ordering of significant life events (Hogan 1980).

These two concepts are related: "the interlocking nature of trajectories and transitions, within and across life stages . . . may generate turning points or a change in course " (Elder 1985, p. 32). Adaptation to life events is crucial: "The same event or transition followed by different adaptations can lead to different trajectories" (Elder 1985, p. 35). This perspective implies both a strong connection between childhood events and experiences in young adulthood, and that transitions or turning points can modify life trajectories—they can "redirect paths."

Criminology and the Life Course

Criminology has been slow to recognize the importance of the life-course perspective (Hagan and Palloni 1988). Not only are the data needed to explore such relationships sparse (see Blumstein, Cohen, Roth, and Visher 1986), some researchers argue that ordinary life events (e.g., getting married, becoming a parent) have little effect on criminal behavior. Gottfredson and Hirschi argue that crime rates decline with age "whether or not these events occur" and note "that the longitudinal/developmental assumption that such events are important neglects its own evi-

dence on the stability of personal characteristics" (1987, p. 604; see also Hirschi and Gottfredson 1983).

The extent of stability and change in behavior and personality attributes over time is one of the most complex and hotly debated issues in the social sciences (Brim and Kagan 1980; Dannefer 1984). The research literature in criminology contains evidence for both continuity *and* change over the life course. Reviewing over 16 studies on aggressive behavior, Olweus (1979, pp. 854-5) found "substantial" stability: The correlation between early aggressive behavior and later criminality averaged .68 for the studies reviewed. . . .

Other work has also demonstrated the effects of early life experiences on adult behavior (McCord 1979; Farrington 1986; Robins 1966, 1978).

At the same time, there is evidence for change over the life course. While studies show that antisocial behavior in children is one of the best predictors of antisocial behavior in adults, "most antisocial children do not become antisocial as adults" (Gove 1985, p. 123). . . .

In the context of personality characteristics, Caspi (1987) found that although the tendency toward explosive behavior in childhood was "re-created across the age-graded life course, especially in problems with subordination (e.g., in education, military, and work settings) and in situations that required negotiating interpersonal conflicts" (e.g., marriage), "invariant action patterns did not emerge across the age-graded life course" (1987, p. 1211). . . .

Some criminological research also suggests that salient life events influence behavior and modify trajectories. . . .

Childhood Behavior and Informal Social Control Over the Life Course

Recognizing the importance of both stability and change in the life course, our model focuses on two propositions. First, we contend that childhood antisocial behavior (e.g., juvenile delinquency, conduct disorder, violent temper tantrums) is linked to a wide variety of troublesome adult behaviors including criminality, general deviance, offenses in the military, economic dependency, educational failure, employment instability, and marital discord. These long-term relationships are posited to occur independent of traditional variables such as social class background and race/ethnicity. As Hagan and Palloni (1988) argue (see also Hagan 1989, p. 260), delinquent and criminal events "are linked into life trajectories of broader significance, whether those trajectories are criminal or noncriminal in form" (p. 90). . . .

Second, we argue that social bonds to adult institutions of informal social control (e.g., family, education, neighborhood, work) influence criminal behavior over the life course despite an individual's delinquent and antisocial background. We seek to identify the transitions embedded in individual trajectories that relate to adult informal social control, and contend that childhood pathways to crime and deviance can be significantly modified over the life course by adult social bonds.

The important institutions of social control vary across the life span: in childhood and adolescence these are the family, school, and peer groups; in the phase of young adulthood they are higher education and/or vocational training, work, and marriage; and in later adulthood, the dominant institutions are work, marriage, parenthood, and investment in the community.

Within this framework, our organizing principle derives from social control theory (Durkheim 1951; Hirschi 1969; Kornhauser 1978): crime and deviance result when an individual's bond to society is weak or broken. We argue that changes that strengthen social bonds to society in adulthood will thus lead to less crime and deviance; changes that weaken social bonds will lead to more crime and deviance. Unlike most life-course research, we emphasize the *quality* or *strength* of social ties more than the occurrence or timing of specific life events. . . . Therefore, we maintain that it is the *social investment* or social capital (Coleman 1988) in the institutional relationship, whether it be in a family, work, or community setting, that dictates the salience of informal social control at the individual level.

Our model assumes that life-event transitions and adult social bonds can modify quite different childhood trajectories. . . .

Data

We are currently engaged in a long-term project analyzing data from Sheldon and Eleanor Glueck's *Unraveling Juvenile Delinquency* (1950) and their subsequent follow-up studies (Glueck and Glueck 1968). . . .

The Gluecks' research design began with samples of delinquent and nondelinquent boys born between 1924 and 1935. The *delinquent* sample comprised 500 10- to 17-year-old white males from Boston who, because of their persistent delinquency, were committed to one of two correctional schools in Massachusetts. The *nondelinquent* sample, or what they called a "control-group" (Glueck and Glueck 1950, p. 14), was made up of 500 10- to 17-year-old white males from the Boston public schools. Nondelinquent status was determined on the basis of official record checks and interviews with parents, teachers, local police, social workers and recreational leaders, as well as the boys themselves. . . . The nondelinquent boys were different from the Boston youth remanded to reform school, "but compared with national averages the men in this study did *not* represent a particularly law-abiding group" (Long and Vaillant 1984, p. 345). Although clearly not a random selection, the samples appear to be representative of their respective populations at that time.

Boys in the two samples were matched on a case-by-case basis according to age, race/ethnicity, general intelligence, and neighborhood socioeconomic status (for details see Glueck and Glueck 1950, pp. 33-9; Laub and Sampson 1988). These classic variables are widely thought to influence both delinquency and official reaction. Boys in each sample grew up in high-risk environments characterized by poverty, social disorganization, and exposure to delinquency and antisocial conduct (Glueck and Glueck 1950, pp. 30-2).

From 1940 to 1965, the Gluecks' research team collected data on these individuals. They were originally interviewed at an average age of 14, at age 25, and again at age 32. On average, then, the original subjects were followed for 18 years. Data were collected for all three time periods for 438 of the 500 delinquents and 442 of the 500 nondelinquent controls (88 percent). . . .

During the first wave, a wide range of biological, psychological, and sociological information concerning each boy and his life from birth until adolescence was gathered. The second wave field investigation and interview began as each subject approached his 25th birthday and concerned the period from age 17 to 25 (the juvenile court in Massachusetts had jurisdiction up to the 17th birthday). The third wave interview covered the period from age 25 to 32. The second and third wave interviews concentrated on social factors, including criminal histories. . . .

The data were gathered through detailed investigations by the Gluecks' research team and included interviews with the subjects and their families, employers, teachers, and neighbors, as well as criminal justice and social welfare officials. The field investigation involved meticulously culling information from the records of public and private agencies that had any involvement with the family. . . .

Measures of Childhood Antisocial Behavior and Adult Crime

We measure antisocial behavior during childhood and adolescence in three ways: (1) official delinquency status as determined by the sampling design of the Glueck study; (2) a composite scale (ranging from 0 to 30) of self, parent, and teacher reports of delinquency and other misconduct that captures both unofficial delinquency as well as incidents known to the police; and (3) temper tantrums—indicating the extent to which a child engaged in violent and habitual temper tantrums while growing up. . . .

Adult crime and deviance was investigated in the follow-up interviews for both groups, including excessive use of alcohol and/or drugs as well as general deviance (e.g., frequent involvement in gambling, illicit sexual behavior, use of prostitutes). . . .

From the official criminal history, we determined whether the subject had an arrest during each follow-up period. . . .

Since the period of the study included World War II and the Korean War, a majority of the men served in the military (67 percent). At the first follow-up, data were collected on the official military experience of each subject using interviews and records from the appropriate military service, Selective Service, State Adjutant General, Veterans Administration, and Red Cross. Our measure of the subject's criminal/deviant behavior in the military (e.g., AWOL, desertion, theft, etc.) captures illegal conduct that came to the attention of authorities.

Measures of Adult Social Bonds

Our key independent variables are *job stability*, *commitment*, and *attachment to spouse*, measured at both follow-ups. Information for these measures was collected during the home interview and corroborated whenever possible by record checks.[1] Job stability is measured by a standardized, composite scale of three intercorrelated variables—employment status, stability of most recent employment, and work habits. . . .

An individual's commitment to occupation-related goals may influence job stability. Our measure of commitment at Time 2 is derived from interviews with the subject and significant others and combines three related variables: work, educational and economic ambitions (Glueck and Glueck 1968, pp. 124-6). . . . At Time 3, commitment is a composite scale combining work ambitions and ambitions generally. . . .

The third key independent variable in our analysis is attachment to spouse. At Time 2, we use a composite measure derived from interview data describing the general conjugal relationship between the subject and his spouse during the period plus the subject's attitude toward marital responsibility (Glueck and Glueck 1968, pp. 84-8). . . . At Time 3, attachment to spouse is a composite scale derived from interview data describing the general conjugal relationship during the follow-up period plus a measure of the cohesiveness of the family unit. . . .

Taken together, these measures capture the quality or strength of an individual's ties to important institutions of informal social control—family, work, and the community at large. . . .

Patterns of Stability and Change

Combining data from the two Glueck samples, we first examine the long-term relationship between childhood delinquency and antisocial behavior and a wide range of later adult behaviors. . . .

In short, childhood delinquent behavior has a significant relationship with a wide range of adult criminal and deviant behaviors, including charges initiated by military personnel, reports of involvement in deviance and excessive drinking, and arrest by the police. The same childhood antisocial behaviors are also predictive of economic, fam-

ily, educational, and employment problems up to eighteen years later. These results are robust as to measurement of delinquency. Because of the matched design, they cannot be explained in terms of original differences between delinquents and nondelinquents in age, intelligence, socioeconomic status, and race/ethnicity—variables often associated with stratification outcomes. Clearly, the boys in the Gluecks' delinquent and nondelinquent samples exhibited behavioral consistency well into adulthood (Glueck and Glueck 1968).

Adult Social Bonds

In Table 18.1 we examine how the social factors of *job stability*, *commitment* to educational, work, and economic goals (i.e., aspi-

Table 18.1
Relationship Between Adult Social Bonds and Adult Crime and Deviance, Controlling for Official Delinquency Status in Childhood

Adult Crime and Deviance	Delinquent Group			Control Group		
	Job Stability, Ages 17-25					
	Low	Medium	High	Low	Medium	High
% Excessive alcohol, ages 17-25	57	24	15*	32	8	5*
% Excessive alcohol, ages 25-32	53	19	11*	27	6	4*
% General deviance, ages 17-25	31	13	9*	12	4	3*
% General deviance, ages 25-32	47	17	8*	17	7	2*
% Arrested, ages 17-25	91	62	60*	36	17	17*
% Arrested, ages 25-32	74	47	32*	36	11	9*
	Occupational Commitment, Ages 17-25					
	Weak	Strong		Weak	Strong	
% Excessive alcohol, ages 17-25	50	21*		21	5*	
% Excessive alcohol, ages 25-32	43	16*		15	4*	
% General deviance, ages 17-25	29	15*		10	3*	
% General deviance, ages 25-32	37	14*		8	5	
% Arrested, ages 17-25	82	64*		34	12*	
% Arrested, ages 25-32	70	47*		221	0*	
	Attachment to Spouse, Ages 17-25					
	Weak	Strong		Weak	Strong	
% Excessive alcohol, ages 17-25	53	17*		46	4*	
% Excessive alcohol, ages 25-32	47	11*		32	6*	
% General deviance, ages 17-25	31	8*		12	4*	
% General deviance, ages 25-32	54	16*		36	7*	
% Arrested, ages 17-25	87	58*		61	15*	
% Arrested, ages 25-32	76	34*		39	12*	

*P < .05

ration), and *attachment* to spouse among those ever married (all measured for ages 17-25) modify the tendency to persist in deviant and troublesome behaviors over the life span. . . .

Job stability in young adulthood has a large inverse relationship with each measure of adult crime and deviance for both the delinquent and nondelinquent samples.[2] Moreover, young-adult job stability has substantial *predictive* power, exhibiting very large negative effects on alcohol use, general deviance, and arrest in the subsequent 25-32 age period. For both samples, subjects with low job stability at ages 17-25 were at least four times more likely to have severe alcohol problems in later adulthood and at least five times more likely to have engaged in deviant behavior compared to those with high job stability. It thus seems unlikely that adult crime itself can account for the patterns observed. . . . Rather, it appears that job stability in adulthood significantly modifies trajectories of crime and deviance regardless of strong differences in childhood delinquent and antisocial conduct.

Adult commitment to conventional educational and occupational goals results in a similar pattern. Subjects with high aspirations and efforts to advance educationally and occupationally were much less likely to engage in deviant behavior, use alcohol excessively, or be arrested at ages 17-25 and 25-32.

The pattern is consistent for the relationship between attachment to spouse and adult crime among those ever married (approximately 50 percent of each sample). . . . As with job stability and commitment, the influence of attachment to wife at ages 17-25 is salient not only in the concurrent period but in the later 25-32 period as well.

The evidence strongly suggests that informal social controls in young adulthood are significantly and substantially related to adult antisocial behavior, regardless of childhood delinquency. . . . Social bonds to the adult institutions of work, education, and the family exert a powerful influence on adult crime and deviance.

Models of Adult Crime Among Original Delinquents

A major question may be raised concerning these results—do individual differences in crime within the delinquent and control groups confound the results? The most delinquent subjects in the delinquent group may have self-selected themselves into later states of job instability, conflict-ridden marriages, and crime (Caspi 1987). Similarly, despite the absence of an official record, the nondelinquent subjects were not equally nondelinquent.

We address this question through a multivariate strategy that controls for prior delinquency and crime in four ways. . . .

The results for all men are consistent across samples—independent of juvenile delinquency, the largest significant influence on overall adult crimes is job stability. . . . [Results] based on ever-married men confirms previous analyses—income and commitment are unimportant in the presence of job stability and marital attachment. Job stability has significant and essentially identical negative effects on adult crime. . . . Furthermore, the largest effect on overall adult criminal and deviant behavior for both groups is marital attachment—ever-married men with close ties to their spouses in young adulthood were much less likely to engage in adult crime and deviance than men with weak ties, net of other factors. . . .

Conclusion

Sociological explanations of crime and delinquency have recently come under strong attack. In probably the most widely cited critique, Wilson and Herrnstein (1985) chastise sociologists for ignoring the fact that crime and delinquency can be traced to early childhood. They argue that high-rate offenders begin deviant behavior very early in their lives, "well before" traditional sociological variables (e.g., labor markets, community, peer groups, marriage) "could play much of a role" (p. 311). We have offered a life-course model that does not deny early childhood differences, but at the same time recognizes that adult life events matter. The basic organizing principle derived from linking the life course perspective with social control theory is that both continuity and change are evident, and that trajectories of crime and deviance are systematically modified by social bonds to adult institutions of informal social control.

This thesis found broad support in a strict test. . . . Consistent with a model of adult development and informal social control, we have shown that job stability and marital attachment in adulthood are significantly related to changes in adult crime—the stronger the adult ties to work and family, the less crime and deviance among both delinquents and controls. The results were strong, consistent, and robust over a wide variety of measures and analytical techniques. The effects of job stability were independent of prior and concurrent levels of commitment (i.e., aspirations and ambitions), suggesting that labor-market instability rather than weak occupational commitment is a key factor in understanding adult crime and deviance.

Sociologists need not be hostile to research establishing early childhood differences in delinquency and antisocial behavior—influences that may persist well into adulthood. Indeed, the other side of continuity is change, and the latter appears to be systematically structured by adult bonds to social institutions. . . .

Finally, early childhood differences should not be ignored as a source of sociological explanation. Just because criminal tendencies emerge early in life does not mean they derive from psychological and/or constitutional differences. Family, school, and neighborhood processes (Laub and Sampson 1988; Sampson and Laub, forthcoming) may provide a sociological link to a complete life-course explanation of crime.

Discussion Questions

1. Sampson and Laub discuss the "life-course perspective." What is this perspective? What do their results suggest with regard to the use of this perspective in criminology?

2. According to Sampson and Laub, social bonds in adulthood have important implications for offending over time. How

do these scholars extend Hirschi's social control theory? Do Sampson and Laub's findings suggest that this extension is useful? Why or why not?

3. According to Sampson and Laub's findings, what is the importance of social bonds in adulthood for former "non-delinquents" with regard to offending? What is the importance of social bonds in adulthood for former "delinquents"?

Notes

1. Descriptive statistics on key source variables collected during each follow-up period for both delinquent and control groups are found in Glueck and Glueck (1968, pp. 71-130). Further descriptive data on constructed variables are available from the authors upon request.

2. In Table 18.1, job stability is trichotomized to permit visual display of the pattern and magnitude of the relationships. Because of skew, the attachment and commitment measures are dichotomized. The number of cases ranges from a minimum of 224 for the ever-married subsample at Time 2 to 437 for occupational commitment at Time 2. All of the percentages are based on at least 30 cases.

References

Allison, Paul. 1984. *Event History Analysis*. Beverly Hills, CA: Sage.

Baltes, Paul and John Nesselroade. 1984. "Paradigm Lost and Paradigm Regained: Critique of Dannefer's Portrayal of Life-Span Developmental Psychology." *American Sociological Review* 49:841-46.

Blumstein, A., J. Cohen, J. Roth, and C. Visher (Eds.). 1986. *Criminal Careers and "Career Criminals"*. Washington, DC: National Academy Press.

Brim, Orville G. and Jerome Kagan. 1980. "Constancy and Change: A View of the Issues." Pp. 1-25 in *Constancy and Change in Human Development*, edited by Orville G. Brim and Jerome Kagan. Cambridge: Harvard University Press.

Caspi, Avshalom. 1987. "Personality in the Life Course." *Journal of Personality and Social Psychology* 53:1203-13.

Caspi, Avshalom, Darryl J. Bem, and Glen J. Elder, Jr. 1989. "Continuities and Consequences of Interactional Styles Across the Life Course." *Journal of Personality* 57:375-406.

Cline, Hugh F. 1980. "Criminal Behavior over the Life Span." Pp. 641-74 in *Constancy and*

Change in Human Development, edited by Orville G. Brim and Jerome Kagan. Cambridge: Harvard University Press.

Coleman, James S. 1988. "Social Capital in the Creation of Human Capital." *American Journal of Sociology* 94:S95-120.

Crutchfield, Robert D. 1989. "Labor Stratification and Violent Crime." *Social Forces* 68:489-512.

Dannefer, Dale. 1984. "Adult Development and Social Theory: A Paradigmatic Reappraisal." *American Sociological Review* 49:100-16.

Durkheim, E. 1951. *Suicide* (translated by J. Spaulding and G. Simpson). New York: Free Press.

Elder, Glen H., Jr. 1974. *Children of the Great Depression*. Chicago: University of Chicago Press.

———. 1985. "Perspectives on the Life Course." Pp. 23-49 in *Life Course Dynamics*, edited by Glen H. Elder, Jr. Ithaca, NY: Cornell Univ. Press.

Farrington, David P. 1986. "Stepping Stones to Adult Criminal Careers." Pp. 359-84 in *Development of Antisocial and Prosocial Behavior*, edited by Dan Olweus, Jack Block, and Marian Radke-Yarrow. New York: Academic Press.

———. 1989. "Later Adult Life Outcomes of Offenders and Nonoffenders." Pp. 220-44 in *Children at Risk: Assessment, Longitudinal Research, and Intervention*, edited by M. Brambring, F. Losel, and H. Skowronek. New York: Walter de Gruyter.

Farrington, David P., Bernard Gallagher, Lynda Morley, Raymond J. St. Ledger, and Donald J. West. 1986. "Unemployment, School Leaving, and Crime." *British Journal of Criminology* 26:335-56.

Featherman, David, Dennis Hogan, and Aage Sorenson. 1984. "Entry in Adulthood: Profiles of Young Men in the 1950s." Pp. 160-203 in *Life-Span Development and Behavior*, edited by Paul Baltes and Orville Brim, Jr. Orlando: Academic Press.

Featherman, David and Richard Lerner. 1985. "Ontogenesis and Sociogenesis: Problematics for Theory and Research About Development and Socialization Across the Lifespan." *American Sociological Review* 50:659-76.

Fisher, Joseph and Robert Mason. 1981. "The Analysis of Multicollinear Data in Criminology." Pp. 99-125 in *Methods in Quantitative Criminology*, edited by James A. Fox. New York: Academic.

Gibbens, T.C.N. 1984. "Borstal Boys After 25 Years." *British Journal of Criminology* 24:49-62.

Glueck, Sheldon and Eleanor Glueck. 1950. *Unraveling Juvenile Delinquency*. New York: Commonwealth Fund.

———. 1968. *Delinquents and Nondelinquents in Perspective*. Cambridge: Harvard University Press.

Gottfredson, Michael and Travis Hirschi. 1987. "The Methodological Adequacy of Longitudinal Research on Crime." *Criminology* 25:581-614.

———. 1990. *A General Theory of Crime*. Stanford, CA: Stanford University Press.

Gove, Walter R. 1985. "The Effect of Age and Gender on Deviant Behavior: A Biopsychosocial Perspective." Pp. 115-44 in *Gender and the Life Course*, edited by Alice S. Rossi. New York: Aldine.

Hagan, John. 1989. *Structural Criminology*. New Brunswick, NJ: Rutgers University Press.

Hagan, John and Alberto Palloni. 1988. "Crimes as Social Events in the Life Course: Reconceiving a Criminological Controversy" *Criminology* 26:87-100.

Hirschi, Travis. 1969. *Causes of Delinquency*. Berkeley, CA: University of California Press.

Hirschi, Travis and Michael Gottfredson. 1983. "Age and the Explanation of Crime." *American Journal of Sociology* 89:552-84.

Hogan, Dennis P. 1980. "The Transition to Adulthood as a Career Contingency." *American Sociological Review* 45:261-76.

Huesmann, L. Rowell, Leonard D. Eron, and Monroe M. Lefkowitz. 1984. "Stability of Aggression Over Time and Generations." *Developmental Psychology* 20:1120-34.

Kessler, Ronald and David Greenberg. 1981. *Linear Panel Analysis*. New York: Academic Press.

Knight, B.J., S.G. Osborn, and D. West. 1977. "Early Marriage and Criminal Tendency in Males." *British Journal of Criminology* 17:348-60.

Kornhauser, Ruth. 1978. *Social Sources of Delinquency*. Chicago: University of Chicago Press.

Laub, John H. and Robert J. Sampson. 1988. "Unraveling Families and Delinquency: A Reanalysis of the Gluecks' Data." *Criminology* 26:355-80.

Laub, John H., Robert J. Sampson, and Kenna Kiger. 1990. "Assessing the Potential of Secondary Data Analysis: A New Look at the Gluecks' *Unraveling Juvenile Delinquency* Data." Pp. 244-57 in *Measurement Issues in Criminology*, edited by Kimberly Kempf. New York: Springer-Verlag.

Loeber, Rolf. 1982. "The Stability of Antisocial Child Behavior: A Review." *Child Development* 53:1431-46.

Long, Jancis V.F. and George E. Vaillant. 1984. "Natural History of Male Psychological

Health, XI: Escape from the Underclass." *American Journal of Psychiatry* 141:341-46.

Markus, G. 1979. *Analyzing Panel Data*. Beverly Hills, CA: Sage.

Matsueda, Ross. 1989. "The Dynamics of Moral Beliefs and Minor Deviance." *Social Forces* 68:428-57.

McCord, Joan. 1979. "Some Child-Rearing Antecedents of Criminal Behavior in Adult Men." *Journal of Personality and Social Psychology* 37:1477-86.

———. 1980. "Patterns of Deviance." Pp. 157-65 in *Human Functioning in Longitudinal Perspective*, edited by S.B. Sells, Rick Crandall, Merrill Roff, John S. Strauss, and William Pollin. Baltimore: Williams and Wilkins.

Olweus, Daniel. 1979. "Stability of Aggressive Reaction Patterns in Males: A Review." *Psychological Bulletin* 86:852-75.

Osborn, S.G. 1980. "Moving Home, Leaving London, and Delinquent Trends." *British Journal of Criminology* 20:54-61.

Plewis, Ian. 1985. *Analysing Change: Measurement and Explanation Using Longitudinal Data*. New York: Wiley.

Robins, Lee. 1966. *Deviant Children Grown Up*. Baltimore: Williams and Wilkins.

———. 1978. "Sturdy Childhood Predictors of Adult Antisocial Behaviour." *Psychological Medicine* 8:611-22.

Rutter, Michael. 1988. "Longitudinal Data in the Study of Causal Processes: Some Uses and Some Pitfalls." Pp. 1-28 in *Studies of Psychosocial Risk: The Power of Longitudinal Data*, edited by Michael Rutter. Cambridge: Cambridge University Press.

Sampson, Robert J. and John H. Laub. Forthcoming. *Crime and Deviance Over the Life Course*. New York: Springer-Verlag.

Stolzenberg, Ross and Daniel Relles. 1990. "Theory Testing in a World of Constrained Research Design: The Significance of Heckman's Censored Sampling Bias Correction for Non-experimental Research." *Sociological Methods and Research* 18:395-415.

Vaillant, George E. 1977. *Adaptation to Life*. Boston: Little, Brown, and Co.

Wilson, James Q. and Richard Herrnstein. 1985. *Crime and Human Nature*. New York: Simon and Schuster.

Wolfgang, Marvin, Terrence Thornberry, and Robert Figlio. 1987. *From Boy to Man: From Delinquency to Crime*. Chicago: University of Chicago Press.

19

A Sociological Theory of Criminal Behavior

Edwin H. Sutherland

Differential association, sometimes referred to as learning theory, considers the issue of how criminal or delinquent behavior is acquired. Edwin Sutherland's 1947 classic statement of differential association is the source of this selection.

According to Sutherland, criminal behavior is learned the same way other behaviors are learned. He delineates nine propositions that outline the process of learning criminal behavior. The process involves learning both the techniques and drives necessary for committing the offense. The drives and motives for offending are learned from the definitions concerning whether legal codes are to be obeyed or whether it is acceptable to violate them. The "principle of differential association" indicates that it is when there is an excess of definitions favorable to law violation relative to those unfavorable to law violation that crime occurs. Learning to view laws as favorable or unfavorable to violate is determined by the definitions of the law provided by people with whom an individual associates, which in turn is impacted by the community in which one lives. As Sutherland notes, some groups in society provide more definitions in favor to law violation than other groups do. Variations in crime rates across communities reflect this differential social organization.

The average citizen is confronted by a confusing and conflicting complex of popular beliefs and programs in regard to crime. Some of these are traditions from eighteenth-century philosophy; some are promulgations of special interest groups; and some are blind emotional reactions. Organized and critical thinking in this field is therefore peculiarly difficult and also peculiarly necessary....

... The following statement refers to the process by which a particular person comes to engage in criminal behavior.

1. Criminal behavior is learned.

Negatively, this means that criminal behavior is not inherited, as such; also, the person who is not already trained in crime does not invent criminal behavior, just as a person does not make mechanical inventions unless he has had training in mechanics.

2. Criminal behavior is learned in interaction with other persons in a process of communication.

This communication is verbal in many respects but includes also "the communication of gestures."

3. The principal part of the learning of criminal behavior occurs within intimate personal groups.

Negatively, this means that the impersonal agencies of communication, such as picture shows and newspapers, play a relatively unimportant part in the genesis of criminal behavior.

4. When criminal behavior is learned, the learning includes (a) techniques of committing the crime, which are sometimes very complicated, sometimes very simple; (b) the specific direction of motives, drives, rationalizations, and attitudes.

5. The specific direction of motives and drives is learned from definitions of the legal codes as favorable or unfavorable.

In some societies an individual is surrounded by persons who invariably define the legal codes as rules to be observed, while in others he is surrounded by persons whose definitions are favorable to the violation of the legal codes. In our American society these definitions are almost always mixed and consequently we have culture conflict in relation to the legal codes.

6. A person becomes delinquent because of an excess of definitions favorable to violation of law over definitions unfavorable to violation of law.

This is the principle of differential association. It refers to both criminal and anti-criminal associations and has to do with counteracting forces. When persons become criminal, they do so because of contacts with criminal patterns and also because of isolation from anti-criminal patterns. Any person inevitably assimilates the surrounding culture unless other patterns are in conflict; a Southerner does not pronounce "r" because other Southerners do not pronounce "r." Negatively, this proposition of differential association means that associations which are neutral so far as crime is concerned have little or no effect on the genesis of criminal behavior. Much of the experience of a person is neutral in this sense, e.g., learning to brush one's teeth. This behavior has no negative or positive effect on criminal behavior except as it may be related to associations which are concerned with the legal codes. This neutral behavior is important especially as an occupier of the time of a child so that he is not in contact with criminal behavior during the time he is so engaged in the neutral behavior.

7. Differential associations may vary in frequency, duration, priority, and intensity.

This means that associations with criminal behavior and also associations with anti-criminal behavior vary in those respects. "Frequency" and "duration" as modalities of associations are obvious and need no explanation. "Priority" is assumed to be important in the sense that lawful behavior developed in early childhood may persist throughout life, and also that delinquent behavior developed in early childhood may persist throughout life. This tendency, however, has not been adequately demonstrated, and priority seems to be important principally through its selective influence. "Intensity" is not precisely defined but it has to do with such things as prestige of the source of a criminal or anti-criminal pattern and with emotional reactions related to the associations. In a precise description of the criminal behavior of a person these modalities would be stated in quantitative form and a mathematical ratio can be reached. A formula in this sense has not been developed and the development of such a formula would be extremely difficult.

8. The process of learning criminal behavior by association with criminal and anti-criminal patterns involves all of the mechanisms that are involved in any other learning.

Negatively, this means that the learning of criminal behavior is not restricted to the process of imitation. A person who is seduced, for instance, learns criminal behavior by association but this process would not ordinarily be described as imitation.

9. While criminal behavior is an expression of general needs and values, it is not explained by those general needs and values since non-criminal behavior is an expression of the same needs and values.

Thieves generally steal in order to secure money, but likewise honest laborers work in order to secure money. The attempts by many scholars to explain criminal behavior by general drives and values, such as the happiness principle, striving for social status, the money motive, or frustration, have been and must continue to be futile since they explain lawful behavior as completely as they explain criminal behavior. They are similar to respiration, which is necessary for any behavior but which does not differentiate criminal from non-criminal behavior.

It is not necessary, at this level of explanation, to explain why a person has the associations which he has; this certainly involves a complex of many things. In an area where the delinquency rate is high a boy who is sociable, gregarious, active, and athletic is very likely to come in contact with the other boys in the neighborhood, learn delinquent behavior from them, and become a gangster; in the same neighborhood the psychopathic boy who is isolated, introvert, and inert may remain at home, not become acquainted with the other boys in the neighborhood, and not become delinquent. In another situation, the sociable, athletic, aggressive boy may become a member of a scout troop and not become involved in delinquent behavior. The person's associations are determined in a general context of social organization. A child is ordinarily reared in a family; the place of residence of the family is determined largely by family income; and the delinquency rate is in many respects related to the rental value of the houses. Many other factors enter into this social organization, including many of the small personal group relationships.

The preceding explanation of criminal behavior was stated from the point of view of the person who engages in criminal behavior. It is possible, also, to state theories of criminal behavior from the point of view of the community, nation, or other group. The problem, when thus stated, is generally concerned with crime rates and involves a comparison of the crime rates of various groups or the crime rates of a particular group at different times. One of the best explanations of crime rates from this point of view is that a high crime rate is due to social disorganization. The term "social disorganization" is not entirely satisfactory and it seems preferable to substitute for it the term "differential social organization." The postulate on which this theory is based, regardless of the name, is that crime is rooted in the social organiza-

tion and is an expression of that social organization. A group may be organized for criminal behavior or organized against criminal behavior. Most communities are organized both for criminal and anti-criminal behavior and in that sense the crime rate is an expression of the differential group organization. . . .

Discussion Questions

1. Discuss Sutherland's nine propositions and describe the processes through which he suggests criminal behavior is learned.

2. According to Sutherland's framework, what specifically is meant by the term "differential association"? When does criminal behavior occur? From whom are the definitions favorable to law violation learned? Why are peers an important part of this process?

3. What is differential social organization? What role does it play with regard to learning definitions favorable to law violation?

Reprinted from: Edwin H. Sutherland, "A Sociological Theory of Criminal Behavior." In *Criminology*, 4th Edition, pp. 3, 6-9. Copyright © 1947 by New York: J.B. Lippincott. Reprinted by permission from the Cressey Estate. ◆

20

The Influence of Delinquent Peers: What They Think or What They Do?

Mark Warr
Mark Stafford

Much of the empirical research involving differential association has focused on the role of peers in the learning process. Because of the impreciseness in Sutherland's statement of the theory, and the difficulty in measuring some of his concepts (for example, how does one determine when there is an excess of definitions favorable to law violation?), research has tended to focus on issues related to the frequency, priority, duration, and intensity of differential associations, usually involving peers.

Mark Warr and Mark Stafford, however, examine one of the key components of Sutherland's theory, that of peers' attitudes toward delinquency. They demonstrate, through use of data from the National Youth Survey, that peers' attitudes do have an impact on an individual's delinquency, a finding consistent with differential association. They also find, however, that in some cases, particularly when there is a conflict in peers' attitudes and behavior (such as approval of delinquency but little delinquent behavior), it is peers' behavior rather than their attitudes that affects an individual's delinquent behavior. Overall, Warr and Stafford provide some support for Sutherland's theory of differential association, but they may actually provide more support for social-learning approaches, which argue that the learning

of behavior, not attitudes, is the key component for engaging in delinquency.

Among the most consistent findings of delinquency research is the association between delinquent friends and delinquent behavior. Numerous investigations over several decades have repeatedly found that the more delinquent friends an adolescent has, the more likely he or she is to engage in delinquent behavior (e.g., Akers et al., 1979; Elliott et al., 1985; Erickson and Empey, 1965; Hepburn, 1977; Jensen, 1972; Johnson, 1979; Matsueda and Heimer, 1987; Reiss and Rhodes, 1964; Short, 1957; Tittle et al., 1986; Voss, 1964).

Although the association between delinquent friends and delinquent behavior is well established, the mechanism by which delinquency is socially transmitted remains unclear. The most commonly invoked explanation is Sutherland's theory of differential association, a theory that "has had a massive impact on criminology" (Vold and Bernard, 1986:225). According to this well-known theory, delinquency is learned through intimate social relations among peers, relations in which attitudes, or "definitions," favorable to the violation of law are acquired. In Sutherland's (1947:7) words, "A person becomes delinquent because of an excess of definitions favorable to violation of law over definitions unfavorable to violation of law." To Sutherland, then, the social transmission of delinquency occurs specifically through the dissemination or transference of attitudes about such conduct through peer networks.[1]

Sutherland's theory is appealing because it rightly stresses the importance of peers in adolescent development and culture. Notwithstanding the importance of peers, however, the theory is open to question on at least two grounds. First, the theory assumes that favorable attitudes toward delinquency are a necessary condition for delinquent behavior. Yet the link between attitudes and behavior is notoriously tenuous (e.g., Deutscher, 1973), and it is not difficult to imagine that adolescents commonly engage in delinquent behavior for social or situational reasons without personally condoning or approving of the behavior in which they engage. Moreover, even if pro-delinquent attitudes are a necessary condition for delinquency, it does not follow that they are a sufficient condition. For example, criminologists largely agree that delinquent behavior is dependent on both motivation and opportunity (e.g., Cloward and Ohlin, 1960; Cohen and Felson, 1979). Where opportunities for delinquency are scarce or absent, even the most staunch pro-delinquent attitudes will not be readily transformed into actual behavior.

Second, the most commonly cited evidence for differential association—the association between delinquent peers and delinquent behavior—is at best only indirect evidence for the theory. Although such evidence clearly speaks to the relevance of peers, it says nothing about the mechanism through which delinquency is socially transmitted. More specifically, the association cannot be uniquely construed as evidence of attitude transmission from one adolescent to the next.

Attitudes Versus Actions

Whereas Sutherland's theory emphasizes the *attitudes* of peers in the transmission of delinquency, other theories stress the *behavior* of peers. According to social learning theorists (see especially Akers, 1985), delinquent behavior may be adopted through imitating or modeling the behavior of peers or by observing the positive consequences of the model's behavior (vicarious reinforcement).[2] In contrast to Sutherland's theory, neither of these processes requires the transference of attitudes from the model to the observer. The emphasis on peers' behavior is also present, if often only implicitly, in theories that stress collective behavior, situational inducements, or group process in the production of delinquency (cf. Briar and Piliavin, 1965; Gold, 1970; Liska, 1981; Short and Strodtbeck, 1965).

The central distinguishing feature of Sutherland's theory, then, is its insistence on attitude transference as the mechanism by which delinquency is socially transmitted. Accordingly, the contrast between Sutherland's theory and other theories ultimately comes down to this question: Is delinquency a consequence of what peers think, or what they do? The answer is not evident at this time because investigators have largely failed to distinguish or separately measure the attitudes and behavior of peers or have simply accepted one as a proxy for the other.

In this chapter, we compare the relative effects of peer attitudes and peer behavior on adolescents' own behavior. We first present some preliminary evidence on the question and then expand the analysis to determine whether peer influences operate directly on adolescents' behavior or whether, as Sutherland argues, they are mediated by adolescents' own attitudes. Finally, we examine the congruence between peers' attitudes and behavior as it affects the delinquent behavior of others.

Data and Measures

Our analysis employs data from the National Youth Survey (NYS). The NYS is a five-year panel study of a national probability sample of 1,726 persons aged 11-17 in 1976 (see Elliot and Ageton, 1980). The NYS is especially well suited for our purpose because it contains a unique set of questions concerning both the attitudes and behavior of peers. Unlike most questions about peers, the NYS questions refer to specific, concrete persons rather than some ill-defined set of friends. That is, respondents were asked to individually name the friends they "ran around with," and were instructed to think of those persons in subsequent questions. The first portion of our analysis employs data from wave III of the NYS, which contains data from interviews conducted in 1979 about events that occurred in 1978.[3]

Respondents' own attitudes toward a variety of delinquent acts were measured using the question, "How wrong is it for someone your age to (act)?" (1—not wrong at all, 2—a little bit wrong, 3—wrong, 4—very wrong). To measure friends' attitudes (as perceived by the respondent), respondents were asked whether their friends would approve or disapprove (1—strongly approve, 2—approve, 3—neither approve nor disapprove, 4—disapprove, 5—strongly disapprove) if they (the respondent) were to commit each of a set of delinquent acts. To simplify the analysis that follows, the direction of these two attitude scales has been reversed so that higher scores indicate approval of the acts in question.

Friends' participation in delinquent behavior was measured by this question, "Think of your friends. During the past year, how many of them (act)?" (1—none of them, 2—very few of them, 3—some of them, 4—most of them, 5—all of them). Respondents' own delinquent behavior was measured by the question, "How many times in the last year have you (act)?" Responses were coded as raw frequencies and as rates (number per day, week, or month). The two measures are highly correlated, and for present purposes we employ raw frequencies with the highest category scored as 5+.

Each of the four questions above asked respondents about a set of offenses, but the set varied from one question to the next. Six offenses, however, were common to all four questions. Of the six, three were felonies with extremely low self-reported frequencies (no more than 3% of respondents committed any of the acts). The three offenses that we analyze here—using marijuana, larceny (stealing something worth less than $5), and cheating on school tests—were each committed by a relatively large proportion (from 15% to 42%) of respondents.[4]

Findings

Regression Analysis

Table 20.1 reports some initial evidence on the relative effects of peer behavior and peer attitudes. The table shows, for each offense, the regression of respondents' behavior (RB) on friends' attitudes (FA) and friends' behavior (FB). In each case, the standardized coefficients for friends' attitudes and friends' behavior are both highly significant ($p < .001$). However, the relative effects of the two variables are quite different. The effect of friends' behavior is much more pronounced than that of friends' attitudes, on the order of 2.5 to 5.0 times greater. Accordingly, although the attitudes of friends are clearly important in determining the delinquent behavior of adolescents, the behavior of friends appears to be the dominant factor.

The evidence from Table 20.1 is simple and straightforward, but it leads to a much larger

Table 20.1
Regression of Respondent's Behavior on Friends' Attitudes and Friends' Behavior

CHEATING
$RB = .13^{***}FA + .47^{***}FB$ $R = .54$ $N = 1,577$

MARIJUANA
$RB = .22^{***}FA + .58^{***}FB$ $R = .76$ $N = 1,612$

LARCENY
$RB = .09^{***}FA + .44^{***}FB$ $R = .49$ $N = 1,596$

NOTE: RB = respondent's behavior; FA = friend's attitudes; FB = friend's behavior.
*** $p < .001$.

question. Granted that the attitudes and behavior of friends influence adolescents, how exactly does this process operate? Does the influence of friends operate by altering adolescents' own attitudes and thus, in turn, their behavior? Or do the attitudes and behavior of friends affect adolescents' behavior directly, that is, independently of their own attitudes? As it is conventionally interpreted, Sutherland's theory is quite clear on this matter: The attitudes of friends affect their associates by altering their attitudes. Thus, the theory implies a simple recursive model, that is, $FA \Rightarrow RA \Rightarrow RB$, where RA is respondent's attitude, and FA and RB are as above.

The issue is more complicated however, when it comes to the behavior of friends. On the one hand, it is entirely possible that the behavior of friends influences adolescents by changing their own attitudes toward delinquency, meaning that the effect of peer behavior, like peer attitudes, is mediated by adolescents' attitudes. Recall, however, that the learning mechanisms stipulated by social learning theory are not dependent on attitude transference, suggesting that the effect of peers' behavior may be direct rather than indirect.

Path Models

To investigate these possibilities, we estimated a path model for each offense incorporating four variables: the attitudes and behavior of friends, and respondents' own attitudes and behavior. The models permit not only a direct test of Sutherland's theory, but also an examination of the effects of peer behavior as well as those of peer attitudes.

Figure 20.1 shows the fitted model for each offense.[5] In general, the models are strikingly similar, and they point to a number of conclusions. First, the models portray a more complicated process than Sutherland envisioned, but they are nonetheless consistent with his theory. Friends' attitudes do affect adolescents' behavior, and the effect is mediated almost entirely by adolescents' own attitudes. Friends' attitudes do not have a significant direct effect on respondent's behavior in two of the models and they have only a small direct effect for one offense (marijuana). The transference of attitudes about delinquency through peer networks, then, does appear to play an important part in the production of delinquency.

If the models provide support for Sutherland's theory, however, they also reveal its limitations. Quite apart from the *attitudes* of friends, the *behavior* of friends exerts a strong influence on respondents' behavior. Part of this influence, as we anticipated, is indirect:

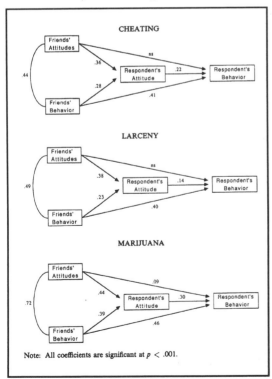

Figure 20.1
*Path Models of Peer Influence
for Three Offenses*

Note: All coefficients are significant at $p < .001$.

The behavior of friends affects adolescents' behavior through their attitudes about delinquency. The effect of peer behavior on respondents' attitude is not as strong as that of peer attitudes, but the effect is nonetheless substantial. Still the single most striking feature of all three models in Figure 20.1 is the strong *direct* effect of peers' behavior on respondent's behavior. No other variable in the models exerts a stronger influence on adolescents' behavior than the behavior of their friends, and the effect of friends' behavior is both direct and substantially greater than that of respondent's attitude or (indirectly) friends' attitudes. Notwithstanding their own attitudes toward delinquency, then, adolescents are strongly influenced by the behavior of their friends. . . .

Congruence Between Peer Behavior and Attitudes

Earlier we noted that delinquent behavior and delinquent attitudes are not necessarily congruent, and we presented evidence that the attitudes and behavior of friends have independent or separable effects on the attitudes and behavior of their associates. Still, the issue of congruence gives rise to some interesting questions. First, is the probability of delinquency enhanced when the attitudes and behavior of one's friends are congruent? Put another way, is the influence of peers greatest when those peers do what they say (or think)? Second, when the attitudes and behavior of friends are inconsistent, which of the two exerts a greater influence on adolescents' behavior? Or does such incongruence cancel or mitigate the influence of peers?

Answering such questions requires some measure of congruence between friends' attitudes and friends' behavior, but constructing such a measure is not as simple as it might appear. The reason is that congruence and incongruence can take different forms, with quite different consequences. In the present case, congruence occurs when friends both approve of and engage in delinquent behavior or when friends disapprove and refrain from such behavior. In the same way, incongruence may take two forms: Friends may approve of delinquent acts but not engage in them, or they may disapprove of such acts but nevertheless commit them.

To capture these distinctions, we first recoiled our measures of friends' attitudes and friends' behavior.[6] We collapsed friends' attitudes into two categories—those who approved of the act (scores 4 and 5) and those who disapproved or were indifferent toward the act (scores 1-3). Likewise, friends' behavior was collapsed into two categories—those who said that "most" or "all" of their friends had committed the act during the past year (scores 4 and 5) and those who said that "none," "very few," or "some" of their friends had done so (scores 1-3). Next, dummy variables were constructed to represent the four combinations of these variables—high approval/high involvement (henceforth *HH*), low approval/low involvement (*LL*), high approval/low involvement (*HL*), and low approval/high involvement (*LH*).

. . . The general features of the are quite similar across the three offenses, and they paint an intriguing picture. First, congruence between the attitudes and behavior of friends does indeed have an effect above and beyond the main effects of the two variables. The coefficient for *HH* is positive and statistically significant in each case.

The most striking features of the models, however, are those that pertain to *in*congruence. The coefficient for *HL* is not statistically significant in any of the models, meaning that there is no significant difference between the *HL* and *LL* groups. In other words, having friends who approve of delinquency has no effect on respondent's behavior when those friends do not also engage in delinquency. On the other hand, the coefficient for *LH* is significant in each case. That is, friends' involvement in delinquency has a significant effect on respondent's behavior even when those friends do not approve or are indifferent toward those acts.

These findings, then, support two conclusions. First, the effect of friends' attitudes and friends' behavior is in fact enhanced when the two are consistent. Friends who behave as well as think in a delinquent fashion produce the most delinquent associates. However, when the attitudes and behavior of peers are inconsistent, the behavior of peers ap-

pears to outweigh or override the attitudes of peers. The actions of peers, it seems, speak louder than their attitudes.

Discussion and Conclusion

The results of our analysis provide both positive and negative evidence for Sutherland's theory of differential association. On the one hand, our findings indicate that attitude transference does indeed play a part in the social transmission of delinquency. The attitudes of adolescents are influenced by the attitudes (and behavior) of their peers, and those attitudes in turn affect delinquency. At the same time, however, our findings suggest that Sutherland's theory is ultimately incomplete. Quite apart from the attitudes of adolescents and those of their friends, the *behavior* of friends has a strong, independent effect on adolescents' behavior.

This finding may appear to be unique, but a careful reading of the literature on differential association over the past several decades shows that we are not the first to come upon this result. In a study of alcohol and marijuana use, Jaquith (1981) found strong effects of both peer use and personal attitudes on adolescents' use of those drugs. However, Jaquith reported the "unexpected" finding that respondent's attitude did *not* mediate the effect of peer behavior. . . . Precisely the same results were reported by Jensen (1972) in a test of differential association theory using data from the Richmond Youth Project. "Association with delinquents and definitions [of delinquency] are independently related to delinquent involvement. . . . It is clear that the effect of the number of delinquent friends on delinquency is not solely a product of socialization into competing normative standards" (1972:568). More recently, Matsueda and Heimer (1987:831) reported that "The number of delinquent friends . . . does have a substantial and statistically significant influence on delinquency," even after controlling for delinquent definitions, attachment to peers and parents, and family structure.[7]

Taken in conjunction with our results, these findings cast serious doubt on the ability of differential association theory to explain fully the influence of delinquent peers.

There can be little doubt that peers are a critical factor in the production of delinquency, but the notion of attitude transference on which differential association theory rests does not appear to be a sufficient explanation of peer influence.

Proponents of differential association may object to that conclusion on the grounds that we have failed to identify the appropriate attitudes or definitions that give rise to delinquent behavior. The meaning of Sutherland's "definitions" has been endlessly debated, but surely an adolescent's approval or disapproval of delinquent acts constitutes one element of such definitions. We note in that connection that our measure of delinquent attitudes is in fact related to delinquency, and it does at least partially mediate the effect of peer behavior. Yet we readily concede that there may be other definitions that fully account for peer influence. But until those definitions are identified and assessed, proponents of differential association cannot claim strong support for the theory.

If our analysis underscores the importance of peer behavior, however, it does not explain exactly how delinquent behavior is transferred or transmitted from one adolescent to the next. As we observed earlier, two of the prime suspects are mechanisms stipulated by social learning theory, that is, imitation and vicarious reinforcement. Measuring these processes in natural settings is likely to prove a difficult task, but several strategies are promising. In addition to questioning adolescents about the delinquent behavior of their friends, investigators should ask questions about the consequences of friends' behavior, both positive (e.g., increases in prestige, friendships, or income) and negative (e.g., social ostracism, arrest) (see Akers et al., 1979, for an example). Such a strategy would not only illuminate the process of vicarious reinforcement, but might also help to integrate differential association and deterrence theory. Although deterrence theorists have scarcely acknowledged the possibility, individuals' perceptions of legal sanctions may be heavily influenced by the perceptions and experiences of their friends. Indeed, the process of general deterrence may be singularly potent within the context of peer networks.

The process of imitation or modeling is more difficult to detect, since there are no external indicia of imitation other than congruence between the model and observer's behavior. The process of modeling might be better understood, however, if investigators were to examine peer influence in domains other than (or in addition to) delinquency, such as school (grades, extracurricular activities), work, and leisure activities. That strategy might help in identifying the most influential models for adolescents and place delinquency within a larger context of social learning.

Finally, investigators should distinguish between adolescents who are merely aware of their friends' behavior and those who have actually witnessed or participated in delinquency with their friends (i.e., as co-offenders). The distinction is critical because it speaks to quite different conceptions of peer influence. To illustrate, whereas differential association emphasizes the learned nature of delinquency, there is nothing in the theory that requires the actual presence of companions in delinquent episodes. By contrast, theories of delinquency that emphasize collective behavior, situational inducements, or group process clearly regard the immediate presence of companions as a necessary stimulus for delinquency. The distinction is no less important for social learning theory, especially if the processes of imitation and vicarious reinforcement are contingent on direct observation of delinquent behavior.

Whatever the mechanism of transmission may ultimately prove to be, our findings suggest that investigators must take care to differentiate the attitudes and behavior of peers in examining the production of delinquency. Sutherland notwithstanding, what peers do appears to be at least as important as what they think.

Discussion Questions

1. According to Warr and Stafford's article, what role do peers' attitudes have for an individual's delinquent behavior? What

role do peers' behaviors have for an individual's delinquent behavior?

2. Do Warr and Stafford consider peers' attitudes or behaviors to be more important overall for an individual's involvement in delinquency? What might be some of the reasons for this?

3. What factor differentiates differential association from social learning approaches? Do Warr and Stafford's results find support for differential association? For social learning approaches?

Notes

1. Differential association is not limited to peer influence; it may be extended to include parents, teachers, and other significant others (see, e.g., Jensen, 1972). Most tests and discussions of the theory, however, have concentrated on peers.

2. Social learning theory contains other mechanisms of learning, including both intrinsic and extrinsic positive and negative reinforcement (Akers, 1985). Imitation and vicarious reinforcement, however, are the two processes that seem to bear most directly on peer influence because they are the most purely *social* mechanisms of learning.

3. Wave III data were the most recent data available at the time this study was undertaken. Waves IV and V have subsequently been released.

4. All of the questions pertaining to marijuana in the NYS refer to both marijuana and hashish. Interviewers were free to use common names ("grass," "pot," "hash") to describe these drugs.

5. All coefficients in the models are significant at $p<.001$. The nonsignificant paths have probabilities $\geq.05$.

6. All analyses in this section are based on wave III data.

7. For another example, see Akers et al., 1979.

References

Akers, Ronald L. 1985. *Deviant Behavior: A Social Learning Approach*. Belmont, Calif: Wadsworth.

Akers, Ronald L., Marvin D. Krohn, Lonn Lanza-Kaduce, and Marcia Radosevich. 1979. "Social learning and deviant behavior: A specific test of a general theory." *American Sociological Review* 44:636–655.

Briar, Scott and Irving Piliavin. 1965. "Delinquency, situational inducements, and commitment to conformity." *Social Problems* 13:35–45.

Cloward, Richard A. and Lloyd E. Ohlin. 1960. *Delinquency and Opportunity*. Glencoe, Ill.: Free Press.

Cohen, Lawrence E. and Marcus Felson. 1979. "Social change and crime rate trends: A routine activity approach." *American Sociological Review* 44:588–608.

Deutscher, Irwin. 1973. *What We Say/What We Do: Sentiments and Acts*. Glencoe, Ill.: Scott, Foresman.

Elliott, Delbert S. and Suzanne S. Ageton. 1980. "Reconciling race and class differences in self-reported and official estimates of delinquency." *American Sociological Review* 45:95–110.

Elliott, Delbert S., David Huizinga, and Suzanne S. Ageton. 1985. *Explaining Delinquency and Drug Use*. Beverly Hills, Calif: Sage.

Erickson, Maynard L. and Lamar T. Empey. 1965. "Class position, peers, and delinquency." *Sociology and Social Research* 49:268–282.

Gold, Martin. 1970. *Delinquent Behavior in an American City*. Belmont, Calif.: Brooks/Cole.

Hepburn, John R. 1977. "Testing alternative models of delinquency causation." *Journal of Criminal Law and Criminology* 67:450–460.

Jaquith, Susan M. 1981. "Adolescent marijuana and alcohol use: An empirical test of differential association theory." *Criminology* 19:271–280

Jensen, Gary F. 1972. "Parents, peers, and delinquent action: A test of the differential association perspective." *American Journal of Sociology* 78:562–575.

Johnson, Richard E. 1979. *Juvenile Delinquency and Its Origins*. New York: Cambridge University Press.

Liska, Allen E. 1981. *Perspectives on Deviance*. Englewood Cliffs, N.J.: Prentice-Hall.

Matsueda,Ross L. and Karen Heimer. 1987. "Race, family structure, and delinquency: A test of differential association and social control theories." *American Sociological Review* 52:826–840.

Paternoster, Raymond. 1987. "The deterrent effect of the perceived certainty and severity of punishment: A review of the evidence and issues." *Justice Quarterly* 4:173–217.

Reiss, Albert J., Jr., and A. Lewis Rhodes. 1964. "An empirical test of differential association theory." *Journal of Research in Crime and Delinquency* 1:5–18.

Short, James F. 1957. "Differential association and delinquency." *Social Problems* 4:233–239.

Short, James F. and Fred L. Strodtbeck. 1965. *Group Process and Gang Delinquency.* Chicago: University of Chicago Press.

Sutherland, Edwin H. 1947. *Criminology.* 4th ed. Philadelphia: Lippincott.

Tittle, Charles R., Mary Jean Burke, and Elton F. Jackson. 1986. "Modeling Sutherland's theory of differential association: Toward an empirical clarification." *Social Forces* 65:405–432.

Vold, George B. and Thomas J. Bernard. 1986. *Theoretical Criminology.* 3rd ed. New York: Oxford University Press.

Voss, Harwin L. 1964. "Differential association and reported delinquency behavior: A replication." *Social Problems* 12:78–85.

Williams, Kirk R. and Richard Hawkins. 1986. "Perceptual research on general deterrence: A critical review." *Law and Society Review* 20(4):545–572.

21

Foundation for a General Strain Theory of Crime and Delinquency

Robert Agnew

Strain theories posit that crime results from attempts to deal with stressful situations, that is, "strain." Although the source of strain varies according to different theorists in this tradition, strain often is considered to be the result of factors or conditions in the larger social structure, such as a disjunction between culturally acceptable goals (e.g., financial success) and socially approved means of achieving these goals (e.g., hard work). It is the individual's responses to such a strain that may result in crime. Robert Agnew, author of this selection, has recently reconceptualized strain theory in social psychological terms.

The extensions of strain theory delineated by Agnew may allow this approach to be a more successful explanation of individual-level criminal and delinquent behavior than earlier versions of strain theory. Agnew's theory goes beyond earlier versions by including a more comprehensive set of strains that may lead to crime or delinquency. Indeed, he argues that there are three major sources of strain. The first is "failure to achieve positively valued goals," which may involve a disjunction between one's aspirations and expectations or actual achievements or a disjunction between just or fair outcomes and actual outcomes. The second is "the removal of positively valued stimuli," such as job loss. The third is "the presentation of negative stimuli," such as adverse situations. In Agnew's framework, the emotion of anger plays a key role. However, criminal behavior does not automatically result when strain is experienced. Instead, Agnew discusses various coping mechanisms—cognitive, behavioral, and emotional—that may be used when strain is experienced so that it does not result in crime. The likelihood of an individual responding to strain by delinquency is related to individual-level factors, such as a person's goals, values or identities, coping resources, and social support.

After dominating deviance research in the 1960s, strain theory came under heavy attack in the 1970s (Bernard, 1984; Cole, 1975), with several prominent researchers suggesting that the theory be abandoned (Hirschi, 1969; Kornhauser, 1978). Strain theory has survived those attacks, but its influence is much diminished (see Agnew, 1985a; Bernard, 1984; Farnworth and Leiber, 1989). In particular, variables derived from strain theory now play a very limited role in explanations of crime/delinquency. Several recent causal models of delinquency, in fact, either entirely exclude strain variables or assign them a small role (e.g., Elliott et al., 1985; Johnson, 1979; Massey and Krohn, 1986; Thornberry, 1987; Tonry et al., 1991). Causal models of crime/delinquency are dominated, instead, by variables derived from differential association/social learning theory and social control theory.

This paper argues that strain theory has a central role to play in explanations of crime/delinquency, but that the theory has to be substantially revised to play this role. Most empirical studies of strain theory continue to rely on the strain models developed by Merton (1938), A. Cohen (1955), and Cloward and Ohlin (1960). In recent years, however, a wealth of research in several fields has questioned certain of the assumptions underlying those theories and pointed to new directions for the development of strain theory. . . . This paper draws on the above literatures, as well as the recent revisions in strain theory, to present the outlines of a general strain theory of crime/delinquency.

The theory is written at the social-psychological level: It focuses on the individual and his or her immediate social environment—although the macroimplications of the theory are explored at various points. . . . This general theory, it will be argued, is capable of overcoming the theoretical and empirical criticisms of previous strain theories and of complementing the crime/delinquency theories that currently dominate the field. . . .

Strain Theory as Distinguished From Control and Differential Association/Social Learning Theory

Strain, social control, and differential association theory are all sociological theories: They explain delinquency in terms of the individual's social relationships. Strain theory is distinguished from social control and social learning theory in its specification of (1) the type of social relationship that leads to delinquency and (2) the motivation for delinquency. First, strain theory focuses explicitly on *negative relationships with others*: relationships in which the individual is not treated as he or she wants to be treated. Strain theory has typically focused on relationships in which others prevent the individual from achieving positively valued goals. Agnew (1985a), however, broadened the focus of strain theory to include relationships in which others present the individual with noxious or negative stimuli. Social control theory, by contrast, focuses on the *absence of significant relationships with conventional others and institutions*. In particular, delinquency is most likely when (1) the adolescent is not attached to parents, school, or other institutions; (2) parents and others fail to monitor and effectively sanction deviance; (3) the adolescent's actual or anticipated investment in conventional society is minimal; and (4) the adolescent has not internalized conventional beliefs. Social learning theory is distinguished from strain and control theory by its focus on *positive relationships with deviant others*. In particular, delinquency results from association with others who (1) differentially reinforce the adolescent's delinquency, (2) model delinquent behavior, and/or (3) transmit delinquent values.

Second, strain theory argues that adolescents *are pressured into delinquency by the negative affective states—most notably anger and related emotions—that often result from negative relationships* (see Kemper, 1978, and Morgan and Heise, 1988, for typologies of negative affective states). This negative affect creates pressure for corrective action and *may* lead adolescents to (1) make use of illegitimate channels of goal achievement, (2) attack or escape from the source of their adversity, and/or (3) manage their negative affect through the use of illicit drugs. Control theory, by contrast, denies that outside forces pressure the adolescent into delinquency. Rather, the absence of significant relationships with other individuals and *groups frees the adolescent to engage in delinquency*. The freed adolescent either drifts into delinquency or, in some versions of control theory, turns to delinquency in response to inner forces or situational inducements (see Hirschi, 1969:31-34). In differential association/social learning theory, the adolescent commits delinquent acts because group forces lead the adolescent to *view delinquency as a desirable or at least justifiable form of behavior* under certain circumstances.

Strain theory, then, is distinguished by its focus on negative relationships with others and its insistence that such relationships lead to delinquency through the negative affect—specially anger—they sometimes engender. . . .

Phrased in the above manner, it is easy to see that strain theory complements the other major theories of delinquency in a fundamental way. While these other theories focus on the absence of relationships or on positive relationships, strain theory is the only theory to focus explicitly on negative relationships. And while these other theories view delinquency as the result of drift or of desire, strain theory views it as the result of pressure.

The Major Types of Strain

Negative relationships with others are, quite simply, relationships in which others are not treating the individual as he or she would like to be treated. The classic strain theories of Merton (1938), A. Cohen (1955), and Cloward and Ohlin (1960) focus on only one type of negative relationship: relationships in which others prevent the individual from achieving positively valued goals. In particular, they focus on the goal blockage experienced by lowerclass individuals trying to achieve monetary success or middle-class status. More recent versions of strain theory have argued that adolescents are not only concerned about the future goals of monetary success/middle-class status, but are also concerned about the achievement of more immediate goals such as good grades, popularity with the opposite sex, and doing well in athletics (Agnew, 1984; Elliott and Voss, 1974; Elliott et al., 1985; Empey, 1982; Greenberg, 1977; Quicker, 1974). The focus, however, is still on the achievement of positively valued goals. Most recently, Agnew (1985a) has argued that strain may result not only from the failure to achieve positively valued goals, but also from the inability to escape legally from painful situations. . . .

Three major types of strain are described—each referring to a different type of negative relationship with others. Other individuals may (1) prevent one from achieving positively valued goals, (2) remove or threaten to remove positively valued stimuli that one possesses, or (3) present or threaten to present one with noxious or negatively valued stimuli. These categories of strain are presented as ideal types. . . .

Strain As the Failure to Achieve Positively Valued Goals

At least three types of strain fall under this category. The first type encompasses most of the major strain theories in criminology, including the classic strain theories of Merton, A. Cohen, and Cloward and Ohlin, as well as those modem strain theories focusing on the achievement of immediate goals. The other two types of strain in this category are derived from the justice/equity literature and have not been examined in criminology.

Strain As the Disjunction Between Aspirations and Expectations/Actual Achievements. The classic strain theories of Merton, A. Cohen, and Cloward and Ohlin argue that the cultural system encourages everyone to pursue the ideal goals of monetary success and/or middle-class status. Lower-class individuals, however, are often prevented from

achieving such goals through legitimate channels. In line with such theories, adolescent strain is typically measured in terms of the disjunction between *aspirations* (or ideal goals) and *expectations* (or expected levels of goal achievement). These theories, however, have been criticized for several reasons (see Agnew, 1986, 1991b; Clinard, 1964; Hirschi, 1969; Kornhauser, 1978; Liska, 1987; also see Bernard, 1984; Farnworth and Leiber, 1989). . . .

As a consequence of these criticisms, several researchers have revised the above theories. The most popular revision argues that there is a youth subculture that emphasizes a variety of immediate goals. . . . This version of strain theory, however, continues to argue that strain stems from the inability to achieve certain ideal goals emphasized by the (sub)cultural system. As a consequence, strain continues to be measured in terms of the disjunction between *aspirations and actual achievements* (since we are dealing with immediate rather than future goals, actual achievements rather than expected achievements may be examined). . . .

Strain As the Disjunction Between Expectations and Actual Achievements. . . . .Here the focus is on the disjunction between *expectations and actual achievements* (rewards), and it is commonly argued that such expectations are existentially based. In particular, it has been argued that such expectations derive from the individual's past experience and/or from comparisons with referential (or generalized) others who are similar to the individual (see Berger et al., 1972, 1983; Blau, 1964; Homans, 1961; Jasso and Rossi, 1977; Mickelson, 1990; Ross et al., 1971; Thibaut and Kelley, 1959). Much of the research in this area has focused on income expectations, although the above theories apply to expectations regarding all manner of positive stimuli. The justice literature argues that the failure to achieve such expectations may lead to such emotions as anger, resentment, rage, dissatisfaction, disappointment, and unhappiness—that is, all the emotions customarily associated with strain in criminology. Further, it is argued that individuals will be strongly motivated to reduce the gap between expectations and achievements—

with deviance being commonly mentioned as one possible option.

Strain as the Disjunction Between Just/Fair Outcomes and Actual Outcomes. . . . A third conception of strain, also derived from the justice/equity literature, makes a rather different argument. It claims that individuals do not necessarily enter interactions with specific outcomes in mind. Rather, they enter interactions expecting that certain distributive justice rules will be followed, rules specifying how resources should be allocated. The rule that has received the most attention in the literature is that of equity. An equitable relationship is one in which the outcome/input ratios of the actors involved in an exchange/allocation relationship are equivalent (see Adams, 1963, 1965; Cook and Hegtvedt, 1983; Walster et al., 1978). Outcomes encompass a broad range of positive and negative consequences, while inputs encompass the individual's positive and negative contributions to the exchange. Individuals in a relationship will compare the ratio of their outcomes and inputs to the ratio(s) of specific others in the relationship. If the ratios are equal to one another, they feel that the outcomes are fair or just. This is true, according to equity theorists, even if the outcomes are low. If outcome/input ratios are not equal, actors will feel that the outcomes are unjust and they will experience distress as a result. Such distress is especially likely when individuals feel they have been underrewarded rather than overrewarded (Hegtvedt, 1990).

The equity literature has described the possible reactions to this distress, some of which involve deviance (see Adams, 1963, 1965; Austin, 1977; Walster et al., 1973, 1978; see Stephenson and White, 1968, for an attempt to recast A. Cohen's strain theory in terms of equity theory). In particular, inequity may lead to delinquency for several reasons—all having to do with the restoration of equity. Individuals in inequitable relationships may engage in delinquency in order to (1) increase their outcomes (e.g., by theft); (2) lower their inputs (e.g., truancy from school); (3) lower the outcomes of others (e.g., vandalism, theft, assault); and/or (4) increase the inputs of others (e.g., by being incorrigible or

disorderly). In highly inequitable situations, individuals may leave the field (e.g., run away from home) or force others to leave the field.[1]

Summary: Strain As the Failure to Achieve Positively Valued Goals. . . .Three types of strain in this category have been listed: strain as the disjunction between (1) aspirations and expectations/actual achievements, (2) expectations and actual achievements, and (3) just/fair outcomes and actual outcomes. Strain theory in criminology has focused on the first type of strain, arguing that it is most responsible for the delinquency in our society. Major research traditions in the justice/equity field, however, argue that anger and frustration derive primarily from the second two types of strain. To complicate matters further, one can list still additional types of strain in this category. Certain of the literature, for example, has talked of the disjunction between "satisfying outcomes" and reality, between "deserved" outcomes and reality, and between "tolerance levels" or minimally acceptable outcomes and reality. . . .

Given these multiple sources of strain, one might ask which is the most relevant to the explanation of delinquency. This is a difficult question to answer given current research. The most fruitful strategy at the present time may be to assume that all of the above sources are relevant—that there are several sources of frustration. . . . One would expect strain to be greatest when several standards were not being met, with perhaps greatest weight being given to expectations and just/fair outcomes.[2]

Strain As the Removal of Positively Valued Stimuli From the Individual

Drawing on the stress literature, then, one may state that a second type of strain or negative relationship involves the actual or anticipated removal (loss) of positively valued stimuli from the individual. . . . The actual or anticipated loss of positively valued stimuli may lead to delinquency as the individual tries to prevent the loss of the positive stimuli, retrieve the lost stimuli or obtain substitute stimuli, seek revenge against those responsible for the loss, or manage the negative affect caused by the loss by taking illicit drugs. . . .

Strain As the Presentation of Negative Stimuli

The literature on stress and the recent psychological literature on aggression also focus on the actual or anticipated presentation of negative or noxious stimuli.[3] . . . Noxious stimuli may lead to delinquency as the adolescent tries to (1) escape from or avoid the negative stimuli; (2) terminate or alleviate the negative stimuli; (3) seek revenge against the source of the negative stimuli or related targets, although the evidence on displaced aggression is somewhat mixed (see Berkowitz, 1982; Bernard, 1990; Van Houten, 1983; Zillman, 1979); and/or (4) manage the resultant negative affect by taking illicit drugs.

A wide range of noxious stimuli have been examined in the literature, and experimental, survey, and participant observation studies have linked such stimuli to both general and specific measures of delinquency—with the experimental studies focusing on aggression. Delinquency/aggression, in particular, has been linked to such noxious stimuli as child abuse and neglect (Rivera and Widom, 1990), criminal victimization (Lauritsen et al., 1991), physical punishment (Straus, 1991), negative relations with parents (Healy and Bonner, 1969), negative relations with peers (Short and Strodtbeck, 1965), adverse or negative school experiences (Hawkins and Lishner, 1987), a wide range of stressful life events (Gersten et al., 1974; Kaplan et al., 1983; Linsky and Straus, 1986; Mawson, 1987; Novy and Donohue, 1985; Vaux and Ruggiero, 1983), verbal threats and insults, physical pain, unpleasant odors, disgusting scenes, noise, heat, air pollution, personal space violations, and high density (see Anderson and Anderson, 1984; Bandura, 1973, 1983; Berkowitz, 1982, 1986; Mueller, 1983). . . .

The Links Between Strain and Delinquency

Three sources of strain have been presented: strain as the actual or anticipated failure to achieve positively valued goals, strain as the actual or anticipated removal of positively valued stimuli, and strain as the actual or anticipated presentation of negative stimuli. While these types are theoretically distinct from one another, they may sometimes overlap in practice. So, for example, the insults of a teacher may be experienced as adverse because they (1) interfere with the adolescent's aspirations for academic success, (2) result in the violation of a distributive justice rule such as equity, and (3) are conditioned negative stimuli and so are experienced as noxious in and of themselves. Other examples of overlap can be given, and it may sometimes be difficult to disentangle the different types of strain in practice. Once again, however, these categories are ideal types and are presented only to ensure that all events with the potential for creating strain are considered in empirical research.

Each type of strain increases the likelihood that individuals will experience one or more of a range of negative emotions. Those emotions include disappointment, depression, and fear. Anger, however, is the most critical emotional reaction for the purposes of the general strain theory. Anger results when individuals blame their adversity on others, and anger is a key emotion because it increases the individual's level of felt injury, creates a desire for retaliation/revenge, energizes the individual for action, and lowers inhibitions, in part because individuals believe that others will feel their aggression is justified (see Averill, 1982; Berkowitz, 1982; Kemper, 1978; Kluegel and Smith, 1986: Ch. 10; Zillman, 1979). Anger, then, affects the individual in several ways that are conducive to delinquency. Anger is distinct from many of the other types of negative affect in this respect, and this is the reason that anger occupies a special place in the general strain theory.[4] It is important to note, however, that delinquency may still occur in response to other types of negative affect—such as despair, although delinquency is less likely in such cases.[5] The experience of negative affect, especially anger, typically creates a desire to take corrective steps, with delinquency being one possible response. Delinquency may be a method for alleviating strain, that is, for achieving positively valued goals, for protecting or retrieving positive stimuli, or for terminating or escaping from negative stimuli. Delinquency may be used to seek revenge; data suggest that vengeful behavior often occurs even when there is no possibility of eliminating the adversity that stimulated it (Berkowitz, 1982). And delinquency may occur as adolescents try to manage their negative affect through illicit drug use (see Newcomb and Harlow, 1986). The general strain theory, then, has the potential to explain a broad range of delinquency, including theft, aggression, and drug use.

Each type of strain may create a *predisposition* for delinquency or function as a *situational event* that instigates a particular delinquent act. . . . Strain creates a predisposition for delinquency in those cases in which it is chronic or repetitive. Examples include a continuing gap between expectations and achievements and a continuing pattern of ridicule and insults from teachers. Adolescents subject to such strain are predisposed to delinquency because (1) nondelinquent strategies for coping with strain are likely to be taxed; (2) the threshold for adversity may be lowered by chronic strains (see Averill, 1982:289); (3) repeated or chronic strain may lead to a hostile attitude—a general dislike and suspicion of others and an associated tendency to respond in an aggressive manner (see Edmunds and Kendrick, 1980:21); and (4) chronic strains increase the likelihood that individuals will be high in negative affect/arousal at any given time (see Bandura, 1983; Bernard, 1990). A particular instance of strain may also function as the situational event that ignites a delinquent act, especially among adolescents predisposed to delinquency. . . .

Adaptations to (Coping Strategies for) Strain

The discussion thus far has focused on the types of strain that might promote delinquency. Virtually all strain theories, however, acknowledge that only *some* strained individuals turn to delinquency. Some effort has been made to identify those factors that determine whether one adapts to strain through delinquency. The most attention has been focused on the adolescent's commitment to legitimate means and association with other strained/ delinquent individuals (see Agnew, 1991b). . . .

Adaptations to Strain

What follows is a typology of the major cognitive, emotional, and behavioral adaptations to strain, including delinquency.

Cognitive Coping Strategies. Several literatures suggest that individuals sometimes cognitively reinterpret objective stressors in ways that minimize their subjective adversity. Three general strategies of cognitive coping are described below; each strategy has several forms. These strategies for coping with adversity may be summarized in the following phrases: "It's not important," "It's not that bad," and "I deserve it." . . .

Ignore/Minimize the Importance of Adversity. The subjective impact of objective strain depends on the extent to which the strain is related to the central goals, values, and/or identities of the individual. As Pearlin and Schooler (1978:7) state, individuals may avoid subjective strain "to the extent that they are able to keep the most strainful experiences within the least valued areas of their life." Individuals, therefore, may minimize the strain they experience by reducing the absolute and/or relative importance assigned to goals/values and identities (see Agnew, 1983; Thoits, 1991a). . . .

Maximize Positive Outcomes/Minimize Negative Outcomes. In the above adaptation, individuals acknowledge the existence of adversity but relegate such adversity to an unimportant area of their life. In a second adaptation, individuals attempt to deny the existence of adversity by maximizing their positive outcomes and/or minimizing their negative outcomes. This may be done in two ways: lowering the standards used to evaluate outcomes or distorting one's estimate of current and/or expected outcomes.

Lowering one's standards basically involves lowering one's goals or raising one's threshold for negative stimuli (see Suls, 1977). Such action, of course, makes one's current situation seem less adverse than it otherwise would be. . . .

In addition to lowering their standards, individuals may also cognitively distort their estimate of outcomes. As Agnew and Jones (1988) demonstrate, many individuals exaggerate their actual and expected levels of goal achievement. In addition to exaggerating positive outcomes, individuals may also minimize negative outcomes—claiming that their losses are small and their noxious experiences are mild.

The self-concept literature discusses the many strategies individuals employ to accomplish such distortions (see Agnew and Jones, 1988; Rosenberg, 1979). Two common strategies, identified across several literatures, are worth noting. In "downward comparisons," individuals claim that their situation is less worse or at least no worse than that of similar others (e.g., Brickman and Bulman, 1977; Gruder, 1977; Pearlin and Schooler, 1978; Suls, 1977). . . . In a second strategy, "compensatory benefits," individuals cast "about for some positive attribute or circumstance within a troublesome situation . . . the person is aided in ignoring that which is noxious by anchoring his attention to what he considers the more worthwhile and rewarding aspects of experience" (Pearlin and Schooler, 1978:6-7). Crime victims, for example, often argue that their victimization benefitted them in certain ways, such as causing them to grow as a person (Agnew, 1985b).

Accept Responsibility for Adversity. Third, individuals may *minimize* the subjective adversity of objective strain by convincing themselves that they *deserve* the adversity they have experienced. There are several possible reasons why *deserved* strain is less adverse than undeserved strain. Undeserved strain may violate the equity principle, challenge one's "belief in a just world" (see Lerner, 1977), and—if attributed to the malicious behavior of another—lead one to fear that it will be repeated in the future. Such reasons may help explain why individuals who make internal attributions for adversity are less distressed than others (Kluegel and Smith, 1986; Mirowsky and Ross, 1990).

Behavioral Coping Strategies. . . .There are two major types of behavioral coping: those that seek to minimize or eliminate the source of strain and those that seek to satisfy the need for revenge.

Maximizing Positive Outcomes/Minimizing Negative Outcomes. Behavioral coping may assume several forms, paralleling each of the major types of strain. Individuals, then, may seek to achieve positively valued goals,

protect or retrieve positively valued stimuli, or terminate or escape from negative stimuli. Their actions in these areas may involve conventional or delinquent behavior. . . .

Vengeful Behavior. Data indicate that when adversity is blamed on others it creates a desire for revenge that is distinct from the desire to end the adversity. A second method of behavioral coping, then, involves the taking of revenge. Vengeful behavior may also assume conventional or delinquent forms, although the potential for delinquency is obviously high. Such behavior may involve efforts to minimize the positive outcomes, increase the negative outcomes, and/or increase the inputs of others (as when adolescents cause teachers and parents to work harder through their incorrigible behavior).

Emotional Coping Strategies. Finally, individuals may cope by acting directly on the negative emotions that result from adversity. Rosenberg (1990), Thoits (1984, 1989, 1990, 1991b), and others list several strategies of emotional coping. They include the use of drugs such as stimulants and depressants, physical exercise and deep-breathing techniques, meditation, biofeedback and progressive relaxation, and the behavioral manipulation of expressive gestures through playacting or "expression work." In all of these examples, the focus is on alleviating negative emotions rather than cognitively reinterpreting or behaviorally altering the situation that produced those emotions. . . . Emotional coping is especially likely when behavioral and cognitive coping are unavailable or unsuccessful.

It should be noted that individuals may employ more than one of the above coping strategies (see Folkman, 1991).

Predicting the Use of Delinquent Versus Nondelinquent Adaptations

The above typology suggests that there are many ways to cope with strain—only some of which involve delinquency. And data from the stress literature suggest that individuals vary in the extent to which they use the different strategies (Compas et al., 1988; Menaghan, 1983; Pearlin and Schooler, 1978). These facts go a long way toward explaining the weak support for strain theory. . . .

The existence of the above coping strategies poses a serious problem for strain theory. If strain theory is to have any value, it must be able to explain the selection of delinquent versus nondelinquent adaptations. . . .

Constraints to Nondelinquent and Delinquent Coping. While there are many adaptations to objective strain, those adaptations are not equally available to everyone. Individuals are constrained in their choice of adaptation(s) by a variety of internal and external factors. The following is a partial list of such factors.

Initial Goals/Values/Identities of the Individual. If the objective strain affects goals/values/identities that are high in absolute and relative importance, and if the individual has few alternative goals/values/identities in which to seek refuge, it will be more difficult to relegate strain to an unimportant area of one's life (see Agnew, 1986; Thoits, 1991a). This is especially the case if the goals/values/identities receive strong social and cultural support (see below). As a result, strain will be more likely to lead to delinquency in such cases.

Individual Coping Resources. A wide range of traits can be listed in this area, including temperament, intelligence, creativity, problem-solving skills, interpersonal skills, self-efficacy, and self-esteem. These traits affect the selection of coping strategies by influencing the individual's sensitivity to objective strains and ability to engage in cognitive, emotional, and behavioral coping (Agnew, 1991a; Averill, 1982; Bernard, 1990; Compas, 1987; Edmunds and Kendrick, 1980; Slaby and Guerra, 1988; Tavris, 1984). . . .

Conventional Social Support. The major types of social support, in fact, correspond to the major types of coping listed above. Thus, there is informational support, instrumental support, and emotional support (House, 1981). Adolescents with conventional social supports, then, should be better able to respond to objective strains in a nondelinquent manner.

Constraints to Delinquent Coping. The crime/delinquency literature has focused on certain variables that constrain delinquent

coping. They include (1) the costs and benefits of engaging in delinquency in a particular situation (Clarke and Comish, 1985), (2) the individual's level of social control (see Hirschi, 1969), and (3) the possession of those "illegitimate means" necessary for many delinquent acts (see Agnew, 1991a, for a full discussion).

Macro-Level Variables. The larger social environment may affect the probability of delinquent versus nondelinquent coping by affecting all of the above factors. First, the social environment may affect coping by influencing the importance attached to selected goals/values/identities. For example, certain ethnographic accounts suggest that there is a strong social and cultural emphasis on the goals of money/status among certain segments of the urban poor. . . .

Second, the larger social environment may affect the individual's sensitivity to particular strains by influencing the individual's beliefs regarding what is and is not adverse. The subculture of violence thesis, for example, is predicated on the assumption that young black males in urban slums are taught that a wide range of provocations and insults are highly adverse. Third, the social environment may influence the individual's ability to minimize cognitively the severity of objective strain. Individuals in some environments are regularly provided with external information about their accomplishments and failings (see Faunce, 1989), and their attempts at cognitively distorting such information are quickly challenged. Such a situation may exist among many adolescents and among those who inhabit the "street-corner world" of the urban poor. Adolescents and those on the street corner live in a very "public world"; one's accomplishments and failings typically occur before a large audience or they quickly become known to such an audience. Further, accounts suggest that this audience regularly reminds individuals of their accomplishments and failings and challenges attempts at cognitive distortion.

Fourth, certain social environments may make it difficult to engage in behavioral coping of a nondelinquent nature. Agnew (1985a) has argued that adolescents often find it difficult to escape legally from negative stimuli, especially negative stimuli encountered in the school, family, and neighborhood. Also, adolescents often lack the resources to negotiate successfully with adults, such as parents and teachers (although see Agnew, 1991a). Similar arguments might be made for others, and they often find it difficult to escape legally from adverse environments—by, for example, quitting their job (if they have a job) or moving to another neighborhood.

The larger social environment, then, may affect individual coping in a variety of ways. And certain groups, such as adolescents and the urban underclass, may face special constraints that make nondelinquent coping more difficult. This may explain the higher rate of deviance among these groups.

Factors Affecting the Disposition to Delinquency. The selection of delinquent versus nondelinquent coping strategies is not only dependent on the constraints to coping, but also on the adolescent's disposition to engage in delinquent versus nondelinquent coping. This disposition is a function of (1) certain temperamental variables (see Tonry et al., 1991), (2) the prior learning history of the adolescent, particularly the extent to which delinquency was reinforced in the past (Bandura, 1973; Berkowitz, 1982), (3) the adolescent's beliefs, particularly the rules defining the appropriate response to provocations (Bernard's, 1990, "regulative rules"), and (4) the adolescent's attributions regarding the causes of his or her adversity. Adolescents who attribute their adversity to others are much more likely to become angry, and as argued earlier, that anger creates a strong predisposition to delinquency. . . .

A key variable affecting several of the above factors is association with delinquent peers. It has been argued that adolescents who associate with delinquent peers are more likely to be exposed to delinquent models and beliefs and to receive reinforcement for delinquency (see especially, Akers, 1985). It may also be the case that delinquent peers increase the likelihood that adolescents will attribute their adversity to others.

The individual's disposition to delinquency, then, may condition the impact of adversity on delinquency. At the same time,

it is important to note that continued experience with adversity may create a disposition for delinquency. This argument has been made by Bernard (1990), Cloward and Ohlin (1960), A. Cohen (1955), Elliott et al. (1979), and others. In particular, it has been argued that under certain conditions the experience of adversity may lead to beliefs favorable to delinquency, lead adolescents to join or form delinquent peer groups, and lead adolescents to blame others for their misfortune. . . .

Conclusion

. . . The general strain theory builds upon traditional strain theory in criminology in several ways. First, the general strain theory points to several new sources of strain. In particular, it focuses on three categories of strain or negative relationships with others: (1) the actual or anticipated failure to achieve positively valued goals, (2) the actual or anticipated removal of positively valued stimuli, and (3) the actual or anticipated presentation of negative stimuli. Most current strain theories in criminology only focus on strain as the failure to achieve positively valued goals, and even then the focus is only on the disjunction between aspirations and expectations/actual achievements. The disjunctions between expectations and achievements and just/fair outcomes and achievements are ignored. The general strain theory, then, significantly expands the focus of strain theory to include all types of negative relations between the individual and others.

Second, the general strain theory more precisely specifies the relationship between strain and delinquency, pointing out that strain is likely to have a cumulative effect on delinquency after a certain threshold level is reached. The theory also points to certain relevant dimensions of strain that should be considered in empirical research, including the magnitude, recency, duration, and clustering of strainful events.

Third, the general strain theory provides a more comprehensive account of the cognitive, behavioral, and emotional adaptations to strain. This account sheds additional light on the reasons why many strained individuals do *not* turn to delinquency, and it may prove useful in devising strategies to prevent and control delinquency. Individuals, in particular, may be taught those nondelinquent coping strategies found to be most effective in preventing delinquency.

Fourth, the general strain theory more fully describes those factors affecting the choice of delinquent versus nondelinquent adaptations. The failure to consider such factors is a fundamental reason for the weak empirical support for strain theory. . . .

Strain theory is the only major theory to focus explicitly on negative relations with others and to argue that delinquency results from the negative affect caused by such relations. As such, it complements social control and differential association/social learning theory in a fundamental way. It is hoped that the general strain theory will revive interest in negative relations and cause criminologists to "bring the bad back in."

Discussion Questions

1. According to Agnew's framework, what are the three major sources of strain? Why is each a potential source of strain?

2. According to Agnew, why may strain lead to crime or delinquency? What are some of the noncriminal responses to strain?

3. What are some of the factors involved in determining whether one's response to strain will be non-criminal or criminal? Why might one choose criminal responses over non-criminal responses and vice versa?

Notes

1. Theorists have recently argued that efforts to restore equity need not involve the specific others in the inequitable relationship. If one cannot restore equity with such specific others, there may be an effort to restore "equity with the world" (Austin, 1977; Stephenson and White, 1968; Walster et al., 1978). That is, individuals who feel they have been inequitably treated may respond by inequitably treating peers. The concept of "equity with the world" has not been the subject of much empirical research, but it is intriguing because it provides a novel explanation for displayed ag-

gression. It has also been argued that individuals may be distressed not only by their own inequitable treatment, but also by the inequitable treatment of others (see Crosby and Gonzalez-Intal, 1984; Walster et al., 1978.) We may have, then, a sort of vicarious strain, a type little investigated in the literature.

2. This strategy assumes that all standards are relevant in a given situation, which may not always be the case. In certain situations, for example, one may make local comparisons but not referential comparisons (see Brickman and Bulman, 1977; Crosby and Gonzales-Intal, 1984). In other situations, social comparison processes may not come into play at all; outcomes may be evaluated in terms of culturally derived standards (see Folger, 1986).

3. Some researchers have argued that it is often difficult to distinguish the presentation of negative stimuli from the removal of positive stimuli (Michael, 1973; Van Houten, 1983; Zillman, 1979). Suppose, for example, that an adolescent argues with parents. Does this represent the presentation of negative stimuli, (the arguing) or the removal of positive stimuli (harmonious relations with one's parents)? The point is a valid one, yet the distinction between the two types of strain still seems useful since it helps ensure that all major types of strain are considered by researchers.

4. The focus on blame/anger represents a major distinction between the general strain theory and the stress literature. The stress literature simply focuses on adversity, regardless of whether it is blamed on another. This is perhaps appropriate because the major outcome variables of the stress literature are inner-directed states, like depression and poor health. When the focus shifts to outer-directed behavior, like much delinquency, a concern with blame/anger becomes important.

5. Delinquency may still occur in the absence of blame and anger (see Berkowitz, 1986; Zillman, 1979). Individuals who accept responsibility for their adversity are still subject to negative affect, such as depression, despair, and disappointment (see Kemper, 1978; Kluegel and Smith, 1986). As a result, such individuals will still feel pressure to take corrective action, although the absence of anger places them under less pressure and makes vengeful behavior much less likely. Such individuals, however, may engage in inner-directed delinquency, such as drug use, and if

suitably disposed, they may turn to other forms of delinquency as well. Since these individuals lack the strong motivation for revenge and the lowered inhibitions that anger provides, it is assumed that they must have some minimal disposition for deviance before they respond to their adversity with outer-directed delinquency (see the discussion of the disposition to delinquency).

References

Adams, J. Stacy. 1963. "Toward an understanding of inequity." *Journal of Abnormal and Social Psychology*, 67:422-436.

——. "Inequity in social exchange". In Leonard Berkowitz (ed.), *Advances in Experimental Social Psychology*. New York: Academic Press.

Agnew, Robert. 1983. "Social class and success goals: An examination of relative and absolute aspirations." *Sociological Quarterly*, 24:435-452.

——. 1984. "Goal achievement and delinquency." *Sociology and Social Research,"* 68:435-451.

——. 1985a. "A revised strain theory of delinquency." *Social Forces*, 64:151-167.

——. 1985b. "Neutralizing the impact of crime." *Criminal Justice and Behavior*, 12:221-239.

——. 1986. "Challenging strain theory: An examination of goals and goal-blockage." Paper presented at the annual meeting of the American Society of Criminology, Atlanta.

——. 1989. "A longitudinal test of the revised strain theory." *Journal of Quantitative Criminology*, 5:373-387.

——. 1990. "The origins of delinquent events: An examination of offender accounts." *Journal of Research in Crime and Delinquency*, 27:267-294.

——. 1991a. "Adolescent resources and delinquency." *Criminology*, 28:535-566.

——. 1991b. "Strain and subculture crime theory." In Joseph Sheley (ed.), *Criminology: A Contemporary Handbook*. Belmont, Calif.: Wadsworth.

Agnew, Robert and Diane Jones. 1988. "Adapting to deprivation: An examination of inflated educational expectations." *Sociological Quarterly*, 29:315-337.

Aiken, Leona S. and Stephen G. West. 1991. *Multiple Regression: Testing and Interpreting Interactions*. Newbury Park, Calif.: Sage.

Akers, Ronald L. 1985. *Deviant Behavior: A Social Learning Approach*. Belmont, Calif.: Wadsworth.

Alves, Wayne M. and Peter H. Rossi. 1978. "Who should get what? Fairness judgments of the distribution of earnings." *American Journal of Sociology*, 84:541-564.

Alwin, Duane F. 1987. "Distributive justice and satisfaction with material well-being." *American Sociological Review*, 52:83-95.

Anderson, Elijah. 1978. *A Place on the Corner*. Chicago: University of Chicago Press.

Anderson, Craig A. and Dona C. Anderson. 1984. "Ambient temperature and violent crime: Tests of the linear and curvilinear hypotheses." *Journal of Personality and Social Psychology*, 46:91-97.

Austin, William. 1977. "Equity theory and social comparison processes." In Jerry M. Suls and Richard L. Miller (eds.), *Social Comparison Processes*. New York: Hemisphere.

Averill, James R. 1982. *Anger and Aggression*. New York: Springer-Verlag.

Avison, William R. and R. Jay Turner. 1988. "Stressful life events and depressive symptoms: Disaggregating the effects of acute stressors and chronic strains." *Journal of Health and Social Behavior*, 29:253 -264.

Bandura, Albert. 1973. *Aggression: A Social Learning Analysis*. Englewood Cliffs, N.J.: Prentice-Hall.

——. 1983. "Psychological mechanisms of aggression." In Russell G. Geen and Edward Donnerstein (eds.), *Aggression: Theoretical and Empirical Reviews*. New York: Academic Press.

——. 1989. "Human agency and social cognitive theory." *American Psychologist*, 44:1175-1184.

Berger, Joseph, Morris Zelditch, Jr., Bo Anderson, and Bernard Cohen. 1972. "Structural aspects of distributive justice: A status-value formulation." In Joseph Berger, Morris Zelditch, Jr., and Bo Anderson (eds.), *Sociological Theories in Progress*. New York: Houghton Mifflin.

Berger, Joseph, M. Hamit Fisck, Robert Z. Norman, and David G. Wagner. 1983. "The formation of reward expectations in status situations." In David M. Messick and Karen S. Cook (eds.), *Equity Theory: Psychological and Sociological Perspectives*. New York: Praeger.

Berkowitz, Leonard. 1978. "Whatever happened to the frustration-aggression hypothesis?" *American Behavioral Scientist*, 21:691-708.

——. 1982. "Aversive conditions as stimuli to aggression." In Leonard Berkowitz (ed.), *Advances in Experimental Social Psychology*. Vol. 15. New York: Academic Press.

——. 1986. *A Survey of Social Psychology*. New York: Holt, Rinehart & Winston.

Bernard, Thomas J. 1984. "Control criticisms of strain theories: An assessment of theoretical and empirical adequacy." *Journal of Research in Crime and Delinquency*, 21:353-372.

——. 1987. "Testing structural strain theories." *Journal of Research in Crime and Delinquency*, 24:262-280.

——. 1990. "Angry aggression among the 'truly disadvantaged'." *Criminology,* 28:73-96.

Blau, Peter. 1964. *Exchange and Power in Social Life.* New York: John Wiley & Sons.

Brewin, Chris R. 1988. "Explanation and adaptation in adversity." In Shirley Fisher and James Reason (eds.), *Handbook of Life Stress, Cognition and Health.* Chichester, England: John Wiley & Sons.

Brickman, Philip and Ronnie Janoff Bulman. 1977. "Pleasure and pain in social comparison." In Jerry M. Suis and Richard L. Miller (eds.), *Social Comparison Processes.* New York: Hemisphere.

Clarke, Ronald V. and Derek B. Cornish. 1985. "Modeling offenders' decisions: A framework for research and policy." In Michael Tonry and Norval Morris (eds.), *Crime and Justice: An Annual Review of Research.* Vol. 6. Chicago: University of Chicago Press.

Clinard, Marshall B. 1964. *Anomie and Deviant Behavior.* New York: Free Press.

Cloward, Richard A. and Lloyd E. Ohlin. 1960. *Delinquency and Opportunity.* New York: Free Press.

Cohen, Albert K. 1955. *Delinquent Boys.* New York: Free Press.

——. 1965. "The sociology of the deviant act: Anomie theory and beyond." *American Sociological Review,* 30:5-14.

Cohen, Ronald L. 1982. "Perceiving justice: An attributional perspective." In Jerald Greenberg and Ronald L. Cohen (eds.), *Equity and Justice in Social Behavior.* New York: Academic Press.

Cole, Stephen. 1975. "The growth of scientific knowledge: Theories of deviance as a case study." In Lewis A. Coser (ed.), *The Idea of Social Structure: Papers in Honor of Robert K. Merton.* New York: Harcourt Brace Jovanovich.

Compas, Bruce E. 1987. "Coping with stress during childhood and adolescence." *Psychological Bulletin,* 101:393-403.

Compas, Bruce E., Vanessa L. Maicame, and Karen M. Fondacaro. 1988. "Coping with stressful events in older children and young adolescents." *Journal of Consulting and Clinical Psychology,* 56:405-411.

Compas, Bruce E. and Vicky Phares. 1991. "Stress during childhood and adolescence: Sources of risk and vulnerability." In E. Mark Cummings, Anita L. Greene, and Katherine H. Karraker (eds.), *Life-Span Developmental Psychology: Perspectives on Stress and Coping.* Hillsdale, N.J.: Lawrence Eribaum.

Cook, Karen S., and Karen A. Hegtvedt. 1983. "Distributive justice, equity, and equality." *Annual Review of Sociology,* 9:217-241.

——. 1991. "Empirical evidence of the sense of justice." In Margaret Gruter, Roger D. Masters, Michael T. McGuire (eds.), *The Sense of Justice: An Inquiry into the Biological Foundations of Law.* New York: Greenwood Press.

Cook, Karen S. and David Messick. 1983. "Psychological and sociological perspectives on distributive justice: Convergent, divergent, and parallel lines." In David M. Messick and Karen S. Cook (eds.), *Equity Theory: Psychological and Sociological Perspectives.* New York: Praeger.

Cook, Karen S. and Toshio Yamagishi. 1983. "Social determinants of equity judgments: The problem of multidimensional input." In David M. Messick and Karen S. Cook (eds.), *Equity Theory: Psychological and Sociological Perspectives.* New York: Praeger.

Crittenden, Kathleen S. 1983. "Sociological aspects of attribution." *Annual Review of Sociology,* 9:425-446.

——. 1989. "Causal attribution in sociocultural context: Toward a self-presentational theory of attribution processes." *Sociological Quarterly,* 30:1-14.

Crosby, Faye and A. Miren Gonzales-Intal. 1984. "Relative deprivation and equity theories: Felt injustice and the undeserved benefits of others." In Robert Folger (ed.), *The Sense on Injustice: Social Psychological Perspectives.* New York: Plenum.

Cummings, E. Mark and Mona El-Sheikh. 1991. "Children's coping with angry environments: A process-oriented approach." In E. Mark Cummings, Anita L. Greene, and Katherine H. Karraker (eds.), *Life-Span Developmental Psychology: Perspectives on Stress and Coping.* Hillsdale, N.J.: Lawrence Eribaum.

Della Fave, L. Richard. 1974. "Success values: Are they universal or class-differentiated?" *American Journal of Sociology,* 80:153-169.

——. 1980. "The meek shall not inherit the earth: Self-evaluations and the legitimacy of stratification." *American Sociological Review,* 45:955-971.

Della Fave, L. Richard and Patricia Klobus. 1976. "Success values and the value stretch: A biracial comparison." *Sociological Quarterly,* 17:491-502.

Deutsch, Morton. 1975. "Equity, equality, and need: What determines which value will be used as the basis of distributive justice." *Journal of Social Issues,* 31:137-149.

Dohrenwend, Bruce P. 1974. "Problems in defining and sampling the relevant population of stressful life events." In Barbara Snell Dohrenwend and Bruce P. Dohrenwend (eds.), *Stress-*

ful Life Events: Their Nature and Effects. New York: John Wiley & Sons.

Dohrenwend, Barbara Snell and Bruce P. Dohrenwend. 1974. "Overview and prospects for research on stressful life events." In Barbara Snell Dohrenwend and Bruce P. Dohrenwend (eds.), *Stressful Life Events: Their Nature and Effects*. New York: John Wiley & Sons.

Donnerstein, Edward and Elaine Hatfield. 1982. "Aggression and equity." In Jerald Greenberg and Ronald L. Cohen (eds.), *Equity and Justice in Social Behavior*. New York: Academic Press.

Edmunds, G. and D.C. Kendrick. 1980. *The Measurement of Human Aggressiveness*. New York: John Wiley & Sons.

Elliott, Delbert and Harwin Voss. 1974. *Delinquency and Dropout*. Lexington, Mass.: Lexington Books.

Elliott, Delbert, Suzanne Ageton, and Rachel Canter. 1979. "An integrated theoretical perspective on delinquent behavior." *Journal of Research in Crime and Delinquency*, 16:3-27.

Elliott, Delbert, David Huizinga, and Suzanne Ageton. 1985. *Explaining Delinquency and Drug Use*. Beverly Hills, Calif.: Sage.

Empey, LaMar. 1956. "Social class and occupational aspiration: A comparison of absolute and relative measurement." *American Sociological Review*, 21:703-709.

——. 1982. *American Delinquency: Its Meaning and Construction*. Homewood, Ill.: Dorsey.

Farnworth, Margaret and Michael J. Leiber. 1989. "Strain theory revisited: Economic goals, educational means, and delinquency." *American Sociological Review*, 54:263-274.

Faunce, William A. 1989. "Occupational status-assignment systems: The effect of status on self-esteem." *American Journal of Sociology*, 95:378-400.

Folger, Robert. 1984. "Emerging issues in the social psychology of justice." In Robert Folger (ed.), *The Sense of Injustice: Social Psychological Perspectives*. New York: Plenum.

——. 1986. "Rethinking equity theory: A referent cognitions model." In Hans Wemer Bierhoff, Ronald L. Cohen, and Jerald Greenberg (eds.), *Justice in Social Relations*. New York: Plenum.

Folkman, Susan. 1991. "Coping across the life-span: Theoretical issues." In E. Mark Cummings, Anita L. Greene, and Katherine H. Karraker (eds.), *Life-Span Developmental Psychology: Perspectives on Stress and Coping*. Hillsdale, N.J.: Lawrence Eribaum.

Garrett, James and William L. Libby, Jr. 1973. "Role of intentionality in mediating responses to inequity in the dyad." *Journal of Personality and Social Psychology*, 28:21-27.

Gersten, Joanne C., Thomas S. Langer, Jeanne G. Eisenberg, and Lida Ozek. 1974. "Child behavior and life events: Undesirable change or change per se." In Barbara Snell Dohrenwend and Bruce P. Dohrenwend (eds.), *Stressful Life Events: Their Nature and Effects*. New York: John Wiley & Sons.

Gersten, Joanne C., Thomas S. Langer, Jeanne G. Eisenberg, and Ora Smith-Fagon. 1977. "An evaluation of the etiological role of stressful life-change events in psychological disorders." *Journal of Health and Social Behavior*, 18:228-244.

Greenberg, David F. 1977. "Delinquency and the age structure of society." *Contemporary Crises*, 1:189-223.

Gruder, Charles L. 1977. "Choice of comparison persons in evaluating oneself. In Jerry M. Suis and Richard L. Miller (eds.), *Social Comparison Processes*. New York: Hemisphere.

Hawkins, J. David and Denise M. Lishner. 1987. "Schooling and delinquency." In Elmer H. Johnson (ed.), *Handbook on Crime and Delinquency Prevention*. New York: Greenwood.

Healy, William and Augusta F. Bonner. 1969. *New Light on Delinquency and Its Treatment*. New Haven, Conn.: Yale University Press.

Hegtvedt, Karen A. 1987. "When rewards are scarce: Equal or equitable distributions." *Social Forces*, 66:183-207.

——. 1990. "The effects of relationship structure on emotional responses to inequity." *Social Psychology Quarterly*, 53:214-228.

——. 1991a. "Justice processes." In Martha Foschi and Edward J. Lawler (eds.), *Group Processes: Sociological Analyses*. Chicago: Nelson-Hall.

1991b. "Social comparison processes." In Edgar F. Borgotta and Marie E. Borgotta (eds.), *Encyclopedia of Sociology*. New York: Macmillan.

Hirschi, Travis. 1969. *Causes of Delinquency*. Berkeley: University of California Press.

——. 1979. "Separate and unequal is better." *Journal of Research in Crime and Delinquency*, 16:34-38.

Hirschi, Travis and Michael Gottfredson. 1986. "The distinction between crime and criminality." In Timothy F. Hartnagel and Robert A. Silverman (eds.), *Critique and Explanation*. New Brunswick, N.J.: Transaction Books.

Hochschild, Jennifer L. 1981. *What's Fair: American Beliefs about Distributive Justice*. Cambridge, Mass.: Harvard University Press.

Homans, George C. 1961. *Social Behavior: Its Elementary Forms*. New York: Harcourt, Brace and World.

House, James S. 1981. *Work Stress and Social Support*. Reading, Mass.: Addison-Wesley.

Hyman, Herbert. 1953. "The value systems of the different classes: A social-psychological contribution to the analysis of stratification." In Reinhard Bendix and Seymour Martin Lipset (eds.), *Class, Status, and Power*. New York: Free Press.

Jasso, Guillermina. 1980. "A new theory of distributive justice." *American Sociological Review*, 45:3-32.

Jasso, Guillermina and Peter H. Rossi. 1977. "Distributive justice and earned income." *American Sociological Review*, 42:639-651.

Jensen, Gary. 1986. "Dis-integrating integrated theory: A critical analysis of attempts to save strain theory." Paper presented at the annual meeting of the American Society of Criminology, Atlanta.

Johnson, Richard E. 1979. "Juvenile Delinquency and Its Origins." London: Cambridge University Press.

Kaplan, Howard B. 1980. *Deviant Behavior in Defense of Self*. New York: Academic Press.

Kaplan, Howard B., Cynthia Robbins, and Steven S. Martin. 1983. "Toward the testing of a general theory of deviant behavior in longitudinal perspective: Patterns of psychopathology." In James R. Greenley and Roberta G. Simmons (eds.), *Research in Community and Mental Health*. Greenwich, Conn.: Jai Press.

Kemper, Theodore D. 1978. *A Social Interactional Theory of Emotions*. New York: John Wiley & Sons.

Kluegel, James R. and Eliot R. Smith. 1986. *Beliefs about Inequality*. New York: Aldine De Gruyter.

Kornhauser, Ruth Rosner. 1978. *Social Sources of Delinquency*. Chicago: University of Chicago Press.

Labouvie, Erich W. 1986a. "Alcohol and marijuana use in relation to adolescent stress." *International Journal of the Addictions*, 21:333-345.

——. 1986b. "The coping function of adolescent alcohol and drug use." In Rainer K. Silbereisen, Klaus Eyfeth and Georg Rudinger (eds.), *Development as Action in Context*." New York: Springer.

Lauritsen, Janet L., Robert J. Sampson, and John Laub. 1991. "The link between offending and victimization among adolescents." *Criminology*, 29:265-292.

Lerner, Melvin J. 1977. "The justice motive: Some hypotheses as to its origins and forms." *Journal of Personality*, 45:1-52.

Leventhal, Gerald S. 1976. "The distribution of rewards and resources in groups and organizations." In Leonard Berkowitz and Elaine Walster (eds.), *Advances in Experimental Social Psychology: Equity Theory: Toward a General Theory of Social Interaction*. New York: Academic Press.

Leventhal, Gerald S., Jurgis Karuzajar, and William Rick Fry. 1980. "Beyond fairness: A theory of allocation preferences." In Gerald Mikula (ed.), *Justice and Social Interaction*. New York: Springer-Verlag.

Lind, E. Allan and Tom R. Tyler. 1988. *The Social Psychology of Procedural Justice*. New York: Plenum.

Linsky, Arnold S. and Murray A. Straus. 1986. *Social Stress in the United States*. Dover, Mass.: Auburn House.

Liska, Allen E. 1987. *Perspectives on Deviance*. Englewood Cliffs, N.J.: Prentice-Hall.

McClelland, Katherine. 1990. "The social management of ambition." *Sociological Quarterly*, 31:225-251.

MacLeod, Jay. 1987. *Ain't No Makin' It*. Boulder, Colo.: Westview Press.

Mark, Melvin M. and Robert Folger. 1984. "Responses to relative deprivation: A conceptual framework." In Philip Shaver (ed.), *Review of Personality and Social Psychology. Vol. 5*. Beverly Hills, Calif.: Sage.

Martin, Joanne. 1986. "When expectations and justice do not coincide: Blue collar visions of a just world." In Hans Weiner Bierhoff, Ronald L. Cohen, and Jerald Greenberg (eds.), *Justice in Social Relations*. New York: Plenum.

Martin, Joanne and Alan Murray. 1983. "Distributive injustice and unfair exchange." In David M. Messick and Karen S. Cook (eds.), *Equity Theory: Psychological and Social Perspectives*. New York: Praeger.

——. 1984. "Catalysts for collective violence: The importance of a psychological approach." In Robert Folger (ed.), *The Sense of Injustice: Social Psychological Perspectives*. New York: Plenum.

Massey, James L. and Marvin Krohn. 1986. "A longitudinal examination of an integrated social process model of deviant behavior." *Social Forces*, 65:106-134.

Mawson, Anthony R. 1987. *Criminality: A Model of Stress-Induced Crime*. New York: Praeger.

Menaghan, Elizabeth. 1982. "Measuring coping effectiveness: A panel analysis of marital problems and coping efforts." *Journal of Health and Social Behavior*, 23:220-234.

——. 1983. "Individual coping efforts: Moderators of the relationship between life stress and mental health outcomes." In Howard B. Kaplan (ed.), *Psychosocial Stress: Trends in Theory and Research.* New York: Academic Press.

Merton, Robert. 1938. "Social structure and anomie." *American Sociological Review*, 3:672-682.

Messick, David M. and Keith Sentis. 1979. "Fairness and preference." *Journal of Experimental Social Psychology*, 15:418-434.

——. 1983. "Fairness, preference, and fairness biases." In David M. Messick and Karen S. Cook (eds.), *Equity Theory: Psychological and Sociological Perspectives.* New York: Praeger.

Michael, Jack. 1973. "Positive and negative reinforcement, a distinction that is no longer necessary; or a better way to talk about bad things." In Eugene Ramp and George Semb (eds.), *Behavior Analysis: Areas of Research and Application.* Englewood Cliffs, N.J.: Prentice-Hall.

Mickelson, Roslyn Arlin. 1990. "The attitude-achievement paradox among black adolescents." *Sociology of Education*, 63:44-61.

Mikula, Gerold. 1980. *Justice and Social Interaction.* New York: Springer-Veriag.

——. 1986. "The experience of injustice: Toward a better understanding of its phenomenology." In Hans Wemer Bierhoff, Ronald L. Cohen, and Jerald Greenberg (eds.), *Justice in Social Relations.* New York: Plenum.

Mirowsky, John and Catherine E. Ross. 1990. "The consolation-prize theory of alienation." *American Journal of Sociology*, 95:1505-1535.

Morgan, Rick L. and David Heise. 1988. "Structure of emotions." *Social Psychology Quarterly*, 51:19-31.

Mueller, Charles W. 1983. "Environmental stressors and aggressive behavior." In Russell G. Geen and Edward I. Donnerstein (eds.), *Aggression: Theoretical and Empirical Reviews.* Vol. 2. New York: Academic Press.

Newcomb, Michael D. and L. L. Harlow. 1986. "Life events and substance use among adolescents: Mediating effects of perceived loss of control and meaninglessness in life." *Journal of Personality and Social Psychology*, 51:564-577.

Novy, Diane M. and Stephen Donohue. 1985. "The relationship between adolescent life stress events and delinquent conduct including conduct indicating a need for super-vision." *Adolescence*, 78:313-321.

Pearlin, Leonard I. 1982. "The social contexts of stress." In Leo Goldberger and Shlomo Berznitz (eds.), *Handbook of Stress.* New York: Free Press.

——. 1983. "Role strains and personal stress." In Howard Kaplan (ed.), *Psychosocial Stress: Trends in Theory and Research.* New York: Academic Press.

Pearlin, Leonard I. and Carmi Schooler. 1978. "The structure of coping." *Journal of Health and Social Behavior*, 19:2-21.

Pearlin, Leonard I. and Morton A. Lieberman. 1979. "Social sources of emotional distress." In Roberta G. Simmons (cd.), *Research in Community and Mental Health. Vol. I.* Greenwich, Conn.: Jai Press.

Pearlin, Leonard I., Elizabeth G. Menaghan, Morton A. Lieberman, and Joseph T. Mullan. 1981. "The stress process." *Journal of Health and Social Behavior*, 22:337-356.

Quicker, John. 1974. "The effect of goal discrepancy on delinquency." *Social Problems*, 22:76-86.

Rivera, Beverly and Cathy Spatz Widom. 1990. "Childhood victimization and violent offending." *Violence and Victims*, 5:19-35.

Rosenberg, Morris. 1979. *Conceiving the Self.* New York: Basic.

——. 1990. "Reflexivity and emotions." *Social Psychology Quarterly*, 53:3-12.

Ross, Michael, John Thibaut, and Scott Evenback. 1971. "Some determinants of the intensity of social protest." *Journal of Experimental Social Psychology*, 7:401-418.

Schwinger, Thomas. 1980. "Just allocations of goods: Decisions among three principles." In Gerald Mikula (ed.), *Justice and Social Interaction.* New York: Springer-Verlag.

Shepelak, Norma J. 1987. "The role of self-explanations and self-evaluations in legitimating inequality." *American Sociological Review*, 52:495-503.

Shepelak, Norma J. and Duane Alwin. 1986. "Beliefs about inequality and perceptions of distributive justice." *American Sociological Review*, 51:30-46.

Short, James F. and Fred L. Strodtbeck. 1965. *Group Process and Gang Delinquency.* Chicago: University of Chicago Press.

Slaby, Ronald G. and Nancy G. Guerra. 1988. "Cognitive mediators of aggression in adolescent offenders: 1." *Developmental Psychology*, 24:580-588.

Sprecher, Susan. 1986. "The relationship between inequity and emotions in close relationships." *Social Psychology Quarterly*, 49:309-321.

Stephenson, G.M. and J.H. White. 1968. "An experimental study of some effects of injustice on children's moral behavior." *Journal of Experimental Social Psychology*, 4:460-469.

Straus, Murray. 1991. "Discipline and deviance: Physical punishment of children and violence and other crimes in adulthood." *Social Problems*, 38:133-154.

Sullivan, Mercer L. 1989. *Getting Paid*. Ithaca, N.Y.: Cornell University Press.

Suls, Jerry M. 1977. "Social comparison theory and research: An overview from 1954." In Jerry M. Suls and Richard L. Miller (eds.), *Social Comparison Processes*. New York: Hemisphere.

Suls, Jerry M. and Thomas Ashby Wills. 1991. *Social Comparison: Contemporary Theory and Research*. Hillsdale, N.J.: Lawrence Erlbaum.

Tavris, Carol. 1984. "On the wisdom of counting to ten." In Philip Shaver (ed.), *Review of Personality and Social Psychology: 5*. Beverly Hills, Calif.: Sage.

Thibaut, John W. and Harold H. Kelley. 1959. "The Social Psychology of Groups." New York: John Wiley & Sons.

Thoits, Peggy. 1983. "Dimensions of life events that influence psychological distress: An evaluation and synthesis of the literature." In Howard B. Kaplan (ed.), *Psychosocial Stress: Trends in Theory and Research*. New York: Academic Press.

——. 1984. "Coping, social support, and psychological outcomes: The central role of emotion." In Philip Shaver (ed.), *Review of Personality and Social Psychology*: 5. Beverly Hills, Calif.: Sage.

——. 1989. "The sociology of emotions." In W. Richard Scott and Judith Blake (eds.), *Annual Review of Sociology. Vol. 15*. Palo Alto, Calif.: Annual Reviews.

——. 1990. "Emotional deviance research." In Theodore D. Kemper (ed.), *Research Agendas in the Sociology of Emotions*. Albany: State University of New York Press.

——. 1991a. "On merging identity theory and stress research." *Social Psychology Quarterly*, 54:101-112.

——. 1991b. "Patterns of coping with controllable and uncontrollable events." In E. Mark Cummings, Anita L. Greene, and Katherine H. Karraker (eds.), *Life-Span Developmental Psychology: Perspectives on Stress and Coping*. Hillsdale, N.J.: Lawrence Erlbaum.

Thornberry, Terence P. 1987. "Toward an Interactional Theory of Delinquency." *Criminology*, 25:863-891.

Tonry, Michael, Lloyd E. Ohlin, and David P. Farrington. 1991. *Human Development and Criminal Behavior*. New York: Springer-Verlag.

Tornblum, Kjell Y. 1977. "Distributive justice: Typology and propositions." *Human Relations*, 30:1-24.

Utne, Mary, Kristine and Robert Kidd. 1980. "Equity and attribution." In Gerald Mikula (ed.), *Justice and Social Interaction*. New York: Springer-Verlag.

Van Houten, Ron. 1983. "Punishment: From the animal laboratory to the applied setting." In Saul Axelrod and Jack Apsche (eds.), *The Effects of Punishment on Human Behavior*. New York: Academic Press.

Vaux, Alan. 1988. *Social support: Theory, Research, and Intervention*. New York: Praeger.

Vaux, Alan and Mary Ruggiero. 1983. "Stressful life change and delinquent behavior." *American Journal of Community Psychology*, 11:169-183.

Walster, Elaine, Ellen Berscheid, and G. William Waister. 1973. "New directions in equity research." *Journal of Personality and Social Psychology*, 25:151-176.

Walster, Elaine, G. William Waister, and Ellen Berscheid. 1978. *Equity: Theory and Research*. Boston: Allyn & Bacon.

Wang, Alvin Y. and R. Stephen Richarde. 1988. "Global versus task-specific measures of self-efficacy." *Psychological Record*, 38:533-541.

Weiner, Bernard. 1982. "The emotional consequences of causal attributions." In Margaret S. Clark and Susan T. Fiske (eds.), *Affect and Cognition: The Seventeenth Annual Carnegie Symposium on Cognition*. Hillsdale, N.J.: Lawrence Erlbaum.

Williams, Carolyn L. and Craige Uchiyama. 1989. "Assessment of life events during adolescence: The use of self-report inventories." *Adolescence*, 24:95-118.

Wylie, Ruth. 1979. *The Self-Concept. Vol. 2*. Lincoln: University of Nebraska Press.

Zillman, Dolf. 1979. *Hostility and Aggression*. Hillsdale, N.J.: Lawrence Erlbaum.

22

General Strain Theory and Delinquency: A Replication and Extension

Raymond Paternoster
Paul Mazerolle

Although Agnew's general strain theory has only recently been developed, research is beginning to examine the utility of his approach for explaining crime and delinquency. The results suggest that this framework has much potential, but may require some modifications. This selection, by Raymond Paternoster and Paul Mazerolle, is one example of an empirical test of Agnew's strain theory.

Paternoster and Mazerolle have conducted what is perhaps the most comprehensive test of general strain theory to date. They examine different types of strain, particularly the presentation of negative stimuli, and a measure of "traditional" strain involving a disjunction between aspirations and expectations. In addition, they include measures of social control and differential association to determine if strain theory still has important effects on delinquency once these factors are taken into account. The main finding is that some elements of general strain theory help explain crime and delinquency. In particular, strain related to adverse stimuli or life events is associated with greater involvement in delinquency. Paternoster and Mazerolle also demonstrate that general strain theory is important for explaining delinquency even when considering the effects of social control and differential association, with strain weakening social bonds and in-

creasing associations with delinquent peers. However, as these scholars note, the empirical evidence does not provide unequivocal support for strain theory. In addition, they were unable to test some of strain theory's key elements, particularly the roles of anger and frustration as responses to strain.

In recent years, sociologists and criminologists have been witness to a host of theoretical rebirths, including ecological theory (Bursik and Webb 1982; Heitgard and Bursik 1987; Bursik 1988; Smith and Jarjoura 1988; Sampson and Groves 1989), utility-based theories (Cornish and Clarke 1986), and labeling theory (Link 1982, 1987; Link, Cullen, Frank, and Wozniak 1987; Link, Cullen, Struening, Shrout, and Dohrenwend 1989; Matsueda 1992). In addition to these, there has been a recent theoretical revitalization of Merton's classic strain theory of delinquency.

In a series of articles, Agnew has presented a revised version of strain theory that includes, but in important ways goes beyond, the original strain formulation (Merton 1938; Agnew 1985, 1989, 1992; Agnew and White 1992). Rather than one source of strain, Agnew suggested three. In addition, he has conducted a detailed set of studies, which provided some empirical support for his theory and seemed to indicate that previous dismissals of strain theory may have been premature. Agnew's revitalized version of strain, general strain theory (GST), may therefore be a potentially important theoretical restatement that promises to complement extant criminological theory. . . .

Traditional and General Strain Theory

Traditional Strain Theories

In what we will call traditional strain theory, youths are motivated to commit delinquent acts because they have failed to achieve desired goals, such as middle-class status (Cohen 1955) or economic status (Merton 1938; Cloward and Ohlin 1960). In operationalizing this type of strain, most researchers have measured it in terms of conventional aspirations, conventional expectations, or as a discrepancy between the two (Gold 1963; Hirschi 1969; Liska 1971; Elliott and Voss 1974; Quicker 1974; Johnson 1979). Moreover, initial tests of traditional strain theory have focused on long-range (educational/occupational) goals. Although some studies found that educational aspirations/expectations were positively related to delinquency (Bordua 1961; Hirschi 1969; Short and Strodtbeck 1965; Quicker 1974), support for strain theory has not generally been particularly strong. With few exceptions, measured discrepancies between occupational/educational aspirations and expectations have generally been found to be unrelated to delinquent behavior. Additionally, the possession of conventional aspirations has frequently been found to be inversely related to self-reported delinquency, which is contrary to theoretical expectations. Although traditional strain theory enjoyed a long tenure within the criminological community, its popularity slowly waned in large measure because of these consistently null findings.[1] An exception to these generally null findings was a recent reconceptualization by Farnworth and Leiber (1989). They found support for strain when it was measured as the disjunction between economic goals and educational expectations. In general, however, the empirical evidence has not been supportive of these versions of strain theory.

Rather than departing entirely from the criminological scene, however, strain theory underwent a brief reconceptualization in the 1970s. These revised strain theories adopted the traditional assumption that strain is due to the failure to achieve desired and valued goals, but altered the temporal nature of these goals. Rather than aspiring to long-range goals, adolescents were now conceived as being motivated toward the satisfaction of more short-term and immediate wants, such as athletic success, good grades, and popularity with peers (Quicker 1974; Elliott and Voss 1974; Greenberg 1977). These revisions of the theory suggested that strain is produced whenever adolescents fail to achieve their more immediate goals. These revised versions of strain theory, however, met the same fate as their earlier counterpart; weak empirical support existed for the presumption that

those adolescents who failed to achieve their immediate goals were more likely to be delinquent than those who were more successful (Reiss and Rhodes 1963; Elliott and Voss 1974; Greenberg 1977; Agnew 1984).

Agnew's GST

In response to the lack of empirical support for strain theory, Agnew has developed a more comprehensive version (see Agnew 1992, 1994 for the most complete explication of his theory). In his GST, Agnew suggested that previous versions of the theory have been unduly narrow in their conceptualization of the sources of strain. In addition to the failure to achieve desired goals, he contends that strain can also be brought about when others take away from us something that we value and when we are confronted with negative or disagreeable circumstances. One sense in which GST is general, then, is that the sources of strain are far more pervasive and extensive than previous strain theorists have articulated—strain is a more general phenomena than the discrepancy between aspirations and expectations.

Although strain is a necessary cause of delinquency, it is not sufficient. A critical intervening variable in GST is the psychological state of "negative affect," which includes disappointment, frustration, and most importantly, anger (Agnew 1992). As a solution to the undesirable affective state of anger, delinquency can be instrumental (as one tries to regain what one has lost or obtain what one has been prevented from obtaining), retaliatory (as one strikes back at the source of strain), and escapist (as one attempts to seek solace from the disagreeable states of anger and strain). In response to strain and its attendant negative emotional states, therefore, adolescents can respond with acts of theft, violence, vandalism, and drug/alcohol use. A second sense in which GST is general, then, is that it can potentially explain a diverse range of delinquent behaviors.

In addition to describing the antecedent (strain) and intervening (negative affect) causes of delinquency, Agnew (1992) has offered a detailed discussion of possible conditional factors. Agnew first notes that not all strain is equally disagreeable, that is, strain is not a discrete experience but varies in its magnitude (how much discomfort is inflicted), its recency (recent events are more stressful and unpleasant than older ones), its duration (strain experienced over longer time periods is more stressful), and its clustering (many stressful events experienced over a short time period are more unpleasant because coping resources become taxed). Second, Agnew notes that in some instances strain does not result in delinquent solutions because stress and consequent negative affective states can be effectively handled or managed.

Even when strain is perceived to be a particularly unpleasant experience that one can neither cope with nor manage, there are various constraints to delinquent and nondelinquent adaptations. Agnew (1992) suggests that a delinquent adaptation to strain is more likely for those with a disposition to engage in delinquency because of "certain temperamental variables" (perhaps, self-control; see Gottfredson and Hirschi 1990) and those with delinquent peers. Conversely, a delinquent adaptation is less likely for those high in self-efficacy, those with conventional social support, and those with strong moral restraints. Strain, then, is likely to lead to a delinquent solution when it cannot be managed, when constraints to nondelinquent solutions are strong, and when constraints to delinquent solutions are weak.

Initial Empirical Tests of GST

In addition to formulating a new version of strain theory, Agnew (1985) has been at the forefront in empirically testing his theory. In the first of several reported tests in the literature, Agnew found that negative relationships with parents and teachers and dissatisfaction with school were each positively related to adolescents' feelings of anger, which in turn were positively related to three forms of delinquent behavior (serious delinquency, aggression, school deviance). In a second, longitudinal study, Agnew (1989) found a relationship between these negative experiences and subsequent delinquency, further corroborating key features of his proposed causal mode of delinquency.

The most comprehensive empirical test do date of GST was recently conducted by Agnew and White (1992). Using longitudinal data from the Rutgers Health and Human Development Project (HHDP), they constructed eight different measures of strain, eight social control/differential association measures, and two measures of deviance (delinquency and drug use). In a cross-sectional regression analysis, they found that even with controls for social control/differential association variables, four measures of strain were significantly related to prior delinquency and drug use. They also found that a composite measure of general strain was as strongly related to prior delinquency as a composite scale of social control. They reported that this composite strain measure had a significantly stronger effect on the delinquency and drug use measures at higher levels of delinquent peers and a significantly weaker effect for youths with high levels of self-efficacy.

Although these initial empirical finding from the Rutgers HHDP were consistent with GST, they do not provide unequivocal evidence. . . .

Encouraged by Angew and White's (1992) initial findings, in the present research we conduct what we believe to be a more comprehensive test of GST. Essentially, we attempted to both replicate and extend Agnew and White's original work. Based on Agnew's (1985, 1992) theoretical discussions, we have constructed several different types or sources of general strain, some of which directly parallel those used by Agnew and White. In addition to capturing several different types of strain, we were able to measure variations in their magnitude and duration, as well as adolescents' attempts to manage or cope with strain by diminishing its importance. We also constructed measures of several variables discussed by Agnew that could interact with strain. We are able to determine if the effect of strain on delinquency is greater for those youths with a large proportion of delinquent peers, with low self-control, with weak self-efficacy, who have weak conventional social support, and with weak moral inhibitions against offending.

Like Agnew and White (1992), our data are longitudinal. Unlike their data, however, the recall period for our delinquency and strain items was a consistent 1-year time period. We also pursue a suggestion of Agnew's (1992, p. 75) that general strain may have an indirect effect on delinquency by weakening the social bond and strengthening involvement with delinquent peers. We present and test a very rudimentary causal model that connects general strain to social control and differential association variables.

Data and Measures

Sample

The data for our empirical test come from the first and second waves of the National Youth Survey (NYS), a longitudinal study of the correlates of delinquency and drug use (see Elliott, Huizinga, and Ageton 1985; Elliott, Huizinga, and Menard 1989). . . .

Measures of Exogenous Variables

Strain Measures. It should be kept in mind that both the loss of positive stimuli and the presence of negative stimuli have a central conceptual role in Agnew's GST (1985, 1992; Agnew and White 1992). In his discussion of these aversive events and experiences, Agnew has included such things as residence in an unappealing and unsafe neighborhood, stressful life events, and disagreeable relationships with adults and peers (Agnew and White 1992):

> The loss of positive stimuli might include such things as the loss of a boyfriend/girlfriend, moving from one's neighborhood, or the death of a parent. The presentation of noxious or negative stimuli might include criminal victimization of various types; a wide assortment of stressful life events; and negative relations with parents, teachers, and others—with such relations involving insults, verbal threats, and other noxious behavior. (P. 477)

In our operationalization of strain, we have attempted to measure these aversive features of persons' lives. Many of our concepts are operationalized in a manner similar to Agnew's measures (Agnew and White 1992)

in his most comprehensive empirical test of the theory.

Neighborhood Problems. This is a composite, summated scale reflecting the degree to which respondents lived in a stressful physical environment. . . .

Negative Life Events. Those who score high on this 13-item scale experienced more stressful events in the past year, such as the divorce/separation of a parent, death or serious injury to a family member, parental unemployment, or changing schools. . . .

Negative Relations With Adults. This is a 17-item summate scale that measures the degree to which respondents feel that they have poor relations with their parents ("I am an outsider with my family," "My parents think I am messed up," "My family is not interested in my problems") and teachers ("Teachers don't call on me," "My teachers think I am messed up," "Teachers don't ask me to work on projects"). . . .

School/Peer Hassles. This is a seven-item summated scale that measures the degree to which respondents feel hassled and isolated by peers or disappointed and dissatisfied with their daily dealings with peers, teachers, and other students . . . .

Traditional Strain. This is a summated measure of traditional strain in terms of perceived limitations on goal attainment. Respondents were asked to estimate the chance that they would "get the job you'd like" and "complete a college degree" . . . .

Conceptual Overlap of General Strain and Other Theories. A question may arise concerning the unique standing of GST because its central theoretical concepts may overlap with other theories of delinquency. For example, our measures of Negative Relations with Adults and Negative Life Events might be seen as indicators of social attachments from Hirschi's (1969) control theory because they both concern the social bonds between persons. In addition, the measure of Neighborhood Problems might be seen as a measure derived from routine activities or social disorganization theory rather than GST.

In response to such questions, Agnew (1992, 1994; Agnew and White 1992), in his own work, has devoted considerable attention to the issue.

With regard to the role of social relationships with others, Agnew is explicit in distinguishing general strain from control theory in terms of the negative valence of the social attachments. In social control theory, delinquency is made possible by the absence of positive relationships with conventional others. In this case, the lack of good social experiences acts to relax inhibitions to delinquency. In contrast, general strain theory focuses on the significance of negative relationships/experiences with others. Such negative relationships do not loosen inhibitions; rather, they serve as motivators for delinquent acts. For general strain theory, then, the fact that young people have negative social experiences is more important in explaining and understanding delinquency than whether they lack favorable ones.[2]

Regarding the more general issue of conceptual overlap with other theories, Agnew (1994) believes, and we concur, that the ultimate "proof of the pudding" lies in the relationship between GST's variables that may conceptually overlap with those from other theories and its unique set of intervening variables. Although GST may share some antecedent variables with other theories, such as negative relationships with conventional others, the experience of disruptive life events, and residence in crime-filled and deteriorated neighborhoods, it has a distinctive set of intervening mechanisms that are hypothesized to lead to crime and delinquency. Strain theory, unlike social control, social disorganization or routine activities theory, stipulates that aversive experiences and relationships result in specific negative affective states (anger, frustration, disappointment) that ultimately lead to delinquency. A full account of GST (and we do not pretend that ours is such a full account) will require the measurement of all of the causal links raised by the theory. . . .

Social Control Measures. *Moral Beliefs.* A nine-item summated scale, which reflects the extent to which youths thought it was morally wrong to commit each of nine different deviant/delinquent offenses (cheat on school tests, destroy property, use marijuana, theft under $5, hit someone, use alcohol, break into a vehicle, sell hard drugs, theft over $50). . . .

Delinquent Peers. Each respondent was asked what proportion of their friends had committed each of nine different deviant/delinquent offenses (listed above). . . .

Delinquent Disposition. This 11-item summated scale reflects respondents' inclination to act impulsively and to exhibit low self-control (Gottfredson and Hirschi 1990; Wilson and Herrnstein 1985). Those scoring high on the scale indicated more approval of non-criminal but inappropriate behaviors. . . .

Grades. Consistent with Agnew and White (1992), we assume that grades in school is a social control theory variable. . . .

Family Attachment. Our measure of attachment to the family is a composite scale that combines three dimensions: (a) time spent with family, (b) importance of parental influence, and (c) parents' involvement in youths' lives. . . .

Delinquency Measures. At both Time 1 (Wave 1, 1977) and Time 2 (Wave 2, 1978) respondents were asked about their involvement during the previous 12 months in an extensive list of delinquent behaviors. The Time 1 measure of self-reported delinquency, then, reflects delinquent acts committed in the year before the first interview, whereas the Time 2 measure reflects delinquent acts committed in the year after the Time 1 interview. Because Agnew claims that GST can explain involvement in a wide range of offenses, a composite scale of general delinquency was constructed from these self-reports. Composite scales of Time 1 Delinquency and Time 2 Delinquency were constructed by summing the reported frequencies for 20 specific offenses.[3] . . .

Findings

Effects of Strain—Preliminary Results. The point of departure for our analysis was to conduct both a cross-sectional and panel analysis, regressing Time 1 and Time 2 delinquency on the Time 1 strain and social control/differential association variables. . . .

The cross-sectional analysis indicates that four of the five strain measures are significantly related to delinquency (Time 1) in the theoretically expected direction. Because this analysis reflects the relationship between current levels of strain and prior delinquency (those acts committed during the previous 12 months), we interpret these coefficients to suggest that involvement in delinquency may lead to greater strain. These results are consistent with Agnew and White's (1992) own cross-sectional analysis. They found that four of their indicators of general strain were positively and significantly related to a measure of prior delinquency.[4]

. . . Because a lagged measure of delinquency is included in our model, the coefficients reported there reflect the Time 1 exogenous variables on Time 1-Time 2 changes in delinquency. Four of the five measures of general strain (Neighborhood Problems, Negative Life Events, School/Peer Hassles, and Negative Relations With Adults) have a positive and significant effect on delinquency. Our panel analysis does, then, reveal support for some components of Agnew's GST. Those who live in neighborhoods beset with many social problems (including crime and physical deterioration), who have in the past year experienced stressful life events, who have problems fitting in with peers and with school, and who have bad relationships with their parents and teachers, commit significantly more delinquent acts than those experiencing less strain. It should be noted that this relationship exists while controlling for social control/differential association variables. In addition, we found that having conventional moral beliefs and earning good school grades effectively inhibits delinquent involvement whereas having delinquent peers significantly contributes to delinquency.

Variations in the Magnitude of and Coping Strategies for Strain

We have thus far found some support for Agnew's (1985, 1989, 1992) GST. Experiencing a variety of negative stimuli does have a positive effect on subsequent involvement in delinquency net of one's prior level of delinquency and other determinants. In addition to suggesting more general sources of strain, Agnew also alluded to the fact that negative stimuli will produce more strain and presumably have a greater effect on delinquency, under particular conditions. . . . Because of data limitations (the NYS was not designed

as a test of GST) our examination of these issues was not as comprehensive as we would like. Nevertheless, we were able to examine some of Agnew's hypotheses about the conditions under which the adverse conditions of strain may be amplified or muted.

For example, in addition to respondents' perceptions about problems of crime and general deterioration where they live (Neighborhood Problems), they were also asked about the length of time they have lived in their neighborhood. Agnew's notion of duration suggests that those who have lived in unpleasant neighborhoods for a longer period of time would experience more stress than recent arrivals and that this stress would produce more delinquency. There was, however, no support for this duration hypothesis. The interaction of neighborhood problems with length of time in the neighborhood was not significant; no matter how long or how recently one lived in a disagreeable neighborhood, it had a positive effect on self-reported involvement in general delinquency.[5]

Agnew (1992, p. 67) also argued that if the unpleasant effects of strain can be managed or coped with, it will be expected to have a diminished effect on behavior. One of the ways that strain can be managed, he suggests, is by individuals' minimizing the importance of the goal/value or area of life affected by the strain. With respect to the measures of strain employed here, we would expect that Negative Relations With Adults would be less strongly related to delinquency for those youths who thought that adults' approval or acceptance was unimportant; we would similarly expect that School/Peer Hassles would have a diminished effect for those youths who viewed having close friends and doing well in school as unimportant; and we would expect that Traditional Strain would be weakly related to delinquency for those who thought that achieving the two future goals (a college education and a good job) was not important. Unfortunately, none of these hypotheses were confirmed. . . . Although ours is not a comprehensive analysis, we failed to find any support for the notion that the duration or importance of strain affected its impact on delinquent behavior.

Constraints to Delinquent and Nondelinquent Responses to Strain

Like Merton (1938), Agnew (1992) did not hypothesize that involvement in delinquent behavior was an inevitable response to strain; rather, there are both delinquent and nondelinquent adaptations. Only some strained adolescents turn to the delinquent option, and this response is affected by such factors as the availability of delinquent peers, the strength of moral inhibitions, the individual's level of self-control (delinquent disposition), coping resources (self-efficacy), and conventional social support.[6] Supporting evidence for Agnew's hypothesis would take the form of a significant interaction effect between the indicators of strain and each relevant conditional variable. . . .

[We] created a composite scale of general strain, which was a weighted sum of the four significant strain predictors of Time 2 delinquency.[7] . . . The effect of the general strain scale on subsequent delinquency is both positive and significant, net of other predictors. . . .

[C]ontrary to Agnew's (1992) theoretical expectations, only one of the interaction effects is statistically significant. The interaction between strain and self-efficacy is significant, but in the opposite direction as that predicted. The positive sign of the interaction term suggests that strain has a more pronounced effect on delinquency at higher levels of self-efficacy. Agnew had suggested that for individuals high in self-efficacy, strain would be responded to with nondelinquent coping strategies because they are likely to perceive themselves as capable and empowered. . . . Strain does not have a more substantial effect for those youths whose delinquent coping strategies are more abundant (delinquent peers, delinquent disposition), nor does it have a less pronounced effect among those with constraints to delinquent coping (strong moral beliefs, high in self-efficacy, and conventional social support). . . .

Relationship Between General Strain and Other Variables

Although we have not found any evidence to suggest that strain interacts with other variables in its effect on delinquency, we do have evidence to suggest that the kind of general strain theorized by Agnew (1992) is significantly related to subsequent delinquency. This is true even when there are controls for other relevant factors, such as those derived from social control and differential association theory. The next question to be addressed, then, is the relationship between the strain and social control/differential association variables. Agnew (1992; Agnew and White 1992) has hypothesized that one effect of strain may be to weaken the individual's social bond to conventional people and institutions and strengthen the bond with unconventional ones. If individuals find their current relationships stressful and unpleasant, it seems reasonable that they would disassociate themselves from these conventional relationships and institutions (either by breaking off the relationship or, if unable to do that, as in the case of parents and teachers, to at least distance themselves emotionally from them) and find more satisfying (although possibly more delinquent) ones. . . .

Social Control is inversely related to delinquency and both General Strain and Delinquent Peers are positively related to subsequent delinquency. . . .

Consistent with Agnew's conjecture, general strain is negatively related to Social Control and positively related to Delinquent Peers. Strain leads to involvement in delinquency, then, because it in part weakens adolescents' ties to conventional sources of social control and strengthens their ties to delinquent others. These are not the only two factors intervening in general strain's effect on delinquency, however, because it still has a significant direct effect on delinquency with social control and Delinquent Peers controlled. It would appear, then, that general strain affects involvement in delinquency through processes in addition to its effect in weakening conventional social control and increasing ties to delinquent others. Agnew (1985, 1992) has theorized and empirically shown that two additional intervening variables between strain and delinquency are the negative affective states of anger and frustration. Unfortunately, we were not able to measure these important theoretical constructs. It is entirely conceivable that feelings of anger and resentment are an additional component of the process connecting general strain with delinquency. . . .

Summary and Conclusions

In a series of recent papers, Agnew has offered a revitalized version of strain theory. His formulation of GST expands the scope of traditional strain theory by suggesting sources of strain other than the failure to achieve desired goals. In addition, he stipulates that strain varies in its effect on delinquency according to such factors as its magnitude, duration, and recency. Finally, explicitly recognizing that only some of those who experience strain respond by committing delinquent acts, he offers several possible factors that account for why delinquent and nondelinquent strategies might be chosen. Not only does Agnew present a very detailed conceptualization of his expanded GST, he begins the difficult task of examining its empirical validity. In the most definitive study to date, he and a colleague (Agnew and White 1992) find some support for the hypothesis that strain is related to involvement in delinquency.

In our article, we have attempted a more comprehensive test of the GST. . . .

Our findings provide partial support for GST. Consistent with Agnew and White's (1992) research, we found that negative relationships with adults, feelings of dissatisfaction with friends and school life, and the experience of stressful events (family breakup, unemployment, moving) were positively related to delinquency. We also found evidence that living in an unpleasant neighborhood (one where social problems and physical deterioration were perceived to be a problem) was positively related to delinquency. When conceived of more broadly as exposure to negative stimuli, then general strain is significantly related to involvement in delinquency. Contrary to Agnew's (1992) hypothesis, we found no evidence that this effect for strain was enhanced when it was experienced for a longer time period or diminished when adolescents considered the dimension of their life in which they experienced strain as "unimportant."

We also did not find any evidence to suggest that impediments to delinquent or nondelinquent strategies interact with strain. Consistent with Agnew and White's (1992) own findings, feelings of general strain were positively related to subsequent delinquency regardless of the level of delinquent peers, delinquent dispositions, moral beliefs, self-efficacy, and conventional social support. It is possible that the feelings of distress that accompany strain can be managed by other strategies not examined here (escapism through drug use, compensatory success is school activities, athletics, or out-of-school employment).

Finally, we found some support for Agnew's (Agnew and White 1992) conjecture that, at least in part, general strain leads to delinquent involvement by weakening the conventional social bond and strengthening the unconventional bond (with delinquent peers). In his own research, Agnew found that the strain process is mediated by a negative affective state (anger). Our findings here suggest, that strain also contributes to delinquency through the mechanisms discussed by social control and differential association theory. . . .

Discussion Questions

1. According to Paternoster and Mazerolle, what are the important ways in which Agnew's "general strain theory" extends "traditional strain theory"?

2. In general, what are the relevant findings from Paternoster and Mazerolle's study? What are the implications for future research in this area? What are some of the limitations of their study that the authors identify?

3. Overall, do you think that Paternoster and Mazerolle's study provides adequate support to warrant future research involving Agnew's "general strain theory"? Why or why not?

Notes

1. The empirical failure of strain theory was not the only factor responsible for its fall from grace. Kornhauser (1978) discusses in detail some theoretical weaknesses of the theory,

and other criticisms can be found in Clinard (1964) and Cohen (1965).

2. The implication of this is that those who have negative social experiences/attachments should have higher levels of delinquency than others. Our data bear this out. When youths were divided into three equal groups on the Negative Relations With Adults scale, the mean on the Time 2 delinquency measure was 8.76 for those at the lowest level, 11.93 for those at the mid-level, and 31.34 for those with the most negative relations with adults. The same monotonically increasing pattern was found for the measure of School/Peer Hassles.

3. For many of these self-report items, the distribution was skewed to the right with a few respondents reporting very high offending frequencies. We truncated the upper 10% of these distributions by recoding all frequencies above the 90th percentile to the frequency at the 90th percentile.

4. They found a significant relationship with their measures of Negative Life Events, Life Hassles, Negative Relations With Adults, and Parental Fighting. Their Negative Life Events and Negative Relations With Adults scales are very comparable to our own.

5. As one reviewer noted, the failure to find an effect for length of time in the neighborhood may reflect the fact that recent arrivals to bad neighborhoods may have moved there from a similarly bad community.

6. The measures of self-efficacy and conventional social support have not yet been described because they were not included in the specification of the general model. Theoretically, Agnew (1992, Agnew and White 1992) describes self-efficacy as an attitudinal state wherein persons feel in control of their own lives and can rely on their own capabilities to be successful. Our measure of self-efficacy was a nine-item summated scale (Cronbach's alpha = .52) designed to capture the extent to which respondents felt that they were in control of things and were capable beings. Those who scored high on this scale perceived that they were doing well in school and were successful in their social lives. Conventional social support was measured by a nine-item summated scale (Cronbach's alpha = .85), which reflected the degree to which respondents thought that their mother, father, and friends would be supportive of them if they got into trouble at school, with police, and in the neighborhood. Higher scores mean more conventional social support. Both scales had an inverse (but nonsignificant) correlation with the measure of Time 2 delinquency.

7. The composite measure of strain was constructed as follows: GENERAL STRAIN = .062 X Neighborhood Problems + .036 X Negative Life Events + .088 X School/Peer Hassles + .096 X Negative Relations With Adults. We used this weighted approach to the construction of the combined general strain measure because we wanted to compare our results with those reported by Agnew and White (1992), who used a weighted scale in their analyses. In a supplemental analysis, we used a simple unweighted sum of the significant strain measures and our findings are virtually the same as those reported here.

References

Agnew, Robert. 1984. "Goal Achievement and Delinquency." *Sociology and Social Research* 68:435-51.

——. 1985. "A Revised Strain Theory of Delinquency." *Social Forces* 64:151-67.

——. 1989. "A Longitudinal Test of the Revised Strain Theory." *Journal of Quantitative Criminology* 5:373-87.

——. 1992. "Foundation for a General Strain Theory of Crime and Delinquency." *Criminology* 30:47-87.

——. 1994. "The Contribution of Social-Psychological Strain Theory to the Explanation of Crime and Delinquency." In *Advances in Criminological Theory*. Vol. 6. New York: Transaction Books.

Agnew, Robert and Helene Raskin White. 1992. "An Empirical Test of General Strain Theory." *Criminology* 30:475-99.

Aiken, Leona S. and Stephen G. West. 1991. *Multiple Regression: Testing and Interpreting Interactions*. Beverly Hills, CA: Sage.

Bordua, David J. 1961. "Delinquency Subcultures: Sociological Interpretations of Gang Delinquency." *Annals* 338:119-36.

Bursik, Robert J. 1988. "Social Disorganization and Theories of Crime and Delinquency: Problems and Prospects." *Criminology* 26:519-51.

Bursik, Robert J. and Jim Webb. 1982. "Community Change and Patterns of Delinquency." *American Journal of Sociology* 88:24-42.

Clinard, Marshall B. 1964. *Anomie and Deviant Behavior*. New York: Free Press.

Cloward, Richard A. and Lloyd E. Ohlin. 1960. *Delinquency and Opportunity*. New York: Free Press.

Cohen, Albert K. 1955. *Delinquent Boys*. New York: Free Press.

——. 1965. "The Sociology of the Deviant Act: Anomie Theory and Beyond." *American Sociological Review* 30:5-14.

Cornish, Derek B. and Ronald V. Clarke. 1986. *The Reasoning Criminal*. New York: Springer-Verlag.

Elliot, Delbert and Harwin Voss. 1974. *Delinquency and Dropout*. Lexington, MA: Lexington Books.

Elliot, Delbert, David Huizinga, and Suzanne Ageton. 1985. *Explaining Delinquency and Drug Use*. Beverly Hills, CA: Sage.

Elliot, Delbert, David Huizinga, and Scott Menard. 1989. *Multiple Problem Youth: Delinquency, Substance Use, and Mental Health Problems*. New York: Springer-Verlag.

Farnworth, Margaret and Michael J. Leiber. 1989. "Strain Theory Revisited: Economic Goals, Educational Means, and Delinquency." *American Sociological Review* 54:263-74.

Gold, Martin. 1963. *Status Forces in Delinquent Boys*. Ann Arbor, MI: Institute for Social Research.

Gottfredson, Michael and Travis Hirschi. 1990. *A General Theory of Crime*. Stanford, CA: Stanford University Press.

Greenberg, David F. 1977. "Delinquency and the Age Structure of Society." *Contemporary Crises* 1:189-223.

Heitgard, Janet and Robert J. Bursik. 1987. "Extracommunity Dynamics and the Ecology of Delinquency." *American Journal of Sociology* 92:775-87.

Hirschi, Travis. 1969. *Causes of Delinquency*. Berkeley: University of California Press.

Johnson, Richard E. 1979. *Juvenile Delinquency and Its Origins: An Integrated Theoretical Approach*. New York: Cambridge University Press.

Kornhauser, Ruth R. 1978. *Social Sources of Delinquency*. Chicago: University of Chicago Press.

Link, Bruce. 1982. "Mental Patient Status, Work and Income: An Examination of the Effects of a Psychiatric Label." *American Sociological Review* 47:202-15.

——. 1987. "Understanding Labeling Effects in the Area of Mental Disorders: An Empirical Assessment of the Effects of Expectations of Rejection." *American Sociological Review* 52:96-112.

Link, Bruce, Francis T. Cullen, James Frank, and John F. Wozniak. 1987. "The Social Rejection of Former Mental Patients: Understanding Why Labels Matter." *American Journal of Sociology* 92:1461-500.

Link, Bruce, Francis T. Cullen, Elmer Struening, Patrick E. Shrout, and Bruce P. Dohrenwend. 1989. "A Modified Labeling Theory Approach to Mental Disorders: An Empirical Assessment." *American Sociological Review* 54:400-23.

Liska, Allen. 1971. "Aspirations, Expectations, and Delinquency: Stress and Additive Models." *Sociological Quarterly* 12:99-107.

Matsueda, Ross L. 1992. "Reflected Appraisals, Parental Labeling, and Delinquency: Specifying a Symbolic Interactionist Theory." *American Journal of Sociology* 97:1577-611.

Merton, Robert K. 1938. "Social Structure and Anomie." *American Sociological Review* 3:672-82.

Quicker, John. 1974. "The Effect of Goal Discrepancy on Delinquency." *Social Problems* 22:76-86.

Reiss, Albert J. and Albert L. Rhodes. 1963. "Status Deprivation and Delinquent Behavior." *Sociological Quarterly* 4:135-49.

Sampson, Robert J. and W. Byron Groves. 1989. "Community Structure and Crime: Testing Social-Disorganization Theory." *American Journal of Sociology* 94:774-802.

Short, James, F. and Fred L. Strodtbeck. 1965. *Group Process and Gang Delinquency*. Chicago: University of Chicago Press.

Smith, Douglas A. and G. Roger Jarjoura. 1988. "Social Structure and Criminal Victimization." *Journal of Research in Crime and Delinquency* 25:27-52.

Thornberry, Terence P. 1987. "Toward an Interactional Theory of Delinquency." *Criminology* 25:863-91.

Wilson, James Q. and Richard Herrnstein. 1985. *Crime and Human Nature*. New York: Simon & Schuster.

Reprinted from: Raymond Paternoster and Paul Mazerolle, "General Strain Theory and Delinquency: A Replication and Extension." In *Journal of Research in Crime and Delinquency* 31, pp. 235-263. Copyright © 1994 by Sage Publications. Reprinted by permission. ✦

23

Formal Characteristics of Delinquency Areas

Clifford R. Shaw
Henry D. McKay

Neighborhoods have long been important for the study of sociological processes. It is little wonder, then, that they have also played a key role in criminology. The theory that focuses on the role of neighborhoods and neighborhood organization on crime is the social-disorganization (or social-ecology) perspective. This perspective developed largely from the work of Clifford R. Shaw and Henry D. McKay in Chicago in the 1920s, 1930s, and 1940s. This selection is an excerpt from their work.

Shaw and McKay show that delinquency rates remained fairly stable over time (between 1900 to 1920) in different areas of Chicago. Applying Park and Burgess's model of "The City" to delinquency, Shaw and McKay demonstrated that the highest delinquency rates were found in neighborhoods in the "zone of transition," an area located immediately outside the industrial area. The zone of transition was characterized by severe economic hardships as evidenced by physical deterioration, changes in population size, high poverty, economic dependency, and a host of other social ills. The low rent and easy access to industrial areas (and therefore jobs) attracted poor newcomers to the zone of transition; many were either first-generation or second-generation immigrants or African Americans. When people living in these areas were financially able, they moved out to zone Three and beyond. Because of continuous in-and-out migration and the heterogeneity of people, the zone of transition was socially disorganized, that is, lacking strong informal social-control mechanisms, such as strong churches and interested neighbors, which are important for controlling crime and delinquency.

The lack of social controls in disorganized areas allowed the development and perpetuation of delinquent traditions, which resulted in continuously high rates of delinquency, even when the former residents moved out and new people moved in. Further, the delinquency rates of each group declined as its members gradually moved away from zone Two and into more organized and stable neighborhoods. This fact demonstrates that it is not the nativity or race/ethnicity of the residents that is associated with high crime and delinquency rates, but rather the lack of social organization in some neighborhoods.

The study of the distribution of juvenile delinquents . . . revealed wide variations in the rates of delinquents in the 113 areas of the city. Likewise it was found that the areas of low and high rates of delinquents assume a typical configuration with regard to the center of the city and also that this configuration of low and high rate areas has remained relatively unchanged over a long period of time. In attempting to interpret these findings, certain questions invariably arise: (1) What are the characteristics of these areas of high rates and how may they be differentiated from the areas with low rates? (2) Why do the low and high rate areas assume this configuration in relation to the center of the city? (3) Why have the rates in most of the areas of the city remained relatively constant over a long period of time? Any attempt to answer these questions must take into consideration the organic nature of the city and the processes of segregation and differentiation that take place in its growth and expansion.

Students of social problems have repeatedly pointed out that there are marked differences between areas within the city. The business center, the foreign districts, the slum, the industrial centers, and many other districts have been differentiated. Of these, the slum has probably received the most attention. This term has been used in a general way to designate areas where such conditions as physical deterioration, bad housing, overcrowding, poverty, and crime are prevalent. Attempts have been made to explain these conditions in terms of the other conditions existing in the same area and in terms of the local situation. Upon further analysis, however, it appears that all of these conditions of the local situation are products of the more general processes of expansion and segregation within the city.

The nature of these processes has been the subject of considerable study during recent years. Students of the city, comprehending its unity and noting its organic nature, have described these processes in natural science terms by suggesting that every American city of the same class tends to reproduce, in the course of its expansion, all the different types of areas. The areas produced by this process are natural in the sense that they are not planned; they are typical in the sense that they tend to exhibit, from city to city, the same physical, social, and cultural characteristics. The natural process involved in the creation of these natural areas within the city is summarized in the following quotation from Robert E. Park:

> The city plan establishes metes and bounds, fixes in a general way the location and character of the city's constructions, and imposes an orderly arrangement with the city area, upon the buildings which are erected by private initiative as well as by public authority. Within the limitations prescribed, however, the inevitable processes of human nature proceed to give these regions and these buildings a character which it is less easy to control. . . . Personal tastes and convenience, vocational and economic interests, infallibly tend to segregate and thus to classify the populations of great cities. In this way the city acquires an organization and distribution of population which is neither designed nor controlled. . . .
>
> Physical geography, natural advantages and disadvantages, including means of transportation, determine in advance the general outlines of the urban plan. As the city increases the population, the subtler influences of sympathy, rivalry, and economic necessity tend to control the distribution of population. Business and industry seek advantageous locations and draw around them certain

portions of the population. There spring up fashionable residence quarters from which the poorer classes are excluded because of the increased value of the land. Then there grow up slums which are inhabited by great numbers of the poorer classes who are unable to defend themselves from associations with the derelict and vicious.

In the course of time every section and quarter of the city takes on something of the character and qualities of its inhabitants. Each separate part of the city is inevitably stained with the peculiar sentiments of its population. The effect of this is to convert what was at first a mere geographical expressions into a neighborhood, that is to say, a locality with sentiments, traditions, and a history of its own. Within this neighborhood the continuity of the historical processes is somehow maintained. The past imposes itself upon the present, and the life of every locality moves on with a certain momentum of its own, more or less independent of the larger circle of life and interests about it.[1]

In his description of the processes of radial expansion, Prof. E. W. Burgess has advanced the thesis that, in the absence of counteracting factors, the modern American city takes the form of five concentric urban zones. This ideal construction, applied to the city of Chicago, is presented graphically in Figure 23.1. Burgess characterized in the following manner the areas which are differentiated in the process of radial expansion from the center of the city:

Zone I: *The central business district.*—At the center of the city as the focus of its commercial, social, and civic life is situated the central business district. The heart of this district is the downtown retail district with its department stores, its smart shops, its office buildings, its clubs, its banks, its hotels, its theaters, its museums, and its headquarters of economic, social, civic and political life. Encircling this area of work and play is the less well-known wholesale business district with its market, its warehouses, and storage buildings.

Zone II: *The zone in transition.*—Surrounding the central business district are areas of residential deterioration caused

Figure 23.1
Urban Zones and Areas

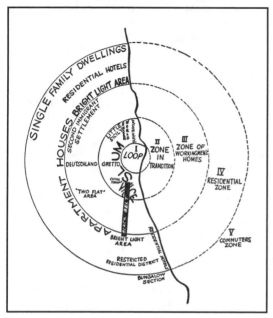

by the encroaching of business and industry from Zone I.

Thus it may therefore be called a zone in transition, with a factory district for its inner belt and an outer ring of retrogressing neighborhoods, of first-settlement immigrant colonies, of rooming-house districts, of homeless men areas, of resorts of gambling, bootlegging, sexual vice, and breeding places of crime. In this area of physical deterioration and social disorganization our studies show the greatest concentration of cases of poverty, bad housing, juvenile delinquency, family disintegration, physical and mental disease. As families and individuals prosper, they escape from this area into Zone III beyond, leaving behind as marooned a residuum of defeated, leaderless, and helpless.

Zone III: *The zone of independent workingmen's homes.*—This third broad urban ring in Chicago, as well as in northern industrial cities, largely constituted by neighborhoods of second immigrant settlement. Its residents are those who desire to live near but not too close to their work.

Zone IV: *The zone of better residences.*—Extending beyond the neigh-borhoods of second immigrant settlements, we come to the zone of better residences in which the great middle classes of native-born Americans live, small business men, professional people, clerks, and the salesmen. Once communities of single homes, these are becoming in Chicago apartment-house residential-hotel areas. Within these areas at strategic points are found local businesses called satellite Loops. The typical constellation of business and recreational units includes a bank, one or more United Cigar Stores, a drug store, a high-class restaurant, an automobile display row, and a so-called "wonder" motion-picture theater. . . .

Zone V: *The commuters' zone.*—Out beyond the areas of better residence is a ring of encircling small cities, towns, hamlets, which, taken together, constitute the suburbs, because the majority of men residing there spend the day at work in the Loop (central business district), returning only for the night. The communities in this commuters' zone are probably the most highly segregated of any in the entire gamut from an incorporated village run in the interests of crime and vice, such as Burnham, to Lake Forest, with its wealth, culture, and public spirit.[2]

The actual situation in any given city is, of course, somewhat different from this ideal presentation of city growth. In every city there are disturbing factors, such as lake fronts, rivers, elevations, railroads, and other barriers which affect the actual configuration that the city takes in its growth. Nevertheless, such an ideal construction furnishes a frame of reference from which the processes of city growth may be studied. It presents not only a general picture of the location of types of areas in a city at any given time, but it draws attention to one of the most significant characteristics of expansion, namely, succession, or the tendency of each inner zone to extend its area by invading the next outer zone.

It is the purpose of this chapter to present a picture of the structure of Chicago and to locate and characterize, by means of indices of organization and disorganization, the areas which have been produced by these processes of expansion and succession acting within this structure. These indices, it is hoped, will afford a basis for differentiating between the areas of low and high rates of delinquents, and will serve as a partial explanation of the location of the high-rate areas and the constancy of the rates in these areas over a long period of time.

The effect of Lake Michigan on the configuration of Chicago is seen in the fact that the business district, which has remained at the point of original settlement, is on the lake shore and not in the center of the city. The study of the growth of Chicago in terms of concentric circles is at once modified to a study in terms of semicircles.

As elevation is a negligible factor in Chicago, the only other natural barrier which has interfered significantly with the free movement of population according to the radial pattern of expansion is the Chicago River. Although not a large river, its two branches, which extend almost diagonally out from the center of the city, have rather effectively divided Chicago into three divisions, each one of which may be thought of as being somewhat distinct from the others. These two branches of the river have also complicated the transportation problem and thus affected the movement of population in near-by areas.

Very early in the history of Chicago industry was attracted to the areas along both branches of the river. This development was accompanied by settlements of early immigrants in the surrounding areas, while high-class residential districts developed north, south, and west of the central business district. . . .

In the course of the growth of Chicago marked changes in the character of the areas around the central business district have taken place. Residential districts close to the center of the city were forced to give away to industrial and commercial developments, while other areas of single-family dwellings along the main transportation lines have become apartment-house districts. The high-class residential districts formerly located on the near west side and near south side have disappeared, but it is interesting to note that a high-class residential district on the near north side, locally known as the Gold Coast, has as yet withstood the invasion of industry.

South Chicago, an outlying business center on the Lake front, which developed almost as early as Chicago proper, was at the time of its founding, and still is, the center of a large industrial development. Likewise the district of Pullman, located just west of Lake Calumet, has always been an industrial center. Outer districts such as Lake View on the North Shore and Hyde Park on the South Shore, which also became a part of Chicago through annexation, have largely retained their strictly residential character.

Distribution of Industrial and Commercial Centers

One index which may be used to distinguish the types of areas that have been differentiated in the process of the growth of Chicago is the configuration of its major industrial and commercial developments. Figure 23.2, gives an outline of the areas zoned for industry and commerce by the Chicago zoning ordinance of 1923. The central commercial and light industrial district is indicated by the cross-hatched sections of this figure. The Loop is almost entirely occupied by commercial houses. In the zoned areas adjacent to the Loop, but not occupied by heavy industry, are slight industrial plants, warehouses, and similar buildings. Some of this area is still used for residential purposes but it is subject to occupancy by industry and commerce as the central district expands.

In contrast with the commercial and light industrial developments in and adjacent to the center of a city, heavy industry tends to be located where there are natural advantages such as rivers, along the trunk lines of railroads, or on the Lake front.

Thus the heavy industrial districts in Chicago, which are indicated in solid black on Figure 23.2, are quite widely dispersed throughout the city. The largest developments are along the banks of the Chicago River and extend outward from the point where the first industries were established. The north extension follows the north branch about three miles from the central district, while the southern extension follows the south branch of the river to the city limits and includes a large portion of the Union Stock

Figure 23.2
Zoning Map of Chicago (Adapted)

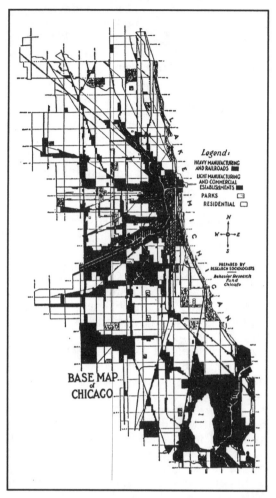

Yards and the central manufacturing district. The other major industrial areas outlined on this figure are in the South Chicago and Calumet district where, as previously indicated, more or less independent industrial communities developed early in the history of Chicago.

When the maps showing the distribution of delinquents in Chicago are compared with this industrial map, it will be noted that most of the concentrations of delinquent and most of the high-rate areas of delinquents are either included in or are adjacent to the districts zoned for industry and commerce. The high-rate areas along the two branches of the Chicago River on the west side, on the south

side, in the stockyard district, and in South Chicago are either completely or in part included in the shaded areas. On the other hand, the areas with low rates of delinquents are, generally speaking, quite far removed from the major industrial developments.

From the foregoing it may be said that, in general, proximity to industry and commerce is an index of the areas of Chicago in which high rates of delinquents are found. It is not assumed that this relationship exists because industry and commerce are in themselves causes of delinquency. But it is assumed that the areas adjacent to industry and commerce have certain characteristics which result from this proximity and which serve to differentiate them from the areas with low rates of delinquents. An effort will be made, therefore, to show how these areas are affected by industry and commerce and to present some of their more significant characteristics.

Physical Deterioration

As the city grows, the areas of light industry and commerce near the center of the city expand and encroach upon the areas used for residential purposes. The dwellings in such areas, already undesirable because of age, are allowed to deteriorate under the threat of invasion, because further investment in them is unprofitable. Others are junked to make way for new industrial or commercial structures. The effect of the changes is that the areas become increasingly undesirable through general depreciation. . . .

Likewise, the areas adjacent to heavy industrial centers, but not yet occupied by industry, are subject to invasion. While the threat of invasion is not so great as in the areas close to the center of the city, first-class residences are not constructed in these areas and there is a definite tendency toward physical deterioration. Furthermore, the areas that are near heavy industrial developments are often rendered more undesirable for residential purposes because of noise, smoke, odors, or the general unattractiveness of the surroundings. The total result is, therefore, that both the areas adjacent to commercial and light industrial properties near the center of the city and those adjacent to centers of heavy industrial development in the outlying sections are in general almost equally unattractive and undesirable for residential areas.

Areas of Increasing and Decreasing Population

Further evidence of the process of deterioration and rapid change in the areas adjacent to commerce and industry is seen . . . in the percentage increase and decrease of the population in each of the 113 areas during the period from 1910 to 1920. . . . Twelve areas, all of them near the center of the city, decreased more than 20 percent in this 10-year period; and a total of 23 areas, either near the central business district of the heavy industrial sections, showed some decrease. . . .

Most of the heavy concentrations of delinquents and most of the high-rate areas are included in those sections of the city which show a decreasing population. Likewise, the areas that are slowly increasing in population tend to be the areas with medium rates of delinquents, while the areas of more rapid increases tend to be the low-rate areas. . . .

The reader is cautioned against attaching causal significance to the correspondence between rates of delinquents and percentage increase and decrease of population . . . or to any of the variables considered in relation to rates of delinquents in this chapter. All the variables considered in this chapter are used solely to indicate differences between community backgrounds. The facts concerning increasing and decreasing population serve as a basis for differentiating between the areas of high rates and those of low rates. It is probable that decreasing population, rather than contributing to delinquency, is a symptom of the more basic changes that are taking place in those areas of the city that are subject to invasion by industry and commerce. . . .

Despite the fact that the districts near the center of the city show a decreasing population, the net density of population, as measured by the number of inhabitants per acre in the area not occupied by industry, is greatest in the areas within 2 miles of the central district and tends to decrease with considerable regularity out from the inner zone. In general the areas with the highest rates of delinquents fall within those sections of the city having the greatest density of population. The notable exceptions to this tendency are found in the high-class apartment districts, where the density is relatively high but the rates of delinquents are low, and in a few outlying areas where the rates of delinquency are comparatively high but the density is low because of the presence of considerable unoccupied waste land.

Economic Dependency

The areas adjacent to industry and commerce are also characterized by low rents and low family income. These are complementary characteristics. The rents in old, dilapidated buildings in deteriorated neighborhood are naturally low and these low rents attract the population group of the lowest economic status.

. . . These rates of dependency are based upon the total number of families which received financial aid from the United Charities and the Jewish Charities during 1921.[3] The rates represent the percentage of the families in each area that received financial aid from these two agencies during the year. While it is not assumed that this series of dependency cases furnishes an ideal index of the economic status of all of the families in these areas, it is probably that, with the exception of some Negro communities, it outlines the poverty areas quite accurately.

The areas of highest rates of dependency, are concentrated . . . around the central business and industrial section and in the stockyards district. The second class of areas— that is, those with rates of dependency ranging from 1.5 to 2—are concentrated just outside the highest-rate areas in the center of the city, in the "back-of-the-yards" district, and in the South Chicago industrial district. On the other hand, the areas of lowest rates are in the outlying residential communities. . . .

It will be observed that the variation in rates of delinquents as between the areas with highest rates of dependency and those with the lowest rates of dependency is 11 to 2.2 in the police series, 9.2 to 2.9 in the juvenile court series, and 3.2 to 0.8 in the juvenile court commitment series. These facts indicate that there is a marked similarity in the variation of rates of family dependency and rates of juvenile delinquents, since for each decrease in rates of dependency there is a corresponding decrease in rates of delinquency for each of the three series of delinquents. . . .

Distribution of Foreign and Negro Population

Another characteristic of the areas of decreasing population, physical deterioration, and economic dependency is the high percentage of foreign and Negro population. The process of selection and segregation, operating on both economic and cultural bases, attract into these areas the population groups of the lowest economic status. These groups, include, for the most part, the newest immigrants and the Negroes. . . . [T]he Negroes and the immigrants are of somewhat comparable economic status; both are unaccustomed to the conditions of a modern urban community and are faced with the problem of making an adjustment in a situation with which they are not familiar. The cultural backgrounds of both groups are largely rural. . . .

[T]he highest percentages of foreign and Negro population are in the areas around the center of the city, in the stockyards district, and in South Chicago. . . . [T]hese are the areas of high rates of delinquents.

A further analysis of the population by square-mile areas revealed that the percentage of aliens among the foreign born was disproportionately large in the areas where the percentage of foreign born in the total population was highest. . . . [N]ear the center of the city, the percentage of aliens in the foreign-born population was 40.0. . . . Thus it is clear that in the areas of high rates of delinquents a much smaller proportion of the foreign born are naturalized than in the outlying areas where the rates are low. This fact suggests that the newest immigrants are concentrated, for the most part, in the areas of highest rates of delinquents.

As distinguished from the other indices of community organization and disorganiza-

tion, the variation in the percentage of the combined foreign and Negro groups in the total population is of additional interest since the children of these two groups have, for a long period of time, constituted a disproportionate percentage of the delinquents in the juvenile court. This is indicated when the 8,141 delinquents included in our 1917-1923 juvenile court series are classified on the basis of the nativity of the father and compared either with the nativity distribution of the male adults in the total population or the nationality distribution of the total aged 10 to 16 male population as recorded in the 1920 census. Of the total number of delinquents classified in the 1917-1923 juvenile court series, 9.1 percent were Negroes, and of the total number of white delinquents. 24.4 percent had native-born fathers and 75.6 percent had foreign-born fathers. The distribution of the male adults in Chicago shows quite different proportions in each of these groups. Of the total population in 1920, 4.9 percent of the male adults (21 years and over) were Negroes, and of the total male white population, 48.3 percent were foreign born and 51.7 percent were native born. Thus, although 75.6 percent of the white delinquents had foreign-born fathers, only 48.3 percent of the total male white population were foreign born.

A comparison of the nationality distribution of the boys in the juvenile court series with that of the aged 10 to 16 male population for the city as a whole also revealed certain significant differences between these two groups. Of the total 10 to 16 white male population. 64.6 percent had foreign-born fathers[4] as against 75.6 percent of the white boys in the 1917-1923 juvenile court series. Interesting differences between the extent of delinquency among the children of native parentage and foreign parentage are revealed when actual rates are computed for each of these groups. The rate for the delinquents with native fathers was 2.9 against 5.0 for the delinquents with foreign-born fathers. Thus the rate for the children with foreign-born fathers is 72 percent greater than that for the delinquents with native-born fathers. The rate in the native group for the single year 1920 was 0.8 and for the native white of foreign parentage 1.3. Thus for this single year the rate of the delinquents of foreign parentage was 62 percent greater than that for the native white of native parentage.

The Negro group shows a somewhat higher rate of delinquents than either the native white of native parentage or the native white of foreign parentage. While the aged 10 to 16 male Negro population was only 2.5 percent of the total aged 10 to 16 male population, 9.9 percent of the delinquents in the 1917-1923 series were Negroes. For this series as a whole the rate for the Negro group was 15.6 and for the single year 1920 the rate was 4.6.

It is significant to note that the presence of a large Negro and foreign-born population in the areas having high rates of delinquents was not a unique situation in 1920. A study of the distribution of racial and national groups in both the school census of 1898 and the Federal census of 1910 showed that the highest percentage of the Negro and foreign born was in the areas having the highest rates of delinquents in the 1900-1906 juvenile court series. . . .

Succession of Cultural Groups in Delinquent Areas

Before attempting to interpret the fact that a disproportionately large number of boys brought before the juvenile court are of foreign born and Negro parentage, or that the highest percentage of foreign born and Negro population is found in the areas having the highest rates of delinquents, it is necessary to consider two complementary changes that have taken place in the history of Chicago. In the first place, during the period between 1900 and 1920 marked changes took place in the racial and national composition of the population which inhabited the areas with the highest rates of delinquents. In the second place, this change in the composition of the population was paralleled by a corresponding change in the racial and nationality groupings among children brought before the juvenile court of Cook County during the 20-year period.

. . . [T]he relative magnitude of the rates of delinquent boys in 1920 has changed relatively little since 1900. In view of this fact, the above-mentioned changes in the composition of the population in these areas are of great significance in the study of juvenile delinquency and will therefore be considered in greater detail. . . .

The movement of the immigrant groups from the areas of the first immigrant settlement to the areas of the second and third settlement, and the succession of nationalities in the areas adjacent to the center of the city, are matters of great significance when considered in relation to the process of city growth and the distribution of juvenile delinquents. Attracted by the low rents and accessibility to employment, the newer immigrants settle in the areas adjacent to industry and commerce, force out the older immigrants, and then in turn give way to still newer immigrant groups. It is in these deteriorated areas, therefore, that the members of each nationality have been forced to make their first adjustments to the new world and to rear their children.

The rate of movement of immigrants out of the areas of first settlement depends, among other things upon the rapidity of growth of the city. In cities that are growing very slowly this movement is less marked both because there is less pressure from incoming groups and because the areas of first settlement are not seriously threatened by the invasion of industry and commerce. In Chicago, because of the vary rapid increase of the population through immigration and the tremendous industrial development, the older groups have been under constant pressure to move out of the areas of first settlement to make way for the newer immigrant groups.

The result has been a continuous change in the composition of the population in the areas of first immigrant settlement, which have been shown to be the areas of highest delinquency rates. . . .

The changes in the distribution of racial and national groups both in the population and the delinquents . . . are paralleled by very similar changes in all of the areas of first immigrant settlement, as well as those that have been invaded by the Negroes. An analysis of the changes in all of the areas in which there has been a succession of foreign groups reveals that, with few exceptions, the older immigrant groups have replaced the newer immigrant groups, and that these changes have been accompanied by little variation in the rates of delinquents.

Changes in the Nationality Distribution Among Juvenile Court Delinquents for the City as a Whole

The movement of the German, Irish, English, and Scandinavian groups out of the areas of first settlement into the areas of second settlement has been paralleled by a corresponding decrease in the percentage of delinquent boys in these nationalities in the Cook County Juvenile Court. Likewise, the increase of Italians, Polish, Russians, Lithuanians, and Negroes in the areas of first settlement has been paralleled by an increase in the percentage of boys in these groups in the juvenile court. This fact is indicated both in the nationality classification of the delinquents in our two series of court delinquents and in the nationality classification published in the annual reports of the juvenile court.[5] For the purpose of making the present comparisons, the classifications in the reports of the court will be used, since they give the

nationality distribution by single years for a period of 30 years. The nationality distribution of the delinquents in the juvenile court, as shown by the annual reports, is presented for each fifth year from 1900 to 1930 in Table 23.1.

Only the cases classified by nationality or race were included in the computations of the percentages. This table indicates that of the 1,035 cases of male delinquents brought to the court during 1900, the German and Irish groups showed the highest percentage, the former 20.4 and the latter 18.7. The percentages in these two groups had decreased to 1.9 and 1.3, respectively, by 1930. Of equal consistency, but opposite in tendency, is the increase in the percentage of Italians and Poles, the former having increased from 5.1 percent in 1900 to 11.7 percent in 1930, and the latter from 15.1 percent to 21.0 percent in 1930.

While these changes were taking place in the foreign group, the percentage of cases in the white American group show relatively little increase. The percentage of American Negroes, on the other hand, increased from 4.7 percent in 1900 to 9.9 percent in 1920, and to 21.7 percent in 1930.

In order to interpret the changes in the percentage of juvenile court delinquents

Table 23.1
Nationality of delinquent boys based on the nativity of their parents expressed in percentages of the total number of cases classified by race and nationality for each fifth year since 1900

Nationality	1900	1905	1910	1915	1920	1925	1930
Total number of cases classified	1,035	1,828	1,123	2,215	1,829	1,910	2,307
American:							
White	16.0	19.0	16.5	16.5	23.0	21.7	19.5
Negro	4.7	5.1	5.5	6.2	9.9	17.1	21.7
German	20.4	18.5	15.5	11.0	6.3	3.5	1.9
Irish	18.7	15.4	12.3	10.7	6.1	3.1	1.3
Italian	5.1	8.3	7.9	10.1	12.7	12.8	11.7
Polish	15.1	15.7	18.6	22.1	24.5	21.9	21.0
English-Scotch	3.4	3.0	2.5	2.6	.9	.7	.6
Scandinavian	3.8	5.6	2.9	2.8	2.3	.5	.8
Austrian	.1	.3	.9	1.3	.8	2.2	1.7
Lithuanian	.1	.3	1.1	2.9	2.2	3.9	3.8
Czechoslovakian	4.6	4.3	5.5	3.0	2.2	2.8	4.2
All others	8.0	4.5	11.8	10.8	9.1	9.8	11.8
Total	100.0	100.0	100.0	100.0	100.0	100.0	100.0

among the various racial and national groups, it is necessary to take into consideration the changes in the proportion of each group in the total population of the city. The extent to which population change is responsible for the decrease in the percentage of the early immigrant groups among the juvenile court delinquents, may be illustrated by a special analysis of the German and Irish groups.

When the percentages of persons of Irish and German nativity in the total population in 1900 and 1920 were compared with the percentages of these nationalities in the juvenile court delinquents for the same years, it was found that the relative decrease in these two nationalities in the total population accounted for 51.8 percent of the decrease in the Irish, and 43.3 percent of the decrease in the German group. In other words, it was found that there was a 48.3 percent decrease in the relative number of delinquents of Irish parentage, and 56.7 percent decrease in the relative number of delinquents of Irish parentage, and 56.7 decrease in the relative number of delinquents of German parentage in the juvenile court cases after corrections were made for the changes in the ratio of each of these nationalities to the total population. On the other hand, calculations revealed that the increase in the percentages of Italian and Polish delinquents in the juvenile court was greater than the increase in the proportion of these groups in the total population.

The above facts indicate that without question the decrease from 1900 to 1920 in the proportion of the German and Irish in the delinquent group is much greater than the decrease in the proportion of these groups in the total population of the city. It is probable that this disproportionate decrease in the percentage of German and Irish delinquents in the juvenile court from 1900 to 1920 is due to the movement of these groups out of the area of first immigrant settlement and of high rates of delinquents during the 20-year period.

It is important to observe that the descendants of the early immigrant groups that have moved out of the areas of highest rates are not appearing in the juvenile court in great numbers. This fact is clearly indicated in the German and Irish groups when the probable number of their descendants in the population is considered. For while the absolute number of persons in Chicago of German and Irish nativity decreased between 1900 and 1920, the actual number of persons of German and Irish nationality, when defined to include the members of the third and fourth generations, probably grew through natural increase at a rate almost in proportion to the growth of the population of the city as a whole. If these descendants were appearing in the juvenile court in the same proportion in 1920 as did the children of German and Irish parentage in 1900, the percentage of delinquents among the white Americans would have increased between 1900 and 1920 in proportion to the decrease of the German and Irish group, since the descendants of these groups would be classified as Americans in 1920. Table 23.1 shows that, while the percentage of Germans and Irish decreased from almost 40 percent of the total number of delinquents in 1900 to 3.2 percent in 1930, the percentage of white Americans failed to show any consistent increase. This indicates that the rate of delinquency among the descendants of the German and Irish in 1920 was relatively insignificant as compared with the rate of delinquents in these two groups when they resided in the high-rate areas near the center of this city.

This same difference is indicated by the aforementioned fact that the rate of delinquents is more than 70 percent greater among the boys of foreign-born parents. All of the children of immigrants would be included in the first group, while all of the descendants after the second generation would be included in the latter.

The decrease in the rates of delinquents in the nationality groups that moved out of the areas of high rates during the period is established quite apart from the nationality classification of cases in the juvenile court by the fact that the rates of delinquents in the areas of second and third settlement are much lower than the rates in the areas of first settlement. . . .

It has been pointed out in this section that there has been a succession of nationalities in the areas of the first settlement near the central business district and the important industrial centers in Chicago, and that while this change was taking place there were few significant changes in the relative rates of delinquents in the same areas. In other words, the composition of the population changed; the relative rates of delinquents remained unchanged.

It was found also that as the older immigrant group moved out of the areas of first settlement there was a decrease in the percentage of these nationalities among the cases in the juvenile court. This fact, which suggests that the high rate of delinquents in these national groups was at least in part due to residence in these areas of high rates, is substantiated by the fact that the rates of delinquents are much lower in the areas of second and third immigrant settlement.

Similarly, it was pointed out in this section that for a long period of time there had been a disproportionate number of delinquents of foreign-born parents in the juvenile court in Chicago. This fact has attracted attention to the foreign-born population in the study of delinquency. One reason for this disproportion, as suggested by these materials, is that a disproportionate percentage of the foreign-born live in the areas of high rates of delinquents. These high rates of delinquents can not be explained in terms of population, for as has been shown in this section the population has changed in many of these areas while the rates of delinquents remained relatively unchanged. All of this material, therefore, suggests, the need for further analysis of the neighborhood situation in these areas of high rates of delinquents.

Disintegration of Neighborhood Organization

Thus far in this chapter we have presented certain formal indices of community organization and disorganization which serve to differentiate the areas of high and low rates of delinquents. When considered collectively these indices imply certain important variations in the community life in the areas adjacent to the central business district and the large industrial centers as compared to the outlying residential neighborhoods. They suggest that certain areas are characterized by great mobility, change, disintegration of the social structure and lack of stability, while in other areas, the neighborhood is more settled, stable, and highly integrated. Decreasing population implies that the security of the neighborhood is threatened; poverty implies bad housing, lack of sanitation, and a dearth of facilities for maintaining adequate neighborhood agencies and institutions; while the presence of a high percentage of foreign-born populations, comprising many divergent cultures and types of background, implies a confusion of moral standards and lack of social solidarity. Where such conditions prevail, the community is rendered relatively ineffective as an agency of control. There is little effective public opinion, community spirit, and collective effort to meet the local problems of the neighborhood.

. . . Under the disintegrative forces of city life many of the traditional institutions of the community are weakened or destroyed. While this tendency is to be observed in the city as a whole, it is particularly accentuated in certain sections of the city. It is obvious that there are tremendous differences between sections of the city in the extent to which the community is vital and effective and concerns itself with the solution of its local problems.

As suggested by Thomas, an effective community life is dependent upon the solidarity and stability of the social organization. In the areas close to the central business district, and to a less extent in the areas close to industrial developments, the neighborhood organization tends to disintegrate. For in these areas the mobility of population is so great that there is little opportunity for the development of common attitudes and interests. This fact is suggested by the difference between the percentage of families owning their homes in the areas close to the center of the city and in the outlying districts. For example, along Radial II the percentages of home ownership by square-mile areas from the Loop outward show the following variation: 6, 13, 25, 34, 44, 47, and 60. The low percentage of home ownership in the areas near the center of the city indicates, among other things, that there is not sufficient permanence to encourage the buying of homes, while the high percentage in the outlying areas indicates that a much larger proportion of the families are settled and permanently established.

It is a significant fact that many of the traditional institutions of society disintegrate under the influence of the rapidly changing conditions that prevail in the deteriorated areas of the large city. . . . If the institution attempts to perpetuate itself in the area, it becomes dependent upon subsidy or endowments from persons or organizations outside of the local area; it ceases to be a spontaneous and self-supporting agency of the neighborhood life. . . .

The inability of the inhabitants of the "slum" to act collectively with reference to their local problems has long been recognized. For example, the settlement movement was a response to the recognized need for establishing in these disintegrated sections of the city, neighborhood agencies and institutions.

A study of the distribution of social settlements and similar agencies in Chicago in 1925 revealed that of the 59 such institutions, 19 or 32.2 percent were located within two miles of the heart of the Loop, and a total of 50 or 84.8 percent were located within four miles of the center of the central business district. Of the remaining eight, three were in the Negro district and two were in South Chicago. Presumably, the concentration of settlements indicate those areas in which the local neighborhood organization is least effective and where there is the greatest need for assistance from other communities.

Apart from the social institutions which are supported and controlled by persons from more prosperous communities, there are few agencies in delinquency areas for dealing with the problems of delinquent behavior. The absence of common community ideals and standards prevents cooperative social action either to prevent or suppress delinquency. In some of the more stable integrated communities in the outlying districts any increase in the amount of delinquency is responded to by mass meetings and other indications of collective action among women's clubs, business men's organizations, church societies, and fraternal orders. On the other hand there is little such spontaneous and concerted action on the part of the inhabitants of the areas of high rates of delinquents to deal with the delinquent.

The neighborhood disorganization in the areas outside of the central business district is probably common to all rapidly growing American cities. However, in northern industrial cities, such as Chicago, the disorganization is intensified by the fact that the population in these areas is made up largely of foreign immigrants who are making their first adjustment to the complex life of the modern city. This adjustment involves profound and far-reaching modification of the whole structure of the cultural organization of the immigrant group. . . .

The problem of assimilation among them differs as regards the extent to which national attitudes are involved and the extent to which cultural backgrounds differ from our own; it involves a more or less complete change from a stable rural life to a rapidly changing and complex industrial urban community. In this situation, as Thomas and Znaniecki point out, demoralization takes place in both the first and the second generation:

> In order to reorganize his life on a new basis he needs a primary group as strong and coherent as the one he left in the old country. The Polish-American society gives him a few new schemes of life, but not enough to cover all of his activities. A certain lowering of his moral level is thus inevitable. Though it does not always lead to active demoralization, to anti-social behavior, it manifests itself at least in what we may call passive demoralization, a partial or a general weakening of social interests, a growing narrowness or shallowness of the individual's social life.

Of course the second generation, unless brought in direct and continuous contact with the better aspects of American life than those with which the immigrant community is usually acquainted, degenerates further still, both because the parents have less to give than they had received themselves in the line of social principles and emotions, and because the children brought up in American cities have more freedom and less respect for their parents. The second generation is better adapted intellectually to the practical conditions of American life, but their moral horizon grows still narrower on the average and their social interests still shallower. One might expect to find fewer cases of active demoralization of antisocial behavior, than in the first generation, which has to pass through the crisis of adaptation to new conditions. And yet it is a well-known fact that even the number of crimes is proportionately much larger among the children of immigrants than among the immigrants themselves.[6]

The disorganization among the foreign immigrants is paralleled by a similar disorganization among the Negroes. More than one-half of the Negroes in Chicago in 1920 were born outside of the State of Illinois; probably most of them in the rural districts in the Southern States. In any event, like the peasants from Europe, they are largely unaccustomed to the life in a large urban community.

But in one respect the background of the Negro is different from that of the foreign immigrant as described by Thomas and Znaniecki. Unlike the immigrant, the Negro has relatively few stabilizing traditions extending back over "hundreds of years." Neither does he have as a background a stable community organization which has remained unchanged over a long period of time. His institutions are very new and inadequately developed. Consequently they break down completely as agencies of social control in the process of adjustment to the complex life on an urban community. This social disorganization is accompanied by a large amount of personal disorganization and demoralization among Negro adults as well as among Negro children.[7]

No doubt this absence of stabilizing tradition in the Negro group is a very important factor underlying the high rates of delinquents already noted among Negro boys. As a whole their situation is much less constructive than that of the children of foreign immigrants, both because there is less tradition in their own group, and because a larger proportion of them live in areas of high rates of delinquents. These conditions are probably important factors in determining the dispro-

portionate number of Negro delinquents in the juvenile court.

Adult Offenders

In concluding this study of the formal characteristics of the delinquency areas of Chicago, it is important to point out that these areas also show the greatest concentration and highest rates of adult offenders.

In the absence of an effective neighborhood organization delinquency gains a foothold in the disorganized areas, despite the efforts of settlements and other social agencies to combat and suppress it. In this situation large numbers of the juvenile delinquents from these areas continue in adult crime. . . .

Summary

In this chapter an attempt has been made to locate and characterize the areas which have been differentiated in the process of the growth of the city and to indicate the variation in the rate of juvenile delinquents among these areas. Particular effort has been made to show the differences between the areas with the highest rates and those with the lowest rates of delinquents. These types of areas represent the two extremes of a continuum between which there are areas with all the intermediate grades of variation.

It was found that the areas of high rates of delinquents are adjacent to the central business district and the major industrial developments. Generally speaking, these areas were found to be characterized by physical deterioration, decreasing population, high rates of dependency, high percentage of foreign-born and Negro population, and high rates of adult offenders.

One of the most significant findings in this part of the study is the fact that, while the relative rates of delinquents in these high-rate areas remained more or less constant over a period of 20 years, the nationality composition of the population changed almost completely in the interval. As the older national groups moved out of these areas of first immigrant settlement, the percentage of juvenile delinquents in these groups showed a consistent decrease.

It was indicated, also, that the areas of high rates of delinquents are characterized by marked disintegration of the traditional institutions and neighborhood organization. In this type of area, the community fails to function effectively as an agency of social control. . . .

Discussion Questions

1. What does "social disorganization" mean? According to Shaw and McKay, why is it important for the study of crime and delinquency?

2. Why do socially disorganized areas remain disorganized over time? Why does the zone of transition have the highest rates of crime and delinquency regardless of the nativity or race/ethnicity of the group living there? Based on this information, what conclusion do Shaw and McKay make concerning the importance of nativity and race/ethnicity for explaining crime and delinquency rates?

3. What are some of the characteristics, identified by Shaw and McKay, of the zone of transition? Are these characteristics directly related to crime and delinquency rates or do they reflect the social and economic circumstances of the neighborhood's residents? What are the implications of the characteristics of the zone of transition for developing strong social controls?

Notes

1. Park, R. E.: "Human Behavior in Urban Environment;" in *The City*, by R. E. Park, E. W. Burgess et al., Chicago, the University of Chicago Press, 1925, pp. 4-6.

2. Burgess, E. W.: *Urban Areas in Chicago: An Experiment in Social Science Research*. Edited by T. V. Smith and L. D. White, Chicago, University of Chicago Press, 1929, pp. 114-117.

3. This series of dependency cases was secured by Prof. Earle Fisk Young and Faye B. Karpf under the direction of Prof. Robert E. Park.

4. The total aged 10 to 16 white male population with foreign-born fathers for the city was secured by combining the native white of foreign parentage, the foreign born, and one-half of the native white of mixed parentage (the latter division was made on the assumption that one-half of the parents were native born and one-half foreign born). While this population is available for the city as a whole it could not be secured for local areas within the city.

5. In the Cook County Juvenile Court Reports through 1920 the delinquents were classified on the basis of the nationality of the parents. It is impossible to ascertain exactly the extent to which nationality represents nativity. Probably in some instances foreign-born parents give their nationality as American, while others who were native born give as their nationality the country from which their ancestors came. In our study of the court records we attempted to make all classification on the basis of the nativity of the father. When our results are compared with the published records of the court the percentage distribution for nationalities are quite similar.

6. Thomas, William I., and Znanieckik, Florian: *The Polish Peasant in Europe and America*. New York, Alfred A. Knopf, 1927, Vol. II, p. 1650.

7. This point of view is quite fully developed by Prof. E. Franklin Frazier, of Fisk University, in an excellent study. This study was prepared as a doctor's dissertation in the Department of Sociology at the University of Chicago and is as yet unpublished.

Reprinted from: Clifford R. Shaw and Henry D. McKay, "Formal Characteristics of Delinquency Areas." In *National Commission on Law Observance and Enforcement, Report on the Causes of Crime, Vol. II*, pp 60-108. United States Government Printing Office, 1931. ✦

24

Economic Deprivation and Neighborhood Crime Rates, 1960–1980

Robert J. Bursik, Jr.
Harold G. Grasmick

Although it experienced a period of decline, Shaw and McKay's social-disorganization perspective has recently received renewed attention and continues to influence theoretical and empirical work in criminology. Some scholars have reformulated the theory in an attempt to account for numerous social and economic changes that cities have experienced in recent decades, primarily as a result of deindustrialization, and that render portions of the theory unable to account for present-day neighborhood level crime patterns. Current efforts in this area are evidenced in the work of Robert Bursik and Harold Grasmick.

In this selection Bursik and Grasmick discuss past and present efforts in the study of social disorganization, particularly noting some of the problems involved in applying Shaw and McKay's framework and the problems that Wilson's research on the underclass pose for traditional formulations of the theory. These scholars also examine crime rates in Chicago for years 1960 to 1980. Their research suggests that by 1960, extreme economic deprivation was concentrated in some neighborhoods and the economic conditions of most neighborhoods declined between 1960 and 1980. Economic deprivation is associated with both higher crime rates and reduced regulatory capacities of neighborhoods; regulatory capacity of neighborhoods is the strongest predictor of crime rates. Bursik and Grasmick conclude that these results offer partial support for Shaw and McKay's original social disorganization theory.

Equally important as the empirical findings are the theoretical innovations that Bursik and Grasmick suggest. They discuss the importance of considering larger social, economic, and political contexts of neighborhoods to understand social control processes. Further, they suggest that social control should be conceptualized at three levels (private, parochial, and public) and that all three need to be considered in social disorganization perspectives. The modifications they propose incorporate changes in the economic structure and residential patterns of urban areas that have occurred since the original studies in the 1920s through the 1940s.

The presumed relationship between economic deprivation and the number of crimes committed by the residents of a particular neighborhood is one of the lasting legacies of the research of Clifford Shaw, Henry McKay, and associates (1929, 1942, 1969). As noted by the theoretical explications of Kornhauser (1978), Tittle (1983), and Bursik and Grasmick (1993), their social disorganization framework assumed that this relationship was an indirect one, mediated in turn by the residential instability and heterogeneity of the neighborhood and by the regulatory capacity of the area. Nevertheless, despite the indirect nature of its effect on crime rates, the economic composition of local urban communities was the key ecological factor that set in operation the dynamics associated with social disorganization.

The pivotal role of economic factors in the development of social disorganization is derived from the Park and Burgess (1924) model of human ecology which assumed that residential mobility was a function of the degree of assimilation of local populations into the occupational structure of urban areas. Since the initial occupations of immigrant groups were assumed to be relatively low paying, these groups tended to be concentrated in economically deprived areas. However, over time, occupational mobility would lead to resettlement in more desirable neighborhoods characterized by higher economic status, greater stability, and less heterogeneity.[1]

The availability of unskilled jobs in goods-production industries played an important role in shaping these ecological dynamics, for they provided a relatively open entree into the occupational structure. Unfortunately, as industries have been enticed into suburban and rural locations, many residents of modern central-city neighborhoods no longer have easy access to the type of jobs that traditionally provided the opportunity for occupational mobility, especially in the older, Northern cities. Wilson (1987:100), for example, notes that the number of manufacturing jobs declined by 701,700 in the Northeast and North Central regions of the United States between 1970 and 1980.

At the same time, dramatic changes have occurred in the racial composition of many cities. For example, while Wilson (1987:101) notes that the black population of the 33 largest central cities increased by more than 5,000,000 between 1950 and 1980, the white population declined by more than 9,000,000 during the same period. The coupling of such demographic shifts with the noted trend in urban economies has resulted in the concentration and isolation of the most disadvantaged segments of minority populations in the central-city neighborhoods of older industrial cities (p. 58), leading to the emergence of an extremely poor "underclass" population that is structurally prohibited from any significant degree of residential upgrading (see Sampson & Wilson 1991). Such dramatic alterations in the ecological structures and dynamics of many urban areas suggest that the relationship between economic deprivation and crime rates may have changed significantly from the indirect effect envisioned by Shaw and McKay. On the other hand, the association may have remained fairly stable despite these new ecological dynamics. We here compare the structure of relationships between the ecological dynamics associated with crime in Chicago during 1960 and 1980 and interpret the results within the contemporary systemic reformu-

lation of the social disorganization framework (Sampson & Groves 1989; Bursik & Grasmick 1993).

The Role of Economic Deprivation in Social Disorganization Models

The literature that has considered the degree to which neighborhood economic composition is related to crime has been characterized by two conceptually distinct approaches. The first has emphasized the degree of economic inequality within local communities. While such internal variation in the availability of economic resources has been recognized within urban sociology at least since the publication of Zorbaugh's classic *The Gold Coast and the Slum* in 1929, surprisingly few recent studies have examined the effects of economic inequality at the neighborhood level.[2] The important exceptions, Messner and Tardiff (1986) and Patterson (1991), have failed to find a significant relationship between inequality and crime. Given Wilson's (1987) argument concerning the flight of affluent families from the central city, such findings are not theoretically unexpected since these dynamics should lead to a decreasing level of inequality within urban neighborhoods over time.

Many more studies have focused on a conceptually different approach to the economic issue that operationalizes deprivation relative to some fixed physical or physiological standards of well-being (Braithwaite 1979; Messner 1982) rather than to the overall distribution of economic status. Whereas the inequality frameworks generally are referred to as relative approaches, the fixed-standard orientation typically is referred to as an absolute approach. Not only do we consider such an orientation to be much more consistent with Wilson's underclass hypothesis, but it is identical to the conceptualization underlying Shaw and McKay's traditional social disorganization framework.

Many contemporary discussions of the relationship of absolute deprivation to crime entail neighborhood dynamics much like those found in Shaw and McKay and, therefore, represent variations of the indirect effect hypothesis. Wacquant and Wilson

(1989), for example, argue that the economic marginalization and deterioration of black neighborhoods has had devastating effects on the ability of local communities to act as agents of social control. In support of this position, they present data (pp. 22-24) suggesting that there is a decline in attachment to and identification with the neighborhood, fewer social ties with other community residents, and an overall loss of strength within such economic contexts. Similarly, Bluestone and Harrison (1982) note that the closing of manufacturing plants typically is accompanied by strained family and social relationships and a general decline in social cohesion in the affected communities.[3]

On the other hand, a growing body of work suggests that the economic and political dynamics associated with the emergence of the underclass are reflected in a direct effect of absolute deprivation on crime. The possibility that deprivation has such an effect presents a historically fascinating challenge to the traditional social disorganization model, for it suggests that it may be necessary to supplant Park and Burgess's "desirable space" ecological model with the "sustenance activity" orientation found in the ecological theory of Amos Hawley (1944, 1950).[4] While Hawley acknowledged that the dynamics emphasized by Park and Burgess should be part of a general ecological model (see, e.g., Hawley 1944:404), and discussed the regulatory capacities of commensualistic relationships (1950: 219), he expanded their orientation by emphasizing the distribution of sustenance activities that give rise to an urban structure of interdependent relationships (ibid., p. 180). From this perspective, crime is an alternative means of gaining economic and social sustenance from the environment (see Bursik & Grasmick 1993:65-70).

Sullivan's (1989) discussion of a Brooklyn neighborhood during the late 1970s and early 1980s provides a rich description of how attempts to derive economic sustenance from the social environment can lead directly to criminal involvement. Many youths in that community were skeptical of the relevance of education to their future in the labor market and left school to obtain work prior to graduation. However, given their relative lack of conventional employment credentials, the positions that were available tended to be unstable, with undesirable working conditions and no chance for advancement. Since a significant proportion of these jobs were never officially recorded, many of these youth did not qualify for unemployment compensation if a position was terminated suddenly (Sullivan 1989:60-64). As a result, many of the local youths became involved in a systematic series of thefts and other economically motivated illegal activities that were coordinated through membership in local gangs (p. 117).

Moore (1988:8) also has argued that the shrinking number of employment opportunities can lead to the institutionalization of gang activities in economically deprived neighborhoods. While a significant proportion of gang members may mature out of such behavior (as also noted by Sullivan), some fraction retain their gang affiliation well into adulthood due to the lack of financial alternatives. Some of the children from this fraction are recruited into gangs during adolescence, and the process of gang formation and maintenance continues to reproduce itself.

The findings of recent studies testing the viability of the direct effect hypothesis are inconsistent.[5] Curry and Spergel (1988) conclude that the degree of poverty in a neighborhood is directly related to both the general delinquency rate and the rate of gang-related homicides; these findings are supported by the research of Taylor and Covington (1988) concerning homicides in general. Yet the direct relationship between percentage poor and the homicide rate presented in Messner and Tardiff (1986) is not significant. Likewise, Sampson and Groves (1989) present evidence that the socioeconomic composition of a local community has no direct effect on community rates of personal violence and property theft/vandalism. Therefore, there has been a great deal of divergence in the findings of studies that have examined this issue. . . .

Data and Measurement

Our examination of the viability of the direct and indirect hypotheses within the context of contemporary urban economies is based on the rates of male referrals to the Cook County, Illinois, juvenile court (computed per 1,000 male juveniles ages 10-17) for the years 1960 and 1980 in each of Chicago's officially recognized local community areas.[6] The years 1960 and 1980 were chosen because they seem to bracket nicely the development of the economic processes discussed by Wilson (1987:3-7) and a wide variety of consistently defined variables were available for these periods.

Our measures of socioeconomic composition and deprivation were selected to be as congruent with Wilson's argument as possible. The indicators of general socioeconomic status (SES) are identical to those that often have been used in past research; the percentage of the population with professional/managerial occupations, the median education level, and the median family income. Three of the measures of severe economic deprivation (DEP) are also straightforward: the percentage of families with incomes below the poverty level (for 1960 this is measured as the percentage with incomes below $3,000), the unemployment rate, and the rate of public assistance allocations per 100 residents.[7]

We have included one other indicator in our scale of economic deprivation, although it does not represent financial considerations per se: the percentage of the population that is black. Wilson has argued that this minority population tends to be concentrated in economically deprived neighborhoods, and as will be seen in the subsequent analyses, a very large proportion of its individual variation is shared in common with the other economic indicators. Therefore, its separate incorporation into the model would have led to an intolerably high level of multicollinearity and very unstable estimates of its effects.

Unfortunately, the selection of indicators to represent the regulatory capacity (RG) element of the social disorganization model was limited by the same paucity of data that other studies have confronted; information on the breadth and depth of relational networks in all these neighborhoods during 1960 and 1980 is not available. Therefore, we have been forced to rely on more indirect measures drawn from census data. Two of these,

the rates of owner occupancy and residential mobility, have often appeared in other research within this tradition. However, the mobility indicator is somewhat problematic given the way the variable is defined by the Bureau of the Census (the percentage of residents who have not lived at the same address for five or more years). While this gives some sense of the rate of turnover, it is possible for very unstable communities to have scores nearing 0% on this item. Such a situation would occur when a large number of residents have left a neighborhood, essentially abandoning those who cannot (or will not) leave. If the remaining population has resided in the area for more than five years, the neighborhood will appear to be highly stable, even if a majority of the population has left the area. To compensate for this source of inferential complexity, we have also included community-specific measures of net migration, defined as the percentage change in population size during the preceding decade that cannot be accounted for by births or deaths, as an additional indicator of stability.[8] The final indicator of regulatory capacity is the percentage of children who live in husband-wife households, for Sampson (1987) has argued persuasively that this compositional element is intrinsically related to a neighborhood's ability to supervise the nature of the activities occurring within its borders.

Each set of variables was combined into the relevant scale.... These findings confirm Wilson's argument concerning the pronounced concentration of these social characteristics within urban neighborhoods.

Second, the factor structures underlying these three dimensions during 1960 and 1980 are strikingly similar. Therefore, the generally invariant ecological structure described by Bursik (1984) for Chicago during 1960 and 1970 appears to also characterize the city during 1980. This finding calls for a slight modification of Wilson's (1987) argument, which implies that recent trends in urban economies have led to an increasing concentration of "the most disadvantaged segments of the urban black population" (p. 58). Rather, our findings suggest that the five indicators of economic deprivation we have used in our analysis generally have been concentrated in particular neighborhood settings since at least 1960.

However, while the nature of concentration is similar for these two decades, the number of neighborhoods characterized by extreme economic deprivation has increased dramatically and in a fashion consistent with Wilson's discussion. Table 24.1 presents the univariate statistics for the variables that formed the basis of our three scales. A simple inspection of these distributions confirms Wilson's argument concerning recent urban dynamics. There appears to have been a bifurcated process of economic change during this 20-year period: while there was an increase in the percentage of residents employed in professional occupations, there also were significant increases in the poverty and unemployment rates, and a more than fivefold jump in the rate of public aid.

It is also interesting that the mean levels and variations of owner occupancy did not change significantly between 1960 and 1980 even though the levels of residential mobility significantly decreased. In addition, note that while the in- and out-migration flows tended to balance one another between 1950 and 1960, Chicago's neighborhoods on the average suffered a net loss of more than 13% in their residential populations between 1970 and 1980 due to migration. In fact, an inspection of the frequencies for the 1980 levels of this variable indicates that only 5 of the 74

neighborhoods were characterized by a positive level of immigration (compared to 21 growing neighborhoods during 1960). When this trend is placed in the context of the noted patterns for owner occupancy and residential mobility, the findings suggest that Chicago's real estate market stagnated during this period and that the central city during 1980 was populated to a large degree by residents who had been "abandoned" in their neighborhoods.

The full extent of Chicago's economic transformation can be provided by examining the changes in the neighborhood levels of economic deprivation during this 20-year period. Unfortunately, this relatively simple analytic question is trickier than it appears....

Table 24.2 provides two very clear indications of the general economic decline of Chicago's neighborhoods. First, note from the marginal distributions that nearly 70% of the areas had the same level of economic deprivation during 1980 as the lowest 25% of the 1960 neighborhoods. In fact, over one-fifth of the least deprived 1960 neighborhoods were in the most deprived category by 1980. Second, economic decline during this period was a unidirectional process; none of the neighborhoods could be classified as moving from a more deprived to a less deprived status during this period.

In sum, Chicago is a city that clearly has undergone the economic transformations

Table 24.1
Chicago Neighborhood Characteristics, 1960–1980

	1960		1980		
	Mean	S.D.	Mean	S.D.	t[a]
Delinquency rate	15.57	12.12	56.83	36.93	11.55
% professional	8.67	5.12	18.05	10.20	10.40
Median education	10.39	1.59	11.02	1.14	3.71
Median income	$6,913	$1,595	$19,180	$6,136	$22.05
% below poverty	13.30	10.46	16.54	14.31	4.04
Unemployment rate	5.09	3.61	10.61	6.12	11.72
Rate of public aid	6.62	10.33	37.89	38.02	9.11
% black	20.06	33.76	39.69	42.86	5.36
% owner-occupancy	45.45	27.31	45.58	24.78	0.21
Residential mobility	50.46	10.73	38.42	11.25	8.34
Net migration (%)	0.34	52.11	-13.44	15.30	2.41
% children with parents	84.49	12.45	65.88	22.06	12.61

[a]N= 74 for all variables. The t-test was computed on the basis of a paired comparison between years.

Table 24.2
Changes in Neighborhood Economic Deprivation, 1960–1980

			1960				
			Low Deprivation			High Deprivation	
			1	2	3	4	Row %
	Low Deprivation	1	21.1	0.0	0.0	0.0	5.4
		2	31.6	11.8	0.0	0.0	10.8
1980		3	26.3	29.4	11.1	0.0	16.2
	High Deprivation	4	21.1	58.8	88.9	100.0	67.6
	Total		100.1	100.0	100.0	100.0	100.0
	Column %		25.7	23.0	24.3	27.0 $N=74$	

Wilson discussed. This is an important difference from the image of Chicago envisioned by Shaw and McKay and by Park and Burgess, in which the functional role of the neighborhood in the ecological system was assumed to be in a general state of equilibrium. The central question facing contemporary social disorganization research, therefore, is the degree to which these changes may have affected the viability of the basic hypothesis that economic deprivation has a primarily indirect, rather than direct, effect on the crime rate.

Findings

. . . In both 1960 and 1980, SES has a nonsignificant effect on both the delinquency rate and regulatory capacity that characterize Chicago's neighborhoods. The level of economic deprivation, on the other hand, plays a major role in shaping these two aspects of the local community even after the effects of the other variables in the model are controlled for. . . .

Nearly as important a finding is that despite the dramatic changes in the distribution of economic deprivation that occurred between the beginning and end of this 20-year period, the patterns of relationships for 1960 and 1980 are strikingly similar, including the magnitudes of the significant standardized coefficients. . . .

Most important, the predictions of the traditional social disorganization model receive strong but mixed support during both periods. As expected, economic deprivation is strongly associated with the regulatory capacity of an area, which in turn has the strongest direct effect on delinquency during both periods. . . . Therefore, our findings indicate that economic factors affect delinquency, at least primarily, in a manner consistent with the traditional Shaw and McKay framework.

Nevertheless, economic deprivation has a significant direct effect on delinquency during both periods. It certainly is possible that this effect would have been further attenuated if we had incorporated additional indicators of the internal regulatory capacity of these neighborhoods into the model. Yet, on the basis of these findings, we must consider the possibility that there are additional neighborhood dynamics relevant to delinquency that are not reflected in the traditional theoretical specification of social disorganization. . . .

Discussion

. . . The viability of the framework as a whole was prematurely dismissed by many criminologists because of its notorious inability to account for the presence of stable, working-class communities that nonetheless were characterized by relatively high rates of crime and delinquency. Likewise, the existence of a direct effect of economic deprivation on delinquency is inconsistent with the core assumptions of the model. In addition, many observers have criticized its general failure to consider the political and economic contexts of the larger urban systems in which local neighborhoods are embedded.

Recently, however, there have been several attempts to reformulate the social disorganization framework in terms of a broader systemic approach that emphasizes the breadth and depth of institutional and personal relational networks within a community and the capacities of such networks as sources of social control (see Sampson & Groves 1989; Bursik & Grasmick 1993). These capacities have been most fully addressed by Hunter (1985), who identifies three dimensions of neighborhood social order. The *private* level is grounded in the intimate, informal primary groups in a community, and control is exerted primarily through the allocation or threatened withdrawal of sentiment, social support, and mutual esteem (Hunter 1985:233). The second, *parochial* level of control reflects the nonintimate relationships among neighbors who do not have a deep sentimental attachment and the interlocking of local institutions such as schools, churches, and voluntary organizations (ibid.). At this level, the regulatory capacity of an area reflects the ability of residents to supervise activities within the community and the degree to which local institutions are integrated into the fabric of everyday community life.

While the concepts of private and parochial control formalize several of the key dynamics of the social disorganization model that were left implicit by Shaw and McKay, we do not feel that they totally can account for our observed direct effect of economic deprivation on delinquency. Likewise, they are totally unable to account for the existence of stable, high-delinquency areas. In our opinion, this is due to the primary emphasis of these two levels of control on the internal dynamics of the community. Spergel and Korbelik (1979:109) have shown that there are externally determined contingencies that mediate the ability of local networks and institutions to control the threat of crime. In fact, some local associations initially arise due to the intervention of external organizations who may seek legitimacy for projects they are considering in a particular community (Taub et al. 1977). Therefore, it is also necessary to consider the *public* level of social control (Hunter 1985:233), which focuses on a community's ability to secure the public goods and services allocated by agencies located outside the neighborhood that are necessary for the development of an effective regulatory capacity. . . .

Such resources are necessarily monetary or even tangible. Molotch (1976; see also Logan & Molotch 1987) characterizes cities as a system of competing neighborhood-based land interests that are capable of strategic coalition and action vis-a-vis other neighborhoods in that system. Therefore, the development of broad-based networks of association can also increase the capacity of local communities to influence the processes of urban political decisionmaking so that the outcomes foster their regulatory capacities. For example, Bursik (1989) has presented evidence suggesting that political decisionmaking about the location of the public housing constructed in Chicago between 1970 and 1980 were not made on the basis of market considerations relating to the costs of acquiring the necessary tracts of land. Rather, the projects were most likely to be located in neighborhoods that already were unstable and presumably unable to organize and negotiate an effective defense against their construction. It is important to note that the construction that resulted from these externally generated decisions tended to increase the existing rate of residential turnover and, in turn, delinquency.

We feel that the greatest shortcoming of the traditional social disorganization model has been the failure to consider the relational networks that pertain to this public sphere of control, for as many urban analysts have noted (see, e.g., Lewis & Salem 1986), it is very difficult to significantly affect the nature of neighborhood life solely through indigenous neighborhood processes. Therefore, a central assumption underlying the systemic reformulation of social disorganization is that crime is more likely in areas in which the networks of public control cannot effectively provide services to the neighborhood.

Therefore, we would argue that the effect of economic deprivation on crime and delinquency is, in fact, an indirect one, mediated by the capacity of a neighborhood to solicit human and economic resources from external institutional actors. Such an assumption is supported by the work of Moore (1978:21-26), who notes the general absence of political "brokers" who can intercede between underclass Chicago communities with relatively high rates of gang behavior and major institutional agencies, such as those connected with health and welfare, education, migration, and most importantly, criminal justice. Thus, she concludes that residents of such neighborhoods are poorly equipped to deal with such institutions. As a result, the potential ability of an economically marginal neighborhood to exercise public control is very limited.

Unfortunately, it is very difficult to collect the requisite data concerning the relational networks implicit to the public-level control of crime on a large scale basis (i.e., for every neighborhood in a large urban system). However, there is at least anecdotal evidence to illustrate the powerful potential for these trans-neighborhood networks to foster a community's capacity for the control of crime. . . .

In sum, we do not feel that the findings pertaining to economic deprivation presented here and in other related research necessarily contradict the assumptions of a systemic model of social disorganization. Rather, we believe that a simultaneous consideration of all three levels of control—the private, the parochial, and the public—can account for these patterns in a logically consistent manner. . . .

Discussion Questions

1. What are the three levels of social control that Bursik and Grasmick argue

need to be included in social disorganization theory? What is the potential relevance of each, according to these scholars, for explaining crime rates in urban areas?

2. What important changes have occurred in urban areas since the 1920s through the 1940s? What are the implications of these changes for Shaw and McKay's social disorganization perspective? What is the importance of the "underclass" for ecological processes in cities?

3. According to Bursik and Grasmick, do their findings support Shaw and McKay's original hypothesis with regard to the relationship between economic deprivation and crime rates? In what ways are their findings consistent with this hypothesis? In what ways are their findings inconsistent with this hypothesis?

Notes

1. The Park and Burgess model assumed the existence of an open market in which housing was available to anyone with sufficient financial resources or credit. However, this has never been the case for many minority groups (see Bursik 1986) and declined generally as a valid assumption since World War II (see Bursik 1989).

2. There certainly are many more studies of neighborhood inequality in the corpus of criminological literature. However, since the underclass argument of Wilson is highly period dependent, we have restricted our attention to the most recent work. The same consideration will be reflected in our discussion of absolute deprivation.

3. Taylor and Covington (1988) present an alternative indirect model in which absolute deprivation is assumed to increase the levels of perceived relative deprivation. However, they do not include measures of the prevalence of such perceptions in their model. Therefore, it is impossible to determine whether their data more fully support the existence of a primarily indirect or direct effect of absolute deprivation on crime rates.

4. Despite the ecological intellectual heritage of the social disorganization perspective, the theoretical implications of the urban dynamics that underlie Hawley's model of human

ecology rarely have been considered from within the disorganization context, although they lie at the heart of the routine activities model as developed by Felson and Cohen (1980).

5. A number of studies have examined the effect of economic deprivation on neighborhood rates of victimization (see, e.g., Smith & Jarjoura 1988; Sampson & Groves 1989; Patterson 1991). However, since the focus of this article is on rates of offending behavior, these findings are not considered in detail.

6. Chicago had 76 community areas during 1960 and 77 during 1980. Since the additional neighborhood for 1980 was created by splitting one of the original 76, we reaggregated the data to make the two decades comparable. Of these 76 units of analysis, two had very small juvenile populations (the Loop and O'Hare), thereby making the estimated rates highly unreliable. They have been eliminated from the analysis, resulting in our use of 74 consistently defined neighborhoods in the analysis.

7. This indicator represents all financial allocations made through the tax-supported programs of Aid to Dependent Children, Aid to the Blind, Disability Assistance, and General Assistance. Since residents can qualify simultaneously under more than one program, it is possible that the total number of allocations provided by these four programs is greater than the number of residents (and this is the case in several neighborhoods). Therefore it is more appropriate to consider it to represent a rate rather than a percentage. All noncensus materials have been drawn from Kitagawa and Taeuber (1963) and the Chicago Fact Book Consortium (1984).

8. Although it would be desirable to have such information on a race-specific basis, the material available to us suppressed the data if the population during the base year (i.e., 1950 for 1960 estimates, and 1970 for 1980 estimates) was less than 1,500. This especially was the case for the size of the black population in many of Chicago's neighborhoods during the 1950–60 period.

References

Bailey, William C. 1985. "Aggregation and Disaggregation in Cross-sectional Analyses of Crime Patterns." Presented at Annual Meetings of American Society of Criminology, San Diego.

Bluestone, Barry, and Bennett Harrison. 1982. *The De-industrialization of America: Plant Closings, Community Abandonment, and the Dismantling of Basic Industry*. New York: Basic Books.

Braithwaite, John. 1979. *Inequality, Crime, and Public Policy*. London: Routledge & Kegan Paul.

Bursik, Robert J., Jr. 1984. "Urban Dynamics and Ecological Studies of Delinquency," 63 *Social Forces* 393.

——. 1986. "Ecological Stability and the Dynamics of Delinquency," in A.J. Reiss and M. Tonry, eds., *Communities and Crime*. Chicago: University of Chicago Press.

——. 1989. "Political Decisionmaking and Ecological Models of Delinquency: Conflict and Consensus," in S.F. Messner, M.D. Krohn, and A.E. Liska, eds., *Theoretical Integration in the Study of Deviance and Crime*. Albany: State University of New York Press.

Bursik, Robert J., Jr., and Harold G. Grasmick. 1993. *Neighborhoods and Crime: The Dimensions of Effective Community Control*. New York: Lexington Books.

Chicago Fact Book Consortium, ed. 1984. *Local Community Fact Book: Chicago Metropolitan Area*. Chicago: Chicago Review Press.

Clelland, Donald, and Timothy J. Carter. 1980. "The New Myth of Class and Crime," 18 *Criminology* 319.

Curry, G. David, and Irving A. Spergel. 1988. "Gang Homicide, Delinquency and Community," 26 *Criminology* 381.

Dawley, David. 1992. *A Nation of Lords*. 2nd edition. Prospect Heights, IL: Waveland Press.

Erlanger, Howard S. 1979. "Estrangement, Machismo, and Gang Violence," 60 *Social Science Quarterly* 235.

Felson, Marcus, and Lawrence E. Cohen. 1980. "Human Ecology and Crime: A Routine Activity Approach," 8 *Human Ecology* 389.

Frey, William H., and Alden Speare. 1988. *Regional and Metropolitan Growth and Decline in the United States*. New York: Russell Sage Foundation.

Gordon, Robert A. 1967. "Issues in the Ecological Study of Delinquency," 32 *American Sociological Rev.* 927.

Hawley, Amos H. 1944. "Ecology and Human Ecology," 23 *Social Forces* 398.

——. 1950. *Human Ecology: A Theory of Community Structure*. New York: Ronald Press.

Hunter, Albert J. 1985. "Private, Parochial and Public Social Orders: The Problem of Crime and Incivility in Urban Communities," in G.D. Suttles and M.N. Zald, eds., *The Challenge of Social Control: Citizenship and Institution*

Building in Modern Society. Norwood, NJ: Ablex Publishing.

Jankowski, Martin Sanchez. 1991. *Islands in the Street: Gangs and American Urban Society*. Norwood, NJ: Ablex Publishing

Kitagawa, Evelyn M., and Karl E. Taeuber, eds. 1963. *Local Community Fact Book. Chicago Metropolitan Area, 1960*. Chicago: University of Chicago Press.

Kornhauser, Ruth Rosner. 1978. *Social Sources of Delinquency*. Chicago: University of Chicago Press.

Land, Kenneth C., Patricia L. McCall, and Lawrence E. Cohen. 1990. "Structural Covariates of Homicide Rates: Are There Any Invariances Across Time and Social Space?" 87 *American Journal of Sociology* 413.

Lewis, Dan A., and Greta Salem. 1986. *Fear of Crime, Incivility, and the Production of a Social Problem*. New Brunswick, NJ: Transaction Books.

Logan, John R., and Harvey L. Molotch. 1987. *Urban Fortunesrontiers: The Political Economy of Place*. Berkeley: University of California Press.

Mayer, Neil S. 1983. "How Neighborhood Development Programs Succeed and Grow: A Survey," in P.L. Clay and R.M. Hollister, eds., *Neighborhood Policy and Planning*. Lexington, MA: Lexington Books.

McCarthy, John D., and Mayer N. Zald. 1987. "Resource Mobilization and Social Movements: A Partial Theory," in M.N. Zald and J.D. McCarthy, eds., *Social Movements in an Organizational Society*. New Brunswick, NJ: Transaction Books.

Messner, Steven F. 1982. "Poverty, Inequality, and the Urban Homicide Rate," 20 *Criminology* 103.

Messner, Steven F, and Kenneth Tardiff. 1986. "Economic Inequality and Levels of Homicide: An Analysis of Urban Neighborhoods," 24 *Criminology* 297.

Molotch, Harvey. 1976. "The City as a Growth Machine: Toward a Political Economy of Place," 82 *American Journal of Sociology* 309.

Moore, Joan W. 1978. *Homeboys*. Philadelphia: Temple University Press.

——. 1988. "Introduction: Gangs and the Underclass: A Comparative Perspective," in J.M. Hagedorn, ed., *People and Folks: Gangs, Crime and the Underclass in a Rustbelt City*. Chicago: Lake View Press.

Park, Robert E., and Ernest W. Burgess. 1924. *Introduction to the Science of Sociology*. 2nd edition. Chicago: University of Chicago Press.

Patterson, E. Britt. 1991. "Poverty, Income Inequality, and Community Crime Rates," 29 *Criminology* 755.

Sampson, Robert J. 1987. "Communities and Crime," in M.R. Gottfredson and T. Hirschi, eds., *Positive Criminology*. Beverly Hills, CA: Sage Publications.

Sampson, Robert J., and W. Byron Groves. 1989. "Community Structure and Crime: Testing Social-Disorganization Theory," 94 *American Journal of Sociology* 774.

Sampson, Robert J., and William Julius Wilson. 1991. "Toward a Theory of Race, Crime, and Urban Inequality." Presented at Annual meetings of American Society of Criminology, San Francisco.

Shaw, Clifford R., Frederick M. Zorbaugh, Henry D. McKay, and Leonard S. Cottrell. 1929. *Delinquency Areas*. 2nd edition. Chicago: University of Chicago Press.

——. 1969. *Juvenile Delinquency and Urban Areas*. 2nd edition. Chicago: University of Chicago Press.

Shaw, Clifford R., Frederick M. Zorbaugh, Henry D. McKay, and Leonard S. Cottrell. 1929. *Delinquency Areas*. Chicago: University of Chicago Press.

Smith, Douglas A., and G. Roger Jarjoura. 1988. "Social Structure and Criminal Victimization," 25 *Journal of Research in Crime & Delinquency* 27.

Spergel, Irving A., and John Korbelik. 1979. "The Local Community Service System and ISOS: An Interorganizational Analysis." Executive Report to the Illinois Law Enforcement Commission. Chicago: Illinois Law Enforcement Commission.

Sullivan, Mercer L. 1989. *"Getting Paid": Youth Crime and Work in the Inner City*. Ithaca, NY: Cornell University Press.

Taub, Richard P., George P. Surgeon, Sara Lindholm, Phyllis Betts Ottim, and Amy Bridges. 1977. "Urban Voluntary Associations, Locality Based and Externally Induced," 83 *American Journal of Sociology* 425.

Taylor, Ralph B., and Jeanette Covington. 1988. "Neighborhood Changes in Ecology and Violence," 26 *Criminology* 553.

Tittle, Charles R. 1983. "Social Class and Criminal Behavior: A Critique of the Theoretical Foundation," 62 *Social Forces* 334.

U.S. Bureau of the Census. 1972. *County and City Fact Book 1972*. Washington, D.C.: U.S. Department of Commerce.

——. 1984. *County and City Fact Book 1983*. Washington, D.C.: U.S. Department of Commerce.

Wacquant, Loic J.D., and William Julius Wilson. 1989. "The Cost of Racial and Class Exclusion in the Inner City," 501 *Annals of the American Academy of Political and Social Science* 8.

Wilson, William Julius. 1987. *The Truly Disadvantaged*. Chicago: University of Chicago Press.

Zorbaugh, Harvey W. 1929. *The Gold Coast and the Slum*. Chicago: University of Chicago Press.

Section V

Types of Crime

Although the question "What is crime?" appears to be a simple one, it has a very complex answer. Crime is not only a social construction, varying and changing across jurisdictions and time; it is also a legal concept, defined by the laws of a state or jurisdiction. Once an action is legally defined as a crime, it becomes more precise, specific, tangible, and measurable, and is therefore generally more amenable to the scrutiny of research. The study of crime is aided by the use of crime typologies, or groupings of similar types of offenses. Although there is no single list of typologies with which every scholar agrees, there are a number of broad categories, such as violent crime and property crime, and a number of specific typologies, such as murder and burglary, about which there is a general, if not detailed, consensus. For example, most if not all scholars would agree that there is a category of crime referred to as rape, although some would define the action much more broadly than others.

Marshall B. Clinard and Richard Quinney (1973) attempt to define or distinguish types of criminal behavior because, as they observe, placing events into categories allows us to reduce them to a level of commonality in which they can be compared and studied systematically. Types, they say, help us create hypotheses and give direction to our research, based on the similar characteristics of all the actions that fall into a particular category. According to Clinard and Quinney, typologies can be based on many different variables or assumptions. Legalistic typologies, for example, are based on the seriousness of the crime (felonies, misdemeanors) or the type of punishment received. Individualistic typologies, by contrast, are based on characteristics of individual offenders, such as genetics, personality, or psychological traits. Social typologies classify criminals by such characteristics as whether they are occasional, infrequent offenders or habitual, repeat offenders, or whether they are professional offenders who make their living from crime or accidental offenders who seem to stumble into criminal behavior. The reason for the great number of typologies, according to Clinard and Quinney, is that they are based on the "purposes they are to serve" and are needed to accommodate crime definitions and criminological theories, both of which change over time. Six commonly agreed-upon types of crimes will be considered here: violent crime, property crime, public-order crime, professional crime, organized crime, and white-collar crime.

Violent Crime

Violent crimes are only a small portion of the nation's total crime. They are murder, forcible rape, robbery, and assault. Some criminologists believe that the term should also include automobile gas tanks that explode upon impact; factory accidents occurring as a result of employers' blatant disregard for worker safety, often in violation of laws regulating working conditions; or the foreign marketing of pharmaceuticals that have been banned domestically because of known serious side effects. But there is no consensus on that point. Violence on the streets is given more publicity and is more widely feared than violence created in corporate suites. Indeed, street violence is more widely feared than violence in the home, though people are more likely to be murdered or assaulted in their own homes or the homes of someone they know than they are to be on the street (Hagan 1998). Thus, "violent crimes" typically refers to the four "street" violent crimes.

The United States has always experienced violence; indeed, violence is an integral part of our heritage. As a nation, we gained our independence through a revolution. We fought Native Americans, foreign foes, and even against one another in a bloody civil war. We have seen violence expressed in slavery, in such groups as the Ku Klux Klan, in labor protests, and in Old West vigilante groups. We are fascinated by it in the newspapers and even pay to see it on the silver screen. So much violence is portrayed on television and in the theaters that it is feared that we as a society are becoming desensitized.

Violence, like other crime, experiences trends (see reading 25). Homicide, for example, has peaked and declined several times throughout the past century (Reiss and Roth 1993). During the 1960s, urban rioting and looting, seizure of campus and government buildings by militant students, and assassinations were of primary concern (Moynihan 1969). At the present time special attention seems to focus on drug related violence, gang related violence, spousal and child abuse, serial murders, domestic terrorists, workplace violence, juvenile violence, and acquaintance rape.

Violent crime is predominantly, though not always, an urban problem. It is typically committed by males, aged fifteen to twenty-four, from lower socioeconomic levels, in minority inner-city areas. Traits of the victims are similar to those of the offenders, except in the case of robbery, whose victims tend to be older and white (Gabor et al. 1988). With the exception of robbery, crimes of violence are likely to be motivated by passion and other emotions among people who know each other, even intimately. It is not unusual for violent offenders to have a history of previous violence.

Homicides, though relatively small in number, capture the attention of the public perhaps more than any other crime. Homicide includes a wide range of categories, from vehicular homicide to manslaughter, and from single crimes of passion to various types of multiple murder. It often involves the use of alcohol, precipitation by the victim, and some level of social interaction. For example, James Bourdouis (1974) has identified a number of common social interactions in which murder is quite likely to occur. Among them are domestic relations, circles of friends and acquaintances (roommates, neighbors, coworkers), love affairs (couples, triangles), business relations (doctor-patient, professor-student, landlord-tenant), criminal transactions, and suicide-murder.

Multiple homicides do not occur often, but when they do they capture a great deal of media attention and public concern. Serial killings seem to be the most frequent type of multiple homicides. A serial killer murders three or more victims, usually unknown to him, in separate instances separated by long intervals, sometimes even years. Serial killers are generally white, middle-aged men from all social classes, who maintain a low profile and are usually employed. Their victims tend to be females with whom they are not or are only slightly acquainted, and they kill for reasons that would not make sense to a normal person (Voigt et al. 1994). Unlike other types of murder, serial killings have a very low clearance rate. Often in cases where serial killings are suspected, FBI agents construct a profile of the killer, in which they attempt to determine the personality, age, occupation, and pattern of killing, in order to increase the chances of identifying the killer and stopping him or her.

Forcible rape is another dreaded but common form of violence. Victims of rape often know their assailants. According to research findings (Hagan 1998), half of rape victims are under eighteen years of age; the younger the victim, the more likely it is that he or she knows the rapist. When the victim knows the rapist, the crime is less likely to be reported to the police. For many years, forced sexual relations involving spouses were not regarded as rape (Russell 1982), although that has now changed. In instances of date or acquaintance rape, the victim was often viewed by the courts as a willing participant or was thought to have led the man on through provocative dress or behavior, by going to a bar, or by entering his apartment, room or vehicle. Victims, when they pressed charges, were often treated as if they were on trial, as their past sexual experiences were used to discredit their character and their account of the incident. Some people have suggested that this treatment resulted in the victim's being victimized a second time by the criminal justice system. Much of this attitude has now changed, however, with the implementation of laws and policies designed to protect victims of rape, such as rape-shield laws. Nevertheless, Susan Estrich (1987) has characterized the general attitude toward rape with the terms "real rape" (rape involving violence) and "simple rape" (which does not involve violence). Real rape is taken seriously by the courts, while simple rape is not.

Three types of rapists have been described in the literature on rape, giving some insight into why it is considered a violent crime rather than a sex crime (Voigt et al. 1994). The angry rapist shows displaced aggression, expressing anger toward a wife or woman friend by hurting someone else. The power rapist uses rape to assert his manhood. The sadistic rapist, the worst type, becomes sexually excited by hurting his victim. Feminists contend that dominant attitudes toward rape are extensions of a paternalistic society's differential socialization for males and females, in which males are taught to dominate and be aggressive, while females are taught to be submissive and subservient. This pattern of gender socialization is the result of historical capitalistic notions of women being the property of men (Brownmiller 1975).

Another area, according to feminists, that reflects the cultural mores of male dominance, control, aggression, and intimidation is domestic abuse. Domestic abuse consists of spousal abuse, child abuse and neglect, and abuse of parents and siblings. Recent data conclude that as many as 2,500 people are killed annually as a result of domestic abuse (Federal Bureau of Investigation 1997). Partly because of changing attitudes and partly because of laws requiring certain professionals such as doctors and school teachers to report suspected cases of child abuse, many more cases are reported now than in the past. Based on known cases, men are usually the abusers in cases of spousal abuse. Although some criminologists contend that women are abusive nearly as often as men, it is women who sustain the most serious and life-threatening injuries, because of men's superior physical strength. Children who have experienced or witnessed abuse have a greater chance of growing up to be abusers themselves, as well as having an adult criminal record (see reading 26).

People often wonder why abused wives do not leave their abusers. There are many reasons, from economic dependence, learned dependence (in which the wife is emotionally battered into thinking it is her fault and she deserves no better), to the cycle of violence. In the cycle of violence, there is an escalation period in which stress and pressure build, finally culminating in the violent act. The abuser then becomes very repentant, begging forgiveness, and swearing never to do it again; a sort of honeymoon period ensues, in which he tries to compensate for his behavior. A woman who still loves her husband or partner has high hopes that he means it this time. As stress and pressures mount, however, the partner, with his poor self-concept, his dependence on his wife, and his traditional view of male and female roles, does batter again, and each incident becomes more violent than the last. Some wives, afraid to leave but unable to take any more abuse, may resort to killing their battering spouse, usually when he is vulnerable and weak, such as when he is sleeping. Battered-wife syndrome is sometimes used in court as a defense similar to self-defense (Monahan and Walker 1994).

Robbery, which may seem to be a property offense, is considered a violent offense because it involves a confrontation and the use or threat of violence, causing victims to fear for their safety. Although most crimes are predominantly intraracial, robbery is often interracial, because many robbers are poor, young, African American males, and many of their victims are older white males perceived to be more affluent. A small portion of robbers are professionals who depend upon robbery to make a living. The majority, however, are opportunistic, unskilled, with no advanced plan for the offense. Many adult robbers indicate that financial need is their motivation (Petersilia 1980).

Assaults can be differentiated into two types: aggravated, which involves serious bodily injury and usually involves a weapon, and simple, which does not involve a weapon. Albert J. Reiss and Jeffrey A. Roth (1993) point out that in 1990, 67 percent of assaults were attempts, almost half of reported assaults were simple (involving no weapon and no injury), and the least common assaults were those involving injuries. They conclude, however, that the costs of violence involve more than just physical injury. There are psychological effects on the victim, the family, and the neighborhood, such as fear, decreased cohesion, and impaired ability to live one's life as before. There are also economic consequences, such as medical and rehabilitation costs, loss of income for the victim, and economic costs for society, such as law enforcement and corrections expenses.

Property Crime

The largest proportion of street crimes in the United States are property crimes committed for monetary gain (see reading 27 and Section Two). These crimes involve the illegal acquisition of, and sometimes the destruction of, various types of property, including money, tangible goods, other property, and, more recently, data. Property index crimes listed in the Uniform Crime Reports are burglary, motor vehicle theft, larceny-theft, and arson. Advances in technology, such as automated banking, widespread use of credit and debit cards, and computer-accessed databases have provided new opportunities for both professional and unskilled property offenders, although the latter are in the major-

ity. It is not uncommon for both amateur and professional thieves to assume the identity of others by entering computer databases and using that information to obtain access to bank accounts and credit cards.

Motor vehicle theft includes the theft of automobiles, trucks, buses, and vans. Many states also include the theft of motorcycles, snowmobiles, and motorscooters (Voigt et al. 1994). There are a number of possible motives for vehicle theft, which range from teenage joyriding, in which the offenders intend only to take the vehicle temporarily, to stealing the vehicle for resale, stripping it for parts, or using it in the commission of a crime. With hundreds of millions of automobiles available in the United States and deterrence devices unreliable, the rate of motor vehicle theft is rising, while clearance rates remain low. Most stolen vehicles are eventually recovered, however.

Burglary involves the unlawful entry of a structure (residences, businesses, even boats and trailers) for the purpose of committing a felony. Most burglars are male, and the majority are under the age of twenty-five (Voigt et al. 1994). Some burglars are inexperienced, while others plan their crimes carefully and have been committing them for a number of years. More than half of all burglaries occur during the daytime, and two-thirds occur in residences; about 21 percent are cleared by arrest (Hagan 1998). Those more likely to become victims of burglaries include African Americans, younger people, those in lower socioeconomic levels, and renters (Voigt et al. 1994). Suburban burglaries have increased because suburbs are more affluent than cities, homes are unoccupied during the day, police forces are smaller, and urban dwellers are moving to the suburbs. This increase is consistent with a routine-activities explanation of crime, which views offenses as resulting from everyday behavior (Felson 1998). In other words, those motivated to commit crime (e.g., persons in need of money) find suitable targets (e.g., homes or businesses believed to contain things of value) that are vulnerable (e.g., not well protected).

Larceny-thefts are perhaps the most common property crimes in the nation. Larceny is the wrongful taking of another's property by physically removing it or by means of fraud or deceit. This broad category includes employee theft, shoplifting, purse snatching, bicycle theft, credit card theft, picking pockets, and a host of other thefts that do not involve force or intimidation. Shoplifting (see reading 28) is one of few crimes in which females are substantially represented, constituting as much as 58 percent of those arrested (Lindquist 1988). In addition, it is a crime that more and more senior citizens are committing (Alston 1986). Although most shoplifters are amateurs, there are a number of professional rings that shoplift for great profit, often working in teams and using sophisticated methods and devices.

It has been estimated that one-third of all employees commit employee theft (Voigt et al. 1994), taking items for personal use, robbing the employer of company time by taking long breaks, making personal phone calls, using computers and other equipment for personal reasons, and so on. Some criminologists believe the biggest problems come from lower-level, young, disgruntled employees, while others think they occur among management-level employees. James Tucker (1989) suggests that employee theft is the result of employees seeking "justice" against what they perceive to be a deviant employer, a way of evening the score, of getting what they think they deserve.

Some types of property crimes are destructive. Arson, the willful or malicious burning of property, is one example. There are a number of types of arson based on the arsonist's underlying motives (Voigt et al. 1994). There is profit-motivated or insurance-claim arson, often committed by professionals, wherein property is burned in order to collect the insurance. Excitement arson is committed by pyromaniacs, who derive some excitement or pleasure from setting and watching fires. Revenge arson is committed to get even with someone. Vandalism arson refers to setting fires for fun, and crime-concealment arson is committed to hide another crime.

Vandalism is another destructive form of property crime. It is a willful destruction of property and includes such things as graffiti, the destruction of library materials, the trashing of buildings, breaking of windows, and so forth. It can be vindictive, predatory, or wanton (Hagan 1998). Vindictive vandalism is fueled by hatred of some group, such as people of another race. Predatory vandalism is for gain, such as the destruction of vending machines in order to steal the contents. Finally, wanton vandalism is committed for no purpose other than to have fun.

Public-Order Crime

Public-order crimes differ from all the others because they are the so-called "victimless crimes" (see reading 29). Public-order crimes include (among others) prostitution, pornography, sex offenses (flashing, voyeurism, fetishism), drug offenses, gambling, drunkenness, disorderly conduct, and vagrancy. They are the *mala prohibita* crimes in which it appears that the state is attempting to legislate morality, the morality that binds us together as a society. As Victoria Swigert (1984) points out, these are the crimes in which people willingly engage, the crimes without complainants. They are the crimes about which a society has mixed feelings. Although laws prohibiting sin look good on the books, many people do not hesitate to indulge in the prohibited behavior; law enforcement officials often hesitate to make arrests for such actions, and judicial systems typically deal lightly with them (with the exception of many drug offenses which now carry mandatory sentences).

On the one hand, some people argue that these are not really victimless crimes. For example, prostitutes are brutalized and women and children are exploited by pornography (Swigert 1984). The children of prostitutes, alcoholics, and drug addicts suffer from a diminished quality of life. Society pays for drug rehabilitation and law enforcement, and individuals become victims of robberies, burglaries, and other crimes committed to support drug and alcohol habits. On the other hand, other people point out that without prostitution, for example, some women would lead lives that were economically even more marginal, because they have no other way to support themselves or their children (Reynolds 1986).

Some public-order laws, such as those prohibiting prostitution, are enforced selectively, often based on political decisions. In any given city, prostitutes may be left alone for a period of time and then arrested when neighbors complain or when the mayor is running for reelection. Public order offenses by their very nature and the ambiguity with which we regard them are a breeding ground for police corruption. Because there are few complainants, police officers must be proactive instead of reactive in their handling of such offenses (Swigert 1984). Individual officers may take payoffs to ignore behavior such as illegal gambling, for example. Because many members of the neighborhood frequent gambling establishments, they are not concerned that the police are turning their backs instead of enforcing law. During Prohibition, even FBI Director J. Edgar Hoover was known to frequent establishments serving illegal liquor.

Prostitution is a good example of society's mixed feelings toward public-order crimes, and it also serves as an example of a double standard between males and females in terms of law enforcement. As already noted, prostitution laws are sometimes enforced rigorously and at other times they are ignored or prostitutes are given only a slap on the wrist, depending upon the political climate. Because most (but not all) prostitutes are women, selective enforcement of the law has a greater impact on women than on men. In addition, although there are two parties involved in the act itself, the prostitute and the john (customer), it is usually only the prostitute who is arrested. Johns, by contrast, particularly when they are considered upstanding members of the community, are often allowed to slip away with no embarrassing arrest. Periodically, cities arrest johns or publish their names in newspapers, but these campaigns are usually short-lived.

Prostitutes (both female and male) are often underage runaways, attempting to survive on the streets. Some young girls have been ensnared by street pimps, who sexually abuse them, control them, and get them hooked on drugs and alcohol. Prostitutes are at great risk of contracting AIDS and other sexually transmitted diseases and are often

targets of serial killers and men with various psychological problems (Lane and Gregg 1992; Diana 1985).

Before the Harrison Act of 1914, drug use and sale were not considered to be crimes. Narcotic drugs were commonly found in elixirs and patent medicines, and the original Coca-Cola even contained cocaine. This situation was far different from the current "law and order" campaign against possession, use, and sale of drugs. With the 1980s' "war on drugs," federal drug-related convictions increased by 134 percent (Voigt et al. 1994: 420). Many current convictions are for possession of drugs, with no intent to use. A number of states have mandatory sentences for those convicted of drug possession. These sentences have been a major cause of prison overcrowding and the growing cost of maintaining correctional facilities (see reading 40). In this regard, society may be the biggest victim of enforcing laws against the possession and use of drugs.

There is a great racial disparity in drug arrests and in the perception of drug use (see reading 30). Though drug use is more prevalent among white suburban teenagers than among African American urban teenagers, suburban use occurs in the privacy of homes, clubs, and cars, while urban use is often in-your-face, street-corner transactions that make the six o'clock news, thus giving the perception that drug abuse is a particularly African American problem. Laws governing the use of crack, a drug used predominantly by African Americans, are more stringent than laws governing cocaine, a similar drug used predominantly by whites. Federal guidelines stipulate a sentence as severe for 1 gram of crack as for 100 grams of cocaine. Such disparities in the law and its enforcement lead some people to charge that public-order laws are less concerned with what is being done than with who is doing it.

Professional Crime

Professional crime can be defined as much by the characteristics of its perpetrators as by the types of crime involved (see reading 31). Professional criminals, unlike amateurs, choose crime as their livelihood, and engage in it purely for economic gain (Inciardi 1987). They identify themselves as criminals, regard themselves as professionals, and become highly skilled in their trades (Staats 1977). Often having been selected and taught by other criminals, they tend to associate with others of similar status, avoiding and looking down upon amateurs. Because of their high level of skill, they are less likely to be arrested or incarcerated and thus enjoy relatively long criminal careers. They may come from many social classes and are often drawn from legitimate peripheral occupations, rather than working their way up through a hierarchy of petty crimes. Where amateur criminals may still subscribe to societal values, professional criminals often hold values different from those of the rest of society; they believe people deserve to be victimized (Staats 1977). Within their culture, there are expected standards of behavior (such as not informing on a peer), typically reinforced by their own argot, or language, which enhances group identity and status and provides a measure of protection (Nash 1985). Professional criminals may work alone or in teams and tend to engage in nonviolent crimes (Staats 1977). They often specialize in one type of offense (see reading 32), although there are those who contend that professionals are not as likely to specialize now as much as they have in the past. In order to be successful and avoid apprehension, shoplifters, pickpockets, and confidence swindlers must also be transient, working new territory where they are not known and staying ahead of the law (Inciardi 1987).

Of the many types of professional crime, one of the most intriguing is the confidence game. Confidence swindles, big and small, depend upon the ability of the criminal to gain the confidence of the victim, a matter of great skill. Anyone, even savvy investors, can be caught up in a fraudulent scheme. Victims are often motivated by greed; they forget that if it sounds too good to be true, then it probably is. Because they have been duped and may suffer from both embarrassment and guilt, victims are reluctant to report these crimes to the authorities.

Ponzi schemes, named after the infamous con artist Charles Ponzi, involve inducing people to invest their money by promising them big returns. The first investors do receive big returns, and they tell their friends, who also invest. Early investors are paid with the money of later investors ("robbing Peter to pay Paul"), and the con artist keeps large amounts of money for himself or herself. Eventually, there is no money left and the investors have lost everything. Such a Ponzi scheme was perpetrated in Philadelphia, by the foundation for New Era Philanthropy. John G. Bennett, Jr. duped universities, museums, philanthropists, and others (Hagan 1998). These individuals and organizations would generally be more knowledgeable and cautious about investing than most ordinary citizens, clearly illustrating the fact than anyone can be duped.

Professional pickpockets work in teams of two or three people. The first person distracts the victim; the second one lifts the wallet or other item; and may pass it off to a third person, who is nowhere around by the time the police are summoned. A training "school" in Colombia, called the School of the Seven Bells, trains pickpockets, who must lift an item from a coat without ringing any of the bells (Hagan 1998).

Other forms of professional crime include shoplifting, burglary, sneak theft, extortion, forgery, and counterfeiting (Inciardi 1977). Professional burglars generally work in teams, although the composition of teams may change from job to job. Such burglars may operate in residences, warehouses, hotel rooms, or other locations. They generally receive tips from hotel employees, household help, and other insiders regarding good targets. Many burglars are experienced at picking locks; some are licensed locksmiths. Stolen merchandise is then passed to another type of professional criminal, a fence, to be sold.

Organized Crime

One of the most enduring beliefs regarding organized crime, both on the part of the media and on the part of many law enforcement agencies (Morash 1984), is what is commonly referred to as the alien-conspiracy theory. According to this theory, a group of foreigners, Italians or Sicilians to be exact, emigrated to the United States and brought with them an organized crime syndicate. Further, this syndicate has conspired to control most if not all of the organized crime in this country. The problem with this theory is that it is in direct contradiction with the evidence.

Examining organized crime allows us to see that it has existed for a long time and has involved people from many different ethnic backgrounds (see reading 33). Organized crime is a profit-motivated crime that provides illegal goods and services that the public wants. It involves a number of people who are associated for a long period in a hierarchy and who conspire together to commit illegal acts. This type of crime occasionally involves violence and coercion and relies on political corruption for protection from investigation and prosecution (Voigt et al. 1994).

Throughout most of this nation's history, urban gangs, often formed along ethnic lines, have attempted to improve their political status and financial well being. Gangs have been composed of German, Irish, Italian, Jewish, Greek, African American, Hispanic, Asian, Russian, and a host of other ethnic groups (Morash 1984; Potter 1994). During the late 1890s and early 1900s, at about the same time that corporations began to see the value of mergers, urban gangs did, too. During Prohibition, from 1920 to 1933, due to the great market for illegal alcohol, gangs merged and organized further and expanded into syndicates. After the end of Prohibition, these syndicates moved into providing other illegal goods, including narcotics. Many of these organized-crime gangs have continued to operate since then, adapting to changing conditions and product demands.

One explanation for organized crime is ethnic-succession theory (Potter 1994). This theory holds that different ethnic groups dominated organized crime at different times. As new ethnic groups arrived in the country or migrated to urban areas, they utilized marginalized means (such as crime) to gain a foothold in the economy. As new groups came in, they replaced old groups, which were now better equipped to achieve success legitimately. From this perspective, Italian Americans dominated organized crime longer than most groups because restrictive immigration policies prevented new groups from quickly taking their place. So many groups now participate in organized crime that the word *Mafia*, once used to refer to Italian organized-crime groups, has become a generic label, and one now hears of the Russian mafia, the Colombian mafia, the Vietnamese mafia, and so forth.

Another theory of organized crime is the market-model, or enterprise, theory, in which organized crime is compared to legitimate business operations. Crime syndicates create markets, work to retain them, and try to extend their markets in much the same way that large corporations selling cars or toothpaste do (Potter 1994). In fact, scholars have drawn attention not only to organized crime's similarities to legitimate business but also to its relationships with legal enterprises. Merry Morash (1984) describes organized crime as relationships between the underworld and the upper world that involve criminal activities, violence and extortion at both levels, and infiltration into legitimate businesses. It is not unusual for organized-crime racketeers to join with seemingly legitimate business and corporate leaders to engage in enterprises that are mutually beneficial (see reading 34).

Efforts by federal and state law enforcement agencies to attack organized crime have occurred throughout the twentieth century, with only modest success. Recently, however, the federal government has been more successful in prosecuting traditional organized crime because of the Racketeer Influenced and Corrupt Organizations Act, or RICO (Kenney and Finckenauer 1994). Created in 1970, this law subjects to prosecution any enterprise that shows a pattern of racketeering, as well as members of the enterprise committing two or more crimes related to the organization's work. Further, membership in such criminal organizations is defined as a crime. Conviction of any of the specified violations of the RICO law may result in the forfeiture of assets and a long prison term. Using this law, prosecutors have convicted a significant number of the leaders of the older, established crime groups and have undermined the operations of their illegal syndicates. It has yet to be seen if these tactics will be equally successful against the newly emerging organized-crime syndicates.

White-Collar Crime

Developed as a concept by Sutherland in 1939, white-collar crime describes crimes committed by middle-class and upper-class people during the normal course of their business life. These crimes involve some violation of the implicit trust that is placed in the offenders and their positions (see reading 35). Sutherland developed this concept in conjunction with his differential association theory, a theory based on social learning and therefore able to account for both street crime and upper-level crimes (Geis 1984) (see reading 17).

Some common types of white-collar crime include insider stock trading, advertising fraud, violations of antitrust law, environmental pollution, restraint of trade, misuse of trademarks, and the manufacture of unsafe foods and drugs (Clinard and Quinney 1973). According to Gilbert Geis, these types of crimes, being "an extension of regular practices," involve less risk than street crimes. Unlike burglars, who have no excuse to be prowling where they do not belong, white-collar criminals are operating where they belong (at work) and are engaging in the general type of activities one expects of them due to their positions (Geis 1984: 137).

Emile Durkheim said in the 1890s that a certain amount of crime is functional for a society. Crimes committed by a few strengthen the group solidarity of the rest, pulling society together and defining its boundaries of right and wrong. White-collar crime, on the other hand, has just the opposite effect. Because it breaks down the implicit trust necessary for a society to function and undermines social solidarity, it causes anomie, or normlessness, and threatens our solidarity. Instead of scorning white-collar criminals, however, many people in society tend to emulate them. The collective "we" tends to think the white-collar criminal is shrewd and wonders if we can get away with similar acts. Prosecutors, judges, and others often think of white-collar criminals as just

like them, "respectable" people from the middle and upper classes.

Part of the reason white-collar crimes are often not considered to be "crimes" is that few people are aware of the harms to society they cause, nor do they necessarily feel directly affected or victimized by such crimes, as they would by an assault, for example. And yet, white-collar crime is the most expensive kind of crime, costing society many times more each year than street crime possibly could, because white-collar crime is committed on such a large scale (see reading 36). Imagine the far-reaching harm that could result if a community's drinking water were contaminated with toxic wastes (Geis 1984). A number of years ago, some Ford Pinto automobiles exploded in rear end collisions, a dangerous situation the manufacturer knew about before selling the vehicle. Death and destruction resulting from these collisions caused a great deal more harm to society than petty crimes committed by a number of street criminals. Unsafe work conditions and failure to comply with occupational health and safety standards causes widespread harm and even death. Brown lung disease has been contracted by 85,000 cotton textile mill workers; 100,000 miners have been killed and another 265,000 disabled by black lung disease; there are 8,000 deaths per year in this country from asbestos-related cancer, and over the next 30 years, another 240,000 are expected to die (Mokhiber 1989). James W. Coleman (1989) attributes half of all asbestos-caused deaths to direct workplace exposure. Although the personal harm and financial costs of such actions by corporations and their executives are evident, they are typically treated as normal business practices rather than violations of criminal statutes.

Two types of white-collar crimes can be distinguished: occupational and corporate. Occupational crimes involve an act of deceit or fraud against one's own company or employer. Perhaps the most common crime of this type is embezzlement. A chief executive officer who violates the trust placed in him or her by stockholders by embezzling from the company is guilty of occupational crime. So is the employee who steals from the company, whether it is a clerk pilfering office supplies or an executive stealing thousands of dollars in raw materials. Crime of this type is solely for personal gain. Corporate crime is that committed for the benefit of the corporation. Although there may well be some personal gain for the offender, it is indirect and not the main purpose of the misdeed. Workers may lie, cheat, violate safety standards, or otherwise break the law in order to give the company a competitive edge or enhance corporate profits. These types of violations seldom bring criminal charges against corporate officers. Instead, the corporation itself is likely to be charged or, more likely, sued in civil court or brought before a regulatory agency rather than face criminal charges. Why is this so?

In 1890 the Sherman Antitrust Act was passed to prevent industries from merging into monopolies. The act also bestowed upon the corporation the legal rights of an individual; the corporation became a legal entity, which could be held responsible for illegal action. This provision tends to absolve those who run the corporation from being charged with wrongdoing, instead allowing the corporation to be charged and taken to court. It is very rare that a chief executive or manager goes to trial for a corporate crime. Therefore, when a corporation is charged and convicted of some infraction, it is usually fined, and the fine is included in the cost of doing business and passed on to its customers.

Corporations are so complex that it is difficult to place the blame for a decision or action on any particular individuals. Susan P. Shapiro (1990) discusses the interworkings of organizations and how they (purposefully and otherwise) hinder the processes of law enforcement. In complex corporate structures, paper or electronic trails can be easily hidden, altered, or falsified, making it easy to commit illegal acts but difficult to detect them. The structure of the organization, the internal networks, the hierarchy, the specialization, the internal diversification, and the task segregation all tend to work together to disguise illicit acts and block the flow of information from both insiders and outsiders. Illicit activities can be divided among many workers or divisions, widely separated by

time and place, and may appear to be part of the ordinary routine. Therefore, it is hard to determine who is guilty and hard to put together a prosecution case.

From crimes of violence to white-collar crimes, it has been shown that criminal typologies are helpful in allowing us to understand the nature of criminal offenses. Although this section has reviewed only a few types of major crimes, it is apparent that crime is more than a violation of the legal code. It is a social phenomenon that has many nuances and extensive ramifications. The following readings were selected to shed more light on the types of crimes discussed in this section.

References

Alston, Letitia T. 1986. *Crime and Older Americans*. Springfield, IL: Charles C. Thomas.

Bourdouis, James. 1974. "A Classification of Homicide." *Criminology*, 11, pp. 525-540.

Brownmiller, Susan. 1975. *Against Our Will: Men, Women, and Rape*. New York: Simon and Shuster.

Clinard, Marshall B. and Richard Quinney. 1973. *Criminal Behavior Systems: A Typology* (2nd Edition). New York: Holt, Rinehart and Winston.

Coleman, James W. 1989. *The Criminal Elite: The Sociology of White Collar Crime* (2nd Edition). New York: St. Martins.

Diana, Lewis. 1985. *The Prostitute and Her Clients: Your Pleasure is Her Business*. Springfield, IL: Charles C. Thomas.

Durkheim, Emile. 1893. *The Division of Labor in Society*. New York: Free Press.

Estrich, Susan. 1987. *Real Rape*. Cambridge: Harvard University Press.

Federal Bureau of Investigation. 1997. *Uniform Crime Reports–1996*. Washington, DC: U.S. Government Printing Office, p. 19.

Felson, Marcus. 1998. *Crime and Everyday Life*. Thousand Oaks, CA: Pine Forge.

Gabor, Thomas, Micheline Baril, Maurice Cusson, Daniel Elie, Marc LaBlanc and Andre Normandeau. 1988. *Armed Robbery: Cops, Robbers, and Victims*. Springfield, IL: Thomas.

Geis, Gilbert. 1984. "White-Collar and Corporate Crime," in R. S. Meier (ed.) *Major Forms of Crime*. Beverly Hills: Sage.

Hagan, Frank E. 1998. *Introduction to Criminology: Theories, Methods, and Criminal Behavior* (4th Ed.). Chicago: Nelson-Hall.

Inciardi, James. 1987. "In Search of the Class Cannon: A Field Study of Professional Pickpockets." In R. Weppner (ed.), *Street Ethnography*. Beverly Hills: Sage.

Kenney, Dennis J. and James O. Finckenauer. 1994. *Organized Crime in America*. New York: Wadsworth.

Lane, Brian and Wilfred Gregg. 1992. *The Encyclopedia of Serial Killers*. London: Headline Book Publishing.

Lindquist, J. 1988. *Misdemeanor Crime*. Newbury Park, CA: Sage.

Mokhiber, Russell. 1989. *Corporate Crime and Violence: Big Business Power and the Abuse of the Public Trust*. San Francisco: Sierra Club Books.

Monahan, John and Laurens Walker. 1994. *Social Science in Law: Cases and Materials*. Westbury, NY: Foundation Press.

Morash, Merry. 1984. "Organized Crime," in R. S. Meier (ed.), *Major Forms of Crime*. Beverly Hills: Sage.

Moynihan, Daniel P. 1969. *Violent Crime: Homicide, Assault, Rape, Robbery: The Report of the National Commission on The Causes and Prevention of Violence*. New York: George Braziller.

Nash, Jeffrey. 1985. *Social Psychology: Society and Self*. St. Paul: West Publishing Company.

Petersilia, Joan. 1980. "Criminal Career Research: A Review of Recent Evidence." *Crime and Justice* (2), pp. 321-379.

Potter, Gary W. 1994. *Criminal Organizations: Vice, Racketeering, and Politics in an American City*. Prospect Heights, IL: Waveland Press.

Reiss, Albert J. Jr. and Jeffrey A. Roth. 1993. *Understanding and Preventing Violence*. Washington, DC: National Academy Press.

Reynolds, Helen. 1986. *The Economics of Prostitution*. Springfield, IL: Charles C. Thomas.

Russell, Diana E. H. 1982. *Rape in Marriage*. New York: Macmillan.

Shapiro, Susan P. 1990. "Collaring the Crime, Not the Criminal: Reconsidering the Concept of White-Collar Crime," *American Sociological Review*, 55 (June), pp. 346-365.

Staats, Gregory R. 1977. "Changing Conceptualizations of Professional Criminals: Implications for Criminology Theory," *Criminology*, 15, pp. 49-65.

Swigert, Victoria. 1984. "Public-Order Crime," in R. S. Meier (ed.), *Major Forms of Crime*. Beverly Hills: Sage.

Tucker, James. 1989. "Employee Theft as Social Control," *Deviant Behavior*, 10, pp. 319-334.

Voigt, Lydia, William E. Thornton, Jr., Leo Barrile, and Jerrol M. Seaman. 1994. *Criminology and Justice*. New York: McGraw-Hill. ✦

25

Violent Crime in the United States

Albert J. Reiss, Jr.
Jeffrey A. Roth

Anyone watching the evening news on television in any American city must conclude that violence is rampant in our nation. Stories abound of shootings, stabbings, murders, rapes, abuse, and other forms of injury or death. Is this a true representation of American criminal violence or a distorted interpretation by the mass media to attract viewers or readers? What is the extent of violence in our society and what patterns of such behavior can be discovered from systematic study? These questions and others are addressed by Albert J. Reiss and Jeffrey A. Roth in the following excerpt taken from an exhaustive study of violence sponsored by the National Academy of Science. Using all available data sources, these authors present the most comprehensive study of violent crime ever undertaken in the United States.

Many of the findings of this study confirm what we have learned from other research. Both victims of homicide and their killers tend to be young men of the same ethnic group living in urban areas. In fact, age is the characteristic most likely to predict one's being a victim of violence. Minorities, especially African Americans, are overrepresented among those arrested for all violent crimes, and men far outnumber women as violent offenders. It is quite difficult to predict an act of violence, although persons with long criminal careers usually commit at least one such act.

Among the relevant information on violent crimes presented in this selection is a discussion of violent bias, or "hate," crimes. The authors note the increased concern for such crimes as manifested in new federal and state statutes, and the requirement that the Uniform

Crime Reports collect and publish statistics on such crimes. It is often difficult to discern the motive of many violent crimes, however. Such knowledge is a necessary prerequisite to classifying an act of violence as a "hate" crime or one motivated by other emotions.

How much crime is violent? The technical problems discussed above preclude any precise estimate of how much of all crime in the United States is violent. We report below some crude estimates, which are useful mainly to establish relative magnitudes among the types of crime and to discern overall trends. Comparisons focus primarily on the 1990 reporting year, the latest available at this writing.

National Estimates

In 1990 the National Crime Survey reported an estimated 34,403,610 personal and household crime victimizations.[1] Of these, 17 percent were attempted or completed violent crimes—8 percent if one excludes simple assault.[2] In considering only the 18,984,120 attempted or completed *personal* victimizations reported, about 32 percent were violent—just over 6 million. Of these, just over half were simple assaults, the least serious violent offense (Bureau of Justice Statistics, 1992:Table 1a).

The bulk of personal victimizations reported are theft from persons, which includes larceny with and without contact with the victim.[3] Together with the violent act of simple assault,[4] these nonviolent thefts constitute the large majority of personal victimizations.

In 1990 UCR estimated that the nation's police departments received reports of 14,475,600 index crimes, excluding arson; of these, about 1.8 million, or 13 percent, were attempted or completed violent crimes.[5] Police departments reports a smaller proportion of all offenses as violent than the NCS reports, excluding simple assault (13 compared with 15 percent). This is in part due to the fact that victims were somewhat more likely to report property crimes than crimes of violence to the police. In 1988 victims reported a higher fraction of household victimizations of burglary, household larceny, and motor vehicle theft (40 percent) than violent personal victimizations (36 percent) to the police (Bureau of Justice Statistics, 1990:Table 92).[6]

Prototype Pattern

The NCS program reported 6,008,790 violent victimizations in 1990, and the UCR program counted 1,820,127 violent index crimes reported to police agencies. Despite their differences, the prototype violent event that emerges from the two systems is an assault, either aggravated or simple. Of the violent victimizations, aggravated and simple assault account for nearly 8 of every 10. By excluding homicide from the UCR and simple assault from the NCS counts to achieve rough comparability, aggravated assaults account for almost 6 of 10 violent crimes reported in both systems. Robbery, which is an assault or threat of assault for the purposes of taking valuables, accounts for most of the rest—which means that at least 9 of every 10 acts reported as violent crimes or victimizations in the United States are either assaults or robberies. Sexual assaults account for most of the remaining violent offenses, and homicides account for just over 1 percent—23,438 of the violent crimes counted by the UCR. . . .

The various types of assault show the expected inverse relationship between frequency and seriousness. In 1990, 67 percent of assaults were attempts. Of all aggravated and simple assaults, 46 percent were attempted simple assaults without a weapon and without injury; 21 percent were attempted aggravated assaults with a weapon, but without injury; 20 percent were simple assaults with injury; and 13 percent were aggravated assaults with injury (Bureau of Justice Statistics, 1992: Table 1a). Assaults with injury are least frequently reported; attempted simple assaults without a weapon and without injury constitute almost half of all reported assaults.

Violent victimizations are more likely than nonviolent ones to involve multiple simultaneous victims. Therefore, on average, every 100 aggravated assault victimizations occurred in 80 events and every 100 simple assaults in about 90 events.

Victims of Violence

Although the rhetoric of campaigns against violence suggests that victims and offenders are distinct populations, in fact there is great similarity in their demographic profiles. Generally, both groups—those at the highest risk of violent offending as well as those at highest risk of violent victimization—tend to be young, black males of low socioeconomic status who live in the nation's central cities. . . . Victim characteristics are discussed in this section, and offender characteristics in the next.

Risks of Violent Victimization

. . . The annual risk of becoming a victim of personal violence—of homicide, forcible rape, robbery, or assault—is well below that of victimization from property crimes. As judged by victim reports to NCS, the risk of becoming a victim of personal violence in 1990 was 1 in 34 for people age 12 and older. That risk is less than half the risk of becoming a victim of a personal theft, which was 1 in 16 in 1990 for people age 12 and older (Bureau of Justice Statistics, 1992: Table 1a). In 1990 the risk of household victimization through burglary, household larceny, or motor vehicle theft was 1 in 6 households (Bureau of Justice Statistics, 1992: Table 1a).

For many purposes, the lifetime risk of violent victimization would be a more informative description than the annual risk for any single age range. The Bureau of Justice Statistics, drawing on the annual prevalence rates from the National Crime Survey, estimated that about 83 percent of the people now age 12 will be violently victimized in their lifetimes (Koppel, 1987). There is good methodological reason to conclude that this is a substantial overestimate (Lynch, 1989). However, because information is unavailable on the proportion of victims in any year who have also been victimized in previous years, we were unable to determine the degree to which it is overestimated. . . .

Homicide. Usable estimates of lifetime risk have been calculated for homicide (Loftin and Wiersma, 1991). In 1987 and 1988, the *annual* risk of becoming a victim of a homicide was about 1 in 12,000, although by 1990 it had risen close to 1 in 10,600. The *lifetime* risk of being a homicide victim is of course much greater (Figure 25.1). Of the six demographic subgroups shown in the figure—male and female whites, blacks, and American Indians—black males are at the highest lifetime risk: 4.16 per 100 black males, which is equivalent to a 1 chance in 24.1 of dying by homicide. American Indian males are also at high risk (1.75 per 100 American Indian males, 1 chance in 57), as are black females (1.02 per 100 black females, 1 in 98.1). For white males and females and for American Indian females, chances of dying by homicide are substantially less than 1 in 100.[7]

This figure also makes clear that, despite media attention to the killings of adolescents and young adults, *less than one-fourth of one's lifetime homicide risk is experienced before the twenty-fifth birthday*. For five of the six subgroups (the exception is American Indian males), the ratio of homicide risk by age 24 to lifetime risk lies in a narrow range, between 0.21 and 0.26. Murders of American Indian males occur later in life on average; the corresponding ratio is only 0.14.

Recent media attention has focused on homicides of young black males. The rate for black males ages 15-24 rose during the late 1980s, approaching levels not observed since a previous peak around 1970 (see Figure 25.2). However, Figure 25.1 makes clear that, although a sizable fraction of black males die of murder by age 24, the high homicide rate for young black males must be viewed in light of the high homicide rate for black males at *all* ages. One major unresolved question is why the homicide death rate is so high for blacks at all ages, especially black males (see Griffin and Bell, 1989). Another is to understand why, for this age category, the trends for blacks and white males have moved in different directions during several periods since 1940, as Figure 25.2 shows. . . .

Figure 25.1
Cumulative Homicide Rate in Five-Year Age Intervals by Race and Gender, 1987

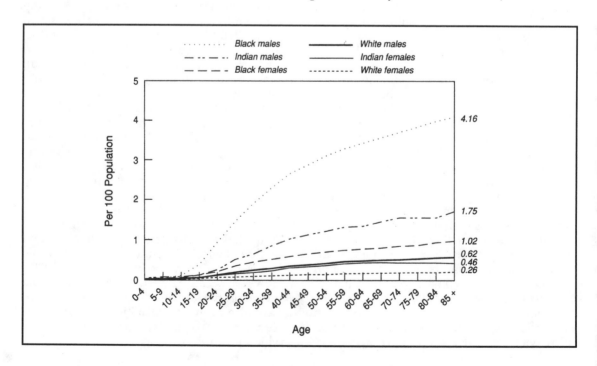

Figure 25.2
Homicide Rates, Persons Ages 15–24 Years, by Race and Sex, 1940–1988

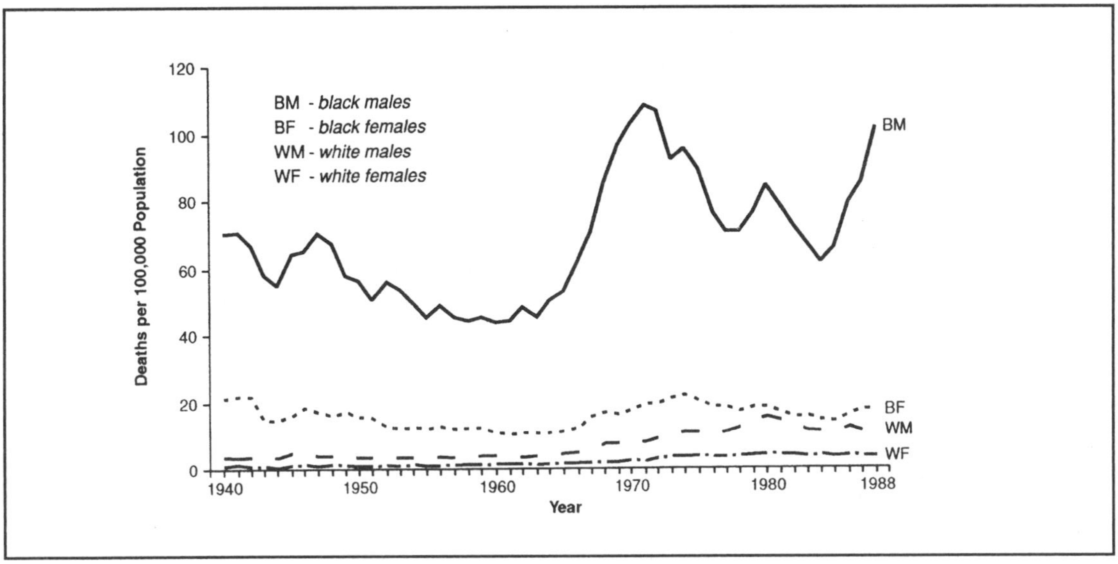

There is considerable variation in homicide mortality by gender and age. In 1988, for example, the homicide mortality rate ranged from 4.2 for females to 14.2 for males, and from 5.3 for whites to 34.4 for blacks. The variation by age and sex within these groups was, for example, from 2.7 for black males age 5 to 9 to 128.2 for black males age 20-24. The range for white males was from 0.8 for age 5 to 9 to 14.6 for white males 20-24 (National Center for Health Statistics, 1991).

The UCR Supplementary Homicide Report discloses that most victims in single offender-single victim homicides are slain by an offender of the same ethnic status:[8] 86 percent of white victims and 93 percent of black victims in 1990. In this kind of homicide, only 6 percent of white victims were slain by black offenders (calculated from Federal Bureau of Investigation, 1992:11).

Multiple homicides by one offender in a single event (so-called mass murders) account for only a very small proportion of all homicides. Similarly, in projecting from data on homicides by known offenders, instances of serial homicide by one offender also appear to be quite infrequent—on the order of 1 percent of all homicides, according to esti-

mates prepared by Fox and Levin for the panel (J. Fox and J. Levin, personal communication, 1990). . . .

Individual Risks of Nonfatal Violent Victimizations

In this section we examine how the risks of violent victimization differ according to people's age, gender, ethnic status, marital status, and socioeconomic status. Two- and three-way associations for age, gender, and ethnic status suggest that the relationships among these factors are generally additive. . . . For some subgroups of the population, the relative risk of violent victimization is higher than expected because of interaction effects. Age has the largest independent effect, followed by gender; ethnic status has the smallest effect of the three.

The rates reported are based on statistical information for the 1990 National Crime Survey (Bureau of Justice Statistics, 1992) unless another source is specified.

Age. Age is one of the most important single predictors of an individual's risk of violent victimization (Hindelang et al., 1978). The annual risk of victimization by violent crime peaks at age 16 to 19 for both men (95 per

1,000 population) and women (54 per 1,000) and declines substantially with age, to 3-4 per 1,000 at age 65 and older. This declining risk of victimization by age holds for the major violent crimes of forcible rape, robbery, aggravated assault, and simple assault, with substantially higher rates below than above age 25. Although the risk of violent victimization is highest at the younger ages, there is evidence that juvenile victimization is less likely to involve serious injury (Garofalo et al., 1987).

Gender. Except for forcible rapes and partner assaults, the risk of a woman becoming a victim of a violent crime is lower than that of a man. Among all female murder victims in 1990, however, 30 percent were slain by husbands or male friends compared with 4 percent of male victims killed by wives or women friends (Federal Bureau of Investigation, 1992:13). The lifetime risk of homicide is three to four times greater for men than for women. Gender differences are much smaller for robbery (Bureau of Justice Statistics, 1992: Table 3).

Women are substantially less likely than men to report being victims of aggravated or simple assault or attempted assault with a weapon. The risk of injury for assault victims is somewhat greater for women than men (38 per 1,000 for women and 30 for men). Women have a higher rate of both simple and aggravated assault by relatives than do men. Their vulnerability to assault by relatives is greater for simple than aggravated assault: the 1990 rate of simple assault by relatives was six times greater for women than men; the rate for aggravated assault was only roughly twice that for men (Bureau of Justice Statistics, 1992: Appendix V).

The reported forcible rape rate for women[9] in 1990 was 1.0 for every 1,000 women age 12 and over (Bureau of Justice Statistics, 1992: Table 3), well below their rates of aggravated assault (4.5) and simple assault (12.7). Female children are three times more likely than male children to be sexually abused (Sedlak, 1991:5-7).

Ethnic Status. Americans of minority status are at greater risk of victimization by violent crime than are those of majority status. The overall 1990 violent victimization rate reported by the NCS was 39.7 for blacks and 37.3 for Hispanics compared with a rate of 28.2 for whites (Bureau of Justice Statistics, 1992: Tables 6 and 8). Simple assaults are a substantially larger proportion of all violent crimes for whites (56%) than for blacks or Hispanics (35%), but the risk of simple assault is about the same for these ethnic groups (16 per thousand whites, 14 for blacks, 13 for Hispanics). Excluding simple assaults from the violent crime rate, the rate of violent crime (forcible rape, robbery, and *aggravated* assault) for blacks and Hispanics is roughly twice that of whites—13 for whites, 26 for blacks, 24 for Hispanics. For reasons discussed early in this chapter, it is not possible to report victimization rates for other ethnic groups.

As noted above, blacks, especially black males, are disproportionately the victims of homicide. Although variations have occurred over time in rates by ethnic status and sex, black rates of homicide have exceeded white rates since at least 1910. In 1990 half of all homicide victims were black, and blacks were homicide victims at a rate six times that of whites (Federal Bureau of Investigation, 1992). Several studies using subnational data have found that the black-white homicide differential is attenuated substantially at high income levels. . . .

American Indians and Alaska natives are also at greater risk of homicide than are white Americans, though exact comparisons are lacking. In a recent special report, the Indian Health Service (1991) placed their age-adjusted rate at 14.1 per 100,000 in 1988—above that for the total population at 9.0 but half the 28.2 rate for all groups other than white. According to the Indian Health Service (1988:Chart 4.21) the rate for Native Americans has substantially exceeded the white rate, but has not exceeded the rate for the entire nonwhite population, since at least 1955.

Socioeconomic Status. Family income,[10] the primary indicator of socioeconomic status measured by the NCS, is inversely related to the risk of violent victimization. In 1988 the risk of victimization was 2.5 times greater for individuals in families with the lowest income (under $7,500) as the highest ($50,000 and over). Of all violent crimes, this negative relation is strongest for robbery.

Table 25.1
Percentage Distributions of All Persons Arrested for Violent Crimes, by Ethnic Status, 1990

Offense Charged	Ethnic Status				
	White American	Black American	American Indian or Alaskan Native	Asian or Pacific Islander	Total
Murder and nonnegligent manslaughter	43.7	54.7	0.7	0.9	100.0
Forcible rape	55.1	43.2	0.8	0.9	100.0
Robbery	37.7	61.2	0.4	0.8	100.0
Aggravated assault	59.9	38.4	0.9	0.8	100.0
Other assaults	64.1	33.9	1.2	0.8	100.0

Source:Federal Bureau of Investigation (1991:Table 38).

The net effect of family income is less than that for age, gender, race, and marital status (Sampson and Lauritsen, Volume 3). Its contribution relative to these other factors may be negligible; consequently it remains unclear just how much and in what ways poverty contributes to the risk of violent victimization. . . .

Violent Offenders

There is more uncertainty about the perpetrators of violent crimes than about their victims because of measurement errors in arrest records and sampling errors in surveys of offenders' self-reports. Because the two data sources are subject to different sources of error, one can be fairly confident about the conclusions on which they converge. The panel cautions readers against interpreting annual statistics on arrestees as an indicator of the distribution of the people actually committing crimes: because persons arrested more than once in any year are disproportionally represented in arrest statistics, there are doubts that the arrest population is representative of the offender population.

Personal Characteristics

Ethnic Status. Blacks are disproportionately represented in all arrests, and more so in those for violent crimes than for property crimes. In terms of violent crimes, blacks constitute 45 percent of all arrestees. They are most overrepresented in the most serious violent crimes of homicide, forcible rape, and robbery (Table 25.1). Particularly striking is their substantial overrepresentation in the crime of robbery, a crime that is both a person and a property crime.

Other minorities are also overrepresented among all arrestees and among those arrested for violent crimes. Particularly striking is the relatively high representation of American Indians and Alaska natives, especially for aggravated and other assaults, given their proportions in the U.S. population (Federal Bureau of Investigation, 1990: Table 38).

It is not possible to calculate annual arrest rates for violent crimes for most demographic categories; however, rates of arrest can be calculated separately for whites, blacks, and others.[11] Thus: 1 white was arrested for every 576 whites in the population; 1 black for every 94 blacks; and 1 "other" for every 739 "others." This arrest rate for violent crimes is about six times greater for blacks than whites. However, because data are not available on repeat arrests during the year, these arrest incidence figures do *not* reflect the annual prevalences of arrest for the different subgroups.

Gender and Age. Men make up 89 percent of all people arrested for violent crimes (Federal Bureau of Investigation, 1991: Table 37). Women accounted for only 10 percent of all arrestees for murder and nonnegligent manslaughter, 8 percent of those for robbery, and 1 percent of arrestees for forcible rape. They accounted for a higher proportion of those ar-

Figure 25.3
Violent Crimes: Percentage Distribution of Co-Offenders by Type of Violence, 1990

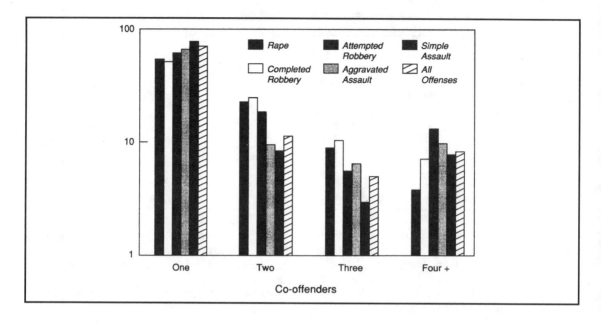

rested for assaults: 13 percent for aggravated assault and 16 percent for simple assaults.

In 1990, arrestees for violent crimes were somewhat older on average than victims, with more falling in the age range of 25-29 than in any other. The age distribution for female arrestees is similar to that of males. Males under age 18, who constituted 16 percent of the U.S. population in 1988, represented roughly comparable portions of male arrestees for murder and nonnegligent manslaughter (14%), forcible rape (15%), aggravated assault (14%), and other assault (15%); they were overrepresented among arrestees for robbery at 24 percent (Federal Bureau of Investigation, 1990: Table 34).

The only major gender-age interaction of note is that the male arrest rate declines beginning at ages 45-49, while the female arrest rate remains fairly constant after age 45. After age 65, the female arrest rate approaches half that of males with both rates at their lowest for any age—comparable to their arrest rate for murder at age 14 and under. . . .

Patterns of Offending

Violent Co-offending. Nearly three-fourths of all violent crimes are committed by lone of-

fenders. Forcible rape was most likely to be committed alone: in 1990 only 12 of every 100 forcible rapes involved co-offenders. Robbery was most likely to be committed with others: in 1990 about 48 of every 100 completed robberies involved co-offenders.

Although the majority of violent crimes involve a single offender, co-offending substantially increases the number of people involved in violent victimizations. For example (using Figure 25.3 and Bureau of Justice Statistics, 1992: Table 70), for every 100 completed robberies, there will be a minimum of 182 offenders. That means that 182 people would have to be apprehended to clear all 100 robberies by arrest. Because a fair number of these offenders are also involved in other robberies or/and in other offenses with other co-offenders, they are linked in a much larger offending network that recruits and selects offenders (Reiss and Farrington, 1991).

Criminal Careers A question asked by policy makers and others is whether criminals specialize in committing violent crimes or if "careers" in crime show a pattern of escalation from nonviolent to violent crimes. If either of these situations were the case, it would have implications for the effectiveness of selective incarceration strategies to reduce levels of violence. The evidence, however, shows otherwise.

Studies of various American and European cohorts have found that no more than 1 in 5 persons ever arrested had an arrest for a violent crime. Furthermore, such arrests were likely to be embedded in long careers dominated by arrests for nonviolent crimes, so that arrests for violence accounted for no more than 1 in 8 of all arrests in the group studied (see for example Farrington, 1991). There is a clear tendency for adult criminals to specialize in various kinds of property crimes or in various kinds of violent crimes rather than to switch between the two types (Blumstein et al., 1986; Farrington et al., 1988).

Although few criminal careers begin with a violent crime, most lengthy careers contain at least one. This pattern is sometimes erroneously interpreted as evidence of escalation from nonviolent to violent crime, or as a demonstration that certain arrest patterns predict subsequent violent crimes. In fact, by most measures, predictions of future violent behavior from arrest records have proven highly inaccurate (Monahan, 1988; Piper, 1985). This is true in part because officially recorded violent crimes are committed largely in the course of lengthy, versatile criminal careers rather than by specialized violent career criminals who could be easily targeted in a strategy of incarceration.

Victim-Offender Relationships

Overlap Between Offenders and Victims. National-level estimates are available on social and personal relationships between victims and offenders that may affect the distribution and consequences of violent events. By social relationship, we mean whether the offender and victim are of the same or different categories—defined in such terms as gender, ethnic status, and sexual preference. By personal relationship we mean the connections between victim and offender as *individuals*—strangers, drinking partners, lovers, spouses, custodian and inmate, and others.

Social Relationships. Clear-cut statements can be made about social relationships defined in terms of characteristics such as

gender and ethnic status, which are easily observable and traditionally recorded in counting systems. When characteristics are more ambiguous, there is greater error in classification. As an example of the latter, violent bias crimes, which have recently attracted substantial public attention, are subject to greater error in reporting.

Gender. Violence frequently crosses gender lines. Sexual assaults are disproportionally committed by males against females. Homicides by both men and women are more likely to involve male victims. Assaults, in contrast, are more likely to involve an offender and a victim of the same gender. Like assaults against women generally, cross-gender violence has more serious consequences for female victims. . . .

Ethnic Status. For violent crimes that involve blacks and whites, one can construct a "chance-encounter" race mix by assuming that each individual's chances of violent offending and victimization are independent of race, so that the probability of any offender-victim race combination depends only on the prevalence of each race in the U.S. population. In these hypothetical circumstances, 78 percent of all violent events would involve a white offender and victim, 21 percent would cross racial lines, and only 1 percent would involve a black offender and victim.

According to the 1987 National Crime Survey (calculated from Bureau of Justice Statistics, 1989b: Table 43), in single-offender victimizations, whites assault whites at about the chance-encounter rate, blacks assault whites at about 72 percent of that rate, and whites assault blacks at about 56 percent of the chance-encounter rate. In contrast, blacks assault blacks at about 800 percent of the chance-encounter rate.

Violent Bias Crimes. One type of violent behavior that has been recently defined in the criminal law is referred to as *hate* or *bias* crimes. Bias crimes are distinguished from other crimes by the presumed role of social relationships in their motivation. The Hate Crime Statistics Act of 1990 requires the UCR program to begin counting bias crimes and specifies that violent attacks, intimidation, arson, and property damage "that manifest evidence of prejudice based on race, religion, sexual orientation, or ethnicity" are all considered to be violent bias crimes. New state and local statutes that prescribe enhanced sentences for bias crimes define them in fairly similar terms.

Documenting and analyzing patterns of violent bias crimes is difficult, because these crimes are sometimes hard to recognize. Absent such signals as graffiti, organizational identity, or lifestyle of victims, classifying some violent act as a bias crime makes it necessary to determine the perpetrator's motivation—a difficult task subject to uncertainty, especially when the prejudice serves only to aggravate a conventional robbery with a gratuitous shooting, beating, or mutilation, for example.

The available statistics have generally been developed by advocacy organizations. Such organizations often lack the resources and infrastructure for regularly counting incidents and classifying them according to rigorous criteria but, by increasing awareness of bias crimes, they may encourage the designation of ambiguous events as bias crimes. Thus, for example, Montgomery County, Maryland, reported 196 bias crimes during 1989. This count constitutes between 14 and 81 percent of various advocacy groups' recent *national* counts (compiled by Ellis, 1990, for the panel), a share that is severely disproportionate to Montgomery County's 0.2 percent share of the U.S. population.

Most of the available data do not distinguish between violent and nonviolent bias crimes. An exception is a synthesis of 10 available victimization surveys of gay men and lesbians (Berrill, 1990). Between 24 and 48 percent of the gay men and lesbians surveyed reported having been threatened by violence related to their sexual orientation at some time in their lives. Similarly, between 9 and 23 percent reported having been punched, hit, or kicked, and between 4 and 10 percent reported having been assaulted with a weapon. In most of the surveys, the victimization rates for gay men exceed the rates for lesbians by factors of 2-4 to 1— slightly greater than the difference by gender for assault victimization in the general population, according to the National Crime Survey (Aurand et al., 1985; Gross et al., 1988).

Personal Relationships. About half of all homicide victims are murdered by neither intimate family members nor total strangers, but rather by people with some kind of preexisting relationship; friends, neighbors, casual acquaintances, workplace associates, associates in illegal activities, or members of their own or a rival gang. . . . The high prevalence of such preexisting relationships between victims and their killers suggests that most people's fears of being killed by strangers overestimate the risk; by the same token, people underestimate the probability of being killed by someone with a close or a known relationship to them.

As discussed earlier in this chapter, women face only about one-third the homicide risk faced by men (4.2 and 14.2 per 100,000, respectively). However, among homicide victims, women are about four times as likely as men to have been killed by intimate partners, and 50 percent more likely to be killed by other family members.

For violent crimes that do not end in death, a preexisting relationship between victim and offender is less likely, yet there is variation by type of crime. Of all nonfatal violent crime types, forcible rapes are most likely to involve intimates or acquaintances (61%), and attempted robbery is least likely (14%). . . .

Discussion Questions

1. With regard to race/ethnicity, gender, age, and other demographic characteristics, who is more at risk of becoming the victim of a violent crime? What crimes is a person more likely to be a victim of? Is violent crime likely to be interracial or intraracial?

2. What are the characteristics of violent offenders? What are the patterns of offending? What can be said about the "criminal careers" of violent offenders?

3. What are the most common victim-offender relationships? What is a bias crime? What are its characteristics? Is there a relationship between the victims and offenders of bias crimes?

Notes

1. The NCS classifies all victimizations as either personal- or household-sector victimizations. Burglary, household larceny, and motor vehicle theft are household-sector victimizations. Personal-sector victimizations are classified as crimes of violence (rape, robbery, and assault) or crimes of theft (personal larceny with contact and personal larceny without contact). NCS violent victimizations are only roughly comparable to UCR index crimes of violence, for reasons discussed earlier in this chapter.

2. The calculation excludes an estimated 3,128,130 simple assaults for crude comparisons with UCR. Their exclusion reduces the number of violent victimizations from 6,008,790 to 2,880,660.

   Aggravated assaults are attacks by one person on another for the purpose of inflicting severe or aggravated bodily injury. Attempts are included since it is not necessary that an injury result when a gun, a knife, or another weapon, including hands, fists, and feet, are used that could, and probably would, result in serious personal injury were the crime successfully completed. Both UCR and NCS classify injuries as serious when they result in broken bones, lost teeth, internal injuries, and loss of consciousness. The NCS also classifies any injury as serious if it requires two or more days of hospitalization.

3. Personal larcenies or personal crimes of theft include two subgroups. *Personal larceny with contact* involves personal contact between the victim and the offender and includes such crimes as purse snatching and pocket picking. *Personal larceny without contact* is theft of property of the victim without personal contact from any place other than the home or its immediate vicinity. The crime differs from household larceny only in the location in which the theft occurs.

4. The panel recognizes that the division between simple and aggravated assault involves considerable classification error and also that there are valid reasons for including simple assault as a violent crime, especially given its prevalence in domestic violence.

5. UCR violent index crimes are offenses of murder, forcible rape, robbery, and aggravated assault (Federal Bureau of Investigation, 1990: Table 1).

6. The inclusion of commercial and nonresidential offenses in the UCR but not the NCS also accounts for some of the difference, as it disproportionally increases the base for property crimes. . . .

7. Loftin and Wiersma (1991) could not calculate risks for Hispanics because, at the time their data were collected, death certificates in only five states provided for that demographic category.

8. Single victim-single offender homicides account for only 54 percent of all homicides in which the ethnic status of victims was reported in 1990 (calculated from Federal Bureau of Investigation, 1990:11). . . .

9. Until 1990, the NCS had reports of fewer than 10 sample cases of sexual assaults on males classified as forcible rape. The 1990 rate was reported as 0.2 per 1,000 males. There is a substantial underreporting of sexual assault on both males and females, but especially so for males at younger ages. Efforts should be made to secure more reliable measures of sexual assaults for both men and women at all ages.

10. Family income in the NCS includes the income of the household head and all other related persons residing in the same housing unit. The income of persons unrelated to the head of household is excluded (Bureau of Justice Statistics, 1990: Glossary).

11. Numerators are counts of violent crime arrests in Federal Bureau of Investigation (1992: Table 38). Denominators are estimated populations, 12 years of age and over by race in Bureau of Justice Statistics (1992: Table 6).

References

1. Aurand, S. K., R. Adessa, and C. Bush. 1985. "Violence and Discrimination Against Philadelphia Lesbian and Gay People." (Available from Philadelphia Lesbian and Gay Task Force, 1501 Cherry Street, Philadelphia, PA 19102).

2. Berrill, K. T. 1990. "Anti-gay Violence and Victimization in the United States: An Overview." *Journal of Interpersonal Violence* 5(3, September):274-294.

3. Blumstein, A., J. Cohen, J. A. Roth, and C. A. Visher. 1986. *Criminal Careers and 'Career Criminals.'* Vol. I. Washington, D.C.: National Academy Press.

4. Bureau of the Census. 1990. *Statistical Abstract of the United States: 1990.* Washington, D.C.: U.S. Government Printing Office.

5. Bureau of Justice Statistics. 1989a. *Injuries From Crime: Special Report.* Washington, D.C.: U.S. Government Printing Office.

——. 1989b. *Criminal Victimization in the United States, 1987*. Washington, D.C.: U.S. Government Printing Office.

——. 1990. *Criminal Victimization in the United States, 1988*. A National Crime Survey Report, December 1990, NCJ-122024.

——. 1992. *Criminal Victimization in the United States, 1990*. Washington, D.C.: U.S. Government Printing Office.

Ellis, W. W. 1990. "Bias Crime." Commissioned paper for the Committee on Research on Law Enforcement and the Administration of Justice, National Research Council.

Farrington, D. P. 1991. "Childhood Aggression and Adult Violence: Early Precursors and Later-life Outcomes." Pp. 5-29 in D. J. Pepler and K. H. Rubin, eds., *The Development and Treatment of Childhood Aggression*. Hillsdale, N.J.: Erlbaum.

Farrington, D., H. Snyder, and T. Finnegan. 1988. "Specialization in Juvenile Court Careers." *Criminology* 26:461-488.

Federal Bureau of Investigation. 1969. *Uniform Crime Reports: Crime in the United States, 1968*. Washington, D.C.: U.S. Government Printing Office.

——. 1974. *Uniform Crime Reporting Handbook*. Washington, D.C.: U.S. Government Printing Office.

——. 1990. *Uniform Crime Reports: Crime in the United States, 1989*. Washington, D.C.: U.S. Government Printing Office.

——. 1991. *Uniform Crime Reports: Crime in the United States, 1990*. Washington, D.C.: U.S. Government Printing Office.

——. 1992. *Uniform Crime Reports: Crime in the United States, 1991*. Washington, D.C.: U.S. Government Printing Office.

Garofalo, J., L. Siegel, and J. Laub. 1987. "School-Related Victimizations Among Adolescents: An Analysis of National Crime Survey Narratives." *Journal of Quantitative Criminology* 3:321-338.

Griffin, Ezra E. H., and Carl C. Bell. 1989. "Recent Trends in Suicide and Homicide Among Blacks." Special Communication. *Journal of the American Medical Association* 282(16):2265-2269.

Gross, L., S. Aurand, and R. Adessa. 1988. "Violence and Discrimination Against Lesbian and Gay People in Philadelphia and the Commonwealth of Pennsylvania." (Available from Philadelphia Lesbian and Gay Task Force, 1501 Cherry Street, Philadelphia, PA 19102).

Gurr, T. R. 1989. "Historical Trends in Violent Crime: Europe and the United States." In T. R. Gurr, ed., *Violence in America. Vol. 1: The History of Crime*. Newbury Park, CA: Sage Publications.

Haenazel, W. 1950. "A Standardized Rate for Mortality Defined in Units of Lost Years of Life." *American Journal of Public Health* 40:17-26.

Hindelang, M., M. Gottfredson, and J. Garofalo. 1978. *Victims of Personal Crime: An Empirical Foundation for a Theory of Personal Victimization*. Cambridge, MA: Ballinger.

Holinger, Paul C. 1987. *Violent Deaths in the United States: An Epidemiologic Study of Suicide, Homicide, and Accidents*. New York: Guilford Press.

Indian Health Service. 1988. *Regional Differences in Indian Health*. Washington, D.C.: U.S. Department of Health and Human Services.

——. 1991. *Regional Differences in Indian Health*. Washington, D.C.: U.S. Department of Health and Human Services.

Jencks, Christopher, and Susan E. Mayer. 1990. "The Social Consequences of Growing Up in A Poor Neighborhood." Pp. 111-186 in Laurence E. Lynn, Jr. and Michael G.H. McGeary, eds., *Inner-City Poverty in the United States*. Washington, D.C.: National Academy Press.

Koppel, Herbert. 1987. "Lifetime Likelihood of Victimization." Bureau of Justice Statistics Technical Report NCJ-104274. U.S. Department of Justice.

Lane, Roger. 1979. *Violent Death in the City: Suicide, Accident, and Murder in Nineteenth Century Philadelphia*. Cambridge, MA: Harvard University Press.

Loftin, Colin, and Ellen J. MacKenzie. 1990. "Building National Estimates of Violent Victimization." Draft paper presented at the Symposium on the Understanding and Control of Violent Behavior. Destin, FL. April 1-4.

Loftin, Colin, and Brian Wiersma. 1991. "Lifetime Risk of Violent Victimization from Homicide." Unpublished memo to the Panel on the Understanding and Control of Violent Behavior.

Lynch, James P. 1989. "An Evaluation of Lifetime Likelihood of Victimization." *Public Opinion Quarterly* 53:262-264.

Maxfield, M. G. 1989. "Circumstances in Supplementary Homicide Reports: Variety and Validity." *Criminology* 27(4):671-695.

Monahan, J. 1988. "Risk Assessment of Violence Among the Mentally Disordered: Generating Useful Knowledge." *International Journal of Law and Psychiatry* 11:249-257.

Monkkonen, Eric H. 1989. "Diverging Homicide Rates: England and the United States, 1850-1875." Pp. 80-101 in T. R. Gurr, ed., *Violence in America. Vol. 1: The History of Crime*. Newbury Park, CA: Sage Publications.

National Center for Health Statistics. 1991. *Vital Statistics of the United States 1988. Volume II: Mortality*. Washington, D.C.: U.S. Government Printing Office.

Piper, E. 1985. "Violent Recidivism and Chronicity in the 1958 Philadelphia Cohort." *Journal of Quantitative Criminology* 1:319-344.

Pyle, G .F. 1980. "Systematic Sociospatial Variation in Perceptions of Crime Location and Severity." Pg. 226 in D. Georges-Abeyie and K. D. Harries, eds., *Crime: A Spatial Perspective*. New York: Columbia University Press.

Reiss, A. J., Jr. 1985. "Some Failures in Designing Data Collection that Distort Results." Pp. 161-177 in L. Burstein, H. E. Freeman, and P. H. Rossi, eds., *Collecting Evaluation Data: Problems and Solutions*. Beverly Hills, CA: Sage Publications.

Reiss, A. J., Jr., and D. P. Farrington. 1991. "Advancing Knowledge About Co-offending: Results From a Prospective Longitudinal Survey of London Males." *Journal of Criminal Law and Criminology* 82(2):360-395.

Sedlak, Andra J. 1991. *National Incidence and Prevalence of Child Abuse and Neglect: 1988*. Washington, D.C.: Westat, Inc. (Revised September 5, 1991).

U.S. Department of Health and Human Services. 1990. *Health United States, 1989*. Hyattsville, MD: Public Health Service.

van Dijk, Jan J. M., Pat Mayhew, and Martin Killias. 1990. *Experiences of Crime Across the World: Key Findings From the 1989 International Crime Survey*. Deventer, The Netherlands: Kluwer Law and Taxation Publishers.

26

The Cycle of Violence

Cathy Spatz Widom

One of the most distressing types of violent behavior is child abuse. Every year millions of children are abused by a parent or guardian, sometimes so seriously that the child is left with permanent physical injury. Even when that does not occur, most child-development experts believe that child abuse leaves the victim with emotional scars. Does the emotional impact of being abused by one's parent or other responsible adult help determine later behavior? Some think the answer is yes and that behavior may well be violent criminal behavior. This "cycle of violence" hypothesis has been debated for some time, but testing it has proved difficult. Cathy Spatz Widom attempts to do just that, however, and comes up with some sobering findings.

Comparing two large samples of abused and nonabused children after they had grown to adulthood, she discovered that the abused subjects had a higher rate of having an adult criminal record and had been arrested more frequently than the controls. The abused subjects also had a rate of arrests for violent crimes that was greater than the nonabused group. This was particularly true for men, especially the oldest, African American males. She concludes that "These findings indicate that abused and neglected children have significantly greater risk of becoming delinquents, criminals, and violent criminals."

Although abused females were less likely than males to engage in adult criminality, they did so more often than their nonabused counterparts. When they did engage in crime they tended to violate property and public-order statutes, similar to the patterns of female offenders in general. Interestingly, Widom concludes that abused girls tend to experience adult depression and mental hospitalization as a consequence of their early life experiences. Whatever the outcome, it is clear that experiencing childhood violence has long-term and detrimental effects on the victims.

The scholarly literature on family violence has grown enormously during the last 20 years. One of the most pervasive claims that appears in both academic and popular writings refers to the cycle of violence: abused children become abusers and victims of violence become violent offenders. Over 25 years ago, in a brief clinical note entitled "Violence breeds violence—perhaps?" Curtis expressed the concern that abused and neglected children would "become tomorrow's murderers and perpetrators of other crimes of violence, if they survive."[1]

Indeed, the notion of an intergenerational transmission of violence has become the premier developmental hypothesis in the field of abuse and neglect. In this article I review the current empirical status of this hypothesis, drawing on data from different disciplines—psychology, sociology, psychiatry, social work, and nursing; comment on methodological problems; and describe new research developments in the field. Although people maintain strong feelings about this topic, they ought to be aware of those aspects of the cycle of violence hypothesis that have received support and of areas where unresolved questions remain.

Literature Review

Researchers and professionals have used the phrases "cycle of violence" and "intergenerational transmission of violence" loosely to refer to assumptions or hypotheses about the consequences of abuse and neglect in relation to a number of different outcomes. Some writers refer exclusively to the hypothesized relation between abuse as a child and abuse as a parent.[2] Others focus on the relations between child abuse and neglect and later delinquent, adult criminal, or violent behaviors.

Because there are difficult methodological problems confronting social science research, most investigations of child abuse have been criticized as methodologically flawed and limited in how the results can be generalized, their scientific validity, and ultimately their policy relevance.[3-5] There remains considerable debate about the definition of child abuse[6] and, consequently, much uncertainty about its prevalence. Even less is known about its effects. For children who have been abused or neglected, the immediate consequences may involve physical injuries or psychological trauma. In addition, the emotional and developmental scars of these children and those who witness severe family violence may persist. Furthermore, because many other events in the child's life may mediate the effects of child abuse or neglect, the long-term consequences of such childhood victimization are difficult to determine.

Abuse leads to abuse. In a recent review of empirical studies relevant to the intergenerational transmission of violence hypothesis, Widom[5] noted that there is surprisingly little empirical evidence to support the claim that abuse leads to abuse. Existing studies suggest that there is a higher likelihood of abuse by parents if the parents were themselves abused as children. Among abusing parents, estimates of a history of abuse range from a low of 7 percent[7] to a high of 70 percent.[8] Among adults who were abused as children, between one-fifth and one-third abuse their own children.[9, 10]

Many studies are methodologically weak and limited because of an overdependence on self-report and retrospective data, inadequate documentation of childhood abuse and neglect, and infrequent use of baseline data from control groups. In a comprehensive review of this literature, Kaufman and Zigler[2] concluded that the unqualified acceptance of the intergenerational transmission hypothesis from abuse as a child to becoming an abusive parent is unfounded.

Small-scale clinical reports. A number of frequently cited writings describe prior abuse in the family backgrounds of adolescents who attempted or succeeded in killing their parents,[11] and of murderers,[12] or of those charged with murder.[13] These reports, offered as support for the cycle of violence, present provocative clinical accounts by as-

tute observers; yet their own statistical usefulness is limited because of small sample sizes, weak sampling techniques, questionable accuracy of information, and lack of appropriate comparison groups.

As Monahan[14] argued, the most important piece of information researchers can have in the prediction of violence is the base rate of violent behavior in the population with which they are dealing. Particularly in the areas of abuse and neglect, there is a tendency to overemphasize individual case information at the expense of base rates. Appropriate control groups are necessary to assess the independent effects of early childhood victimization because many of the same family and demographic characteristics found in abusive home environments also relate to delinquency and later criminality.[15] Without control groups to provide an estimate of such base rates, it is difficult to assess the magnitude of relationships.

In the United States, for example, groups with different demographic characteristics (males/females, blacks/whites, rural/urban) have different base rates of arrest for violent crimes.[16] Thus, base rates—from the same general population of people at the same time period—must be taken into account in assessing the cycle of violence.

Delinquency. Another facet of the cycle of violence hypothesis refers to the relation between abuse and neglect and delinquency. The majority of studies that address this relation are retrospective ones[17, 18] in which the researcher typically asks delinquents about their early backgrounds. Estimates of abuse from these retrospective studies generally range from 9 to 29 percent. In prospective studies that follow up individuals who had been abused or neglected as children, the incidence of delinquency was between 10 and 17 percent. Of three prospective studies,[19-21] two lacked control groups (nonabused comparisons). Most studies of delinquents report that the majority were not abused as children. In at least one study,[21] rejected children had the highest rates of delinquency. However, without appropriate control groups and improved methodology, any conclusions remain highly ambiguous.

Violent behavior. Several studies involving delinquents [18, 19, 22, 23] and psychiatric patients[24] suggest that abuse and neglect are related to violent criminal behavior. However, findings are contradictory. Some provide strong support for the cycle of violence hypothesis; in others, abused and nonabused delinquents did not differ; and in at least one study, abused delinquents were less likely to engage in aggressive crimes later. Each of these studies has methodological problems, not the least of which is the universal lack of normal comparison groups providing baseline data. Furthermore, since existing studies focus primarily on violence among delinquents and adolescents, whether these childhood experiences have direct and lasting consequences for the commission of violent crimes into adulthood is unknown.

Aggressive behavior in young children. Another body of studies focuses on the relation between abuse, neglect, and aggressive behavior in young children. This work is based on experimental research and laboratory observations. Age groups vary, as do definitions of child abuse and outcome measures. However, these studies indicate with some consistency that abused children, as young as infants and toddlers, manifest significantly more aggressive and problematic behavior than nonabused or neglected children.[25]

These studies also suggest the need to consider neglect as distinct from abuse, because in some reports[26] neglected children appeared more dysfunctional than those abused. With one exception,[21] only these developmental psychology studies have systematically examined and reported differences between separate samples of abused and neglected children. By combining abused and neglected groups, or by studying only physically abused children, important differences in consequences may be obscured.

Observing violence. In addition to studies of children directly victimized, the indirect effects on children observing family violence have also been investigated in two types of studies. First, large-scale self-report surveys have found a modest, although fairly consistent, association between exposure to family violence and approval of violence or marital violence as an adult.[27] Second, studies of the children of battered women suggest that observing abuse or extreme marital discord may be as harmful to the development of the child as physical abuse, although other factors might contribute to these findings.[28]

Despite widespread belief in the intergenerational transmission of violence, methodological limitations substantially restrict our conclusions about the long-term consequences of early childhood victimization.[5] The research described here was designed to overcome some of the methodological problems that have hindered the empirical documentation of the cycle of violence.

New Research Developments

During a two-year research project, I examined a number of basic questions about the relationship between child abuse and neglect and later violent criminal behavior. This research was designed to incorporate methodological improvements. These included a relatively unambiguous operational definition of abuse and neglect; a prospective design; separate abused and neglected groups; a large sample to allow for subgroup comparisons and to allow for conclusions with respect to violent criminal behavior; a control group matched as closely as possible for age, sex, race, and approximate social class background; and assessment of the long-term consequences of abuse and neglect beyond adolescence or juvenile court into adulthood.

The purpose of this project was to identify a large sample of substantiated and validated cases of child abuse and neglect from approximately 20 years ago, to establish a matched control group of nonabused children, and to determine the extent to which these individuals and the matched control group subsequently engaged in delinquent and adult criminal and violent criminal behavior. At present, this research involves (and is limited to) the collection, tabulation, and analysis of official records.[29]

The decision to use official arrest records for the dependent variable was made for several reasons. Arrest records are relatively easy to locate, and reasonably complete information on arrests in official records can be collected retrospectively.[30] Results of self-report studies and research with the use of official records have been fairly consistent in terms of the correlates of crime.[31] Although self-reports are basically reliable and valid for relatively minor offenses, more serious offenses are more efficiently revealed (and with fairly little bias) by some official data.[32] Arrest records were also chosen because interviewing a large number of abused and neglected cases would be extremely costly. Compared to a good survey by interviewers, a register study such as the one described here tends to be much less expensive per case.[33]

Design. This study is based on a standard design referred to as specialized cohorts[33] or observational cohorts.[34] In a matched cohort design, both groups are free of the "disease" in question (violent or delinquent behavior) at the time they are chosen for the study and, because of matching, are assumed to differ only in the (risk) attribute to be examined (having experienced child abuse or neglect). Because it is not possible to randomly assign subjects to groups, the assumption of equivalence for the groups is an approximation.

In studies of the relation between child abuse and neglect and later delinquency or criminality, it is important to avoid ambiguity in the direction of causality of the events. Specifically, cases occur where delinquency precedes abuse or neglect in time and cases where delinquency itself may actually provoke the abuse or neglect of the child. Thus, to minimize this ambiguity and to maximize the likelihood that the temporal direction is clear (that is, abuse or neglect leading to delinquency or criminality), abuse and neglect cases were restricted to those in which children were less than 11 years of age at the time of the abuse or neglect.

In comparisons of delinquent or violent behavior, it is also difficult to judge what portion of the differences is due to the experience or factors under study and what portion is due to being labeled a delinquent or violent offender. My research does not totally avoid this problem, but by use of a prospective design, with data collection started at the point of abuse or neglect and before the onset of delinquency and violent behavior, the problem is minimized.

Abuse and neglect cases. All cases of physical and sexual abuse and neglect processed during the years 1967 through 1971 in the county juvenile court (situated in a metropolitan area in the Midwest) and validated and substantiated by the court were initially included. Abuse and neglect cases from the adult criminal courts were also included. In these cases, a criminal charge was filed against the adult defendant. During 1967 through 1971, there were 140 cases (physical and sexual abuse and neglect) processed in adult criminal court in which the victim was 11 years of age or less. After examining 2623 abuse and neglect petitions, a total of 908 cases were retained for this study.[35]

Definitions. Physical abuse refers to cases in which an individual had "knowingly and willfully inflicted unnecessarily severe corporal punishment" or "unnecessary physical suffering" upon a child or children (for example, striking, punching, kicking, biting, throwing, or burning). Sexual abuse refers to a variety of charges, ranging from relatively nonspecific charges of "assault and battery with intent to gratify sexual desires" to more specific and detailed charges of "fondling and touching in an obscene manner," sodomy, and incest. Neglect refers to cases in which the court found a child to have no proper parent care or guardianship, to be destitute, homeless, or to be living in a physically dangerous environment. The neglect petition reflects the judgment that the behavior represents a serious omission by the parents—beyond acceptable community and professional standards at the time—to provide to children needed food, clothing, shelter, medical attention, and protection from hazardous conditions.

Matched control group. One of the critical elements of this research design is the establishment of a control group, matched as closely as possible on the basis of sex, age, race, and approximate family socioeconomic status during the time period under study (1967 through 1971). To accomplish this matching, the sample of abused and neglected cases was first divided into two groups on the basis of their age at the time of the abuse or neglect incidents: those under school age and those of school age.[36]

Children who were under school age at the time of abuse or neglect were matched with children of the same sex, race, date of birth (±week), and hospital of birth through the use of county birth record information. Of the 319 abused and neglected children under school age, there were matches for 229 (72 percent).

For children of school age, records of more than 100 elementary schools for the same time period were used to find matches with children of the same sex, race, date of birth (±6 months), same class in same elementary school during the years 1967 through 1971, and home address, preferably within a five-block radius of the abused or neglected child. Out of 589 school-age children, there were matches for 438, representing about 74 percent of the group. Overall, there were 667 matches (73.7 percent) for the abused and neglected children.[37]

This cohort design involves the assumption that the major difference between the abused and neglected group and the controls is in the abuse or neglect experience. Official records were checked to determine if the proposed control subject had been abused or neglected. If there was evidence that a control subject had been abused, then he or she was excluded from the control group. This situation occurred in 11 cases.[38]

Demographic characteristics of the groups. Among the abused and neglected group, there are about equal numbers of males and females (49 versus 51 percent) and more whites than blacks (67 versus 31 percent). The mean age for the abused and neglected subjects is 25.69 years (SD = 3.53 years). The majority of the sample are currently between the ages of 20 and 30 years (85 percent), with about 10 percent under age 20 (the youngest is 16) and 5 percent older than 30 (the oldest is 32). The current age distribution of the sample indicates that our design has allowed sufficient time for most of the subjects to come to the attention of authorities for delinquent, adult criminal, and violent behavior.[23, 39]

The controls are well matched to the abused and neglected subjects in terms of age, sex, and race. Controls are equally divided between males and females. The racial composition of the group is quite similar to that of the abused and neglected group, although slightly more controls are black (35 percent). Their mean age is 25.76 years (SD = 3.53 years; range, 16 to 33 years).

Data collection. Detailed information about the abuse or neglect incident and family composition and characteristics was obtained from the files of the juvenile court and probation department, the authority responsible for cases of abused, neglected, or dependent and delinquent children. Juvenile court and probation department records were also examined for the control subjects. Detailed delinquency and detention information was recorded for both groups. Adult criminal histories for all subjects were compiled from searches at three levels of law enforcement: local, state, and federal. Searches also extended to the Bureau of Motor Vehicles and (for all females) marriage license records to find social security numbers to assist in tracing subjects through criminal records.

The Cycle of Violence: Findings

Abused and neglected children have a higher likelihood of arrests for delinquency, adult criminality, and violent criminal behavior[40] than the matched controls. Table 26.1 presents the percentage of individuals in the abused and neglected and control groups who have official records for delinquency, adult criminality, and violent criminal behavior.[41] In comparison to controls, abused and neglected children overall have more arrests as a juvenile (26 versus 17 percent), more arrests as an adult (29 versus 21 percent), and more arrests for any violent offense (11 versus 8 percent).

In addition to the extent of involvement, criminality is often described in terms of the number of offenses committed, the age at first arrest, and the repetitiveness (or chronicity) of a person's criminal activity. In comparison to controls, abused and neglected children as a group have a larger mean number of offenses (2.43 versus 1.41, t = 4.49, $P<0.001$); an earlier mean age at first offense (16.48 versus 17.29, t = 2.38, $P<0.05$); and a higher proportion of chronic offenders, that is, those charged with five or more offenses [17 versus 9 percent; X^2 (1) = 28.865, $P<0.001$].

Differences related to demographic characteristics. To illustrate the independent effects of demographic characteristics, the results of separate analyses for sex and race are included in Table 26.1.

Sex. Males have higher rates of delinquency, adult criminality, and violent criminal behavior than females (Table 26.1). Within each sex, a history of abuse or neglect also significantly increases one's chances of having an official criminal record. Thus, despite the fact that women generally have lower rates of arrests for criminal behavior, abused or neglected females are significantly more likely to have an adult arrest (15.9 percent) than control females (9.0 percent), although the difference for females in these groups is not significant for violent crimes.

Race. Although blacks are statistically more likely to have official criminal records than whites,[16] the same pattern exists across the abused and neglected and the control group for all three levels of criminal activity (delinquency, adult criminal, and violent criminal behavior). For blacks and whites, being abused or neglected increases the likelihood of having a criminal record as a juvenile and as an adult. However, for whites, being abused or neglected does not significantly increase the risk of an arrest for violent criminal behavior.[42]

Age. Dividing our sample (ages 16 to 33 years) into four age groups of equal size, older subjects in both groups have higher frequencies of an adult criminal record than younger subjects [x^2 (3) = 36.17, $P<0.001$] and of violent criminal behavior [X^2 (3) = 14.05, $P<0.01$]. Although this finding may simply reflect the number of years available for the subjects to accumulate criminal records, it also illustrates the complexity of dealing with criminal behavior and the need to control for age.

Continuity. As seen so far, victims of early child abuse and neglect differ from nonabused and nonneglected children on a number of indices of delinquency, adult criminality and violent criminal behavior; however, not all aspects of criminal activity differentiate the groups. One example of such a similarity between the groups is provided by findings about the continuity between antisocial behavior as a juvenile and criminal behavior as an adult.

Of those with juvenile offenses, roughly the same proportion of abused and neglected children and controls go on to commit offenses as an adult (53 versus 50 percent). Similarly, of those with violent offenses as juveniles, approximately the same proportion go on to commit violence as an adult in the abused and neglected group (34.2 percent) as in the controls (36.8 percent). Thus, despite significant differences in the extent of involvement in criminal activity, nonabused and nonneglected subjects are just as likely as abused and neglected individuals to continue criminal activity once they have begun.

These findings are interesting in light of recent literature in criminology, particularly the current debates on criminal careers.[30, 43] Although my findings indicate that officially recorded abuse and neglect increase one's likelihood of having an official criminal record and speed up the age at entrance into officially recorded delinquent activities, early childhood victimization does not appear to place one at increased risk for continuing in a life of crime. These findings reinforce the notion[30] that it is important to distinguish factors that may stimulate an individual to become involved in crime from the factors that affect whether the person continues or desists in a criminal career.

Does Violence Beget Violence?

In a direct test of the cycle of violence hypothesis, violent criminal behavior was examined as a function of the type of abuse or neglect experienced as a child. According to the cycle of violence hypothesis, individuals who experienced childhood physical abuse only should show higher levels of violence than individuals victimized by other forms of abuse or neglect. Table 26.2 shows the percentage of subjects in each abuse group who have an arrest for any violent offense[40] (juvenile or adult record). As expected, victims of physical abuse had the highest level of arrests for violent criminal behavior, followed by vic-

Table 26.1

Extent of involvement in delinquency, adult criminality, or violent criminal behavior among abused and neglected (n = 908) and control (n= 667) groups. NS, not significant.

Demographic characteristic	Abused and neglected (%)	Controls (%)	x^2	p
		Juvenile record (delinquency)		
Overall	26.0	16.8	18.91	<0.001
Sex				
Male	33.2	22.2	11.38	<0.001
Female	19.1	11.4	8.66	<0.01
Race				
Black	37.9	19.3	21.29	<0.001
White	21.1	15.4	5.36	<0.05
		Adult criminal record		
Overall	28.6	21.1	11.38	<0.001
Sex				
Male	42.0	33.2	6.18	<0.05
Female	15.9	9.0	8.16	<0.01
Race				
Black	39.0	26.2	9.46	<0.01
White	24.4	18.4	5.26	<0.05
		Any violent criminal record		
Overall	11.2	7.9	4.68	<0.05
Sex				
Male	19.4	13.5	4.79	<0.05
Female	3.4	2.4	0.72	NS
Race				
Black	22.0	12.9	7.22	<0.01
White	6.5	5.3	0.70	NS

tims of neglect. However, types of abuse and neglect are not distributed randomly in the sample across age, sex, and race groups, and thus bivariate analyses present an overly simplistic picture.

Need for multivariate models. Since sex, race, and age are independently related to differences in rates of violent criminal behavior, it is necessary to control for the effects of these factors in examining the hypothesized cycle of violence. Thus, data analysis and interpretation of these findings must incorporate and control for sample demographic characteristics.

One statistical technique for analyzing the influence of a set of explanatory variables on a "response" variable that takes a binary form is logistic regression or linear logistic response models. This technique models the log-odds of the presence or absence of re-sponse as a linear function of the independent variable. Models were estimated with the use of iterative maximum likelihood methods,[44] with any arrest for a violent crime as the response variable and race, sex, age, and group status (physical abuse, sexual abuse, neglect, and controls) as explanatory variables.

The estimated coefficients in the resulting fitted model for predicting the log-odds of an arrest for any violent crime are presented in Table 26.3. Group contrasts are with the control group, so that each pure type of abuse (omitting cases with more than one type of abuse) is compared to the control group, holding other factors constant. The results of this analysis indicate that, controlling for age, sex, and race, the physical abuse and neglect groups have a significantly higher likelihood of having an arrest for a violent offense than the controls.[45] Thus, in the most direct and stringent test of the cycle of violence hypothesis, being physically abused as a child does increase one's propensity to commit further criminal violence. Although being neglected also increases one's likelihood of violent behavior, the type of abuse or neglect is not as powerful a predictor of violent criminal behavior as the demographic characteristics of sex, race, and age.

Caveats

My research was explicitly designed to examine the relation between abuse, neglect, and later violent behavior and to overcome methodological shortcomings in previous literature. However, this research has limitations because of its exclusive reliance on official records. Thus, one should be circumspect about these findings [3, 4] and not generalize inappropriately.

Much child abuse and neglect that occurs does not come to the attention of welfare departments, police, or courts. This fact especially applies to official data from the late 1960s and early 1970s, when it is generally believed that only a fraction of all maltreatment cases were reported. The abuse and neglect cases studied here are those in which agencies have intervened and those processed through the social service systems.[46] These cases were dealt with before most states had adopted mandatory child abuse reporting laws and before the Federal Child Abuse Treatment and Prevention Act was passed.

Child abuse researchers have argued that there is bias in the labeling and reporting of child abuse cases and that lower income and minority groups are overrepresented in official reports of child abuse and neglect.[47] The design discussed here does not generally include instances of abuse in higher level socioeconomic families in which such abuse may be more likely to be labeled an accident. On the other hand, national surveys of family violence have found that those with the lowest income are more likely to abuse their children.[10] Even though most poor people do not abuse or neglect their children, there is a greater risk of abuse and neglect among the

lowest income groups.[48] Regardless, one cannot generalize from these findings to unreported cases of abuse and neglect, such as those cases handled unofficially by private medical doctors.[4] Similarly, because of the exclusions,[35] these findings are not generalizable to abused and neglected children who were adopted in early childhood.

Table 26.2
Does violence breed violence? Any arrest for a violent offense as function of type of abuse [$x^2(5) = 13.85$, $P = 0.02$].

Abuse group	n	Arrest for any violent offense (%)
Physical only	76	15.8
Neglect	609	12.5
Physical and neglect	70	7.1
Sexual and other abuse	28	7.1
Sexual only	125	5.6
Controls	667	7.9

Other potential biases may be introduced by relying on official records for exposure to abuse or neglect and criminality. Pagelow[49] suggested that the process of intervening and labeling abused and neglected children, disrupting their residence with their family and stigmatizing the parents (who often received little or no assistance to improve), may create a self-fulfilling prophecy that can be difficult to resist or overcome. This implies that it is the official response to abuse, rather than the abuse itself, which begets later criminal behavior. On the basis of this reasoning, strong evidence for the long-term ill-effects of childhood victimization would be expected because the children in our abused and neglected sample were processed through the courts and presumably suffered all the negative effects associated with such a process.

On the other hand, because individuals in the control group could have been abused, but not officially reported as abused, the extent of the differences between the abused and neglected group and the controls might be suppressed. Thus, the findings here may represent an underestimate because the differences between the abused and neglected group and the control group may be smaller than would be the case for a "pure nonabused and nonneglected" control group.

In the case of the dependent variable, reliance on official arrest records for violent criminal behavior also represents an underestimate of potential violent behavior. These findings do not describe violent behavior, but rather violent criminal behavior. Whether these findings extend to violence in general, to spousal violence, and to violence directed at children is unknown at this time.

Therefore, it is important to locate and conduct a follow-up study with these individuals to determine the extent to which the abused and neglected subjects and the controls report having experienced child abuse or neglect and to determine the extent of delinquency, criminality, and violent criminal behavior not disclosed in official records. Eventually, further intergenerational transmission of violence to the offspring of these individuals (currently in their 20s and 30s) should be examined.

Conclusions and Implications

Early childhood victimization has demonstrable long-term consequences for delinquency, adult criminality, and violent criminal behavior. The results reported here provide strong support for the cycle of violence hypothesis. The experience of child abuse and neglect has a substantial impact even on individuals with otherwise little likelihood of engaging in officially recorded criminal behavior. My findings are consistent with previous empirical data; however, there is now baseline data with which to assess the significance and magnitude of the association, and there is an assessment of the consequences of childhood victimization beyond adolescence into adulthood.

In a direct test of the violence breeds violence hypothesis, physical abuse as a child led significantly to later violent criminal behavior, when other relevant demographic variables such as age, sex, and race were held constant. However, being neglected as a child also showed a significant relation to later violent criminal behavior, and type of abuse was not as powerful a predictor of this behavior as demographic characteristics.

These findings indicate that abused and neglected children have significantly greater risk of becoming delinquents, criminals, and violent criminals. These findings do not show, however, that every abused or neglected child will become delinquent, criminal, or a violent criminal. The linkage between childhood victimization and later antisocial and violent behavior is far from certain, and the intergenerational transmission of violence is not inevitable. Although early child abuse and neglect place one at increased risk for official recorded delinquency, adult criminality, and violent criminal behavior, a large portion of abused or neglected children do not succumb. Twenty-six percent of child abuse and neglect victims had juvenile offenses; 74 percent did not. Eleven percent had an arrest for a violent criminal act, whereas almost 90 percent did not. These findings mean that prevention programs and intervention strategies aimed at buffering at-risk children play a potentially important role in the reduction of further violent criminal behavior.

In addition, alternative manifestations of the consequences of these early abusive experiences should be examined. For example, the effects of early abusive experiences may be manifested in different ways from those already discussed, in particular in withdrawal or self-destructive behavior.[50] Thus, one possible explanation for the lack of a more substantial relation between childhood victimization and later delinquency, adult criminality, or violent criminal behavior may lie in more subtle indications of emotional damage such as depression, withdrawal, or more extreme behavior, as in suicide. Given the attrition that typically occurs in longitudinal studies, examination of cases lost because of early death would be particularly revealing. In some ways, studies that focus on violence and criminal behavior may be shortsighted.

Most likely, the long-term consequences of child abuse and neglect for females are manifest in more subtle ways. Abused and neglected females may be more prone to suffer depression and perhaps undergo psychiatric hospitalization as a consequence of these early childhood experiences, rather than direct their aggression "outwardly." Interpretation of results is also complicated because the type of abuse and neglect suffered by females and males differs (more females are sexually abused than males), which in turn may differentially affect the long-term consequences.

Table 26.3

Predictors of any violent crime: coefficients from linear logistic response model. Likelihood ratio x^2 (3) = 10.28, P = 0.016. Number of response subjects was 1455.

Predictor variable	Coefficient	Z value*
Sex (male)	2.08	8.32
Race (black)	1.35	7.11
Age	0.11	3.67
Sexual abuse	0.54	1.20
Physical abuse	0.94	2.47
Neglect	0.53	2.65
Constant	-7.48	-0.84

*Z values are computed by dividing the coefficient by the standard error. Values of Z greater than 2.0 are regarded as statistically significant.

Abused and neglected children are generally at "high risk" for social problems. It is important to understand the potential protective factors that intervene in the child's development and to compare the development of those who succumb and those who are "resilient" and do not. Although one can speculate on why child abuse and neglect should have various outcomes, the substance of what is learned and the intervening linkages that transpire to produce aggression and violent criminal behavior are not well understood. For example, child abuse or neglect may not directly cause delinquency or violent criminal behavior. Rather, these outcomes may be an indirect by-product of these early abusive experiences. There are suggestions in the empirical literature about possible intervening variables.[51] [A discussion of possible pathways and some of the potentially relevant variables is presented by Widom.[5]] However, more research is needed to look at possible mediating variables that act to buffer or protect abused or neglected children from developmental deficits and later delinquent and adult criminal behavior. Studies must be

undertaken to examine the role of what Garmezy[52] has called protective factors—dispositional attributes, environmental conditions, biological predispositions, and positive events—that act to mitigate against early negative experiences.

The scientific issue should not be the "box score" (the magnitude of the association between childhood victimization and later delinquent or criminal behavior), but rather the goal should be further knowledge of the processes involved.[53] Research should be directed at understanding how these early experiences relate to later violent behavior, recognizing the likelihood of multiple pathways, and noting how possible protective factors act to buffer some children from the long-term negative effects of these early childhood experiences.

Discussion Questions

1. Studies of the relationship between child abuse and violent criminal behavior are problematic. What are some of the problems with these studies?

2. What characteristics appear in females who have experienced long-term abuse and neglect? How do their actions differ from those of abused males?

3. Did the author conclude that there is a relationship between childhood abuse and adult violence? How was this study different than previous studies with regard to method? Was this methodology sound?

References and Notes

1. G. C. Curtis, *Am. J. Psychiatry*, 120, 386 (1963).

2. J. Kaufman and E. Zigler, *Am. J. Orthopsychiatry*, 57, 186 (1987).

3. J. Besharow, *Child Abuse Negl.*, 5, 383 (1981).

4. C. S. Widom, *Am. J. Orthopsychiatry*, 58, 260 (1988).

5. ——, *Pathways to Criminal Violence*, N. Weiner and M. E. Wolfgang, Eds. (Sage, Newbury, CA, 1989).

6. The literature on child abuse and neglect encompasses several different phenomena: physical abuse, sexual abuse, neglect, severe physical punishment, and psychological maltreatment. Despite occasional references to

the destructive impact of psychological abuse, the focus here is primarily on physical abuse and neglect. Excluded are medical reports that describe immediate or long-term physical consequences of early childhood trauma.

7. D. Gil, *Violence Against Children: Physical Child Abuse in the United States* (Harvard Univ. Press, Cambridge, MA, 1973).

8. B. Egeland and D. Jacobvitz, "Intergenerational continuity of parental abuse: Causes and consequences," presentcd at the conference on BioSocial Perspectives on Abuse and Neglect, York, ME, 1984.

9. L. R. Silver, C. C. Dublin, and R. S. Lourie, *Am. J. Psychiatry*, 126, 152 (1969); J. J. Spinetta and D. Rigler, *Psychol. Bull.*, 77, 296 (1972); B. J. Steele and C. B. Pollock, in *The Battered Child*, R. E. Helfer and C. H. Kempe, Eds. (Univ. of Chicago Press, Chicago, 1974), pp. 103-147; R. S. Hunter and N. Kilstrom, *Am. J. Psychiatry*, 136, 1320, (1979); E. C. Herrenkohl, R. C. Herrenkohl, L. J. Toedter, in *The Dark Side of Families*, D. Finkelhor, R. J. Gelles, G. T. Hotaling, M. A. Straus, Eds. (Sage, Beverly Hills, CA, 1983), pp. 305-316.

10. M. Straus, R. Gelles, S. K. Steinmetz, *Behind Closed Doors: Violence in the American Family* (Anchor, Garden City, NY, 1980).

11. W. M. Easson and R. M. Steinhilber, *Arch. Gen. Psychiatry*, 4, 27 (1961); E. Tanav, *Austr. N.Z.J. Psychiatry*, 7, 263 (1973); C. H. King, *Am. J. Orthopsychiatry*, 45, 134 (1975); I. B. Sendi and P. G. Blomgren, *Am. J. Psychiatry*, 132, 423 (1975); J. M. Sorrels, *Crime Delin.*, 23, 312 (1977).

12. J. W. Duncan and G. M. Duncan, *Am. J. Psychiatry*, 127, 74 (1971); R. K. Ressler and A. W. Burgess, *FBI Law Enforc. Bull.*, 54, 2 (1985).

13. M. Rosenbaum and B. Bennett, *Am. J. Psychiatry*, 143, 367 (1986).

14. J. Monahan, *Predicting Violent Behavior* (Sage, Newbury, CA, 1981).

15. W. H. Friedrich and A. J. Einbender, *J. Clin. Child Psychol.*, 12, 244 (1983); R. Loeber and T. Dishion, *Psychol. Bull.*, 94, 68 (1983); R. Loeber and M. Stouthamer-Loeber, in *Crime and Justice*, M. Tonry and N. Morris, Eds. (Univ. of Chicago Press, Chicago, 1986), vol. 7, pp. 219-339.

16. Department of Justice, *Crime in the United States—1985*, (Government Printing Office, Washington, DC, 1986), pp. 166-67 and 182-184.

17. S. Glueck and E. Glueck, *Unraveling Juvenile Delinquency*, (Cambridge Univ. Press, Cambridge, 1950); D. 0. Lewis and S. S. Shanok, *Am. J. Psychiatry*, 134, 1010 (1977); C. M. Mouzakitis, in *Explaining the Relationship Between Child Abuse and Delinquency*, R. J. Hunner and Y. E. Walker, Eds. (Allanheld, Osman, Montclair, NJ, 1981) pp. 220-232; S. C. Wick, *ibid,*. pp. 233-239.

18. P. C. Kratcoski, *Child Welf.* 61, 435 (1982).

19. J. Alfaro, in *Exploring the Relationship Between Child Abuse and Delinquency*, R. J. Hunner and Y. E. Walker, Eds. (Allanheld, Osman, Montclair, NJ, 1981) pp. 175-219.

20. F. G. Bolton, J. Reich, S. E. Gutierres, *J. Fam. Iss.*, 2, 531 (1981).

21. J. McCord, *Child Abuse Negl.*, 7, 265 (1983).

22. R. L. Jenkins, *Am. J. Psychiatry*, 124, 1440 (1968); D. O. Lewis, S. S. Shanok, J. H. Pincus, G. H. Glaser, *J. Am. Acad. Child. Psychiatry*, 18, 307 (1979); S. Gutierres and J. A. Reich, *Child Welf*, 60, 89 (1981); M. Geller and L. Ford-Somma, *Violent Homes, Violent Children*, (report to National Center for Child Abuse and Neglect, Washington, DC, 1984); D. O. Lewis et. al., *Am. J. Psychiatry*, 142, 1161 (1985).

23. E. Hartstone and K. Hansen, in *Violent Juvenile Offenders: An Anthology*, R. A. Mathias, Ed. (National Council on Crime and Delinquency, San Francisco, CA, 1984), pp. 83-112.

24. C. E. Climent and F. R. Ervin, *Arch. Gen. Psychiatry*, 27, 621 (1972); H. T. Blount and T. A. Chandler, *Psychol. Rep.*, 44, 1125 (1979); M. Monane, D. Leichter, D. O. Lewis, *J. Am. Acad. Child Psychiatry*, 23, 653 (1984); R. E. Tarter, A. M. Hegedus, N. E. Winsten, A. I. Alterman, *ibid.*, p. 668.

25. T. J. Reidy, *J. Clin. Psychol.*, 33, 1140 (1977); R. L. Burgess and R. D. Conger, *Child Dev.*, 49, 1163 (1978); C. George and M. Main, *ibid.*, 50, 306 (1979); E. M. Kinard, *Am. J. Orthopsychiatry*, 50, 686 (1980); R. M. Barahal, J. Waterman, and H. P. Martin, *J. Consult. Clin. Psychol.*, 49, 508 (1981); M. A. Perry, L. D. Doran, E. A. Wells, *J. Consult. Clin. Psychol.*, 12, 320 (1983); D. A. Wolfe and M. D. Mosk, *J. Consult. Clin. Psychol.*, 51, 702 (1983); D. M. Bousha and C. T. Twentyman, *J. Abnorm. Psychol.*, 93, 106 (1984).

26. C. A. Rohrbeck and C. T. Twentyman, *J. Consult. Clin. Psychol.*, 54, 231 (1986).

27. D. J. Owens and M. A. Straus, *Aggressive Behav.*, 1, 193 (1975); D, Kalmuss, *J. Marriage Fam.*, 46, 11 (1984); P. C. Kratcoski, *J. Adolesc.*, 8, 145 (1985).

28. D. A. Wolfe, P. Jaffe, S. K. Wilson, *J. Consult. Clin. Psychol.*, 53, 657 (1985); P. Jaffe, D. A. Wolfe, S. Wilson, and L. Zak, *Am. J. Orthopsychiatry*, 56, 142 (1986).

29. A complete description of the design of this study and details of the subject selection criteria are given by C. S. Widom (*Am. J. Orthopsychiatry*, in press).

30. A. Blumstein, J. Cohen, D. P. Farrington, *Criminology*, 26, 1 (1988).

31. T. Hirschi, *Causes of Delinquency* (Univ. of California Press, Berkeley, 1969).

32. M. J. Hindelang, T. Hirschi, J. G. Weis, *Measuring Delinquency* (Sage, Berkeley Hills, CA, 1981).

33. F. Schulsinger, S. A. Mednick, and J. Knop, *Longitudinal Research: Methods and Uses in Behavioral Sciences* (Nijhoff, Boston, 1981).

34. J. M. Leventhal, *Child Abuse Negl.*, 6, 113 (1982).

35. Excluded were juvenile court cases that represented: (i) adoption of the child as an infant (n = 322), (ii) "involuntary" neglect only (n = 319), (iii) placement only (n= 72), and (iv) cases of "failure to pay child support" (FTPCS) (n = 898). "Involuntary neglect" refers to cases in which the mother or other legal guardian is temporarily unable to provide for child (children) because of institutionalization in a girls' school, jail, prison, mental hospital, or medical facility. In FTPCS, there was no indication of neglect on the part of the caretaking parent. These cases represented a neccessary step in seeking financial support from the noncustodial parent. There were 76 other exclusions, for the same and one additional reason (a morals charge against a mother with no evidence of abuse or neglect). Cases that involved adoption of an abused or neglected child were also excluded. Because of name changes concurrent with adoption and moves away from the county and state, the ability to locate official criminal histories for these individuals was seriously impaired. Thus, these 162 cases involving adoption were eliminated from the final sample. These findings, then, are not generalizable to adoptive cases of abused or neglected children.

36. Matching for social class is important in this study because it is theoretically plausible that any relation between child abuse or neglect and later delinquency or adult criminality is confounded or explained by social class differences. It is difficult to match exactly for social class because higher income families could live in lower class neighborhoods and vice versa. The matching procedure used here is based on a broad definition of social class that includes neighborhoods in which children were reared and schools they attended. Similar procedures, with neighborhood school matches, have been used in studies of schizophrenics [for example, N. F. Watt, *J. Nerv. Ment. Dis.*, 155, 42 (1972)] to match approximately for social class. Busing was not operational at this time, and students in elementary schools in this county were from small, socioeconomically homogeneous neighborhoods. After inspecting the home addresses of abused and neglected children and their matches, often the same street a few houses apart, it appeared as if the school matches might be closer than the birth record matches in terms of social class. To determine whether this matching procedure produced groups not evenly matched (hospital and school record matches), the analyses were repeated for the two subsets (abused and neglected children and their birth record matches and abused and neglected children and their school record matches), and they yielded essentially the same results. Although it would be surprising if social class had no effect on these results (arrest rates), given the matching procedure used here, there are good grounds for supposing that social class cannot explain all or possibly even most of the disparity in crime rates between the abused and neglected and the control groups.

37. The goal was to have a control group of approximately 700 subjects and to start with two matches (the second was backup in case the first was eliminated) for as many of the abused and neglected children as possible (up to 700). Non-matches occurred for a number of reasons. For matches through birth records, non-matches occurred in situations where the abused or neglected child was born outside the county or state or when date of birth information was missing. For school records, non-matches occurred because class registers were unavailable because of the closing of the elementary school over the last 20 years or lack of adequate indentifying information for the abused and neglected children.

38. An obvious limitation of this study is that the number in the control group who were actually abused, but not reported as such, is unknown. If the control group included subjects who had been officially reported as abused, at some earlier or later time period, this would jeopardize the design of the study.

Thus, any child who had an offical record of abuse or neglect occurred before or after the time period of the study. An alternative was to include these subjects and treat them as a separate group in the analyses. However, because the number of these subjects was small, this was not done.

39. M.E. Wolfgang, R.M. Figlio, and T. Sellin, *Delinquency in a Birth Cohort* (Univ. of Chicago Press, Chicago 1972); P. Strasburg *Violent Delinquents* (Monarch, New York, 1978); D. Rojek and M. Erikson *Criminology* 20, 5 (1982).

40. Violent Crimes include arrest for robbery, assault and battery, battery with injury, battery, aggravated assault, manslaughter/involuntay manslaughter/reckless homocide, murder/attempted murder, rape/sodomy, and robbery and burglury with injury.

41. A reanalysis of these findings was done, excluding abuse and neglect cases who did not have matches. Thus, the number of individuals in each group was 667. The results do not change with this smaller sample size. In cases where differences were significant, they became even more significant. In the few cases where differences were not significant, these results remained the same.

42. Because these findings are based on offical records and official records overrepresent minority groups, the most obvious explanation for the higher rates of arrests for violent crimes among blacks would be the bias and discriminatory treatment by the criminal justice system. However, this explanation does not seem to explain the differences among blacks and the lack of difference for the whites, unless we postulate a "double jeopardy" theory. Another possible explanation is that parental violence is more severe among blacks than whites or that nonwhites are more physically abusive with their children and within their homes than whites; however, the data indicate that this is not the case. Among whites, approximately 20% suffered physical abuse, compared to less than 9% for blacks. Blacks suffered more neglect, relative to whites in the sample.

43. M. Gottfredson and T. Hirschi, *Criminology* 26, 37 (1988).

44. R.J. Baker and J.A. Nelder, *The GIMM System. Release 3.77: Generalized Interactive Modeling Manual* (Numerical Algorithms Group, Oxford, 1986).

45. Separate logit analyses were done by using different methods of dividing the abuse and neglect groups in addition to the one presented here, which is based on pure groups. In these analyses, the same pattern emerged, indicating the importance of physical abuse only and neglect. One exception was in replicating the logit analysis by using only those abused or neglected cases with matches. Here, in addition to physical abuse and neglect as significant predictors, sexual abuse only was also significant.

46. L.P. Groeneveld and J.M Giovanni, *Soc. Work Res. Absr. 13* 24 (1977).

47. R.J. Gelles, *Am. J. Orthopsychiatry* 45, 363 (1975); E.H. Newberger, R.B. Reed, J.H. Daniel, J.N. Hyde, M. Kotelchuck, *Pediatrics* 60, 178 (1977).

48. R.J. Gelles and C.P. Cornell, *Intimate Violence in Families* (Sage, Beverly Hills, CA 1985)

49. M.D. Pagelow, "Child abuse and delinquency: Are there connections between childhood violence and later deviant behavior?" Presented at the Tenth World Congress of the International Sociological Association, Mexico City, Mexico, 1982.

50. G. Bach-y Rita and A. Veno, *Am. J. Psychiatry* 131, 1015 (1974); J. Kagan, *Daedalus* (Boston) 106, 33, (1977); H.P. Martin and P. Beezley, *Dev. Med. Child Neurol.* 19, 373 (1977). A.H. Green, *Am. J. Psychiatry*, 135, 579 (1978).

51. A. Frodi and J. Smetana, *Child Abuse Negl.* 8, 459 (1984); M.A. Lynch Roberts, *Consequences of Child Abuse* (Academic Press, Lonon, 1982).

52. N. Garmczy, in *Further Explorations in Personality*. A.I. Robin, J. Aronoff, A.M. Barclay, R.A. Zucker, Eds. (Wiley, New York, 1981), pp. 196-269.

53. K. Heller, personal communication,

54. Supported in part by the National Institute of Justice grant, 86-IJ-CX-0033, by Indiana University Biomedical Research grant S07 RR07031, and by a Talley Foundation grant while the author was a visiting scholar in the Psycholoy Department at Harvard University, Cambridge, MA. I thank A. Ames, J. Lindsay, B. Rivera, and B. Tshantz for assistance with the data collection and B. Ross for assistanse with the data analysis.

Reprinted from: Cathy Spatz Widom, "The Cycle of Violence." In *Science* 244, pp. 160-166. Copyright © 1989 American Association for the Advancement of Science. Reprinted by permission. ✦

27

The Motivation to Commit Property Crime

Kenneth D. Tunnell

Why do criminals break the law? What motivates them to violate norms protecting the security of one's person and property? These are the questions that Kenneth D. Tunnell asks in his study of sixty "repetitive property criminals." Through in-depth interviews with convicted felons, Tunnell probes their motives and rationalizations for various property offenses. Often using their own words, he demonstrates that property offenders are not all alike in what motivates their crime. They are, however, articulate in explaining their motives.

Tunnell is not the first scholar to attempt to understand common property criminals. Other researchers have attributed their crimes to economic motives, a search for thrills and excitement, or revenge. Since there are literally millions of property offenders among the criminal population, finding some common motivating factor could be an important step toward developing an effective crime prevention strategy. Tunnell's work demonstrates that will not be easy.

Eighty-eight percent of the interviewed offenders committed a property crime because they "just wanted money." They perceived that stealing was an easier way of obtaining money for their needs than working. With relatively little effort they could finance their drugs, alcohol, partying, and generally having a good time with relatively little risk of detection. Some study participants did attribute their crime to a sense of accomplishment, sport, vengeance, or power, but in most cases these motivations were secondary to the criminal's desire for quick and easy money.

Although these findings should not be surprising, since stealing what one wants has always been a viable if illegal alternative to earning it, they show the necessity of providing everyone with employment opportunities and the skills needed to earn a living. With a skill and a real job, it is possible that many property offenders would fulfill their needs in a legitimate way.

Rational choice theorists assume that individual decision makers analytically resolve decision problems through a logically calculated series of steps that culminate in a rational decision. As a way of situating this research within a larger theoretical tradition, this study relied on social-psychological variables indicative of these steps that lead to rational decisions. The process of deciding and the various steps involved constitute the focus of this study and the components of such processes served as lines of inquiry.

During the in-depth interviews, I had each of the 60 participants reconstruct specific criminal decision problems and their resolutions. To this end, each participant was asked to recall the most recent typical crime he had committed and could remember clearly.[1] Once they had selected the most recent crime, all of the daily events, conversations, and thoughts which occurred during the decision to commit the crime were reconstructed through conversation. The conversations produced 60 crime-specific decision problems, and the way they were framed and resolved.

One of the earliest factors in the temporal process of deciding to commit a crime is the dimension of motivation. During the interviews, I occasionally posed the question simply as, "Why did you break into that house that day?" Sometimes I arrived at the information in less direct ways, by deducing motivation from the various topics of conversation about the day of the crime and its events.

As I describe the motivations to commit crime among this sample of repetitive property criminals in this chapter, decision-making theorists might be rather disappointed that the accounts offered by these prisoners are neither complex nor analytically sophisticated. But, these criminals may not be the most reflective individuals, who rational choice theorists may desire studying. They may have given little thought to motivational forces in their lives, and in this way are not unlike "normal," law-abiding individuals, who might also be hard-pressed to explain the reasons for their actions and the choices they have made. Nonetheless, with this type of self-reporting retrospective research, we are left with little choice but to rely on the respondents for enlightening us as to motivation.

Motivations: Framing the Decision Problem

Social psychologists inform us that motivation is inseparable from goal attainment. Motivation research focuses primarily on the various factors that determine what psychologists call "goal-directed behavior," which is of central importance in understanding motivated behavior. "Motivated behavior can perhaps best be described by its purposefulness and persistence until the goal is reached" (Van Doren, 1972: 369) and such behavior usually will continue if the results are beneficial or positive. An attempt at goal attainment generally is preceded by the expectation of an end product—the perception of expected benefits from a particular act—and is the motivation for engaging in such an act. However, to analytically understand individuals' motivations is difficult, for motivation cannot be observed directly and must be inferred from either observed behavior or individuals' self-reporting of prebehavioral thoughts and perceptions of goals.

Table 27.1
Motivations to Commit Crime

Motivation Type	Number	Percent
Money	53	88
A sense of accomplishment	3	5
Crime as sport	2	3
Vengeance	2	3
Crime as power	2	5

The total number is greater than the N of 60 and the total percent is greater than 100 due to some overlap among the members' reporting.

Motive is considered an essential component of criminality by both jurists and investigators of criminal decision making. Jurists are interested in motivation because to them it represents an integral part of intent or *mens rea*. Decision-making researchers are interested in motivation because it represents a component of the decision problem: the benefits and calculable results the decision maker anticipates from engaging in a particular act.

It's Money that Matters

The motivating force among this sample of repetitive property criminals was nearly uniform—money—"quick, easy money," which they believed they would obtain from committing crimes. Table 27.1 illustrates the motivations to commit crime among this sample.

In fact, 53 of the 60 (88 percent) reported that money was their primary motivating force for committing property crimes, as the following conversation with a twenty seven-year-old high-rate burglar illustrates.[2]

Q: Why do think you did the armed robbery?

A: For the money.

Q: Any other reason?

A: I just wanted money.

The financial payoff from crime was defined as especially attractive when compared to the wages they would have expected, perhaps from past experience, to legally earn. The following brief excerpts from conversations with three of the 60 participants are illustrative of this primary motivation. I asked the following of a 31-year-old high-rate burglar who was quite aware of the possibility of his earning a decent legitimate wage.

Q: What about crime is attractive to you or appealing?

A: It doesn't take very long, the profit is quick. If I worked construction I would make a week what I could make in fifteen minutes. That's pretty much why it's appealing.

The following dialogue with a 29-year-old burglar illustrates how money acted as the only benefit that he and others like him believed they would obtain from committing crimes.

Q: So, when you were doing these burglaries then, what benefits did you see coming from them?

A: The money to make it from day to day, to pay me gas, pot, party money. To have a good time.

Q: Some people say they break into places for the thrill of it or the excitement or the accomplishment of it.

A: It never gave me no thrill and I really wasn't accomplishing nothing but putting money in my pocket. So, I didn't get no thrill because of it.

The attractive benefits of criminality are illustrated in the following conversation with a high-rate burglar.

Q: So it sounds like you're saying that the money you've made illegally far outweighs the money you can make—

A: Far outweighs. I don't mind working, but it's hard to work all day and kill yourself for really nothing.

And the following conversation with a 38-year-old armed robber who began his criminal activities with shoplifting also illustrates the benefits of earning money through crime.

Q: What benefit did you see coming from shoplifting and committing other crimes?

A: Just getting money to run around on the weekends with and buy some beer and whiskey and shit like that.

The financial attractiveness, coupled with the perception that threats of formal sanction were not serious, explains a significant part of the decision-making processes found among many of these respondents, particularly the high-rate persistent offenders.

Benefits identified other than money included the excitement of committing crime, the enjoyment of "getting over on" the powers that be, respect from peers for committing crime, and the control over crime situations

and crime victims.[3] These anticipated benefits, however, represent *latent* benefits and not the prime objective considered as these men resolved criminal decision problems. The following dialogue with a 28-year-old high school dropout who had committed dozens of burglaries and auto thefts illustrates this point.

Q: What was the reason you did the burglary?

A: Well, for the money, for the money. That's the only reason I did any burglaries. Really, any crime at all would be for the money. And the excitement, you know, it was always there, but it was for the money, more or less.

Q: Did you see any other benefits coming from doing burglaries or was it just the money?

A: Just the money.

Q: You didn't do it because it was exciting or—

A: It was fun, I guess it was kind of exciting in a way.

We can see from the above dialogue that money represented the primary motivation and expected benefit from this crime. Excitement was present but only as a latent benefit—a byproduct of the criminal act.

Although excitement did contribute to the motivation for some of these offenders, the burglar in the following dialogue claimed that for him excitement was not an issue.

Q: Why did you do it, for the money, or excitement, or—

A: Oh, for the money and no, I don't think it was for the excitement, it was just for the money.

Although some of these criminals had very few living expenses (they lived either at home with their parents, with a spouse or a lover who worked, or with a series of lovers), they wanted "easy money" to spend on leisure and recreational activities. This 29-year-old burglar, who rarely worked a legitimate job, reported this when I questioned him about motivation:

Q: Why did you do the burglary?

A: Broke and needed money and wasn't working. And just needed money to drink and party. It wasn't for bills.

As previous research has likewise shown (e.g., Petersilia et al., 1978), money represents the most common motivation. In fact, 53 reported that money was nearly the only element that motivated them to commit crimes. However, nearly a third of the sample (N = 17 or 32 percent) sought money because they had severe physical drug addictions. Their motive was to obtain money to purchase a drug to which they were literally physically addicted (or they defined their situation as such) and they committed crimes to sustain an addiction to a very expensive drug, not necessarily as a "way of life." The following conversation with a 33-year-old individual who committed a wide variety of crimes, but tended to specialize in a particular crime type for a period of time, sheds light on the motivating power of money for drugs.

Q: Why did you commit forgeries at that time?

A: The reason was to get money to buy the drugs with.

Q: That was the main reason?

A: That was the only reason.

Q: Did you use a lot of drugs?

A: Constantly. It was money for drugs. Now I know if I didn't have that drug habit I wouldn't be in this prison. It had got to the point that I really wasn't out there for nothing but just to do drugs.

And the following conversation with a 30-year old high-rate armed robber illustrates how a drug-addiction propelled him to commit crimes.

Q: Why did you do it, at that time?

A: I was doing drugs real heavy, powerful drugs, and I liked it and by me liking that I took them chances. I really didn't think about the risks period then hardly. All I though about was just getting dope and I'd go to any lengths to get it. The urge for that dope is stronger than getting caught so I'd go ahead and do it. I was doing it just to get money and it was for that damn dope.

I didn't really think about all the trouble I'd end up in or anything. I was just wanting to get the money for dope.

Clearly, money for 53 of these participants represents the most significant motivating factor in their criminal calculus. Two-thirds needed money for either living expenses or miscellaneous expenses and considered crime a relatively easy way to maintain their lifestyles. A third, however, were driven to commit crimes because they needed money to regularly obtain physically addictive drugs (e.g., cocaine, heroin, and Dilaudid.)[4]

A Sense of Accomplishment

A second and less-often-stated motivation for committing crimes was for the sense of accomplishment. From the respondents' self-reporting, this was the primary motivation only rarely. In fact, only three of the 60 reported "sense of accomplishment" rather than "easy money" as their motivation. The following dialogue with Floyd, a high-rate shoplifter and later a high-rate armed robber, well illustrates this motivation in the case of shoplifting.

Q: Why would you do it?

A: Because I enjoyed it and the people with me enjoyed it. I'm the type of person, man, if I could steal something from way in the back row or if the store manager is standing here and I could take something right under his nose, that's what I'd get.

Q: Why would you prefer that?

A: Because it was more of an accomplishment.

Although for some this motivation was primary, it nearly always was coupled with the desire for easily obtainable money or a sense of enjoyment, as the following comments from Floyd illustrate.

Q: What do you think the major motivations were to commit shoplifting?

A: Because it's easy money, it's exciting to do it, it ain't never hard to sell the stuff. But wanting to do it man, wanting to do it. Love to do it. *Love* to do it would be the word.

Those who committed crimes for the sense of accomplishment represent the segment that was very committed to a criminal lifestyle. They reported to me that crime was their job, their profession, and a way of obtaining both pecuniary and nonpecuniary benefits that they could not have earned from a "square-john" lifestyle. Although the sense of accomplishment was not a widespread motivational force among this sample, it did represent a significant factor in a few cases.

Crime as Sport

Two sample members reported in vivid detail a motivation for their crimes unlike those of others. Both individuals committed burglaries at a very high frequency and considered crime a fun and exciting game. The game-like rewards served as motivation to commit crimes. The easy money, which was motivating, paled in significance to beating the opponent of the game, or as they called it, "getting over on the law," which they considered a risky, yet psychologically fulfilling, act. I asked a 29-year-old, rather flamboyant, and very high-rate burglar why he committed the particular burglary he described to me. He described his motivation to commit burglaries in general.

A: If I had to write a damn paper on the reason I steal, there would be one sentence—it was for the game. It's a high, now, I mean it's exhilarating. I mean, some people like racquetball and some people like tennis, but I get off going through doors.

Successfully completing a crime provided them with a sense of accomplishment and purpose, and reinforced their belief that they had "won the game." They functioned with the knowledge that in this game, like others, there emerges a winner and a loser. And whenever they were arrested and convicted, they simply admitted to having lost the game, but only temporarily.

The following dialogue with a 28-year-old high-rate offender clearly illustrates this motivation. This particular individual was a burglar who went on "burglary binges" much like drunks go on drinking binges. During those times he would burglarize nonstop in a rather blatant way, with the belief that he was untouchable. He fancied himself an outlaw, a modern day John Dillinger. Coming from a small town where law enforcement officers were few in number and lagged behind in investigative and detective skills, he considered himself beyond the law, as his willingness to boast about just how good he thought he was proves.

A: It got to be a game. I've been locked up since I was sixteen. I've wasted the best years of my life. I can never get them back because I've played this game of 'I'm going to beat them.' And then you get to that stage, you wonder, 'Who in the hell is it I'm trying to beat?' But it got to be a game. I played the game and lost. You got me. Let's go ahead and run it and start it over.

Q: Did you feel like you were winning the game?

A: Well, it starts, it's just like the trumpets at a horse race. I mean that sounds a silly way to sum it up, but now, that's the damn, that's just about it. It's like a starting gun at a swim meet that starts the game. And it's not ended until you stand before that judge or you beat it. It's just like a chess game. I'm trying to stay a step ahead. I mean, fuck, it's a challenge. I mean, by God, it gets down to where it's just me against them and that's the way it is. To me, getting over on him or beating him at this game is 90 percent of it. The fucking money ain't nothing. Getting over on them is what it is. It got to where I just liked it.

Q: What did you like about it?

A: The excitement and the feeling of, you know, I fucked them, I mean, I had got over on them. They put their best investigators on me and I fucked them, man. I sit back and laugh thinking. Really. Basically, and you know yourself, it's a sorry mother-fucking thing, but I mean it provides that damn challenge. Crime was a game . . . with a whole lot of reality to it.

Thus, we can see from the two individuals who felt this motivation for committing crimes that the financial payoffs were rather insignificant compared to the psychologically fulfilling rewards of beating the opponent of the criminal game, a game with "a whole lot of reality to it." Ironically, they considered the years they spent incarcerated punishment for losing the game and not necessarily for breaking the law. One of the two individuals made the statement that going to prison was analogous to violating a rule in the board game *Monopoly*—go directly to jail, do not pass go, do not collect two hundred dollars. Again, this motivation was rare among this sample of repeat offenders but a very real factor in explaining why these few individuals committed crimes repetitively and what types of benefits they believed they would obtain from committing crimes.

Vengeance is Mine

The fourth type of motivation found among this sample, and only used by two armed robbers, was the desire for retaliation and vengeance. These armed robbers claimed to have suffered severely due to official governmental decision making, or lack of it. Both claimed to have lost legitimate earnings, both believed the government had done them an injustice, and one was homeless at the time that he committed his most serious crime of armed robbery. They acted criminally for revenge, generalizing and striking out at others as a representation of government and legitimate society. Although their crimes were individualistic, expressive acts and had no anti-systemic impact, they believed they were getting even with the status quo and the state that had caused them such harm.

Such motivation has been described by previous researchers. Becker, for example, wrote of revenge as both motivation and rationalization for committing crimes for individuals who believe they have been wronged and are entitled to such revenge. Revenge can also motivate individuals who believe their lives are out of control or that they are in the grips of "an uncontrollable force" (Becker, 1970: 332). Thus, individuals who commit crimes out of vengeance often define their situation as one imposed on them, over which they have little control.

The motivation of one of the two armed robbers clearly was shaped by his definition of his situation. He believed that some of his legal earnings from early in life had been wrongfully collected from him by the Internal Revenue Service. He claimed to have lost nearly all of his legally earned capital due to the collection of back taxes and legal fees. It was then that he decided to enter crime as a way of life to retaliate against the system and legitimate society. Crime as work also became a matter of principle to him since he had come to define legitimate work, where individual workers end up with little to show for their labor, as unfair. I had the following conversation with him about when he first began committing crimes in the early 1950s. He was 58 years old and serving his third prison sentence.

Q: Did you try and find a job?

A: I was determined then that I wasn't going to work and make a living. I wasn't going to go out and work all day and week after week and pay the government for working. I mean this is the way I felt then. I felt that if I went out and got a job and they took federal tax out, they took state tax out, they took medicare out, they took Social Security out and by the time I got my check they had already took out 30 dollars or 40 dollars. So why would I work to pay the government for working? That's the way I felt.

The second armed robber expressed similar rebellion against a government that he believed had done him an injustice by refusing to assist him with his physical and emotional problems in a time of serious need. During the interview he certainly looked the part of a man in questionable health. He looked much older than his 42 years, favored his bent back, and had some difficulty breathing. Although serving his third prison sentence, he claimed that he had committed relatively few crimes. He had committed the most serious, armed robbery, only twice and admitted he was motivated by frustration and a desire for vengeance. His words provide an inside view of his world.

A: The government did this somewhat to me too by denying me benefits.

Q: Your Social Security?

A: Yeah. I mean I was desperate. I didn't know what the hell I was going to do because I couldn't even keep the roof over my head. I moved into my car and I didn't have much of a car, but I slept in my car for a long time. I've had three back surgeries and now I've got heart trouble on top of the back surgery, so how in the hell am I going to get a job? My wife took me to _____ Mental Hospital because I did have an alcoholic problem and drugs and I asked her to take me there. And she did and I got turned away from over there, saying they didn't have the funds or money to help me and there was no room for me. No place for me there.

Q: And it was before that that you had gotten turned down for Social Security?

A: Right. I had many problems, mental problems. It got to the point where I knew I needed help and I couldn't get it. And that whole chain of events got me right in prison. I was on my Social Security and they cut it out and when they cut it out it like to cut my life off. I lost my Social Security, I lost my truck and I didn't know what the hell I was going to do. I done it out of desperation and frustration at life, no help, no money, living in a car. I couldn't even take a bath. Nowhere to take a bath. I felt less than worthless.

Those who committed crimes out of vengeance calculated their crimes emotionally rather than logically, as the following comment from the 58-year-old robber illustrates.

A: When you're mad like that and a person did something to you, you be in a mental state of mind, you don't give a damn about no police, or being locked up, or a judge, or no damn nobody else.

This vengeance motivation was rare among this sample. These two individuals made their decisions and then committed their crimes using emotionally charged reasoning processes and modes of behavior. They were not that methodical in their planning, understandings of benefits and risks, or target selections. They typically robbed spontaneously and selected targets without rhyme or reason.

Crime as Power

A fifth and particularly important latent motivation found among armed robbers was the exertion of power and the control of victims and of the crime situation. The following conversation with a 30-year-old, very experienced and seasoned armed robber illustrates how control and power were important elements to him, although money was obviously the primary benefit from the crime.

Q: Is that a pretty scary experience when you walk in with a gun pulled asking for money?

A: No, it's not really scary because you know you've got control of the situation, you know? It's a surprise, an element of surprise. You go in and you throw a gun on the table and everybody flips out. But it never did scare me because I always just put myself in their position. But it's just getting in that door. After you get through that door it ain't nothing, it's like you're running, like you own that place.

Q: You said like you own the place?

A: Yeah, you are ruling everything because everybody, whoever is in there is going to pay attention to you, I didn't want to hurt nobody. The only thing I wanted was the money. If you go in there you've got to play that act all the way out whether you get hurt or not.

Q: I think you're saying you were also prepared to do whatever to get the money?

A: Right. It wouldn't be that they'd try to harm me, it would be that they wouldn't give up the money. Because, you see, if you go in there and then let them tell you what to do, then there ain't no sense in you going in there at all.

Armed robbers who expressed this type of psychological benefit from and motivation for armed robbery were few in number (N = 3). The armed robbers almost universally reported the desire for quick cash as the single motivating factor in their decisions to commit crime. And even the very few who reported this expressive benefit of power and control indicated that it was not as significant in motivating them as the desire or necessity of money.

Conclusion

Although the majority of these repetitive criminals reported one primary motivation, many reported one primary and other less important or latent motivations. But, not surprisingly, the goal-directed behavior among this sample was nearly entirely for monetary gain. The other motivational forces found among this group of chronic offenders pale in significance to money. Monetary gain, for whatever reason (e.g., for drugs, for living expenses, for pleasurable commodities) represents the most significant and most widely reported source of motivation among this sample of repetitive property criminals. The benefits that these offenders believed they would obtain by committing crimes was a significant component of the process of deciding to commit a crime.

Such findings from this sample of repetitive offenders are both similar and dissimilar to those from previous research. For example, this study differs from that of Frazier and Meisenhelder (1985), who reported that many of their 95 property offenders found crime to be exciting and believed they were "getting over on" someone or away with something. Many respondents in my sample reported the same. In fact, nearly all 60 found it exciting. But, excitement was a latent benefit neither primarily nor objectively sought after. Very few respondents reported excitement as a reason for committing crime. Rather, "quick, easy money" was the most common reason for doing crime. If committing crime was also exciting, then that added more pleasure to a financially rewarding activity. But, few entered crime motivated primarily by a desire for excitement.

These findings are similar to those of Reppetto (1974), who interviewed 97 burglars and found money to be the primary benefit of crime. Excitement was mentioned most often among the young and least often among the old. This age-related difference is similar for the 60 men of my research. Motivation responses were measured across three different age periods of these men's lives.[5] These data show that excitement was often a primary motivator among the young, but its importance lessened with age until it typically became, at most, a latent benefit and motivating force.

Discussion Questions

1. What are the motivations for committing crime, as expressed in this article? Are some motivations stronger than others? Do you think these same motivations would be present in most crimes committed by females? Why or why not?

2. For those who regard "crime as sport," what are the rewards of crime? What does incarceration mean to them? What is their attitude toward the law? Do you think this motivation would ever be present in the commission of white collar/corporate crimes?

3. After reading their responses, would you say that criminals use the same rational choice, logical decision-making process that non-criminals use? Why or why not? What is a jury's interest in an offender's decision-making process?

Notes

1. The respondents typically would recall and begin to describe an exceptional crime that stood out in their minds for one reason or another. Knowing the types of crimes they committed and something about their frequency, I would remind them that I was interested in a typical crime that they had committed. They would then discontinue their description of the outstanding crime and begin describing a more typical crime for them. In this way, I was able to learn about the various events, conversations, and thoughts (as they reconstructed them) for a crime that they most frequently committed and the type most often committed by serious repetitive property criminals.

2. "High rate" as used in this work refers to those individuals in this sample who committed the most property crimes of the 60. As an arbitrary cutoff point, high-rate criminals are those who committed more than 100 property felonies during their lives in the "free world" and low-rate criminals, among this sample, are those who committed fewer than 100 felony crimes during their lives in the "free world." These high-rate felons are classified as persistent decision makers. . . . High-rate criminals represent those criminals who are very committed to a criminal

way of life and criminal profession. Such high-rate criminals clearly make decisions differently than low-rate repetitive criminals, who are classified as sporadic criminals in the taxonomy of decision makers among this sample.

3. "Getting over on" the law is a phrase used by criminals to describe successfully committing a crime and often refers to committing a crime with law enforcement officials nearby. "Getting over on" gives criminals satisfaction and is an expressive benefit derived from crime commission.

4. According to the *Physicians Desk Reference,,* Dilaudid is a "hydrogenated ketone of morphine . . . a narcotic analgesic." The PDR has this to say about this widely used and very addictive drug:

> Small doses of Dilaudid produce effective and prompt relief of pain usually with minimal disturbance from nausea and vomiting. Generally, the analgesic action of Dilaudid is apparent within 15 minutes and remains in effect for more than five hours. May be habit forming. The relative addiction potential does not exceed that of morphine with equianalgesic doses (Physicians Desk Reference, 1977: 871).

Dilaudid was certainly a drug of choice among the very serious drug users and addicts among this sample. Dilaudid was preferred over heroin because the users claimed that they felt safe with Dilaudid, knowing that it was clean, laboratory produced and

had not been "stepped on" (i.e., cut with an additive).

5. Each of the 60 was asked about motivation and benefit perceptions for three different age periods—juvenile (under age 18), young adult (ages 18 to 26), and adult (age 27 and older). Their responses reveal that excitement as a motivational force and as a perceived benefit lessened with age.

References

Becker, Howard S. 1970. "Conventional crime: Rationalizations and punishments." Pp. 329-39 in *Sociological Work: Method and Substance*. Chicago: Aldine.

Frazier, Charles E. and Thomas Meisenhelder. 1985. "Criminality and emotional ambivalence: Exploratory notes on an overlooked dimension." *Qualitative Sociology* 8:266-84.

Petersilia, Joan, Peter Greenwood, and Marvin Lavin. 1978. *Criminal Careers of Habitual Felons*. Washington, DC: U.S. Department of Justice.

Reppetto, T. A. 1974. *Residential Crime*. Cambridge, MA: Ballinger.

Van Doren, Bob. 1972. *Psychology Today*. 2d ed. Del Mar, CA: CRM Books.

28

Economic Motivators for Shoplifting

JoAnn Ray
Katherine Hooper Briar

One of the most prevalent property crimes is shoplifting. A number of studies of shoplifting indicate that women are overrepresented in this crime compared to other property offenses. A number of explanations have been offered. Women do much of the shopping and are exposed to the opportunity of theft from stores, according to some scholars. Shoplifting is consistent with women's nature, say others, and helps satisfy certain emotional characteristics of females. Depression, for example, is frequently cited as a motivator of female shoplifting. In this selection, JoAnn Ray and Katherine Hooper Briar challenge many of these assumptions and examine an idea that we have already learned is important in explaining other types of property crimes. Is it possible that shoplifters, including women thieves, steal because they need the merchandise they take?

Comparing a sample of self-reported shoplifters with those arrested for such crime, Ray and Briar found many interesting similarities and differences. More women report shoplifting, but more men are arrested as shoplifters. The typical shoplifter is apt to be young; ethnic minorities are more frequently arrested and taken to court. One out of three shoplifters report some sort of family problem, many more than shoppers who report no shoplifting behavior.

Regarding the main focus of this study, the authors report that "Economic hardships appear to be strongly related to shoplifting." Unemployment was a significant problem, as was a low or inadequate family income. Compared to other shoppers, shoplifters manifested more stress related to economic well-being and security. It appears that the psychological stress caused by economic marginality was related to the decision to steal merchandise from a retail establishment. These findings are consistent with other research findings pertaining to property crime. Shoplifters, male or female, are motivated by economic needs and steal to obtain what they cannot acquire legitimately.

Shoplifting is one of the most prevalent crimes in society. As its incidence has been associated primarily with psychological attributes or character defects, responses involve either correctional or mental health services. Little is known about the extent to which economic need may shape or contribute to shoplifting behavior.

While economic factors may cause or contribute to shoplifting, this has not been empirically established. In fact, many studies have ignored the obvious possibility that people may be shoplifting because they need the merchandise and have little money. Absence of attention to economic factors may not only limit the appropriateness of interventions such as psychological treatment strategies but may prevent systematic problem solving required to address economic factors and economic need. While historically the social work profession has acknowledged that economic conditions may influence behavior, the extent to which economic factors are addressed in practice remain debatable. As few social workers have skills and resources which explicitly respond to the economic correlates of their clients' behavior, it is understandable that psychologically oriented interventions and assumptions may predominate. Nevertheless, inattention to economic factors may reinforce victim-blaming strategies while protecting economic structures and statuses that may be contributing to the problem behavior. Drawing on research findings of two studies of shoplifters, this article addresses the significance of economic variables in contributing to shoplifting behavior. In addition, the article examines the need for expanded assumptions about human behavior and shoplifting, as well as more appropriate preventive, correctional, and treatment interventions. Finally, the social policy implications of the findings are explored.

Why Do People Shoplift?

Despite considerable research on why people shoplift, a number of studies suffer from methodological problems. Most are based on shoplifters who have been arrested, however, and the few who get caught may not be representative of all shoplifters. In fact, store detectives may watch certain types of people, thereby increasing their likelihood of being detected, while overlooking others. Moreover, because an estimated 60 percent to 80 percent of arrested shoplifters have been women, shoplifting has been attributed to women's nature (Cameron 1964; Robin 1963; Walsh 1978). Economic and related societal factors such as unemployment have received much less attention.

Most of the writings impugning women's nature as the motivational source for shoplifting are not based upon empirical research; the few studies that exist have used small samples of women only. The roles of women as wives and mothers have been searched for explanatory clues, and variables relating physiological and hormonal changes during adolescence and menopause have been used to understand shoplifting dynamics. Shoplifting has been presumed to be related to a number of physical factors including menopause, pregnancy, and psychosomatic illnesses (Applebaum and Klemmer 1974; Rourke 1957). The most frequently cited emotional problem associated with shoplifting is depression, especially for middle-aged women (Gibbens 1962; Neustatter 1954; Russell 1973). Other psychological factors associated with shoplifting, include low self-concept, symbolic sexual gratification, feelings of guilt, loneliness, fright, confusion, and conflict (Beck and McIntire 1977; Beers 1974; Gibbens 1962; Neustatter 1954; Rourke 1957; Russell 1973; Woodis 1957).

Other explanations of shoplifting are based upon stress and environmental factors. Some studies assume that shoplifting may be related to the failure of the shoplifter to internalize the dominant values of society (Cameron 1964; Kraut, 1976; Shave 1978). A high stress level has recently been identified as a contributing factor in shoplifting by mental health centers providing special services to shoplifters (Free 1982; Shave 1978). Society may condone or encourage shoplifting by stressing the importance of material possessions, thus creating a feeling of "perceived deprivation" among people with limited budgets. Shoplifting is made easy by few clerks, the ready availability of merchandise, and the impersonality of stores (Cameron 1964; Kraut 1976; Won and Yamamoto 1968).

While economic factors and their relationship to shoplifting have been relatively unaddressed, those studies that have focused on economic variables merit review. One study concluded that shoplifting might be related to lower income; Thomas found higher shoplifting rates in census tracts with lower median family income and housing in Lincoln, Nebraska (Thomas 1980). Findings of two other studies using archival data concluded that there was a little relationship between shoplifting and socioeconomic status. Won and Yamamoto found that the shoplifters with incomes under $5,000 are underrepresented in a study of grocery store shoplifting in Hawaii (Won and Yamamoto 1968). Cameron, who conducted a seminal shoplifting study in a Chicago Department Store, noted a high unemployment rate among the male shoplifters (Cameron 1964). Instead of viewing unemployment as an important indicator, the researcher questioned the reliability of the data arguing that the men may have lied about their employment to protect their employers from embarrassment. After analyzing the occupations of the employed shoplifters, Cameron concluded that the shoplifters reflected the socioeconomic pattern of the other customers involving few impoverished and few privileged shoplifters.

The contradictory findings may be explained partially by the noncomparability in the three data bases. While Cameron, Won, and Yamamoto studied store arrests, the differences in the types of stores might affect shoplifting patterns. Department and grocery stores may attract different kinds of shoppers and shoplifters. Thomas' study was based on city arrest data and may provide a wider cross section of persons arrested for shoplifting, however the data may reflect the referral biases of store personnel. Thus, such studies lead to the conclusion that the relationship of socioeconomic status to shoplifting has not yet been established.

Methodology

To address the influence of economic variables two data bases were used. Data Base I provided information from police and court records on personal characteristics, crime characteristics, and treatment of shoplifters by the criminal justice system. A one-sixth systematic sampling (200 cases) with a random start was completed on shoplifting cases filed with a municipal court in an urban area in the Northwest, between September 1981 and October 1982.

Data Base II was derived from a shopping center survey designed to obtain shoplifting self-report rates, shoplifting profiles by age, attitudes toward shoplifting, and perception of motivational factors for shoplifting. Questionnaires were anonymous as there were no names or identifying numbers. The questions were stated in a nonjudgmental manner to elicit the most honest response possible.

One thousand questionnaires were distributed—100 at each of ten shopping centers. Shopping centers were selected purposively to provide for socioeconomic differences in the city. Times and days during the week were randomly selected for each of the ten sites. Members of a research team approached shoppers randomly, introduced themselves, explained the research briefly, and asked shoppers whether they would complete the questionnaire. A questionnaire and stamped return envelope were given to those persons stating they would be willing to participate in the study.

Multiple measures of shoplifting motivations were included. For example, measures relating to economic factors were derived from both data bases including demographic data, items shoplifted, attitudinal factors, stress levels, and motivations. The following Shoplifting Motivation Scales were developed: (a) economic factors, (b) negative attitudes toward the system, (c) value of possessions, (d) perceived low-risk attitude, (e) psychological factors, (f) social stress factors, and (g) other stresses. Two hundred court records and 382 usable self-report questionnaires form the basis for analysis.

The limitations of the study must be considered when reviewing the findings. The major limitations are the low return rate of 38 percent of the questionnaires, the small number of shoplifters studied, and the large number of statistical tests performed. The truthfulness of self-reports by respondents is unknown. The study is exploratory and descriptive, thus it is designed to identify variables for further study rather than to offer conclusive evidence.

Description of the Sample

The two data bases produced differing shoplifting profiles. The Self-Report Study suggests that shoplifters are apt to be young, white, and female. The Court Sample Study, which may reflect observer bias, indicates that men, ethnic minorities, the young, and the elderly may be more frequently arrested and referred to court.

The typical shoplifter was apt to be young, although the respondents' ages ranged from 18 to over 65. Persons aged 25–34 were overrepresented in the Self-Report Sample, and then again along with persons over 65 were overreported in the Court Sample.

More women reported recent shoplifting, but this higher percentage of female shoplifters reflects the larger proportion of women shoppers. Fifty-nine percent of the self-reported shoplifters were women, but 63 percent of the respondents were women. Men, however, were overrepresented in the Court Sample as 67 percent of the arrested shoplifters were men.

Ethnic minorities were more apt to appear in the Court Sample than in the Self-Report shopping center sample. While 21 percent of those referred to the court were ethnic minorities, only 8 percent of the shopping center sample and 8 percent of the population were ethnic minorities. None reported recent shoplifting.

Shoplifters reflected a wide variety of occupations in the Self-Report Study, ranging from blue collar to white collar workers. Approximately one out of three shoplifters was experiencing family disruptions while 13 percent of other shoppers were separated, divorced, or widowed. Most shoplifters indicated that religion was "somewhat important" in their lives, while other shoppers rated religion as "very important." Shoplifters did not identify as criminals or as being dishonest and did not have friends who shoplift.

Shoplifting Motivating Factors

Economic Factors

Economic hardships appear to be strongly related to shoplifting. The economic problems of some shoplifters are perhaps most dramatically indicated by their employment and family income. Eighteen percent of the shoplifters, compared with 7 percent of the other shoppers, reported unemployment during the previous year. The court data indicated an even higher percentage of unemployed shoplifters, however the category of unemployed in the court sample includes housewives, retired persons, and students. Sixty-four percent of the court sample compared to 36 percent of the shopping center sample were identified as unemployed.

Although the family income of shoplifters varied widely, shoplifters more often indicated a lower family income than did other shoppers. Almost one-fourth of the current shoplifters had an income under $5,000 compared to 8 percent of the other shoppers. As shown in Table 28.1, another 30 percent of the shoplifters reported family incomes over $25,000, however, many of these people indicated on their questionnaires that they were experiencing economic problems.

The economic problems of the shoplifters are further indicated in their responses to stress-related questions. Stress inventory responses strongly suggest that many shoplifters are experiencing economic hardships and insecurity as depicted in Table 28.2. The Economic Stress Subscale and four individual items on this scale differed significantly between the shoplifters and other shoppers. Shoplifters more frequently indicated that they had been laid off or out of work during the previous year. Almost 40 percent of the shoplifters claimed that unemployment had

been a stressor. Shoplifters also experienced more problems finding employment than did the other shoppers. Two items relating to a shortage of money were answered differently by shoplifters and shoppers. Shoplifters are more concerned about having money for basic necessities and for repaying debts.

Table 28.1
Comparison of Family Income by Shoplifting Behaviors

Family Income	Shoplifters		Other Shoppers	
	N	%	N	%
Under $5,000	8	23.5	23	7.6
$5,001 to $10,000	2	5.9	30	9.5
$10,001 to $15,000	6	17.6	49	16.1
$15,001 to $20,000	2	5.9	42	13.8
$20,001 to $25,000	6	17.6	59	19.4
Over $25,000	10	29.4	101	33.2

Chi Square = 10.7, 5 d.f., $p \leq .0573$ (borderline)

Table 28.2
Comparison of Shoplifters and Other Shoppers on the Economic Stress Subscale

*Economic Stress Subscale	(Percent)		$p \leq .016$
	Shoplifters	Other Shoppers	
Concerns about owing money	70.6	50.2	$p \leq .037$
Not enough money for basic necessities	35.3	14.4	$p \leq .004$
Laid off or out of work	38.3	15.4	$p \leq .002$
Problems finding employment	32.4	12.9	$p \leq .005$

*Scale or subscale statistically significant (t-test).
All items statistically significant (corrected Chi Square).

Further support for the influence of economic need on shoplifting is provided by responses to attitudinal questions. The difference in the attitudes of the shoppers and shoplifters indicate that shoplifters are much more apt to identify "lack of money" and "being poor" as reasons why adults shoplift as shown in Table 28.3. Included on the list of reasons why adults shoplift was the item,

"They are unable to pay." Shoplifters more frequently than other shoppers perceived that people shoplift because they have insufficient funds.

Table 28.3
Comparison of Shoplifters and Other Shoppers on Economic Attitude Scale and Items

*Attitudes Toward Economic Factors Scale p ≤ .001	
If you don't have money for something you really need like food, it's OK to shoplift.	p ≤ .016
People shoplift because they are too poor to buy the things they need.	p ≤ .010
There are many things that I would like to own that I cannot afford.	p ≤ .020

*Scale statistically significant (ANOVA).
All items statistically significant (Mann-Whitney U Test).

A review of the kind of merchandise stolen further highlights the economic motivations of shoplifting. Food, an obvious basic necessity, was the top ranking category of stolen merchandise in the court sample. Over one out of three shoplifters was arrested for stealing food.

The write-in comments of the shoppers gave further insight into the motivations for shoplifting. Economic hardships are poignantly expressed in some of these comments. A 31-year-old housewife reflected on her shoplifting in the past: "My main reason for shoplifting was because I didn't have the money to buy the things I needed. At the time, it seemed as though we barely had enough money to buy formula for the baby." A 24-year-old woman recalled the painful memories:

> I shoplifted because my parents died and it took me over six months before we could receive financial help of any kind. I have two brothers and we were all under 19. It was either shoplift or we would have gone without food and clothing.

A 40-year-old unemployed male stated: "I'm out of work. But a dollar saved is still a dollar." Two shoplifters in the court sample were arrested for shoplifting clothing needed for job interviews.

Other Motivations

Multiple measures of the relationship between shoplifting and shopper's economic status suggest that shoplifting is strongly related to economic and employment variables. Shoplifting, however, was related to several other factors. Some of these other factors may be correlates and consequences of economic stress reaffirming the pervasive influence of economic factors as potential shapers of behavior and attitudes. However, further study is warranted before definitive statements can be made on the extent to which these measures are in fact by-products of economic stress. The following is a summary of factors other than economic related to shoplifting behaviors:

People who shoplifted recently were more apt to check the following items as stressors:

Personal (Psychological Factors) Stresses
regrets over past decisions
feeling sad and blue

Social Stresses
being lonely
watching too much TV

Family Stresses
problems with divorce or separation

Physical Stresses
personal use of drugs
sexual problems

People who shoplifted recently were more apt to answer differently the following items:

Attitudes toward Psychological Factors Scale
When I get feeling blue, going shopping makes me feel better. (agree)

Attitudes toward the Retail System Scale
People shoplift because items are overpriced. (agree)
The item stolen will never be missed. (agree)

Attitudes toward Perceived Low Risk Scale
If I shoplifted, I would get caught. (disagree)

It's not worth the risk of getting caught to shoplift. (disagree)

Attitudes toward Possessions Scale
Wearing designer clothes is important to me. (agree)
I like to keep up with the latest fads and trends in clothes. (agree)
People shoplift luxuries they feel they cannot afford. (disagree)

A more accurate picture of shoplifting is obtained by taking into account the combination of several factors, rather than only one motivator. The frequent occurrence of the combination of economic and psychological factors was documented in this study. One-half of the shoplifters were experiencing economic hardships as well as depression or other emotional stress. The psychological consequences of unemployment and economic stress are well documented (Briar 1978).

Discussion

Economic need appears to be related to shoplifting. People who shoplifted are more apt to have a lower family income, to be unemployed, and to believe that the economic need causes shoplifting. Not all jobless, economically insecure, or poor people shoplift, of course, and conversely, not all people who shoplift are poor.

Shoplifting and its relationship to the depressed economy is unknown. The unemployment rate in the area in which the research was conducted hovered around 13 percent and may have contributed to who shoplifts and why. Whether different or more people shoplift during hard times than in more prosperous economic conditions is unknown. That crime is a correlate of unemployment is well documented even though still disputed (Chaiken and Chaiken 1983). Shoplifters indicated that they were more likely than other shoppers to be experiencing economic stresses, social stresses, and depression. Shoplifters, too, were more apt than other shoppers to highly value possessions and to hold negative attitudes toward the system. The attachment and high value on possessions may be related to the loss of possessions associated with downward economic skidding caused by unemployment (Gordus 1984). Likewise, economic insecu-

rity and joblessness contribute to disenchantment with the system.

While the findings of this study are correlational and tentative, they do suggest that some of the previous research on shoplifting may need to be reinterpreted. While psychological and social stresses do appear to be related to shoplifting, these factors appear to be present for both women and men. Other factors, especially economic need, appear to be related to shoplifting. Many researchers have limited the scope of their research questions to factors related to women's roles, and therefore, have overlooked the realities of their economic dependence, insecurity, and inequality. Underemployment and economic insecurity are by-products of the caregiver, household role of some women (Briar and Ryan 1986). The fact that underlying economic problems and stress factors were not assessed may have resulted in limited interpretations and even sexist interpretations of motivations. Moreover, these interpretations fail to explain shoplifting among men and do not adequately explain shoplifting in women.

Implications

The appropriateness of referring shoplifters for psychological treatment is questioned. Such referral is based upon the assumption that the primary motivation behind shoplifting is emotionally based. Exploring only the emotional factors related to shoplifting may result in treating only symptoms since shoplifting appears to arise from multiple motivators for most people. Economic distress has been found to be a correlate of shoplifting and it is very often accompanied by emotional stress. When unemployment or other economic distresses are present, these variables need to be addressed in treatment and criminal justice responses.

Social workers need to develop a broader skill repertoire to work with clients with economic problems. Recognizing the potential devastating impact of unemployment, underemployment, and economic insecurity, practitioners might become more skilled in occupational problem solving, job development, and economic reform. While mental health treatment may address some of the emotional symptoms of economic and employment problems, few shoplifting treatment groups offer job development or job clubs. The shoplifter who is experiencing financial problems may benefit from an income treatment repertoire that addresses the conditions that cause or contribute to shoplifting behavior. Similarly, job placement diversion programs with the criminal justice system might be developed for shoplifters with economic and employment problems. Social workers have major roles to play in redressing some of the systemic conditions that contribute to shoplifting and in building a knowledge base for practice which ensures that systemic variables are included in research as well as inform clinical program and policy responses.

Discussion Questions

1. What are the non-economic-related stressors associated with shoplifting? Do these stressors characterize the typical shoplifter?

2. What have been some of the weaknesses of previous studies of shoplifting? How would this problematic research design affect policy-making? What would constitute effective policy to combat shoplifting?

3. Discuss the economic-related motivational factors related to shoplifting. Would these factors be consistent across gender, age, race/ethnicity and socioeconomic lines?

References

Applebaum, A. W. and Klemmer, H. 1974. "Shoplifting." *Menninger Perspectives*, 5(3), 16-19.

Beck, E. A. and McIntire, S. C. 1977. "MMPI patterns of shoplifters within a college population." *Psychological Reports*, 41 (3 pt.2), 1035-1040.

Beers, J. S. 1974. "A comparison of shoplifters and nonshoplifters: A study of student self-concepts." *Dissertation Abstracts International*, 34(7-B), 3455-3456.

Briar, K. H. 1978. *The effect of long-term unemployment on workers and their families*. San Francisco: R & E Research Press.

Briar, K. H. and Ryan, R. 1986. "The anti-institution movement and women." *Affilia Women and Social Work,(I) 1(1)*, 20-31.

Cameron, M. O. 1964. *The booster and the snitch*. London: The Free Press of Glencoe.

Chaiken, J. M. and Chaiken, M. R. 1983. Crime trend and targets. *The Wilson Quarterly*, 7(2), 102-115.

Free, P. 1982. Personal communication.

Gibbens, T. C. 1962. "Shoplifting." *Medico-Legal Journal*, 30(l), 6-19.

Gordus, J. P. 1984. *Economic change, physical illness, mental illness and social change*. Washington, DC: Congressional Research Service.

Kraut, R. 1976. "Deterrent and definitional influences in shoplifting." *Social Problems*, 23(3), 358-368.

Neustatter, W. L. 1954. "The psychology of shoplifting." *Medico-Legal Journal*, 22(4), 118-130.

Robin, G. D. 1963. "Department store shoplifting." *Crime and Delinquency*, 9(2), 163-172.

Rourke, F. L. 1957. "Shoplifting, its symbolic motivation." *Crime and Delinquency*, 3(1), 54-58.

Russell, D. H. 1973. "Emotional aspects of shoplifting." *Psychiatric Annals*, 3(5), 77-86.

Shave, P. L. 1978. *Shoplifting in the state of Washington*. Washington: State Office of the Attorney General.

Thomas, D. J. 1980. "The demographics of shoplifting." *Dissertation Abstracts International*, 40 (11-A—), 5931.

Walsh, D. J. 1978. *Shoplifting: Controlling a major crime*. London: The Macmillan Press, Ltd.

Won, G. and Yamamoto, G. 1968. "Social structure and deviant behavior, a study of shoplifting." *Sociology and Social Research*, 53(1), 44-55.

Woodis, G. M. (1957). "Depression and crime." *British Journal of Delinquency*, 8(2), 85-94.

Reprinted from: JoAnn Ray and Katherine Hooper Briar, "Economic Motivators for Shoplifting." In the *Journal of Sociology and Social Welfare* 15, pp. 177-189. Copyright © 1988 by the Journal of Sociology and Social Welfare. Reprinted by permission. ✦

29

Public Order Crime

Robert F. Meier
Gilbert Geis

No group of criminal statutes cause as much controversy as those variously labeled public order crimes or victimless crimes. Offenses such as drug use, prostitution, and gambling appear not to hurt anyone or threaten anyone's property. Any risk, physical or financial, involved in such behaviors is incurred by the persons initiating the action. If those persons are responsible adults, does the state have the right to label them criminals because they choose to use drugs, engage in prostitution as a buyer or seller, or gamble with their own money? These questions, and many others, are examined in this selection by Robert F. Meier and Gilbert Geis. While examining these and other victimless crimes, they explore some of the philosophical and historical roots of society's banning certain behaviors that appear to do no clear harm.

Clearly, criminalizing certain behaviors that do not appear directly to harm others enforces a morality that is shared by those who make society's laws. They argue that a civilized society must have a common morality that upholds a certain level of decency and decorum. In addition, such a society is obligated to protect its members from harm, even harm they might inflict upon themselves. Lastly, calling the prohibited behaviors victimless is to mislabel it, because they cause indirect harm to families, communities, and society in general.

Meier and Geis address issues of harm and morality and how they are related to criminal law. They introduce the term "victims without crimes," referring to those who have been harmed by actions not defined as crime. And, lastly, they ask the question, "What should be against the law?" Obviously, there is no clear answer to that question, since it varies with time and place, especially the public order crimes, whose harm is often difficult to discern.

This selection is concerned with one broad area in which criminal law has grappled with the problem of reconciling ideas of justice, principles of harm, and state intervention into our private lives and practices. Our interest centers on . . . behaviors . . . about which American moral codes have historically dictated the imposition of penalties by the state. . . .

Those who favor criminalization of such behaviors insist most fundamentally that all societies need to enforce a common morality and that such behaviors fall inside the limits of what should be permitted by law. They further maintain that these behaviors inflict harm on those who engage in them, and that a decent society has the obligation to protect its less careful members from their own self-destructive impulses.

Those who oppose the inclusion of these behaviors within the boundaries of criminal law say that they do not represent a threat to the integrity of the society and that they should not be the business of the law. They often call attention to analogous kinds of acts that are regarded with indifference by criminal law. The use of outlawed narcotics, for instance, they consider to be no different and perhaps even less serious a personal and social problem than drinking alcoholic beverages or smoking cigarettes.

The trend has distinctly favored those who have campaigned for the removal of some of these offenses from the criminal law roster. Gambling, once forbidden, is now part of everyday life, with lottery tickets on sale in some states at many local grocery stores. Homosexuality has been buried away in the criminal law closet. And in a particularly dramatic development, the United States Supreme Court declared that abortion was legally permissible during the first trimester of pregnancy.

However, disputes over the proper legal response to these behaviors did not abruptly end with the removal of some of them from the statute books. The subject of abortion continues to arouse fierce passions in many people, and there exists a concerted, organized effort to reverse the Supreme Court's ruling. Homosexuality for some people remains a carnal sin that must not be implicitly sanctioned just because it is no longer defined as criminal. Many disputes today focus on the question of whether same-sex partners ought to be allowed to marry and enjoy the same legal advantages (such as tax and inheritance breaks) that marriage provides. After the Walt Disney Corporation extended health benefits to same-sex partners, delegates to the Southern Baptist Conference in June 1996, representing a membership of 16 million people, voted to "boycott Disney Company stores and theme parks if they continue this anti-Christian and anti-family trend" (Niebuhr, 1996: A10).

Controversy also abounds regarding the way the law should define narcotic use. Those favoring decriminalization believe that longstanding law enforcement efforts have proven to be a failure and only encourage the underground traffic in drugs by raising the risks and therefore the price. On the other side, those opposing decriminalization maintain that things would be even worse if the law was no longer able to at least nibble away at the edges of narcotics use and narcotics traffic.

Criminal law is a political product, and there are disagreements about most aspects of law, including which acts should be illegal, how severely violators should be punished, and which powers should be given to the police and under what circumstances should they be exercised.

The disagreements are acted out in political debates, arguments before courts and legislatures, and even conversations among neighbors. And because law is enacted within a political context, controversy about criminal law is virtually guaranteed. . . .

We are aware that all laws are controversial, but we have become increasingly sensitive to the fact that there is a complex relationship between criminal law and the problems it addresses.

Consider two questions: What kinds of problems can the law solve? What kinds of

problems can the law create? The questions themselves suggest that the law can do both, although most conceptions of law give little consideration to the fact that the law can sometimes make matters worse. Our starting point is the observation that law creates as well as solves problems and often requires other sources of social control to deal with them. The law is far from impotent, but it is limited. As we shall see, the most effective use of law requires a social consensus on which problems are deemed appropriate for legal intervention. In the absence of such agreement, the law is often ineffective.

Crimes Without Victims: Victims Without Crimes

The behaviors that we will address—as well as some similar kinds of behavior—have come to be known in shorthand as "crimes without victims." The term first gained widespread attention in social science circles when it was used as the title of a monograph by Edwin Schur (1965). Graduating from Yale Law School, Schur earned a Ph.D. at the London School of Economics, where he wrote his dissertation on British drug policies. He subsequently taught sociology at Tufts University, then at New York University until his retirement in 1994. Schur wrote his monograph while on leave at the Center for the Study of Law and Society at the University of California, Berkeley The draft was titled "Nonvictim Crimes," but Sheldon Messinger, a colleague of Schur's at Berkeley, thought that term was too awkward. The result was *Crimes Without Victims* (Schur, 1996).

Legal historians had earlier discussed somewhat parallel concepts, such as "public welfare offenses," which made criminal such activities as merchandising intoxicating liquors that the seller was unaware were alcoholic (*Commonwealth v. Boynton*, 1861; Sayre, 1933). Sumptuary crimes, which forbade people of lesser social standing to wear more elegant kinds of clothing, were another kind of predecessor to the idea of "crimes without victims" (McManus, 1993). There are also offenses called "inchoate crimes," which tend to be vague catch-all statutes designed to give police the power to arrest persons whom they suspect of something untoward or whom they merely consider to be cluttering the landscape in an unappetizing way. Loitering was a quintessential inchoate crime; it was so vaguely defined that the Supreme Court, ruling on a Jacksonville, Florida ordinance, found it unconstitutional (*Papachristou v. City of Jacksonville*, 1972). Other such crimes are disorderly conduct and vagrancy, the definitions of which are often loose and differ from jurisdiction to jurisdiction.

For Schur, *crimes without victims* concern behaviors about which there is no complaining witness. The prostitute and the customer transact their business like any other merchant and customer; so do drug users and drug sellers. Homosexual couples mutually agree to do what they do, just as heterosexual couples do. When abortions were illegal, a female sought out a service that would satisfy her and unless there were dire complications, she would not complain to the authorities about what had happened to her.

But the concept of *crimes without victims* aroused early and strong opposition, primarily on the grounds that it failed to take into account the eddying kinds of harms surrounding different behaviors that could result from such crimes. Opponents argued that prostitutes rob and spread venereal diseases, narcotics make many users incapable of satisfactory social contributions, male homosexuals have a tendency to be promiscuous and (in more recent times) register a high rate of AIDS, a serious crisis which today drains public resources. The assumption was that outlawing these behaviors and arresting their perpetrators would alleviate some of the harm they were said to cause.

A recent attempt in the *Concise Dictionary of Sociology* to define the term *victimless crime* explains particularly well the semantic confusion that sometimes surrounds the term:

An activity classified as a crime in the laws of a country which may therefore be prosecuted by the police or other public authorities, but which appears to have no victim in that there is no individual person who could bring a case for civil damages under civil laws.

Unlike (say) a case of theft where the damage is to society as a whole, and to notions of morality, proper conduct, and so on. Examples might be drinking alcoholic beverages, reading Marxist literature, homosexuality, gambling, or drug-taking in societies where such activities are prohibited. . . . The concept is polemical, arguing in effect that certain crimes should not be prosecuted by the police, or should be decriminalized (Marshall, 1994:555-356).

This is a rather eccentric definition, but it offers a good basis for scrutinizing more closely some aspects of what commonly is and is not regarded as falling within the realm of crimes without victims, at least in the United States. Whether or not a victim can collect civil damages has never been seen as germane to the idea: its essence is that the offense is statutorily a crime. Also, although reading Marxist literature may be a victimless crime in some jurisdictions (most notably pre-Mandela South Africa, though it was not the reading but the possession of such material that was outlawed), it remains a protected constitutional right in the United States.

The second segment of the previous definition is quite on target: crimes without victims is a polemical concept and most commonly is invoked to persuade others that such offenses should not be outlawed, even if they are believed to be morally despicable. It is not unreasonable to suppose that Schur himself believed that decriminalization should probably be considered seriously in regard to the behaviors that he reviewed. In another writing, for instance, he favorably quotes Robert Lynd's (1939:283) observation that "research without an actively selected point of view becomes the ditty bag [a carryall used by sailors] of an idiot, filled with bits of pebbles, straws, feathers, and other random hoardings."

. . . We will . . . introduce a new term—*victims without crimes*—to include those behaviors that some people believe have been unreasonably eliminated from criminal law. Again, the focus here will be on behaviors in which there would be no complaining witness, such as in the cases of homosexuality and abortion. It might be argued that there is no true distinction between abortion and murder, because in both cases the object of the event no longer can enter a legal objection. For traditional homicides, however, the state assumes the role of complainant, usually on the assumption that survivors of the victim (unless, of course, they themselves are the perpetrators) demand redress. For abortion, the law assumes that the fetus is not a human and that the pregnant woman possesses the right to either eliminate it during the first trimester or to carry it to term.

The concept of *victims without crimes* inherently encompasses a broad reach to embrace acts that allegedly or in fact cause harm and create victims who would complain if they had a legal basis in criminal law. Many of the behaviors that would fit into a more expanded category fall under the heading of *white-collar crime*. The claim is often made that the corporations and industrialists of America are so powerful that by means of campaign contributions and other leverage they are able to inhibit the legislature from passing laws that might circumscribe some of their harmful behaviors. A corporation, for instance, is perfectly free to relocate a manufacturing plant (even out of the country), throwing thousands of people out of work so that it can secure cheaper labor elsewhere and thereby obtain a higher return for its stockholders.

Obviously then, neither harm nor Judeo-Christian moral precepts dictate totally what will or will not be included within criminal law. We continue to uphold by the use of criminal law countless such requirements imposed upon believers in the country's religious heritage. But we also pay little or no attention to some Biblical positions. Cursing at one's parents, for example, is a death penalty offense in the Bible, as it was in colonial times, though the penalty was never exacted. Adultery and fornication, now almost totally outside the scope of criminal law, are discussed today with gregarious exuberance on television talk shows. In early America, however, both were serious criminal offenses.

That there are remnants of these earlier statutory injunctions—ready to become manifest under certain circumstances—was demonstrated in 1996 by a wave of prosecution against those who impregnated unmar-

ried Idaho teenage females. By invoking a long-dormant statute, the prosecuting attorney in one county justified his action by noting, "It's a sad thing for a child to only know his or her natural father as someone who had a good time with his mother in the back seat of a car." Typically, the boy and girl are given a three-year term of probation and required to attend parenting classes together, to complete high school, and to not use drugs, alcohol, or cigarettes. Civil rights advocates have objected that the law is enforced only against teenagers, which they insist is discriminatory (Brooke, 1996).

Opponents of the ideological position that calls for minimum interference with human choices believe that a civilized society has a right to enforce a "common morality." In a forceful argument for this position, Patrick Devlin (1965:13), then a British high court judge, maintained that social harm will result if we fail to secure adherence to a general standard of morality, and that such harm threatens a society's survival:

> Societies disintegrate from within more frequently than they are broken up by external pressure. There is disintegration when no common morality is observed and history shows that the loosening of moral bonds is often the first stage of disintegration, so that society is justified in taking the same steps to preserve a moral code as it does to preserve its governmental and other institutions.

The same position found its way into the 1996 presidential race when Senator Robert Dole, defending his opposition to allowing abortions in the later months of pregnancy, raised this issue to the level of a more general commentary on contemporary American life: "As a society, we can't shake the feeling that our culture is in trouble and our values are under assault." Not surprisingly, Dole blamed the incumbent president for this unfortunate state of affairs (Nagourney, 1996).

Much better known, because it became the basis for the title of a novel by Ernest Hemingway, is the seventeenth-century dictum of John Donne (1624, No. 7):

> No man is an island of itself; every man is a piece of the continent, a part of the

main.... Any man's death diminishes me, because I am involved in mankind, and therefore never send to know for whom the bell tolls: It tolls for thee.

This position suggests that the injury or death of any of us, such as the narcotic addict or the prostitute, diminishes us all. Counterarguments insist that nothing is all good or bad, that laws must represent a position that balances costs and outcomes.

History demonstrates that the use of criminal law to enforce moral positions on crimes without victims sometimes takes a cyclical form. Gambling was outlawed in colonial times except in some cases for gentleman who were allowed to place wagers on horse races. Criminal law took the moral position that to bet was to substitute human judgment for divine will. Nonetheless, public lotteries soon became common in the United States until the 1830s. Many universities, including Columbia, Harvard, and Yale, were financed in part by lotteries. But a moral upsurge and a large number of scandals led to the outlawing of gambling (Ezell, 1960).

The initial break with this criminalization tradition came in the state of Nevada in 1869 (Skolnick, 1978). Today, legal gambling is permitted in some form in every state except Utah and Hawaii. State lotteries began in 1964 in New Hampshire and now have spread to 36 additional states (Berry and Berry, 1990); voters typically prefer a lottery to a tax increase. Riverboat gambling, an old American tradition, has been revived, and gambling is now permitted on most Native American reservations, where it has often been said that it rips asunder traditional tribal values yet makes significant amounts of money for tribal coffers (Vizenor, 1992).

The Notion of Harm

The idea of *harm* is one of the key elements involved in an understanding of why certain behaviors are forbidden by criminal law and are subject to punishment by the state. The concept also plays a prominent role in arguments about whether certain kinds of behaviors are regarded as *victimless crimes* or whether they involve *victims without crimes*. Outlawed harms typically take the form of a loss of property which the owner has a legal right to possess, or they involve physical injury or death. There are also some offenses, most notably treason, where the damage is regarded as falling upon the state, which is said to represent the best interests of all—or at least, most—of its citizens.

If the harm that results from a behavior injures the person who has committed the act, this is usually considered to be that person's own private problem and not the concern of criminal law. But arguments are made that private harm can have obvious public consequences. People who hurt themselves, even if they can personally bear the medical costs, tie up facilities that might be employed otherwise. Nonetheless, the law typically allows most "reasonable" risktaking to remain beyond its concern.

Though criminal law, taken as a whole, can be regarded as protection against harm, it is neither consistent nor comprehensive in affording such protection. The harm need not be inflicted; it need only be seen as reasonably related to the act that is outlawed. Attempted rape may be charged, even though the overt act involved no more than light touching of a woman's shoulder (Chappell et al., 1971). Nor does criminal law usually attend to more subtle kinds of harm, most notably those that create psychological damage. Also, there may not be any harm at all created by some acts that are declared to be criminal, only the statistical probability that some harm might result. Driving under the influence of alcohol or drugs is a serious criminal offense, even though most drivers in such a condition navigate their way home uneventfully. The behavior is outlawed because, compared to other motorists, a higher percentage of intoxicated or drug-high drivers will not be in adequate control of their vehicles and may injure or kill other people. Also, such drivers who are arrested may serve as a warning to others to avoid driving when not in full control of their faculties.

Morality and Criminal Law

Criminal law draws its dictates from the moral preferences of those in a position to determine its content. Beliefs about morality interact with beliefs about harm in determining the roster of "victimless" offenses. Moral precepts that ruled early American colonial life were derived from Biblical roots, and many of them had found their way into English common law and hence into American criminal law. In fact, virtually every criminal statute in the Massachusetts Bay Colony appended a Biblical reference to indicate its irrefutable authority (Elliott, 1952:22). If behavior was not covered in the *Laws and Liberties of Massachusetts,* issued in 1648, it was declared that it should be dealt with according to biblical doctrine (McManus, 1993).

In early Maryland, for instance, the law called for penalties against a person who was a "common swearer, blasphemer, or curser." There are records of a number of prosecutions, including one against Captain Thomas Bradnox, who was charged with having uttered at least "100 oaths" (Semmes, 1936:162). It was only in 1969 that the 246-year-old Maryland law against blasphemy was finally declared unconstitutional in *West v. Campbell,* a case involving a man who had been charged with swearing at a police officer following his arrest. The judge noted that in England in 1656, a hole could be bored in the offender's tongue for the first offense of blasphemy. A second offense could result in burning the letter "B" on the culprit's forehead. Fear of blasphemy charges underlay the taboo nature of such English expressions as "bloody" (a corruption of "By Our Lady") and "zounds" (a corruption of "God's wounds").

Biblical justice was responsible for the hanging of a considerable number of colonial defendants for the crime of bestiality, that is, sexual intercourse with animals. Adultery, though consensual, was also a capital crime, but the letter of the law was almost invariably tempered with mercy. The only time the death penalty was used in New England occurred in 1644 in Massachusetts, when James Britton and Mary Latham were sent to the gallows (McManus, 1993). The Puritans adopted the Old Testament rule that adultery could be committed only with a married woman. The marital status of the male partner did not count. A married man could not be punished for sexual relations with a single woman, unless she was engaged to be married; nor could an unmarried woman be punished for relations with a married man. The underlying doctrine in this case involved the use of criminal law to seek to protect the male's bloodline (McManus, 1993).

Suicide and Attempted Suicide

Perhaps the most extraordinary intermingling of moral dictates and criminal law involved the outlawing of the "victimless" act of suicide in the United States and England. Attitudes in earlier civilizations toward suicide were contradictory. The Athenians prohibited it, showing their disapproval by cutting off the hand of the person who committed suicide and refusing to bury it with the body. In ancient Rome, the philosopher Seneca summarized what appears to have been the prevalent Stoic view regarding suicide with the observation, "As I choose the ship in which I will sail and the house I will inhabit, so I will choose the death by which I will leave life" (Lecky, 1904:220).

Those who committed suicide in medieval times could not be buried in hallowed ground but were instead interred at a crossroads with a stake driven through their body, a tactic designed to prevent the tainted soul from escaping (Radzinowicz, 1948-1953:I, 196-197). As Edmond Cahn (1959:236) has noted with both bemusement and sarcasm, there is no record of "whether this mode of burial did more to reduce the incidence of suicide than to disrupt vehicular traffic." Obviously, the suicide could not be punished personally, but the state confiscated the offender's property, an arrangement which gave rulers considerable incentive to keep the criminal prohibition in place.

The Bible contains no injunction against suicide. During the Council of Arles in 452 A.D., the Catholic Church adopted such a position, supporting it with the thesis that "whoever kills himself, thereby killing an innocent person, commits homicide." Suicide is seen in Christian doctrine as thwarting God's will, given that it is a divine prerogative to determine when life shall end. Later, when the law against suicide was removed from the statute books, there still remained a prohibition against "attempted suicide." This law has largely been employed to provide the state with the authority to take into custody persons whom its officials believe constitute a danger to themselves.

Physician-Assisted Suicide

The controversy surrounding the issue of criminal law's proper role in regard to some behaviors defined in moral terms is clearly demonstrated in the intense debate today about the question of doctor-assisted suicide and the broader issue of euthanasia. If sane people formally declare their desire to die, and if it can be shown that they are in pain—perhaps terminally ill—and there is little likelihood that their condition will improve, should they be allowed to enlist a doctor to assist them in leaving this life? If so, how far should such a "right" extend? If a physician is accorded the right to assist in suicide, why should that right be withheld from those close to the person, such as a husband or wife, if they are given the sufferer's written permission which is witnessed by a court official? On the other hand, is it not possible that a person, forced to live and given succor, might change his or her mind about suicide? If the person consents to die, is the act "victimless" and/or should it be a matter of criminal law concern? (For opposing viewpoints of two doctors see Angell, 1997, and Foley, 1997.)

Studies show that about 15 percent of American doctors annually receive one or more requests for help in suicide; they grant about one-quarter of such requests, despite the legal risks. In the past, most requests were from people with intractable pain from cancer and other diseases. Today, such pain can largely be controlled. What patients most fear now is loss of control and dignity and the dependence and financial burden often associated with the end state of a fatal illness (Back, Wallace, Starks, and Pearlman, 1966).

Two recent federal court decisions both struck down attempts by state legislatures to outlaw doctor-assisted suicide. The Ninth Circuit Appeals Court overturned by an 8-3 vote a Washington state statute against assisted suicide. Inferentially, this ruling also endorsed the terms of Oregon's Death with Dignity Act, which was passed after a referendum vote, then ruled unconstitutional by a federal district court on the grounds that it constituted discrimination against the terminally ill (*Lee v. Oregon*, 1995; see also Previn, 1996).

The Ninth Circuit decision outlined one of the tragedies that formed the basis of the lawsuit, that of a 69-year-old pediatrician who since 1988 had suffered from a cancer that had metastasized throughout her body. Chemotherapy and radiation had offered temporary relief, but she had been bedridden for the past three years and in constant pain. The court noted that she was mentally competent to determine that she preferred physician-assisted suicide to the condition she found herself in. The decision relied on the following reasoning:

> A competent terminally ill adult, having lived nearly the full measure of his life, has a strong liberty interest in choosing a dignified and humane death rather than being reduced at the end of his existence to a childlike state of helplessness, diapered, sedated, and incompetent. (*Compassion in Dying v. Washington*, 1996:812)

That court heard two hours of oral arguments during the second week of January 1997, and left little doubt that the justices would overturn the circuit court rulings and leave the issue to be debated and decided state by state. As a news reporter noted: "It was clear that the Justices were fascinated by the issue and deeply engaged by the arguments—but at the same time eager to keep the Court out of yet another momentous question of life and death" (Greenhouse, 1997:A1).

No one on the bench spoke in favor of the idea of physician-assisted suicide, while several justices raised strong objections to the practice. "You are asking us in effect to declare unconstitutional the law of all 50 states," said Justice Anthony Kennedy. Justice Sandra Day O'Connor maintained that deciding who would have the right to die and who would not "would result in a flow of cases through the court system for heaven knows how long." Justice David H. Souter appeared to be speaking for the large majority of his colleagues when he noted during the oral argument: "This is all fairly recent.

Twenty years ago, we weren't even discussing the issue. Would it be better to leave it to the political process?" (*Washington v. Glucksberg*, 96-110, 1997; *Vacco v. Quill* 95-1858, 1997) Sauter's observation is, of course, a bit disingenuous. The Supreme Court itself is an integral part of the country's political process, as its decision on the right to abortion patently demonstrated.

The Dutch Experience. The situation in the Netherlands offers the most dramatic illustration of a political jurisdiction that has adopted a position on physician-assisted suicide that is much less restrictive than anything contemplated in the United States. Fears of a slippery slope decline once any door is opened for physician-assisted suicide also have been realized in the Netherlands. In a recently published study, Hendin (1996:44) claims that "The Netherlands has moved from assisted suicide to euthanasia, from euthanasia for people who are terminally ill to euthanasia for those who are chronically ill, from euthanasia for physical illness to euthanasia for psychological distress, and from voluntary euthanasia to involuntary (called 'termination of the patient without explicit request')."

A 1991 case in the Dutch city of Assen involved a healthy 50-year-old woman who asked her physician to help her die. One of her sons had committed suicide, another had died of cancer. She wanted to be with them. After an extended period of consultation, the doctor consented. He prescribed lethal pills and was at the woman's side when she died from taking them.

The doctor was tried on criminal charges because his patient was not terminally ill. Nor was she psychiatrically ill; only inconsolable. The doctor was acquitted by the trial court, the appellate court, and the country's Supreme Court (Hendin, 1996). Obviously, the country's law, as interpreted by its courts, now grants doctors the right to aid those who want to commit suicide for reasons that make sense to the person and to a doctor.

Usury

The practice of usury provides a further example of the manner in which Biblical morality was initially embalmed in criminal law,

despite its consensual elements, but was subsequently removed from the statute books in the face of what proved to be the more compelling requirements of capitalist machinery. Usury refers to the lending of money at exorbitant rates of interest. John Noonan, Jr. describes the evolution of social and legal concern with usury from medieval to current times:

> How can we appreciate the intensity of intellectual interest in usury in the sixteenth and seventeenth centuries, when its nature and extent were as lively an issue, and as voluminously discussed by reflective observers of commerce, as the nature and cure of business cycles are today? How much less can we grasp the spirit of a yet earlier age whose most perspicacious moralists describe usury as a great vice which corrupted cities and Church alike and held all men of property in bondage? Usury today is a dead issue, and except by plainly equivocal use of the term, or save in the mouths of a few inveterate haters of the present order, it is not likely to stir to life (Noonan, 1957:1).

Particularly significant in determining policies about usury were the ideas of Aristotle, the first major figure to oppose usury on theoretical grounds: "The term usury, which means the birth of money from money, is applied to the breeding of money because the offspring resembles the parent." Continuing, Aristotle wrote in *Politics* (Bk. I, Ch. 10): "Wherefore of all modes of making money this is the most unnatural."

Sanctions against usury were first leveled by church authorities against the clergy, based on the Biblical text of *Psalms* 15:5, which declared that a person who, among other things, "takes no interest on a loan" may dwell on God's sacred hill. The ban was extended from the clergy to laypersons by Pope Leo the Great, who wrote around 450 A.D., inveighing against the *turpe Iucrum*, or the shameful gain, of usury. Finally, for the first time, the theological principle was translated into secular law when the capitularies of Charlemagne outlawed usury in the Holy Roman Empire in the ninth century, defining it as the financial act in which "more is asked than given."

Between 1050 and 1175, the elements of usury were more carefully stipulated. The term was extended to embrace credit sales, which today would have included the interest charged on the use of credit cards, as a criminal offense. Dante, the principal poet of the medieval church, in his *Divine Comedy* (Canto VII), relegated usurers to the outer edge of the seventh circle of Hell, calling them "the melancholy folk," their eyes "gushing forth their woe." Later, usury was seen as an offense against the words of Christ: "Lend freely, hoping to gain nothing thereby" (*Luke* 6:35). Professional usurers were excommunicated by the church and prosecuted in state courts.

John Calvin, the Protestant leader, was the first major theologian to have insisted on the "fertility of money." Calvin believed that moneylending should be judged by the Golden Rule: It would be sinful only if it injured one's neighbor; otherwise, it was desirable. Each person's conscience was to be the guide. Loans to poor people would clearly be wicked, whereas loans to the rich or to business people were no different from profit on a sale. "Biting usury," or usury that sucks the substance of another while the usurer runs no risk, and charges of interest above certain limits were both condemned by Calvin, whose ideas gradually found their way into criminal law.

It is striking to note how the legal denotation of what is considered to be criminal varies with the economic conditions and social conscience of the times. In the Middle Ages, the average annual interest rate was about 43-1/2 percent, a figure not much higher than that prevalent for small commercial businesses in the United States during the 1930s (Robinson and Nugent, 1935:248-265).

Today in the United States, there is neither a total ban on usury nor unrestricted freedom. Policies tend to show a crazy-quilt pattern. Most states impose some ceiling on interest rates, but on the theory that usury laws are designed to protect only small, individual borrowers, loans to corporations are usually exempted from legal limits. The early conceptions of the theological immorality and illegality of usury have obviously given way in our times to a very different point of view.

Bad Samaritans

Suicide and usury laws indicate that the tie between Biblical morality and criminal law can be readily broken if secular concerns come to dominate discourse, as they have most notably in recent developments in regard to major "crimes without victims." The "bad Samaritan" condition illustrates that criminal law sometimes pays no heed to certain matters of morality that most of us would regard as essential elements of a decent society. The situation also illustrates the occasional absence of consistency in arguments based on moral precepts that appear in discussions of acts regarded as *crimes without victims*.

"Bad Samaritanism" reflects the fact that American law does not require a person to aid another human being, even when this can be done easily and with no risk to the rescuer. For instance, a bystander has no legal obligation to intervene if a blind man walking without a cane is going to step off the edge of a cliff to his death (Geis, 1991).

American law traditionally takes the position that one need not be burdened with the responsibility of aiding another. The reigning legal principle was cold-bloodedly set forth by the Chief Justice of New Hampshire almost a century ago:

> Suppose A, standing close by a railroad, sees a two-year old babe on the track and a car approaching. He can easily rescue the child with entire safety to himself. And the instincts of humanity require him to do so. If he does not, he may perhaps justly be styled a ruthless savage and a moral monster, but he is not liable in damage for the child's injury or indictable under the statutes for its death. (*Buch v. Amory Manufacturing Co.*, 1898:809)

The legal doctrine goes a step further and indicates that a person compassionate or foolhardy enough to intervene becomes liable thereafter for the consequences; in the absence of such intervention, the person remains juridically unassailable. A few exceptions to this basic rule do exist. If the bystander has made an initial effort to assist, then that effort must be carried through. The bystander must also help those with whom there is a pre-existing relationship, such as a spouse or kin, as well as help those to whom there is owed a contractual duty.

This laissez-faire approach is based on the idea that a free citizen should have no personal obligation to keep the public order and uphold public well-being, though there have been a few statutory efforts to encourage such behavior. Vermont and Minnesota laws now insist that bystanders must intervene or face criminal penalties, Massachusetts has decreed that persons on the site must report crimes of violence, and Rhode Island's legislature enacted a law that declared that the authorities must be notified of crimes of sexual assault. These last two acts came in the wake of a 1993 episode in New Bedford, Massachusetts, in which a woman was raped by at least four men over the course of an hour, while bystanders failed to intervene or notify the authorities.

In contrast, virtually all European countries have provisions in their criminal codes that demand bystander intervention under reasonable circumstances, and prosecutions, particularly in France, are not uncommon. Doctors, for instance, may be criminally charged if they fail to stop at the scene of an accident to render aid. In 1979, the body of Jean Seberg, a prominent American actress, was found in a car on a Paris side street. It was presumed that she had died of an overdose of alcohol and pills. But since Seberg could not drive without her glasses (which were found in her apartment), it was believed that her body, when there might have remained a chance to save her life, had been transported to the site where it was discovered. Criminal charges were filed against those who had been in the apartment with her (Richards, 1981). In addition, a surgeon was criminally charged in France as a bad Samaritan when he refused to perform a caesarian section on the dead body of a woman eight months pregnant (Feldbrugge, 1965-1966).

Pornography

The debates over pornography involve well-etched positions. Many people maintain that pornography routinely depicts scenes of the male brutalization of women and thus encourages acts of rape and sadism directed against them. They also find pornography involving children (tagged "kiddie-porn") to be a particularly despicable form of sexual exploitation. On these grounds, they insist that the purveyance of pornography should be made a criminal act (MacKinnon, 1993).

Those on the other side, while they may be hard-pressed to say much good about the product, believe that the First Amendment of the U.S. Constitution protects unpopular forms of expression, including pornography (Hawkins and Zimring, 1988). They argue that not all pornography portrays women as victims: there is, for example, a thriving industry in pornography directed toward homosexual men. Others (Paglia, 1994) insist that pornography is tied to aggressive masculinity, a requisite trait in nature's plan for human reproduction. They maintain that feminists are engaged in a power struggle in which their constant portrayal of women as "victims" rather than as persons who must take control of their own fate does a disservice to their gender.

The debate over pornography also centers on the consequences of exposure to it and whether it possibly reflects social malaise rather than introduces it (Linz and Malamuth, 1993). Pornography is a common staple on Japanese television and an integral element in religious art in India, two countries with low rates of violence directed at women. It has also been pointed out that there is no shortage of violent content in "mainstream" literature, even for children. Nobody apparently wants to criminalize the sale of the classic stories of childhood, for example, though many are grim and gory. Diverse forms of homicide occupy a prominent position in classical literature. Theatergoers need only count the corpses in Shakespeare's *Hamlet* to appreciate the extent of violence in the theater.

As with other victimless crimes and crimes without victims, the fundamental question here is whether pornography and the depiction of violence produce harmful consequences for innocent people. Regardless of how this question is answered, a key issue remains: whether a free society should have to tolerate these activities, because they are part of a spectrum of constitutionally protected rights; that is, if they are harmful, is it harm that we should bear as part of the price of our guaranteed freedoms?

Motorcycle Helmets

Ideological dispute today also includes the riding of a motorcycle without a helmet, one of the relatively few victimless crimes that does not have a strong sexual component.

Studies show that of the 47,000 automobile fatalities in the United States every year, about 8 percent involve motorcycle drivers and 1 percent motorcycle passengers. The total number of such deaths has been declining, from 3,189 in 1975 to 2,394 in 1992, though the death rate of about 64 per 100,000 registered motorcycles has remained fairly constant. This rate compares with 15.7 per 100,000 for automobile drivers and their passengers. About half of the motorcycle deaths resulted from a crash with another vehicle, usually an automobile; in 42 percent of the cases, the motorcyclist had been drinking more than the legal minimum, a far higher percentage than is true for automobile fatalities. If helmets had been worn, it is estimated that about 30 percent of the deaths could have been prevented. Twenty-three states, as well as the District of Columbia and Puerto Rico now require that all motorcyclists wear helmets (Council on Scientific Affairs, 1994).

Opponents of these laws insist that the statutes penalize behavior that endangers only the persons engaged in it. They say that the choice should be that of the motorcyclists: if they elect not to wear a helmet, that is nobody else's business. They also challenge the validity of the statistical claims about the safety of helmets and note that "helmets, especially, full-face models, suppress the normal sensations of wind and speed and thus can give riders a false sense of invulnerability and can lead to excessive risk-taking and dangerous riding habits." Statistics that demonstrate a significant decrease in deaths of motorcyclists in the wake of laws that mandate helmets are rejected on the basis that the helmet requirement has cut dramatically into motorcycle riding and that this drop is responsible for the decline in the number of deaths. They also insist that the more important place for helmets is in automobiles, as

car crashes inflict a higher percentage of head injuries than those resulting from motorcycle accidents (Teresi, 1995:15).

Responding to this position, the president of the Advocates for Highway and Auto Safety argued that motorcycle enthusiasts may delight in "feeling the wind in their hair" but that the rest of us "are feeling their hands in our pockets" because "bikers without helmets cost the rest of us big money" (Stone and Davis, 1995). Or, as Laurence Tribe (1988:1372), a leading constitutional authority, has put the matter: "In a society unwilling to abandon bleeding bodies on the highway, the motorcyclist or driver who endangers himself plainly imposes costs on others."

Another part of the argument about motorcycle helmets is that all human existence is filled with risks and that we cannot handcuff every exercise of freedom in an attempt to eliminate or reduce risks. After all, nobody would seriously suggest that we cut down the awful toll of highway deaths by banning automobiles, or even by putting mechanical governors on them that would restrict their speed to 45 miles an hour or less, though the savings in life and limb would be impressive.

In places where helmet wearing is mandatory for motorcyclists, the general supporting rationale is that the inconvenience to the rider is hardly so burdensome as to constitute an intolerable deprivation of personal liberty. It is noted that there has been an almost universal acceptance of the requirement to fasten seat belts. As one eminent legal scholar argued, "Any new law at all is some restriction on liberty, but not all restrictions are threats to it" (Woozley, 1983).

During the 1960s and early 1970s, a number of state courts heard motorcycle helmet law challenges. A New York court ruled that "to hold that a citizen may be required to protect his health alone would be an enlargement of the police power beyond traditional limits" (*People v. Carmichael*, 1967). State courts in Michigan (*American Motorcycle Association v. Davids*, 1968) and Illinois (*People v. Fries*, 1969) ruled that it was unconstitutional to demand under threat of criminal penalty that motorcyclists wear helmets. Shortly following these decisions, appeals and new cases occupied the courts, and many of the earlier decisions were reversed (see, for example, *People V. Kohrig*, 1986), including the *Carmichael* case. Finally in 1989, a federal circuit court put a likely end to anti-helmet claims by ruling that a Florida statute mandating helmets violates no right to privacy nor any privilege of a kind that the appellants labeled "the right to be left alone" (*Picou v. Gillum*, 1989).

What Should Be Against the Law?

Determining the problems that law should solve and those that it should avoid is a difficult task, but there have been suggested standards against which the appropriateness of law has been measured. Many believe that official action may legitimately be taken against a behavior if some substantial harm to others can be demonstrated to result from it. John Stuart Mill said in a classic statement (1859/1892:6):

> The sole end for which mankind are warranted, individually or collectively, in interfering with the liberty of action of any of their number, is self-protection. . . .

> The only purpose for which power can rightfully be exercised over any member of a civilized community, against his will, is to prevent harm to others. His own good, either physical or moral, is not a warrant.

The Mill statement, however, is not definitive enough when an attempt is made to use it as a guide to public policy. The terms, "self-protection" and "to prevent harm to others" allow so many interpretations that honest people may disagree on the same issue when confronted by the same set of facts. Mill does not tell us how serious the harm has to be and how directly it can be tied to the given act before the act can be reasonably banned. Would the harm be sufficient enough, for example, if it could be shown that homosexuality is producing a decline in the population that leads to inadequate numbers for economic growth and satisfactory military defense?

Nor is there any uniform agreement regarding Mill's views about official action to protect individuals from, as it were, themselves. There are those who insist that the state has the right or obligation to interfere in a situation where an individual is likely to be "exploited," such as in the case of twelve-year-old children who take factory jobs because their families sorely need funds. The difficulty of relying on Mill's guidelines to advocate or oppose public policy is illustrated by three recent articles, each of which argued that Mill would have adopted a different position regarding the law and pornography (Dyzenhaus, 1992; Skipper, 1993; Vernon, 1996).

. . . One useful approach to determine what should be the proper attitude of criminal law toward such action was offered by Herbert Packer (1968), then a law professor at Stanford University. The conditions that Packer believed should be present before criminal sanctions are invoked against conduct include: (1) the conduct must be regarded by most people as socially threatening and must not be approved by any significant segment of society; (2) the conduct can be dealt with through evenhanded and non-discriminatory law enforcement; (3) controlling the conduct through the criminal process will not expose that process to severe qualitative or quantitative strain; and (4) no reasonable alternatives to the criminal sanction exist for dealing with the behavior. These criteria are not, of course, the last word on the subject. There are those who would take issue with them, but they can be useful for drawing out some of the concerns that we face in determining what ought to be done—and not done—about [such] behavior. . . .

Discussion Questions

1. Why do some believe that we must enforce "common morality"? Why do others believe we should not enforce a "common morality"? How does the breakdown or extinction of common morality threaten society's survival?

2. What did the authors mean when they said "the law creates as well as solves problems"? How does criminalization of "immoral" behavior affect citizens? Police?

3. The authors discuss how riding a motorcycle without a helmet is a victimless crime. Explain why officials require cyclists to wear helmets by law. What are the arguments of those who oppose it?

References

American Motorcycle Association v, Davids. 1968. 11 Mich. App. 351.

Angell, Marcia. 1977. "The Supreme Court and Physician-Assisted Suicide—the Ultimate Right." *New England Journal of Medicine* 336:50-53.

Back, Anthony L., Jeffrey I. Wallace, Helene E. Starks, and Robert A. Pearlman. 1996. "Physician-Assisted Suicide and Euthanasia in Washington State: Patient Requests and Physician Responses." *Journal of the American Medical Association* 275:919-925.

Berry, Francis S. and William D. Berry. 1990. "State Lottery Adaptation as Policy Innovation: An Event History Analysis." *American Political Science Review* 84:395-415.

Bopp, James J. and Richard E. Coleson. 1995. "The Constitutional Case Against Permitting Physician-Assisted Suicide for Competent Adults with 'Terminal Conditions'." *Issues in Law and Medicine* 11:239-268.

Brooke, James. 1996. "Idaho County Finds Ways to Chastise Pregnant Teens: They Go To Court." *New York Times*, October 28:A26.

Buch v. Amory Manufacturing Co. 1898. 44 Atl. 809 (N.H.)

Cahn, Edmond. 1959. *The Moral Decision*. Bloomington: Indiana University Press.

Chappell, Duncan, Gilbert Geis, Stephen Schafer, and Larry Siegel. 1971. "Forcible Rape: A Comparative Study of Offenses Known to the Police in Boston and Los Angeles." Pp. 169-190 in James M. Henslin, ed., *Studies in the Sociology of Sex*. New York: Appleton-Century-Crofts.

Commonwealth v. Boynton. 1861. 84 Mass. (2 Allen) 160.

Compassion in Dying v. Washington. 1996. 79 F.3d 790 (9th. Cir.).

Council on Scientific Affairs. 1994. "Helmets and Preventing Motorcycle- and Bicycle-Related Injuries." *Journal of the American Medical Association* 272:1535-1538.

Devlin, Patrick. 1965. *The Enforcement of Morals*. London: Oxford University Press.

Donne, John. 1624. *Devotions Upon Emergent Conditions and Several Steps in My Sickness*. London: Augustine Matthewes.

Dyzenhaus, David. 1992. "John Stuart Mill and the Harm of Pornography." *Ethics* 102:534-551.

Elliott, Mabel A. 1952. *Crime in Modern Society*. New York: Harper.

Ezell, John. 1960. *Fortune's Merry Wheel: The Lottery in America*. Cambridge: Harvard University Press.

Feldbrugge, Ferdinand J. M. 1965-1966. "Good and Bad Samaritans: A Comparative Study of Criminal Law Provisions Concerning Failure to Rescue." *American Journal of Comparative Law* 14:630-667.

Foley, Kathleen M. 1997. "Competent Care for the Elderly Instead of Physician-Assisted Suicide." *New England Journal of Medicine* 336:54-55.

Geis, Gilbert. 1991. "Sanctioning the Selfish: The Operation of Portugal's New 'Bad Samaritan' Statute." *International Review of Victimology* 1:297-313.

Greenhouse, Linda. 1997. "High Court Hears Two Cases Involving Assisted Suicide." *New York Times*, January 9:AI,A10.

Hawkins, Gordon, and Franklin E. Zimring. 1988. *Pornography in a Free Society*. New York: Cambridge University Press.

Hendin, Herbert. 1996. *Seduced by Death Doctors, Patients, and the Dutch Cure: A Study of Euthanasia and Suicide in the Netherlands*. New York: Norton.

Lecky, William E. H. 1904. *History of European Morals from Augustus to Charlemagne*. 3rd ed. New York: Appleton.

Lee v. Oregon. 1995. 891 F. Supp. 1429.

Linz, Daniel, and Neil Malamuth. 1993. *Pornography*. Newbury Park, CA: Sage.

Lynd, Robert S. 1939. *Knowledge for What?: The Place of Social Science in American Culture*. Princeton: Princeton University Press.

MacKinnon, Catharine A. 1993. *Only Words*. Cambridge: Harvard University Press.

Marshall, Gordon, ed. 1994. *The Concise Dictionary of Sociology*. New York: Oxford University Press.

McManus, Edgar J. 1993. *Law and Liberty in Early New England: Criminal Justice and Due Process, 1620-1692*. Amherst: University of Massachusetts Press.

Mill, John Stuart. [1859]/1892. *On Liberty*. London: Longmans, Green.

Nagourney, Adam. 1996. "Heatedly, Dole and Clinton Escalate a Split on Abortion." *New York Times*, May 24:Al, A8.

Niebuhr, Gustav. 1996. "Baptists Censure Disney on Gay-Spouse Benefits." *New York Times*, June 13:A10.

Noonan, John T., Jr. 1957. *The Scholastic Analysis of Usury*. Cambridge: Harvard University Press.

Packer, Herbert L. 1968. *The Limits of the Criminal Sanction*. Stanford: Stanford University Press.

Paglia, Camille. 1994. *Vamps & Tramps*. New York: Vintage Books.

Papachristou v. City of Jacksonville. 1972. 405 U.S. 156.

People v. Carmichael. 1967. 279 N. YS. 272 (New York).

People v. Fries. 1969. 250 N.E.2d 149 (Illinois).

People v. Kohrig. 1986. 498 N.E. 2d 1158 (Illinois).

Picou v. Gillum. 1989. 874 F.2d 1519 (11th Cir.), cert. den., 493 U.S. 920.

Previn, Matthew P. 1996. "Assisted Suicide and Religion: Conflicting Conceptions of the Sanctity of Human Life." *Georgetown Law Journal* 94:589-616.

Quill, Timothy E. 1996. *A Midwife Through the Dying Process*. Baltimore: Johns Hopkins University Press.

Quill v. Vacco. 1996. 80 F.3d 716 (2d Cir.).

Radzinowicz, Leon. 1948-1953. *A History of English Criminal Law*. London: Macmillan.

Reitman, James S. 1995. "The Debate on Assisted Suicide: Redefining Morally Appropriate Care for People with Intractable Suffering." *Issues in Law and Medicine* 11:299-329.

Richards, David. 1981. *Played Out: The Jean Seberg Story*. New York: Random House.

Robinson, Louis N., and Rolf Nugent. 1935. *Regulation of the Small Loan Business*. New York: Russell Sage.

Sayre, Francis B. 1933. "Public Welfare Offenses." *Columbia Law Review* 33:55-88.

Schur, Edwin H. 1965. *Crimes Without Victims: Deviant Behavior and Public Policy*. Englewood Cliffs, NJ: Prentice-Hall.

Schur, Edwin H. 1996. Telephone Interview (June 6).

Semmes, Raphael. 1936. *Crime and Punishment in Early Maryland*. Baltimore: Johns Hopkins University Press.

Skipper, Robert. 1993. "Mill and Pornography." *Ethics* 103:726-730.

Skolnick, Jerome H. 1978. *House of Cards: The Legalization and Control of Casino Gambling*. Boston: Little, Brown.

Stone, Judith Lee, and Don Davis. 1995. "Bikers Without Helmets Cost Us Big Money." [Letter to the Editor], *New York Times*, June 24:14.

Stone, T. Howard, and William J. Winslade. 1995. "Physician-Assisted Suicide and Euthanasia in the United States." *Journal of Legal Medicine* 16:481-507.

Teresi, Dick. 1995. "The Case for No Helmets." *New York Times*, June 15:15.

Tribe, Laurence H. 1988. *American Constitutional Law*. 2nd ed. Mineola, NY: Foundation Press.

Vernon, Richard. 1996. "John Stuart Mill and Pornography: Beyond the Harm Principle." *Ethics* 106:621-632.

Vizenor, Gerald. 1992. "Gambling on Sovereignty" *American Indian Quarterly* 16:411-413.

West v. Campbell. 1969. Case No. 2814 (Criminal), Circuit Court, Carroll County, Maryland (May 1).

Woozley, Anthony D. 1983. "A Duty to Rescue: Some Thoughts on Criminal Liability." *Virginia Law Review* 69:1273-1300.

30

Homeboys, Dope Fiends, Legits, and New Jacks

John M. Hagedorn

Ever since drug use was criminalized in 1914, numerous myths have arisen about those who use illegal substances. These myths have proliferated in recent years as drug availability and use have increased, and the criminal justice system declared a "war on drugs." Among the myths created largely by official policy and media sensationalism are those of the "drug fiend," the extensive use of drugs in urban gangs, and the blatant disregard for conventional morality by gang members who use and sell illegal substances. This selection, by John M. Hagedorn, addresses these popular beliefs and uses research data to characterize young, urban gang members, their relationship with drugs, and the social circumstances of their daily lives.

Hagedorn's research indicates that most young, male gang members are not committed to dealing drugs. They move in and out of legitimate and illegitimate employment (dealing drugs) on an irregular basis depending on opportunities and circumstances. For most, dealing drugs is a short-term expedient measure, a way to make more money than they can make from unskilled service jobs. Most do not reject conventional values but share many of the aspirations of the legitimate working class. If they could secure them, they would accept full-time jobs and lead conventional lives. Being trapped in a cycle of poverty and hopelessness makes drug using and occasional drug dealing attractive options.

Hagedorn concludes that most urban gang members "are selling in order to survive." When arrested, prosecuted, and incarcerated on drug charges, they are "being punished for the 'crime' of not accepting poverty or of being addicted to cocaine." Rather than arresting and prosecuting them for this method of coping with their circumstances, a better strategy would be to train them in marketable job skills, assist them in finding jobs, and provide those who need treatment with the opportunity to overcome their drug dependency.

This paper addresses issues that are controversial in both social science and public policy. First, what happens to gang members as they age? Do most gang members graduate from gangbanging to drug sales, as popular stereotypes might suggest? Is drug dealing so lucrative that adult gang members eschew work and become committed to the drug economy? Have changes in economic conditions produced underclass gangs so deviant and so detached from the labor market that the only effective policies are more police and more prisons?

Second, and related to these questions, are male adult gang members basically similar kinds of people, or are gangs made up of different types? Might some gang members be more conventional, and others less so? What are the implications of this "continuum of conventionality" within drug-dealing gangs for public policy? Data from a Milwaukee study on gangs and drug dealing shed some light on these issues.

Gang Member, Drugs, and Work

An underlying question is whether the drug economy provides sufficient incentives to keep gang members away from legal work. If drug sales offer highly profitable opportunities for all who are willing to take the risks, we might expect many adult gang members to be committed firmly to the drug economy. On the other hand, if drug dealing entails many risks and produces few success stories, gang members might be expected to have a more variable relationship to illicit drug sales. In that case we could look at variation within the gang to explain different behaviors.

The research literature contains few empirical studies on the pull of the drug economy away from licit work. On the more general level, Carl Taylor (1990:120) asserts that "when drug distribution becomes the employer, $3.65 or $8.65 can't compare with drug business income." Martin Sanchez Jankowski (1991:101), in his study of gangs in three cities, found an "entrepreneurial spirit" to be the "driving force in the world view and behavior of gang members." This "entrepreneurial spirit" pushes gang members to make rational decisions to engage in drug sales. Jerome Skolnick (1990) and his students argue that gangs are centrally involved with profitable mid-level drug distribution, although these findings have been challenged by researchers (Klein and Maxson, 1993; Waldorf, 1993).

Others have found that gang involvement in drug sales varies substantially (see Cummings and Monte, 1993; Huff, 1990). Klein et al. (1991) remind us that not all gangs are involved with drug sales, a point that is often overlooked in the discussion of an invariant gang/drug nexus. Among those who sell drugs, actual income varies. Fagan (1991) points out that earnings from drug dealing in two Manhattan neighborhoods ranged from about $1,000 to nearly $5,000 per month. Although most drug sellers had little involvement with the formal economy, 25 percent of Fagan's dealers also worked in conventional jobs, and most reported both illegal *and* legal income for each month. This finding suggests that incentives from drug sales were not always sufficient to make dealing a full-time job.

Similarly, a Rand Corporation study (MacCoun and Reuter, 1992:485) found that the typical Washington, D.C. small dealer made about $300 per month and the typical big dealer $3,700, with an average of about $1,300. Sullivan (1989) found illicit economic activities in Brooklyn to be a youthful enterprise, quickly outgrown when "real" jobs offered themselves. The seriousness of criminal activity varied with the intactness of networks providing access to legitimate work. Most of Williams's (1989) New York "cocaine kids" matured out of the drug business as they became young adults and their drug-dealing clique broke up. Padilla's (1992:162) "Diamonds" became "disillusioned" with the empty promises of street-level dealing and aspired to legitimate jobs.

These few studies suggest substantial variation in the degree and duration of gang involvement in drug dealing. The drug economy is not an unquestionably profitable opportunity for gang members; rather, its promise appears to be more ambiguous. If that conclusion is valid, research must examine both the actual amounts of money earned by adult gang drug dealers and variation within the gang to understand gang involvement in drug dealing. We have a few studies on how much money gang members make from selling drugs, but hardly any contemporary data on different types of gang members.

Variation Within the Gang

Some research has portrayed gang members as relatively invariant. Walter Miller (1969) viewed gang delinquents as representative of a lower-class cultural milieu; his six "focal concerns" are persistent and distinctive features of the entire American "lower class." Similarly, Jankowski (1991:26-28) said that male gang members were one-dimensional "tough nuts," defiant individuals with a rational "social Darwinist worldview" who displayed defiant individualism "more generally" than other people in low-income communities.

Other research, however, has suggested that gang members vary, particularly on their orientation toward conventionality. Whyte (1943) classified his Cornerville street corner men as either "college boys" or "corner boys," depending on their aspirations. Cloward and Ohlin (1960:95), applying Merton's (1957) earlier typology, categorized lower-class youths in four cells of a matrix, depending on their aspirations and "criteria for success." Many of their delinquents repudiated the legitimacy of conventional society and resorted to innovative solutions to attain success goals. Cloward and Ohlin took issue with Cohen (1955) and Matza (1964), whose delinquents were internally conflicted but, as a group, imputed legitimacy to the norms of the larger society.

Some more recent researchers also have found variation in conventionality within gangs. Klein (1971), echoing Thrasher (1927), differentiated between "core" and "fringe" members, a distinction that policy makers often use today as meaning more or less deviant. In the same view, Taylor (1990:8-9) saw gang members as "corporates," "scavengers," "emulators," "auxiliaries," or "adjuncts," mainly on the basis of their distance from gang membership. Fagan (1990:206), like Matza and Cohen, found that "conventional values may coexist with deviant behaviors for gang delinquents and other inner city youth." MacLeod (1987:124) observed surprising variation between ethnic groups. The white "hallway hangers" believed "stagnation at the bottom of the occupational structure to be almost inevitable" and were rebellious delinquents, whereas the African American "brothers" reacted to similar conditions by aspiring to middle-class status.

Joan Moore is one of the few researchers who have looked carefully at differentiation within gangs. In her early work (1978), she discovered both square and deviant career models among East Los Angeles gang members. In an impressive restudy (1991) she found that most adult gang members were working conventional jobs, but those who had been active in the gang in recent years had more difficulty finding employment as job networks collapsed. Many veteran gang members had been addicted to heroin for years, but by the 1990s few were dealing drugs to support themselves. Moore found that both male and female Chicano gang members could be categorized as "tecatos," "cholos," or "squares," a typology similar to those suggested for the nongang poor by Anderson (1978, 1990) and Hannerz (1969).

If gang members in fact vary on orientation to conventionality, and if the drug economy itself offers only an ambiguous lure, jobs and other programs that strengthen "social capital" (Coleman, 1988) might be effective means of integrating many adult gang members into the community (see Sampson and Laub, 1993). On the other hand, if adult gang members are look-alike criminals who are dazzled by the prospect of vast profits in the drug trade, jobs and social programs would have little effect, and our present incarceration strategy may be appropriate.

This paper provides quantitative and qualitative data on the conventional orientations of young adult gang members in Milwaukee. First we report on the licit work and illicit drug-dealing patterns of adult gang members. Then we offer a typology, drawn from Milwaukee data, that demonstrates a "continuum of conventionality" between core members of drug-dealing gangs. In conclusion, we discuss research and public policy consequences of the study.

Research Methods and Sources of Data

The interpretations presented here draw on observation and extensive fieldwork conducted over a number of years, specifically from two funded interview studies, in 1987 and in 1992. During the early 1980s I directed the first gang diversion program in the city and became acquainted with many leaders and other founders of Milwaukee's gangs. I have maintained a privileged relationship with many of these individuals.

In the 1987 study, we interviewed 47 members of 19 Milwaukee male and female gangs (Hagedorn, 1988). These "founders" were the core gang members who were present when their gangs took names. Founders are likely to be representative of hard-core gang members, not of peripheral members or "wannabes." As time has passed, the gang founders' exploits have been passed down, and younger Milwaukee gang members have looked up to them as street "role models." Our research design does not enable us to conclude how fully our sample represents subsequent groups of adult gang members.

As part of our current study, we conducted lengthy audiotaped interviews with 101 founding members of 18 gangs in the city; 90 were male and 11 female. Sixty percent were African American, 37 percent Latino, and 3 percent white. Their median age was 26 years, with 75 percent between 23 and 30. Twenty-three respondents also had been interviewed in the 1987 study; 78 were interviewed here for the first time. Members from two gangs interviewed in the earlier study could not be located. Each respondent was paid $50.

The interview picks up the lives of the founding members since 1987, when we con-

378 Section V ✦ Types of Crime

ducted our original study, and asks them to recount their careers in the drug business to discuss their pursuit of conventional employment, and to reflect on their personal lives. The respondents also were asked to describe the current status of their fellow gang members. In the 1987 study, we collected rosters of all members of each gang whose founders we interviewed. In the current study, we asked each respondent to double check the roster of his or her gang to make sure it was accurate. In both studies, we asked respondents to tell us whether the other members were still alive, had graduated from high school, were currently locked up, or were working. In the 1992 study, we also asked whether each of the founding members was selling or using dope (in our data "dope" means cocaine), had some other hustle, or was on the run, among other questions.

To understand more clearly the variation between and within the gangs, we interviewed nearly the entire rosters of three gangs and about half (64 of 152) of the original founding members from eight male gangs in three different types of neighborhoods. In each of these gangs, we interviewed some who still were involved with both the gang and the dope game and some who no longer were involved. This paper reports on data on all of the 90 males we interviewed and on their accounts of the present circumstances of 236 founders of 14 male gangs.

The interviews in this most recent study were conducted in late 1992 and early 1993.[1] As in the original study, the research follows an inductive and collaborative model (see Moore, 1978), in which gang members cooperate with the academic staff to focus the research design, construct interview schedules, conduct interviews, and interpret the findings.

Findings: Drug Dealing and Work

As expected, gang members appear to be working more today than five years ago, but participation in the formal labor market remains quite low (see Table 30.1).[2]

These low levels of labor market participation apply to more than gang members. A recent Milwaukee study revealed that in 1990, 51 percent of jobs held by all African American males age 20 to 24, slightly younger than our study population, lasted less than six weeks. The average *annual* income in retail trade, where most subjects held jobs, was $2,023; for jobs in service, $1,697; in education, $3,084 (Rose et al., 1992). African American young adults as a whole (and probably nongang Latinos) clearly were not working regularly and were not earning a living wage.

Selling cocaine seems to have filled the employment void. In 1987 only a few gang members dealt drugs, mainly marijuana. Within African American gangs, at least, cocaine dealing was not prevalent. By 1992, however, cocaine had become a major factor in Milwaukee's informal economy, evolving into widespread curbside sales and numerous drug houses (see Hamid, 1992). Of the 236 fellow gang founders, 72 percent reportedly had sold cocaine at some time in the last five years.[3]

That involvement has not been steady, however. We collected detailed data on the length of involvement in the drug economy and the amount of money made by those we interviewed. We asked our respondents to indicate how they had supported themselves in each month of the past three years, and then asked how much money they made in both legal and illegal employment. For most respondents, selling cocaine was an on-again, off-again proposition. About half (35) of those who had sold cocaine sold in no more than 12 months out of the past 36; only 12 percent (9) sold in more than 24 of the past 36 months. Latinos sold for slightly longer periods than African Americans, 17.7 months to 13.1 months (p=.07).

When gang members did sell dope, they made widely varying amounts of money. About one-third of those who sold reported that they made no more than they would have earned if they worked for minimum wage. Another one-third made the equivalent of $13 to $25 an hour. Only three of the 73 sellers ever made "crazy money," or more than $10,000 per month, at any time during their drug-selling careers. Mean monthly income from drug sales was approximately $2,400, or about $15 per hour for full-time work. By contrast, mean monthly income for legal work was only $677; Latinos made more than African Americans ($797 per month to $604 per month, p=.08; table not shown). The *maximum* amount of money earned monthly by any gang member from legal income was $2,400, the *mean* for gang drug sales (see Table 30.2).[4]

Table 30.1
1992 Status of Male Gang Founders, 236 Founding Members of 14 Male Groups

Predominant Activity/Status	African American	White	Latino	Total
Work: Part-Time or Full-Time	22.2%	68.8%	27.6%	30.5%
Hustling: Nearly All Selling Cocaine	50.4	15.4	56.3	47.9
Deceased	7.7	6.3	5.7	6.8
Whereabouts Unknown	19.7	9.4	10.3	14.8
Total N=100%	N=117	N=32	N=87	N=236

NOTE: Column percentages may not equal 100 percent because of rounding.

Qualitative data from our interviews support the view that for some respondents, the dope game indeed lives up to its stereotype. One dealer credibly reported income from his three drug houses at about $50,000 per month for several months in 1989. Another told how he felt about making so much money:

Q: Did you ever make crazy money?

R#220: Yeah . . . one time my hands had turned green from all that money, I couldn't wash it off, man, I loved it. Oh man, look at this . . . just holding all that money in my hand turned my hands green from just counting all that money. Sometimes I'd sit back and just count it maybe three, four times, for the hell of it.

Even for big dealers, however, that money didn't last. Some "players" were "rolling" for several years, but most took a fall within a year or so. As with Padilla's Diamonds, disap-

pointments with the drug trade seemed to exceed its promise for most gang members. Prison and jail time frequently interrupted their lives. More than three-quarters of all gang founders on our rosters had spent some time in jail in the past five years, as had two-thirds of our respondents. Even so, our respondents had worked a mean of 14.5 months out of the last 36 in legitimate jobs, had worked 14.5 months selling dope, and had spent the remaining seven months in jail. Twenty-five percent of our respondents had worked legitimate jobs at least 24 of the past 36 months.

Table 30.2
Mean Monthly Income from Drug Dealing: 1989-1991, 87 African American and Latino Respondents

Average Monthly Income from Drug Sales	African American	Latino*	Total
Never sold	15.8%	23.3%	18.4%
Less Than $1,000 Monthly (Equivalent to Less Than $6/Hour)	28.1	30.0	28.7
Between $1,000 and $2,000 Monthly (Equivalent to $7-$12/Hour)	28.1	6.7	20.7
Between $2,000 and $4,000 Monthly (Equivalent to $13-$25/Hour)	25.3	33.3	28.7
More Than $10,000 Monthly	1.8	6.7	3.4
Total N=100%	N=57	N=30	N=87

* Three whites were excluded from the analysis. One white founder never sold, and the other two made less than $2,000 monthly.

NOTE: Column percentages may not equal 100 percent because of rounding.

Yet an anomaly confronted us as we analyzed our data on work. As might be expected, nine out of 10 of those who were not working at the time of our interview had sold dope in the past three years. We also found, however, that three-quarters of those who were working in 1992 had sold dope as well within the previous five years (see Table 30.3).

These findings lend themselves to alternative explanations. It may be that three-quarters of those who were working had sold cocaine in the past, but had stopped and were getting their lives together. A second interpretation is that full-time employment is nothing more than an income supplement or "front" for continuation in the drug game. Some gang founders indeed fit into one or the other of these categories.

A third interpretation evolved as we received reports from our staff and respondents about the current status of their fellow gang members. A few days after an interview with "Roger," one of our staff members would report that "Roger" was no longer working for a temporary agency, as he had reported, but was "back in the dope game." The next week "Roger" might call us from jail. A week or so later, we would learn that he was out on bail, his "lady" had put pressure on him, and he was now working full-time in construction with his brother-in-law. Our offices were flooded with similar reports about dozens of people on our rosters. Working and selling drugs were both part of the difficult, topsy-turvy lives led by our respondents. Elliot Liebow's (1967:219) colorful description of the confused lives on Tally's Corner also fits our data: "Traffic is heavy in all directions."

Table 30.3
1992 Work Status by Involvement in Cocaine Sales, 220 Surviving Founding Members of 14 Male Gangs

Sold Dope Last Five Years?	Not Working Now	Working Now*	Work Status Unknown	Totals
Have Sold Dope	75.0%	91.2%	40.0%	77.7%
Have Not Sold Dope	16.7	5.3	2.9	8.6
Unknown	8.3	3.5	57.1	13.6
Total N=100%	N=72	N=113	N=35	N=220

*Includes selling cocaine, being "on the run," being locked up, and being involved in other street hustles.

These vicissitudes became too complicated for us to track, so we "froze" the status of founders on our rosters at the time of the last and most reliable interview. Some of our founders seemed to be committed to the dope business and a few had "gone legit," but most

of those we were trying to track appeared to be on an economic merry-go-round, with continual movement in and out of the secondary labor market. Although their average income from drug sales far surpassed their income from legal employment, most Milwaukee male gang members apparently kept trying to find licit work.

To help explain this movement in and out of the formal labor market, we created a typology of adult gang members, using constant comparisons (Strauss, 1987). This categorization has some similarities to earlier typologics, but it differs in that it intends to account for the different orientations of gang members in an era of decreased legitimate economic opportunities and increased drug-related, illicit opportunities.

A Typology of Male Adult Gang Members

We developed four ideal types on a continuum of conventional behaviors and values: (1) those few who had gone *legit,* or had matured out of the gang; (2) *homeboys,* a majority of both African American and Latino adult gang members, who alternately worked conventional jobs and took various roles in drug sales; (3) *dope fiends,* who were addicted to cocaine and participated in the dope business as a way to maintain access to the drug; and (4) *new jacks,* who regarded the dope game as a career.

Some gang members, we found, moved over time between categories, some had characteristics of more than one category, and others straddled the boundaries (see Hannerz, 1969:57). Thus a few homeboys were in the process of becoming legit, many moved into and out of cocaine addiction, and others gave up and adopted a new jack orientation. Some new jacks returned to conventional life; others received long prison terms or became addicted to dope. Our categories are not discrete, but our typology seemed to fit the population of gang members we were researching. Our "member checks" (Lincoln and Guba, 1985:314-316) of the constructs with gang members validated these categories for male gang members.

Legits

Legits were those young men who had walked away from the gang. They were working or may have gone on to school. Legits had not been involved in the dope game at all, or not for at least five years. They did not use cocaine heavily, though some may have done so in the past. Some had moved out of the old neighborhood; others, like our project staff, stayed to help out or "give back" to the community. These are prime examples of Whyte's "college boys" or Cloward and Ohlin's Type I, oriented to economic gain and class mobility. The following quote is an example of a young African American man who "went legit" and is now working and going to college.

Q: Looking back over the past five years, what major changes took place in your life—things that happened that really made things different for you?

R#105: I had got into a relationship with my girl, that's one thing. I just knew I couldn't be out on the streets trying to hustle all the time. That's what changed me, I just got a sense of responsibility.

Today's underclass gangs appear to be fundamentally different from those in Thrasher's or Cloward and Ohlin's time, when most gang members "matured out" of the gang. Of the 236 Milwaukee male founders, only 12 (5.1 percent) could be categorized as having matured out: that is, they were working full time *and* had not sold cocaine in the past five years. When these data are disaggregated by race, the reality of the situation becomes even clearer. We could verify only two of 117 African Americans and one of 87 Latino male gang founders who were currently working and had not sold dope in the past five years. One-third of the white members fell into this category.[5]

Few African American and Latino gang founders, however, were resigned to a life of crime, jail, and violence. After a period of rebellion and living the fast life, the majority of gang founders, or "homeboys," wanted to settle down and go legit, but the path proved to be very difficult.

Homeboys

"Homeboys" were the majority of all adult gang members. They were not firmly committed to the drug economy, especially after the early thrill of fast money and "easy women" wore off. They had reached an age, the mid-twenties, when criminal offenses normally decline (Gottfredson and Hirschi, 1990). Most of these men were unskilled, lacked education, and had had largely negative experiences in the secondary labor market. Some homeboys were committed more strongly to the streets, others to a more conventional life. Most had used cocaine, some heavily at times, but their use was largely in conjunction with selling from a house or corner with their gang "homies." Most homeboys either were married or had a "steady" lady. They also had strong feelings of loyalty to their fellow gang members.

Here, two different homeboys explain how they had changed, and how hard that change was:

Q: Looking back over the past five years, what major changes took place in your life—things that happened that really made things different for you?

R#211: The things that we went through wasn't worth it, and I had a family, you know, and kids, and I had to think about them first, and the thing with the drug game was, that money was quick, easy, and fast, and it went like that, the more money you make the more popular you was. You know, as I see it now it wasn't worth it because the time that I done in penitentiaries I lost my sanity. To me it feels like I lost a part of my kids, because, you know, I know they still care, and they know I'm daddy, but I just lost out. Somebody else won and I lost.

Q: Is she with somebody else now?

R#211: Yeah. She hung in there about four or five months after I went to jail.

Q: It must have been tough for her to be alone with all those kids.

R#211: Yeah.

Q: What kind of person are you?

R#217: Mad. I'm a mad young man. I'm a poor young male. I'm a good person to my kids and stuff, and given the opportunity to have something nice and stop working for this petty-ass money I would try to change a lot of things . . .

. . . I feel I'm the type of person that given the opportunity to try to have something legit, I will take it, but I'm not going to go by the slow way, taking no four, five years working at no chicken job and trying to get up to a manager just to start making six, seven dollars. And then get fired when I come in high or drunk or something. Or miss a day or something because I got high smoking weed, drinking beer, and the next day come in and get fired; then I'm back in where I started from. So I'm just a cool person, and if I'm given the opportunity and if I can get a job making nine, ten dollars an hour, I'd let everything go; I'd just sit back and work my job and go home. That kind of money I can live with. But I'm not going to settle for no three, four dollars an hour, know what I'm saying?

Homeboys present a more confused theoretical picture than legits. Cloward and Ohlin's Type III delinquents were rebels, who had a "sense of injustice" or felt "unjust deprivation" at a failed system (1960:117). Their gang delinquency is a collective solution to the failure of institutional arrangements. They reject traditional societal norms; other, success-oriented illegitimate norms replace conventionality.

Others have questioned whether gang members' basic outlook actually rejects conventionality. Matza (1964) viewed delinquents' rationalizations of their conduct as evidence of techniques meant to "neutralize" deeply held conventional beliefs. Cohen (1955:129-137) regarded delinquency as a nonutilitarian "reaction formation" to middle-class standards, though middle-class morality lingers, repressed and unacknowledged. What appears to be gang "pathological" behavior, Cohen points out, is the result of the delinquent's striving to attain core values of "the American way of life." Short and Strodtbeck (1965), testing various gang theories, found that white and African American gang members, and lower- and middle-class youths, held similar conventional values.

Our homeboys are older versions of Cohen's and Matza's delinquents, and are even more similar to Short and Strodtbeck's study subjects. Milwaukee homeboys shared three basic characteristics: (1) They worked regularly at legitimate jobs, although they ventured into the drug economy when they believed it was necessary for survival. (2) They had very conventional aspirations; their core values centered on finding a secure place in the American way of life. (3) They had some surprisingly conventional ethical beliefs about the immorality of drug dealing. To a man, they justified their own involvement in drug sales by very Matza-like techniques of "neutralization."

Homeboys are defined by their in-and-out involvement in the legal and illegal economies. Recall that about half of our male respondents had sold drugs no more than 12 of the past 36 months. More than one-third never served any time in jail. Nearly 60 percent had worked legitimate jobs at least 12 months of the last 36, with a mean of 14.5 months. Homeboys' work patterns thus differed both from those of legits, who worked solely legal jobs, and new jacks who considered dope dealing a career.

To which goal did homeboys aspire, being big-time dope dealers or holding a legitimate job? Rather than having any expectations of staying in the dope game, homeboys aspired to settling down, getting married, and living at least a watered-down version of the American dream. Like Padilla's (1992:157) Diamonds, they strongly desired to "go legit." Although they may have enjoyed the fast life for a while, it soon went stale. Listen to this homeboy, the one who lost his lady when he went to jail:

Q: Five years from now, what would you want to be doing?

R#211: Five years from now? I want to have a steady job, I want to have been working that job for about five years, and just with a family somewhere.

Q: Do you think that's gonna come true?

R#211: Yeah, that's basically what I'm working on. I mean, this bullshit is over now, I'm twenty-five, I've played games long enough, it don't benefit nobody. If you fuck yourself away, all you gonna be is fucked, I see it now.

Others had more hopeful or wilder dreams, but a more sobering outlook on the future. The other homeboy, who said he wouldn't settle for three or four dollars an hour speaks as follows:

Q: Five years from now, what would you want to be doing?

R#217: Owning my own business. And rich. A billionaire.

Q: What do you realistically expect you'll be doing in five years?

R#217: Probably working at McDonald's. That's the truth.

Homeboys' aspirations were divided between finding a steady full-time job and setting up their own business. Their strivings pertained less to being for or against "middle-class status" than to finding a practical, legitimate occupation that could support them (see Short and Strodtbeck, 1965). Many homeboys believed that using skills learned in selling drugs to set up a small business would give them a better chance at a decent life than trying to succeed as an employee.

Most important, homeboys "grew up" and were taking a realistic look at their life chances. This homeboy spoke for most:

Q: Looking back over the past five years, what major changes have taken place in your life—things that made a difference about where you are now?

R#220: I don't know, maybe maturity. . . . Just seeing life in a different perspective . . . realizing that from 16 to 23, man, just shot past. And just realizing that it did, shucks, you just realizing how quick it zoomed past me. And it really just passed me up without really having any enjoyment of a teenager. And hell, before I know it I'm going to hit 30 or 40, and I ain't going to have nothing to stand on. I don't want that shit. Because I see a lot of brothers out here now, that's 43, 44 and ain't got shit. They's still standing out on the corner trying to make a hustle. Doing this, no family, no stable home and nothing. I don't want that shit. . . . I don't give a fuck about getting rich or nothing, but I want

a comfortable life, a decent woman, a family to come home to. I mean, everybody needs somebody to care for. This ain't where it's at.

Finally, homeboys were characterized by their ethical views about selling dope. As a group, they believed dope selling was "unmoral"—wrong, but necessary for survival. Homeboys' values were conventional, but in keeping with Matza's findings, they justified their conduct by neutralizing their violation of norms. Homeboys believed that economic necessity was the overriding reason why they could not live up to their values (see Liebow, 1967:214). They were the epitome of ambivalence, ardently believing that dope selling was both wrong and absolutely necessary. One longtime dealer expressed this contradiction:

Q: Do you consider it wrong or immoral to sell dope?

R#129: Um-hum, very wrong.

Q: Why?

R#129: Why, because it's killing people.

Q: Well how come you do it?

R#129: It's also a money maker.

Q: Well how do you balance those things out? I mean, here you're doing something that you think is wrong, making money. How does that make you feel when you're doing it, or don't you think about it when you're doing it?

R#129: Once you get a (dollar) bill, once you look at, I say this a lot, once you look at those dead white men [*presidents' pictures on currency*], you care about nothing else, you don't care about nothing else. Once you see those famous dead white men. That's it.

Q: Do you ever feel bad about selling drugs, doing something that was wrong?

R#129: How do I feel? Well a lady will come in and sell all the food stamps, all of them. When they're sold, what are the kids gonna eat? They can't eat the dope cause she's gonna go smoke that up, or do whatever with it. And then you feel like "wrong." But then, in the back of your mind, man, you just got a hundred dollars worth of food stamps for thirty dollars worth of dope, and you can sell them at the store for seven dollars on ten, so you got seventy coming. So you get seventy dollars for thirty dollars. It is not wrong to do this. It is not wrong to do this!

Homeboys also refused to sell to pregnant women or to juveniles. Contrary to Jankowski's (1991:102) assertion that in gangs "there is no ethical code that regulates business ventures," Milwaukee homeboys had some strong moral feelings about how they carried out their business:

R#109: I won't sell to no little kids. And, ah, if he gonna get it, he gonna get it from someone else besides me. I won't sell to no pregnant woman. If she gonna kill her baby, I want to sleep not knowing that I had anything to do with it. Ah, for anybody else, hey, it's their life, you choose your life how you want.

Q: But how come—I want to challenge you. You know if kids are coming or a pregnant woman's coming, you know they're going to get it somewhere else, right? Someone else will make their money on it; why not you?

R#109: 'Cause the difference is I'll be able to sleep without a guilty conscience.

Homeboys were young adults living on the edge. On the one hand, like most Americans, they had relatively conservative views on social issues and wanted to settle down with a job, a wife, and children. On the other hand, they were afraid they would never succeed, and that long stays in prison would close doors and lock them out of a conventional life. They did not want to continue to live on the streets, but they feared that hustling might be the only way to survive.[6]

Dope Fiends

Dope fiends are gang members who are addicted to cocaine. Thirty-eight percent of all African American founders were using cocaine at the time of our interview, as were 55 percent of Latinos and 53 percent of whites. African Americans used cocaine at lower rates than white gang members, but went to jail twice as often. The main focus in a dope fiend's life is getting the drug. Asked what

they regretted most about their life, dope fiends invariably said "drug use," whereas most homeboys said "dropping out of school."

Most Milwaukee gang dope fiends, or daily users of cocaine, smoked it as "rocks." More casual users, or reformed dope fiends, if they used cocaine at all, snorted it or sprinkled it on marijuana (called a "primo") to enhance the high. Injection was rare among African Americans but more common among Latinos. About one-quarter of those we interviewed, however, abstained totally from use of cocaine. A majority of the gang members on our rosters had used cocaine since its use escalated in Milwaukee in the late 1980s.

Of 110 gang founders who were reported to be currently using cocaine, 37 percent were reported to be using "heavily" (every day, in our data), 44 percent, "moderately" (several times per week), and 19 percent "lightly" (sporadically). More than 70 percent of all founders on our rosters who were not locked up were currently using cocaine to some extent. More than one-third of our male respondents considered themselves, at some time in their lives, to be "heavy" cocaine users.

More than one-quarter of our respondents had used cocaine for seven years or more, roughly the total amount of time cocaine has dominated the illegal drug market in Milwaukee. Latinos had used cocaine slightly longer than African Americans, for a mean of 75 months compared with 65. Cocaine use followed a steady pattern in our respondents' lives; most homeboys had used cocaine as part of their day-to-day life, especially while in the dope business.

Dope fiends were quite unlike Cloward and Ohlin's "double failures," gang members who used drugs as part of a "retreatist subculture." Milwaukee dope fiends participated regularly in conventional labor markets. Of the 110 founders who were reported as currently using cocaine, slightly more were working legitimate jobs than were not working. Most dope fiends worked at some time in their homies' dope houses or were fronted an ounce or an "eightball" (3.5 grams) of cocaine to sell. Unlike Anderson's "wineheads," gang dope fiends were not predominantly "has-beens" and did not "lack the ability and motivation to hustle" (Anderson, 1978:96-97). Milwaukee cocaine users, like heroin users (Johnson et al., 1985; Moore, 1978; Preble and Casey, 1969), played an active role in the drug-selling business.

Rather than spending their income from drug dealing on family, clothes, or women, dope fiends smoked up their profits. Eventually many stole dope belonging to the boss or "dopeman" and got into trouble. At times their dope use made them so erratic that they were no longer trusted and were forced to leave the neighborhood. Often, however, the gang members who were selling took them back and fronted them cocaine to sell to put them back on their feet. Many had experienced problems in violating the cardinal rule, "Don't get high on your own supply," as in this typical story:

> R#131: . . . if you ain't the type that's a user, yeah, you'll make fabulous money but if you was the type that sells it and uses it and do it at the same time, you know, you get restless. Sometimes you get used to taking your own drugs. . . . I'll just use the profits and just do it . . . and then the next day if I get something again, I'd just take the money to pay up and keep the profits. . . . You sell a couple of hundred and you do a hundred. That's how I was doing it.

Cocaine use was a regular part of the lives of most Milwaukee gang members engaged in the drug economy. More than half of our respondents had never attended a treatment program; more than half of those who had been in treatment went through court-ordered programs. Few of our respondents stopped use by going to a treatment program. Even heavy cocaine use was an "on-again, off-again" situation in which most gang members alternately quit by themselves and started use again (Waldorf et al., 1991).

Alcohol use among dope fiends and homeboys (particularly 40-ounce bottles of Olde English 800 ale) appears to be even more of a problem than cocaine use. Like homeboys, however, most dope fiends aspired to have a family, to hold a steady job, and to find some peace. The wild life of the dope game had played itself out; the main problem was how to quit using.[7]

New Jacks

Whereas homeboys had a tentative relationship with conventional labor markets and held some strong moral beliefs, new jacks had chosen the dope game as a career. They were often loners, strong individualists like Jankowski's (1991) gang members, who cared little about group norms. Frequently they posed as the embodiment of media stereotypes. About one-quarter of our interview respondents could be described as new jacks: they had done nothing in the last 36 months except hustle or spend time in jail.

In some ways, new jacks mirror the criminal subculture described by Cloward and Ohlin. If a criminal subculture is to develop, Cloward and Ohlin argued, opportunities to learn a criminal career must be present, and close ties to conventional markets or customers must exist. This situation distinguishes the criminal from the violent and the retreatist subcultures. The emergence of the cocaine economy and a large market for illegal drugs provided precisely such an opportunity structure for this generation of gang members. New jacks are those who took advantage of the opportunities, and who, at least for the present, have committed themselves to a career in the dope game.

> Q: Do you consider it wrong or immoral to sell dope?
>
> R#203: I think it's right because can't no motherfucker live your life but you.
>
> Q: Why?
>
> R#203: Why? I'll put it this way . . . I love selling dope. I know there's other niggers out here love the money just like I do. And ain't no motherfucker gonna stop a nigger from selling dope . . . I'd sell to my own mother if she had the money.

New jacks, like other gang cocaine dealers, lived up to media stereotypes of the "drug dealer" role and often were emulated by impressionable youths. Some new jacks were homeboys from Milwaukee's original neighborhood gangs, who had given up their conventional dreams; others were members of gangs that were formed solely for drug dealing (see Klein and Maxson, 1993). A founder of one new jack gang described the scene as his gang set up shop in Milwaukee. Note the strong mimicking of media stereotypes:

> R#126: . . . it was crime and drug problems before we even came into the scene. It was just controlled by somebody else. We just came on with a whole new attitude, outlook, at the whole situation. It's like, have you ever seen the movie *New Jack City*, about the kid in New York? You see, they was already there. We just came out with a better idea, you know what I'm saying?

New jacks rejected the homeboys' moral outlook. Many were raised by families with long traditions of hustling or a generation of gang affiliations, and had few hopes of a conventional future. They are the voice of the desperate ghetto dweller, those who live in Carl Taylor's (1990:36) "third culture" made up of "underclass and urban gang members who exhibit signs of moral erosion and anarchy" or propagators of Bourgois's (1990:631) "culture of terror." New jacks fit the media stereotype of all gang members, even though they represent fewer than 25 percent of Milwaukee's adult gang members.

Discussion: Gangs, The Underclass, and Public Policy

Our study was conducted in one aging postindustrial city, with a population of 600,000. How much can be generalized from our findings can be determined only by researchers in other cities, looking at our categories and determining whether they are useful. Cloward and Ohlin's opportunity theory is a workable general theoretical framework, but more case studies are needed in order to recast their theory to reflect three decades of economic and social changes. We present our typology to encourage others to observe variation within and between gangs, and to assist in the creation of new taxonomies and new theory.

Our paper raises several empirical questions for researchers: Are the behavior patterns of the founding gang members in our sample representative of adult gang members in other cities? In larger cities, are most gang members now new jacks who have long given up the hope of a conventional life, or

are most still homeboys? Are there "homeboy" gangs and "new jack" gangs, following the "street gang/drug gang" notion of Klein and Maxson (1993)? If so, what distinguishes one from the other? Does gang members' orientation to conventionality vary by ethnicity or by region? How does it change over time? Can this typology help account for variation in rates of violence between gang members? Can female gang members be typed in the same way as males?

Our data also support the life course perspective of Sampson and Laub (1993:255), who ask whether present criminal justice policies "are producing unintended criminogenic effects." Milwaukee gang members are like the persistent, serious offenders in the Gluecks' data (Glueck and Glueck, 1950). The key to their future lies in building social capital that comes from steady employment and a supportive relationship, without the constant threat of incarceration (Sampson and Laub, 1993:162-168). Homeboys largely had a wife or a steady lady, were unhappily enduring "the silent, subtle humiliations" of the secondary labor market (Bourgois, 1990:629), and lived in dread of prison. Incarceration for drug charges undercut their efforts to find steady work and led them almost inevitably back to the drug economy.

Long and mandatory prison terms for use and intent to sell cocaine lump those who are committed to the drug economy with those who are using or are selling in order to survive. Our prisons are filled disproportionately with minority drug offenders (Blumstein, 1993) like our homeboys, who in essence are being punished for the "crime" of not accepting poverty or of being addicted to cocaine. Our data suggest that jobs, more accessible drug treatment, alternative sentences, or even decriminalization of nonviolent drug offenses would be better approaches than the iron fist of the war on drugs (see Hagedorn, 1991; Reinarman and Levine, 1990; Spergel and Curry, 1990).

Finally, our typology raises ethical questions for researchers. Wilson (1987:8) called the underclass "collectively different" from the poor of the past, and many studies focus on underclass deviance. Our study found that some underclass gang members had embraced the drug economy and had forsaken conventionality, but we also found that the *majority* of adult gang members are still struggling to hold onto a conventional orientation to life.

Hannerz (1969:36) commented more than two decades ago that dicthotomizing community residents into "respectables" and "disrespectables" "seems often to emerge from social science writing about poor black people or the lower classes in general." Social science that emphasizes differences within poor communities, without noting commonalities, is one-sided and often distorts and demonizes underclass life.

Our data emphasize that there is no Great Wall separating the underclass from the rest of the central-city poor and working class. Social research should not build one either. Researchers who describe violent and criminal gang actions without also addressing gang members' orientation to conventionality do a disservice to the public, to policy makers, and to social science.

Discussion Questions

1. What are some of the different empirical findings regarding gangs? In what ways do gangs differ from each other? How are gang membership and (un)employment related? Is one a substitute for the other?

2. Are gang members less committed to conventionality than other people? Is the level of conventionality consistent from gang to gang? Is it the same for "core" members as it is for "fringe" members? Is there a difference between races?

3. Based on the findings of this research, is it your opinion that the availability of good jobs would reduce the number of drug-dealing gang members? Why or why not? Do gang members prefer dealing drugs or legitimate employment? Or both?

Notes

1. This study was funded by NIDA Grant ROI DA 07218. The funding agency bears no responsibility for data or interpretations presented here.

2. Rosters of gangs in 1992 were refined and new gangs were added; thus it was difficult to make comparisons with 1987 rosters. In 1987, with $N=225$, 20 percent of white male gang members, 10 percent of Latinos, and 27 percent of African Americans were working.

3. Selling cocaine is not only a gang-related phenomenon. Half of those who were reported as no longer involved with the gang also had sold cocaine within the last five years.

4. We asked respondents to report on the number of months they worked legitimate jobs, worked selling dope, and were in prison. We then asked them to tell us the average amount of money they made in those months working or selling dope. Hourly estimates are based on the monthly average divided by 160 hours. Most respondents reported that they worked selling dope "24/7," meaning full time.

5. About 15 percent of the founders' whereabouts were not known by our informants, but "unknown" status was no guarantee that the missing member had gone legit. One founder of an African American gang was reported to us in a pretest as having "dropped from sight," but later we learned that he had been a victim of one of serial killer Jeffrey Dahmer's grisly murders. Others, with whom our respondents no longer have contact, may be heavy cocaine users who left the gang and the neighborhood because they were no longer trustworthy.

6. Homeboys varied as well. Some were entrepreneurs or "players"; typically they were the "dopemen" who started a "dopehouse" where other gang members could work. Others worked only sporadically in dopehouses as a supplement to legitimate work or during unemployment. Finally, some, often cocaine users, worked most of the time at the dopehouse and only sporadically at legitimate jobs. Although homeboys also varied over time in their aspirations to conventionality, as a group they believed that the lack of jobs and the prison time were testing their commitment to conventional values. We found no significant differences between Latino and African American homeboys.

7. It is too early to tell how many persons will succeed at freeing themselves from cocaine use. Ansley Hamid (1992) found that by the 1990s, most New York crack users were in their thirties and poor; their heavy drug in-

volvement had ruined their chances for conventional careers.

References

Anderson, Elijah. 1978. *A Place on the Corner*. Chicago: University of Chicago Press.

——. 1990. *Streetwise: Race, Class, and Change in an Urban Community*. Chicago: University of Chicago Press.

Blumstein, Alfred. 1993. "Making rationality relevant." *Criminology*, 31:1-16.

Bourgois, Phillippe. 1990. "In search of Horatio Alger: Culture and ideology in the crack economy. *Contemporary Drug Problems*, 16:619-649.

Cloward, Richard and Lloyd Ohlin. 1960. *Delinquency and Opportunity*. Glencoe, Ill: Free Press.

Cohen, Albert. 1955. *Delinquent Boys*. Glencoe, Ill.: Free Press.

Coleman, James S. 1988. "Social capital in the creation of human capital." *American Journal of Sociology*, 94:S95-Sl2O.

Cummings, Scott and Daniel J. Monte. 1993. *Gangs*. Albany: State University of New York Press.

Fagan, Jeffrey. 1990. "Social processes of delinquency and drug use among urban gangs." In C. Ronald Huff (ed.), *Gangs in America*. Newbury Park: Sage.

——. 1991. "Drug selling and licit income in distressed neighborhoods: The economic lives of street-level drug users and dealers." In Adele V. Harrell and George E. Peterson (eds.), *Drugs, Crime, and Social Isolation*. Washington: Urban Institute Press.

Glueck, Sheldon and Eleanor Glueck. 1950. *Unraveling Juvenile Delinquency*. New York: Commonwealth Fund.

Gottfredson, Michael and Travis Hirschi. 1990. *A General Theory of Crime*. Stanford: Stanford University Press.

Hagedorn, John M. 1988. *People and Folks: Gangs, Crime, and the Underclass in a Rustbelt City*. Chicago: Lakeview.

——. 1991. "Gangs, neighborhoods, and public policy." *Social Problems*, 38:529-542.

Hamid, Ansley. 1992. "The developmental cycle of a drug epidemic: the cocaine smoking epidemic of 1981-1991." *Journal of Psychoactive Drugs*, 24:337-348.

Hannerz, Ulf. 1969. *Soulside: Inquiries into Ghetto Culture and Community*. New York: Columbia University Press.

Huff, C. Ronald. 1990. *Gangs in America*. Newbury Park: Sage.

Jankowski, Martin Sanchez. 1991. *Islands in the Street: Gangs and American Urban Society*. Berkeley: University of California Press.

Johnson, Bruce D., Terry Williams, Kojo Dei, and Harry Sanahria. 1985. *Taking Care of Business: The Economics of Crime by Heroin Abusers*. Lexington, Mass.: Heath.

Klein, Malcolm W. 1971. *Street Gangs and Street Workers*. Englewood Cliffs, N.J.: Prentice-Hall.

——. 1992. "The new street gang . . . or is it?" *Contemporary Sociology*, 21:80-82.

Klein, Malcolm W. and Cheryl L. Maxson. 1993. "Gangs and cocaine trafficking." In Craig Uchida and Doris Mackenzie (eds.), *Drugs and the Criminal Justice System*. Newbury Park: Sage.

Klein, Malcolm W., Cheryl L. Maxson, and Lea C. Cunningham. 1991. "Crack, street gangs, and violence." *Criminology*, 29:623-650.

Liebow, Elliot. 1967. *Tally's Corner*. Boston: Little, Brown.

Lincoln, Yvonna S. and Egon G. Guba. 1985. *Naturalistic Inquiry*. Beverly Hills: Sage.

MacCoun, Robert and Peter Reuter. 1992. "Are the wages of sin $30 an hour? Economic aspects of street-level drug dealing." *Crime and Delinquency*, 38:477-491.

MacLeod, Jay. 1987. *Ain't No Makin' It: Leveled Aspirations in a Low-Income Neighborhood*. Boulder: Westview.

Matza, David. 1964. *Delinquency and Drift*. New York: Wiley.

Merton, Robert K. 1957. *Social Theory and Social Structure*. 1968. New York: Free Press.

Miller, Walter B. 1969. "Lower class culture as a generating milieu of gang delinquency." *Journal of Social Issues*, 14:5-19.

Moore, Joan W. 1978. *Homeboys: Gangs, Drugs, and Prison in the Barrios of Los Angeles*. Philadelphia: Temple University Press.

——. 1991. *Going Down to the Barrio: Homeboys and Homegirls in Change*. Philadelphia: Temple University Press.

Padilla, Felix. 1992. *The Gang as an American Enterprise*. New Brunswick: Rutgers University Press.

Preble, Edward and John H. Casey. 1969. "Taking care of business: The heroin user's life on the street." *International Journal of the Addictions*, 4:1-24.

Reinarman, Craig and Harry G. Levine. 1990. "Crack in context: politics and media in the making of a drug scare." *Contemporary Drug Problems*, 16:535-577.

Rose, Harold M., Ronald S. Edari, Lois M. Quinn, and John Pawasrat. 1992. *The Labor Market*

Experience of Young African American Men from Low-Income Families in Wisconsin. Milwaukee: University of Wisconsin-Milwaukee Employment and Training Institute.

Sampson, Robert J. and John H. Laub. 1993. *Crime in the Making: Pathways and Turning Points through Life*. Cambridge: Harvard University Press.

Short, James F. and Fred L. Strodtbeck. 1965. *Group Process and Gang Delinquency*. Chicago: University of Chicago Press.

Skolnick, Jerome H. 1990. "The social structure of street drug dealing." *American Journal of Police*, 9:1-41.

Spergel, Irving A. and G. David Curry. 1990. "Strategies and perceived agency effectiveness in dealing with the youth gang problem." In C. Ronald Huff (ed.), *Gangs in America*. Beverly Hills: Sage.

Strauss, Anselm L. 1987. *Qualitative Analysis for Social Scientists*. Cambridge: Cambridge University Press.

Sullivan, Mercer L. 1989. *Getting Paid: Youth Crime and Work in the Inner City*. Ithaca: Cornell University Press.

Taylor, Carl. 1990. *Dangerous Society*. East Lansing: Michigan State University Press.

Thrasher, Frederick. 1927. *The Gang*. 1963. Chicago: University of Chicago Press.

Waldorf, Dan. 1993. *Final Report of the Crack Sales, Gangs, and Violence Study: NIDA Grant 5#RO1DA06486*. Alameda: Institute for Scientific Analysis.

Waldorf, Dan, Craig Reinarman, and Sheigla Murphy. 1991. *Cocaine Changes: The Experience of Using and Quitting*. Philadelphia: Temple University Press.

Whyte, William Foote. 1943. *Street Corner Society*. Chicago: University of Chicago Press.

Williams, Terry. 1989. *The Cocaine Kids*. Reading, Mass.: Addison-Wesley.

Wilson, William Julius. 1987. *The Truly Disadvantaged*. Chicago: University of Chicago.

Reprinted from: John M. Hagedorn, "Homeboys, Dope Fiends, Legits, and New Jacks." In *Criminology* 32, pp. 197-219. Copyright © 1994 by the American Society of Criminology. Reprinted by permission. ✦

31

The Nature and Historical Roots of Professional Crime

James A. Inciardi

The *professional criminal, who chooses to earn a living from illegal enterprise, is a rare breed. Specializing in a highly skilled form of crime, he or she is a nonviolent property offender whose sole desire is to maximize his or her financial reward as efficiently and effectively as possible, just as any career professional would go about an occupational task. Becoming a professional criminal usually requires learning necessary skills over a long period of time and being recognized by others for one's achievement. Many experts believe that the number of professional criminals is diminishing, as the current generation of young criminals is too impatient to learn sophisticated skills and turns readily to strong-arm methods. Nevertheless, those professional criminals who continue to practice their trade are representative of an important type of criminality.*

James A. Inciardi tells about the history and nature of the most common types of professional crimes in this selection. Placed within the parameters of professionalism set out by Edwin Sutherland, Inciardi systematically explores five categories of professional crime: burglary, sneak theft, confidence swindling, forgery and counterfeiting, and extortion. Each type requires unique skills that were often developed long ago and have been adapted to modern conditions over the years. Pickpockets continue to lift wallets, for example, but now often find credit cards rather than cash. Using stolen credit cards has become a new type of professional crime.

Knowledge of professional crime and criminals allows us to understand the complex nature of criminality. While most crime, including property crime, is committed by offenders who do not make a career of it (although they may be repeat violators), those who meet the criteria of professional criminal bring a unique challenge to crime prevention and law enforcement.

Professional crime traditionally refers to the nonviolent forms of criminal behavior that are undertaken with a high degree of skill for monetary gain, and that exploit interests which tend to maximize financial opportunities and minimize the possibilities of apprehension. It is a specialized variety of career crime, reflecting an occupational structure similar to many of the "learned" professions and other vocational pursuits, and as noted in the introduction, typical forms of professional crime include pickpocketing, burglary, shoplifting, forgery and counterfeiting, extortion, sneak theft, and confidence swindling.

Although professional crime has existed for many centuries and in numerous countries, its unique character has remained essentially hidden from the society at large for the better part of its long history. The publication of Edwin H. Sutherland's *The Professional Thief* in 1937 represented an unforgettable moment for the disciplines of criminology, police science, and correctional administration. For the first time, a systematic analysis of a behavior system that heretofore had remained unstudied from the perspective of social science was available. It revealed the details of a "profession," which was not typically recognized as a "profession" at that time, and it made manifest the nature and complexity of a criminal career. Further, *The Professional Thief* was a contribution to general sociology and history. Sutherland's effort demonstrated the relationships between the culture of the underworld and general social institutions. He pointed out how the "profession" of theft had originated and was perpetuated in social disorganization, and why it would continue to persist in the absence of modifications in the basic social order. The characterization offered by Sutherland suggested the following:

1. The professional thief makes a regular business of stealing. It is his occupation and means of livelihood, and as such, he devoted his entire working time and energy to stealing.

2. The professional thief operates with proficiency. He has a body of skills and knowledge that is utilized in the planning and execution of his work. He has contempt for the amateur thief.

3. The professional thief is a graduate of a developmental process that includes the acquisition of specialized attitudes, knowledge, skills, and experience.

4. The professional thief makes crime his way of life. He organizes his life around his criminal pursuits, and develops a philosophy regarding his activities and profession.

5. The professional thief identifies himself with the world of crime. There, he is a member of an exclusive fraternity that extends friendship, understanding, sympathy, congeniality, security, recognition, and respect.

6. The professional thief is able to steal for long periods of time without going to prison. He commits crimes in a manner that reduces the risks of apprehension, and he is able to effectively cope with confrontations with the criminal justice system.

Finally, Sutherland's analysis referenced the notions that the profession of theft was centuries old, having originated in the disintegration of the feudal order, which occurred during the early centuries of the current millennium, and that the characteristics of twentieth-century professional thieves were strikingly similar to those apparent during earlier historical periods.

In brief, Sutherland's pioneer effort represents a unique contribution. Yet, in retrospect, since the finalization of his work almost forty years ago, little has been done to expand, test, or update his findings. A limited selection of specialized endeavors has appeared during recent years descriptive of pickpockets, shoplifters, forgers, and confidence swindlers. Beyond these, however, only a minimum of significant empirical data can be found in the annals of scholarly research. Analysis of the broadest fields of professional criminality in a contemporary setting continues to be avoided, and finally, a comprehensive historical assessment of this criminological phenomenon, as urged by Sutherland even prior to the publication of his *The Professional Thief*, still awaits initiation. This spectrum of historical and sociological inquiry represents the tasks of this current effort.

The Categories of Professional Crime

The categories of contemporary professional crime in the United States are, for the most part, centuries old, having been transmitted from one generation of criminals to another since the days of the Elizabethan rogues. Modifications in techniques, newer varieties of crime, and more efficient methods of committing old crimes, however, have appeared concurrently with changes in technology and social conditions. An overview of the history of professional crime in Britain and America suggests, nevertheless, that the more common types of professional crime have tended to remain limited to the following areas:

1. Burglary
    Safe burglary
    House burglary

2. Sneak Theft
    Bank sneak theft
    House sneak theft
    Shoplifting
    Pennyweighting
    Pickpocketing
    Lush-working

3. Confidence Swindling
    The short con
    The big con
    Circus grifting

4. Forgery and Counterfeiting

5. Extortion

Burglary

Safe Burglary. Safe burglary was a rare phenomenon prior to the Civil War. During the 1860s, however, the federal government began circulating millions of "greenbacks" and securities "payable to the bearer," and by the close of that decade the breaking and entering of safes had become a major undertaking of the professional underworld. *Safeblowers* were considered to be among the elite of this segment of the profession, but their techniques were rarely exercised without some assurance that the high risk would be rewarded. Safe doors were readily blown apart by powder and fuses positioned in precision-drilled holes after the safes were wrapped in wet blankets to muffle such explosions. The initial entry to the banks was gained through keys produced from wax impressions.

The safe-blowers of the 1870s maintained an extensive knowledge of explosives as well as the mechanical aspects of safe construction. Black (1927:109) referred to one practitioner whose career began as an apprentice to a village blacksmith, followed by instruction in the uses of explosives as a soldier during the Civil War. Finally, he was employed for one year in a safe factory, and was allegedly among the first to *thrash out the soap* (extract nitro from sticks of dynamite).

Blowing has always been a less desirable form of safe opening due to the noise created and attention attracted, and elaborate measures for sound concealment have been common. During the latter part of the last century, for example, a division of the Hell's Kitchen gangs from New York City's West Side coordinated their explosions with community-organized Fourth of July fireworks and pyrotechnic displays (O'Connor, 1958:60-61). And during the 1920s and 1930s, thieves successfully robbed butcher shops by pushing the safes into iceboxes prior to detonation, or by hauling away the small 5-ton units found in country towns (Martin, 1952:125-27).

The use of explosives for opening safes was noted as early as 1853 (Clark & Eubank, 1927:36), but a sharp decline has been apparent since the turn of the century. In addition to the severe penalties imposed for the use of nitroglycerine, even the most skillful blasting techniques became outdated when the magic flame of the acetylene torch allowed thieves to cut rapidly through metal. *Combination-safe pickers* have also been among the safe burglars since the last century, and other enduring methods have included drilling and *peeling* the metal with chisels.

The story of safe burglary has been characterized by industry's continued effort to produce the burglar-proof safe, and the underworld's ability to keep pace with modern technology. Safe robbery, particularly of banks, began to decline at the beginning of this century with the inception of time locks and electrical alarm systems, leaving the trade open to none but the mechanical genius as modern bank vaults became virtually impregnable. In 1962, for example, when the building located at 15 Broad Street in New York City was being prepared for demolition, the task of dismantling the 10 by 20 foot vault of the Morgan Guarantee Trust Company occupied two thousand man-hours of labor. The door to the vault alone weighed some forty tons. Modern money fortresses are far too expensive for all but the largest firms, and tens of thousands of smaller and older safes remain in use, allowing the experts in explosives, acetylene work, or straight lock-picking to pursue their careers.

House Burglary. House burglary, or housebreaking, has been a persistent form of criminality for centuries. Within the context of professional crime, it was thoroughly noted in the rogue pamphlets, and later manifestations of a similar nature were described by numerous observers who were contemporary to these periods. As such, the ancient methods of forcing passage with iron wedges endured. Technological change, however, did offer some refinements and defined the context of burglary for the past fifteen decades.

As early as 1821, the expert London *cracksman* or professional housebreaker had already developed a notable reputation (Egan, 1905b:179), and by 1854 skeleton keys and jimmys of different types, somewhat advanced over the Elizabethan black art, were used as major forms of burglars' tools in this country. In 1862 Mayhew's *London Labour*

and the London Poor reported that the manufacture and use of skeleton keys had already
become a fine art, and the more experienced
burglars had methods for opening any lock.
In a discussion of criminal activities from
1925 to 1950, a contemporary thief commented on various housebreaking techniques, which were not unlike the methods
used by his predecessors (Martin, 1952).
Modern professional burglars rely less upon
skeleton keys and other mechanical devices
and more upon their own mechanical ability.
The more lucrative burglaries have rarely
been haphazard operations based on a random selection of homes as potential targets.
Many burglars are *tipped off* as to the location
of homes with valuable contents and when
the occupants will be away from their residences.

Sneak Theft

The sneak thief has been referred to as "all
that is determined, patient, plausible, schem-
ing, thoroughly educated and able in ro-
guery" (Crapsey, 1872:15). As such, the sneak
is an outlaw who does not, at the outset of his
crime, proclaim his intentions by some work
or act; he is a thief who has the ability to
remain unnoticed, blending with his environment while stealing in the proximity of the
awake and active victims.

Bank Sneaks. In a historical perspective,
the bank sneak was considered the most skillful and the "highest possible criminal development" (Crapsey, 1872:15). As a *bond robber*
or *damper sneak*, he entered banking institutions with an appearance of respectability to
engage in financial discussions within reach
of an open safe. The theft would occur when
the attention of bank personnel was diverted
to some other situation. Thieves of this type
extracted large amounts of money, and the
losses often remained unnoticed for many
hours. Bank sneaks often worked in gangs
composed of a lookout, a conversationalist to
distract the banker's attention, and a small-
sized man who could "sneak" behind a
counter and quickly gather cash or bonds.

Groups such as these prowled the financial areas of large cities dressed as honest
merchants or stockbrokers, always alert for
an opportunity to steal. After banking hours,

they often frequented the hotels and haunts
of the financial leaders to learn their interests
and weaknesses, and whatever else might be
useful in later distracting conversations.

Bank sneak-thieving was a lucrative enterprise in New York in the 1870s and 1880s.
Immediately prior to the Civil War, there
were fifty-three banks in the city of New York
with capital totaling some $66 million (Gib-
bons, 1858:9). During the reconstruction period, when investments and industry were increasing, the number of banking institutions
multiplied and most were concentrated in
New York's financial district. Sneak thieves
loitered in that area on a daily basis and cash-
filled boxes disappeared from tellers' cages
regularly and within the view of special detectives. In response to this situation,
Thomas Byrnes, the city's chief of detectives
during the 1880s and later chief of police,
instituted a special patrol system in 1889 in
the Wall Street area that virtually eliminated
thefts by bank sneaks. The new system involved a detective subsquad in the financial
district with special patrols during business
hours, and telephone connections between
the Wall Street substation and the banks. The
activities of bank sneak thieves persisted in
this country until World War II. In New York
City, for example, the newspapers reported
three large thefts of this type between 1932
and 1935 with losses totaling $2 million
(Sutherland, 1937:52). Since 1940, however,
efforts have been made by banking institutions to increase security measures, and in
contemporary banks with electronically controlled doors and cages, photoelectrically operated alarm systems, and closed-circuit television, such thefts are almost impossible.

The procedures used by the bank sneak
thief, when applied to small stores, were
called *till-tapping*. Barney Coogarty, a member of a gang of clever sneak thieves in New
York City during the 1880s, practiced the
more typical form of till-tapping: as one of his
group lured a proprietor from his store on
one pretext or another, his confederates
would enter from a rear door and remove
whatever money was in the till or cash register. Till-tapping continues to exist, although
not necessarily under the same label. A shoplifter, paroled from Sing Sing prison in 1966,

indicated to me that owing to the carelessness of shopkeepers regarding open cash registers, the profession continues to have a bright future:

> During the busy hours of the day and busy seasons of the year, you can always find an open register within the reach of the customer. Down here [the financial district of New York City], coffee shops are good targets at lunch hour. People are rushing in and out; the cashier wants to see that everyone pays; she looks to see if the chap leaving paid his check, and bang, you've got it. Christmas is a good season too. Store cops are looking for shoplifters or just trying to keep order. They don't watch the registers. They don't watch the crooks who make a legitimate purchase to get near the money box. One time I walked right into the cage in the refund department and counted out the money, no one even looked at me—it was a busy day.

Similarly, another contemporary professional thief reported:

> Taking cash from a till is the easiest kind of stealing. If you're alert and fast, you have a good income. I kept away from the big stores—too many people to watch. The busy specialty shops on 34th Street or Nassau Street always have a lot of customers, a lot of confusion, and few employees. Liquor stores are not good though, the owner is there, and it's *his* money, and he's more careful. Besides, he's suspicious to start with.

House Sneaks. The art of the Elizabethan *curbers*, when contrasted with that of the *morning, evening,* and *upright* sneaks of the eighteenth century (see Parker, 1781), varied only minimally from the more recent house sneaks. These types, however, employed techniques somewhat different from the more daring thefts from banks. The *bed-chamber sneak*, an ally of the early bank burglar, entered the homes of bank owners or officers as they slept and made wax impressions of their keys. This gave safe-blowers easy access to banking institutions, businesses, and stores. *Second-story sneaks* were similar to burglars in that they entered dwellings and removed various articles of value, but they were sneaks in that they accomplished their art while the

buildings were occupied and the inhabitants were awake.

Little is known regarding the evolution of the house sneak or *porch climber* of the nineteenth century. Contemporary literature does not refer to him specifically, yet many of his methods appear in the efforts of modern burglars. The status of the second-story man is less certain. The newer varieties of residential housing, including the small one- and two-family units and large apartment buildings, offer difficult settings for daytime prowling and entry. On the other hand, fire escapes have expanded the access to some living quarters. Explaining the existence of modern sneak thieves, an ex-pickpocket turned narcotic addict said:

> I haven't heard the term *sneak thief* in a long time, maybe ten or twenty years. Most of the old timers have died off or are in jail. Many of 'em are dead. You still have them though, but they're called something else. Most of the good ones specialize. The guy that steals coats is a "coat thief"; or if he steals from the butchers or the stock yards he's a "ham thief." I met one about five years ago at Rikers. He was a "hotel thief." He looked for open rooms and made a lot of hits, but it never amounted to anything.

Shoplifting. Shoplifting, the later variant of Elizabethan lifting law, can also be regarded as a variant of sneak theft. Although the shoplifter has isolated his theft to specific locations and employs devices and techniques peculiar only to his own trade, the basic pattern of "theft by sneaking" is characteristic.

The history of shoplifting indicates only minor changes in operation. During the late 1800s, shoplifters were of two types, "the regular criminal professional and the kleptomaniac" (Byrnes, 1895:25). The professional practitioners usually worked in large groups or in pairs, and the more common method involved the distraction of the storekeeper with idle conversation by one thief while another filled his pockets with merchandise. Female shoplifters used the same procedure with the addition of large pockets under their dresses, sustained by girdles about their waists, and many females of this type often specialized in the theft of expensive lace handkerchiefs. Sutherland (1937:48) reported two types of professional shoplifters: the *booster* and the *heel*. The booster contacted salesmen and stole from the articles displayed; the heel operated without the assistance of the salesman. Both types were daring and confident, and appeared in the dress of the normal upstanding customer. Cameron (1964) divides modern shoplifters into *boosters*, the professional commercial shoplifters, and *snitches*, the pilferers who steal for their own consumption. The booster steals for profit, while the snitch steals for use. Cameron indicated that boosters seem to gravitate toward New York City, preferring the large number of small stores. This preserves their anonymity for greater lengths of time since in other major cities large stores, protected by detectives who become familiar with the well-known professionals, seem to predominate. *Booster skirts* or *bloomers*, garments designed especially for holding stolen merchandise, have been common forms of concealment for more than a century, and were observed as early as the 1820s:

> The pregnancy was assumed, the better to evade suspicion; her undergarments were completely lined with hooks, to which were suspended, in vast variety, articles of stolen property, including not only those of light weight, viz. handkerchiefs, shawls, stockings, etc., but several of less portable description, amongst which were two pieces of Irish linen. These articles had been conveyed through an aperture in her upper habiliment of sufficient dimensions to admit an easy access to the general repository. The ingenuity of this invention created much surprise, and as it greatly facilitated concealment and evaded detection, there is no doubt of its having frequently produced a rich harvest (Egan, 1905b:136).

There is no accurate index of the number of shoplifters in operation today. Cameron (1964:58) suggested that about 10 percent of those arrested in department stores are professionals, yet this figure reflects only a small segment of the thefts. Not all shoplifters are detected, and of those who are, many are not approached since management does not wish to run the risk of arresting a respectable customer. The value of goods taken from retailers annually has been estimated from $100 million to $1,700 million (Edwards, 1958:v), with no less than $250 million representing the losses of supermarkets (Reckless, 1967:165). Other estimates have ranged from $200 million to $3 billion, not including the $5 million per day losses from employee pilferage. These thefts, furthermore, can be attributed to four distinct groups: (1) the professional *boosters* and *heels*; (2) the amateur *pilferers* who steal for their own use; (3) store employees who steal for their own consumption; and (4) narcotic addicts who shoplift merchandise for resale as a means of supporting their drug habits. As indicated by one of my informants, a pickpocket and shoplifter retired due to old age and the onset of arthritis, several of these categories may overlap one another:

> Women always make better shoplifts. Their sex gives them the advantage. They have more places to hide the stuff and they can always dangle a bag between their legs. They also get more sympathy or holler louder if they're caught. Lots of addicts are shoplifts, and lots of pros become addicts and shoplift. So many of the old timers have fallen that way.

Pennyweighting. Pennyweighting, which involves the substitution of spurious jewelry or gems for the genuine, is a highly sophisticated form of shoplifting requiring knowledge of precious stones. Chicago May, a prostitute and extortionist, indicated that the pennyweighter had to be familiar with the weight, size, and color of gems, have the ability to appraise them instantly, and carry a perfect mental image of the jewelry or stone (Sharpe, 1928:239). Typical pennyweighting operations are undertaken as follows:

> Pennyweighting is a very "slick" graft. It is generally worked in pairs, by either sex or both sexes. A man, for instance, enters a jewelry store and looks at some diamond rings on a tray. He prices them and notes the costly ones. Then he goes to a fauny shop (imitation jewelry) and buys a few diamonds which match the real ones he has noted. Then he and his pal, usually a woman, enter the jewelry store and ask to

see the rings. Through some little "con" they distract the jeweler's attention, and then one of them . . . substitutes the bogus diamonds for the good ones; and leaves the store without making a purchase (Hapgood, 1903:56-57).

Pennyweighting has suffered a decline over the past three decades. Contemporary jewelers are extremely careful about leaving their goods unattended, and jewelers' exchanges are protected by security guards and closed-circuit television. As one informant indicated: "The pennyweighter went out with the end of the Depression, or at least there hasn't been any new ones since then. I guess it's because easy targets are few and far between nowadays, making the profession unprofitable."

Similarly, I conducted interviews during 1969 with forty-four independent jewelry shop operators on Manhattan's Fifth Avenue, Broadway, and Bowery; Brooklyn's Fifth Avenue, Flatbush Avenue, and Fulton Street; and Bronx's Fordham Road, as well as with twenty-seven jewelers in three "exchanges" in New York's diamond center. Of the seventy-one operators, only one had been victimized since they had been in business, or since World War II if they were established prior to 1950; three had employees who had been victimized on one occasion, although in two cases the employees were suspected and consequently fired; and seven had recollections of hearing about it during the period under study. The respondents attributed the scarcity of offenses to the difficulty of obtaining perfectly matched substitutes, the jewelers' personal precautions, and the presence of closed-circuit television, security guard, and locked display cases. Fifty-six jewelers or 81 percent of the sample has observed "suspicious characters" during the period, and attributed the lack of victimization in those cases to their own diligence.

Pickpocketing. Pickpocketing is a form of sneak theft, for as Maurer (1964:59) has pointed out, it involves the successful robbery of money from a person without his cooperation or knowledge.

Methods of picking pockets have remained unchanged for thousands of years, and reference to the practitioners of this profession, as noted earlier, can be found in literature dating back to the days of Nero. Elizabethan literature highlighted the way of life of the pickpocket and closely observed the nature of his trade, but except for slight modifications in technique made necessary by changing clothing fashions, the pickpocket of centuries ago differs little from his contemporary counterpart. Beyond minor changes in argot, past discussions of pickpocketing by numerous observers in the United States and Great Britain show little variation from the depth analysis by Maurer (1964). The process of pickpocketing includes: (1) the selection of a victim, (2) the locating of the money on the victim's person, (3) the maneuvering of the victim into the proper position, (4) the act of theft, and (5) the passing of the stolen property. Pickpockets usually work in groups of two or more, each member playing a specific role in the total operation.

Professional pickpockets seek only those victims who appear to have money enough to make the theft worthwhile. The ability to select the proper victim (*mark*) is an occupational intuition and is based upon many years of experience. The money is then located on the victim's person by feeling his pockets (*fanning*). This operation is done by one mob member (*the tool*), while another (*the stall*) closely watches the victim's movements. This operation is not necessary if the location of the pocketbook or wallet (*the loot*) is known. The stall maneuvers the victim into proper position, and the tool removes the wallet. The success of the operation is due to the distractions by the stall, the dexterity of the tool, and their combined teamwork. As a safety precaution, the tool usually passes the pocketbook or wallet to another mob member, for in the event that he is suspected he will be *clean* when approached by the victim or police. As soon as possible, the stolen wallet is emptied of its contents and discarded.

Modern pickpockets seem to thrive in crowds, a situation not unlike the Elizabethan foists and nips who plundered the countrymen that filled the streets of London during the terms of court. The workshop and arena of theft are the city street, the railroad station, the bus depot, the amusement park, any places where there are people who are likely to have money. Yet the pickpocket does not need a large crowd to work in. The experienced pickpocket can successfully operate in areas of sparse population, a situation which will catch the victim off guard.

The profession of picking pockets has been able to survive for centuries, undergoing little alteration, and seemingly untouched by technological change. In spite of the use of checks, charge accounts, and credit cards, which reduce the need for carrying cash, people still carry valuables and currency on their person. Fashion tends to alter the course of the profession periodically, but rather than increasing or lessening, it merely influences the shifting of techniques. On the other hand, the profession has suffered a decline due to a lack of new recruits. Maurer (1964:171) estimated that in 1945 there were about five or six thousand *class cannons* (expert pickpockets), while that number was reduced to approximately one thousand by 1955. By 1965, according to one expert pickpocket from Times Square, the total number suffered even further reduction:

> Most of the ones left are old timers, and I say that there are probably no more than six or seven hundred in the whole country—if that much. There are plenty of amateurs, young ones, old ones, prostitutes, addicts, but they were never associated with the old time mobs. The kids are just not interested in it as a profession. Probably 'cause there's no money in it. And they're right.

Similarly, a member of the Pickpocket and Confidence Squad of the New York City Police Department indicated: "You see very few of the real experts these days. They have either quit, died, or are in jail, and they are rarely replaced. Most of the newer boys are from Harlem, and you can spot them a block away."

Lush Workers. Lush workers, known in this country since before the Civil War, are low-status pickpockets who prowl dark halls and alleys and steal from sleeping drunks or frequent public places and rob sleepers. The lush worker is not usually a *professional* criminal. Muggers, prostitutes who steal from their customers, and the vagrants from other criminal enterprises are found among them. Lush-working has usually been undertaken by professionals only when they are in desperate need of money or working without the protection (and good graces) of a pickpocket mob. The common lush workers, or *jack rollers*, work alone or in two's and three's in subways, railroad and bus terminals, and in parks during the warm months. Criminals of this type are found also on the back streets of the waterfront, the skid rows, and the amusement districts. Campion (1957:34) has noted specific techniques used by lush workers. One method involves two workers sitting at either side of a drunk in a subway or on a park bench, and unfolding a newspaper between them as if the three were reading it together. Shielded by the paper, the lush workers empty the victim's pockets and remove whatever jewelry he may have. A lush worker can also be a type of con man who approaches a potential victim in a bar, buys him drinks, and volunteers to take him home when he has had too much, robbing him somewhere along the way.

Confidence Swindling

Swindling or confidence games refers to any operations in which advantage is taken of the confidence placed by the victim in the swindler or confidence man. A swindle or confidence game is fraud: any misrepresentation by trickery or deceit, any false representation by word or conduct.

Activities of confidence swindlers have been known for centuries, perhaps even before the efforts of the Elizabethan rogues. The varieties and types of this form of criminality are as numerous as social situations, for a con game can be accomplished under any circumstances where one individual may place trust in another. The confidence operator is a smooth, adroit talker and has the ability to "size up" and manipulate people. Furthermore, he has a winning personality, is shrewd and agile, and is an excellent actor. The two classes of confidence games, the *big con* and the *short con*, are differentiated by the amount of preparation needed and the quantity of benefits reaped. *Circus grifting* is a type of short con, but is treated separately since its occupational setting is considerably different from other con games. All confidence operations, whether large or small, usually involve the following steps (see Maurer, 1940:17-18):

1. Locating and investigating the victim (*putting up the mark*);

2. Gaining the victim's confidence (*playing the con*);

3. Steering him to meet the insideman (*roping the mark*);

4. Showing the victim how he can make a large amount of money, most often dishonestly (*telling the tale*);

5. Allowing the victim to earn a profit (*the convincer*)—this is not always present in short-con games;

6. Determining how much the victim will invest (*the breakdown*);

7. Sending the victim for his money (*putting him on the send*);

8. Fleecing him (*the touch*);

9. Getting rid of him (*the blowoff*); and,

10. Forestalling action by the law (*putting in the fix*).

The Short Con. The short con is designed to obtain whatever money the victim may have on his person at the time he is approached. It can be operated at almost any place, and in a short period of time. Virtually thousands of rackets of this type have been undertaken over the years, but most of these have been variations of a few basic ideas. The success of the short-con racket depends upon a combination of four factors: (1) the existence of an opportunity, namely, a victim with money; (2) the easy, convincing manner of the confidence operator; (3) the gullibility of the victim; and (4) the desire of the victim to gain something dishonestly. Numerous writers suggest that it is the intrinsic dishonesty of the victim that makes the confidence game possible. Maurer (1940:15) maintained that the success of a confidence scheme depended upon the "fundamental dishonesty" of the victim, or as Chic Conwell, a professional thief, indicated, "it is impossible to beat an honest man in a confidence game" (Suther-

land, 1937:69). All professional thieves seem to agree on this point: the victim must have "larceny in his heart" before a swindle can be effected. Sutherland cites numerous comments by professional criminals on this point, and "Yellow Kid" Weil, perhaps the most famous of con men, stated that the men he fleeced were no more honest than he was (Brannon, 1948:293).

One of the more common rackets, called *ring falling* by John Awdeley in his *The Fraternity of Vagabonds*, published in 1552, was reported again by Egan (1905a:358-59) in the early nineteenth century as *ring-dropping*. A variety of ring-dropping might involve a pair of earrings, a ring, or some other jewelry along their path. After informing them that they were entitled to half the value of the articles, since they were in his presence when he found them, a second operator would appear, observe the goods, and declare that they were pure gold. The ensuing conversation would induce the women to provide money to the first operator for his share. When offered later to a jeweler, the women would learn that the jewelry was worthless. Another variation of this same idea exists now as the *pigeon drop*. This short con is similar to high-pressure salesmanship. After securing the victim, his gullibility is played upon by the manipulative abilities of the operator. And as many observers have indicated, con men are usually well dressed, exuding an air of real or fictitious prosperity, and their smooth flow of conversation is wonderfully soothing to the vanity of the proposed victim.

The number of swindles would be difficult to calculate, yet in every arena of social activity, numerous varieties exist. In 1873, sixty-four different types of swindles were listed by Lening (1873:168), and some years later, MacDonald (1939) described no less than one hundred varieties. The more common short-con rackets include the selling of worthless articles, allegedly stolen or of a high value but "discounted"; the legitimate purchase of goods with worthless checks; and swindles with dice or cards. Descriptions and explanations of numerous short-con enterprises in all types of literature in the last few centuries indicate a fascination with the offense. In 1841 Douglas Jerrold, a journalist for *Punch* magazine, described the offense as it appeared in England at that time. Much of the anti-urban literature, which launched a hostile attack upon city life from 1850 through the turn of the century, explored every phase of swindling and confidence operations. Greiner (1904) wrote an illustrated guidebook specifically designed as a warning to rural folk. It outlined more than two hundred and fifty swindles, the majority of which continue to exist.

The Big Con. Big-con games involve greater preparation than the short con, and the profits reaped are larger. The big-con men are uppermost in the professional underworld, and appear to be businessmen of the highest caliber. Their rackets include stock and real estate swindles, fraudulent business deals, and securing money under false pretenses from wealthy people. The three major big-con games are *the rag, the wire,* and *the payoff,* all of which follow the basic framework of confidence swindling in general. Perhaps the most well known of the big-con men was "Yellow Kid" Weil, mentioned earlier, who is said to have acquired about $8 million in various swindles and was a master at taking an everyday situation and turning it into a lucrative swindle.

Confidence men often dream about the rarely obtained "big one." It may be the fixed telegraph message that delays the results of a horse race, allowing one to bet heavily on a "sure thing"; it may be a land swindle that permits thousands of acres of worthless desert to earn millions of dollars; or it may be a fraud that disposes of millions of shares of worthless stock. This confidence game usually enables the professional to leave the rackets, and the execution of any such elaborate scheme is possible only with the accumulated wealth of knowledge obtained as a long-term operator. Among the more unique examples was the perpetual motion machine of John Ernest Worrell Keely. Keely, an ex-carnival pitchman, began a hoax in 1874 that reaped many fortunes and lasted for a quarter of a century. His nonexistent perpetual motion machine, "which would produce a force more powerful than steam and electricity," involved the financiers of many cities,

the public of two continents, and the United States secretary of war. Before his career ended, Keely had a 372-page volume written on his "discovery," over a million dollars in cash, a life of luxury for twenty-five years, and an international reputation.

The story of John Keely is an unusual one, but the methods of his operation were not. The basic ingredients of the con were at work, a complex of factors that are still present in our social system. The practitioners of such operations may be less colorful than Keely, but the profits of many stock and land swindles often approach the size of his earnings.

Forgery and Counterfeiting

Forgery and counterfeiting are varieties of fraud, although differing from confidence operations, since the thief is in a less face-to-face relationship with the victim. Furthermore, the victim is not involved with the forger for the purpose of winning or earning money dishonestly. Forgery and counterfeiting are fraud in that the act of forging a name or note carries an intent to deceive. Legally, these categories refer to the "making, altering, uttering, or possessing, with intent to defraud, anything false which is made to appear true," and bonds, stocks, checks, and currency are the items most often made or altered in the acts of forgery and counterfeiting (F.B.I., 1968:57).

Even before the Elizabethan era, forgery and counterfeiting were highly skilled crafts on British soil. The 1300s had a high incidence of forgeries of charters, deeds, bonds, letters, writs and returns in courts of law, pardons, and exchequer bills. In addition, counterfeiters produced false seals for the Pope and British nobles, alderman's marks, paper currency, and coins. These avenues of fraud endured through the emerging professional underworld in London, Exeter, and Bristol. Although forgery and counterfeiting continued to flourish, *versing law,* or the passing of counterfeit coins, was characteristic of the Elizabethan professional thief, and *coining,* the manufacture of false coins, represent the most widespread form of counterfeiting. Early in the nineteenth century, Colquhoun

(1806:113) described the unique character of the counterfeiter:

> The great qualifications, or leading and indispensable attributes, of a *Sharper*, a *Cheat*, a *Swindler*, or a *Gambler*, are, to possess a genteel exterior, a demeanor apparently artless, and a good address.

Like the more violent depredators upon the public, this class who are extremely numerous) generally proceed upon a regular system, and study as a *trade* all those infamous tricks and devices by which the thoughtless, the ignorant and the honest are defrauded of their property.

Forgery. Nineteenth-century forgeries included imitations of handwriting, duplication of corporate bonds and securities, printing of currency, and raising the values of bank checks. While forgers duped the operators of small businesses on countless occasions, the large banking institutions were the major targets. Byrnes reported one gang of forgers that netted $160 thousand in a single year (Campbell et al., 1892:719), and the Bank of England forgery in 1873 involved the passing of over one million pounds of forged bills (Hamilton, 1952:58-59). Many of the early forgers had elaborate schemes that brought them hundreds of thousands of dollars during their careers.

In the early part of this century, Roger Benton, a master check forger by profession, devised numerous methods of fraud that he operated simultaneously in different parts of the country. In one scheme Benton set up a fictitious business in New Haven while his partner established himself in Pittsburgh. Four lawyers were contacted for the purpose of collecting an unpaid bill of $4,000 from an alleged client in Pittsburgh. The lawyers forwarded collection notices to Pittsburgh, where Benton's partner received them and answered that he had only $3,200 to send as full payment. Benton instructed the lawyers to demand certified checks, easily forged by his partner. Upon receipt of the checks, the lawyers deposited them in their accounts, kept an agreed commission of $800 and gave Benton a check for the remaining $2,400. This operation, which took relatively little time to consummate, would net the pair a total of $9,600.

The counterfeiter or forger was not always a member of the professional underworld. The engraver who made false securities and bank notes operated in secrecy, and passed his bogus bills through agents. Sutherland (1937:77) reported that many a professional thief became involved in this complex of illegality by either purchasing and passing counterfeit money, by robbing post offices of money orders and subsequently passing them throughout the country, or by forging travelers' checks acquired by pickpocketing. Members of counterfeit mobs have little contact with professional thieves, making their participation in the professional underworld difficult.

The acts of counterfeiting and check forgery in large denominations have steadily drifted from the purview of the professional criminal since the turn of the century. The early thieves effectively committed serious assaults upon banking institutions as a result of unsophisticated methods of detection and apprehension, as well as the inferior quality of the materials being forged. As technological improvements were made in the production of inks, papers, check protectors and check-writing machines, and in the processes of printing and engraving, those who were committed to forgery and counterfeiting as a profession found their occupation more risky. Lemert (1958) has suggested that the vulnerability of forgery as a profession has been heightened in recent years by the persons engaged in passing the worthless goods, including bar waitresses, unattached women, drug addicts, alcoholics, petty thieves, and transient unemployed thieves—types who might readily inform on one another if threatened with long-term incarceration. Furthermore, with the widespread use of personal checks, which are easily forged and passed, the habitual and systematic forger can operate as a lone wolf, unattached to other thieves. Such isolation inhibits the incorporation of the professional criminals' conceptions of conformity and deviance, and encourages an identification with the middle-class value system. One informant, paroled after a three-year incarceration for forgery, suggested that few "true" professionals exist today. Although arrested over eighty times in all parts of America, his fifty years of professional forgery indicate a long and highly mobile career with only a few years spent in prison:

> I have been arrested over fifty times, almost always for forgery. And I think I'm one of a kind. There are few good forgers any more, and they don't work in mobs as they did fifty years ago. I've worked alone so long that I only see familiar faces on the T.V. set—and I don't even *know* those people.

Modern forgery is seemingly undertaken by solitary thieves with blank checks stolen from individuals or corporations. Losses from such forgery, furthermore, have been of greater magnitude than in the past. In 1966, for example, one estimate was placed at $800 million per year, or approximately $2 million per day or $1,500 per minute (Gentry, 1966:230). The American Bankers Association, in a more conservative frame of reference, indicated economic losses of $70 million for 1968, representing a 16 percent increase from the previous year (Gartner, 1968:82). What percentage of these figures represents the efforts of the professional forger is not known. That most modern forgers are a "lone-wolf" type, however, does not necessarily suggest a decline in the number of professionals. Some of the more celebrated personalities in the annals of professional forgery have been "lone wolves" for all or part of their careers, including Austin Bidwell, notorious for the $11 million Bank of England forgery in 1873; Harry Eastwood Hooper, the clever forger and actor who convinced San Francisco financiers that he was an English nobleman; and William Hamilton Harkins, once called the greatest lone-wolf bank bilker the world has ever produced. These individuals worked in concert with other professional criminals in spite of the fact that their acts of forgery may not have been group affairs. Jackson's (1969) account of a professional forger and safe robber depicts similar situations in which solo operators would purchase counterfeit checks and identification from thieves who produce

blank checks, secure legitimate personal checks from burglars, or set up dummy businesses with others for the purpose of having banks print official checks for them. Evidence does suggest, however, that some organized forgery groups may exist that are equipped with printing plants to prepare counterfeit checks with magnetically encoded account numbers that will pass computer inspection.

Check-kiting. is a swindle related to forgery that is directed against banks. This fraudulent operation involves the covering of bad checks with other bad checks. A professional bank swindler might open a series of checking accounts at scattered banks with deposits of $25. At *Bank Z* he cashes a $100 check drawn on *Bank X*, depositing $25 and pocketing $75. He then covers the *Bank X* check with a $250 check on *Bank Y*, depositing $125 and pocketing $125. This latter check on *Bank Y* is made good with a $500 check on *Bank Z*, with $300 deposited and $200 pocketed. Manipulations of this type have been executed by both individuals and organized groups of bank swindlers, with single operations accumulating thefts in excess of half a million dollars. *Double-pledging* is similar to kiting, and is undertaken with false collateral on loans. The more common types involve selling a mortgage to several different banks, or securing loans based on fraudulent insurance policies. Travelers' checks also provide an arena for the forger's operations, as well as the theft or illicit production of credit cards.

Counterfeiting. Counterfeiting is related to forgery in that it represents an alternative method of producing illegal tender. Although the most common form of counterfeiting involves the manufacture of false treasury notes, early twentieth-century methods also included the raising of legitimate $10 bills to $50 denominations. Contemporary counterfeit operations range from solitary entrepreneurs who produce and distribute only a few bills at a time to large organizations undertaking currency fraud running into millions of dollars. These large counterfeit organizations employ a variety of individuals: artists, engravers, draftsmen, and photographers who produce the currency, and professional thieves, hustlers, and pickpockets who pass the finished products. Such organizations may also include middlemen who make arrangements for the sale and distribution of large quantities of the false money. In addition to treasury notes, the larger counterfeiting gangs also manufacture and distribute passports, share scrip, visa stamps, legal agreements, documents of all types, travelers' checks, and sometimes paintings, sculpture, and china. As an enterprise of the professional criminal, counterfeiting is usually limited to the hustling levels since the large operations require substantial investments for equipment and staffing. Furthermore, without sufficient financial backing, it is difficult to induce essentially legitimate printers and engravers to prostitute their arts to counterfeit uses.

Extortion

Extortion essentially refers to securing money or property from an individual by means of an illegal use of fear. Within the professional underworld, extortion, or *blackmail*, is usually perpetrated when a victim is accused of, or found engaged in, some illegal or immoral act. Such acts are more commonly of a sexual nature, and the victims are forced to pay for the silence of the extortionists. The common extortion rackets are the *shake* or *shakedown*, and the *badger* and *panel* games.

Extortion within the framework of illicit sexual acts appears in the writings of the Elizabethan pamphleteers as crossbiting law. As described by S.R. in his 1610 publication, *Martin Markall, Beadle of Bridewell* (Judges, 1930:383-427), crossbiting was undertaken in the following manner:

> . . . Some base rogue . . ., that keepeth a whore as a friend, or marries one to be his maintainer, consents or constrains those creatures to yield the use of their bodies to other men, that so, taking them together, they may strip the lecher of all the money in his purse or that he can presently make (p. 418).

Although this form of solicitation has likely been associated with prostitution for thousands of years, its invention was attributed to Laurence Crossbiter in 1491.

The Elizabethan crossbiter's pretense of the outraged husband of a whore represents the basis of the *badger, panel*, and *shakedown* rackets of nineteenth- and twentieth-century United States. The term *badger* seems to derive from the Anglo *badge*, first referred to in 1725. A *badge* was a "malefactor burned in the hand," or a tormented person. With the meanings of "torment," "annoy," or "malign," *badger* then appeared in John O'Keeffe's *Wild Oats* (published in 1798), and Dickens's *Pickwick Papers* and *Great Expectations* (published in 1836 and 1860). During the middle 1800s, badger had also become part of American underworld slang, referring to a *panel thief*—a fellow who robs a man's pocket after he has been enticed into bed with a woman.

The panel game was the basis of much of the professional criminals' extortion rackets. There were several variations, usually involving the collective efforts of sneak thieves, prostitutes, and other types of criminals. In the more typical situation, an attractively dressed female approached a country gentleman, explaining that she was a victim of circumstances and was thus forced for the first time in her life to accost a man. After naming a modest sum for her charms, he would accompany her to her room, bolting the door. While he engaged in sexual relations with the young female, a wall panel would slide open from which a thief would enter, replace the money in the victim's pocket with paper, and silently exit. After the theft had taken place, a sound was heard which the woman claimed to be her husband. The gentleman would quickly dress and hastily leave through a rear door, unaware that he had been robbed. Variations of this practice were known in most of the larger cities in the last century.

As early as 1848, a prostitute's room was known as a *panel-crib*, perhaps from the fourteenth-century *parnel*, meaning prostitute, found in William Langland's *The Vision of William Concerning Piers Plowman*. A panel-crib was also known as a *shakedown*, hence, the shakedown racket. And the meaning of this term seems to be rooted in the descriptive context of an impoverished resting place. Egan (1821:164) described a shakedown as a temporary substitute for a bed, "a two-penny layer of straw"; Mayhew (1861) used the term with reference to the poor mattresses in lodging houses, as did Dickens in his *Great Expectations*. In an alternative setting, a *shake* was either a whore or a theft from one's pocket. The twentieth-century badger games rarely use the sliding panel. Rather, the "wronged husband" confronts the embracing couple, threatening to make the matter public, suggesting that money be paid in return for his silence. Although the use of the sliding panel seems to have disappeared, the panel man or sneak thief is still used. Known to some as *creeps*, they sneak from under a bed, from an adjoining room, closet, or even a large trunk.

Extortion rackets similar to the badger game still exist, often employing the use of a photographer who will "sell" his pictures of the compromising situation. The contemporary analysis of prostitution by Winick and Kinsie (1971:27-28) notes the current usage of creeps and panel houses.

Sutherland (1937) described two variations of the shake: the *muzzle* and the *income tax*. The muzzle allegedly began as a professional racket around 1909 at a poolroom near Broadway and West 43rd Street in New York City. The first operation involved waiting until two men entered a nearby subway toilet. When they were interrupted and found in a compromising situation, money was demanded in lieu of a report to the police. Later applications involved impersonation of police officers, or the use of a *steerer* who played the role of the homosexual. Numerous subway-station toilets in that same area have maintained their status as meeting places for homosexuals, especially within the Times Square station at 42nd Street, and the Columbus Circle station at 59th Street. Evidence suggests that this practice has maintained a place in the professional underworld since the time of Sutherland's description.

By contrast, the *income tax* extortionist accused the more hidden deviant of falsifying his income tax returns, and threatens exposure. This shakedown operator usually impersonates a revenue officer, and since many individuals do indeed submit incorrect returns, guilt is readily admitted and payment for the officer's silence is made. In other cases, the shakedown operator may examine a businessman's stock, often taking "evidence" of undeclared goods (perhaps uncut diamonds), leaving the merchant a receipt. The thief is never heard from again.

Discussion Questions

1. What are the general characteristics of "professional crime"? What types of crime can be included in this category? What are the characteristics of the professional thief?

2. How do the various professional criminals described in this article benefit from the "appearance of respectability" or the ability to blend in? How has advancing technology changed the usefulness of these characteristics? How has the profile of the shoplifter changed over the years?

3. What steps are involved in confidence swindling? What is the difference between the short con and the big con? Does this type of crime exist to any great degree today? What factors, together, determine the success of a short con?

References

Black, Jack. 1927. *You Can't Win*. New York: Macmillan.

Brannon, W. T. 1948. *'Yellow Kid' Weil*. Chicago: Ziff-Davis.

Byrnes, Thomas. 1895. *Professional Criminals of America*. New York: G. W. Dillingham.

Cameron, Mary Owen. 1964. *The Booster and the Snitch*. New York: Free Press of Glencoe.

Campbell, Helen, Thomas W. Knox, and Thomas Byrnes. 1892. *Darkness and Daylight; or, Lights and Shadows of New York Life*. Hartford: A. D. Worthington.

Campion, Daniel. 1957. *Crooks Are Human Too*. Englewood Cliffs, NJ: Prentice-Hall.

Clark, Charles L. and Earle E. Eubank. 1927. *Lockstep and Corridor: Thirty-five Years of Prison Life*. Cincinnati: University of Cincinnati Press.

Colquhoun, Patrick. 1806. *A Treatise on the Police of the Metropolis*. London: J. Mawman, et al.

Crapsey, Edward. 1872. *The Nether Side of New York*. New York: Sheldon.

Edwards, Loren E. 1958. *Shoplifting and Shrinkage Protection in Stores*. Springfield, IL: Thomas.

Egan, Pierce. 1821. *Real Life in London*, vol. 2. London: Jones.

——. 1905a. *Real Life in London*, vol. 1. London: Metheun (reprint of 1821 edition).

——. 1905b. *Real Life in London*, vol. 2. London: Metheun (reprint of 1821 edition).

Federal Bureau of Investigation. 1968. *Crime in the United States: Uniform Crime Reports—1967*. Washington, DC: U.S. Government Printing Office.

Gartner, Michael (ed.) 1968. *Crime and Business*. Princeton: Dow Jones.

Gentry, Curt. 1966. *The Vulnerable Americans*. Garden City, NY: Doubleday.

Gibbons, J. S. 1858. *The Banks of New York, Their Dealers, The Clearing House, and The Panic of 1857*. New York: D. Appleton.

Greiner, A. J. 1904. *Swindles and Bunco Games, in City and Country*. St. Louis: Sun.

Hamilton, Charles. 1952. *Men of the Underworld: The Professional Criminals' Own Story*. New York: Macmillan.

Hapgood, Hutchins. 1903. *The Autobiography of a Thief*. New York: Fox, Duffield.

Jackson, Bruce. 1969. *A Thief's Primer*. London: MacMillan.

Judges, Arthur V. (ed.) 1930. *The Elizabethan Underworld*. London: George Routledge.

Lemert, Edwin M. 1958. "The behavior of the systemic check forger." *Social Problems*, 6 (Fall): 141-148.

Lening, Gustav. 1873. *The Dark Side of New York Life and Its Criminal Classes*. New York: Fred'k Gerhard.

MacDonald, J. C. R. 1939. *Crime Is a Business: Buncos, Rackets, Confidence Schemes*. Stanford: Stanford University Press.

Martin, John Bartlow. 1952. *My Life in Crime: The Autobiography of a Professional Criminal*. New York: Harper.

Maurer, D. W. 1947. "The argot of the three-shell game." *American Speech*, 22 (October): 161-170.

——. 1964. *Whiz Mob: A Correlation of the Technical Argot of Pickpockets with their Behavior Pattern*. New Haven, CT: College and University Press.

Mayhew, Henry. 1861. *London Labour and the London Poor. Vol. I, The London StreetFolk (partial)*. New York: Dover Publications (1968 edition).

——. 1862. *London Labour and the London Poor. Vol. IV, Those That Will Not Work, comprising Prostitutes, Thieves, Swindlers and Beggars*, by several contributors. New York: Dover Publications (1968 Edition).

O'Connor, Richard. 1958. *Hell's Kitchen*. New York: Lippincott.

Parker, G. 1781. "A view of society of manners in high and low life." Pp. 627-631 in J. C. Ribton-Turner (ed.) *A History of Vagrants and Vagrancy*. London: Chapman & Hall, 1887.

Reckless, Walter C. 1967. *The Crime Problem*. New York: Appleton-Century-Crofts.

Sharpe, May Churchill. 1928. *Chicago May: Her Story*. New York: Macaulay.

Sutherland, Edwin H. 1937. *The Professional Thief*. Chicago: University of Chicago Press.

Winick, Charles and Paul M. Kinsie. 1971. *The Lively Commerce: Prostitution in the United States*. Chicago: Quadrangle.

Reprinted from: James A. Inciardi, "The Nature and Historical Roots of Professional Crime." In *Careers in Crime*, pp. 5-6, 12-30. Copyright © 1975 by Rand McNally. Reprinted by permission of James A. Inciardi. ✦

32

The Stooper: A Professional Thief in the Sutherland Manner

John Rosecrance

In the last twenty years, Sutherland's conceptualization of professional crime has been criticized as too narrow and not applicable to modern criminal activity. Some researchers contend that today's criminals do not usually undergo the tutoring and apprenticeship that Sutherland saw as essential qualities of professional criminals. Others claim that thieves do not specialize but are generalists who do whatever they can for illegal profit. Still others view professional criminals as a dying breed whose ranks are not being replenished by young recruits. John Rosecrance, the author of this selection, disagrees. His study of racetrack stoopers shows that professional thieves in the Sutherland tradition continue to exist and are even prospering.

'Racetrack stoopers' are people who frequent racetracks in order to find winning tickets that have been mistakenly discarded. Although this nonviolent activity is seemingly harmless, it is a violation of law and stoopers may be arrested if caught. Therefore, like all professional thieves, stoopers develop particular skills that allow them to commit their crimes successfully. They are accorded a certain status and admiration by police and track officials, and they respect one another as professionals. As a group, stoopers develop similar values and outlooks, sharing rationalizations for their criminal behavior. Their shared code demands mutual respect and helpfulness. As with other professional criminal types, they maximize differential association by allowing only others like themselves into their social worlds. Within that social world, stoopers cooperate, divide turf, and work together.

The racetrack stooper is an excellent example of a professional criminal meeting the characteristics laid out by Sutherland. At times his earnings are modest, but the lifestyle is alluring and keeps him hooked on his criminal career.

The professional criminal is traditionally defined as one who obtains a major portion of his or her income from illegal activity (Blumberg 1981, p. 46). Professional crime generally refers to nonviolent patterns of criminal behavior undertaken with skill and planning, the execution of which minimizes the possibility of apprehension (Inciardi, 1975: 5). Sutherland was the seminal source of a systematic analysis of professional crime. In 1937, he advanced the concept of a behavior system to explain the existence of this form of criminal activity. Typically, members of such a system shared a distinct argot, an ideology of legitimation, normative expectations, a specialized activity, and a degree of technical expertise (Sutherland 1937, pp. 197-216). Sutherland's model gained acceptance by many criminologists and police officials as an accurate representation of professional crime.

Since his pioneering work, there have been various criticisms of Sutherland's concept of professional crime. Criticisms have coalesced around three issues: (1) the existence of an established professional criminal organization, (2) the specialized character of professional crime, and (3) the contention that Sutherland's model is either too narrow or outdated. Lemert (1958) and Einstadter (1969), after investigating check forgers and armed robbers respectively, concluded that these offenders, who otherwise met the criteria of professional criminals, worked alone, were not part of a criminal system, and had not been tutored by other criminals. After conducting studies for a president's commission on crime, researchers (Gould, Bittner, Messinger, Powledge, and Chaneles 1966) concluded that professional thieves were not specialists but instead were generalists—that is, "hustlers" who sought available opportunities for illegal gain. Other criminologists (Shover 1973; Klein 1974; Inciardi 1974, 1975) have indicated that professional criminals are not reproducing themselves and their behavior systems are dying out: "Professional theft will continue to atrophy until its unique qualities become only references within the history of crime" (Inciardi 1975, p. 82). Walker (1981, p. 171) has argued that Sutherland's model is unnecessarily narrow and can be applied accurately only to highly successful professionals who represent a criminal elite (for example, class cannons or jewel thieves).

The research discussed here considers a group of contemporary thieves whose behavior patterns closely resemble the Sutherland model of professional crime. Following an analysis of this striking resemblance, the conclusion reached is that Sutherland's concept of professional crime is still applicable and can serve as a useful guide in depicting a modern criminal behavior system. The criminal group studied is that of racetrack stoopers. A stooper has been defined as "someone who looks through the litter of discarded [racetrack] tickets for a winner mistakenly thrown away" (Martinez, 1983, p. 222). Although this group has been acknowledged by prior researchers (Scott 1968; Maurer 1974; Surface 1976), their criminal activities have apparently never been delineated.

Those who frequent racetracks for the purpose of stooping are in violation of pandering laws. Stoopers are subject to both criminal prosecution and administrative banishment by track officials. They fit the general criteria of a sneak thief as one "who does not, at the outset of his crime, proclaim his intentions by some work or act; he is a thief who has the ability to remain unnoticed, blending with his environment while stealing in the proximity of his awake and active victims" (Inciardi, 1974, p. 306).

This paper describes the activities of professional stoopers and demonstrates how their behavior closely parallels the original Sutherland model of professional crime. This will demonstrate that in this case, the major criticisms of Sutherland's concept have not lessened its applicability to a contemporary criminal behavior system. The accumulated data reveal that this group is reproducing itself, a finding that belies the contention that Sutherland's professional thief should be considered merely a historical reference. This research is in general accord with that of Chambliss (1972, p. 168):

> the overwhelming evidence is that professional theft is no more dead today than it has ever been. There have always been a small cadre of devotees who consider themselves professional thieves; who plan their capers carefully; who develop their craft through apprenticeship and with planning.

Chambliss's finding is extended by applying Sutherland's concept of professional crime to a heretofore unresearched criminal system.

Methodology

It is always difficult to collect data about professional criminals (Clinard and Quinney 1967, p. 429; Cressey 1967, p. 102; Letkemann 1973, p. 165-166; Abadinsky 1983, p. 4). By design, professional thieves are secretive and take elaborate steps to remain unobtrusive. This was certainly the case with the group under investigation. Stoopers attempt to mingle with other race-goers in a chameleon-like deception. Professional stoopers have achieved virtual anonymity and conduct their business unnoticed by even longtime racing fans. The author began his investigation of stoopers by first interviewing racetrack officials and security personnel. After learning how to identify stoopers, he observed their actions in racetracks in California, Louisiana, Maryland, and West Virginia. Because most stoopers refuse to discuss their activities, he was unable to interview any of them until he located a stooper in California who agreed to be an informant. This stooper introduced him to others and he was able to conduct interviews with eight stoopers in California. In Louisiana the author developed a relationship with another informant and was able to interview five stoopers in that area. The stoopers who consented to be interviewed were all male, ranged in age from 25 to 55, and generally had minor criminal records. The author did not use a structured questionnaire, but asked such questions as the following:

(1) How did you get into stooping?

(2) Why do you remain a stooper?

(3) Can you support yourself by stooping?

(4) Do you follow the horses from track to track?

(5) Have you done time in jail?

(6) Do you know other stoopers?

(7) Do you work with other stoopers?

(8) What steps do you take to avoid detection?

(9) What do your family or friends think of your stooping?

During the study the author was guided by the principles of grounded theory (Glaser and Strauss 1967) and sought to develop analyses that were generated directly from the data gathered from the interviews with stoopers, racetrack officials, and personnel.

Findings

An analysis of the research data revealed that, in most respects, the behavior system of racetrack stoopers corresponds to that described by Sutherland in his classic work, *The Professional Thief*. This finding will be clarified by describing their demonstrated behavior in terms of the five characteristics of professional crime outlined by Sutherland (1937, p. 198): (1) technical skill, (2) status, (3) consensus, (4) differential association, and (5) organization.

Technical Skills

In 1984 at California racetracks over three million dollars worth of winning tickets were not cashed.[1] At one track alone (Belmont Park, New York) during a single racing season, tickets worth more than one and a half million dollars were not redeemed (Surface 1976, p. 183). In most states these unclaimed winnings subsequently revert to state treasuries. Racing patrons, who for various reasons lose their winning tickets, create a source of illegal income for stoopers. In the racing argot, live tickets (those that can be cashed) are there for the taking. However,

actually finding and retrieving discarded winning tickets involves the application of skillful techniques.

The development and implementation of technical skills among stoopers closely resembles Sutherland's conceptualizations. According to Sutherland (1937, p. 197), "the professional thief has a complex of abilities and skills, just as do physicians, lawyers, or bricklayers." He indicated that these abilities were based upon cleverness and stealth, not upon strength or physical dexterity. Sutherland conceived of professionals as specialists who concentrated their talents in a particular form of criminal activity.

Professional stoopers are definitely specialists. They devote their efforts to finding winning tickets and rarely participate in other illegal endeavors. The time, commitment, and specialization involved in becoming a successful stooper precludes active participation in other illegal activities. The comment of a veteran stooper reflects this situations:

I have to work so hard at stooping I just don't have the time for other capers. Some guys I know are into stealing and fencing. I suppose I could get in on their action. But with busting my ass six days a week at the track I gotta pass. Besides, even though I know how to make it at the track, I don't know diddly shit about heavy-duty thieving.

The skills involved in stooping are not related to unusual physical abilities; moderate eyesight and normal mobility comprise the basic physical requirements.

The process of stooping is divided into four stages: (1) blending (2) hunting, (3) identifying, and (4) cashing. During each of these stages the use of skillful techniques is required. Remaining unobtrusive while also looking for discarded tickets is the stooper's most basic skill. Stoopers often talk of the necessity of blending.

You become part of the crowd—just like any other guy at the track. Security won't hassle you as long as you don't call attention to yourself. You're OK if you just act natural. First, last, and always you have to blend.

Stoopers are careful to dress like other racing fans. Those who "work" the grandstand, where blue-collar patrons congregate, dress in jeans or work clothes. Appropriately, stoopers who situate themselves in the clubhouse, where middle-class patrons are in the majority, wear jackets, dress slacks, and polished shoes. Most stoopers are not active gamblers. A stooper explained: "I haven't got the time to look at a Racing Form—too busy hustling tickets. Half the time I don't even know who's running." However, in order to blend they occasionally wager on races. "I throw away a few bucks every day just to look the part. I never saw a racing man who didn't bet some." Professional stoopers refrain from drinking or arguing while on the job to avoid "sticking out."

While remaining unnoticed is essential, the stooper must also develop an aptitude for finding discarded winning tickets. "Hunting" is a commonly used term to describe this search. Although stoopers maintain a continuing vigil, they usually do not begin a serious search until the middle of the racing day when a significant number of discarded tickets has accumulated. A stooper described this practice, "I can't bear down and go all out after each race. I'd get bummed out. I usually don't get serious until after the fifth race when the losers start to go home."

Certain kinds of race results and betting situations dictate an extensive search. Just after a disqualification (when the actual order of finish is changed) is considered by many stoopers to be an excellent time for locating cashable tickets. Although gamblers are always cautioned by the track announcer to "hold all tickets until the race is declared official" they often disregard this warning and throw their tickets away before the official winners are posted. Frequently, when betters discover that a disqualification has made their seemingly worthless tickets winning ones, they're unable to locate the discarded ticket. Often the tickets have been picked up by an alert stooper who has blended into the crowd. Other situations that are conducive to mistakenly throwing away winning tickets occur when, for betting purposes, more than one horse is combined to form an entry (horses trained by the same

person) or a field (more than 12 horses are entered in a single race). When such situations arise, stoopers must redouble their efforts in order to take advantage of a potential windfall.

If stoopers are to be successful, they must identify those mutuel tickets that can eventually be cashed. This must be accomplished quickly to avoid being noticed. A veteran stooper related, "Instant recall is required in this business. You can't linger over a ticket trying to remember whether it's live." Such identification necessitates that stoopers be able to recall a multitude of winning ticket numbers. They must remember numbers of the win, place, and show horses in each of nine races plus daily double, exacta, and quinella combinations. This form of mental acuity is often facilitated by development of a memory system. One stooper related that he used the childhood nursery rhyme "One-two, buckle my shoe; three-four, shut the door" to remember the winning numbers. Others have used color combinations or personally significant codes such as their age, social security number, and birthdate as recall keys.

Patience and persistence are important during the hunting and identification phases. Some days stoopers "come up empty," while other days tickets they locate result in payoffs between $2 and $20. On occasion, tickets worth over $100 or even $1,000 have been found. One of the informants indicated, "I find a lot of two-buck show tickets but every once in awhile I make a big score. Those big ones are out there for the taking—keeps me coming back."

Once a live ticket has been retrieved, it must be redeemed at one of the cashier windows. Stoopers employ skillful techniques to achieve this end. Tickets with a low monetary amount can be routinely cashed by presenting them at varied cashier locations. However, tickets that will result in large payoffs must be handled more circumspectly. Stoopers are aware that most security personnel and track officials know them on sight. Collecting a large payoff could attract unwanted attention and might cause the security department to more closely monitor their activities. In order to avoid notoriety, stoopers hire beards or accomplices to cash large-value tickets. These beards are usually "straight types" who are not regular track patrons. To the track cashier the beard appears as a solid citizen and is able to receive large payouts without incident.

Status

Accomplished stoopers, in common with Sutherland's professional thieves, have achieved status. This status is drawn from the attitudes of racetrack authorities, especially security personnel and other track insiders. Stoopers, like other professional thieves, are "contemptuous of amateur thieves and have many epithets which they apply to amateurs" (Sutherland 1937, p. 200).

Security personnel and local police assigned to the track expressed a grudging admiration for successful stoopers.

Such respect works to the advantage of stoopers. The observation of a security chief reflects this situation.

The pros are really something else. They don't even bend over until they spot a live ticket. Once they stoop you can bet they will come up with something good. These guys don't cause anyone any trouble and they go out of their to avoid a hassle. They are real pros. I could bust 'em, but what's the point? As long is they keep out of everybody's way we don't bother them.

Others who work at the racetrack—for example, trainers, jockeys, grooms, and ticket sellers—also acknowledge the professional status of stoopers. A long-time horse trainer commented, "I don't know how those boys do it, but they sure can find live tickets. I guess it's because they're real professional about what they do."

At every racetrack there are people who attempt to find live tickets. Most of these searchers are not professional in their manner or technique and are considered amateurs by track insiders. A popular method used by nonprofessional stoopers involves picking up all the tickets they can find and then openly culling through them. Some amateurs send their children around the grandstand area to scoop loose tickets into a bag. Children who engage in obvious ticket collection are less likely to arouse the ire of

security forces than are adults. Other track bustouts will steal tickets from pockets, wallets, and purses, or take tickets directly from a winning bettor. One technique is grabbing and running with tickets taken from bar patrons who have waved them about while happily proclaiming, "I've got a winner." Security personnel report that many of these "snatch and grab" (Sutherland 1937, p. 201) thieves have tried stooping but did not have the skill or practice to be successful and instead have turned to more visible or violent criminal activities.

Professional stoopers heap scorn and ridicule upon amateurs "who give stooping a bad name" and disdain methods deemed "unprofessional." Such perspectives can be illustrated by the statement of an accomplished stooper.

Those assholes who run around the track with shopping bags while grabbing tickets off the floor are pathetic. They never find anything and security runs 'em off quick. The jokers who roll drunks or grab purses are just thugs and deserve to be put in the slammer. If I ever resort to those tactics I hope someone locks me up.

By most standards, stoopers are not financially successful. Because earnings fluctuate drastically, it is difficult to estimate their annual incomes. However, estimates among ten of the stoopers interviewed ranged from $6000 to $20,000 per year. But most were quick to point out "it's all tax-free." An important source of status among stoopers is their independence and ability to operate outside the system. They frequently talked of the "uptight assholes" who lead a routine, structured life. Stoopers pride themselves on their ability to function without bureaucratic support.

It's a heady feeling living without a safety net. There's no Blue Cross, dental plan, company retirement plan, sick days, or paid vacations to fall back on. On the other hand, there's no forms to fill out, supervisors to suck up to, or time clocks to punch. I don't want to work for wages. I can come and go as I want. I live by my wits alone. Sure bets being a scared little pencil-pusher.

Consensus

As a group, stoopers because of their common endeavor have developed similar attitudes and values. Share feelings include rationalizations for their type of criminal activity as well as perspectives concerning their victims. Consensus among stoopers has fostered an informal but extant "code of helpfulness" (Sutherland 1937, p. 203).

Professional stoopers are able to rationalize much of their criminal activity by adhering to a prevailing societal attitude subsumed within the popular expression, "finders, keepers; losers, weepers." Such an attitude holds that careless persons should not expect to have their property returned by good samaritans. The responsibility to adequately safeguard one's personal property is a basic America tenet. Stoopers contend that by thoughtlessly throwing away winning tickets, racing patrons have forfeited their right to those tickets. They maintain that "If the sucker is not sufficiently smart enough to protect himself, his rights are gone" (Sutherland 1937, p. 173). Security personnel, while acknowledging that stooping is theft, also feel little sympathy for the victim. A security guard expressed that view: "Any jerk who throws away a live ticket gets what's coming to him—a lost ticket." Stoopers do not conceive of their activities as victimless crimes. They all have seen the frantic look of desperation on the faces of those searching for the discarded winning tickets that are already in the stoopers's possession. Notwithstanding the victim's understandable anguish, there is a consensus among professionals that the victim's carelessness absolves the stooper of moral responsibility.

There is an implicit code among stoopers which stipulates that other professional stoopers should be treated with respect, protected from being apprehended and given financial aid when needed. Adherence to this code, while not always absolute, does add to the consensual relationship among group members. Stoopers relate to one another in a generally friendly manner and are careful not to openly criticize each other. If stoopers are apprehended or detained, they do not attempt to curry favor from the authorities by "ratting on a buddy." Stoopers are constrained to follow their code since their numbers are few and their professional reputations are at stake. An informant succinctly described this phenomenon: "I wouldn't screw other stoopers. It wouldn't be professional. Besides, I need their help later on. The track's a small world."

Differential Association

Stoopers are separated from larger society both by the racetrack milieu in which they operate and by their own specialized illegal activity. This pattern of differential association tends to form social barriers which further accentuate the differences between them and nongroup members. They are often reluctant to discuss their stooping with those outside their social world, even with family members and close friends. Stoopers believe that "outsiders would never understand what we do." Frequently they tell their significant others that they are working at the track as cashiers, trainers, or even security worker. The stoopers' behavior system fits Sutherland's (1937, p. 207) characterization that the "group defines its own membership." Only accomplished stoopers who act professionally are fully accepted into the inner world of this group. Those considered amateurs or part-timers must function on their own, without assistance from professional stoopers. Once accepted by other professionals, social contacts are generally contained within this group.

Although separated by differential association, stoopers are not totally isolated from the larger society. During their stooping efforts they must mingle and associate with the general population, even while planning to fleece them. Occasionally they need the assistance of those in conventional society—for example, beards, lawyers, and bail bondsmen. Stoopers, while engaged in an illegal endeavor, share many of society's basic values. They tend to be conservative, to strongly favor a capitalistic system, and to believe that hard work will ultimately be rewarded.

Social Organization

Even though stoopers are informally organized to help one another, they are not part of a larger criminal underworld. They do not have ties with either organized crime or large mobs, and typically do not associate or hang out with the general body of criminals. Consequently, they have little contact with traditional criminal organizations. In this respect, the stoopers' behavior patterns do not fit precisely the Sutherland model.

Stoopers prefer instead to consider themselves as a special breed of thief. Among themselves they cooperate and work together to increase their financial opportunities. The supply of discarded winning tickets in not inexhaustible, and most tracks cannot support more than four to six full-time stoopers. Professional stoopers divide the racetrack into work areas and then do not infringe on one another's territory.

The stoopers' pattern of tutelage closely resembles that described by Sutherland (1937, p. 211-213). In most cases, stoopers have learned the business from an older and more accomplished professional. As tyros, they were introduced to the complex of skills that make up professional stooping by a already established thief. "In the course of this process a person who is not a professional may first become a neophyte and then a recognized thief" (Sutherland 1937, p. 212). Older, more established stoopers indicated that there was no shortage of potential recruits, and they could choose carefully their apprentices. One such professional said, "I don't know where these young guys come from, but every few months one comes around and wants to learn the business. Most of them I can't help but every once in awhile I take a liking to a guy and show him the ropes."

Summary and Conclusions

This paper has described and analyzed the criminal system of a little-known group of professional thieves. Accomplished racetrack stoopers are few in number, and their illegal activity does not represent a serious threat to society. For the most part, police officials are unaware of their existence, and knowledgeable security personnel have shown little interest in apprehending or prosecuting them. The victims, careless bettors, and the state treasuries that are entitled to the uncashed winnings have not demanded that action be taken to halt their loss. While stoopers are involved in illegal activity and their victims do incur financial loss, their interest to the criminology community rests upon the theoretical implications of the stoopers' empirically demonstrated behavior patterns, not the scope of their criminal activity.

Sutherland's (1937) original conceptualization of professional crime has been hailed as "an unforgettable moment for the disciplines of criminology, police science, and correctional administration," and has been said to have "made manifest the nature and complexity of a criminal career" (Inciardi 1975, p. 5). However, in the intervening years there has been a host of criticisms of Sutherland's definition of professional crime (Lemert 1958; Gould et al. 1966; Einstadter 1969; Jackson 1969; Klein 1974; Walker 1981). Researchers have also contended that a rapidly changing, modern technology has rendered the Sutherland model obsolete (Shover 1973; Inciardi 1974, 1975; Wickman and Whitten 1980). Sutherland's perspective of professional crime has been labeled traditional (Staats 1977), and there is a suggestion that the professional thief may be "more the creation of journalism, romanticism, and commercialism than an empirically demonstrable social type" (Turk 1969, p. 15).

The research findings here demonstrate that the Sutherland model is still visible and that it has relevance to contemporary criminal activity. These findings still lend support to Chambliss's (1972, p. 168) contention that "professional theft is not about to become extinct." The ongoing behavior system of racetrack stoopers manifests the major characteristics of professional crime delineated by Sutherland. A consideration of these characteristics has demonstrated that, with respect to this group, the major criticisms of Sutherland's concept of professional crime (enumerated in the introduction) have not detracted from its applicability.

Professional stoopers employ a specialized complex of skills to perpetrate a unique form of criminal behavior. Although not financially successful by most standards, stoopers derive status from their professional manner, and in turn are contemptuous of amateur practioners. Due to a common endeavor and the specialized nature of their activity, stoopers have developed a consensus which includes shared rationalization, attitudes toward victims, and an informal code of behavior. Through a process of differential association, stoopers are separated but not isolated from traditional society. While not belonging to a larger criminal network, stoopers are informally organized and tutelage is necessary to become part of that organization.

Professional crime as described by Sutherland should not be relegated to the status of a romanticized footnote. While modern technology may have drastically altered some forms of professional crime, in the case of racetrack stoopers it has not radically changed their behavior system. Contemporary stoopers go on plying their trade in much the same manner as their earlier counterparts. There is no evidence of a diminution of skills or that modern stoopers ignore the tenets of their code. Novice stoopers are being tutored, and there are many indications that stooping will provide a regular source of income for a determined cadre of skilled thieves. Racetrack patrons show no signs of becoming more careful, and a continuing supply of discarded live tickets seems assured. In this instance, a group of professional criminals continues to behave in the Sutherland manner.

Discussion Questions

1. What is a professional criminal, according to the article? In what three areas does Sutherland's concept of a professional crime come under attack?

2. Do you agree that professional criminals are dying out? If so, what are some of the reasons that this might be the case?

3. What is stooping? Why is it considered to be a crime? In what ways does stooping correspond to Sutherland's description of professional crime? In what ways, if any, does it fail to correspond to Sutherland's description?

Notes

1. The figure of three million dollars was given to the author by John Regan of the California Horse Racing Board during a phone conversation of August 14, 1985.

References

Abadinsky, Howard. 1983. *The Criminal Elite*. Westport, CT: Greenwood.

Blumberg, Abraham S. 1981 "Typologies of criminal behavior," in Abraham Blumberg (ed.), *Current Perspectives on Criminal Behavior*. New York: Knopf.

Chambliss, William. 1972. *Box Man: A Professional Thief's Journal*. New York: Harper Torchbooks.

Clinard, Marshall B. and Richard Quinney. 1967. *Criminal Behavior Systems: A Typology*. New York: Holt, Rinehart, and Winston.

Cressey, Donald. 1967. "Methodological problems in the study of organized crime as a social problem." *Annals of American Academy of Political and Social Sciences*, 374: 98-120.

Einstadter, Werner J. 1969. "The social organization of armed robbery." *Social Problems*, 17: 64-83.

Glaser, Barney and Anselm L. Strauss. 1967. *The Discovery of Grounded Theory*. Chicago: Aldine.

Gould, Leroy C., Egon Bittner, Sheldon Messinger, Fred Powledge, and Sol Charles. 1966. *Crime as a Profession*. Washington, DC: U.S. Government Printing Office.

Inciardi, James. 1974. "Vocational crime," in Daniel Glaser (ed.), *Handbook of Criminology*. Chicago: Rand McNally.

——. *Careers in Crime*. Chicago: Rand McNally.

Jackson, Bruce. 1969. *A Thief's Primer*. Englewood Cliffs, NJ: Prentice-Hall.

Klein, John F. 1974. "Professional theft: The utility of a concept." *Canadian Journal of Criminology and Corrections*, 16: 133-144.

Lemert, Edwin. 1958. "The behavior of the systemic check forger." *Social Problems* 6: 141-148.

Letkemann, Peter. 1973. *Crime as Work*. Englewood Cliffs, NJ: Prentice-Hall.

Martinez, Tomas. 1983. *The Gambling Scene*. Springfield, IL: Thomas.

Maurer, David W. 1974. *The American Confidence Man*. Springfield, IL: Thomas.

Rosecrance, John D. 1985. *The Degenerates of Lake Tahoe: A Study of Persistence in the Social World of Horse Race Gambling*. New York: Lang.

Scott, Marvin B. 1968. *The Racing Game*. Chicago: Aldine.

Shover, Neal. 1973. "The social organization of burglary." *Social Problems*, 20: 499-514.

Staats, Gregory R. 1977. "Changing conceptualization of professional criminals." *Criminology*, 15: 49-65.

Surface, Bill. 1976. *The Track*. New York: Macmillan.

Sutherland, Edwin H. 1937. *The Professional Thief*. Chicago: University of Chicago Press.

Turk, Austin. 1969. *Criminality and the Legal Order*. Chicago: Rand McNally.

Walker, Andrew. 1981. "Sociology and professional crime," in Abraham Blumberg (ed.), *Current Perspectives on Criminal Behavior*. New York: Knopf.

Wickman, Peter and Phillip Whitten. 1980. *Criminology: Perspectives on Crime and Criminality*. Lexington, MA: Heath.

33

Organized Crime

Frank R. Scarpitti

What American has not heard of organized crime? From tales of Prohibition-era gangsters to the Godfather books and movies, organized crime has become part of the nation's folk legends. It has been romanticized unlike any other type of criminality but remains an enigma to many people. Organized crime is another form of career crime to which participants become committed and around which a unique lifestyle develops. Understanding organized crime allows us to see the often intricate relationships that exist among law, morality, vice, ethnicity, social mobility, and politics. No other form of criminality blends so many social dynamics; perhaps that is what makes it such an intriguing and romantic subject.

In this selection, Frank R. Scarpitti presents a short history of organized crime in the United States and its current nature. Beginning with the pirates of the seventeenth and eighteenth centuries, there have always been groups of criminals willing to provide the public with goods and services that were desired but forbidden by law. Although the groups changed over the centuries, their mission did not. In the twentieth century organized crime groups were identified with immigrant groups searching for the American dream but using illegal means to attain it. Although this pattern has led some observers to speculate that an alien conspiracy controls U.S. organized crime, most scholars see ethnic succession and enterprise theory as more reasonable explanations of its origin and permanence.

As this selection makes clear, controlling organized crime has been difficult. Because law enforcement has traditionally seen this type of crime as the product of evil persons or groups, emphasis has been placed on prosecuting individuals rather than on systemic change. Denying organized crime access to illegal profits by legalizing some of the goods and services it pro-vides would be one alternative. The likelihood of such change, however, is not very great. So, as individuals and groups are successfully prosecuted, they are replaced by others, and illegal goods and services continue to be provided to willing consumers.

Any consumer of popular culture is exposed to a great deal of information about organized crime. Books, articles, news reports, movies, television shows, all feature numerous stories about this form of criminal behavior and those who engage in it. These fictional and nonfictional accounts of crime syndicates and their operators have, unfortunately, created a number of myths about organized crime and made some organized criminals virtual folk heroes. Despite this public and media attention, there remains significant disagreement about the exact nature of organized crime, its etiology, and the role it plays in contemporary American society.

Defining Organized Crime

Controversy begins with attempting to define organized crime. Although criminologists have offered numerous definitions, several common features are noted in most. Organized crime is profit-motivated,[1] provides illegal goods and services,[2] involves planning and conspiracies among group members,[3] uses violence and coercion,[4] and relies on political corruption to protect itself.[5] It is violation of the law that involves more than one person, a group that intends to remain associated with one another in an identifiable hierarchy of authority in order to commit additional crimes.[6]

These attributes of organized crime groups allow us to see that they are *organized* because they are hierarchically arranged conspiracies of like individuals designed to provide goods and services to buyers at substantial profits. They are prone to using violence and corruption to maintain monopolistic control of markets and to achieve their illegal goals. In addition, organized crime groups are self-perpetuating and engage in ongoing criminal activity.

Although this definition of organized crime is generally accepted by law enforcement agencies, they have placed greater emphasis on several key characteristics than most criminologists believe to be accurate. The model of organized crime perpetuated by the U.S. Justice Department and its enforcement agencies suggests that a single national syndicate (Cosa Nostra), sometimes working with other national or international groups, controls most organized criminal activities.[7] Such groups, it is believed, are highly structured and tightly controlled by ruthless bosses who have great power. As two investigators have commented:

They [the government] picture a secret organization of ruthless and violent men bound by a common interest in illicit gain, ordered by a rigid code of rules, rights, and obligations, and maintained by the constant threat of death to informers or defectors.[8]

While this conception of organized crime and criminals has been questioned by numerous scholars, it is still popular among social control agents and continues to shape the public image.

History of Organized Crime

Although some believe that American organized crime began to emerge early in the twentieth century, others contend that its origin can be traced to the pirates of the seventeenth and eighteenth centuries.[9] Highly organized and subscribing to hierarchical authority, these bandits of the seas earned their livings from crime. Their loot was sold to otherwise lawful consumers who valued the bargains, and their wealth ingratiated them with government officials. In nearly every way, these early criminal organizations possessed the attributes of organized crime groups as defined earlier.

Pirates were not the only organized criminal groups in the colonies, however. In all of the major port cities, gangs stole from docked ships, raided warehouses, smuggled, and provided sex and liquor to sailors and others willing to pay. Following the American Revolution, huge land frauds were perpetrated by officials in high office and their henchmen,

setting the stage for the great "robber barons" of the nineteenth century. Called "financial pirates"[10] by one writer, they were determined to make their fortunes by whatever means necessary, often using illegal methods of the most callous type. These early crooks, Anglo-Saxon and Protestant, served as role models for immigrants who arrived later and also bent upon making their fortunes in the new land. It has been pointed out that:

. . . with the wealth of the "robber barons" now institutionalized and their progeny firmly in control of the economy, there . . . [was] little opportunity for the poor but ambitious adventurers of our urban frontiers. These later immigrants, Irish, Jewish, Italian, sought to innovate, not on the grand scale of the Vanderbilts, the Rockefellers, and the Morgans, but in a manner more consistent with available opportunity.[11]

Largely German and Irish before the Civil War and Italian and Jewish after, these later immigrants settled in the cities of the new country, usually in ethnic neighborhoods with others like themselves. Poor and uneducated, but fiercely ambitious, they searched for ways to achieve the promises of their adopted society. The young formed gangs which frequently saw crime as a means to attain the riches promised by their new life. Their crimes, of course, were those, with their limited skills, to which they had access, typically providing countrymen with the vices forbidden by the law. Urban political machines, usually corrupt, appealed to the immigrants for their support, often by giving tacit approval and protection to the gangs and their illegal activities. The collaboration between local gangs engaged in organized criminality and political operatives offering support in exchange for payoffs was simply an extension of the system that originated with the Colonial pirates.

The magnitude and nature of the problem changed after 1920, however, with the advent of Prohibition.[12] Although outlawed, Americans still wanted to drink liquor, and organized crime groups were ready to provide for their needs. Anticipating huge revenues, local gangs expanded their bootlegging activities by importing liquor, financing clandestine breweries and distilleries, and establishing speakeasies and other places where liquor could be purchased. Profits from such operations provided capital for expansion as well as for the financing of other illegal enterprises. Local, neighborhood crime groups soon began to grow well beyond their original boundaries.

In New York City, the most influential organized crime groups were dominated by Jewish and Italian gangsters. Often the groups cooperated, but just as frequently they fought for control of territory and enterprises. In Chicago, the second hub of organized crime activity, most gangs were controlled by Irish and Italian criminals, although here as in other places groups of various ethnic and racial origins were also involved in organized criminal activities. After bitter conflict, however, the group led by Al Capone eventually dominated organized criminality in Chicago.

By the time World War II ended, the prevalence of Italian-Americans in organized crime activities was attracting increased attention. Many experts attributed this to an international conspiracy known as the Mafia (later to be called La Cosa Nostra), manned by Italian immigrants from Sicily and now in control of organized crime activities across the nation.[13] Others disputed the notion of an Italian-dominated conspiracy, pointing out there was scant evidence of such a scheme and that the belief was based largely on myth often supplied by low-level syndicate members. In addition, little attention was paid during this period to the organized crime activities of other ethnic and racial group members, creating a false notion of ethnic and racial homogeneity among all organized crime groups. To both law enforcement and the public, however, organized crime in America was controlled by Italian-Americans.

Whatever the extent of Italian-American control and domination of organized crime, it began to diminish in the late 1960s.[14] Members of the old crime "families" were targeted by law enforcement, especially at the federal level, with intense scrutiny, investigation, and prosecution, resulting in the imprisonment of many. As members of the ethnic group attained middle class status, fewer of the young saw organized crime as a legitimate avenue for mobility, and leadership roles were not being filled with new recruits as vacancies occurred. Other groups became more brazen in challenging the old "families" for a share of the illegal markets. Clearly, changes began to take place that have continued since, with the old Italian-American gangs or "families" having very limited power in organized crime today.[15]

Since the 1970s, new organized crime groups have assumed power in certain geographical areas or over specific types of criminal activities. Many are identified by their ethnic affiliation, and, like the Irish, Jews, and Italians before them, usually representing the nation's newest immigrants. Thus, there are now recognized Mexican, Jamaican, Colombian, Asian, Israeli, and Russian crime groups, as well as those held together by other loyalties, like motorcycle gangs.[16] While most of these groups engage in a variety of crimes, the illegal drug business seems to be one criminal enterprise shared by many. Importing and distributing drugs has become so profitable that it attracts numerous groups to organized crime activity, making them rich and powerful very quickly, as well as increasingly violent as they fight to establish and retain their share of the market.

Role of Organized Crime in Society

Organized crime is a business, and like any business its objective is to maximize profits. It is different than legitimate businesses in that it operates in the illegal market which imposes certain conditions that do not pertain to legal enterprises. Nevertheless, organized crime is motivated by the same fundamental assumptions that control conventional business activities, namely, the need to create, retain, and extend a share of the market.[17] Organized crime becomes more understandable when it is seen as entrepreneurship that is defined as illegal.

Since no business survives without customers, it is obvious that a considerable market exists for the goods and services that organized crime provides. These goods and services—drugs, gambling, sex, usurous loans, waste dumping, to name a few—are in demand by a significant portion of the population but are not provided by legitimate businesses. In most cases they are forbidden by law because they are contrary to moral principles to which a substantial number of us subscribe, although in practice both principle and law are violated with enough frequency to create a lucrative market for illicit suppliers. Without public demand, organized crime would have little or no function.

Providing goods and services that are wanted by consumers but are illegal allows crime groups to make substantial profits. The amount of profit is determined by the risk involved for the provider and the fact that the commodity is in short supply. Such profit has been referred to as "the crime tariff,"[18] or the cost consumers pay for illegal goods or services which are unavailable in the legitimate market and which may cause the supplier to be arrested and prosecuted. The crime tariff assures profitability and makes the business of organized crime worthwhile. Because risk varies by activity, however, the tariff is greater for some activities than for others. Heroin importation and distribution is better policed and more heavily sanctioned than growing and selling marijuana, for example; therefore, it is more profitable. While the cost of each substance reflects the risk involved to the supplier, the market for each is assured since there are no legal alternative sources for the drugs.

Organized crime groups devote considerable time and attention to minimizing risk. One way to do this is to operate within a limited area in order to control the operating environment.[19] Because new risks are encountered with growth, organized crime groups tend not to expand too widely nor to acquire new markets, as profitable as this might be. The transportation of illegal goods, communication among accomplices, protection from the law, all become more difficult and riskier with growth and territorial expansion. As one observer states, this "helps to explain why most organized crime groups operate in a small and limited area. . . . Effective and efficient organization guarantees a continuation of significant profits; greed and overexpansion may well spell the end of the enterprise all together."[20]

Risk is also diminished through the corruption of public officials. Without such corruption, organized crime would have a difficult time carrying on its illegal activities. Because there is considerable public ambivalence about the illegal nature of some organized crime activities forbidden by law (gambling, for example), social control agents are often able to justify lax enforcement and even outright bribery. In addition, the availability of huge amounts of money to offer public officials makes it very difficult for them to resist requests from organized criminals to assist their enterprises in various subtle ways. Police officers may selectively enforce laws to favor an organized crime group, or deliberately overlook criminal activity on the part of syndicate operators. Politicians may use their political clout to assist criminals in the courts, before zoning boards, or in legislatures. All this, of course, is in exchange for direct payoffs, campaign contributions, or even the delivery of votes.

Collusion among organized criminals, the police, and politicians appears to be as old as such crime itself and essential to its strength and profitability.[21] As we have seen, organized crime has endured over a long period of time despite repeated efforts by law enforcement and congressional committees to eradicate it. It has survived by being a part of the political establishment and by continuing to provide goods and services wanted by a willing public. Although some commodities have changed over time, those that exist today continue to make organized crime a powerful force in our society.

Experts agree that the illegal drug trade is organized crime's most profitable business. Revenues from drug sales have been estimated to be between $81[22] and $100[23] billion each year. Processing and importing drugs, especially heroin and cocaine, are done by large crime groups, usually with international connections. The distribution of drugs on the streets is typically controlled by local, neighborhood groups which operate as retailers in the marketing process. Law enforcement attempts to curb the drug trade have been largely unsuccessful, since the crime bosses are virtually immune from arrest and prosecution and street pushers are easily replaced if arrested.

Organized crime has been supplying illegal drugs to consumers since the implementation of the Harrison Act in 1914, the original federal law outlawing narcotic drugs. Criminalizing drug use created a black market which organized crime quickly satisfied. Later, in 1937, when marijuana was added to the list of prohibited substances, the market enlarged, as it did again in 1970 when synthetic drugs (amphetamines and barbiturates, for example) were included. Ironically, legal attempts to deter use have expanded organized crime's market and make the drug trade more profitable.

Another lucrative service provided by organized crime groups is gambling. A Presidential Commission has estimated that Americans spend more than $59 billion a year on illegal gambling.[24] While this may appear surprising when legal gambling is increasingly available, it is understandable when one remembers that illegal gains are not taxed, telephoned bets are accepted, and credit may be extended to the gambler. The most popular forms of illegal gambling are betting on sporting events (bookmaking) and playing the numbers (a form of lottery). Each of these appeals to working class people who tend to believe that winning will make their lives easier.

Since the 1940s, organized crime groups have been involved in Las Vegas gambling, often as the hidden owners of large casinos.[25] In addition to making legal profits from casino gambling, they also engage in "skimming," the practice of stealing part of the money spent by patrons before it is tallied for tax purposes. While the presence of organized crime groups in Atlantic City is not debated, their relationship to that city's casino industry is unclear.[26] It is known that they are involved with many of the industries that support and service the hotels and casinos, and in that way exert an unhealthy influence on the gambling industry.

It is estimated that organized crime groups earn between $2 and $3 billion each year from interest on loans for which they charge very high and illegal rates of interest.[27] Known as loansharking, this activity caters to those who are unable to secure a legitimate loan and are desperate for cash. Customers include those with bad credit records, or persons in need of quick cash, perhaps to cover a failing business or a gambling debt. The services of the loanshark are popular because they are secret, informal, and convenient.[28] Transactions are not subject to public scrutiny or credit checks, no applications need be completed, and cash is available immediately. For this, borrowers may pay as much as 20 percent a week in interest on the principal. Although failure to pay may lead to violence, that consequence is quite rare and exists more in stereotype than in reality. Loansharks tend to deal with customers who pay off their loans and often return to borrow again.[29]

Another commodity provided by organized crime groups is illicit sex. According to one study, "Sex services run the gamut from prostitution, after-hours clubs catering to solicitation of various sexual preferences, and pornography outlets, to the production of pornographic films."[30] Providing sex to willing customers is nothing new for organized crime, although its nature and organization has changed. At one time, large and profitable prostitution rings were operated under the direction of organized criminals and their associates. Brothel prostitutes, streetwalkers, and call girls were often recruited and employed by crime groups which ran the business and offered the women protection. More recently, with changing sexual mores and the decline of organized prostitution, other sex services have become more profitable, and now seem to occupy more of the attention of organized crime groups. Clubs featuring exotic dancers, sex shops with live shows sometimes viewed through peepholes, pornographic book and film stores, and the production of pornographic films are now more profitable ventures, and may even be legal.

When American labor unions were attempting to organize workers, they sometimes turned to crime groups for help in combatting the hired thugs of management. Thus marked the entry of organized crime into what has come to be called "labor racketeering." By controlling certain unions, organized criminals have placed themselves in a position to have a powerful impact on the economy and on the lives of thousands of working men and women. They have negotiated "sweetheart contracts" that benefit themselves more than their union members, accepted kickbacks, drained union pension funds for their own enrichment, and driven up the cost of many goods and services essential to the national economy. Often, legitimate union members have been killed or beaten when they have opposed their corrupt leadership. While this pattern of labor crime has been found in several industries and the unions associated with them, the worst case may well be the Teamsters Union, one of the country's largest and most powerful. Until recently, a pattern of illegality involving organized criminals has existed in the national Teamsters Union and its locals that have been the subject of countless investigations and indictments.

Just as organized crime groups have infiltrated legitimate trade unions, they have also entered many legal businesses, often bringing their illegal tactics with them. A good example of this is the waste industry.[31] In many areas of the country, especially the large metropolitan regions of the Northeast, trash hauling has been controlled by organized crime since the 1940s. During that time, this essential business was marked by unfair trade practices, rigged bids, kickbacks to officials, and even violence among competitors. Profits are huge for company owners and their protectors in the mob, with consumers paying inflated prices for garbage removal. But the illegality of many of these companies has gotten even worse. They have recently moved into the collection and disposal of toxic wastes, bringing with them the same tactics used for years in the solid waste business. In addition, the difficulty associated with the disposal of toxic waste has led to their dumping it in sanitary landfills, sewers, waterways, fields, and on highways from the back of tanker trucks. While some have argued that there are few "victims" of organized crime since most of the consumers of their goods and services are willing participants, this cannot be said for those innocent persons adversely affected by the contamination of the land and water around them.

In addition to waste disposal, organized crime has entered numerous other legitimate businesses, using the huge profits made from illegal activities to gain entry. This not only helps clean their "dirty" money, it gives them vast new opportunities to use illegal techniques to gain market advantage and increase profits. One commentator has indicated that organized crime groups have already entered many areas of big business, including banking, construction, credit cards, entertainment, real estate, securities, and various others.[32] Sometimes, a reciprocal relationship develops between the legitimate and illegitimate participants in a business, with their coming to rely on each other for services and favors. In this way, organized crime becomes integrated into a community's business structure and criminals assume a powerful role in its economic and political life.

Explanations of Organized Crime

At least three explanations of the origins and perpetuation of organized crime have been offered: alien conspiracy theory, ethnic succession theory, and enterprise theory. While each recognizes the existence of organized crime in American society, they differ greatly in their interpretations of its meaning and function.

The alien conspiracy theory views organized crime as an evil imposed on our society by a foreign conspiracy.[33] According to this theory, these foreigners, usually Italians of Sicilian extraction, have infiltrated our society and created a secret organization, the Mafia, that is undermining the American way of life; the Mafia, controlling all organized crime in the United States, is governed by a national commission of gang leaders who coordinate a well-orchestrated attack on our traditional values. This explanation of organized crime seems to have arisen in the 1950s and was quickly adopted by law enforcement agencies, especially at the federal level. It provided a simple explanation by creating a conspicuous scapegoat who transplanted this type of criminality from another culture. This concept of organized crime gained popularity in the media as well as with the public.

Often referred to as the "Mafia myth,"[34] this explanation is no longer accepted by either law enforcement officials or social scientists. In addition to being unable to explain organized crime before the arrival of the ominous foreigners, this idea fails to recognize that organized crime groups simply respond to the needs or desires of customers who want the goods or services that are for sale. Before the arrival of the Italians other groups furnished them, and in recent years, non-Italian groups and independent entrepreneurs have played a larger role in such activities. This is not to say, of course, that many organized crime groups have not been ethnically similar. They have, but more for reasons having to do with kinship, friendship, patterns of recruitment, and trust than with an alien conspiracy.

The ethnic nature of many organized crime groups has also supported the notion that disadvantaged minorities have used such criminality to achieve upward social mobility.[35] Francis Ianni states, "How do you escape poverty through socially approved routes when such routes are often foreign to the ghetto life? Crime resolves the dilemma because it provides a quick if perilous route out."[36] He notes that every major ethnic group has faced the problem and has chosen organized crime as one solution. While each group quickly assimilates the goals of the new society, it takes some time for it to achieve the legitimate means to attain those goals. In the meantime, groups must "innovate" or devise whatever means work to share the rewards of the new society.[37] Organized crime may be considered to be one such innovation.

As the assimilation process progresses and legitimate means to attain society's goals are achieved, later generations of each group find less need to use organized crime as a vehicle for upward mobility. Just as one ethnic group has succeeded the other in its involvement in crime groups, so too one has followed the other in its attainment of education, legitimate jobs, and respectability. While this theory cannot account for those who experience the deprivations of ethnic groups but do not become criminals, or those who become organized criminals although they are not members of deprived ethnic groups, it does demonstrate that deprived social status may contribute to crime causation.

Clearly, neither conspiracy nor ethnic succession theories appear to be adequate in explaining the etiology of organized crime. Instead, modern scholars have turned increasingly to enterprise theory,[38] or some modification of it. In fact, the basic tenets of that perspective had been used throughout this discussion of organized crime. Enterprise theorists maintain that there is no evidence of a nationwide conspiracy to control organized crime activities, that such activities are not limited to members of certain ethnic groups, and that the use of violence by organized crime groups is exaggerated. Instead, organized crime groups are local in nature, typically have shifting and overlapping memberships, and can often achieve their goals because they are believed to be violent and benefit from their bad reputation.[39]

The essence of enterprise theory, however, is that organized crime groups and legitimate business groups are engaged in similar activities, providing goods and services to consumers. Organized crime exists because the legitimate market does not meet the needs of a substantial number of buyers. While one type of business deals with legal products, the other deals with illegal products. The behaviors, ideas, beliefs and values that motivate the legitimate business person are the same as those that motivate the organized criminal. Markets must be found and maintained, goods and services provided, risk reduced, and competition controlled, all good business objectives whether the product is textbooks or illegal drugs. Organized crime, then, is like any other business.

Combatting Organized Crime

Because law enforcement and political leaders have traditionally viewed organized crime as the product of evil persons or groups imposing their criminality on a law-abiding society, typical control techniques have focused on the prosecution of individuals.[40] Assuming that the crimes would disappear if the criminals were removed from society, local and federal law enforcement agencies have launched countless investigations over the years, often resulting in the arrest, prosecution, and imprisonment of organized crime figures. These efforts have been aided by special congressional hearings, federal strike forces, a witness protection program, local crime commissions, investigative grand juries, the use of informants, and a variety of other methods and programs designed to attack organized crime.[41]

Among the most comprehensive efforts directed at organized crime groups was the 1970 Organized Crime Control Act, in particular its provision creating the Racketeer Influence and Corrupt Organizations Act (RICO).[42] RICO imposes stiff penalties on those convicted in federal court of various racketeering offenses, requires those convicted to forfeit any property acquired by or used in criminal activity, and allows the federal government to bring civil action against suspected criminals. The latter provision of the Act is important because the standard of proof is not as great in civil court as it is in criminal court, and allows the opportunity to extract large monetary judgments from defendants. Since the inception of RICO, a large number of reputed crime bosses and their underlings, principally members of the old Italian-American gangs, have been convicted under its provisions, but the activities of other organized crime groups have not been diminished.

Some critics have suggested that the only effective way to control organized crime is to take away its access to illegal profits.[43] This could be done by legalizing many of the illegal goods and services that are in demand but legally unavailable. This is particularly true of gambling and drugs, both of which could be legalized, taxed, and controlled by the government, thereby divesting crime groups of those markets. Deprived of the revenue from its two chief money makers, organized crime would have less capital to fund other illegal activities and to corrupt public officials. Since organized crime has become an integral part of our social structure, as proponents charge, only real change in the definition of victimless or consensual crimes will be effective in controlling it. Opponents argue, however, that organized crime would continue to offer advantages that the legitimate market could not match and that it would continue to operate. In addition, legalizing the so-called victimless crimes would legitimize them and encourage their use by some who would otherwise not consider them.

At the present time, major social policy reform appears unlikely, and controlling organized crime groups will remain a law enforcement function. Even though this approach has not proven to be very effective, that seems to be how Americans want it.

Conclusion

Organized crime groups have operated in America since Colonial days, filling a market niche by providing certain goods and services defined by law as illegal but coveted by consumers nevertheless. Whatever the illegal goods and services, the fact that they are outlawed means that lucrative profits can be attached to making them available. Driven by the profit motive, groups of criminals have organized to satisfy consumer demand and protect their markets from competitors as well as from social control agents. Violence, or at least its threat, and political corruption are common mechanisms used by these groups to achieve their goals. Seen in this way, there is nothing very mysterious about organized crime. The stratified and heterogenous nature of our society encourages socially marginal groups to use organized crime activities as a means of achieving material goals and even some social standing within the community. The makeup of organized crime groups has changed over time, however, and continues to change today, as legitimate opportunities for social mobility become available and replace organized crime as a ladder toward upward mobility.

Because organized crime is built into our social, economic, and political structures, it has survived repeated attempts to eradicate it. As local gang leaders and even entire gangs fall, others replace them, and control shifts to a new group of organized criminals. Illegal goods and services continue to be provided, needs of otherwise good citizens continue to be met, and corruption continues to be part of the legal and political systems. In this sense, organized crime appears to be "an American way of life."[44]

Discussion Questions

1. What are the characteristics of organized crime? Which model of organized crime is perpetuated by the U.S. Justice Department and remains popular among the public, but is questioned by criminologists?

2. Trace the history of organized crime. How did it begin in the seventeenth and eighteenth centuries? What caused small gangs to grow, then solidify into large crime groups? What part did race and ethnicity play in this process? What ethnic groups are involved in organized crime today?

3. In what ways is organized crime similar to large organizations or businesses? What goods/services does it provide? How is the amount of profit determined? What is a crime tariff?

Notes

1. Howard Abadinsky, *Organized Crime*, Chicago, Nelson-Hall, 1985; Joseph L. Albini, *The American Mafia: Genesis of a Legend*, New York, Appleton-Century-Crofts, 1971.

2. Gary W. Potter, *Criminal Organizations: Vice, Racketeering, and Politics in an American City*, Prospect Heights, IL, Waveland, 1994.

3. National Advisory Committee on Criminal Justice Standards and Goals, *Organized Crime: Report of the Task Force on Organized Crime*, Washington, D.C., U.S. Department of Justice, 1976.

4. Abadinsky, op. cit.; Albini, op. cit.

5. Ibid.

6. Michael Maltz, "On Defining 'Organized Crime': The Development of a Definition and a Typology," *Crime and Delinquency* 22:336-348, 1976.

7. Potter, op. cit., p. 173.

8. Francis A.J. Ianni and E. Reuss-Ianni, *A Family Business: Kinship and Social Control in Or-*

ganized Crime, New York, Russell Sage Foundation, 1972, p. 5.

9. Dennis J. Kenney and James O. Finckenauer, *Organized Crime in America*, New York, Wadsworth, 1994, chap. 3.

10. Abadinsky, op. cit., p. 53.

11. Ibid.

12. Kenney and Finckenauer, op. cit., chap. 6.

13. Ibid., chap. 9.

14. Humbert S. Nelli, "A Brief History of American Syndicate Crime," in T. Bynum, ed., *Organized Crime in America: Concepts and Controversies*, Monsey, N.Y., Criminal Justice Press, pp. 15-29.

15. Ibid.; Kenney and Finckenauer, op. cit., pp. 252-255.

16. President's Commission on Organized Crime, *Organized Crime Today*, Washington, D.C., U.S. Government Printing Office, 1985, pp. 58-128.

17. Dwight C. Smith, Jr., "Paragons, Pariahs, and Pirates: A Spectrum-Based Theory of Enterprise," *Crime and Delinquency*, 26:358-386, 1980.

18. Stuart Hills, *Crime, Power and Morality: The Criminal Law Process in the United States*, Scranton, PA, Chandler, 1971.

19. Potter, op. cit., pp. 130-131.

20. Ibid., p. 131.

21. Mark Haller, *History of Organized Crime: 1920-1945*, Washington, D.C., National Institute on Law Enforcement and Criminal Justice, U.S. Government Printing Office, 1976.

22. Alan A. Block and William Chambliss, *Organizing Crime*, New York, Elsevier, 1981.

23. Erich Goode, *Drugs in American Society*, New York, McGraw-Hill, 1989.

24. President's Commission on Organized Crime, *Organized Crime and Gambling*, Washington, D.C., U.S. Government Printing Office, 1985.

25. Humbert S. Nelli, *The Business of Crime*, New York, Oxford, 1976.

26. Ovid Demaris, *The Boardwalk Jungle*, New York, Bantam, 1986.

27. James Cook, "The Invisible Enterprise," *Forbes*, September 29, 1980.

28. John Seidl, "Loan-sharking," in L. Savitz and N. Johnson, eds., *Crime in Society*, New York, Wiley, 1978.

29. Jonathan Rubenstein and Peter Reuter, *Bookmaking in New York*, New York, Policy Sciences Center, Inc., 1978.

30. Potter, op. cit., p. 91.

31. Alan A. Block and Frank R. Scarpitti, *Poisoning for Profit: The Mafia and Toxic Waste in America*, New York, Morrow, 1985.

32. Ralph Salerno, as cited in Alan A. Block, "Thoughts on the History of Organized Crime: In Praise of Revisionist Criminology," paper presented at the annual meeting of the American Society of Criminology, 1990, p. 16.

33. Dwight C. Smith, Jr., *The Mafia Mystique*, New York, Basic Books, 1975; and "Mafia: The Prototypical Alien Conspiracy," *The Annals of the American Academy of Political and Social Science* 423:75-88, January 1976.

34. Gordon Hawkins, "God and the Mafia," *The Public Interest* 14:24-51, 1969; Kenney and Finckenauer, op. cit., pp. 230-250.

35. Ianni and Reuss-Ianni, op. cit.; Francis A.J. Ianni, *Ethnic Succession in Organized Crime*, Washington, D.C., U.S. Department of Justice, Law Enforcement Assistance Administration, December 1973.

36. Ianni, Ibid., p. 13.

37. Robert K. Merton, "Social Structure and Anomie," *American Sociological Review* 3:672-682, 1938.

38. Smith, op. cit., 1980; Dwight C. Smith, Jr., "Organized Crime and Entrepreneurship," *International Journal of Criminology and Penology* 6:161-177, 1978.

39. Peter Reuter, "The Value of a Bad Reputation," Santa Monica, CA, Rand Corporation, 1982.

40. Smith, op. cit., 1978.

41. Kenney and Finckenauer, op. cit., pp. 324-341.

42. Ibid., pp. 317-323.

43. Ibid., pp. 364-369.

44. Daniel Bell, *The End of Ideology*, Glencoe, IL, Free Press, 1964.

34

Casinos and Banking: Organized Crime in the Bahamas

Alan A. Block
Frank R. Scarpitti

Revenues derived by organized crime from its many illegal enterprises total billions of dollars each year. In many instances it is necessary to "clean" the "dirty" money by laundering it through a legitimate enterprise. Money laundering may be accomplished in a number of ways, but perhaps the most common technique is to invest in legitimate enterprises. Using its tainted money from drugs, prostitution, pornography, gambling and other criminal activities, organized crime has invested in real estate, construction, entertainment, the food industry, and other areas of commerce. Often bringing their usual business tactics to these endeavors, crime syndicates gain an unfair advantage while corrupting entire markets.

In this selection Alan A. Block and Frank R. Scarpitti examine the relationship between offshore banks and gambling casinos in the Bahamas. Caribbean casinos have been used by U.S. organized crime figures to launder money since the 1940s, while being a source of new profits as well. Since many countries in that area have strict bank secrecy laws, local banks have also been established for the purpose of tax evasion. In the Bahamas, these interests merged as local developers and politicians worked to attract casinos through favorable legislation, especially regarding gambling and banking. The resort town of Freeport, for example, was developed largely through the efforts

of organized criminals and their business and government supporters.

The influence of organized crime on the Bahamas has been dramatic and long lasting. Government corruption has been noted by many commentators, and the islands of that nation continue to be used as a transshipment point for drug money from South to North America. Numerous investigations of the offshore banks have turned up cases of tax fraud and evasion by U.S. citizens. No island paradise is exempt from the effects of organized crime.

Within the past few years, both the President's Commission on Organized Crime and the U.S. Senate's Permanent Subcommittee on Investigations have reported on the extensive use of offshore banks and businesses by American criminal interests to launder money and evade taxes (Permanent Subcommittee on Investigations, 1983; President's Commission on Organized Crime, 1984). A recent government report "concludes that the use of so-called 'secret' offshore facilities has become so pervasive that it challenges basic assumptions regarding the ability of federal and state authorities to enforce the laws" (Permanent Subcommittee on Investigations, 1983:1). Such enterprises are established in tax haven countries around the world, but for a number of reasons, those in the Caribbean have grown fastest in recent years and now appear to control billions of dollars of illegally gained and untaxed money. Although the Caribbean's proximity to the United States makes it especially attractive to Americans wanting to hide money, its development as an important stop in the South American drug traffic and the fact that some countries have stringent bank secrecy laws also contribute to its contemporary popularity. In fact, a few Caribbean nations have been so corrupted by illegal foreign dollars that they have virtually offered themselves as crime havens (Permanent Subcommittee on Investigations, 1983:49-95).

Among the Caribbean nations active in hosting offshore enterprises owned by Americans have been the Bahamas. Like all tax havens, the Bahamas are characterized by the essential elements of strict rules of bank secrecy and little or no taxes. Since 1965 bank secrecy has been based on legislation which prohibits and punishes the disclosure by a bank employee of an account holder's name or financial situation (the 1965 legislation increased the severity of the crime of disclosure). The strict secrecy associated with banks also applies to the activities and ownership of corporations. In addition, there are no income, profit, capital gains, gift, inheritance, estate or withholding taxes in the Bahamas. Although the nation does tax imports and some real property, this has little effect on those who own or use its many banks and corporations. Hence, for a small initial cost and annual fee, one may own a bank or company that can receive and disburse large sums of money in complete secrecy and without the threat of taxation. These advantages, of course, are available to bank depositors as well.

Even though offshore tax havens may provide legitimate investment opportunities for American citizens wishing to avoid taxes, a practice recognized as lawful by U.S. courts, it is the evasion of taxes by using tax haven services that now concerns law enforcement authorities. "Tax evasion . . . involves acts intended to misrepresent or to conceal facts in an effort to escape lawful tax liability" (Workman, 1982:667). Tax havens may be used to hide income or to misrepresent the nature of transactions in order to put the taxpayer in a more favorable tax position. A corollary problem concerns the "laundering" of illegal money gained from strictly criminal activity. This "is the process by which one conceals the existence, illegal source, or illegal application of income, and then disguises that income to make it appear legitimate" (President's Commission on Organized Crime, 1984:1). Off-shore tax havens, with their strict secrecy laws, dependence on foreign deposits, and disregard for the sources of overseas cash, provide ideal vehicles for assorted racketeers, drug dealers and financial manipulators to hide "dirty" money while it is being cleaned for further use. For both the tax evader and money launderer, the offshore haven guarantees that any paper trail will be blocked.

The popularity of the Bahamas as an offshore tax haven may be seen in the amount of corporate and bank activity which it hosts. This small island nation of just over 200,000 inhabitants has some 15,000 active companies and 330 chartered banks, or one bank for ever 600 residents (Lernoux, 1984:85). Nevertheless, Bahamian banks held over $95 billion of foreign assets in 1978 (Workman, 1982:680) and a 1979 Ford Foundation study estimated that the flow of U.S. criminal and tax evasion money into the Bahamas was $20 billion per year (Blum and Kaplan, 1979).

Even though the accuracy of these figures may be questioned, due largely to the Bahamian government's and banking industry's reluctance to provide reliable data, it seems obvious that the American contribution to these questionable assets constitutes a considerable resource for the Bahamas and a substantial loss in taxes for the United States.

The Bahamas evolved into an offshore haven for tax evaders and money launderers in a very short period of time. The process included receptive public officials, international entrepreneurs and American racketeers entering into formal and informal relationships designed to serve their respective financial positions. A partial examination of the history of the Bahamas reveals the extent of the collusion among political, business, and criminal interests to serve their illicit purposes.

This history also demonstrates the important relationship between offshore banks and gambling casinos. In fact, key Bahamian offshore banks were formed by or for individuals deeply involved in Nevada casinos and who subsequently played big roles in developing the first large-scale, modern casinos in the Bahamas. Most likely, the relationship between the casinos and banks emerged in order to hide the casinos' "skim," that portion of casino profits unreported to taxing authorities. The historical material which follows discusses those individuals whose mutual interests embraced both casino gambling and haven banking and who were instrumental in providing organized criminal elements with both an economic bonanza and sanctuary.

The Making of Freeport

The process started on Grand Bahama Island located about 60 miles from the Florida coast. The prime mover on Grand Bahama was an American named Wallace Groves who first came to the Bahamas in the 1930's. Groves' background had been in investment trusts administered through a firm called Equity Corporation which he sold for $750,000. Following this, he became affiliated with a company known as the General Investment Corporation. After these deals were in place, Groves sailed to the Bahamas, started two Bahamian companies (Nassau Securities Ltd. and North American Ltd.), and purchased an island, Little Whale Cay, about 35 miles from Nassau, the capital of the country. During this first, eventful trip, Groves met Stafford Sands, a member of the local political elite known as the Bay Street Boys. This elite was composed of certain merchants and attorneys who met on a regular basis after work in a club located on Bay and Charlotte Streets in Nassau. They were invariably white and, by the standards of the Bahamas, wealthy and influential. The Bay Street Boys controlled Bahamian development, both the licit and illicit, until 1967 when the first black Prime Minister was elected (United Kingdom, 1971).

Unfortunately for Groves, in the late fall of 1938 he was indicted on numerous counts of mail fraud and looting the General Investment Corporation of almost one million dollars. Eventually, Groves was convicted and sentenced to two years in prison. He was released in 1944 and returned to the Bahamas. During Groves' time of troubles, his associate, Stafford Sands, was busy arranging a way for casinos to operate legally. Sands successfully sponsored a bill in the Assembly which allowed casinos under certain circumstances. By securing a Certificate of Exemption from the local government, a gambling casino could operate with what amounted to a government license. The bill passed in 1939 and certificates of exemption were granted to two small casinos which had been operating illegally for years.[1]

It was in the 1950's that Groves, Sands, and others to be discussed shortly put their talents together on Grand Bahama Island. They created a new city, Freeport, which soon had a casino and several significant "haven" banks. Stafford Sands, who had become Chairman of the Bahamas Development Board (equivalent to Minister of Tourism) in the 1950's, crafted legislation "to establish a port and an industrial complex" on Grand Bahama Island (United Kingdom, 1971:6). The Hawksbill Creek Act, as the legislation was entitled, was signed on August 4, 1955. The deal called for Groves to "organize a company, to be called the Grand Bahama Port Authority Limited, which would undertake to dredge and construct a deep water harbour and turning basin at Hawksbill Creek as a preliminary aid for factories and other industrial undertakings to be set up there" (United Kingdom, 1971:6). In return, the government made available thousands of acres of Crown Land to the Port Authority for one pound per acre (equivalent then to around $2.80 an acre). In fact, by 1960 Groves' company had acquired a total of 138,296 acres which was officially "designated as a town (Freeport) in Grand Bahama" (United Kingdom, 1971:6).

The terms of the initial Hawksbill Creek Act allowed "that the whole of Freeport was to be the private property of the Port Authority in whom was vested the supreme right to its administration and control" (United Kingdom, 1971:16). An analysis of the legislation by a Royal Commission in 1971 commented on this extraordinary transfer of authority noting that the company had "exclusive responsibility" for traditional governmental services such as education, health, communications, energy "and all other public utilities and services and services and the performance of all aviation activities." The Commission also wrote that no one was allowed to interfere with the Port Authority's decisions, especially in awarding licenses or otherwise controlling firms doing business in Freeport.

The major shareholders of The Grand Bahama Port Authority in 1959 included Wallace Groves and his wife, Georgette, who individually held a small amount of shares but whose company, Abaco Lumber, held almost one million. Other significant owners were Variant Industries which represented the interests of Charles W. Hayward, an English entrepreneur, and held just over one half million shares; Charles Allen, whose family's financial interests in New York and Hollywood (especially motion picture companies) were very extensive and who held over a quarter million shares; Arthur Rubloff, a Chicago real estate agent, who had over 70,000 shares; and Charles C. Goldsmith, who owned about 100,000 shares and listed his affiliation in 1959 as the New York Cosmos Bank. Wallace Groves was the company's Director and Charles Hayward and his son, Jack, were other important officers (Grand Bahama Port Authority, 1959). Although Allen and Goldsmith appeared to play no managerial role in the company, they "were well aware that the major partner in the enterprise . . . was . . . a convicted stock manipulator who had served time in federal prison for mail fraud and conspiracy" (McClintick, 1982:89).

Even with his new financiers, Groves' project was barely limping along in 1960. Because the industrial development of Freeport was extremely far off, perhaps far-fetched, Groves and others decided that Freeport could best be developed around tourism. Hence, an amendment to the original Hawksbill Creek Act was enacted which, among other things, allowed the Port Authority to build a "first-class deluxe resort hotel" (United Kingdom, 1971:7). By the time the hotel was completed in 1963, it had the added attraction of a casino, and the Bahamas had become the new Caribbean headquarters of Meyer Lansky's underworld gambling enterprise.

Lansky had operated in the Caribbean for quite some time, of course, running casinos in Cuba with the full cooperation of that country's government. With the overthrow of Battista, however, American organized crime figures and their gambling operations were no longer welcomed and were soon thrown out of the country by Fidel Castro. Even before that actually happened, Lansky was looking around for another site in the Caribbean, a place where tourists from the United States would come for the sun and the gambling, where local officials would be cooperative, and where he could establish a worldwide gambling empire (Messick, 1971:225). The Bahamas appeared to be the ideal spot.

According to Lansky biographer, Hank Messick, the gambling czar moved quickly once he decided to seek additional fortunes in the Bahamas. Early in 1960 he dispatched an associate, Louis Chesler, to the islands to meet with

Groves and Sands, presumably to discuss plans by which the Port Authority would be salvaged and gambling established in Freeport (Messick, 1971:228). In order to accomplish the first part of the plan, the Port Authority formed a company called Grand Bahama Development Corporation (known as DEVCO). DEVCO immediately placed Chesler on its Board of Directors, giving him an official position in the Bahamas from which he could supervise the development of casino gambling. Another Lansky associate, Max Orovitz, was also placed on the DEVCO board (Grand Bahama Development Corporation, 1964). But it was Chesler who would protect Lansky's interests and serve as a dominant force in the early development of Bahamian gambling.

Chesler's earliest known contacts with organized crime began in 1942 when he had as partners in several businesses John Pullman and Pullman's brother-in-law. A.C. Cowan (McClintick, 1982:87-93). Pullman, an important associate of Meyer Lansky for a number of decades, had served a prison term for bootlegging in the early 1930's. By the mid-1950's, Pullman had moved to Canada and been granted Canadian citizenship (Charbonneau, 1976). Chesler, also Canadian, had a series of dealings with Lansky and Lansky's associates prior to the formation of DEVCO which are revealing. He hired, for instance, a key Lansky operative, Mike McLaney, as the manager of a Miami Beach dinner club which Chesler owned.

In 1958, Chesler's association with Lansky became more visible through the financial machinations of Maxwell Golhar, another of his partners. Golhar became Chairman of the Board of an enterprise called New Mylamaque Explorations Ltd. A well-known Lansky associate, Sam Garfield, purchased 100,000 shares of New Mylamaque which he divided in the following manner: Edward Levinson, 50,000 shares; Moe Dalitz, former Cleveland racketeer, 25,000; and Allard Roen, 25,000. Roen's shares were then divided further with Ben Siegelbaum receiving 15,000 and Meyer Lansky 10,000. Finally, 50,000 more shares of New Mylamaque were parceled out, with 10,000 going to Dalitz, 15,00 to Siegelbaum, and 25,000 to Lansky. This same group of investors also provided capital for Miami's new international airport hotel in

1958. Other investors in the hotel (brought in by Lansky and Chesler) were Bryant B. Burton, connected to the Sands and Freemont Hotels in Las Vegas, and Jack Cooper, who owned a highly successful dog track in Miami (New York State Senate, n.d.a.).

With the formation of DEVCO there was only one hurdle left to transform Freeport into a center for casino gambling run by organized crime. That hurdle was acquiring the necessary Certificate of Exemption. The second Certificate ever granted in the Bahamas was offered on March 27, 1963, to a new company called Bahamas Amusement Ltd., which had been formed only the previous week. The Certificate allowed Bahamas Amusement to operate a casino at the Lucayan Beach Hotel in Freeport. In order to secure the Certificate a considerable amount of money had been passed to key members of the government by DEVCO. Stafford Sands acted as the financial intermediary between DEVCO and Sands' political cronies who were hired as "consultants" and paid very handsome fees (United Kingdom, 1967). The original directors of Bahamas Amusement included Chesler, Georgette Groves, and a member of the Hayward family.

Less than a week after the Certificate was granted, there were meetings attended by Meyer Lansky and his brother, Jake, Lou Chesler, Max Orovitz, and others to discuss issues concerning both the hotel and the casino, called the Monte Carlo. A number of important Lansky racketeers were hired to work in the casino, including Dino Cellini, George Saldo, Charles Brudner, Max Courtney, and Frank Ritter. Other subjects discussed at this time included the purchase of casino equipment from Las Vegas and probably the Beverly Hills Club in Newport, Kentucky, and the establishing of a casino training school in London, England (United Kingdom, 1967; Messick, 1971; Block and Klausner, 1985-86). About ten months after the Certificate was granted, the hotel and casino formally opened with the Lansky men firmly entrenched in casino management as well as overseers of all credit arrangements.

Bahamian Banks

Let us now turn to those banks formed by or for individuals with multi-million dollar invest-

ments in Nevada casinos and deeply involved in the Freeport development. John Pullman, mentioned above as a Chesler associate since 1942 and, in effect, an important member of Meyer Lansky's organized crime syndicate, was responsible for putting the banks and casinos together. Pullman, recently identified as a "Canadian organized crime figure" (Pennsylvania Crime Commission, 1980:195), was instrumental in forming two banks (with subsequent numerous off-shoots) created to handle the skim from the Monte Carlo and most likely the Sands and Frontier casinos in Nevada (New York State Senate, n.d.a).

The bank connected to the Monte Carlo was the International Credit Bank (ICB) which was formed by John Pullman in partnership with Dr. Tibor Rosenbaum (New York State Senate, n.d.c). The bank was located in Geneva, Switzerland, with branches in the Bahamas. The major shareholder was a trust (international Credit Trust) resident in Vaduz, Lichtenstein. At least part of the Monte Carlo skim undoubtedly traveled from the casino to the Bahamian branch of Pullman's ICB, then to Switzerland, and ultimately to the obscurity of Lichtenstein. Other more direct but clumsy avenues for the skim no doubt existed. For instance, a Royal Commission reported that "large quantities of cash up to $60,000, and in one case $120,000, were being despatched by the Amusements Company to the Marine Midland Grace Trust Co., of New York. They were being parceled up in Pauli Girl beer cartons" (United Kingdom, 1967:19).

Although formed as a conduit for unreported casino profits, the ICB quickly developed additional interests. One of the early major clients for ICB Geneva, for example, was Investor Overseas Services, the infamous mutual fund operation run by Bernard Cornfeld and later looted by Robert Vesco. The relationship between the fund and the bank became exceptionally close when ICB people were used to smuggle money out of various countries into Switzerland on behalf of mutual fund clients. One of the principal ICB money couriers, Sylvain Ferdman, was identified as an organized crime money mover by Life magazine in 1967. Ferdman performed the same function for another Bahamian bank called Atlas Bank. Actually, Ferdman and Dr. Rosenbaum were two of the directors of Atlas. A close scrutiny of both Atlas and ICB indicates they were virtually identical in ownership, management and function. Furthermore, there is some evidence to suggest that ICB and Atlas, which both had several branches or permutations, were also linked to another bank located in Beirut, Lebanon, which, in turn, appeared to own a major Lebanese casino (*Fortune*, 1966:93).

The ICB and Atlas banks are two primary examples of the links between organized crime gamblers and the offshore banking industry put together in the Bahamas. Another major example involving the same cast was the Bank of World Commerce, formed on September 21, 1961, most likely to launder the skim from Nevada casinos (New York State Senate, n.d.c; Wall Street Journal, 1976). John Pullman was the president and director, while the former Lieutenant Governor of Nevada, Clifford A. Jones, was one of the larger shareholders, holding about 8% of the total. The other directors included Alvin I. Malnik and Philip J. Matthews who owned about 32 percent of the shares.

Malnik was believed to have been one of Meyer Lansky's closest associates and, when Lansky died in 1982, some speculated that Malnik may have inherited much of Lansky's action (New York State Senate, n.d.a). In 1980, the Pennsylvania Crime Commission detailed a series of shady transactions involving Caesars World, Inc., which owned casinos in Las Vegas and Atlantic City, and "Alvin I. Malnik and Samuel Cohen, who have ties to Meyer Lansky, a major financial advisor to organized criminals" (Pennsylvania Crime Commission, 1980:252). The Crime Commission also stated that "Vincent Teresa, a former Cosa Nostra capo, said that, in the underworld, dealing with Malnik is the same as dealing with Lansky and that the purpose of Malnik's association with Lansky is to launder illegal cash by investing it in real estate" (Pennsylvania Crime Commission, 1980:252). Other reports cited by the Crime Commission had Malnick with Lansky and members of the Carlo Gambino crime syndicate discussing "the construction and/or ownership of two or three casinos in Florida if a gambling referendum passed. Some $20 million to $25 million was to be invested in the casinos and

profits were to be skimmed off the top and channeled back to the investors" (Pennsylvania Crime Commission, 1980:255).

The relationships among Malnik, Pullman, and Matthews (the largest single shareholder in the bank) preceded the formation of the Bank of World Commerce (New York State Senate, n.d.c). Several years earlier, Malnik and Matthews had been involved with two closely connected firms, including one called Allied Empire, Inc. When the Bank of World Commerce started, Allied Empire showed up as a shareholder and then as the recipient of a large loan from the new bank. Furthermore, Malnik, Matthews and a former racketeer associate of Louis Buchalter (executed by the State of New York in 1944 for murder) had worked together long before the founding of the Bank of World Commerce to purchase a small, "brass plate," Bahamian bank from one of Lou Chesler's associates.

Chesler, Pullman, Lansky, Malnik, Matthews, and other gamblers and racketeers from New York, Miami, Newport, Kentucky, Montreal, Toronto, Las Vegas, and Los Angeles formed both gambling casinos and offshore Bahamian banks, the latter to solve the problem of "washing" the money generated by the former. Stock manipulators like Wallace Groves, allied with well-known financiers from the United States and the United Kingdom, organized crime figures, and, of course, important local politicians, turned Grand Bahama Island into an experimental station for money gathering and laundering. To help the scheme along, the Bahamian government actually relinquished part of its sovereign territory to this mixed group.

Some Consequences

The impact the developers had on the original inhabitants of Grand Bahama Island was hardly beneficial. Prior to the Bahamian government's enacting the Hawksbill Creek Agreement, the island was described by a Royal Commission as nothing more than "a pine barren with less than 5,000 inhabitants" (United Kingdom, 1971:5). After the Agreement and the building of Freeport, most of the island remained a pine barren with the exception of the area around Freeport which the Royal Commission found to be "predominantly non-Bahamian" (United Kingdom, 1971:31). Bahamians made up only 34 percent of the population of Freeport in 1968, as compared with about 84 percent on New Providence Island where the capital, Nassau, is situated. And although some held DEVCO's many construction projects to be a benefactor for Bahamian labor, in fact DEVCO turned to Haiti for a supply of cheap labor whenever it could. Through 1968, the percent of Haitians in Freeport was over four times that of New Providence Island (United Kingdom, 1971:31). The Port Authority, of course, contributed to the pattern of exploitation engaged in by its creation, DEVCO. About 30 percent of the licenses granted by the Port Authority to people wishing to do business in its part of Grand Bahama went to non-Bahamians (United Kingdom, 1971:33).

The combination of Certificates of Exemption, bank secrecy laws, and the Hawksbill Creek Agreement set more than Freeport into motion. It stamped the Bahamas as a center for organized crime activities. Indeed, as we noted earlier, the Bahamas has been recognized as one of the principal transshipment points for drug traffickers moving cocaine and marijuana from South America to the U.S. and Canada (Royal Canadian Mounted Police, 1983:42-46). In one recent narcotics case, the defendants were charged with buying and using "the Darby Islands, a group of five islands in the Bahamas, as a trans-shipment point," and using Bahamian companies including banks and a major Bahamian Trust Company to launder their money (U.S. District Court, 1981). In another case, an officer of the Columbus Trust Company, Nassau, has been charged with using the trust company, a Bahamian corporation named Dundee Securities, Barclays Bank International (The Bahamas), and the Southeast First National Bank of Miami in a complicated scheme to wash millions of dollars for a drug syndicate (U.S. District Court, 1980).

The symbiotic relationships among casinos, offshore banks and professional criminals are complex, to say the least. In numerous contemporary cases, professional criminals utilize both casinos and banks to launder money. An IRS Special Agent reporting on a major drug and tax case gave an example of this as he detailed how a financial services corporation served drug racketeers. The "laundering" method included (1) exchanging the smugglers's initial small denomination cash (mostly tens and twenties) for $100 bills in a Las Vegas casino; (2) moving the new "casino" money from the U.S. to offshore banks and depositing it in secret accounts; (3) returning the money to the U.S. "disguised as offshore loans"; and (4) investing the phony loans in businesses through blind trusts and fictitious corporate fronts (U.S. District Court, n.d.).

Even without the use of offshore banks, casinos themselves perform many clandestine banking services for professional criminals. Drug Enforcement Administrator, Gary D. Liming, testified that casinos "exchange small bills for large bills, travelers' checks or money orders; wire transfer money overseas to associate casinos; provide safety deposit boxes; and make loans . . . without being required to report the transactions to the Department of the Treasury" (Judiciary Committee, 1984:8-9). Casinos, therefore, are acting like offshore banks providing anonymity for depositors (players) and various "laundering" options. Consequently, there are enforcement agents who are convinced that certain casinos have been built solely to launder the proceeds of drug transactions.[2]

However, long before the full potential of casinos working either alone or with offshore banks and other shady financial institutions was realized by drug traffickers, developers in the Bahamas had started the process of bringing casinos and banks together. Within less than a decade, the groundwork for organized crime's penetration of the Bahamas was established. Networks of banks, trust companies, holding companies, casinos, hotels, marinas, mutual funds, and so on representing illicit interests all across the U.S. and many other countries were, and most importantly remain, paramount.

Discussion Questions

1. What is money laundering? How does it affect our tax base? How does it affect our government's ability to enforce the law? What characteristics of a country make it a favorable place to launder money? What makes the Caribbean such an attractive money laundering location?

2. What is the relationship between the Bahamas and Nevada casinos? How does the relationship benefit the casinos? How does the relationship benefit the Bahamas?

3. What was the Hawksbill Creek Act? What was its stated purpose? What rights of authority did it confer upon the company (the Grand Bahama Port Authority)? How did gambling begin in Freeport? Why?

Notes

1. The two illegal casinos included one opened by American Frank Reid for private membership in 1920. By 1923, Reid's club was joined by another called the Bahamian Club, run by a gambler known as Honest John Kelly. Over the course of the Prohibition Era, the Bahamian Club was managed first by Kelly, then Herbert McGuire, and then purchased by Willard McKenzie and Frank Dineen. Like all Bahamian tourist-supported establishments, it was only open during the three winter months when the wealthy arrived to escape the seasonal rigors. At least one other casino was opened during Prohibition. On a privately-owned island close by the Bahamian fishing resort of Bimini, New Yorker Louis Wasey opened a private membership casino called the Cat Cay Club. Authors' interviews conducted in the Bahamas, 1984.

2. Authors' interview with Special Agent, Department of Labor, June, 1985.

References

Block, Alan A. and Patricia Klausner. 1985-86. "Masters of Paradise Island, part 1: Organized Crime, Neo-Colonialism and the Bahamas." *Dialectical Anthropology*. Winter.

Blum, Richard and John Kaplan. 1979. "Offshore Banking: Issues With Respect to Criminal Use." Report submitted to the Ford Foundation.

Charbonneau, Jean-Pierre. 1976. *The Canadian Connection*. Montreal: Optimum Publishing Company.

Fortune. 1966. "Business Around the Globe." 77:93-99.

Grand Bahama Development Corporation. 1964. Letter to the Registrar in the Bahama Registry.

Grand Bahama Port Authority. 1959. "Annual Report." Bahamas Registry.

Judiciary Committee. 1984. U.S. House of Representatives. "Statement of Gary D. Liming on Casino Money Laundering." Washington, D.C.: Government Printing Office.

Lernoux, Penny. 1984. *In Banks We Trust*. New York: Anchor/Doubleday.

McClintick, David. 1982. *Indecent Exposure: A True Story of Hollywood and Wall Street*. New York: Dell.

Messick, Hank. 1971. *Lansky*. New York: Putnam.

New York State Senate. n.d.a. Select Committee on Crime. Bahamian File: Lansky Folder.

——. n.d.b. Select Committee on Crime. Bahamian File: ICB Folder.

——. n.d.c. Select Committee on Crime. Bahamian File: Bank of World Commerce Folder.

Pennsylvania Crime Commission. 1980. *A Decade of Organized Crime: 1980 Report*. Commonwealth of Pennsylvania.

Permanent Subcommittee on Investigation. 1983. Committee on Government Affairs, U.S. Senate. *Crime and Secrecy: The Use of Offshore Banks and Companies*. Washington, D.C.: Government Printing Office.

President's Commission on Organized Crime. 1984. *The Cash Connection: Organized Crime, Financial Institutions, and Money Laundering*. Interim Report to the President and the Attorney General.

Royal Canadian Mounted Police. 1983. *National Drug Intelligence Estimate*, 1982. Ottawa: Minister of Supply and Services.

U.S. District Court. 1980. Western District of Pennsylvania, Indictment. *U.S. Versus Thomas E. Long*, et al.

——. n.d. Southern District of Mississippi. Affidavit for Search Warrant, *U.S. Versus Offices and Premises of Red Carpet Inns International*, Biloxi, Mississippi.

United Kingdom. 1967. Commission on Inquiry into the Operation of the Business of Casinos in Freeport and in Nassau. Report published in the Nassau Guardian.

——. 1971. Royal Commission Appointed on the Recommendation of the Bahamas Government to Review the Hawksbill Creek Agreement. Report, Volume 1. Her Majesty's Stationery Office.

Wall Street Journal. 1976. "Empire Builder." December 15.

Workman, Douglas J. 1982. "The Use of Offshore Tax Havens for the Purpose of Criminally Evading Income Taxes." *The Journal of Criminal Law and Criminology* 73:675-706.

35

White Collar Crime

Edwin H. Sutherland

This selection by Edwin H. Sutherland had a profound impact on criminology when it was originally published in 1949. Prior to that time, the type of crime Sutherland defines, white collar crime, was seldom considered by criminologists. The rule infractions by businesses, corporations, and their executives were usually part of civil actions or heard by regulatory boards or agencies. Persons violating laws applying to businesses and the professions, generally of upper socioeconomic status, were seldom prosecuted as common criminals. Because they were not considered criminals, they were not considered in theoretical statements about the causes of crime.

Sutherland wanted to end all that and show that poverty and lower-class status were not necessarily prerequisites for criminality. It certainly was not the cause of white collar crime, "crime committed by a person of respectability and high social status in the course of his occupation." If factors common to crime by the poor as well as that by the rich could be isolated, a more general theory of criminality would be possible. First, though, he had to establish that the rich committed frequent crimes that established a pattern of criminality.

To this end, he examined the history of 70 major corporations, noting charges of criminal behavior where a court or commission decision went against the company. He found 980 such decisions, an average of 14 per corporation. Corporations in some industries had far more convictions than those in other industries, probably due to the amount and rigor of regulations. The conclusion, however, was that white collar crime was extensive and its financial cost is probably several times larger

than that of all the crimes customarily regarded as the "crime problem."

Although Sutherland's original work is now dated, the principles he espoused have spawned an ever growing field of criminology. Researchers have gone far beyond his early work, using his seminal conceptualizations to explore new avenues of white collar criminality.

The thesis of this [selection], stated positively, is that persons of the upper socioeconomic class engage in much criminal behavior; that this criminal behavior differs from the criminal behavior of the lower socioeconomic class principally in the administrative procedures which are used in dealing with the offenders; and that variations in administrative procedures are not significant from the point of view of causation of crime. The causes of tuberculosis were not different when it was treated by poultices and bloodletting than when treated by streptomycin.

These violations of law by persons in the upper socioeconomic class are, for convenience, called "white collar crimes." This concept is not intended to be definitive, but merely to call attention to crimes which are not ordinarily included within the scope of criminology. White collar crime may be defined approximately as a crime committed by a person of respectability and high social status in the course of his occupation.[1] Consequently it excludes many crimes of the upper class such as most cases of murder, intoxication, or adultery, since these are not a part of the occupational procedures. Also, it excludes the confidence games of wealthy members of the underworld, since they are not persons of respectability and high social status.

The significant thing about white collar crime is that it is not associated with poverty or with social and personal pathologies which accompany poverty. If it can be shown that white collar crimes are frequent, a general theory that crime is due to poverty and its related pathologies is shown to be invalid. Furthermore, the study of white collar crime may assist in locating those factors which, being common to the crimes of the rich and the poor, are most significant for a general theory of criminal behavior.

A great deal of scattered and unorganized material indicates that white collar crimes are very prevalent. The "robber barons" of the last half of the nineteenth century were white collar criminals, as practically everyone now agrees. Their behavior was illustrated by such statements as the following. Colonel Vanderbilt asked, "You don't suppose you can run a railway in accordance with the statutes, do you?" A.B. Stickney, a railroad president, said to sixteen other railroad presidents in the home of J.P. Morgan in 1890, "I have the utmost respect for you gentlemen individually, but as railroad presidents, I wouldn't trust you with my watch out of my sight." Charles Francis Adams said, "One difficulty in railroad management . . . lies in the covetousness, want of good faith, low moral tone of railway managers, in the complete absence of any high standard of commercial honesty." James M. Beck said in regard to the period 1905-17, "Diogenes would have been hard put to it to find an honest man in the Wall Street which I knew as a corporation attorney."

The present-day white collar criminals are more suave and less forthright than the robber barons of the last century but not less criminal. Criminality has been demonstrated again and again in reports of investigations of land offices, railways, insurance, munitions, banking, public utilities, stock exchanges, the petroleum industry, the real estate industry, receiverships, bankruptcies, and politics. When the airmail contracts were canceled because of graft, Will Rogers said, "I hope they don't stop every industry where they find crookedness at the top," and Elmer Davis said, "If they are going to stop every industry where they find crookedness at the top they will have to stop them all." The Federal Trade Commission reported in 1920 that commercial bribery was a prevalent and common practice in many industries. In certain chain stores the net shortage in weight was sufficient to pay 3.4 percent on the investment, while no net shortage in weights was found in independent stores and cooperative stores. The Comptroller of the Currency reported in 1908 that violations of banking laws were found in 75 percent of the banks examined in a three-month period. Lie detector tests of all employees in certain Chicago banks, supported in almost all cases by subsequent confessions, showed that 20 percent of them had stolen bank property, and lie detector tests of a cross-section sample of the employees of a chain store showed approximately 75 percent had stolen money or merchandise from the store.[2] Investigators for the *Reader's Digest* in 1941 drove into a garage with a defect in the car, artificially produced for this experiment, for which a proper charge would be 25 cents, and learned that 75 percent of the garages misrepresented the defect and the work which was done; the average charge was $4 and some garages charges as much as $25. Similar frauds were found in the watch-repair and the typewriter-repair businesses.[3]

White collar crime in politics, which is popularly supposed to be very prevalent, has been used by some persons as a rough gauge by which to measure white collar crime in business. James A. Farley, who had experience both in business and in politics, said, "The standards of conduct are as high among office-holders and politicians as they are in commercial life." Cermak, mayor of Chicago and a businessman, said, "There is less graft in politics than in business." And Walter Lippmann wrote, "Poor as they are, the standards of public life are so much more social than those of business that financiers who enter politics regard themselves as philanthropists."

In the medical profession, which is used here as an example because it is probably less criminal than other professions, are found illegal sale of alcohol and narcotics, abortion, illegal services to underworld criminals, fraudulent reports and testimony in accident cases, extreme instances of unnecessary treatment and surgical operations, fake specialists, restriction of competition, and fee splitting. Fee splitting, for instance, is a violation of a specific law in many states and a violation of the conditions of admission to the profession in all states. The physician who participates in fee splitting tends to send his patients to the surgeon who will give the largest fee rather than to the surgeon who will do the best work. The report has been made that two-thirds of the surgeons in New York split fees and that more than half of the physicians in a central western state who answered a questionnaire on this point favored fee splitting.

The financial cost of white collar crime is probably several times as great as the financial cost of all the crimes which are customarily regarded as the "crime problem." An officer of a chain grocery store in one year embezzled $800,000, which was six times as much as the annual losses from 500 burglaries and robberies of the stores in that chain. Public enemies numbered one to six secured $130,000 by burglary and robbery in 1938, while the sum stolen by Krueger is estimated at $250 million, or nearly 2,000 times as much. The *New York Times* in 1931 reported four cases of embezzlement in the United States with a loss of more than $1 million each and a combined loss of $9 million. Although a million dollar burglar or robber is practically unheard of, the million dollar embezzler is a small-fry among white collar criminals. The estimated loss to investors in one investment trust from 1929 to 1935 was $580 million, due primarily to the fact that 75 percent of the values in the portfolio were in securities to affiliated companies, although the investment house advertised the importance of diversification in investments and its expert services in selecting safe investments. The claim was made in Chicago about 1930 that householders lost $54 million in two years during the administration of a city sealer who granted immunity from inspection to stores which provided Christmas baskets for his constituents. This financial loss from white collar crime, great as it is, is less important than the damage to social relations. White collar crimes violate trust and therefore create distrust, and this lowers social morale and produces social disorganization on a large scale. Ordinary crimes, on the other hand, produce little effect on social institutions or social organization.

Statements such as those made above do little more than provide a justification for further investigation. Obviously they are not precise. For that reason, a detailed investigation of violations of certain laws by a sample of the large corporations has been made and is reported in the following [pages].

The Statistical Record

In order to secure more definite information regarding the crimes of persons of the upper socioeconomic class, an attempt has been made to tabulate the decisions of courts and administrative commissions against the 70 largest manufacturing, mining, and mercantile corporations. The 70 largest corporations used in this analysis are, with two exceptions, included in each of two lists of the 200 largest nonfinancial corporations in the United States. One of these lists was prepared by Berle and Means in 1929 and the other by the Temporary National Economic Committee in 1938. From these lists were excluded the public utility corporations, including transportation and communications corporations, and also the petroleum corporations. This left 68 corporations common to both lists. To these were added two corporations which appeared in the list for 1938 but not in the list for 1929. One of these was Standard Brands, which was organized by the merger of preexisting corporations in 1929 and had grown to the dimensions of the other large corporations by 1938. The other was Gimbel Brothers, which was not far below the other corporations in 1929, and which was added to the present list in order to secure a larger representation of mercantile corporations. The list of 70 corporations is, therefore, unselected except as to size and type of specialization, with the two exceptions mentioned, and neither of these exceptions was selected with knowledge of its rank among large corporations as to violations of laws.

The present analysis covers the life careers of the 70 corporations. The average life of these corporations is approximately 45 years, but decisions as to the date of origin are arbitrary in a few cases. The analysis, also, includes the decisions against the subsidiaries of the 70 corporations, as listed in the standard manuals, for the period these subsidiaries have been under the control of the parent corporation.

The analysis is concerned with the following types of violations of laws: restraint of trade, misrepresentation in advertising, infringement of patent, trademarks, and copyrights; "unfair labor practices" as defined by the National Labor Relations Board and a few decisions under other labor laws; rebates; financial fraud and violation of trust; violations of war regulations; and some miscellaneous offenses. All of the cases included in the tabulation are defined as violations of law, most of them may properly be defined as crimes, and the others are closely allied to criminal behavior. . . .

The sources of information regarding these violations of law are the decisions of the federal, state, and, in a few cases, municipal courts, as published in the *Federal Reporter* and the *American State Reports*; the published decisions of the Federal Trade Commission, the Interstate Commerce Commission, the Securities and Exchange Commission, the National Labor Relations Board, and, for the period 1934-37, of the Federal Pure Food and Drug Administration. These official reports have been supplemented, as to infringement, by the reports on infringement cases listed in the *Official Gazette* of the Patent Office, and as to violations of law in general by reports of decisions in newspapers. The *New York Times* has been used, especially, because its material has been indexed since 1913. The name of each of the 70 corporations and its subsidiaries was checked against the index of each of these series of reports and of the *New York Times*.

The enumeration of decisions as reported in these sources is certainly far short of the total number of decisions against these 70 corporations. First, many of the decisions of the lower courts are not published in the series of federal and state reports, and many of them are not published in the newspapers. Second, many suits are settled out of court and no outcome is reported in the series of reports or in newspapers. The number of suits initiated against the 70 corporations which dropped out of sight after preliminary motions and were presumably settled out of court is approximately 50 percent of the number included in the tabulation in this [selection]. Presumably many of these involved violations of law and could have been tabulated as such if more complete information were available. Third, the Pure Food and Drug Administration has not published its decisions by names of offenders except during the years 1924-47. Fourth, many of the decisions are indexed under names such as "The John Doe Trade Association," or "John Doe et al." Consequently, many of the 70 corporations which have been defendants in those suits were not discovered because their names did not appear in the indexes, and often were not even mentioned in the published reports. Finally, many of the subsidiaries of these corporations are not listed in the financial manuals and could not be identified for the present study.

A decision against one of the 70 corporations is the unit in this tabulation. If a decision is made in one suit against 3 of the 70 corporations, that decision is counted three times, once against each of the 3 corporations. Also, if a criminal suit and an equity suit are initiated against one corporation for essentially the same overt behavior and a decision is made against the corporation in each of those suits, two decisions are counted. This, obviously, involves some duplication. On the other hand, one decision may contain scores of counts, each of which charges a specific violation of law and, also, may refer to a policy which has been in operation for a decade or longer. These are some of the reasons why these decisions are not an accurate index of the comparative amounts of illegal behavior by the several corporations.

The term "decision" is used here to include not only the formal decisions and orders of courts, but also the decisions of administrative commissions, stipulations accepted by courts and commissions, settlements ordered or approved by the court, confiscation of food as in violation of the Pure Food Law, and, in a few cases . . . [the] opinion of courts that the defendant had violated the law at an earlier time even though the court then dismissed the suit.

The . . . decisions which have been discovered . . . show that each of the 70 large corporations has 1 or more decisions against it, with a maximum of 50. The total number of decisions is 980, and the average per corporation is 14.0. Sixty corporations have decisions against them for restraint of trade, 53 for infringement, 44 for unfair labor practices, 43 for miscellaneous offenses, 28 for misrepresentation in advertising, and 26 for rebates.

Armour & Company and Swift & Company stand at the top of the list in the total number of adverse decisions, with 50 each. General Motors has third rank with 40, and Sears Roebuck ties with Montgomery Ward for fourth rank with 39 each. These five corporations are decidedly in excess of the other corporations in the number of decisions, for Loew's in sixth rank has only 31. These totals, however, are not a precise measure of the comparative amounts of illegal behavior by these corporations. Armour and Swift, for instance, are subject to the Pure Food and Drug Law, which does not apply to many other corporations. If the laws explicitly declared that any defects in shoes, electrical equipment, tobacco, films, or automobiles were misdemeanors, as they do in regard to foods, the number of decisions against the other corporations might be as high as the number against Swift and Armour. . . . Armour and Swift would be in the highest ranks even if decisions under the Pure Food Law were disregarded. General Motors, which stands in third rank, has more than half of the decisions against it on charges of infringements, while Sears Roebuck and Montgomery Ward have decisions concentrated in "misrepresentation in advertising" and "infringements."

The corporations in one industry frequently cluster in one part of the distribution and have ranks which are not far apart, considering the possible spread of 70 ranks. Three meat-packing corporations in the list of 70 corporations have ranks of 1, 2, and 17. The two mail order corporations tie for fourth ranks. The two dairy corporations tie for 33rd ranks. The ranks of the three motion picture corporations are: Loew's sixth, and Paramount and Warner tied for tenth position. On the other hand, the corporations in one industry are sometimes scattered more widely. The four rubber manufacturers have ranks as follows: Goodyear 25th, U.S. Rubber 35th, Firestone 43rd, and Goodrich 48th. The nine steel corporations range between ninth and 58th positions.

. . . An analysis of the 980 decisions by types of jurisdictions of the courts and commissions which rendered the decisions . . . shows that 158 decisions were made against 41 of the 70 corporations by criminal courts, 296 decisions against 57 of the corporations by civil courts, and 129 decisions against 44 corporations by courts under equity jurisdiction. This gives a total of 583 decisions which were made by courts. The administrative commissions made 361 decisions, and approximately one-fourth of these were referred to courts and were sustained by the courts. The commissions, also, confiscated goods in 25 cases as in violation of the Pure Food law. Eleven cases are tabulated as "settlements," and all of these were civil suits in which the settlements were approved or ordered by the courts. In hundreds of other cases, settlements were reached outside of courts but these have not been included in the tabulation in this chapter.

This analysis shows that approximately 16 percent of the decisions were made by criminal courts. . . . Even if the present analysis were limited to these decisions by criminal courts, it would show that 60 percent of the 70 large corporations have been convicted in criminal courts and have an average of approximately four convictions each. In many states persons with four convictions are defined by statute to be "habitual criminals." The frequency of these convictions of large corporations might be sufficient to demonstrate the fallacy in the conventional theories that crime is due to poverty or to the personal and social pathologies connected with poverty.

One of the interesting aspects of these decisions is that they have been concentrated in the last decade. . . . In this analysis the date of the first adverse decision in a particular suit was used. The case was not counted, of course, unless the final decision was against the corporation. Relatively few cases initiated after 1944 have been included in this study. Consequently, it is approximately correct to conclude that 60 percent of the adverse decisions were rendered in the 10-year period 1935-44, while only 40 percent were rendered in the 35-year period 1900-34.

One possible explanation of this concentration is that violations of laws by large corporations have increased and are much more prevalent in recent years than in earlier years. Since several other possible explanations may be equally significant, they are considered first.

First, the number of corporations has not remained constant during the period under consideration. Although the 70 corporations have had an average life of 45 years, only 63 of these corporations were in existence in 1920 and only 53 in 1910. This factor, however, seems to be relatively unimportant. A separate tabulation of the 53 corporations which originated prior to 1910 shows that 57.4 percent of the decisions were rendered in the period 1935-44, as contrasted with 59.7 percent for the entire list of 70 corporations.

Second, some of the laws which have been violated by these corporations were enacted during the last decade. The National Labor Relations Law was enacted in 1935, with a similar law under the National Industrial Recovery Act of 1934, and decisions under this law are necessarily concentrated almost entirely in the period 1935-44. If this law is disregarded, 52.5 percent of the decisions under the other laws were made in the ten-year period 1935-44. The enactment and amendment of other laws applying to corporations provide some explanation of this concentration in the last decade. Although this influence cannot be measured with precision, it certainly accounts for a very small part of the concentration.

Third, vigorous prosecution of violations of law by corporations has been concentrated in the period since 1932. Budgets have been increased and additional assistants provided, so that violations were acted upon in the last decade which were neglected in the earlier decades. Probably both the enactment of laws and the enforcement of laws during this period are explained by the fact that businessmen lost much prestige in the depression which began in 1929. The increase in the number of decisions on restraint of trade and misrepresentation in advertising, especially, can be explained in this manner.

Fourth, businessmen are resorting to an increasing extent to "policies of social manipulation" in contrast with the earlier concentration on efficiency in production. With emphasis on advertising and salesmanship, as policies of social manipulation, have gone increased attention to lobbying and litigation. This is shown especially in the trend in decisions regarding infringements. Since these are civil suits, initiated by persons who regard their rights as infringed, they are not a direct reflection of governmental policies. They are, however, presumably affected somewhat by governmental policies in an indirect manner. The increase in the number of prosecutions on charges of restraint of trade, frequently involving patent manipulations, has given the general public and the owners of patents insight into the policies of these large corporations and has stimulated efforts of patent holders to protect their rights.

Of these possible explanations, the increased vigor of and facilities for prosecution are probably the most important. It is probable, also, that the frequency of violations of some of the laws has increased significantly, although this does not appear to be true of all laws.

Of the 70 corporations, 30 were either illegal in their origin or began illegal activities immediately after their origin, and 8 additional corporations were probably illegal in origin or in initial policies. Of the violations of law which appeared in these early activities, 27 were restraint of trade and 2 were patent infringements; of the 8 origins which were probably criminal, 5 involved restraint of trade, 2 patent infringements, and 1 fraud. The evidence for this appraisal of the origins of corporations consists in court decisions in 21 cases, and other historical evidence in the other cases.

Discussion Questions

1. What is white collar crime? Who commits it? In what way is it different from other crime? In what ways is it similar to other types of crime? How prevalent is it? What are some specific examples of white collar crimes?

2. How are white collar crimes and criminals usually treated? What agencies are responsible for regulation of white collar offenses?

3. Are white collar crimes as serious as other types of crimes? Should white col-

lar offenders be criminally prosecuted? Would prosecution be an effective deterrent to white collar crime? Why or why not? What are some problems associated with the prosecution of white collar criminals?

Endnotes

1. The term "white collar" is used here to refer principally to business managers and executives, in the sense in which it was used by a president of General Motors who wrote "An Autobiography of a White Collar Worker."

2. F. P. McEvoy, "The Lie Detector Goes Into Business," *Reader's Digest*, February 1941, p. 69.

3. Roger W. Riis and John Patric, *The Repairman Will Get You if You Don't Look Out* (Garden City, 1942).

Reprinted from: Edwin H. Sutherland, "The Problem of White Collar Crime." In *White Collar Crime*, pp. 7-25. Copyright © 1983 by Yale University Press. Reprinted by permission. ✦

36

The State and White-Collar Crime: Saving the Savings and Loans

Kitty Calavita
Henry N. Pontell

One of the many facts Sutherland pointed out in his original statement on white collar crime was the lack of prosecution of offenders. Many law violations by business and professional persons were overlooked by state agents, handled by civil court authority, or processed before a regulatory commission or agency. Indeed, many criminologists argued that such matters should not be considered criminal unless they were processed by criminal courts. Although Sutherland's view has prevailed, studies of white collar crime have consistently noted the differential implementation of justice concerning alleged crimes of business and professional persons committed in pursuit of their occupational objectives.

Against this backdrop, the nation faced a pattern of white collar crime of enormous magnitude in the late 1980s and early 1990s. After being freed of numerous government regulations (deregulation), institutions of the savings and loan industry began to engage in an unparalleled number of frauds amounting to billions of dollars. Corrupt institutions and their officers perpetrated frauds that ruined individual investors, bankrupted pension funds, and threatened to destroy the federal agency that insures savings and loan facilities. A crisis of this magnitude, caused by criminal activities, had never been faced before.

In this selection Kitty Calavita and Henry N. Pontell examine the federal government's re-

sponse. Rather than the lax and half-hearted attitude observed in other cases of business corruption, they claim the response was unprecedented in terms of the resources used to investigate and prosecute the offenders and the number brought to trial and convicted. Although some have hailed this reaction as a new governmental aggressiveness toward white collar criminals, the authors believe differently. They point out that the new crackdown is very selective, focusing largely on fraud that threatens institutional solvency and financial stability while continuing to ignore traditional corporate crimes that enhance profits at the expense of workers and consumers. A large portion of white collar crime will continue, then, to be treated with the same indifference Sutherland pointed out.

In early 1989, news reports began to reveal evidence of widespread fraud in the U.S. savings and loan (S&L) industry, in what has turned out to be the costliest white-collar crime scandal in U.S. history.[1] Shortly after his election, President Bush announced a plan to bail out the crippled industry and investigate and prosecute theft crime. Several months later, Congress passed the Financial Institutions Reform, Recovery and Enforcement Act of 1989 (FIRREA). This law authorized $75 million annually for three years to fund the Justice Department's efforts to prosecute financial fraud. The FBI budget for these cases went from less than $60 million for fiscal year 1990 to over $125 million in 1991, and FBI personnel dedicated to financial fraud almost doubled (U.S. Senate 1992:45). By 1992, over 800 savings and loan offenders had been convicted, with 77% receiving prison sentences (U.S. Department of Justice 1992b:66).

Edwin Sutherland in 1949 documented the pervasiveness of white-collar crime and highlighted the lenient treatment received by elite offenders compared to perpetrators of street crimes. Since Sutherland's lead, a vast literature has developed attesting to the differential treatment of white-collar criminals (Geis 1967; Carson 1970, 1982; Clinard et al. 1979; Clinard & Yeager 1980; Ermann & Lundman 1978, 1982; Barnett 1982; Levi 1984; Pearce &

Tombs 1988; Snider 1978, 1991). Recently, however, a number of scholars have questioned the conventional wisdom that white-collar offenders are favored by the legal system (Katz 1980; Hagan & Nagel 1982; Hagan 1985; Wheeler & Rothman 1982; Wheeler et al. 1992). While the empirical and theoretical foci of these latter studies vary, they all argue that a crackdown on white-collar crime is underway.

The government effort to ferret out and prosecute S&L criminals seems inconsistent with the longstanding argument of legal favoritism of elite offenders, and might seem to substantiate these more recent arguments that white-collar criminals have been put on notice by an outraged public and "enterprising" law enforcement officials (Katz 1980:170-71). We argue here, however, that the issue is more complex than this "either/or" debate implies. Pointing out that the official response to white-collar crime is decidedly *selective* (e.g., regulators continue a policy of lenience toward violators of labor standards and occupational safety and health laws), we use the S&L case to explore the patterns of that response and the conditions under which it is likely to include a crackdown on corporate offenders.

In an effort to make sense of the enforcement response to the S&L debacle and the broader pattern of white-collar crime enforcement of which it is a part, we borrow a number of concepts from the state theory literature, thereby bringing together two traditions that have much in common but have largely remained distinct. While state theorists generally focus on the role of the state and public policy in *subsidizing* specific capitalists, or the capitalist class collectively, with favorable public policies, corporate crime scholars focus on government action (or inaction) in the *punishment* of capitalist actors. Yet, the way a state punishes (or does not punish) capitalist offenders must be related to the nature of the relationship between the state and capital and the degree to which the offenses in question jeopardize that relationship. This article represents an effort to synthesize the white-collar crime and state theory traditions in order to understand the U.S. government response to savings and loan crime, as well as the current selective crackdown on white-collar crime more generally.

We first provide a brief overview of the scholarship defining white-collar crime and locate thrift fraud within this context. We then outline the government reaction to thrift crime and pose alternative explanations for the crackdown, including the possibility that it reflects a growing intolerance of white-collar crime in the post-Watergate era. We further argue that the highly selective nature of the crackdown on white-collar crime suggests that the explanation must lie elsewhere. In searching for a viable explanation for the aggressive response to thrift fraud, we place it within the context of state theory, focusing on the notion of "relative autonomy" posited by structuralist theories of the state. We point out that the assertive posture of the government in pursuing thrift fraud—and financial crime more generally—seems compatible with the structuralist position that the state must work to preserve economic stability, and that in doing so it enjoys a measure of autonomy vis-á-vis individual elites. Having illustrated the utility of these structuralist insights for explaining the pattern of the response to thrift crime by the late 1980s, we turn next to the shortcomings of a pure structuralist model. In particular, we note the inadequacy of any model that attributes to the state a coherence of purpose and collective rationality that were conspicuously absent in the early (mis)handling of the thrift disaster. We argue here that the indecision and active struggle among policymakers and regulators during the mid-1980s over how to respond to early signs of thrift fraud reveal a state that neither is monolithic nor unilaterally enjoys relative autonomy. After offering some suggestions for an alternative synthetic model, we conclude that just as it is necessary to unpack "the state," so too the concept of corporate crime must be unpacked to reveal its various dimensions and its relationship to the modern state whose job it is to preserve the stability of the economic and financial system.

Our data come from a variety of sources, including government documents, congressional hearings and reports, and interviews with key policymakers, investigators, and regulators. The interviews with FBI investigators and officials in the Federal Deposit Insurance Corporation (since 1989, the thrift insurance agency), the Office of Thrift Supervision (the federal thrift regulatory agency since 1989), and the Resolution Trust Corporation (the new agency charged with managing and selling insolvent thrifts' assets), were tape-recorded and open-ended. They took place in Washington, DC, and in field offices in California, Texas, and Florida, and generally lasted between one and two hours, with some key respondents being interviewed several times over the course of two and a half years. Secondary sources and journalistic accounts of specific cases supplement the primary and archival material.

"White-Collar Crime" Revisited

Sutherland (1949:9) defined white-collar crime as "crime committed by a person of respectability and high social status in the course of his [*sic*] occupation." Recognizing that the concept includes a broad range of behaviors and motivations, later scholars have attempted further classification. One broad distinction is that between "corporate" or "organizational" crime which is committed by executives and managers acting as representatives of their institutions on behalf of those institutions versus white-collar "occupational" crime perpetrated by employees acting independently of their organizations and victimizing them for personal gain (Clinard & Quinney 1973; Coleman 1985; Hagan 1985; Schrager & Short 1978; Shapiro 1980; Wheeler & Rothman 1982).[2] There are a myriad of other ways of categorizing and labeling white-collar crime, and indeed some (e.g., Wheeler et al. 1982) include in the concept any crime committed by a white-collar individual, whether or not it occurs within the context of his or her occupation. The white-collar crime definitional debate is beyond the scope of this article and, in any case, has generally resulted in an intellectual cul-de-sac (see Geis 1992). For our purposes here, the important distinction is that between "corporate" and "occupational" crime, as defined above.

Following Sutherland, numerous researchers have found that corporate crimes are treated differently by law enforcement than are common street crimes. Clinard et al.'s (1979) study of legal actions taken against 582 of the largest corporations in the United States supports Sutherland's contention that not only is corporate crime extensive but law enforcement and regulatory systems tend not to take it very seriously. Case studies of specific industries and/or specific corporate violations corroborate these findings. Whether the focus is on the great electrical company conspiracy (Geis 1967), the Pinto case (Dowie 1979), the Firestone tire scandal (Coleman 1985), occupational safety and health violations (Carson 1970, 1982; Berman 1978; Calavita 1983), or environmental crimes (Gunningham 1974; Barnett 1982), a substantial literature documents the anemic legal response to corporate crime.

These empirical studies of corporate crime have focused primarily on the manufacturing sector. These *manufacturing* crimes are perpetrated for the purpose of maximizing corporate profits and/or cutting production costs and therefore are in a sense consistent with the logic of capital accumulation. Increasingly, however, a qualitatively different type of "corporate" crime has attracted headlines. As financial services replace industrial production as the primary locus of economic activity in late capitalism, more corporate crime scandals involve *financial* fraud. Many of these crimes are distinct in important ways from the manufacturing crimes described above. Unlike corporate crimes in the manufacturing sector, financial fraud is often perpetrated by corporate executives for their own personal gain. More important, while manufacturing crimes tend to advance corporate profits and thus follow the logic of capital, financial fraud undermines that logic, jeopordizing the stability of the financial system and/or institutional survival.

Such financial frauds may thus be thought of as a hybrid. Like traditional corporate crime, the fraud is often carried out by management as part of company policy, not by isolated individuals acting independently of institutional prescriptions. Indeed, many thrift kingpins operated within institutions whose primary purpose was to provide a "cash cow" to management. Unlike traditional corporate crime, however, these financial frauds ultimately erode the viability of the corporation itself. In this sense, it is crime *by* the organization *against* the organization; or to use a variation of Wheeler and Rothman's (1982) conceptual scheme, the organization is both weapon *and* victim. Thus, these financial frauds combine aspects of both traditional "corporate" crime—in which the offenses are company policy and are committed via company trasactions—and "occupational" crime perpetrated by individuals for personal gain, in which the institution itself is victimized.

While thrift fraud is unusual in its scope and impact, it is by no means unique in combining aspects of corporate and occupational crime. As we have shown elsewhere (Calavita & Pontell 1991), some insurance industry fraud is similar to this thrift fraud, as is much crime in other financial institutions, such as pension funds and credit unions. What these crimes have in common is that they are committed *by management, against the institution*. As we will see, the government response to the thrift crisis hinges in part on the peculiar nature of this hybrid form of corporate crime.

'Throw the Crooks in Jail': A Crackdown on White-Collar Crime?

In a speech to U.S. Attorneys in June 1990, President Bush promised, "We will not rest until the cheats and the chiselers and the charlatans [responsible for the S&L disaster] spend a large chunk of their lives behind the bars of a federal prison" (quoted in U.S. Department of Justice 1990:1). Announcing his plans for attacking financial institution fraud, the president was unequivocal: "[W]e aim for a simple, uncompromising position. Throw the crooks in jail" (quoted in U.S. House of Representatives 1990a: 128).

President Bush undoubtedly hoped to gain political mileage from an emphatic response to the worst financial fraud epidemic in U.S. history. However, this was not empty political rhetoric—at least not entirely. By 1989, both the legislative and executive branches were devoting considerable attention to savings and loan fraud. FIRREA allocated $225 million over three years to the Justice Department's financial fraud efforts. Almost immediately, FBI personnel assigned to financial fraud investigations climbed from 822 to 1,525. The total Department of Justice budget for financial institution fraud went from $80,845,000 to $212,236,000 (U.S. Senate 1992:45). The 1989 law also provided for increased penalties for financial institution crimes and extended the statute of limitations for such crimes from 5 to 10 years. The Comprehensive Thrift and Bank Fraud Prosecution and Taxpayer Recovery Act of 1990 raised maximum statutory penalties from 20 to 30 years in prison for a range of specific violations, reserving the most severe sanctions for "financial crime kingpins."

The number of prosecuted S&L offenders grew quickly. Major financial institution fraud investigations increased 54% from 1987 to 1991, when the FBI opened over 260 investigations every month. By early 1992, it had over 4,300 major financial fraud investigations underway, of which about 1,000 involved savings and loans (U.S. Senate 1992). From October 1988 to April 1992, more than 1,100 defendants were formally charged in "major" savings and loan cases,[3] and 839 were convicted (for completed prosecutions, the conviction rate was 92.6%). Of the 667 offenders who had been sentenced by the spring of 1992, 77% received a prison sentence (U.S. Department of Justice 1992b:64).

At no time in its history has the U.S. government allocated so many resources and concentrated so much of its law enforcement effort on pursuing white-collar criminals and sending them to prison.[4] The question is, Why? Two explanations come to mind. The first possibility is that this assault on financial fraud is an indication of the erosion of official tolerance for white-collar crime postulated by a number of recent scholars. Katz (1980), for example, notes an increased emphasis on the criminal prosecution of business and political elites. Arguing that while earlier in this century journalists, populists, and other "lay catalysts" spearheaded the movement against business and political corruption, beginning in the 1970s prosecutors and public officials began to take the initiative, rendering the general public a "passive audience" (p. 169). Katz notes that the potential for *institutional* reform has been eroded by the "case" approach taken by law enforcement and that the movement against white-collar crime may be in decline since its peak in the 1970s. He nonetheless concludes that "some degree of institutionalization of the increased emphasis on white-collar crime has been achieved" (p. 178). Hagan (1985:286) similarly argues that in the post-Watergate era, the prosecution of white-collar and corporate crime has been stepped up. And Braithwaite and Geis (1982:292-93), on the eve of Ronald Reagan's presidency, observed that the post-Watergate era had seen a "surge of governmental . . . interest in corporate crime" and warned against reversing the trend.

While not distinguishing among different types of white-collar crimes, a number of empirical studies report an increased willingness to prosecute and sanction white-collar offenders in general. Focusing on prosecutorial patterns in the Southern District of New York from 1963 to 1976, Hagan and Nagel (1982) point to "proactive" policies, including an increase in resources for white-collar prosecutions and an "activist" approach to successful completion of these cases. According to this study, while there was a general tendency for white-collar offenders to receive favorable sentencing, this depended on the nature of the offense, with those convicted of mail fraud being most likely to be sent to prison (60 percent) and those convicted of illegal restraint of trade the least likely to be incarcerated (2.4 percent). Hagan and Palloni (1983) similarly report an increased tendency to sentence white-collar criminals to prison, albeit with relatively short sentences.

Wheeler, Weisburd, and Bode (1982) investigated eight types of white-collar crime in seven federal districts for the years 1976, 1977, and 1978 in order to determine the effect of a number of variables on white-collar sentencing. Surprisingly, they found that higher-status perpetrators of white-collar crime received prison sentences more often than did their lower-status counterparts.[5] Although they observe that in the aftermath of Watergate judges may be sensitized to the seriousness of elite deviance, Wheeler et al.

(p. 658) speculate that heavier penalties for higher-status individuals is not a new phenomenon but is "anchored in historical patterns that link greater social obligation with higher social status."

These arguments contesting the notion that white-collar criminals receive more lenient treatment are complicated by a number of issues. Some (e.g., Katz 1980; Hagan 1985) suggest, for example, that there has been a *shift* toward greater intolerance of white-collar crime since the Watergate revelations; others (such as Wheeler et al. 1982, who subtitle their article "Rhetoric and Reality") contend that the assumed favorable treatment of higher-status offenders has always been a myth. Further, to a large extent, the empirical studies focus on the status of the offenders rather than the nature of the offenses. Despite the fact that embedded in these data are revelations that certain offenses continue to be dealt with leniently and almost never result in prison sentences, the cumulative effect of this research has been to buttress the increasingly common refrain that we are witnessing a "crackdown on white collar crime."[6] The government reaction to thrift crime might, then, simply be part of a larger pattern of decreasing official tolerance for white-collar crime.

The second possible explanation for the vigorous response to thrift fraud is that the unprecedented epidemic of fraud has quite naturally required a corresponding unprecedented response. There is, however, a common flaw in both of these explanations: The "crackdown" on white-collar crime is highly *selective*. While Congress, the Justice Department, and the thrift regulatory agencies take an aggressive approach to financial institution fraud, corporate and business crime in other sectors is virtually ignored. Further, the regulatory response to crime in these other sectors seems unrelated to the frequency or scale of the crimes involved. Since the Reagan administration began dismantling the Occupational Safety and Health Administration in the early 1980s (Calavita 1983), sanctions against employers who violate safety and health standards have plummeted. Despite the fact that hundreds of thousands of U.S. workers are killed and disabled annually from work-related accidents and illnesses, employers are rarely prosecuted criminally for safety and health violations. (The production of asbestos will result in 170,000 deaths from lung cancer and other related diseases; yet none of the corporate executives who deliberately concealed the dangers have been criminally charged.) The U.S. Food and Drug Administration continues to be reluctant to recommend criminal prosecution of corporate executives who conceal the hazards of their products or deliberately fabricate data to attest to their safety (Coleman 1985:44-45). Indeed, if we focus on traditional forms of corporate crime in the manufacturing sector, there is no evidence of any crackdown. The point here is that if the aggressive response to thrift fraud were simply a reflection of a broader crackdown on white-collar crime or a straightforward response to the scale of thrift crime, then we would expect to see similar patterns in other sectors where regulatory violations are frequent and egregious. The laxity that characterizes much regulatory enforcement contrasts markedly with the aggressive response to thrift fraud, however, and suggests that the answer must lie elsewhere.

To understand the government response to thrift misconduct, particularly in conjunction with the lenient reaction to other regulatory violations, we need to examine the nature of the state itself and its relationship to the industrial and financial sectors it is charged with regulating.

A Structuralist Perspective on Regulatory Enforcement

Sociologists have long made a distinction between "social" regulations (such as occupational safety and health standards) which are aimed at controlling production processes, and "economic" regulations (such as insider trading restrictions) which regulate the market and stabilize the economy (Barnett 1981; Cranston 1982; Snider 1991; Stryker 1992; Yeager 1991). While the former protect workers and consumers against the excesses of capital—and tend to cut into profits—the latter regulate and stabilize the capi-

tal accumulation process and historically have been supported by affected industries.

This distinction is based on a structuralist approach to the state, which emphasizes the "objective relation" (Poulantzas 1969) between the state and capital (see also Althusser 1971; O'Connor 1973). This objective relation guarantees that the capitalist state will operate in the long-term interests of capitalists independent of their direct participation in the policymaking process or mobilization of resources. Central to this objective relation under capitalism, the state must promote capital accumulation since its own survival depends on tax revenues derived from successful profit-making activity, as well as the political sensibility that is contingent on economic growth. In addition, it must actively pursue "political integration" (Friedland et al. 1978), "legitimation" (O'Connor 1973), or "the cohesion of the social formation" (Poulantzas 1969) in the interest of political survival and the economic growth on which it depends. As O'Connor (1973) has pointed out in his seminal work on the capitalist state's fiscal crisis, the state's capital accumulation and legitimization functions are often mutually contradictory: efforts to promote and project capital accumulation favor the capitalist class and may jeopardize the state's legitimacy by alienating the other classes who inevitably pay the price. From this perspective, state institutions must continually grapple with this contradiction and its various forms of fallout, which according to O'Connor is at the base of the state's "fiscal crisis."

In this structuralist rendition, the state enjoys "relative autonomy" in its efforts to realize these potentially contradictory functions. In direct contrast to the instrumentalist model espoused by Domhoff (1967, 1978) and others (Kolko 1963, 1965; Milliband 1969), structuralists argue that state managers are not captive to individual capitalist interests and indeed are capable of violating those interests in order to pursue the broader and more long-term interests of capital accumulation and political legitimacy. Nonetheless, its autonomy is "relative." While the state may be free from the manipulation of individual capitalists or even the business community as a whole, it is by no means autonomous from the structural requirements of the political economy within which it is embedded and which it must work to preserve (see Poulantzas 1969, 1973).

Most of the corporate crime literature that borrows from this structuralist perspective focuses on social—rather than economic—regulation. This literature addresses the generally lax enforcement of these regulations and ties that laxity to the capital accumulation function of the state and the perceived costs of interfering with profitable industry (Barnett 1979; Calavita 1983; Snider 1991; Yeager 1988). These scholars also note, however, that the legitimation mandate of the state periodically requires that it respond to political demands to shore up worker safety, reduce environmental hazards, or enforce labor standards. Thus, when there is a politically powerful working-class movement, or in the face of high public visibility of the social costs of nonenforcement, the state may mount correspondingly visible enforcement campaigns. The point is, however, that active enforcement of social regulation occurs primarily in response to public pressure and is usually short-lived, receding once political attention has shifted elsewhere and state legitimacy is no longer threatened. Whether the issue is occupational safety and health standards (Carson 1982; Walters 1985; Calavita 1986; Gunningham 1987; Tucker 1987), environmental regulation (Adler & Lord 1991; Barnett 1979, 1981; Yeager 1991), or U.S. Office of Surface Mining enforcement (Shover et al. 1986), empirical studies consistently confirm that social regulation ebbs and flows with public pressure; in the absence of such pressure and the related challenges to state legitimation, enforcement dwindles.[7]

In contrast, when the goal is economic regulation, the state tends to assume a more rigorous posture. Despite occasional protest from the individual capitalists at whom sanctions are directed, the state rather vigorously enforces regulations that stabilize the market and enchance economic viability. Unlike social regulations which are implemented primarily in response to on-again/off-again legitimation needs, economic regulations are integral to the capital accumulation process and are thus more consistently and urgently pursued (Barnett 1981; Snider 1991; Yeager 1991). While case studies are far fewer in this area, some excellent research has focused on the U.S. Securities and Exchange Commission (SEC). As Yeager (1986) and Shapiro (1984) have shown, while the SEC is by no means omnipotent in the face of its powerful Wall Street charges, nonetheless it rather routinely seeks criminal sanctions and stiff monetary fines for elite offenders.

Extensive comparative research documents this enforcement discrepancy. Clinard et al.'s (1979) comprehensive analysis of enforcement actions against the 582 largest corporations in the United States during 1975 and 1976 found a strong relationship between level of enforcement and type of violation. While over 96% of "manufacturing violations" (involving social regulations concerning such things as product safety and food and drug standards) were handled entirely at the administrative level, only 41.5% of "trade violations" (involving economic regulations controlling bid rigging and other unfair trade practices) were disposed of administratively. Further, while over 21% of trade violations were processed criminally, less than 1% of manufacturing violations were criminally processed, and *no* labor standard violations were prosecuted criminally. Clinard et al. (p. 147) conclude, "Corporate actions that directly harm the economy were more likely to receive the greater penalties, while those affecting consumer product quality were responded to with the least severe sanctions. Although over 85 percent of all sanctions were administrative in nature, those harming the economy were most likely to receive criminal penalties."

Surveying enforcement efforts across a variety of regulatory areas, Barnett (1981:17) similarly concludes that enforcement is directly correlated with whether the regulation in question protects or impedes capital accumulation. Regulations perceived as "anti-capital" received the least enforcement and those protecting markets or economic stability elicited the most enforcement.

This empirical discrepancy in the enforcement of social and economic regulations is consistent with the structuralist depiction of the state, and the concept of relative autonomy in particular. While social regulations potentially cut into profits and interfere with the capital accumulation process, the function of economic regulations is to stabilize and shore up that process. In pursuing this economic function, the state inevitably encounters individual opposition and periodic attempts to neutralize enforcement, but overall its successes in this area dwarf its halting efforts at social regulation.

In the next section, we draw from this structural analysis of the state, and the distinction between social and economic regulation, to explain the vigorous response to thrift fraud by the late 1980s. As we will see, the pattern of that response confirms the utility of these structuralist insights and seems to contradict competing models of public policy such as instrumentalism, pluralism, or public interest/consensus theory. . . .

The Thrift Cleanup, Capital Accumulation, and Relative Autonomy

At first glance, the details of the crackdown on thrift fraud seem to fit well with the structural model described above. Most important, the law enforcement response is consistent with the logic of the state's capital accumulation function and its relative autonomy in realizing that function. For if we look at the pattern of enforcement, we find that it varies with the degree to which the fraud jeopardizes financial stability. It is noteworthy, for example, that priority is placed on financial institutions on the verge of failure or already insolvent and in which fraud played a significant role in the collapse.

The official definition of a "major case," or cases to which top priority is assigned, refers to dollar losses, the role of insiders, and the like (see note 3 above). Yet, government officials consistently specify another factor as among the most important ingredients: *whether the alleged fraud contributed to insolvency*. Ira Raphaelson, at the time Special Counsel for Financial Fraud in the Deputy Attorney General's Office, told a Senate subcommittee that cases are treated as "major" depending on dollar losses and whether the

fraud played a role in an institution's failure (U.S. Senate 1992:10-11; emphasis added):

> Senator Dixon: "How do you define a major case?"
>
> Mr. Raphaelson: "If it involves an alleged loss of more than $100,000 or involves a failed institution."
>
> Senator Dixon: "There are at least 4300 cases over $100,000?"
>
> Mr. Raphaelson: "Or involving a failed institution, it might be less than $100,000. But *because it is linked to a failure, we still consider it a major case*."

At the same hearing, Harold A. Valentine, Associate Director for General Government Programs of the U.S. General Accounting Office (U.S. Senate 1992:55), defined major cases as "those involving failed institutions or alleged losses of $100,000 or more." Referring to their prioritization of cases, as well as sentence severity, one FBI agent in Flordia gave an example: "If you steal over $5 million and you make a bank fail, you've popped the bubble on the thermometer there!" (personal interview). The same Florida agent tied the influx of federal resources for financial fraud investigations to the economic importance of these cases. He explained that a few years ago:

> We as financial crimes or financial institution fraud investigators were vying for manpower in this office along with [drugs and public corruption] squads. We had to share the white-collar crime staffing . . . with these people. *Now that we've had such dramatic increases in the number of failed institutions in the last year and a half, they're being investigated here and Congress has appropriated huge amounts of funds to target that.* (Emphasis added)

In addition to the "major case" specification, in June 1990 the Office of Thrift Supervision, the Resolution Trust Corporation, and the Federal Deposit Insurance Corporation developed a matrix with which to prioritize thrift fraud investigations and used the matrix to draw up a list of the "Top 100" thrift institutions to be investigated. Among the most important ingredients in this prioritization were the financial health of the institution, whether fraud had contributed to insolvency, and the economic effect on the larger community (personal interviews).

Enforcement statistics confirm these priorities. A General Accounting Office report (U.S. Senate 1992:8) reveals that of the approximately 1,000 major thrift cases under investigation in fiscal year 1991, *one-third* involved failed institutions, and the other two-thirds were for investigations of fraud that contributed to major losses. The Dallas Bank Fraud Task Force handles *only* failed financial institution fraud cases. Indeed, the task force was established in 1987 when it was brought to the attention of officials that 18 thrifts in the Dallas area were on the verge of collapse.

When alleged fraud does *not* result in demonstrable losses, no further investigation is pursued. In response to a query from Congress about criminal referrals made in connection with Silverado Savings and Loan, the Justice Department explained that one of the referrals in question was dropped: "This matter involved no demonstrable loss; prosecution was declined in the United States Attorney's Office, District of Colorado" (quoted in U.S. House of Representatives 1990a:121).

The emphasis of the regulatory and law enforcement community is thus on fraud in failed, or failing, "problem" institutions in which the alleged fraud undermines the thrift's financial health. This selective focus suggests that *the crackdown on financial fraud represents less an effort to control crime per se than it is a desperate effort to contain the damage in a fraud-ridden and ailing industry.*[8] While crime in one financial institution might elicit relatively little concern, the epidemic of crime in the thrift industry in the 1980s threatened the survival of the industry itself and, indeed, the stability of the whole financial system. The law enforcement reaction was thus meant both to incapacitate the offenders and as a deterrent to curb the epidemic of fraud. The unprecedented crackdown on this form of white-collar crime conveyed the deterrent message that this fraud will be dealt with seriously; and defining fraud de facto as including only those activities that might lead to insolvency highlights the "damage control" basis for this crackdown. Together with the reregulation of thrifts under FIRREA, the aggressive prosecution of thousands of thrift offenders was designed to stop the hemorrhage of public dollars and stabilize the industry.[9]

The General Accounting Office's Harold Valentine (U.S. Senate 1992:19) called bank and thrift fraud and the financial collapse to which they contributed "perhaps the most significant financial crisis in this nation's history." The Justice Department (1990:2) referred to it as "the unconscionable plundering of America's financial institutions." A senior staff member of the Senate Banking Committee explained the attention being given to thrift fraud: "This industry is very close to the heart of the American economy! We teetered on the edge of a mjor, major problem here. . . . [W]e got a major problem, but we teetered on the edge of a major collapse. . . . You know, all these [financial] industries could bring down the whole economy" (personal interview).[10]

Bank and thrift fraud are of course not new. Investigators and regulators report that abuse by thrift insiders was frequent in the 1960s and 1970s but attracted little attention since the institutions were generally thriving (personal interview). One regulator who said that fraud has always existed in thrifts claimed that "[hot prices in real estate are] the only thing that pulled everybody's asses out for years" (personal interview). A staff member of the Senate Banking Committee explained it this way, "People basically bet on the come. If the market goes up, we all win. And if the market goes down, you begin to look back and see what corners were cut. But you don't look back if the market goes up" (personal interview). The current response to thrift fraud thus has less to do with punishing criminal activity per se than it does with preventing further damage to financial institutions that lie "close to the heart of the American economy."[11]

A number of studies have noted the role of regulatory agencies in minimizing uncertainty and risk and generally stabilizing the financial system. Shapiro's (1984) study of the Securities and Exchange Commission is exemplary. As Shapiro reports, SEC officials see their function as protecting the securities and exchange system rather than as its adversaries. Similarly, Reichman (1991) underlines the stabilizing effect of regulating risks in the stock market. Abolafia (1984) observes a similar dynamic in the commodities futures market, where regulations "structure anarchy." And Yeager (1986) draws attention to the fact that the Reagan administration, while virtually dismantling the worker safety and health system and eroding environmental protections, was relatively aggressive in pursuing insider trading and stock market fraud in an effort to restore confidence in the integrity of the market and encourage investment. As Snider (1991:224) explains, "Controlling this type of corporate crime turns out to be in the interests of the corporate sector overall, as well as being compatible with state objectives. Such laws protect the sanctity of the investment market, which is central to the ability of corporations to raise money by issuing shares."

The U.S. government's mission to salvage the thrift industry is consistent with this literature. And the mission is all the more urgent since this industry—and the capital it stands to lose—are government-insured. This, then, is an effort directed less at penalizing wrongdoers for their misdeeds than at limiting damage to the industry, preventing comparable damage in other financial sectors, and containing the hemorrhage of government-insured capital. An upper-echelon Washington official, when asked to comment on this interpretation, said simply, "You hit the nail right on the head" (personal interview).

The crackdown on thrift crime thus begins to make sense. As we have seen, savings and loan fraud is not new. What is new is the devastating effect it has had on the industry and the billions of dollars of government liability for losses. The need to contain the damage precipitated the unprecedented response and explains the priority accorded failed and failing institutions. So consistent is this pattern that the very criminality of an act is defined not only in terms of whether it violates the law but also in terms of the effect it has on an institution's financial health. Thus, a regulator explained that violations of bank statutes and agency regulations—such

as misapplication of bank funds, violations of loan-to-one-borrower restrictions, and nominee loan schemes—are often treated by regulators as illegal *only* if they result in a loss for the institution. "If you're good for the money," he explained, referring to various types of loan fraud, "You're not defrauding the banks" (personal interview).

This pattern of the government response to thrift crime seems to confirm the utility of the structuralist model of the state, in particular, the notion of relative autonomy. Despite the vast resources available to these corporate offenders, an unprecedented campaign was launched to prosecute and penalize their frauds. Further, enforcement is focused on frauds that jeopardize the stability of the financial system. Thrift fraud was not taken seriously until it began to undermine one institution after another in the 1980s, and as we have seen, the current prosecutorial effort still aims only to curb fraud that causes demonstrable losses.

This pattern is inexplicable from a straightforward instrumentalist position, which would predict that these affluent offenders could shield themselves from prosecution and/or conviction by mobilizing their extensive resources. Neither is it explicable from a traditional interest group model, according to which public policy is the result of pressure from any of a plurality of special interests. The U.S. Savings and Loan League—the thrift industry's major association and during the 1980s one of the most successful lobbying groups in Washington—was certainly the most powerful political actor in this arena; yet it was incapable of derailing the Financial Institution Reform, Recovery, and Enforcement Act of 1989 and the enforcement campaign that it unleashed—a failure that triggered intense controversy and recriminations within the association (O'Connell 1992). Further, the *public's* knowledge of the scope of the thrift disaster was minimal before President Bush's announcement of the bailout and enforcement effort following the 1988 election. Media attention to the scandal quickly intensified, but only *after* the state response was well underway, suggesting that it was not public pressure that triggered the vigorous government reaction.[12] While this reaction is inexplicable from either an instrumentalist or an interest group model of public policy, it is consistent with the structuralist notion of the capital accumulation function of the state and its ability to sacrifice individual capitalists' interests to long-term economic survival.

Furthermore, these structuralist insights offer the only viable explanation for the pattern of the current crackdown on white-collar crime more generally. The increased intolerance of corporate crime noted by Katz (1980), Hagan (1985), and others is in fact a *selective* intolerance—directed at financial fraud and similar violations of economic regulations that undermine the stability and viability of the economic system. This intolerance of risky financial fraud, in combination with the absence of a corresponding response to traditional corporate crimes that violate social regulations, cannot be explained by instrumentalism or by any general theory of post-Watergate reformism. It is, however, precisely what structuralists would predict. . . .

Conclusion

We have argued here that the aggressive reaction to thrift fraud in the late 1980s is not indicative of a general crackdown on corporate crime, recently postulated by some white-collar crime scholars. The timing of the response, the almost exclusive focus on fraud that leads to institutional insolvency, and the selective nature of the crackdown—targeting financial fraud while virtually ignoring traditional corporate crime in the manufacturing sector—all suggest that it is not an increased intolerance of white-collar crime that motivates the reaction but a concern with economic stability. . . .

Just as it is important to reexamine the monolithic concept of the state, the concept of corporate crime must be unpacked if we are to understand the pattern of the state's response to corporate offenders. To explain the current response to thrift fraud, side by side with the official tolerance of other corporate offenses, an important distinction was made here. White-collar crime research generally defines corporate crime as crime committed by corporate offenders *on behalf of the organization*; but thrift fraud *undermines* the financial viability of the institution and ultimately the industry itself. Thus, it is important to distinguish between traditional corporate crimes in the manufacturing sector that enhance profits at workers' or consumers' expense, and financial fraud that enriches individuals at the expense of the economic system. The state is likely to tolerate the former, taking action primarily in response to grassroots political demands and to shore up its own legitimacy, while treating the latter with more urgency.

The current response to thrift fraud makes sense within this context. As we have seen, the way the state punishes corporate offenders depends on the nature of the relationship between the state and capital at various points in time and across agencies, and the way the offenses in question jeopardize that relationship or undermine the economic process around which the relationship revolves. In attempting to explain the crackdown on financial fraud, we thus bring together two traditions that have remained relatively distinct—state theory and white-collar crime research. It is hoped that the analysis will contribute not just to a better understanding of the government response to white-collar crime but to a more integrated and empirically grounded approach to the state.

Discussion Questions

1. What is a structuralist state theory? What is "relative autonomy"? How do these concepts define the role of government in business? What are the problems with a pure structuralism model?

2. What is the difference between organizational or corporate crime and occupational crime? How does the concept of capital accumulation affect the way in which white collar criminals are treated? Which types of white collar crime is the state more likely to crack down on? Which types is it more likely to ignore?

3. What may have caused the government to get tougher on white collar crime? What is wrong with the possible expla-

nations? What types of sentences are white collar criminals getting?

Notes

1. For a description of the epidemic of savings and loan fraud and the conditions that facilitated it, see Calavita & Pontell 1990, 1991.

2. It is of course possible for lower-level employees to commit occupational crime. Clinard & Quinney (1973), for example, point to a variety of occupational crimes by blue-collar workers, such as embezzlement and theft.

3. "Major" cases are those in which "a) the amount of fraud or loss was $100,000 or more, or b) the defendant was an officer, director, or owner [of the S&L]. . , or c) the schemes involved multiple borrowers in the same institution, or d) involves [*sic*] other major factors" (U.S. Department of Justice 1992a:9).

4. The law enforcement response to the S&L crisis is of course not without its critics. Public interest groups as well as Congress, citing backlogs and unworked cases, have questioned the job the Justice Department is doing in prosecuting thrift offenders (see, e.g., U.S. House of Representatives 1990a; U.S. Senate 1992). Whether or not the Justice Department could pursue these cases more efficiently is beyond the scope of this article. White-collar crime cases are notoriously difficult to investigate and prosecute (Katz 1980; Braithwaite & Geis 1982). It is worth noting that S&L fraud cases are among the most difficult and time-consuming with which the FBI has ever had to deal, dependent as they often are on intricate financial schemes involving "daisy chains" of participants (personal interviews). The more important point here, however, is that the U.S. government has launched an unprecedented attack on this form of white-collar crime.

5. It is noteworthy that the Wheeler et al. study included few of what could be called "corporate" or "organizational" crimes and indeed contained a large contingent of very low-status violators, including significant numbers of the unemployed. Geis (1991) has suggested that the type of offenses and offenders included in this study do not fit particularly well Sutherland's original definition of "white collar crime."

6. Tillman and Pontell (1992) have recently contested this crackdown hypothesis. Presenting data on Medicaid provider fraud in Califor-

nia, they found that Medi-Cal offenders were less likely to be sentenced to prison than comparable street criminals, and conclude, "Our findings provide considerable support for the white-collar leniency thesis" (p. 423).

7. As Yeager (1991:28) points out, there may be cases in which social regulation and its enforcement are the product of "intraindustry competition" and the desire of some segments of capital to use regulations to enhance their own competitive edge. For example, Kolko (1963) demonstrates that the Meat Inspection Act of 1906 was spearheaded by large meatpackers to eliminate smaller companies that could not comply with the new social regulation of the industry. Far more common, however, is the scenario depicted above, in which social regulation is opposed by industry and enforced by the state primarily to further its legitimation needs.

8. A continuum of law enforcement motivations might be devised in which pure "crime control" lies at one extreme and "damage control" at the other. Thus, victimless crimes and statutory offenses are prosecuted to penalize the offender for having violated the law: it is the *fact* of law violation in and of itself that is at issue in this kind of "crime control." At the other extreme is "damage control," in which the primary motive for enforcement is to contain the effects of the violation. It follows that, as in the case of thrift fraud prior to the 1980s, little response will be elicited in the absence of perceived effects from the offense. Between these two extremes, there is considerable overlap and, it could be argued, it is in this middle region that much day-to-day law enforcement lies.

9. We are not suggesting here than an aggressive law enforcement response is the most effective deterrent to fraud. (It might be argued that reversing the deregulation that in the early 1980s set the stage for the fraud epidemic was the more potentially effective deterrent strategy.) The point instead is to determine the motives for the crackdown.

10. One official spoke of the "havoc ratio"—the amount of havoc that a given thrift crime wreaks on the institution, the community, and the general economy. The reason these crimes are so serious, she said, is that they have the potential to wreak havoc far beyond the millions that the offender actually steals. She explained, "Using a thrift to go on a shopping spree is a lot like a fellow who wants to rob a teller at a bank. . . . In order to get the

$20,000 dollar cash drawer, he blows up the entire building" (personal interview).

11. It might be argued that the vigorous prosecution of thrift offenders has to do also with the fact that the "villains" are identifiable individuals, not corporations. This certainly makes prosecution and conviction easier. Nonetheless, it is also the case that in a number of notorious corporate crime scandals in the manufacturing sector—the great electrical company conspiracy comes to mind here—individual offenders have been identified as the responsible parties yet have received notoriously lenient treatment. The central ingredient here seems to be that in the thrift case, the institutions—and ultimately the industry—were victims, not beneficiaries, of the offenses.

12. It has been consistently alleged that during the 1988 presidential campaign, both Michael Dukakis and George Bush deliberately avoided any discussion of the S&L issue since both political parties shared responsibility for the disaster (Mayer 1990:260–61; Pilzer 1989:208–9; Wardman 1990:90). The dearth of new reports on the subject before the election is indeed striking, particularly in comparison to the rapid escalation of media attention beginning in 1989, suggesting that the candidates' strategy may have been successful in keeping the issue out of the public eye.

References

Abolafia, Mitchel Y. 1984. "Structured Anarchy: Formal Organization in the Commodities Futures Markets," in P. Adler & P. Adler, eds., *The Social Dynamics of Financial Markets*. Greenwich, CT: JAI Press.

Adler, Robert W., & Charles Lord. 1991. "Environmental Crimes: Raising the Stakes," 59 *George Washington Law Rev.* 781.

Althusser, Louis. 1971. *Lenin and Philosophy and Other Essays*. New York: Monthly Review Press.

Barnett, Harold. 1979. "Wealth, Crime, and Capital Accumulation," 3 *Contemporary Crises* 171.

——. 1981. "Corporate Capitalism, Corporate Crime," 27 *Crime & Delinquency* 4 (Jan.).

——. 1982. "The Production of Corporate Crime in Corporate Capitalism," in P. Wickham & T. Dailey, eds., *White Collar and Economic Crime*. Lexington, MA: Lexington Books.

Berman, Daniel M. 1978. *Death on the Job: Occupational Health and Safety Struggles in the United States*. New York: Monthly Review Press.

Block, Fred. 1987. *Revising State Theory: Essays in Politics and Postindustrialism*. Philadelphia: Temple Univ. Press.

Braithwaite, John, & Gilbert Geis. 1982. "On Theory and Action for Corporate Crime Control," 28 *Crime & Delinquency* 292.

Calavita, Kitty. 1983. "The Demise of the Occupational Safety and Health Administration: A Case Study in Symbolic Action," 30 *Social Problems* 437.

——. 1986. "Worker Safety, Law, and Social Change: The Italian Case," 20 *Law & Society Rev.* 189.

——. 1992. *Inside the State: The Bracero Program, Immigration, and the INS*. New York: Routledge, Chapman & Hall.

Calavita, Kitty, & Henry N. Pontell. 1990. "'Heads I Win, Tails You Lose': Deregulation, Crime, and Crisis in the Savings and Loan Industry," 36 *Crime & Delinquency* 309.

——. 1991. "'Other People's Money' Revisited: Collective Embezzlement in the Savings and Loan and Insurance Industries," 36 *Crime & Delinquency* 309.

Carson, W.G. 1970. "White Collar Crime and the Enforcement of Factory Legislation," 10 *British J. of Criminology* 383.

——. 1982. "Legal Control of Safety on British Offshore Oil Installations," in P. Wickham & T. Dailey, eds., *White Collar and Economic Crime*. Lexington, MA: Lexington Books.

Chambliss, William J., & Robert Seidman. 1982. *Law, Order, and Power*. Reading, MA: Addison-Wesley Publishing Co.

Clinard, Marshall B., & Richard Quinney. 1973. *Criminal Behavior Systems*. 2d ed. New York: Holt, Rinehart & Winston.

Clinard, Marshall B., & Peter Yeager. 1980. *Corporate Crime*. New York: Free Press.

Clinard, Marshall B., Peter C. Yeager, Jeanne Brissette, David Petrashek, & Elizabeth Harries. 1979. *Illegal Corporate Behavior*. Washington, DC: National Institute of Law Enforcement & Criminal Justice, Department of Justice.

Coleman, James W. 1985. *The Criminal Elite: The Sociology of White Collar Crime*. New York: St. Martin's Press.

Cranston, R. 1982. "Regulation and Deregulation: General Issues," 5 *Univ. of New South Wales Law J.* 1.

Domhoff, G. William. 1967. *Who Rules America?* Englewood Cliffs, NJ: Prentice-Hall.

——. 1978. *The Powers That Be*. New York: Random House.

Dowie, Mark. 1979. "Pinto Madness," in J. Skolnick & E. Currie, eds., *Crisis in American Institutions*. 4th ed. Boston: Little, Brown.

Ermann, M. David., & Richard J. Lundman. 1978. *Corporate and Governmental Deviance: Problems of Organizational Behavior in Contemporary Society*. New York: Oxford Univ. Press.

——. 1982. *Corporate Deviance*. New York: Holt, Rinehart & Winston.

Friedland, Roger, Frances Fox Piven, & Robert R. Alford. 1978. "Political Conflict, Urban Structure, and the Fiscal Crisis," in D. Ashford, ed., *Comparing Public Policies: New Concepts and Methods*. Beverly Hills, CA: Sage Publications.

Geis, Gilbert. 1967. "White Collar Crime: The Heavy Electrical Equipment Antitrust Cases of 1961," in M. Clinard & R. Quinney, *Criminal Behavior Systems: A Typology*. New York: Holt, Rinehart, & Winston.

——. 1991. "The Case Study Method in Sociological Criminology," in J.R. Feagin, A.M. Orum, & G. Sjoberg, eds., *A Case for the Case Study*. Chapel Hill: Univ. of North Carolina Press.

——. 1992. "White-Collar Crime: What Is It?" in K. Schlegel & D. Weisburd, *White Collar Crime Reconsidered*. Boston: Northeast University Press.

Gunningham, Neil. 1974. *Pollution, Social Interest and the Law*. London: M. Robertson.

——. 1987. "Negotiated Non-Compliance: A Case Study of Regulatory Failure," 9 *Law & Policy* 69.

Hagan, John. 1985. *Modern Criminology: Crime, Criminal Behavior, and Its Control*. New York: McGraw-Hill Book Co.

Hagan, John L., & Ilene H. Nagel. 1982. "White-Collar Crime, White-Collar Time: The Sentencing of White-Collar Offenders in the Southern District of New York," 20 *American Criminal Law Rev.* 259.

Hagan, John, & Alberto Palloni. 1983. "The Sentencing of White Collar Offenders before and after Watergate." Presented at American Sociological Association annual meeting, Detroit.

Hooks, Gregory. 1990. "From an Autonomous to a Captured State Agency: The Decline of the New Deal in Agriculture," 55 *American Sociological Rev.* 29.

Jackson, Brooks. 1988. *Honest Graft: Big Money and the American Political Process*. New York: Alfred A. Knopf.

Katz, Jack. 1980. "The Social Movement against White-Collar Crime," 2 *Criminology Rev. Yearbook* 161.

Kolko, Gabriel. 1963. *The Triumph of Conservatism*. New York: Free Press.

——. 1965. *Railroads and Regulations, 1877-1916*. Princeton, NJ: Princeton Univ. Press.

Krasner, Stephen D. 1984. "Approaches to the State: Alternative Conceptions and Historical Dynamics," 16 *Comparative Politics* 223.

Levi, Michael. 1984. "Giving Creditors the Business: The Criminal Law in Inaction," 12 *International J. of the Sociology of Law* 321.

Lowi, Theodore J. 1969. *The End of Liberalism*. New York: W.W. Norton.

Mayer, Martin. 1990. *The Greatest Even Bank Robbery: The Collapse of the Savings and Loan Industry*. New York: Charles Scribners' Sons.

Milliband, Ralph. 1969. *The State in Capitalist Society*. London: Weidenfield & Nicolson.

O'Connell, William B. 1992. *America's Money Trauma: How Washington Blunders Crippled the U.S. Financial System*. Winnetka, IL: Conversation Press.

O'Connor, James. 1973. *The Fiscal Crisis of the State*. New York: St. Martin's Press.

Pearce, Frank, & S. Tombs. 1988. "Regulating Corporate Crime: The Case of Health and Safety." Presented at American Society of Criminology annual meeting, Chicago.

Pilzer, Paul Zane. 1989. *Other People's Money: The Inside Story of the S&L Mess*. New York: Simon & Schuster.

Pizzo, Stephen, Mary Fricker, & Paul Muolo. 1989. *Inside Job: The Looting of America's Savings and Loans*. New York: McGraw-Hill Publishing Co.

Poulantzas, Nicos. 1969. "The Problem of the Capitalist State," 58 *New Left Rev.* 67.

——. 1973. *Political Power and Social Classes*, trans. T. O'Ryan. London: New Left Books.

Reichman, Nancy. 1991. "Regulating Risky Business: Dilemmas in Security Regulation," 13 *Law & Policy* 263.

Rueschemeyer, Dietrich, & Peter B. Evans. 1985. "The State and Economic Transformation: Toward an Analysis of the Conditions Underlying Effective Intervention," in P. Evans, D. Rueschemeyer, & T. Skocpol, eds., *Bringing the State Back in*. New York: Cambridge Univ. Press.

Schrager, Laura Shill, & James F. Short, Jr. 1978. "Toward a Sociology of Organizational Crime," 25 *Social Problems* 407.

Shapiro, Susan. 1980. *Thinking about White-Collar Crime: Matters of Conceptualization and Research*. Washington, DC: National Institute of Justice.

——. 1984. *Wayward Capitalist: Target of the Securities and Exchange Commission*. New Haven, CT: Yale University Press.

Shover, Neal, Donald A. Clelland, & John Lynx-wiler. 1986. *Enforcement or Negotiation: Constructing a Regulatory Bureaucracy*. Albany: State Univ. of New York Press.

Skocpol, Theda, & Kenneth Finegold. 1982. "State Capacity and Economic Intervention in the Early New Deal," 97 *Political Science Q.* 255.

Snider, Laureen. 1978. "Corporate Crime and Canada: A Preliminary Report," 20 *Canadian J. of Criminology* 142.

———. 1991. "The Regulatory Dance: Understanding Reform Processes in Corporate Crime," 19 *International J. of the Sociology of Law* 209.

Stryker, Robin. 1992. "Government Regulation," in E.F. Borgatta & M.L. Borgatta, eds., 2 *Encyclopedia of Sociology*. New York: Macmillan Publishing Co.

Sutherland, Edwin H. 1949. *White Collar Crime*. New York: Dryden.

Tillman, Robert, & Henry N. Pontell. 1992. "Is Justice 'Color Blind'? Punishing Medicaid Provider Fraud," 30 *Criminology* 547.

Tucker, Eric. 1987. "Making the Workplace 'Safe' in Capitalism: The Enforcement of Factory Legislation in Nineteenth Century Ontario." Presented at Canadian Law & Society Association annual meeting, Hamilton, ON, 3-6 June.

U.S. Department of Justice. 1990. *Attacking Savings and Loan Institution Fraud*. Report to the President. Washington, DC: U.S. Department of Justice.

———. 1992a. *Attacking Financial Institution Fraud, Fiscal Year 1992 (First Quarterly Report)*. Washington, DC: U.S. Department of Justice.

———. 1992b. *Attacking Financial Institution Fraud, Fiscal Year 1992, Second Quarterly Report*. Washington, DC: U.S. Department of Justice.

U.S. House of Representatives. 1987. *Adequacy of Federal Efforts to Combat Fraud, Abuse, and Misconduct in Federally Insured Financial Institutions*. Hearings before the Committee on Government Operations, Subcommittee on Commerce, Consumer, & Monetary Affairs, 19 Nov. 1987. 100th Cong., 1st sess.

———. 1988. *Combatting Fraud, Abuse, and Misconduct in the Nation's Financial Institutions: Current Federal Efforts Are Inadequate*. House Report No. 100-1088, Committee on Government Operations. 100th Cong., 2d sess.

———. 1989. *Report of the Special Outside Counsel in the Matter of Speaker James C. Wright, Jr.* Committee on Standards of Official Conduct. Washington, DC: GPO.

———. 1990a. *When Are the Savings and Loan Crooks Going to Jail?* Hearing before the Subcommittee on Financial Institutions Supervision, Regulation & Insurance of the Committee on Banking, Finance & Urban Affairs, 28 June 1990. 101st Cong., 2d sess.

———. 1990b. "Effectiveness of Law Enforcement against Financial Crime." Field Hearing before the Committee on Banking, Finance & Urban Affairs, Dallas, TX, 11 April 1990. 101st Cong., 2d sess.

U.S. Senate. 1992. *Efforts to Combat Criminal Financial Institution Fraud*. Hearing before the Subcommittee on Consumer & Regulatory Affairs, Committee on Banking, Housing, & Urban Affairs, 6 Feb. 1992.

Waldman, Michael. 1990. *Who Robbed America: A Citizen's Guide to the S& L Scandal*. New York: Random House.

Walters, Vivienne. 1985. "The Politics of Occupational Health and Safety: Interviews with Workers' Health and Safety Representatives and Company Doctors," 22 *Canadian Rev. of Sociology & Anthropology* 97.

Wheeler, Stanton, & Mitchell Lewis Rothman. 1982. "The Organization as Weapon in White-Collar Crime," 80 *Michigan Law Rev.* 1403.

Wheeler, Stanton, David Weisburd, & Nancy Bode. 1982. "Sentencing the White-Collar Offender: Rhetoric and Reality," 47 *American Sociological Rev.* 641.

Yeager, Peter. 1986. "Managing Obstacles to Studying Corporate Offences: An Optimistic Assessment." Presented at 1986 American Society of Criminology Annual Meetings, Atlanta.

———. 1988. "The Limits of Law: State Regulation of Private Enterprise." Presented at the 1988 American Society of Criminology annual meetings, Chicago.

———. *The Limits of Law: The Public Regulation of Private Pollution*. Cambridge: Cambridge Univ. Press.

Statutes Cited

Comprehensive Thrift and Bank Fraud Prosecution and Taxpayer Recovery Act of 1990.

Financial Institutions Reform, Recovery and Enforcement Act of 1989 (FIRREA).

Section VI

Responses to Crime

Crime consists of those acts codified into the criminal law, and therefore thought to be potentially disruptive to the social order. They are considered threatening enough to individual and group security to call for state responses, rather than relying on private citizens to respond. When a crime is committed, the state, acting on behalf of all the citizens, reacts by mobilizing agencies of the government to assess responsibility, to apprehend, and, ultimately, to punish the guilty party. Known as the criminal justice process, this state-sponsored response to crime consists of police, court, and correctional personnel and procedures intended to control crime and make law breakers accountable for their acts. How the agents and agencies of government carry out these important responsibilities is determined by the rule of law and the interpretation of relevant laws by those charged with implementing them. Both making law and implementing them are influenced by the social context, which in the last ten years has been hostile to conventional law violators.

There are, in effect, two responses to crime, the official and the unofficial. The official response includes all of the institutionalized elements of the criminal justice process; the unofficial response includes the public's feelings and attitudes about crime, especially the fear of it. It is these unofficial sentiments that determine the context within which criminal statutes and their penalties are framed and within which the agents of

the justice system carry out their responsibilities. Society's fear of crime has certainly increased by the steady rise in crime, especially violent crime, in the 1970s and 1980s: widespread drug use, drive-by shootings, and other urban dangers. Because of these conditions, city dwellers are often frightened to leave their homes, worry about the safety of their children, and feel compelled to use extraordinary security measures. In an environment of such fear and concern, the public often expresses its anger about the way crime is being addressed by the government and the way criminals are handled by the justice system. One commentator claims that " . . . Americans are increasingly alarmed at news stories of violent crimes committed by individuals who had received long sentences for other crimes and yet were released after serving only a small fraction of their time" (Wooten 1995: 150). Even in the 1990s, the fear of crime appears to be rising, although the crime rate, especially for serious crime, has steadily declined (Kappeler, Blumberg, and Potter 1996).

Three factors appear to be responsible for the difference between the diminishing amount of crime and the perception of the rising amount of crime: media reporting, law enforcement warnings, and the politicalization of crime (Kappeler, Blumberg, and Potter 1996). For example, the number of investigative television shows that portray sensational but atypical crimes, and the entertainment programming which provides a steady diet of violence, influence our public perception and subsequent fear of crime. In addition, the obvious financial benefit to various branches of the criminal justice system (police, courts, and prisons) of keeping crime in the public's view as a serious problem and the politicians who use the issue of crime to garner public support also contribute to the exaggerated picture the public has of the severity of the crime problem.

Of these factors, it may well be that media coverage of crime is the most important in shaping our fear and determining the public agenda. Some contend that when the media speak, the government and others listen (Mead 1994). Moreover, it is not really the content of the coverage but the extent of it that makes people think an issue is important (Johnson et al. 1994). If this logic is applied to crime and its constant portrayal in the news and in the entertainment field, it becomes clear why people are convinced that crime is a serious problem and one that needs to be dealt with effectively.

An important myth about crime is the distinction between criminals and noncriminals, a kind of us-and-them mentality that ignores the fact that many Americans have committed crimes for which they could be incarcerated at some time in their lives (Kappeler, Blumberg, and Potter 1996). When all of these factors—exaggerated exposure to crime, the resulting fear of crime and altered lifestyles, the us-and-them distinction, and public outrage at the seemingly lenient treatment of offenders—are combined, they form the basis for the public's punitive attitude toward offenders. Indeed, Victor E. Kappeler and his colleagues suggest that the public's desire for punishment outweighs its concern for fair judicial treatment of the offender. Although the philosophy of the American correctional system has vacillated among a number of goals, such as retribution (vengeance), incapacitation (the removal of an offender from society), rehabilitation (treatment for the offender), and deterrence (both specifically aimed at the offender, and generally aimed at using the offender as an example to society), the public in recent years has cried for greater vengeance. Evidence of this

attitude can be seen in the growing public support for the death penalty, longer sentences, mandatory sentences, the abolition of parole in many states, and new "three strikes and you're out" legislation. Both the public and its lawmakers seem to be less interested in rehabilitation or the general welfare of inmates than in punitive sentences and scapegoats to bear the brunt of public outrage and fear.

Within this context of rising public fear of crime, the official agents of the criminal justice system work to ensure public safety and protect the established social order. How these goals are accomplished has varied over time, but at each point in history the roles of the police, the courts, and the correctional system have been debated and argued. The debate continues today.

Policing Society

For most people, our first response to knowledge of a crime is to call the police. It is the responsibility of the police to protect us from those who would break the law by enforcing codes of conduct found in criminal statutes. But the police do more than just protect us; they engage in many activities that have little to do with enforcing the law (see reading 37). Although the police are often held responsible for rising crime rates and are accused of not being able to prevent crime, the truth is that the public has misconstrued the true nature of police work. Policing actually involves little crime control and almost no crime prevention. James A. Inciardi (1996: 196) claims that only a small percent of police activities are related to law enforcement; other criminologists are more specific, placing the amount of law enforcement activity as low as 10 to 20 percent (Kappeler, Blumberg, and Potter, 1996). Instead, large portions of the work day are given to peacekeeping (control of disorderly crowds and individuals, directing traffic, providing directions, and so forth), and mundane activities such as filling out reports and testifying in court. A majority of police work is reactive, not proactive. Police respond when they are called, and the manner and nature of the response have often generated controversy.

Although policing society is arguably the justice system's most important function, it is also the one fraught with the gravest problems and the most sensitive issues, including police discretion, coercive force, brutality, and corruption. Interestingly, policing is one area of work in which the amount of discretion increases as one goes from the top of the organization down to patrol officers (Glaser 1972). Police discretion is the ability to make quick, on-the-spot decisions, sometimes contrary to official rules. An important discretionary decision is whether or not to make an arrest. If every instance of law violation known to the police led to an arrest, the system would be overwhelmed and paralyzed. Discretion allows some screening of whom the police react to and process officially. Some factors that influence the decision to arrest, for example, include the seriousness of the offense, how well the victim and offender know each other, department policy, and the demeanor of the offender toward the police (Voigt et al. 1994). One important problem with police discretion is the potential for institutionalized discrimination. Even with problems associated with discretion, many scholars agree that it is a necessary and integral part of police work and should be controlled (not eliminated) by formal rules created within the agencies themselves (Walker 1993).

An important detail that sets the police apart from the rest of society is that they have the "legitimate right to use [coercive] force" in situations where it may be required (Inciardi 1996: 196). Sometimes the use of force is carried too far and turns into police brutality, as in the 1991 beating of Rodney King by Los Angeles police officers. Police brutality is most likely to take place when an individual shows disrespect for the police or when the police want information.

One factor that contributes to police brutality, as well as to corruption, is the police subculture, which "provide[s] officers with a shared cognitive framework from which to view the world . . . the beliefs, values, definitions and manners of expression necessary to depart from society's expectation of acceptable behavior" (Kappeler, Blumberg, and Potter 1994: 124). Police officers, who are generally exposed to the negative aspects of society, feel isolated, sometimes even hostile toward much of society, and they soon learn to trust very few people except fellow officers. Not only are they dependent upon one another for safety on the job, but they find that fellow officers are the only ones who can understand and relate to the stresses, strains, and alienation associated with police work. As a result, they tend to associate with one another and maintain an us-and-them attitude. One consequence is that few officers will implicate a fellow officer in any wrongdoing, preferring instead to maintain a "code of silence."

According to Daniel Glaser, there are three types of policing: the watchman style, the legalistic style, and the service style. Officers in "watchman" departments, typically located in older cities with strong political machines, have little education, little training and receive low pay. Most police efforts in the watchman style are for the benefit of people of high status; lower-class people are served grudgingly. Officers in legalistic departments stress a high level of law enforcement and have somewhat more education. Most of their efforts are directed against those of lower status. Officers in the service-style departments stress courtesy and neighborhood relations; compared to outsiders, residents receive preferential treatment from the police.

In the last 20 years, efforts have been made to professionalize police departments. Many now have higher standards of admission, requiring applicants to have at least an Associate's degree. In 1988 almost 23 percent of police officers had four or more years of college; not quite 35 percent of officers had no college education, down from 80 percent in 1960 (Walker 1993). In many jurisdictions, rates of pay have been increased substantially in order to attract and keep higher-level officers on the force and to reduce temptations for corruption. Officers receive better training than in the past; training hours have almost doubled from 340 hours to 633 hours in the 30-year period from 1952 to 1982, and training has been expanded to cover more topics.

Closer attention is also being paid to police-community relationships, with community-based and problem-oriented policing becoming trendy options.

Although there is substantial agreement on the need to professionalize the police and make them more responsive to their local communities, some methods used to achieve these objectives are not well accepted by rank-and-file officers. In order to combat brutality and corruption, most urban police departments have internal-affairs departments, which attempt to monitor, review, and at times discipline inappropriate police behavior. These units are sometimes seen as violations of the unofficial police subculture, which expects officers to keep silent about one another's transgressions. In a number of communities, citizen review boards have been formed to hear and investigate citizen complaints against police officers. These boards have typically been opposed by the police, who see them as an unwarranted intrusion into their departmental affairs.

In response to past injustices and abuses, the behaviors of police are bound (or limited) by a number of Supreme Court rulings. In 1914 the Court found in *Weeks v. United States* that evidence seized illegally, in violation of the Fourth Amendment's unreasonable search-and-seizure clause, could not be used in federal courts. In 1961, the Supreme Court's ruling in *Mapp v. Ohio* extended the exclusionary rule to state courts as well. Unfortunately, this ruling was viewed by many as tying the hands of police officers in their fight against crime. *Escobedo v. Illinois* (1964) guaranteed a suspect the right to an attorney when police questioning becomes accusatory. The implications of *Miranda v. Arizona* (1966) included protection from self-incrimination. Suspects must be informed of their Miranda rights, a process now familiar to most of society: the right to remain silent, the right to an attorney, and the warning that any statements can be used against the accused in a court of law. In 1985 in *Tennessee v. Garner*, the Supreme Court affirmed the step that most police departments had already taken by invalidating the "fleeing felon" rule in favor of the "defense of life" standard in police decisions involving

whether or not to shoot (Walker 1993). Some states have adopted laws requiring police departments to develop rules governing high-speed pursuits. There are, of course, varying opinions on whether these limitations improve or hinder policing.

The Judicial System

The judicial system in the United States is an accusatorial, or adversarial, system, unlike inquisitorial systems found elsewhere. In an adversarial system, two opposing sides (the prosecution and the defense) argue their cases before an impartial referee (the judge) and a jury of the accused's peers. In an inquisitorial system, the judge is a part of the fact-finding mission, and all sides cooperate to bring forth the truth, regardless of whether or not it benefits the side that discloses the evidence.

Prosecutors enjoy some of the broadest discretionary powers of any criminal justice personnel (see reading 38). They decide when and whom to prosecute, the nature and degree of the charges, and whether or not to offer a plea bargain. Their decisions are often based on such arbitrary considerations as their win-lose court record, the credibility of the victim (taking into consideration a victim's character and background), or the relationship between an offender and a victim (Voigt et al. 1994). The wishes of a victim or victim's family to avoid trial (for various reasons such as fear or inconvenience), bargains in which the defendant agrees to testify against others, the strength or absence of societal pressure to prosecute, and the ego of the prosecutor may also determine whether a deal is struck (Holten and Lamar 1991).

Although the U.S. Constitution guarantees the right to trial by a jury of one's peers, in reality, a trial is not what generally happens. Ninety percent of all cases are decided through plea bargaining, an informal procedure in which the prosecution or the state makes an offer to lower the charges or set a limit on the punishment imposed in exchange for a plea of guilty from the defendant (Inciardi 1996: 346). There are many advantages and some disadvantages to the widespread use of plea bargaining. One of the biggest advantages is that it greatly reduces the number of cases being tried on already over-crowded court dockets. Plea bargaining is particularly advantageous to prosecutors who have weak cases, poor witnesses, and small staffs; it allows them to win a case that might otherwise be lost or require too much preparation time and manpower.

Plea bargains are also advantageous for overworked defense attorneys, particularly public defenders or court-appointed attorneys, who are assigned huge work loads and who may have only a few minutes to spend with each defendant. Defense attorneys often succumb to "work group pressures," knowing that giving judges and prosecutors too much flack on one case may jeopardize the treatment of their other clients (Holten and Lamar 1991). Some public defenders may not want to rock the boat if they aspire to higher-level jobs in the system. Public defenders have been described as "double agents," giving the appearance of representing the defendant but in actuality working for the court and coming to regard guilty pleas as the most cost-effective way to run the system (Voigt et al. 1994). Public defenders often approach their cases with the assumption that their clients are guilty of *something* (Voigt et al. 1994), and they work from that assumption.

Plea bargaining has several disadvantages. There is always a chance that innocent persons will take a plea bargain for fear of going to prison if they are found guilty in a trial. In addition, those who plead guilty give up their constitutional rights to a trial by jury, the right to confront and cross-examine witnesses against them, and so forth. Nevertheless, the public often feels that plea bargaining lets criminals off easy with less punishment than they deserve. This effect erodes the public's confidence in the criminal justice system and may fuel a punitive, "get tough" attitude toward offenders.

Even cases that go to trial are fraught with the possibility of unfair and discriminatory treatment and outcomes. Defendants are guaranteed a right to a trial by a jury of their peers. For many years, however, African Americans and other minorities, even females, could not serve on juries, so it was

highly questionable whether a defendant from one of these groups was tried by a jury of peers. Defendants and jurors often come from different social classes, further reducing the likelihood of facing a jury of one's "peers." During *voir dire*, the jury screening process, each side (defense and prosecution) may eliminate a certain number of candidates it thinks are unsuitable. But today, it is perfectly legal for those with enough money to hire professional jury consultants to help select a "winning" jury. That practice negates the idea of random jury selection and puts those who cannot afford consultants at a disadvantage. Juries are often unpredictable. In jury nullification, or jury pardons, for example, juries often refuse to convict a person they think is guilty, because they do not believe he or she deserves the punishment (Holten and Lamar 1991).

Another area in which there is disparity in treatment of defendants is that of bail. Judges set bail based on a number of factors, such as the seriousness of the crime and the likelihood that the defendant will appear in court as ordered. Little consideration is given to the defendant's ability to post bail. Therefore, upper-class and well-to-do defendants are often freed on bail, while poor, lower-class defendants often languish in jail or detention centers awaiting hearings or trials. Consequently, those accused of petty offenses may be jailed while those with more serious offenses are allowed to remain free until their cases come to trial because of differing economic circumstances. Innocent people have been incarcerated (sometimes for a long period of time) while awaiting hearings or trials. Those in jail have no opportunity to participate in the preparation of their defense. Often families of lower-class and middle-class jailed defendants experience great financial hardship in their absence.

Punishment

Earlier, it was stated that all criminal laws contain a penalty, or a specification of the punishment that one deserves for breaking the law. The provision of punishment is society's way of attempting to prevent and control crime, the overall goals of the criminal justice system. Punishment is not, of course, the only objective of the correctional system (see reading 39). Indeed, social control theorists generally identify four goals of American corrections: retribution, deterrence (general and specific), incapacitation, and rehabilitation (or treatment). Retribution is akin to vengeance, a situation in which the severity of the punishment is equal to the severity of the crime. Specific deterrence reflects the idea that offenders will find the punishment unpleasant enough that they will refrain from committing the crime again in the future. General deterrence involves the punishment of an offender serving as an example to the rest of society not to engage in a particular activity. Incapacitation simply means that an offender is not able to commit other illegal acts while incarcerated. Rehabilitation seeks to change offenders in some way that will encourage them to engage in legal activities and stay away from crime.

Deterrence, incapacitation, and rehabilitation are forward-looking goals with an eye toward preventing future crime, while retribution is backward-looking, intent only on punishment, with no thought for crime prevention (Travis, Schwartz, and Clear 1983). Looking at the goals from this perspective illuminates a flaw in the public desire for retribution at the expense of other goals, especially treatment: it offers no hope of a solution, no possibility of change or improvement in the problem of crime, and it may actually worsen the situation. The large number of recidivists seem to illustrate that our correctional facilities are doing little to facilitate change, except perhaps change for the worse.

Correctional goals should be based on the "least drastic alternative," that is, the least severe punishment necessary to obtain the desired result (Travis, Schwartz, and Clear 1983: 230). Why incarcerate those who pose no physical threat to society? This can only be answered when society has a clear idea of what its goals of punishment are. If the goal is retribution, then incarceration fulfills that goal. If the goals include the prevention of future crime, incarceration alone does not address this goal. There is a need for some form of rehabilitation, either within the process of incarceration or perhaps instead of it.

Not everyone agrees, of course, that the U.S. system incarcerates too many people for too long. For example, James Wooten discusses the costs of letting people out of prison early. They include the commission of new crimes, the cost of private protection (lights, locks, guards) against criminals, and the cost of insurance. Victims, he says, experience a loss of property and wages, and altered lifestyles. In addition, costs of crime include medical costs, business losses passed on to consumers, and urban blight. From this perspective, keeping a large number of offenders, especially chronic offenders, under state supervision might even be considered cost effective.

Although punishment is an integral and often used element of our criminal justice system, it is not always administered fairly or effectively. There is racial, class, and gender disparity in punishment. As noted previously, penalties for possession and sale of crack, a drug used primarily by African Americans, are stiffer than penalties for possession and sale of cocaine, a very similar drug used primarily by whites. Capital punishment discriminates against minorities, males, and the lower class. One study found that over a 60-year period, 13 percent of murders were committed by women, but they made up less than 1 percent of the executions (Lee 1995). During the same 60-year period, almost half of those executed were people of color (Stephens 1995). It has been found that a person of any race is more likely to be executed if the victim was White (Kappeler, Blumberg, and Potter 1996). Eighty-five percent of those executed during one recent 20-year period had white victims (Stephens 1995).

Prisons

In 1997, more than 1 million adults were incarcerated in federal and state prisons and more than 500,000 were imprisoned in local jails (Donziger 1996). This is the largest number of incarcerated men and women in the history of the country, and it ranks the United States second only to Russia in number of persons locked up. In addition, several million more are under the supervision of a correctional system (on probation or parole or serving a sentence in a community facility). The rates of incarceration and correctional supervision have grown significantly since 1980 for members of all racial and ethnic groups, although African American males have experienced the largest growth.

Although they do not receive as much public attention as prisons, there are more than 3,300 local jails in the United States. Jails hold persons who are awaiting a court appearance or sentencing as well as those serving sentences of one year or less. Between 1989 and 1997, the jail population rose 43 percent (Bureau of Justice Statistics, 1998). The inmates of the nation's jails are typically poor men, largely of a racial minority, who were using drugs, alcohol, or both at the time of their arrest. Sometimes characterized as the "ultimate ghetto" of the criminal justice system, jails are often unsafe, brutal places where inmate services are lacking and rehabilitation programs nonexistent (Inciardi 1996).

The number of prisoners and the composition of prison populations change as a result of two factors: changes in criminal activity and changes in responses of the system (Beck and Brien 1995). Such changes in the last 20 years are well documented. One of the most striking changes has been in the number of drug-related offenses coming to the attention of authorities. The number of inmates in prison for a drug crime has risen to the point where they now make up approximately 50 percent of those in federal prisons and 23 percent of those in state prisons (Office of National Drug Control Policy 1998). As drug-related offenses have increased, legislatures have cracked down by passing laws that increase the likelihood of incarceration upon conviction, impose mandatory sentences, and make early release more difficult. At the same time, several offenses not necessarily related to drugs, such as weapons possession, drunk driving, and some sexual assaults, also carry stiffer prison sentences. Although the advent of sentencing guidelines has allowed greater uniformity in sentencing, it has also increased the overall time served in prison.

Although we keep building new prisons, we fill them almost as fast as they can be built (see reading 40), and overcrowding continues to be a major problem. In 1993 "state prisons were estimated to be operating at between 18 and 29 percent above capacity [and] the federal system . . . 36 percent over capacity" (Crouch et al. 1995: 66). Overcrowding and its resulting stress, coupled with the almost total loss of privacy, can lead to violence and abuse and is conducive to the spreading of illness.

The cost of prisons is great. It costs $160,000 per "bed" (not including interest paid on borrowed money) to build a maximum-security prison (Irwin and Austin 1997) and $25,000 a year to support one inmate (DiIulio and Piehl 1995). Additional costs include loss of tax revenue from inmates, loss of property taxes from prison grounds, and payment of social services to inmates' families; these costs add up to another $21,000 per inmate (Irwin and Austin 1997). Money used to build and support prisons is money taken from some other service, such as education.

There are other costs to society besides monetary, however. Since prisons are a breeding ground for crime, many first-time petty offenders who end up in prison turn into hardened criminals who commit more heinous crimes upon their eventual release. A prison record and a lack of educational opportunities and job-/training programs make it difficult for many prison releasees to find employment, thus increasing their chances of becoming recidivists. Society pays a steep price for their continued criminal activities.

Prisons are "total institutions," with involuntary residents; the institution controls every area of the inmates' lives. Upon entering prison, inmates suffer a number of losses, first and foremost the loss of liberty and personal space. They are separated from family and friends, are deprived of heterosexual relationships, and lose their sense of security. Their movements are restricted, and the goods and services that they are allowed are limited primarily to basic needs, unless obtained through prison gangs or "service providers." Inmates are not allowed to make many decisions and are reduced to a dependent state, a situation that does nothing to help them cope with common problems of living when they are released.

There are a number of less severe and less costly alternatives to prisons. Many of these fall into the category of community-based corrections, half-way houses, work-release programs, and community service (Voigt et al. 1994). Individuals may be diverted from the system by entering rehabilitation programs, counseling programs, or drug and alcohol treatment programs, or by such innovations as house arrest with electronic surveillance devices. Drug courts, an increasingly popular option, stipulate drug treatment with parole in lieu of incarceration; successful completion of this sentence results in the original charges being dropped.

Probation is another alternative to prison sentences. Probation allows an offender to be under supervision while continuing to live in the community, thus creating only minor disruptions in his or her life. The probationer is expected to follow certain rules (different for each person), such as visiting or calling the probation officer at regular intervals, avoiding the use of alcoholic beverages, or staying away from criminal acquaintances. Not only is probation less expensive than incarceration, but it allows an offender to keep his or her job, maintain family relationships, and avoid the violent and corrupt prison setting. Also, the typical probationer experiences less social stigma than a convict who has served time in prison. For many first-time or nonviolent offenders, probation is often a viable option.

Decriminalization

As a result of the get-tough-on-crime policy, which now characterizes this nation's reaction to the perceived growth in law-violating behavior, U.S. prisons and jails are filled beyond capacity, and probation and parole caseloads are unmanageably large. In 1992, the latest year for which data are available, nationwide spending on corrections exceeded $31 billion (*Seeking Justice* 1997). "Between 1987 and 1993, state spending increases for corrections outpaced higher education by 41 percent nationwide" (ibid, p. 9). Since then, there have been no indications that the rate of commitment to correctional programs or the cost of such policies has slowed. How long can the nation continue to spend more on incarcerating its citizens than on educating them?

One way of reducing the burden now being shouldered by the police, courts, and correctional facilities is to eliminate some behaviors from the criminal statutes. If a behavior were no longer considered a crime, it would not be of concern to the police, and those engaging in the activity would not be sent to overcrowded prisons and jails. Decriminalization is repealing a law or laws governing some type of behavior that should no longer be labeled as criminal (see reading 41). Admittedly applicable to a limited number of offenses, generally public-order crimes about which there is ambivalent moral consensus, decriminalization could be an important alternative response to some criminal activity, since much of the current criminal justice crisis has resulted from the enforcement of substance-abuse laws. Decriminalization of drug offenses, for example, would drastically reduce the number of individuals incarcerated in prisons and alleviate the problem of overcrowding without building more prisons or letting serious felons out the back door as new offenders come in the front door. It would also reduce court dockets substantially.

Using drugs as an example, arguments for and against decriminalization may be analyzed. From Arnold Trebach's point of view (see Trebach and Inciardi 1993), the war against drugs has filled prisons with small-time drug offenders; invaded personal privacy and violated constitutional rights; provoked hatred of racial minorities; wasted large sums of money; encouraged violent drug traffickers and police corruption; diverted resources and attention from other pressing problems such as racial hatred, criminal violence, and AIDS; and pushed crime and violence levels higher. Furthermore, Trebach points out, there is really no scientific basis for distinguishing legal and illegal drugs as far as potential harm to users, inasmuch as annual deaths from alcohol and cigarettes far outstrip those from illicit substances. He claims that for most simple cases of drug possession (the majority of which are for marijuana), prison is an entirely inappropriate punishment, because the punishment far exceeds the crime.

It is Trebach's contention, therefore, that the legalization of drugs would help curb the problems of massive drug abuse, high levels of crime and violence (such as murders and maimings), the spread of AIDS, the collapse of cities, and vicious racial conflict. He believes we should have addict-maintenance programs in conjunction with the legalization of drugs.

Inciardi, by contrast, is against the legalization of drugs. He refutes Trebach's contention that legalization would probably not increase drug use, and he also refutes the idea that drugs such as marijuana are harmless (Trebach and Inciardi 1993). Although Inciardi is careful to point out that for most individuals criminal activities begin long before drug use, he does believe that drugs intensify criminal careers. The drug-crime interaction may be seen in each of three types of drug-related violence delineated by Paul Goldstein: the psychopharmacologic, the economically compulsive, and the systemic. The psychopharmacologic type results from drug-induced irrational behavior; cocaine psychosis fits this type. In the economically compulsive type, some users support their habit through economically oriented violent crime. Finally, the systemic type results from interactions involving drug trafficking, such as fights over turf. Inciardi believes that any decrease in systemic violence that might occur as a result of legalization would be compensated for by an increase in psychopharmacologic violence. Therefore, he does not see legalization as a means of decreasing crime and, in fact, thinks that it may create more addicts (hence, more psychopharmacologic crime), because unlike Trebach, he believes that current laws do limit access to drugs for many groups, especially teenagers. He contends that the legalization of currently illegal drugs will not discourage their use but will most likely encourage it.

Perhaps the best response to crime is to prevent it from occurring in the first place. Crime prevention is often discussed but seldom implemented. The reason for that may be the difficulty in knowing precisely what to do to prevent crime. Programs designed to improve social conditions, to deliver more effective policing, to "get tough" on violators have all claimed some success in reducing the crime rate, but empirical verification of such claims is scarce. In the meantime, responses to crime after it has occurred continue to be the principal way in which society handles crime and criminals.

The readings that follow deal in some detail with the topics discussed in this section: the police, courts, corrections, the efficacy of punishment, and the possibility of decriminalization.

References

Beck, Allen J. and Peter M. Brien. 1995. "Trends in the U.S. Correctional Populations: Recent Findings from the Bureau of Justice Statistics," in Kenneth C. Haas and Geoffrey P. Alpert (eds.), *The Dilemmas of Corrections: Contemporary Readings* (3rd. ed.). Prospect Heights, IL: Waveland Press.

Bureau of Justice Statistics. 1998. *Profile of Jail Inmates 1996.* Washington, DC: U.S. Department of Justice.

Crouch, Ben M., Geoffrey P. Alpert, James W. Marquart, and Kenneth C. Haas. 1995. "The American Prison Crisis: Clashing Philosophies of Punishment and Crowded Cellblocks," in Kenneth C. Haas and Geoffrey P. Alpert (eds.), *The Dilemmas of Corrections: Contemporary Readings* (3rd ed.), Prospect Heights, IL: Waveland Press.

DiIulio, John J. Jr. and Anne Morrison Piehl. 1995. "Does Prison Pay? The Stormy National Debate Over the Cost-Effectiveness of Imprisonment," in Kenneth C. Haas and Geoffrey P. Alpert (eds.), *The Dilemmas of Corrections: Contemporary Readings* (3rd. ed.). Prospect Heights, IL: Waveland Press.

Donziger, Stephen R., ed. 1996. *The Real War on Crime.* New York: Harper Perennial.

Glaser, Daniel. 1972. *Adult Crime and Social Policy.* Englewood Cliffs, NJ: Prentice-Hall.

Goldstein, Paul (1985). "The Drugs/Violence Nexus: A Tripartite Conceptual Framework," *Journal of Drug Issues,* (fall), pp. 493-506.

Heineman, Robert A., Steven A. Peterson, and Thomas H. Rasmussen. 1995. *American Government* (2nd ed.). New York: McGraw-Hill.

Holten, N. Gary and Lawson L. Lamar. 1991. *The Criminal Courts: Structures, Personnel, and Processes.* New York: McGraw-Hill.

Inciardi, James A. 1996. *Criminal Justice* (5th. ed.) San Diego: Harcourt Brace Jovanovich.

Irwin, John and James Austin. 1997. *It's About Time: America's Imprisonment Binge* (2nd ed.). Belmont, CA: Wadsworth.

Johnson, Paul E., Gary J. Miller, John H. Aldrich, David W. Rohde, and Charles W. Ostrom, Jr. 1994. *American Government: People, Institutions, and Policies* (3rd. ed.). Boston: Houghton Mifflin.

Kappeler, Victor E., Mark Blumberg, and Gary W. Potter. 1996. *The Mythology of Crime and Criminal Justice* (2nd ed.). Prospect Heights, IL: Waveland Press.

Kappeler, Victor E., Richard D. Sluder, and Geoffrey P. Alpert. 1994. *Forces of Deviance: Understanding the Dark Side of Policing*. Prospect Heights, IL: Waveland Press.

Lee, Robert W. 1995. "Deserving to Die," in George McKenna and Stanley Feingold (eds.), *Taking Sides: Clashing Views on Controversial Political Issues* (9th ed.). Guildford, CN: Dushkin.

Mead, Timothy D. 1994. "The Daily Newspaper as Political Agenda Setter: The Charlotte Observer and Metropolitan Reform," *State and Local Government Review,* 26 (Winter), pp. 27-37.

Office of National Drug Control Policy. 1998. Drug Policy Information Clearinghouse, *Fact Sheet* (March).

Seeking Justice: Crime and Punishment in America. 1997. New York: Edna McConnell Clark Foundation.

Stephens, Matthew L. 1995. "Instrument of Justice or Tool of Vengeance?" in George McKenna and Stanley Feingold (eds.), *Taking Sides: Clashing Views on Controversial Political Issues* (9th ed.). Guildford, CN: Dushkin.

Travis, Lawrence F. III, Martin D. Schwartz, and Todd R. Clear. 1983. *Corrections: An Issues Approach* (2nd ed.). Cincinnati, OH: Anderson.

Trebach, Arnold S. and James A. Inciardi. 1993. *Legalize It?: Debating American Drug Policy*. Washington, DC: The American University Press.

Voigt, Lydia, William E. Thornton, Jr., Leo Barrile, and Jerrol M. Seaman. 1994. *Criminology and Justice*. New York: McGraw-Hill.

Walker, Samuel. 1993. "Beyond the Supreme Court: Alternative Paths to the Control of Police Behavior," in Chris W. Eskridge (ed.), *Criminal Justice: Concepts and Issues*. Los Angeles: Roxbury.

Wooten, James. 1995. "Truth in Sentencing: Why States Should Make Violent Criminals Do Their Time," in George McKenna and Stanley Feingold (eds.), *Taking Sides: Clashing Views on Controversial Political Issues* (9th ed.). Guilford, CN: Dushkin. ✦

37

Police

Carl B. Klockars

W̲hy do we have police in our society and what do they do? Are they the first line of defense against lawlessness and anarchy? Or do they serve the larger, more subtle function of protecting the status quo and those who have a vested interest in it? Questions such as these have been debated by scholars and social critics for a long time, with few clear-cut answers emerging from the discussion. What we do know, however, is that all societies have some sort of social control agency charged with enforcing laws and maintaining order. Although the nature and organization of such agencies may vary, their functions are generally similar. For most citizens, the police represent the criminal justice system, and for most law violators, the police are their first contact with the process of justice.

In this selection Carl B. Klockars examines the roles of police in modern American society. He demonstrates that the police do much more than fight crime, that their roles are so varied and complex it is difficult to offer a precise definition of their function. Nevertheless, the common element in all police roles and functions is the right to use legitimate coercive force. Such force may be used immediately in responding to one of the situations police are expected to handle. Obviously, this gives the police enormous discretionary authority that must be supervised by government agents who are responsive to the people.

Klockars demonstrates the origins and background of some of the unique features of American police. The uniform, for example, links the police to a military model of organization, which helps account for their believing they are engaged in a "war on crime." Winning such a war cannot be done by the police, because crime results from factors over which the police have no control. The best that might be achieved is controlling crime more effec-

tively with nontraditional tactics. Two ideas that have recently emerged as part of the reform movement of policing are community-oriented policing and problem-oriented policing. These techniques, targeting "hot spots" and working more closely with the community, may well be the models of policing for the future. But this selection shows that they, too, are not without shortcomings and potentially serious problems.

F̲or modern sociology the core problem of police has been, and continues to be, the extrication of the concept *police* from the forms and institutions in which it has been realized and the symbols and concealments in which it has been wrapped. Doing so is essential to the interpretive understanding of the idea of police and is prerequisite to mature answers to the question of what policing means, has meant, and can mean. In one form or another it is the project that has occupied sociologists of police since the early 1960s, and although there is occasional overlap and interchange, attention to it is primarily what distinguishes contributions to the sociology of police from scholarly efforts in the study of police administration, jurisprudence, criminalistics, and police science.

The Police: A Sociological Definition

By the end of the 1960s a small number of now-classic empirical studies of police had made it apparent that conventional understandings of the idea of police were fundamentally and irreparably flawed. In the face of large-scale studies by Reiss (1971) and Black (1971) which showed that the model tour of duty of a patrol officer in the high-crime areas of the nation's largest cities did not involve the arrest of a single person, it became impossible for sociologists to continue to speak of police as "law enforcers" or of their work as "law enforcement." Likewise, both Skolnick's *Justice Without Trial* (1966) and Wilson's *Varieties of Police Behavior* (1968) illustrated dramatic differences in the way police were organized and the relationships they elected to enjoy with courts and law. Similarly, early studies of both the exercise of patrol officer discretion (Bittner 1967a, 1967b) and requests for police service (Cumming et al. 1965; Bercal 1970) cast substantial doubt on the notion that as substantial, much less a defining, activity of police was "fighting crime."

Police Role and Functions

The task of extricating the concept of police from these common misconceptions was assumed by Egon Bittner in his *The Functions of Police in Modern Society* (1970). A fundamental theme of Bittner's work was that to define police as "law enforcers," "peacekeepers," "agents of social control," "officers of the court," or, indeed, in any terms that suppose what police should do, confuses police role and function. Throughout history, in this country and in others, police have performed all sorts of functions. In fact, the functions, both manifest and latent, which police have performed are so numerous and so contradictory that any attempt to define police in terms of the functions they are supposed to perform or the ends they are supposed to achieve is doomed to failure.

Force as the Core of the Police Role

Sociologically, policing cannot be defined in terms of its ends; it must be defined in terms of its means. In *Functions* Bittner advanced an approach to understanding the role of the police that was based on the single means which was common to all police, irrespective of the ends to which they aspired or were employed. The means Bittner found to define police was a right to use coercive force. Police, said Bittner, are "a mechanism for the distribution of non-negotiable, coercive force" (1971). No police had ever existed, nor is it possible to conceive of an entity that could be called police ever existing, that did not claim the right to use coercive force.

Sociologically, Bittner's formulation has three major virtues. First, it was universal. It was applicable to police everywhere as diverse as the sheriff's posse of the old West, the London bobby, the FBI, or the police of Hitler's Third Reich or Castro's Cuba. Second, it was politically, and morally neutral. It could be used to refer to police whose behavior was exemplary as readily as it could be applied to police whose behavior was appalling. And, third, it made it possible to make explicit and to probe in systematic ways a host of questions about the role of police that could not previously be explored because they had been concealed in the confusion between role and function: Why do all modern societies, from the most totalitarian and most tyrannical to the most open and democratic, have police? What does having police make available to society that no other institution can supply? What functions are appropriate to assign to police and what are best left to other institutions?

These questions are of such enormous consequence and so fundamental to an understanding of the role of the police that it is difficult to conceive of a sociology of police existing prior to their recognition.

Why Police?

If police are a "mechanism for the distribution of non-negotiably coercive force," why should all modern societies find it necessary to create and sustain such a mechanism? What does having such a mechanism make available to modern societies that no other institution can provide?

Bittner's answer is that no other institution has the special competence required to attend to "situations which ought not to be happening and about which something ought to be done NOW!" (1974, p. 30). The critical word in Bittner's careful formulation of the role of the police is "now." What the right to distribute coercive force gives to police is the ability to resolve situations that cannot await a later resolution. The crucial element is time. Turning off a fire hydrant against the wishes of inner-city street bathers, preventing the escape of a serial murderer, halting the escalation of a domestic dispute, or moving back the curious at the scene of a fire so that emergency equipment can pass—these and hundreds of other tasks fall to police because their capacity to use force may be required to achieve them "now."

This view of police radically inverts some conventional conceptions. While popular opinion holds that police acquire their right to use coercive force from their duty to enforce the law, the sociology of police holds that police acquire the duty to enforce the law because doing so may require them to invoke their right to use coercive force. Similarly, focus by police on the crimes and misdemeanors of the poor and humble, and their relative lack of attention to white-collar and corporate offenders, is often promoted as reflecting a class or race bias in institutions of social control. While not denying that such biases can exist and do sometimes influence the direction of police attention, if such biases were eliminated entirely, the distribution of police effort and attention would undoubtedly remain unchanged. It would remain unchanged because the special competence of police, their right to use coercive force, is essential in enforcement efforts in which offenders are likely to physically resist or to flee. In white-collar and corporate crime investigations, the special competence of lawyers and accountants is essential, while the special competence of police is largely unnecessary.

Institutional Forms

Although all modern societies have found it necessary to create and maintain some form of police, it is obvious that any institution which bears the right to use coercive force is extraordinarily dangerous and highly subject to abuse and corruption. The danger of the institution of police would appear to be magnified when it gains a monopoly or a near monopoly on the right to use coercive force and those who exercise that monopoly are almost exclusively direct and full-time employees of the state. Appearances and dangers notwithstanding, these are nevertheless the major terms of the institutional arrangement of police in every modern democracy. Some comment on the sociology of this institutional uniformity may be helpful.

Avocational Policing

For most of human history most policing has been done by individuals, groups, associations, and organizations in the private sector. This type of private-sector policing, done by citizens not as a job but as an avocation, may be classified into at least three types, each of which offered a somewhat different

kind of motivation to private citizens for doing it (Klockars 1985). Historically, the most common type is *obligatory avocational policing*. Under its terms private citizens are compelled to police by the threat of some kind of punishment if they fail to do so. In American police history the sheriff's posse is perhaps the most familiar variety of this type of policing. The English systems of frankpledge (Morris 1910) and parish constable (Webb and Webb 1906) were also of this type.

A second type of private-sector policing, *voluntary avocational policing*, is done by private citizens not because they are obliged by a threat of punishment but because they, for their own reasons, want to do it. The most familiar American example of this type of policing is vigilante groups, over three hundred of which are known to have operated throughout the United States up to the end of the nineteenth century (Brown 1975).

A third type, *entrepreneurial avocational policing*, includes private citizens who as English thief takers, American bounty hunters, French agents provocateurs, and miscellaneous paid informants police on a per-head, per-crime basis for money.

The institutional history of these avocational forms of policing is thoroughly disappointing, and modern societies have largely abandoned these ways of getting police work done. The central flaw in all systems of obligatory avocational policing is that as the work of policing becomes more difficult or demanding, obligatory avocational policing takes on the character of forced labor. Motivated only by the threat of punishment, those who do it become unwilling and resistant, a situation offering no one any reason to learn or cultivate the skill to do it well. All forms of voluntary avocational policing suffer from the exact opposite problem. Voluntary avocational police, vigilantes and the like, typically approach their work with passion. The problem is that because the passionate motives of voluntary avocational police are their own, it is almost impossible to control who and where and what form of police work they do and on whom they do it. Finally, the experience with entrepreneurial forms of avocational policing—thief takers, bounty hunters, and paid informants—has been the most disappointing of all. The abuse and corruption of entrepreneurial avocational police has demonstrated unequivocally that greed is too narrow a basis on which to build a police system.

Sociologically, the shortcoming of all forms of avocational policing is that none of them offers adequate means of controlling the police. This observation leads directly to the question of why one might have reason to suspect that a full-time, paid police should be easier to control than its avocational precedents. What new means of control is created by establishing a full-time, paid, police vocation?

The answer to this problem is that only when policing becomes a full-time, paid occupation is it possible to dismiss, to *fire*, any particular person who makes his or her living doing it. The state can only hire entrepreneurial avocational police, bounty hunters, paid informants, and thief takers; it cannot fire them. Vigilantes are driven by their own motives and cannot be discharged front them. Obligatory avocational police are threatened with punishment if they don't work; most would love to be sacked. Because the option to fire, to take police officers' jobs away from them, is the only essential means of controlling police work that separates the police vocation from all avocational arrangements for policing, how that option is used will, more than anything else, determine the shape and substance of the police vocation.

The Police Vocation

The English, who in 1829 created the first modern police, were intimately familiar with the shortcomings of all forms of avocational policing. They had, in fact, resisted the creation of a paid, full-time police for more than a century, out of fear that such an institution would be used as a weapon of political oppression by the administrative branch of government. To allay the fears that the "New Police" would become such a weapon, the architects of the first modern police, Home Secretary Robert Peel and the first commissioners of the New Police, Richard Mayne, and Charles Rowan, imposed three major political controls on them. Peel, Mayne, and Rowan insisted that the New Police of London would be unarmed, uniformed, and confined to preventive patrol. Each of these features shaped in profound ways the institution of the New Police and, in turn, the police of the United States and other Western democracies that explicitly copied the English model.

Unarmed

Politically, the virtue of an unarmed police is that its strength can be gauged as a rough equivalent of its numbers. Weapons serve as multipliers of the strength of individuals and can increase the coercive capacity of individuals to levels that are incalculable. One person with a rifle can dominate a dozen citizens; with a machine gun, hundreds; with a nuclear missile, thousands. One person with a police truncheon is only slightly stronger than another, and that advantage can be quickly eliminated by the other's picking up a stick or a stone. In 1829 the individual strength of the three thousand-constable, unarmed New Police offered little to fear to London's 1.3 million citizens.

While this political virtue of an unarmed police helped overcome resistance to the establishment of the institution, the long-run sociological virtue of an unarmed police proved far more important. Policing is, by definition, a coercive enterprise. Police must, on occasion, compel compliance from persons who would do otherwise. Force is, however, not the only means to compel compliance. Sociologically, at least three other bases for control are possible: authority, power, and persuasion.

Unarmed and outnumbered, the New Police "bobby" could not hope to police effectively on the basis of force. Peel, Mayne, and Rowan knew that if the New Police were to coerce successfully, they would have to do so on the basis of popular respect for the authority and power of the institution of which they were a part. The respect owed each constable was not owed to an individual but to a single, uniform temperament, code of conduct, style of work, and standard of behavior that every constable was expected to embody.

In order to achieve this uniformity of temperament, style, conduct, and behavior, the architects of the New Police employed the option to dismiss with a passion. "Between

1830 and 1838, to hold the ranks of the New Police of London at a level of 3300 men required nearly 5000 dismissals and 6000 resignations, most of the latter not being altogether voluntarily" (Lee 1971, p. 240). During the first eight years of its organization, every position on the entire force was fired or forced to resign more than three times over!

Unlike their earlier London counterparts, the new American police were undisciplined by the firing option. What prevented the effective use of the firing option by early American police administrators was that police positions were, by and large, patronage appointments of municipal politicians. In New York, for example, the first chief of police did not have the right to fire any officer under his command. So while London bobbies were being dismissed for showing up late to work or behaving discourteously toward citizens, American police were assaulting superior officers, taking bribes, refusing to go on patrol, extorting money from prisoners, and releasing prisoners from the custody of other officers.

In New York, Boston, Chicago, and other American cities the modern police began, in imitation of London's bobbies, as unarmed forces; but, being corrupt, undisciplined, and disobedient, they could not inspire respect for either their power or their authority. In controlling citizens they had no option but to rely on their capacity to use force. The difficulty with doing so unarmed is that someone armed with a multiplier of strength can always prove to be stronger. Gradually, against orders, American police armed themselves, at first with the quiet complicity of superior officers and later, as the practice became widespread, in open defiance of departmental regulations. Eventually, in an effort to control the types of weapons their officers carried, the first municipal police agencies began issuing standard service revolvers.

The long-run sociological consequence of arming the American police can be understood only by appreciating how it shaped American police officers' sense of the source of their capacity to control the citizens with whom they dealt. While the London bobbies drew their capacity for control from the profoundly social power and authority of the institution of which they were a part, American police officers understood their capacities for control to spring largely from their own personal, individual strength, multiplied if necessary by the weapon they carried on their hips. This understanding of the source of their capacity for control led American police officers to see the work they did and the choices they made in everyday policing to be largely matters of their individual discretion. Thus, the truly long-run sociological effect of the arming of the American police has been to drive discretionary decision making to the lowest and least public levels of American police agencies. Today how an American police officer handles a drunk, a domestic disturbance, an unruly juvenile, a marijuana smoker, or a belligerent motorist is largely a reflection not of law or agency policy but of that particular officer's personal style. This is not to say that law or agency policy cannot have influence over how officers handle these types of incidents. However, one of the major lessons of recent attempts by sociologists to measure the impact of changes in law or police policy in both domestic violence and drunken driving enforcement is that officers can resist those changes vigorously when the new law or policy goes against their views of proper police response (see Dunford et al. 1990; Mastrofski et al. 1988).

Uniformed

Politically, the requirement that police be uniformed is a guarantee that they will not be used as spies; that they will be given information only when their identity as police is known; that those who give them information, at least when they do so in public, are likely to be noticed doing so; and that they can be held accountable, as agents of the state, for their behavior. The English, who had long experience with uniformed employees of many types, understood these political virtues of the uniform completely. In fact, an incident in 1833 in which a police sergeant assumed an un-uniformed undercover role resulted in such a scandal that it nearly forced the abolition of the New Police.

By contrast, the early American understanding of the uniform was totally different. Initially it was seen to be a sign of undemocratic superiority. Later it was criticized by officers themselves as a demeaning costume and resisted on those grounds. For twelve years, despite regulations that required them to do so, early New York policemen successfully refused to wear uniforms. In 1856 a compromise was reached by allowing officers in each political ward to decide on the color and style they liked best.

Despite the early resistance to the uniform and the lack of appreciation for its political virtues, American police eventually became a uniformed force. But while the London bobby's uniform was explicitly designed to have a certain "homey" quality and reflect restraint, the modern American police officer's uniform is festooned with the forceful tools of the police trade. The gun, ammunition, nightstick, black-jack, handcuffs, and Mace, all tightly bolstered in shiny black leather and set off with chromium buckles, snaps, badges, stars, flags, ribbons, patches, and insignia, suggest a decidedly military bearing. The impression intended is clearly one not of restraint but of the capacity to overcome the most fearsome of enemies by force.

The Military Analogy and the War on Crime

To understand the sociology of the American police uniform, it is necessary to see in it a reflection of a major reform movement in the history of the American police. Around 1890 American police administrators began to speak about the agencies they administered as if they were domestic armies engaged in a war on crime (Fogelson 1977).

The analogy was powerful and simple. It drew upon three compelling sources. First, it sought to connect police with the victories and heroes of the military and to dissociate them from the corruption and incompetence of municipal politics. Second, it evoked a sense of urgency and emergency, in calls for additional resources. From the turn of the century to the present day, the war on crime has proved a useful device for getting municipal governments and taxpayers to part with money for police salaries and equipment. And, third and most important, the war on crime and the military analogy sought to create a relationship between police administrators and politicians at the municipal level that was similar to the relationship enjoyed by military generals and politicians at the national level. At the national level Americans have always conceded that the decision on whether to fight a war was a politicians' decision, but how that war was to be fought and the day-to-day discipline of the troops was best left to the generals. By getting the public and the politicians to accept these terms of the police-politics relationship, the early police administrators found a way to wrest from the hands of politicians the tool they needed to discipline their troops: the option to fire disobedient officers.

The uniform of the war-ready American police officer is testimony to the fact that since the 1940s, American police administrators have won the battle to conceive of police as engaged in a war on crime. And in doing so then, have gained control of the option to fire for administrative purposes. However, the cost of that victory has been enormous.

A major problem is the idea of a war on crime and the expectation police have promoted that they can, in some sense, fight or win it. In point of fact, a war on crime is something police can neither fight nor win for some fundamental sociological reasons. It is simply not within the capacity of police to change those things—unemployment, the age distribution of the population, moral education, civil liberties, ambition and the social and economic opportunities to realize it—that influence the amount and type of crime in any society. These are the major social correlates of crime, and despite presentments to the contrary, police are but a small tail on a gigantic social kite. Moreover, any kind of real "war on crime" is something that no democratic society would be prepared to let its police fight. No democratic society would be able to tolerate the kinds of abuses to the civil liberties of innocent citizens that fighting any real "war" on crime would necessarily involve. It is a major contribution of the sociology of police since the 1960s to demonstrate that almost nothing police do can be shown to have any substantial effect on reducing crime.

The problems of policing in the name of crime when one cannot do much of anything about it are enormous. It is not uncommon for patrol officers to see their employers as hypocritical promoters of a crime-fighting image that is far removed from what they know to be the reality of everyday police work. They may seek to explain what they know to be their failure to do much about crime in terms of the lack of courage of their chief, the incompetence of police administration, or sinister political forces seeking to "handcuff" the police. They often close off what they regard as the disappointing reality of what they do in cynicism, secrecy, and silence—the "blue curtain," the occupational culture of policing.

Equally problematic as a spoil of the early chiefs' victory in their war on crime is the quasimilitary police administrative structure. Although once heralded as a model of efficiency, it is now regarded as an organizationally primitive mode of management. It works, to the extent that it works, by creating hundreds and sometimes even thousands of rules and by punishing departures from those rules severely. The central failing of such an administrative model is that it rests on the unwarranted assumption that employees will not discover that the best way to avoid punishment for doing something wrong is to do as little as possible. The administration can, in turn, respond by setting quotas for the minimum amount of work it will tolerate from employees before it moves to punish them, but if it does so, that minimal amount of work is, by and large, all it will get.

Preventive Patrol

The third major mechanism with which architects of the New Police sought to neutralize their political uses was to confine police to preventive patrol. This restriction was understood to have the effect of limiting the uniformed, patrolling constable to two relatively apolitical types of interventions: situations in which constables would be called upon for help by persons who approached them on the street and situations that, from the street, constables could see required their attention. These political virtues of patrol impressed the architects of the New Police, par-

ticularly Sir Richard Mayne. Mayne postponed the formation of any detective unit in the New Police until 1842, and for his 40 years as commissioner held its ranks to fewer than 15 detectives in a force of more than 3,500.

In the early American experience uniformed patrol served the principal purpose of imposing some semblance of order on unruly officers. Patrol offered some semblance of assurance that officers could be found at least sometime near the area to which they were assigned. And while American police created detective forces almost immediately after they were organized, patrol has become in the United States, as in Britain and other modern democracies, the major means of getting police work done.

Sociologically, patrol has had tremendous consequences for the form and substance of policing. It has, for example, been extraordinarily amenable to the three most profound technological developments of the past century: the automobile, the telephone, and the wireless radio. And while there is no evidence that increasing or decreasing the amount of patrol has any influence whatsoever on the crime rate, each of these technological developments has made police patrol more convenient and attractive to citizens who wish to call for police service. It is not an exaggeration to say that the vast majority of the activity of most modern police agencies is driven by a need to manage citizen demand for patrol service.

In recent years attempts to manage this demand have taken many forms. Among the most common are the creation of computer-aided dispatch systems that prioritize the order in which patrol officers are assigned to complaints and increasingly stringent policies governing the types of problems for which police will provide assistance. Also increasingly common are attempts to handle complaints that merely require a written report, by taking that report over the telephone or having the complainant complete a mail-in form. In no small part, such efforts at eliminating unnecessary police response and making necessary police response efficient have produced some of the increasing cost for police labor.

Reorienting Policing

Despite efforts at prioritization, limitation of direct police response, and development of alternative ways of registering citizen complaints, demand for police service continues to grow. And despite the fact that individual citizens appear to want this form of police service more than any other, some contemporary approaches suggest that the entire idea of "dial-a-cop," "incident-driven" policing requires reconsideration. Two such approaches, "community-oriented policing" (Skolnick and Bayley 1986) and "problem-oriented policing" (Goldstein 1979, 1990), have been advanced as the next generation of "reform" movements in American policing (Greene and Mastrofski 1988).

As theories of police reform, both "problem-oriented" and "community-oriented" policing are grounded in the suspicion that the traditional police response of dispatching patrol officers in quick response to citizen complaints does little to correct the underlying problem that produced the complaint. To some degree at least, this suspicion is confirmed by studies which tend to show that a fairly small number of addresses tend to generate disproportionate numbers of calls for police service, and that patrol officers commonly return to such "hot spots" again and again to attend to similar problems (Sherman et al. 1989).

Both problem-oriented and community-oriented policing offer strategies to deal with such problems that go beyond merely dispatching an officer to the scene. Problem-oriented policing offers a generic, four-step, problem-solving strategy—scanning, analysis, response, and assessment—that police can use to identify problems and experiment with solutions. Community-oriented policing, by contrast, does not offer a mechanism for problem analysis and solution. It is, however, committed to a general strategy that calls for cooperative, police-community efforts in problem solving. In such efforts it encourages the employment of a variety of police tactics—foot patrol, storefront police stations, neighborhood watch programs— that tend to involve citizens directly in the police mission.

While both approaches to reorienting policing have been heralded as revolutionary in their implications for the future of policing, both confront some major obstacles to their realization. The first is that neither problem-oriented nor community-oriented police efforts have been able to reduce the demand for traditional patrol response. Unless that demand is reduced or police resources are increased to allow it to be satisfied along with nontraditional approaches, the community- and problem-oriented policing approaches will most likely be relegated, at best, to a secondary, peripheral role.

The second problem confronting both community- and problem-oriented policing stems from the definition of police and the role appropriate to it in a modern democratic society. The special competence of police is their capacity to use force, and for that reason all modern societies find it necessary and appropriate to have them attend to situations that cannot await a later resolution. Reactive, incident-driven, dial-a-cop patrol is a highly popular, extremely efficient, and, as near as possible, politically neutral means of delivering that special competence. To expand the police role to include responsibility for solving the root problems of neighborhoods and communities is an admirable aspiration. But it is a responsibility that seems to go beyond the special competence of police and to require, more appropriately, the special competence of other institutions.

Discussion Questions

1. Why do societies have police? What is the key operative word in Bittner's explanation of why we have police? Explain how this word separates policing from other methods of societal problem-resolution.

2. Define obligatory avocational policing, voluntary avocational policing, and entrepreneurial avocational policing. What are examples of each model? What are the problems with each of these models?

3. Describe the evolution of policing with regard to arms (weapons), clothing, and patrol. What was the reasoning behind the changes? What is the military anal-

ogy of policing? What strengths and weaknesses are associated with it?

References

Bercal, T. E. 1970 "Calls for Police Assistance: Consumer Demand for Governmental Service." *American Behavioral Scientist*, 13, no. 2 (May–August): 221-238.

Bittner, E. 1967a "Police Discretion in Apprehension of Mentally Ill Persons." *Social Problems*, 14 (Winter): 278-292.

——. 1967b "The Police on Skid Row: A Study of Peace Keeping." *American Sociological Review*, (October): 699-715.

——. 1970. *The Functions of Police in Modern Society*. Washington, DC: U.S. Government Printing Office.

——. 1974. "Florence Nightingale in Pursuit of Willie Sutton: A Theory of Police." In H. Jacob, ed., *The Potential for Reform of Criminal Justice*. Beverly Hills, CA: Sage.

Black, D. 1971 "The Social Organization of Arrest." *Stanford Law Review*, 23 (June): 1087-1111.

Brown, R. M. 1975 *Strain of Violence: Historical Studies of American Violence and Vigilantism*. Oxford: Oxford University Press.

Cumming, E., I. Cumming, and L. Edell. 1965. "Policeman as Philosopher, Guide, and Friend." *Social Forces*, 12, no. 3: 276-286.

Dunford, F. W., D. Huizinga, and D. S. Elliott. 1990. "The Role of Arrest in Domestic Assault: The Omaha Police Experiment." *Criminology*, 28, no. 2: 183-206.

Fogelson, R. 1977. *Big City Police*. Cambridge, MA: Harvard University Press.

Goldstein, H. 1979 "Improving Policing: A Problem-Oriented Approach." *Crime and Delinquency*, 25 (April): 236-258.

——. 1990. *Problem-Oriented Policing*. New York: McGraw-Hill.

Greene, J. and S. Mastrofski. 1988. *Community Policing: Rhetoric or Reality*. New York: Praeger.

Klockars, C. B. 1985. *The Idea of Police*. Beverly Hills, CA: Sage.

Lee, M. 1971. *A History of Police in England*. Montclair, NJ: Patterson Smith.

Mastrofski, S., R. R. Ritti, and D. Hoffmaster. 1988. "Organizational Determinants of Police Discretion: The Case of Drunk Driving." *Journal of Criminal Justice*, 15: 387-402.

Morris, W. A. 1910. *The Frankpledge System*. New York: Longmans, Green and Co.

Reiss, A. J., Jr. 1971. *Police and the Public*. New Haven, CT: Yale University Press.

Sherman, L. W., P. Gartin, and M. E. Buerger. 1989. "Hot Spots of Predatory Crime: Routine Activities and the Criminology of Place." *Criminology*, 27: 27-55.

Skolnick, J. K. 1966. *Justice Without Trial*. New York: John Wiley.

——, and D. Bayley. 1986 *The New Blue Line*. New York: Free Press.

Webb, S. and B. Webb. 1906. *English Local Government from the Revolution to the Municipal Corporations Act: The Parish and the County*. York: Longmans, Green and Co.

Wilson, J. Q. 1968. *Varieties of Police Behavior: The Management of Law and Order in Eight Communities*. Cambridge, MA: Harvard University Press.

Reprinted from: Carl B. Klockars, "Police." In Edgar F. Borgatta and Marie L. Borgatta (eds.), *Encyclopedia of Sociology*, Vol. 3, pp. 1463-1471. Copyright © 1992 by Edgar F. Borgatta and Marie L. Borgatta. Reprinted with permission of Macmillan Library Reference, a Simon & Schuster Company. ✦

38

The Decision to Prosecute

George F. Cole

What happens after an arrest has been made in a criminal case? An uninformed observer might assume that the arrestee is soon given his or her day in court, an opportunity to have innocence or guilt established before an impartial panel of peers, the jury. The more informed student of criminal justice realizes that the process is not quite that simple. The quality of justice depends upon many factors, not the least of which are the decisions made by judicial officers, including prosecutors and judges. It also involves the police, defense attorneys, and community values and attitudes.

George F. Cole explores many of these variables in his examination of the decision to prosecute. It is the prerogative of the prosecutor's office to decide whether or not to prosecute a case. That decision is usually the product of a series of exchange relationships among justice-system personnel and even members of the community. Police try to influence prosecutors, defense attorneys negotiate for plea bargains or reductions in charge, and the lead prosecutor is sensitive to the feelings of judges and potential leaders. In addition, courts are congested, dockets are full, prosecutors are overburdened, and, in general, resources are scarce. What would happen to the courts if every person arrested were prosecuted before a jury?

The answer, of course, is paralysis and a denial of justice. Fortunately, prosecutors have a number of options they may employ throughout the proceedings that are designed to expedite the process of justice. Some cases are rejected for prosecution, others are plea bargained, and still others plead guilty. But the prosecutor's office must be careful about using these options because each decision has possi-

ble political ramifications. Justice-system constituencies cannot be alienated, and the public cannot believe that justice is not being served. Thus, the decision to prosecute is complex, involving more than perceived guilt or innocence.

This paper is based on an exploratory study of the Office of Prosecuting Attorney, King County (Seattle), Washington. The lack of social scientific knowledge about the prosecutor dictated the choice of this approach. An open-ended interview was administered to one-third of the former deputy prosecutors who had worked in the office during the ten year period 1955-1965. In addition, interviews were conducted with court employees, members of the bench, law enforcement officials, and others having reputations for participation in legal decision-making. Over fifty respondents were contacted during this phase. A final portion of the research placed the author in the role of observer in the prosecutor's office. This experience allowed for direct observation of all phases of the decision to prosecute so that the informal processes of the office could be noted. Discussions with the prosecutor's staff, judges, defendant's attorneys, and the police were held so that the interview data could be placed within an organizational context.

The primary goal of this investigation was to examine the role of the prosecuting attorney as an officer of the legal process within the context of the local political system. The analysis is therefore based on two assumptions. First, that the legal process is best understood as a subsystem of the larger political system. Because of this choice, emphasis is placed upon the interaction and goals of the individuals involved in decision-making. Second, and closely related to the first point, it is assumed that broadly conceived political considerations explained to a large extent "who gets or does not get—in what amount— and how, the good (justice) that is hopefully produced by the legal system" (Klonski and Mendelsohn, 1965:323). By focusing upon the political and social linkages between these systems, it is expected that decision-making in the prosecutor's office will be viewed as a principal ingredient in the authoritative allocation of values.

The Prosecutor's Office in an Exchange System

While observing the interrelated activities of the organizations in the legal process, one might ask, "Why do these agencies cooperate?" If the police refuse to transfer information to the prosecutor concerning the commission of a crime, what are the rewards or sanctions which might be brought against them? Is it possible that organizations maintain a form of "bureaucratic accounting" which, in a sense, keeps track of the resources allocated to an agency and the support returned? How are cues transmitted from one agency to another to influence decision-making? These are some of the questions which must be asked when decisions are viewed as an output of an exchange system.

The major findings of this study are placed within the context of an exchange system (Evan, 1965:218).[1] This serves the heuristic purpose of focusing attention upon the linkages found between actors in the decision-making process. In place of the traditional assumptions that the agency is supported solely by statutory authority, this view recognizes that an organization has many clients with which it interacts and upon whom it is dependent for certain resources. As interdependent subunits of a system, then, the organization and its clients are engaged in a set of exchanges across their boundaries. These will involve a transfer of resources between the organizations which will affect the mutual achievement of goals.

The legal system may be viewed as a set of interorganized exchange relationships analagous to what Long (1962:142) has called a community game. The participants in the legal system (game) share a common territorial field and collaborate for different and particular ends. They interact on a continuing basis as their responsibilities demand contact with other participants in the process. Thus, the need for the cooperation of other participants can have a bearing on the decision to prosecute. A decision not to prosecute a narcotics offender may be a move to pressure the United States' Attorney's Office to cooperate on another case. It is obvious that bargaining occurs not only between the major actors in a case—the prosecutor and the defense attorney—but also between the clientele groups that are influential in structuring the actions of the prosecuting attorney.

Exchanges do not simply "sail" from one system to another, but take place in an institutionalized setting which may be compared to a market. In the market, decisions are made between individuals who occupy boundary-spanning roles, and who set the conditions under which the exchange will occur. In the legal system, this may merely mean that a representative of the parole board agrees to forward a recommendation to the prosecutor, or it could mean that there is extended bargaining between a deputy prosecutor and a defense attorney. In the study of the King County Prosecutor's Office, it was found that most decisions resulted from some type of exchange relationship. The deputies interacted almost constantly with the police and criminal lawyers, while the prosecutor was more closely linked to exchange relations with the courts, community leaders, and the county commissioners.

The Prosecutor's Clientele

In an exchange system, power is largely dependent upon the ability of an organization to create clientele relationships which will support and enhance the needs of the agency. For, although interdependence is characteristic of the legal system, competition with other public agencies for support also exists.

Since organizations operate in an economy of scarcity, the organization must exist in a favorable power position in relation to its clientele. Reciprocal and unique claims are made by the organization and its clients. Thus, rather than being oriented toward only one public, an organization is beholden to several publics, some visible and others seen clearly only from the pinnacle of leadership. As Gore (1964:23) notes, when these claims are "firmly anchored inside the organization and the lines drawn taut, the tensions between conflicting claims form a net serving as the institutional base for the organization."

An indication of the stresses within the judicial system may be obtained by analyzing its outputs. It has been suggested that the administration of justice is a selective process in which only those cases which do not create strains in the organization will ultimately reach the courtroom (Chambliss, 1969:84). As noted in Figure 38.1, the system operates so that only a small number of cases arrive for trial, the rest being disposed of through reduced charges, *nolle pros.*, and guilty pleas.[2] Not indicated are those cases removed by the police and prosecutor prior to the filing of charges. As the focal organization in an exchange system, the office of prosecuting attorney makes decisions which reflect the influence of its clientele. Because of the scarcity of resources, marketlike relationships, and the organizational needs of the system, prosecutorial decision-making emphasizes the accommodations which are made to the needs of participants in the process.

Police

Although the prosecuting attorney has discretionary power to determine the disposition of cases, this power is limited by the fact that usually he is dependent upon the police for inputs to the system of cases and evidence. The prosecutor does not have the investigative resources necessary to exercise the kind of affirmative control over the types of cases that are brought to him. In this relationship, the prosecutor is not without countervailing power. His main check on the police is his ability to return cases to them for further investigation and to refuse to approve arrest warrants. By maintaining cordial relations with the press, a prosecutor is often able to focus attention on the police when the public becomes aroused by incidents of crime. As the King County prosecutor emphasized, "That [investigation] is the job for the sheriff and police. It's their job to bring me the charges." As noted by many respondents, the police, in turn, are dependent upon the prosecutor to accept the output of their system; rejection of too many cases can have serious

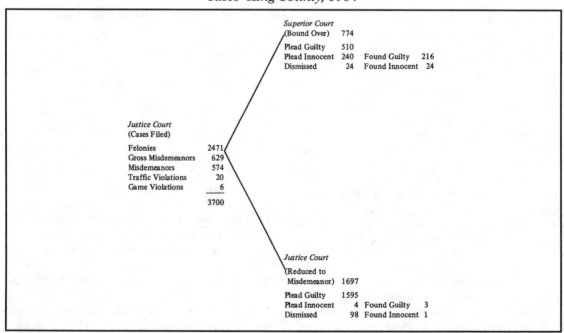

Figure 38.1
Desposition of Felony
Cases–King County, 1964

repurcussions affecting the morale, discipline, and workload of the force.

A request for prosecution may be rejected for a number of reasons relating to questions of evidence. Not only must the prosecutor believe that the evidence will secure a conviction, but he must also be aware of community norms relating to the type of acts that should be prosecuted. King County deputy prosecutors noted that charges were never filed when a case involved attempted suicide or fornication. In other actions, the heinous nature of the crime, together with the expected public reaction, may force both the police and prosecutor to press for conviction when evidence is less than satisfactory. As one deputy noted, "In that case [murder and molestation of a six-year-old girl] there was nothing that we could do. As you know the press was on our back and every parent was concerned. Politically, the prosecutor had to seek an information."

Factors other than those relating to evidence may require that the prosecutor refuse to accept a case from the police. First, the prosecuting attorney serves as a regulator of case loads not only for his own office, but for the rest of the legal system. Constitutional and statutory time limits prevent him and the courts from building a backlog of untried cases. In King County, when the system reached the "overload point," there was a tendency to be more selective in choosing the cases to be accepted. A second reason for rejecting prosecution requests may stem from the fact that the prosecutor is thinking of his public exposure in the courtroom. He does not want to take forward cases which will place him in an embarrassing position. Finally, the prosecutor may return cases to check the quality of police work. As a former chief criminal deputy said, "You have to keep them on their toes, otherwise they get lazy. If they aren't doing their job, send the case back and then leak the situation to the newspapers." Rather than spend the resources necessary to find additional evidence, the police may dispose of a case by sending it back to the prosecutor on a lesser charge, implement the "copping out" machinery leading to a guilty plea, drop the case, or in some instances send it to the city prosecutor for action in municipal court.

In most instances, a deputy prosecutor and the police officer assigned to the case occupy the boundary-spanning roles in this exchange relationship. Prosecutors reported that after repeated contacts they got to know the policemen whom they could trust. As one female deputy commented, "There are some you can trust, others you have to watch because they are trying to get rid of cases on you." Deputies may be influenced by the police officer's attitude on a case. One officer noted to a prosecutor that he knew he had a weak case, but mumbled, "I didn't want to bring it up here, but that's what they [his superiors] wanted." As might be expected, the deputy turned down prosecution.

Sometimes the police perform the ritual of "shopping around," seeking to find a deputy prosecutor who, on the basis of past experience, is liable to be sympathetic to their view on a case. At one time, deputies were given complete authority to make the crucial decisions without coordinating their activities with other staff members. In this way the arresting officer would search the prosecutor's office to find a deputy he thought would be sympathetic to the police attitude. As a former deputy noted, "This meant that there were no departmental policies concerning the treatment to be accorded various types of cases. It pretty much depended upon the police and their luck in finding the deputy they wanted." Prosecutors are now instructed to ascertain from the police officer if he has seen another deputy on the case. Even under this more centralized system, it is still possible for the police to request a specific deputy or delay presentation of the case until the "correct" prosecutor is available. Often a prosecutor will gain a reputation for specializing in one type of case. This may mean that the police will assume he will get the case anyway, so they skirt the formal procedure and bring it to him directly.

An exchange relationship between a deputy prosecutor and a police officer may be influenced by the type of crime committed by the defendant. The prototype of a criminal is one who violates person and property. However, a large number of cases involve "crimes without victims" (Schur, 1965). This term refers to those crimes generally involving violations in moral codes, where the general public is theoretically the complainant. In violations of laws against bookmaking, prostitution, and narcotics, neither actor in the transaction is interested in having an arrest made. Hence, vice control men must drum up their own business. Without a civilian complainant, victimless crimes give the police and prosecutor greater leeway in determining the charges to be filed.

One area of exchange involving a victimless crime is that of narcotics control. As Skolnick (1966:120) notes, "The major organizational requirements of narcotics policing is the presence of an informational system." Without a network of informers, it is impossible to capture addicts and peddlers with evidence that can bring about convictions. One source of informers is among those arrested for narcotics violations. Through promises to reduce charges or even to *nolle pros.*, arrangements can be made so that the accused will return to the narcotics community and gather information for the police. Bargaining observed between the head of the narcotics squad of the Seattle Police and the deputy prosecutor who specialized in drug cases involves the question of charges, promises, and the release of an arrested narcotics pusher.

In the course of postarrest questioning by the police, a well-known drug peddler intimated that he could provide evidence against a pharmacist suspected by the police of illegally selling narcotics. Not only did the police representative want to transfer the case to the friendlier hands of this deputy, but he also wanted to arrange for a reduction of charges and bail. The police officer believed that it was important that the accused be let out in such a way that the narcotics community would not realize that he had become an informer. He also wanted to be sure that the reduced charges would be processed so that the informer could be kept on the string, thus allowing the narcotics squad to maintain control over him. The deputy prosecutor, on the other hand, said that he wanted to make sure that procedures were followed so that the action would not bring discredit on his office. He also suggested that the narcotics

squad "work a little harder" on a pending case as a means of returning the favor.

Courts

The ways used by the court to dispose of cases is a vital influence in the system. The court's actions effect pressures upon the prison, the conviction rate of the prosecutor, and the work of probation agencies. The judge's decisions act as clues to other parts of the system, indicating the type of action likely to be taken in future cases. As noted by a King County judge, "When the number of prisoners gets to the 'riot point,' the warden puts pressure on us to slow down the flow. This often means that men are let out on parole and the number of people given probation and suspended sentences increases." Under such conditions, it would be expected that the prosecutor would respond to the judge's actions by reducing the inputs to the court either by not preferring charges or by increasing the pressure for guilty pleas through bargaining. The adjustments of other parts of the system could be expected to follow. For instance, the police might sense the lack of interest of the prosecutor in accepting charges, hence they will send only airtight cases to him for indictment.

The influence of the court on the decision to prosecute is very real. The sentencing history of each judge gives the prosecutor, as well as other law enforcement officials, an indication of the treatment a case may receive in the courtroom. The prosecutor's expectation as to whether the court will convict may limit his discretion over the decisions on whether to prosecute. "There is great concern as to whose court a case will be assigned. After Judge_____ threw out three cases in a row in which entrapment was involved, the police did not want us to take any cases to him." Since the prosecutor depends upon the plea-bargaining machinery to maintain the flow of cases from his office, the sentencing actions of judges must be predictable. If the defendant and his lawyer are to be influenced to accept a lesser charge or the promise of a lighter sentence in exchange for a plea of guilty, there must be some basis for belief that the judge will fulfill his part of the arrangement. Because judges are unable formally to announce their agreement with the details of the bargain, their past performance acts as a guide.

Within the limits imposed by law and the demands of the system, the prosecutor is able to regulate the flow of cases to the court. He may control the length of time between accusation and trial; hence he may hold cases until he has the evidence which will convict. Alternatively, he may seek repeated adjournment and continuances until the public's interest dies; problems such as witnesses becoming unavailable and similar difficulties make his request for dismissal of prosecution more justifiable. Further, he may determine the type of court to receive the case and the judge who will hear it. Many misdemeanors covered by state law are also violations of a city ordinance. It is a common practice for the prosecutor to send a misdemeanor case to the city prosecutor for processing in the municipal court when it is believed that a conviction may not be secured in justice court. As a deputy said, "If there is no case—send it over to the city court. Things are speedier, less formal, over there."

In the state of Washington, a person arrested on a felony charge must be given a preliminary hearing in a justice court within ten days. For the prosecutor, the preliminary hearing is an opportunity to evaluate the testimony of witnesses, assess the strength of the evidence, and try to predict the outcome of the case if it is sent to trial. On the basis of this evaluation, the prosecutor has several options: he may bind over the case for trial in Superior Court; he may reduce the charges to those of a misdemeanor for trial in Justice Court; or he may conclude that he has no case and drop the charges. The President Judge of the Justice Courts of King County estimated that about seventy percent of the felonies are reduced to misdemeanors after the preliminary hearing.

Besides having some leeway in determining the type of court in which to file a case, the prosecutor also has some flexibility in selecting the judge to receive the case. Until recently the prosecutor could file a case with a specific judge. "The trouble was that Judge _____ was erratic and independent, [so] no one would file with him. The other judges

objected that they were handling the entire workload, so a central filing system was devised." Under this procedure cases are assigned to the judges in rotation. However, as the chief criminal deputy noted, "the prosecutor can hold a case until the 'correct' judge came up."

Defense Attorneys

With the increased specialization and institutionalization of the bar, it would seem that those individuals engaged in the practice of criminal law have been relegated, both by their profession and by the community, to a low status. The urban bar appears to be divided into three parts. First, there is an inner circle which handles the work of banks, utilities, and commercial concerns; second, another circle includes plaintiff's lawyers representing interests opposed to those of the inner circle; and finally, an outer group scrapes out an existence by "haunting the courts in hope of picking up crumbs from the judicial table" (Ladinsky, 1963:128). With the exception of a few highly proficient lawyers who have made a reputation by winning acquittal for their clients in difficult, highly publicized cases, most of the lawyers dealing with the King County Prosecutor's Office belong to this outer ring.

In this study, respondents were asked to identify those attorneys considered to be specialists in criminal law. Of the nearly 1,600 lawyers practicing in King County only eight can be placed in this category. Of this group, six were reported to enjoy the respect of the legal community, while the others were accused by many respondents of being involved in shady deals. A larger group of King County attorneys will accept criminal cases, but these lawyers do not consider themselves specialists. Several respondents noted that many lawyers, because of inexperience or age, were required to hang around the courthouse searching for clients. One Seattle attorney described the quality of legal talent available for criminal cases as "a few good criminal lawyers and a lot of young kids and old men. The good lawyers I can count on my fingers."

In a legal system where bargaining is a primary method of decision-making, it is not surprising that criminal lawyers find it essential to maintain close personal ties with the prosecutor and his staff. Respondents were quite open in revealing their dependence upon this close relationship to successfully pursue their careers. The nature of the criminal lawyer's work is such that his saleable product or service appears to be influence rather than technical proficiency in the law. Respondents hold the belief that clients are attracted partially on the basis of the attorney's reputation as a fixer, or as a shrewd bargainer.

There is a tendency for ex-deputy prosecutors in King County to enter the practice of criminal law. Because of his inside knowledge of the prosecutor's office and friendships made with court officials, the former deputy feels that he has an advantage over other criminal law practitioners. All of the former deputies interviewed said that they took criminal cases. Of the eight criminal specialists, seven previously served as deputy prosecutors in King County, while the other was once prosecuting attorney in a rural county.

Because of the financial problems of the criminal lawyer's practice, it is necessary that he handle cases on an assembly-line basis, hoping to make a living from a large number of small fees. Referring to a fellow lawyer, one attorney said, "You should see _____. He goes up there to Carroll's office with a whole fist full of cases. He trades on some, bargains on others and never goes to court. It's amazing but it's the way he makes his living." There are incentives, therefore, to bargain with the prosecutor and other decisionmakers. The primary aim of the attorney in such circumstances is to reach an accommodation so that the time-consuming formal proceedings need not be implemented. As a Seattle attorney noted, "I can't make any money if I spend my time in a courtroom. I make mine on the telephone or in the prosecutor's office." One of the disturbing results of this arrangement is that instances were reported in which a bargain was reached between the attorney and deputy prosecutor on a "package deal." In this situation, an attorney's clients are treated as a group; the outcome of the bargaining is often an agreement whereby reduced charges will be achieved for some, in exchange for the unspoken assent by the lawyer that the prosecutor may proceed as he desires with the other cases. One member of the King County Bar has developed this practice to such a fine art that a deputy prosecutor said, "When you saw him coming into the office, you knew that he would be pleading guilty." At one time this situation was so widespread that the "prisoners up in the jail had a rating list which graded the attorneys as either 'good guys' or 'sell outs.'"

The exchange relationship between the defense attorney and the prosecutor is based on their need for cooperation in the discharge of their responsibilities. Most criminal lawyers are interested primarily in the speedy solution of cases because of their precarious financial situation. Since they must protect their professional reputations with their colleagues, judicial personnel, and potential clientele, however, they are not completely free to bargain solely with this objective. As one attorney noted, "You can't afford to let it get out that you are selling out your cases."

The prosecutor is also interested in the speedy processing of cases. This can only be achieved if the formal processes are not implemented. Not only does the pressure of this caseload influence bargaining, but also the legal process with its potential for delay and appeal, creates a degree of uncertainty which is not present in an exchange relationship with an attorney with whom you have dealt for a number of years. As the Presiding Judge of the Seattle District Court said, "Lawyers are helpful to the system. They are able to pull things together, work out a deal, keep the system moving."

Community Influentials

As part of the political system, the judicial process responds to the community environment. The King County study indicated that there are differential levels of influence within the community and that some people had a greater interest in the politics of prosecution than others. First, the general public is able to have its values translated into policies followed by law enforcement officers. The public's influence is particularly acute in those gray areas of the law where full enforcement is not expected. Statutes may be enacted by legislatures defining the outer limits of criminal conduct, but they do not necessarily mean that laws are to be fully enforced to these limits. There are some laws defining behavior which the community no longer considers criminal. It can be expected that a prosecutor's charging policies will reflect this attitude. He may not prosecute violations of laws regulating some forms of gambling, certain sexual practices, or violations of Sunday Blue Laws.

Because the general public is a potential threat to the prosecutor, staff members take measures to protect him from criticism. Respondents agreed that decision-making occurs with the public in mind—"will a course of action arouse antipathy towards the prosecutor rather than the accused?" Several deputies mentioned what they called the "aggravation level" of a crime. This is a recognition that the commission of certain crimes, within a specific context, will bring about a vocal public reaction. "If a little girl, walking home from the grocery store, is pulled into the bushes and indecent liberties taken, this is more disturbing to the public's conscience than a case where the father of the girl takes indecent liberties with her at home." The office of King County Prosecuting Attorney has a policy requiring that deputies file all cases involving sexual molestation in which the police believe the girl's story is credible. The office also prefers charges in all negligent homicide cases where there is the least possibility of guilt. In such types of cases the public may respond to the emotional context of the case and demand prosecution. To cover the prosecutor from criticism, it is believed that the safest measure is to prosecute.

The bail system is also used to protect the prosecutor from criticism. Thus it is the policy to set bail at a high level with the expectation that the court will reduce the amount. "This looks good for Prosecutor Carroll. Takes the heat off of him, especially in morals cases. If the accused doesn't appear in court the prosecutor can't be blamed. The public gets upset when they know these types are out free." This is an example of exchange where one actor is shifting the responsibility and potential onus onto another. In turn, the court is under pressure from county jail officials to keep the prison population down.

A second community group having contact with the prosecutor is composed of those leaders who have a continuing or potential interest in the politics of prosecution. This group, analogous to the players in one of Long's community games, are linked to the prosecutor because his actions affect their success in playing another game. Hence community boosters want either a crackdown or a hands-off policy towards gambling, political leaders want the prosecutor to remember the interests of the party, and business leaders want policies which will not interfere with their own game.

Community leaders may receive special treatment by the prosecutor if they run afoul of the law. A policy of the King County Office requires that cases involving prominent members of the community be referred immediately to the chief criminal deputy and the prosecutor for their disposition. As one deputy noted, "These cases can be pretty touchy. It's important that the boss knows immediately about this type of case so that he is not caught 'flat footed' when asked about it by the press."

Pressure by an interest group was evidenced during a strike by drug store employees in 1964. The striking unions urged Prosecutor Carroll to invoke a state law which requires the presence of a licensed pharmacist if the drug store is open. Not only did union representatives meet with Carroll, but picket lines were set up outside the courthouse protesting his refusal to act. The prosecutor resisted the union's pressure tactics.

In recent years, the prosecutor's tolerance policy toward minor forms of gambling led to a number of conflicts with Seattle's mayor, the sheriff, and church organizations. After a decision was made to prohibit all forms of public gaming, the prosecutor was criticized by groups representing the tourist industry and such affected groups as the bartenders' union which thought the decision would have an adverse economic effect. As Prosecutor Carroll said, "I am always getting pressures from different interests—business, the Chamber of Commerce, and labor. I have to try and maintain a balance between them."

In exchange for these considerations, the prosecutor may gain prestige, political support, and admission into the leadership groups of the community.

Summary

By viewing the King County Office of Prosecuting Attorney as the focal organization in an exchange system, data from this exploratory study suggests the market-like relationships which exist between actors in the system. Since prosecution operates in an environment of scarce resources and since the decisions have potential political ramifications, a variety of officials influence the allocation of justice. The decision to prosecute is not made at one point, but rather the prosecuting attorney has a number of options which he may employ during various stages of the proceedings. But the prosecutor is able to exercise his discretionary powers only within the network of exchange relationships. The police, court congestion, organizational strains, and community pressures are among the factors which influence prosecutorial behavior.

Discussion Questions

1. Why do the various criminal justice agencies cooperate with each other? Who are the prosecutor's clientele?

2. How is the prosecuting attorney dependent upon the police? What tools does the prosecutor have to motivate the police to be more effective on behalf of the prosecutor? How can police influence the prosecuting attorney's office? How are the police dependent upon the prosecutor?

3. What are the different types of defense attorneys? What is the relationship between the prosecutor and the defense attorney? What are the advantages of this relationship to each one? What are the disadvantages of this system, if any, to the concept of "justice for all"?

Notes

1. See also Levine and White (1961:583) and Blau (1955).

2. The lack of reliable criminal statistics is well known. These data were gathered from a number of sources, including King County (1964).

References

Blau, P. M. 1955. *The Dynamics of Bureaucracy*. Chicago: University of Chicago Press.

Chambliss, W. J. 1969. *Crime and the Legal Process*. New York: McGraw-Hill.

Evan, W. M. 1965. "Towards a Theory of Inter-organizational Relations." *Management Sci.* 11 (August): 218-230.

Gore, W. J. 1964. *Administrative Decision Making*. New York: John Wiley.

King County (1964) Annual Report of the Prosecuting Attorney. Seattle: State of Washington.

Klonski, J. R. and R. I. Mendelsohn. 1965. "The Allocation of Justice: A Political Analysis." *Journal of Public Law* 14 (May): 323-342.

Ladinsky, J. 1963. "The Impact of Social Backgrounds of Lawyers on Law Practice and the Law." *Journal of Legal Education* 16, 2:128-144.

Levine, S. and P. E. White. 1961. "Exchange as a Conceptual Framework for the Study of Inter-Organizational Relationships." *Administrative Sci. Q.* 5 (March): 583-601.

Long, N. 1962. *The Polity*. Chicago: Rand McNally.

Schur, E. M. 1965. *Crimes Without Victims*. Englewood Cliffs, N.J.: Prentice-Hall.

Skolnick, J. E. 1966. *Justice Without Trial*. New York: John Wiley.

39

The Evidence in Favor of Prisons

Richard A. Wright

Once the accused has been arrested by the police, tried in a criminal court before a jury of peers or pleaded guilty, and sentenced by a judge, the state imposes some type of punishment as retribution for the misdeed. Although the state-imposed punishments may vary in type, ranging from death to a simple reprimand, crimes always call for a punishment. Criminal laws, as we saw earlier, are based on the principle of penalty. Through the years, this principle has been questioned as shortsighted and contrary to rehabilitative efforts. What should the state's objective be, then, to punish for past misdeeds or to resocialize for a future, noncriminal role in society? Does punishment play any positive role in making us more law abiding?

In the next selection Richard A. Wright examines the objectives of punishment and, more specifically, the role of prisons in deterring crime. He concludes that prisons are not successful as either instruments of retribution or rehabilitation. Their use also fails to restore social solidarity to conformists who are demoralized by criminality. Prisons do, however, have beneficial functions. They "are effective agents of general deterrence, specific deterrence and incapacitation," he claims. In other words, the use of prisons has some effect on preventing crime among conformists and reducing future crimes among offenders. While to cannot be argued that imprisonment prevents crime among those who are locked up (except, of course, for some prison behavior that is illegal), it remains uncertain that the fear of being sent to prison prevents the average person from committing an offense.

Is imprisonment an effective means of punishment? That appears to be a question that

may be answered in several ways, depending on one's objectives. It is certain, however, that a large number of citizens and policy makers believe it is, as the just deserts of those who violate the law and as a means of making us all more law abiding.

Of all the institutions in American society, prisons are perhaps the most vilified. The critics of prisons come in all shapes, sizes, political persuasions, and walks of life. Criticisms have been raised by political radicals (Wright, 1973), liberals (Currie, 1985) and neoconservatives (von Hirsch, 1976), and by attorneys (Stender, 1973), journalists (Wicker, 1975), novelists and playwrights (Shaw, 1946; Wilde, [1898] 1973), television scriptwriters (Bello, 1982), psychologists (Sommer, 1976), psychiatrists (Menninger, 1968), sociologists (Goffman, 1961), religious groups (American Friends Service Committee, 1971), ex-correctional officials (Fogel, 1975; Murton and Hyams, 1969; Nagel, 1973), ex-convicts (Johnson, 1970), current convicts (Abbott, 1982; Hassine, 1996) and criminologists far too numerous to list. Among academicians, only a handful of conservatives (see DiIulio and Logan, 1992; van den Haag, 1975; Wilson, 1985; Wright, 1994) staunchly support prisons.

The criticisms of prisons range from cautious reservations to virtual hysteria. Currie (1985:52) moderately concludes that "although imprisonment is all too often an unavoidable necessity, it is not an effective way to prevent crime." (One must wonder, though, why Currie considers prisons necessary if they are so ineffective.) Among the less moderate, Menninger (1968:89) bluntly reviles prisons as "monuments to stupidity." He continues:

> [Prison] is a creaking, groaning monster through whose heartless jaws hundreds of American citizens grind daily, to be maimed and embittered so they emerge [as] implacable enemies of the social order and confirmed in their "criminality" (1968:89).

The title of Menninger's book—*The Crime of Punishment* (1968)—conveys the view that the injuries committed by criminals are relatively innocuous compared to the far more harmful social response of imprisonment.

I contend that the critics of prisons are wrong in their assessments (see Wright, 1994). Recent empirical research shows that punishments prevent crime and that prisons are at least modestly successful as a means of social control.

The Objectives of Punishment

Philosophers of punishment offer contradictory justifications—*retributive* and *utilitarian*—for inflicting pain on offenders (Wright, 1994). Retributivists (e.g., Fogel, 1975; Hospers, 1977; Lewis, [1948] 1971; von Hirsch, 1976, 1985) argue that the objective of punishment involves the repayment by the offender for his or her wrongs; the severity of punishment should be carefully calibrated to fit the seriousness of the offense. Retribution is considered a desirable end in itself: punishments are justly deserved by offenders as a consequence of the wrongfulness of their criminal acts. In addition, by seeking to right prior wrongs, retribution is directed toward punishing past offenses rather than toward preventing future crimes.

Utilitarians (e.g., Andenaes, 1974; Bentham, [1811] 1930; Hawkins, 1971; Wilson, 1985) are less concerned about offenders repaying their past "debts" to society; instead, they endorse punishment as a means (or instrument) to achieve certain desirable social ends (or benefits) in the future. In particular, utilitarians believe that punishment should prevent crime, through promoting such beneficial social outcomes as *rehabilitation, social solidarity, general deterrence, specific deterrence* and *incapacitation*. Correctional rehabilitation refers to the treatment of inmates through various counseling, educational, vocational, industrial and recreational programs. Those who claim that punishment promotes social solidarity argue that punishing the law-breaking minority reinforces and strengthens the commitment of the law-abiding majority to the dominant cultural norms, values and beliefs. General deterrence is the use of the threat of punishment to convince those who are not being punished not to commit future crimes. Specific deterrence is the use of punishment to convince those who actually are being punished not to commit future crimes. (In general deterrence, Peter is punished as an example to Paul that crime does not pay; in specific deterrence, Peter is punished as an example to convince Peter himself that crime does not pay.) Finally, incapacitation prevents crime in society-at-large through the use of punishment to remove criminals from uninhibited circulation in free society.

Here I briefly survey what modern research shows about the effectiveness of prisons in achieving the retributive and utilitarian objectives of punishment (for a much more extensive review of this evidence, see Wright, 1994). In general, research suggests that prisons are mostly ineffective as instruments of retribution, rehabilitation and social solidarity, but are moderately effective in promoting general deterrence, specific deterrence and incapacitation. I conclude with a policy recommendation based on this evidence.

The Failure of Prisons: Retribution, Rehabilitation and Social Solidarity

The critics of prisons usually depict them as total failures, or as Nagel (1973:177) contends, institutions that are "grossly ineffective [and] grossly dehumanizing." While Nagel's claims are grossly exaggerated, empirical evidence indicates that prisons do not effectively accomplish all their retributive and utilitarian objectives.

Retribution demands the equivalence of crimes and punishments, where the seriousness of crimes and the severity of punishments are closely matched (Fogel, 1975; von Hirsch, 1976). Certainly this is a laudable principle in the abstract, but probably impossible to accomplish in the real world of crime and imprisonment. For retributive-based sentencing to be successful, policymakers must be able to rank *both* the seriousness of crimes and the severity of punishments, and match them by degree. To date, though, empirical research shows that there is little public consensus on the seriousness of many crimes (especially vice, public order and white-collar offenses; see Miethe, 1982;

Cullen et al. 1985; Warr, 1989); without basic social consensus in seriousness of crime rankings, it is impossible to fit punishments neatly to crimes.

There are other problems with using prisons as instruments of retribution. For example, retribution is modeled on the ancient rabbinical principal of *lex talionis* ("an eye for an eye and a tooth for a tooth"). But what about the offender who has a long history of eye-gouging and tooth bashing? Do we take into consideration his or her past record, or simply sentence on the basis of the current offense? Retributivists have never offered a satisfactory answer to this question (but for an attempt, see von Hirsch, 1985).

Retribution also ignores the social and personal contexts of crime and punishment. Variations in social class, demographic factors and personal backgrounds "mean that two different offenders guilty of similar crimes may experience the severity of supposedly identical punishments in very dissimilar ways" (Wright, 1994:45). A $50 fine is not the same thing to a millionaire as it is to a homeless person; likewise, a 65-year-old corporate executive would perceive a 10-year prison sentence much differently than a 20-year-old unemployed construction worker. For these and other reasons (see Wright, 1994), it is difficult to justify the use of imprisonment for the objective of retribution.

It is also sensible to be skeptical of the effectiveness of prisons as instruments of rehabilitation. The debate about the effectiveness of rehabilitation has been waged primarily through meta-evaluation (also called meta-analysis) studies, which judge the effectiveness of social programs by summarizing the findings of many individual studies (for longer reviews of meta-evaluation studies of correctional rehabilitation programs, see Wright, 1994, 1995). The most famous meta-evaluation study of rehabilitation is the "Martinson Report" (Lipton, Martinson and Wilks, 1975; Martinson, 1974), an analysis of 231 studies of the effectiveness of criminal justice treatment programs implemented between 1945 and 1967. This study found that rehabilitation programs have little to no effect on recidivism (defined as the percent of ex-convicts who commit subsequent offenses). Numerous other meta-evaluations of the impact of rehabilitation programs on offender recidivism have reached similar negative conclusions (for example, see Bailey, 1966; Greenberg, 1977; Lab and Whitehead, 1988; Sechrest, White and Brown, 1979; Whitehead and Lab, 1989; but see Andrews et al., 1990 for a more positive assessment of the effectiveness of rehabilitation programs). The balance of evidence seems to show that correctional rehabilitation programs are an ineffective means of preventing crime.

A number of prominent sociologists (see Durkheim, [1893] 1964; Erikson, 1966; Garfinkel, 1956) speculate that crime and punishment promote social solidarity by drawing law-abiding citizens together in a spirit of consensual outrage and indignation. For example, Erikson (1966:4) argues the crime and punishment create "a climate in which the private sentiments of many separate persons are fused together into a common sense of morality." He believes that the defense of moral boundaries that occurs through the punishment of criminals not only reinforces respect for the law among the already law-abiding, but also assists in the socialization of new generations.

Unfortunately, those who make this argument apparently underestimate the immense social injury that crime inflicts on communities. Current research shows that crimes and punishments tear us apart far more than they bring us together (Conklin, 1975; Lewis and Salem, 1986; Tittle, 1980). For example, Conklin's (1975:99) analysis of the impact of crime on 266 families in two Boston neighborhoods demonstrates that the fear of crime contributes to social disorder by promoting interpersonal suspicion, "insecurity, distrust, and a negative view of the community." Furthermore, there is no empirical evidence to suggest that even when offenders are apprehended by the police and eventually imprisoned, their punishments on balance restore *more* social solidarity than their crimes initially disrupted. In general, the empirical evidence suggests that prisons fail as instruments of retribution and as utilitarian agents promoting rehabilitation and social solidarity.

The Success of Prisons: General Deterrence, Specific Deterrence and Incapacitation

In his summary of research on deterrence and incapacitation, Currie (1985:52) argues that only "the more extreme proponents of an 'economic' view of crime" believe that crime can be prevented by incarceration. At the risk of being labeled an extremist, I think there is clear and compelling evidence to suggest that prisons are effective agents of general deterrence, specific deterrence and incapacitation.

Before discussing the research evidence relating to deterrence and incapacitation, it is necessary to define some key terms. Since the days of Cesare Beccaria ([1764] 1963) and Jeremy Bentham ([1843] 1962), scholars have argued that the effectiveness of punishments as deterrents depends on three properties: *celerity* (the promptness of punishment following a crime), *certainty* (the probability or likelihood that an offender will be arrested and punished) and *severity* (the painfulness of the punishment to an offender). More recently, deterrence theorists have distinguished between *actual deterrence* (or one's real probability of experiencing prompt, certain and severe punishments at the hands of criminal justice officals) and *perceptual deterrence* (or one's subjective estimation of the likelihood of experiencing prompt, certain and severe punishments; see Chiricos and Waldo, 1970; Jensen, 1969; Tittle, 1980; Wright, 1994). One other important distinction made by deterrence researchers concerns the relative effect of *formal social controls* (exerted by criminal justice agencies) and *informal social controls* (exerted by one's family, friends, neighbors, teachers and employers) in deterring criminal behavior (see Tittle, 1980; Williams and Hawkins, 1986; Wright, 1994).

Punishment researchers distinguish between two forms of incapacitation, *collective* and *selective* (see Blumstein et al., 1986; Blumstein, Cohen and Nagin, 1978; Greenwood, 1982; Wright, 1994). Collective incapacitation refers to preventing crime by removing criminals from society-at-large through traditional forms of prison sentencing, which mostly emphasize the seriousness of the current offense, and to a lesser extent, one's prior criminal record. Selective incapacitation targets repeat offenders for removal from society-at-large.

General Deterrence

Many criminologists still dispute the idea that prisons can achieve the objective of general deterrence (see Biles, 1979; Brodt and Smith, 1988; Currie, 1985; Wright, 1996). These critics often cite research which shows that incarceration rates and crime rates frequently rise simultaneously; for example, Biles' (1979) historical study of the levels of imprisonment and crime rates in the United States, Canada and Australia shows a positive relationship between the variables.

Interestingly, these same critics conveniently ignore other bivariate evidence that suggests that punishment sometimes promotes general deterrence. For example, the United States faced a dramatic rise in bank robberies in the early 1930s (MacDonald, 1975). The FBI chose to attack this problem by pursuing a well-publicized "get tough" policy in which particularly notorious bank robbers (e.g., John Dillinger, Bonnie Parker and Clyde Barrow) were ambushed and shot to death. The result was a sharp drop in bank robberies, from a high of 609 in 1932 to 129 in 1937 (see MacDonald, 1975; Wright, 1994).

More important are two methodological shortcomings that render suspect any criticism of general deterrence that merely associates incarceration rates with crime rates. First, the causal order of the relationship must be specified: do higher incarceration rates cause higher crime rates, or vice versa? Only the former suggests the failure of general deterrence. Also, bivariate studies that simply relate incarceration and crime rates ignore many possible rival causal factors (e.g., the percent of the population unemployed and the percent of the population in crime-prone age groups) that might confound the relationship.

In my extensive survey of hundreds of deterrence studies published over the last 25 years (see Wright, 1994), I discerned a few clear trends about the effectiveness of punishments as general deterrents:

1. A moderate inverse relationship exists between crime rates and both the actual and perceived certainties of punishment.

2. The perceived certainty of punishment is more significant than actual certainty in deterring crime.

3. "Get tough" criminal justice policies that increase the perceived certainty of punishment to potential offenders have a moderate initial (immediate) deterrent effect on crime rates, but little residual (long-term) deterrent effect.

4. Little relationship exists between crime rates and either the actual and perceived severities of punishment.

5. Celerity plays little role in the effectiveness of punishments as general deterrents, because there is no logical reason why timeliness in the punishment of offenders should influence others.

6. Empirical evidence suggests that general deterrence effects vary for different types of offenders: for example, lower-class persons and older persons appear to be deterred more by the certainty of punishment than the affluent and the young (see Wright, 1994:90).

To mention a few specific studies showing the effectiveness of prisons as general deterrents, Gibbs (1968) and Tittle (1969) analyzed admissions to prisons to examine the effect of the probability of imprisonment (certainty) and the length of prison sentences (severity) on the rates of FBI index crimes in different states. Both of these early studies supported the argument that the certainty of punishment promotes general deterrence by showing that the probability of imprisonment, although not the length of time served, is inversely related to statewide crime rates for most index crimes.

More recently, in a methodologically sophisticated multivariate study that used advanced economic techniques, McGuire and Sheehan (1983) again found an inverse relationship between state imprisonment rates for one year and crime rates for subsequent years. In analyzing imprisonment and crime rate data for the years 1960 to 1979, these authors conclude that a one percent increase in incarceration rates results in a 0.48 to 1.1 percent reduction in crime rates.

Glassner et al.'s (1983) qualitative study of an unspecified number of older juvenile offenders from upstate New York suggests that imprisonment threats help to deter youth from committing adult crime. The authors try to explain why those interviewed usually curtailed their criminal activities at approximately age 16. Two-thirds of their subjects noted the fear of the harsher penalties (especially imprisonment) imposed by the criminal justice system on adults (compared to the lenient punishment of younger offenders by the juvenile justice system) as the reason for quitting crime. Glassner et al. (1983:221) conclude that most older youth make a "conscious decision" to abandon crime based on a rational calculation of risk, largely "because they fear being jailed if apprehended as adults."

Specific Deterrence

Critics who contend that prisons are ineffective agents of specific deterrence usually rely on recidivism to support their arguments. For example, Currie (1985) produces what he claims is "astonishing" evidence that between one-third and two-thirds of all released inmates eventually return to prison. He concludes: "High recidivism rates are a troubling, stubborn prima facie case that if imprisonment deters individual criminals at all, it clearly doesn't do so reliably or consistently" (Currie, 1985:70).

Simple recidivism rates, however, are invalid measures of the specific deterrent effect of prisons for three reasons. First, simple recidivism rates offer no comparisons of offenders who are arrested and incarcerated with those who avoid apprehension. While undoubtedly a large percent of those arrested and incarcerated continue to commit crimes, it is likely that a far larger percent of offenders who avoid arrest persist in crime (Packer, 1968).

In addition, for recidivism to be a valid indicator of specific deterrence, criminal justice personnel need to randomize the assignment of punishments to those apprehended

(Sherman and Berk, 1984; Wilson, 1985). Otherwise, studies that compare various forms of intervention—e.g., arrest and detention versus nonarrest and informal mediation—may mistakenly conclude that the former fail only because higher risk offenders (who are more likely to recidivate) are arrested and detained.

Finally, simple recidivism rates ignore the "suppression effects" of various forms of punishment (Farrington, 1987; Murray and Cox, 1979). Using only one arrest after incarceration as an indicator of recidivism ignores the fact that the "recidivist" may be committing fewer or less serious crimes following imprisonment. To analyze suppression effects, researchers must have measures of the number and the seriousness of an offender's crimes both *before* and *after* incarceration. In a survey of the specific deterrence literature (see Wright, 1994), a number of conclusions emerge:

1. Formal social controls—including arrest, court processing, and brief periods of confinement—appear to have a moderate inverse relationship to subsequent individual offending.

2. No evidence exists to suggest that long prison sentences are more effective as specific deterrents than shorter prison terms.

3. Formal and informal social controls apparently work together as specific deterrents. Punishments are more effective in deterring future individual offending, the more one worries about reprisals from one's family and friends, or the loss of one's job and good reputation in the community.

4. Even when punishments fail to prevent simple recidivism, they may be effective in suppressing the number and the seriousness of future offenses (see Wright, 1994:104-105).

Unquestionably, the most important evidence relating to specific deterrence is a cluster of studies on domestic assault sponsored by the National Institute of Justice (for a summary of this research, see Sherman, 1992). These studies offer considerable insight into the effect of punishments on individual offenders because all use research designs in which males apprehended for misdemeanor domestic assault are randomly assigned to alternative law enforcement strategies: advice or mediation, ordering offenders to leave the premises for a few hours, or arrest and short-term detention. The pioneering study in this area is Sherman and Berk's (1984) evaluation of the effectiveness of these three apprehension strategies in 314 domestic assault cases processed by the Minneapolis Police Department in the early 1980s. The cases were followed for six months to determine whether male offenders experienced a subsequent police contact for domestic assault and/or interviewed female victims reported subsequent assaults. In both the police and victim data, arrest/detained offenders were significantly less likely to recidivate than those who were informally processed.

Numerous studies attempted to replicate these findings in such widely dispersed places as Colorado Springs, Colorado (Berk et al., 1992), Miami (Pate and Hamilton, 1992), Milwaukee (Sherman et al., 1991; Sherman and Smith, 1992), Omaha, Nebraska (Dunford, Huizinga and Elliott, 1990) and San Diego (Berk and Newton, 1985). Although these studies have a less straightforward interpretation, they tend to show that an arrest/detention strategy only deters women batterers in conjunction with informal social controls, or the offenders' attachments and commitments to the community. Specifically, arrest/detention significantly decreases recidivism in domestic assault cases involving males who are employed and married, but has little effect on the recidivism of men who are unemployed and unmarried (see Sherman, 1992). It is crucial to note, though, that even when punishment fails as a specific deterrent, it still can have a beneficial effect as a general deterrent.

Incapacitation

Although there is fairly compelling evidence that arrest and short-term confinement can deter many potential and actual offenders, some types of criminals clearly are unafraid of punishment. The existence of "career" or "chronic" offenders—or a small number of criminals who commit a great number of crimes—shows that deterrence clearly is no panacea for the problem of crime in America. Researchers have for some time noted the problem of the career offender; for example, in their study of the arrest records of 9,945 Philadelphia boys born in 1945 and followed until their eighteenth birthdays, Wolfgang, Figlio and Sellin (1972) found that 6.3 percent of the cohort was responsible for 51.9 percent of the total arrests. A Rand Corporation study of 2,190 prison inmates in California, Michigan and Texas revealed that the most active 10 percent of burglars and robbers reported committing, respectively, 232 and 87 of these crimes in their last year on the streets (Chaiken and Chaiken, 1982; Greenwood, 1982). In a thorough survey of career offender studies, Blumstein et al. (1986) estimate that the most active 10 percent of offenders nationally commit about 100 crimes each per year. The career criminal problem suggests that the use of prisons for incapacitation is an important crime control strategy.

In an extensive review of the research evidence relating to collective incapacitation (see Wright, 1994), I estimate that current imprisonment strategies annually result in about a 20 percent reduction in the national crime rate. One way to estimate the overall effectiveness of collective incapacitation policies is to project this figure into the total number of offenses committed in the United States in any given year. For example, National Crime Victimization survey data show that 34,800,000 serious (FBI index) offenses were committed in the United States in 1990 (Bureau of Justice Statistics, 1991), so that an estimated 20 percent reduction in the crime rate would mean that collective incapacitation via imprisonment averted 6,960,000 offenses during the year. Certainly this suggests that prisons are at least moderately effective in reducing the amount of crime through collective incapacitation.

Policies of selective incapacitation—in which career criminals are specifically targeted for long-term imprisonment—may hold additional promise for reducing crime. The effectiveness of selective incapacitation on crime prevention depends on the accuracy of risk assessment instruments, or composites of factors that can predict an offender's future criminality. Greenwood (1982) and Forst (1984) have devised two important risk assessment instruments for selective incapacitation purposes. Based on the Rand Corporation study of 2,190 prisoners in three states, Greenwood (1982) discerned seven factors that could be used to predict high-rate offending: (1) conviction for offenses as a juvenile (before age 16); (2) time served in a facility for juvenile delinquents; (3) the use of illegal drugs as a juvenile; (4) the use of illegal drugs during the past two years; (5) unemployment for more than 50 percent of the last two years; (6) incarceration for more than 50 percent of the last two years; and (7) a previous conviction for the current offense. Using these factors, Greenwood (1982) originally estimated that California could reduce burglaries by 20 percent by pursuing a selective incapacitation sentencing strategy, but reanalyses of Greenwood's data have cut these burglary reduction estimates in half (Blumstein et al., 1986).

In his study of 1,708 parolees from the federal prison system, Forst (1984) reached conclusions similar to Greenwood's. Forst's (1984) risk assessment instrument includes two factors not considered by Greenwood: polydrug abuse (specifically alcohol and heroin) by an offender, and a recent conviction for a crime of violence. If federal sentencing were based on his instrument, Forst (1984) estimates that career offenders could be targeted for imprisonment with sufficient success to prevent five to 10 percent of all federal offenses (or as many as 45,000 serious crimes annually).

Despite evidence suggesting that prisons can be effective agents of selective incapacitation for career offenders, these proposals have been sharply criticized (see Currie, 1985; von Hirsch, 1985, 1988). The standard criticism is that risk assessment instruments used for selective incapacitation sentencing will produce an unacceptable number of false positives (or persons predicted to become career criminals who subsequently offend at low rates). False positives are certainly a problem in risk assessment instruments; various studies suggest that between

15 and 50 percent of those predicted to become career criminals by these instruments will not recidivate at high rates (see Wright, 1994). Still, Forst's (1984) analysis shows that traditional nonstatistical, "intuitive" prediction strategies for sentencing result in higher numbers of false postives than strategies using risk assessment instruments. Forst (1984:157-158—emphasis in the original) concludes that risk assessment instruments "not only do not 'cause' false positives where none existed before," but more importantly "generally *reduce* the rate of false positives." In the future, more sophisticated risk assessment instruments using additional prediction factors will undoubtedly further reduce the number of false positives (Wright, 1994).

Retributivists argue that selective incapacitation sentencing is unjust because the severity of the sentence will exceed the seriousness of the current offense (von Hirsch, 1985, 1988). Von Hirsch (1988) raises the disturbing specter of the trivial offender who receives a long prison term simply because of the diagnostic label of a risk assessment instrument. Ignoring such concerns, state legislatures recently have abandoned the logic of retribution by enacting "three-strikes-and-you're-out" laws (that mandate life sentences for a third felony conviction). Selective incapacitation sentences based on risk assessment instruments offer a more scientific and rational sentencing alternative to these draconian statutes.

Summary and a Policy Recommendation

On balance, the research evidence suggests that prison critics are wrong in their assessment that prisons have failed as a form of punishment. Although prisons are apparently ineffective in promoting the objectives of retribution, rehabilitation and social solidarity, they appear to be moderately effective in reducing the crime rate through general deterrence, specific deterrence and incapacitation. Elected officials who wish to implement a rational correctional policy should deemphasize the former three objectives of imprisonment in favor of the latter three.

Furthermore, deterrence and incapacitation seem to be complementary objectives of imprisonment: sentencing strategies based on deterrence appear to be most effective in preventing crimes among nonoffenders and occasional offenders; incapacitation is ideally suited for career criminals. This suggests that a rational crime-reduction policy should involve a combination of *selective deterrence* sentencing (emphasizing the certainty of brief periods of detention) to threaten nonoffenders and occasional offenders and *selective incapacitation* sentencing (emphasizing severity through long-term incarceration) for career criminals (Wright, 1994). In practical terms, this means that the length of a convict's prison sentence should be determined primarily by the number of his or her prior offenses, and not by the seriousness of the current offense. This is my policy recommendation based on the evidence in favor of prisons.

Discussion Questions

1. What types of people are critical of prisons? Why? What are some of the criticisms?

2. According to Wright, do punishments prevent crime? Do prisons prevent crimes? Are they an effective means of social control?

3. Describe the various justifications for punishment. What are the problems associated with each? Which one is dominant in society today? Why? What is the difference between specific and general deterrence? Do they work?

References

Abbott, J. H. 1982. *In the Belly of the Beast: Letters from Prison*. New York: Vintage.

American Friends Service Committee. 1971. *Struggle for Justice*. New York: Hill and Wang.

Andenaes, J. 1974. *Punishment and Deterrence*. Ann Arbor: University of Michigan Press.

Andrews, D. A., I. Zinger, R. D. Hoge, J. Bonta, P. Gendreau and F. T. Cullen. 1990. "Does Correctional Treatment Work? A Clinically Relevant and Psychologically Informed Meta-Analysis." *Criminology* 28(3):369-404.

Bailey, W. C. 1966. "Correctional Outcome: An Evaluation of 100 Reports." *Journal of Criminal Law, Criminology and Police Science* 57(2):153-160.

Beccaria, C. ([1764]1963). *On Crimes and Punishments*. Indianapolis, IN: Bobbs-Merrill.

Bello, S. 1982. *Doing Life*. New York: St. Martin's Press.

Bentham, J. ([1843] 1962). *The Works of Jeremy Bentham, Volume 1*. New York: Russell and Russell.

———. ([1811]1930). *The Rationale of Punishment*. London: Robert Howard.

Berk, R. A., A. Campbell, R. Klapp and B. Western. 1992. "The Deterrent Effect of Arrest in Incidents of Domestic Violence: A Bayesian Analysis of Four Field Experiments." *American Sociological Review* 57(5):698-708.

Berk, R. A. and P. J. Newton. 1985. "Does Arrest Really Deter Wife Battery? An Effort to Replicate the Findings of the Minneapolis Spouse Abuse Experiment." *American Sociological Review* 50(2):253-262.

Biles, D. F. 1979. "Crime and the Use of Prisons." *Federal Probation* 43(2):39-43.

Blumstein, A., J. Cohen and D. Nagin (eds.). 1978. *Deterrence and Incapacitation: Estimating the Effects of Criminal Sanctions on Crime Rates*. Washington, DC: National Academy of Sciences.

Blumstein, A., J. Cohen, J. A. Roth and C. A. Visher (eds.). 1986. *Criminal Careers and "Career Criminals," Volume 1*. Washington, DC: National Academy Press.

Brodt, S. J. and J. S. Smith. 1988. "Public Policy and the Serious Juvenile Offender." *Criminal Justice Policy Review* 2(1):70-85.

Bureau of Justice Statistics. 1991. *National Update*. Washington, DC: U.S. Department of Justice, Office of Justice Programs.

Chaiken, J. M. and M. R. Chaiken. 1982. *Varieties of Criminal Behavior*. Santa Monica, CA: Rand Corporation.

Chiricos, T. G. and G. P. Waldo. 1970. "Punishment and Crime: An Examination of Some Empirical Evidence." *Social Problems* 18(2):200-217.

Conklin, J. E. 1975. *The Impact of Crime*. New York: Macmillan.

Cullen, F. T., B. G. Link, L. F. Travis III and J. F. Wozniak. 1985. "Consensus in Crime Seriousness: Empirical Reality or Methodological Artifact?" *Criminology* 23(1):99-118.

Currie, E. 1985. *Confronting Crime: An American Challenge*. New York: Pantheon.

DiIulio, J. and C. Logan. 1992. "The Ten Deadly Myths about Crime and Punishment in the U.S." *Wisconsin Interest* 1(1):21-35.

Dunford, F. W., D. Huizinga and D. S. Elliott. 1990. "The Role of Arrest in Domestic Assault: The Omaha Police Experiment." *Criminology* 28(2):183-206.

Durkheim, E. ([1893] 1964). *The Division of Labor in Society*. New York: The Free Press.

Erikson, K. T. 1966. *Wayward Puritans: A Study in the Sociology of Deviance*. New York: Wiley.

Farrington, D. P. 1987. "Predicting Individual Crime Rates." In D. M. Gottfredson and M. Tonry (eds.), *Crime and Justice: An Annual Review of Research, Volume 9*, pp. 53-101. Chicago: University of Chicago Press.

Fogel, D. 1975. ". . . We Are the Living Proof. . ." *The Justice Model for Corrections*. Cincinnati: Anderson Publishing Co.

Forst, B. 1984. "Selective Incapacitation: A Sheep in Wolf's Clothing?" *Judicature* 68(4 and 5):153-160.

Garfinkel, H. 1956. "Conditions of Successful Degradation Ceremonies." *American Journal of Sociology* 61(5):420-424.

Gibbs, J. P. 1968. "Crime, Punishment, and Deterrence." *Southwestern Social Science Quarterly* 48(4):515-530.

Glassner, B., M. Ksander, B. Berg and B.D. Johnson. 1983. "A Note on the Deterrent Effect of Juvenile Versus Adult Jurisdiction." *Social Problems* 31(2):219-221.

Goffman, E. 1961. *Asylums: Essays on the Social Situation of Mental Patients and Other Inmates*. Garden City, NY: Anchor.

Greenberg, D. F. 1977. "The Correctional Effects of Corrections: A Survey of Evaluations." In D.F. Greenberg (ed.), *Corrections and Punishment*, pp. 111-148. Beverly Hills, CA: Sage Publications.

Greenwood, P. W. 1982. *Selective Incapacitation*. Santa Monica, CA: Rand Corporation.

Hassine, V. 1996. *Life Without Parole: Living in Prison Today*. Los Angeles: Roxbury.

Hawkins, G. 1971. "Punishment and Deterrence: The Educative, Moralizing, and Habituative Effects." In S.E. Grupp (ed.), *Theories of Punishment*, pp. 163-180. Bloomington: Indiana University Press.

Hospers, J. 1977. "Retribution: The Ethics of Punishment." In R. E. Barnett and J. Hegel III (eds.), *Assessing the Criminal: Restitution, Retribution, and the Legal Process*, pp. 118-209. Cambridge, MA: Ballinger.

Jensen, G. F. 1969. " 'Crime Doesn't Pay:' Correlates of a Shared Misunderstanding." *Social Problems* 17(2):189-201.

Johnson, L. D. 1970. *The Devil's Front Porch.* Lawrence: University of Kansas Press.

Lab, S. P. and J. T. Whitehead. 1988. "An Analysis of Juvenile Treatment." *Crime and Delinquency* 34(1):60-83.

Lewis, C. S. ([1948]1971). "The Humanitarian Theory of Punishment." In S. E. Grupp (ed.), *Theories of Punishment*, pp. 301-308. Bloomington: Indiana University Press.

Lewis, D. A. and G. Salem. 1986. *Fear of Crime: Incivility and the Production of a Social Problem.* New Brunswick, NJ: Transaction.

Lipton, D., R. Martinson and J. Wilks. 1975. *The Effectiveness of Correctional Treatment: A Survey of Treatment Evaluation Studies.* New York: Praeger.

MacDonald, J. M. 1975. *Armed Robbery: Offenders and Their Victims.* Springfield, IL: Charles C. Thomas.

Martinson, R. 1974. "What Works? Questions and Answers about Prison Reform." *The Public Interest* 35(Spring):22-54.

McGuire, W. J. and R. G. Sheehan. 1983. "Relationships Between Crime Rates and Incarceration Rates." *Journal of Research in Crime and Delinquency* 20(1):73-85.

Menninger, K. 1968. *The Crime of Punishment.* New York: Viking.

Miethe, T. D. 1982. "Public Consensus on Crime Seriousness: Normative Structure or Methodological Artifact?" *Criminology* 20(2-4):515-526.

Murray, C. A. and L. A. Cox, Jr. 1979. *Beyond Probation: Juvenile Corrections and the Chronic Delinquent.* Beverly Hills, CA: Sage Publications.

Murton, T. and J. Hyams. 1969. *Accomplices to the Crime.* New York: Grove.

Nagel, W. G. 1973. *The New Red Barn: A Critical Look at the Modern American Prison.* New York: Walker.

Packer, H. L. 1968. *The Limits of the Criminal Sanction.* Stanford, CA: Stanford University Press.

Pate, A. M. and E. E. Hamilton. 1992. "Formal and Informal Deterrents to Domestic Violence: The Dade County Spouse Assault Experiment." *American Sociological Review* 57(5):691-697.

Sechrest, L., S. O. White and E. D. Brown (eds.). 1979. *The Rehabilitation of Criminal Offenders: Problems and Prospects.* Washington, DC: National Academy of Sciences.

Shaw, G. B. 1946. *The Crime of Imprisonment.* New York: Philosophical Library.

Sherman, L. W. 1992. *Policing Domestic Violence: Experiments and Dilemmas.* New York: The Free Press.

Sherman, L. W. and R. A. Berk. 1984. "The Specific Deterrent Effects of Arrest for Domestic Assault." *American Sociological Review* 49(2): 261-272.

Sherman, L. W., J. D. Schmidt, D. P. Rogan, P. R. Gartin, E.G. Cohn, D. J. Collins and A. R. Bacich. 1991. "From Initial Deterrence to Long-Term Escalation: Short-Custody Arrest for Povery Ghetto Domestic Violence." *Criminology* 29(4):821-850.

Sherman, L. W. and D. A. Smith. 1992. "Crime, Punishment, and Stake in Conformity: Legal and Informal Control of Domestic Violence." *American Sociological Review* 57(5):680-690.

Sommer, R. 1976. *The End of Imprisonment.* New York: Oxford University Press.

Stender, F. 1973. "Violence and Lawlessness at Soledad Prison." In E. O. Wright (ed.), *The Politics of Punishment: A Critical Analysis of Prisons in America*, pp. 222-233. New York: Harper Torchbooks.

Tittle, C. R. 1980. *Sanctions and Social Deviance: The Question of Deterrence.* New York: Praeger.

——. 1969. "Crime Rates and Legal Sanctions." *Social Problems* 16(4):409-423.

van den Haag, E. 1975. *Punishing Criminals: Concerning a Very Old and Painful Question.* New York: Basic Books.

von Hirsch, A. 1988. "Selective Incapacitation Reexamined: The National Academy of Sciences' Report on *Criminal Careers and 'Career Criminals.'"* *Criminal Justice Ethics* 7(1):19-35.

——. 1985. *Past or Future Crimes: Deservedness and Dangerousness in the Sentencing of Criminals.* New Brunswick, NJ: Rutgers University Press.

——. 1976. *Doing Justice: The Choice of Punishments.* New York: Hill and Wang.

Warr, M. 1989. "What Is the Perceived Seriousness of Crimes?" *Criminology* 27(4):795-821.

Whitehead, J. T. and S. P. Lab. 1989. "A Meta-Analysis of Juvenile Correctional Treatment." *Journal of Research in Crime and Delinquency* 26(3):276-295.

Wicker, T. 1975. *A Time to Die.* New York: Ballantine.

Wilde, O. ([1898]1973). "The Ballad of Reading Gaol." In *De Profundis and Other Writings*, pp. 229-252. Middlesex, England: Penguin.

Williams, K. R. and R. Hawkins. 1986. "Perceptual Research on General Deterrence: A Critical Review." *Law and Society Review* 20(4):545-572.

Wilson, J. Q. 1985. *Thinking about Crime*. New York: Vintage.

Wolfgang, M. E., R. M. Figlio and T. Sellin. 1972. *Delinquency in a Birth Cohort*. Chicago: University of Chicago Press.

Wright, E. O. (ed.) 1973. *The Politics of Punishment: A Critical Analysis of Prisons in America*. New York: Harper Torchbooks.

Wright, R. A. 1994. *In Defense of Prisons*. Westport, CT: Greenwood Press.

——. 1995. "Rehabilitation Affirmed, Rejected, and Reaffirmed: Assessments of the Effectiveness of Offender Treatment Programs in Criminology Textbooks, 1956 to 1965 and 1983 to 1992." *Journal of Criminal Justice Education* 6(1):21-39.

——. 1996. "The Missing or Misperceived Effects of Punishment: The Coverage of Deterrence in Criminology Textbooks, 1956 to 1965 and 1984 to 1993." *Journal of Criminal Justice Education* 7(1):1-22.

40

Prisons

Steven R. Donziger

Although there are many ways to punish the convicted offender, the public and their lawmakers consider imprisonment the most appropriate for an increasing number of offenses. The United States now incarcerates more than 1.5 million men and women in its federal and state prisons and jails, a more than 212 percent increase since 1980. This selection, excerpted from the Report of the National Criminal Justice Commission (1996) and edited by Steven R. Donziger, explores the many ramifications of those startling numbers.

It is difficult to understand why the United States leads all other nations in the rate of imprisonment. Ironically, much of the recent increase has resulted from the incarceration of non-violent offenders, primarily low-level drug users and dealers. There is no evidence that the recent incarceration frenzy has reduced the amount of crime in U.S. society. There is ample evidence, however, that it has a disproportionate impact on African Americans. When probation, parole, and awaiting trial are added to being in jail or prison, as many as one-third of African-American men between eighteen and thirty-four are under the supervision of the criminal justice system.

Jail and prison conditions have continued to worsen as overcrowding, violence, boredom, and fear mitigate any effects that scarce rehabilitation or employment training programs might have. More than two-thirds of all state correctional systems are under federal court orders to improve their conditions. The cost of

Figure 40.1
U. S. Incarceration Rate of Sentenced Prisoners in State and Federal Institutions, 1860–1993

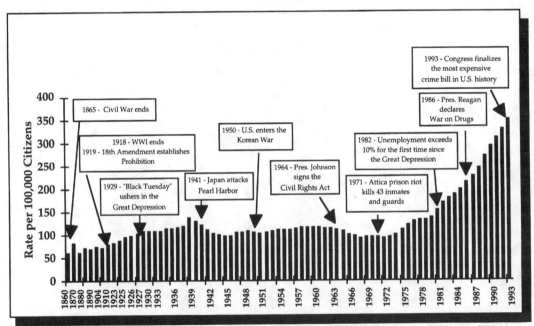

Sources: **U.S. Department of Justice, Bureau of Justice Statistics (1994),** *Sourcebook of Criminal Justice Statistics—1993,* **p. 600; U.S. Department of Justice, Bureau of Justice Statistics (June 1994),** *Prisoners in 1993,* **p. 2; U.S. Department of Justice, Bureau of Justice Statistics (December 1986),** *Historical Corrections Statistics in the United States, 1850–1984,* **p. 34.**

supporting the current system is billions of dollars annually, and the future includes only increasing financial burdens for taxpayers. As this report concludes, there must be a better way to rehabilitate while punishing offenders than committing so many to the futility of imprisonment.

Since 1980, the United States has engaged in the largest and most frenetic correctional buildup of any country in the history of the world. During this time the number of Americans imprisoned has tripled to 1.5 million. About 50 million criminal records—enough to cover nearly one-fifth of the entire U.S. population—are stuffed into police files. Hundreds of billions of dollars have poured from taxpayers' checking accounts into penal institutions and the businesses that service them. Several million people have come to depend on the criminal justice system for employment.

The hidden side of the growth of the criminal justice system is its direct effect on how much less money Americans spend on education, parks, libraries, recreation centers, highways, and universities. With a significant percentage of the potential male workforce in prison, our high rates of incarceration also act as a drag on economic growth. One estimate has the nation's jobless rate rising from 5.9 percent to 7.5 percent if male prisoners were counted as part of the labor force.[1]

One would think that the extraordinary expansion of the criminal justice system would have made at least a small dent in the crime rate. The increase in the prison population did not reduce crime, nor did it make Americans feel safer. In fact, some criminologists have argued that the overuse of the penal system for so many small-time offenders has actually created more crime than it has prevented, a topic we will explore shortly.

The Numbers

In order to appreciate this development, it is necessary to examine the size and recent growth of the criminal justice system.

More Than 1.5 Million Americans Are Behind Bars

The United States now has 1.5 million people behind bars—one million in state and federal prisons and another half million in local jails.[2] Compared to other countries, this is by far the highest rate of incarceration relative to population in the Western world. The

Table 40.1
Who Is in Jail and Prison

	Jails	Prisons (State)	Prisons (Federal)
Number of Inmates	490,442	958,704	100,438
Jurisdiction	Cities, counties	States	U. S. Government
Characteristics of Facility	Usually holds persons awaiting trial and sentenced under 1 year.	Usually holds persons sentenced to 1 year or more.	Persons convicted of federal offenses regardless of sentence length.
Characteristics of Inmate Population	Two-thirds in custody for nonviolent offenses. Half are awaiting trial. 10 million admissions to jails every year.	53% of inmates are serving sentences for nonviolent offenses.	89% of inmates sentenced for nonviolent offenses. Nearly 2 of 3 inmates convicted of a drug offense.

Sources: U.S. Department of Justice, Bureau of Justice Statistics (August 1995), *Prisoners in 1994*, p. 3, Table 2; U.S. Department of Justice, Federal Bureau of Prisons (September 4, 1995), *Monday Morning Highlights*; U.S. Department of Justice, Bureau of Justice Statistics (April 1995), *Jails and Jail Inmates 1993–94*.

Table 40.2
Change in the State and Federal Prison and Local Jail Populations 1980–1994

Year	State & Federal Prisons	Jails	Total	Annual Percent Change	Percent Change Since 1980
1980	329,821	163,994	493,815	n/a	n/a
1981	369,930	195,085	565,015	14.4%	14.4%
1982	413,806	209,582	623,388	10.3%	26.2%
1983	436,855	223,551	660,406	5.9%	33.7%
1984	462,002	234,500	696,502	5.5%	41.0%
1985	502,507	256,615	759,122	9.0%	53.7%
1986	544,972	274,444	819,416	7.9%	65.9%
1987	585,084	295,873	880,957	7.5%	78.4%
1988	627,600	343,569	971,169	10.2%	96.7%
1989	712,364	395,553	1,107,917	14.1%	124.4%
1990	773,919	405,320	1,179,239	6.4%	138.8%
1991	825,619	426,479	1,252,098	6.2%	153.6%
1992	883,656	444,584	1,328,240	6.1%	169.0%
1993	948,881	459,804	1,408,685	6.1%	185.3%
1994	1,053,738	490,442	1,544,180	9.6%	212.7%

Note: A small number of inmates who are held in local jails under state sentence are included in both the prison and jail counts. As a result, the totals are slightly inflated.
Source: U.S. Department of Justice, Bureau of Justice Statistics.

population of Americans incarcerated on any given day would qualify as the sixth-largest city in the country and is equal to the combined populations of Seattle, Cleveland, and Denver. The Rikers Island Correctional Facilities in New York City and the Los Angeles County Jail system are the two largest penal colonies in the world and by themselves have budgets larger than many cities.

Five Million Americans Are Under Correctional Supervision

In addition to the 1.5 million Americans behind bars, there are also an additional 3.6 million persons on probation or parole.[3] There are thus over 5 million citizens—or almost 3 percent of the U.S. adult population— under the supervision of the criminal justice system. One in thirty-eight adults in our country, and one in twenty-one men, live under the supervision of the criminal justice system.[4]

Over 11 Million People Admitted to Locked Facilities

Even this staggering sum does not reflect the reach of the criminal justice system. Each year, prisons and jails across the country admit 11 million individuals for booking. Most of these admissions are in local jails at the city or county level and lead to at least one night of incarceration.[5] The number of people admitted to a locked facility in a single year surpasses the combined populations of Alaska, Delaware, Hawaii, Idaho, Maine, Montana, Nevada, New Hampshire, North Dakota, Rhode Island, South Dakota, Vermont, and Wyoming. Enough people are locked up every two days to fill the New Orleans Superdome to capacity.

Most People Admitted to Jail for Minor Offenses

Nationally, many citizens arrested and imprisoned in county jails have committed public order or misdemeanor offenses—crimes such as drunkenness, being a nuisance, traffic violations, shoplifting, and drug possession.[6] The average length of stay in local jails for these offenses is a few days. The jail in one Florida city is typical of national trends. Of the thousands of people booked each year into the Duval County (Jacksonville) Jail, 70 percent faced misdemeanor charges and only 5 percent were convicted of a felony.[7] The jail held people for offenses that included letting a dog on the beach without a leash and shoplifting candy bars.

Table 40.3
The Reach of the Criminal Justice System

Adult Correctional Populations	Adults (18 and over) Pop.=192.6 million	Male Adults (18 and over) Pop.=92.4 million	African-American Male Adults (18 and over) Pop.=10.1 million	Young African-American Male Adults (18 - 34) Pop.=4.5 million
Incarcerated on any given day	1 in 128	1 in 68	1 in 17	1 in 10
Under correctional supervision on any given day	1 in 38	1 in 21	1 in 6	1 in 3
Admitted to prisons or jails in the course of a year	1 in 25	1 in 14	1 in 4	1 in 3

Note: Population estimates are as of July 1, 1994.
Sources: U.S. Department of Justice, Bureau of Justice Statistics; U.S. Bureau of the Census.

Fifty Million Criminal Records

Police create a criminal record each time an individual is arrested and fingerprinted, be it for trespassing or murder. It is the huge number of arrests for nonviolent crimes that explains why 50 million criminal records are on file in the United States.[8] Some individuals have a criminal record in more than one state or have committed more than one offense, so there are *not* 50 million separate people with criminal records. Nevertheless, we estimate that there are at least 30 million individuals in the United States with a criminal record on file—or about one-ninth of the entire U.S. population. Since most of the 50 million criminal records are of men (80 percent of arrests are of men), and there are 92.6 million adult males in the country, we conservatively estimate that one-fourth of all men in the Unites States have a criminal record on file with the police.

Toward a Prison Population of 7.5 Million

One research organization has projected that the prison population will rise to 7.5 million if several "get tough" measures are implemented on a national scale.[9] The projection—made by the National Council on Crime and Delinquency, a respected research organization in San Francisco—is based upon the enactment of anti-crime proposals such as "three strikes and you're out," truth in sentencing, adding 100,000 police officers, increasing the conviction rate, and increasing the proportion of defendants who get sentenced in prison. Under this scenario, annual criminal justice costs in America will increase to almost $221 billion. In comparison, the entire defense budget for 1995 was $269 billion.[10]

Prison and jail construction in the United States continues at a rapid pace despite evidence that the increase in rates of incarceration has failed to reduce crime. More than 600 new prisons have been constructed in the United States since 1980 at a cost of tens of billions of dollars, and this does not include modifications of existing facilities.[11] The 1994 federal crime bill allocated nearly $10 billion for states to build prisons.[12] Many states, including Texas and California, are carrying out ambitious prison-building programs.

Comparing Imprisonment Across Countries

One way to understand the scale of imprisonment in the United States is to compare it to other industrialized nations with similar rates of crime. The United States leads the Western world by imprisoning 555 out of every 100,000 of its citizens.[13] The imprisonment rate in the United States is about five times the rate of Canada and Australia and seven times the rate of most European democracies. Yet as we have seen, the overall crime rate in America is no higher than it is in comparable nations. The reason more peo-

Figure 40.2
Criminal Justice System Growth, 1980–1993

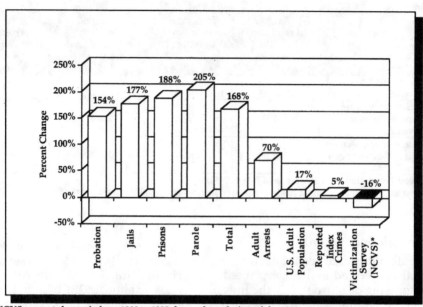

*NCVS percent change is from 1980 to 1992 due to the redesign of the 1993 survey.

Sources: U.S. Department of Justice, Bureau of Justice Statistics (1994), *Criminal Victimization in the United States: 1973–1992 Trends;* U.S. Department of Justice, Federal Bureau of Investigation (1994), *Crime in the United States—1993* and (1981) *Crime in the United States—1980;* U.S. Department of Justice, Bureau of Justice Statistics Press Release (September 11, 1994), *Parole and Probation Populations Reach New Highs;* U.S. Bureau of the Census (February 1993), *U.S. Population Estimates, By Age, Sex, Race, and Hispanic Origin: 1980 to 1991;* U.S. Bureau of the Census (March 1994), *U.S. Population Estimates, By Age, Sex, Race, and Hispanic Origin: 1990 to 1993.*

ple are in prison in the United States is because our sentences are so much longer for lesser crimes. In most other countries, people who commit nonviolent offenses receive shorter prison terms or noncustodial sanctions such as fines or community service.

African-Americans in the Criminal Justice System

A race crisis of disastrous proportions is unfolding in the American criminal justice system. A racial breakdown of the inmate population in the United States reveals that African-Americans are incarcerated at a rate more than six times that of whites—1,947 per 100,000 citizens compared to 306 per 100,000 citizens for whites.[14] This disparity exists for two reasons: African-Americans tend to get arrested at higher rates than

whites *and* they tend to be treated more harshly than whites as they move through the criminal justice system. That said, it is still true that the majority of violent crime nationwide is committed by whites. . . . For now, it is important to remember that in many cities one-third of all African-American men aged eighteen to thirty-four are under the supervision of the criminal justice system—either in jail or prison, on probation or parole, or awaiting trial.[15]

Rates of Imprisonment and Crime

Academic research has shown little or no correlation between rates of crime and the number of people in prison. States with high rates of imprisonment may or may not have high rates of crime, while states with low rates of crime may or may not have high rates

Figure 40.3
International Rates of Incarceration, 1992–1993

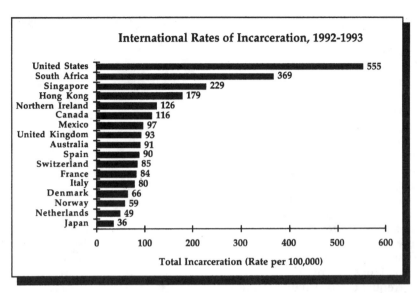

International Rates of Incarceration, 1992-1993

Country	Rate per 100,000
United States	555
South Africa	369
Singapore	229
Hong Kong	179
Northern Ireland	126
Canada	116
Mexico	97
United Kingdom	93
Australia	91
Spain	90
Switzerland	85
France	84
Italy	80
Denmark	66
Norway	59
Netherlands	49
Japan	36

Total Incarceration (Rate per 100,000)

Note: Russia's incarceration rate is estimated to be 558; it has been omitted because of questions of reliability. The incarceration rates include both prison and jail populations.

Sources: Mauer, Marc (September 1994), *Americans Behind Bars: The International Use of Incarceration, 1992–1993* (Washington D.C.: The Sentencing Project); Austin, James (January 1994), *An Overview of Incarceration Trends in the United States and Their Impact on Crime* (San Francisco: The National Council on Crime and Delinquency).

of imprisonment. North Dakota and South Dakota, which are virtually identical in terms of demographics and geography, provide an example. South Dakota imprisons its citizens at three times the rate of North Dakota, but crime between the two states is roughly the same and has been for several decades.[16] This point can also be illustrated by comparing the homicide and incarceration rates in most states. Louisiana, for example, puts more of its citizens in prison per capita than almost any other state—yet it also had the highest homicide rate in 1994. Oklahoma had the third highest incarceration rate but ranked twentieth in its rate of homicide.[17] Dramatic increases in incarceration are not necessarily followed by declines in crime.

The link between crime and imprisonment creates a great deal of confusion. Because increasing rates of imprisonment will sometimes occur at the same time as declining rates of crime (though sometimes not), those who use the data selectively can make it appear that prisons work to lower crime. In California, the prison population rose in 19 of the past 21 years. In 15 of those 19 years, violent crime rose as well. This would seem to indicate that prisons did not reduce violent crime in California. Yet some elected officials point to the few years that crime fell and claim that additional prison construction is necessary to reduce crime.

This kind of claim is becoming more frequent in the debate over crime policy, particularly since crime rates have declined slightly in each of the last three years. Though we are gratified crime is dropping, it is impossible to point to an increase in the prison population as the primary reason. In fact, nobody can conclusively explain this drop by pointing to one factor. Many experts believe the decline has resulted from a combination of demographic changes (there are fewer criminally active young males), more effective law enforcement, and greater stability in the drug trade (which leads to less violence among drug gangs).

The Effects of Incarceration

Sending such a high number of Americans through the jailhouse door each year has wide ramifications. Anyone who has been handcuffed by police knows how deeply humiliating the experience can be. Imagine the effects of spending even a night in the bizarre and violent subculture of most jails. Literature abounds with examples of people traumatized by the experience. Each person booked is fingerprinted and photographed for their criminal record (the record remains with them even if the charges are later dropped). Basic survivial tactics are necessary to endure even a short stay. Inmates learn to strike first and seek strength in gangs often comprised of dangerous offenders. Sexual assaults are frequent and usually go unpunished.[18] The prison experience is one in which the code is survival of the fittest, in which weakness is a crime, and in which the expression of vulnerable feelings can jeopardize the survival of the prisoner. As ever more young men and women are socialized to the cell blocks and then returned to the streets, the violent subculture of the correctional facility increasingly acts as a vector for spreading crime in our communities. Prisons and jails thus have a dual effect: They protect society from criminals, but they also contribute to crime by transferring their violent subculture to our community once inmates are released.

In many communities, spending time locked up is such a natural part of life that correctional facilities have lost their ability to scare people into good behavior. In California, 40 percent of youths in custody have a parent who had done time. Experts on the inner city point out that many young men do not mind going to prison because they see it as a glamorous rite of passage that earns respect and status.[19] The *New York Times* described a scene on the South Side of Chicago where neighborhood youth surrounded an ex-inmate who came home "as if he were a rap star passing out concert tickets."[20]

Table 40.4
Prison Incarceration Rate by State, 1994

Rank	State	Rate (per 100,000)
1	Texas	636
2	Louisiana	530
3	Oklahoma	508
4	South Carolina	494
5	Nevada	460
6	Arizona	459
7	Georgia	456
8	Alabama	450
9	Michigan	428
10	Mississippi	408
11	Florida	406
12	Maryland	395
13	Virginia	395
14	Delaware	393
15	California	384
16	Ohio	377
17	New York	367
18	Arkansas	353
19	Missouri	338
20	North Carolina	322
21	Connecticut	321
22	Alaska	317
23	Illinois	310
24	New Jersey	310
25	Colorado	289
26	Kentucky	288
27	Tennessee	277
28	Indiana	258
29	Idaho	258
30	Wyoming	254
31	Kansas	249
32	South Dakota	240
33	Pennsylvania	235
34	New Mexico	220
35	Hawaii	202
36	Washington	201
37	Montana	194
38	Iowa	192
39	Wisconsin	187
40	Rhode Island	186
41	New Hampshire	177
42	Oregon	175
43	Massachusetts	171
44	Vermont	168
45	Nebraska	159
46	Utah	155
47	Maine	118
48	West Virginia	106
49	Minnesota	100
50	North Dakota	78

Source: **U.S. Department of Justice, Bureau of Justice Statistics** (August 1995), *Prisoners in 1994,* p. 3, Table 2.

. . . Joanne Page has worked with ex-offenders for years as the director of The Fortune Society in New York City. She compares the impact of incarceration to post-traumatic stress disorder, which often afflicts soldiers who return home from war. Many offenders emerge from prison afraid to trust, fearful of the unknown, and with their vision of the world shaped by the meaning that behaviors have in the prison context. For a recently released prisoner, experiences like being jostled on the subway, having someone reach across them in the bathroom to take a paper towel, or staring can be taken as the precursor to a physical attack. Professionals who work with ex-offenders have said it appears prison damages a person's mid-range response to the environment, leaving the choice of gritting one's teeth and enduring, or full-fledged attack to protect oneself from perceived danger. In a relationship with a loved one, this socialization means that problems will not easily be talked through but are more likely to result in a blowup or an absence of communication. In a job situation, this means tensions are more likely to result in a loss of temper or in the failure to show up for work.

Jail and Prison Conditions

A few elected officials have sought to rid correctional facilities of amenities such as television and air conditioning.[21] These demands have an intuitive appeal because no taxpayer wants to fund a comfortable lifestyle for prisoners. Yet the reality in prison is different from the one described by many of those who want to toughen conditions. Three out of four inmates in the United States are housed in overcrowded facilities where the living space for two people is the size of a walk-in closet.[22] Some inmates suffer physical abuse in prison: In the high-security wing of an Oregon state prison, an inmate was stripped naked, placed in full mechanical restraints, and locked in a "quiet cell" with the lights on for twenty-four hours a day.[23] He was not permitted out-of-cell exercise for five years. Others suffer sexual abuse: It has been estimated that almost one-quarter of all inmates are victims of a sexual assault each year during incarceration.[24] Other prison systems are corrupt: Between 1989 and 1994, fifty correctional staff in the District of Columbia were convicted of serious crime, eighteen of them for smuggling drugs into prison for inmates.[25] Many prisons are clean and well-administered, but no prison is luxurious. In some, life is so wretched that the courts have ordered authorities to improve conditions or face jail time themselves. For example, in 1994, thirty-nine states plus the District of Columbia were under court order to reduce overcrowding or improve prison conditions.[26] It is partly because of these conditions that many offenders have such a difficult time making the transition to freedom.

The debate over prison conditions is often used to distract voters from the real problems facing the criminal justice system. In Mississippi, a law was passed banning individual air conditioners for inmates even though not a single inmate had an air conditioner.[27] A Louisiana law forbids inmates from taking classes in karate or martial arts, even though there were no such training classes available. The governor of Connecticut blasted a prison for providing "country club" landscaping on the outside of the facility. In reality, the planting had been done at the request of nearby residents annoyed by the ugly prison wall.[28] It appears that other new laws are intended to humiliate inmates. Mississippi recently began requiring inmates to wear striped prison suits with the word "convict" on the back. In Alabama, the governor recently reinstituted prison chain gangs. Inmates shackled together in groups of five "work" on state roadways chipping away at rocks, with no apparent purpose except to convince passersby something is being done about the crime problem.

For those concerned with public safety as well as vengeance, the issue of jail and prison conditions becomes more complicated. We all want inmates to feel the sting of punishment and loss of freedom. On the other hand, it does not serve public safety to so frustrate inmates that they return to the streets embittered and angry. Jail and prison conditions exert a significant influence on whether an inmate becomes productive upon release or resumes criminal behavior. More than nine out of ten inmates currently in prison will be released at some point.[29] Although prisons cannot become "country clubs" without losing their deterrent effect, they also cannot become gulags without jeopardizing public safety. The best correctional facilities strike a balance between punishment and the opportunity for inmates to become self-sufficient, particularly as they get closer to release.

One way to strike this balance and save tax dollars is to make offenders more responsible for their upkeep. One of the best-kept secrets in American corrections is that most inmates *want* to work, but prison jobs are scarce. Work opportunities should be provided for all inmates, and that work should be geared toward maintaining the institution at minimal cost to taxpayers. At one prison in Washington state, inmates produce blue jeans, and most of the profits are put back into the facility. In a prison in Denmark, inmates were given a budget to purchase food and then made to cook it in small kitchens in their living units.[30] Inmates quickly formed cooperatives where they pooled their money and cooked together. In the end, prisoners learned social skills and the prison saved money on food and staffing. Life skills for youthful offenders are also critical: A juvenile facility in Utah requires youths to write checks and balance a checkbook if they want to purchase food from the canteen. Before they can obtain a prison job, the youths have to prepare a resume and be formally interviewed. We squander money by not allowing prisoners the chance to work productively. Simple measures such as work can lower costs and teach inmates the skills they will need to function on the outside.

Rates of Incarceration: The Effect on the Family

Although we know that a stable family is one of the strongest bulwarks against a life of crime, so many men in our inner cities are incarcerated that it has become increasingly difficult there to create and sustain a two-parent family. For many young women in the inner city, there is a scarcity of available men of marriage age because so many are going in and out of jails and prisons. Moreover, about three out of four women in prison have children. Only 22 percent of these women say they can count on the fathers of their children to care for them while they are incarcerated.[31] In some inner-city areas, virtually every resident has a close relative and over 50 percent have a parent who is in prison, on probation, on parole, in jail, or in hiding because there is a warrant out there for their arrest.[32]

Many advocates of continued prison construction argue that longer sentences are necessary to protect families from crime. It is certainly appropriate to remove violent offenders from our streets. But the flip side of our crime policy is that the injudicious use of prison to incarcerate so many nonviolent offenders can undermine family structure by removing a large portion of the male popula-

tion from community life. This reality must be weighed carefully by those who make criminal justice policy.

The Costs

States all over the county are trimming and reorganizing their budgets, but taxpayers continue to pour money into prison construction and operations in a way that competes with funding for education and other quality-of-life programs. Five states have a corrections budget of over one billion dollars.[33] California, which has the largest prison system of any state, spends $3.6 billion per year on prison operations and another $500 million per year on new prison construction.[34] Nationwide, spending on corrections at the state level has increased faster than any other spending category. Preliminary data for fiscal year 1996 show average increases in appropriations for corrections over the previous year to be 13.3 percent, more than twice the increase for education.[35] Prison has become a modern public works program: in Texas, the government spent more than $1 billion to add over 76,000 prison beds in two years and in 1995 planned to hire 12,000 employees to staff its new prisons. Spending on corrections at a national level has risen three times as fast as military spending over the last twenty years.

In order to fund jails and prisons, state and local governments have been forced to divert money from education and welfare spend-

Table 40.5
Trends in State Spending, 1976–1989

Spending Category	Percent Change
Corrections	+95%
Medicaid	+85%
Health and hospitals	+5%
Elementary-secondary education	-2%
Higher education	-6%
Highways	-23%
Welfare (non-Medicare)	-41%

Source: Gold, Steve (July 1990), *The State Fiscal Agenda for the 1990's,* **p. 16.**

Figure 40.4
Percent Increase in Correctional Costs, 1979–1990

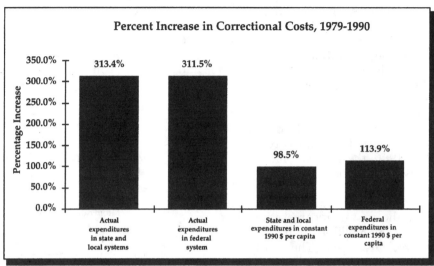

Percent Increase in Correctional Costs, 1979-1990

Note: **Measuring expenditures in constant 1990 dollars per capita corrects for both population growth and inflation.**

Source: **U.S. Department of Justice, Bureau of Justice Statistics (1993),** *Sourcebook of Criminal Justice Statistics—1992,* **p. 3, Table 1.3.**

ing.[36] California is typical of the trend. Fifteen years ago, 3 percent of the state budget in California went to prisons while 18 percent was allocated for higher education. In 1994, the state spent 8 percent of its budget on prisons and 8 percent on higher education. Between 1994 and 1995 the *overrun* in corrections spending (an 11.1 percent actual increase compared to a 7.1 percent budgeted increase) was more than the entire increase in higher education (2.3 percent).[37] From 1979 to 1990, state government expenditures nationwide rose 325 percent for prison operations and 612 percent for prison construction.[38] Some states that have built prisons find they cannot afford to run them. In South Carolina, two prisons that cost $80 million recently stood empty because of a shortage of money.[39]

The Costs of Incarceration

Many correctional facilities are built without a full understanding of the actual costs involved. What follows is a summarized breakdown of prison costs. It helps explain why many prisons—just like many projects

for the Department of Defense—end up costing the public more than originally planned.

Construction Costs. The average cost of building a new cell is $54,000.[40] Because states usually pay for prison construction by borrowing money, debt service often doubles or even triples the original construction costs. With interest on the debt, the real cost of a new cell is usually well over $100,000.

Operating Costs. The capital outlay for prison construction represents only the beginning of a long-term financial commitment. According to the Justice Department, every $100 million a legislature spends on new prison construction commits the taxpayers of the state to $1.6 billion in expenditures over the next three decades.[41] The cost of operating a state prison bed averages $22,000 per prisoner per year, and this cost often does not include food and medical services that are provided by private companies under contract with the prison.[42] In the federal system, all of the taxes paid each year by three average families is equal to the cost it takes to keep one inmate in prison for one year.[43] In Delaware, all of the annual taxes paid by eighteen average residents are needed to house one prisoner for a single year.[44]

Many costs of the criminal justice system are hidden because they do not appear on criminal justice budgets. They include:

Off-Budget Items. The budget for a corrections agency often does not count the large sums of money paid to for-profit businesses that provide services to the prison. These services can include everything from the cafeteria to medical care. An independent audit of the Indiana prison system found the actual expenditures to be one-third higher than the costs reported by the corrections authority.[45] In 1986, the Correctional Association of New York found that the corrections budget would increase by 29 percent if off-budget items were counted.[46] Off-budget items increase the cost of incarceration by about 25 percent or $8 billion annually.[47]

Construction Overruns. The cost of prison construction is often much higher than promised. A survey of 15 states found that cost overruns came in at an average of *40 percent* over the original budget. In many states, this adds tens of millions of dollars to the final tab.[48]

Child Support. Inmates have nearly a million children. Many of these children are in foster care or are supported by taxpayers in some manner.

Lost Tax Revenues. Because they are often barred from working, inmates cannot contribute to the government revenues that their incarceration depletes.

Public Health Costs. Prisons and jails are high-risk settings for the spread of infectious diseases, largely because of the close quarters and poor ventilation. By the end of 1992, there were more than 48,000 tuberculosis cases reported in the state and federal prison systems.[49] The rate of AIDS infection in the prison population is nearly fourteen times higher than that of the general population.[50] New York recently committed $250 million over four years to treat the growing population of AIDS-infected inmates.[51]

The High Cost of Elderly Prisoners. One effect of longer sentences is that many prisoners now house an increasing number of elderly inmates who require medical care at enormous cost to taxpayers. With the passage of "three strikes" laws in California and other states, the number of elderly inmates is expected to rise sharply in the coming years. In California alone, it is estimated that the "three strikes" law will increase the number of geriatric inmates from 5,000 in 1994 to 126,400 in the year 2020. In 1993, there were 25,000 inmates over 55 years of age in state and federal prisons.[52]

Table 40.6
Medical Problems of Elderly Inmates

Medical Problems of Elderly Inmates
• 80% have at least one chronic health condition
• 38% suffer from hypertension
• 28% suffer from heart disease
• 16% suffer from cataracts

Source: Zimbardo, Philip G. (November 1994), *Transforming California's Prisons into Expensive Old Age Homes for Felons: Enormous Hidden Costs and Consequences for California's Taxpayers* (San Francisco, CA: Center on Juvenile and Criminal Justice).

The chance that a typical elderly prisoner will commit a violent crime upon release is almost nil. Yet we have seen that because of health care costs, the upkeep of an elderly inmate can run triple that of a younger inmate.[53] The Louisiana State Penitentiary in Angola has an "old folks" ward where inmates are allowed to roam about with virtually no restrictions. Others lay in bed because of severe medical conditions. Frank Blackburn, who served as warden of the prison, said he "personally knew of 25 to 50 longtermers that I would release immediately because there is no doubt they are rehabilitated. . . . There are just too many people in prison today as tax burdens who do not need to be there."[54]

Other costs of Crime. Lost business revenues from inner-city crime have been estimated to cost $50 billion annually.[55] Health care costs associated with injuries caused by crime have been estimated at $5 billion annually.[56] Individuals and business spend about $65 billion each year on private security systems.[57] This so-called "security tax" is added to the actual taxes spent to finance the formal justice system—a cost incurred at least partly by the failure of the criminal justice system to achieve its ends.

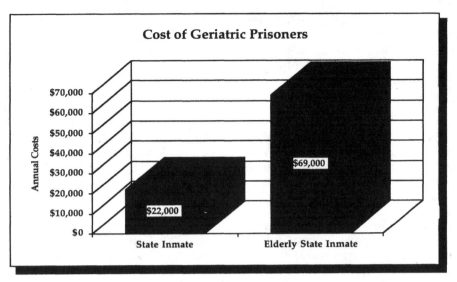

Figure 40.5
Cost of Geriatric Prisoners

Sources: Camp, Camille G., and George M. Camp (1994), *The Corrections Yearbook—1994; Adult Corrections,* pp. 48–49; U.S. Department of Justice, Bureau of Justice Statistics (August 1995), *Prisoners in 1994,* p. 4, Table 3.

Sentencing

Many Americans believe that convicted criminals get off easy, and they are partially right. Some offenders get off lightly for serious crimes while others pay too great a price for lesser offenses. A vivid illustration of this phenomenon can be seen by comparing the time served of murderers to that of first-time drug offenders in the federal system. In 1992, federal prisons held about 1,800 people convicted of murder for an average time served of 4 1/2 years.[58] That same year, federal prisons held 12,727 nonviolent first-time drug offenders for an average time served of 6 1/2 years.[59] No other nation treats people who commit nonviolent crimes as harshly as the United States.[60] A national survey of prison wardens revealed that the wardens felt that on average, half of the offenders under their supervision could be released without endangering public safety.[61]

Intermediate Sanctions Between Prison and Probation

Intermediate sanctions provide a means of responding strongly to a criminal act without having to rely on prisons as the primary means of punishment. For nonviolent offenders and some lesser violent offenders, it is useful to consider a wide variety of punishment options other than prison. Many are less expensive and more effective at reducing recidivism than locking up an offender in a small cell. The principle of choosing an appropriate punishment from a variety of options makes sense because most Americans do it in their daily lives. When a child disobeys his parents, they may order him to go to his room. For other infractions, he may be grounded for a night or lose his allowance. Parents recognize these as different punishments that can be tailored to the infraction. There is no reason that courts should not have as many options in sentencing offenders as parents do in disciplining their children.

More importantly for American taxpayers, non-prison sanctions are often less expensive than prison as long as they do not pose an increased risk to public safety. Each time an offender is sentenced to prison, it costs on average $22,000 per year. Including hidden costs of incarceration—construction over-runs and debt service—the average inmate consumes an amount significantly higher than the salary of the typical American worker. Most non-prison sanctions cost less than half as much as prison. Taxpayers can pocket the savings.

Following is a list of currently available noncustodial punishments. None of these programs is pleasant for the offender. While all involve hardship and some encroachment on liberty, they also are designed to advance the interests of society by making it less likely that the offender will commit new crimes. Typically, the programs require the offender to work, pay fines, repay victims, and un-dergo substance abuse treatment if neces-sary. These punishments can be combined with traditional prison sentences. The reader should keep these non-prison sanctions in mind as we examine the criminal justice sys-tem. These intermediate sanctions include:

Probation. This is the most common sanction in the criminal justice system. About three million people are on probation. Probation is largely considered ineffectual because there are not enough probation offi-cers to assist offenders to find jobs or, if nec-essary, receive treatment for a drug addic-tion. . . .

Intensive Probation. This usually in-cludes five meetings per week with each of-fender, costs about one-seventh of prison, and usually leads to much lower rates of of-fending down the road.

Day Reporting Centers. Usually a part of probation, reporting centers are a place where offenders must check in on a daily ba-sis, provide a schedule of the day's planned activities, and participate in programs. Of-fenders are subject to random telephone checks to ensure they are where they are sup-posed to be.

Halfway Houses. Halfway houses are used as a transition between prison and free-dom. Most offenders who live there work and pay rent. They are usually allowed to leave only to report to their job, and they must re-

Figure 40.6
Costs of Sentencing Alternatives

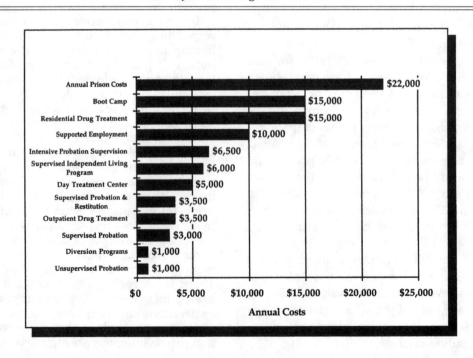

turn promptly at the end of the workday. The residents are under much closer control and supervision than people living entirely on their own, but they have a far greater degree of independence and cost taxpayers far less than people in prison. Treatment services and educational programs are usually provided.

Boot Camps. One of the most publicized intermediate sentencing options, boot camps require offenders to undergo military-style training designed to foster a sense of discipline and respect for authority. What is often missing from most boot camps are services to assist the offender to adjust to life on the outside. When military boot camp is completed, the new soldier is at least assured of a job. In boot camps for inmates, there usually are not even services to help the offender look for a job. It is unrealistic to expect that a few weeks of rigorous physical training will prepare offenders to avoid or overcome the problems that led to their conviction.

Boot camps cost less than prison, and their rates of recidivism (i.e., the number of offenders who commit new crimes upon release) are no worse than those of prison.[62] There is reason to believe that better techniques will yield better results—especially if training is combined with intensive aftercare.

Fines and Restitution. These are especially appropriate for property offenses. The money collected can be used to help fund the court system and to repay crime victims for the cost of their hardship. Less affluent offenders can pay a proportional amount.

Community Service. Community service requires offenders to work without pay for a designated number of hours, usually for public or nonprofit organizations. Tasks can include cleaning up streets and public parks, maintenance work in old age homes, and clerical work in public offices. Offenders with professional skills can be ordered to put their skills to work for those who ordinarily could not afford them. The community receives services while the offender works off the punishment and, it is hoped, develops a sense of right and wrong.

Home Detention. Much cheaper than prison, this requires the offender to remain at home except for carefully controlled excursions to work or treatment.

Drug Treatment. For those with an addiction, successful drug treatment can return enormous savings to taxpayers over the long term. A study by the state of California found that each dollar spent on drug treatment saved seven dollars in reduced crime and health care costs.

What Polling Data Reveal About Crime Policy

Our attitudes toward punishment are widely considered by elected officials and the media to be far more punitive than they actually are. Most polls that gauge attitudes toward crime ask simplistic questions that produce predictable conclusions about cries for "vengeance" against criminals. More serious polling reveals a much more complex set of public concerns about crime. While we naturally want to punish offenders and hold them responsible for their actions, we also want to be *smart* about that punishment so money is not wasted and criminals do not reoffend when released.[63]

Most Americans agree with the notion that serious violent offenders need to be incarcerated to protect public safety. But public attitudes toward imprisoning nonviolent offenders and less violent offenders are decidedly different. When the issues are broadly presented, most Americans are willing to consider alternative approaches to criminal justice policy that rely much less on prison as the first response to crime control.

Research of public opinion about crime clearly demonstrates the following:

Polling Questions Can Distort Findings

We are bombarded with simplistic polling questions on crime that virtually guarantee an answer that will "prove" public support for more prisons. Consider the following polling question, which for years has been used to gauge public attitudes toward sentencing: "Are sentences too harsh, about right, or not harsh enough?" Most people consistently respond to this question by saying that sentences are *not harsh enough*.

We live in a nation where polls like these make for political platforms. From this simple response, some pollsters have suggested, and many politicians have been quick to adopt, policies that lengthen prison sentences.

This interpretation of the polling data fails to consider three additional findings from more in-depth polls. First, when answering a question like this, most of us automatically think of violent offenders who have criminal histories. Second, the public has little idea of the actual severity of sentencing practices. Most of us actually *underestimate* the length of sentences for crimes, especially those for nonviolent offenders. Finally, this question fails to take into account limited public awareness of punishments other than prison punishments that are often more effective at preventing crime and less costly to implement.

The Public Prefers a Balanced Approach to Crime Control

Polling techniques that present crime issues squarely demonstrate that there is much less support for prison than is commonly believed. Most Americans prefer punishments outside of prison for many types of nonviolent offenders *if they are available*. Such sanc-

tions include boot camps, intensive probation, house arrest, community service, and restitution.[64] The nonprofit Public Agenda Foundation conducted focus groups in Alabama and Delaware to determine what would happen to public attitudes if people were given information about punishments other than prison.[65] In the first phase of the research, groups of people were given brief descriptions of crimes and then asked to choose between prison and probation for the offenders. At that point, most people in the group heavily favored prison.

The participants then viewed a videotape describing five sanctions outside of prison: intensively supervised probation; restitution; community service; house arrest; and boot camp. After receiving information about sentencing alternatives, the group was asked to "re-sentence" the offender. *Support for imprisonment declined dramatically for a number of offenses*. A juvenile with no prior convictions who committed an armed robbery was sent to prison 80 percent of the time in the first phase, but only 38 percent of the time after the alternatives were discussed. In Delaware, participants in the first phase of the study wanted to incarcerate seventeen out of twenty-three offenders. This dropped to only five out of twenty-three in the second phase.

Table 40.7
Support for Incarceration Before and After Receiving Information About Sentencing Alternatives

Offense	Alabama		Delaware	
	Before	After	Before	After
Theft (5th Offense)	90%	46%	83%	47%
Armed Robbery	78	47	72	47
Shoplifting	74	22	71	19
Burglary	68	19	70	22
Drunk Driving	13	2	16	4
Embezzlement	71	30	71	31

Source: Doble, John, and Josh Klein (1989). *Punishing Criminals, The Public's View—An Alabama Survey* (New York: The Edna McConnell Clark Foundation).

In Alabama, incarceration was favored in eighteen out of twenty-three cases in the first phase and in only four cases afterward.

Conclusion

One has to wonder whether a further expansion of the criminal justice system will reduce crime. Crime is a complex phenomenon that derives from a combination of personal choice, family circumstance, economic condition, and much more. We should not expect the criminal justice system to correct all antisocial behavior or to solve all (or even any) of our social problems—it is simply too blunt an instrument for such complicated tasks. We cannot expect the criminal justice system to create strong families, deliver jobs, or provide hope to young people. The only service that we should expect from the criminal justice system is the one it was set up to deliver—crime control that makes all Americans safe. And in the course of delivering that service, we should expect that our tax dollars will not be wasted.

Imprisonment is a politically appealing response to fear because a person who is locked up obviously cannot commit a crime against a person on the outside. But the simplicity can be deceptive. Take the example of the typical small-time drug dealer. This offender has helped fuel the jail and prison expansion in recent years, yet it is also this offender who is most easily replaceable in the drug trade. Somebody else almost always steps in to take the place of the dealer when he or she goes to prison. Incarcerating the second drug dealer costs just as much as incarcerating the first. By the time the criminal justice system has passed through several generations of drug dealers, billions of dollars have been spent and the corner is still scattered with empty vials of crack cocaine.

Our rate of incarceration is the highest in the world. Two percent of the potential male workforce is behind bars. In some urban areas, close to half of the young African-American men are in the criminal justice system. Yet crime nationally has not been reduced significantly, and most of us do not *feel* safer. . . .

Discussion Questions

1. Why do you think America has such a high incarceration rate, compared to other countries? What measures might push our numbers of incarcerated offenders even higher?

2. What effect has high incarceration rates had on the rate of crimes committed? How can data be manipulated to make it appear as though incarceration has a great effect on crime rates?

3. What effects does incarceration have on individuals in the system? How do these individuals affect crime rates upon their release from prison? Why, according to the author, doesn't the threat of incarceration scare people? What effect does incarceration have on the inmates' loved ones?

Notes

1. Zachary, G. Pascal. September 29, 1995. "Economists Say Prison Boom Will Take Toll." *Wall Street Journal*: B1.

2. U.S. Department of Justice, Bureau of Justice Statistics. April 1995. *Jails and Jail Inmates 1993-1994*. Washington, D.C.: U.S. Government Printing Office; *Prisoners in 1994*. August 1995. Washington, D.C.: U.S. Government Printing Office.

3. U.S. Department of Justice, Bureau of Justice Statistics. August 27, 1995. *The Nation's Correctional Population Tops 5 Million*. Press release.

4. U.S. Bureau of the Census. November 1993. *Population Projections of the United States, by Age, Sex, Race, and Hispanic Origin: 1993 to 2050*. Washington, D.C.: U.S. Government Printing Office: 14, Table 2.

5. The total number of admissions, including transfers and readmissions, is 13,245,000. U.S. Department of Justice, Bureau of Justice Statistics. April 1995. *Jails and Jail Inmates 1993-1994*. Washington, D.C.: U.S. Government Printing Office.

6. Miller, Jerome G. March 1994. *African-American Males in the Criminal Justice System*. Unpublished paper presented at the National Criminal Justice Commission Conference, Alexandria, Virginia.

7. ———. June 1, 1993. *The Duval County Jail Report*. Alexandria, VA: National Center on Institutions and Alternatives.

8. The number of criminal records as of December 31, 1993, was 47,833,600, and in 1993 alone the FBI received almost 4.2 million fingerprint records. U.S. Department of Justice, Bureau of Justice Statistics. January 1995. *Survey of Criminal History Information Systems, 1993*. Washington, D.C.: U.S. Government Printing Office: 19.

9. Austin, James, and John Irwin. 1994. *It's About Time: America's Imprisonment Binge*. Belmont, CA: Wadsworth: 160.

10. Office of the Comptroller of the Department of Defense. March 1994. *National Defense Budget Estimates for FY 1995*. Washington, D.C.: Department of Defense.

11. Camp, Camille G., and George M. Camp. Various years. *The Corrections Yearbook; Adult Corrections 1981* through *1994*. South Salem, NY: Criminal Justice Institute.

12. Violent Crime Control and Law Enforcement Act of 1994. Public Law 103-322. September 13, 1994.

13. The Sentencing Project reports the incarceration rate in Russia to be 558 per 100,000. Mauer, Marc. September 1994. *Americans Behind Bars: The International Use of Incarceration, 1992-93*. Washington, D.C.: The Sentencing Project: 4. However, data from Russia suffers from serious problems of reliability. Austin, James. March 1994. *An Overview of Incarceration Trends in the United States and Their Impact on Crime*. Unpublished paper presented at the National Criminal Justice Commission Conference, Alexandria, Virginia.

14. Mauer, Marc. September 1994. *Americans Behind Bars: The International Use of Incarceration, 1992-93*. Washington, D.C.: The Sentencing Project.

15. Ibid.

16. U.S. Department of Justice, Bureau of Justice Statistics. August 1994. *Prisoners in 1994*. Washington, D.C.: U.S. Government Printing Office.

17. Ibid.

18. See for example July 1995. "Breaking the Silence on Prison Rape and AIDS." *Corrections Compendium*. Vol. XX, no. 7, p. 14.

19. Terry, Don. September 13, 1992. "More Familiar, Life in a Cell Seems Less Terrible." *New York Times*: 1; also see generally Miller, Jerome G. 1996. *Search and Destroy*. Cambridge, MA: Cambridge University Press.

20. Terry, Don. September 13, 1992. "More Familiar, Life in a Cell Seems Less Terrible." *New York Times*: 1.

21. See, e.g., Nossiter, Adam. September 17, 1994. "Making Hard Times Harder: States Cut Jail TV and Sports." *New York Times*.

22. Clark, Charles S. February 4, 1994. "Prison Overcrowding." *The Congressional Quarterly Researcher*. Vol. 4, no. 5, p. 100; U.S. Department of Justice, Bureau of Justice Statistics. April 1992. Bulletin. *Prisons and Prisoners in the United States*. Washington, D.C.: U.S. Government Printing Office: 8.

23. *LeMaire v. Maass*, 745 F. Supp. 623 (D. Or. 1990).

24. Donaldson, Stephen. 1995. *Rape of Incarcerated Prisoners: A Preliminary Statistical Look*. New York: Stop Prisoner Rape, Inc.

25. Editorial. September 21, 1994. "Blunt talk from U.S. attorney." *Washington Post*.

26. ACLU National Prison Project. January 1, 1995. *Status Report: State Prisons and the Courts*. Washington, D.C.: American Civil Liberties Union.

27. Nossiter, Adam. September 17, 1994. "Making Hard Times Harder: States Cut Jail TV and Sports." *New York Times*.

28. Bass, Paul. May 26, 1994. "Hit and Run." *New Haven Advocate*.

29. U.S. Department of Justice, Bureau of Justice Statistics. October 1994. *National Corrections Reporting Program, 1992*. Washington, D.C.: U.S. Government Printing Office: 39; Camp, Camille G., and George M. Camp, 1994. *The Corrections Yearbook 1994: Adult Corrections*. South Salem, NY: Criminal Justice Institute, Inc.: 18; U.S. Department of Justice, Bureau of Justice Statistics. October 27, 1994. Press release. *State and Federal Prison Population Tops One Million*.

30. Anderson, Eric. Winter 1985. Denmark's Radical Approach to Super-Max Yields Success. *The National Prison Project: A Project of the American Civil Liberties Union Foundation*. No. 6:8-9.

31. U.S. Department of Justice, Bureau of Justice Statistics. March 1994. Special Report. *Women in Prison*. Washington, D.C.: U.S. Government Printing Office: 6-7.

32. Miller, Jerome G. 1992. *Search and Destroy: The Plight of African-American Males in the Criminal Justice System*. Unpublished paper. Alexandria, VA: National Center on Institutions and Alternatives.

33. Camp, Camille G., and George M. Camp. 1994. *The Corrections Yearbook 1994: Adult Corrections.* South Salem, NY: Criminal Justice Institute: 48-49.

34. Ibid., pp. 37, 48-49.

35. Proband, Stan. October 1995. Corrections Leads State Appropriations Increases for '96. *Overcrowded Times.*

36. Gold, Steve. 1990. *Trends in State Spending.* Albany, NY: Center for the Study of the States, Nelson A. Rockefeller Institute of Government.

37. Proband, Stan. October 1995. "Corrections Leads State Appropriations Increases for '96." *Overcrowded Times.*

38. U.S. Department of Justice, Bureau of Justice Statistics. September 1992. Bulletin. *Justice Expenditure and Employment, 1990.* Washington, D.C.: U.S. Government Printing Office: 2.

39. Moore, John W. July 30, 1994. "Locked In." *National Journal*: 1785.

40. The Edna McConnell Clark Foundation. April 1993. *Americans Behind Bars.* New York: The Edna McConnell Clark Foundation: 4.

41. Moore, John W. July 30, 1994. "Locked In." *National Journal*: 1785.

42. This is arrived at by dividing the FY94 total operating and capital costs of $20.1 billion by the number of inmates in the state systems on June 30, 1994, 919, 143. See Camp, Camille G., and George M. Camp, 1994. *The Corrections Yearbook 1994: Adult Corrections.* South Salem, NY: Criminal Justice Institute: 1, 48-49; U.S. Department of Justice, Bureau of Justice Statistics. October 27, 1994. Press release. *State and Federal Prison Population Tops One Million.* Washington, D.C.: U.S. Government Printing Office. 1993 median household after-tax income is $26,112. U.S. Bureau of the Census. 1993. Unpublished data. Current Population Survey.

43. The average family will pay $6,498 in federal taxes per year in 1992 (provided by the Congressional Budget Office. January 1994. *An Economic Analysis of the Revenue Provisions of OBRA-93:32*). The most recent published figure on the annual cost of an inmate in the federal system is $20,885. See Federal Bureau of Prisons. 1995. *State of the Bureau, 1993.* Sandstone, MN: Federal Prisons Industry: 63.

44. Branham, Lynn S. April 1992. *The Use of Incarceration in the United States: A Look at the Present and the Future.* Chicago, IL: American Bar Association: 21.

45. See Cory, Bruce, and Stephen Gettinger. 1984. *Time to Build? The Realities of Prison Construction.* New York: The Edna McConnell Clark Foundation.

46. The Edna McConnell Clark Foundation. April 1993. *Americans Behind Bars.* New York: The Edna McConnell Clark Foundation: 5. Also see Loeb, Carl M., Jr. October 1978. "The Cost of Jailing in New York City." *Crime and Delinquency.*: 446-52.

47. Irwin, John, and James Austin. 1994. *It's About Time: America's Imprisonment Binge.* Belmont, CA: Wadsworth: 144; see also McDonald, D. 1980. *The Price of Punishment.* Boulder, CO: Westview Press; and Loeb, Carl. October 1978. "The Cost of Jailing in New York City." *Crime and Delinquency*: 446-52.

48. See Cory, Bruce, and Stephen Gettinger. 1984. *Time to Build? The Realities of Prison Construction.* New York: The Edna McConnell Clark Foundation.

49. U.S. Department of Justice, Bureau of Justice Statistics. *Tuberculosis in Correctional Facilities, 1993.* Washington, D.C.: U.S. Government Printing Office.

50. Sennott, Charles M. May 2, 1994. "AIDS Adds a Fatal Factor to Prison Assault: Rape Behind Bars" (second of three parts). *Boston Globe*; January 1994. Prison and AIDS. *Stanford Law Review* 44:1541.

51. Hanlon, Sean M. December 24, 1993. "State Prisons Taking a Hit from AIDS." *Washington Times.*

52. U.S. Department of Justice, Bureau of Justice Statistics. 1993. *Sourcebook of Criminal Justice Statistics 1992.* Washington, D.C.: U.S. Government Printing Office: 609, Table 6.69.

53. See, e.g., Cromwell, Paul. June 1994. "The Greying of America's Prisons." *Overcrowded Times.*

54. Wikberg, Ron. May/June 1988. "The Longtermers." *The Angolite* Vol. 13, no. 3, p. 40.

55. Mandel, Michael J., Paul Magnusson, James E. Ellis, Gail DeGeorge, and Keith L. Alexander. December 13, 1993. "The Economics of Crime." *Business Week*: 74.

56. Ibid., p. 78.

57. Ibid., p. 73.

58. U.S. Department of Justice, Bureau of Justice Statistics. November 1993. *Federal Criminal Case Processing, 1982-1991: With Preliminary Data for 1992.* Washington, D.C.: U.S. Government Printing Office: 18, Table 18.

59. U.S. Department of Justice. February 4, 1994. *An Analysis of Nonviolent Drug Offenders with Minimal Criminal Histories*. Washington, D.C.: U.S. Government Printing Office.

60. See generally Killias, Martin, Andre Kuhn, and Simone Ronez. June 1995. Sentencing in Switzerland. *Overcrowded Times*. Vol. 6, no. 3.

61. Simon, Paul. December 21, 1994. *In New Survey, Wardens Call for Smarter Sentencing, Alternatives to Incarceration, and Prevention Programs*. Washington, D.C.: Office of Senator Paul Simon, U.S. Senate.

62. See generally MacKenzie, Doris Layton. August 1994. Boot Camps: A National Assessment. *Overcrowded Times*: Campaigh for an Effective Crime Policy. March 1994. *Evaluating Boot Camp Prisons*. Washington, D.C.: Campaign for an Effective Crime Policy; U.S. Department of Justice, National Institute of Justice. November 1994. *Multisite Evaluation of Shock Incarceration*. Washington, D.C.: U.S. Government Printing Office.

63. Roberts, Julian V. April 1992. "American Attitudes About Punishment: Myth and Reality." *Overcrowded Times*. Vol. 3, no. 2, p. 1.

64. Ibid.

65. Doble, John, and Josh Klein. 1989. *Punishing Criminals. The Public's View—An Alabama Survey*. New York: The Edna McConnell Clark Foundation; Doble, John, Stephen Immerwahr, and Amy Richardson. 1991. *Punishing Criminals: The People of Delaware Consider the Options*. New York: The Edna McConnell Clark Foundation.

41

Decriminalization

Samuel Walker

One certain way of reducing crime is to reduce the number of behaviors that are defined as crime. This process, decriminalization, would not only lower the number and rate of crimes but would free police and judicial officers to concentrate on more serious offenses, while prisons and other correctional programs would be less crowded and capable of doing a better job rehabilitating convicted offenders. Advocates of decriminalization typically suggest it apply to victimless or public order crimes, those that seem to hurt no one but consume a great deal of the time and resources of the criminal justice system. But if the process were so simple, it probably would have been tried by now. In fact, this is an enormously complex issue that raises passions on both sides.

In this selection Samuel Walker explores some of the arguments for and against the decriminalization of certain public order offenses. He points out that this is essentially a moralistic debate, with opponents of decriminalization believing that certain behaviors are simply wrong and needs to be deterred by threat of criminal penalty. Although the various rationales for decriminalization appear logical and reasoned, they cannot overcome the differences concerning moral standards that exist between proponents and opponents. Walker reaches no conclusion about the efficacy of decriminalization, concluding that predatory crimes, those that threaten us with harm or loss, would not be affected by removing public order offenses from the criminal statutes. Interesting though it may be, decriminalization is not the answer to America's crime problem.

... In their 1970 book, *The Honest Politician's Guide to Crime Control*, Norval Morris and Gordon Hawkins called decriminalization a "first principle." Specifically, they call for removing criminal penalties for (1) public drunkenness; (2) purchase, possession, and use of all drugs; (3) all forms of gambling; (4) disorderly conduct and vagrancy; (5) abortion; (6) private sexual activity between consenting adults; and (7) juvenile "status" offenses.[1]

It is important to clarify exactly what kinds of behavior are involved in this proposal. Public drunkenness is included but not drunk driving. The person drunk on the street may be a nuisance but poses no threat of harm to anyone else. The drunk driver does pose such a threat. Sexual activity between consenting adults is covered, but not sex between an adult and a child. In short, the standard decriminalization proposal covers a limited range of activity and not a general repeal of all criminal laws governing drinking or sex.

At this point in history there are two different approaches to decriminalization. We can call the items on Morris and Hawkins's agenda the "old" decriminalization. Something new arose in the 1980s: the notion of decriminalizing or legalizing drugs, including even those long considered the most dangerous drugs, heroin and cocaine. We can call this the "new" decriminalization. . . . In this chapter let's examine the "old" decriminalization agenda to see what impact it might have on serious crime.

The Rationale for Decriminalization

Decriminalization was a response to what many liberals saw as the problem of the "overreach" of the criminal law. As Morris and Hawkins explained, too many different kinds of behavior are criminalized. The criminal law in America has traditionally been highly moralistic, covering gambling, many forms of sexual behavior, and alcohol-related problems.

According to the advocates of decriminalization, the broad reach of the criminal law has several undesirable consequences. First, it overburdens the justice system. The police spend too much time on relatively unimportant events, leaving them with less time for the really serious crimes of murder, rape, robbery, and burglary. These arrests fill the jails and clog the courts. In 1989 there were over 800,000 arrests for drunkenness. Since many of the 770,000 disorderly conduct arrests involved drunken people, the total number of alcohol-related arrests (not including drunk driving) is over a million a year.[2]

Second, there is not a strong public consensus about many of these crimes. In fact, the public is very ambivalent. We have many laws restricting gambling, but millions of people want to gamble and do so illegally. The laws prohibiting certain kinds of sexual activity hardly deter people from engaging in those forms of sex.

Ambivalent public attitudes send mixed signals to law enforcement officials, who are simultaneously told to enforce and not to enforce certain laws. The result is a pattern of selective and often arbitrary law enforcement. This violates the principle of equal protection of the law and leads to cynicism about law enforcement among the public and among police offenders.

Third, making various forms of recreation illegal brings into being criminal syndicates that provide the illegal goods and services that people want. Gambling was historically the principal source of revenue for organized crime, and America's demand for illegal drugs sustains vast international networks and neighborhood drug gangs. In this sense, the laws are criminogenic; they create forms of criminal behavior.

Fourth, the criminal syndicates corrupt both the justice system and the political system. The Knapp Commission investigation into police corruption in New York City found that police officers were receiving a weekly "pad" of between $300 and $1,500 a month for protecting illegal gambling.[3] In the 1980s the vast profits from the drug trade began to corrupt the banking system, as banks became involved in laundering drug profits.

Fifth, criminal penalties violate the right to engage in activities that many people believe are a matter of private choice among consenting adults. The overwhelming majority of Americans believe that sex between two adults of the opposite sex should not be a crime. About half of all Americans today now believe that sex between two adults of the same sex should not be a crime. About 80 percent of Americans believe that there is a right to terminate a pregnancy by abortion.[4]

Sixth, many criminal justice and public health experts believe that we have mistakenly attempted to deal with social, psychological, and medical problems through the criminal law. Arrest and prosecution do nothing to help the chronic alcoholic deal with his or her drinking problem, and in many cases they make matters worse. Medical and social services would be a far more effective response.[5] . . .

The Terms of the Debate

Debate over the old decriminalization has generally been framed in moralistic terms. Advocates of criminal penalties see certain kinds of behavior as wrong. The basic function of the criminal law, after all, is to define the boundaries of acceptable conduct. Robbery is a crime because taking something from another person by force violates our basic standards. Taking another person's life is also wrong. As Patrick Devlin put it, "the criminal law as we know it is based upon moral principle."[6]

Decriminalization is a bitterly controversial issue because of fundamental differences of opinion over moral standards. Opponents of abortion, for example, believe that human life begins at conception and therefore abortion is murder. Abortion rights supporters, on the other hand, believe that life begins at birth and therefore that abortion is a legitimate medical procedure. The same is true for sexual activities traditionally prohibited by the criminal law. Many people believe that adultery and homosexuality are wrong. Others believe that these are "victimless crimes," private matters that are none of the law's business.[7]

Decriminalization is also debated in terms of the personal and social consequences of certain kinds of behavior. We have always regulated drinking (restricting the place and hours of alcohol sale) on the grounds that the person who drinks to excess harms himself, his family, and his employer. Devlin argues that "Society is entitled by means of its laws to protect itself from dangers, whether from within or without."[8] The sum of all these harms damages society as a whole. Many people believe that public drunkenness harms society by lowering the quality of neighborhood life. Dealing with disorder problems of this kind is one of the central premises of community policing.

Advocates of decriminalization reply with a pragmatic argument of their own. The practical effect of criminalizing behavior is to make things worse. Arrest of the chronic alcoholic overburdens the justice system, doesn't help the problem drinker, and may actually aggravate the problem.[9]. . .

Public Drunkenness, Disorderly Conduct, and Vagrancy

Public drunkenness, disorderly conduct, and vagrancy are public nuisances rather than predatory crimes. They may offend the sensibilities of many people, but they do not inflict harm in the way that robbery and burglary do.

The crime control strategy underlying decriminalization in this area is indirect. The argument is that freeing the police from enforcing these laws will give them more time to concentrate on serious crime. These public order offenses do consume a great deal of police time and resources. In the nineteenth century they represented about 80 percent of all arrests, and they still make up the largest single group of arrests. In 1975 there were 1.2 million arrests for drunkenness, representing 13 percent of all arrests and three times the number of arrests for all violent crimes.[10]

The basic assumption about freeing up more police resources is flawed—that if the police quit making public drunkenness arrests and concentrated on serious crimes such as robbery and burglary, the availability of more time and resources would help to reduce crime. . . . We learned that simply adding more patrol officers will not prevent more crime. Adding more detectives will not produce higher clearance rates. The liberal crime control strategy behind decriminalization is ultimately identical to the traditional "more cops" proposal offered by conservatives. The proposal is just as unlikely to reduce serious crime.

In fact, we have already gone quite a ways in decriminalizing public nuisance offenses. Between 1975 and 1989 the total number of arrests for drunkenness, disorderly conduct, and vagrancy fell from 2 million to 1 million (the 2 million figure included drunkenness and a certain number of disorderly conduct and vagrancy arrests).[11] Several factors accounted for this drop. First, some court decisions held that arresting someone because of a medical condition—as opposed to some behavior—was unconstitutional. Second, some states decriminalized public intoxication. Third, the decline in public order arrests reflects informal decisions by police departments across the country to deemphasize minor crimes and concentrate on the more serious ones. In large part, this shift was in response to the high rate of serious crime. . . .

Conclusions

There are many arguments for and against criminal penalties for the various forms of behavior we have discussed. Many people have serious moral objections to decriminalizing these behaviors. The anticipated advantages of decriminalization—reducing system overload, reducing corruption, and so on—may or may not be achieved. In either event, decriminalization will not necessarily have any effect on the predatory crimes of robbery and burglary that we are concerned about. If we are serious about reducing predatory crime, we have to keep our eyes focused on those crimes. . . .

Discussion Questions

1. What is decriminalization? How does "old" decriminalization differ from "new" decriminalization? Why are some in favor of decriminalization? Why do some oppose it?

2. What problems are associated with criminalizing too many behaviors? How does criminalization of trivial matters affect equal protection of law? What effect does it have on the right to privacy?

3. How do laws such as the ones discussed by Walker create forms of criminal behavior? For actions such as drinking (al-

coholic beverages), what might be a more effective policy than arrest?

Notes

1. Norval Morris and Gordon Hawkins, *The Honest Politician's Guide to Crime Control.* (Chicago: University of Chicago Press, 1970), p. 3.

2. Federal Bureau of Investigation, *Crime in the United States*, 1989 (Washington, D.C.: Government Printing Office, 1990).

3. *The Knapp Commission Report on Police Corruption* (New York: George Braziller, 1973).

4. Bureau of Justice Statistics, *Sourcebook of Criminal Justice Statistics, 1990* (Washington, D.C.: Government Printing Office, 1991), pp. 195, 248.

5. Raymond T. Nimmer, *Two Million Unnecessary Arrests* (Chicago: American Bar Foundation, 1971).

6. Patrick Devlin, *The Enforcement of Morals* (London: Oxford University Press, 1965), p. 7.

7. Edwin M. Schur, *Crimes without Victims* (Englewood Cliffs, N.J.: Prentice-Hall, 1965).

8. Devlin, *The Enforcement of Morals*, p. 13.

9. Morris and Hawkins, *The Honest Politician's Guide to Crime Control.*

10. Federal Bureau of Investigation, *Crime in the United States, 1975* (Washington, D.C.: Government Printing Office, 1976), p. 179.

11. Nimmer, *Two Million Unnecessary Arrests.*

Index

S